P9-BJR-551

JA '87

FOR REFERENCE

Do Not Take From This Room

Twentieth-Century Literary Criticism

Guide to Gale Literary Criticism Series

When you need to review criticism of literary works, these are the Gale series to use:

If the author's death date is: **You should turn to:**

After Dec. 31, 1959
(or author is still living)

CONTEMPORARY LITERARY CRITICISM

for example: Jorge Luis Borges, Anthony Burgess,
William Faulkner, Mary Gordon,
Ernest Hemingway, Iris Murdoch

1900 through 1959

TWENTIETH-CENTURY LITERARY CRITICISM

for example: Willa Cather, F. Scott Fitzgerald,
Henry James, Mark Twain, Virginia Woolf

1800 through 1899

NINETEENTH-CENTURY LITERATURE CRITICISM

for example: Fedor Dostoevski, George Sand,
Gerard Manley Hopkins, Emily Dickinson

1400 through 1799

LITERATURE CRITICISM FROM 1400 TO 1800
(excluding Shakespeare)

for example: Anne Bradstreet, Pierre Corneille,
Daniel Defoe, Alexander Pope,
Jonathan Swift, Phillis Wheatley

SHAKESPEAREAN CRITICISM

Shakespeare's plays and poetry

Antiquity through 1399

CLASSICAL AND MEDIEVAL LITERATURE CRITICISM

for example: Dante, Plato, Homer, Sophocles, Vergil,
the Beowulf poet

(Volume 1 forthcoming)

Gale also publishes related criticism series:

CHILDREN'S LITERATURE REVIEW

This ongoing series covers authors of all eras.
Presents criticism on authors and author/illustrators
who write for the preschool to junior-high audience.

CONTEMPORARY ISSUES CRITICISM

This two volume set presents criticism on
contemporary authors writing on current issues.
Topics covered include the social sciences,
philosophy, economics, natural science, law, and
related areas.

ISSN 0276-8178

Volume 17

Twentieth-Century Literary Criticism

**Excerpts from Criticism of the
Works of Novelists, Poets, Playwrights,
Short Story Writers, and Other Creative Writers
Who Died between 1900 and 1960,
from the First Published Critical Appraisals
to Current Evaluations**

**Dennis Poupard
James E. Person, Jr.
Editors**

**Thomas Ligotti
Associate Editor**

**Gale Research Company
Book Tower
Detroit, Michigan 48226**

STAFF

Dennis Poupard, James E. Person, Jr., *Editors*

Thomas Ligotti, *Associate Editor*

Lee Fournier, Marie Lazzari, Serita Lanette Lockard, *Senior Assistant Editors*

Sandra Giraud, Paula Kepos, Sandra Liddell,
Claudia Loomis, Jay P. Pederson, *Assistant Editors*

Lizbeth A. Purdy, *Production Supervisor*
Denise Michlewicz Broderick, *Production Coordinator*
Eric Berger, *Assistant Production Coordinator*
Robin Du Blanc, Kelly King Howes, Sheila J. Nasea, *Editorial Assistants*

Victoria B. Cariappa, *Research Coordinator*
Jeannine Schiffman Davidson, *Assistant Research Coordinator*
Vincenza G. DiNoto, Daniel Kurt Gilbert, Maureen R. Richards,
Filomena Sgambati, Valerie J. Webster, Mary D. Wise, *Research Assistants*

Linda M. Pugliese, *Manuscript Coordinator*
Donna Craft, *Assistant Manuscript Coordinator*
Colleen M. Crane, Maureen A. Puhl, Rosetta Irene Simms, *Manuscript Assistants*

Jeanne A. Gough, *Permissions Supervisor*
Janice M. Mach, *Permissions Coordinator*
Patricia A. Seefelt, *Permissions Coordinator, Illustrations*
Susan D. Nobles, *Assistant Permissions Coordinator*
Margaret A. Chamberlain, Sandra C. Davis, Mary M. Matuz, *Senior Permissions Assistants*
Kathy Grell, Josephine M. Keene, *Permissions Assistants*
H. Diane Cooper, Dorothy J. Fowler, Yolanda Parker, Mabel C. Schoening, *Permissions Clerks*
Margaret Mary Missar, *Photo Research*

Frederick G. Ruffner, *Publisher*
Dedria Bryfonski, *Editorial Director*
Christine Nasso, *Director, Literature Division*
Laurie Lanzen Harris, *Senior Editor, Literary Criticism Series*

Since this page cannot legibly accommodate all the copyright notices,
the Appendix constitutes an extension of the copyright notice.

Copyright © 1985 by Gale Research Company

Library of Congress Catalog Card Number 76-46132
ISBN 0-8103-0231-4
ISSN 0276-8178

Computerized photocomposition by
Typographics, Incorporated
Kansas City, Missouri

Printed in the United States

Contents

Preface

It is impossible to overvalue the importance of literature in the intellectual, emotional, and spiritual evolution of humanity. Literature is that which both lifts us out of everyday life and helps us to better understand it. Through the fictive lives of such characters as Anna Karenina, Jay Gatsby, or Leopold Bloom, our perceptions of the human condition are enlarged, and we are enriched.

Literary criticism can also give us insight into the human condition, as well as into the specific moral and intellectual atmosphere of an era, for the criteria by which a work of art is judged reflects contemporary philosophical and social attitudes. Literary criticism takes many forms: the traditional essay, the book or play review, even the parodic poem. Criticism can also be of several types: normative, descriptive, interpretive, textual, appreciative, generic. Collectively, the range of critical response helps us to understand a work of art, an author, an era.

Scope of the Series

Twentieth-Century Literary Criticism (TCLC) is designed to serve as an introduction for the student of twentieth-century literature to the authors of the period 1900 to 1960 and to the most significant commentators on these authors. The great poets, novelists, short story writers, playwrights, and philosophers of this period are by far the most popular writers for study in high school and college literature courses. Since a vast amount of relevant critical material confronts the student, *TCLC* presents significant passages from the most important published criticism to aid students in their location and selection of criticism on authors who died between 1900 and 1960.

The need for *TCLC* was suggested by the usefulness of the Gale series *Contemporary Literary Criticism (CLC)*, which excerpts criticism on current writing. Because of the difference in time span under consideration (*CLC* considers authors who were still living after 1959), there is no duplication of material between *CLC* and *TCLC*. For further information about *CLC* and Gale's other criticism series, users should consult the Guide to Gale Literary Criticism Series preceding the title page in this volume.

Each volume of *TCLC* is carefully compiled to include authors who represent a variety of genres and nationalities and who are currently regarded as the most important writers of this era. In addition to major authors, *TCLC* also presents criticism on lesser-known writers whose significant contributions to literary history are important to the study of twentieth-century literature.

Each author entry in *TCLC* is intended to provide an overview of major criticism on an author. Therefore, the editors include approximately twenty authors in each 600-page volume (compared with approximately sixty authors in a *CLC* volume of similar size) so that more attention may be given to an author. Each author entry represents a historical survey of the critical response to that author's work: some early criticism is presented to indicate initial reactions, later criticism is selected to represent any rise or decline in the author's reputation, and current retrospective analyses provide students with a modern view. The length of an author entry is intended to reflect the amount of critical attention the author has received from critics writing in English, and from foreign criticism in translation. Critical articles and books that have not been translated into English are excluded. Every attempt has been made to identify and include excerpts from the seminal essays on each author's work. Additionally, as space permits, especially insightful essays of a more limited scope are included.

An author may appear more than once in the series because of the great quantity of critical material available, or because of a resurgence of criticism generated by events such as an author's centennial or anniversary celebration, the republication of an author's works, or publication of a newly translated work or volume of letters. A few author entries in each volume of *TCLC* feature criticism on single works by major authors who have appeared previously in the series. Only those individual works that have been the subjects of vast amounts of criticism and are widely studied in literature classes are selected for this in-depth treatment. Leo Tolstoy's *Anna Karenina* is the subject of such an entry in *TCLC*, Volume 17.

Organization of the Book

An author entry consists of the following elements: author heading, biographical and critical introduction, principal works, excerpts of criticism (each followed by a bibliographical citation), and an additional bibliography for further reading.

- The *author heading* consists of the author's full name, followed by birth and death dates. The unbracketed portion of the name denotes the form under which the author most commonly wrote. If an author wrote consistently under a pseudonym, the pseudonym will be listed in the author heading and the real name given in parentheses on the first line of the biographical and critical introduction. Also located at the beginning of the introduction to the author entry are any name variations under which an author wrote, including transliterated forms for authors whose languages use nonroman alphabets. Uncertainty as to a birth or death date is indicated by a question mark.

- The *biographical and critical introduction* contains background information designed to introduce the reader to an author and to the critical debate surrounding his or her work. Parenthetical material following many of the introductions provides references to biographical and critical reference series published by Gale. These include *Children's Literature Review, Contemporary Authors, Dictionary of Literary Biography, Something about the Author,* and past volumes of *TCLC.*

- Most *TCLC* entries include *portraits* of the author. Many entries also contain illustrations of materials pertinent to an author's career, including holographs of manuscript pages, title pages, dust jackets, letters, or representations of important people, places, and events in an author's life.

- The *list of principal works* is chronological by date of first book publication and identifies the genre of each work. In the case of foreign authors where there are both foreign language publications and English translations, the title and date of the first English-language edition are given in brackets. Unless otherwise indicated, dramas are dated by first performance, not first publication.

- *Criticism* is arranged chronologically in each author entry to provide a useful perspective on changes in critical evaluation over the years. All titles by the author featured in the critical entry are printed in boldface type to enable the user to ascertain without difficulty the works being discussed. Also for purposes of easier identification, the critic's name and the publication date of the essay are given at the beginning of each piece of criticism. Unsigned criticism is preceded by the title of the journal in which it appeared. When an anonymous essay is later attributed to a critic, the critic's name appears in brackets at the beginning of the excerpt and in the bibliographical citation.

- Important critical essays are prefaced by *explanatory notes* as an additional aid to students using *TCLC.* The explanatory notes provide several types of useful information, including: the reputation of a critic; the importance of a work of criticism; the specific type of criticism (biographical, psychoanalytic, structuralist, etc.); a synopsis of the criticism; and the growth of critical controversy or changes in critical trends regarding an author's work. In many cases, these notes cross-reference the work of critics who agree or disagree with each other. Dates in parentheses within the explanatory notes refer to a book publication date when they follow a book title and to an essay date when they follow a critic's name.

- A complete *bibliographical citation* designed to facilitate location of the original essay or book by the interested reader follows each piece of criticism. An asterisk (*) at the end of a citation indicates that the essay is on more than one author.

- The *additional bibliography* appearing at the end of each author entry suggests further reading on the author. In some cases it includes essays for which the editors could not obtain reprint rights. An asterisk (*) at the end of a citation indicates that the essay is on more than one author.

An appendix lists the sources from which material in each volume has been reprinted. It does not, however, list every book or periodical consulted in the preparation of the volume.

Cumulative Indexes

Each volume of *TCLC* includes a cumulative index to authors listing all the authors who have appeared in *Contemporary Literary Criticism, Twentieth-Century Literary Criticism, Nineteenth-Century Literature Criticism,* and *Literature Criticism from 1400 to 1800,* along with cross-references to the Gale series *Children's Literature Review, Authors in the News, Contemporary Authors, Contemporary Authors Autobiography Series, Dictionary of Literary Biography, Something about the Author,* and *Yesterday's Authors of Books for Children.* Users will welcome this cumulated author index as a useful tool for locating an author within the various series. The index, which lists birth and death dates when available, will be particularly valuable for those authors who are identified with a certain period but whose death date causes them to be placed in another, or for those authors whose careers span two periods. For example, F. Scott Fitzgerald is found in *TCLC,* yet a writer often associated with him, Ernest Hemingway, is found in *CLC.*

Each volume of *TCLC* also includes a cumulative nationality index. Author names are arranged alphabetically under their respective nationalities and followed by the volume numbers in which they appear.

A cumulative index to critics is another useful feature in *TCLC.* Under each critic's name are listed the authors on whom the critic has written and the volume and page where the criticism may be found.

Acknowledgments

No work of this scope can be accomplished without the cooperation of many people. The editors especially wish to thank the copyright holders of the excerpted criticism included in this volume, the permissions managers of many book and magazine publishing companies for assisting us in securing reprint rights, and Jeri Yaryan for assistance with copyright research. We are also grateful to the staffs of the Detroit Public Library, the Library of Congress, University of Detroit Library, University of Michigan Library, and Wayne State University Library for making their resources available to us.

Suggestions Are Welcome

In response to various suggestions, several features have been added to *TCLC* since the series began, including: explanatory notes to excerpted criticism that provide important information regarding critics and their work; a cumulative author index listing authors in all Gale literary criticism series; entries devoted to criticism on a single work by a major author; and more extensive illustrations.

Readers who wish to suggest authors to appear in future volumes, or who have other suggestions, are cordially invited to write the editors.

Authors to Be Featured in *TCLC*, Volumes 18 and 19

James Agee (American novelist and journalist)—Agee's *Let Us Now Praise Famous Men* and *A Death in the Family* are harshly realistic treatments of the moral crises and moral triumphs of mid-twentieth-century America. In addition, Agee's film criticism is recognized as the first serious consideration in English of film as a modern art form.

Hilaire Belloc (English poet and essayist)—One of turn-of-the-century England's premier men of letters, Belloc has been the subject of renewed critical and biographical interest in recent years.

Arnold Bennett (English novelist)—Bennett is credited with introducing techniques of European Naturalism to the English novel. Set in the manufacturing district of the author's native Staffordshire, Bennett's novels tell of the thwarted ambitions of those who endure a dull, provincial existence.

Hermann Broch (Austrian novelist, poet, and essayist)—Broch was a philosophical novelist whose works are considered profound reflections upon the social and moral disintegration of modern Europe. His major works, which include his masterpiece *The Sleepwalkers*, have been compared to James Joyce's *Ulysses* and *Finnegans Wake* for their contribution to the Modernist exploration of language.

Robert Cunninghame Graham (Scottish fiction writer, travel writer, and historian)—Called "the most singular of English writers" by the novelist W. H. Hudson, Cunninghame Graham was a world traveler, a socialist member of Parliament, and a friend of such authors as Joseph Conrad and George Bernard Shaw. Cunninghame Graham's works, both fiction and nonfiction, are based on the often dramatic experiences of his life.

John Gray (English poet and fiction writer)—Reputed to be the model for the title character of Oscar Wilde's *The Picture of Dorian Gray*, Gray is best known for his poetry collection *Silverpoints*, which is often considered one of the high-points of Decadent verse during the 1890s. His futuristic novel *Park: A Fantastic Story* has recently been reissued.

Thomas Hardy (English novelist)—Hardy's novel *Tess of the d'Urbervilles* was controversial in the late nineteenth century for its sympathetic depiction of an independent female protagonist. *TCLC* will devote an entire entry to the critical reception of this classic work of English fiction.

O. Henry (American short story writer)—O. Henry (William Sydney Porter) was one of America's most popular short story writers. His stories, known for their inventiveness and characteristic surprise endings, are widely anthologized and often compared to the works of Guy de Maupassant.

Julia Ward Howe (American poet and biographer)—A famous suffragette and social reformer, Howe was also a popular poet who is best known as the composer of "The Battle Hymn of the Republic."

T. E. Hulme (English poet)—A major influence on the work of T. S. Eliot, Ezra Pound, and other important twentieth-century poets, Hulme was the chief theorist of Imagism and Modernism in English poetry.

James Weldon Johnson (American novelist and poet)—One of the most prominent black leaders of his time, Johnson is also regarded as the principal forerunner of the Harlem Renaissance. His novel *The Autobiography of an Ex-Colored Man* was one of the first works of fiction to explore the complexity of race relations in America and profoundly influenced such writers as Ralph Ellison and Richard Wright.

Lionel Johnson (English poet and critic)—Johnson is considered one of the most important figures associated with the Decadent and Aesthetic movements of the 1890s. Like many of his contemporaries, he lived an eccentric life and died young, producing a small but distinguished body of works that reflect his most personal preoccupations while also representing many of the typical concerns of his generation.

T. E. Lawrence (English autobiographer)—Lawrence is more popularly known as Lawrence of Arabia, a sobriquet received for his campaign against the Turks during World War I. His chronicle of this period in what has been described as "perhaps the strangest, most adventurous life of modern times" is contained in *The Seven Pillars of Wisdom*. *TCLC* will present excerpts from the entire range of criticism on this classic modern work, along with commentary on Lawrence's diary, his letters, and *The Mint*, an account of his experiences following his enlistment as a private in the Royal Air Force.

Ludwig Lewisohn (American novelist and critic)—An important man of letters during the first quarter of the twentieth century, Lewisohn made a notable contribution to modern literature through his critical writings and his translations from German and French literature. Many of Lewisohn's later works of fiction and nonfiction reflect his concern for the plight of European Jews during the 1930s and 1940s.

Detlev von Liliencron (German poet)—The author of works in several genres, Liliencron is most renowned for his lyric poetry, which is praised for its forcefulness and vivid detail.

Rainer Maria Rilke (German poet and novelist)—Rilke's *The Notebooks of Malte Laurids Brigge*, a loosely autobiographical novel that explores the angst-ridden life of a hypersensitive man in Paris, is considered the author's most accomplished prose work. To mark a new translation of this novel, *TCLC* will devote an entire entry to critical discussion of this important work.

Jacques Roumain (Haitian novelist, poet, and essayist)—One of the most militant and influential Haitian intellectuals of this century, Roumain was the author of the novel *Masters of the Dew*, which was widely praised for its haunting stylistic beauty as well as its powerful social message.

Raymond Roussel (French novelist and dramatist)—Roussel was a wealthy eccentric who staged expensive but entirely unsuccessful productions of his own plays and published elaborate but ignored editions of his novels. He was claimed as a forerunner by the Surrealists for the extravagant and often shocking imagination demonstrated in his works and is today recognized as one of the oddest and most ingenious authors in modern literature.

John Ruskin (English critic)—Most renowned for his critical writings on art and architecture, particularly *Stones of Venice* and the five-volume series *Modern Painters*, Ruskin was also an important social critic. His advocacy of various reforms and his association with the Pre-Raphaelite circle of artists, writers, and thinkers place him at the intellectual and cultural center of Victorian England.

Lincoln Steffens (American journalist and autobiographer)—Steffens was one of a group of writers in the early twentieth century who were described as "muckrakers" by President Theodore Roosevelt. Steffens's call for radical reforms in American government and society form the substance of his best works, including *The Shame of the Cities* and *The Struggle for Self Government*, and serves as the background to his highly readable *Autobiography*.

Mark Twain (American novelist)—Twain is considered by many to be the father of modern American literature. Breaking with the genteel literary conventions of the nineteenth century, Twain endowed his characters and narratives with the natural speech patterns of the common person and wrote about subjects hitherto considered beneath the consideration of serious art. He is renowned throughout the world for his greatest novel, *Huckleberry Finn. TCLC* will devote an entry solely to critical discussion of that controversial work. Included will be works of criticism written from the late nineteenth century through 1985, the centenary year of *Huckleberry Finn*'s American publication and the one hundred-fiftieth anniversary of Twain's birth.

Robert Walser (Swiss novelist and short story writer)—Considered among the most important Swiss authors writing in German, Walser was praised by such major figures of German literature as Franz Kafka and Robert Musil. His fiction is distinguished by a grotesque imagination and black humor suggestive of the Expressionist and Surrealist movements.

Beatrice and Sydney James Webb (English social writers)—Prominent members of the progressive Fabian society, the Webbs wrote sociological works significant to the advent of socialist reform in England and influenced the work of several major authors, including H. G. Wells and George Bernard Shaw.

H. G. Wells (English novelist)—Wells is best known today as one of the forerunners of modern science fiction and as a utopian idealist who foretold an era of chemical warfare, atomic weaponry, and world wars. *The Time Machine, The Invisible Man, The War of the Worlds, The Island of Doctor Moreau,* and several other works among Wells's canon are considered classics in the genres of science fiction and science fantasy. *TCLC* will devote an entire entry to Wells's accomplishments as a science fiction writer.

Owen Wister (American novelist)—Considered the founder of modern fiction about the Old West, Wister is best known as the author of *The Virginian,* a novel that established the basic character types, settings, and plots of the Western genre.

Andrei Zhdanov (Soviet censor)—As Secretary of the Central Committee of the Soviet Communist Party from 1928 until 1948, Zhdanov formulated the official guidelines for all writing published in the Soviet Union. He was instrumental in establishing the precepts of Socialist Realism, which for decades severely circumscribed the subjects deemed suitable for Soviet literature.

Emile Zola (French novelist, dramatist, and critic)—Zola was the founder and principal theorist of Naturalism, perhaps the most influential literary movement in modern literature. His twenty-volume series *Les Rougon-Macquart* is one of the monuments of Naturalist fiction, and served as a model for late nineteenth-century novelists seeking a more candid and accurate representation of human life.

Additional Authors to Appear
in Future Volumes

Abbey, Henry 1842-1911
Abercrombie, Lascelles 1881-1938
Adamic, Louis 1898-1951
Ade, George 1866-1944
Agustini, Delmira 1886-1914
Akers, Elizabeth Chase 1832-1911
Akiko, Yosano 1878-1942
Aldanov, Mark 1886-1957
Aldrich, Thomas Bailey 1836-1907
Aliyu, Dan Sidi 1902-1920
Allen, Hervey 1889-1949
Archer, William 1856-1924
Arlen, Michael 1895-1956
Austin, Alfred 1835-1913
Austin, Mary 1868-1934
Bahr, Hermann 1863-1934
Bailey, Philip James 1816-1902
Barbour, Ralph Henry 1870-1944
Barreto, Lima 1881-1922
Benét, William Rose 1886-1950
Benjamin, Walter 1892-1940
Bennett, James Gordon, Jr. 1841-1918
Benson, E(dward) F(rederic) 1867-1940
Berdyaev, Nikolai Aleksandrovich
    1874-1948
Beresford, J(ohn) D(avys) 1873-1947
Bergson, Henri 1859-1941
Binyon, Laurence 1869-1943
Bishop, John Peale 1892-1944
Blackmore, R(ichard) D(oddridge)
    1825-1900
Blake, Lillie Devereux 1835-1913
Blum, Leon 1872-1950
Bodenheim, Maxwell 1892-1954
Bosschere, Jean de 1878-1953
Bowen, Marjorie 1886-1952
Byrne, Donn 1889-1928
Caine, Hall 1853-1931
Campana, Dina 1885-1932
Cannan, Gilbert 1884-1955
Chand, Prem 1880-1936
Churchill, Winston 1871-1947
Coppée, Francois 1842-1908
Corelli, Marie 1855-1924
Croce, Benedetto 1866-1952
Crofts, Freeman Wills 1879-1957
Crothers, Rachel 1878-1958
Cruze, James (Jens Cruz Bosen) 1884-
    1942
Curros, Enriquez Manuel 1851-1908
Dall, Caroline Wells (Healy) 1822-1912
Daudet, Leon 1867-1942
Davidson, John 1857-1909
Day, Clarence 1874-1935
Delafield, E.M. (Edme Elizabeth Monica
    de la Pasture) 1890-1943

Deneson, Jacob 1836-1919
DeVoto, Bernard 1897-1955
Douglas, (George) Norman 1868-1952
Douglas, Lloyd C(assel) 1877-1951
Dovzhenko, Alexander 1894-1956
Drinkwater, John 1882-1937
Drummond, W.H. 1854-1907
Durkheim, Emile 1858-1917
Duun, Olav 1876-1939
Eaton, Walter Prichard 1878-1957
Eggleston, Edward 1837-1902
Erskine, John 1879-1951
Fadeyev, Alexander 1901-1956
Ferland, Albert 1872-1943
Feydeau, Georges 1862-1921
Field, Rachel 1894-1924
Flecker, James Elroy 1884-1915
Fletcher, John Gould 1886-1950
Fogazzaro, Antonio 1842-1911
Francos, Karl Emil 1848-1904
Frank, Bruno 1886-1945
Frazer, (Sir) George 1854-1941
Freud, Sigmund 1853-1939
Froding, Gustaf 1860-1911
Fuller, Henry Blake 1857-1929
Futabatei, Shimei 1864-1909
Futrelle, Jacques 1875-1912
Gladkov, Fydor Vasilyevich 1883-1958
Glaspell, Susan 1876-1948
Glyn, Elinor 1864-1943
Golding, Louis 1895-1958
Gosse, Edmund 1849-1928
Gould, Gerald 1885-1936
Guest, Edgar 1881-1959
Gumilyov, Nikolay 1886-1921
Gyulai, Pal 1826-1909
Hale, Edward Everett 1822-1909
Hall, James 1887-1951
Harris, Frank 1856-1931
Hawthorne, Julian 1846-1934
Hernandez, Miguel 1910-1942
Hewlett, Maurice 1861-1923
Heyward, DuBose 1885-1940
Hilton, James 1900-1954
Hope, Anthony 1863-1933
Hudson, W(illiam) H(enry) 1841-1922
Huidobro, Vincente 1893-1948
Hviezdoslav (Pavol Orszagh) 1849-1921
Ilyas, Abu Shabaka 1903-1947
Imbs, Bravig 1904-1946
Ivanov, Vyacheslav Ivanovich 1866-
    1949
Jacobs, W(illiam) W(ymark) 1863-1943
James, Will 1892-1942
Jammes, Francis 1868-1938
Jerome, Jerome K(lapka) 1859-1927

Johnson, Fenton 1888-1958
Johnston, Mary 1870-1936
Jorgensen, Johannes 1866-1956
Kaye-Smith, Sheila 1887-1956
Khlebnikov, Victor 1885-1922
King, Grace 1851-1932
Kirby, William 1817-1906
Kline, Otis Albert 1891-1946
Kohut, Adolph 1848-1916
Korolenko, Vladimir 1853-1921
Kuzmin, Mikhail Alexseyevich 1875-
    1936
Lamm, Martin 1880-1950
Lawson, Henry 1867-1922
Ledwidge, Francis 1887-1917
Leipoldt, C. Louis 1880-1947
Lemonnier, Camille 1844-1913
Leverson, Ada 1862-1933
Lima, Jorge De 1895-1953
Locke, Alain 1886-1954
Long, Frank Belknap 1903-1959
Louys, Pierre 1870-1925
Lucas, E(dward) V(errall) 1868-1938
Lyall, Edna 1857-1903
Maghar, Josef Suatopluk 1864-1945
Manning, Frederic 1887-1935
Maragall, Joan 1860-1911
Marais, Eugene 1871-1936
Martin du Gard, Roger 1881-1958
Masaoka Shiki 1867-1902
Masaryk, Tomas 1850-1939
McClellan, George Marion 1860-1934
McCoy, Horace 1897-1955
Mirbeau, Octave 1850-1917
Mistral, Frederic 1830-1914
Molnar, Ferenc 1878-1952
Monro, Harold 1879-1932
Moore, Thomas Sturge 1870-1944
Morley, Christopher 1890-1957
Morley, S. Griswold 1883-1948
Mqhayi, S.E.K. 1875-1945
Murray, (George) Gilbert 1866-1957
Nansen, Peter 1861-1918
Nathan, George Jean 1882-1958
Nobre, Antonio 1867-1900
Nordhoff, Charles 1887-1947
Norris, Frank 1870-1902
Obstfelder, Sigborn 1866-1900
O'Dowd, Bernard 1866-1959
Ophuls, Max 1902-1957
Orczy, Baroness 1865-1947
Owen, Seaman 1861-1936
Page, Thomas Nelson 1853-1922
Papini, Giovanni 1881-1956
Parrington, Vernon L. 1871-1929
Peck, George W. 1840-1916

Peret, Benjamin 1899-1959
Phillips, Ulrich B. 1877-1934
Pickthall, Marjorie 1883-1922
Pinero, Arthur Wing 1855-1934
Pontoppidan, Henrik 1857-1943
Prem Chand, Mushi 1880-1936
Prévost, Marcel 1862-1941
Quiller-Couch, Arthur 1863-1944
Quiroga, Horacio 1878-1937
Randall, James G. 1881-1953
Rappoport, Solomon 1863-1944
Read, Opie 1852-1939
Reisen (Reizen), Abraham 1875-1953
Remington, Frederic 1861-1909
Riley, James Whitcomb 1849-1916
Rinehart, Mary Roberts 1876-1958
Ring, Max 1817-1901
Rohmer, Sax 1883-1959
Rolland, Romain 1866-1944
Rozanov, Vasily Vasilyevich 1856-1919
Saar, Ferdinand von 1833-1906
Sabatini, Rafael 1875-1950
Saintsbury, George 1845-1933
Sakutaro, Hagiwara 1886-1942
Sanborn, Franklin Benjamin 1831-1917

Santayana, George 1863-1952
Sardou, Victorien 1831-1908
Schickele, René 1885-1940
Seabrook, William 1886-1945
Seton, Ernest Thompson 1860-1946
Shestov, Lev 1866-1938
Shiels, George 1886-1949
Skram, Bertha Amalie 1847-1905
Smith, Pauline 1883-1959
Sodergran, Edith Irene 1892-1923
Solovyov, Vladimir 1853-1900
Sorel, Georges 1847-1922
Spector, Mordechai 1859-1922
Spengler, Oswald 1880-1936
Squire, J(ohn) C(ollings) 1884-1958
Stavenhagen, Fritz 1876-1906
Stockton, Frank R. 1834-1902
Subrahmanya Bharati, C. 1882-1921
Sully-Prudhomme, Rene 1839-1907
Talev, Dimituv 1898-1966
Thoma, Ludwig 1867-1927
Tolstoy, Alexei 1882-1945
Trotsky, Leon 1870-1940
Tuchmann, Jules 1830-1901

Turner, W(alter) J(ames) R(edfern)
   1889-1946
Vachell, Horace Annesley 1861-1955
Van Dine, S.S. (William H. Wright)
   1888-1939
Van Doren, Carl 1885-1950
Van Dyke, Henry 1852-1933
Vazov, Ivan Minchov 1850-1921
Veblen, Thorstein 1857-1929
Villaespesa, Francisco 1877-1936
Wallace, Edgar 1874-1932
Wallace, Lewis 1827-1905
Walsh, Ernest 1895-1926
Webb, Mary 1881-1927
Webster, Jean 1876-1916
Whitlock, Brand 1869-1927
Wilson, Harry Leon 1867-1939
Wolf, Emma 1865-1932
Wood, Clement 1888-1950
Wren, P(ercival) C(hristopher) 1885-
   1941
Yonge, Charlotte Mary 1823-1901
Zecca, Ferdinand 1864-1947
Zeromski, Stefan 1864-1925

Readers are cordially invited to suggest additional authors to the editors.

Stella Benson

1892-1933

English novelist, essayist, short story writer, memoirist, and poet.

Benson was an early twentieth-century novelist who explored the isolation and alienation of contemporary women in her fiction. Her novels provide perceptive and sympathetic investigations into the inner selves of characters who lead solitary lives, either by choice or because they are unable to communicate effectively with others. It has been suggested that her most original contribution to the examination of these themes was her introduction of elements of fantasy into otherwise naturalistic stories with modern settings. R. Meredith Bedell has written that Benson used "the supernatural to insist upon the realities of our own world," offering paranormal explanations for the problems faced by her characters.

Benson was the third of four children born to a financially comfortable family whose wealth came from her father's inherited holdings in the Indies. She was plagued by respiratory problems that limited the activities she was permitted as a child. Consequently, she pursued such quiet, introspective diversions as writing fiction and verse, some of which appeared in *St. Nicholas* magazine. The death of an older sister increased her parents' concern about Benson's precarious health, and she was raised in virtual isolation by a succession of nannies and tutors. At eighteen, when her health had improved, Benson went to Freiburg, Germany, to study music and languages. However, she suffered a physical collapse almost at once and was taken by her mother to recuperate in Arosa, Switzerland. There she underwent a sinus operation that left her partially deaf; she was eventually to lose her hearing completely. In 1912 she left Switzerland for a cruise to Jamaica with her mother, and on this trip began working on her first novel, *I Pose*. Upon her return to England, Benson—young, unmarried, and in frail health—was expected to return to her family's estate. Desiring independence, however, she moved to the "Brown Borough" slum district of Hoxton in London, supporting herself with a variety of odd jobs that included secretarial work, professional gardening, vocational training, and the establishment of a business manufacturing paper bags. She thrived on this unconventional way of life and was not seriously ill again until 1916, after which poor health often required hospitalization and long periods of convalescence. She refused to live as an invalid, however, and when not actually incapacitated she enjoyed diverse and strenuous activities that included hiking, camping, horseback riding, mountain climbing, and world travel.

In 1918 Benson took an extended trip to the United States, seeking to escape the grimness of postwar England. With California as her destination, she spent five months making her way across the country from New York, taking jobs when her funds ran low, and meeting longtime correspondents such as Harriet Monroe, the editor of *Poetry* magazine. Benson lived and worked for a year in San Francisco and Berkeley before returning to England via Hawaii, Hong Kong, Japan, and China. During her journey home, civil strife in China disrupted transportation and communications, leaving Benson stranded in Chungking, where she was helped by a customs official named

Mary Evans Picture Library

Shaemas O'Gorman Anderson. They met again in England and were married late in 1921. Their honeymoon was spent crossing the United States by automobile—the first that either had ever driven. They subsequently lived in the various small provincial outposts of China to which Anderson's government sent him. For reasons which Benson's biographer, R. Ellis Roberts, has left deliberately vague, her marriage was an unhappy one. Deeply regretting that she had no children, Benson lavished her devotion—to what she cheerfully admitted was an excessive degree—on dozens of pet dogs, whom she named after popes, brands of typewriters, and makes of automobiles. Benson continued to travel extensively, often without her husband, returning several times to the United States, England, the Carribbean, and to different parts of Europe, recording her experiences in numerous travel essays first published in newspapers and magazines and later collected in the volumes *The Little World* and *Worlds within Worlds*. While it was common to extol the broadening, educational aspects of travel, Benson maintained, perhaps facetiously, that what she saw of the world only served to reinforce her own prejudices. As she grew older, Benson's bouts of respiratory illness increased in frequency and severity. She died at forty-one.

Benson's first novel, *I Pose,* received largely favorable reviews, tempered with some objections that recur in much of the later commentary about her works. Though commending her wit and cleverness, early reviewers noted that these qualities were often prominently and self-consciously displayed. Somewhat overt didacticism was noted as well in the feminist philosophizing of the character of the suffragette, who experiences social pressure to marry. The otherwise unremarkable story of the suffragette and an unemployed gardener who meet and agree to marry for wholly pragmatic reasons was distinguished by an unusual ending—the suffragette kills herself at the altar. Benson continued throughout her career to depict characters making choices that often varied from the traditional ones of marriage and family. After *I Pose*, the alternatives to conventional marriage as well as the complexities of marital relationships were explored by Benson in two different ways represented by two groups of novels. In three of her novels, *This Is the End*, *Living Alone*, and *Goodbye, Stranger*, Benson utilized elements of the fantastic, while in the rest of her works she relied on the techniques of the realistic novel.

This Is the End and *Living Alone* are sympathetically told stories that engage the reader in the inner lives of solitary female protagonists who seek to remain alone and self-sufficient. In both novels, Benson incorporated elements of fantasy into otherwise straightforward narratives. Joseph Collins has written that Benson used fantasy as "a sort of delicate symbolism for getting over a very sane attitude toward certain social foibles and trends." *This Is the End* deals with the imaginary world in which Benson's protagonist seeks refuge from the unpleasant realities of her life. At the novel's end she agrees to marry only because her solitary life of the imagination has been destroyed. Similarly, *Living Alone* "confronts an unromantic reality," in Bedell's words, "through the medium of fantasy." Sarah Brown, a plain and not particularly talented young woman trying to make a living in London, encounters various supernatural beings including a broomstick-riding witch, a warlock, and a dragon employed as foreman of a cooperative farm. In the novel, *Goodbye, Stranger*, a husband's self-absorption and lack of interest in his wife is explained as a case of fairy possession—a changeling has occupied the man's body, altering his behavior. Benson used fantasy to distance the reader from the sometimes didactic points she wished to stress. She sought to explain the bleakness and loneliness of life in the real world by looking beyond the purely rational and positing the interaction of an imaginative fairyland of her own creation with the events of everyday life. This provided a comfortable distance that eased both the readers' and the authors' personal involvement with her sometimes painful subject matter. For example, the English and German witches battling above London in *Living Alone* illustrate the dangers of blind patriotism, while the hypocrisy of Sarah Brown's ostensibly charitable work is revealed to her after she eats a magic sandwich.

With her fourth novel, *The Poor Man*, Benson shifted the focus from her sensitive portrayals of the inner lives of characters— all based to some extent on herself—to more objective and ironic character studies. *The Poor Man* was characterized by reviewers as a psychological study or slice of life, presented without authorial intrusion. Benson wrote that *The Poor Man* represented her first deliberate "refusal to imply an *ought* or *ought not* . . . the withholding of comment." This distanced approach was important to the construction of her subsequent novels. *Pipers and a Dancer* was the first of Benson's novels to conclude with the idea that her self-sufficient female protagonist might have found happiness with another person. Typically for Benson, this ending departed from tradition as the central character rejects marriage to form a close relationship with her fiancé's sister. Benson's last novel, *Tobit Trans-*

planted, published in the United States as *The Far-Away Bride*, is generally considered her best work. In *Tobit Transplanted* Benson recast in modern terms the story of Tobit from the apocryphal books of the Bible. The Book of Tobit, one of two short historical books following the Book of Nehemiah in the Roman Catholic version of the Bible, is named for the central character of Tobit, a Jew persecuted by the Assyrians and afflicted with cataracts. Benson's novel is based on a section of the story in which Tobit's son Tobias, aided by the angel Raphael, overcomes the demon that prevented the successful marriage of Tobit's niece Sara, marries her himself, and subsequently cures Tobit's blindness. *Tobit Transplanted* provides rational explanations for the seemingly miraculous or supernatural events. It is the only one of Benson's novels to conclude with two contented, solitary characters happily choosing the commitment of marriage. While all of Benson's novels have been noted for wit and humor, in *Tobit* she achieved some highly comic scenes. Benson believed that working within the frame provided by the existing story from the Apocrypha enabled her to write more easily with a detached outlook, a characteristic that had been increasingly important to her fiction since the novel *The Poor Man*. Despite the attention given *Tobit*, most critical notice of Benson's works ended with her death.

Benson's overfondness for the unusual word and the smart, epigrammic phrase were the faults most often noted by early critics of her novels. Too-frequent authorial intrusiveness, as well as sometimes overt didacticism, were also commonly noted flaws. Though frequently mentioned, these faults were often attributed to Benson's youth and inexperience as a novelist. *Stella Benson* by Bedell, the only major critical study of Benson's career since her death, found that a chronological study of her novels shows a clear development of her skills as a writer and a decrease in her early errors of inexperience. Cyril Connolly, however, found the same kind of clever pretentiousness in Benson's posthumously published unfinished novel *Mundos* as her earlier critics had found in her first novel. It should be noted, though, that Benson had requested that none of her incomplete works be printed after her death. Although Benson's works never became well known or widely popular, they did attract the notice and praise of a few prominent critics, including Katherine Mansfield, who applauded Benson's "exuberant fancy" and "love of life", and Christopher Morley, who noted at her death that Benson was one of the three or four novelists to whom he looked for "the cobweb strictures of perfection."

PRINCIPAL WORKS

I Pose (novel) 1915
This Is the End (novel) 1917
Twenty (poetry) 1918
Living Alone (novel) 1919
The Poor Man (novel) 1922
Pipers and a Dancer (novel) 1924
The Awakening (short stories) 1925
The Little World (travel essays) 1925
Goodbye, Stranger (novel) 1926
The Man Who Missed the Bus (short stories) 1928
Worlds within Worlds (travel essays and short stories) 1928
The Far-Away Bride (novel) 1930; published in England as *Tobit Transplanted*, 1931

Hope against Hope, and Other Stories   (short stories)
     1931
Christmas Formula, and Other Stories   (short stories)
     1932
Pull Devil, Pull Baker [with Count Nicolas De Toulouse
     Lautrec De Savine]   (essays and memoirs)   1933
Mundos   (unfinished novel)   1935
Collected Short Stories   (short stories)   1936

THE SPECTATOR   (essay date 1915)

[*The following excerpt, an anonymous review of Benson's first novel,* I Pose, *notes her talent and wit as a novelist, but criticizes the author's sometimes excessive intrusions into the narrative.*]

The entrance of a new writer of undoubted talent into the arena of fiction is a welcome incident at all times, and Miss Benson's talent is beyond question. But while she inspires admiration for her wit, her attitude and method render it hard to welcome her without reserves. To begin with, she represents an acute revolt against the theory which regards self-effacement on the part of the author as a supreme virtue. She not only lets us know what she thinks of her *dramatis personae,* but constantly intervenes with comments and asides and nods and nudges, and even recitals of her own experiences. . . . Passages in brackets abound in the earlier part of [*I Pose*]—*e.g.,* "You need not be afraid. There is not going to be so very much about the cause in this book"; or "Yes, I know that made you tremble, but there are not many more paragraphs of it." As a matter of fact, there is a good deal about "the [feminist] cause" in the book, and when we are told on the opening page that there are to be no deathbed scenes, the sequel prompts one to observe that there are other modes of distressing the reader which are quite as effective. For Miss Benson, though she states her aim to be that of amusing herself and instructing her reader, is not to be reckoned amongst those whose view of the function of the novelist is that of providing a sedative or an anodyne. And her method of instruction is not based on Montessorian methods. Her love of her fellow-creatures—and she confesses that she loves her heroine, the militant suffragette, "perhaps a good deal"—is combined with a remarkable capacity for exhibiting them in their most unlovely and unlovable aspects. The only "healthy and human" person in the story is greedy, fat, and vulgar. The principal male character is an insufferable egoist, and a coward into the bargain. There is no one in the book who inspires affection; for at most one can only feel compassion for the heroine; and some of the characters are designed to excite contempt or derision. . . . It may be urged that to criticize *I Pose* seriously is to break a butterfly on the wheel, if not indeed to misinterpret its aim entirely. And the objection would hold good if the tone of the opening pages were maintained throughout. *I Pose* begins as an extravagantly fantastic comedy, but it is not long before we discover a vein of deadly earnest behind a mask of somewhat feverish levity. This is foreshadowed in the poem which serves as prologue, and confirmed in the verses which precede the last chapter, which glorify the ecstasy of loneliness, proclaim a sovereign contempt of those in whom the "precious venom" in their veins has run dry to merge themselves in the infinite. Miss Benson is careful to assure us in one of her asides that no militant society has commissioned her to write this book, and we can readily believe it. For while a strong undercurrent of sympathy with advanced feminism may be detected, she does not refrain from some mordant remarks at the expense of the self-protecting attitude of the nominal leaders who exploit the self-sacrifice of such fanatics as the heroine of *I Pose.* And, again, her love does not prevent her from exhibiting the heroine in moments of weakness, when she is magnetized by the personality of a wholly unworthy young man and for the time being sinks the militant in the woman. (p. 795)

A review of "I Pose," in The Spectator, *Vol. 15, No. 4562, December 4, 1915, pp. 795-96.*

THE TIMES LITERARY SUPPLEMENT   (essay date 1917)

[*In the following excerpt, an anonymous reviewer of* This Is the End *finds fault with Benson's tiresome cleverness and her sometimes incoherent ideas, but praises her imagination and descriptive powers.*]

"There is no reason in tangible things and no system in the ordinary ways of the world." This is the "unfinal conclusion" at which Miss Stella Benson has arrived; and hence the cryptic title, *This Is the End* . . . , which she has chosen for her book. What she is concerned to describe is not so much the doings of her characters as the day-dreams in which they seek refuge, when their little bodies are a-weary of this great world; it is not necessary to say more about them, as their business is to expound the author's views rather than their own.

A book about day-dreams by a writer with no belief in system is not the place to look for the well-knit tale or the coherent ideas which make for easy reading. In other ways, too, what Miss Benson writes ties the attention, she is too fond of the dramatic word to confine it to the important, with the result that her sentences are so uniformly clever that the reader will tire of her cleverness; indeed, if he is one of those dull arrogant fellows, he may say that phrases like "When you feel as tired as the night" and "Sentences of such pure construction that they were extremely difficult to understand" are too clever by half. We feel, in fact, that Miss Benson has either not yet found her medium or is protesting that a medium has no more existence than a system. Her smart phrases seem an incongruous dress for the longings and aspirations which are at the back of her thought, and at times they make us doubt her sincerity. Yet she is so sincere that she will insist on her conceptions to the point of defiance. For instance, "If I'm too poetic—like a swan—don't report me too accurately," purports to be the dying utterance of a youngster with a horror of romance. What rings false here is not so much that the speech itself is romantic, for dying men say strange things, but that it is too self-conscious for the speaker, whom the writer describes as simple and straightforward. . . .

It follows that Miss Benson often irritates when she means to stimulate; and if we have dwelt on this at some length it is because the irritation spoils our enjoyment of gifts of fancy and expression not often met with. There is an imaginative tenderness in what she writes about certain dead soldiers which shows her sensibility to be delicate, rare, and true; in one of the poems with which her chapters are interspersed, she finds just the right music for this feeling, and when she is describing coast scenery she makes us see it with her own seeing eyes. . . .

A review of "This Is the End," in The Times Literary Supplement, *No. 793, March 29, 1917, p. 152.*

THE TIMES LITERARY SUPPLEMENT   (essay date 1918)

[*In the following excerpt Benson's volume of poetry,* Twenty, *is criticized for obscurity and overriding cleverness. These faults, however, are considered to be those of youth and inexperience that the reviewer hopes Benson will overcome.*]

These three volumes [*Twenty,* by Stella Benson; *The Wind on the Downs,* by Marian Allen; and *Demeter,* by Eleanor Deane Hill] have little in common but their appearance at the same time and the sex and apparent ages of their writers. The cleverest is certainly Miss Benson's, as will be expected by the readers of her two novels. Several, indeed, of the twenty poems appeared in **This Is the End.** They attempt to express a depth of thought and feeling which in the prose pages of the novels is generally concealed by the almost horrible cleverness of what is on the surface. But even they do not escape the writer's besetting sin, of which she is not old enough to have seen the folly—that of wanting, before all things, to prove her own cleverness and daze and dumbfounder the slower brains of ordinary mortals. Several of these poems are intolerably obscure, with the obscurity of a riddle of which it is the maker's intent and pleasure to be sure that it will not be guessed. . . .

Now poetry is more than prose. It says what prose cannot say. . . . But every poem has, or should have, its logical anatomy or framework, bare in itself and lifeless, perhaps even ugly, but essential: the hard rock on which the house beautiful is built. This is often absent in Miss Benson's verses; and the consequent obscurity is a defect, and not what she has an air of fancying it to be—a merit. There are other defects of youth in the book. The desire to be independent and defiant produces such outbursts of the emancipated schoolgirl as "damned Philistine" addressed to the middle-aged and conventional. . . . But these are not very great matters. What is of more importance is that Miss Benson's little volume shows, with all its faults, real quality not only of brain, but of heart and imagination. Not one of her poems is a mere exercise; not one is commonplace mediocrity; in all she both succeeds and fails, and rouses the hope that presently she will succeed without failing. Her most ambitious poem, and perhaps her finest, **"The Slave of God,"** gives us once more the moon as the prize of romance for which the poet and the lover are ready to be wrecked on any seas. But the treatment of the theme is quite original; and it is perhaps characteristic of the poet and of our day that, when the impossible quest had failed, God gave the seeker not madness, not death, but "vulgar love and speech, and gave him threescore years and ten."

> *"Three Poetesses," in* The Times Literary Supplement, *No. 860, July 11, 1918, p. 333.**

KATHERINE MANSFIELD   (essay date 1919)

[*Mansfield was a pioneer in stream-of-consciousness literature and among the first English authors whose fiction depended upon incident rather than plot, a development that significantly influenced the modern short story form. Throughout 1919 and 1920, Mansfield conducted a weekly book-review column in* The Athenaeum, *a magazine edited at the time by her husband, John Middleton Murry. In the following excerpt from an approbatory review of* Living Alone *originally published in* The Athenaeum *in 1919, Mansfield hails Benson as "a born writer."*]

Whereas Miss Stella Benson declares that [*Living Alone*] is not a real book—it does not deal with real people nor should it be read by them—we feel that Miss Romer Wilson would say the exact opposite of her novel, 'If All these Young Men.' Both

are about the war. We suppose it will be long and long before the novelist, looking about him for a little wood wherewith to light his fire, does not turn instinctively to that immense beach strewn with wreckage. But Miss Stella Benson gives us the impression of having found herself there by chance, and being there she has picked up her charming broomstick, Harold. . . . (p. 108)

Miss Wilson's theme is the effect the war has upon the minds and hearts of a number of highly modern young persons living in England during the terribly critical months of 1918. There is no plot, but there is a principal character, Josephine Miller, the 'star' of the company, who, at a word from here, a wave from there, and a glance at the scenery, gathers the scattered emotions of the moment into her bosom and pours them forth in song. (pp. 108-09)

The heroine of Miss Stella Benson's novel is as subject to flights as Josephine, but she has her justification. She is a witch. She has also her broomstick, Harold, a very faithful, helpful creature. 'Witches,' according to Miss Benson, 'are people who are born for the first time. . . . Remembering nothing, they know nothing and are not bored. . . . Magic people . . . are never subtle, and though they are new they are never Modern.' Their common behaviour is, in fact, like that of people who are in love for the first time and for ever.

This little alien book describes the adventures of Angela and the adventures of those with whom she comes in contact while she is caretaker of a small general shop which is also part convent and monastery, part nursing home and college, and wholly a house for those who wish to live alone. She is an out-and-out, thorough witch, a trifle defiant, poor, always hungry, intolerant of cleverness and—radiant. It is her radiance above all which pervades everything, chasing over the pages like sunlight. For the minority who are magically inclined it is impossible to resist, and, since she has expressly told the real people that they are not invited to her party, what does it matter if they pass the lighted windows with a curl of the lip? We have said that **Living Alone** is a book about the war. There is an Air Raid described, from below and from above, together with a frightful encounter which Harold has with a German broomstick, and one of the inmates of the house of Living Alone is Peony, a London girl who is drawing her weekly money as a soldier's wife—unmarried. The story that Peony tells her fellow-lodger Sarah Brown of how she found the everlasting boy is perhaps the high-water mark of Miss Benson's book. It is full of most exquisite feeling and tenderness. We hardly dare to use the thumb-marked phrase, a 'born writer'; but if it means anything Miss Stella Benson is one. She seems to write without ease, without effort; she is like a child gathering flowers. And like a child, there are moments when she picks the flowers which are at hand just because they are so easy to gather, but which are not real flowers at all, and forgets to throw them away. This is a little pity, but exuberant fancy is rare, love of life is rare, and a writer who is not ashamed of happiness rarer than both. (pp. 111-12)

> Katherine Mansfield, *"A 'Real' Book and an Unreal One," in her* Novels and Novelists, *edited by J. Middleton Murry, Alfred A. Knopf, 1930, pp. 108-12.*

R. BRIMLEY JOHNSON   (essay date 1920)

[*Johnson surveys Benson's early career, noting her skilled presentation of an imaginative "fairyland" or dream world in her second and third novels,* This Is the End *and* Living Alone. *John-*

son contends that with these works, Benson has supplied "a new landscape in fiction, a new creation of art."]

Our first impressions of Miss Stella Benson are rather bewildering: bewildering, because while she has an exceptionally firm grip of realities, her heart dwells with the unreal.

"I Pose" was principally concerned with plain men and women, playing a part indeed, but subject to the ordinary limitations of humanity. **"This Is the End"** revealed a strange commingling of war-time flesh and blood characters with a marvellous dream-life of the sea-shore: of **"Living Alone"** she writes frankly: "This is not a real book. It does not deal with real people, nor should it be read by real people."

The pioneer women-novelists all practised realism, as their contribution to the historical development of English fiction: realism, again, was certainly the prevalent note of late nineteenth century writers. Those of the twentieth have not escaped the tradition: but some of them have imposed thereon a new mysticism (perhaps the most interesting aftermath of war-mentality) which seems to indicate at once looking backward and straining ahead. At present this does not amount to a new philosophy of life; though Miss Benson, for example, can reflect and generalise. She declares that "one dies as one lives, in a little ordinary way, and that there is no glory between people who don't lie to one another." She sees "the whole world as a thing running away from its thoughts": and . . . she finds "nothing in the world but second bests." (pp. 163-64)

It would be obviously unreasonable to expect any complete or ordered philosophy from youth: while the world is in the melting-pot. Miss Benson, indeed, is not essentially a revolter—like her "suffragette"; though she does not accept convention, authority, or tradition. A complete view of her attitude leaves rather the impression of one dissatisfied, though sympathising, with average humanity—as represented by "the Family": a wanderer not without hope: seeking somewhere in the "Parish of Faery" (with which she is not altogether unfamiliar) for something that may prove at least more satisfying, if not actually an interpretation.

It is possibly to emphasize the beautiful possibilities of this beautiful dream-world, that she has introduced (in all three novels) the vivid atmosphere of Brown Borough; where true "palliness" means "a drop and a jaw together." And here, strangely enough, she seems thoroughly at home. Whether it be through the Suffragettes' honest attempt at uplifting (poisoned by clerical interference); through Jay's genial ambition to "'urry and get drunk" with Mrs. Love, and "keep 'and in 'and all the time"; or through the "Committee" and Sarah Brown's office for "collecting evidence from charitable spies about the naughty poor"; Miss Benson knows these people and those, officially or unofficially, at work among them. Just as always and everywhere, despite a flavour of aloofness or inhumanity, she loves children with understanding; she is equally at home with East End Girls' Clubs, the men and women of the "mean streets," or the Vicar who honestly regards Trade Unions (at least for women) as a wile of the devil. It is, I think, really an admirable study in understanding to compare Jay's true comradeship in the joys of the slum-life, with the sorrows and tragedies which the Suffragette strives to relieve. To understand Happiness is more difficult, and quite as helpful, as to sympathise with grief. It is a rare gift.

One may notice, in passing, that Miss Benson has, no doubt unconsciously, followed the wisdom of the pioneers. Like Jane Austen and other great early women novelists, she only attempts to exhibit this rare insight for her own sex. Here she writes as a woman for women, and the limitation is most prudent. It ensures success. We do not, indeed, claim for her any power that is positively unique. Other writers understand "the Poor"—individually. But it is remarkable in Miss Benson, because of her strong leanings towards mysticism, and the curious position of her other character-types. She can observe and reflect.

The persons in **"I Pose,"** indeed, cannot be fitted into any pigeon-hole. They are, fortunately, as far removed from the typical "modern" (with its obsession for sex and its passion for ugliness) as from the Victorian "sentimental." But, superficially, they live much like ordinary folk: their experiences are human, if unusual. They are, indeed, born tramps—though more addicted to "passing by" than to adventure; having no special interest in Savages, Super-men or the Antique; no craving for Wild Lands or Lone Seas.

In **"This is the End"** and **"Living Alone,"** Miss Benson seems to have discovered a new century and, if one may so express her, a new humanity. . . . We meet here with horses and suit cases, dogs and broomsticks, who can talk: and at least one dragon, strangely employed as foreman to faery farm-labourers. The unconventional witch rides a conventional broomstick: the man of magic produces thunderstorms, and travels "by flash of lightning": a mayor is rendered invisible.

Speaking generally, the human characters here are happier than most; because they possess the secret of two lives—one material, the other visionary. And it is in their dreams they are most themselves. (pp. 164-67)

Miss Benson has given us something which we cannot find, and never have known, elsewhere: a new landscape in fiction, a new creation of art: which, if not normal, is yet a positive contribution to human experience and the possible developments of human nature; a new hint towards the Mystery of the Soul—not like the frankly inhuman legends of faery, the idle vision of a dream.

To such unconventional material, obviously, it is not easy to apply the ordinary critical tests. Like all reformers, Miss Benson adopts certain mannerisms which really deform her art. (p. 169)

The majority of modern writers do not aim at style in the conventional sense; and . . . Miss Benson may have a specific reason, quite justifiable, for adopting the colloquial jerkiness which her contemporaries seem to have learnt from America. Nevertheless, she would be none the worse for more careful grammar, and for some of that composed dignity which we of the older days have been used to consider essential to good writing. This she could clearly accomplish with ease, as one sees from the poetry interspersed and from several poetic passages of description. The truly imaginative have always—style.

Miss Benson, however, does not neglect construction. **"I Pose"** is put together and completed with a vigorous feeling for drama. It is a finished tale, the record of characters developed consistently to an inevitable denouement. Even in **"This Is the End"** we have a *contained* episode, and **"Living Alone"** leaves off at the end. Nevertheless, the conventionality, here, may be more apparent than real. Certainly, the gardener and the suffragette pass through the stages proper to fiction, or drama:—antipathy, attraction, misunderstanding, and tragedy—on the eve of an happy ending. Like the ordinary hero and heroine, they suffer mainly from the (well-meaning or malicious) interference of outsiders. In **"This Is the End,"** again, Jay has her dreams (amid sordid surroundings, following the Family split) and, after the shock of her brother's death, marries the rather "impossible" lover—a thoroughly good sort—whom in her moments of exaltation, she had found inadequate. **"Living Alone,"** too, is a complete episode—of magic, vividly war-inspired. . . . (pp. 170-71)

Miss Benson is less independent than many of her contemporaries. Having handled a topic, she finishes with it: having exhibited a character, or an episode, she closes it. She does not merely stop. Only her sense of proportion is rather uncertain. The central figure wanders, rather frequently, into a bye-path. Important issues are introduced, and remain ragged.

Miss Benson, however, is well-equipped in what may be called the paraphernalia of fiction. She has very considerable humour—on original methods; and much aptness in turning a phrase. Even her generalities, which as a rule the novelist does well to avoid, often suggest real thought. She is sympathetically observant—for all her waywardness—and her dialogue is dramatic. If you accept the characters (and criticism should rather accept than demand) you will admit that their talk is revealing and, nearly always, inevitable. Constantly we come upon the epigram that arrests. . . . Everywhere the point of view is quite clear and quite individual.

And finally I would maintain the apparent paradox that Miss Benson derives her strength from her humanity. However unusual her characters, however unique their experience, they are real people. Whether or no she would repudiate the applause, she does fulfil the true functions of all art—which are to tell a tale and to give pleasure. And part of that pleasure is (consciously or unconsciously) produced by good art; pervading and overmastering the superficial perversities of artifice. (pp.171-72)

Her emotions are poignant, because they are neither over-analysed nor naked. She is, of course, introspective, or she would not be modern: but, on the other hand, she is not morbid or uncouth. At times, she would seem out of touch with the actual and, in moments of egoism, loses her sense of proportion: but she responds at once to simplicity and the kind act. (p. 173)

It would not, in fact, be at all just to speak of Miss Benson as an unhealthy writer. Being fortunately quite feminine, she—still more fortunately—does not worry herself about the Decadent or the Super-man. There is a spring, a flush, and a gusto about her work which is positively refreshing. Without ignoring, or failing in sympathy with, the world's heart ache; she has given us a new youth, hopeful for all its puzzlement over cheap ugliness, wasted chances, and cruel stupidity. Missing the full-blooded Chestertonian optimism, she is yet mistress of secret occasions for happiness, somewhat akin to J. M. Barrie's. Though, may be, a little vague about right and wrong, rather uncertain about the whence and the whither; because she dreams of real men and of real women, her dreams are strong. (p. 174)

R. Brimley Johnson, "Stella Benson," in his *Some Contemporary Novelists (Women), 1920. Reprint by Books for Libraries Press; distributed by Arno Press, Inc., 1967, pp. 161-74.*

JOSEPH COLLINS (essay date 1923)

[*Collins is a physician and essayist who has written the literary studies* The Doctor Looks at Literature *(1923),* Taking the Literary Pulse *(1924), and* The Doctor Looks at Biography *(1925). In the following excerpt Collins briefly surveys Benson's career, praising her development and concluding that she is becoming one of England's most interesting female novelists.*]

Miss Stella Benson and Mrs. Virginia Woolf are young women who have come to the fore very rapidly. The former, who lived in this country for two years after the war, published in 1915, when she was barely out of her teens, a novel called **"I Pose"** which revealed an unusual personality with an uncommon outlook on life, and an enviable capacity to describe what she saw, felt, and fabricated. Until the appearance of her last novel it might be said that she created types which symbolised her ideas and attitudes and gave expression to them through conveniently devised situations, rather than attempting to paint models from life and placing them in a realistic environment.

"I Pose" is a story of allegorical cast lightened with flashes of whimsical sprightliness. A pensive Gardener who likes to pose as "original," a Suffragette who disguises romance under a mask of militancy, a practical girl, Courtesy, and a number of others take an ocean voyage and have many adventures. . . .

For the setting of her two succeeding books, **"This Is the End,"** and **"Living Alone,"** Miss Benson created a world of her own. . . . (p. 181)

Her world is not the traditional fairyland of the nursery, nor are the supernatural endowments of some of the characters the classic equipment of witches and fairies, although her *dramatis personæ* include both who function under the law of Magic. Rather is her dramatic machinery in these books a vehicle in the form of a sort of delicate symbolism for getting over a very sane attitude toward certain social foibles and trends of today. Incidentally it gives her opportunity of expressing this attitude in frequent witticisms and epigrammatic sayings for which she has a gift. In **"Living Alone"** social service and organised charity are the targets for her irony. (p. 182)

Miss Benson gives the artist in her what is called "rope." She doesn't ask herself, "Will people think I am mad, or infantile?" She doesn't care what "people think." And that is an encouraging sign. Women writers will come to their estates more quickly and securely the more wholeheartedly they abandon themselves to portraying instincts as they experience them, behaviour as they observe it, motives and conduct as they sense and encounter them, accomplishments and aspirations as they idealise them, the ideals being founded, like the chances of race horses, on past performances.

In her last novel, **"The Poor Man,"** Miss Benson's art shows tremendous development. This story is characterisation in the finest sense. Edward, the poor man, as a psychological study, is living, vivid, almost tragically real in the reactions which betray his inherent defects—a poor devil who never gets a chance. Miss Benson preaches no sermon, points no moral, makes no plea. She gives us a slice of life—and gives it relentlessly, but justly. It is the Old Testament justice which visits the iniquity of the father upon the third and fourth generations, and leaves the reader with the congenial task of finishing the sentence by supplying the mercy without which this old world could hardly totter under the weight of this Commandment. The story, however, makes no reference either to eugenics or to religion. The application is for the reader to supply—if he is so inclined. The author is not concerned with "science," but with art. She does not bore us with a history of Edward's heredity or of his early life. (p. 185)

If one were obliged to confine himself to backing one entry in the Fiction Sweepstakes now being run in England (entries limited to women above ten and under forty), he would do well to consider carefully the Stella Benson entry. (p. 186)

> Joseph Collins, "Two Lesser Literary Ladies of London: Stella Benson and Virginia Woolf," in his The Doctor Looks at Literature: Psychological Studies of Life and Letters, George H. Doran Company, 1923, pp. 181-90.*

THE SATURDAY REVIEW OF LITERATURE   (essay date 1925)

[In the following excerpt, Benson's first volume of collected travel essays, The Little World, is praised for its originality and wit.]

Have no fears that **"The Little World"** is not interesting and well-written and clever and alive. Stella Benson is never, in any of these respects, a disappointment; she is too expert a journalist to fail the readers who for her sake alone will wander through India and China, and go across the American continent, and touch Africa, and swelter in Aden. She makes these wanderings, usually so banal, as absorbing exhibitions as they could be, and more absorbing than probably any other contemporary writer could make them. Her publishers are justified in saying that she avoids the commonplace and sees things in a new and original light. For one thing, she is often wise enough not to see things steadily and see them whole. In sketches of travel the whole of a view or an experience or an exotic impression is not likely to be half so attractive as a certain few of its details; beyond question only a few of the details can be original. Miss Benson goes in for these details, for oblique views, for undiscovered stances, for personality-plus handlings of the situation. She is personal, and she is what can best be termed impressionistic.

At the same time her keen journalistic sense prevents her from being tenuous and jerky and indeterminate: she is not a creator of the familiar variety of "vignette." . . . Also, she gives us, however individual the presentation, what she actually sees. She has imagination, and poetry, and style, and color, and second-sight; but in distinction to writers who can meet the world of concrete loveliness only with abstract descriptions, and the world of beauty only with rhapsody, she presents what she actually sees, and the reader sees what she presents. This is how she conducts one through Yunnan, and Indo-China, and Aden, and New Mexico.

Miss Benson has whipped **"The Little World"** together with an abundance of cleverness. Its gaily satiric bits, its witty observations, its expert garnering of humorous details, make the brine salty enough to prevent the possibility of failure from other sources. . . . [This] is neither a boring nor an insipid book. It is, as it should be, good journalism, for most of it first saw print in newspapers and periodicals. Not that Miss Benson has not half an eye on the *literati*, as when she calls three young egrets Edith, Osbert, and Sacheverell. Of sketches which were born separately, and first printed so, it is not unfair to say that even now one will enjoy them best reading a few at a time. They have about them too much of Miss Benson's personality, and they are too much of a geographical *pot-pourri*, to captivate at a single sitting.

> "Lively Sketches," in The Saturday Review of Literature, Vol. II, No. 1, December 5, 1925, p. 364.

L. P. HARTLEY   (essay date 1926)

[Author of the acclaimed novel trilogy Eustace and Hilda (1944-47), Hartley was an English novelist and short story writer whose fiction is unified by the theme of the search for individuality and meaning in the modern world. In his examination of moral dilemmas he is often compared to Nathaniel Hawthorne, while his effective use of symbolism and close attention to craft and plot unity evoke frequent comparisons to the works of Henry James. A literary critic as well, Hartley contributed reviews for many years to The Saturday Review, Time and Tide, The Spectator, and other periodicals. In the following excerpt, Hartley finds that all of Benson's novels exhibit richness, delicacy, wit, and insight. Goodbye, Stranger, which he does not rank with her best novels, is nevertheless found to be full of vitality.]

Miss Stella Benson is an *enfant terrible* among contemporary novelists; charming, naughty, angelic, tiresome by turns: but rarely "good." Goodness is a quality for which, in her last book, she seems to be making a haphazard search; but whenever she comes upon its likeness she points rudely and makes faces at it. Her mind is still occupied with the enigma of modern American civilization. Her heroine [in *Goodbye, Stranger*], Daley Cotton, is an American married to an Englishman, Clifford Cotton, who is apparently crazy. He is obsessed by the desire to be like an ordinary man, a desire which, as anyone familiar with Miss Benson's work will know, is scarcely likely to be gratified between the covers of her books. . . .

As the incarnation of America, radiating kindliness and longing wistfully to have safe, good thoughts, [Daley] is excellent; and she says some very good things. It is one of Miss Benson's shortcomings that she cannot bring herself to let the stupid stew quietly in their stupidity; ever and again a bubble of wit disturbs their viscous surface. Even the idiotic Mrs. Lorne must have been very good company. But the weakness of the book lies in the fundamental restlessness of Miss Benson's mind. It is a brilliant, provocative mind, quick as a needle, impatient of checks. But it is always in a high fever and Miss Benson never waits to let the temperature go down. All "values," relationships, events are keyed so high that the attention, straining after them, can only take in isolated effects, and wearies of this dazzling pointillism. One could not read *Goodbye, Stranger* without being disturbed and excited; one could hardly read it without laughter, one might read it with tears. It has enough vitality in one page to galvanize a dozen ordinary novels. But it has not solidity enough to absorb its own recoil. National differences, the contrast between Lena's starved nature and Daley's rich one, these themes, considerable as they are, are not substantial enough to bear the racket that takes place upon them. But what richness, what delicacy, what wit, what insight does not Miss Benson always exhibit! *Goodbye Stranger* has all these qualities, even if it is not quite in the fore-front of her novels.

> L. P. Hartley, in a review of "Goodbye, Stranger," in The Saturday Review, London, Vol. 142, No. 3711, December 11, 1926, p. 737.

V. S. PRITCHETT   (essay date 1933)

[Pritchett is a highly esteemed English novelist, short story writer, and critic. Considered one of the modern masters of the short story, he is also considered one of the world's most respected and well-read literary critics. Pritchett writes in the conversational tone of the familiar essay, a method by which he approaches literature from the viewpoint of a lettered but not overly scholarly reader. A twentieth-century successor to such early nineteenth-

century essayist-critics as William Hazlitt and Charles Lamb, Pritchett employs much the same critical method: his own experience, judgment, and sense of literary art are emphasized, rather than a codified critical doctrine derived from a school of psychological or philosophical speculation. His criticism is often described as fair, reliable, and insightful. In the following excerpt, Pritchett reviews Pull Devil, Pull Baker, *which purports to be Benson's edition of the reminiscences of a deposed White Russian count. The periodical* Transition, *mentioned in the essay, was a monthly "little magazine" founded in Paris by Eugene Jolas and Elliot Paul. Believing that the literary imagination of the time was too photographic, they sought new ways of expressing such states of mind as dream and hallucination through the use of new words and arbitrarily imposed rules of grammar.*]

One has heard fantastic stories about the White Russian refugees who beg, borrow or steal a living in places like Hong Kong and Shanghai, but it would be difficult for any of his wildest compatriots to surpass the adventures and above all the style of the Count Toulouse de Lautrec de Savine, as edited by Miss Stella Benson [in ***Pull Devil, Pull Baker***].

It may be that the Count is a preposterous humbug and it is certain that, like the gentleman who sang of Agib Prince of Tartary, he is "shaky in his dates." He would, for example, be quite equal to describing how he met Napoleon. But if he is a humbug, he is one of the inspired, the splendid creatures who without a penny in their pockets (which has long been the aged Count's lot) live in an imaginary world of dashing romance, adventure and "loving stories," made all the more Romantic, Adventurous and Loving by the passage of time. It is doubtful, even if he had avoided politics, as he says Tolstoy advised him to do, that he would have been a Munchausen or a Cellini; but as it is, if the editor of *Transition* really does found a new language, Count Nicolas's fragmentary reminiscences stand a chance . . . of being a classic, a kind of *Beowulf,* of a new and not unpleasantly dubious literary age. Later, quotation will illustrate our meaning.

In the meantime we must accept Miss Benson's assurance that the Count is a real person. . . . He is a Russian who claims to be descended from the Kings of Toulouse, and the Savine is the Russianized Sévigné, the family having fled to Russia after the revocation of the Edict of Nantes. His main point, insisted upon throughout this narrative, is that he is of "hyg aristocratic famelys of Russia, who had nothing in commun with the pepels" and that his arrival everywhere "make Grand Sansation."

[Now] he lives down and out in China, on his gorgeous past, telling stories for food, and filling them with denunciations or eulogies of everything and everybody. He is one of those delightful people who, as Miss Benson points out, Know Where Everybody Is Wrong. If Kerensky had only taken his advice, if Lenine had listened, if the Tsar had thought, if Tolstoy and Karl Marx had only realized—in the middle of even the most "lovely story" these views may leap from the mouth of any character. The whole narrative may cease in order that nine pages in praise of his ancestry may see the light. . . .

To attempt the plots of his "loving stories," to outline his travels and catalogue his catastrophes, to deal with delights like "Shemful Story of Ant Ema" would be cruelty to such a stylist. The type has slipped and his tall stories become round, rich, naive and human. Miss Benson's part has been to play an acid Sancho to his Quixote, to sandwich between chapters a commentary of her own. Some of this is very amusing, some rather tiresome. Her chapter on his spelling is excellent. She tells us that she first discovered the old gentleman lying in a

Hong Kong hospital denouncing "the commun peopels" to the disgust of the neighboring poor, and that she persuaded him to write down these memories on odd bits of paper which she has stitched, patched and put into shape in a manner fitting to his "hyg aristocratic" past—"the story of a man who never got tired of anything—least of all himself."

V. S. Pritchett, "Trader Nicholas," in The Christian Science Monitor, *April 29, 1933, p. 8.*

STELLA BENSON   (essay date 1933)

[*In the following excerpt, Benson summarizes her literary career. Maintaining that as time passes an author's motivations for writing change, Benson lists her own novels and briefly explains her mood while writing and her reasons for writing each.*]

If one could live on a consistent plan, I suppose it would be possible to write on a consistent plan. But short of this ideal— if it be an ideal—I do not know how anyone can discuss his or her work as though it had followed any definite, conscious path of development through the changes of youth and middle age. I wonder if many writers, as they approach middle age, feel that all the writings of their youth were written by mistake, or under the influence of moods that seemed to lead nowhere and to prove nothing. Actually, I suppose, there is no inconsequence and no dislocation in the development of a human mind; the sequence exists, though not in that realm of conscious intelligence that our vanity would like to analyse.

My first book, *I Pose,* was written in order to Show Off; it was an exercise in deliberate self-revelation, as I imagine all books by authors in their early twenties are—except books by those rare persons whose minds spring into the world fully armed in serenity and detachment.

This Is the End was written in a mood of innocent and bloodless romance—a mood in which visions seem to be things in themselves, not symbols of reality or escapes from reality. I wrote *Twenty,* my book of verses, in the same mood—the mood in which one puts one's trust in (fairy) princes.

Living Alone was a rather more sophisticated approach to fairies—and this was the first of my books the writing of which interested me impersonally—the first, in fact, that was in some measure a book about *other people,* not only about myself in different masochistic or romantic or inverted guises. *Now,* I think that no novel is worth reading unless it is about *other people*—with oneself (if oneself must enter at all) only as one centre among many centres.

The Poor Man was written in a mood of revulsion against visions, and for this reason was a very formless and—in a sense—an even more immature book than its predecessors. In writing, one returns to immaturity in the same way as a little boy, who leaves his private school as a confident senior, finds himself again a trembling little boy at his public school—and yet, though at first he may not appreciate it, he is an older little boy in an older world; his tremblings and hesitancies now are induced by bogeys more nearly real and more difficult to placate. The approach to *The Poor Man* himself, I think, shows the first admission on my part of a principle that now seems important to me—the refusal to imply an *ought* or an *ought not* . . . the withholding of comment.

Pipers and a Dancer is, I think, written more as a whole than those books of mine that preceded it. I do not know how to make a really shapely frame for a book, so to speak, but *Pipers and a Dancer* was given a kind of shape by the fact that it was written rather coldly and deliberately—much more coldly than was *The Poor Man.*

In writing *Goodbye, Stranger,* I forgot my dislike of taking sides—and the book is unfortunately full of personal bias and personal appeals, with a refrain of This is Right, and This is Wrong which I now think most unnecessary.

The two travel-books—*The Little World,* and *Worlds Within Worlds*—were simply magazine articles and sketches brought together, only a few of which particularly interested me to write. It always, however, amuses me to write down any experience or incident in words as exact as I can find; probably most other journalists share my illusion that a happening is not complete—has not quite finished happening—until words for it have been found. (pp. 39-41)

My last novel, *Tobit Transplanted,* being written within a fixed frame (the frame provided by the apocryphal story), allowed me greater scope than usual for detachment of outlook. It is my first really consistent attempt to record, as honestly as was possible to me the point of view of people *as other people*—not as people seen by me or seen through myself, but people *seeing* by themselves—each from the vantage point of his own identity. If there be any *ought* or *ought not*—any *right* or *wrong*—implied in this book, it is a mistake. People in themselves and things in themselves, I think, are a study that has no limits at all, and, speaking for myself, I am convinced that to write *what I think* of people and things, in novel writing, is to place an arbitrary limit upon such vision as I have. (p. 42)

> Stella Benson, *"About My Books,"* in Ten Contemporaries: Notes Toward Their Definitive Bibliography, *by John Gawsworth, Joiner and Steele Ltd., 1933, pp. 39-42.*

VIRGINIA WOOLF   (diary date 1933)

[*Woolf is considered one of the most prominent literary figures of twentieth-century English literature. Like her contemporary James Joyce, with whom she is often compared, Woolf is remembered as one of the most innovative of the stream-of-consciousness novelists. Concerned primarily with depicting the life of the mind, she revolted against traditional narrative techniques and developed her own highly individualized style. Woolf's works, noted for their subjective explorations of characters' inner lives and their delicate poetic quality, have had a lasting effect on the art of the novel. A discerning and influential critic and essayist as well as a novelist, Woolf began writing reviews for The Times Literary Supplement at an early age. Her critical essays, which cover almost the entire range of English literature, contain some of her finest prose and are praised for their insight. Along with Lytton Strachey, Roger Fry, Clive Bell, and several others, Woolf and her husband Leonard formed the literary coterie known as the "Bloomsbury Group." In the following journal entry, Woolf reflects on hearing of Stella Benson's death.*]

I was walking through Leicester Square—how far from China—just now when I read "Death of Noted Novelist" on the posters. And I thought of Hugh Walpole. But it is Stella Benson. Then why write anything, immediately? I did not know her; but have a sense of those fine patient eyes: the weak voice; the cough; the sense of oppression. She sat on the terrace with me at Rodmell. And now, so quickly, it is gone, what might have been a friendship. Trusty and patient and very sincere—I think of her; trying to cut through, in one of those difficult evenings, to some deeper layer—certainly we could have reached it, given the chance. I'm glad I stopped her at the door as she got into her little car and asked her to call me Virginia—to write to me. And she said: "There's nothing I should like better." But it's like the quenching—her death out there in China; and I sitting here and writing about her and so fugitive and yet so true; and no more to come. How mournful the afternoon seems, with the newspaper carts(?) dashing up Kingsway, "Death of Noted Novelist" on the placard. A very fine steady mind: much suffering; suppressed;—there seems to be some sort of reproach to me in her death, as in K. M.'s [Katherine Mansfield's]. I go on; and they cease. Why? Why not my name on the posters? And I have a feeling of the protest each might make: gone with their work unfinished—each so suddenly. Stella was 41. "I am going to send you my book" and so on. A dreary island she lived on, talking to colonels. A curious feeling, when a writer like S. B. dies, that one's response is diminished: *Here and Now* won't be lit up by her: it's life lessened. My effusion—what I send out—less porous and radiant—as if the thinking stuff were a web that were fertilised only by other people's (her that is) thinking it too: now lacks life. (pp. 206-07)

> Virginia Woolf, in a diary entry of December 7, 1933, in her A Writer's Diary: Being Extracts from the Diary of Virginia Woolf, *edited by Leonard Woolf, 1953. Reprint by Harcourt Brace Jovanovich, 1954, pp. 206-07.*

CYRIL CONNOLLY   (essay date 1935)

[*Connolly was an English novelist and critic who reviewed books for the* New Statesman, The Observer, *and* The Sunday Times *from 1927 until his death in 1974. He was also the founding editor of the respected literary monthly* Horizon *(1939-50) and was considered a remarkably hard-to-please critic. In the following excerpt, Connolly criticizes* Mundos, *a posthumously published novel fragment, for the same fault that early reviewers found in Benson's first novels—"the pretentiousness of a clever woman showing off."*]

Mundos . . . acknowledges a debt to Mrs. Woolf. *Mrs. Dalloway,* in fact, in her vague way, must have originated as much pretension and unhappiness as Greta Garbo. Apart from that, a posthumous novel is always a disappointment, partly because the inflation which publicity now ensures a living author is matched by a corresponding intensity of oblivion when he is dead—such writers as Arnold Bennett, Galsworthy and Edgar Wallace are now sleeping off their Ballyhoo—and partly because there is usually a good reason why the posthumous work was not previously published. *Mundos* is both unfinished and a not very good example of the work of the author. It is a novel about a small West Indian island, where a doctrinaire governor, with a deformed intelligent son and a silly wife, tries to enforce unwanted reforms on a refractory population. There is a murder, a love-affair, the beginnings of a ruritanian revolution. Miss Benson was highly gifted and sometimes wrote exceedingly well. *Mundos* is often readable and amusing, but on the whole reveals only the faults of cleverness—the affectation, the febrility, the pretentiousness of a clever woman showing off. All the images are too far-fetched, and the sentiment is slightly rancid. The publishers explain that Miss Benson left a wish that none of her half-finished work should be published after her death, and that they thought otherwise.

> Cyril Connolly, in a review of "Mundos," in The New Statesman & Nation, n.s. Vol. IX, No. 218, April 27, 1935, pp. 594.

GEORGINA BATTISCOMBE   (essay date 1947)

[In the following excerpt, Battiscombe summarizes Benson's career, tracing the growth of her central theme "of the difficulty of making contact between person and person" and her later development of the theme of detachment, defined by Battiscombe as "the respect due to the unalienable right of every person, every sentient creature, to be itself." In attempting to determine Benson's place in literature, Battiscombe finds that a judgment based solely on the earlier novels earns Benson the reputation of an "entertaining, original writer," while her final works, Tobit Transplanted *and the uncompleted novel* Mundos *demonstrate that Benson had considerably developed her novel-writing talents and was at "the beginning and not the peak of her possible achievement" when she died.]*

In spite of the handicap of constant ill-health [Stella Benson] filled her short but eventful life with adventure, teaching in a mission school in Hongkong, watching tiger-shoots in Bengal, peddling school books in California, experiencing the excitement of an earthquake in the West Indies, and several times escaping narrowly from dangers of battle, murder and sudden death during the Chinese civil wars; yet all the time she remained the same Stella Benson, an observer who stood a little to one side of life, at once acutely sensitive and profoundly detached.

But if in essentials she remained the same the balance of her character changed, a change which is clearly reflected in her writing. Time and circumstances deepened her detachment, teaching her perhaps to use it as a shield for her too-sensitive spirit. Every artist is of necessity a person set slightly apart, but in the small circle of a remote Chinese station or the official and commercial society of such a place as Hongkong this isolation is inevitably stressed and exaggerated. Her early novels, *I Pose, This Is the End,* and *Living Alone,* are the work of some one young and romantic who has not yet learnt to be afraid of giving herself away. In these modern fairy-stories Stella Benson gives herself away with both hands, her dreams, her fantasy, her ideals, her youthful disillusionment. She underlines her points with reflections addressed direct to the reader, she sandwiches self-revealing verses in between her chapters of prose, she crams the whole of herself into the book without selection or discrimination. The result is, of course, an undisciplined and unsatisfactory novel; those who attempt to say everything at once end by saying nothing clearly.

Gradually, however, one or two characteristics develop and dominate the rest. In 1919 she spent several months in California, a period which greatly influenced the development both of her character and of her art. *The Poor Man,* published in 1923, is the fruit of her Californian experience. This novel marks the beginning of a new stage when she turns away from fairies and romance, though she remains fantastical. Edward and Emily of *The Poor Man* are not quite creatures of this earth. Yet Edward at least is bitterly real. He is the 'I,' the despicable 'I' that each one of us greets with horrified recognition in our rare moments of clearsightedness. . . . The early fairy-stories have their cynical moments but *The Poor Man* is Stella Benson at her most disillusioned. The book is a probing psychological operation performed under only the lightest anæsthetic of fantasy. Written as a realistic novel it would have been unbearable; in its present form it is only just to be borne because it stands at one remove from ordinary life. In the character of Edward, Stella Benson exposes to public view that self-distrust which is the most carefully concealed of all the skeletons hidden away in the cupboards of the soul. He suffered

those agonies which we all know but to which few of us ever admit. (pp. 208-09)

'It is simple and human,' Stella Benson once wrote, 'to pose a bit and not know you are posing. When you try to know yourself too well you devastate yourself.' She herself was the last person to act upon that piece of kindly wisdom. Forever striving to know herself down to the last unexplored corner of her brain (in the secret places of her heart she took much less interest), she would not let herself off the necessity for facing up to anything and everything that she might find in her explorations, and the result would have been devastating to her sensitive nature had it not been for her saving humour. Though she analysed herself and other people so acutely she took nobody entirely seriously, least of all Stella Benson. A curiously individual wit plays over all her books, not least *The Poor Man,* and makes tolerable a bitterness that could not otherwise be borne. And the very acuteness of her analytical mind has compensations. At times you may wriggle unavailingly beneath the probing knife but at others you cry out for pleasure at the unexpected and delightful accuracy of her description of your symptoms. Time and again you exclaim, 'Yes, of course, that is true; that is how *I* feel. But no one else has ever noticed.' . . . Incidentally, Stella Benson's deafness probably explains her preoccupation with the theme of shyness and embarrassment, her constant reiteration of the difficulty of making contact between person and person. (pp. 209-10)

Wit and perception help to lessen the acid taste of *The Poor Man,* and descriptive passages of a curious beauty act as a relief to the general bitterness of the novel. In Stella Benson's earlier books the descriptions are all too obviously purple, but in *The Poor Man* they have a lyrical character that contrasts oddly with their setting of satire. (pp. 210-11)

Brilliant though *The Poor Man* may be the fire of its brilliance burns with a cold flame that can never warm the heart. Stella Benson does not quite succeed in blending her strangely-assorted ingredients into a satisfactory whole; the mixture lacks the essential touch of humanity. The same criticism applies to *Goodbye Stranger* and *Pipes and a Dancer,* two books in which she makes a not entirely successful attempt to combine the 'fairy' manner of her earlier novels with the satire of *The Poor Man.* Then in 1931 she published *Tobit Transplanted,* and with this book came to the full height of her stature as a novelist. Hitherto she had not found a wholly satisfactory medium of expression; even the best of her previous books had been in the nature of promise rather than performance, leaving the reader with a sense of pleasurable expectancy as to what she might one day produce. In *Tobit Transplanted* promise is fulfilled, expectancy satisfied. The novel tells the Apocrypha story of Tobias and the Angel transposed into modern times and imagined as taking place among a colony of White Russians in Manchuria. The limits of the fable set a pattern for the story, a convention exactly suited to Stella Benson's talent, which was inventive of byepaths, but not particularly happy when confronted with the necessity of constructing a plot. Here at last she has combined comedy and romance, wit and lyricism into a harmonious whole, lit with understanding and sympathy for poor human beings in whose lives humour and tragedy are so inextricably mixed. The book met with great success, winning the Femina Vie Heureuse prize, but it is doubtful whether it was, or is likely to be, generally popular, in spite of the plaudits with which it was greeted. *Tobit Transplanted* is that rare thing, a witty novel, and there is nothing that the British and American public distrust more than wit, as opposed to humour, unless it be a story with an exotic setting, a drawback from which *Tobit* also suffers. (pp. 211-12)

Some of the best chapters in the book are pure comedy and many of the characters are figures in the grand comic tradition. . . . But the main theme of the book is a serious one, the urge that is in all human beings towards detachment, the quality which Stella Benson valued beyond anything except truth. By detachment she did not mean a chilly lack of feeling but the respect due to the unalienable right of every person, every sentient creature, to be itself. (p. 212)

This problem of detachment came to occupy Stella Benson's mind more and more, appearing even in her next book, which was in the nature of a *jeu d'esprit*. *Pull Devil, Pull Baker* was the result of an incongruous collaboration between Stella Benson and a disreputable old vagabond known as the Count of Toulouse-Lautrec de Savine. Stella Benson found this new Baron Munchausen stranded in hospital in Hongkong, penniless but rich in stories. 'Stories are his currency; he pays—or tries to pay—for everything with stories.' Partly from amusement, partly from a characteristic desire to help a 'down and out,' a generosity ill-repaid by the Count, Stella Benson conceived the idea of editing some of the stories for publication, the profits to be shared between the two oddly assorted collaborators. Interspersed among the Count's more incredible adventures, his *Loving Stories of My*, all written in his highly individual version of the English language, are Stella Benson's reflections on life in general and literature in particular. The Count is good fun for his own sake but the chief interest of the book lies in these comments by his editor. In *Tobit Transplanted* Stella Benson claims detachment as a right; now she admits it as a necessity of nature. Man cannot be otherwise

than detached because he can hold no real communication with his fellows. (pp. 212-13)

Pull Devil, Pull Baker was the last book that Stella Benson lived to complete, but she left behind her an unfinished novel entitled *Mundos,* published two years after her death. In this fragment, which touches, if it does not surpass, the high level she set herself with *Tobit Transplanted* she is again concerned with the problem of detachment, though superficially the book might pass as a piece of brilliant satire. Mundos is an island administered by the Colonial Office and any reader familiar with the smaller Crown Colonies or Dependencies will recognise with glee the wicked accuracy of Stella Benson's sketch. She is at her best and wittiest in such passages as her portrait of Sir Victor Cole, Governor of Mundos, 'a really excellent man who from first to last wanted the best for the colony in his charge,—but unfortunately it was always a different best from the one the colony wanted for itself,' her description of Lady Cole's tea-party, typical of all tea-parties given by Governors' wives the Empire over, her account of the chess-board of official society where

> as long as the pieces stay on the chess-board, treading their safe and consistent measure, refusing to try anything that has no precedent, they are exquisitely safe—safe from impertinence—safe from intrusion—above all, safe from challenge.

The real subject of the book, however, is not Sir Victor, who 'never thought but only planned; the impulses of his excellent brain were all outwards, the results of his private soliloquies were always public works,' nor even his ineffectual, endearing Phoebe, whose hat was 'always the first to break faith with

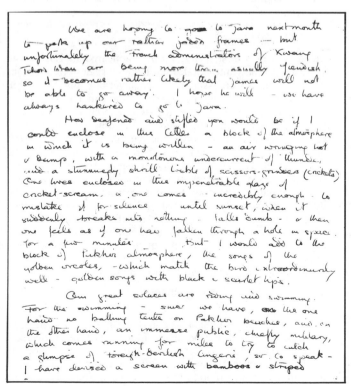

Facsimile of a letter from Benson to Winifred Holtby. From Portrait of Stella Benson, *by R. Ellis Roberts. Macmillan & Co. Ltd, 1939. Copyright. By permission of Macmillan, London and Basingstoke.*

the angle that bedroom mirrors had sanctioned' and whose son found her most enchanting 'when she behaves like an old goose.' The book's hero is that same son, Francis, a dwarf, whose physical deformity inevitably shuts him away from contact with his fellows. He is detachment personified. In **Pull Devil, Pull Baker** Stella Benson wrote, 'perhaps bodies are the only sanity. The machinery of my neighbour's body I can count on with a fair degree of confidence. . . . His body and my body are our common hold on sanity.' But what if the body be the insanely inadequate body of a dwarf? If bodies alone can meet and make contact on grounds of common likeness, spirits being for ever separate, a dwarf must be of all human beings the most detached. Yet to Francis alone, and not to any of the characters possessed of a normal body, comes the nearest approach to contact possible on this earth, that rare moment of perception when one human being sees in another 'the one real thing— the bone—shut away from clamour and thought, resentment and preference.' (pp. 213-14)

Being himself inevitably detached Francis respects and values this detachment in other people. Man is born to be lonely and he has a right to his loneliness. And not man only; everything in the heaven above and the earth beneath has a separate inviolable identity which must be accepted and valued for itself alone. (p. 214)

Stella Benson asks to be judged as an artist and nothing but an artist.

Her place in literature is hard to determine because she left behind her so little work that can be called mature. She was only forty-one when she died. Jane Austen died at forty-two, Charlotte Brontë at thirty-nine, Emily at thirty, and among the moderns, Katherine Mansfield at thirty-five, yet all these authors, even Emily Brontë, are far more easy to assess than Stella Benson. They had already found the right expression for their particular gifts at an age when she was still experimenting with her material. Coming late to artistic maturity she only 'found herself' with **Tobit Transplanted**. A direct line of succession can be traced from *Northanger Abbey* to *Persuasion*, but no such kinship exists between **Tobit** and **I Pose**, and the unfinished **Mundos** gives ample proof that **Tobit** was only the beginning and not the peak of her possible achievement. If she is to be judged on the greater part of her work she must be counted an entertaining, original writer, but no more; if it is possible to assess her only on her performance in **Tobit Transplanted** and her promise in **Mundos** she attains to a small but secure place in the front rank of modern novelists.

A comparison inevitably arises between Stella Benson and her contemporary Katherine Mansfield, a writer who was perhaps unduly praised in her own day and who is certainly unduly neglected now. The circumstances of their lives were curiously similar. Both had a natural talent for painting and for music as well as for literature, both were dogged by ill-health, both were obliged to spend a great part of their lives separated from their husbands and to forego that normal home life for which they craved, both were childless to their great sorrow, both died young. They never met in the flesh, but they knew and appreciated each other's work. Judging only from her books Katherine Mansfield describing Stella Benson as 'a very attractive creature,' adding, however, that 'she seems to me just to miss it.' (It must be remembered that this criticism is written twelve years before the publication of **Tobit Transplanted**.) (pp. 214-15)

Stella Benson was greatly influenced by Katherine Mansfield's Letters and Journal, recognising in them the mind of a writer who appeared to attain that integrity which was the goal of all her own effort. Higher than anything else in life or in art both of these writers valued truth. (p. 215)

It was in her method of seeking truth that Stella Benson differed from Katherine Mansfield. Detail for its own sake is one of the great characteristics of Katherine Mansfield's writing; she believed that the truth of a subject resided somehow in its detail. . . . Stella Benson saw only significant detail but Katherine Mansfield saw all detail as significant.

This absorption in detail is a manifestation of Katherine Mansfield's passion for life. She loved life, and in spite of the illness which cut her off from ordinary people and their interests, condemning her to a remote and almost frustrated existence, she touched life far more immediately than Stella Benson. 'She put her wits between herself and me,' says one of the characters in **The Poor Man**, 'a shining armour.' Stella Benson put the shining armour of her wit and her intelligence between herself and the intrusive world. (pp. 215-16)

> *Georgina Battiscombe, "Stella Benson," in* The Nineteenth Century and After, *Vol. CXLI, No. 842, April, 1947, pp. 208-16.*

R. MEREDITH BEDELL   (essay date 1983)

> [*Bedell's* Stella Benson *is the first book-length critical study of Benson's career. Bedell provides insightful and highly approbatory examinations of all of Benson's literary works, including the novels, travel books, and the lesser-known poetry and short stories, and concludes that Benson's contribution to literature is both original and significant. In particular, Bedell focuses on the role of women and feminist sympathies in Benson's novels. While writing her study, Bedell had access to Benson's unpublished correspondence and used this as the basis for an introductory biographical chapter that she claims corrects inaccuracies in the earlier biography of Benson by R. Ellis Roberts (see Additional Bibliography).*]

Stella Benson's first novel, *I Pose,* appeared in England in 1915 and in the United States the next year. In both countries women's rights were issues that, whatever one might have felt about them, one could not ignore. Nor can the subject be ignored in this novel. One of the two main characters is identified simply as "the Suffragette" (the other is simply "the Gardener"), and though only one episode is devoted to overt political activity (a women's march in London), the suffragette *does* repeatedly threaten to blow up property in protest for women's rights. However, the essential question in the novel is not, What can be done to improve society? The essential question is explicitly articulated in the final lines of the novel as the narrator confronts the problem of establishing identity: "Yes, I pose of course. But the question is—how deep may a pose extend?" As the smoke of the final explosion clears, the concerns of the narrator rise as the haunting question of identity and individual significance in an imperfect world.

The "I" of the title is the unnamed narrator of the story. . . . (p. 24)

I Pose, witty and indignant, is entertaining while offering criticism of the social and political order of its time. Organized causes, commercialized art, and institutionalized religion are castigated because they evince a failure of belief and an absence of commitment to a moral purpose. However, one of Benson's strengths is her ability to remind us that "they" are people. The suffrage movement is a movement of individual men and women; not all are selflessly devoted to the cause. Organized charity requires the efforts of individuals to carry out charitable missions; individual charity workers overlook the emotional needs of the recipients of charity. Finally, God's stewards in the world are after all human: an individual priest whose prayers are empty formulas, whose parishioners are expected to accept their secular lot and not try to improve it, whose bad advice to a well-intentioned man causes a worthy young girl to despair, is not the best recommendation for organized religion.

The novel is most obviously concerned with the problem of women's place in society, yet it is neither a panegyric to the nobility of women nor a diatribe against the depravity of men. Two of the three most devastating potraits in the novel are of women. In a book that advocates women's rights, the Chief Militant Suffragette, the leader of this organized cause, is mercilessly revealed in her limited commitment to that cause. Further, a novelist who might be able to affect the values of her audience is shallow and egotistical. Finally, however, the most contemptible character in the novel is a man: Father Christopher, the religious head of the Brown Borough.

Although most individuals working for reform may be sincere and committed, there is little hope expressed in the novel that effective change will ever occur. (pp. 26-7)

The life of women without men in *I Pose* is far from idyllic. In a world in which a woman's sphere is the home, a woman's identity seems dependent upon her association with men. If she is not a wife she may be identified by her association with a brother . . . , a nephew . . . , or a brutal boyfriend. . . . (p. 32)

Shy, ill, drunk, hypocritical, or immature, the men in the novel seem weak pillars indeed to support the world of women. The gardener is likable, or would be if he were about fourteen. His infatuation for the suffragette is her first, and in all likelihood would be her only, opportunity to secure the position of wife, to find identity and occupation through submission to male dominance. Marriage to the gardener would produce the standard "happy ending" for the reader who refuses to speculate about what life would be after the closing of the book. However, the life of the wife of the gardener would be certain to be far from easy. A soft touch who is unable to manage his own finances, an impractical man of no apparent skill (it is a poor recommendation for a gardener that his only plant, a nasturtium, dies), a romantic who never considers seriously the person that the suffragette is (in spite of the fact that she is undistinguished in appearance, he affectionately asserts that anyone seeing her would notice her instantly), his first act upon meeting her is to thwart her plans by imposing his judgment, and his determination to make her his wife would thwart any possibility of her being her own woman. The gardener, younger than the suffragette and uncommitted to any single ideal, is ill equipped to protect anyone from the vicissitudes of life. Yet, if he were to marry the suffragette, it is his vision of her before a fire caring for their children that both of them accept as the future reality. Younger, less introspective, more selfish, less experienced, and more romantic than the suffragette, the gardener will dominate. The suffragette's physical suicide [at the novel's close] is more dramatic than the emotional and intellectual suicide of marriage, but perhaps no more final. (p. 33)

The character of the suffragette contains the contradiction that determined individualists face when operating in a world of cause and effect. If the suffragette is a suffragette by a choice circumscribed by the social fact that her choices were limited (she could have been simply a spinster, or a governess perhaps, but not, until she met the gardener, a wife), is the self that she

chooses any less her true self because the number of roles available to her was limited? *I Pose* seems to assert, like Oscar Wilde, that the pose becomes the reality. A pose maintained establishes individual identity. But the novel also reveals the pitfalls that await those who attempt to give an exclusive focus to their lives, who believe that they can embrace only one role and that any admission of other characteristics is detrimental to the preservation of individual identity. The suffragette attempts to maintain her identity as suffragette by denying her basic identity as woman. When finally confronted with the acceptance of a facet of her person that she has tried to ignore, she is unable to reconcile what she perceives to be conflicting roles. (p. 34)

I Pose emphasizes the total isolation of the gardener and the suffragette. They have no names and barely even a hint of a past. The novel highlights the universal isolation of individuals and emphasizes the inescapable destruction that finally resolves the problem of estrangement. Raising questions about personal identity and individual integrity, Stella Benson's first novel is built around the issue of women's rights, but it is the more universal concern for individual life in a world opposed to individuality that makes its theme timeless. (p. 39)

I Pose ended with a question. *This Is the End* opens with a declaration, an assertion of belief in the nonfactual. The narrator is explicit: there is a life of the heart accessible to everyone, which is more important than the external world confronting the body. The narrator's assertion would sound like frightened whistling in the dark were it not for the impossible and improbable facts the reader accepts while reading the novel. The story of Jay in *This Is the End* emphasizes the fragility of the inner life, while revealing that it exists, or existed at one time, in everyone. Irreconcilable inconsistencies within the novel support the world view that there *is* a truth that all the reasoning in the world cannot verify but that may be discovered by anyone.

The third novel, *Living Alone,* reiterates the idea of the reality of fantasy, but both inner and outer worlds seem bleak and lonely. Paradoxically, *Living Alone* is both more fantastic and more realistic than its predecessors. (p. 40)

The protagonist of [*This Is the End*] has . . . lived a life of the imagination; not until the fairy adventures of her heart have been exiled by facts does she surrender to marriage and the everyday, reasonable world.

Jay (Jane Elizabeth Martin) is a "Suffragetty" sort of girl "wasting an expensive education" working in London as a bus conductor. She sends her Family (Benson's capitalization) letters describing her dream life in a house on a cliff by the sea, but writes about this life as though it were fact. (p. 41)

Both the theme and the characters in this novel are developed through gentle but highly effective irony. For instance, the significance of the "Anti-Climax" may be missed if the reader forgets the narrator's initial assertion that it is her faith in the insubstantial nature of fact that allows her to continue living. The dichotomy between the opening and closing sentiments must be recognized. The narrator's assertion denies the inevitability as well as the desirability of the complete capitulation to reality which seems to be the final fate of each of the characters in this novel.

The narrator discusses the characters with precisely controlled omniscience. Statements that initially appear to be reflections of the narrator's opinion often prove to be, upon careful reading, her transmission of the impression the characters make upon others. When she makes factual observations about the characters, the facts are demonstrably accurate in light of the character's actions; however, what often becomes apparent is that these facts are not the *truth* of these people. The real people cannot be understood through memorization of a list of facts. (p. 43)

In *This Is the End* Benson offers . . . "word vignettes," rather than what the modern critic would call well-rounded characters. Yet these characters are dynamic enough to throw the reader repeatedly off balance when he believes he understands them. The reader is constantly forced to recognize the "unfinal" nature of his own conclusions. (p. 45)

The suffragette in *I Pose* committed suicide rather than succumb to the temptation of a marriage that she feared would become a tomb for her personal identity. Instead of rejecting the conventional ending for a heroine who has not behaved immorally, *This Is the End* reveals the threadbare reward that marriage can be. But Benson is not content with simply demonstrating the absence of passion with which a young girl sinks into matrimony; . . . she attacks a pervasive romantic myth of the ideal husband: the kindly, experienced, older man. (pp. 49-50)

Benson's point was not that marriage is inevitably bad, but that marriage is not inevitably good. It is a tribute to her accomplishment that without offering any suggestion that Bill Martin will be a bad husband, she nonetheless conveys the sense of loss that accompanies the acceptance of the standard role for a woman. It would have been quite easy to give this fine young man a hint of vice or unworthiness; few would doubt that a bad husband can bring a lifetime of grief to a woman. But Benson develops the realistic observation that husbands (or wives) do not necessarily bring happiness and contentment. (p. 50)

Benson's third novel [*Living Alone*], populated with witches, wizards, flying broomsticks, fairies, and dragons is more emphatically a fantasy than the first two. Yet the novel confronts an unromantic reality in a way the others do not. The heroines in Benson's first two novels are allowed an unusual choice. The usual dilemma of women in fiction was not *whether* to marry but whom to marry or how to marry. By permitting the heroines of her first two novels to elect not to marry, Benson was departing from the approved conventional plot. However, she was unable to offer a vision of the life of an unmarried woman. A pleasant life for a woman of no particular talent (usually in novels the talent was novel writing) who had chosen not to marry was unimaginable. Significantly, the suffragette had to eliminate herself altogether if she were to resist marriage. Jay, on the other hand, once rejected marriage, then finally relented. In *Living Alone* Benson explores the life of a single woman who does not regret her husbandless condition. Like Graham Greene's Major Scobie in *The Heart of the Matter*, some people—women included—might prefer the peace of loneliness to the pain that often attends intimate relationships. Such a woman is Sarah Brown. She is unmarried and neither particularly attractive nor particularly attracted to anyone, man or woman.

Living Alone is the story of Sarah Brown's life after she meets a witch. Sarah Brown is a faceless and nearly nameless member of a charity committee; the witch is the superintendent of a store and boarding house known as the House of Living Alone. Boarders in the House of Living Alone pay no rent, but must agree to observe rules enforcing almost complete seclusion and

must resist any temptation to make their lodging "homey." Sarah Brown moves into the House of Living Alone with her one companion, David the Dog. (pp. 53-4)

Under the influence of a magic sandwich, Sarah Brown quits her job "in a small office, collecting evidence from charitable spies about the Naughty poor," and leaves to seek love in the world outside. Needing to support herself, she finds a job working on a farm superintended by an ineffectual dragon whose weak commands are blithely ignored by the fairy fieldhands. Unused to strenuous activity, Sarah is soon conquered by the physical pain attendant upon the unfamiliar outdoor work and is returned to the House of Living Alone by the wizard Richard. Meanwhile, the witch has been seen battling a German witch over London and is sought by the police. Believing the witch in danger of arrest, Sarah Brown insists the witch accompany her to the United States. Just as their ship passes the Statue of Liberty, the witch returns to England. The novel ends as Sarah Brown, deaf and alone, enters the United States, "the greater House of Living Alone." (pp. 54-5)

Living Alone is a novel of fantasy; yet it addresses the real issue of isolation in the real world. The heroine has no resource beyond herself; she looks forward to no significant future work for which she is sacrificing or even enduring now; she has no warm memories of any specific past accomplishment to which her life has been devoted. She is a less dramatic version of the suffragette in *I Pose*. True, she is the doer of committees: she, like the suffragette, performs the tedious and unromantic chores required for any movement to move. But, unlike the suffragette, she seems to work not out of any sense of deliberately submitting her pride, but out of a sense that such tasks are the only ones appropriate for her. Furthermore, she has neither the dedicated sense of mission of the suffragette nor the despondent sense that all is not as it should be which haunted Jay in *This Is the End*. Sarah Brown seems to move through a world in which she neither feels she is a citizen nor desires to be one. (p. 55)

This third novel is about isolation, but not all the isolation is voluntary and not all the isolation is permanent. (p. 58)

Living Alone emphasizes the pervasiveness of isolation and establishes magic as a reality. The presence of magic, of fairies, wizards, and dragons, does not in any way detract from the seriousness of this novel. Writers as diverse as Jonathan Swift, Oscar Wilde, H. G. Wells, Jorge Luis Borges, Stanislaw Lem, Ursula K. Le Guin and Harold Bloom, to name but a very few, have all employed the "unreal" or fantastic to develop their visions of a truth. Reasonable readers are much quicker to perceive the error of excessive rationality in Houyhnhnms much admired by Gulliver than they would be to acknowledge the same error in themselves. Fantasy serves paradoxically to distance the reader from the action of the story while encouraging him to recognize the personal truth of the fantastic world. For instance, when Benson uses two witches to demonstrate the shallows of unreflecting patriotism and unexamined prejudice, the reader can see the problem more quickly because he is less personally involved with witches than with people. This same technique will be useful later in *Goodbye, Stranger* when Benson defuses resentment of her characterization of an insensitive husband by attributing his personality to the fact that he is a fairy in a man's body.

The fantasy in *Living Alone* reaffirms the idea that complete accurate communication is impossible. We see normal people failing to understand each other and their world; we also see beings with unusual abilities who are no better able to communicate than mere mortals. (pp. 59-60)

Like all of Benson's novels, *Living Alone* is primarily concerned with the situation of isolated individuals. Although the chapters are given titles that seem to call attention to a pattern of organization, the reader may emerge less with a sense of having read a well-designed novel than with the feeling of having completed a collection of loosely connected short stories. In spite of this weakness in structure, the novel achieves a telling effect through the ambivalence with which it leaves the reader at its conclusion. In tension with the conventional pity for Sarah Brown, deaf and alone in a strange land, is an almost resentful recognition that Sarah Brown does not need anyone's pity: she manages quite well alone and prefers not to be bothered even by well-intentioned concern.

Recognizing the inadequacy of rationality as a means of coping with an incomprehensible and seemingly indifferent universe, Stella Benson's first three novels assert an extra-reality and defend the necessity for individuality even if a unique identity ensures isolation. These works are fundamentally concerned with depreciating the immediacy of observable external reality. Yet they are not simple fantasies. While encouraging fantasy as an escape, these novels not only have an anti-convention bias which often characterizes the outlook of the young, but also recognize human fallibility with a compassion found in the mature. (p. 61)

Stella Benson's last four completed novels focus not on alternative realities, nor on the inner life at odds with outer activities, but on the nature of individual reality. The novels reflect a sensibility finely attuned to the human weaknesses that contribute to individual unhappiness. Benson herself was not unfamiliar with unhappiness during this time: her fourth novel, *The Poor Man,* was begun in the aftermath of a California sojourn that had been emotionally exhausting, and the last three novels were written while she lived what she believed to be an intellectually barren life in China. . . . [Her] novels reveal an increasing inclination to search for the possible and positive in human relations and to de-romanticize loneliness.

The Poor Man marks an important change in Benson's art. The earlier novels give the reader the feeling that he is being included in the world of a witty and determinedly hopeful narrator. The narrator's observations have assumed a common disinclination on the part of the reader to bow to an external reality. And the reader gets caught up in that assumption. The fact that none of the early novels end on a note of resounding optimism paradoxically encourages the acceptance of the ideals of the narrator because there is no simple assertion that these ideals will ever truly prevail in the world. The omniscient narrator in *The Poor Man,* on the other hand, does not include the reader in a comfortable spectator's box with a reassuring voice reminding him that the world needn't really be as bad as all that. (p. 62)

This novel is an early salvo in Benson's continuing battle against what she saw as leveling mediocrity and crass commercialism breeding out from the United States. She spent a lifetime decrying the sentimentality and the mindless acceptance of clichés, slogans, and advertisements that she believed characteristic of many Americans. Several of her short stories focus specifically on this theme. But the main business of *The Poor Man* is not to vent anti-American prejudice; the novel has broader aims. It remorselessly strips the defensive facade from imperfect humans and reveals the wretchedness within. In their bigotry

and ignorance [the American family] the Webers seem quite content. Afflicted with a different type of selfishness, it is the introspective characters in the novel who are far from happy.

The Poor Man directs the reader's attention to a reality that is almost totally devoid of romance. . . . (p. 65)

Pipers and a Dancer was written after Benson had suffered the criticism of her California friends for her unflattering picture of Californians in *The Poor Man* and after she had come to realize how devastatingly arid life could be even in a physically beautiful setting. She began her married life in Mengtsz, China, and her letters written during the time spent there reflect a total disenchantment with her few European neighbors and an increasing tendency to question her own personal worth. (p. 72)

With *Pipers and a Dancer* Benson makes some interesting changes in the standard formula for women in novels. Unmarried women were supposed to be dissatisfied with their husbandless condition. When occasionally the reader ran across a woman not pining for a husband, the woman was usually strident, abrasive, and generally unpleasant—and of course somehow corrupt because content with the company of women. Women who did not consider marriage their life's goal had been easily dismissed from much literature by the suggestions that if they were not being punished for past indiscretions, for too much love of men, they were lesbians. (pp. 74-5)

Benson's young heroine [Ipsie] is not deflected from the embrace of an aggressive female; she welcomes the alliance for the range of experience it offers her. Furthermore, her fragmented personality characterized by the feeling that her essential identity was lost at birth is caused not by an absence of identity but by a rejection of an identity that is socially unacceptable and biologically impossible. The diminutive Ipsie seeking safety as Mrs. Jacob Heming recognizes perfection in the idea of her dead brother Conrad. In fact, there are in each of her moods and poses slight impersonations of specific traits of her three dead brothers. Unable to live her masculine identity, she is driven by it (her Show*man*) to reflect the expectations of others.

As the novel opens, Ipsie seems destined to have to choose, and the choice initially seems to be between her miserable fiancé Jacob and the pleasant Rodd Innes. (p. 75)

Pipers and a Dancer is not an apology for homosexuality; Benson merely claims for women what has earlier been the right of men. The ideal of perfect friendship had long been assumed to exist only between men. The true understanding of strong minds could be found among men—not between men and women, no matter how wise the woman, and certainly not between women. Benson's development of the bond between Pauline and Ipsie is handled quite skillfully: the sexual element is deemphasized and the emotional and social basis clarified. Thus, her handling of the bond between two women is quite different from D. H. Lawrence's as he develops the sensual nature of the bond between men in *Women in Love,* a novel published about the same time as *Pipers and a Dancer.* (p. 79)

Pipers and a Dancer is the first Benson novel to end with even a hint that the protagonist may find contentment through a union with another human being. Jay's marriage in *This Is the End* marks the surrender of what she believed to be her essential identity; hers is not a union of promise. Furthermore, the final chapter of that novel underscores the pathos of the empty, solitary Mr. Russell. *Pipers and a Dancer,* on the other hand, concludes with both Ipsie and Pauline anticipating a pleasant future and even Rodd, his vanity wounded, will be safe from the dangerous introspection that would have altered his own amiable self-image which he protects with his superficiality.

Benson's novels focus increasingly on the problem of women isolated in ill-fitting feminine roles. This is not a problem newly conceived, but its development has become more explicit. As early as *I Pose* the character of the suffragette, working for the improvement of the lot of women, claiming a right to the prerogatives of men, had been unable to join her life with the gardener's in a traditional effort to encourage mutual comfort. In *Pipers and a Dancer* Ipsie and Pauline seem well suited for each other, and their early ambivalence toward each other would not be at all unusual in a male-female relationship. Ipsie's rejection of Rodd and her conscious decision to accept Pauline may startle the reader into a closer examination of Ipsie's sense of absent identity. With this unconventional ending Benson encourages a questioning of convention. The determined preservation of individuality, even individuality characterized by an absence of defined identity, may ultimately make possible alliances against isolation. (pp. 83-4)

Benson's last two novels are her finest work. They both continue to develop the subject of isolation in the world, and they both hold two worlds in suspension, but they are in fact quite different from each other in technique and theme. *Goodbye, Stranger* insists again that the reader enter a world of uncommon reality. The male central character is a changeling, a fairy in a man's body; but the reader is almost forced to consider the novel as a commentary on the sufficiency, or insufficiency, of stereotypes. *Tobit Transplanted,* on the other hand, is presented as a recording of mundane fact, but constructed as it is on the plot from the Apocrypha—a plot which contains an angel of God, a demon-haunted young woman, and miraculous cures—it prods the reader toward awe for the power of the human being to transcend usual physical and emotional rules.

William Frierson has observed [in *The English Novel in Transition 1885-1940* (1942)], that the authors of the 1920s "cared little that [their] writing was true *to* life so long as it was true *of* life." Stella Benson's *Goodbye, Stranger* illustrates this principle well. Concerned with problems of identity and isolation, the novel calls upon the world of fairies to demonstrate the truth of the human world. . . . *Goodbye, Stranger,* like good poetry, turns the reader back upon himself and reveals an increased complexity with each reading.

The novel covers a thirty-six hour period while three female English performers are in a Chinese town. The town boasts, in addition to a few Frenchmen, an English missionary family named Lorne, Clifford Cotton and his American wife Daley and his mother, and three single men: Lion, Mr. Diamond, and a doctor. Lena, one of the performers, has an attack of pleurisy during the evening performance and is taken to the house of Daley and Clifford Cotton. Daley is shallow but pretty, pleasant, and kind. Her husband Clifford believes that he is a changeling, a fairy who has inhabited a man's body for seven years. His goal in life is to be at home in the world, and he believes Lena has a wisdom that she can share with him and that will allow him to attain his goal. Clifford makes no secret of his fascination with Lena. . . . (pp. 85-6)

[Daley sees Clifford] embracing Lena, and he unabashedly announces that he loves her but would like Daley to remain with them. Daley runs out of the house, and Clifford the changeling is sent away by Lena.

Daley returns home by dinner time, but Clifford remains absent. Soon most of the local community is trying to protect Daley from their suspicion that Clifford has either gone mad or been murdered. His clothes have been found in a bamboo grove, and he has been seen running naked in the woods. What actually happened was that the changeling discarded his clothing and was reclaimed by his fairy people. The person who finally returns late at night to Daley is her seven-years-absent husband. Lena discovers the changeling's departure when old Mrs. Cotton enters Lena's room to bemoan the return of the ''*so* manly—*so* practical—*so* good-hearted . . . fool'' who is her son, and the departure of the fairy who had occupied her son's body.

Benson believed that her thesis was quite clear. It was, in her later opinion, too clear: ''In writing *Goodbye, Stranger,* I forgot my dislike of taking sides—and the book is unfortunately full of personal bias and personal appeals, with a refrain of This is Right, and This is Wrong which I now think most unnecessary'' [see excerpt dated 1933]. But with this remark she was underestimating her accomplishment. The simplistic thesis Benson seems to have believed she was developing, a thesis which asserts that there is a Right and a Wrong, is contrary to the thesis that in fact emerges. . . . Studying what life offers, she always discovers some qualifying element which will not allow her to believe that she has at last discovered an absolute good. Thus, what is true of life is true of the novel: general observations are easy to make, but precise, accurate, comprehensive judgments are quite difficult.

Goodbye, Stranger is a more mature presentation of Benson's earlier preoccupations. There is a world-weary response to the dilemma of identity which strips away any shred of optimism in the reader's response, yet offers a more positive, realistic assessment of the world. Any reader of Benson's earlier novels will recognize in the character of Lena the later life of earlier heroines. Lena is alone, and apparently alone by choice, and she reaffirms that choice after her experience with the changeling Clifford. True, just before learning that the changeling has been returned to his fairy people, Lena looks to the mountains and wills Clifford to return to her. However, she makes absolutely no physical move to encourage him to come to her. Furthermore, she does not pretend to herself that she is being swept by a strong emotion. She is in command of herself and would like Clifford on her terms, but she will not risk any shadow over her independence by pursuing him or even overtly indicating her interest in him. Her independence may seem comfortless, and indeed Lena is cold and dry herself, but, again, it is worth stressing that the life she leads is a life she chooses.

Benson's heroines, unlike Virginia Woolf's upper-class or upper-middle-class women, are not totally divorced from the need for money. Nor are they, though, driven to act because of a need for money. Even Lena, who is closer to destitution than any of Benson's earlier heroines, seems indifferent to her financial situation. Benson's women all seem to come from that genteel class that assumes their daughters will dutifully marry but that finds many of their young women husbandless in the work force. These women are not faced with the choice of husbands or sweatshops, although the decision to work is probably assumed to be an admission of failure to secure a proposal. One always has the feeling that if Benson's women did not choose to work there would be families, heretofore ignored, ready to reembrace the prodigal daughter. But it is the reader's vague sense of the safety net beneath these solitary women that places emphasis on the fact of their choice. In this novel above all else Benson makes the point of the possibility of female independence.

This is not, however, a one point book. While insisting upon the possibility of female independence, Benson demonstrates the inadequacy, indeed the destructiveness, of the feminine stereotype both for the women who strive to embody it and the men who must then live with women intent upon passivity, submission, and rejection of their physical or intellectual natures. Meanwhile, as she explores the recesses of isolation in the world, Benson weaves in a criticism of commercialism and the cult of mediocrity spreading out from the United States.

It is the disinclination or inability to accept the combined physical, emotional, and intellectual components of a relationship or even of one's own personality that contributes most significantly to the pervasive sense of isolation in the novel. For instance, the missionary couple, the Lornes, are finally isolated from each other because Mr. Lorne cannot share the emotional life of his wife and Mrs. Lorne cannot find beauty in their sexual life. (pp. 86-8)

On the other hand, Daley and Clifford Cotton enjoy the union of their bodies, but for seven years there has been no mutual emotional and intellectual commitment in their marriage. It is because of the absence of anything but physical pleasure in Clifford's response to her, that Daley is so bewildered when she sees her husband attracted to the unfeminine Lena. . . .

The critic for the *Saturday Review* thought Daley an "amiable but not very consistent character." He went on to explain, "It is one of Miss Benson's shortcomings that she cannot bring herself to let the stupid stew quietly in their stupidity; ever and again a bubble of wit disturbs their viscous surface" [see excerpt by L. P. Hartley dated 1926]. But the reviewer missed the point. Although Daley is not an introvert inclined to self-doubt or intellectual pondering, she is not stupid. She has a mind but does not bother to use it. (p. 89)

While developing [a] broad comment on fragmented identity and individual isolation, *Goodbye, Stranger* follows the pattern of the quest myth to comment on the threat that women who are not passive and demure pose to men. This story makes perfect sense as an allegory criticizing society's roles for men and women. Daley seems the perfect wife and woman, but the shallows of her mind tire her husband. Clifford Cotton, secure in the approval of his mother (who seems to encourage his less-than-loving treatment of his wife) and the loyalty of his wife, is free to test the role of seeker. As a man he may openly demand more from life than what he has. Tired of seeing his reflection in the adoring gaze of his wife, he may search for a more critical view, a more complex image. During this time he is not the contented man he was but a man callous to the feelings of his wife. However, his chafing at his sane and sensible marriage and his adoring wife evaporates once he has glimpsed life with a woman who does *not* reflect his desires. Finally meeting a woman who does not consider him all-important—a sexually experienced, economically independent, emotionally ambivalent, and physically weak woman who, attracted to his wife, does not abandon herself to him—he withdraws from the search for wisdom. The wisdom he would find would diminish his stature in his own eyes. He has been all-important to his wife and mother: he is not even able to give Lena self-forgetting pleasure. The wisdom that comes with the realization that one is not all-perfect requires more strength than many men have. Clifford becomes again the happily married man, content to see himself reflected in Daley's uncritical eyes.

In addition to the problems of sex stereotypes, the phenomenon of modern commercial America disturbed Benson greatly. Her concern is reflected in both her professional writing and her personal correspondence. She made no secret of her distaste for the "modern expression of democracy—especially intellectual democracy"; earlier criticism is found in *The Poor Man* and several of her short stories. But one of the great strengths of *Goodbye, Stranger* is the fact that she does not encrust any single character with so much criticism that he or she loses all sympathy. Benson is evenhanded in her criticism if restrained in her admiration. (p. 94)

Although her sympathies are with Lena, Benson is not uncritical, and she emphasizes that there is much in life that Lena misses. To develop that point Benson creates a claustrophobic setting for Lena. All the action in Lena's life seems to take place in the evening and at night, and an imprisoning rain seems to surround her. Daley, on the other hand, moves outside and searches the world around her for beauty and comfort. (p. 96)

The pervasive isolation of individuals is apparent when the identity of the stranger of the title is sought. The most obvious candidate is the changeling Clifford, the fairy stranger in the real world who, after his contact with Lena, returns to his fairy world. The title could be a farewell to the changeling. A second possibility is that the title could refer to Lena, who is from the beginning of the novel a stranger. When the man Clifford Cotton returns to his wife he is someone to whom the frail boyish body of Lena will be forever a stranger. Lena, a stranger to life who has erected so many defenses that the extremes of joy and sorrow are lost to her, will leave the house and lives of the Cottons. Her physical intimacy with the body of the fairy Clifford Cotton will be unremembered by the man, and her attraction to Daley will never even have been recognized by anyone other than herself. Thus, the novel's title may be a sardonic farewell to a woman who has been and will be everywhere a stranger. There is a third possibility. With the return of the human Clifford who disappeared seven years earlier, Daley is no longer a stranger among cynics. Her husband is not seeking wisdom, and he is delighted with his pretty, child-like wife. He may bridge the gap between Daley's innocence and her neighbors' disillusion. The title may allude to the renewed bond between husband and wife which banishes the confused and estranged Daley and replaces her with a contented and loved woman. These three possibilities are not mutually exclusive; indeed, they are held simultaneously.

Still Benson demonstrates that women *can* be independent; they can be sufficient unto themselves. She makes no attempt to suggest that the life of the single woman is gay or that it is tragic; it is lonely and even dangerous, but it is an alternative that women are capable of electing and preferring.

Goodbye, Stranger is a truly remarkable book which draws upon the supernatural to insist upon the realities of our own world. The element of fantasy enables Benson to emphasize the situation of the women while minimizing a reader's desire to defend the man involved. The fact that Daley's husband is temporarily non-human frees the reader from any inclination to discover a misunderstood or much suffering husband. And of course the fact that he is non-human establishes a disequilibrium in the reader. The constant necessity of trying to place this odd creature finally underscores the external ordinariness of the situation: a man insensitive to the emotions of his pleasant, boring wife rediscovers her value after his experience with a woman of more independent mind. Because Benson supplies an excuse for the man, the reader can more readily sympathize with the woman. The exotic setting and the intrusion of fairies and changelings in the lives of mortals develop a criticism of blind adherence to approved roles and acknowledge the difficulty of independence.

Tobit Transplanted (published in America as *The Far Away Bride*) was critically and financially Stella Benson's most successful novel. In 1932 it won both the A. C. Benson silver medal for "services to literature" and the Vie Heureuse Prize—a French honor which thrilled her more than the English recognition. For *Tobit Transplanted* Benson transformed the story of Tobit in the Apocrypha, with its magic, devil, and angel, and produced a rationally explicable tale in which there is no necessarily supernatural power; there is only the awesome and mysterious power of each individual mind upon itself, upon the body that houses it, and upon the lives that swirl around it. (pp. 96-7)

In a rather long introduction to the novel Benson gives a complete historical, demographic, and linguistic account of the area and the people of Manchuria and Korea. She assures the reader that the problems with language—which require a Russian and a Chinese to communicate in English, which leave Koreans misunderstood in their own country, and which reduce Chinese to writing to each other because their respective dialects are unintelligible—do in fact exist. The historical accuracy of the confusion of tongues reinforces its strength as a symbol of the essential loneliness of the individuals isolated within themselves by their individual limitations.

The limitations are not simply linguistic. As men grow and become aware of new ideas they may easily become exiles in their own lands. (p. 102)

Indispensable to the success of all of Benson's novels has been the wit and humor with which she treats even the most serious subjects. With few exceptions, most of the humor in her novels is derived from the ironic commentary of the narrator. In *Tobit Transplanted,* however, irony gives way to outright comedy. . . .

It is perhaps belaboring the obvious to point out that a reader's perception of comedy, irony, pathos or tragedy is dependent upon a standard against which the reader may measure events. This self-evident fact must be recognized if any of Benson's work is to be properly appreciated. Benson always strives to puncture easy answers, and nowhere is this more apparent than in *Tobit Transplanted.* (p. 109)

Before their publication in the posthumous *Collected Short Stories* . . . , quite a few of Benson's short stories had appeared before the public at least twice. They would appear first in magazines, then be issued in small, limited editions. There were in all four of these small collections: *The Awakening* (1925), *The Man Who Missed the Bus* (1928), *Hope Against Hope and Other Stories* (1931), and *Christmas Formula and Other Stories* (1932). More than a collection but not exactly a novel is *Pull Devil, Pull Baker.* . . .

In her introduction to *Pull Devil, Pull Baker* Benson explains that she is acting as editor for autobiographical "Love Stories of My" written by Count Nicolas De Toulouse Lautrec De Savine, K. M., an old man in a hospital ward in Hong Kong. He describes himself as "a very good-known men, who belong

to one of the most distinguiched aristocratic famelys of Europe—pretty well known all the world other." His stories, recorded in his own English and his own spelling, are told with the amoral innocence of the utterly self-centered. To the "moral confectionery" of his baker, the devil, in the guise of the editor Stella Benson, contrasts tales stripped of sentimentality and bathetic indulgence. (p. 111)

In the final analysis *Pull Devil, Pull Baker* is closer to an arrangement of short stories than to a novel. By the arrangement the stories lend each other support and become stronger. **"The Man Who Fell in Love with the Cooperative Stores"** succeeds in *Pull Devil, Pull Baker* but is quite weak when standing alone in *Collected Short Stories.* The story taken by itself seems to be the kind of attack on materialism that sounds good when first conceived but is too outrageous to be effective. The language conforms precisely to what is expected of the lovelorn. The story is of a man in love with a store—not with buying or the process of acquisition but with the store itself. The analogy to the business of love sounds good, but it does not quite work. Although the story demonstrates well the narrator's concluding observations and the tone of the parody of the love lament is well maintained, the elements do not cohere as an imaginative whole which wins the emotional assent of the reader. It is the sort of idea that Benson's detractors might term "too cute." However, when placed beside the cream puffery of the Count in *Pull Devil, Pull Baker,* its literal preposterousness fades rather quickly as the reader automatically compares the situation in the love stories.

The opposite malady afflicts another of the stories in *Collected Short Stories.* **"A Dream"** powerfully evokes a nightmare world of desolation punctured by a distant clanging. But having entered so completely the experience of a woman with a brain tumor, the reader is disappointed with the ending. Benson began the story with the explanation that it is the transcription of a dream, but as she had observed elsewhere, other people's dreams seem pointless. The reader's disappointment springs from the fact that he has *felt* the dream, but the flat ending diminishes the entire experience. . . . The reader knows long before [the narrator's nurse] Zillah's announcement that both women are dead; the unease has given it away. But *why* is Zillah uneasy? Surely not because she has to break the news of death! There must be more to it.

Stella Benson's short stories are very uneven in quality. Most do give a strong sense of a story told; there is a completeness about them that is not always present in this form which lends itself so readily to recounting incident with no sense of finality. However, although a few stories don't quite come off, most are good and four are extremely good.

"Hope Against Hope" is a moving attack on conventional attitudes toward women. The limited omniscience in the third-person point of view is restricted to the thoughts and actions of the convalescing man who is attended in his recovery by a plain but pleasant, and as it turns out imaginative and lonely, nurse. In spite of her patience with him, her unfailing good humor, and her professional attentiveness, Ward Clark "felt justified in despising her, since he thought of himself as a reasonable-looking and still-young man, in spite of the fact that he was older than she was." . . . Miss Hope has committed the unpardonable sin of being an unmarried female over the age of thirty. Throughout the story thirty-six year old Ward Clark is disgusted by Miss Hope's enjoyment of conversation with a fifty-year old schoolteacher who has an annoying sniff. While Clark is being rude to and contemptuous of Miss Hope, he is basking in the light of the schoolteacher's daughter's infatuation. This nineteen-year old girl finds Clark extremely attractive, his age enhances his romance in her innocent eyes. The story ends with Clark, utterly incredulous that Miss Hope has attempted suicide, sending her away. Clark will send for his sister to come care for him (she is a woman and therefore will have no other duty apparently!); he neither inquires into nor cares about the reason for the suicide attempt.

Since the focus is on the man's perceptions, the reader sees his irritation with every suggestion, however unconscious, that Miss Hope is a person. He prefers to consider her a dull background whose conscientious pleasantries deserve no more than rudeness. It never crosses his mind that she could be interesting for herself, or that any man might find her so. Ward accepts as his due, on the other hand, the empty-headed adoration of a nineteen-year old girl. The story not only exposes a double standard—an expectation that women must remain pure, and a contempt for those who do—but also criticizes society's treatment of unmarried women who are no longer young. To accomplish this Benson insists upon the ordinariness of Miss Hope. Like Clark, the reader sees her as a bit ridiculous in her humble vanities. Therefore, the shock of surprise is especially sharp at the realization that her capacity for love has been completely ignored. The reader has been guilty of the same prejudice—perhaps in a milder form—that Ward Clark has.

"Submarine" is a mood piece, conveying quite effectively the growing terror in a woman's mind as guilt for an earlier heartlessness rises to haunt her. The action of the story is beneath the surface of the ocean as a couple go diving. Their air hoses are controlled by a man who the wife becomes convinced is the son of her former nana. The nana had been with the wife for twenty years, but when the new husband suspected that she had embezzled money, he fired her instantly. Beneath the surface of the water long-submerged guilt floats back to the wife. Regretting that she had not defended her nana, that she had not opposed her husband's will, the wife becomes convinced that the man controlling their air lines intends to exact vengeance by drowning them for the injury done years ago to his mother. Her mounting panic is played against the incongruity of the appearance of her husband. Looking like a rhinoceros in his diving suit, the man bumbles about like a clown. When they are finally safe again above water the reader understands from the final lines that the wife feels not just guilt but also resentment: resentment toward her husband who so completely changed her life years ago by assuming control of her household, who had been so oblivious to her recent heart-stopping terror. (pp. 113-15)

One of the best of all Benson's short stories, **"The Desert Islander"** pits the determined individualist against the ingrained organization man. The antagonists are a Russian deserter from the Foreign Legion in China and an Englishman from whom he seeks assistance. The deserter insists upon being an individual, a unique individual. He bristles whenever compared to anyone else or considered as part of any group. It is his article of faith that anything he does, because he does it, must be original and therefore good. The Englishman, on the other hand, does always what he should. At the risk (indeed finally at the cost) of his life he behaves decently. Because the Russian's infected leg must receive medical attention, the Englishman drives him through a war to get help. The recipient of the automatic assistance, far from being grateful, grows to hate his benefactor because he has seen too much of the deserter's fears and weakness for the Russian soldier to maintain his self-image as a fearless individualist. . . . [The English-

man's] life is senselessly taken by a stray bullet as he waves goodbye to a man who despises him. The individualist survives but the world seems no better for the loss of the convention-loving man.

"Story Coldly Told" addresses more broadly the weakness of unexamined conventions. The title suggests detachment, and detachment suggests an absence of caring. But while criticizing sentimental caring, the story itself demonstrates that there is something in the world other than reason. The narrator, Palmer, lives in an isolated city in an out-of-the-way country and is the last representative of a dying commercial activity. He seems mildly interested in the goings-on around him but personally uninvolved. Even his sense of identity is ambiguous as he describes himself "like the blessed Damosel" watching a scene below him. Few men would liken themselves to the image of a woman, no matter what the circumstance. A native who works for him, but for whom he feels no sense of friendship, rescues Palmer, an English vice-consul, and a seventy-five year old woman missionary from revolutionaries by turning the three of them over to a band of brigands.

During their captivity the vice-consul, who had been full of admiration for the noble savages among whom he lived, is insulted by them and comes to fear them. The missionary, who has lived in the country for thirty-five years without ever bothering to learn anything about its culture, preaches love to men who believe she is a eunuch dedicated to a special god. The first sign that her missionary efforts are effective is the return of a stolen sweater. The next sign comes from the leader of the band who tells Palmer that if the woman doesn't stop talking he will cut out her tongue—several of his men have abandoned their life of crimes because of her. Before the resolve of the leader can be tested, a rescue party arrives. As the party approaches, three of the brigands offer final proof of Miss Sims's effectiveness. They murder their leader in front of everyone. This murder is supposed to demonstrate the sincerity of their newfound faith in the religion of love; with the killing they reject their sinful past. . . . Palmer, who believes he lives without sentimentality, is the only person to try to make the dying man's last moments comfortable.

This story of misunderstanding and death ends on a quietly positive note. In spite of sentimental blindness (the vice-consul's belief in idealized noble savages instead of living people), fanatic ignorance (Miss Sims's lack of interest in the realities of the world around her), and religious misunderstanding (the converts' murder of their leader in the name of the religion offered by what they believe is a eunuch), communion is possible. A man who cultivates detachment respects the integrity of life and can be moved, against all reason, to a gesture of brotherhood through an act of impractical sympathy. It is the possibility of sympathy through an unsentimental respect for life that Benson's entire work insists upon. (pp. 115-17)

Benson's poems do not cover a wide range of subjects or styles, but they do glow with a quiet loveliness. Yearning for belief, resolute in isolation, glorying in beauty, they speak for the lonely who have felt life's splendor. Whereas in her novels and travel articles Benson never strays far from the light touch, in her poetry she exposes emotion without the protective covering of humor or playful irony. What irony there is compresses the pain of empathy. . . . (p. 117)

Benson does tend to an elevated diction and occasional archaisms which obscure meaning. For instance, in **"Christmas, 1917"** the use of the archaic "holden" seems to have nothing to speak for it other than that it rhymes with "golden"—and everything going against it including the fact that it does not make much sense in the stanza. In the next stanza "stoned" is rhymed with "enthroned," but why the extra syllable in each word? But these are her worst offenses. In a collection revealing so honestly a sense of isolation and betrayal in the world, there are precious few slips into sentimentality. (pp. 117-18)

Many of Benson's travel articles are collected in two books. The first, *The Little World* . . . , includes pieces written between 1919 and 1924 during travels in the United States, China, and India. *Worlds Within Worlds* . . . reflects an appreciation for the humor and beauty of the world through close observation of the details of the life around her. Observations made when she was feeling particularly unsympathetic to the missionaries, French officials, and Chinese who surrounded her offer an excellent tonic for the reader who is satiated with accounts of the "Mystic Withdrawn Orient, Shot with the Glances of Dark Almond Eyes that See Beyond Mere Human Wisdom." It is the human that unfailingly attracts Benson, and the human that she seeks. Her descriptions entertain and the entertainment instructs. (pp. 118-19)

Benson interweaves the humor and sadness of mortality with the beauty of a living response. After all, if the Orient is inscrutible, then one need not consider the people within it, there is no point of identification. Above all, common life unites us. (p. 119)

In some moods Benson can treat hostilities between Japan and China or the civil war in China lightheartedly; she makes men sound like children squabbling. But this tone is not indicative of callous indifference to human suffering. A description of a trip up a river can encompass criticism of war by calling quiet attention to the human cost of war—any war. (p. 120)

But Benson's concern about physical death is transitory. She returns over and over again to incidents that suggest the failure of intellectual communication, while the very success of her imagery nurtures the sympathetic communication between individuals that she found so often lacking. For example, in a Korean train she accidentally dropped a cigarette down the padded back of a Korean's coat. Alas, she was unable to make the man understand his problem. With no common language she resorted to trying a charade to point out his danger. However, since she was not only a foreigner but a woman as well, her audience decided to ignore her before perplexity could change to annoyance. The serious consequences of the smoldering cigarette are overshadowed in the amusing final scene of a man walking off unaware of the thin wisp of smoke rising behind his neck. With no explicit generalization, Benson adds one more tile to the mosaic of her enduring theme. Isolated man may be, and inconsequential to others, yet there is grandeur as man, determinedly blind to the potential pain always with him, goes on with the business of living.

Stella Benson's travel articles can bear comparison to any of the best, to those of Rebecca West or Graham Greene. She always gives the reader the feeling of immediate participation in vivid experience. Perhaps more important, she manages to make the exotic believable. While comparing the strange with the familiar, she encourages an appreciation of the beauty and variety of life and universal individuality, and thus opens the reader's eyes anew to the familiar world around him. (pp. 120-21)

Benson's novels are witty and haunting. Her poetry complements them in its seriousness. Her accomplishment is original and significant. Christopher Morley once said that lazy and contented people will never appreciate her work. That is probably true, but for those who dare the disarming challenge she waits to be appreciated. (p. 125)

> *R. Meredith Bedell, in her* Stella Benson, *Twayne Publishers, 1983, 141 p.*

ADDITIONAL BIBLIOGRAPHY

Bottome, Phyllis. *Stella Benson.* San Francisco: Albert M. Bender, 1934, 13 p.
  Tribute to Benson, praising her character as well as her fiction.

Brandon, William. "Stella Benson: Letters to Laura Hutton, 1915-1919." *The Massachusetts Review* XXV, No. 2 (Summer 1984): 225-46.
  Partial texts of letters from Benson to an old friend, interspersed with biographical data supplied by Brandon. Most of the material deals with the period Benson spent living and working in California.

Collins, Joseph. "Charge of the Amazons in Current English Fiction." *The New York Times Book Review* (28 January 1923): 7, 31.*
  Review of Benson's novel *The Poor Man*, incorporating an overview of popular women fiction writers and ranking Benson high among them.

Daiches, David. "Fiction: The Age of Experiment." In his *The Present Age in British Literature*, pp. 264-301. Bloomington: Indiana University Press, 1958.*
  Calls Benson "a highly original novelist whose tragic view of life is artfully disposed behind a facade of remarkable comic wit."

Estcourt, Doris. "Stella Benson." *The Bookman* London LXXXII, No. 488 (May 1932): 103-04.
  Highly approbatory biographical and critical essay by an old friend of Benson. Estcourt notes especially the literary awards and prizes won by Benson.

Holden, Raymond. "Stella Benson's Latest." *The Saturday Review of Literature* I, No. 1 (25 October 1924): 223-24.
  Review of *Pipers and a Dancer*. Although he calls Benson "a writer of great ability" possessed of wit and verbal facility, Holden finds the novel seriously flawed by authorial intrusiveness.

Kelly, Florence Finch. "Firstlings in Fiction: 'I Pose'." *The Bookman* London XLIII, No. 3 (May 1916): 325.
  Review of Benson's first novel, calling it "clever and amusing," with frequent and occasionally strained sallies of wit.

Morley, Christopher. "Stella Benson." *The Saturday Review of Literature* X, No. 22 (16 December 1933): 354.
  Brief reminiscence praising the sophisticated observations of human nature in Benson's novels.

Roberts, R. Ellis. *Portrait of Stella Benson.* London: Macmillan & Co., 1939, 416 p.
  Largely noncritical biography by a friend of Benson. R. Meredith Bedell, author of the only book-length critical study of Benson, has claimed that *Portrait* is a poorly documented work containing many unsupported authorial suppositions. Roberts frequently quotes from Benson's fiction to make points about her life.

"Miss Stella Benson: Originality and Imagination." *The Times*, London, No. 46,622 (8 December 1933): 9.
  Obituary. Benson's wide-ranging world travels and her literary career are briefly outlined.

Wylie, I. A. R. "Chapter 5." In her *My Life with George: An Unconventional Autobiography*, pp. 260-72. New York: Random House, 1940.*
  Contains a brief reminiscence of encounters with Benson in California and later in England. Wylie calls *The Far-Away Bride* "one of the best novels" of her lifetime.

Christopher John Brennan

1870-1932

Australian poet, critic, and philosopher.

Brennan is considered the most accomplished poet Australia has produced, as well as that country's greatest classical scholar. However, due to the inferior status often assigned writers from less-established literary traditions, he remains an obscure figure in world literature. An admirer of French Symbolist poet Stéphane Mallarmé, Brennan strove to develop a poetic system that would enable him to express humankind's intellectual, emotional, and spiritual quest for ultimate truth. Enforced by a heavily architectonic and allusive style, Brennan's greatest work, *Poems 1913,* is viewed as a powerful record of human experience and has led some critics to rank Brennan's poems among the finest written in the English language between 1890 and World War I.

Brennan was born in Sydney to a lower middle-class Irish Catholic family. He received his early education in Catholic schools, where he acquired a strong command of Latin, one of several languages that he mastered during his lifetime. Recognized as an unusually intelligent student, Brennan was awarded a scholarship to Riverview College, which he entered in 1885 at the age of fifteen. Impressed by the cultured, saintly demeanor of Father Patrick Keating, a preeminent classicist there, Brennan developed a lifelong interest in the spiritual and intellectual perfection of the individual. During his years at Riverview, he read widely in Greek and Latin and composed poetry in both languages in addition to writing several English verse dramas, though none of these early works has survived. In 1888 he enrolled at Sydney University, where he consistently won high honors and spent much of his time on independent projects, his most notable being textual research on Aeschylus's dramas. By the age of eighteen, Brennan challenged the generally accepted theory concerning the origin of Aeschylus's seven surviving tragedies. His published study, "On the Manuscript of Aeschylus," received little consideration at the time by ranking classicists but has since been accorded high importance for its informed and original conclusions.

A major turning point in Brennan's life came in 1890. Until then he had adhered to the Roman Catholic faith; however, following his study of Herbert Spencer's *First Principles* (in which Spencer espoused "a belief in an Absolute that transcends not only human knowledge but human conception"), Brennan became an agnostic. An early poem entitled "Farewell, the pleasant harbourage of faith" arose from this transformation in world view. Critics now assume that the theme of spiritual quest that unifies *Poems 1913* is actually the documentation of Brennan's search for a philosophical system to replace the religious faith he abandoned. After graduating from Sydney University, Brennan taught for a short time at a Catholic boys' school, and while there began seriously to write poetry. Although his early verses are deemed of little merit, they display the Victorian sensibility which characterizes Brennan's later work. During this period, Brennan also completed his master's thesis in philosophy, "The Metaphysic of Nescience," which presents a monist view of existence through its assertion of one ultimate, yet unknowable truth. However, Brennan knew that his essay represented only an unsubstan-

tiated hypothesis and consequently, though he maintained a keen interest in metaphysical theories, he turned increasingly to poetry to express his view of life. Awarded a traveling scholarship in 1892 after receiving special honors for his thesis, Brennan elected to study in Berlin, as that city's university possessed a renowned classics department. But shortly after his arrival there, Brennan became engrossed in modern European literature, particularly in the works of Stéphane Mallarmé, then a relatively unknown French poet. In Mallarmé's conception of poetry as suggestive expression rather than overt statement, and his utilization of the *livre composé* ("composed book")—a thematically unified sequence of individual works—Brennan discovered an aesthetic approach and literary vehicle which he adopted in the following years to communicate his monist convictions and belief in the perfectibility of humanity.

Engaged to a young German woman whom he eventually married, Brennan returned to an economically depressed Australia in 1894. Because he had not earned his doctorate, his prospects for academic employment were unpromising and he eventually settled for a position as tutor and librarian's assistant. During this time he also occupied himself with refining and organizing his poetry and in 1897 privately issued his first collection, *XVIII Poems.* The favorable attention the volume received prompted Brennan to publish an enlarged edition titled *XXI Poems: MDCCCXCIII-MDCCCXCVII Towards the Source.*

Critical reaction ranged from disparagement of what some considered its imprecise language and unconventional punctuation to enthusiastic praise by others for what they perceived as Brennan's admirable command of imagery and poetic construction. During the next five years, Brennan wrote more poetry than during any other period in his life and attained high status in Sydney's literary circles, magnifying this position in later years when he became the dominant force in the weekly clubs Les Compliqués and the Casuals. Yet domestic problems, misgivings about the relevance of his poetry to his life, and his assumption of teaching duties at Sydney University, deterred him from composing poetry for several years, until he began revising *Towards the Source* and other verse in 1911 for inclusion in *Poems 1913*. Now considered his masterwork, this volume received very little acclaim during his lifetime, primarily due to its detachment from the regional and national issues that preoccupied many of his contemporaries. His greatest notoriety came with his publication during World War I of the fervently anti-German poems in one of his least-regarded works, *A Chant of Doom, and Other Verses*.

During the early 1920s Brennan's family problems worsened, contributing to a progressive lapse in his academic and poetic performance and exacerbating an already chronic alcoholic condition. A three-year love affair with a New Zealand woman inspired Brennan to resume literary and scholarly projects, but her accidental death in 1925 depressed Brennan severely, and he never completely recovered. Long after his dismissal from the university for indecorous behavior, a personal maintenance fund was established for Brennan by friends and colleagues to assist a scholar whom they believed still possessed an enormous amount of knowledge and critical insight. Gradually, Brennan resumed academic work, offering periodic university lectures and teaching classical and romance languages at a convent school. After a brief period of hospitalization in 1932, he died of stomach cancer.

Shortly after Brennan had completed the main body of his poetry he delivered a series of lectures in 1904 titled "Symbolism in Nineteenth Century Literature." In these lectures he submitted that all serious poetry, as exemplified by the verse of Arthur Rimbaud, Charles Baudelaire, and Mallarmé, reflected a yearning for an equivalent of the biblical Eden—a perfect, harmonious reality beyond the immediate world. *Poems 1913* was Brennan's attempt to base a work on this Symbolist-inspired poetic theory. The poem sequence is comprised of three major sections—"Towards the Source," "The Forest of Night," and "The Wanderer"—which respectively document the narrator's initial Edenic delight with the visible world, his eventual rejection of this world and intellectual search for a theory of absolute reality, and his final stoic return to the material sphere after failing to discover, or fully accept, any such theory. "Lilith," a subsection of "The Forest of Night," has been viewed as the core of the entire work. An elusive goddess of darkness which Brennan derived from Jewish legend and the works of German Romanticist Novalis, the Lilith of the title emerges as a symbol of lost love and lost paradise, contrasting with the Eve-like companion of the narrator in "Towards the Source." This subsection concludes in a solipsistic despair which links itself with the acquiescent mood of "The Wanderer," in which the narrator declares himself "the wanderer of the ways of all the worlds, / to whom the sunshine and the rain are one / and one to stay or hasten, because he knows / no ending of the way, no home, no goal. . . ."

Whether Brennan achieved the epic unity of theme he strove for in *Poems 1913* has been the topic of considerable debate among scholars. Charges that he created an ambiguous symbolic system through confusion of three separate Edens—the biblical, the sensual, and the gnostic—have been met by contentions that of these three, the gnostic is the central unifying element in the poem's emphasis on the intellectual and spiritual evolution of the narrator. This argument, however, is challenged by one of the most compelling criticisms of *Poems 1913* and of Brennan's work in general—that it contains such unorthodox and perplexing syntax and such a profusion of inferior poetical styles as to preclude any effective thematic development. Consequently, a few critics have dismissed Brennan's poetry as a hodgepodge of the lesser qualities of English Romantic and Victorian poetry, a body of verse that Brennan admired perhaps even more than Mallarmé's work. In general, critics concede the greatness of Brennan's endeavor in *Poems 1913*, but question whether the poetry of those he chose to emulate—Alfred Lord Tennyson, Algernon Charles Swinburne, Coventry Patmore, and others—was best suited for the philosophical, Symbolist work he envisioned, despite the occasional appearance of astonishing, incantatory verse in the work.

Yet *Poems 1913* is upheld by Brennan admirers as a unique literary experiment of lasting significance and the powerful spiritual autobiography of a profound individual. In addition, Brennan's critical writings, although less studied, have been consistently recognized for their comprehensive, erudite scholarship anticipating that of modern, multilingual critics such as René Wellek. Although he has had little direct influence on later Australian writers, Brennan is nonetheless revered in his country as an outstanding literary figure worthy of far wider consideration than he has received.

PRINCIPAL WORKS

"On the Manuscript of Aeschylus" (essay) 1894; published in *Journal of Philology*
XVIII Poems (poetry) 1897
XXI Poems: MDCCCXCIII-MDCCCXCVII; Towards the Source (poetry) 1897
Poems 1913 (poetry) 1914
A Chant of Doom, and Other Verses (poetry) 1918
The Burden of Tyre (poetry) 1953
The Verse of Christopher Brennan (poetry) 1960
The Prose of Christopher Brennan (criticism) 1962
"The Uncollected Verse of C. J. Brennan" (poetry) 1963; published in journal *Southerly*

RANDOLPH HUGHES (essay date 1934)

[*As a student at Sydney University, Hughes often conversed with then professor Brennan on a wide range of literary and aesthetic topics. In the following excerpt from one of the most adulatory estimates of Brennan, Hughes discusses both the Symbolist nature and structural brilliance of Brennan's work. In this essay Hughes mentions Brennan's affinity with the Symbolist poet Stepháne Mallarmé; for a more detailed discussion of Mallarmé's influence on Brennan's work, see the excerpt by A. R. Chisholm (1961-62).*]

[Brennan's] was essentially a brooding, a deeply and continuously brooding mind, that easily withdrew itself from the petty things with which the ordinary world solicits the attention; frequently it seemed to be masterfully delving its way towards some far-off issue: and this is the most permanent impression one retains of it. Even in the most casual conversations, it seemed to be ready to go off into some profound reverie, or into some arduous excogitation. One would never have been surprised to see Brennan standing stock-still, in a trance or ecstasy or travail of thought, as Socrates did at the blockade of Poteidæa . . . , from the light of earliest dawn until the approach of evening, following out the spoor of some idea, or pursuing the intricacies of a whole system of ideas; making a philosophy, or, better still, a poem that should be adequate to the cosmos, and should extend in suggestion beyond it. . . . He had all the dialectical pertinacity of Socrates, but he had the gift of beauty as well. (p. 24)

In especial, his knowledge of what may be called esoteric French Symbolism (to distinguish it from other lesser and perfectly banal things to which the word symbolism is also applied or misapplied) was full at all points; it was the knowledge of a master, of a past-master, or better still of a grand-master, whose competence on this matter was absolute, and from whose authority there could be no appeal. All that was most profound in him as a poet was attracted by the aspirations and doctrines of the French esoteric Symbolist school, particularly as formulated and put into practice by Stéphane Mallarmé, whom he probably reverenced more than he did any other artist who had ever lived; (this is not to say of course that there were not others whom he considered greater, Aeschylus, for example; but there was something almost personal in the regard he had for Mallarmé.) . . . The best of his own poetry in its general feeling and atmosphere, and in several, and the most important, of its distinctive technical procedures, is definitely and intentionally Symbolist, to a much greater extent than any other poetry in English; in fact, it is the only example of thorough-going and fully maintained Symbolism that exists in English literature. In this connexion, it may be said that Brennan rendered a notable (and as yet quite unrecognized) service to English poetry by importing into it, and, as far as was necessary, acclimatizing in it the spirit and principles of that kind of Symbolism which I have called esoteric. For in doing so he endowed that poetry with further resources, he pointed the way to the creation in it of what is on the whole a new species of beauty—a beauty that is more essentially poetical than the various sorts secured in writing mainly governed by the older, more canonical, principles of aesthetic. (pp. 62-3)

Brennan is . . . practically the only writer who has essayed (principally in large sections of his later work) to introduce Symbolist art in an unadulterated and consistently pure form into English poetry, and this fact alone should render him worthy of attention; if he was successful in the attempt, it will be readily allowed that he is entitled to the most serious consideration, and I shall hope before the conclusion of this study to indicate that he actually was successful in a most remarkable degree. I will only say at this point that I think his writing, when it comes to be known as it deserves to be, will exercise a decisive influence in certain quarters, and will help to guide the movement of English poetry. (p. 69)

To begin with, it is well to proceed by a few negatives, by making it perfectly clear that there are certain things which Brennan's poetry most definitely is *not*, one at least of which many people might well expect it to be, and which Australians in general will probably consider it a pity, if not actually a crime, that it is not; and others again which the great majority of people, and not only Australians, would very much rather that it were. To put the matter briefly, it is not Australian, it

is not artless and unlettered, it does not contain messages, or other things meant for one's instruction, encouragement or general edification, and it is not crystal-clear, limpid or pellucid. These four things more or less hang together, and any one of them, in some measure, implies the others; they all issue from the fact that his preoccupations and intentions as a poet were predominantly and increasingly those of a Symbolist. . . . (p. 72)

We choose Mallarmé as being the most thorough-going, the most authoritative and the most influential of the Symbolists, and also and more particularly because he was the master of Brennan's special election, and hence the chief force determining Brennan's aesthetic theory and his practice as a poet. (p. 94)

The very title of Brennan's first published collection of verses— *Towards the Source*—is significant as showing the aim he had deliberately proposed to himself at the stage of his poetic career of which these verses are representative; his design is to move away from descriptive and otherwise external literature, with its divers "developments", towards the remote springs where poetry rises in its most original and purest essence—where, free of all that is extraneous or foreign to itself, it is absolute. . . . *Towards the Source*, it must be admitted (in spite of Mallarmé's approving pat), is not very successful as an essay in Symbolist poetry; but it is interesting as very definitely marking a departure on Brennan's part, and as indicating the line of his future progress. In this connexion, it should be noted that at this date Brennan was only imperfectly acquainted with Mallarmé's doctrine, and even with what was most revolutionary in his poetry; for much of Mallarmé's aesthetic philosophy had not yet been given to the world in a developed or extended form. . . . When this later verse and prose finally did come to Brennan's knowledge—after he had completed *Towards the Source*—it had a great, an enormous, influence on him, and made him very much more of a Symbolist than he had previously been. This is clearly shown in his later poetry, which, in all respects, is altogether superior to *Towards the Source*, and is the work of a man fully possessed of the principles of Symbolism. (pp. 103-05)

It is not to *Towards the Source*, then, but to later work (and especially work written in the five years between 1897 and 1902) that we must turn if we wish to see Brennan as a fairly complete and on the whole very successful symbolist. In this later poetry, he is constantly abandoning the world of external reality (or perhaps one should say of external appearances), and is moving in "the devious and covert ways of dream", to use one of his own phrases (and all the quotations in this section will be taken from one or another of his own poems). He is constantly now following shifting "cortèges of dream" that "fill imaginary avenues of gloom", and he is more intent on these than on any immediate presences, hard and clear-cut and well-defined. It will be his object more and more to evoke elusive visions in far-receding spiritual avenues, and to create a gloom of mystery around them; more and more he will temper the light, and subdue it to a twilight, and secure an effect of dimness in which things are suggested rather than seen. . . . And the mystery is reinforced by an inner undertone of music, which, as Mallarmé would have it do, acts on the mind with incantatory effect; at times it might be part of the music of Baudelaire's Thessalian sorcerers, which brings the moon down from the sky, and makes it dance upon the terrified turf. In poetry of this sort we have the "enticing strain" of supra-logical magic which Brennan, as a good Symbolist, valued above all other forms of song; and the "hint of nameless things revealed" which was more precious to him than any precise presentation of the definite things of everyday life. In this poetry there is disturbing reminiscence, the obsessing sense of another existence, it is full of:

> the haunting years
> this life has never known.

Here we have the Edenic mood, which is one of the major elements in Brennan's work, as it is in that of Baudelaire and Mallarmé. (pp. 106-07)

But the hints by which he will create an impression of something lost and absent must necessarily be delicate, evanescent and fragile; for any insistence or development would at once call up the concrete. And so, once again, more and more, like Mallarmé, he will be in quest of an utterance that shall as far as possible partake of the condition of silence. Hence the title *The Quest of Silence,* given to one of the subdivisions of the greatest section of his poetry, which itself has for covering title *The Forest of Night,* no less significant of the ideals he pursued as a poet. (p. 110)

If one wishes to look for real weaknesses in Brennan's work, then, one must look for them elsewhere, and no fair-minded critic could deny that they exist. In general, it may be said that there is very little singing quality in his verse; there is most decidedly absence or defect of singing quality of the Shelleyan or Swinburnian sort.... This is of course not necessarily a derogation, for there are certain poets of genuine and very great singing powers, but who have not the particular singing faculty of which we are speaking, the faculty that is pre-eminently Swinburne's and Shelly's, and for which it were desirable that the word lyrical should be reserved . . . ; Keats is perhaps the most notable example of the poets of this class. No-one would deny that in iambic measures Keats makes music of a very high order, music that rises into a rhapsodic cry. But Brennan's poetry, which never passes into music of the lyrical, the Shelleyan, kind, never passes into music of this latter kind either, for which the word elegiac might be reserved; or, if it does, it is so infrequently that the result almost seems to be out of keeping with the character of his verse as a whole. Once or twice, in the earliest of his published verses, there is music of this latter kind, and it seems to give promise of better things to come . . . but there is not much of this even in his early poetry, and it diminishes markedly with time, until at last there is practically none of it; this part of the earnest of his beginnings—fitful and faltering in any case—was never redeemed by anything that came later. But of course there are other things, which provide no small compensation. These are in the domain of what might be called the architecture of verse, rather than in that of music in the strict sense of the word. Brennan's poetry, apart from its penumbral and twilight effects of mystery, is chiefly remarkable for its structure, its build, its considerable achievements in architectonics. At its best it has impressive and almost overwhelming weight and mass and amplitude; it is monumental like mountains, and has the sublimity of mountains; to use one of his own phrases, it is "builded enormously", and this gives it greater powers of mystery. I have mentioned Aeschylus as one of Brennan's masters, and here, if anywhere, I think, is the influence of Aeschylus felt; it is hard to lay one's finger on any point of detail . . . and say 'this obviously is a reminiscence or echo of Aeschylus'; it is only in this more general matter of the architecture, of the structure of the verse, that one can trace any affiliation with Aeschylus; and here too is to be sought any influence that

Pindar may have had on Brennan. This structure of course is not without music; but the music is in a profound, a brooding monotone, it does not rise into song; it is a species of recitative, and one might almost say that it was talking that passes into crooning if this last word had not been vulgarized and cheapened by injudicious use or misuse.

I have somewhere used the word frustration in speaking of Brennan's poetry, and have more than once suggested that it is not uniformly successful or happy; not even those who love his poetry best, I think, will demur to this judgment. There is sometimes—there is frequently indeed—a lapse or failure of inspiration in it, a giving out of powers, a sudden cessation of what the French call *souffle*. In these cases it becomes laborious, jejune, anemic, thin, sterile, turbid, pebbly, metallic—if one may be allowed such a mixture of metaphors; there is no gathering volume of sound in it, none of that resonance that rises as it were from profound spiritual sources within, and seems to be prolonged infinitely; there is not even so much harmony of sound in it as would inevitably attend upon the presence of life of the most ordinary kind; and there is not even a harmony of mass, of architectural design; its constituent elements are independent of each other, and not bound together into a vital unity; as so often in Baudelaire's poetry, they bear the signs of hesitation and tinkering, and give the effect of pieces stuck together into a mosaic that is only verse because it scans. This is no doubt partly due to that conflict of contraries in Brennan to which we have more than once alluded: he was not always able to achieve even so much of a synthesis as would enable him to command a living stream of poetry. Some critics of course (not necessarily malignant) will bluntly say that it is due simply and solely to impotence, to sheer defect of creative power; and they will doubtless point to cases (Sully Prudhomme, for example) of men who have painfully laboured under the handicap of a divided personality, and yet have not sunk below a tolerable level of excellence as artists. Whatever the cause of Brennan's weaknesses may be, the fact remains that they exist, and it is best to admit it quite frankly. There is also the other offsetting and much more important fact that he wrote some very great poetry, in which he transcended these weaknesses, and that should be consolation enough for anybody. (pp. 139-43)

[For Brennan] was a scholar of poetry, in the same way as Henry James, for example, may be called a scholar of the novel. Both men had made a profound study of, and meditated deeply on, the craft which they practised; they had the most delicate sensibilities as well as encyclopedic knowledge in the matter of its resources; and to this extent at least their competence was masterly. (p. 159)

> *Randolph Hughes, in his* C. J. Brennan: An Essay in Values, *P. R. Stephensen & Co. Limited, 1934, 165 p.*

G. A. WILKES   (essay date 1953)

[*Wilkes's* "New Perspectives on Brennan's Poetry" *is considered a seminal essay in the history of Brennan scholarship. In the following excerpt from the concluding section of that study, Wilkes discusses* Poems 1913 *as a conceptually and artistically unified sequence and offers guidelines for future critics to follow when analyzing Brennan's work. The unity or lack of unity of this poetic sequence is one of the most extensively debated topics in Brennan criticism. For further discussion of the unity of* Poems 1913, *see the excerpt by A. R. Chisholm (1967/1970); for discussions of the lack of unity of the sequence, see the excerpts by Robert Ian Scott (1957) and Annette Stewart (1970).*]

"The great poet has not arrived yet," Brennan assured an interviewer in 1909, "but Australia will welcome him—when he is dead, probably." Today he has arrived and been welcomed, but there are so many needs still to be satisfied—a definitive text, a biography, a reliable exegesis—that even now it is not time for a final assessment of Brennan. The purpose of this . . . article, therefore, will be not to say the last word in a critical estimate, but to suggest . . . the lines that future criticism might properly take, and to anticipate some of its findings.

First, the study of the "conceptual framework" of Brennan's poetry—as revealed in his prose—must remove any doubt as to what *Poems (1913)* is about. It has one preoccupation, and one only—the author's quest for Eden. Whether one concedes the validity of the Eden concept or not, one must concede that it was valid for Brennan. Eden was his term for the "paradisal instinct" in humanity, and his verse records his pursuit of the vision from the youthful hopes of *Towards the Source,* through the soul-searching of *The Forest of Night,* to the secure confidence of *The Wanderer.* There is no other theme.

As a study of the manuscripts of the unfolding cycle makes plain, it is this unity of theme that has imposed on *Poems (1913)* its coherence of form. We are no longer at liberty to mistake the character of this volume: patterned on the symbolist *livre composé,* it is "a book of verse conceived and executed as a whole, a single concerted poem". This must be the datum for criticism, not some other datum. We must give up estimating Brennan's poetry from isolated lyrics, and begin to evaluate it as a whole. (p. 160)

As *Poems (1913)* is read . . . , the *modulation* of the versecraft to the varying demands of the theme is one of the most striking impressions received. Each specific form is wrung (there is no other word) to achieve, at its highest intensity, the particular effect attainable through its media, and is also made to fulfil a function in the unitary scheme. The moods of yearning and despair that contend in *Towards the Source* are caught and held in the moulds of heroic quatrain, rondel, *vers libre* and Patmorian ode as the movement presses on; the drama of **"Lilith"** is unfolded majestically through heroic couplets with a sliding caesura, the sense overflowing from verse to verse; in **"The Labour of Night"** the inexorable doom Lilith lays on man is reflected in the rigidity of the sonnet form iterated throughout; and the emancipation that comes with *The Wanderer* is felt in the turbulence of its blank verse. At all stages the versification is subtly adjusted to the theme, the elasticity of the form permitting comprehensiveness without disorder, the attainment of multiplicity within the single design.

Of course falterings may be detected here and there, occasional strains and fissures in the structure. Brennan himself felt "the marks of forced work" in *The Forest of Night,* and the "rhetoric" which he castigated as "the inherent evil of my flesh" at times permits the stateliness of **"Lilith"** to pass into magniloquence. The basic cause of such inequality as does occur, however, is that it seems a condition of the success of Brennan's writing that it should be refracted through some personal experience. Secure in *Toward the Source,* he wavers when, in the later series, he begins to objectify his quest. It is impossible not to feel the synthetic quality of parts of **"Secreta Silvarum"**, or of the passages in **"Lilith"** representing the impersonal aspects of the myth-Lilith as sphinx, as serpent, as wrought in

metal or carven in stone. **"The Labour of Night"**, because it is so objectified, also gives the impression of being written by force.

How far discord and infelicity were part of Brennan's intention in *Poems (1913),* as rhythms in its complex harmony, is hard to ascertain; but strictures which arise from attending to particular segments of the cycle do lose significance when it is experienced as a unit. It is as a whole that the volume demands appraisal, and it is only when it is so appraised that one discovers that for Brennan the *livre composé* held possibilities even richer than modulation of style.

For he adopted the form not only for its flexibility, but also because it possessed an *indirection* denied to outright narrative. The inner variations of structure permitted a suggestiveness akin to that sought by Eliot in *Four Quartets,* the effect described by Brennan as "symphonic". The analogy with the symphony is not exact, and need not be pressed. But *Poems (1913)* is no simple continuum: the diversity of its parts, its rhythmic development, and the balance of statement and obliquity within the design in concert give a disclosure of significance that reaches beyond the sum of the components. The cycle is inherently a *progression,* of course, rather than a structure of "movements" posed one against the other, with the true meaning to be found in the development relation amongst them—but it is still a progression so ordered and varied that a larger allusiveness is achieved.

Achieved in part by the "general arrangement of responsive divisions", it is also achieved, more subtly, by the iterative imagery that Brennan plies throughout. It is rather in this, than in its broad structural disposition, that the "symphonic" character of the book resides. (pp. 161-62)

Brennan's characteristic method with iterative imagery is to repeat and vary a motif for a time, then to allow it to be absorbed by a larger rhythm, which is duly absorbed by another farther on, giving a sense of deepening resonance as the cycle advances. (p. 163)

[As these] systems of imagery are developed and interwoven through the cycle, giving richer expression to the history it traces, it becomes apparent that in Brennan's hands the *livre composé* is not simply unitary in its effect, but rather cumulative. The slow breaking of significance as understanding deepens: this is the calculated effect. Most readers of *Poems (1913),* feeling the operation of this principle, have used the wrong word to describe it—"obscurity". Yet it was not Brennan's purpose that the book should be completely understood at a first reading. "An obscure beauty luring to long reverie over its complex significance," he explained, "is the symbolic ideal." The allusions of the cycle, its subtle evolutionary sequence, and the secret harmony of its parts were not to be instantly apprehended: they were to be at first obscurely sensed, and then, with successive readings, gradually discovered. It is only when *Poems (1913)* is experienced in this way, as its author intended, that one may hear the strains of a deeper harmony as the myth unfolds. This is Brennan's triumph in the *livre composé* form.

The mention of "obscurity" points to the second critical reorientation now imperative: the place of symbolism in Brennan's poetry must be defined afresh. (pp. 163-64)

At the outset, major confusions may be avoided by distinguishing (as Brennan himself distinguished) between symbolism as a metaphysic, and symbolism as a literary technique.

Metaphysically, symbolism is an illimitable subject, but so far as professed by Brennan, it is contained in the doctrine of correspondence. In its bearing on art, this doctrine is subsidiary to his philosophy of Eden. The connection has already been demonstrated. Eden is the ideal synthesis, the "last Unity of World and Human" towards which the universe is toiling, but to which it has not yet attained. While consummation delays, art, as the embodiment of a "correspondence", a *rapport* between man and nature achieved by the perceptive imagination, may pass ahead of the time-process and exhibit a pledge of the perfected world. Operating in the creative act, the imagination at once accomplishes a fusion of all the powers of mind at their highest pitch, and through its perception of "correspondence", effects a union between man and the outer world. Embodied in the poem, this harmony—limited as it is—becomes an earnest of the ultimate harmony that is promised, becomes (in a word) *symbolic* of Eden.

This is the symbolist philosophy of art, as distinct from the symbolist technique, as it figures in the thought of Chris Brennan. I have already argued that *Poems (1913)* cannot be interpreted as a series of attempts to traffic with Eden in this way. . . . Brennan's philosophy of symbolism, explaining the value assigned to art in his metaphysical scheme, has little bearing on his own composition.

His symbolist technique, however, is more relevant. The link between the conceptual and the technical levels of Brennan's theory is his conception of the *image*. (pp. 164-65)

To Brennan, a complete lyric, or a drama, may constitute an image, just as may a painting or a sculpture. . . . The image, to Brennan, is not merely pictorial or sensory: it is the resultant of an interaction between man and the outer universe, expressed in artistic form of any character or dimension.

What are the implications for literary technique? The crucial feature of Brennan's theory here is that the image must be a *direct* embodiment of the union between soul and nature, without intervening matter of any kind. It was for this that he prized the work of Mallarmé. (p. 166)

How far does Brennan pursue this ideal in his own work? He once assured Stephens "I'm NOT a symbolist". The statement is quite true, taken in its entirety: "I've simply some tendencies that way & of my contemporaries—for one must live in one's own age—I get on best with the so-called . . . symbolists." His poetry has tendencies toward and affiliations with symbolism, but is not universally governed by the technique.

The successive **"Lilith"** manuscripts are enough to show that Brennan strove always for condensation. The motive of his rewriting was always to take in the slack, to excise any passage that could possibly be spared. This exacting compression is even more apparent in the constricted form of the Brennan lyric, wherein the associated principle of suggestion is most finely exemplified. (p. 167)

Yet his symbolist "tendencies" are tendencies only. Adopting some principles, Brennan rejected others. He opposed the view that poetry should approximate to the condition of music, insisting that "each art, if it would reach the infinity of suggestiveness, must first rigorously confine itself to the effects attainable by its media". He also censured Rimbaud's proclivity to write verse as a series of disconnected images, like the later "automatic writing" of the surrealists. . . . For all his cultivation of suggestiveness, Brennan will not surrender the logical signification of poetry to it.

This refusal leads directly to the central rift between Brennan and the symbolists. He does not write poetry to disengage essences or to achieve a mystic unity of sounds, perfumes, and colours. He writes for *self-expression*. "We use poetry—to refer again to his manifesto—to express not the perfect Beauty, but our want of it, our aspiration towards it. Setting it far off in some imagined empyrean, the poet may even by a paradox, treat with fierce irony of life devoid of all shadow of it or desire for it. More often his theme will be the tragedy of such beauty as this world affords, or the fate that dogs the soul intoxicated with perfection." From the personal cry of *Towards the Source* to the defiant challenge of *The Wanderer,* Brennan's poetry (as has often been remarked) has the characteristics of a monologue. Poems so rigorously symbolist as "I saw my life as whitest flame" constitute but a fraction of his work. Again and again the urgent pressure of self-expression drives Brennan to direct utterance. The symbolist technique is always influential in chiselling the form of his poetry, but the character of the poetry itself is confessional.

Criticism in the future must recognize the unity of theme and structure in *Poems (1913),* and reconsider the symbolism of its method. My third suggestion, hesitantly advanced, implies the need for a new definition of the *nature* of Brennan's poetic achievement.

Since the "dissociation of sensibility" which Milton is held to have accomplished in the seventeenth century, poets (it is claimed) have been capable of expressing only one side of their experience at a time—feeling has been severed from thought, sensation from feeling. The attempt to recover the synthesis has come only with T. S. Eliot and his fellows. Looking back to Donne and the metaphysicals, they have given currency to such notions as "the sensuous apprehension of thought" and the "amalgamating of disparate experience", rediscovering poetry as "the expression of the whole man".

The anticipation of this movement in Brennan, even before the turn of the century, has passed unnoticed. A student of Donne, he was also well versed in Coleridge's theory of the imagination, with its similarities to the seventeenth-century conception of wit. But the influences are unimportant: Brennan's effort to "unify experience" arose from his private metaphysic of Eden, already described. (pp. 168-70)

It is in poetry that this living synthesis may be achieved. Poetry is the product of the imagination, which is "an intensive union and fusion of all the modes of mental activity", an absorption of all the separate faculties in the one perceptive act. "In all high imagination every one of them is implied, sensation, emotion, intellect: all work together." While Brennan did not regard poetry as a means of realizing Eden through such moments of stress, the theory has its consequences in the texture of his verse.

The distinctive Brennan lyric is indeed a "union and intension of all mental forces". It does not report a simple emotional agitation; Brennan is usually at the same time presenting an ordered statement of an idea. (p. 170)

The effort to unify sensibility in *Poems (1913)* nevertheless reaches beyond Eliot's notion of amalgamating disparate experience into new wholes. The "expression of the whole man" may be perceived in the texture of the individual poem, but it is better observed, on the grand scale, in the "texture" of the complete cycle. . . . "The sublimation of a whole imaginative life and experience into a subtly ordered series of poems"—this was the objective Brennan held before him.

Perhaps the aim was higher still. Brennan once described Baudelaire, in his aspiration to some ideal "that should be the consummation of all desire", as making of himself "the test-case of humanity". The test-case of humanity—the phrase might well apply to Brennan himself. He saw Eden as a possession offered to all, the "desire of the infinite" that has tortured man down the centuries, shaping his theogonies and dominating him in thought, passion and deed. Although Brennan's own saga is personal, its reverberations are infinite: he casts it in the form of a myth—inclusive of all myths—to magnify its dimensions, and applies an allusive technique which is constantly bringing the experience of other ages and other nations into the compass of his own. . . . Does *Poems (1913)* essay even more than the expression of the whole man: the expression, might it be, of all men? No one poem could achieve such an aim—only literature, as a whole, could achieve it—but it is still possible for the single poem to be touched by the grandeur of the attempt. (p. 171)

> G. A. Wilkes, "New Perspectives on Brennan's Poetry: Conclusion," in Southerly, Vol. 14, No. 3, 1953, pp. 160-71.

ROBERT IAN SCOTT (essay date 1957)

[*In the following excerpt, Scott discusses the interplay of myth and symbol in* Poems 1913. *Although he notes the ambiguous, disunified, and artistically uneven nature of the poetic cycle, Scott nonetheless affirms the ambitiousness of Brennan's attempt to define the essence of humanity's perpetual sense of discontent. For a more detailed discussion of the lack of unity of* Poems 1913, *see the excerpt by Annette Stewart (1970); for contrasting discussions of the mythic and symbolic unity of the work, see the excerpts by G. A. Wilkes (1953) and A. R. Chisholm (1967/1970).*]

Probably few poets writing in English anywhere, and certainly no other Australian poets, have attempted so ambitious a work as Christopher John Brennan's book *Poems* . . . or have brought to their work so comprehensive a theory of what poetry should be. . . .

[His] book is more than the autobiography of an exceptionally intelligent and unhappy man, because Brennan attempts to give his book a mythic stature and significance by making it suggest why our lives will not content us, and why this must be so. Brennan was the first Australian poet of more than local importance, and is still in some ways the most considerable, but his poems present almost nothing of Australia. Brennan's concern was with his own, and all human, emotional states, and with what they may mean, rather than with his own environment or the material world outside himself.

Brennan planned his book to be one manifold poem about his and our desire for, loss of, and search for Beauty, by which Brennan meant some perfect and permanent happiness and calm: some Eden. He believed this to be the subject of all true poetry. His definition of poetry is essentially Coleridge's, for whom beauty was the goal of poetry. Beauty is achieved, Coleridge said, by "the simultaneous intuition of the relation of parts, each to each, and of all to a whole". (p. 125)

[The first major part of *Poems*], "**Towards the Source**", describes his desire for the perfect beauty and ecstasy. The second, "**The Forest of Night**", provides a myth to explain why we are not happy here on earth, and the third part, "**The Wanderer**", concerns a "soul intoxicated with perfection" on this imperfect earth; and these three are what T. S. Eliot's *The Waste Land* and *Four Quartets* also present, in other ways.

Brennan and Coleridge both regarded poetry as a linking of the material or objective correlatives that are symbols of spiritual truths which hint at what these ultimately inexpressible truths are by means of what Brennan called "correspondences". These are comparisons of specific, concrete things on earth in time with those universal limits which shape human life. For Brennan, these correspondences are the essence of poetry, hints of another, more perfect world. . . .

Brennan's correspondences link his emotional life (the untranslated feeling) with dreams or images of what he wants that life to be. Because he turns from the concrete things we all see to a private world within himself, what is seen in his poems is increasingly abstract and vague, and in them earthly life is seen more and more as a dream-haunted twilight in which the dreams are most important and are of imagined other worlds. (p. 126)

For Brennan, turning to himself as his only subject, man (he) is the measure of all things and the whole truth, all in one within his mortal skin. Beauty is found by fully realizing man's self. In this quest symbols are articulations of parts of human experience, and corroborations of spiritual truths. Poetry is, for Brennan, ideally the birth of new worlds of, or by means of, uncommon insights into our human condition, which make us feel that there are two lives, ours now, here on earth, and another, better life we want. Symbols spawn myths, and the myth of some better life recurs repeatedly in poetry. And, Brennan wrote, the fall from Eden is the birth of the soul into matter, which cages it and is what it would escape. (p. 127)

[The] second and central part [of *Poems*] is the most intricate, and core and key to the whole book. The four main sections of it progress from gloomy dreaming to a desolate disillusionment. In the first section, "**The Twilight of Disquietude**", Brennan searches for happiness within himself, and finds himself unhappily chaotic. In the second, "**The Quest of Silence**", he tries to find peace in old poems, written when the world was younger, and in his own childhood, but finds the world a wasteland, and made so by sin. "**The Shadow of Lilith**" provides a myth, a most protean symbol, to explain why our lives are unhappy and chaotic. The last part, "**The Labour of Night**", lists human miseries in ancient history, and might well have been left out.

As G. A. Wilkes has shown [see excerpt dated 1953], Brennan began the plan of his book with the Lilith myth and accumulated about it an increasingly involved structure of subordinate poems, which he had in most cases already written and only afterwards fitted into his scheme. These other poems depend upon this central myth to make explicit and universally applicable what is true for Brennan, so that we may see how his fate involves, or is like, our own. Brennan employed the myth-figure Lilith as the central symbol of his book, to organize many disparate parts of his experience into one coherent whole, and to make it meaningful to us. In this way he anticipates T. S. Eliot's *The Waste Land, Ash-Wednesday,* and *Four Quartets,* which are also collections of various aspects of a world-view more or less organized by, or about, a central myth. Like *Four Quartets*—which is, like *The Waste Land* and Brennan's *Poems,* about our desire for some better life than this earth in time affords—Brennan repeats what he has to say in different ways to develop different aspects of his subject. The first part shows the hope held and disappointed which leads Brennan to despair; the second, more general and abstract, shows why he (and we) must despair, and the third, "**The Wanderer**", shows what effect this despairing search for happiness has on him. The two short tail-sections bring us from the desolate world of Brennan's soul to the Sydney of 1893-1913 in which he lived.

In **"The Forest of Night,"** Brennan first dreams of his bride, who will melt and end his winter dreams and discontent. He wants to be consumed by love and when that ends so does the world he wants. He seeks the fiery rose (Eden) in this world, where is no fire and no love, but only stifling smoke. To reach the fire, he would freeze within the lucid crystal of his winter dream of wanted summer. This is more than a lover's hyperbole. In these paradoxes are a deep-rooted discontent with earth and a desire for a happier realm of experience. Earth is sad and dreary, but while we live we have no other place. Earthly love is no help. Life has left Brennan self-haunted, seeking what he cannot reach. He knows only himself and that he is unhappy. This is the twilight of his disquietude, turning now to a darker despair. (pp. 130-31)

[In **"The Wanderer"** section] Brennan writes of himself as a homeless wanderer in this dreary twilight life. He has no hopes but will not stop, is far from his heart's desire but was not always. If only he could dream of someone to save him all this pain; but he cannot, knowing such dreams are delusions. He sees the narrowness of other men, and pities them if they should come to know his sort of misery. Yet their stifling lives are worse than his, for times wears them like weather, leaving them without memory or desire. Unless they save themselves they will die "a death that is never soften'd with sleep".

Brennan is disillusioned but still dream-haunted. He would that his love and he had gained peace, for all his peace is now lost with her. This memory and whatever glory he can win by continuing his foredefeated quest sustain him in his wind-bitten world. He cannot remember who he was and, realizing this, reaches peace. (p. 132)

This Eden-cycle tends to fall apart and fail because the relation of its parts, each to each, and of all to the whole, is not clear or inevitable, and because the Lilith myth is too ambiguous to make it obvious why Brennan says what he does or why it concerns us. This and his all too often awkward, artificial and verbose style make the book neither all one manifold poem, as Brennan planned, nor what he said poetry should be. Instead, the book is a chaos of fragments, some of them self-sufficient, even magnificent poems, and some only muddled empty bombast, "poetical" in the worst sense, which clogs the sense and movement of the whole book.

But some of his poems express as emotion candling our own emotional anatomies and unborn Edens to us, albeit darkly; and darkly because of the way in which Brennan writes what he had to say. His thought is sound at its root, for what emotions spurred it spur us all. We are all concerned with earth and time, which begin and end us all. Brennan says nothing of this in any clear, curt, concrete way. A Miltonic splendour of sound and subject can at times carry us past lapses of meaning in these verses and, perhaps, suggest moods no words catch, but this vague splendour alone is not basis enough on which to build a poem a fourth again as long as *Macbeth,* with neither a narrative nor some clear formal structure to sustain our attention.

In his Eden-seeking, his world-weariness, and his use of such symbols as the wasteland, the fiery rose, the seasons of life and of death, etc., Brennan employs what many poets have employed before and after him. In this, and in his debt to the French symbolist poets, Brennan anticipated T. S. Eliot, but Eliot took not Milton but Webster as a model, and wrote tersely

with concrete imagery to express his moods and abstract thought, using allusion as a means of compression and to make his poems more manifold and meaningful. Brennan employed a vaguer imagery and the sounds and side-associations of words more to cast spells which may sound deep within our emotions than to say anything prose can paraphrase. Like music, this poetry is emotive but not explicit. Brennan's 1913 **Poems** remains an isolated, obscure and uneven work, anticipating but apparently contributing little to more recent poetry. The book is only spasmodically what Brennan indicated poetry could be at its best. His failure is not that his first conception of his book was wrong, but that his writing was inadequate to the great work he set himself. (pp. 133-34)

> Robert Ian Scott, "Christopher Brennan's 1913 'Poems'," in Southerly, Vol. 18, No. 3, 1957, pp. 125-34.

FRANK KERMODE (essay date 1961)

[*Kermode is an English critic whose career combines modern critical methods with expert traditional scholarship, particularly in his work on Shakespeare. In his critical discussions of modern literature, Kermode has embraced many of the conceptions of structuralism and phenomenology. Kermode characterizes all human knowledge as poetic, or fictive: constructed by humans and affected by the perceptual and emotional limitations of human consciousness. Because perceptions of life and the world change, so does human knowledge and the meaning attached to things and events. Thus, there is no single fixed reality over time. Similarly, for Kermode, a work of art has no single fixed meaning, but a multiplicity of possible interpretations; in fact, the best of modern writing is constructed so that it invites a variety of interpretations, all of which depend upon the sensibility of the reader. Kermode believes his critical writings exist to stimulate thought, to offer possible interpretations, but not to fix a single meaning to a work of art. True or "classic" literature, to Kermode, is thus a constantly reinterpreted living text, "complex and indeterminate enough to allow us our necessary pluralities." In the following excerpt Kermode, assessing Brennan's poetry from a European standpoint, notes the unevenness of the Australian's work but predicts that despite this Brennan will be highly regarded among all English poets who wrote during his period.*]

By a happy accident of war I found myself, at the beginning of 1945, in Sydney; more good luck acquainted me with poets, and the poets told me about Brennan. I got to know one or two poems—they were not easy to find—and heard a great deal about the man and the myth. People were already talking about a collected edition, though not, as I remember it, with much hope. Now [*The Verse of Christopher Brennan*] has appeared, and I can imagine the rejoicing, there being no sign visible from here that Brennan is less venerated among the intelligentsia than he was fifteen years ago. But in that interval I have often tried him out on suitable Englishmen without much response, and this despite the appearance of *The Wanderer* in *The Penguin Book of Australian Verse*. As a matter of fact, the only non-Australian I ever met who had the vaguest idea of Brennan was the German polymath Kurt Wais, who had come across him in his Mallarmé studies.

I mention these matters by way of presenting my credentials; so far as expert knowledge goes I write of Brennan as a complete outsider, but a more interested outsider than most of the others. At any rate I am in no danger of underestimating his importance, which is clearly fundamental, in the development of modern Australian intellectual life.

Brennan himself believed, perhaps erroneously, that there was little specifically Australian about his poems, that he might as well have written them in China, and I suppose this view has importance as basic to a poetic tradition against which Australian poets occasionally revolt. Certainly he could have worked in Paris, in a circle that contained many expatriates, and he would have been at ease with the conversation of the *mardistes*. He might have flourished in England; cultural estrangement seems to be a condition of modernism, of extreme technical experiment, and modern English poetry is the work of non-English English speakers founding their own traditions. But the achievement of Brennan is so indissolubly bound to his place in Australian history that it is useless to abstract him from that context, however speculatively. Some of his failures might be attributed to an uncertainty in his communications with Europe—with the Paris of, say, Apollinaire and the London of Pound and Hulme—but nobody can be certain of this (least of all I, who lack information as to the contents of the promised volume of prose) and everybody can be certain that whatever difference this book may make to his international reputation, Brennan will remain the great *Australian* poet.

Mr. Chisholm, on whom the considerable weight of this important enterprise has fallen, presents the text with only the more important variants, and does not claim to be definitive. He offers, in this work at any rate (I have not seen his book on Brennan) little help towards interpretation, though outsiders will need it. And his biographical introduction, though deft and thorough, does not set out to provide a substitute for that aura of legend—I mean the stories of Brennan's social life and his learning—that invest him in the minds of Australians. (The observation that he 'was one of the world's greatest scholars' will probably seem excessive on the evidence provided.) Such passages of more or less supererogatory information as Mr. Chisholm finds space for are very valuable; for example, it exactly confirms one's historical 'placing' of the poet that the pictures in his study included not only the Nadar Mallarmé but a Puvis de Chavannes, drawings by Rossetti and Blake, and the woodcuts for Thornton's Virgil. They are what, without improbability, you might have expected to find in the rooms shared by Symons and Yeats in Fountain Court during the brief but glorious life of *The Savoy*. He knew the growing-point of modern literature.

Brennan certainly understood Mallarmé well—better than Yeats, of course, and perhaps better than Symons. His debt is very great, and aptly so, for this is where a modern poetry ought to begin. It is the second step, not the first, that introduces the idea of failure. Despite his admiration for Dante ('every line, nay every word, pure muscle, nothing superfluous') Brennan—unlike the American poets in London—did not find in other French poetry examples of a diction less idiosyncratic, less distorted by syntactical strain, less farded, that might have pointed him forward to criteria of exactitude which he seems to have needed. To some extent he doubles back from Mallarmé into the language of English heterodox mysticism—to Shelley, for instance. When he is writing badly the eye bounces off his lines as off some of Shelley's. Throughout his most productive period he clung to, perhaps saw no need to dispose of, an archaistic diction which would have served Francis Thompson. He had a dreadful passion for the Shakespearian-Keatsian 'viewless'. Tennyson constantly obtrudes. With a slight change in the sense of the noun one might apply to Brennan what Verlaine said of Tennyson, that when he should have been broken-hearted he had many reminiscences. Too often in these poems one sees the metal of a distinguished imagination run

off into banal moulds, and always, of course, with a reduction of that very complexity of effect for which Brennan was trying. On the other hand, when writing his taut, syntactically complex quatrains and evidently aiming at 'muscular strength', he frequently produces only a hollow Kiplingesque roar, and the reverberations confound the sense. *The Burden of Tyre,* which comes first in the new book, one reads with something approaching dismay; it is shot through with those Eden-images that are a vital constituent of Brennan's verse, and occasionally, as in VIII, these are made to match the public theme of the poem; but the tense bellowing destroys all their quality. In the end both these faults—the archaism and the hollow roaring—may proceed from the same cause: uncertainty, isolation, oracular concealment of these.

But it is with *Poems 1913* that the outsider has chiefly to deal. (pp. 57-9)

A degree of instability is what might be expected of any poet in Brennan's precarious position; yet as one turns over these pages one becomes aware of something that is happening steadily and impressively. Brennan, in short, is writing a characteristically 'modern' sequence of poems, united by elements of iteration, by the cohesion not of thoughts but of images. The root-image is of the lost paradise. I do not know whether the Sydney of his lifetime could offer Brennan ritual satisfactions for his occult tastes; one would, given the period, suppose it could. He certainly writes like an adept, and in London would have found his way into something like the Golden Dawn. (Sad to reflect that the impact of Australian poets on London in the Nineties seems to have been confined to a disastrous evening at the Rhymers' Club.) His Rose symbolism may owe something to Yeats, and is certainly indebted to the systematic esotericism disseminated by Mathers (in whose *Kabalah Unveiled* the rose 'with its mysterious centre, its nucleus, the central Sun, is a symbol of the infinite and harmonious separations of nature'). The Paradise image itself is part of the vast, untidy heap of lore accumulated by students of Neo-Platonic Hermetic and alchemical writing, and rearranged by the secret societies; but it also goes straight back to Blake, and has a place in the French tradition. Perhaps all this has been studied. I should be surprised to find that Milton was of the first importance to Brennan, as the Penguin editors affirm. But the very ubiquity of such an image, though it helps the Symbolist poet, can obviously be dangerous as derivative as the young Brennan. In fact he is sometimes almost too direct in his handling of it ('Ah, who will give us back our long-lost innocence') and sometimes a good simplicity ('And shall the living waters heed') degenerates into *Yellow Book simplesse* ('I am shut out of mine own heart').

By 1898 ('**The Forest of the Night'**) the image had gone deep, and the opening sonnet to Mallarmé, though very poor, is a hint of the increased obliquity of what follows. I can find no good word to say of the long '**Liminary'**; but with '**The Twilight of Disquietude'** there begins a series of variations radically associated with the basic theme, the task of art in the restoration of Eden: 'I seek the word/That shall become the deed of might.' This is the Word sought beyond good and evil and in the teeth of dark opposition. The experimentation goes on—Keatsian couplets, Tennysonian reminiscences, even glances, I think, at Yeats and Symons—but here one nevertheless does feel the man's peculiar strength, as in '**Fire in the heavens,'** and notably in '**A gray and dusty daylight,'** where he is precisely the occult-symbolist he wanted to be. The sequence numbered 56-62, followed by '**The Window and the Hearth'** is unmistakeably the work of a big poet; and this takes us to *Lilith*.

Here there is all the Symbolist dark one could wish, witness the obscure and yet brilliant *terza rima* poem **'Cloth'd now with dark alone'**. . . . Lilith, in short, is a figure of the fallen, divided world, and also of the forces that restore it. She is a characteristic late-Romantic image, and Brennan does not entirely avoid the dangers of such a theme; there is too much merely rhapsodical agonising in the poem. There are also conceptions of great strength and originality; the speech of Adam (ix), the Mallarméan comment of x ('cool'd of his calenture, elaborate brute') and the superb prosopopeia of Lilith ('Terrible if he will not have me else'). Yet the final section of this remarkable poem suggests ultimate failure; it has fine lines, but is too 'Symonsy'—Brennan's own word of another poem— and brings to its conclusion a work deprived of classic status only because it is trapped in the iconography and the diction of an age too early.

I have not space to speak of the night-poems that follow *Lilith,* nor of *The Wanderer,* which I understand is regarded as an experiment in sprung rhythm, but seems nearer to the less radical 'wavering organic rhythms' of Yeats; he is certainly a somewhat too substantial presence in 'How old is my heart,' fine as that section is:

> my garment and my home shall be the
>   enveloping winds
> and my heart fill'd wholly with their
>   old pitiless cry.

Of the war poems the least said the better, though it is interesting to see the Germans getting identified with Ancient Night. (pp. 59-60)

It is much too early for those of us who do not know Brennan well to attempt dispassionate, non-Australian estimates. We should now, however, be clear that there is no preposterous degree of self-delusion in the highest claims of his countrymen, and that Brennan will claim a distinguished place among poets writing in English between 1890 and the first world war. (p. 61)

> *Frank Kermode, "The European View of Christopher Brennan,"* in Australian Letters, *Vol. 3, No. 3, March, 1961, pp. 57-61.*

A. R. CHISHOLM   (essay date 1961-62)

[*Editor of* The Verse of Christopher Brennan *and* The Prose of Christopher Brennan, *Chisholm is considered a pioneering Brennan scholar. In the following excerpt he compares and contrasts the poetic methods of Brennan and his French counterpart, Stéphane Mallarmé.*]

It is easy to make mistakes when estimating the extent of Mallarmé's influence on Christopher Brennan. The latter denied that he was a Symbolist, and was no doubt justified in doing so; but that does not wipe out his debts to the greatest of the French Symbolists. On the other hand, like a few others who are familiar with the work of both poets, I have been taxed with reading too much Symbolism into Brennan's poetry; and to some extent the present study is a defence of my position.

Perhaps it is best to begin by saying that Brennan was a poet in his own right, with a strongly individual style and plenty of native temperament, so that he would have been a poet of major importance even if Mallarmé's writings had not existed, or if Brennan had never come in contact with them. But it is equally true that his poetry would have been very different

from what it is if he had not been influenced by the poetic theory and practice of Stéphane Mallarmé. (p. 2)

I am convinced that Brennan was a major star in the poetic firmament; that he learnt much from Mallarmé and benefited greatly from what he learnt; that this did not take away from his originality; and that the intellectual relationship between the two poets was one of the most fruitful examples of elective affinity in the history of literature. Moreover, Brennan's indirect participation in a great European poetic movement, in which Mallarmé was a dominant figure, lifts him out of his Australian limits and gives him a place in world literature. (p. 3)

Brennan and Mallarmé postulated an Eden beyond the banal realities of the world. But in the case of both poets this Eden took various forms, and those taken by Brennan's Eden do not always coincide with those conceived by Mallarmé. A notable example of this divergence is seen in what we might call the Eden of the heart.

Brennan, for one thing, was more sensual than his predecessor, and behind the visionary idealism of *Towards the Source* we discern an ardent desire for *possession*: the beloved woman is very much a woman, a creature of flesh and senses, inspiring passion and stirring a lover's hot blood. I do not hold this against Brennan, of course: he was a whole man, and he loved in a man's way. Nor do I suggest that his passion is always explicit in *Towards the Source*: often it expresses itself through the warmth (or wistfulness) of the imagery rather than through passionate statement. . . . (p. 6)

Art for Mallarmé was concerned with beauty, and Brennan had the same outlook. Neither of the two men would ever have accepted the idea, not uncommon today, that the ugly is as important as the beautiful. But in their working definition of beauty we find them at variance in several respects. Beauty, as Mallarmé saw it, was not in perceptible objects but in their effect on the mind of the observer: hence his dictum, 'Peindre non la chose, mais l'effet qu'elle produit'—the artist must paint not the thing, but what he experiences when looking at it. Beauty, in other words, is purely psychological; and I doubt whether Brennan instinctively subscribed to this belief. For him, beauty is partly external, and a landscape exists in its own right. . . .

Mallarmé's idealism led him to postulate the Absolute as the only real and timeless beauty. . . . (p. 7)

Brennan, on the other hand, has this in common with the French Romantics, that he is vitally concerned with time, with the past, even with his ancestral past. His Eden of beauty is not one that is concealed by the illusory splendour of things so much as an Eden that once existed and has now been lost. . . . I am strongly inclined to believe that this idea of an Eden once possessed and now lost has some connection with Brennan's loss of his Catholic faith, found again only towards the end of his life. Even in his long period of estrangement from his Church, he never ceased to regret what he had lost. . . . And both his nostalgias, the ancestral and the spiritual, persist in the two Epilogues to *Poems 1913*.

His preoccupation with the past is also, no doubt, part of his Celtic make-up; whereas Mallarmé had no ancestral nostalgias. He took the view, explicitly stated in the sonnet *Surgi de la croupe et du bond,* that a man's mind has nothing in common with the mind of his forebears; that the union of his two parents had produced only his body, in as much as no couple can ever dream the same dream, and there is, consequently, no creative affinity between them. He believed (see the sonnet beginning 'Une dentelle s'abolit') that ideally a man should create his own true self, which is not an ego at all but an aspect of the Absolute. Curiously enough, he is here much closer than Brennan to the Christian belief that men are made in God's image, and to the New Testament dictum that we must be born again.

The questions just discussed bring us to an important poetic doctrine which Brennan undoubtedly shared with Mallarmé and which, to some extent, he owed to him: the doctrine of correspondences.

Mallarmé did not invent the idea of correspondences, which reaches back a long way, through Swedenborg, Blake, Jakob Boehme and others, and which was enunciated as a poetic doctrine in Baudelaire's well-known sonnet *Correspondances*. But the great French Symbolist was the first to make it the very basis of poetry.

Briefly, the theory of correspondences, as it was practised by Mallarmé, is this: all Reality is one; but, though total Reality is present even in the smallest object (cf. Blake), the object itself only symbolises it, gives it a visible form, which, however, is too individual to be perfect. Baudelaire had postulated an obscure unity, of which all things are symbols, but he did not make very clear what this unity was. (pp. 7-8)

But we do not need to go into all the philosophical ramifications of this theory: the most important thing, in the present context, is its implications for poetry. If Reality is mind, then it follows (and Mallarmé put this corollary into practice) that the real concern of poetry is not objects but mental experiences, and the means of conveying these experiences to the reader. This obviously cannot be done by the *description* of objects or by *statements* about what is happening in one's mind: description would keep us in the physical domain, and statement would arrest our mental processes, which can really never stand still while we are alive and conscious. Incidentally, Brennan uses statement and description much more than Mallarmé does, and some passages in *The Forest of Night* are sheer arguments.

Now, just as things are the correspondences of Reality, so too mental experiences can be conveyed to others only by correspondences and suggestions; and since objects yield their inner Reality only when they are transformed into mental experiences, what is conveyed to the reader by means of suggestive correspondences is much more real than mere appearances.

Brennan sometimes adopts Mallarmé's practice and uses correspondences and suggestion; but, particularly in *The Forest of Night*, the mind that he thus reveals is very different from the mind that Mallarmé reveals to us. The very symbol used by Brennan for a covering title, the **'Forest of Night'**, tells its own tale. Mallarmé conceived his mind as a flux, situated not in space but in time; but Brennan's is conceived by himself as a forest enveloped in night, situated in both time and space (space plays a still more important role in *The Wanderer*). His symbols thus tend to be more complex than Mallarmé's, which are difficult rather than obscure; and they play with space in a way that occasionally almost bewilders the reader. (pp. 8-9)

Mallarmé could pack ["a wealth of correspondence"] into a few lines; and this is a path along which Brennan did not follow him; did not, and perhaps could not, because he was too preoccupied with philosophical ideas to devote as much time as Mallarmé did to pure form. (p. 11)

· · · · ·

Though difficult, Mallarmé's poetry is not obscure: it always says something. But it says it in such a way as to produce an incantation. . . .

Unlike Mallarmé, who produces incantation by means of compression, packing a wealth of imagery into a short poem (even *Hérodiade* and *L'Après-midi d'un Faune* are not conspicuously long), Brennan achieves his effect by means of an architectural massiveness. Such massiveness is characteristic of him, and manifests itself not only in his verse but in the architectonic and coherent immensity of his scholarship. His incantations, consequently, seem for the most part Miltonic rather than Mallarmean. But really they are neither: they are native, individual, pure Brennan. . . . (p. 26)

I open a parenthesis here to remark that Brennan's poetry never yields the fullness of its beauty unless it is read aloud. I realised this on the rare occasions when I induced him to repeat some of his own lines—which he could do with amazing facility, thanks to his infallible memory. He did not actually recite them: he intoned them, with that deep, resonant voice that still haunts me . . . Intone 'O thou that achest', and you will *hear* the images emerging and disappearing, each serving its individual purpose and yet being subordinated to the incantatory structure of the whole; you will hear how the very sound of the words is echoed, not only in the rather intricately woven rhymes but even in passages far removed from each other.

There are passages also, in [*The Forest of Night*], where both the sonority of the words and the cosmic character of the images lift the architecture of the lines up into the far dimensions of the universe, in much the same way as the tremendous chords in Wagner's well-known *Lohengrin* overture. (p. 27)

It is Brennan's resonant voice that is here heard singing, louder and more desperately than Mallarmé's; for behind it, like a tragic orchestra, is the cosmic voice of Night, the voice of the terrible Absence, the voice of the shadowy but relentless and inescapable Lilith.

And there, I think, is the answer to a critic who, reviewing the volume of collected *Verse* published in 1960, affirmed that Brennan's idiom was out of date and conveyed little meaning to the reader of today. If that were true (which I cannot believe), it would be a sad reflection on the poverty of our modern idiom, and would banish not only Brennan but Aeschylus, Milton, Beethoven, Wagner—and how many other incantatory voices of the past? (p. 28)

Mallarmé was a born poet, and became a great one because he sat down and thought rigorously about poetry; Brennan was a born poet, and was at the same time one of the greatest scholars of his age. In both men, intellect reached a stage where it took command of emotion without destroying it, disciplined imagination, coordinated private nostalgias and temperamental sensibilities and transformed them into pure incantation.

Of the two, Mallarmé was the more fortunate, in that he was born in a Europe where poetry was ripe for a fundamental transformation; whereas Brennan was born in an Australia that was only beginning to pass out of its pioneering stage. Small wonder that he experienced a cosmic loneliness, a desperate sense of exile. For he wore the royal mantle of poetry but knew no kingdom. (p. 35)

A. R. Chisholm, "Brennan and Mallarmé: Part One" and "Brennan and Mallarmé: Part Two," in Southerly, Vol. 21, No. 4, & Vol. 22, No. 1, 1961 & 1962, pp. 2-11; 23-35.*

SYBILLE SMITH   (essay date 1963)

[In the following excerpt Smith places Brennan at the forefront of Australian literary criticism, in large part for his expositions on German Romanticism and French Symbolism.]

One's first tendency, now that Brennan's prose is available, is perhaps to focus it back on his poetry, to look for revelations of his thought which will throw light on the more problematical aspects of his work. Certainly there are such glimpses and glosses, in his remarks on symbolism, on the search for Eden, or in his interpretation of Lear as man the wanderer whose home is 'built upon the winds and under them upon the storm . . . which strips from him, like so many vain garments, the laws, the order, the convention in which he has sheltered his life'. It is obvious, however, that while such a statement may illuminate **'The Wanderer'** it primarily illuminates the work in question. From [*The Prose of Christopher Brennan*] we receive a powerful complementary image to that of Brennan the poet; the image of Brennan the critic and interpreter. Where Brennan's poetry at its best—in **'Towards the Source'** and **'The Wanderer'**—is experience become idea, Brennan's criticism at its best is idea become experience.

Brennan reveals a combination of powers necessary to, but rare in, the critic: range and depth of scholarship together with sensitivity of response; a sense for patterns of development and relationship together with the ability for close textual comment which safeguards him from the arbitrariness or abstraction which sometimes accompany a literary-historical approach; a basic good-will; and finally, scrupulous honesty and commitment. (p. 65)

His criticism is both interpretive and evaluative, and he has also a craftsman's approach, a professional interest which gives added solidity to his judgments.

One rather surprising aspect of this approach is Brennan's attack on poetic diction (examples he gives are 'resilient boughs' and 'ensanguined cross')—surprising in view of the glimmer and glamour, the 'whelmed quiring, which are a feature of the pre-Raphaelite vocabulary which he commends, and of his own work. A certain obtuseness to words, which flaws some of his poetry, emerges for instance in two lines of his otherwise lovely translation from Verlaine:

> My God, my God, and yon is life
> Simple, sans soil;

On the other hand, Brennan emphasises throughout these essays the poet's need for intellectual control of his language. He is particularly sensitive to that point where words acquire an impetus of their own, where they take over and begin to re-shape what they are to express instead of being controlled by it.

Brennan's mastery of the basic critical 'positions' can be seen already in the shorter essays on contemporary English poets. In attack (as on William Watson) he is pungent, agile and witty, but also fair. He does not score off his author by creating a critical context in which the quotations he gives will inevitably seem ridiculous, but analyses them with devastating precision. In appreciation (for instance, of Henley) he is generous but discriminating. He does not give with one hand and take with the other, but makes clear what he considers to be Henley's achievement as well as his limitations.

In marked contrast to the general fairness and responsibility of his criticism are the essays on Heine and on the *Nibelungenlied*. Here the tone is not critical but vindictive.

Brennan's attacks come so much at a tangent to the real nature of the works, and are in such contrast to his normal accuracy of response and impartiality, that they seem to be the expression of his war-inspired anti-Germanism rather than of a critical attitude. This hostility is expressed explicitly in another essay attacking the apologists and defenders of Germany. Not the fact of Brennan's attack, which could have force and relevance, but the tone is objectionable; as in **'Chant of Doom'** an obsessive note intrudes—what expresses itself is not revulsion that controls and points what is said, but a resentment which remains impotent.

The most sustained and interesting sections of the book are those on German Romanticism and French Symbolism. Brennan perceptively recognizes the affinity between these two movements, which is a much more essential affinity than that between German and French romanticism. (pp. 65-6)

In his essays on aesthetics Brennan formulates the theory on which his interpretation of the two movements is based. He rejects the unhelpful definition of poetry as the expression of emotion, pointing out that emotion is a directing power but that the expression does not constitute poetry, which is 'the expression of the imagination in language'. This definition leads to his central theory: 'Imagination is a perceptive act; the perception of analogies and correspondences, whereby things which in ordinary consciousness led a separate existence are fused into a unity, so that sensuous facts become symbols.' From this, in itself basically Romantic view (Romantic in that it takes as perception of objective fact what is an essentially subjective act of synthesis), Brennan goes on to develop the, again essentially Romantic, idea of the mystical and religious nature of art: 'There is only one subject of all art and that is the thought of Eden, which is only another name for harmony.' (p. 67)

Following up the implications of his theory Brennan arrives ultimately at the identification of art and religion. 'From the fact that the world is capable of spiritual interpretation all special religion is an inference.' Man, he continues, can live by poetry as by religion because it constitutes a revelation of his true self and its relationship to the world. Here the heritage of Romanticism present in the aestheticism of the turn of the century, with its assumption that 'spiritual' and 'religious' are synonymous, emerges as clearly in Brennan as in Stefan George and, to a certain extent, in Rilke. This view of art seems to imply, not a clearly developed aesthetic system but the simplified substitution of art for God at the centre of a system based on, and inextricably intermeshed with, the premise of the existence of God. The throne of God, advertised as vacant by Nietzsche, is filled, paradoxically, by a successor whose lack of legitimacy Nietzsche himself was the first to proclaim.

Unlike many systems of aesthetics which are persuasive in the abstract and disappointing when applied to specific works, Brennan's theory, with all its weaknesses, becomes more illuminating and compelling when used to interpret concrete examples. It is already valuable in that it takes into account the special nature of poetic utterance and in that it focuses attention on the work as a unity. (p. 68)

In the study of Mallarmé (a remarkable achievement, in itself, and even more for its time) Brennan's theory has its fullest application—and, presumably, its source. The textual analysis here is masterly, and the discussion of obscurity in poetry as good as anything Eliot has written on the subject.

What makes Brennan's series of essays on German Romanticism particularly interesting—and accounts also for any limitations—is that he is speaking to a remarkable degree from within Romanticism, from a basically Romantic temperament. Passing comments in various other contexts already begin to indicate this—'Man's task is to spiritualize, idealize and humanize'—'The arts should be kindred phases of one vital culture'—'I hold it impossible to conceive reality otherwise than in terms of the spirit.' His definition of Symbolism has many affinities with Friedrich Schlegel's famous definiton of Romantic poetry: *'Die romantische Poesie ist eine progressive Universalpoesie . . .'* His remarks on Goethe show a typical Romantic edginess; and his defence of Romantic restlessness, inefficiency and yearning is in part almost a paraphrase of certain passages from Tieck and Novalis. His attempt to defend the *Hymnen an die Nacht* against the charge that they glorify death and sickness comes so much from within the spirit of Romanticism that it remains ineffectual: 'What they proclaim is that the dead are not dead but alive . . . more alive than we.' This, in answer to attacks like that of Nietzsche, is simply playing with words, the very point of the attack being that the sense of life's ultimate value is diminished by the positing of a higher transcendent existence, whatever its name. (p. 69)

One may question certain theories and details of interpretation, but throughout this book Brennan's opinions command respect and attention. He stands, not only at the beginning of, but unrivalled in, Australian literary criticism. His range, covering the literatures of six countries, is unique, but even more remarkable is his grasp of the essential nature of European writers and movements a decade and sometimes more before real critical attention turned to them in their own countries. His interpretations foreshadow and are in no way invalidated by later developments. One has, from this volume, not only the impression of contact with a sympathetic and creatively intelligent mind, but that constantly renewed sense of the importance of the work being discussed which only great criticism can give. (p. 70)

> Sybille Smith, *"Brennan's Stature as Critic,"* in Quadrant, *Vol. VII, No. 1, Summer, 1963, pp. 65-70.*

JUDITH WRIGHT   (essay date 1965)

[*Wright is an Australian writer who has received international attention for her traditional lyric poetry which evokes love for her native land through remarkably descriptive imagery. In the following excerpt Wright discusses Brennan's representation of man's search for enlightenment in* Poems 1913—*an artistic undertaking which Wright believes failed when Brennan abandoned, in* "The Wanderer," *his conviction that the human soul could attain spiritual perfection through prolonged, conscientious introspection.*]

Brennan's chief poetic preoccupation was with the relationship between man's thought and his universe, and hence with the supposed dichotomy between mind and matter. His statement of the philosophical position as he saw it is to be found in its most condensed form in his paper **'Fact and Idea'**. . . . (p. 81)

In **'Fact and Idea'**, Brennan's conclusion is that consciousness 'has broken up its own unity, that it might become more fully aware of its interests, each by each, and use them in turn as means to remodel the world'. This fragmentation or analysis, however, is 'just so much preparation to some greater synthesis—the complete humanization of the Universe. . . .'

Only, then, in the final 'Unity of World and Human' that the journey of consciousness implies, can that journey find its end. This state, 'where thought would be like quivering flame, inseparable from sense, emotion and imagination', is Brennan's foreseen Eden, the second Eden in which God and man, mind and matter, flesh and soul, and all dichotomies, are reconciled.

Since it is only the increase of consciousness that can lead to this apotheosis of man-in-world, Brennan's position here might seem to point him rather in the direction of philosophy than of art. But, in his paper delivered in 1903 and titled **'Philosophy and Art'** he states his view of the function of the artist in the world-process. In this paper, too, a number of ideas important to his poetry are to be found; especially his statement of the dilemma of thought deprived of any absolute basis. For Brennan, only the increase of knowledge, i.e. of consciousness, could lead to the union of man with his universe; but knowledge is seen to be founded, not on absolute referents, but on human experience and human consciousness itself, and, says Brennan, 'all concepts (are) teleological instruments, the creatures of attention and of attention obeying the hest of interest . . .' 'Here was the whole foundation cut away from under all the splendid shrines erected on the eternal rock of reason and its ideas: ideas were man's tools and eternal only if he found them most fitting.'

This is the very crux of his **'Lilith'** series, in the poem from **'The Watch at Midnight'**, 'The plumes of night, unfurl'd', and the point on which Brennan himself seems to have been finally impaled. (p. 82)

The Absolute that Brennan felt humanity to be in search of was, in fact, not to be known by intellect alone, but by the fullest possible power of human experience, deployed in the function of imagination and 'mediated by the symbol', the point at which inner experience and outer reality find their expression and unity.

It is at this point that Symbolist theory becomes crucial for Brennan. Yet there are important differences between his use of it, and that of Mallarmé. Brennan's notion of the symbol is as a form through which a dynamic current flows in two directions; from the inner toward the outer, and back again. The symbol itself may cease to mediate one particular current (the Rose's meaning changes with time, but the form of the Rose remains and may be reanimated by new insights). What is important is that meaning though it may alter, is a real relationship between inner and outer—that the 'correspondences' between inner and outer which are mediated through the symbol form a guarantee that human experience is truly connected with, and can assimilate, a true reality. . . . (pp. 83-4)

There is a sense, in fact, in which Brennan's whole exploration and achievement stem from his religious upbringing—it is an attempt at reconciliation and reanimation of his early religious experiences. And, if there is one note in his writing that is unmistakable, it is the habit of mind and even of diction that his early experience left in him. His mind is not secular; his vision and the imagery he used are constantly coloured by, and refer back to, his early training. And it may be that the somewhat *ex cathedra* tone of many of the poems, the assumption of a kind of timeless experience in the speaker (as though, like Eliot, Brennan were assuming a Tiresian mantle) is traceable to Brennan's early ambition toward the impersonal authority of the priesthood. (p. 84)

From one point of view, the whole structure of *Poems 1913* is a personal testament to Brennan's own 'fall' from the Church in which his youth found fulfilment, and from the love that symbolized Eden to him in later years, and to his search through the whole recorded conscious history of man, from the Cabbala to Swedenborg and beyond, for a rebirth of faith. But if it is in essence the story of Brennan's spiritual movement away from Catholicism, it is also a great deal more. It is also a history—a symbolic history—of the whole movement of consciousness through recorded time, and its successive attempts at embodying itself in absolutes that themselves become lifeless and give way to other absolutes, whether religions or systems of thought.

For Brennan, all such systems (pantheism, sun-god religions, the Mars-worship of empires, even the pursuit of ultimate wisdom) are themselves no more than symbols—symbols of man himself and of his never-ending search. This is why the section **'The Forest of Night',** which deals with this search, is dense, difficult and cyclic: it is an attempt to deal symbolically with the history of consciousness seen as a succession of symbolic embodiments. It is like a series of Chinese puzzle-boxes, but the series is infinite—Eden is as far off at the end, as at the beginning.

And yet it is not, after all, as far off. The history that Brennan tells is a history with direction; the search is, seen rightly, a search for self-consciousness. This self-consciousness, this knowledge of the self and of its correspondent harmonies in the reality of the universe, is nearer at the end than at the beginning of the poem, because man has at last become conscious that this is what he seeks, and that the search is a human search for full human stature. The gods, the religions, the attempts at absolute systems, that strew the path behind us, can at last be seen, according to Brennan, for what they are—symbols, forms, which man has used to mediate his own experience—crystals that he has used to polarize the universe. Now he is sufficiently conscious to discover the reality of his own humanity; he can cease to dream that he is a king for whom the universe has been created, and can realize that the creation is his own—that it is for him to accept responsibility for his own journey towards consciousness and for the 'humanizing of the universe'. (pp. 86-7)

In the final section, **'The Wanderer',** the rose image has disappeared. What is left is only the bleak light of consciousness and the winds of time. 'The deathless rose of gold'—the final fulfilment, the realization in full consciousness of man's own unity with the universe—was glimpsed only as a vision, no more than momentary; the final poem of the Lilith sequence marks its disappearance. The poem is one of Brennan's most ambiguous and negative statements. . . .

The whole sonnet, in its hesitating movement and its repetitive negations, seems to close off the Lilith-experience, almost to dismiss it as meaningless. The long wrestle with that subtle and ambiguous figure seems to have ended not even in defeat, but in inconclusiveness. At the end of **'The Forest of Night'** we seem no nearer the 'deathless rose' than at the beginning, even less so. The wanderer seems even to have lost his belief in its possibility. Perhaps by now Brennan believed that the fight was indeed 'foredoom'd disastrous'.

It seems as though, in spite of his glimpses of the positive side of his night-goddess, Brennan was never in fact able after his encounter with her to give full credence to his earlier assertion that 'the road does lead somewhere'. She is his Muse, but she is also his Medusa, and his poem was not shield enough to protect him against her. (p. 90)

'The Wanderer' sequence, though it has been greatly admired, and with justice, has in fact a note not only of uncertainty but at times of hollow vaticination. It is where the Wanderer is most clearly speaking through Brennan's own experience that it is at its best, and perhaps only here is it really convincing. Where, in the persona of **'The Wanderer',** Brennan addresses 'the souls that serve', or cries 'Dawns of the world, how I have known you all', it is right for the reader to feel a little uneasy. It is too like Brennan's own voice under the prophet's mantle; it is somehow inflated, hollow, not sufficiently human. The 'I' who speaks is not intended to be personal: this is the voice of the figure from the Cabbala: 'man is a wanderer from his birth . . . his house is builded upon the winds, and under them upon the storm'. But it is dangerous to assume too far a symbolic and universal persona—and I cannot help feeling that Brennan in this series identifies himself a little too closely with this vast generalized archetype of man—that this is less the Wanderer speaking through Brennan's lips than Brennan speaking with the voice of the Wanderer. The individual should not assume the universal; it is a dangerous expansion. The personality can disintegrate under the strain.

It is possible, I think, to argue that this is in one sense what happened to Brennan. His long and involved struggle with his Lilith—which ended inconclusively—perhaps stretched his powers beyond their limit, and allowed an over-identification with his Lear-like protagonist. In an essay he speaks of Lear as a form of the Cabbala-figure, himself a Wanderer. Shakespeare, however, who was so often right in these matters, was clear enough that Lear's wanderings were too much for his humanity: Lear was, after all, mad. To humanize the Universe is only a step away from the attempt to universalize the human; and the individual, however great his capacities, cannot become Man. If he tries to do so, he assumes an impossible burden, and loses in the end his own humanity.

Perhaps this is the explanation of the fact that during the years after the publication of *Poems 1913* Brennan so curiously failed his own vision. The war poems published as *A Chant of Doom* contain some of the most unpleasant and inflated verse produced by any war. In them Brennan's worst weaknesses come to the fore—indeed, they seem for the time to take over the whole of Brennan's carefully built-up poetic personality. . . . No abuse, no condemnation, no hatred seemed enough; these poems hurl every possible curse at the German 'monster-birth of man and fiend'. . . . (pp. 91-2)

The role of hanging judge is dangerous for any man; that is why the judge is appointed by society as instrument, not as person. Here Brennan takes it on himself, without appointment, and without qualms. This is distasteful enough in any man, even in those too ignorant of moral responsibility to know what they are doing. But we cannot believe that Brennan was ignorant of the issues involved. We can only watch in horror while he pulls the whole structure of his own thought about his ears. This is no abstract judgement on the principle of Evil (and even that he would once have disowned, with Blake); this is a personal judgement on a human foe.

It is just here that I think the nature of Brennan's failure to measure up to the demands of his own vision becomes clear. He has fallen into his Lilith's most obvious trap; he has made the mistake of identifying the eternal foe with the temporary wrong, as he identified the Eternal Wanderer with himself. It is dangerous for anyone to live too long with universal symbols.

If there is truth in this explanation, if in his attempt at 'humanizing the Universe' Brennan faces an antagonist far too strong for him, and succeeds only in making himself inhuman, it ought also to be an explanation of the sense we have that his poetry is at too far a remove from the real immediate world of happenings, things, and persons. In effect, his Symbolism is not really symbolism at all; it much more resembles allegory. For the symbols with which he is working are already symbols before he reaches them; they are not transformations of Brennan's own, they are already one step beyond the perceived world and are conceptual. Brennan escaped at a bound from the first poetic necessity—that of seeing, hearing, feeling and undergoing the immediate flow of personal experience, before the transformation process can begin. His process of thought led him, logically and correctly, to the belief that 'the progress of art is the continual victory over matter which had been rejected as ignoble and unfit for art'. . . . But his choice of the 'Edenic myth', of the figure of Lilith, and of the figure of the Wanderer, as the symbols through which he sets out his theme, was a choice not of the intractable matter of his personal experience, but of what had already been tamed and made 'noble and fit for art' by other artists; his poem is synthesis of already-existing symbols, through which Brennan expounds his philosophy of man and the universe. The poem that he writes has, in a sense, already been written; the transformation has already taken place. He has inherited its riches, he has not worked for them.

This is not to deny that the great figures and the great myths have their continual part in our temporal circumstances; nor that they need to be re-experienced, re-embodied and reinterpreted by every poet and every age. This is a very obvious truth about art. The figure of Lilith and the figure of the Wanderer are part of the whole human inheritance; the myth of Eden never loses its meaning. But such myths and figures ought never to be used as pieces in a kind of poetic chess-game, or an illustration in a philosophic history of man-versus-universe. They must be come upon by the poet—not seized upon; they must be rediscovered, always in a new and revelatory form, if they are to act as true transformers of experience. They must never be plot-characters; they must grow of themselves out of the struggle with raw experience. And I think that in an important sense ***Poems 1913*** is a plotted poem, a chess game, with symbols whose meaning Brennan already knew, or thought he knew. (pp. 93-4)

This is not to say that Brennan plotted the poem with its protagonists as little more than dramatis personae. Clearly his imagination had been deeply involved in recreating the figures and the landscape of the Great Myth; and clearly too, he had a much wider and deeper grasp of their implications than might have been expected. Rather, it seems to me, the poem began in Brennan's conscious intelligence, but as it progressed took him farther and farther from his own intentions, into regions he had not forseen. The disproportion of the Lilith sequence (which is both longer and much more complex than the other sections), and the unexpectedly hopeless note that rings through the Wanderer sequence (unexpectedly, when we remember Brennan's comparative optimism in his earlier lectures) seem unambiguously to point in this direction.

In the last of his six lectures on ***Symbolism in Nineteenth Century Literature***, summing up the implications of earlier lectures, Brennan makes use of the philosophy of F.C.S. Schiller as a demonstration that 'philosophy is driven in the same direction as poetry'. Comparing Schiller's 'principle of postulation' with the Symbolist theory of correspondence, he says:

> But if the principle of postulation has any meaning at all, it means that the process has a goal. Man . . . is on a way but not an endless one: he is on the way to himself.
>
> (pp. 95-6)

It is reasonable to conclude that **'The Wanderer'** series was intended to symbolize this task of man, the wanderer 'on the way to himself', and that the Wanderer himself, as symbol of the search, might be expected to have had at least a glimpse of the possibility of the way's not 'being an endless one'. In fact, however, the whole tone of **'The Wanderer'** series is that man's fight is 'foredoom'd disastrous'; that man is

> the wanderer of the ways of all the worlds,
> to whom the sunshine and the rain are one
> and one to stay or hasten, because he knows
> no ending of the way, no home, no goal. . . .

Whatever may have happened to alter Brennan's attitude, between 1904 when the lectures were delivered, and 1913, it does seem clearly to have altered in the direction if not of actual

Holograph copy of a manuscript page from Prose Marine. *From* A Brennan Collection, *by Harry F. Chaplin. Wentworth Press, Sydney, 1966. Courtesy of Harry F. Chaplin.*

despair, at least of pessimism; the Eden vision seems to have been swallowed up by the encounter with darkness. All that seems to be left of it is the search itself; and the searcher, the Wanderer so far from being identified with man himself, seems now to be visualized as a somewhat arrogant, somewhat overweening figure, whose task apparently is that of arousing the less enlightened from their comfortable ignorance and driving them forth on a journey that even the Wanderer acknowledges to have 'no ending' and 'no goal'.

There is no overt mention at all of the 'transcendent self' which is to be made explicit and to introduce harmony; man is not even given that hope and consolation for his loss of hearth and home. We cannot help feeling that the Wanderer is not merely a somewhat uncongenial and rhetorical figure, but that he is sometimes even an over-inflated preacher, with little more than a sense of superiority over others to prove him an eternal and archetypal symbol.

It seems to me, in fact, that the poem, taken as a whole, represents a second loss of faith, this time in the possibility of man's attaining by his own powers, the realization of self and the humanization of the universe, to which Brennan had turned as a substitute for his early Catholicism; and that this second disillusionment has something to do with the violence of his later reaction to the German aggression.

The poems written between 1923 and 1932, first under the influence of his brief and tragic second love affair, later from the depths of his unhappiness after 'Vie's' death, and his own personal poverty, are much more immediately human and even lyrical than *Poems 1913*. Few as they are, they make Brennan much more real to us as a man, and more sympathetic, than do the earlier poems. The final brief **'A Jingle or Drowsy Chime'**, written in 1932, not long before his death, closes the circle that his whole work draws, in a gentleness and quiet acceptance of both 'the antient woe' and its transcending. It is a final note or epigraph perhaps, to a life whose dominant note was of recurring attainment and loss, but which seems to have closed, if not in happiness, at least in all-embracing peace. (pp. 96-7)

> Judith Wright, "Christopher Brennan," in her Preoccupations in Australian Poetry, Oxford University Press, Melbourne, 1965, pp. 80-97.

A. R. CHISHOLM (essay date 1967/1970)

[*In the following excerpt (the first portion of which was published in* Meanjin *in 1967) Chisholm discusses the various forms Brennan's ideal of Eden takes in* Poems 1913 *and analyzes the Latin epigraph to "The Forest of Night" section of that work, which he believes embodies the core of the poet's metaphysical quest and compels the reader to approach* Poems 1913 *as a spiritual autobiography.*]

G. A. Wilkes published a valuable monograph in *Southerly*, 'New Perspectives on Brennan's Poetry' [see excerpt dated 1953] . . . , in which he set out to examine the conceptual framework of *Poems 1913* and the evolution of Brennan's metaphysic as expounded in his prose writings from *Fact and Idea* . . . onwards. He explained very clearly the cyclic character of these poems and the need to study them as *livre composé*.

Professor Wilkes also affirmed that **'Lilith'** is the very core of *The Forest of Night;* that *Towards the Source* constitutes a lyrical prelude to the latter, and that Lilith became a symbol of Eden. He completed this extremely useful survey by discussing the transition from *The Forest of Night* to the more widely read section of *Poems 1913*, which is *The Wanderer*.

All this pioneering work is so well done that I should hardly have undertaken the present study if Dr Wilkes had not stressed the need for defining the *nature* of Brennan's poetry.

No planning and conceptual framework can ever suffice to produce poetry, which, as Dr Wilkes clearly recognizes, is not versified philosophy. It is, I believe, the product of mood, the expression of something deeply and at times painfully felt. Scholarship and philosophy may help to induce the creative mood or to modify it; for mood, in the case of a significant poet, is not mere emotion—there is even, as Paul Valéry has demonstrated in his poetry, such a thing as sensibility of the intellect. But the creative mood, whatever its nature may be, or to whatever extent it may utilize or discard the raw material of emotion, has to be native and compulsive.

Consequently we need to be on our guard when we base our study of a poet's work on the assumption (quite correct in Brennan's case) that it constitutes a *livre composé*. This assumption does not or should not imply that the *composition* of the work is chronologically systematic, or that one mood alone dominates and shapes one or more of the parts. Mood fluctuates, fades away, is replaced by another mood, comes back, yields once more to other compulsions . . .

What I have just said really amounts to this: poetry, whether it is lyrical or discursive or even narrative, is a personal matter, the exteriorization of a man's inner self, and so a poet can never subordinate himself wholly to a predetermined plan. . . . I propose to examine, above all, Brennan's spiritual experiences and the fluctuations of his sensibility; his lofty aspirations and many disappointments; the loss of his first Eden and its replacement by Edens of a different kind—always remembering that although an Eden may be lost, its memory haunts the mind that once dwelt in, or surmised, its ineffable perfection.

The first of Brennan's Edens was bequeathed to him, we might say, by his Irish Catholic forebears. (pp. 1-2)

This Eden had its literal, Biblical meaning for the boy; and it was illumined no doubt by the mysterious light that an imaginative young mind sheds upon its emotional experiences. (p. 2)

Eden, then, for the young Brennan was an ideal of innocence, the memory of a perfect state which was surrendered (but not forgotten) by man thanks to the promptings of the Serpent. It was the garden of man's 'long-lost innocence'. . . . (p. 3)

That early Eden, though Brennan turned his back on it as a young man, was not only unforgotten but subtly obsessive; it continued to be a fundamental factor in the evolution of his poetic thought. It left in him a yearning for the ideal and thus brought about the conception of two other Edens, which dominate in their turn *Towards the Source* and *The Burden of Tyre*.

The Eden which Brennan had known as a boy was not only a state of innocence: it was also a garden of love, in which Eve was given to Adam. And this special aspect of the Biblical Eden was elaborated into a new Eden when Brennan fell in love with Anna Elisabeth Werth in Berlin.

There is nothing unusual in this. Practically every young man who falls in love idealizes the object of his affection. For him she wears a magical aura; she is something infinitely greater than herself. She is wrapped in a tissue of imagination, in a Veil of Maya through which her glory shines, whether she is a lady of high degree or a kitchen-maid. All her defects are hidden by that transfiguring veil and she becomes Eve, ideal love, ideal beauty, an embodiment of the Eternal Feminine that leads us on ('zieht uns hinan'), as Goethe says at the end of *Faust*. (pp. 4-5)

It was partly, but not entirely, Brennan's enthusiasm for the poetry and doctrines of Mallarmé that led him towards a third Eden (I do not use 'third' in a chronological sense) quite different from the other two.

His discovery of Mallarmé's work while he was in Berlin made him realize, or appreciate in a new way, the poetic value of 'correspondences', which are based on the concept that the realities revealed by the senses are only symbols or correspondences of a deeper Reality, imperfect echoes or reflections of a perfect and eternal unity. (p. 6-7)

With Mallarmé's aesthetic Brennan seems to have combined a philosophical concept in which there was a strong Gnostic element. Eden is no longer the result of a creation; Creation itself is only an imperfect reflection of something greater. . . .

Brennan's third, largely Gnostic, Eden finds its most definite expression in *The Burden of Tyre,* where God, the perfect Spirit, is distinguished from the demiurge who created the material world and whom men often worshipped as the God of Battles.

There have been many varieties of Gnosticism, European and Oriental, and many sects. But there are certain elements common to most of them, of which the most important in the present context are these:

1. The demiurge who created the world is not the true God; the latter is the source of being, not of the phenomenal world.

2. No worlds, but only some emanations, issue from the true God. These emanations are usually designated, in Gnostic writings, as æons—ages or eternities. (p. 7)

To come back to *The Burden of Tyre:* Eden, in this poem, is the domain of the Gnostic God. It is an Eden of perfection, set high above the imperfections of the phenomenal world; and in his Prologue Brennan asserts that this true Eden can be safeguarded if we realize that the Creation is only a mass of 'senseless dust'. . . . (p. 8)

This explains Brennan's diatribes, in various sections of *The Burden of Tyre,* against the God of Battles, the Old Testament deity; his ironical quotations from, and allusions to, the poet who commended this demiurge to us: Rudyard Kipling.

The Eden of perfection evoked in this poem continued to beckon to him, but again in a fluctuating fashion. One of the most striking fluctuations can be discovered if we look at the date of composition of *The Burden of Tyre* and the first of the *Wanderer* poems. They fall roughly into the same period; and yet *The Wanderer* is a forsaking of Eden for a quest of a different kind, though both works are inspired by Brennan's persistent search for Reality.

I think he realized at an early date that the Eden of perfection was unattainable; and *The Wanderer* is not so much a definite abjuration of Eden as a conviction that, since Eden is inaccessible, he must follow a hard road of his own.

This is only one of many fluctuations. The following of the Wanderer's bleak road was preceded by another quest: the search for Lilith. It was an even more hopeless search than that of *The Wanderer*, for Lilith was not, like the *'annus peregrinationis meae'*, on the hither side of Eden, but beyond it.

Brennan tells us in the Argument, no. 68 (i) in the **Verse** volume, that Lilith is the Lady of Night. And despite his lapse from his early faith and his estrangement from the most youthful of his Edens, he could not escape the Biblical idea that night preceded Eden; night was the matrix from which the *Fiat lux* created Eden and the world.

Lilith was not only night but (according to a Hebrew legend) Adam's first wife. And therein lies, I think, the source of the anguish we find in this longest of Brennan's poems.

Adam (who is sometimes identical with Brennan in the poem) could not forget Lilith, and this incapacity to forget marred his enjoyment of Eden and his love for Eve. For Eve was visible; that is to say, she was part of the phenomenal world, and this phenomenal world was imperfect. Lilith, on the other hand, was invisible. She could be found, not in the earthly Paradise, but only in 'the mire-fed writhen thicket of the mind'; and the mind, which in the Argument becomes the mind of humanity, transformed her into a monster, so that she was seen

> later as Lamia and Melusine,
> and whatsoe'er of serpent-wives is feign'd

Brennan did not, of course, accept the primitive superstitions of 'the folk', in whose 'scant fireside lore' Lilith was 'misread'. But he saw himself as a mind with shadowy depths, in which monsters as well as ideas of perfection could be found. 'Lilith' is thus to some extent an elaborate piece of self-analysis.

Self-analysis is not the same thing as psycho-analysis, although like the latter it entails an examination of the relationship between consciousness and the subconscious mind. Freud did not invent the subconscious; he only gave it a special twist, making it a repository of complexes and therefore a dangerous territory whose demons have to be, by analysis, dragged out into the light, which exterminates them and sets the mind free.

He may have been right with regard to the morbid aspects of the subconscious in some ill-adjusted minds. But his implications have been disastrous in the case of a few critics who have applied his theories to the study of certain poets. (pp. 8-10)

Wishing to dissociate the present study from that particular school of literary criticism, I shall keep clear of the special psychiatric overtones that the term 'subconscious' is apt to give off.

The subconscious mind and the conscious mind are really two aspects of the same thing. The basic difference between them is almost a linguistic one, in the widest sense of that adjective. The subconscious mind has no power of speech and is non-analytic, whereas lucid consciousness has a peculiar analytic power, strengthened by the ability to relate one experience to another by the use of language—which of course includes painting, musical notation and other co-ordinated means of expression.

Brennan himself practically made this basic distinction when he wrote, in the final passage of 'Lilith':

> deepen'd with all the abysm that under speech
> moves shudderingly

'Shudderingly', an intrinsically cumbersome adverb, does not chime with what I am going to say, but 'abysm' has a close affinity with it.

The mind undoubtedly has two strata (I realize, of course, that 'strata' is a spatial term, whereas the mind does not exist in space, but I have to accommodate myself to the limitations of language). The 'upper' stratum gives the individual his contacts with the outer world, his ability to analyse and classify phenomena, and even to analyse his own acts of classification, to watch himself watching. It can also become aware of its own depths and put form into the wordless communications that come from it. Such communications are, I believe, a major source of poetry. No man can sit down and write a real poem, with its magic and its inner form, by using his analytic, conscious and self-conscious powers alone, as poets laureate have too often been obliged to do. (pp. 10-11)

There is nothing uncanny about the subconscious mind, though it is sometimes taken as a starting-point for various kinds of hocus-pocus. It is, above all, a repository wherein are stored multitudinous memories which the conscious mind cannot house, though it often dips into this storehouse, or rather, feels the storehouse overflowing into it.

I doubt whether anything that we experience, from the very beginning of our individual existence, is ever wholly forgotten. People, events, fears, moments of misery or exultation, are recorded in that illimitable repository; and we all know how, quite unexpectedly, an item that our conscious mind had forgotten will emerge.

This storing of memories by the subconscious mind is of great importance for poetry. Having all its memories stored and, in its own hazy but tenacious fashion, collocated and classified, the subconscious mind does not need to seek analogies: they are always at hand, always 'visible'. For this reason, subconscious memory plays a major role in Symbolist poetry; for the symbol, as Brennan remarks, 'is the meeting point of many analogies'. . . . Where the conscious mind sees one thing at a time, or recalls one memory, the deeper stratum of mind has the means of relating one memory to another, or one experience to another, in a kind of instantaneous vision.

Even in non-literary fields, the subconscious mind is able to pick out from its memories two items that are really, though not conspicuously, related to each other; or it can seize on an item that has just been passed down from the upper stratum, and relate it to one of its own accumulated memories. That is, in fact, how genius works; and it is this capacity for swift collocations of perceptions and memories that distinguishes the man of genius from the laborious but unillumined investigator, who, admittedly, often does a vast amount of useful spadework, but, for lack of promptings from his subconscious mind, does not see beyond his spade. (pp. 11-12)

The lengthy poem [*The Forest of Night*] . . . is part of a trilogy, of a *livre composé* generally known as *Poems 1913*. Any doubts about this are dispelled by Brennan himself, not only in the [concluding sonnet of the section], but also, and still more definitely, in the Latin epigraph to *The Wanderer*.

This epigraph is not a mere frontispiece or ornament, but a carefully thought out and admirably condensed compendium of Brennan's spiritual autobiography, and is at the same time an important interlude between *The Forest of Night* and the *Wanderer* poems:

> *Quoniam cor secretum concupivi*
> *factus sum vagus inter stellas huius revelationis:*
> *Atque annus peregrinationis meae*
> *quasi annus ventorum invisibilium.*

How much care the poet actually devoted to the writing of this epigraph is demonstrated by his emendation of the first line,

which, in the version published in *Hermes* (Jubilee Number, 1902), had been:

> *Quia cor secretum concupivi*

Quoniam considerably improves the euphony of the line, by getting rid of the harsh juxtaposition of gutturals in *Quia cor*.

The opening line, 'Because I ardently yearned for a heart that was apart', might tempt the reader to suppose that Brennan had wanted to be a lonely heart. But actually, the *cor secretum* to which he had aspired was the Heart of Night, Lilith, and the long story of this aspiration was told in *The Forest of Night*. His desire was frustrated; he found that Lilith was inaccessible and that he, like all men, and all things, was nothing more than one of the evanescent gleams thrown out by Lilith's 'scatter'd hair'.

And so he became (*factus sum*) an aimless wanderer (*vagus*), like the stars whose true, futile nature had been revealed to him during his search for Lilith (*inter stellas huius revelationis*). Their true nature, like his own, was as nothing in comparison with the formidable greatness of Lilith; they were wanderers without any attainable goal.

Annus, in this epigraph, is not, of course, a short period of twelve months. The primary meaning of the word in Latin is 'circuit', or 'cycle', and its use here brings out the cyclic character of Brennan's poetry. The first segment of the cycle is found in *Towards the Source*. The second is *The Forest of Night*. The third is that brave but hopeless sequence, *The Wanderer*; it is the *annus peregrinationis meae*.

Annus ventorum is an important and, I think, revealing phrase, and may well be a key to the inner form of Brennan's *livre composé*. We know from his lectures on *Symbolism in Nineteenth Century Literature* (1904) that he recognized and approved an affinity between symbolism and mysticism; and it is therefore legitimate to expect an occultist element in the planning of his poetic work. As I remarked in my Introduction, we should not assume that the *composition* of his work is chronologically systematic, or that one mood alone dominates and shapes one or more of the parts. The plan is not consciously predetermined, but evolves as the work progresses. Nevertheless there is, I believe, a general shaping that is partly subconscious, inspired to a large extent by Brennan's familiarity with the work of certain outstanding mystics and visionaries.

Further, two of these visionaries, at least, Jakob Boehme and Swedenborg, were influenced by the philosophy of the idealistic alchemists, and even Blake's mind was to some extent in tune with alchemical philosophy. Mr C. A. Burland, in his erudite and illuminating book, *The Arts of the Alchemists* (London, 1967), vouches for this in the case of Boehme and Swedenborg, adding that 'the visionary world of William Blake had some affinity with them [the alchemists], although Blake formed his own mythology as his visions developed'.

I would go even further, and suggest that there is, somewhere, a point where mysticism, gnosticism, alchemical philosophy and nineteenth century symbolism meet.

Now, among the seven major volumes of alchemical writings listed by Mr Burland is the *Musaeum Hermeticum reformatum et amplificatum*, published at Frankfurt-on-Main in 1678, and made available in English by A. E. Waite in 1893. In the *Musaeum* is a sort of cosmic chart, which could also be taken as a chart of the mind's evolution. This chart, reproduced on the jacket of Mr Burland's book, is extraordinarily interesting to any serious student of Brennan's work.

In it, a symbolic and characteristically alchemical landscape is surmounted by a dial. The circumference of the dial is divided into three equal segments, labelled in Latin. Beginning at the top (as the eye tends to do when looking at a clock) and reading clockwise, the segments are: *Annus Solaris—Annus Stellatus—Annus Ventorum.*

It seems to be more than a mere coincidence that the structure of *Poems 1913* corresponds to this division into *anni.* ***Towards the Source,*** though it has some gloomy patches, is essentially the poem of Brennan's 'solar' period, during which he thought he had found his earthly paradise when he met and courted Anna Elisabeth Werth, with her 'summer-storm of hair'. (This latter phrase is not in ***Towards the Source,*** of course, but in the liminary poem of ***The Forest of Night.***)

The second *annus* in *Poems 1913* is Brennan's *annus stellatus,* during which he probes the night in search of the *cor secretum,* only to be disillusioned. And then, naturally and inevitably, he plunges into his *annus ventorum,* depicted in ***The Wanderer.***

It would obviously be childish to suggest that Brennan ordered his life in conformity with alchemical or occultist theories about the chart of the mind. But it is highly probable, I think, that while he was working on his poems he progressively recognized a concordance between the occultist chart and the plan of his own work, and that he had this in mind when he wrote the phrase 'annus ventorum invisibilium'. 'Invisibilium' is not a piece of padding, but stresses the difference between the two earlier cycles (***Towards the Source*** and ***The Forest of Night***) and ***The Wanderer.*** In the first of the three cycles there was sunlight; the phenomenal world was both visible and attractive. In the second, though night prevailed, there was the light of the stars, however deceptive it might be. But in ***The Wanderer*** the phenomenal world is reduced to its most nebulous manifestation: the viewless winds.

I am not an occultist, and certainly not an alchemist! But it seems to me that there is nothing unduly fantastic in the idea that Brennan's mind evolved according to a pattern recognized by visionaries and alchemical philosophers. That very broad-minded and lively psychologist, C. J. Jung, did not hesitate to believe that alchemical and similar theories about the evolution of the mind were by no means crazy, and that they led by unscientific ways to some conclusions that are not refuted by the scientific psychology of the modern period. (pp. 107-10)

For my part, I admit that ***The Forest of Night*** is extremely difficult. . . . But if parts of this long poem are obscure, I feel that this obscurity is not deliberate. Brennan, in his conversation, often assumed that his interlocutor knew as much as he knew himself about the subject under discussion. This assumption gave his monologues at the lunches of the Compliqués part of their charm, and though it did not make them easy to follow, it was always possible to ask him bluntly what he meant. But when he makes a similar assumption with regard to readers of his poetry, he leaves himself open to the charge of being obscure.

This obscurity stems also, in ***The Forest of Night,*** from the fact that Brennan had an idiom of his own, not deliberately acquired, but instinctively adopted, or brought about by his familiarity with classical texts. . . . (pp. 110-11)

And for readers belonging to a later generation, this semantic difficulty is increased by the fact that most of the poems in

The Forest of Night were written a good seventy years ago. I do not mean that the English of that distant Australian period was abysmally remote from the English of today, but the background of the educated Australian was different. Latin practically always, and in many cases Greek as well, constituted a basic part of higher education. Further, people read the English classics more spontaneously and enthusiastically, perhaps, than they usually do nowadays. Even in my own school days, which began some twenty years later than Brennan's, we were steeped in these older poetic idioms.

It is not surprising, therefore, that some contemporary critics have complained of Brennan's 'old-fashioned' idiom. Of course it is old-fashioned! But so is the idiom of Shakespeare—which none the less the man in the street often quotes without being aware of his debt.

The greatest defect that I notice in ***The Forest of Night*** is not its idiom, but its unevenness; a defect which is inevitable in any very long poem. It is sometimes uneven in its planning, the most conspicuous example being, in my opinion, the falling back upon the legendary and mythological miscellany that we find in the **'Twilights'** sequence.

This unevenness manifests itself also, unfortunately, in Brennan's poetic style. Too often we find a splendid line followed by a phrase or a line that falls flat. For instance, that awful line . . . 'him shaped that pluck'd the golden apple low' (no. 73), follows a line that is quite lapidary. Moreover, Brennan far too often resorts to padding, throwing in such dead wood as 'ay', 'hark', 'yon', 'lo'. And he really tortures English syntax at times. . . . (p. 111)

But Homer nods now and then, mainly because his two poems are so long; and Brennan slips occasionally for a similar reason. And in ***The Forest of Night*** there are enough outstanding passages to make its composition as a whole extraordinarily impressive.

Possibly the most important fact of all that we have to bear in mind when assessing the value of ***The Forest of Night*** is that this poem is to a large extent . . . a spiritual autobiography. The latter term implies not a mere narration of biographical events, but a sincere (and therefore tragic, for there is tragedy in any man's inner life) exteriorization of the multitudinous experiences through which any distinguished mind passes. ***The Forest of Night*** is the picture of a mind that lost God and sought Him in every remote corner of the universe, in occult lore, in various philosophies, only to find that night was unfathomable and that night's emblem, Lilith, was the sole truth: inaccessible, insensible, as self-sufficient as death and no less enduring.

At the same time, it is night's immensity itself that provides the most adequate background for the spectacle of the beckoning but meaningless stars, for the story of man's titanic futility. Only the monumental character of ***The Forest of Night*** as a whole could put into their true perspective such magnificent poems as **'The window is wide'** and **'O thou that achest'.** (p. 112)

A. R. Chisholm, "Introduction" and "Epilogue," in his A Study of Christopher Brennan's "The Forest of Night," *Melbourne University Press, 1970, pp. 1-14, 107-12.*

ANNETTE STEWART   (essay date 1970)

[*In the following excerpt, Stewart disagrees with G. A. Wilkes's argument (see excerpt dated 1953) that* Poems 1913 *is a "single concerted poem'' unified through its central theme of the quest for Eden. Instead, Stewart contends that the presence of several various kinds of Edens, a generally fragmented structure, and the fact that only a few of the poems in the collection are centrally concerned with the quest theme, precludes the work's existence as a unified entity. For a discussion of the various Edenic ideals in the sequence, see the excerpt by A. R. Chisholm (1967/1970).]*

G. A. Wilkes published a series of articles in *Southerly* [see excerpt dated 1953] which were later reprinted as *New Perspectives on Brennan's Poetry.* This work is now considered to be basic to an appreciation of Christopher Brennan and I have found, as all students of Brennan will find, that it is of invaluable assistance, especially as an illumination of the way in which the poet thought and as an interpretation of his frequently obscure writings in prose. But there is one view that Professor Wilkes expresses about *Poems 1913* which seems to me to present certain difficulties (I choose a typical example):

> *Poems 1913* has not only two themes or three or four, it has one theme only—the quest for Eden. . . . *Poems 1913* is not a simple assembly of verses, to be individually interpreted and appraised: it is a unitary structure, an organism complete in itself—a poem.

In another place he speaks of it as a 'single concerted poem'. *Poems 1913* is very far from being a 'single' poem: it consists of one hundred and five individual pieces that were fitted, as well as might be, into a frame devised only after most of them had been written. There were, of course, a handful of interludes and poems deliberately added for 'architectural' reasons. One would admit, too, on the evidence of Brennan's prose writings, that he might have had it in mind to emulate the kind of loose poetic unity we find in *Les Fleurs du Mal.* . . . But even if we decide to regard *Poems 1913* as such an attempt, we still need not regard it as an achieved 'single poem'. Professor A. R. Chisholm has shown recently, in an authoritative article, that the *livre composé* is not necessarily conducive to poetic unity, or even to a synthesis of themes and moods [see excerpt dated 1967/1970].

The initial reasons for disagreeing with the 'unitary view' are structural and bibliographic ones; however, it breaks down not merely on these grounds but on a thematic issue as well. The 'Eden-quest' which Wilkes proposes as the single theme of the poems does not provide the unifying thread that such a widely-assorted group of poems requires—if, that is, we are to consider them as an organic whole. The final resort is the symbolic framework: does the creation of a few outstanding motifs, and correspondence of imagery and setting, provide evidence of another kind of unity, of a looser kind than the structural attempt? Again, when the symbolism of the poems is inspected closely it seems only to increase our sense of the final disunity of the work. Indeed my investigation of the structure, themes and symbolism leads me to believe that the qualities of *Poems 1913* are best appreciated if we regard them as a series of fragments that have essentially separate origins. (pp. 281-82)

Obviously when Brennan came to the point of collecting all these many poems and sections together, he must have found he had an enormous problem of organization. How were all the poems, scattered over a considerable period and written for a variety of reasons, going to look as if they had been intended for a single work? The problem was only partially overcome by the invention of an elaborate structure with sections, divisions and subdivisions which, rather than creating harmony, seems to have increased the fragmentation of the work.

The way in which *Poems 1913* developed suggests that Brennan felt a self-consciousness and a lack of assurance about the final design. Early rejected versions and rearrangements only gave rise to an unnatural pretentiousness. The poems are, as it were, over-organized. The numerous sections and sub-sections that make up 'The Forest of Night': 'The Twilight of Disquietude', 'The Quest of Silence', 'The Shadow of Lilith', and 'The Labour of Night' (with its further sub-sections), tend to obscure what is intended to be the real centre of the poems ('Lilith'). Some of the sections, too, contain a mere handful of poems: 'The Shadow of Lilith' (which previously consisted of five poems) has only two.

Fortunately we can also look at this fragmentation in a more positive way. In 'The Forest of Night' there are many excellent little pieces and groups, seemingly complete in themselves, which we can interpret without relating them to other poems at all. Such a poem is 'Red autumn in Valvins' (31). It can be related, in ways that I will show, to a symbolic scheme—but its qualities are perhaps better appreciated if we look at it individually. Written to celebrate a special occasion which had moved Brennan profoundly—the death of Mallarmé—it is a unique imitation of Mallarmé's own 'tombeau' poems, and a careful development of his ideas about absence and silence in the creative process—a theme which finds no correspondence in the whole of *Poems 1913*.

On the other hand, in the poem which begins 'The Quest of Silence' (49), we find a lamentable diffuseness, a failure to integrate image, mood and theme. When this is placed against (31) it certainly pales. Yet Brennan obviously attempted to fit (49) into the whole sequence; in the first stanza he carries on the mood of silvery enchantment already established in the Prelude (48). However, this is followed by some strange syntactical dislocation. I quote the first two stanzas:

> What tho' the outer day be brazen rude
> not here the innocence of morn is fled;
> this green unbroken dusk attests it wed
> with freshness, where the shadowy breasts are nude,
> her's guess'd whose looks, felt dewy-cool, elude—
> save this reproach that smiles on foolish dread:
> wood-word, grave gladness in its heart, unsaid,
> knoweth the guarded name of Quietude.

We might well wonder what happened to produce this curiously crippled verse. If we go back to the original version of the poem . . . , we find that it is the direct result of Brennan's attempt to improve the piece, to polish it and make its place in the sequence more apparent. Ironically, the original poem makes smoother reading. Thus neither the structural nor the bibliographic approach to the poems can greatly affect our opinion of their success.

When larger groups of the poems are taken into account we can see that a comparative degree of unity was achieved in 'Towards the Source'. In an earlier article called 'The Art of "Towards the Source"', Wilkes demonstrated how the poems grew out of a mere assembly of pieces into the more ordered arrangement, *XXI Poems,* and from there developed into an arrangement which he called 'not an assembly of poems in chronological order but a single poem in three movements with an envoi'.

Certainly we can see that in **'Towards the Source'** a loose kind of order has been attempted. As Wilkes points out, the poems are more or less organized into three movements with an envoi which was added to give each group a greater direction. However, the amount of unity achieved within the sections varies considerably. The first section, for instance, is much less ordered than the last, though it contains some of the best poems, while many of the pieces in the third section are more atmospheric 'ephemera' added to the original body (as in *XXI Poems*) to enhance the impression of the 'dream of love' that he wants to create.

A scrutiny of the structural and bibliographic background of the poems does not seem to offer much evidence of unity. However, Wilkes attaches more importance to the Eden-theme and indeed I take the main basis of his argument to be that *Poems 1913* centres around a single quest which is also to be found running, in Brennan's parallel fashion, through the prose writings. He claims that the clue to Brennan's whole system of thought is found if we compare certain passages of the prose with the poetry, up to the point where in **"Philosophy and Art"** Brennan speaks of man as 'a wanderer' who is 'on the way to himself'. For Wilkes this forms a 'triumphant conclusion' to the Eden-quest which is recorded also in the final section of *Poems 1913*.

While I would not deny that in places a kind of vague metaphysical quest is going on in *Poems 1913*, it is not clear to me that it is precisely the same quest that Brennan deals with in his lectures and essays which come, we must remember, a little after the poetry and might therefore logically be expected to provide us with greater clarity. The lectures on nineteenth-century symbolism, which contain his most important ideas, were written in 1904 when the main body of the poems had been completed. But the central issue is to determine whether Brennan is essentially concerned with the same quest, 'Eden', both in poetry and prose and I think there is little evidence to show that he was. The possible exception is **'The Wanderer'** poems, which deal more specifically with a philosophic issue than the rest of the poems, and which therefore I will consider as a separate case.

The kind of quest that Brennan discusses in the prose writings is defined clearly, in two or three places, as a quest for 'Eden' and this quest is also related to a poet's search for perfection. . . . (pp. 283-85)

To what extent is 'Eden' present as a generalizing concept in *Poems 1913*? When we look here for evidence of a single Eden-theme, we encounter the difficulty that there is not just one Eden for Brennan but in fact several, of different kinds. A. R. Chisholm has already explored this difficulty [see excerpt dated 1967/1970]. (p. 285)

When we take a final collective view of the Eden-theme in *Poems 1913* we find merely a confirmation of Chisholm's thesis that not just one, but five or six Edens, are involved. Further to this, we see that only about six poems treat Eden as a central theme, and without vagueness. It would not be necessary, of course, for very many of the poems to deal with this theme alone, for a dominant theme of Eden to emerge, but a close examination shows that even the few poems directly involved with it have only the faintest connection with one another. The Eden that is being sought by the lover in **'Towards the Source'** has little to do with the Eden that is the setting for Lilith.

I believe most readers of *Poems 1913* have accepted the idea of Eden as central, perhaps too readily, because they have hoped to find some principle of unity, some section to follow in the poems, which the structure fails to provide. Certainly a quest can provide a spurious argument for relating some poems to others, but when looked at more closely the so-called 'quest' really only increases our sense of a general fragmentation. It is disappointing that the quest falls short of full poetic realization. The theme of Eden, which could have been central to *Poems 1913*, does not unite or clarify its other themes. The concerted singleness which Brennan may have hoped for is not achieved by thematic or structural means. (pp. 290-91)

> Annette Stewart, *"Christopher Brennan: The Disunity of 'Poems 1913',"* in Meanjin Quarterly, *Vol. 29, No. 3, September, 1970, pp. 281-302.*

JAMES McAULEY (essay date 1973)

[*McAuley is a prominent contemporary Australian poet and an important literary and social critic. In an unexcerpted portion of the following work, McAuley places Brennan soundly within the tradition of English prosody. In the following excerpt, he underscores the depth and range of Brennan's verse, which he finds firmly sustained by "the burn and ache of personal experience," yet reluctantly concludes that Brennan failed to achieve greatness because he was unable to attain a unique development of his style or themes.*]

Brennan's poetry is a brooding monody. No one else is there but the figures of his inner dream. Yet in its *range of reference*, Brennan's poetry is not narrow. Concentric to the myth or symbol are bands of possible meaning: beyond the intimately personal lie the social and historical and even cosmic levels of significance.

In its *method*, the poetry is willed to be difficult, but not finally inaccessible. We should, I suggest, approach it by the most simple, trusting, co-operatively alert attention to Brennan's basic symbolic script, allowing its elements to develop their imaginative possibilities in our minds.

These elements fall into certain recurring contrasts: Eden and the fallen world; bright dawn and sinister dark; garish day and mysterious beautiful night; stars and constellations, fixed or perishing; silence and noise; the forest and the lea. There are also recurring words; images, symbols, which carry a range of suggestion: the seasons; sexual union; ice—glass—mirror; the rose; Chimera and other monsters; city, ocean, hearth; dream; the hero-king and the folk; the last fight and world-ruin.

These key-elements cohere in one underlying subject which Wilkes has designated thus: '*Poems (1913)* has not two themes or three or four; it has one theme only—the quest for Eden' [see excerpt dated 1953]. (pp. 14-15)

Brennan's *Poems 1913* attempts an order that goes beyond the individual poems. As Wilkes has shown, it has a design. Brennan was interested in 'a new ideal of the concerted poem in many movements'. . . . (p. 15)

This does not mean that every poem was originally written to fit into its place in the *livre composé:* clearly the scheme is to some extent an ordering of pre-existent materials. Nor does it mean that the scheme is a static one, framed on a stable system of ideas. Brennan's scheme embraces changing views. Almost all his poetry that matters was written between 1894 and 1902 (with revisions and completions extending for another decade, and a small renewal of inspiration in 1923-25 under the stimulus of 'Vie'). Within the period 1894-1902 his mind and feelings underwent great and rapid changes. This should warn us not to seek a greater degree of order and coherence in the scheme of *Poems 1913* than it actually possesses. It really represents only a broken arc of his whole life-cycle; and even that arc is constituted by the careful mosaic-work of fitting disparate pieces into a frame.

To speak of Eden is to imply a Fall, and also a desire to recover from the Fall and win back Eden. In the first section of *Poems 1913*, 'Towards the Source', Brennan writes of man's intrinsic longing for the paradisal condition, and how this 'paradisal instinct' is frustrated in our modern industrial cities of damnation. (pp. 19-20)

One of the most interesting of the poems in this group is one which was written before his marriage. It originally bore the title: '*Ero sicut deus*' (I shall be as a god). The title seems to refer to the hope for a divinized state to be attained through love; and presumably contains a sidelong reference to the false promise of the serpent in Eden, '*eritis sicut dei*' (Genesis 3:5). The poem confesses that the fire of love has not had the unifying and transfiguring effect he had hoped for.... The poem is thus an anticipation of the post-nuptial disillusion—so much so that if we did not know the approximate date we might err in placing it.

A poem published in 1906 and presumably a relatively late production is placed as No. 64, near the Lilith sequence. In it the poet very explicitly abandons the hope that life will ever fulfill the promises it seems to offer.... (p. 20)

In the second (No. 67) of the two poems grouped together under the title 'The Shadow of Lilith' the poet says:

> Eve's wifely guise, her dower that Eden lent,
> now limbeck where the enamour'd alchemist
> invokes the rarer rose, phantom descent;
>
> thy dewy essence where the suns persist
> is alter'd by occult yet natural rite:
> among thy leaves it was the night we kiss'd.

The 'Adam' of this poem says that the flesh-and-blood wife who temporarily wore the promise and attraction of Eden ('her dower that Eden lent') is now of no value in herself but only as a vessel from which the imagination can extract an ideal beauty and passion ('the rarer rose'). Lilith is the personification of this ideal beauty: she is the real bride, for whom Eve is an illusory substitute; she is also the Lady of Night, so that when Adam and Eve embrace, it is her mystery into which they are plunged.... (p. 21)

Thus in Brennan we have a symbolic system which is ambivalent. Eden is light, complete consciousness, full self-realization. But, after the fall, Eden has vanished from our sight. From the point of view of our fallen state, Eden is a mysterious darkness beyond our ken; the daylight that we know is not that supernal glory of the endless day of paradise, but the little round of fallible sense-knowledge and reason which is all that is left to us.

Lilith, the Lady of Night, is thus presented from one aspect as the ultimate beauty, desire of man's heart. On the other hand, man also fears and flees from total absorption in the Absolute: he fears to go out beyond his little day and face the vast outer mystery, the cosmic darkness. His fears breed strange imaginings, he wanders far astray in the trackless darkness, he encounters monsters and nightmares no less real for being of his own devising. Night, even though it be the promise of

Eden, is also the realm of horror and death. Lilith is also terrible in her aspect. (p. 23)

This ambivalence is clearer if the symbolism is taken in its psychological application, as Brennan increasingly did. At this level, night is the subconscious self. To regain the Eden-state, one must leave the small area lit by consciousness and venture into the mysterious night-world of the subliminal self. There we encounter shapes of dread, fantastic terrors, and we are threatened in this inward exploration by mental disaster if we are overwhelmed by these monsters. But, if we can overcome our fear and come to terms with the inner denizens, we find the subconscious is also the source of the primal energies of the self. We become fully masters of ourselves, our conscious self is now harmonized with the subconscious, and invigorated by its tremendous powers: day and night are reconciled; there is a marriage of heaven and hell; man regains the divinized state of perfection.

Brennan thus shows us Lilith as supremely beautiful and desirable in herself, the very principle of joy and delight, but, as it were, clothed in darkness, surrounded by phantoms and monsters, fearful to approach, apparently evil in the influence she exercises upon fallen man. All this is summed up in the hymn to Lilith, which has claims to being considered his finest single poem.... (pp. 24-5)

To sum up this central phase of Brennan's poetry: the conscious ego (the 'diamond-probe of thought') must venture into the night-realm to overcome its fears and fantasies and achieve a nuptial union with the cosmic creative spirit.

But the Lilith section ends in defeat. Night remains dark and silent, and the paradisal instinct frustrated. Hope is deferred—and failing. (pp. 25-6)

The next section, called 'The Labour of Night', reiterates the themes of sterility, defeat, dissolution. Night seems in labour to bring forth the promise, but the labour is worse than in vain.... (p. 26)

Now comes the sequence called 'The Wanderer', the most uniform and sustained single utterance of Brennan—and the end of his major poetical work, except for a few significant pieces written at long intervals. 'The Wanderer' represents a movement of thought beyond the Lilith-complex. The idea of a transcendental fulfilment seems to be given up: the poet claims that he looks no further than the time-process. He seeks somehow an acceptance of, a unity with, the restlessness of the actual. Thus the idea of a divine overlordship of the world is dismissed:

> nay, there is none that rules: all is a strife of the
>   winds ...

and man must live accordingly.... (pp. 26-7)

The last poem in *Poems 1913*, No. 105 named '1908', is a valedictory review of the quest thus preluded. It begins with explicit reference back to No. 10 in particular. The poet is sitting in a tram going up George St West to the University. Electric light is now beginning to replace gas-light in the streets. He sees the wanderers on the pavement seeking their banal pleasures which are delusive substitutes for the lost Eden. The poet is one with them except that he knows what really drives them, and himself, while they do not. He thinks back to when he first contemplated the city crowds in this way:

> so, in my youth, I saw them flit
> where their delusive dream was lit ...

(p. 38)

The poet goes on to say how he came to renounce the Christian form of the metaphysical quest. He did so because he could not accept the doctrine of damnation, by which the final perfected and eternal state of creation would include an eternal hell. So he stepped out of the 'choiring tent' of the church and sought a different goal: one in which all men might in the end be saved and gathered up into harmonious happiness: 'a sphere appeas'd and undistraught', 'no grim eternal cell'. (p. 39)

Brennan closes by saying that he has . . . in his own fashion remained faithful to the two great sources of inspiration he experienced in youth, symbolized by the two spires, that of St Benedict's church and that of the clock-tower of the University. He has pursued the metaphysical quest which began in baptism, and he has brought to it the intellectual culture which gave him 'the lucid diamond-probe of thought' and opened 'the mines of magian ore divined / in rich Cipangos of the mind'.

Again in this interesting poem one has to ask how much of it is 'would-be' writing, an attempt to make the words appear valid tokens of a spiritual realization which has not really taken place. It is a problem not absent from other poets, Yeats for example, and Rilke; and these names can remind us that a rather sceptical answer on this point does not necessarily prevent a poem being a significant achievement in other ways. We may not feel well instructed about occult gnosis, and may doubt Brennan's claim to have it, but we still have parts of an inner history of some interest. (p. 40)

It is only reluctantly that I bring myself to some critical judgement, finally, on Brennan. His appeal for me has been partly that his poetic presence was originally more congenial to me than any other Australian writer of the generation before mine. And the complexities of his poetry can generate an interest which, while essential for the formation of a sound critical judgement, is not a substitute for it.

In the end, it is the reluctance I have felt that has indicated to me the measure of the critical approval I could give. Brennan has the ambition, the seriousness, and some of the gifts needed for major poetry; but his performance is good only exceptionally, the sense of greatness he communicates is the sense of a potentiality more than a realization. The labour and complication of his art too often remain labour and complication for the reader: he does not rise often enough above the routines and vices of a period style.

Yet as soon as one begins to make these negative judgements one feels that they do not do justice to the real power of expression, and to the fact that so much of the work is alive with the burn and ache of personal experience.

Personal experience is the vital core of Brennan's work. But his personal content is expressed only in accordance with the canons of art which he maintained. . . . (p. 41)

With all its faults 'Lilith' provides the dense central weight of Brennan's 1913 volume. It offers much work yet for the interpreter. For Brennan is of the modern race of 'difficult' writers whose work will partially defeat all but those who are prepared to spend a long time and effort in deciphering it. It is useless to complain of this: it is what the writer has intended; and for the reader who is attracted to the work it is part of his pleasure in it. It may be that only in Australia can Brennan command this degree of continued work upon him, but here he will receive it.

'The Wanderer' is generally given the highest praise. This is a view which I do not share. It is true that 'The Wanderer' is

exceptionally well sustained as a sequence. It is true also that the five-stress and six-stress metres are handled with a vigour and flexibility that are admirable. It is true that the personal note emerges with poignancy, while the theme is more readily accessible to the reader. But it is also true that the content is attenuated, that the rhythm carries us forward through a rhetoric that does not really *explore* the experiences implied, but slips too loosely over them. (p. 47)

Brennan's work . . . has for the most part the limitations of a monody. One can make an interesting comparison with Milton, however different the stature of the two poets. Like Milton, Brennan was a man of vast literary culture, with a mind built for the greater magnitudes of cosmic vision and utterance. Like Milton, he wrote at the very end of a period, essaying a kind of work that was about to go out of date. Like Milton's, Brennan's work is ultimately solipsistic; it really contains only one living being, one powerful consciousness projecting its inner agonies into 'myth'. Both poets try to explain and overcome the exile of the human ego from the primal paradisal state, to salve the wounds of nuptial failure, and to assert the innate force of a baffled powerful mind whose ideas the world seems willing to crush or ignore.

But the differences are no less significant. Brennan's artistic powers are, of course, far less; and were exercised only for a short time; and the cosmos his imagination can work in, though it should be vaster because of our more recent cosmology, seems smaller, and certainly darker and more incoherent, because instead of a unified world scheme Brennan had to make do with a 'void dismantled universe' (81); a 'dwindling realm' (71) lighted by wrecked drifting constellations and furnished only with miscellaneous symbolist bric-à-brac.

Nevertheless, the fact that it is not absurd to consider Brennan in relation to Milton, in order to bring out likenesses and differences, is a measure of his flawed but genuine power. (pp. 49-50)

[We] come back in the end to the fact that he is a late nineteenth century poet; an assessment will most naturally measure him against others of his time. And when one tries to do this, it does not seem possible to avoid the conclusion that Brennan achieved nothing like the sustained and unified artistry of Rossetti or Thompson or Patmore or the early Yeats. Whatever our view be of the achievement of these, our view of Brennan's poetic achievement must be decisively lower, because he could not fuse and unify his styles and influences into a new and stable compound with sufficiently distinctive and valuable properties. Still more damaging is the reflection that the best work of Bridges and Hardy and Hopkins and Housman bears witness to the fact that a poet of sufficiently authentic inspiration did not have to be so tightly bound within period limits at that time.

There are only two things that might be set against this. In the first place, we must allow that Brennan was trying to unify a wider range of styles and influences than the others, if only because of his deeper immersion in European romanticism. In the second place, Brennan's subject-matter has a wider and deeper range in the social and historical order. I have insisted on the way in which he extends his vision from his personal quest to the nature of human civilization and the history of mankind. This gives a weight and largeness to Brennan's work which one must acknowledge even while seeing to what degree the artistic struggle was foiled. It was foiled because he inherited worn-out and vicious poetic styles; and because he practically gave up at about the age of thirty-two when he should have gone on to transcend his heritage; and perhaps he gave up because he knew he did not, for all his gifts, have the final thing necessary: that force of poetic genius which overcomes and subdues everything to its own sure purpose. The sign of this is that there is not a Brennan style: there is simply a period conglomerate, which can be separated into its components. He was not without fire and imaginative power, and a core of urgent feeling needing expression. One can see how he must loom large on the threshold of modern Australian poetry, and continue to elicit interest and respect and appreciation from those who are concerned with the Australian tradition. But while his style and tone and matter challenge us to consider whether he may not rank with the major poets of his time, that comparison is bound to end to his disadvantage. I hope I have at least indicated some of the positive qualities in his work that have made me slow to come to this conclusion, and reluctant and regretful in stating it. (pp. 50-1)

> *James McAuley, in his* Christopher Brennan, *Oxford University Press, Melbourne, 1973, 56 p.*

AXEL CLARK   (essay date 1980)

[*In the following excerpt from the most comprehensive biographical study of Brennan, Clark examines the strongly introspective nature of* "Lilith," *a poem he considers Brennan's greatest expression of the soul's inward journey. Clark concludes with an assessment of Brennan's position in Australian literature.*]

By early in the twentieth century, Brennan knew most of the important literary figures in Sydney, but though he grew very fond of some of them, and they of him, their work generally meant little to him, and had little effect on his own. (p. 82)

But perhaps it did not matter much to Brennan that he drew little on the writings of his compatriots: probably the kind of writer he was could not have done so. His interests were idiosyncratic, which may have reflected his position as a metropolitan in the colonies: no one else in Australia was so alive to the movements of contemporary western literature. It is hard to imagine that a writer of his learning and interests might have found, in his own society's short cultural tradition, a spiritual or imaginative depth which could match the mighty tradition from which he chose to draw. A comparison with Russia of the later nineteenth century suggests Brennan started his literary career with a handicap. Dostoevsky and other authors of his generation had grown up in an age when western values commonly made Russians believe their country had no history, no tradition. And yet that generation found in the Russian tradition—in spite (even because) of the irrationality, the excesses, the terrible suffering—a spiritual strength which could match the material and intellectual values of the west. The Russian and the western could not easily be reconciled or fused, but the effect of their meeting on the Russian creative imagination was momentous. In the progress of Myshkin from Switzerland to Russia, and back to Switzerland; in the relation of Ivan Karamozov and Alyosha Karamazov (with, behind the latter, the figure of Father Zosima); in Levin's struggle to establish a socially just and agriculturally efficient order on his estates, while he also attempted to satisfy his religious needs—in such things Dostoevsky and Tolstoy advanced towards new perceptions, not only of western values and of what was involved in being a Russian, but also of what it meant to be a man, of the possibilities in life.

Australian writers could not draw on a national tradition in this way, as a counterpoise to the western thought and manners at that time steadily asserting their superiority in every corner of the globe. No white writers could properly draw on Aboriginal culture, the only Australian tradition of a depth and richness matching the European. (pp. 82-3)

[For] all his obvious references to and borrowings from the literature of other languages, that literature has been absorbed by a poet whose sensibility was basically Victorian, and its influence is subsumed into a basically Victorian style of expression. The basically Victorian character of Brennan's sensibility did not have a totally—perhaps not even predominantly—unfortunate effect on his poetry. At times identifiably Victorian elements make a decisive contribution to some of his best work. But ... he consciously attempted to attach himself, at least to a significant degree, to a poetic tradition from which his choice of poetic diction ensured that he must remain detached. His idea of his relation to that poetic tradition, and consequently his idea about the sort of poetry he wrote, meant that his great undertaking in poetry, his 'solitary emprise', was perhaps fundamentally misconceived: he ran the risk of producing an unrecognized confusion in the basic conception of his work. (pp. 106-07)

In the early nineties, he had encountered in Pater's *Marius the Epicurean* the suggestion that 'the individual is to himself the measure of all things'; he had gathered from Baudelaire the idea that the self might be adequate to the universe—might, in his own words, humanize the universe—if it could perceive the correspondences between things; and in Mallarmé he had found a refined expression of Angelism, the recourse to the individual spirit as the sole source of explanations of the universe. So now, in his attempted recovery of Eden, in his search for the *cor secretum*, he looked principally within his own 'unbounded hermit-heart'. He returned to that region within himself, deep in his hidden country, where he believed neither marriage, nor friendship, nor any bond with other people or the outside world in general, could reach.

But the journey into self did fundamentally represent some retreat, some renunciation of human responsibility, some abnegation of the poetic task. Brennan, in attempting to follow the principles of Count Axël in the drama by Villiers ('Vivre? les serviteurs feront cela pour nous'), began to prepare for himself a fate more like that of another Axel, the Axel Heyst of Conrad's *Victory*. Brennan liked to stand aside from or to express scorn for everyday life; for the 'imperfect world' which he felt to be 'vexed with its own littleness and meanness', for the norms, the morality and the behaviour that were expected of him at home and at work. But the people who upheld this morality marked him down with disapproval, impeded his academic progress, and in the end brought about his disgrace.

The journey into the self reached its poetical climax in the composition of **'Lilith'**. (p. 130)

The impulse to write **'Lilith'** apparently arose out of radically contradictory circumstances and feelings. These included the contradictions evident in the poetry Brennan wrote in 1897: on the one hand, the ardent expectation of romantic, sexual and metaphysical fulfilment through union with another person; on the other, the intense introspection based on (or leading to) his hope that he could find within himself everything that he most desired. But, in addition, out of these contradictions arose fresh complications, directly related to Brennan's experience in the first months of his marriage. He felt deeply that man's capacity for natural love becomes perverted by society, and especially by the false morality and artificial institutions of modern civilization: this idea (which we might trace back to the poem he wrote in 1894, **'Threnos',** and to the tangled inconsistencies of his sexual and romantic behaviour at Goulburn in 1891 which lay behind that poem) became a leading theme in **'Lilith'.** It showed that Brennan was in a significant way moving out of the nineteenth century; it linked him, however incompletely, with our own century, and especially with writers such as D. H. Lawrence.

But Brennan gave Lilith, the symbolic object of this natural love, two other symbolic functions which stand in unrecognized and unresolved contradiction to this one. Firstly, she symbolized the truth and the satisfaction which Brennan hoped to find within himself; secondly, she was a central point of reference in his elaborate quest for magian knowledge. The notions of sexuality and morality implied in these two symbolic aspects of Lilith conflict fundamentally with those implied in the search for natural love. Natural love is a relation free of guilt or complication, but Brennan, in describing Adam's attempts to grasp imaginatively the nature of Lilith, draws heavily on various occult traditions, which give the poem the appearance of dealing more with exotic subjects, for a coterie of initiates, than with something basic to all humanity. In particular, at the start of section ix he draws directly on the Manichean myth of the creation, and the conflict between the light and the darkness: this Gnostic dualism makes Lilith an interestingly ambiguous, volatile figure, but it also gives her a highly uncertain symbolic function in the poem. She offers man a way back to primary consciousness, where 'life is whole and one'. But she is also a manifestation of the dualistic Manichean view of man's deeply, permanently divided nature.

On this contradictory basis, Brennan created in **'Lilith'** a moving, challenging and original work, but one which ultimately lacks coherence. . . . Brennan appears to have believed that, in the attempt to give poetic shape to the elusive Lilith, he was directly confronting the reality that could either liberate or blight mankind; but perhaps the poem represents more of an evasion or retreat than a genuine undertaking of such a colossal task. Certainly, though one of his aims in composing **'Lilith'** was unblinking self-exploration, the finished product represents, to a significant degree, a retreat from contact with exterior reality into a world of self-absorption.

The classic type of the man who makes this type of retreat is Narcissus; perhaps **'Lilith'** most nearly approaches coherence if we read it as both an expression of the Narcissistic temperament, and an account of Narcissistic experience. Perhaps, also, Brennan's own life in this period, and the history of the gradual disintegration of his marriage, become more intelligible if we consider him as a kind of Narcissus. He was certainly very interested, in the middle and late 1890s, in the myth of Narcissus, and at about the time he wrote **'Lilith'** he described the malady of Narcissism quite acutely: 'the soul, if it yield to the delight of absorption in its own essential beauty, is led away from life and its beauty becomes a flower of malady and death.'

Ironically, the malady of Narcissism as Brennan describes it here resembles the choice he took in writing **'Lilith',** and in some of the most powerful and profound parts of the poem he explores the imaginative and moral consequences of that choice. The Narcissist 'led away from life', the man who feels the 'littleness and meanness' of 'things ''as they are'', things with

Notes made by Brennan regarding his poem Lilith.

the poetry dissolved out', finds that his dream becomes a compulsive headlong flight into a region of fear:

> the wingless soul . . . flees
> along the self-pursuing path, to find
> the naked night before it and behind.
> (**'Lilith'**, section x)

'The self-pursuing path' is one of those phrases that occur intermittently in *Poems,* where Brennan gives untypically concise and precise expression to a very complex idea. (Indeed, it is untypical enough to raise the question whether the following account is the charitable elaboration of a verbal accident.) The phrase means, firstly, a path which pursues the self: this suggests a path which compels exploration, a course of action which cannot be avoided; it also suggests a path which disappears behind as one follows it, a path which offers only a way forward and no return. From the context, we deduce that it leads nowhere, to a place which gives the soul no bearings, only a fearful sense of being unprotected, of loss and desolation.

The phrase has a second meaning associated with the first, and with the immediate and the larger context. The path is followed in pursuit of the self. But the pursuit is in reality an arduous, involuntary, fearful retreat ('the *wingless* soul *flees*'); the path leads to a spiritual state in which the soul is lost within itself, and from which there appears to be no exit. Brennan, in making Lilith the object of man's deepest yearning, commits his emotional energy to a figure who, as well as being explicitly a phantom, is essentially an interior, private projection. The quest for fulfilment in these circumstances bears some of the marks of spiritual onanism . . . and in the end leads naturally to barren waste.

Even the most powerful and suggestive passages in **'Lilith'** seem to point 'away from life' in the direction of ultimate barrenness:

> Nightly thy tempting comes, when the dark breeze
> scatters my thought among the unquiet trees
> and sweeps it, with dead leaves, o'er widow'd lands
> and kingdoms conquer'd by no human hands . . .
>
>   **('Lilith', section ix)**

The reader confronted with these lines cannot easily deny sympathy for Brennan's need of something other, of something more than what he derisively used to call 'Life' offered him. And he undoubtedly believed that, by turning away from life, he might gain access to a superior, transcendent reality. It was a hope he shared with many literary men of his age, such as Arthur Symons, who expressed it in a passage that might have served as a prefatory credo to **'Lilith'**: 'As we brush aside the accidents of daily life, in which men and women imagine that they are alone touching reality, we come closer to humanity, to everything in humanity that may have begun before everything in the world and may outlast it'. But in his atempt to 'brush aside the accidents of daily life', Brennan turns to what he can offer himself: when he speaks of 'thy tempting . . . my thought', he is really speaking of his tempting of himself, he is playing at his kind of emotional shadow-boxing. In turning 'away from life' he makes final disappointment of his greatest need inevitable. The pain of his frustrated desire is overwhelming; and perhaps partly for that very reason it perpetuates itself, it immobilizes him:

> I sicken with the long unsatisfied
> waiting . . .
>
>   **('Lilith', section ix)**

The poem does offer an experience that it claims to be a form of union with Lilith. But the 'bliss' of momentary, fragmentary union with her is achieved in a state of high tension, in the imagination only, privately, secretly:

> . . . the tense lips towards her bliss
> in secret cells of anguish'd prayer
> might know her in the broken kiss
> she prompts nor, prompting, fails to share.
>
>   **('Lilith', section vii)**

If this experience represents fulfilment, it seems peculiarly disabling; after it there is an inevitable loss of vitality and hope, and in **'The Labour of Night'** we enter the region of deserts, ice and lost peoples.

There is something incongruously furtive and wretched about **'Lilith'**, which complements and helps to account for the strongly introverted temper of the poem. This is not merely the wretchedness of Adam, who is 'born into dividual life', and does not accept the gift of love and wholeness that Lilith offers. The stanza quoted above, for example, which suggests an uncertain, agitated state of religio-sexual ardour and frustration, is not uttered by Adam but by the stars, disdainful of those who fail to find Lilith in their own anguished yearning. Thus by design it has the status of something like editorial com-

mentary, yet the stanza—indeed the whole of the stars' song—seems the product of one who, like the timorous 'man' of this poem, 'withheld his hand from life', one who withdrew his poetic interest from the world around him, and created a symbolic drama in which different figures within his private imaginative world sought fulfilment only of each other.

'Lilith' is essentially a poem of introversion, but it is not unequivocally a poem of retreat. At times Brennan confronts quite directly the emptiness he finds within himself, and the frustration he experiences in seeking fulfilment there. . . . (pp. 131-34)

But this open acknowledgement of and attempt to accommodate the abyss of despair is not typical of **'Lilith'** as a whole. (p. 135)

As the living memory of Brennan has faded, the 'Brennan legend' and the conviction that 'Brennan was greater than his work' have to a degree yielded to the continuing examination of what he wrote, and above all of his verse. Opinions about its worth have ranged from the declaration of Randolph Hughes [see excerpt dated 1934] that it was the equal of anything written in English this century, to A. L. French's dismissal of it [see excerpt dated 1964]: 'Brennan's stature as a poet is so small as to be, by International standards, negligible'. A more circumspect but quite favourable opinion has been expressed by Kenneth Slessor and Frank Kermode [see Kermode's excerpt dated 1961], who have placed Brennan among the leading poets who wrote in English between 1890 and the Great War. But outside Australia Brennan has met the fate common to nearly every Australian writer, and is almost unknown. His interest in human psychology and sexuality, and his attempts to use the French Symbolists as a basic model for his own poetry, link him to writers such as T. S. Eliot, W. B. Yeats and D. H. Lawrence; but he has attracted little attention in Britain, or America, or the continent, no doubt partly because his literary achievement hardly matches theirs. So in spite of the essentially European manner and interests of Brennan's poetry (and in spite of the colossal range of the scholarship, the originality of the criticism, which underpin his poetry), his audience has been, and remains, almost exclusively Australian.

Brennan's place in Australian literature is as paradoxical as his character. He drew little from distinctively Australian experience, or from the work of his Australian predecessors and contemporaries. With his clotted diction and extreme Victorian poeticism he could not represent a model to be followed by the generations of poets who succeeded him. Nevertheless some of the most important Australian poets of this century, such as R. D. Fitzgerald, A. D. Hope, Judith Wright and James McAuley, have found in his work a point of reference and departure, because he was the first Australian poet to write within (and be worthy of) the great European philosophico-poetic tradition. Brennan in fact stands at the head of a remarkably vigorous Australian tradition of intellectual poetry. At the same time, the similarities between Brennan's career and the careers of other gifted but blighted Australian writers, such as Marcus Clarke and Henry Lawson, help to make him in some ways a representative figure in the Australian literary tradition. His poetry will certainly receive continued, detailed study in this country. Even if he failed both in his quest for magian enlightenment through poetic symbol, and in his related attempt to create a 'livre composé', he wrote many fine individual pieces. In works such as **'Lilith'**, most of the poems in the **'Wanderer'** sequence, and some love poems written for Vie, his poetry remains challenging, and deeply moving. (pp. 297-98)

Axel Clark, in his Christopher Brennan: A Critical Biography, *Melbourne University Press, 1980, 341 p.*

ADDITIONAL BIBLIOGRAPHY

Bavinton, Anne. "The Darkness of Brennan's 'Lilith'." *Meanjin Quarterly* XXIII, No. 1 (1964): 63-9.
  Determines that "Brennan uses well the techniques of vagueness, analogy, and symbol; his failure is a lack of wholeness in the basic presentation of spiritual reality. Yet only a poet of stature could invite such a criticism; and Brennan is a poet of stature."

Chaplin, Harry F. *A Brennan Collection: An Annotated Catalogue of First Editions, Inscribed Copies, Letters, Manuscripts, and Associated Items.* Sydney: Wentworth Press, 1966, 81 p.
  Catalogue of works by and about Brennan designed primarily for the serious book collector.

Dobrez, L.A.C. "Christopher Brennan: *The Wanderer.*" *Australian Poems in Perspective: A Collection of Poems and Critical Commentaries,* ed. by P. K. Elkin, pp. 11-36. St. Lucia, Queensland: University of Queensland Press, 1978.
  Posits that *The Wanderer*, regarded as a single unit, is Brennan's best poem, but emphasizes that its fullest significance is realized only through a thorough examination of the entire *Poems 1913* sequence. From his analysis of the sequence, Dobrez concludes that Brennan "had the boldness to compete on equal terms with the finest European talent—and this is something no Australian before him or since has been able to do."

Foulkes, John. "Mallarmé and Brennan: Unpublished Letters and Documents from the Moran Collection in St. John's College, Cambridge." *French Studies* XXXII, No. 1 (January 1978): 34-45.*
  Includes copies of letters from Stéphane Mallarmé to Brennan and a bibliographic discussion of Brennan's private collection of Mallarmé works and related manuscripts.

Green, Dorothy. "Towards the Source." *Southerly* 37, No. 4 (1977): 363-81.
  Traces several influences present in Brennan's verse, including the poet's Catholic upbringing, his study of the writings of Walter Pater and Edward Maitland, and his interest in alchemy. Green prefaces her investigation by remarking, "I doubt whether any final interpretation is possible, simply because the poetry seems to issue from a deep personal compulsion, whose origin has been deliberately and carefully disguised."

Green, H. M. *Christopher Brennan: Two Popular Lectures Delivered for the Australian English Association.* Sydney: Angus & Robertson, 1939, 77 p.
  Overview of Brennan's poetry, which Green considers the lyrical embodiment of a truly great mind.

Heseltine, H. P. "'Cyrus Brown of Sydney Town': Christopher Brennan and Dowell O'Reilly." In *Bards, Bohemians, and Bookmen: Essays in Australian Literature,* ed. by Leon Cantrell, pp. 136-52. St. Lucia, Queensland: University of Queensland Press, 1976.*
  Explores the tumultuous friendship of Brennan and fellow poet Dowell O'Reilly.

Macainsh, Noel. "Christopher Brennan and 'Die Romantik'." *Southerly* 23, No. 3 (1963): 150-63.
  Underscores the importance of Brennan's aesthetic affiliations with the German romantics, particularly Novalis.

——. "Brennan and Nietzsche." *Southerly* 26, No. 4 (1966): 259-61.*
  Supports the view that Brennan "was familiar with Nietzsche's work but was firmly opposed to Nietzsche from his own romantic standpoint."

——. "Christopher Brennan's Poetic." *Southerly: A Review of Australian Literature* 44, No. 3 (September 1984): 306-28.
  Postulates that Brennan's literary perspective was rooted in German neo-romantic theory. Macainsh believes Brennan "interpreted the course of Western literature, from the Greeks onward, as an ever-repeated striving for the ideal of Symbolic literature. He greeted Stéphane Mallarmé as the latest high embodiment of this striving."

Marsden, Robin B. "New Light on Brennan." *Southerly* 31, No. 2 (1971): 119-35.
  Collections of Brennan's essays and letters, many previously unpublished, which shed light on his intellectual development during the 1890s.

McAuley, James. "The Erotic Theme in Brennan." *Quadrant* XII, No. 6 (November-December 1968): 8-15.
  Analysis of the relationship between Brennan's romantic life and his poetry.

Penningston, Richard. *Christopher Brennan: Some Recollections.* Sydney: Angus and Robertson, 1970, 54 p.
  Recalls Brennan's later years, from 1925 through 1932.

Quadrant XXI, No. II (November 1977): 36-46.
  Special Brennan issue which includes a discussion of the poet's Berlin years and his studies of Aeschylus.

Smith, Vivian. "Christopher Brennan and Arthur Symons." *Southerly* 27, No. 3 (1967): 219-22.*
  Explores the influence of Arthur Symons's poetry on Brennan's work.

Stone, Walter W., and Anderson, Hugh. *Christopher John Brennan: A Comprehensive Bibliography with Annotations.* Cremorne, Australia: Stone Copying Co., 1959, 55 p.
  Catalogues Brennan's published poetry, criticism, and translations and furnishes a list of articles on his works, from the first reviews of *Towards the Source* in 1897.

Sturm, T. L. "The Social Context of Brennan's Thought." *Southerly* 28, No. 4 (1968): 250-71.
  Understands *Poems 1913* as an expression of the individual's relation to the external world. Sturm speculates that "Australia provided the most immediate context for [Brennan's] sense of the external world, not only as something felt to be insubstantial, but as a positive hindrance to the attainment of self-knowledge."

Wilkes, G. A. "Brennan and His Literary Affinities." *The Australian Quarterly* XXX, No. 2 (June 1959): 72-84.
  Examines the influence of such figures as Herbert Spencer, Algernon Swinburne, and Coventry Patmore on the literary development of Brennan.

——. "The 'Wisdom' Sequence in Brennan's Poems." *Journal of the Australian Universities Languages & Literature Association,* No. 14 (November 1960): 47-51.
  Regards the "Wisdom" poems in "The Forest of Night" as a continuation of the motif of mankind's futile search for knowledge.

——. "The Art of Brennan's *Towards the Source.*" *Southerly* 21, No. 2 (1961): 28-41.
  Explication of *Towards the Source* which traces the speaker's development from a state of wordly innocence through experience to a disenchantment with the romantic outlook.

——. "Brennan's *The Wanderer*: A Progressive Romanticism?" *Southerly* 30, No. 4 (1970): 252-63.
  Considers *The Wanderer* Brennan's critical reappraisal of all romantically inspired quests. Wilkes also contends that *Poems 1913* demonstrates the pursuit of an external form of perfection that is ultimately revealed to be meaningless because the attainment of transcendental unity from within the self has been neglected.

Wright, Judith. "Christopher Brennan." *Southerly* 30, No. 4 (1970): 243-51.

Discusses Brennan's long-deserved recognition as a significant poet. Wright submits that "Brennan stands or falls by the *whole* of *Poems 1913,* not by a few anthology-extracts robbed of half their meaning by the extraction. . . . He remains monumental, perhaps the most worthy antagonist and lover of his Lilith that she has recently had to deal with."

Zwicky, Fay. "Gallic Sanction, Kiss of Death: Another Look at Brennan's Reputation." *Westerly* 23, No. 3 (October 1978): 77-83.
An examination of Brennan, his prose, and his poetry, in which Zwicky concludes: "he was capable of contemplating the unified movement of the mind through feeling, will, and intellect," yet "he could never get all three together in his own work."

Stephen Crane

1871-1900

(Also wrote under pseudonym of Johnston Smith) American novelist, short story and novella writer, poet, and journalist.

Crane was one of America's foremost realistic writers, and his works have been credited with marking the beginning of modern American Naturalism. His Civil War novel *The Red Badge of Courage* is a classic of American literature which realistically depicts the psychological complexities of fear and courage on the battlefield. Influenced by William Dean Howells's theory of Realism, Crane utilized his keen observations, as well as personal experiences, to achieve a narrative vividness and sense of immediacy matched by few American writers before him. While *The Red Badge of Courage* is acknowledged as his masterpiece, Crane's novella *Maggie: A Girl of the Streets* is also acclaimed as an important work in the development of literary Naturalism, and his often-anthologized short stories "The Open Boat," "The Blue Hotel," and "The Bride Comes to Yellow Sky" are considered among the most skillfully crafted stories in American literature.

Born in Newark, New Jersey, Crane was the youngest in a family of fourteen children. His desire to write was inspired by his family: his father, a Methodist minister, and his mother, a devout woman dedicated to social concerns, were writers of religious articles, and two of his brothers were journalists. Crane began his higher education in 1888 at Hudson River Institute and Claverack College, a military school which nurtured his interest in Civil War studies and military training, knowledge which he later used in *The Red Badge of Courage*. During two indifferent semesters at Lafayette College and Syracuse University he was distinguished more for his prowess on the baseball diamond and the football field than for his ability in the classroom. Throughout his college years, however, Crane was writing; he worked as a "stringer" for his brother's news service, and it is thought that he wrote the preliminary sketch of *Maggie* while still at Syracuse. In 1891, deciding that "humanity was a more interesting study" than the college curriculum, Crane quit school to work full time as a reporter with his brother and part time for the New York *Tribune*. In New York he lived a bohemian existence among the local artists and became well acquainted with life in the Bowery; from his firsthand knowledge of poverty during this period he was able to realistically depict tenement life in his writings. In 1893 Crane privately published his first novella, *Maggie*, under a pseudonym after several publishers rejected the work on the grounds that his description of slum realities would shock readers. According to Crane, *Maggie* "tries to show that environment is a tremendous thing in the world and frequently shapes lives regardless." Critics suggest that the novel was a major development in American literary Naturalism and that it introduced Crane's vision of life as warfare: influenced by the Darwinism of the times, Crane viewed individuals as victims of purposeless forces and believed that they encountered only hostility in their relationships with other individuals, with society, with nature, and with God. Also prominent in his first novel is an ironic technique that exposes the hypocrisy of moral tenets when they are set against the sordid reality of slum life. Although it received the support of

such literary figures as Hamlin Garland and Howells, *Maggie* was not a success. It was not until 1896, after Crane tempered the brutalities in a second edition, that the work received wide recognition.

Crane's second novel, *The Red Badge of Courage*, won him international fame. His vision of life as warfare is uniquely rendered in this short, essentially plotless novel. Often compared to Impressionist painting, *The Red Badge of Courage* is a series of vivid episodes in which a young soldier, Henry Fleming, confronts a gamut of emotions—fear, courage, pride, and humility—in his attempt to understand his battlefield experiences; in this respect, Fleming represents the "Everyman" of war. Crane's work employs a narrative point of view which distinctively offers both an objective panorama of the war as well as the more subjective impressions of the young soldier. Since he had never been to war when he wrote *The Red Badge of Courage*, Crane claimed that his source for the accurate descriptions of combat was the football field; when he finally experienced battle as a war correspondent, he said of the novel, "It was all right." Critics have long debated whether *The Red Badge of Courage* should be considered a product of any specific literary movement or method. The work has been claimed by several schools and referred to as Realistic, Naturalistic, Symbolistic, and Impressionistic. Proponents of Realism view

The Red Badge of Courage as the first unromanticized account of the Civil War and find Fleming's maturation from an inexperienced youth to an enlightened battle-worn soldier to be truthfully depicted. Defenders of a Naturalistic reading contend that the youth's actions and experiences are shaped by social, biological, and psychological forces and that his "development" as a character is incidental to Crane's expert depiction of how these forces determine human existence. Stylistically, Crane's novel contains elements of both Impressionism and Symbolism. For example, some critics note that *The Red Badge of Courage* is laden with symbols and images, while others explain that Crane's episodic narrative structure and his consistent use of color imagery are indicative of an Impressionistic method. A succinct estimate of this debate is offered by Edwin H. Cady, who writes: "The very secret of the novel's power inheres in the inviolably organic uniqueness with which Crane adapted all four methods to his need. *The Red Badge*'s method is all and none. There is no previous fiction like it."

Shortly after the publication of *The Red Badge of Courage* in 1895, Crane published the poetry collection *The Black Riders, and Other Lines*. Although he is not widely recognized for his poetry, this volume of free verse is important because it foreshadowed the work of the Imagist poets with its concise, vivid images. During this time Crane continued to work as a journalist, traveling throughout the American West and Mexico for a news syndicate, and later using his experiences as the basis for fictional works. Returning to New York, Crane wrote *The Third Violet*, a story of bohemian life among the poor artists of New York. This novel is considered one of his least accomplished works and some early critics believed that it was an indication of Crane's failing talent.

In 1897 Crane met Cora Taylor, the proprietor of the dubiously named Hotel de Dream, a combination hotel, nightclub, and brothel. Together as common-law husband and wife they moved to England, where Crane formed literary friendships with Joseph Conrad, H. G. Wells, and Henry James. Shortly after this move, Crane left to report on the Spanish-American War for the New York *World,* an assignment he accepted, in part, to escape financial debts he and Cora had accrued. Although Crane was ill when he returned to England, he continued writing fiction in order to satisfy his artistic needs and to earn money. With *Active Service* he produced another flawed work. This war novel, based on his experiences as a war correspondent in the Greco-Turkish War, is often described as an uneven and sprawling work. By 1900, Crane's health had rapidly deteriorated due to general disregard for his physical well-being. After several respiratory attacks, Crane died of tuberculosis at the age of twenty-eight.

Although Crane achieved the pinnacle of his success with the novel *The Red Badge of Courage,* many critics believe that he demonstrated his greatest strength as a short story writer. His major achievements in this genre are "The Open Boat," "The Blue Hotel," and "The Bride Comes to Yellow Sky." "The Open Boat" is based on Crane's experience as a correspondent shipwrecked while on a filibustering expedition to the Cuban revolutionaries in 1897. The Naturalistic story pits a handful of men against the power of the indifferent but destructive sea. Crane's characteristic use of vivid imagery is demonstrated throughout this story to underscore both the beauty and terror of natural forces. According to critics, Crane is at his best in "The Open Boat," maintaining an even tone and fluent style, while conveying a metaphysical identification between God and nature. Crane's facility with imagery is again displayed

with telling effect in the tragic story "The Blue Hotel." In this deceptively simple Western tale, "the Swede," one of Crane's most interesting characters, becomes the inevitable victim of his own preconceptions about the "Wild West"—fearing a lawless, uncivilized world, his violent reactions to Western life result in his own death. Thomas Gullason refers to Crane's depiction of "the Swede" as "almost Dostoevskyean in its psychological penetration." In another Western story, the comic "The Bride Comes to Yellow Sky," Crane parodies the "shoot 'em-up" Western myth as the characters Jack Potter and Scratchy Wilson fail to fulfill romantic illusions through a gunfight. In these short stories, as in most of his work, Crane is a consummate ironist, employing a technique that most critics find consistently suggests the disparity between an individual's perception of reality and reality as it actually exists.

Commentators generally agree that for the most part Crane disregarded plot and character delineation in his work, and that he was unable to sustain longer works of fiction. However, with the proliferation of Crane scholarship during the last twenty years, Crane's literary reputation has grown. Critics contend that despite his minor flaws, Crane's artistry lies in his ability to convey a personal vision based on his own "quality of personal honesty." In so doing, he pioneered the way for a modern form of fiction which superceded the genteel Realism of late nineteenth-century American literature.

(See also *TCLC*, Vol. 11; *Contemporary Authors*, Vol. 109; *Yesterday's Authors of Books for Children*, Vol. 2; and *Dictionary of Literary Biography*, Vol. 12: *American Realists and Naturalists*.)

PRINCIPAL WORKS

Maggie: A Girl of the Streets (A Story of New York) [as Johnston Smith] (novella) 1893; also published as *Maggie: A Girl of the Streets* [revised edition], 1896
The Black Riders, and Other Lines (poetry) 1895
The Red Badge of Courage: An Episode of the American Civil War (novella) 1895
George's Mother (novel) 1896
The Little Regiment, and Other Episodes of the American Civil War (short stories) 1896
The Third Violet (novel) 1897
The Open Boat, and Other Tales of Adventure (short stories) 1898
Active Service (novel) 1899
The Monster, and Other Stories (short stories) 1899
War Is Kind (poetry) 1899
Whilomville Stories (short stories) 1900
Wounds in the Rain: A Collection of Stories Relating to the Spanish-American War of 1898 (short stories) 1900
*The O'Ruddy (novel) 1903
The Collected Poems of Stephen Crane (poetry) 1930
**The Sullivan County Sketches of Stephen Crane (sketches) 1949
Stephen Crane: An Omnibus (poetry, short stories, and novels) 1952
Stephen Crane: Letters (letters) 1960
The Works of Stephen Crane. 10 vols. (poetry, short stories, novels, and journalism) 1969-72
The Western Writings of Stephen Crane (short stories) 1979
Stephen Crane: Prose and Poetry (novels, novellas, short stories, sketches, journalism, and poetry) 1984

*This work was completed by Robert Barr.

**This work was originally published serially in the newspaper *New York Tribune* and the journal *The Cosmopolitan* in 1892.

ROBERT SHULMAN (essay date 1978)

[*In the following excerpt Shulman discusses Crane's thematic concern with the nature of human community, regarding Crane's mastery of the theme in "The Open Boat" as evidence of his development since writing* The Red Badge of Courage.]

The dynamics of Crane's growth are revealing. Consider the situation of extreme isolation and fragmentation Crane had brought to life for himself in the process of creating *The Red Badge*. Crane was in part responding to one of the deepest tendencies of his American society, its tendency to isolate individuals, to fragment selves and relations, and to substitute technological, contractual, and bureaucratic ties for those of human compassion and community. *The Red Badge of Courage* is one of the most self-contained novels in all of literature. Although in a few scenes of brilliant colloquial dialogue a sense of human relatedness emerges, for the most part selves are cut off from one another and grope through the fog. This aura of fragmentation is furthered by the prevailing smoke, the blurring of fixed outlines, and by the dislocating irony and absence of grammatical connectives and explicit evaluations. As in the most intense battle scenes, moreover, the focus in *The Red Badge* is predominantly on the inner responses of a self unaware of others or even of its own "higher" mental powers.

Beginning with **"An Experiment in Misery"** and **"Men in the Storm"** . . . and developing through the major stories of 1897-1898, however, Crane was compelled to test the possibilities and failures of community, an understandable interest since for him the solitary self has limited resources and God and nature are both inaccessible as sources of sustaining power. As an alternative to an intolerable, deadening sense of isolation, human community assumes heightened importance, and in the great works of his maturity Crane understandably explores different dimensions of this concern.

Crane hardly waited until the ink was dry on his final revision of *The Red Badge* before he tentatively began this exploration of community in **"An Experiment in Misery,"** which was published on April 22, 1894. The Depression of 1893-1894 gave an acute topical interest to Crane's enduring concern with the underside of city life and the underside of existence. In **"An Experiment in Misery"** Crane fuses these interests with his incipient concern with community and his basic preoccupation with perception. In **"An Experiment in Misery"** and, through the next few years in story after story—it is a stylistic signature—Crane arranges his opening paragraphs so that clear outlines are blurred and stable relations are undermined. At the start of **"An Experiment in Misery"** Crane thus stresses the "fine rain swirling down," the glistening of light on the pavement, the "quivering glare" on the benches, and "the mists of the cold and stormy night" out of which loom cable cars and elevated trains, embodiments of the "irresistible," "formidable power" of the city. In **"The Open Boat,"** **"An Experiment in Misery,"** and in many other stories, Crane's visually effective experiments with light, motion, and color express different degrees of epistemological uncertainty. They are not arty exercises but rather his unique and extreme version of a common nineteenth-century response. Because absolutes and certainties no longer exist for him, because he does not take for granted the mind's ability to perceive clearly, and because he has strong intuitions about the sheer power of natural and social forces and perhaps a residual longing for a protection that for him no longer exists—for all of these reasons Crane is compelled by blurred forms and powerful shapes emerging from mist or storm, by scenes in which the heavens are beyond us and the storm of existence blows hard on men who can see jagged waves or cold pavement but not the sky.

Another basic move of Crane's imagination is the descent into the depths of the self and of existence, as in *The Red Badge*, *Maggie*, or **"An Experiment in Misery."** As the latter two works show, death, fear, and human misery, the realities Crane repeatedly confronts, are for him often fused with a social world he brings to the test. Thus, after preliminaries in the saloon, "the youth" of **"An Experiment in Misery"** begins a "journey"—the word is his—into "the dark and secret places of the building," . . . a flophouse from the lower depths. (pp. 441-43)

The descent into the interior brings into sharp focus the youth's underlying fears, so that throughout the story Crane gives us the youth's revealing subjective perceptions, not to call their reliability into question, as in *The Red Badge*, but to establish the intense reality of his inner response to a dark world. The visual blurring and gloom, the stress on eyes and seeing, culminating in the youth's confrontation with the eyes of a corpselike being, and the authority of the third person narrator all suggest that at key moments both the inner and outer worlds are dangerously problematic, so that death, social misery, and nightmares are not only on the youth's mind but also have a reality outside of his mind. Death, agony, and loss of identity, moreover, are genuine threats. (p. 444)

In **"An Experiment in Misery"** the setting . . . becomes increasingly hell-like, an effect Crane conveys at the center of the story by intensifying to the tenth power the visual blurring and flickering lights of the opening paragraph. The youth can hardly see "in the intense gloom within," "a small flickering orange hued flame . . . caused vast masses of tumbled shadows in all parts of the place," and the youth struggles violently against "the unholy odors [that] rushed out like fiends" from the closely packed bodies of the sleeping man. In this dark, hell-like cavern, a clothes locker has "the ominous air of a tombstone," the youth's cot is "like a slab," and the sleeping men, far from seeming tranquil, were "lying in a death-like silence, or heaving and snoring with tremendous effort, like stabbed fish," so that even in sleep, because of that startlingly effective simile, there is the threat of horrible, violent death. Matters reach an almost unbearable impasse when the youth stares into the partly open eyes of a "corpse-like being" and feels threatened to the core of his own being by this glimpse of death and misery. . . . (pp. 444-45)

At the climax of the story, the youth, already deeply unsettled, almost immediately hears nightmare shrieks "echoing . . . through this chill place of tombstones, where men lay like the dead." . . . He could easily respond with terror or total despair or he could identify with this tormented man and risk being pulled under with him. Instead, the youth saves himself by finding a grim, life-affirming meaning in these awful sounds. To him they "were not merely the shrieks of a vision pierced man. They were an utterance of the meaning of the room and its occupants. It was to him the protest of the wretch who feels the touch of the imperturbable granite wheels and who then cries with an impersonal eloquence, with a strength not from him, giving voice to the wail of a whole section, a class, a people." . . .

His recognition of community—for him the voice speaks "for a whole section, a class, a people"—and the youth's sense of the protest against death and inexorable social misery: this constitutes one of the most profound of Crane's insights. At stake are the youth's personal identity and his deepest feelings about human mortality. These concerns combine with his sense of social pain to endow the nightmare sound with its full significance. The context, timing, and unfolding psychological drama are fully realized; the issues are personally, socially, and humanly urgent.

At the end of the story, however, these conditions are absent. The youth emerges from the depths of the building and from the intensity of his nighttime experience. In the light of day the story tapers off into observations of the men dressing and the social panorama the youth's tramp companion supplies through the unidealized details of his wandering life. The story ends with the youth's journalistic indictment of a prosperous, materialistic society that ignores the suffering he has seen, a society he feels alienated from. (p. 445)

As his responses in the depths indicate, the youth, like Crane himself, is also open to metaphysical as well as social and moral issues. These metaphysical concerns should not be dismissed as an unreliable distortion of "objective reality," as "strictly a property of the youth's mind," to quote a recent critic, as if Crane somehow neatly divides the universe into a valued and reliable "objective reality" and a suspect and distorting mind. In Crane the relation between perceiver and perceived is much more fluid and shifting than that, and in "An Experiment in Misery" the relation itself is central.

The story centers, then, not on the Bowery or its inhabitants and their moral cowardice, as Crane later suggested, but on the relation between the youth and a new, dark environment, or on his responses to and perceptions of this world. Thus, what gives power to the ending is not the conventional indictment of an indifferent, money-grubbing society but the youth's feeling that he is "an outcast" . . . , a characteristic Crane response but one that at the center of the story the youth has momentarily transcended by recognizing that the nightmare voice speaks in protest against the misery of "a whole section, a class, a people." (pp. 446-47)

[The] acceptance of the youth's perceptions in "An Experiment in Misery" looks ahead, in particular to "The Open Boat." Instead of the human mortality and social misery of "An Experiment in Misery," in "The Open Boat" the impersonal violence of nature is the antagonist that makes the correspondent aware of his involvement in a human community, to focus on two of Crane's other main interests. Similarly, the correspondent's awareness that the brotherhood of the men in the boat is their main resource in the face of the assaults of the elements constitutes a deepening of the insights of "Men in the Storm." (p. 447)

[Written] as he was revising *The Red Badge* during the severe Depression winter of 1893-1894, Crane renders the elemental violence of the fierce blizzard that characteristically blurs clear outlines in a "swirl" of "great clouds of snow." . . . It is within this universe that Crane, without the mediating presence of the youth or the correspondent of "The Open Boat," then sympathetically records the unemployed men huddling together for warmth against the storm and joking and swearing together

at both their social superiors and the fierce winter. In contrast to "An Experiment in Misery," however, Crane does discriminate between the habitual Bowery inhabitants and the temperate, hardworking unemployed, whose pathos is that they uncomplainingly blame themselves for their failure. . . . All of the beleaguered men, those from the Bowery and the working men alike, nonetheless share an American language of profanity and a grim sense of American humor as resources against their natural and social antagonists. Despite their impulse to trample each other as they rush to escape the knives of snow, moreover, they finally enter the refuge of the soup kitchen "three by three, out of the storm." . . . In this echo of the formation of the Biblical community on Noah's Ark, the shift from two to "three by three" stresses a certain human brotherhood opposed to the storm of the universe. (pp. 447-48)

The realizations of "The Open Boat" were implicit but less fully and deeply developed in the earlier sketches. Under the pressure of his own exposure to the elements after the wreck of the *Commodore,* Crane brought into sharp, suggestive focus concerns and a sense of existence he had been growing toward for nearly three years. In Crane's development beyond *The Red Badge of Courage,* "The Open Boat" marks a culmination and turning point.

From the beginning of "The Open Boat" the perspective of the men is totally limited by the violent sea. They come to know it intimately, in the precise detail, wry humor, and sensitivity to color and to the way things look and feel that are major achievements of Crane's narrative art. He develops the point of view of men who "knew the color of the sea" but not "the color of the sky," a distinction that points up simultaneously Crane's accurate rendering of the men's visual perceptions, the inaccessibility of those conventional certainties the sky traditionally represents, and man's inevitable involvement in a situation that conditions his vision and awareness.

The fact that for Crane men cannot achieve absolutely certain, unchanging knowledge, however, does not for him make their perceptions inevitably false in an absurd universe and it does not detract from their remarkable achievements. The fact that the point of view of the men is limited, moreover, does not for Crane discredit their views or make any one perception suspect on principle. (pp. 448-49)

In contrast to *The Red Badge,* from the outset of "The Open Boat" the responses and perceptions of the men are basically convincing and reliable. It is a mistake to assume that what holds for Henry Fleming holds equally for the men in the open boat, as if Crane had not genuinely developed. Even more insistently than in "Men in the Storm," in paragraph after paragraph of "The Open Boat" Crane builds up the drama of the immense power and ferocity of the elements all but destroying the infinitely small men in their shell of a craft. Sometimes like jagged rocks, sometimes like snarling animals, sometimes like white flames, the waves attack and nearly overwhelm the boat. The elements that arbitrarily follow their own uncontrollable rhythms are sometimes more and sometimes less fierce as the ordeal goes on, but immediately before the men jump, as at the beginning, the waves are "furious" and the third one "fairly swallowed the dingey." . . . Like the figurative language throughout the story, this metaphor serves, not to discredit the distorting minds of the men but to render the felt, perceived reality of their situation.

In all of these instances the figurative language is the narrator's. He is close to the men but his role is to go beyond them and to speak in his own convincing voice so as to establish the reality of their world, their views, and their responses. Thus, he sometimes says "seemed," as when he renders their point of view in the famous first paragraph. Sometimes he uses "was" or "raged" or "came," as when he writes of the waves, "they came in silence, save for the snarling of the crests." And sometimes he reconstructs, as when he says "in the wan light, the faces of the men must have been gray. Their eyes must have glinted in strange ways as they gazed steadily astern." . . . This usage—"must have glinted"—establishes both the inevitability of precisely these glints under such circumstances and the credibility of a narrator who catches the most minute nuances of a scene and even discriminates his own reconstructing role, implied in "must have," from direct reports ("was," "came," "raged").

In a story "after the fact," . . . as part of the occasional process of reconstructing, the narrator sometimes recalls other vantage points. For the men the precipices were immense, each ascent was perilous, and then the dinghy had to face the next menace. Then the shift to "viewed from a balcony, the whole thing would doubtlessly have been weirdly picturesque." This line does not imply that several equally tenable views are possible but it does effectively highlight through contrast the reality of "the men [who] . . . had no time to see it, and if they had the leisure there were other things to occupy their minds." . . . (pp. 449-50)

For them, "the wind tore" and mundane matters related to survival, not the aesthetics of the situation, understandably dominate what they see and take into account.

As in this scene, the recurring explicit and implicit references to other points of view—the balcony or a picnicker's, for example—always serve to stress the earned, experienced reality of the men in the boat. After he has endured the night on the ocean, the exhausted correspondent, we recall, can still see an unlikely admirable "speed and power" in the shark's fin that "cut the water like a gigantic and keen projectile." . . . We are not to ask if it is *really* gigantic or to imagine how a detached observer would see it and to praise or blame the correspondent accordingly, praise if he sees it as the detached observer would, blame if he fails to, but in any case to take it in context as evidence of man's shifting, unreliable perceptions, of what James Colvert sees as Crane's dominant theme, that of "faulty perceptions," or of what others have seen as the story's undermining of man's mind, character, and language in an epistemologically absurd universe. Instead, what is remarkable is that tired as he was the correspondent was capable of such complex, precise, and convincing responses and that Crane, as he does time and again, was able to convey so exactly the experienced quality of the situation. . . . [His] night's experience, fatigue, personal sensibility, and deep involvement give the correspondent rather different expectations and responses than a picnicker. Central to the reality of the correspondent's situation, moreover, is his desire for companionship in a world of sharks and sea. The episode appropriately ends on this note, thus carrying into yet another scene the central theme of community, touchingly rendered here because the correspondent does not awaken his exhausted companions. (pp. 450-51)

A further reality for the correspondent, "a man in this situation, impressed with the unconcern of the universe," is that he "should see the innumerable flaws of his life and have them taste wickedly in his mind and wish for another chance." . . . As the passage continues, the narrator's point of view merges with the correspondent's, so that the exposure of the religion

Crane as a student at Hudson River Institute, 1888.

of the foxhole men under stress is prone to suggest a dimension of self-depreciation, a wry awareness on the correspondent's part of his and man's tendencies and pretenses, and an unwillingness to strike noble postures, as in the comic anti-climax of his understanding that, given another chance, "he would mend his conduct and his words, and be better and brighter during an introduction, or at a tea." . . . The correspondent's credibility is furthered, not weakened, by the episode.

As in this context, which includes his well-known reflection on the windmill, the correspondent's occasional emphasis on the individual in an indifferent universe, moreover, does not detract from his and the story's concern with community but rather develops convincingly the reality of the correspondent's situation. The feeling of brotherhood he experiences early in the ordeal the correspondent knew "even at the time was the best experience of his life," . . . a value that is not undercut when circumstances later force the men apart. (pp. 452-53)

Having experienced the sea as they have, they are now in a position to convey some of its inexhaustible meaning to those on shore, to use human speech to communicate suggestively and intelligently with other men, and to make humanly meaningful "the sound of the great sea's voice" and man's relation to it, as **"The Open Boat"** itself does. (p. 455)

As an alternative both to that impersonal order of experts and to the restless, alienated individualism Tocqueville diagnosed, Stephen Crane's vision of human community in **"The Open Boat"** has an irresistably powerful appeal and significance. As with those moments in Twain's novel when Huck and Jim are together with each other and at one with the river, we are fortunate that our most sensitive American writers have been impelled to remind us of the value of relations our society threatens systematically to destroy. (p. 460)

Robert Shulman, "Community, Perception, and the Development of Stephen Crane: From 'The Red Badge' to 'The Open Boat'," in American Literature, Vol. 50, No. 3, November, 1978, pp. 441-60.

BERNARD WEINSTEIN (essay date 1980)

[*In the following excerpt, Weinstein argues that* George's Mother *presents a more realistic picture of Bowery life than* Maggie: A Girl of the Streets, *noting that after completing* Maggie *Crane intentionally roomed in a flophouse, an experience which gave the later work the insight of firsthand knowledge.*]

In a letter, . . . Crane described "the root of Bowery life" as "a sort of cowardice . . . the willingness to be knocked down flat and accept the licking" . . . , and *Maggie* is filled with examples of degradation and the absence of moral responsibility for oneself and for others. Even with his famous and somewhat pompous pronouncement to the reader that the book shows how environment "is a tremendous thing and shapes life," . . . he cuts with rapid and slashing strokes through his characters' veils of illusion and conventional morality to reveal their self-deception, hypocrisy, and brutality. Yet for all its impact, *Maggie* is largely the effort of a clever young man still dwelling on the periphery of experience, and the result is a novel that suffers frequently from brittleness, detachment, generalization (the specific location of Rum Alley, for instance, is never identified), and self-conscious literariness. The characters—with the possible exception of Jimmie Johnson, Maggie's brother—are flattened anonyms, like Maggie herself, or near-grotesques, like her mother. Perhaps because Crane was partly concerned with proving the naturalistic thesis and because he insisted on life as a condition of war, he failed in *Maggie* to probe the processes of individual degradation. We are certain of Maggie's family's conscious culpability, for example, but we are overwhelmed with the arguments and devices of determinism. By the time he finished *George's Mother*, however, Crane understood enough to write "the New York book that leaves Maggie at the post." . . . In *George's Mother*, the process of degradation is traced more carefully, and as a result the novel is shrewder than *Maggie*: more observant about human nature and less inclined to embrace sociological and metaphysical platitudes. Its shaping force is first-hand observation and experience.

The most generally accepted theory about the history of *George's Mother* holds that Crane began writing it before *The Red Badge of Courage*, resumed it in May 1894, and finished it the following November. This suggests that much of the novel was written after he had published his famous Bowery sketch **"An Experiment in Misery."** This sketch and its companion piece, **"The Men in the Storm,"** grew out of Crane's attempt to "eat as a tramp may eat and sleep as the wanderers sleep." . . . In a single twenty-four hour period in February 1894, Crane had stood on a breadline in a blizzard (**"The Men in the Storm"**) and spent a night in a flophouse **"An Experiment in Misery"**). The two sketches signified not only Crane's full immersion in the life of the Bowery, but provided a sharper focus than *Maggie* for analyzing the roots of beggardom. The two sketches fix responsibility more clearly than *Maggie* does. The assassin of **"An Experiment in Misery"** is revealed, for example, as no more than a parasite with a soft, wheedling voice, manipulative and shiftless, fearful and resentful, turned out (perhaps justifiably) by his stern father; the naked men in the flophouse strut about majestically, suggesting previous grandeur and revealing what they could have been had they not capitulated before life; the men on line in the storm huddle together, feed each other's resentment of society, and, as a result, lose their individual identities and become, almost imperceptibly, a mob. Everywhere cowardice, resentment, illusions flourish. These devour man's potential for activity and creativity, reducing him to a surly, cowardly pauper.

"An Experiment in Misery" and **"The Men in the Storm"** describe the lowest point in the descent from moral responsibility; *George's Mother* dramatizes the descent itself. The central theme of the novel is young Kelcey's disintegration to the level of a drunkard and social parasite, the level at which he might well link arms with the assassin of **"An Experiment in Misery"** or any of the jeering paupers of **"The Men in the Storm."** Moral weakness, not alcoholism, causes his disintegration. If in *Maggie* Crane was able to fall back to a large degree on the notion that environment shapes life, here he sees the environment of Rum Alley as far less consequential (it seems gratuitous that the Johnsons and the Kelceys should actually be neighbors!). George's fall results from his cowardice in the face of moral reality.

Elements in *George's Mother* recall Crane's earlier themes and scenes. . . . Like Pete and Jimmy, the self-indulgent egotists of *Maggie,* George is endowed with crippling illusions of power, attainment, and prestige—which reality will never fulfill. He envisions an "indefinite woman" before whom he struts triumphantly in conquest. In his dreams he is "icy and self-possessed," but his dream-woman is "consumed by wild torrential passion. He went to the length of having her display it before the people. He saw them wonder at his tranquility." . . . Like the little man of Crane's *Sullivan County Sketches,* George is heroic in fantasy but hapless and conventional in reality: "He was told [in books] that there was a goddess in the world whose business it was to wait until he should exchange a glance with her. It became a creed subtly powerful. It saved discomfort for him and for the several women who flitted by him. He used her as a standard." . . . (pp. 45-6)

Like Maggie, George Kelcey creates for himself an impossible ideal, doomed to be frustrated by life. But, while all Maggie's dreams are concentrated on Pete, whom she sees as a theatrically heroic and unswerving figure, George's dreams turn outward with devastating innocence to embrace a vaguely romantic world of excitement, pageantry, and multiplicity. . . . Both George and Maggie mistake a shallow facade for substance. George, for example, creates a fantasy in which Maggie is already a possession; he is, therefore, shattered when he realizes that the more aggressive Pete has already conquered her. Bleeker, George's preceptor in the "religion of drink," appears initially like a Bowery Falstaff, jovial and stout, but when George awakens in the morning after a drunken party, he suddenly perceives Bleeker to be "a tottering old beast." . . . The "clever," contemptuous hoodlums whom George initially finds attractive—romantic rebels against work and responsibility—ultimately appear to him a howling, animalistic mob when they reject and scorn him.

His adoring mother, too, is broken on the rack of her own illusions. Even more than her son, she resembles Maggie. George is as much a concentration of her dreams as Pete is of Maggie's, but George's mother remains utterly blind to his failings until . . . she realizes her powerlessness and George's worthlessness. For both the mother and Maggie, a sudden illumination signals an inexorable movement toward death. Though

George has many dreams, his mother has only one, and she cannot live with its failure. She is indeed "A Woman Without Weapons," as Crane's original title made clear. . . . Mrs. Kelcey's affection dwells at periphery of combat, and George is as much her adversary in a battle for psychological power in the family as he is the ultimate object of her crusade. Their relationship is depicted in the imagery of warfare. Frustrated in her desire to get her son to church, she becomes a raging army of one against an impenetrable fortification. "The waves of her desire were puny against the rocks of his indolence. She had a great wish to beat him." . . . George, for his part, takes advantage of his opponent's vulnerability. "He had traced her emotions and seen her fear of his rebellion. He thrust out his legs in the easy scorn of a rapier-bravo." . . . Still she continues to be "a soldier . . . at her post, imperturbable and unyielding." When she realizes she has finally lost control, she throws out her hands "in the gesture of an impotent one. He was the acknowledged victor." . . . Mrs. Kelcey's chief misconception is that she *has* weapons; that she is battling for the causes of virtue, temperance, and obedience; and that she will win her son to her side. Having done so, she will enable him to rise and do holy battle against evil, like the knight who is his namesake. George, however, soon surrenders to the "green dragon" of alcohol.

Even the church is pictured in metallic and militarized images. The pulpit "was surrounded by vague shapes of darkness on which at times was the glint of brass, or of glass that shone like steel until one could feel there the presence of the army of the unknown." . . . In the Asbury Park world of Crane's youth, which included the fanatically Methodist Ocean Grove, the groundwork was laid for *George's Mother*, as it had been for *Maggie*. If Mrs. Kelcey suggests Mrs. Helen Crane in her loving attitude toward her son and in her personal integrity, she also suggests her in her unrelenting militancy in the cause of temperance. . . . Set between "two towering apartment houses," symbols of an encircling materialism, the church offers George little comfort. . . . The multitude of eyes that turn toward him are "implacable in their cool valuations." The minister, "a pale-faced but plump young man in a black coat that buttoned up to his chin," . . . is a living reproach to him. He suggests the pompous man in the frock coat who sidestepped Maggie, and, like the missionaries in the earlier novel who try to convert Rum Alley, this minister confirms to the members of his congregation that they are already damned. Conventional morality—represented by clergy, churchgoers, and temperance crusaders—reproves those who most need tolerance. Even George's mother is changed by the rigid atmosphere of the church; she is strong, calculating, triumphant and, only this once, intimidating to George.

But the brief time between the completion of *George's Mother* and the publication of "An Experiment in Misery" and "Men in the Storm" suggests similarities among them more important than between *George's Mother* and Crane's earlier writings. All three, unlike *Maggie*, are based on actual experience and are considerably refined in theme and technique. The earlier novel's exaggerated tone, its extreme contrast between unbelievable innocence and surrounding depravity, Crane's brittle cleverness and occasionally mock-heroic diction—all are eliminated or considerably muted in the three major Bowery impressions of 1894. *George's Mother* contained none of *Maggie's* incessant repetition of overt violence. In the later novel Crane played upon the psychological, rather than physical, intimidation; only the metaphor of physical battle remains in the contest between Mrs. Kelcey's militantly religious dogma and

fervent crusading in her errant son's behalf and George's manipulation of his mother's weakness and his progressively hardening sense of power over her.

George has advantages Maggie lacks. He has a decent job, at least one person who is not indifferent to his welfare, a clean and reasonably stable physical environment at home, and a moral consciousness that prods him when he refuses to behave decently and responsibly. But, like the assassin of "An Experiment in Misery," who succumbs to whining excuses of parental rejection in order to justify flight from a useful life, George is filled with sullen petulance and self-rationalization whenever someone disappoints or disillusions him. One may infer from *George's Mother* that the real Bowery for Crane was less a place of genuine physical brutality and naturalistic terrors than a metaphor for manipulation, cowardice, and illusion. Like the assassin of "An Experiment in Misery," George lacks aggressiveness. As Eric Solomon pointed out, comparing George with Pete (Kelcey's "successful rival" for Maggie), "Pete actually does what George can only ineffectually dream of, and his fantasies explode as Pete rescues Maggie from a tenement squabble." Yet George is a more interesting character because he evades classification as a mere Bowery type and takes on aspects of the real Bowery inhabitants whom Crane had met. Crane made the point in *Maggie* that Pete's assertiveness, like George's, lacked conviction, yet the novelist made Pete exaggeratedly glamorous and ridiculous in order to portray the Bowery of his imagination. George is freer of his author's need for hyperbolic extremes. As Crane came to know the Bowery, he became convinced that the poles of innocence and depravity, passivity and aggression, victim and tormentor were oversimplifications as dramatized in *Maggie*, sometimes as stagily contrived as Maggie's own illusions. In *George's Mother*, he came to employ greater interest in individual lives, greater care and credibility in plot manipulation and character motivation and stronger control of narrative.

Living on the Bowery emphasized to Crane that degradation was more a process than a result. Maggie's innocence, like her mother's vicious depravity, lacks an adequately explained cause; rather it seems to have been grafted upon her arbitrarily. In *George's Mother*, however, Crane is noticeably more concerned with psychological background. The mother has lost all her family except her son and thus expects more from him than he can possibly give her. His retreat from life stems both from his calculated rage and rebellion against his mother and from the impossible standard set by the books he has read. (pp. 46-8)

Crane's increasing mastery of his Bowery materials also shows in his diction. The animal imagery in *George's Mother* seems far less gratuitous and artificial than in *Maggie*, more attuned to the moral context of the novel. While passages such as the one comparing a brewery and "a great bird flying" recall the excesses of *Maggie*, many of the animal references avoid the inanimate world and focus attention instead on human degradation. From "the tottering old beast," Bleeker, George descends on the moral and social scale to the level of men whose every gesture evokes the jungle: they talk in "growls" and "snarls"; they make for themselves a "den" on a vacant lot surrounded by tenements; in anger they "gibber" like "wounded ape[s]." (pp. 48-9)

Ultimately, *George's Mother* does not convey *Maggie's* dark sense of the world as a cruel, amoral, naturalistic juggernaut demanding the sacrifice of innocence. But the later novel does reveal the world as a void where each human being must existentially grope toward moral responsibility and understanding, where cowardice and brutality are not arbitrarily assigned but chosen. The increasing complexity of Crane's vision likely reflects his experiences, as a journalist, of the authentic life of the Bowery. Without them, even his greatest tale might have remained unfinished. (p. 49)

> Bernard Weinstein, "'George's Mother' and the Bowery of Experience," in The Markham Review, Vol. 9 (Spring, 1980), pp. 45-9.

SUE L. KIMBALL (essay date 1980)

[*Kimball is an American author and essayist who has written extensively on the use and function of games in the works of such authors as Alfred Tennyson and Crane. In the following excerpt, Kimball discusses the symbolic meaning of the many circles, squares, parallel lines, and angles in "The Blue Hotel" as representations of unity, community, and exclusion in the society of the town.*]

In 1882, when Stephen Crane was eleven years old, a German mathematician named Lindemann proved once and for all that the ancient problem of squaring the circle was impossible to solve. Although mathematics was always one of young Stephen's weakest subjects, it is likely that as a pre-engineering student he would have come into contact with Professor Lindemann's findings. Whether or not we can prove that Crane was interested in the mathematical controversy—which goes back to five hundred years before the exodus of the Israelites from Egypt—the fact remains that he made esthetic use of the problem by employing a circle-square dichotomy and by using certain other geometrical figures thematically in his short story **"The Blue Hotel."**

The word "square" appears seven times in the story; once as a verb, once as a noun, and five times as an adjective. The *Oxford English Dictionary* lists over thirty-five distinct meanings of the word, some of them obsolete, and many of them applicable to Crane's tale. . . . (p. 425)

The Palace Hotel's two little windows initiate the right-angular imagery of the story. Like the windows of Beckett's *Endgame*, they are the means through which the hotel's occupants view the world proper; in neither case is the view optimistic, the "profligate fury" of **"The Blue Hotel's"** blizzard appearing only slightly less menacing than *Endgame*'s "muckheap."

The first actual "square" reference appears when Johnny and the farmer resume their game of High Five "destroyed" by Scully on the arrival of the three guests. The two "sat close to the stove and squared their knees under a wide board." The playing board is, of course, also square and serves as the arena for *agon* on at least four occasions. The Swede is not present when Johnny and the farmer play the first game, and he is not invited to participate in the second; nor does he watch "with interest" as do the cowboy and the Easterner. Instead he remains "near the window, aloof, but with a countenance that showed signs of an inexplicable excitement." . . . During the third and fourth games, of which the Swede is a nervous participant, the four players "form a square, with the little board on their knees." While it is true that his ostracism is somewhat self-perpetuated by his silences interrupted by loud, shrill laughs, and by his suspicions, those around the square board refuse to form a communal circle. The Swede, the only one of Scully's newly arrived guests who is immediately excluded from the brotherhood of man, never becomes a true member of the group, even when he becomes a "board-thwacking" player.

During the six o'clock supper, the heretofore reticent Swede, his spirits raised temporarily by the whiskey Scully has insisted that he drink, almost "bursts into riotous song." . . . The Easterner and the cowboy are quiet throughout the meal, but the Swede's voice "rings through the room." He "nearly impales the hand of the Easterner" with his fork and smites Scully a painful blow on his tender shoulder as he remarks, "Well, old boy, that was a good, square meal." While he is not the Swede's "old boy," Scully knows that he alone is responsible for the Swede's affected affability, and that the others understand this. The now-gregarious Swede, however, is still on the outside of the circle he pretends to invade; while the playing board is both literally and figuratively square, the meal is figuratively "square" in the same sense of being non-circular or non-communal. Traditionally a time of fellowship, the meal here emphasizes the isolation of the Swede, whose manner causes Scully's daughters to flee in "ill-concealed trepidation" after they serve the biscuits.

The Swede's attempt to insinuate himself into the hotel's microcosmic community of man having failed, he leaves Scully's place "tacking across the face of the storm as if he carried sails" . . . —which would themselves be triangular or square. Following "a line of little naked, grasping trees," the Swede finally glimpses "a number of square shapes" which he recognizes as "the houses of the main body of the town," squares that represent his exclusion from membership in that populace also.

Upon reaching the saloon, the Swede sees at a table four men, who "in some subtle way encase themselves in reserve." . . . One of them is a "professional gambler of the kind known as 'square'," i.e., "fair" or "honest." In the character of this gambler Crane exercises his irony to the fullest: the townspeople call the gambler a "thoroughbred" because he is so "judicious in his choice of victims." The residents of Fort Romper, like their counterparts in Shirley Jackson's "Lottery" village, condone the gambler's "craft" and "laugh in contempt of the victim," secure in the "knowledge that he would never dare think of attacking their wisdom and courage." . . . The gambler is "square" in the best sense of the word, according to the Romperites, but he too is an isolato, refused admittance to the town's Pollywog Club—fraternity of immature things— "even as a spectator."

The last two "square" references appear in the often-criticized coda of the story. When the Easterner comments, "The Swede might not have been killed if everything had been 'square'," the cowboy questions, "Everythin' square?" . . . Scully's two guests have apparently become friends, but their ideas of squareness differ because of their divergent backgrounds. The cowboy, who is originally from the West, where cheating at cards may be an acceptable way of life—particularly if one does not get caught, and especially when the game is "for fun"—finds the Easterner's willingness to assume a universal guilt for the Swede's murder a "mysterious theory." . . . (pp. 425-27)

What all these varieties of squareness have in common is that they serve to exclude the Swede in one way or another—either literally, in the card games and in the town, or figuratively, in the code of honor acceptable to Fort Romper and the West. The numerous circles imply a community of interest, but never one that admits the Swede. . . . His antagonists, Johnny and the gambler, are both part of conventional family circles: Scully evinces a tenderness when his son is hurt, and Johnny's mother and sisters "bear him away" to minister to him. The gambler leads "an exemplary home life" in a "neat cottage in a suburb," where his "real wife and two real children" complete a "virtuous family circle." . . . (pp. 427-28)

Other circles in **"The Blue Hotel"** also serve to exclude the Swede and to bind other factions together. The hotel itself may even be round since it is named the "Palace Hotel." While its shape is never delineated, the stove, which is at the hotel's center, is probably round also. The guests sit about it, smoking their pipes while it "hums." The Swede remains "aloof" from this cozy group, finally removing himself to pack his bag for departure. When Scully persuades the Swede to rejoin Johnny and the other guests, their "five chairs are formed in a crescent" . . . around one side of the stove. Scully has to force admission of the Swede even to this half-circle. . . .

Another circle—actually a sphere—is the infamous "space-lost bulb" . . . to which the men-lice cling. Instead of being "conquering and elate," says Crane, mankind hangs desperately onto his hostile environment, in which "one is a coxcomb not to die." If there is a hierarchy of the parasitic insects on this globe, however, one suspects that the Swede might be among the lower orders; if there were not enough room for all, he would be pushed off by his fellow vermin.

Circular images include the three basins of cold water offered by Scully in a ritualistic ceremony; the cowboy and the Easterner accept, "burnishing themselves fiery red," . . . but the Swede merely "dips his fingers gingerly and with trepidation," thereby refusing the rites of initiation offered him on his arrival. In turn, the Swede offers, and Scully refuses, three silver pieces—circles which would at least have established for him the status of paying guest. It is likely that Scully, who is nothing if not businesslike, has seldom refused payment from the patrons whom he coerces to his shockingly blue lair. (p. 428)

The "two spots brightly crimson and sharply edged, as if they had been carefully painted," . . . circles on the "deathly pale cheeks" of the Swede—and reminiscent of the famous "red wafer" image of *The Red Badge of Courage*—reflect the Swede's tension. When he does manage to leave Scully's hotel unscathed and moves toward the saloon, the Swede is greeted by "the circumscribed territory of the lamp's shining." . . . The "blood-coloured snowflakes," even if inviting, offer false promise; the Swede passes through the arc, into the saloon, and toward his destiny. (p. 429)

Because the word "square" derives from the Latin *quadrus,* meaning "having four equal sides and four right angles," the various combinations of four in **"The Blue Hotel"** are important underpinnings for the circle-square motif. The four-sided playing board is a major symbol; the foursome around it never become a circle because on one side sits the Swede, who neither chooses nor is chosen to become a bona fide member. And whenever such a square converts to a circle, he becomes the odd-man-out. When the Swede goes to the saloon, he finds four men already seated at a table and is therefore refused admission to their circle. The most significant number four in **"The Blue Hotel,"** however, is to be found in Scully's prophecy that Fort Romper plans to build four churches for the tiny town—eloquent proof that the few citizens cannot agree among themselves ecumenically and must form four mutually exclusive circles even for worship.

Each mention of a corner in **"The Blue Hotel"** suggests a turning point into mounting opposition. The first corner is that rounded by the men who have just observed the fight: they are "fairly blinded by the pelting of the snow." . . . As the Swede travels through the town enroute to the saloon, he is hit at each corner by a "terrific blast." . . . And as the barkeeper "dashes around the corner of his bar," he meets "a great tumult" and "a long blade in the hand of the gambler." . . . (pp. 429-30)

The total effect of **"The Blue Hotel's"** design of circles and squares, cubes and spheres, parallel lines, and right and acute angles is rather like that of a self-designed horror-house maze through which the Swede has walked virtually alone, his destination inevitable. The irony of the Swede's quest is that he is disappointed because he finds order in the West. His presuppositions and his imagination require that he initiate chaos from the design that he discovers. In so doing, he causes circles to become squared—a quadrature that all mathematicians recognize as an impossibility. (p. 430)

Sue L. Kimball, "Circles and Squares: The Designs of Stephen Crane's 'The Blue Hotel'," in Studies in Short Fiction, *Vol. 17, No. 4, Fall, 1980, pp. 425-30.*

WARREN FRENCH (essay date 1981)

[*French is an American author, editor, and essayist who has written several important studies of twentieth-century American writers and literary movements. In addition to his works on celebrated American authors, French also served as an editor of the influential* Twayne Theatrical *series and the* Twayne United States Authors *series. In the following excerpt, he discusses* "The Veteran" *and* "Moonlight on the Snow" *as minor works that serve as companion pieces to and illuminate the central themes and characters of* The Red Badge of Courage *and* "The Bride Comes to Yellow Sky." *French regards these minor stories as exemplars of Crane's "ironic perception of the relationship between the individual and his culture."*]

Although Crane never carried from story to story characters with the pertinacity that William Dean Howells did Basil March or William Faulkner, Ike McCaslin to reflect the artist's growing apprehension about the evolution (*devolution* fits better the picture that emerges) of an increasingly urbanized United States, he did demonstrate a potential for the serial treatment of his conceptions in works about Henry Fleming and the team of Jack Potter and Scratchy Wilson. Although the earlier stories about these figures, the novel *The Red Badge of Courage* and the short story **"The Bride Comes to Yellow Sky,"** are among Crane's most often reprinted and revalued works, the brief sequels **"The Veteran"** and **"Moonlight on the Snow"** have been usually dismissed more summarily than they may deserve. While both are slight, perhaps unartful works, the glosses that they provide on their predecessors offer unique glimpses of Crane's ironic perception of the relationship between the individual and his culture.

Elsewhere I have argued that if we accept the broadest definition of literary modernism, which sees all its varied manifestations as concerned with an individual self-consciously set apart from his society, Crane's *The Red Badge of Courage* is the first substantial manifestation of this sensibility in American fiction. . . . As I have also pointed out, this feeling of breaking away resulted at first in a tremendous exhilaration, in a sense of personal triumph rather than in the alienation that has become the characteristic feeling of the protagonists of most deeply felt fiction since World War I. Before succumbing to existential despair, modernism began militantly with the defiance James Joyce's Stephen Dedalus expresses at the end of *A Portrait of the Artist as a Young Man*—and even earlier in a more arrogantly optimistic version voiced by Henry Fleming in Crane's *The Red Badge of Courage*.

What actually happens to Henry in **Red Badge** has often been misconstrued because generations of readers have accepted the novel as an "initiation" story, like Mozart's *The Magic Flute* or Faulkner's "The Bear," a tale of the perilous rites of passage through which a hitherto immature individual wins a place in a traditional society. In **Red Badge,** however, Henry does not enter society on its own terms; rather he transcends it in order to create a unique place for himself on *his* own terms.

From the point of view from which I am looking at the novel, its twenty-four chapters may be divided at exactly the middle, with Henry Fleming portrayed in the first twelve chapters as a "victim," not so much of society or even the universe (like the voices in many of Crane's poems), but of his own naive illusions and lack of conscious control over his behavior. In the final twelve chapters, on the other hand, we see Henry thinking his own way through to a victory over whatever external or internal forces are inimical to the full realization of himself.

At the beginning of the novel, Henry exercises no control over his environment at all. Crane speaks of Henry's being "in a little trance of astonishment." . . . Although he has often as a youth dreamed of bloody battles and has finally enlisted in the Union Army of his own volition as a result of his unreflective responses to patriotic propaganda, now, trapped in the regiment, "it occurred to him that he had never wished to come to the war. He had not enlisted of his free will. He had been dragged by the merciless government. And now they were taking him out to be slaughtered." . . . (pp. 155-57)

Even before giving away to these excesses of self-pity, however, Henry, faced with the question of whether he might run away from the battlefield, has exhibited a capacity for experimenting with himself. Finding that "in this crisis his laws of life were useless," he sees that "he would again be obliged to experiment as he had in early youth. He must accumulate information of himself and, meanwhile, he resolved to remain close upon his guard lest those qualities of which he knew nothing should everlastingly disgrace him." . . . Even in this moment of confusion, Henry is endowed by Crane with a preternatural concern about controlling the impression that he makes upon others. For the time being, however, he can develop only "a dull, animal-like rebellion against his fellows, war in the abstract, and fate;" . . . and he retreats back into nature, which he conceives of as "a woman with a deep aversion to tragedy." . . . Nature, however, as so often in Crane's writings, is entirely indifferent to man's dilemmas. Henry has already been surprised that "nature had gone tranquilly on with her golden processes in the midst of so much devilment." . . . (p. 157)

At this point, Henry Fleming seems the prototype for the protagonist of the modernist fiction of the 1920s, who, like Ernest Hemingway's Frederic Henry in *A Farewell to Arms*, makes "a separate peace" and takes flight into a nature that also proves indifferent to man's designs. Henry's fortunes turn, however, after chapter 12 of the novel, in which a devastating blow on the head, the result of human cowardice and panic, is verbally transformed into Henry's "red badge of courage" that redeems him in the eyes of his fellows and sets him on the road to a mastery of his surroundings. In chapter 13, the second half of the novel begins with the great turn in Henry's fortunes, when, after a man with a cheery voice, who seems to possess a kind of "magic wand," has led him back to his regiment, he announces, "I got shot." . . .

In the ensuing dialogue Crane subtly employs a reverse of his usual form of irony in which expectations exceed fulfillment. A corporal almost subverts Henry's word magic, when he observes in passing of the wound, "It's raised a queer lump jest as if some feller had lammed yeh on th' head with a club;" . . . but, achieving a fulfillment that outstrips all his expectations, Henry wins the respect of his colleagues for his bravery. Out of this experience and what follows, Henry learns that "many obligations of a life were easily avoided. . . . There was a little flower of confidence growing within him." He learns also that he need not formulate fixed new laws to replace those of his youth for predetermining his behavior: "He could leave much to chance." . . . (p. 158)

The groundwork for this crucial reversal has been carefully laid back in chapter 11 when Crane depicts Henry as realizing that "he could not but know that a defeat for the army this

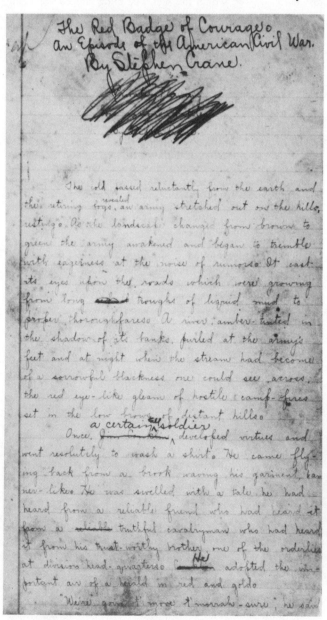

Holograph copy of the first page of The Red Badge of Courage.

time might mean many favorable things for him," as it would provide "a means of escape from the consequences of his fall." . . . Still under the spell at this point, however, of his earlier indoctrination, he dismisses the possibility of the army's defeat, for "his education had been that success for that mighty blue machine was certain," so that he tries "to bethink him of a fine tale which he could take back to his regiment and with it turn the expected shafts of derision;" . . . but its invention proves impossible. Chance, however, plays into his hands and teaches him that one need not be at the mercy of events: one can restructure secret histories to place oneself in a favorable light. The self-made hero structures his history not on what has happened, but on what he conceives would have been the best thing to have happened from his point of view. The full significance of Henry's discovery of the self-conscious manipulation of situations occurs when, as he reviews "the battle-pictures he had seen," he begins to feel "quite competent to return home and make the hearts of people glow with stories of war. He could see himself in a room of warm tints telling *tales* to listeners." . . . (pp. 158-59)

Tales indeed they would be. What we must pause to observe, quite unsentimentally, is that Crane is shaping his heroic Henry Fleming into one of the first public-relations men. What Henry has developed through his military experiences is no sense of patriotic devotion to a socially cohesive group (this is rather one of the illusions that he has shed), nor yet the bitter rejection of society's propaganda that Hemingway's Frederic Henry expresses in *A Farewell to Arms*. Henry has wised up to the world; but he is still self-confident enough to think that he can manipulate it to his own advantage. Crane is quite conscious of what he has depicted as happening to Henry. During a pause in his rush to glory, in the last chapter of the book, Henry "began to study his deeds—his failures and his achievements. Thus fresh from scenes where many of his usual *machines of reflection* had been idle, from where he had proceeded sheeplike, he struggled to marshall all his acts" (. . . my italics). I had thought for a while of titling these remarks "machines of reflection," until I perceived that something less tangible was involved in the pursuit; for the phrase certainly does sum up Crane's conception of the skills that he must call upon to make his way in a world where he has ultimately nothing but the "fine tales" that he can concoct, perhaps with the aid of chance. (Thus *The Red Badge of Courage* turns out also to be finally, as we have learned recently so many great fictions are, another story of the artist's—specifically the taleteller's—discovery of his own vocation. . . . (p. 159)

Thus the ending that some critics have complained does not really fit the novel is indeed the only fitting conclusion for Henry Fleming's *bildungsroman* as Crane has shared it with us. Henry is not speaking ironically nor is Crane condescending to his creation when he writes, "He saw that he was good. He re-called with a thrill of joy the respectful comments of his fellows upon his conduct." . . . And Crane is giving us Henry as his creator sees him when in the next-to-last paragraph, the youth smiles, "for he saw that the world was a world for him though many discovered it to be made of oaths and walking-sticks. . . ." He had been an animal blistered and sweating in the heat and pain of war. He turned now with a lover's thirst, to images of tranquil skies, fresh meadows, cool brooks; an existence of soft and eternal peace." . . . For many people, like the characters in Crane's own novel *Maggie,* the world is indeed made of oaths and walking-sticks. They need crutches of some kind to make their way, curses to support them in

their disappointment and despair; for they are victims of a world that they have not made. But Henry Fleming has learned to make the world work for him, to live in the world that he has made, so that the world is indeed *for* him, not in the rejected sense that "nature was of his mind," but in the sense that it is only raw material for his "machines of reflection." (p. 160)

What plans Stephen Crane might have had for Henry Fleming—or a whole Fleming clan—we cannot know; but the character and his ancestry certainly continued to occupy the author's imagination as late as 1899, for in his plans that year for a new novel about the Revolutionary War in New Jersey, he mentions in the last sentence, "Introduce Henry Fleming's grandfather as first farmer." . . . Henry himself turns up in a comic sketch called **"Lynx Hunting."**

He reappears much more importantly, however, in **"The Veteran,"** which, though appended to a loose collection of war tales called *The Little Regiment,* should regularly be reprinted as a coda to *The Red Badge of Courage* providing the epitaph for a bold grandfather who had as a young man not only survived the Civil War but turned that bloody episode to his own advantage as a means of self-discovery.

Despite its brevity, **"The Veteran,"** read in the light of Henry's triumphant success in learning to reshape reality for his own purposes, offers several important insights into Crane's conception of the hero in a self-conscious age; they are entirely consistent with the final image of Henry in *Red Badge* and tie up the necessarily open end of any tale—about events however unpleasant—that ends in a comic vision.

For one thing, we discover that, as he aged, Henry Fleming retained the ability to recount the past in a way that most impressed his deferential neighbors, even to the extent of admitting that indeed during the war he had been scared at times. Since "their opinion of his heroism was fixed" (. . . one is tempted to add "fixed" in several senses of the word), such modesty, though it scandalizes Henry's adoring grandson, impresses the neighbors even more than would vain boasting.

More important, we learn that Henry had indeed not used his talents for the kind of advancement they might have won him. Fleming was certainly ahead of his times; the manipulative techniques that Crane allows him to master in the early 1860s did not become the tools of the modern advertising business and its offshoots until the end of the century. . . . There would, however, have been bountiful opportunities even during the Gilded Age that followed the Civil War for a character like Henry to turn his talents to cynical self-aggrandizement in politics or land speculation, for example. Henry, however, is satisfied to return home to win the respect of his neighbors; he shows no desire to battle for glory on the sullied fields of peace as he had on the bloody fields of battle. Actually, one of the most specific links betwen *Red Badge* and **"The Veteran"** is forged by Crane in the earlier work, when he foreshadows Henry's future course, by having Henry wind up his already quoted reflections on the tales of war he would tell at home: "He could exhibit laurels. They were insignificant; still, in a district where laurels were infrequent, they might shine. . . . (pp. 161-62)

Most of the sketch, however, despite even the excitement of a barn fire, is so low-keyed that Crane seems to be offering us simply an American pastoral to contrast with the sordid scenes of rural life that had already entered our fiction in the stories of Hamlin Garland and E. W. Howe. In the final paragraph, however, the tone suddenly changes in a way that suggests that the brief account has been only a deceptively modest preparation for a climax that will transcend the bare facts of the incident and place it in a mythological context:

> When the roof fell in, a great funnel of smoke swarmed toward the sky, as if the old man's mighty spirit, released from its body—a little bottle—had swelled like the genie of fable. The smoke was tinted rose-hue from the flames, and perhaps the unutterable midnights of the universe will have no power to daunt the color of this soul. . . .
>
> (pp. 162-63)

In death as in life, Crane suggests that Henry Fleming has risen above the dark circumstances that surrounded him and achieved some kind of celestial light. In *Red Badge*, Henry triumphs over the immediate obstacles to self-realization; but since even such a modern hero is mortal, what is the fitting end for him? Should he simply be laid away in the ground, returned to the nature to which in his moments of defeat he had sought refuge? Such a conclusion would be a victory for the very forces of preordination that Henry had vanquished in *Red Badge*. If Crane were indeed to create a hero for an age which seemed to have little place for heroes, his figure would have to achieve at last an archetypal force. What more appropriate indeed than that Henry Fleming should disappear into fire, immolated in the manner of the Vikings or ancient Nordic demigods who may have been his ancestors? The metaphor of the genie and the bottle forces attention to the way in which Crane is transcending materiality in this paragraph to achieve the magical; and his concluding tribute that "the unutterable midnights of the universe" are powerless against the *color* of this soul not only recalls and spiritualizes the bloody *red* of the novel, but also consciously and deliberately moves Henry Fleming out of any particular place and time, suggesting that his spirit is untouchable by any physical powers. (p. 163)

In the light of the pretensions of the Henry Fleming saga, Crane's other paired tales about Jack Potter and Scratchy Wilson seem an abrupt comedown from the sublime to, if not the ridiculous, distinctly the mundane. **"The Bride Comes to Yellow Sky"** moves in a direction quite contrary to the Fleming stories. If *The Red Badge of Courage* is a tale of the self-transcendence of a victimizing society by a heightened consciousness, **"The Bride"** is deservedly admired as a classic tale of the disappearance of the old Wild West and its replacement by a conformist society. When Jack Potter abandons his guns and brings a bride back to the frontier settlement, law and order asserts itself and the last of the old gang, Scratchy Wilson, must steam off into the sands, symbolizing the triumph of "civilized" institutions over the once wilderness. (p. 164)

"Moonlight on the Snow" has been practically disregarded, although for one reading the works of an author rather than individual stories, it contains one startling surprise—not that Jack Potter has extended his entrepreneurship by expanding the territory to which he brings the law, but that Scratchy Wilson has not disappeared into the desert. Instead he has sobered up and become one of Potter's deputies. The Wild West has not been just defeated, but assimilated. Since Scratchy does nothing at all but appear in **"Moonlight on the Snow,"** the only reason for introducing him is to tie up another loose end in the way Crane had in **"The Veteran."**

This tale is deservedly less well known than **"The Bride,"** for the whole situation of Larpent, the killer whom the evilly re-

garded community of War Post wants to hang so that it may appear as virtuous as neighboring communities, strains credulity as **"The Bride"** never does. . . . Larpent's own willingness to be hanged seems simply like Scratchy Wilson's capitulation in **"The Bride,"** a less convincing symbol of the recognition that the old days are gone. Larpent's apparent escape from his fate also shows within a single story that the West is really only exchanging one form of corruption for another. The easternization of the West will only mean the replacement of irresponsible individuals by dishonest institutions.

Such a portrayal of the defeat of individualism in the two western stories seems superficially inconsistent with Crane's mythologizing of the ultimately self-reliant individual in the Henry Fleming stories. Of course, the tone of the works is different. Everyone—even Jack Potter—in the western stories is being corrupted or at least cowed into submission by the force of neighbors' opinions and the temptation of easy money— the very things that Henry Fleming learns to control once he has learned that "the world was a world for him." (pp. 164-65)

The kind of chaotic disorder existing on frontiers beyond the reach of the law must be displaced by institutionalized society as even such cheerless communities as Yellow Sky and War Post develop because of the violent threat that uncontrolled behavior poses to innocent persons. (Crane sums up the whole matter in a sentence in **"Moonlight on the Snow"** describing a minister's family's reaction to a hanging party: "And the rough West stood in naked immortality before the eyes of the gentle East." . . . But the very institutions that bring stability and perhaps prosperity quickly become corrupted—are corrupted, in fact, even before they arrive and are seized upon, as in War Post, for corrupt purposes from the beginning, so that the individual whose soul might remain undaunted by "the unutterable midnights of the universe," must, like Henry Fleming, transcend the cycle through the efforts of his own consciousness, since assistance seems available from nowhere else.

Crane's Henry Fleming was thus, even before James Joyce's creation of Stephen Dedalus, the first example of the modernist hero who was distanced, detached, but not yet alienated from his society. He was not to provide the model for the future. Stephen Crane, despite the ironic bitterness of much of his work, was both too traditional and too optimistic in his conception underlying the creation of Henry Fleming that the same individual might be both shrewd and unexploitative enough to rise above the victimizing power of institutions, while remaining a functioning and even respected member of his hometown society. His only counterpart in American literature is Vanamee a few years later in Frank Norris's *The Octopus*; and even he was obliged to endure years of pain and isolation before finding a peace that eludes his contentious contemporaries. Even Joyce's Stephen had to fly the "nets" of "home, fatherland, and church" to forge "the uncreated conscience" of his race. By the time of Faulkner's Ike McCaslin, one can save one's self only by renouncing one's birthright—a form of alienation that involves flight in time if not space. (p. 165-66)

*Warren French, "Stephen Crane: Moment of Myth,"
in* Prairie Schooner, *Vol. 55, Nos. 1 & 2, Spring-Summer, 1981, pp. 155-67.*

KHALIL HUSNI (essay date 1981)

[*In the following excerpt, Husni argues that Henry Fleming has neither changed nor matured at the end of* The Red Badge of

Courage. *Husni regards Fleming as a romantic who simply exchanges illusions of glory for illusions of peace.*]

The purpose of this note is to show that the hero of Stephen Crane's *The Red Badge of Courage* is neither more mature as a result of his war experience, nor is he in possession of a "lasting wisdom" at the end of the novel. What has stamped reading the novel as the education of a young man is the expressed emotional change which the "heroic youth," Henry, undergoes when his battle ordeal is over. . . . (p. 16)

The youth's renunciation of his previously cherished Homeric illusions of war as glorious and heroic, and this turning to natural images of peace and tranquility have been taken to underline his newly acquired perspective. When the youth comes to realize that his "earlier gospels" of war are bloody and destructive, he resorts to the gospel of nature which seems to advocate "an existence of soft and eternal peace." His proselytism would have been indicative of his maturity had there been such an "existence," had not such a vision been parodied and undermined in the novel itself.

Through its treatment of war, *The Red Badge of Courage* presents a grim portrait of nature. Following his blood baptism, the youth is astonished at the "golden" indifference of nature:

> As he gazed around him, the youth felt a
> flash of astonishment at the blue, pure sky
> and the *sun-gleamings* on the trees and
> fields. It was surprising that nature had gone
> tranquilly on with her golden process in the
> midst of so much devilment (. . . italics
> added).

The youth fails to perceive the implications of this scene. Fleeing the battlefield, he withdraws into the heart of nature where he seeks the "chapel" in the hope of finding an evidence which would justify his desertion:

> This landscape gave him assurance. A fair
> field, holding life. It was the religion of
> peace. It would die if its timid eyes were
> compelled to see blood. . . .

As the youth probes through the labyrinth of the "fair field," he sees "a small animal pounce in and emerge directly with a *gleaming fish*" (. . . italics added). The youth witnesses the incident without grasping its significance—the correlation between the new recruits [referred to as "Fresh fish" . . .] who are butchered to feed the "red animal—war," and the "animal" that devours the "gleaming fish" in that "fair field" to survive.

Upon reaching the "chapel," the youth is momentarily petrified when he glimpses, through the dazzling rays of a "religious half light," not the sought-after image of life and salvation, but the appalling image of death and decay—a corpse. . . . The youth stares vacantly at "the liquid-looking eyes," the appearance of which, interestingly, but shockingly enough, is likened to "the dull hue to be seen on the side of a dead fish." . . . (pp. 16-17)

The message that the novel brings home (the letters of which the youth remains unable to decipher) is that the deadly and horrifying laws which govern the battlefield are not very different from those which govern nature: Both feed on death; battlefield laws seem to be a startling, ferocious magnification of the deadly principle of survival inherent in the subtle mechanism of nature. If "Nature" has no aversion to the sight of

corpses, it is because at its heart lies a "charnel place," "the house of the dead." . . . (p. 17)

Following his ordeal, the youth rids himself "of the red sickness of battle"; his war dreams which prove nightmarish are replaced by a soothing vision "of tranquil skies, fresh meadows, cool brooks. . . ." His dreams of Homeric glory and grandeur are replaced by an illusory vision of "eternal peace." As the youth drops the "Red Badge of Courage," he puts on the "Green Badge of Peace." Both Badges signify one form or another of romantic enchantment. (pp. 17-18)

> *Khalil Husni, "Crane's 'The Red Badge of Courage',"* in The Explicator, *Vol. 39, No. 4, Summer, 1981, pp. 16-18.*

HOLLIS CATE (essay date 1982)

[*Cate is an American educator who has written studies of nineteenth-century English and American literature. In the following excerpt, he examines Crane's use of visual imagery and ocular symbolism in "The Blue Hotel," and posits that these devices accentuate the compound misconceptions and misunderstandings that exist among the story's characters.*]

Crane's use of ocular references in **"The Blue Hotel"** strongly supports his story's structure and thematic significance. The story turns, for the most part, on what the characters do or do not perceive and on what they think they perceive. The world of **"The Blue Hotel"** is in the eye of the characters as beholders. Crucial incident is created through the act of seeing, of taking in the other (or trying to); and Crane uses these glances (looks) as pivotal points in his story, one situation naturally leading to another. From the first sight reference to the last Crane underscores the idea that his participants constantly perceive falsely at the other's expense, and that seeing truly does not necessarily result in one's acting responsibly.

When the Swede comes into the presence of the others, he immediately begins to concoct a false situation, and to make of the others something which they are not: actively dangerous. He makes "furtive estimates of each man in the room" and "his eyes continued to rove from man to man." To the Swede the others are in a constant state of becoming. Because they are what *he* sees, he will become an enigma to *them*. We read that "they looked at him, wondering and in silence." . . . He further confounds them when he takes a seat to play cards and gazes into the others' faces and inexplicably laughs. When he says he supposes many men had been killed in the room, the men's jaws dropped and "they looked at him." . . . But they do not comprehend what they see. This point is later emphasized when Johnnie says the man is "the dod-dangest Swede I ever see." The cowboy replies, "He ain't no Swede . . . He's some kind of Dutchman." . . . Seeing the man does not help the cowboy and the others to decipher him.

Early in the story the Swede sends an "appealing glance" . . . toward the Easterner, who says outright that he doesn't understand the stranger (at the *end* of the story the Easterner says, however, that all the men were involved in the Swede's death). When "the appealing glance" brings no sympathy for the Swede, he says, "Oh I see you are all against me I see." . . . But his perception is flawed here early in the story, and it becomes progressively worse.

Later the Swede goes upstairs, and Scully, the proprietor, follows him in hope of mollifying him. When he turns and sees Scully, the proprietor's eyes are in shadow. Crane tells us that old Scully resembled a murderer, to the Swede, of course. They stand glaring at each other. But perception is sorely lacking. . . . When Scully offers him a drink of whiskey, the Swede is at first reluctant to accept, casting a "look of horror upon Scully." He does drink, however, keeping "his glance burning with hatred upon the old man's face." . . . Later, Scully says the Swede looked as he did because he thought the proprietor was trying to poison him. Indeed he was poisoned in a sense, for the liquor causes him to lose sight of himself completely and of the others. From that moment on, of course, he is a doomed man. (pp. 150-51)

He does not cast now, as he had earlier, appealing glances in anyone's direction. The collective *other* must be reduced to size. He must stare everyone down. He no longer scans old Scully but turns "a wolfish glare upon him." The Swede's and Johnnie's glances "crossed like blades." . . . In a short while the Swede accuses Johnnie of cheating; the stranger holds his fist in the face of Johnnie, who "looked steadily over it into the blazing orbs of his accuser." Each man reflects the image he sees in the other: "The eyes of the two warriors ever sought each other in glances of challenge that were at once hot and steely." . . . Ironically we learn from the Easterner at the end of the story that Johnnie *was* cheating. But the Swede's accusation at the time receives no corroboration, and the repulsive intruder moves (or is pushed) one step closer to the gambler's knife.

Old Scully says his son Johnnie and the Swede must fight: at the time the proprietor's "eyes glowed." . . . He was warming to the occasion, no doubt thinking Johnnie would thrash the impudent stranger. Outside, the combatants "eyed each other in a calm that had the elements of lionine cruelty in it." . . . Now only the defeat, the submission of the opposing image will suffice; and of course the Swede is the victor. (p. 151)

The Swede is now irrepressible. He swaggers into the hotel, but "no one looked at him." . . . The men will not give him the satisfaction of being recognized. In an existential sense they refuse to create his image by not looking at him. But the Swede does not cooperate by remaining silent. He jeers at and mimicks their urging Johnnie on earlier, "Kill him! Kill him! . . ." The men sit staring at the stove "with glassy eyes." As the Swede leaves, he further controls them with "one derisive glance backward at the still group." . . .

The Swede meets his end at the point of the gambler's knife. In death his eyes are fixed upon the cash register legend, "This registers the amount of your purchase." . . . [The] legend, apt as it is, does *not* register in the lifeless eyes of the Swede. The revelation goes for naught. Sight fails once more, this time with shocking finality. (pp. 151-52)

> Hollis Cate, "Seeing and Not Seeing in 'The Blue Hotel'," in College Literature, *Vol. IX, No. 2, Spring, 1982, pp. 150-52.*

JOHN R. COOLEY (essay date 1982)

[*Cooley is an American author and essayist who has written about contemporary American literature, Harlem Renaissance writers, and the depiction of black characters in the works of white writers. In the following excerpt from his* Savages and Naturals, *Cooley discusses Crane's depiction of the character Henry in "The Monster," finding that while he succeeds as a well-defined character in the early sections of the story, he loses definition in the later sections because of distancing by the author.*]

Crane's portrait of the black coachman Henry Johnson [in **"The Monster"**] is a far cry from the blatantly racist portraits of writers such as Thomas Dixon and Charles Carroll. Crane brings to this work the complexity of theme, finely honed irony, and depths of human compassion associated with the best of his writing. In **"The Monster"** he attempts to distinguish between the savagery of civilized whites in their reaction to a disfigured black man and the very unsavage, unmonsterlike reality of his life.

At the time of its publication William Dean Howells gave the novella high praise, although many other critics have disfavored it. In a perceptive contemporary discussion of the novella, Donald Gibson has termed it "in certain respects . . . the most ambitious piece Crane ever attempted." It is, as Gibson and many others have commented, Crane's most critical portrait of society. Not only does the story reveal the pettiness, the ingrained fears, and prejudices of white America, it provides a dilemma through which to test the moral fiber of a man of principle. This man is Dr. Trescott, physician in the town of Whilomville, New York, and Stephen Crane's portrait of a "good man," a man even Christlike in character. The second hero of the novel is Henry Johnson, Dr. Trescott's black coachman, who saves the good doctor's son by carrying him through the burning inferno of the Trescott house. Charles Mayer expresses the heroic twinship of employer and employee in this way: Trescott's "moral act is the counterpoint of Henry's physical heroism." The thrust of most discussions of **"The Monster,"** however, has been to examine the interplay between Trescott and the Whilomville community and largely to overlook the hero and "villain" of the story, Henry Johnson. (pp. 38-9)

The issue here is how sensitively does this brilliant social realist portray the black servant who is the focal center of his novel? Is Crane able to establish and maintain a counter-distinction between public opinion of his character and the complex, anguished, private reality of this man? It is not enough to say that Crane attempted a difficult task in exploring race relations and moral values; the final test will be of Crane's own integrity to the character of Henry Johnson. One may turn to Ralph Ellison's *Invisible Man* or Richard Wright's *Native Son* for comparison. Ellison and Wright, it should be said, never lose sight of their protagonists while describing the reactions of white society to them.

In the opening pages of **"The Monster"** Crane attempts to provide a detailed and individual portrait of Henry Johnson. Henry and Dr. Trescott's son Jimmy are best of friends. Crane comments, "He grinned fraternally when he saw Jimmy coming. These two were pals. In regard to almost everything in life they seemed to have minds precisely alike." The insertion of "seems" saves the description from racist assumptions. The reader soon learns that Henry is more than a "pal"; he is able to console Jimmy when the boy is in trouble with his father, and even to mediate between the two. In the evenings, when Henry dresses up for town, Crane writes that he "was more like a priest arraying himself for some parade of the church." . . . Forced by society to an inferior position, he can at best imitate white society and pretend he is a gentleman. "There was no cakewalk hyperbole in it. He was simply a quiet, well-bred gentleman of position, wealth, and other achievements out for an evening's stroll." . . . Like "Nigger Jim" and Huck Finn, Henry and Jimmy are pals, but Henry is also seen here as an adult and an actor who shifts roles frequently to make the best of his situation as a black man in a town like Whilomville.

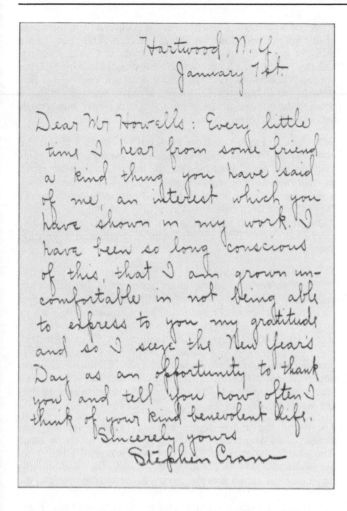

Holograph copy of a letter written by Crane to William Dean Howells on January 1, 1896.

The power of Crane's irony becomes apparent now. Henry's reception by the townsfolk stands in contrast to the portrait of him Crane has just drawn. One white man hails him with, "Hello, Henry! Going to walk for a cake tonight?" Further down the block another comments, "Why, you've got the cake right in your pocket, Henry!" Crane's intention in these comments is not certain until later in the story when his satire of the white townsfolk becomes unmistakable. The whites here are obviously not responding to the Henry Johnson whom Crane has just described but to their ingrained minstrel image of a black man "dressed up" for their entertainment rather than his own. Henry seems accustomed to this treatment; it is the way of Whilomville.

Even though Henry is among the first to reach the burning Trescott house, flames are already "roaring like a winter wind among the pines." He rushes up the flaming staircase, but by the time he has gotten little Jim, the staircase is engulfed in flames. After a moment of hesitation and panic, he recalls the back stairway that leads down and out through Dr. Trescott's laboratory. Once down the stairs, he pushes open the door to confront a garden of burning flowers. . . .

> There was an explosion at one side, and suddenly before him there reared a delicate, trembling sapphire shape like a fairy lady. With a

quiet smile she blocked his path and doomed him and Jimmy. Johnson shrieked, and then ducked in the manner of his race in fights. He aimed to pass under the left guard of the sapphire lady. But she was swifter than eagles, and her talons caught in him as he plunged past her. Bowing his head as if his neck had been struck, Johnson lurched forward, twisting this way and that way. He fell on his back. The still form in the blanket flung from his arms, rolled to the edge of the floor and beneath the window. . . .

(pp. 39-41)

The great horror of the scene comes from the realization that it represents a domestic jungle that Henry, like O'Neill's Emperor Jones, must cross in order to survive. The panther flame that leaps at him, the sapphire flame of the "fairy lady," the ruby-eyed, "scintillant and writhing serpent" . . . may be seen as various manifestations of racism and inhumanity harbored in the "good" people of Whilomville. The jeers and taunts hurled at "supremely good-natured" Henry earlier in the evening were prelude to this scene and are contained in it. The flaming jungle is neither Hell nor Africa, but a white physician's laboratory. The implied savagism refers not to the black man, Henry, but to the townsfolk in their reactions to Henry's disfigurement. Crane's intended effect here is quite the opposite of the jungle portraits presented by Vachel Lindsay and Eugene O'Neill. The "writhing serpent" represents the sin of racial injustice, or more generally, all acts that debase character and subvert honest relations.

At Trescott's insistence, Henry is brought forth, "a thing which he laid on the grass." From this point on, even Crane begins referring to Henry with increasing detachment. It is at first puzzling and disturbing that Henry is maimed in the laboratory of the man whom Crane admires most among the people of Whilomville. Crane chooses to test Trescott precisely because he sees admirable qualities in the man. Trescott is the only character in **"The Monster"** who might have wisdom, humanity, and strength of character sufficient to maintain integrity and understanding during the events that follow.

The "Morning Tribune," which had sent a boy up hourly to see if Henry had yet died, finally goes to press announcing his death. Now that it seems likely he will not live, people begin referring to him as "a saint." Crane implies through this sentiment not only that a society desires to kill its heroes so that it may properly praise them, but that to the white community there is something especially noble in the sacrificial death of a black man while saving a white child. It would be comforting for the whites to believe both that blacks were born to serve and that Henry and "his race" also recognized white superiority and were willing to sacrifice their lives to protect it.

In contrast to the town's hero worship, Crane gives a very different scene at Judge Hagenthorpe's house, where Henry had been taken after the fire. His head and body, frightfully burned, are covered in bandages; all that is visible is "an eye, which unwinkingly stared at the judge." Trescott sleeps and eats at the judge's house, keeping an almost continuous vigil, doing what he can to facilitate Henry's recovery. In his desire to do the medically "right" thing, to save a life, Trescott does not consider the possible mental and physical disfigurement that might attend Henry's survival.

The judge has considered these possibilities, and comments to Trescott: "'He will hereafter be a monster, a perfect monster'.'' . . . Later he adds, as his mind begins to work on the subject, '''He will be your creation, you understand. He is purely your creation. Nature has evidently given him up. He is dead. You are restoring him to life. You are making him, and he will be a monster and with no mind'.'' . . . Perhaps as the judge argues, Trescott errs in struggling to save Henry. It is clear from his reply he is working partially out of self-interest. '''He will be what you like, Judge,' cried Trescott, in a sudden polite fury, 'He will be anything, but, by God! he saved my boy'.'' . . . Not once does he consider the kind of life Henry could have or where he will live and who will care for him. Could the judge's comment that Trescott's act is one of the ''blunders of virtue'' be Crane's criticism of the doctor, despite his admiration for the man? As Hagenthorpe said, the Henry Johnson once known is dead and what emerges from the ashes depends on one's perspective. To the judge he is a blunder of indiscriminate healing; to the doctor he is a savior; to the town he is a monster.

Crane's metaphor of facelessness is analogous to Ralph Ellison's metaphor of invisibility. The former Henry Johnson is no longer, and in his stead society places its desired substitutes. ''He now had no face. His face had simply been burned away,'' and in its place whites and blacks substitute the masks they desire. Yet his physical facelessness also brings into focus that virtual facelessness he quietly tolerated in the white community before the fire. In the passing scenes, as this process occurs, Crane juxtaposes the innocence of Henry with the monstrous inhumanity of Whilomville.

Not only is the doctor's practice dwindling as a result of gossip about Henry, but insults and threats are hurled at the family. One of his neighbors moves away in protest. Next, Trescott is visited by a self-appointed committee of four of the town's ''very active and influential citizens.'' They have come, they say, out of friendship and concern, lest he ''ruin himself'' over this ''silly'' matter. Their message is, in essence: even if there are a lot of fools in Whilomville stirring up this mess, it is senseless for you to ''ruin yourself by opposing them. You can't teach them anything, you know.'' . . . The members of the committee pose a considerable threat to Trescott's position, for they appear as the voices of reason and good sense. Instead, they are the voices of rationalization. Before their scrutiny all issues of moral judgment dissolve into matters of practicality and profitability. (pp. 42-4)

In Crane's world survival is difficult; survival with integrity is almost impossible. The condition of warfare is all-pervasive in his fiction. In fact, it is Crane's richest symbol for man's condition. As in *The Red Badge of Courage* and ''The Open Boat,'' Crane is interested here in studying man under stress. In all three works, as Sy Kahn has observed, ''forging and tempering an answerable courage and code is the repetitive situation.'' If Trescott is as strong as he seems, he and his family will manage with Henry under their care, despite the town.

What is most regrettable about ''The Monster,'' however, is Crane's shift in emphasis in the latter half, from Henry to Dr. Trescott. For all his care to avoid stereotyping Henry, Crane retreats further and further from him as the story progresses. By the end he is almost a forgotten character, totally absent from the last ten pages of the novella. From the time of the fire, neither Crane nor his readers get near Henry again. First an unblinking eye stares out from beneath bandages, then the reader hears reports of what he has done, what he looks like, as observed from windows, open doors, porches, from the

corner of a barn. As a result, Henry is removed from the center of our vision, and almost from our concern. The finely honed irony of contrast between the Henry whom Crane described and the Henry seen by the white townsfolk is lost in the latter half of ''The Monster.'' The reader does not know if his face is really as hideous as described, or what humanity remains beneath the ''faceless'' face. For the reader Henry Johnson has become an invisible man.

Why does Crane retreat from his focus on Henry and shift his attention to Trescott? Had he created a creature he could no longer work with? Had he created, in fact, a monster rather than the outward visage of a monster? Or is Crane, the supreme ironist, not only in control of his craft but intentionally testing the reader's identification and sympathy? Perhaps he intended ''The Monster'' to read us, to see whether his readers sided emotionally with Whilomville, even if intellectually with Dr. Trescott.

The Stallman biography of Crane documents the notion that '''The Monster' was an appeal for brotherhood between white and black.'' In a very limited sense the story achieves this end—the fidelity of Trescott to Henry *is* admirable—but at great expense in its development and handling of black character. Unfortunately, most commentary on ''The Monster'' has forgotten to look at Crane's other black portraits or to consider the novella's treatment of race. Stallman, at least, observed that ''Crane's social irony is that the white man's face is also disfigured—by white society's cruelty to the Negro.'' (pp. 45-6)

The literal fire and disfigurement are to stand for the real, though often disguised, injuries suffered particularly by black Americans. Yet after the fire Crane does not restore Henry for the reader. He does not distinguish between the symbolic disfigurement of Henry represented by the actual injuries and the Henry who must reside beneath the ''monster'' if one is to continue identifying with him. This is where Crane fails. There is nothing left of Henry for the reader to identify with; he is figuratively dead. Consequently one must shift identification and sympathy to Dr. Trescott.

Briefly consider Henry during his visit to the black community after his injury. Crane describes him here and through the remainder of the tale as ''the monster,'' ''it,'' ''the terror''; he has Henry raise a ''deprecatory claw'' while addressing the Farragut women. Although they see him as the monster they have been warned about, Crane presents Henry's speech in minstrel fashion. Henry Johnson makes a succession of low and sweeping bows, scraping his feet and mumbling. . . . Instead of suffering from shock, one sees that Henry has been reduced by Crane to the comic Sambo stereotype. Yet to the other blacks of ''Watermelon Alley'' he has been transformed into a monster. In their desperation to get away from Henry the black residents shriek and screech; one of them even breaks her leg attempting to scale a fence. Regrettably, Crane chose to use familiar stereotypes rather than attempt the much more difficult task of detailing Henry's mental and physical injury while maintaining his humanity and individuality.

Crane's description of Alek Williams, the black man who tended Henry for a time, is even more derisive. Alek is obviously Crane's attempt at a comic black portrait. He is described as obsessively superstitious, inexcusably lazy, and continually amusing. He asks for more money from Judge Hagenthorpe because his frightened children cannot eat. They imagine Henry to be the devil. Alek stands before the judge, ''scratching his wool, and beating his knee with his hat.'' While arguing for a raise, he ''began swinging his head from side to side in the strange racial mannerism.'' . . . The portrait, with its comic touches and its racial generalizations, is unnecessary for the story's development and is inexcusable.

The only other glimpse of the much-altered Henry Johnson occurs in chapter twenty, where Jimmie Trescott leads his companions to the edge of the Trescott barn so they can gape at Johnson. Crane writes that Jim slowly ''sidled into closer relations with *it*,'' referring to Henry, but fails to show even a hint of the old friendship. On a dare, Jim runs up and touches Henry. ''*The monster* was crooning a weird line of negro melody that was scarcely more than a thread of sound, and *it* paid no heed to the boy'' (my italics . . .). This is the reader's last glimpse of Henry Johnson. It is as if in his mental derangement he were slipping back in time, becoming more thoroughly a primitive figure. He croons softly and submits to his condition. Crane made this same point while describing the fire. ''He was submitting, submitting because of his fathers, bending his mind in a most perfect slavery to this conflagration.'' . . . During the fire Henry chose to act and resisted the flames while he could. But now Crane has rendered him incapable of either understanding his plight or of resisting it. Whatever is to be done for Henry must either be done by the Trescotts of Crane's world or it will be done by the fools of Whilomville. (pp. 46-8)

The regrettable, though inescapable conclusion is that Crane's ''monster'' got away from him. He could no longer work with Henry, except at considerable distance, because he had lost the critical distinction he started with—between the monster mask and the man beneath the mask. By the end of the novella there is only mask; somewhere along the way the man had ceased to be. Even though Crane fails to sustain the portrait of Henry, his novella remains a very significant failure. Crane is most skillful, after all, in exposing the potential savagism of Whilomville toward blacks and all scapegoats, and it appears that he intended a fully developed and sustained portrait of Henry. Yet one must judge what is, not what might have been. Crane's portrait of Henry Johnson reflects an artistic maladroitness in handling a character who demanded utmost care, and in a piece of fiction otherwise finely wrought. Further, it reflects a sadly limited racial consciousness, despite all good intentions, in one of America's most astute and compassionate social realists. (p. 49)

John R. Cooley, ''The Savages,'' in his Savages and Naturals: Black Portraits by White Writers in Modern American Literature, *University of Delaware Press, 1982, pp. 37-88.**

ROBERT SHULMAN   (essay date 1983)

[In the following excerpt, Shulman discusses the merits of a recent edition of The Red Badge of Courage *that includes material altered or discarded before the initial publication of the work.]*

Thanks to Henry Binder and Norton, for the first time we can read, think about, and teach *The Red Badge of Courage* in the manuscript version Crane probably wanted published. Binder makes a strong case that Ripley Hitchcock of Appleton insisted on cutting the manuscript and that Crane, to get it into print, went along. The major deletions are in the endings of chapters seven, ten, and fifteen (fourteen in all previously published editions), the elimination of the original chapter twelve, and significant excisions in the original chapter sixteen and the final chapter. These cuts all involve Henry Fleming's inner thoughts—his attacks on nature and his equally unbalanced recantations, his oscillating views about his own superlative goodness and significance in the eyes of God and nature and the pointed undercutting of this unearned optimism and egotism. The cuts, Binder argues, are Hitchcock's attempts to tone down elements that would be offensive to late-nineteenth-century genteel taste. (p. 149)

In the previously excised material Binder includes, Henry Fleming's egotism and intellectual pretensions expand to their farthest limits. For a time he believes he is a new messiah singled out to bring an unworthy world his redemptive philosophy of the doomed. As he rationalizes his flight from battle he sees himself as a martyr and rages against the majority, the unbelievers who will never accept his gospel. His thoughts and moods swing wildly, from self-exaltation to self-contempt. This drama of self-esteem is rooted in what Philip Greven has characterized as the evangelical mode of the Protestant temperament. This influential American character type similarly swings from self-hatred and hatred of others to the sense of absolute power that comes from identification with the will of God. In Binder's text of *The Red Badge,* Henry Fleming as a representative American Everyman is never more American than in his belief that he is either uniquely elected or uniquely insignificant. For the first time, moreover, we can enjoy the spectacle of Henry Fleming as a critic of poets whose ''songs of black landscapes were of no importance to him since his new eyes said that his landscape was not black. People who called landscapes black were idiots.'' . . . This passage at the end of chapter sixteen . . . develops one of the basic patterns in *The Red Badge,* the exposure of the connection between Fleming's state of mind and his perception of the natural world. It bears revealingly on the status of the lush landscape of eternal peace Henry Fleming has in mind at the end, a passage many critics have seen as ironically overwritten, an interpretation the previously cut material confirms.

In Binder's welcome version Henry Fleming's oscillating lack of balance and his unresolved drama of self-esteem continue throughout the novel and emerge with an added intellectual dimension. The controversy about the ending will not be resolved by Binder's edition, although it gives strong support to an ironic view of a self-centered youth who in the final chapter feels death is for others and that peace is eternal. Because the physical and documentary evidence is inconclusive, like any text of *The Red Badge* the Binder-Norton edition is based partly on conjecture, probabilities, and assumptions. As a result, it will not satisfy everybody. But it is an intelligently edited text that many will find more convincing than the Virginia edition and that all of us can now test and enjoy in our studies and classrooms. (p. 151)

Robert Shulman, in a review of ''The Red Badge of Courage: An Episode of the American Civil War,'' in American Literary Realism 1870-1910, *Vol. XVI, No. 1, Spring, 1983, pp. 149-51.*

LAURA HAPKE   (essay date 1983)

[In the following excerpt Hapke discusses the characterization of Nell in Maggie: A Girl of the Streets, *arguing for her importance as a counterpoint to the romantic, self-deprecating Maggie, and as one of the first prostitutes in nineteenth-century American literature to break with the stereotype of the manipulated woman forced to act against her will.]*

Although Stephen Crane's *Maggie: A Girl of the Streets* . . . contains two Girls Who Went Wrong, most critics discuss Maggie and ignore the more successful Nell. Yet Nell, the "woman of brilliance and audacity" who lures the seducer Pete from Maggie, is far from one of the "flattened anonyms" Bernard Weinstein finds peopling the novel [see excerpt dated 1980]. . . . [In] Crane's warring Bowery world she is a "Darwinian super-woman." She survives while Maggie cannot. Maggie, to be sure, is the protagonist, and Nell appears in only two (barroom) scenes, but these scenes expand and satirize the harlot's progress tale on which *Maggie* is based. As the alternate fallen woman, Nell is central to Crane's vision of the urban prostitute.

Maggie, a slum flower, falls because she is victimized by what Larzer Ziff terms a "landscape of hysteria," and by her own naivete and vulnerability. She takes refuge from the brutish disorder of her brawling family and sweatshop life in romantic delusions of a rescuing lover. When lover and family desert her because she has lost her virtue, she turns brokenly to prostitution.

Unlike Nell, Maggie cannot withstand either the ravages of remorse or the unsavory conditions of her trade. The solicitation scene, which was until a recent reissue excised from all but the privately printed 1893 edition, implies that Maggie will not long endure such loathsome customers:

> When almost to the river the girl saw a great figure. On going forward she perceived it to be a huge fat man in torn and greasy garments. . . . His small, bleared eyes. . . . swept eagerly over the girl's upturned face. . . .

With no choice other than this kind of man, Maggie soon falls prey to the prostitute's traditional fate, suicide.

Nell, a sexual politician of the highest order, is a notable contrast to the hapless Maggie. Not for Nell the repulsive street customer or gloomy river death. She is consummate in choosing her clients and playing them off against each other until she finds the highest bidder. Maggie interests customers, but Nell earns a good living from them, as her saloon conversation with Maggie's lover Pete, whom she is sizing up, indicates:

> "When did yeh git back? How did dat Buff'lo business turn out? . . ." [Pete asked.] "Well, he didn't have as many stamps as he tried to make out, so I shook him, that's all." . . .

Whereas in the solicitation scene Maggie reveals her poor self-image by a desperate acceptance of the fat, greasy man, Nell acts with confidence in all senses of the word. Although she is a schemer whose manner is patently phony—evidence of Crane's satiric attitude toward the professional adventuress—her "act" succeeds. She is immune to the dark fate that hounds the more human but less "talented" Maggie.

One source of Maggie's inability to sustain a life of prostitution is dependence on the opinions of others, even after they have condemned and cast her out. Like Jimmie's jilted girlfriend Hattie, Maggie beseeches her rejecting lover and hopes for support. In her despondency, traditionally believed to cause women to fall to prostitution, she no longer cares what happens to her. In this version of a prostitute's fall, Crane was faithful to literary convention and contemporary opinion. . . .

Nell provides an ironic perspective on this traditional view. No seducer breaks her heart and forces her to the streets. Unlike Maggie, she has no guilty ties to the community, no raging family to placate; whatever hardships she may have had in life the reader knows nothing of them. Where Maggie, once fallen, feels powerless to influence any man's low opinion of her, Nell brazenly manipulates. (p. 41)

Just as Pete controls Maggie, Nell commands a "mere" male. Armed with this escort, she sees the dance hall as a combat. She ostentatiously invites Pete and Maggie over to her table, and proceeds to "vamp" Pete. She unscrupulously discredits Maggie by sarcastically referring to her inexperience. Ironically, Pete responds to Nell because she is so experienced and has such "audacity," while he scorns Maggie because he himself has "ruined" her. Crane thus implies that a woman who is going to lose her virtue on the Bowery had better be prepared to become as tough and calculating as Nell, whose audacity is merely the price of her survival.

Nell exits with Pete, leaving a bewildered Maggie at the mercy of Nell's disgruntled and drunken escort, who sees and treats Maggie like a woman for hire: "Nell gone. On'y you left. Not half bad, though." Although she rejects his proposition, by the very helplessness of her situation she is moving closer to the life of prostitution. The entire episode with Nell, indeed, is proleptic of her fate now that Pete has left her, and her family—to whom in panic she will briefly return—has cast her out again.

Nell victimizes Maggie and hastens her fall to prostitution. She also provides a picture of what Maggie herself will first experience as a well-paid prostitute. Crane links Maggie to Nell by suggesting how fascinated she was when Nell first entered the dance hall. When Maggie is in the first flush of success as a well-off woman of the evening, with "handsome cloak," "well-shod feet," and gaze "as if intent on reaching a distant home," she calls up earlier images of Nell's stylish dress and "clear-eyed gaze" through the stares of men. Of course Maggie's successful career will be much shorter than Nell's because, unlike Nell, she will never be able to snatch a customer from another woman or exit laughing scornfully after fleecing a drunken customer.

Nell's conduct with Pete is as traditional as Maggie's preseduction naivete about him. She is the typical "panel house" pickpocket warned against in red-light district guidebooks designed to acquaint the unwary with the perils of the metropolitan painted woman. . . . Like the seasoned adventuresses of anti-vice narrative, Nell stalks her prey with mercenary singlemindedness—"she knew the exact amount of [Pete's] . . . salary," Crane comments satirically.

Writers of Crane's time acknowledged the lure of this pavement *femme fatale* but unlike Crane always tempered their descriptions with a didactic prediction. . . . Crane applies [a] judgmental description to Maggie, who falls quickly. Nell, though slumming in concert halls, shows no other signs of encountering Maggie's fate.

Some precursors of Nell do appear in earlier nineteenth-century fiction, before the tightening of moral and literary codes such as those which prevented Crane from including references to solicitation. . . . Yet such mid-century portraits, if they doom the prostitute, also admit that she may have had a long and lucrative life. Later writers were more cautious and reverted to the "wages of sin is early death" formula. (p. 42)

Thus Nell, despite traditional associations with the temptress and some parallels in fiction of the period, shares nothing of the conventional fate meted out to the fallen woman. Self-sufficient, cruel, and ruthless, she is that rare figure in American literature, the thoroughly unrepentant prostitute. The voice of experience, she scorns innocence. . . . (pp. 42-3)

Nell's bloodless adaptability, "honest" given Crane's definition of the true streetwalker, increases sympathy if not admiration of Maggie. Had Maggie taken Nell's prostitute-as-worker attitude she would have survived. Furthermore, Nell's overblown sense of self and exaggerated pragmatism highlight Maggie's pathetically stunted self-image and absurd romanticism. Nell, who is thus paired and contrasted with Maggie, gives a richer dimension to the traditional story. A counterpoint to the seduced Maggie, Nell is the alternate fallen woman whose success provides a reality more unsettling to nineteenth-century audiences than that of Maggie's fall. (p. 43)

> Laura Hapke, "The Alternate Fallen Woman in 'Maggie: A Girl of the Streets'," in The Markham Review, *Vol. 12 (Spring, 1983), pp. 41-3.*

DONALD PIZER   (essay date 1983)

[*In the following excerpt, Pizer examines Crane's recurring variations on the phrase "What to do?" at pivotal points in* "The Monster" *as an echo of the Christian concern with charity addressed in Leo Tolstoy's essay* "What to Do?"]

Ellen Moers, in her *Two Dreisers,* has written fully and persuasively about the impact of Tolstoy's polemic *What to Do?* on American writers of the 1890s and in particular on the mature William Dean Howells and the youthful Theodore Dreiser. . . . In his work Tolstoy vividly recounts his discovery of urban poverty, the shame and guilt occasioned by this discovery, and his working through to the question which he feels each man must ask himself in the face of poverty in the midst of wealth. . . . Tolstoy's specific explanation of what we must do to relieve human need—that each man must lessen his dependence on the labor of others—had less impact in America than the query itself. (p. 127)

It is almost impossible that Stephen Crane would not have been aware of Tolstoy's tract. He deeply admired Howells, Tolstoy's leading American advocate; *The Red Badge of Courage* owes a good deal to *Sebastopol* and somewhat less to *War and Peace,* and Crane frequently commented positively on Tolstoy as a man, artist, and moralist.

Crane's **"The Monster,"** though often interpreted as a modern Christ story, has not been connected with *What to Do?* But in a key moment of the story Crane echoes the title of Tolstoy's work so clearly, repetitiously, and suggestively that it is difficult to resist the conclusion that he wished his readers to recognize the echo and to respond to its implications. The moment occurs in Chapter XI when the problem presented by the horribly disfigured and deranged Henry Johnson, who has been deformed in his successful effort to rescue young Jimmie Trescott from a fire, is discussed by Judge Hagenthorpe and Dr. Trescott. The Judge, who speaks for the superficially good-hearted but expedient morality of the town, notes that Henry will henceforth be a monster and that it would have been better to let him die. Trescott, who has worked ceaselessly to save Henry, responds:

> "And what am I to do?" said Trescott, his eyes suddenly lighting like an outburst from smouldering peat. "What am I to do? He gave himself for—for Jimmie. What am I to do for him?"

Trescott's question is of course the question which John the Baptist, Christ and Tolstoy demand that we must all ask ourselves. God's love has created us all creatures of God and when we see our fellows in need we must act in response to that need. The question is especially imperative when Christ's model of giving of one's self entirely in response to need is invoked, as it is frequently by Tolstoy and as it is by Crane in this story. Christ gave his all, and Henry Johnson gave his all. And Dr. Trescott, alive to the parallel, echoes both Luke and Tolstoy in his reaching toward the realization that he too must now sacrifice and give of himself. But Judge Hagenthorpe, despite his sympathy for Trescott's dilemma (and in a sense the human dilemma), is left volitionless by the enormity and—from his "rational" point of view—the insolubility of the dilemma. And so in a final and now ironic echoing of Tolstoy's tract, he closes the chapter with the statement, "It is hard for a man to know what to do." (pp. 128-29)

"The Monster" demonstrates the futility of the Christian model of sacrifice despite the powerful thrust of "And what am I to do?" Henry has to be removed from the town, Trescott and his wife are ostracized, and so Christ is in effect again killed. (p. 129)

> Donald Pizer, "Stephen Crane's 'The Monster' and Tolstoy's 'What to Do?': A Neglected Allusion," in Studies in Short Fiction, *Vol. 20, Nos. 2 & 3, Spring & Summer, 1983, pp. 127-29.*

ALICE HALL PETRY   (essay date 1983)

[*Petry is an American author and educator whose interest in American and English literature has been most concerned with local color or regionalist fiction and its combined evocation of universal and particular literary associations. In the following excerpt, Petry examines Crane's symbolic use of names in* "The Bride Comes to Yellow Sky" *and concludes that the names are both illustrative of individual character traits and of the influences affecting a changing American West.*]

Donald B. Gibson has argued that the name of the character "John Twelve" in *The Monster* evidently was designed to send the discerning reader to Chapter 12 of the Gospel according to St. John—a chapter which contains the story of Lazarus and thereby underscores the Christlike aspects of Dr. Trescott. But this sort of inquiry proves fruitful not only with unusual names such as "John Twelve": even Crane's tendency to employ "the commonest possible" names and, for that matter, his "compulsive namelessness," are more significant than one might assume. For example, a consideration of **"The Bride Comes to Yellow Sky"** shows that Crane chose names ideally suited to the revelation of his characters' personalities and situations, to the development of the story's theme, and to the setting of tone.

As the characters of his "hilariously funny parody of neoromantic lamentations over 'The Passing of the West,'" Crane provides us with an anonymous bride, a marshal named Jack Potter, and one Scratchy Wilson, the local hellraiser. In his depiction of the meeting of these three characters in a single anticlimatic scene, Crane is dramatizing the dying of the sentimentalized West with the encroachment of the lifestyle of the civilized East; and nothing better illustrates this rather abstract cultural and demographic concept than his refusal to give Jack Potter's new bride a name. As an individual she is insignificant. She matters only as a representative of the new Eastern order, and to underscore her symbolic status Crane depersonalizes her in the most obvious way: anonymity. Scratchy must be stopped dead in his tracks not by the individual—"The bride was not pretty, nor was she very young"—but by his recognition of the changes in the social order which she represents and, concomitantly, of the imminent death of an already-passing way of life which Scratchy represents.

Although the bride is given only a generic name, her husband is given a specific and seemingly common one, Jack Potter; but in fact Crane chose it for its uncommon capacity to express the marshal's personality and situation, as well as to help convey the theme and tone of the tale. The very blandness of his name stands in immediate contrast to what one would expect of a Texas marshal. By the 1890's, dead or retired were the marshals with such colorful names as Wyatt Earp, Wild Bill Hickok, and Bat Masterson, and with them had died the romantic notion of Boot Hill, the traditional final resting-place of desperadoes and macho marshals. In its place, Crane has subtly substituted a far less appealing entity: the surname "Potter" suggests a "Potter's Field," traditionally a graveyard for the homeless and friendless. As the ranking leader of the Yellow Sky community, Marshal Potter controls it virtually as his domain; indeed, Crane states explicitly that he was "a man known, liked, and feared in his corner, a prominent person." . . . Ultimately the entire town of Yellow Sky—a name indicative of sunsets and death—is one huge cemetery for the dying Westerners: it is, in fine, "Marshal Potter's 'field.'" That Potter functions less as a macho marshal than as the caretaker of a town rapidly turning into a graveyard is also conveyed by other connotations of his surname. Far from being routinely well-groomed à la Earp or Masterson, Potter is so embarrassed by his "new black clothes" (a rather funereal note) that "his brick-colored hands were constantly performing in a most conscious fashion." . . . The surname Potter denotes, of course, one who works with clay, and it is typical of the rich diction of Crane's best fiction that this "potter" has brick-colored hands and lives in an adobe house. His essential earthiness is far more suggestive of a grave-digger or farmer (in nineteenth-century slang, to "plant" someone is to bury him) than of a slick Western marshal. As a final meaning of his name, Jack Potter is a "Jackpot-er"—the "jackpot" being the bride; but in keeping with the ironic, debunking tone of the story, she is far less appealing than one might expect of the woman "won" by a Western marshal: with her "steel buttons abounding" and "plain, under-class countenance," she "had cooked, and . . . expected to cook, dutifully." . . . (pp. 45-6)

Just as complex as the name of Jack Potter is that of his "ancient antagonist," Scratchy Wilson. . . . His name . . . connotes the demonic, for "Old Scratch" is a traditional nickname for the devil. The "y" suffix of "Scratchy," however, nicely deflates Wilson's demonism, his capacity to do real harm—and his harmlessness is in keeping not only with the idea of a Saturnalia (which is ritualized behavior), but also with the systematic debunking of the West which the story achieves. After all, when sober Scratchy is "'all right—kind of simple—wouldn't hurt a fly—nicest fellow in town.'" . . . In fine, his status as the meanest hombre in Yellow Sky belies his actual personality: Scratchy is less brave than pot-valiant ("scratched," in fact, is slang for "tipsy"), and as such his reputation as a Western bad-man merely "scratches the surface" of Wilson. Furthermore, the word "scratchy" signifies both "irritating" and "irritable": the townspeople find his periodic rampages annoying (in the Weary Gentleman saloon, only the "drummer," an out-of-towner, is genuinely excited), and the drunk and frustrated Wilson yells at the sky, shoots at a piece of paper,

and roars "menacing information" to the unresponsive town. . . . As a poet, Crane was peculiarly sensitive to the dense web of connotative and denotative meanings which could be conveyed with a well-chosen word; and, as Berryman and Gibson have recognized, this sensitivity could also be brought to bear upon his choice of fictional names. (pp. 46-7)

Alice Hall Petry, "Crane's 'The Bride Comes to Yellow Sky'," in The Explicator, *Vol. 42, No. 1, Fall, 1983, pp. 45-7.*

JAMES DICKEY (essay date 1984)

[*Dickey is considered one of America's foremost contemporary poets. He is also the author of the bestselling novel* Deliverance *(1970). In the following excerpt, he discusses* Stephen Crane: Prose and Poetry, *finding Crane's style to be the natural, unaffected product of a many-sided personality and talent.*]

[It] is difficult to pin down exactly wherein Crane's uniqueness lies. It is not, despite **"The Open Boat,"** his overall comprehensive or dramatic power as a writer of fiction that gives him value, but his peculiar laconic turn of personality in the single insight or phrase, which can and does occur in anything he put down, from business letters to novels; that is to say, as a fragmentary but authentic poet. The spontaneity is quite real, not a device but a part of Crane's way of going, and gets into his words in a manner that is uncannily involving, though at first it seems to stem from the most extreme detachment. To Crane's unorthodox animism, battleships are thus:

> These great steel animals sat in a little bay,
> menacing with their terrible glances a village
> of three rows of houses and a dock and vast
> stretches of hillsides, whereon there was not
> even a tree to shoot at for fun. A group of
> vicious little torpedo boats also waited impa-
> tiently. To one who did not care to feel that
> there was something in this affair as much as
> a planet it would be a joke of a kind. But it
> was the concert of Europe. Colossi never smile.

Crane's offhandedness would be irritating if it were studied, for affectation dates rapidly, but once the reader surrenders to the odd-angled brilliance he is likely to want more, a lot more. Crane shoots from the hip, but he is deadly accurate. His short, bitterly humorous phrases, tossed off as though in passing, are the kind of thing that somebody ought to be able to do; the effect is that an inspired remark made out of the side of the mouth or to one's self has come to rest on paper as a kind of mistake; that is to say, as a perception threatened by darkness and only by miracle preserved. (pp. 1, 9)

He must surely have understood that a shrugging negligent irony, natural to him, was his strong suit, his full-house, and as an inveterate gambler he knew it to be best that he depend on the luck of that particular draw, which makes the writing of masterpieces, in the accepted sense, unlikely if not impossible; *The Red Badge of Courage* is uneven indeed, and verges on the scrappy, but it is full of fiery revelations. The good side of things is that this gambler's daring also makes everything Crane wrote, even the veriest hack-work, of great interest; there is no telling when he will blindside you with stunning and illuminating force, as though there were nothing to it.

Despite Crane's insistence on the "truth," that he only wrote what he "saw," *The Red Badge of Courage* remains, along with Coleridge's "Rime of the Ancient Mariner," among the most striking examples of works of pure imagination. Its "seeing" is not literalism or naturalism, and it is amusing to note Howells' dismissal of *The Red Badge* as a book based on material which the author did not know at first-hand. The qualities we now esteem are those supplied not by Crane's eyes but by his invention, and it is pertinent here to remember Coleridge's belief that the symptoms of poetic power are most evidenced in depictions of events and actions which the author has not witnessed but summoned up from the depths of himself.

The poetry is not, in the main, as memorable as the prose, though since it is Crane it is still valuable. No one deals with its qualities better than John Berryman ... : "His poetry has the inimitable sincerity of a frightened savage anxious to learn what his dreams mean." And, "Crane's poetry is like a series of primitive anti-spells." This is maybe going it some, but Berryman is right in citing the enigmatic, heavily ironic, allegorical nature of those verses as essentially, "primitive" or not, a casting-out. The source from which they come is not defiance or supplication, but fear, and there is the suspicion that, though compulsively said, they don't work; they are incantatory spin-offs; the genius is incidental. (p. 9)

> *James Dickey, "The Casual Brilliance of Stephen Crane," in* Book World—The Washington Post, *August 19, 1984, pp. 1, 9.*

ADDITIONAL BIBLIOGRAPHY

Beaver, Harold. "Stephen Crane: The Hero as Victim." *Yearbook of English Studies* 12 (1982): 186-93.
> Discusses the changing depiction of the hero and the heroic in the works of Crane and his contemporaries.

Christophersen, Bill. "Stephen Crane's 'The Upturned Face' as Expressionist Fiction." *Arizona Quarterly* 38, No. 2 (Summer 1982): 147-61.
> Discussion of the short story "The Upturned Face" as a remote, complex piece which is difficult to place and analyze among Crane's other works. Christophersen regards the story as the epitome of the Expressionist strain in Crane's work.

Deamer, Robert Glen. "Remarks on the Western Stance of Stephen Crane." *Western American Literature* XV, No. 1 (Spring 1980): 123-41.
> Examines Crane's lifelong attraction to the American West and the importance of Western themes in his works.

Delbanco, Nicholas. *Group Portrait: Joseph Conrad, Stephen Crane, Ford Madox Ford, Henry James, and H. G. Wells.* New York: William Morrow and Co., 1982. 224 p.*
> Relationship of the writers to each other, and as collaborators and influences on each others' works. The chapter "Stephen Crane in England" characterizes Crane as a generous, financially irresponsible man with a weak constitution and a strong desire to live life fully.

Dietze, Rudolf. "Crane's *The Red Badge of Courage.*" *The Explicator* 42, No. 3 (Spring 1984): 36-8.
> Analyzes the critical interpretations of the crucial flight-from-the-battlefield scene in *The Red Badge of Courage*.

Morace, Robert A. "Games, Play, and Entertainments in Stephen Crane's 'The Monster'." *Studies in American Fiction* 9, No. 1 (Spring 1981): 65-81.
> Contends that in "The Monster" adults and children participate in games on both conscious and unconscious levels and in both frivolous and serious matters, perpetuating misconceptions about other characters as well as their own self-delusions.

Nettels, Elsa. "'Amy Foster' and Stephen Crane's 'The Monster'." *Conradiana* XV, No. 3 (1983): 181-90.*
> Comparison of Crane's "The Monster" to Joseph Conrad's "Amy Foster." While Nettels believes it likely that Conrad had read Crane's story before he composed "Amy Foster," she attributes the stories' similarities primarily to the two authors' similar interests, attitudes, and temperaments.

Petry, Alice Hall. "Stephen Crane's Elephant Man." *Journal of Modern Literature* 10, No. 2 (June 1983): 346-52.
> Traces the many possible sources for the character of Henry in "The Monster," drawing particular parallels between the fictional situation in Crane's story and that of "Elephant Man" John Merrick.

———. "Gin Lane in the Bowery: Crane's *Maggie* and William Hogarth." *American Literature* 56, No. 3 (October 1984): 417-26.
> Point-by-point comparison of the visual and literary imagery emphasized in William Hogarth's painting *Gin Lane* and Crane's *Maggie: A Girl of the Streets*.

Proudfit, Charles L. "Parataxic Distortion and Group Process in Stephen Crane's 'The Blue Hotel'." *University of Hartford* 15, No. 1 (1983): 47-53.
> Illustrates how "The Blue Hotel" dramatizes what psychiatrist Harry Stack Sullivan has termed "the parataxic mode" in interpersonal relationships.

Schirmer, Gregory A. "Becoming Interpreters: The Importance of Tone in Crane's 'The Open Boat'." *American Literary Realism: 1870-1910* XV, No. 2 (Autumn 1982): 221-31.
> Examines the narrator's changing voice throughout "The Open Boat" as a reflection of the tension and interplay between the view of man as helpless and insignificant in an indifferent universe, and that of men bound together in the face of that indifference.

Starr, Al. "A 'Blue Hotel' for a 'Big Black Good Man'." *American Notes and Queries* XXI, Nos. 1 & 2 (September/October 1982): 19-21.*
> Notes similarities in plot, theme, and stylistic treatment of names in Crane's story and in Richard Wright's "Big Black Good Man."

Swann, Charles. "Stephen Crane and a Problem of Interpretation." *Literature and History* 7, No. 1 (Spring 1981): 91-123.
> Examines some of the most persistent critical controversies over Crane's work, including the question of Henry Fleming's maturity and the degree of realism in *Maggie: A Girl of the Streets*.

Stig (Halvard) Dagerman

1923-1954

(Born Stig Halvard Andersson; also wrote under pseudonym Qroll) Swedish novelist, dramatist, short story writer, essayist, critic, journalist, and poet.

Dagerman's fiction and dramas made him one of his country's most highly regarded authors during the decade immediately following World War II. He has been praised for the effectiveness with which he expressed a modern angst-ridden temperament and for the conscientiousness which led him to withhold facile solutions to the struggles of human existence. Advocating a literature that worked for social improvement, Dagerman came to be considered a model of the socially committed writer in postwar Sweden.

The illegitimate son of a quarry worker and a telephone operator, Dagerman seldom saw his father and never met his mother until he reached adulthood. Instead, he was cared for by his paternal grandparents on their small farm some fifty miles northwest of Stockholm. At that time in Sweden's history, large numbers of the unemployed in urban areas were forced to search for work in the country. Consequently, Dagerman witnessed at an early age the hard life faced by many working-class people in his country, and in later years he advocated a socialist form of government. In 1929 Dagerman went to live with his father, who had married and settled in Stockholm. He received his education in Stockholm and was there exposed to the political philosophy of anarcho-syndicalism, a type of socialism that denounced central, authoritarian control and promoted the freedom of the common worker. Dagerman joined this burgeoning movement, contributing articles to the syndicalist newspaper *Arbetaren* and later editing the organization's youth journal, *Storm*. However, as he noted later in an autobiographical sketch, his literary career was precipitated not by his political activities, but rather by the profound impact that two sudden deaths had upon him. The first, that of his grandfather in 1940, led him to write his first poem; the second, that of a friend who in 1942 was buried in an avalanche while skiing, caused Dagerman to seriously question the meaning of life and to commit himself to writing of its perils, both actual and imminent. Following brief, sporadic study at Stockholm University, Dagerman was drafted by the army in 1943. His encounter with military life provided the background for *Ormen*, a work that has as its central concern the problem of terror and how to confront it, a theme which reappears in virtually all of Dagerman's works. At this time Dagerman also began composing the first of over one thousand occasional verses, primarily on political topics, that he wrote for *Arbetaren*.

Rising rapidly in Stockholm's literary circles after the publication of *Ormen*, Dagerman became coeditor in 1946 of *40-tal*, a liberal journal that became a forum for the younger generation of Swedish writers. His next two years were characterized by an enormous amount of creative activity, highlighted by his first major success, *Den dödsdömde*, a Kafkaesque drama about a man condemned to death for a murder he did not commit. Now moderately wealthy and publicly hailed as a writer of genius for his accomplished treatment of relevant social themes and uniquely expressive prose, Dagerman was besieged by the media for interviews and received countless requests from editors for more examples of his work. The appearance of his travel volume on Germany, *Tysk höst*, and the novel *Bränt barn (Burnt Child)*, further advanced Dagerman's reputation. But an unhappy marriage and deteriorating psychological health led to a breakdown in 1950. The following year he began living with the famous Swedish actress Anita Björk, whom he eventually married. Although Björk greatly aided his recuperation and afforded him a much happier personal life, Dagerman suffered difficulties with his literary projects, planning many but completing only a few, while simultaneously incurring large debts to publishers and friends. One article written during this difficult period, "Vårt behov av tröst ar omättligt" (which may be translated as "Our Need of Consolation is Boundless"), contains a thinly-disguised wish for self-destruction and expresses Dagerman's conviction that he had somehow failed to realize his potential as a writer and therefore greatly disappointed his country. After several failed attempts at suicide, he finally succeeded in asphyxiating himself in 1954.

Dagerman's first novel, *Ormen*, is typical of all of his later works in that it is concerned with the presence of angst, or acute dread of social, emotional, and moral collapse, in the postwar Swedish consciousness. The novel has occasionally been regarded as a series of short stories rather than a thematically unified work, for its focus shifts from one character to another; however, *Ormen* is generally considered a highly successful novel in which Dagerman—intimately identified as he was with the dark mood of the times—analyzed the Swedish political and social milieu. In this and successive novels and dramas Dagerman communicated his belief that current society was often hypocritical, uncaring, and frequently absurd. Yet he emphasized the necessity of maintaining one's moral integrity and forcibly confronting one's forebodings of widespread disintegration. Critics have questioned Dagerman's faith in the viability of this approach, given his chief protagonist's premature death near the end of the novel; however, this conclusion has been explained not in terms of a complete pessimism, but in accordance with Dagerman's belief that complete security or safety can never be guaranteed in life, no matter how meritorious one's actions might be. In his most overtly pessimistic work, *De dömdas ö*, the mood of angst is given full expression as seven shipwrecked people recall their troubled pasts and then face, in differing ways, the inevitability of their deaths on a desolate island. Imbued with recurrent animal imagery suggesting the precariousness of human existence, *De dömdas ö* is recognized as one of Dagerman's most forceful and symbolically complex works, and one in which anarcho-syndicalist theory is presented as a means toward ordering a desperately chaotic world. Stylistically and structurally, Dagerman's most unified novel is *Burnt Child*. In this work he minimized complex imagery and socialist theory and presented a semiautobiographical story of a boy growing up amidst a troubled home environment. As in his other works, however, a strong existentialist message is primary, demonstrated by the novel's conclusion: "But moments of peace are short. All other moments are much longer. Knowing this is also wisdom. But since they are so short we must live in those moments as if it were only then we were alive.'' Dagerman's stories in *Nattens lekar (The Games of Night)*, many of which recount his early years in the country, are as highly regarded as his novels for their poignant studies of loneliness, frustration, and despair, and have been compared with the films of Ingmar Bergman for their fusion of the real and surreal.

Less acclaimed are Dagerman's dramas and poetry. Contending that an excessive emphasis was being placed on dramatic effects by his contemporaries, Dagerman developed dramas in which dialogue and ideas took precedence over other features. The majority of his plays, however, though concerned with the same trenchant themes as his novels, suffered from a sluggish pace and a tendency to portray one-dimensional characters. His poems, primarily political in import, are considered well-polished but ephemeral exercises which lack the stunning, vivid language which critics have found in his novels and stories.

Today Dagerman's works remain highly respected, concerned as they are with the contemporary issue of the human struggle to survive—economically, emotionally, and spiritually—under unjust social systems and in a war-torn environment—under Thompson has recently written that ''Dagerman's works have a relevance which suggests they are worthy of much wider recognition. The time is ripe to acclaim Stig Dagerman as one of Sweden's most important twentieth-century novelists.''

PRINCIPAL WORKS

Ormen (novel) 1945
De dömdas ö (novel) 1946
Den dödsdömde (drama) 1947; published in *Dramer om döda*, 1948
　[*The Condemned* published in *Scandinavian Plays of the Twentieth Century*, third series, 1951]
Nattens lekar (short stories) 1947
　[*The Games of Night*, 1959]
Tysk höst (travel essay) 1947
Bränt barn (novel) 1948
　[*A Burnt Child*, 1950]
Skuggan av Mart (drama) 1948; published in *Dramer om döda*, 1948
Streber (drama) 1948; published in *Judasdramer*, 1949
Bröllopsbesvär (novel) 1949
Ingen går fri (drama) 1949; published in *Judasdramer*, 1949
Den yttersta dagen (radio drama) 1952
Dagsedlar (poetry) 1954
Vårt behov av tröst (poetry) 1955

S. A. BERGMANN (essay date 1957)

[*In the following excerpt Bergmann discusses the novels* Ormen *and* De dömdas ö, *contending that a close study of the latter work is essential to a complete appreciation of Dagerman as a skilled analyst of individuals under duress.*]

Dagerman was no doubt a fine intelligence, though not at all academically inclined. He had a swift and observant eye. This general receptivity made him also stylistically very alert, and his literary ancestry is a conglomeration of elements which were at the time something new for Swedish literature. Apart

from the natural influences, such as Strindberg, Lagerkvist and Eyvind Johnson, there are strong elements of Kafka, of Faulkner, and also of Hemingway. Later, when Sartre became known, Dagerman could indeed turn to him for confirmation of certain trends; for he can even be said to have anticipated the Frenchman in his first novel. The fact that Dagerman seemed to be able to acquire certain stylistic features almost effortlessly led some critics to question his originality and to regard as suspect his very effortlessness. There is, however, a quality in his language which could never have been taught or imitated. Fresh metaphors and images spring up on every page; they are the fruits of a unique imagination. Another criterion is the constant tendency to symbolisation, brought out at times in almost surrealist patterning, in magnified and distorted projections, and in heightening of colour and tension generally. Only constant poetical preparation and original mind can account for the violent creative outbursts that led up to nearly all his major works. (p. 19)

The novel *Ormen (The Snake)* is remarkably free from tentative fumbling, the redundant matter and the over-explicitness of the typical first work. Based largely on the author's experiences in the military training-camp, and presenting in an expert version the modern young people of the capital, it stands halfway between the psychological study and the symbolic fantasy. The glowing language is teeming with images; the emotions contained in it largely violent or aggressive and swinging readily between extremes. Thus, the scorching summer heat seems, in Faulkner's way, to be full of darkness, and against the heat of the day and the emotions there stands the cold fear radiating from the snake, a living symbol of dread. This snake also serves ingeniously to connect the two parts into which the book irrevocably falls. The first section, Irene, is a display of passions, predominantly sexual; it is charged with dramatic events and swift reactions, touched off as it were half-consciously, such as the girl Irene's murder of her mother and another attempted murder. The boy, Bill, catches a viper and keeps it in his knapsack. When in the climax Bill shows the snake to the orgiastic company, terror triumphs and reveals itself as a major force in life. In the second, deliberately analytical part, a snake has hidden in a barrack-room and its inhabitants are united in the common fear of the faint reptilian tang which penetrates to the bottom of their awareness. The snake again symbolises fear, which cannot be excluded, since it is one of the pillars of existence. To keep vigilant, the servicemen tell stories all night, somewhat in the fashion of the Decamerone, and remarkably well told they are. The overall impression of this section, We cannot sleep, is in some degree strained. It makes an ambitious attempt to round up significant representatives of society and pin-point their relation to the common theme of fear. Here, as the author approaches society at large, one cannot help feeling a lopsidedness and limitation of his vision, or rather, the setting is only half-fictional and not fully integrated. Thus the book ends with an *avant-garde* discussion between fictional type-characters taking the form of an explicit doctrine which, in its remarkable pre-echoes of contemporary, but still unknown, French Existentialism, necessarily leaves the fiction behind. (pp. 19-20)

Whereas the normal reaction would be to remove or to avoid the cause of fear, all Dagerman's characters who have the virtue of intellectual honesty accept their *ångest* (a state which partakes both of dread and anguish, like the German *Angst*). *Ångest* is not only terror of death; more important is the dread of life itself. There is in this doctrine a note of nihilistic optimism, but it is characteristic only of the young militant intellectual, whose special antagonists were "the hard-boiled mystics" who "out of cowardice are set on reducing all problems to the realm of intestines and glands". There *is* no emergency exit; the only remedy is to keep one's eyes wide open in the darkness. If Dagerman had a literary programme it was this: the writer must take the lead in "a new period of intellectualism which can give at least someone the courage to face his fear instead of creeping away into the caves and bedrooms of mysticism".

This was a pledge, and in his next novel, *De dömdas ö (Island of Doom)*. Dagerman set himself the task of keeping his eyes open to the very end. It is what many people would call an inhuman book; from another point of view a suicidal work: there is no relief in it, no hope, only the faint pulse of pity, and in the end nothing but a void. It does not contain one "normal" person; its emotions are stretched to breaking-point; yet its visions shed light on the dark regions of the soul into which we never penetrate willingly. But Dagerman, increasingly aware of his incurable malady, had to write it.

If, therefore, *De dömdas ö* on one level is a tale of destruction, a story of adventure gone all wrong, it is also a vast symbolic fantasy, an enactment of human failure and endurance, despair and self-realisation. Kafka and the French Existentialist writers must have inspired Dagerman with architectonic daring, and for the richness and sombre beauty of the language he is indebted to Faulkner; but the conception is all his own, and so is the passion which informs it. This symbolism, however, is not wholly unquestionable; it is through the creation of the seven people, all, paradoxically, sympathetic or at least fascinating characters, that the book becomes remarkable by any standards. Washed ashore on a small Pacific island, which is inhabited only by a species of blind birds and aggressive lizards, the five men and two women meet their deaths, each in his or her logical way. The waterless island, set in the ocean, with the serene sky vaulting overhead, is the scene of their symbolic annihilation. The intense natural descriptions, especially those devoted to light and cosmic silence, have a cool, sublime beauty which through its absence of concern brings out the inhuman predicament.

Of the seven people, who are all excruciatingly alive till their last breath, each provides a variation on a common theme of guilt and isolation. Each of them represents a human failure of living, and together they make up the greater failure of a meaningful community. Their suffering burns out all dross; nothing is left but a shell round their essential nature. That they do not become lifeless, allegorical figures is due to the virtue of the organic presentation. They exist on many levels, in introspection, in observation, and in action; in the past and in the present; but chiefly in the fevered hallucinatory memories of their failure or treachery, and in their actual suffering and despair. There is nothing accidental in their shipwreck: their lives have been preparations for "the island", the fulfilment of their destinies. There is at last a complete congruence between their external situation and their agonised realisation of guilt and failure: on the verge of destruction a momentary balance is restored.

For a full appreciation of the book nothing, of course, short of reading it will do, but since there is not yet an English translation, I shall say a few words on each character in the hope of conveying at least a fraction of its range and power.

Lucas Egmont, the last of all to die, and, if anyone, the author's special mouthpiece, represents the irrational, impotent sense of social guilt. Though innocent—at that stage—he has felt guilty of the death of every consumptive child in his neighbourhood and of the life of the impoverished old people in his street. So much so indeed that he has had to invent and commit real crimes to ease the pain of self-incrimination (thoroughly whipped in by a sadistic father). He is the most capable of pity and yet he becomes the immediate destroyer of the other six: in a dreamlike frenzy he believes that the universal solution is thirst, and faithful to his thirst, he opens and drains the last fresh-water tank in the sand . . .

Jimmie Baaz, the boxer, is outwardly the champion, the public hero, the pride of his nation; but with every success (and towards the end they were all staged victories) he is only driven further into panic dread of life. He has become a martyr of modern publicity, and his paranoic fear alone has made him brave the enemy. His personality is by now a system of possible escapes, exits and voids. Rescued against his will, severely injured and paralysed in both legs, he can only dream of escaping, and a benevolent fate grants him an early death.

Tim Solider, the simple labourer, is a giant with a dwarfish self-confidence and a refined sensibility; the physically strong man without trust in his own body. Despite his name he stands for the false solidarity: he is no doubt kind-hearted, but he is only capable of cowardly subservience. Too hollow even to seek his own ends, he has constantly refused to commit himself, and is yet haunted by the memory of how he once failed his comrades and by implication became a strike-breaker. His is the sin of "the great refusal".

"Madame", the red-haired middle-aged woman, lives like the boxer in a state of complete introversion. Her whole being is given up to sorrow, all the stages of sorrow ending up in apathy when sorrow has dried up all soft emotion and covers her, as she thinks, with the skin of a lizard. The lizards of the island help her to understand her life. One evening she has killed a big lizard, which represents to her her son, whose death in the shipwreck she hastened, an imbecile child, born of adultery, and covered with hypnotising curses of her crippled husband. She has believed that the fruit of her frustrated dream of love was this child "with the soul of a lizard", but how differently she felt the killing of the real lizard: and she is lost in chaotic, guilt-stricken sorrow.

Boy Larus, the young airman, identifies himself with the Spartan boy with the biting fox under his shirt. He represents obedience, military obedience, total and undivided. Under his clothing he feels deep-seated wounds spreading: he can hardly endure the sight of them, and he has never told anybody. Yet these imagined wounds compensate for the mental wounds inflicted on him by a militarised age. However, the other military man amongst them, the captain, sees through the pretence, and can also tell that Larus is a deserter. Larus's final delusion is that of having freed his will by an act of disobedience when he ravished the English girl, who seemed to have gone out of her mind from the strain. How far removed Dagerman is from the sexual gospellers of the thirties, becomes evident in the study of their relationship: sexual love is incapable of breaking their isolation.

Draga, the English girl, has experienced attempted rape in adolescence, but long before she has become a narcissist, out of hate for her brusque military father and longing for her dead mother. She is consumed by virulent desire, but it is "a longing for nothing", a longing which does not seek satisfaction since it is fundamentally turned upon herself. Indeed, she is so blinded by lust that she does not stop short of necrophil tendencies:

there she lies whispering words of love to the dying boxer, and later to the corpse, as he is the only one who could not reciprocate her advances.

The Captain is the most fascinating character, but his variety of isolation is dangerous also in the sense that it respects life as little in others as in himself. He has had a hard and merciless childhood, and through humiliating experiences in adolescence, such as being seduced by a homosexual, he has over-readily developed a taste for contempt and abasement as a means to reach perverted pleasure in loneliness. For a time, however, he becomes again part of a community; makes a name for himself as a writer, even marries. Then he suffers a relapse. In a hallucination he sees the earth flattened out, and pressed to its glossy surface, he faces the boundless space in which there stands one immobile, hypnotic orb. And then: suddenly he hears "the whole space singing with desolation". He is alone in the universe, and the song, though terrifying, is beautiful beyond anything in life. This ecstasy of solitude makes him leave everything, cut off all relationships; and with brutal logic he embarks on a military career. Everywhere he seeks the renewal of his experience. He becomes an empty shell, a suit of armour, and in the eyes of the world the strong, lonely man. Here on this desolate island he plans the consummation of his life in an ecstatic death. For this he needs the deaths of his fellow-sufferers, and the struggle which follows provides the substance of the second part of the book, The Struggle for the Lion.

In their efforts to cover up the dead body of the boxer the survivors discover a well-defined white rock buried under the sand. They are now all in a state of great exhaustion, but mentally they are not yet incapable. In fact, as their bodies decline, the importance of the purely mental or symbolic looms larger. Regarding the white rock as a gift, they are agreed they must use it in some meaningful way—to commemorate their death on the island. The Captain suggests they carve a lion into the rock. Lucas is instinctively against it, for the Captain wants to carve a lion sitting on a dead man: he has a model for it in the trade mark on his topboot. This lion, which has just killed its last enemy, represents to the Captain "the singing loneliness". Lucas sees through his intentions and, compromising, declares himself ready to carve a lion—but without the man. This would signify to him, if not community, at least strength and harmony. (pp. 20-4)

Lucas Egmont, who is convinced of "the meaninglessness of the whole" but believes in "the unintended meaningfulness of the part", stands for what there is of positive energy in the book. Although he is criminal in the normal sense of the word, his awareness is the only one capable of breaking the guilt and isolation which was the doom the other six carried with them and which placed them beyond rescue. When, therefore, Lucas swims out into the lagoon to meet his death with open eyes, he does so in the conviction that the only possibility for himself and mankind is "faithfulness": "I shall be faithful to my direction and everything within it". Only by his heroically widened awareness and by acceptance of everything human, by a universal responsibility, and by abandoning exclusive faithfulness (exemplified by the seven deadly sins of isolation in the story), does Dagerman believe that the sickness of mankind can be remedied. This is *amor fati* in a universalized, modern version, the story of a deep despair and its possible rejection. (p. 24)

Dagerman once summed up his conception of the novel in a metaphor of bridge-building. There are three aspects which concerned him equally much: the communication problem (involving his isolation and the hoped-for consolation); the construction problem (the span, the daring of his imagination and the scope of his talent); finally, the problem of the view from the bridge (the *milieu*, the new waters which for the first time can be contemplated from above). That the communication aspect was more important in Dagerman's case than is usual we need not doubt. In all his novels we feel a message directed to us, as if he were seeking a comforting communion with his unknown readers. This can be done in a novel, though the risk may be high. When Dagerman turned to the drama, he must have realized that his concern for direct message could no longer be his motivation, that the drama made more rigorous demands on the objective independence of the illusion. But this realization must have been a painful one. There are traces of not fully overcome temptations, and one can feel that the medium imposed limitations on him which he could never adequately turn to profit. Dagerman was a born novelist, but a dramatist only by discipline. He had to learn the craft slowly and was beginning to find his feet, when for other reasons he could not go on. Intense, often impressive as his plays may be, I do not find them by a long way as interesting as his best novels. They are, in fact, a novelist's plays, static, filled with descriptions rather than actions, and seriously flawed, I think, by the lack of sympathetic characters. It is as though Dagerman's effects and people become too crude when they present themselves at first hand in the objectifying illusion of the theatre. (p. 27)

Of Dagerman's work *De dömdas ö* lays the strongest claims to greatness. In its grandiose, obsessive one-sidedness it bears the stamp of urgent necessity. For a purely literary evaluation its chief asset is the harmony of fictional setting and characters and the author's intentions. Beyond the reach of critical jargon lies the question of what Dagerman *knew* while writing this work. It is the heightened awareness and stoical endurance that make the book a truly remarkable achievement. But this takes us beyond the limit of art. Art, confessedly, can be a matter of life and death; but for a work to come wholly into the realm of art, it must side with life and result in a fuller realization of potential life. Only on this principle, it appears, can literary work reach indefinable and unlimited greatness. Dagerman's greatness is of a different order. While his neurosis sapped his vital and creative powers he strove tragically to universalize his private experience. Eventually he broke under the strain. And that is also why, in the last analysis, we are forced to reject his vision, whenever it threatens to become the exclusive truth, whenever his *ångest*, projected on to the outside world, is substituted for reality. It was his tragedy (and may be ours) that such fine gifts could be poisoned by his commitment to truth, and that the very cure of his obsession with death should appear to him like a fraud. (p. 31)

> *S. A. Bergmann, "Blinded by Darkness: A Study of the Novels and Plays of Stig Dagerman," in* Delta, *No. 11, Spring, 1957, pp. 16-31.*

IRVING HOWE (essay date 1961)

[*A longtime editor of the leftist magazine* Dissent *and a regular contributor to* The New Republic, *Howe is one of America's most highly respected literary critics and social historians. He has been a socialist since the 1930s, and his criticism is frequently informed by a liberal social viewpoint. Howe is widely praised for what F. R. Dulles has termed his "knowledgeable understanding, critical acumen and forthright candor." Howe has written: "My work has fallen into two fields: social history and literary criticism. I have tried to strike a balance between the social and the literary; to fructify one with the other; yet not to confuse one with the other. Though I believe in the social approach to literature, it seems to me peculiarly open to misuse; it requires particular delicacy and care." In the following discussion of* The Games of Night, *Howe praises the sensibility that lay behind the stories but concludes that Dagerman failed to fully confront his nihilistic conceptions.*]

Most of the stories in [*The Games of Night*] do not entirely come off, and a few are finger exercises that should not have been published at all, yet one feels that if he had lived, Dagerman would have been an important writer.

His best stories are set in that hard region north of Stockholm which forms a permanent place of the imagination to anyone brought up on the Scandinavian novels that were in fashion 25 years ago. Some of the stories are *genre* pieces of Swedish rural life as seen through the eyes of a lonely boy, and while Dagerman must finally be described as an urban and sophisticated writer, he retained the ability to recall the sensuous elements of his boyhood on a provincial farm, evoking a remembrance of the past that is pictorially strong and objective.

He did not, however, remain content with such limited purposes. In several of the stories one is struck by a sudden nervous tremor, a plunge into distraught reflection which the subject does not quite warrant but which is a sign of his straining to move beyond the material he had already subdued. That straining, I would guess, was toward a confrontation of nihilism, the glacial emptiness of soul behind the thickness of the farms and the men. Dagerman located this nihilism not among intellectuals or criminals, as is the fashion in modern writing, but among ordinary men and even children as they suffer a dizzying sense of the bottomlessness of experience, the terror of the meaningless as it strikes an unprepared imagination. In no single story does Dagerman fully realize this theme, or beginnings of a theme, yet in his sensibility, if not his subjects, he shared that absorption with the void which is a distinguishing mark of so many writers who began to publish after the Second World War. And this may explain the curious tone of his best passages, a mixture of blandness and ferocity, as if to register how the security of appearances can melt into the fright of nothing, and the familiar world of grandfather's farm into the questionings of the Stockholm intelligentsia. (p. 23)

Irving Howe, "Stories: New, Old, and Sometimes Good," in The New Republic, *Vol. 145, No. 20, November 13, 1961, pp. 18-19, 22-3.**

ALRIK GUSTAFSON (essay date 1961)

[*In the following excerpt Gustafson discusses Dagerman's dramatic works.*]

For a brief and brilliant period before his early death Stig Dagerman . . . was the wonderchild in contemporary Swedish literature. When he was but twenty-three his first novel, *Ormen* (*The Serpent*), became the sensation of the autumn book season, and in the immediately following years he wrote two more novels, *De dömdas ö* (*The Isle of the Damned* . . .) and *Bränt barn* (tr. *Burnt Child* . . .), a collection of short stories entitled *Nattens lekar* (tr. *The Games of Night* . . .), an incisive travel book on postwar Germany *Tysk höst* (*German Autumn* . . .), and a number of fascinating plays, most of which have been performed on the Swedish stage with considerable success. In its bulk and its over-all quality this production by such a young

author during a brief span of less than ten years is without a Swedish parallel and is the more astonishing because of the originality of its conception and the variety and range of its form. Dagerman is at his most impressive in the symbolistic and expressionistic forms employed in the two novels *The Serpent* and *The Isle of the Damned* and in the drama *Den dödsdömde* [(*The Condemned*)]. . . . But he has written a gripping psychological study in *Burnt Child* and a number of brilliant realistic short stories, and in *Streber* . . . he has tried his hand with limited success in a traditional problem drama. Whether Dagerman employs symbolistic or expressionistic or realistic forms, or some combination of these, he employs the form which he feels might best express his ideas, his central theme in the work in question. That which is recurrent in nearly all of his work is the terror theme, or, rather, the necessity of overcoming our terror by facing it, grappling with it, and conquering it. This theme is most central in *The Serpent*, but it figures more or less consciously in most of Dagerman's other work, frequently—as in *The Isle of the Damned* and *The Condemned*—in bizarre tragic variations, in situations where the element of terror is so overwhelming that a victory over it seems quite out of the question.

Among those of his generation who wrote in dramatic form Dagerman is on the whole the most notable, particularly in *The Condemned,* his first play. In this play he is dealing with a basic moral problem—the problem of the limitations of human justice. The events which at the beginning of the play provide the point of departure for a consideration of its central moral problem are ordinary enough: a husband has been condemned to death for the murder of his wife, though his wife's lover rather than he is the murderer. But then a queer twist of events occurs: the innocently condemned husband escapes the death penalty when the executioner becomes suddenly ill, and immediately thereafter the real murderer confesses and the hitherto presumed murderer is set free. In the tragic interplay in the drama between the condemned man and various representatives of society, the author is treating symbolically the essentially tragic nature of life itself. We are often condemned through imperfect instruments of so-called justice, Dagerman would say—not because of what we have done or what we are, but rather because of other people's notions of what we have done or what we are, notions frequently based on the thinnest kind of evidence and nurtured by human callousness and the primitive sadistic instincts of the mass eager for "the kill." . . . [Dagerman's recurring theme in this work is] the idea that we shall never overcome evil without facing it squarely, without drinking it to the very dregs.

And in the over-all structure of the play the theme is developed with an astonishing virtuosity and piling-up of dramatic effects: in the first act in a controlled pianissimo with certain restrained grotesque overtones; in the second with a complex obbligato, bizarre and cumulatively furioso; in the third act with a grim, starkly intense intermezzo formulation; and in the fourth with a haunting diminuendo in which the harsh patterns of the thematic development stalk quietly but inexorably toward the tragic denouement. The controlled pianissimo of the opening act introduces the theme of human callousness in the apathetic indifference of the prison doorkeeper, while a half-developed grotesque counterpoint is provided by the moronic newsmongering representatives of a maudlin, sensation-exploiting daily press. The complex obbligato of the second act, rising to a furioso at the end, is developed (with a Satanic fury reminiscent of the Strindberg of the "Chamber Plays") by means of probing grimly the weird motivations of a bizarre group of characters who call themselves The Rescued-Men's Club and who have arranged an evening's fantastic "Symposium" in honor of the recently freed condemned man. The stark intensity of the third-act intermezzo provides a kind of torture-chamber study in the condemned man's impotence, resulting from the terror of his four months' imprisonment. And the starkly haunting diminuendo of the fourth act reintroduces us to the restrained tone of the opening act, recapitulating the theme of the play with a mercilessly quiet note of tragic inevitability.

Despite the general critical acclaim accorded *The Condemned* on its first performance in Stockholm, some critics expressed their enthusiasm with reservations, suggesting particularly that its preoccupation with an ethical problem drove the psychological problem too far into the background, and that the symbolistic form of the play was so rigidly schematic that it tended to force the drama too far in the direction of the abstract and the near-esoteric. That Dagerman himself was aware of these dangers would seem to be clear from an examination of his subsequent plays, each of which in its way apparently seeks to reduce the dangers inherent in the type of symbolistic drama represented in *The Condemned.* Unfortunately, however, Dagerman did not in these later plays succeed in making an entirely satisfactory shift toward either the modern psychological play, which he attempted in *Skuggan av Mart (The Shadow of Mart* . . .) and *Ingen går fri (No One Is Free* . . .), or the realistic play with a carefully observed milieu, which he tried in *Streber (The Climber* . . .). The last of these plays despite its having captured with absolute fidelity the exact quality of everyday living among certain working-class groups, fails finally to impress us on the whole because of certain of its propagandistic excesses, its tendency to depict human character in terms of naïve contrasts, in white and black, good and evil. In developing its plot—the disintegration of an ideally conceived cooperative business venture on the part of a small group of workingmen, in which the vulgar "climber" egotism of one of the partners finally succeeds in destroying the venture—Dagerman satirically trains his Syndicalist sights too obviously on the renegade climber, who becomes reduced simply to the status of the villain in an old-fashioned melodrama with social reform purposes. In *The Shadow of Mart* and *No One Is Free,* on the other hand, where Dagerman joins psychological insights of considerable penetration with a dramatic form which maintains a nice balance between its realistic and symbolistic elements, he is more successful. The former of these plays is a study in the tragic frustrations of a young man who must drag on his existence in the shadow of a brother who had attained the legendary distinction of martyrdom as an under-ground fighter in a recent war, while in the latter play Dagerman adapts to the stage his novel *Burnt Child,* a complex modern study of a young man's brooding mother fixation.

It is not possible for us yet to disentangle the confused skein of circumstances which led to Dagerman's early death, but it is probable that literary frustrations, his momentary inability to quickly fulfill his youthful promise, had something to do with it. His very last years were creatively sterile in comparison with the few short years which had catapulted him to fame. It may be said that he ripened too rapidly, that his reading public came to expect too much of him, and that he could not meet his public's demands. Had circumstances permitted him to lie fallow for a few years before again taking up the pen he might finally have produced with the fullness and maturity which his early brilliance had promised. (pp. 544-48)

> *Alrik Gustafson, "Modernism Triumphant and Its Aftermath," in his* A History of Swedish Literature, *University of Minnesota Press, 1961, pp. 541-66.**

LAURIE THOMPSON   (essay date 1974)

[*In the following excerpt Thompson examines Dagerman's belief that the artist must be politically engaged and discusses how he resolved that belief with his vision of the absurdity of existence.*]

One of the first pieces of Swedish literature read in the original language by foreign students is often Stig Dagerman's **"Att döda ett barn".** The usual reaction is positive, and students are sufficiently inspired to seek out more Dagerman; the work chosen is generally the collection of *noveller* . . . , *Nattens lekar.* The level of difficulty, from a linguistic point of view, varies from reasonably easy to rather difficult, but most students find the effort involved worthwhile. Young people are generally fascinated by the discussions and depictions of *ångest* so typical of Dagerman, and the book has a mixture of humour, violence and sex, spiced with symbolism which can hardly fail to interest the young enthusiast besides giving food for thought and discussion.

It is rather unfortunate, therefore, that the final story in the book, **"Vår nattliga badort",** is difficult linguistically, containing a lot of vocabulary the near-beginner is unlikely to have come across, and difficult also as regards interpretation. The stories that have preceded **"Vår nattliga badort"** can be treated independently, but together they form a picture of a state of mind recognizable as the dilemma of the sensitive person in the post-war era—the familiar Dagerman theme, in fact. In the concluding *novell,* the author paints a picture of the society of his day, pointing to the social and political causes of the unrest and insecurity that have plagued his characters in the previous stories. **"Vår nattliga badort"** is obviously allegorical—too obviously so, perhaps, to make it completely satisfying as a work of art; but it is vital for an understanding of Dagerman's purpose in *Nattens lekar* to be clear about the irony and sarcasm that abound in the story. Only then can the pathos, the force of the concluding sentence be properly appreciated: "Hur smärtsamt vi längtar tillbaka till vår nattliga badort" ["How painful is the longing to return to our nocturnal resort"]. Moreover, to underestimate the importance of Dagerman's political views for an appreciation of his works as a whole would be gravely misleading.

There was no doubt in Dagerman's mind that the writer had to be engaged politically, and that he had to take the part of the humble and oppressed. . . . Dagerman's own views, passionately held, were those of anarcho-syndicalism. . . . Anarcho-syndicalism attempted to combine socialism with a belief in extreme individualism, a refusal to submit to organized authority purporting to have the right to organize the life of the individual for him, irrespective of whether it was claimed to be in the interests of the individual to allow himself to be "organized". For Dagerman, the alleged impossibility of his political beliefs was irrelevant. (pp. 117-18)

The poet must write about society and express his ideological views on it, however ineffective this may be. The resort in **"Vår nattliga badort",** then, is the world; and Dagerman clearly does not think very highly of it—not, that is, in its present state of decadence, corruption, injustice and hypocrisy. To an anarcho-syndicalist, the social and political system in Sweden was dirty: and filth is a characteristic of the resort. The dirt that the slovenly housewife allows to accumulate under the sofa, or brushes under the carpet, is paralleled in the *badort* by the unappetizing crust of egg-shells, tin cans, empty bottles, cartons, old newspapers and similar offal that clings to the water's edge. Society uses things for as long as they are exploitable, then casts off whatever is left of them and allows the remains to gather on the periphery, out of sight for the most part. . . . Society, it is suggested, is there to coddle its members and to lull them into a false sense of the pleasantness and prettiness of the life it orders for them. The cost, in terms of garbage of every kind (human garbage is to be discussed later), is something that should be forgotten about. To the analyst, waste matter is an invaluable source of information as to what is happening in a given process, just as a dustbin is a reliable guide to a family's living habits. What can be learnt from the garbage of the *badort*? Precious little of a positive nature. Tin cans tell tales of pitifully trite dinner conversations, newspapers betray shallow comment and silly, superficial attitudes to everything. . . . Moreover, the newspapers one finds lying around on the beach are from the day before yesterday: yesterday's events are still sufficiently current to be of relevance, those of years ago can be of historical interest; but things that happened the day before yesterday are of no conceivable interest or relevance to anyone or anything at all. The criticism of the kind of reports and articles carried by newspapers is devastating.

If one is disgusted by the resort, takes to a boat and tries to row away to sea, one is soon chased and "rescued" by the vigilant lifeboat. Similarly, modern society recovers its dropouts or objectors and, like some benevolent but firm parent, returns the erring child to the family, irrespective of the child's wishes. . . . The state claims to make life secure and enjoyable for its citizens, and hence is going to make quite sure that they enjoy the provisions it has made. In Dagerman's view, society, its principles, its standards are scandalously inadequate. . . . (pp. 118-20)

In section two of the story, the guide who takes holiday-makers up the lighthouse in order to reveal the squalor skulking behind the apparent beauty below is given the apparently incongruous name of Sisyphus. That the guide has a symbolic function is quite clear and if he had not been named, one might have been content to see him as the truth-seeker, the man who is not blinded by illusion but can see through the attractive veneer of society to the unpleasant reality beneath—not only that, but a man who then considers it his duty in life to point out this truth to others, to jerk his fellow-citizens out of their apathetic acceptance of a superficially acceptable and pleasurable society. In other words, the guide seems to be Dagerman's idea of the poet, and the parallel is so apt and so typical that the conclusion must be largely correct. The name "Sisyphus" adds an extra dimension, however; in Greek mythology Sisyphus, founder of Corinth and clever rogue, was eventually condemned by the gods to eternal punishment. He has to roll a large stone up to the top of a hill and down the other side, but never manages to do so, for as soon as he pushes the stone to the summit, the weight becomes too much for him and it bounces back to the bottom once more; Sisyphus retrieves the stone, and the process begins once again.

In 1942, Albert Camus published his essays on the Absurd, entitled "Le Myth de Sisyphe". In a preface to the English edition, written in 1955, Camus comments:

> The fundamental subject of "The Myth of Sisyphus" is this: it is legitimate and necessary to wonder whether life has a meaning; therefore it is legitimate to meet the problem of suicide face to face. The answer, underlying and appearing through the paradoxes which cover it, is this: even if one does not believe in God,

> suicide is not legitimate . . . this book declares that even within the limits of nihilism it is possible to find the means to proceed beyond nihilism.

The essays appeared in Swedish translation in 1947, although a translation of the central essay concerning the Sisyphus myth itself was published in *40-tal* in the autumn of 1946. Dagerman is clearly referring to this when he names his guide Sisyphus. The job of the poet is hopeless and never-ending, but it must be attempted even so, for if he does not attempt to reform the world, who will? We are reminded of Dagerman's assertion that in a world where all too many are politicians of the possible, he is satisfied to be a politician of the impossible. It may be absurd to be a pedlar of truth in a society where people are only too eager to ignore reality in the interests of comfort and convenience, but it is also an honourable and noble occupation—the only way in fact to make oneself a master of one's situation.

The negative side of Sisyphus's task is described in section two of **"Vår nattliga badort"** as the guide leads his "victims" up the *evighetstrappa* and reveals that the apparently beautiful resort below the lighthouse, compared to a pretty girl, is in fact more like a brashly made-up prostitute: the beauty is superficial, patched-up and misleading. The revelation is so shattering and a natural reaction is such extreme disgust that suicide, a desire to be rid of it all, must inevitably be considered. . . . In section three, Dagerman applies his thesis to society, showing the ugly reality under the apparently enjoyable amusements offered by his seaside resort. . . . It is a bitter piece of writing, passionately sarcastic as Dagerman pleads the case of the young boys manipulated by the feelingless, egocentric monsters masquerading as rich holiday-makers. The setting is exotic but hardly unusual: small boys dive into the water after coins thrown in from the cliff-top by amused guests. The parallel with labour exploited by capital is not difficult to see. . . . The boys are young and do not comprehend the humiliation of their position, the relentless lack of sympathy in their "employers"—in short, they live in a world of innocent illusions and do not understand the realities of their situation. Their mothers merely worry about their safety, while their fathers evidently do understand how the working class is oppressed but they prefer not to think too deeply about the society which has brought the situation about; they go beach-combing and gather what lost or cast-off treasures they can find to form their wages. . . . (pp. 120-22)

It is an absurd world, full of grotesque situations. Section four portrays a nightmarish parody of the Greek myth of Leda and the Swan: instead of a noble god in the guise of a graceful and powerful bird coupling with a beautiful goddess, we are confronted with fat, elderly ladies astride inflatable rubber toys. . . . Equally absurd, suggests the author, are the critics who lounge around on the beach condemning everything they discuss. (pp. 123-24)

When the reader reaches the fifth and final section of **"Vår nattliga badort"**, it may well occur to him that, despite the title, the resort has only been described by day. After all, the whole collection of stories is called *Nattens lekar,* and he will probably recall reading in the opening story (which gives the book its title) that: "Nattens lekar är mycket bättre än dagens" ["The games of night are better than those of the day"] . . . . At last, in section five, we see the resort by night. And although there may be no entirely satisfactory reply to the appeal of the opening sentence: "Finns det någon förlåtelse för oss?" ["Is there any forgiveness for us?''] we find that in Sisyphus's judgement:

> Den enda ursäkten, det enda som ger badorten
> lov att existera är just nätterna, de här underbara
> blåa nätterna. Är det inte vackert, säg? . . .
>
> [''The only excuse, the only thing that justifies
> the existence of the resort, is night-time, those
> wonderful, blue nights. Aren't they beautiful,
> eh?'']

Sisyphus condemns society and admires pure nature, when the noise and activity has subsided and the guests are asleep; this seems to be the world in its natural state, untainted by all the mistakes made by humans so far—the world of dreams and ideals.

In Camus' essay, he wrote of the time when Sisyphus walks back down the hillside to collect the stone which has, inevitably, rolled down to the bottom yet again:

> It is during that return, that pause, that Sisyphus
> interests me. A face that toils so close to stones
> is already stone itself! I see that man going back
> down with a heavy yet measured step towards
> the torment of which he will never know the
> end. That hour like a breathing space which
> returns as surely as his suffering, that is the
> hour of consciousness. At each of those mo-
> ments when he leaves the heights and gradually
> sinks down towards the lairs of the gods, he is
> superior to his fate. He is stronger than his rock.

This descent, as he contemplates his position, may be a time of sorrow, but it may also be a time of joy. . . . (pp. 124-25)

The night games, the dreams, the ideals, the relaxation after the trials and tribulations of a day lived in established society— this is the equivalent of Camus' Sisyphus descending the hill. It is no accident that Dagerman's Sisyphus, contemplating his peaceful resort from afar, sees it as ''en liten blå sten'' [''a little blue stone'']. . . . The earlier reaction to the misery and squalor of life led to thoughts of suicide; now such thoughts are replaced by a love of life, a determination to live in spite of everything. Dagerman's ideals can sustain him at this point in his life, for paradoxically they can help to make him more tolerant of the imperfections of society by their very existence. (p. 125)

The beach-combers are praised for their ability to derive plea-sure from life, to prize beauty as well as gain. They occa-sionally burn a beachful of rubbish merely for the pleasure of enjoying the ''firework display'', even though they know that in so doing they are destroying their means of support for a whole week. Their carefree attitude to money contrasts tellingly with the parsimony of the rich guests throwing small coins from the cliff-tops for the young divers, and the implication is that the ordinary working man has more idea of beauty, pleasure, even art than the capitalist who sees everything in terms of profit and loss.

''**Vår nattliga badort**'' is, then, a story with a paradoxical message. Many of the earlier stories in *Nattens lekar* have shown that life is a struggle, that despair is never far away and that *ångest* is constantly with us. ''**Vår nattliga badort**'' sug-gests that in addition to the psychological factors which create in man a timeless sensation of inadequacy, there are social factors too. Dagerman clearly believes that the capitalist system

is rotten, and that the task of the poet is to point this out untiringly. The author's anarcho-syndicalist standpoint does not make him any more amenable to the social-democratic solution of the welfare state and a secure *folkhem*. Irrespective of the practical possibility of ideals combining socialism with extreme individualism, Dagerman nevertheless finds the strength to continue the struggle, the will to live, in those ideals. The suicide which is always a possible solution to be considered in all Dagerman's books, and which eventually claimed the author's life in reality, is rejected in *Nattens lekar*.

The student will find, if he cares to look, that there is a co-herence about *Nattens lekar* that may be more orderly than first appears likely. He will have noticed, of course, the theme of *ångest* that runs through every *novell*, just as it dominated the author's life. He will have noticed, too, that the violence, frustration, fear, loneliness all stem from an inability to face up to facts, an inability to recognize truth and reality for what they are and to react accordingly instead of living in a state of permanent hypocrisy. It has been pointed out that the collection starts with a series of childish dreams which the reader rec-ognizes as an attempt by the boy Åke to flee from reality; and the final story in the book ends on a dream-like meditation of the realities of the world at night. As happened in *Ormen*, Dagerman has explored the psyche of his characters, and finally justifies his claim to be an *ångestanalytiker* by analysing the society which creates the *ångest* his characters feel.

The question hinted at earlier still remains: is the symbolism of ''**Vår nattliga badort**'' too obviously allegorical, too awk-wardly obtrusive to allow the story to be adjudged a complete artistic success? It probably is. But it does help to demonstrate the care with which Dagerman constructed his books, the im-portance he placed on creating a coherent argument. Some critics feel that Dagerman's style and approach were more suited to the short story genre than to the novel because of what is sometimes felt to be a slapdash, spontaneous way of writing that shows up as more obviously undisciplined in the longer genre. Whereas it may be true that Dagerman's novels are not always perfectly constructed, it is certainly true that more disciplined planning is present than is often realized. It is interesting that the awkward symbolism of ''**Vår nattliga badort**'' seems to be due at least in part to a desire by the author to mould even his collection of short stories into a coherently planned whole. (pp. 125-27)

> *Laurie Thompson, ''Stig Dagerman's 'Vår nattliga*
> *badort': An Interpretation,'' in* Scandinavica, *Vol.*
> *13, No. 2, November, 1974, pp. 117-27.*

LAURIE THOMPSON   (essay date 1983)

[*In the following excerpt, Thompson surveys Dagerman's career.*
Thompson considers Dagerman's novels his most successful works
and claims that the author deserves much wider recognition than
he has received.]

Since Dagerman's suicide it has become generally realized that many of his problems were psychological and can be traced back to his childhood; due to an unfortunate combination of circumstances they were made worse in later life, and he began to have difficulty in writing as early as 1948. (p. 14)

The snake symbol runs through all Dagerman's works, and the intensity of terror which it invoked for the author can be traced back to an incident when he was three years old and out for a walk in the woods with his uncle. The impressionable young boy was terror-stricken when he almost stepped upon a snake coiled on the path in front of him. This encounter triggered one of Dagerman's many phobias, and for him the very word "snake" was synonymous with fear for the rest of his life. (pp. 15-16)

It is a universally applicable symbol, but Dagerman's own snake phobia accounts for the intensity of terror with which any mention of a snake in his writings is always associated. (p. 16)

[The novel *Ormen* (*The Snake*)] has a motto, preceding the text, which relates the central symbol of existential *Angst* to the author's theoretical writings and his view of the role of the author: "If poetry is a drawing-room entertainment, I will go out into the twilight with darkened foot and make friends with the snakes and the little gray desert rat. If poetry is an essential element of life for someone, don't forget your sandals, watch out for piles of stones! Now the snakes are hunting after my heel, now I am disgusted by the desert rat." If this statement seems a little obscure at first sight, the novel makes it clear that Dagerman is maintaining that while one may not be able completely to overcome one's *Angst*, one should not attempt to ignore or suppress it: one is less vulnerable if one accepts its existence and is prepared for its manifestations. The words are ascribed to "My friend Scriver," who is a character in the novel and, like his creator, an army clerk who is also a writer. The status of Scriver as an alter ego of the author becomes more obvious when one realizes that the motto is in fact a quotation from Dagerman's article **"Diktaren och samvetet"** ["**The Poet and His Conscience**"], published in the summer issue of *40-tal,* 1945. In this article Dagerman argues that a modern writer must be politically committed and, writing with deep inner conviction, must point out tirelessly the ills of contemporary society. (pp. 16-17)

In *The Snake* Dagerman created a plot out of events and situations he had experienced personally, and used it to express his views on contemporary Swedish politics and culture. In keeping with the mood of the times, the novel is an expression of *Angst* and explores the existential dilemma of modern man, highlighting the necessity of making a morally right decision in an apparently meaningless, even absurd world.

The structure of *The Snake* is unconventional in that it falls into two distinct halves, each with a completely different set of characters. The first part, entitled "Irène," concerns a young woman of that name and her activities over an approximate twenty-four-hour period at some unspecified date in the early 1940s in Sweden. (pp. 17-18)

The second part of the novel is called "We Cannot Sleep" and concerns the thoughts and experiences of a group of army conscripts—two of them clerks, the rest General Duties men. They are all restless and afraid; although the cause of their anxiety is not made known until quite late in the book, it is eventually revealed that it is due to the presence of a snake which has escaped in their section of the barracks. The origins of the snake are never made unequivocally clear, but the assumption is that it is the same one that Bill captured in the first half of the novel. (p. 19)

The final chapter in *The Snake* is intriguing, not least because the snake was found dead in the previous chapter and life has returned to normal in the barracks. In "The Flight That Didn't Come Off" Scriver, Dagerman's alter ego, never actually returns to camp but instead dies a symbolic death while trying to prove a point. It is a chapter full of theoretical discussions,

this time mainly in the literary and cultural field although there are clear political implications. (p. 30)

"The Flight That Didn't Come Off" can be seen as a sort of epilogue to the whole novel in which all the themes are summarized. *The Snake* ends on a question mark, however: if the analysis of the contemporary situation was correct, why does the author's alter ego die, having failed to prove his point by means of the symbolic climb? To draw the apparently obvious conclusion that Scriver's analysis must have been wrong would be to negate at a stroke the argument developed over the book as a whole. The answer must presumably be that Scriver's death illustrates the point that awareness of one's *Angst* and its causes does not put the individual in a comfortable and secure position—that is the realm of the "philosophy of harmony," which is based on illusions. It is an ironical and pessimistic ending. (p. 32)

Thirty-five years [after its publication] *The Snake* still seems a remarkable first novel, less dated in its appeal than one might expect. It has its faults, of course. There is a tendency to repeat the same message too often and some of the theorizing sits rather awkwardly in context. The whole novel gives a somewhat episodic impression—apart from the division into two parts, the sections in the second part seem to be arranged in an arbitrary order; moreover, the fact that the snake is found dead in the penultimate chapter emphasizes the fact that the final chapter is linked with the rest of the book on a theoretical level but hardly at all in terms of a narrative link. This stresses the intellectual and analytical aspects of the work but adds fuel to the fire of those who feel that *The Snake* is a collection of stories rather than a novel. The unifying factors are surely sufficient to qualify it as a novel, but it was certainly a bold experiment for a young author in his first book. (pp. 32-3)

Stig Dagerman was busy with his second novel [*De dömdas ö* (*The Island of the Doomed*)] in the early part of 1946, and according to an interview given the following year it was intended—on one level, at least—as a political novel and an apologia for anarcho-syndicalism. Dagerman claimed that it was "a defense of individualism. It is also meant to be an attack on the tendency to use ideas as means of instilling terror, as political truncheons. Ideas should be used as toys—as Socrates did in his lectures!" True to his instinct for expressing key ideas in striking symbolism, Dagerman made the climactic section of his novel a struggle between a Fascist and an Anarcho-Syndicalist over the details of a picture featuring a lion to be scratched into a rock. . . . (p. 35)

The Island of the Doomed is a complicated novel of ideas in which situations and actions symbolize states of mind and possible solutions. The basic plot is comparatively simple but hardly begins to indicate the subtleties and richness of this novel. As was the case with parts of *The Snake,* it seems to be made up of an incredible series of disasters and instances of warped behavior; however, there is a surrealistic atmosphere in the novel which makes the exaggerations as acceptable as they would be in a dream. (p. 36)

The novel is divided into two parts: the first part, "The Castaways," which occupies some three-fifths of the total number of pages, takes each of the seven characters in turn and, in subtitled chapters, presents their past lives in a series of flashbacks. All of them bear heavy burdens of guilt and are trying to run away from reality—they are doomed long before the shipwreck takes place. The second part of the book is entitled "The Fight over the Lion" and is subdivided into seventeen numbered chapters. The reactions of the castaways to their plight are recorded, as are ways in which they meet their deaths. (p. 37)

The important characters in the novel from a political point of view are Captain Wilson, the harsh elitist and authoritarian; Lucas Egmont, the man who feels guilty about his supposed social superiority and craves to align himself with the underdog; Tim Solider, the worker with the slave mentality and inadequate feelings of solidarity; and Boy Larus, who seems to be the epitome of a man who has lost his individual freedom thanks to the authoritarian regime under which he has been living. The latter two tend to be the foils of the former, whose opposing political philosophies are represented in detail. (p. 50)

It will be recalled that in *The Snake,* Scriver explained that a writer always takes an extreme case to represent a concept he wishes to symbolize: Captain Wilson is clearly steeped in National Socialism and Fascist ideology, but Dagerman is using him to represent all political philosophies that depend on a centralized system of authority involving the exploitation of some individuals by others. Boy Larus's compulsive submission to the commands of those in authority over him certainly echoes the standard excuse of the SS members accused of war crimes after World War II, "We were only obeying orders"; the link with the Spartan boy surely extends the reference, however—Sparta was the authoritarian Greek state in contrast with democratic Athens—and there are suggestions of Nietzschean master-slave relationships. In *The Snake* and in his theoretical writings such as **"My Views on Anarchism"** Dagerman criticized authoritarian tendencies even in professedly democratic states. Any hint of central authority is anathema to an Anarcho-Syndicalist.

Lucas Egmont clearly has a social conscience. In his early life it manifests itself as irrational guilt feelings, but his awareness of its true character is made quite specific in his arguments with Captain Wilson about the lion symbol. Egmont is not so obviously an Anarcho-Syndicalist as were Scriver and Edmund in *The Snake,* but there are details which indicate that he believes in "free socialism" rather than conventional socialism, quite apart from knowledge of Dagerman's well-known sympathies. In his summary of the development of his social conscience in Chapter 14, Lucas Egmont attacks all political parties for their preoccupation with peripheral questions which results in perpetual postponement of effective measures to put right social injustice. (pp. 51-2)

Tim Solider is an example of the typical working man created by an authoritarian social system. He lacks dignity, he is treated with contempt, and he has an inferiority complex; although his wish is to contribute to the general good, he has little idea of how to do so, the odds are stacked against him and he is hampered by the streak of selfishness which is inevitable in a system which does not encourage the idea of brotherhood and genuine solidarity with the oppressed (even though it may pay lip-service to it).

A number of Swedish critics have questioned the depth of Stig Dagerman's commitment to anarcho-syndicalism, maintaining that it does not figure prominently enough in his creative works. It seems an unfair claim to make when one examines Dagerman's first two novels in detail. To be sure, the specifically Anarcho-Syndicalist nature of the socialism advocated in *The Island of the Doomed* is less obvious than in *The Snake.* On the other hand, one can hardly be very specific about the dogma of a political creed which intentionally avoids dogma. It is true

that the political content of Dagerman's later completed works dwindled, but the Anarcho-Syndicalist elements are strong in his first two novels. (p. 53)

If the novel is difficult to read it is because of the high degree of *Angst*-ridden tension and the density of imagery which forms a network of associations and cross-references which is far from easy to keep track of, especially at a first reading. It was this relentless consistency in the imagery and the complete intellectual control over the various complicated strands of *The Island of the Doomed* which particularly impressed Dagerman's biographer, Olof Lagercrantz, and led him to declare that of all Dagerman's works, this is the greatest and the one which will live longest. (p. 55)

Dagerman's widely praised book [*Tysk höst* (*German Autumn*)] was published in May 1947. After the fantastic "landscape of terror" he had conjured up in *The Island of the Doomed,* he had now become acquainted with a reality of devastation and ruin which was in many ways more horrific than anything his imagination could produce. He depicted the nightmarish landscape with more insight than any ordinary reporter and displayed sympathetic understanding for the state of the bombed-out Germans living in damp cellars and crumbling ruins. He was sarcastic about the ex-Nazis who continued to prosper, and highly critical of the allied approach which seemed indifferent to justice. (p. 56)

An inevitable result of the success of *German Autumn* was that pressure was put on Dagerman to use his more realistic style in his creative works. When his short-story collection, [*Nattens lekar* (*The Games of Night*)] appeared, some reviewers claimed that it was possible to detect which of the stories had been written before the German journey, and which ones afterwards, on the basis that the latter were more realistic in style. It is a fact that Dagerman did move toward a realistic style and *The Games of Night* contains a wide range of variations across the spectrum from realism to expressionism and surrealism—indeed, the author's mastery of such varied styles is one of the chief merits of the book. (p. 57)

The autobiographical stories of childhood at the beginning of the collection illustrate interesting variations in narrative perspective in spite of obvious similarities. In **"Sleet"** the story is told in the first-person form in the present tense by a nine-year-old boy: as a result, the reader is left to draw conclusions about the boy's family and the events of the story since the narrator sees everything through juvenile eyes and does not completely understand all that happens. In **"Salted Meat and Cucumber,"** although the central character is also a nine-year-old boy and the story is in the I-form, the narration is in the past tense and the narrator is clearly an older man looking back on his childhood. He can thus comment on events with the insight of an adult.

A further variation on the first-person narrative is **"Open the Door, Richard!"** which is an exercise in stream-of-consciousness techniques (and also notable because it is the only story in the collection narrated wholly by a woman). It is a skillfully narrated story which stands comparison with most of its type; but it pales into insignificance beside **"Where Is My Iceland Jumper?",** a prolonged and cleverly sustained inner monologue which is generally agreed to be one of Dagerman's most brilliant pieces of writing. The woman in the former story is confused and psychologically disturbed, yet she seems to think quite clearly and logically and expresses herself in rather sophisticated images which can only come from a narrator striving to do her thinking for her in language he imposes onto her speech. Knut in **"Where is My Iceland Jumper?"**, on the other hand, talks and thinks in a mixture of Stockholm slang and Uppland dialect, liberally sprinkled with exclamations and colorful curses. His train of thought is confused and the narrative staggers along beneath a burden of asides, accusations, protests, excuses, and self-deceptions. . . . Knut is a preposterous character, but his weaknesses are so transparent and he is so vividly and entertainingly alive that the reader cannot help but be drawn to him—thanks largely to the tour de force of stream-of-consciousness technique achieved by Dagerman in this story. (pp. 72-3)

[At this point in Dagerman's career the] public was hoping for a novel in the new realistic style they had discerned and appreciated in *German Autumn* and parts of *The Games of Night*. . . . (p. 76)

Of all Dagerman's novels [his next, *Bränt barn* (*A Burnt Child*)] is the most obviously controlled and tightly constructed. It develops in linear fashion over a period of a year and is not split into two distinct halves like his previous novels. The preponderance of short sentences is immediately noticeable and the style is measured, lacking in the mass of imagery which had characterized its predecessors and in what Dagerman's detractors sometimes called his hysteria. (p. 79)

[But] the continuity from Dagerman's previous work to *A Burnt Child* is obvious. Indeed, the thread can be traced back to *The Island of the Doomed*, where frigidity and numbness were depicted in terms of coldness, particularly in connection with Captain Wilson. . . . The problem of numbness, the inability to experience emotion to the full, was one which constantly taxed Dagerman both in his works and in his private life. The constant fear was that guilt feelings and suppressed *Angst* would so confine the senses that eventually one was no longer capable of genuine emotions. That occasionally there should be "volcanic eruptions" of passion was a comforting fact: at least it showed one was emotionally alive.

There is a lot of autobiography in *A Burnt Child*, suitably embellished for fictional purposes. Of considerable interest in view of the mounting psychological problems which were already troubling Stig Dagerman is the maternal theme. A psychologist would no doubt trace many of Dagerman's problems to his lack of a mother, a lack which he obviously felt deeply. (pp. 88-9)

[Yet, interesting] though the autobiographical aspects may be, the more universal significance of *A Burnt Child* must be the reader's primary concern. The reader is invited to question the conventional meaning of concepts such as purity and morality, right and wrong. Perhaps the biggest outrage in the novel to a conventional moralist is the incest theme, the idea of Bengt making love to his mother—his mother in law (i.e., stepmother) rather than his natural mother, but shocking even so. The message seems to be that such facile and conventional ideas of right and wrong are misguided. Being true to oneself, accepting facts irrespective of artificial conventions, seems to be held up by Dagerman as "the right direction," to use a phrase from *The Island of the Doomed*. The concluding sentences of *A Burnt Child* preach an Existentialist message: "But moments of peace are short. All other moments are much longer. Knowing this is also wisdom. But since they are so short we must live in those moments as if it were only then we were alive. They know this, too." . . . (p. 89)

Whereas *A Burnt Child* had been an austere and disciplined book, carefully planned and tightly constructed, [*Bröllopsbesvär* (*Wedding Worries*)] was superficially chaotic. Of course, it has a plan and the chaos is much more meaningful than is immediately apparent, but the novel is intentionally confusing, reflecting the circumstances in which it was written.

The plot of *Wedding Worries* is extremely difficult to summarize. There are a number of subplots and themes which intertwine to give the book its special character and a bald statement of the main action is grossly inadequate to convey the contents of the book, but an attempt will be made here to cover the main points.

The action covers a single day on a farm in rural Uppland. . . . The farm is owned by Viktor Palm, and on the day in question his daughter Hildur marries a butcher, Westlund, from a nearby village. The morning is devoted to preparations, the afternoon is when the ceremony takes place at the local vicarage, and the evening and night are spent celebrating, an occasion which deteriorates into a drunken orgy and ends with the sun rising on a new day with almost everyone sleeping off the effects, many of them in places where they ought not to be, such as under hedges, on floors, or in someone else's bed. It is an amusing novel but with tragic undertones, written in Uppland dialect. (pp. 93-4)

In *Wedding Worries* Dagerman manages to capture a subtle quality which invests simple folk in what are often squalid circumstances with a certain nobility which elevates their fate to one of timeless significance. . . . Characters are steeped in *Angst*, but there is a new air of resignation and a desire for love and tenderness which sometimes seems to be a longing for love in the Christian sense. Apart from the style, a notable difference between *A Burnt Child* and *Wedding Worries*, and Dagerman's previous works, is that the political element has virtually disappeared. In *The Snake* and *The Island of the Doomed* the autobiographical elements were balanced by the author's missionary zeal as a politically committed writer keen to present a case for anarcho-syndicalism. As his private problems increased and the apparently effortless ease with which he had been able to write in 1945-47 began to desert him, it seems that Dagerman concentrated on autobiographical situations and Existentialist messages at the expense of his political enthusiasms. The technical virtuosity is still there in his later novels; indeed, his touch seems more sure than ever. The average reader at the end of the 1940s must have wondered what style Dagerman would next show himself to be master of, and his fifth novel was awaited with great expectations. It never came. (pp. 107-08)

The first play by Stig Dagerman to be performed in public was a one-act sketch, *På tåget* [*On the Train*], which he had written in a couple of hours in 1942 and given to a friend as a Christmas box, being short of cash as usual and unable to afford a "real" present. It was performed in 1943 by an experimental theater group and was sufficiently successful to attract a short notice in the literary journal *Bonniers Litterära Magasin*, where Holger Ahlenius referred to it as "the droll little sketch." The author had forgotten about it and was unaware of the planned production until he was invited to attend rehearsals.

With this "involuntary debut" in mind, Dagerman referred to [*Den dödsdömde* (*The Man Condemned to Death*)] as "my first real play." (pp. 111-12)

The plot of the play is basically the same as that of the short story with the same name. A man found guilty of murdering his wife is reprieved when the executioner is indisposed and at the same time news arrives of a confession by someone else. The man is taken out for a celebratory meal and provided with a whore, but he kills her and is returned to prison, this time unmistakably guilty.

Dagerman was lucky in that Alf Sjöberg's production of *The Man Condemned to Death* was brilliant, creating a mysterious, dreamlike atmosphere appropriate to the Kafkaesque happenings in the play. Later productions elsewhere were generally not nearly so successful, the London production being particularly disastrous. Sjöberg managed to conceal the fact that large portions of the play are static with a strong emphasis on words and ideas rather than on dramatic conflict. (p. 112)

Despite the weaknesses of the play, the subject matter caught the imagination of the theatergoing public—at a time when the Cold War was intensifying and the world was living in constant fear of the atomic bomb, the *Angst* of the man condemned to death found an echo in many people's souls. (p. 114)

[*Upptäcktsresanden (The Explorer)*] was published in *40-tal* in the fall of 1947, subtitled **"Miniature Drama in Four Acts,"** and was not actually performed until October 1949, when it was produced in Hälsingborg with moderate success. It appears to be an offshoot of *The Man Condemned to Death,* in which play an Explorer is chairman of the Reprieved Club. There is an element of social criticism in the play—the Explorer does very little himself, is carried everywhere by native bearers, and has a guide who knows "undiscovered" territory well, indeed, has even lived there: nevertheless, the Explorer receives all the credit and the contribution of the servants is unrecognized. More important, however, are the doubts the Explorer has about his calling, first hinted at in the earlier play but expanded here, which create in him strong feelings of *Angst.* He has a great desire to discover new territory, but although he will not acknowledge it, he is aware of the bogus nature of his discoveries: the territories are there in any case, people have visited them before, and there is even a native population. His "discovery" of a territory has no effect on the existence of the area, the only change takes place in the attitude of people toward it—another echo from *The Man Condemned to Death.* (pp. 114-15)

It is possible to see the Explorer as a representative figure standing for modern man, eager for new experiences but conscious of the fact that they are only "new" from his own point of view. Perhaps most appropriate is an interpretation which sees the Explorer as representing a writer, and more particularly as a projection of Dagerman himself. In "Entrance Lines," Dagerman wrote that "a writer is naturally exposed to constant doubts, as is any traveler (doubts not only about his "calling" but about poetry in general); he is constantly assailed by recriminations which strike at the very core of his existence." (p. 115)

As a play, *The Explorer* is not particularly outstanding: its main interest lies in the fact that it is the most consistently "de-dramatized" of Dagerman's dramas. It is clearly a difficult play to produce satisfactorily: very little actually happens, the title character spends the first two acts asleep and is dead by the time the fourth act begins—his murder having taken place off-stage. The four acts consist of characters talking to each other, discussing ideas and doing very little. The stage settings are expressionistic "landscapes of the soul" rather than realistic places—the directions describe the desert, the jungle and the tropical river as "every member of the audience's idea of

(such a place)" and are clearly not meant to be represented realistically.... An outstanding production and a highly effective climax made the first performance of *The Man Condemned to Death* a success and seemed to suggest that Dagerman's theory of the de-dramatized drama might have much to recommend it; *The Explorer* shows that even a short play constructed consistently and exclusively in accordance with the theory has serious defects when it comes to a stage performance.

Dagerman's next play, [*Streber (The Go-Getter)*], was in his mind even before the first performance of *The Man Condemned to Death* in April 1947, but it was not completed until the middle of December. (pp. 115-16)

The Go-Getter is Dagerman's most overtly political work, written at a time when political divisions were appearing among writers of his generation. The journal *40-tal* had ceased to exist; trouble was brewing in the Writers' Union in connection with attitudes to the Soviet Union and the imminent annexation of Czechoslovakia; anarcho-syndicalism and its organ, *Arbetaren,* were being exposed to severe criticism from more conventional Socialists. It is understandable that at this time Dagerman should be keen to write a play so obviously sympathetic to Socialist ideals, and in particular Syndicalist ones. Nevertheless, judged from an artistic point of view, *The Go-Getter* is one of Dagerman's weaker works. (pp. 117-18)

[*Skuggan av Mart (The Shadow of Mart)*] was written soon after *The Go-Getter.*...

The play is rather short on action. As the title implies, the martyred hero Mart dominates proceedings although he is already dead. His mother, Mme Angelica, reveres his memory and constantly upbraids Gabriel for failing to measure up to the standards set by his elder brother. Gabriel is shortsighted and shy, not to say cowardly. Eventually he can endure no longer the humiliation heaped upon him by his mother and shoots her. The play ends with a long monologue, the closing minutes of which are enlivened by the appearance of Mart's shadow which grows larger and larger until it dominates the whole stage. (p. 118)

Too often and for too long, the characters merely talk and not enough happens in the play: the climactic monologue at the end might work well if it were drastically shortened—as it is, the dramatic tension disperses about halfway through and the attention of the audience is inevitably lost. Dagerman falls into the trap primed for any author who tries to write a play strong on ideas and tends to create caricatures rather than rounded characters.... (p. 119)

The novel *A Burnt Child* was Dagerman's most successful work from the point of view of sales, and a dramatized version of it was completed early in 1949....

In adapting his novel for the stage Dagerman was naturally forced to make changes and simplifications which resulted in significant alterations in character and in the central conflict. The device of interposing letters written by Bengt, usually to himself, between the conventionally narrated chapters, so successful in the novel, was clearly impossible in the theater. Symbols imposed by the narrator in *A Burnt Child* had to be abandoned in the play—the tiger and the gazelle, for instance, and the imagery in the final chapter when the frozen wilderness melts, the desert blooms and Bengt's emotional outbursts are compared to volcanoes. The motifs of heat and coldness were retained, but in simplified form; similarly the subtlety of the dog symbol had to be made more straightforward—being a present from a former lover, it simply represents Gun's loose morals and erotic appeal. These and other enforced changes dictated that Bengt's character should become less complicated, and the maternal theme is greatly reduced in significance. (p. 120)

[*Ingen går fri* (*No One Goes Free*)] was received warmly but not enthusiastically. It has obvious faults—the staccato dialogue seems terse in the extreme, the verbal repetition is frequently tiresome and some of the symbolic action (such as Bengt's staring out of the window at the butcher's shop and refusing to close the blind) is labored. The first two acts tend to drag, but there is dramatic tension and developing interest as more of the extent of the depression and illusion in the play is revealed: the pace quickens after Gun's appearance in Act III and the progress of the relationship between her and Bengt holds the attention of the audience. Despite its faults, however, *No One Goes Free* is one of the more satisfying of Dagerman's plays. While the novel probed more deeply into the psychology of the main characters and provided Dagerman with a vehicle to display his technical virtuosity, the stage version sensibly simplifies the problems and presents them in a way immediately comprehensible to a live audience. Dagerman's ability to do this confirms that he was already a competent dramatist. (p. 121)

[*Den yttersta dagen* (*The Day of Judgment*)] was the last work of creative literature that Stig Dagerman managed to complete. (p. 122)

In an interview given in connection with the Gothenburg production Dagerman commented on the origins of his plot: "I regard peasant society as my home environment. What happens in *The Day of Judgment* goes back to impressions of my youth on Grandfather's farm—he was a father to me in every way. When he was murdered by a lunatic during my formative years, this was far and away the most important incident of my youth."

Despite the happiness connected with the birth of his daughter and his love for Anita Björk, the time when *The Day of Judgment* was written was a period of distress for Stig Dagerman. He had just informed Ragnar Svanström of his inability to complete a planned novel, and a visit to Paris had failed to produce any more articles for *Expressen*. His negotiations with his wife in his efforts to obtain a divorce were entering a critical stage, and his financial affairs were in chaos. The play thus seems to be yet another of Dagerman's highly personal works, set against an autobiographical background and reflecting the author's own mood at the time of writing.

Every character in *The Day of Judgment* bears a heavy burden of guilt. All have failed to offer support and help, and this failure or betrayal gives them extremely guilty consciences. The question is asked: if this were your last day on earth, what would you do? Each character would like to do some good deed, but in fact they fail in their good intentions.

The Day of Judgment is an odd play. The background is an authentic Uppland farming situation, with realistically convincing characters—rough, brusque, even crude at times yet with a countryman's stubborn superstition and a warm-hearted streak. But Dagerman introduces a strong element of mystery, even mysticism. Someone is hovering outside near the farm—stealing tools, eating eggs, opening doors, knocking on windows. . . . Each character sees the ghost created by his or her own particular guilt embodied in the mysterious stranger. There are far too many omens, too much heavy-handed mystery, and the ponderous pace of the play is exaggerated by the static

nature of the scenes. *The Day of Judgment* has its effective parts but it would have benefited by being reduced ruthlessly in length and by the removal of excessive omens.

Dagerman himself seemed to be aware of the unsatisfactory nature of the play and called it "a preliminary rehearsal" for what he called "the real peasant play" he planned to write later. (pp. 122-23)

There is no doubt that Dagerman had considerable potential as a dramatist—indeed, his achievements make him worthy of mention among the leading half-dozen or so Swedish playwrights this century. His instinctive mastery of language enabled him to create remarkable verbal effects, and while his theories of a "de-dramatized drama" tended to work against him, the discipline of writing a play and taking into account all the time what is practicable in the theater was undoubtedly useful in restraining Dagerman from some of the excesses which are sometimes apparent in his novels. It is doubtful, however, whether he would have developed into a dramatist rather than a novelist first and foremost. His plays have distinct weaknesses and his virtuosity as a master of narrative styles was ideally suited to the prose genres: his plays tend to lack the subtlety of his novels. (pp. 123-24)

For several years, Dagerman toyed with the idea of publishing a collection of lyric poetry. He never achieved this ambition although two books published after his death contain a representative selection of his achievements in verse. The volume *Vårt behov av tröst* [**Our Need of Consolation**] has a section containing sixteen poems, almost all of them published previously in various journals and newspapers; the selection includes almost all the best of Dagerman's genuinely lyric poems. The other volume, *Dagsedlar* [**Calendar Pages**], . . . contains 152 of the 1,350 or so "daily verses" published during the years 1943-54 in *Arbetaren*.

The daily verses are a good example of occasional poetry and are often of a high standard. . . . The standard varies, of course, but Dagerman's facility with rhyme and rhythm, his instinctive feeling for the *mot juste* and the striking image shows that he had the potential to develop into a poet of rank.

Most of the daily verses are ephemeral, making a political point with wit and, occasionally, venom on such topics as capitalistic excesses, Communist suppression, bureaucracy, the monarchy, nuclear bombs, anti-Semitism, Franco's Spain. The satire is sometimes crude, but usually to the point and thought-provoking. The better poems are not merely witty and sarcastic but show compassion with the wronged, the oppressed, with ordinary people who have suffered in some way at the hands of Authority. (p. 125)

[In his final year, after] a series of projects that came to nothing, Dagerman began to plan an ambitious novel on a large scale, based on the tragic life of the Swedish Romanticist turned Realist C. J. L. Almqvist (1793-1866), and he actually managed to complete the prologue. . . . Unfortunately, Dagerman was unable to progress any further with the planned novel, and all that remained among his papers when he died were a few sketches for later chapters, notably a few pages about the American Civil War. The prologue, which does not refer directly to Almqvist at all, was published posthumously under the title *Tusen år hos Gud* [**A Thousand Years with God**], and was lavishly praised—excessively so for a fragment which is undoubtedly clever and witty but rather contrived. Be that as it may, the potential for it to develop into a successful novel of high quality is undoubtedly there.

There is a directness and precise simplicity of language in the fragment which suggests a development of the style the author adopted in *A Burnt Child;* however, whereas the earlier novel is predominantly realistic, *A Thousand Years with God* is decidedly surrealistic. The prologue describes a meeting between Sir Isaac Newton and God, who comes to earth in the guise of Claes Jensen, a sailmaker, and has to endure a series of tribulations as an introduction to the human condition. (pp. 136-37)

Humiliation, terror, betrayal, degradation: such is the lot of the mere human. Repeatedly Jensen is given cause to hope—but always his optimism is dashed. The themes are familiar ones in Dagerman's works, the surprise being what Newton calls the "impossibility of Love." (p. 137)

Stig Dagerman could not believe in a god, but the vain search for consolation in religion, noticeable in *Wedding Worries,* is continued with the Almqvist fragment. *A Thousand Years with God* can be read as the desperate assertion of a tortured soul that even if God exists, he is helpless to assist humans in distress. . . .

A Thousand Years with God is a deeply pessimistic fragment, but the mood is not all gloom. There is considerable humor in the basic symbol, which is the reversal of Newton's law of gravitation. Newton's servant enters his master's room and is perturbed to find himself floating up to the ceiling; all dropped objects join the servant up aloft instead of falling to the ground, with amusing consequences. When Newton dies, the English establishment—especially the church—is horrified to discover that although normal gravitation has been restored in general, his body and the coffin in which it is placed rise to a height of about three feet and can only be made to sink to the ground when they are draped with coils of enormously heavy chain. The absurdity and irony of the scene are most appealing. (p. 138)

While few of Dagerman's works end happily, there is more humor in his style than he is generally given credit for, and all his novels abound in irony. Although the satire in his "daily verses" is sometimes crude, it is frequently apposite and effective—and ought to warn the readers of his novels and stories that there is often much more in an apparently straightforward statement or incident than meets the eye. The narrative technique is seldom uncomplicated in a work of Dagerman's and is used to comment or enlarge upon the story being told in such a way that the form becomes inseparable from the content.

Dagerman's novels and the best of his stories can be read on a number of levels. He is always enquiring about the meaning of life; in concluding that there is none he is clearly much influenced by contemporary Existentialist philosophy and the mood of the 1940s, but who can claim that the intervening years have produced evidence to refute such pessimism? True to his Anarcho-Syndicalist politics, Dagerman never falters in his consistent and fierce defense of individual freedom. (pp. 144-45)

Dagerman's mastery of narrative technique and his advocacy of ideas worth considering seriously constitute an important part of his status as a writer; however, he would not be as outstanding as he is were it not for his ability to create convincing, living characters and authentic environments. Dagerman possesses to an unusual degree the natural storyteller's eye for pertinent detail. (p. 145)

It has long been recognized in Scandinavia that Stig Dagerman was a writer of outstanding natural talents, although acknowledgment of the true stature of his actual achievements has been slower in coming. In an age dominated by existential *Angst,* Dagerman's works have a relevance which suggests that they are worthy of much wider recognition. The time is ripe to acclaim Stig Dagerman as one of Sweden's most important twentieth-century novelists. (p. 146)

> *Laurie Thompson, in his* Stig Dagerman, *Twayne Publishers, 1983, 167 p.*

ADDITIONAL BIBLIOGRAPHY

Cook, Bruce A. "Distinctly European Voices." *Commonweal* LXXIV, No. 18 (11 August 1961): 451-52.*
> Review of *The Games of Night*. Cook declares: "These are not the stories of an exhausted talent, but of a writer at the height of his powers."

Cruttwell, Patrick. "Fiction Chronicle." *The Hudson Review* XIV, No. 3 (Autumn 1961): 448-51.*
> Compares the stories of *The Games of Night* to Ingmar Bergman's films for their fusion of "extreme physical and tactual reality with unearthly fantasy."

Hauser, Frank. "New Novels." *The New Statesman and Nation* 40, No. 1009 (8 July 1950): 50-1.*
> Unfavorable review of *A Burnt Child*. Hauser considers the novel "the literary equivalent of a very slow, very bad Swedish film, where the simplest actions are invested with a portentousness which would have dismayed the House of Usher."

Meyer, Michael. Introduction to *The Games of Night*, by Stig Dagerman, pp. 7-16. New York: J. B. Lippincott Co., 1961.
> Biographical summary. Meyer regards Dagerman's inability to reconcile the world of the country with the world of the city as the primary reason behind his creative paralysis in his last years, but declares: "Yet, like his masters Strindberg and Kafka, he photographed his small, split world with a vivid and faithful clarity."

Vance, Thomas. "A Note on Stig Dagerman." *Poetry* CIII, No. 4 (January 1964): 255.
> Acknowledges the superiority of Dagerman's prose to his poetry, but contends that the poem "Birgitta Suite" "stands out for its depth and intensity."

Anne Frank

1929-1945

(Born Annelies Marie Frank) German-born Dutch diarist, fabulist, short story writer, and essayist.

Anne Frank is known throughout the world for her diary *Het Achterhuis* (*Anne Frank: The Diary of a Young Girl*), which documents her adolescence in German-occupied Amsterdam during World War II, as well as the impact of Nazi anti-Semitism on both Jewish and non-Jewish Dutch individuals during that era. Her diary is at once a candid self-portrait, a portrayal of domestic life, an account of people threatened with imminent death, a depiction of experiences and problems common to young adults, and an examination of universal moral issues. This private journal, which she did not live to see published, sheds light on an episode in history that embodied extremes of both the degradation and the nobility of the human spirit.

Frank was born to an upper-class Jewish family in the city of Frankfurt. Her father, Otto Frank, was a respected businessman who had been a German officer in World War I. The early childhood of Frank and her elder sister, Margot, was secure, loving, and comfortable, but the year of Anne's birth also marked the onset of a worldwide economic depression, a catastrophic event that affected the lives of a great number of Europeans. In Germany, economic disaster, combined with the lingering effects of the harsh demands made on Germany after its defeat in World War I, led to the installation of Adolf Hitler as leader of the government. Through policies that stressed rearmament, nationalism, and racism, Hitler sought to restore his country to a position of preeminence in Europe. A primary target for Hitler's condemnation were Jews; by aggravating long-held antisemitic prejudice, Hitler sought to purge Germany of what he considered an exploitive group. In 1933, following Hitler's decree that Jewish and non-Jewish children could not attend the same schools, the Franks left their homeland and by 1934 were settled in Amsterdam, where Otto Frank directed a food import business. Despite the growing threat of war, Frank lived a normal life, much like any Dutch girl, for the next few years. She attended a Montessori school and was an average student, remembered by one teacher as being ordinary in many ways but as having the ability to draw more from her experiences than other children. In many respects, Frank remained absorbed in everyday life even after the Germans invaded Holland in 1940 and imposed harsh anti-Jewish measures. Under the German occupation, Frank was forced to leave the Montessori school and attend the Jewish Lyceum, where she adjusted well and soon became known for her pranks and her incessant talking. However, as Nazi horrors increased, including the roundup of Amsterdam's Jews in 1941 for incarceration in concentration camps, Otto Frank and his business partners secretly prepared a hiding place in some rooms located in the top, back portion of their company's combined warehouse and office building on Prinsengracht Canal. In June 1942, a month before the Franks went into hiding to escape Nazi persecution, Anne celebrated her thirteenth birthday, receiving among her presents a small clothbound diary which she deemed "possibly the nicest of all" her gifts. Several weeks later, Margot Frank was notified to report to the recep-

The Granger Collection, New York

tion center for the Westerbork concentration camp, and the family fled into the "Secret Annex." They were joined shortly thereafter by a Mr. and Mrs. Van Pelz (rendered as "Van Daan" in Anne's diary) and their fifteen-year-old son Peter, and several months later by Albert Dussel, a middle-aged dentist. Together they remained hidden and virtually imprisoned for over two years.

During her confinement, Frank continued her education under her father's guidance, and on her own initiative she wrote the equivalent of two books: in addition to her diary she also wrote a number of fables, short stories, reminiscences, essays, and an unfinished novel. Life in the annex, a common concern in her diary entries, was strained by quarrels and tensions arising from the anxiety inherent in the situation, the frustrations of a monotonous, restrictive life, and personality clashes. The eight annex inhabitants shared cramped, drab quarters and had to remain stiflingly quiet during the day, at times refraining from using water faucets and toilet facilities to avoid being heard by other people in the building. Their very survival depended on remaining undiscovered. Through the generosity of four benefactors who risked their own lives, the annex inhabitants were provided with food and supplies, as well as companionship and news from the outside world. When on June 6, 1944 (D-Day), news came that the tide of war had turned in favor of the Allies, hope increased for the annex group. Then suddenly, on August 4, 1944, their hiding place was raided, and they became prisoners of the Nazis and subjected to their captors' "final solution to the Jewish problem." All were sent first on a passenger train to Westerbork, and then in a cattle car among the last human shipment to Auschwitz. Anne was remembered by a survivor of Auschwitz as a leader and as someone who remained sensitive and caring when most prisoners protected themselves from feeling anything. In March 1945, two months before the German surrender, Anne Frank died of typhoid fever in the Bergen-Belsen concentration camp.

Of the eight inhabitants of the secret annex, only Otto Frank survived. When he returned to Holland from Auschwitz, Anne's diary and papers were given to him. Anne's writings had been left behind by the Secret Police in their search for valuables, and were found in the hiding place by two Dutch women who had helped the fugitives survive. Frank kept her diary for nearly twenty-six months, capturing experiences which range from a visit to the ice cream parlor to her reflections about God and human nature. What emerges from Frank's diary is a multifaceted young person who is at once an immature young girl and a precocious, deep-thinking individual. Yet, her inner world and writing ability had hitherto remained unknown to anyone but herself. After reading her diary, Otto Frank confessed, "I never knew my little Anna was so deep." Shortly after the war's end, he circulated typed copies of the diary among his friends, who quickly recognized it as a meaningful human document which should not remain a private legacy. Published two years after Anne's death, the diary has since been translated into some forty languages and adapted into the Pulitzer Prize-winning play *The Diary of Anne Frank*, which was made into a motion picture.

Although stylistic considerations are of minor importance when compared to the documentary value of the diary, some critics have described Frank as a "born writer," or as someone who could have become a professional writer. Annie Romein-Vershoor has expressed the view that Frank "possessed the one important characteristic of a great writer: an open mind, untouched by complacency and prejudice." Initially, Frank had considered her diary a private work that she might someday show to a "real friend." Motivated by her need for a confidant and by a strong desire to write, she disclosed her deepest thoughts and feelings to her diary, though she sometimes doubted that anyone would be interested "in the unbosomings of a thirteen-year-old schoolgirl." Conceiving of her diary as a friend, she named it "Kitty" and wrote her entries in the form of letters to Kitty. Throughout, the diary reveals Frank's sense of an unseen audience as well as her ambivalence toward the importance of her own experience. She also sensed the need for variety in her writing and was able to achieve it despite the repetitiveness of routine and paucity of stimulation in her life. The vivid, poignant entries range in tone from humorous to serious, casual to intense, and reveal Frank's ability to write narrative and descriptive accounts as well as to write about abstract ideas. The diary, often commended for its engaging style, is full of vitality. Meyer Levin has praised the work for sustaining "the tension of a well-constructed novel," and attributes this to Frank's dramatic psychological development and to the physical dangers that threatened the group.

Frank's personality and character development are the aspects of the diary most commonly discussed by critics. Her circumstances of confinement and enforced silence are considered factors that precipitated a rapid maturation and nurtured a more

introspective, analytical approach to life. Initially, Frank made an exemplary adjustment to life in hiding, seeking the good and amusing aspects of her situation, decorating her room, and remarking, "It is like being on holiday in a very peculiar boarding house." But as the routine and boredom set in, she became increasingly restless, frustrated, and lonely. Under stress, her formerly light-hearted demeanor gave way to a more irritable, defensive nature; she became critical of others, especially her mother, and frequently quarreled with Mr. and Mrs. Van Pelz and Mr. Dussel. These reactions, according to critics, stemmed from her sense of justice, her dislike of anything artificial or pompous, and her desire to be treated like an adult. Gradually, Frank developed more mature attitudes and behavior. Largely because of her determination to do so, she became more self-controlled and inclined toward deliberate rather than spontaneous courses of action. As Frank grew in confidence and self-knowledge, her perspective and writing ability broadened as well. Her simple desire "to write" became an ambition to become a journalist and a famous writer. She considered publishing her diary and other miscellaneous writings after the war, and came to appreciate her talent as a gift from God that might enable her words to live on after her death. She also learned to view herself and life more objectively, and while she grew increasingly self-reliant, she found consolation and inspiration in nature. Amidst all her hardships, she maintained her faith in God and was sensitive to her moral accountability as an individual. On April 11, 1944, Frank wrote: "If God lets me live, . . . I shall not remain insignificant. I shall work in the world and for mankind!" Critics point to Frank's evolving relationships with her parents, sister, and Peter Van Pelz as illustrations of her growing self-knowledge and her longing for a deep, meaningful human relationship. Although at the end of her diary Frank still sees herself as a young woman struggling to maturity, during her years in hiding she underwent a psychological and moral development which a number of critics have deemed remarkable for someone her age.

Like her diary, Frank's creative works reveal that, although she was well acquainted with degradation, persecution, and injustice, she refused to dwell only on the grim aspects of reality. She maintained some personal freedom, despite her confinement, and poured her imagination, wisdom, fears, and deeply religious sense of values into these works. Being tested through confinement and finding consolation in nature are common themes of her stories and fables. Among the subjects addressed in her reminiscences and essays are the Dutch dislike of nudity, memories of her school days, and the possibility of improving the world with kindness and fairness. Of all her creative works, G. B. Stern regards *Cady's Life*, Frank's unfinished novel, as the best example of her writing potential, displaying as it does her wisdom, perceptiveness, and religious nature. Containing an account of a young girl's arrest and "disappearance" through the agency of the Nazis, the work foreshadows Frank's own fate at the hands of the Nazis, and includes a discussion about God which, according to Stern, bears "the essence of so much that one has read in profound theological works of the true nature of God and how He expresses Himself, that one is staggered at its maturity." In her diary, Frank expressed some doubts about finishing *Cady's Life*, asking herself, "At the age of fourteen and with so little experience, how can you write about philosophy?" None of these works has the quality of vivid reality found throughout the diary and, as Frederick Morton points out, they "show an occasional leaning to rhetoric quite inevitable in a fifteen-year-old who sits down 'to write'." Nevertheless, like her diary, they further illustrate her potential as a writer and reaffirm her determination to keep hope alive.

Because Frank's diary was not written as creative literature, and because of the extraordinary circumstances of the author's life, critics most commonly discuss the human and historical importance of the work rather than its aesthetic or structural elements. Most also express their personal responses to the diary, as well as to its worldwide success and its powerful impact on readers. Anne herself and her experiences in growing up are the primary focus of discussions about the diary as a human document. Henry Pommer has stated, "The chief literary merit of the diary is its permitting us to know intimately Anne's young, eager, difficult, lovable self," and other critics express similar opinions. John Berryman has underscored the significance of her diary as a frank account of growing up, explaining that, unlike other books which are merely about adolescence, Frank's diary makes available the mysterious, fundamental process of a child becoming an adult as it is actually happening. In simply being herself, Frank also succeeded in portraying the universalities of human nature and in touching millions. In particular, young people can at once identify with her zest for life and her typical adolescent problems and be inspired by her courage and ideals.

As a historical document the diary is an indictment against the Nazis' destruction of human life and culture. As Ilya Ehrenburg has stated, "One voice speaks for six million—the voice not of a sage or a poet but of an ordinary little girl." Critics have posited that while newsreels and books which explicitly portray Nazi atrocities have had a stupefying effect on people, Frank's story acquaints people with everyday, recognizable individuals, and has thus been phenomenally effective in communicating this enormous tragedy. In postwar Germany, for example, there were widespread expressions of guilt and shame in response to viewing the stage production of *The Diary of Anne Frank,* and an intense interest in Frank among German youth after years of repressive silence regarding Nazi crimes. Anne Birstein and Alfred Kazin have asserted that "the reality of what certain people have had to endure in our time can be grasped humanly and politically only because of the modulation of a document like *The Diary of a Young Girl,* which permits us to see certain experiences in a frame, in a thoroughly human setting, so that we can bear them at all." Recognized by some critics as a portrait of humanity in all of its varied aspects, Frank's diary has been used as a basis for considering other injustices in the world and for assessing moral responsibility in contemporary crises. Frank herself has become a symbol, not only of six million murdered Jews, but of other people who suffer persecution because of race, belief, and color.

Frank's diary, which embodies the triumph of the human spirit in a destructive, dehumanizing system, has outlasted many other books about World War II. Although it has been suggested that her writing is an escape into the ideal, it may be this quality which partially accounts for the universal acceptance of the diary. Frank herself questioned her idealism in an often-quoted passage: "It's really a wonder that I haven't dropped all my ideals, because they seem so absurd and impossible to carry out. Yet I keep them, because in spite of everything I still believe that people are really good at heart." Her story and ideals have inspired many creative and constructive responses which reflect the timeless message of her diary: the importance, as stated by Rabbi Philip S. Bernstein, of keeping "pity and kindness and love alive in the world."

(See also *Contemporary Authors,* Vol. 113.)

PRINCIPAL WORKS

Het Achterhuis   (diary)   1947
   [*Anne Frank: The Diary of a Young Girl,* 1952]
The Works of Anne Frank   (diary, fables, reminiscences, short stories, and essays)   1959
Tales from the House Behind   (fables, reminiscences, short stories, essays, and unfinished novel)   1962
Tales from the Secret Annex   (fables, reminiscences, short stories, and essays)   1984

JAN ROMEIN   (essay date 1946)

[*Prior to the formal publication of his daughter's diary, Otto Frank privately circulated copies of it. He gave one typed copy to a friend, who in turn lent it to Romein, a professor of modern history. To Otto Frank's surprise, the professor wrote an article on the diary for a Dutch newspaper,* Het Parool, *in 1946. In the following excerpt from this article, which has been called "the first serious attempt to evaluate Anne Frank's diary as a historic document," Romein describes his total absorption upon reading the diary, praising Anne Frank for her insight, humor, compassion, and love, while at the same time recognizing her profoundly childlike nature.*]

Purely by chance a diary written during the war years has come into my hands. The Government Institute for War Documentation is in possession of about two hundred similar diaries, but it would amaze me if there was *one* among them as pure, as intelligent, and yet as human as this one. I read it from beginning to end without stopping, forgetting my many responsibilities for several hours. When I finished it was evening, and I was astonished that the light was burning, that there was still bread and tea, that I heard no airplanes droning above and no soldiers' boots shuffling on the streets, so thoroughly had this diary captured me and carried me back to the unreal world, behind us for almost a year now. . . .

For me [Anne Frank's] apparently insignificant diary, this *de profundis* in the stammering voice of a child, embodies the real hideousness of fascism, more than all the trials of Nuremberg. For me the lot of this young girl sums up the worst crime of that abominable spirit. The worst crime is not the destruction of life and culture in itself; these things can also fall victim in a culture-creating revolution. The worst crime is the damming of the sources of culture, the destruction of life and talent only because of a senseless desire to destroy. If all signs do not deceive us, this girl, had she lived, would have become a talented writer. Coming to Holland at the age of four, she was able to write an enviably pure and sober Dutch ten years later, and she exhibited an insight into human nature—including her own—so faultless that it would be surprising in an adult, let alone a child. She also displayed, equally faultlessly, the limitless possibilities for humor, compassion, and love in human nature. These we should admire perhaps even more than her insight, and we might even shy away from them as we sometimes do from something very special, if her rejection and acceptance had not at the same time remained so profoundly childlike. That it was possible for this child to have been taken away and killed is proof for me that we have lost the battle against the beast in man.

We have lost because we have not been able to substitute something positive for it. And that is why we will lose again.

No matter in what form inhumanity may lay traps for us, we will fall into them as long as we are unable to replace that inhumanity with a positive force.

The promise never to forget or forgive is not enough. It is not even enough to keep the promise. Passive and negative defense is almost the same as no defense.

Active, positive, total democracy—political, social, economic, and cultural democracy—is the only means by which we can build a society in which talent is no longer destroyed, oppressed, and driven out, but is discovered, cultivated, and encouraged wherever it may show itself.

And with all our good intentions, we are still as far away from this kind of democracy as we were before the war.

> *Jan Romein, "A Child's Voice," in* A Tribute to Anne Frank, *edited by Anna G. Steenmeijer with Otto Frank and Henri van Praag, Doubleday & Company, Inc., 1971, p. 21.*

ANNIE ROMEIN-VERSHOOR   (essay date 1947)

[*In the following excerpt from the preface to the Dutch edition of Anne Frank's diary, Romein-Vershoor acknowledges the value of the diary as a war document, but is touched primarily by the personal aspect of this work which reveals the rich, abundant inner life of the author.*]

Under the exceptional circumstances of life in the Annex, the growth of the lively, intelligent and impressionable child Anne Frank, from girl to woman, from child to adult, occurred in a remarkably brief time. The relationship of the growing young individual to the outside world, which in normal life is recorded in a great number of more or less fluctuating and varying lines, was here reduced to an extremely simple pattern, forcing her perceptive spirit to expand in depth rather than in width. In a continual process of rapprochement, collision, and wrestling with the seven people around her, in a constant state of inquisitive examination of these seven eternal close-ups, the child's knowledge of human character grew perceptibly. Through introspection forced upon her by circumstances, through a struggle with herself and her limited possibilities, the self-knowledge of the child playing at keeping a diary, evolved with unbelievable speed to sharp analysis, even of her own dreams and illusions, of her reactions to her surroundings, of her fate, and of her abandonment of all the beautiful little girl's dreams which were no longer a part of her life in hiding. . . .

There is much more to say about this diary. It is a war document, a document of the cruelty and heartbreaking misery of the persecution of the Jews, of human helpfulness and treason, of human adjustment and non-adjustment, of the small joys and the great and small miseries of life in hiding, written in a direct, non-literary, and therefore often excellent style, by this child who in any case possessed the one important characteristic of a great writer: an open mind, untouched by complacency and prejudice.

But for me the most important thing about this diary is not the documentation, which so often is and will be recorded elsewhere. When people in the tropics take a young plant from the temperate mountain zone and plant it in a very hot area, it will bloom once, richly and superabundantly, only to die soon after. That feeling is what touches me the most in this diary.

In the same way, this small, plucky geranium stood and bloomed, and bloomed, behind the shuttered windows of the Annex.

> *Annie Romein-Vershoor, "The Book that Started a Chain Reaction: Prefaces to the Diary," in* A Tribute to Anne Frank, *edited by Anna G. Steenmeijer with Otto Frank and Henri van Praag, Doubleday & Company, Inc., 1971, p. 34.*

ELEANOR ROOSEVELT   (essay date 1952)

[*Considered one of the most influential and distinguished women of twentieth-century America, Roosevelt wrote and lectured widely on behalf of various humanitarian and social-welfare causes. After the death of her husband, President Franklin D. Roosevelt, she twice served as the U.S. delegate to the United Nations General Assembly. In the following introduction to Anne Frank's diary, Roosevelt praises the work, stating that the diary addresses what she considers war's greatest evil—"the degradation of the human spirit"—while at the same time making clear the "ultimate shining nobility of that spirit."*]

[*Anne Frank: The Diary of a Young Girl*] is a remarkable book. Written by a young girl—and the young are not afraid of telling the truth—it is one of the wisest and most moving commentaries on war and its impact on human beings that I have ever read. Anne Frank's account of the changes wrought upon eight people hiding out from the Nazis for two years during the occupation of Holland, living in constant fear and isolation, imprisoned not only by the terrible outward circumstances of war but inwardly by themselves, made me intimately and shockingly aware of war's greatest evil—the degradation of the human spirit.

At the same time, Anne's diary makes poignantly clear the ultimate shining nobility of that spirit. Despite the horror and the humiliation of their daily lives, these people never gave up. Anne herself—and, most of all, it is her portrait which emerges so vividly and so appealingly from this book—matured very rapidly in these two years, the crucial years from thirteen to fifteen in which change is so swift and so difficult for every young girl. Sustained by her warmth and her wit, her intelligence and the rich resources of her inner life, Anne wrote and thought much of the time about things which very sensitive and talented adolescents without the threat of death will write—her relations with her parents, her developing self-awareness, the problems of growing up.

These are the thoughts and expression of a young girl living under extraordinary conditions, and for this reason her diary tells us much about ourselves and about our own children. And for this reason, too, I felt how close we all are to Anne's experience, how very much involved we are in her short life and in the entire world.

Anne's diary is an appropriate monument to her fine spirit and to the spirits of those who have worked and are working still for peace. Reading it is a rich and rewarding experience. (pp. ix-x)

> *Eleanor Roosevelt, in an introduction to* Anne Frank: The Diary of a Young Girl *by Anne Frank, translated by B. M. Mooyaart-Doubleday, 1952. Reprint by Pocket Books, 1953, pp. ix-x.*

ANTONIA WHITE   (essay date 1952)

[*An English critic, editor, and translator, White is best known as a Catholic novelist whose works, notably* Frost in May *(1933) and the Clara Batchelor trilogy (1950-54), reflect her troubled life and spiritual struggles. In the following excerpt, she praises*

*Anne Frank for her unusual honesty and self-criticism, and com-
mends her diary for its extraordinary human and historical interest.*]

Anne's journal is not only highly interesting as a vivid factual
record of life in Amsterdam during the most oppressive and
terrifying years of the war, it is also a remarkable study in the
psychology of a small group of people forced to live together
in almost unbearable proximity. (p. 592)

In this unnatural confinement, the personal relations of two
married couples, three adolescents and a peculiarly irritating
elderly bachelor developed a feverish intensity. Even the continual threat of danger and the knowledge of what terrible, half-
guessed fate might be awaiting them did not prevent them from
bickering as fiercely, and over the same trivial things, as any
two ill-assorted couples sharing a house and quarrelling as to
whose turn it was to wash up. Occasionally a major crisis
would quell them into comparative peace, as on one agonizing
night when the police were actually in the building looking for
burglars who had already hacked away part of the secret door.
But the moment the crisis had passed, the bickerings—matrimonial, political and filial—broke out again with new vigour
to be noted by the sharp eye of an irrepressible schoolgirl.

However much sympathy one feels with this bright creature so
hideously trapped, it is impossible not to feel considerable
sympathy with her elders too. It is indeed a tribute to Anne
Frank that one forgets her great courage in the face of the real
horrors of her situation (of which she was perfectly aware) in
an occasional desire to slap her. However exasperating she is
at times with her adolescent mixture of private self-pity and
public bumptiousness, she always disarms one by her quite
unusual honesty. She criticises herself as sharply as she criticises others and she draws one so completely into her family
situation with its classic father-mother-daughter tensions that
one is almost more enraged than pitiful when the record is
brutally broken off for ever. Had Anne survived the concentration camp, there is no doubt she would have become a
professional writer. Yet it is possible that she might never have
written anything so vivid, and, at times, so deeply moving as
this journal. . . . What she has left behind is a book of extraordinary human and historical interest, as living as the mischie-
vous, intelligent face in the photograph which confronts the
middle-aged reader with the same shrewd pertness that must
so often have been turned on her parents and the Van Daans.
(pp. 592-93)

Antonia White, "From the Secret Annexe," in The
New Statesman & Nation, *Vol. XLIII, No. 1106, May
17, 1952, pp. 592-93.*

MEYER LEVIN (essay date 1952)

[*An American Jewish writer whose career spans fifty years, Levin
has been a novelist, playwright, short story writer, editor, journalist, and filmmaker. While on assignment as a war correspondent, he was with the liberators of Buchenwald, Dachau, and
other concentration camps. Despite being an eyewitness to the
horrors of camps, he believed he could not write adequately of
the holocaust because he was not himself a victim. After reading
Anne Frank's diary, he was so moved that he wrote a stage version
of the diary that was ultimately rejected by the producers he
submitted it to, allegedly for not being "theatrical enough." Levin,
however, maintained that there was a campaign against him and
his work for being "too Jewish." The Broadway version of the
play,* The Diary of Anne Frank, *written by Frances and Albert
Hackett, appropriated parts of the staging, dialogue, and action*

*of Levin's play; however, it eliminated all of Anne Frank's ref-
erences to hopes for a Jewish homeland and generalized her
concern for the Jews' suffering to a concern for all races who
have suffered. Levin believed that in addition to this being a
falsification of the diary, it was also a personal injustice, and he
took his case to court. Four years of litigation ended in a verdict
for Levin, but a defense motion for a new trial ultimately resulted
in Levin being forced to agree to a ban on any performance of
his version of the Anne Frank play. In the following excerpt from
a review of* Anne Frank: The Diary of a Young Girl, *Levin praises
the work for successfully communicating, in classic form, the
drama of puberty, and he recommends the diary be read both for
insight and enjoyment. He notes that the diary has the tension of
a well-constructed novel, and that it is freed from the mundane
effects of most diaries by presenting the unfolding psychological
drama of Anne Frank's growth and by the physical dangers that
threaten the inhabitants of the annex.*]

Anne Frank's diary is too tenderly intimate a book to be frozen
with the label "classic," and yet no lesser designation serves.
For little Anne Frank, spirited, moody, witty, self-doubting,
succeeded in communicating in virtually perfect, or classic,
form the drama of puberty. But her book is not a classic to be
left on the library shelf. It is a warm and stirring confession,
to be read over and over for insight and enjoyment.

The diary is a classic on another level, too. It happened that
during the two years that mark the most extraordinary changes
in a girl's life, Anne Frank lived in astonishing circumstances:
she was hidden with seven other people in a secret nest of
rooms behind her father's place of business, in Amsterdam.
Thus, the diary tells the life of a group of Jews waiting in fear
of being taken by the Nazis. . . .

This is no lugubrious ghetto tale, no compilation of horrors.
Reality can prove surprisingly different from invented reality,
and Anne Frank's diary simply bubbles with amusement, love,
discovery. It has its share of disgust, its moments of hatred,
but it is so wondrously alive, so near, that one feels overwhelmingly the universalities of human nature. These people
might be living next door; their within-the-family emotions,
their tensions and satisfactions are those of human character
and growth, anywhere.

Because the diary was not written in retrospect, it contains the
trembling life of every moment—Anne Frank's voice becomes
the voice of six million vanished Jewish souls. It is difficult
to say in which respect her book is more "important," but one
forgets the double significance of this document in experiencing
it as an intimate whole, for one feels the presence of this child-
becoming-woman as warmly as though she was snuggled on
a near-by sofa.

We meet Anne on her thirteenth birthday, "Quicksilver Anne"
to her adored father, but "Miss Chatterbox" and "Miss Quack-
Quack," she tells us, to her teacher—for the family is still at
liberty. Indeed, her teacher makes her write a self-curing essay
on chattering; she turns in a poem that convulses teacher and
class, and is allowed to remain her talkative self without further
reprimand.

Yet, with the moodiness of adolescence, she feels lonesome.
"Let me put it more clearly, since no one will believe that a
girl of 13 feels herself quite alone in the world, nor is it so. I
have darling parents and a sister of 16. I know about thirty
people whom one might call friends—I have strings of boy
friends, anxious to catch a glimpse of me, who . . . peep at
me through mirrors in class. I have relations, aunts, uncles,
who are darlings too, a good home, no—I don't seem to lack

anything. But it's the same with all my friends, just fun and nothing more. We don't seem to be able to get any closer, that is the root of the whole trouble. Hence, this diary. I want this diary itself to be my friend, and shall call my friend Kitty.''

What child of 13 hasn't had these feelings, and resolved to confide in a diary? Anne carried it through, never shrinking from revealing the ugly things about herself. . . .

A born writer, Anne zestfully portrays the Annex inhabitants, with all their flaws and virtues. . . . Anne Frank's diary probes far deeper than [John Hersey's] ''The Wall'' into the core of human relations, and succeeds better than ''The Wall'' in bringing us an understanding of life under threat.

And this quality brings it home to any family in the world today. Just as the Franks lived in momentary fear of the Gestapo's knock on their hidden door, so every family today lives in fear of the knock of war. Anne's diary is a great affirmative answer to the life-question of today, for she shows how ordinary people, within this ordeal, consistently hold to the greater human values.

The Frank's Dutch friends in the office on the other side of the secret door sustained them to the end. ''Never have we heard *one* word of the burden which we certainly must be to them. . . . They put on the brightest possible faces, bring flowers and presents for birthdays, risking their own lives to help others.'' These Dutch friends, Miep, Elli, Kraler, Koophuis, even managed to smuggle in Chanukah gifts, and shyly offered their Christmas remembrances to the hidden Jews. (p. 1)

Most wondrous of all is her love affair. Like a flower under a stone fulfilling itself, she came to her first love in her allotted time. ''I give myself completely. But one thing. He may touch my face, but no more.'' All is told, from her potato-fetching devices for going up to Peter's attic lair, to the first misplaced kiss, on her ear. And the parents worrying about the youngsters trysting up there in the dusk, sitting by the window over the canal. And her fears that her older sister is lonely and jealous, leading to an amazing exchange of letters beween the two girls, in those hidden rooms. Finally, there is even the tender disillusionment with Peter, as Anne reaches toward maturity, and a character understanding replaces the first tug of love. In all this there are perceptions in depth, strivings toward mother, father, sister, containing love-anguish of the purest universality.

As is arch-typical for a girl in this period, her relations with her mother are difficult. Unflinchingly, Anne records each incident. ''Dear Kitty—Oh dear, I've got another terrible black mark against my name. I was lying in bed yesterday evening waiting for Daddy to come and say my prayers with me, and wish me good night, when Mummy came into my room, sat on my bed, and asked very nicely, 'Anne, Daddy can't come yet, shall I say your prayers with you tonight?' 'No, Mummy,' I answered.

''Mummy got up, paused by my bed for a moment, and walked slowly toward the door. Suddenly she turned around, and with a distorted look on her face said, 'I don't want to be cross, love cannot be forced.' There were tears in her eyes as she left the room.

''I lay still in bed, feeling at once that I had been horrible to push her away so rudely. . . . It is hard to speak the truth, and yet it is the truth: she herself has pushed me away, her tactless remarks and her crude jokes, which I don't find at all funny, have now made me insensitive to any love from her side.''

But her understanding grew, until she could write, ''The period when I caused Mummy to shed tears is over. I have grown wiser and Mummy's nerves are not so much on edge.''

It is this unfolding psychological drama of a girl's growth, mingled with the physical danger of the group, that frees Anne's book from the horizontal effect of most diaries. Hers rises continuously, with the tension of a well-constructed novel. On the plane of physical suspense, a series of burglaries in the office-warehouse dreadfully endangers the hidden group. And there is the race of the Nazis' intensified hunt for victims, as against the progress of the Allied campaign, followed over a clandestine radio.

Psychologically, the diary contains the completely rounded story of the development of a social nature; one lives in suspense, watching it unfold: will she understand her mother? will she surmount her perplexities? will she comprehend her body-changes, so frankly described?

The girl's last entries rather miraculously contain a climactic summation, a maturing self-analysis: ''If I'm quite serious, everyone thinks it's a comedy, and then I have to get out of it by turning it into a joke,'' she remarks with typical adolescent self-consciousness. ''Finally I twist my heart around again, so that the bad is on the outside and the good is on the inside. . . . I am guided by the pure Anne within, but outside I'm nothing but a frolicsome little goat who's broken loose.''

This frolicsome little goat could write, ''It's twice as hard for us young ones to hold our ground, and maintain our opinions, in a time when all ideals are being shattered and destroyed, when people are showing their worst side, and do not know whether to believe in truth and right and God.

''It's really a wonder that I haven't dropped all my ideals, because they seem so absurd and impossible to carry out. Yet I keep them, because in spite of everything I still believe that people are really good at heart. I simply can't build up my hopes on a foundation consisting of confusion, misery, and death. I see the world gradually being turned into a wilderness. I hear the ever-approaching thunder, which will destroy us too, I can feel the sufferings of millions and yet, if I look up into the heavens, I think that it will all come right, that this cruelty too will end, and that peace and tranquility will return again . . . .''

''I want to go on living even after my death,'' Anne wrote. ''I am grateful to God for giving me this gift, this possibility of developing myself and of writing, of expressing all that is in me.'' Hers was perhaps one of the bodies seen in the mass grave at Bergen-Belsen, for in August, 1944, the knock came on that hidden door in Amsterdam. After the people had been taken away, Dutch friends found Anne's diary in the debris, and saved it.

There is anguish in the thought of how much creative power, how much sheer beauty of living, was cut off through genocide. But through her diary Anne goes on living. From Holland to France, to Italy, Spain. The Germans too have published her book. And now she comes to America. Surely she will be widely loved, for this wise and wonderful young girl brings back a poignant delight in the infinite human spirit. (pp. 1, 22)

*Meyer Levin, ''The Child behind the Secret Door,''
in* The New York Times Book Review, *June 15,
1952, pp. 1, 22.*

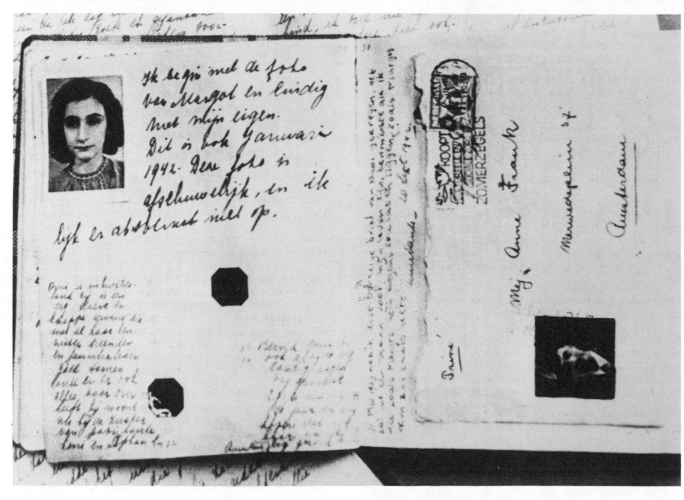

Holograph copy of a portion of Anne's diary. UPI/Bettmann Archive.

DANIEL L. SCHORR   (essay date 1952)

[*Schorr's journalistic career, for which he has received many awards and honors, has included diverse assignments in the United States, Europe, and the Soviet Union. The opening of the CBS news bureau in Moscow, Nikita Khrushchev's first American television interview, and the Watergate investigations have been among his notable assignments. In the following excerpt, Schorr describes the effect of Anne Frank's diary upon the distinguished violinist Isaac Stern after his first reading of the work and after touring the secret annex.*]

Isaac Stern came to town last week for a couple of concerts. He had just finished reading Anne Frank's ***Diary of a Young Girl***. . . . He expressed interest in seeing the house where the Frank family had hidden, and I arranged that for him, going along on the trip. If you've read the book, with its minute details of how the family lived only to be caught by the Gestapo in the end, you'll understand what an emotional experience it was for Isaac and me to be taken through the house by someone who knew the family well and is mentioned in the book. The guide showed Isaac some pictures of the family and gave him one of Anne. Isaac seemed disturbed by the experience, and later, practicing in his hotel room, told me he found it difficult to play that night.

That evening at the Concertgebouw, where he was playing a Beethoven concerto with the Utrecht orchestra, I saw him open

his violin case while looking at Anne Frank's picture, lying next to it. In a rather depressed mood, he went out on the stage to play. The orchestra wasn't very good, but Isaac's playing was consummate; it had a depth and a feeling I'd never heard in him before. He got a tremendous ovation. When he returned to the soloists' room, he glanced at Anne Frank's picture and muttered (I'm sure he didn't know I was listening): "That was for you." (pp. 58-9)

> Daniel L. Schorr, "The Book that Started a Chain Reaction: Later Reactions by Contemporaries," in A Tribute to Anne Frank, *edited by Anna G. Steenmeijer with Otto Frank and Henri Van Praag, Doubleday & Company, Inc., 1971, pp. 58-9.*

ALBRECHT GOES   (essay date 1955)

[*In the following excerpt from his preface to the German translation of Anne Frank's diary, Goes comments upon Frank's intelligence, depth of feeling, and her ability to find a comic element in even the worst situations.*]

Now and then in the course of our life we meet a girl like Anne Frank—not too often, for the level of intelligence, reflectiveness, depth of feeling, and precocity that are revealed in the jottings of this thirteen- or fourteen-year-old are certainly extraordinary. But her cool, keen observation of human beings, and her resolve to be alert to the comic element in even the worst situations, these are familiar to us: they belong to the armor worn by our generation.

We have her diary still, and in that journal a most remarkable document of awakening humanity written down quite without premeditation, and for that very reason absolutely sincere.

It is a dialogue between one "I" and another, between a highly sensitive, thinskinned being and another that seems to be armed with thorns. And it is a dialogue between the one "I" and the surrounding world, a discussion carried on with painstaking exactitude. No one could possibly miss the aggressive note that dominates the dialogue, and no one could miss the second tone that is not dominant and yet is the true keynote of the whole: the note of a genuine ability to love. If the reader is inclined to wonder that we dare to speak of the ability to love in this context, when we are dealing with observations written down by a child—well, there is ample ground for wonder in this book. But at least we must testify that the dialogue between the "I" and the world, set down in these pages, is carried on with almost uncommon instinct for reaching its appointed goal. This young person who loves and hates and struggles and suffers, knows what objectives she must strive towards, what answer is demanded of her by the claims of the hour and those of the nation, which for Anne Frank is Holland—and Israel.

More than a decade has passed now, and life in Amsterdam's Prinsengracht runs its course, as it does everywhere, runs its lively and forgetful course. It is necessary that this voice be heard in the world of 1955, which has not ceased to be a world of concentration camps and persecutions. And one must be ever grateful to the two Hollanders who, in that room ransacked by the Secret Police, hid and kept secure under magazines and newspapers this child's journal—this book that tells the truth without a trace of false ornament, tells the whole truth and nothing but the truth.

> *Albrecht Goes, "The Book that Started a Chain Reaction: Prefaces to the Diary," in* A Tribute to Anne Frank, *edited by Anna G. Steenmeijer with Otto Frank and Henri van Praag, Doubleday & Company, Inc., 1971, p. 35.*

LIES GOSLAR PICK (essay date 1958)

[*The following excerpt is taken from an essay written by a childhood friend of Anne Frank. In the essay, Pick recalls her close friendship with Frank, from their early childhood through the German occupation of Amsterdam, their separation, their reunion at the Bergen-Belsen concentration camp, and her relationship with Otto Frank after the war. The following excerpt contains conversations with Otto Frank and with one of Anne's teachers, who express their surprise at discovering the perceptiveness and writing talent of Anne Frank. Pick concludes her account with some examples of the responses to the dramatized version of the diary in Germany and Amsterdam. For further discussion of Anne by her father, see the excerpt by Otto Frank (1967).*]

One of the questions people often ask me about Anne Frank is whether or not she gave any indication of the remarkable gifts that later illuminated her diary. Millions of readers have marveled that a thirteen-year-old girl, cut off from life before she really experienced it, possessed such mature insight and retained her faith in the essential goodness of humanity.

To be honest, these qualities came as the biggest surprise to the two living people who knew Anne best—her father and me.

"I never realized my little Anna was so deep," Otto Frank sadly admitted to me when her *Diary of a Young Girl* was first published. "Anna developed under our eyes in that room, but we went on treating her as though she still was a giddy little girl. All of us were too wrapped up in our own troubles to give her the understanding she needed." . . .

In desperation Anne turned to young Peter Van Pelz for companionship. But in spite of their tender feelings for each other, in Peter she did not find what she most longed for—"a friend for my understanding." After the first flowering of their romance in the Secret Annexe, she wrote, "Peter hasn't enough character yet, not enough will power, too little courage and strength. He is still a child in his heart of hearts, he is no older than I am. . . ."

Anne might have found the confidante she longed for in her wise and gentle older sister Margot, but her feelings toward Margot were complicated—a mixture of admiration and jealousy.

Anne was especially sensitive to her father's attitude toward Margot. "If he holds Margot up as an example, approves of what she does, praises and caresses her," she wrote early in her days of hiding, "then something gnaws at me inside, because I adore Daddy. He is the one I look up to. . . . He doesn't notice that he treats Margot differently from me. Now Margot is just the prettiest, sweetest, most beautiful girl in the world. But all the same I feel I have some right to be taken seriously too. I have always been the dunce, the ne'er-do-well of the family."

Margot was graduated with honors from school. Anne was an indifferent student. . . .

Serious Margot was studying to be a nurse in Palestine. Frivolous Anne (she calls herself "superficial" in her diary) was interested mainly in dates, clothes and parties. Margot never gave her parents a moment's trouble. Anne was a mischief-maker who annoyed the neighbors with her pranks and continually was in hot water at school for her conduct.

If I had been asked to guess which girl's diary would someday be worth publishing, I would certainly have said Margot's. Oddly enough, Margot's diary was a very average, pedestrian kind of record. I know because by accident I had a chance to read it. The day after the Franks went into hiding, my mother sent me to their apartment just across the street to get a kitchen scale before everything was confiscated by the Germans. As I was leaving, I saw Margot's diary on a table and took it out of sheer curiosity. Although I knew that I shouldnt' read it, I couldn't resist. I was disappointed. Nothing appeared to be terribly important to Margot. . . .

In Amsterdam I went to see Mrs. Kuperus, headmistress at the Montessori School, which has been renamed the Anne Frank School. After we had exchanged tearful reminiscences of Anne, I asked Mrs. Kuperus the question so many people have asked me: Did Anne show any early promise of her unusual talents? Mrs. Kuperus hesitated a long moment.

"In all honesty I cannot say she did," she replied. "In my years of teaching I've never known a child who changed so remarkably in such a short time. The compositions Anne wrote in school were just ordinary, no better than average. Many pupils wrote with more imagination and feeling than Anne. I've reread the diary many times looking for clues to the amazing transformation in her, but I still don't know what caused it."

I myself believe it was a combination of things—the long hours of enforced reflection, the tragic intensity of the situation in which she and her family were living, and the flowering of her own physical maturity and her first love. (p. 109)

It is impossible for people who have not lived under Nazi oppression to appreciate fully the influence of Anne's diary in Germany. When the play opened simultaneously in seven German cities on October 1, 1956, every account reported an identical reaction. Audiences were so stunned they remained in their seats five minutes after the final curtain fell. The reporter from Berlin commented: "When movies actually taken in a concentration camp were shown to German audiences just after the end of the war they were received with derision and disbelief. . . . But the reception . . . given to this play was different. The impact of its portrayal of the horrors of Naziism struck home, as the silence that greeted most of the performance showed." . . .

There was a good deal of opposition to presenting the play in Amsterdam because of the fear that it would revive bitter memories of the German occupation. Queen Juliana and Prince Bernhard abruptly ended those weaseling objections by attending the première and recommending the play to all Dutchmen as an object lesson in the nobility of the human spirit. It made such a profound impression on my former countrymen that they raised a fund to convert the Secret Annexe into the Anne Frank Youth Center.

Since the war many eloquent books have been written denouncing the Nazis for their crimes against humanity. Anne never accused the Germans of atrocities or railed against them for isolating her from life, yet her simple story has moved more people than all the other books combined. The best explanation of this phenomenon I ever have heard came from Otto Frank in New York last November.

"Anna told the gentile world what it meant to be a Jew without preaching propaganda," he said. "The Germans never will admit they knew what happened to six million Jews, but Anna made them feel guilty as individuals by showing what persecution had done to one innocent girl. Anna's diary has been such a force for good in changing German attitudes because she aroused pity rather than anger." . . .

Everyone who has read the diary has been inspired by a favorite passage. The lines quoted most often were written by Anne after she had been in hiding more than two years. "It's really a wonder that I haven't dropped all my ideals, because they seem so absurd and impossible to carry out. Yet I keep them, because in spite of everything I still believe that people are really good at heart. I simply can't build up my hopes on a foundation consisting of confusion, misery, and death. I see the world gradually being turned into a wilderness, I hear the ever approaching thunder, which will destroy us too. I can feel the sufferings of millions and yet, if I look up into the heavens, I think that it will all come right, that this cruelty too will end, and that peace and tranquillity will return again." (p. 110)

Lies Goslar Pick, "I Knew Anne Frank," in McCall's, Vol. LXXXV, No. 10, July, 1958, pp. 30-1, 109-11, 114-15.

RABBI PHILIP S. BERNSTEIN   (essay date 1958)

[In the following excerpt from his address to the annual conference of the National Youth Aliyah Committee of Hadassah in New York City, Bernstein condemns the Nazis, but challenges his audience to go beyond judging the Nazis by realizing their own participation in the Jewish Holocaust through their silence, and to be constructive and humane, in the spirit of Anne Frank, in current crises.]

No one, whether he be a Nazi, or a communist, or a segregationist, has the right to deny life, liberty, or the opportunity for happiness to a child because of some doctrine that he holds. Perhaps there is a special danger in such doctrines in the lives of men who deny God. For a belief in God makes for humility, for charity, for a recognition of the fact that our basic rights coming from God, no man, no group, no state may take them away.

To hold this point of view in today's world takes courage. It takes courage in the South for a Jew to stand up for equal rights for the Negro and particularly for the Negro child. But how can he condemn those who refused to help Jews in Holland or Germany, or applaud those that did, if he himself lacks the courage to display the right attitude in the current color crisis? This brings home the sense of universal responsibility. Of course, the Nazis were beasts and history will never forgive them, but how about the decent Germans who did not stand up against them, how about the German Jews who did not become disturbed when they thought the Nazis were directing their assault only on the Polish Jews? How about the Western governments that summoned phony refugee conferences which only highlighted their unwillingness to let Jews in? How about Americans whose attitude toward emergency immigration was guided by bigotry rather than by Christian charity? And how about the Jews, us, who insisted upon our comforts, our luxuries, our normalcy after which we gave a limited way to the U.J.A. or to Youth Aliyah, or to any of the causes which if supported adequately might have saved many more Jews? No man is an island unto himself, that is what we have learned. And no one can free himself from some responsibility, yes, some guilt. That's what the diary of Anne Frank teaches us. It also says something else which is particularly needed today. We live in a world of mass cruelty in which the H-bomb has broken through the barriers of civilian compassion. We live in a time in which all young people are being trained to kill. We live in a world of potential horrors undreamed of by our primitive ancestors. It is desperately important that we keep pity and kindness and love alive in the world. This is exceedingly difficult in a world of mass cruelty, but is all the more necessary.

Rabbi Philip S. Bernstein, "The Book that Started a Chain Reaction: Later Reactions by Contemporaries," in A Tribute to Anne Frank, *edited by Anna G. Steenmeijer with Otto Frank and Henri Van Praag, Doubleday & Company, Inc., 1971, p. 58.*

ANN BIRSTEIN AND ALFRED KAZIN   (essay date 1959)

[Birstein is a novelist, short story writer, and essayist, while her husband Kazin is a highly respected American literary critic who is best known for his essay collections The Inmost Leaf (1955) and Contemporaries (1962), and particularly for On Native Grounds (1942), a study of American prose writing since the era of William Dean Howells. Having studied the works of "the critics who were the best writers—from Sainte-Beuve and Matthew Arnold to Edmund Wilson and Van Wyck Brooks" as an aid to his own critical understanding, Kazin has found that "criticism focussed many— if by no means all—of my own urges as a writer: to show literature as a deed in human history, and to find in each writer the uniqueness of the gift, of the essential vision, through which I hoped to penetrate into the mystery and sacredness of the individual soul." In the following excerpt from their introduction to The Works of Anne Frank, Birstein and Kazin focus on the sensibility of the

author: her ambivalence toward her own experience, her sense
of an unseen audience, her interpretation of ordinary events, her
emphasis on moral accountability, her compassion for suffering
humanity, and her search for the meaning of life.]

For two years before her arrest [Anne Frank] wrote all the time. She wrote while she was in hiding from the Nazis and could not take one step outdoors or in the daytime speak above a whisper. She wrote although the bombs came down so heavily at night that she fled for comfort into her father's bed. She wrote so steadily that by the time she was fifteen she had finished the equivalent of two books, one the **Diary**, the other a collection of short stories, essays, and reminiscences. (pp. 9-10)

In a certain sense . . . it isn't fair to call **The Diary of a Young Girl** a diary at all, since from the very first it was more to her than a purely personal record of triumphs and defeats. Always she had toward her own experience the marvelous ambivalence of the born novelist, and immediately after claiming that "neither I—nor for that matter anyone else—will be interested in the unbosomings of a thirteen-year-old schoolgirl," on the very same page of her journal she has already chosen a literary form—the entries will be in the shape of letters to an imaginary girl named Kitty—and embarked on a concise sketch, not only of her own life, but of general conditions in Holland. This same uncanny sense of an unseen audience, actually of posterity, prevails throughout her work. Scared out of her wits as she must have been when she went into hiding, one of the first things she writes about it is a detailed description of the hiding place and the bits and pieces of furnishings that went into it. When new people arrive, first the Van Daans and then Dussel, the dentist, she has them down on paper practically the minute they are through the door. With a writer's eye for how much is implied in the ordinary events of an ordinary day, she describes a typical morning, afternoon, and evening in the annexe; how they went to the toilet; where they slept; what they talked about while they peeled potatoes and shelled peas and stuffed sausages. She fell in love with the boy upstairs, yearned desperately for her first kiss, and in the breathless moment before it finally came broke into tears—which she described meticulously: "I sat pressed closely against him and felt a wave of emotion come over me, tears sprang into my eyes, the left one trickled onto his dungarees. Did he notice? He made no move or sign to show that he did. . . . At half past eight I stood up and went to the window, where we always say good-by. . . . He came toward me, I flung my arms around his neck and gave him a kiss on his left cheek, and was about to kiss the other cheek, when my lips met his and we pressed them together."

To everything that happened to her, to everything that she felt, Anne gave a kind of permanence by transcribing it, and day after day she went on adding still another segment to the world she was creating. In the stories, where she chose her subjects, this world is not so real. But in her diary, where her subject chose her, its vividness and poignance are overwhelming. . . . What makes her achievement really amazing is how little, aside from her own natural gifts of observation and her sense of humor, she had to work with. Other people have countrysides and multitudes. For Anne, the one boy upstairs was love; a single chestnut tree seen from her window, nature; a patch of blue sky—heaven. No wonder that soon she began to think of her diary and some of her sketches as the basis for a book after the war. *Het Achterhuis (The House Behind)* she meant to call it—a perfect title for the first book of a young girl, suggesting

mystery and suspense and excitement; she even had a list of pseudonyms for the people in it. . . . (pp. 11-13)

But the duality of Anne's nature, that quality of mind that made her turn to her writing for solace and relief, that made of her diary her "only friend" and the first thing she packed when she went into hiding, was exactly what would not let her rest. Like all young growing things, Anne, forced into a premature ripeness by the terrible intensity of events, yearned and struggled for the light. It was not enough to take her own little part in the day's happenings, to chatter and laugh and cry with everyone else; the spectator in her kept pressing her to ask the meaning of it all, kept goading her into a search that could only take her deeper and deeper into the most painful realms of solitude. We tend to think of Anne now as pure innocence in captivity. But her mind and heart were never held captive by herself or anyone, and as for her innocence—it was the last thing she ever thought about. On the contrary, she wanted to take it all on her own shoulders, she considered herself responsible for everything, not only her own destiny—if she was permitted to live it out—but also the fate of everyone else who suffered. ". . . I believe," she said, "that God wants to try me . . ." And this theme of being tested through confinement is repeated in her stories of Blurry, the Explorer, the bear who goes out to see the world and is locked up instead, and of Dora and Peldron, the two elves who are imprisoned by a wise dwarf and emerge improved by their experience. Somehow, Anne, too, would come out a better person, if only she were good and strong enough. Of course it was hard, agonizingly hard, to keep herself to such a strict moral accounting, especially when everything outside beckoned so sweetly: "The sun is shining, the sky is a deep blue, there is a lovely breeze and I'm longing—so longing—for everything. To talk, for freedom, for friends, to be alone. And I do so long . . . to cry!" . . . But still she kept at it, crying herself out when she could, and then trying to unloose her own pity for herself into a great stream of compassion for all suffering humanity. How could she feel sorry for herself when just outside her door children were running about half naked, begging food from passers-by, and people did not dare leave their homes for fear that when they came back no one would be left in them? It was not enough to be glad of her own precarious safety; one had to ask why even this was denied others. (pp. 13-14)

Child or not, anyone who asks such questions can never find an answer, only the strength of spirit to go on searching. Anne found her strength in her love of the very world which was denied her. (p. 14)

Anne Frank has become a universal legend. Out of the millions who were gassed, burned, shot, hanged, starved, tortured, buried alive, the young girl who died so "peacefully" in Bergen-Belsen, almost in unconscious sympathy with her dead sister Margot, has become a prime symbol of the innocence of all those who died in the middle of the twentieth century at the hands of the most powerful state in western Europe. Perhaps more than any of the known dead, and certainly more than the now nameless ones who died scratching the ceilings of the gas chambers in the last agonized struggle against death, the girl born in Frankfurt of an upper-class Jewish family, whose father was a German officer in World War I, has become the personal example of the heartlessness, the bestiality, the still unbelievable cruelty of Germans in World War II. Upon her, at least, all agree; in her all peoples, in the uneasy peace since 1945 that is no peace, can find a moment's occasion for compassion and awareness. When *The Diary of Anne Frank* was produced on the Dutch stage, royalty wept; and . . . Germans who had wept for no one but themselves, who had not allowed themselves to recognize the horror in their midst, who laughed in derision when they were made to see films of Auschwitz and Buchenwald, have wept in theaters over Anne Frank. (pp. 17-18)

The production of *Das Tagebuch der Anne Frank* coincided with what in certain intellectual circles became a pro-Jewish philosophy, a return to the abstraction of the "noble Jew" among the German intellectuals of the Enlightenment. It is for this reason that Anne Frank has symbolized so much—so peculiarly much—in current German thought. (p. 19)

The figure of universally accepted innocence, a young girl, is so perfect a subject that young people can identify with her; older people can pity her; the world can almost believe that it has made peace with itself over the unknown grave of Anne Frank. During the height of the German emotion over the play, reports Alfred Werner, a few Germans protested that "the play might be letting the Germans off too lightly, that it did not even begin to suggest how frightful were the German actions" [see Additional Bibliography]. Yet it is also a fact that it is impossible to make artistic use of the worst horrors of the concentration camps. *The Diary Of Anne Frank* does not deal with horror—at least not directly; yet this, though it makes it too easy for all of us not to think of the horror at all, is also what makes both book and play *possible*. It was not only Germans who laughed derisively when shown the first films of the concentration camps; so did the English in Piccadilly newsreel theaters. The fact is that certain events in our time, prime and unforgettable images of human suffering and degradation, seem incredible to us even when we remember them, and are ungraspable even when we face them. (pp. 20-1)

Anne Frank's diary has rarely been subjected to criticism. The dramatic economy of the book has moved its readers just as much as the fate of its author has served as an occasion of emotion. Yet it has been suggested that Anne was unable to confront the hideousness of her experience, that her diary was an escape into the ideal. And in one sense this "evasion" of reality, if one may so call it, though improbable coming from people who have never had to face anything like Anne Frank's experience, is perfectly true. It may be that the "ideal" quality of the book accounts for the universal acceptance of the *Diary;* has made it possible for Germans to ease their souls sitting in a theater; for Jews to honor their dead; for the Dutch and the French to remember their suffering under the occupation; for adolescent children to take imaginative refuge from their problems. And yet it is a fact that Anne Frank's wholly domestic picture of life works toward the understanding of her true situation, rather than the other way around. For truthfully direct "war literature," naked shots of the ultimate horror, are hard for everyone to get down—this is as true for the victims' kin as it is for the Germans eager to evade responsibility; they stupefy instead of awakening us. The last shudder of death, the shriek of crucifixion—these really belong to death, not life. If we are still in danger of evading the full truth of Nazism, we are also in danger, when we think we are confronting the truth, of adding to the extreme abstractness and tension of the human spirit which represents Nazism, with its insatiable slogans and its monolithic sense of truth. The enemy of Nazism is its enemy because it is different from Nazism in kind, in intention, in the spirit with which it addresses itself to life. In the "ideal" world of Anne Frank's diary, in the preoccupation with potato peels, a young girl's discovery of puberty, there

is the truth of life as human curiosity and sensitivity and fellowship—while outside, the green and gray German army lorries trundle past bearing their helpless Jewish victims to the slaughter heap.

The Diary of a Young Girl has survived its author and most of her family, as it has already survived so many books about the war, because the faithfulness with which it records an unusual experience reminds us—as opposition to Nazism on its own terms never can—of the sweetness and goodness that are possible in a world where a few souls still have good will. The *Diary* moves us because its author had the strength to see, to remember, to hope. (pp. 22-3)

> *Ann Birstein and Alfred Kazin, in an introduction to* The Works of Anne Frank *by Anne Frank, Doubleday & Company, Inc., 1959, pp. 9-24.*

FREDERIC MORTON   (essay date 1959)

[*In the following excerpt from a review of* The Works of Anne Frank, *Morton posits that the appearance of Frank's creative writings and the passage of time make it possible to focus on and critically appraise Frank the writer. While he commends her for following the platitude "Write whereof you know," he states that none of her essays or works of short fiction has the power of any single entry of her diary.*]

It may well be that the single most enduring thing to be born during the entire course of the Nazi nightmare was a book a young Jewish girl wrote in the occupied Holland of the early Forties. Anne Frank's diary of the years spent in the few cubic feet of her family's hide-out has become familiar to the world as an international best seller, as a dramatization that has moved audiences in every major country, and as a motion picture.

Now Anne is being published again; this time the diary together with all her other writings extant, and a deeply felt introduction by Ann Birstein and Alfred Kazin [see excerpt dated 1959]. The new writings [*The Works of Anne Frank*] consist of stories, fables, essays and reminiscences found by Dutch friends in notebooks.

Today many will be able to extend to Anne Frank that full critical justice they couldn't help withholding earlier. For the shock accompanying the first appearance of the diary was so great that it focused attention only on Anne the victim. It was almost easy to forget Anne the writer, who made her victimization so memorable. . . .

[The] illumination of these new pages is important. They show that Anne followed instinctively the best of all platitudes: Write whereof you know. Not even her little fairy tales are easy escapes into make-believe, but rather pointed allegories of reality—the two elves who are imprisoned together to learn tolerance; or Blurry the Baby who runs away from home to find the great, free, open world, and never does. At the other end of the gamut we find **"My First Article."** It is a thorough journalistic account of Peter Van Daan's small room (the Van Daans shared the hiding place with the Franks). Her infatuation for the boy sets aglow the skimpy catalogue of furnishings. Through her words glimmers the prisoner's secret fondness for the universe that is his cell.

Still none of these places, not even a charming little morality tale like **"The Wise Old Dwarf,"** has the power of any single entry in the diary. Anne's stories show an occasional leaning to rhetoric quite inevitable in a 15-year-old who sits down "to write." And the obligation she seems to have felt to give most efforts a didactic turn reflects her background as a rather stringently brought up child (by American standards) in a German-Jewish home. But the little author's ebullience keeps breaking through her stiffest intentions. In "**Kitty**" she sets out to write a rather formal composition about an imaginary girl next door. Before long she stops composing and simply bubbles on, with an entirely incidental perceptiveness about all girlhood.

Indeed, as I reread the diary in the light of her other works I realized that Anne, like any true writer, was at her best when, without self-consciousness or elaborate device, she poured out her own personality. Such enormously difficult simplicity is the hallmark of her journal. Not even terror or the most painful constraint could deprive her of a wonderfully feminine, young, vital responsiveness.

Somehow she preserved enough of the teen-ager's normal frivolities and irresponsibilities—enough to make her abnormal plight comprehensible to a generation who could read her in an armchair under an open sky. She has shown us that it is possible to remain human as long as we are alive.

Frederic Morton, "Her Literary Legacy," in The New York Times Book Review, *September 20, 1959, p. 22.*

HENRY F. POMMER (essay date 1960)

[In the following excerpt, Pommer surveys the critical response to Anne Frank's diary, and traces Frank's development as a writer, concluding that the chief literary merit of the diary is that it allows readers to intimately know its many-faceted author. Pommer also states that the diary is important for its moral significance.]

The quality of both her death and her life have given Anne Frank an extraordinary status in our culture. Antigone represents a willingness to die for principles; Juliet's is the tragedy of ironic confusion; Marguerite was the victim of her own and Faust's sensuality; St. Joan was martyred by jealous institutions. Anne was destroyed by a pattern of evil perhaps not unique to our century, but at least unique within Western culture of the past two thousand years.

But her fame rests on knowledge of her life as much as of her death. She is not a fictional character like Juliet or Tolstoy's Natasha, nor a girl with wide-spread and immediate effects like St. Joan or the young Cleopatra. Yet she shares with Cleopatra and St. Joan the fact of being historical; and her life is already, like theirs, the source of a legend. As an historical figure relatively unimportant to her immediate contemporaries but affecting a larger and larger circle after her death, she is most like St. Thérèse of Lisieux. But over all these girls from Antigone to St. Thérèse, Anne has the great advantage that she left a diary. Therefore, we need not know her through the documents of her contemporaries or the professional imagination of middle-aged authors. Her legend lacks the support of patriotic and ecclesiastical power, but it has the strength of her authentic, self-drawn portrait. (p. 37)

Some writers have considered the diary as primarily "one of the most moving stories that anyone, anywhere, has managed to tell about World War II." At Oradour-sur-Glane, where Nazis wantonly destroyed the entire population, is printed "Remember," and in the ruins of bomb-destroyed Coventry has been carved "Father Forgive." Anne's diary helps us remember what there is to forgive. (p. 38)

[The] truths of Anne's history, the bitter as well as the sweet, are not about Germans alone or Dutchmen or Jews, but humanity. And these truths must be recalled whenever we try to measure human nature, to estimate its heights and depths, its capacities for good and evil. The extremes of cruelty temper all our hopes. On the other hand, a young person is supposed to have once asked Justice Felix Frankfurter "And how do you know that the human race is *worth* saving?" The Justice replied, "I have read Anne Frank's diary."

A second group of critics has praised the diary as primarily an intimate account of adolescence. For these it is of only secondary importance that Anne hid with her family in an attic of old Amsterdam; of primary importance is her frankness in telling what it is like to grow up. (p. 40)

Often she was difficult to live with. Tensions were almost inevitable for eight people living with so many restrictions in such cramped quarters, but Anne seems to have done more than her share to stir up ill will. She had a temper, and was not always either anxious or able to control it. At times she must have been obnoxiously precocious in telling the other hiders what they were like; she may have appeared very patronizing at times, particularly in dealing with Margot about Peter. She was very critical of her mother, very fond of her father, and from time to time hurt both of them deeply. Her sense of justice, her loathing of whatever was pompous or artificial, and her desire to be treated as an adult led to frequent quarrels with Mr. and Mrs. Van Daan, and with Mr. Dussel.

Bit by bit, however, these evidences of immaturity and of being difficult decrease. Mixed with them, yet gradually replacing them, came the actions and reactions of a more mature young woman. (pp. 40-1)

Any diary of a young girl who hid in Amsterdam during the Nazi occupation, who described her first protracted love affair, and who was a person of breeding, humor, religious sensitivity, and courage might well interest us. But Anne had one further trait of the utmost importance for her own maturity and for what she wrote: an unusual ability for self-analysis. She knew she had moods, and she could write eloquently about them—about loneliness, for example. But she could also step outside her moods in order to evaluate them and herself in them. (p. 43)

One of the clearest evidences of objectivity was her ability to see a moral ambiguity in her enjoying relative security while other Jews suffered worse fates:

> I saw two Jews through the curtain yesterday.
> I could hardly believe my eyes; it was a horrible
> feeling, just as if I'd betrayed them and was
> now watching them in their misery.

This is the honesty concerning oneself out of which are born humor, maturity, and one kind of ability to write well.

Anne could write well. Her self-consciousness and skill as an author receive only implicit acknowledgement if we regard her diary as no more than an educative historical document or an intimate disclosure of adolescence. W. A. Darlington is probably correct in predicting that

> in time to come, when the horrors of Nazi occupation in Europe are no longer quite so fresh in quite so many minds and "The Diary of Anne Frank" comes to be judged purely on its merits as a play, the piece will . . . lose its place on the stage.

But Anne's diary may have a longer life. It is, to be sure, a mixture of good and bad writing—but so, too, are the diaries of Pepys, Samuel Sewall, and William Byrd.

Some people have combed the external record of Anne's life for evidence of her ability as a writer. (pp. 43-4)

It was to be expected that little external evidence of Anne's talent would be found. When she went into hiding, she was not a diarist worthy of much attention. During the twenty-five months in the Secret Annexe, the world of her thought was a secret within a secret—a secret so well kept that even her father confessed, when the diary was first published, "I never realized my little Anna was so deep." After she had left the Annexe, the brutality of guards, shortages of food, epidemics of disease, separation from loved ones, and the prospect of gas chambers must have left Anne little time to think about writing, and certainly gave her companions little interest in what her literary talents might be. Ever so much more important was whether she could beg a piece of zwieback.

When we turn to the diary itself, we find that if her affair with Peter is the most striking measure of her change towards maturity, the second most striking is the clarification of her desire to be a writer. The third entry begins the development.

> I haven't written for a few days, because I wanted first of all to think about my diary. It's an odd idea for someone like me to keep a diary; not only because I have never done so before, but because it seems to me that neither I—nor for that matter anyone else—will be interested in the unbosomings of a thirteen-year-old schoolgirl. Still, what does that matter? I want to write, but more than that, I want to bring out all kinds of things that lie buried deep in my heart. . . .
>
> There is no doubt that paper is patient and as I don't intend to show this . . . "diary," to anyone, unless I find a real friend, boy or girl, probably nobody cares. And now I come to the root of the matter, the reason for my starting a diary: it is that I have no such real friend. . . .
>
> It's the same with all my friends, just fun and joking, nothing more. I can never bring myself to talk of anything outside the common round. . . .
>
> Hence, this diary. In order to enhance in my mind's eye the picture of the friend for whom I have waited so long, I don't want to set down a series of bald facts in a diary like most people do, but I want this diary itself to be my friend, and I shall call my friend Kitty.

After this early entry the diary shows a progressively self-conscious artistry reflected in the beginnings of certain letters to Kitty such as

> Now that we have been in the "Secret Annexe" for over a year, you know something of our lives, but some of it is quite indescribable. . . . To give you a closer look . . . , now and again I intend to give you a description of an ordinary day. Today I'm beginning with the evening and the night. . . . (August 4, 1943).

> I asked myself this morning whether you don't sometimes feel rather like a cow who has had to chew over all the old pieces of news again and again, and who finally yawns loudly and silently wishes that Anne would occasionally find something new. . . . (January 28, 1944).

> Perhaps it would be entertaining for you—though not in the least for me—to hear what we are going to eat today. . . . (March 14, 1944).

That her diary might itself be the basis of a published work may not have occurred to Anne before March 29, 1944, when

> Bolkestein, an M.P., was speaking on the Dutch News from London, and . . . said that they ought to make a collection of diaries and letters after the war. Of course, they all made a rush at my diary immediately. Just imagine how interesting it would be if I were to publish a romance of the "Secret Annexe." The title alone would be enough to make people think it was a detective story.
>
> But, seriously, it would seem quite funny ten years after the war if we Jews were to tell how we lived and what we ate and talked about here.
>
> (pp. 44-5)

After the entry of March 29, Anne's expressed desires to be a journalist, and then a famous writer, grew more numerous. Writing would, she hoped, enable her to live after her death; she wrote short stories, even wanting to submit them for publication. (p. 45)

The chief literary merit of the diary is its permitting us to know intimately Anne's young, eager, difficult, lovable self. We follow the quick alternations of her great gaiety and sometimes equally great depression, and we benefit from the introspections generated by her sharply contrasting moods. Some pages read as though they had been written in the security of a Long Island suburbia; on the next page we are plunged into Nazi terror; and both passages use vivid details. Sometimes our delight is simply in her charm, as in "Daddy always says I'm prudish and vain but that's not true. I'm just simply vain." At other times her wisdom surprises us, as in her distinction that "laziness may *appear* attractive, but work *gives* satisfaction." She sensed the need for variety in reporting, and used effective techniques for achieving it. Life in the Secret Annexe was terribly repetitious, but there is little repetition in the diary itself.

Even if the last entry told of Jews liberated by the arrival of Allied armies in Amsterdam, the book would still have real interest and value. And it would still have its chief moral significance. Both diary and play illustrate D. H. Lawrence's contention that

> the essential function of art is moral. Not aesthetic, nor decorative, not pastime and recreation. But moral. . . . But a passionate, implicit morality, not didactic. A morality which changes the blood, rather than the mind. Changes the blood first. The mind follows later in the wake.

Because of Anne Frank's art, this change in blood and then in mind sometimes takes the direction of brotherhood. At those moments her legend receives fresh life, and her adolescent

The warehouse containing the "secret annex." The Granger Collection, New York.

record of history helps to make history less adolescent. (pp. 45-6)

> Henry F. Pommer, "The Legend and Art of Anne Frank," in Judaism, Vol. 9, No. 1, Winter, 1960, pp. 37-46.

BRUNO BETTELHEIM (essay date 1960)

[*An Austrian-born American psychologist, author, and educator specializing in child development, Bettelheim has written prolifically on the subject of emotional disturbances in children. Considered by many critics to be among the most prominent and innovative of Freudian theorists, he is the author of* The Uses of Enchantment: The Meaning and Importance of Fairy Tales *(1976), a critically acclaimed work which examines the healthy, cathartic aspects of fantasy for children. A survivor of the Nazi concentration camps, in which he was incarcerated from 1938 to 1939, Bettelheim is also renowned for his essay "Individual and Mass Behavior in Extreme Situations," which attracted worldwide attention and is based on his observations of fellow prisoners in the camps. In the following excerpt from a later essay, originally published in 1960, he examines Anne Frank's experience from a psychological and sociological point of view, urging people to learn from her tragedy how to increase their chances of surviving extremely threatening situations. While agreeing that Frank's story is a humane and moving one, and that worldwide compassion for her is well merited, he is alarmed by the uncritical response to the Franks' plan of action and their passivity which, he contends, may have led them unnecessarily to their deaths. He interprets the acclaim for and uncritical response to the story as indications of people's tendency to want to forget the gas chambers and cling to the reassuring, but delusional, notion that people can carry on normal lives amidst horrifying circumstances.*]

The extraordinary world-wide success of the book, play, and movie *The Diary of Anne Frank* suggests the power of the desire to counteract the realization of the personality-destroying and murderous nature of the camps by concentrating all attention on what is experienced as a demonstration that private and intimate life can continue to flourish even under the direct persecution by the most ruthless totalitarian system. And this although Anne Frank's fate demonstrates how efforts at disregarding in private life what goes on around one in society can hasten one's own destruction.

What concerns me here is not what actually happened to the Frank family, how they tried—and failed—to survive their terrible ordeal. It would be very wrong to take apart so humane and moving a story, which aroused so much well-merited compassion for gentle Anne Frank and her tragic fate. What is at issue is the universal and uncritical response to her diary and to the play and movie based on it, and what this reaction tells about our attempts to cope with the feelings her fate—used by us to serve as a symbol of a most human reaction to Nazi terror—arouses in us. I believe that the world-wide acclaim given her story cannot be explained unless we recognize in it our wish to forget the gas chambers, and our effort to do so by glorifying the ability to retreat into an extremely private, gentle, sensitive world, and there to cling as much as possible to what have been one's usual daily attitudes and activities, although surrounded by a maelstrom apt to engulf one at any moment.

The Frank family's attitude that life could be carried on as before may well have been what led to their destruction. By eulogizing how they lived in their hiding place while neglecting to examine first whether it was a reasonable or an effective choice, we are able to ignore the crucial lesson of their story—that such an attitude can be fatal in extreme circumstances.

While the Franks were making their preparations for going passively into hiding, thousands of other Jews in Holland (as elsewhere in Europe) were trying to escape to the free world, in order to survive and/or fight. Others who could not escape went underground—into hiding—each family member with, for example, a different gentile family. We gather from the diary, however, that the chief desire of the Frank family was to continue living as nearly as possible in the same fashion to which they had been accustomed in happier times. (pp. 247-48)

The Franks were unable to accept that going on living as a family as they had done before the Nazi invasion of Holland was no longer a desirable way of life, much as they loved each other; in fact, for them and others like them, it was most dangerous behavior. But even given their wish not to separate, they failed to make appropriate preparations for what was likely to happen.

There is little doubt that the Franks, who were able to provide themselves with so much while arranging for going into hiding, and even while hiding, could have provided themselves with some weapons had they wished. Had they had a gun, Mr. Frank could have shot down at least one or two of the "green police" who came for them. There was no surplus of such police, and the loss of an SS with every Jew arrested would have noticeably hindered the functioning of the police state. Even a butcher knife, which they certainly could have taken with them into hiding, could have been used by them in self-defense. The fate of the Franks wouldn't have been very different, because they all died anyway except for Anne's father. But they could have sold their lives for a high price, instead of walking to their death. Still, although one must assume that Mr. Frank would have fought courageously, as we know he did when a soldier in the first World War, it is not everybody who can plan to kill those who are bent on killing him, although many who would not be ready to contemplate doing so would be willing to kill those who are bent on murdering not only them but also their wives and little daughters.

An entirely different matter would have been planning for escape in case of discovery. The Franks' hiding place had only one entrance; it did not have any other exit. Despite this fact, during their many months of hiding, they did not try to devise one. Nor did they make other plans for escape, such as that one of the family members—as likely as not Mr. Frank—would try to detain the police in the narrow entrance way—maybe even fight them, as suggested above—thus giving other members of the family a chance to escape, either by reaching the roofs of adjacent houses, or down a ladder into the alley behind the house in which they were living.

Any of this would have required recognizing and accepting the desperate straits in which they found themselves, and concentrating on how best to cope with them. This was quite possible to do, even under the terrible conditions in which the Jews found themselves after the Nazi occupation of Holland. (pp. 248-49)

This is not mentioned as a criticism that the Frank family did not plan or behave along similar lines. A family has every right to arrange their life as they wish or think best, and to take the risks they want to take. My point is not to criticize what the Franks did, but only the universal admiration of their way of coping, or rather of not coping. (pp. 249-50)

Many Jews—unlike the Franks, who through listening to British radio news were better informed than most—had no detailed knowledge of the extermination camps. Thus it was easier for them to make themselves believe that complete compliance with even the most outrageously debilitating and degrading Nazi orders might offer a chance for survival. But neither tremendous anxiety that inhibits clear thinking and with it well-planned and determined action, nor ignorance about what happened to those who responded with passive waiting for being rounded up for their extermination, can explain the reaction of audiences to the play and movie retelling Anne's story, which are all about such waiting that results finally in destruction.

I think it is the fictitious ending that explains the enormous success of this play and movie. At the conclusion we hear Anne's voice from the beyond, saying, ''In spite of everything, I still believe that people are really good at heart.'' This improbable sentiment is supposedly from a girl who had been starved to death, had watched her sister meet the same fate before she did, knew that her mother had been murdered, and had watched untold thousands of adults and children being killed. This statement is not justified by anything Anne actually told her diary.

Going on with intimate family living, no matter how dangerous it might be to survival, was fatal to all too many during the Nazi regime. And if all men are good, then indeed we can all go on with living our lives as we have been accustomed to in times of undisturbed safety and can afford to forget about Auschwitz. But Anne, her sister, her mother, may well have died because her parents could not get themselves to believe in Auschwitz.

While play and movie are ostensibly about Nazi persecution and destruction, in actuality what we watch is the way that, despite this terror, lovable people manage to continue living their satisfying intimate lives with each other. The heroine grows from a child into a young adult as normally as any other girl would, despite the most abnormal conditions of all other aspects of her existence, and that of her family. Thus the play reassures us that despite the destructiveness of Nazi racism and tyranny in general, it is possible to disregard it in one's private life much of the time, even if one is Jewish.

True, the ending happens just as the Franks and their friends had feared all along: their hiding place is discovered, and they are carried away to their doom. But the fictitious declaration of faith in the goodness of all men which concludes the play falsely reassures us since it impresses on us that in the combat between Nazi terror and continuance of intimate family living the latter wins out, since Anne has the last word. This is simply contrary to fact, because it was she who got killed. Her seeming survival through her moving statement about the goodness of men releases us effectively of the need to cope with the problems Auschwitz presents. That is why we are so relieved by her statement. It explains why millions loved play and movie, because while it confronts us with the fact that Auschwitz existed, it encourages us at the same time to ignore any of its implications. If all men are good at heart, there never really was an Auschwitz; nor is there any possibility that it may recur.

The desire of Anne Frank's parents not to interrupt their intimate family living, and their inability to plan more effectively for their survival, reflect the failure of all too many others faced with the threat of Nazi terror. It is a failure that deserves close examination because of the inherent warnings it contains for us, the living.

Submission to the threatening power of the Nazi state often led both to the disintegration of what had once seemed well-integrated personalities and to a return to an immature disregard for the dangers of reality. Those Jews who submitted passively to Nazi persecution came to depend on primitive and infantile thought processes: wishful thinking and disregard for the possibility of death. Many persuaded themselves that they, out of all the others, would be spared. Many more simply disbelieved in the possibility of their own death. Not believing in it, they did not take what seemed to them desperate precautions, such as giving up everything to hide out singly; or trying to escape even if it meant risking their lives in doing so; or preparing to fight for their lives when no escape was possible and death had become an immediate possibility. It is true that defending their lives in active combat before they were rounded up to be transported into the camps might have hastened their deaths, and so, up to a point, they were protecting themselves by ''rolling with the punches'' of the enemy.

But the longer one rolls with the punches dealt not by the normal vagaries of life, but by one's eventual executioner, the more likely it becomes that one will no longer have the strength to resist when death becomes imminent. This is particularly true if yielding to the enemy is accompanied not by a commensurate strengthening of the personality, but by an inner disintegration. We can observe such a process among the Franks, who bickered with each other over trifles, instead of supporting each other's ability to resist the demoralizing impact of their living conditions. (pp. 250-52)

Unfortunately the Franks were by no means the only ones who, out of anxiety, became unable to contemplate their true situation and with it to plan accordingly. Anxiety, and the wish to counteract it by clinging to each other, and to reduce its sting by continuing as much as possible with their usual way of life incapacitated many, particularly when survival plans required changing radically old ways of living that they cherished, and which had become their only source of satisfaction. (p. 253)

I have met many Jews as well as gentile anti-Nazis . . . who survived in Nazi Germany and in the occupied countries. These people realized that when a world goes to pieces and inhumanity reigns supreme, man cannot go on living his private life as he was wont to do, and would like to do; he cannot, as the loving head of a family, keep the family living together peacefully, undisturbed by the surrounding world; nor can he continue to take pride in his profession or possessions, when either will deprive him of his humanity, if not also of his life. In such times, one must radically reevaluate all of what one has done, believed in, and stood for in order to know how to act. In short, one has to take a stand on the new reality—a firm stand, not one of retirement into an even more private world. (p. 257)

> Bruno Bettelheim, *"The Ignored Lesson of Anne Frank,"* in his Surviving and Other Essays, *Alfred A. Knopf, 1979, pp. 246-57.*

ILYA EHRENBURG (essay date 1960)

[*A Russian-Jewish novelist, journalist, essayist, and poet, Ehrenburg's prolific writing career spanned five decades, including those of both world wars and the post-Stalin years. During World War II he was one of the most active of Russian writers in war journalism and propaganda; his articles were extremely popular and are considered to have played a large part in inspiring Russian resistance to the German invasion. Following the war, Ehrenburg published many anti-American articles in the Soviet press, as well as* The Storm *(1948), a novel about World War II that is considered a leading example of the postwar anti-American trend in Russian fiction. However, even though Ehrenburg castigated the failures of Western society in his writings, he also perceived the corruption and brutality of revolutionary ideals in the Soviet Union, and often despaired of the course his government was following. After Stalin's death, when the Soviets became more tolerant of certain types of dissent, Ehrenburg publicly rejected the conviction that writers should serve the purposes of the state and asserted that "the writer [is] a servant of the truth." He set out to acquaint the nation's youth with Russia's literary heritage and with its community of thought, spirit, and culture shared with the rest of Europe. He asserted: "The basic task of literature is to throw light on the spiritual world of our contemporaries, on their secret thoughts and emotions, their doubts and hopes, their joys and sorrows." Thus, the essays of his later years reflect his grandiose goal to impress Russia's youth with the moral purposes of art and with the ideals and convictions of the great Russian writers who had been obscured under Stalin's repressive regime, and to inspire his readers to help build a humane Russia. Toward the end of his life, with the periodic recurrence of anti-Semitism within Russia, Ehrenburg became more conscious of his Jewish heritage. It was largely through his influence that, after great delay, a small edition of Anne Frank's diary was published in Moscow in 1960. One year later, on his seventieth birthday, he declared, "I am a Russian writer, and so long as there is even a single anti-Semite in the world I shall answer proudly to the question of nationality: 'I am a Jew.'" In the following excerpt from Ehrenburg's foreword to the Russian edition of the diary, he summarizes Frank's experience and calls her diary "a human document of tremendous importance and an act of indictment," with Frank's voice having "the power of sincerity, of humanity, and also of talent."*]

The history of [*Anne Frank: The Diary of a Young Girl*] is unusual. It appeared in Holland ten years ago, was translated into seventeen languages, and millions of copies have been sold. Plays and films have been made from it; special studies have been written about it.

This is not a novel by a celebrated author, it is the diary of a thirteen-year-old girl; but it affects the reader more profoundly than many masterly works of literature.

Everyone knows that the Hitlerites killed six million Jews, the citizens of twenty countries, rich and poor, famous and unknown. The atom bomb fell on Hiroshima out of the blue, there was no possibility of taking cover. For several years the Hitlerites organized the round-up of millions of people, as wolf battues are organized. The Jews tried to hide; they concealed themselves in quarries, in disused mines, in the holes and corners of towns. They waited days, weeks, months for the final blow to fall. Six million were poisoned in gas chambers, shot in ravines or against fortress walls, condemned to slow death by starvation. They were separated from the world by the walls of ghettos, by the barbed wire of concentration camps. Nobody knows what they felt and thought. One voice speaks for six million—the voice not of a sage or a poet but of an ordinary little girl.

Anne Frank kept a diary as girls of her age so often do; on her birthday she was given a thick exercise book and she began to record the events of her young life. Adults decreed that this childish life soon lose its childishness. The diary of one little girl became a human document of tremendous importance and an act of indictment. (pp. 258-59)

There is nothing in Anne's diary that might not have been written by a Dutch, French, or Italian girl. The Hitlerites pinned a six-pointed star on her girlish dress, and she accepted the fact with deep incomprehension but with great dignity.

Some of the pages of the diary make one smile, but the smile quickly fades: the end of the book is all too clearly foreseeable. The thirteen-year-old girl writes that she will give her children a book that she enjoyed; she remarks that life as depicted in novels is very extraordinary—she, for one, would never stay alone with a strange man. This is written by a child who grows up before one's eyes, grows up in the underground, completely walled in. Now she is fifteen, she wants to fall in love; the boy Peter lives in the "annexe" too, and she persuades herself that she is in love with him.

In prison, in concentration camps, people survived terrible ordeals when they had an aim, when they became absorbed in some activity, however illusory. What could an adolescent girl do? Study? Anne tried to study. Play? Anne played—she played at being a writer. She kept a diary, invented stories, started a novel. This uplifted and saved her: of all games she chose the most difficult one, but perhaps the most humanist. (pp. 260-61)

One voice out of six million has reached us. It is only a child's voice but it has great power, the power of sincerity, of humanity, and also of talent. Not every writer would have been capable of describing both the inhabitants of the "annexe" and his own feelings as Anne succeeded in doing. (p. 262)

Anne Frank confessed that she was not particularly interested in politics. She did not play at tribunals and parliaments. She wanted to live. She dreamed of love; she would have been a good mother. They killed her.

Millions of readers know Anne Frank as if she had been to their homes. Six million perfectly innocent people perished. One clear, child's voice lives on: it has proved stronger than death. (p. 264)

> *Ilya Ehrenburg, "Anne Frank's Diary," in his* Chekhov, Stendhal, and Other Essays, *translated by Tatiana Shebunia and Yvonne Kapp, Alfred A. Knopf, 1963, pp. 258-64.*

G. B. STERN   (essay date 1962)

[*In the following excerpt from her introduction to* Tales from the House Behind, *Stern surveys the minor works of Anne Frank, summarizing and quoting from them, and noting the many qualities they reveal about Anne Frank as a person and as a writer. For further discussion of Anne Frank's minor works, see the excerpt by Stefan Kanfer (1984).*]

Let us for the moment remember Anne Frank as just a delightful child, a chatterbox, a flirt, and even with the characteristic childish need to invent an imaginary friend called Kitty to whom she addressed the now world-famous *Diary* found after she and her family had been taken away by the Nazis to die in concentration camps at Auschwitz and Belsen; and be glad that she lives again in [*Tales from the House Behind,* a] collection of fables, personal reminiscences, and short stories found in a notebook and on odd sheets of paper. . . . (p. 9)

Anne was a writer in embryo. Her title for the book she was planning to write after the war was *Het Achterhuis,* meaning the 'House Behind,' referring of course to the house in Amsterdam where they all lived cooped up and in hiding for over two years, but it could also have stood for an unconsciously symbolic title to indicate that behind her passionate zest for life, we should find wisdom and a deeply religious sense of values. For instance, in one of her fables, the elf who takes Eve on a tour of a big park dismisses the rose as too obviously the queen of flowers, lovely, elegant, and fragrant—"and if she wouldn't always push herself into the foreground, she might be lovable as well," and then completes the lesson by analogy between two of Eve's friends, Lena symbolising the rose, and little Marie, plain and poor, as a bluebell: "This flower is much happier than the rose. It doesn't care about the praise of others." Though the language of this fable may be immature, it reveals nevertheless that amazing sense of values which we have already noticed.

And according to Anne Frank, the overworked little flower-girl, Krista, is never dissatisfied so long as at the end of every day she might have a brief rest "in the field, amid the flowers, beneath the darkening sky. . . . Gone is fatigue . . . the little girl thinks only of the bliss of having this short while alone with God and nature"—as Anne herself found endless compensation in looking up at the sky or at the chestnut tree, from the attic window of *Het Achterhuis.*

And indeed, the more we read of her or by her, the more strange and incongruous it seems that she could combine in one human being the contradictory qualities of extrovert and introvert. In spite of her overflowing exuberance, her reputation as a chatterbox, unable to refrain from pouring out to her companions whatever might have danced into her head, in these fables we are allowed to penetrate into the House Behind—and aware of the end of Anne Frank, we can hardly bear to read the vivid fable called *Fear,* written, according to its date, only a few days before she was taken away to Belsen: she dreamed that bombs were falling and she ran outside the city

and fell asleep in the grass under the sky—"Fear is a sickness for which there is only one remedy. Anyone who is afraid, as I was then, should look at nature and see that God is much closer than most people think." Like all the best fabulists, she applies her own experience to a universal need.

And that brings us to her last fable, of the *Wise Old Dwarf* who keeps captive two elves of widely different temperaments, Dora and Peldron, and would not let them go home until four months later: he explains his motive—"I took you here and left you together to teach you there are other things in this world beside *your* fun and *your* gloom . . . Dora has become somewhat more serious, and Peldron has cheered up a bit, because you were obliged to make the best of having to live together."

We have already seen that Anne Frank was by no means lacking in a subtle vein of humour; she concluded her story of Blurry, the little bear who set off to 'discover the world,' when after all his crowded experiences he had to admit that he had failed to discover it because—"You see, I couldn't find it!"

And so we pass on to the section of personal reminiscences, her school-days in retrospect, gay and entirely youthful, with no heartbreak for the reader until her fervent wish at the end that those happy days could come again. Among these reminiscences is a study of a certain Miss Riegel, a clever woman who gives them lectures in biology "starting with fish and ending with reindeer. Her favourite topic is propagation, which surely must be so because she is an old maid"—satire, pungent and mature, co-dweller in the House Behind with Anne's merry description of her six reprimands for talking incessantly in class, when she pleads that little can be done because her case is hereditary: "My mother, too, is fond of chatting and has handed this weakness down to me"; thus our young extrovert finds a plausible excuse for her fault. In **"Dreams of Movie Stardom"** she lapses again into the child day-dreaming of herself as a movie star—well, she had the looks, the exuberance and animation, but the world would have lost an author revealing already those infallible signs of genius, including the necessary flair for conveying personality; as where in **"My First Article"** she brings her friend Peter vividly before us with every touch.

The essay called **"Give"** strikes a note startlingly up to date and prophetic; since the date of its conception we have all read a hundred essays and leaders, heard a thousand sermons and speeches, on the theme of the true communal spirit of sharing—"Oh, if only the whole world would realise that people were really kindly disposed toward one another, that they are all equal and everything else is just transitory!. . . No one has ever become poor from giving!. . . There is plenty of room for everyone in the world, enough money, riches, and beauty for all to share! God has made enough for everyone. Let us all begin by sharing it fairly."

But more than all the rest of this collection, Anne Frank's fragment of a novel, which she called *Cady's Life,* corroborates all one has said about her potential powers. In it she combines a wisdom beyond her years, a sense of character and a feeling for religion, until at the very end a lapse from fiction into the grim reality of the danger to all Jews under Hitler's régime that autumn of 1942, though she still continues to call her heroine 'Cady' and Cady's friend 'Mary,' foreshadows what was shortly to prove the fate of her own family and herself.

Cady's Life starts straight into the story without unnecessary preliminaries: Cady had been knocked down and injured by a car, and opened her eyes in hospital—"The first thing she saw was that everything around her was white,'' and the first thing she felt was a panic that she would be a cripple for life. When she woke again, her parents had come to visit her, and immediately we get an impression that her father means far more to her than her mother, who—the nurse looking after her noticed—''tired the child out with her incessant nervous prattle.'' After a fortnight, Cady confided in the nursing sister, who was calm and always talked softly, her reactions towards her mother, and here Anne Frank's talent for drawing character emerges clearly: she longs for a mother who, as well as loving her, would truly and sensitively understand how to handle her. (pp. 10-14)

All this is psychologically perceptive to a marked degree; as far as can be surmised, Anne Frank would have developed into a subjective novelist, never objective.

After several weeks Cady's health slowly improves, and for a moment Anne Frank herself intrudes on fiction: ''Her father bought her a diary. Now she often sat up and wrote down her feelings and thoughts.''

In three months they sent her to a sanatorium in the country, where she began to learn to walk without support and then to go out alone into the gardens and grounds or into the wood, where she loved to sit and meditate ''about the world and its meaning,'' and ''suddenly realised that here in the wood and in the quiet hours in hospital she had discovered something new about herself, she had discovered that she was a human being with her own feelings, thoughts, and views, apart from anyone else. . . . What does a child know of the lives of others, of her girl friends, her family, her teachers, what else did she know of them but the outer side? Had she ever had serious talks with any of them?''

Enter romance and a panacea for loneliness both in one—Hans Donkert, a boy of seventeen on holiday from school, who passed by her in the wood every morning on his way to visit his friends in the neighbourhood. For some time they knew each other only by sight, until one day he stopped and introduced himself; after that, he came along earlier and sat and talked with her, though not profoundly . . . until on one occasion they looked at each other longer than they really wanted to and he asked her what she was thinking about. She could not at first bring herself to tell him, and then she suddenly said: ''Do you also often feel lonely, even if you have friends, lonely inside, I mean?'' Hans owned up to it and added that boys confide even less in their friends than do girls, and were even more afraid of being laughed at.

Again neither of them spoke for a long time, until: ''Do you believe in God, Hans?'' ''Yes, I do firmly believe in God.'' And the discussion between them which followed this, although simply phrased, contained the essence of so much that one has read in profound theological works of the true nature of God and how He expresses Himself, that one is staggered at its maturity.

Yes, perhaps Cady and Hans were destined by their author, could she have completed the volume, to be *en route* for a happy marriage in a few years . . . when suddenly, as we noted earlier, Anne Frank was swept away from fiction into stark unbearable reality. (pp. 15-16)

> *G. B. Stern, in an introduction to* Tales from the House Behind: Fables, Personal Reminiscences and Short Stories *by Anne Frank, translated by H.H.B. Moseberg and Michel Mok, The World's Work (1913) Ltd., 1962, pp. 9-16.*

OTTO FRANK   (essay date 1967)

[*The following excerpt is taken from an essay by Anne Frank's father in which he recounts Anne's childhood, the family's life in hiding, their arrest and separation, his liberation and return from the Auschwitz concentration camp, his discovery of his daughters' deaths, and his acquisition of Anne's diary. In the following excerpt, Frank expresses the deep satisfaction he felt because of the public homage paid to his daughter and because of the millions of young people who have shown an interest in her.*]

''It must be a source of deep joy to you, in all your sorrow,'' the head of a girls' school wrote to me, ''to know that your daughter's life is, in the deepest sense, only just beginning.''

In the deepest sense, this is so. My daughter Anne died in a Nazi concentration camp in March, 1945, at the age of 15. But that was not the end, for later in 1945 I first read Anne's diary. It is through her diary that Anne still lives.

I am the child's father, and yet I believe I speak objectively when I say that something extraordinary is happening in the world because of this little book. ''Who would ever think,'' Anne wrote with a trace of humor at the end of a passage in her diary, ''that so much could go on in the soul of a young girl?'' And who, one might add, would ever have thought that a young girl's soul could have such an effect on so many others?

Sometimes the effect is public and apparent: Schools were named after Anne in many countries; the renowned French artist Marc Chagall is moved to do a lithograph of Anne; the young Soviet poet Yevgeny Yevtushenko, in a bold poem attacking anti-Semitism, says: ''It seems to me that I am Anne Frank, / As frail as a twig in April, / And I am full of love . . .'' Heads of state and distinguished citizens pay her tribute—the late President Kennedy, for example, who said: ''Of the multitude who throughout history have spoken for human dignity in times of great suffering and loss, no voice is more compelling than that of Anne Frank.''

Yet, as moving as such homage is, especially to me, Anne's father, more moving still is the intense and unrelenting interest shown in Anne by millions of ordinary young people all over the world. Many of these youngsters cherish Anne privately, in their solitary thoughts; many of them write me letters, and reading them is an astounding experience. In them is the overwhelming evidence of the power of Anne Frank's memory.

Over and over again, in phrases that are sometimes awkward or sentimental but always earnest, the letter writers tell me how Anne's diary first shocked them, then transformed them. ''I will never be the same, having read Anne's book,'' a 12-year-old girl wrote to me from Bayport, N.Y. ''I only hope that in my life I will be able to do some small something so that what happened to Anne will never happen again.''

Often the letters reveal that, through Anne's experience, readers see what prejudice is really like. ''In my country,'' wrote a 16-year-old girl from Gorham, Maine, ''the country that is *supposed* to be for everyone and where everyone is 'equal,' we have the Negro situation. I believe it's all horrible, and . . . I shall do everything I can to help the Negroes and whites live peacefully together.''

This same letter illustrates the uncanny way in which so many teen-agers identify with Anne. ''When I feel troubled,'' wrote the girl from Maine, ''I turn to Anne's picture. I look at those beautiful dark eyes looking at us all. She was *so* in love with life itself. I think of all she endured and it gives me strength to go on, no matter what.'' . . .

Because I was privileged to read Anne's diary, I perhaps know my daughter better than most fathers can know their daughters. Her diary was for me a marvelous gift of intimacy and insight from the child I had lost. (p. 87)

Never had I imagined the depths of her thoughts and feelings. Though I had always felt close to her, I now had to admit to myself [after reading her diary] that I had not known her innermost self.... .

Anne's wish—"I want to publish a book entitled *The Secret Annexe* after the war"—[was] fulfilled. To my surprise, the book turned out to be an extraordinary success and received high praise from the press. How proud Anne would have been.

When the play, and later the film, based on the diary were produced, Anne's name became known all over the world, and she is now regarded as a symbol of all those who were and still are persecuted innocently because of race, belief or color. (p. 154)

> Otto Frank, "The Living Legacy of Anne Frank: The Memory Behind Today's Headlines," in Ladies' Home Journal, *Vol. LXXXIV, No. 9, September, 1967, pp. 87, 153-54.*

JOHN BERRYMAN (essay date 1967)

[*Berryman was probably one of the most important, and certainly one of the most widely read, of modern American poets. His own work developed from an objective, classically controlled poetry into an esoteric, eclectic, and highly emotional type of literature. In his own words, he has called poetry "the means by which the writer can shape from an experience in itself usually vague, a mere feeling or phrase, something that is coherent, directed, intelligible." In the following excerpt from an essay originally published in 1967, Berryman argues that the diary is most important as an account of a child's maturation into an adult. He cites many examples from Frank's diary to illustrate the process*

Entrance to the "secret annex." Courtesy of the Consulate General of The Netherlands.

of her maturation, and analyzes her experiences, sometimes in Freudian terms.]

Suppose one became interested in the phenomenon called religious conversion.... If one wants ... to experience the phenomenon, so far as one can do so at second hand,—a phenomenon as gradual and intensely reluctant as it is also drastic,—there is so far as I know one book and one only to be read, written by an African fifteen hundred years ago. Now in Augustine's *Confessions* we are reckoning with just one of a vast number of works by an architect of Western history, and it may appear grotesque to compare to even that one, tumultuous and gigantic, the isolated recent production of a girl who can give us nothing else. A comparison of the *authors* would be grotesque. But I am thinking of the originality and ambition and indispensability of the two books *in the heart of their substances,*—leaving out of account therefore Book X of the *Confessions,* which happens to award man his deepest account of his own memory. I would call the subject of Anne Frank's *Diary* even more mysterious and fundamental than St Augustine's, and describe it as: the conversion of a child into a person.

At once it may be exclaimed that we have thousands of books on this subject. I agree: autobiographies, diaries, biographies, novels. They seem to me—those that in various literatures I have come on—to bear the same sort of relation to the *Diary* that the works *on* religious conversion bear to the first seven books of the *Confessions.* Anne Frank has made the process itself available.

Why—I asked myself with astonishment when I first encountered the *Diary,* or the extracts that *Commentary* published— has this process not been described before? universal as it is, and universally interesting? And answers came. It is *not* universal, for most people do not grow up, in any degree that will correspond to Anne Frank's growing up; and it is *not* universally interesting, for nobody cares to recall his own, or can. It took, I believe, a special pressure forcing the child-adult conversion, and exceptional self-awareness and exceptional candour and exceptional powers of expression, to bring that strange or normal change into view. This, if I am right, is what she has done, and what we are to study. (p. 93)

Let's distinguish, without resorting to the psychologists, temperament from character. The former would be the disposition with which one arrives in the world, the latter what has happened to that disposition in terms of environment, challenge, failure and success, by the time of maturity,—a period individually fixed between, somewhere between, fifteen and seventy-five, say.... I think we ought to form some opinion of the *temperament* of Anne Frank before entering on her ordeal and thereafter trying to construct a picture of her character.

The materials are abundant, the *Diary* lies open. She was vivacious but intensely serious, devoted but playful. It may later on be a question for us as to whether this conjunction "but" is the right conjunction, in her thought. She was imaginative but practical, passionate but ironic and cold-eyed. Most of the qualities that I am naming need no illustration for a reader of the *Diary:* perhaps "cold-eyed" may have an exemplar: "Pim, who was sitting on a chair in a beam of sunlight that shone through the window, kept being pushed from one side to the other. In addition, I think his rheumatism was bothering him, because he sat rather hunched up with a miserable look on his face ... He looked exactly like some shriveled-up old man from an old people's home." So much for an image of the man—her adored father—whom she loves best in the world. She was self-absorbed but un-self-pitying, charitable but sarcastic, industrious but dreamy, brave but sensitive. Garrulous but secretive; skeptical but eloquent. This last "but" may engage us, too. My little word "industrious," like a refugee from a recommendation for a graduate student, finds its best instance in the letter, daunting to an American student, of 27 April 1944, where in various languages she is studying in one day matters that—if they ever came up for an American student—would take him months.

The reason this matters is that the process we are to follow displays itself in a more complicated fashion than one might have expected: in the will, in emotion, in the intellect, in libido. It is surprising what it takes to make an adult human being.

For one reason in particular, which I postpone for the present, I am willing to be extremely schematic about the development we are to follow. I see it as occupying six stages, surprisingly distinct from each other, and cumulative.

1. *Letter of 10 August 1943:* "New idea. I talk more to myself than to the others at mealtimes, which is to be recommended for two reasons. Firstly, because everyone is happy if I don't chatter the whole time, and secondly, I needn't get annoyed about other people's opinions. I don't think my opinions are stupid and the others do; so it is better to keep them to myself. I do just the same if I have to eat something that I simply can't stand. I put my plate in front of me, pretend that it is something delicious, look at it as little as possible, and before I know where I am, it is gone. When I get up in the morning, also a very unpleasant process, I jump out of bed thinking to myself: 'You'll be back in a second,' go to the window, take down the blackout, sniff at the crack of the window until I feel a bit of fresh air, and I'm awake. The bed is turned down as quickly as possible and then the temptation is removed. Do you know what Mummy calls this sort of thing? 'The Art of Living'—that's an odd expression."

I make no apology for quoting this remarkable passage, as it seems to me, and the crucial later ones, at length, because here there are so many points to be noticed, and because later the excessive length itself of an outburst may prove one of its most significant features. Of course the passages are interesting in themselves, but it is their bearing, in analysis, on our investigation that counts; though I take the reader probably to be acquainted with the *Diary,* a detailed knowledge of it can hardly be expected.

We notice first, then, that this "idea," as she calls it, really is "new"—there has been nothing like it in the diary hitherto—one has an impression, considering it, that she has up till now (over a year) merely been holding her own under the ordeal, assembling or reassembling her forces; and also that it addresses itself strongly to the future. Moreover, it is by no means simply an idea: it is a *program,* and a complicated one, and as different as possible from people's New Year's resolutions ("I will," "I will not," etc.). She describes, and explains, what she *is doing.* Her tone is sober and realistic, the reverse of impulsive.

Now for the burden of the program. It takes place in the Practical Will, and aims at accounting for the two *worst* problems with which her incarceration (let's call it that) confronts her. It has nothing incidental about it. These problems are meals and rising. Meals, because the exacerbated interplay of these huddled persons then is more abusive and dazing even than at other times, and because the fare is so monotonous and taste-

less. Rising, because she is rising to what? the same fear, darkness, slowness, privation, exasperation as on all other days; the tendency of profoundly discouraged men to take to their beds and stay there is familiar, and got dramatic illustration—even to many deaths—in the dreadful record of our fighting men as captives in Korea. The steps taken by her against these problems are exactly opposite but verge on each other. She uses first a refraining (that is, a negative) and then her imagination (that is, a positive). I must comment on both procedures. This girl's imaginativeness—the ability to alter reality, to create a new reality—was one of her greatest mental strengths: it is here put twice, solidly, at the service of her psychological survival and tranquillity. The food, and getting up, change under her hand, in a process which *inverts* what we call daydreaming. As for the refraining, one subsidiary point seems to me so important that I want to reserve it for separate consideration, but I hope that the reader will not undervalue the main point: her decision to keep silent. Examples of garrulous persons undertaking silence are certainly not unknown, but they are spectacularly rare, as programmatic and experimental. (pp. 95-7)

Third, the program is *submitted to her mother*. Whether my word "submitted" is quite right will be questionable. I use it tentatively, looking to an evaluation of the decidedly strange tone of her comment on her mother's comment. Her mother, clearly impressed by her daughter's account of the new administration—as who would not be?—applies an adult label; one, by the way, far from stupid. Anne Frank responds with the automatic doubt of a child about adult labels, say: children are concrete, non-categorical, and no child was ever more so perhaps than this girl. But I cannot feel that we have accounted for the sentences—in terms either of what has been taking place in the diary or in terms of what is to come. I hear *scorn* in her characterization of the mother's formula—"that's an odd expression" (I do *not* hear respect, and the expression is not neutral); and I confess to surprise that she told her mother about the program at all, much less submitted it to her,—she has not been in the habit of doing anything of the sort. I take it that the referral, the telling, contained an element of competitiveness, even aggression—as if to murmur, "You are not mastering your own ordeal in this way"; and that this element emerges even more plainly in the final, almost contemptuous comment. Independence comes hard-won and is not friendly. I hardly think, however, that we can form an opinion about these suggestions except in relation to the second and third stages of the development.

The subsidiary point is this: the refraining is described as embarked on *first* in the interest of *others*—and this will interest us later.

2. Three and a half months later, 27 November: "Yesterday evening, before I fell asleep, who should suddenly appear before my eyes but Lies!

"I saw her in front of me, clothed in rags, her face thin and worn. Her eyes were very big and she looked so sadly and reproachfully at me that I could read in her eyes: 'Oh, Anne, why have you deserted me? Help, oh, help me, rescue me from this hell!'

"And I cannot help her, I can only look on, how others suffer and die, and can only pray to God to send her back to us.

"*I just saw Lies, no one else* [my italics], and now I understand. I misjudged her and was too young to understand her difficulties. She was attached to a new girl friend, and to her it seemed as though I wanted to take her away. What the poor girl must have felt like, I know; I know the feeling so well myself!

"Sometimes, in a flash, I saw something of her life, but a moment later I was selfishly absorbed again in my own pleasures and problems. It was horrid of me to treat her as I did, and now she looked at me, oh so helplessly, with her pale face and imploring eyes. If only I could help her!''

There is as much again as this, in the same strain, but this will have to do.

If we had *only* this letter on this topic, I don't think we should be able to interpret it, but even so, certain observations might be made. We are dealing here with a *vision*, and a vision heavily charged with affect; nothing earlier in the *Diary* resembles it, and this very cool-headed girl seems overwhelmed. It seems, in short, to demand interpretation, as a dream would. Second, the *reason* given for the remorse (in the fourth paragraph) strikes one, I think, as inadequate; one suspects that an operation of the unconscious has thrown up a screen, if Lies is the real subject. But I have to be doubtful, third, that Lies is the real subject, in the light of the phrases that I have taken the liberty of italicizing. Why should the girl so stress the identity of an individual seen in a vision? I once as a young man experienced an hallucination of a senior writer whom I wildly admired, the poet Yeats . . . , and it would never have occurred to me, in describing it, to say "I just saw Yeats, no one else." We seem bound to suppose that the emotion—passionate remorse—is real, but that both its cause (to which it is excessive, and violently so) and its object are not real—are, as we say, *transferred.*

These doubts are confirmed by a very similar letter of a month later, 29 December: "I was very unhappy again last evening. Granny and Lies came into my mind. Granny, oh, darling Granny, how little we understood of what she suffered, or how sweet she was,'' and so on and so on, and then back to an agony over Lies.

Now the actual circumstances—the girl friend's fate being doubtful, and the grandmother having died of cancer—were tragic. The question is whether they account for the strangeness and extremity of these outbursts, *at this point,* of love-and-remorse; and I feel certain that they cannot. Clearly, I would say the real subject is the mother—for whom the friend and the grandmother, also loved and felt as wronged, make eminently suitable screens. But how has Anne Frank wronged her mother? This emerges, *at once,* in the next letter. What I think has happened, in this second stage of the development, is that the girl is *paying beforehand,* with a torrent of affection and remorse, for the rebellion against her mother that then comes into the open.

3. 2 January 1944: "This morning when I had nothing to do I turned over some of the pages of my diary and several times I came across letters dealing with the subject 'Mummy' in such a hotheaded way that I was quite shocked, and asked myself: 'Anne, is it really you who mentioned hate? Oh, Anne, how could you!' . . . (pp. 97-100)

Three days later comes the remarkable letter that winds up, to my sense, this first phase of her development, concerned with her mother. The important passages are three. "One thing, which perhaps may seem rather fatuous, I have never forgiven her. It was on a day that I had to go to the dentist. Mummy and Margot were going to come with me, and agreed that I should take my bicycle. When we had finished at the dentist, and were outside again, Margot and Mummy told me that they were going into the town *to look at something or buy something—I don't remember exactly what.* I wanted to go, too, but was not allowed to, as I had my bicycle with me. Tears of rage sprang into my eyes, and Mummy and Margot began laughing at me. Then I became so furious that I stuck my tongue out at them in the street just as an old woman happened to pass by, who looked very shocked! I rode home on my bicycle, and I know I cried for a long time.'' It is clear that the *meaning* of this experience is not known to the girl, and cannot become known to us, since we do not have her associations; but its *being reported,* and here, is extremely interesting. I notice that censorship has interfered with memory, in the passage I have italicized, just as it interferes with the recollections of dreams, and of course if we were in a position to interpret the account, this is where we would start. But there is no need to interpret. The traumatic incident has served its purpose, for her and for our understanding of her development, *in being recollected:* this is the sort of experience that in persons who become mentally ill is blocked, whereas the fullness here both of the recollection (with very slight blockage) and of the affect testifies to her freedom.

The next passage concerns her periods, of which she has had three, and its unexpressed tenor certainly is that of rivalry, maturity, independence of the mother, while the letter concludes with the one solid passage of physical narcissism in the whole *Diary.*

It is time to say, before we pass into the second phase of her development, that more than a year earlier (7 November 1942) Anne Frank had defined for herself with extraordinary clarity this part of her task. "I only look at her as a mother, and she just doesn't succeed in being that to me; I have to be my own mother . . . I am always making resolutions not to notice Mummy's bad example. I want to see only the good side of her and to seek in myself what I cannot find in her. But it doesn't work . . . Sometimes I believe that God wants to try me, both now and later on; I must become good through my own efforts, without examples and without good advice. Then later on I shall be all the stronger. Who besides me will ever read these letters? From whom but myself shall I get comfort?'' Self-command and strength, virtue and independence: we have seen the struggle for them working itself out through the practical will, the imagination, an agonized vision, a trauma recovered, the physical self. The mother will remain a focus for comparison, and almost that only; not a model.

4. The second phase begins on the night of the day of the traumatic and narcissistic letter, and we hear of it in the letter of the day following—as if to say: Now that that problem's dealt with, let's get on with the next. She has sought out Peter Van Daan, exceptionally for her (he has hardly figured in the *Diary* at all to this point), in the evening in his room, and helped him with crossword puzzles. 6 January: "It gave me a queer feeling each time I looked into his deep blue eyes . . . Whatever you do, don't think I'm in love with Peter—not a bit of it!. . . I woke at about five to seven this morning and knew at once, quite positively, what I had dreamed. I sat on a chair and opposite me sat Peter . . . [these dots are in the original, or at any rate in the English translation] Wessel. We were looking together at a book of drawings by Mary Bos. The dream was so vivid that I can still partly remember the drawings. But that was not all—the dream went. Suddenly Peter's eyes met mine and I looked into those fine, velvet brown

[*sic*] eyes for a long time. Then Peter said very softly, 'If I had only known, I would have come to you long before!' (pp. 100-01)

The rest of this letter, and the next, give the history of her secret calf-love for Peter Wessel,—of whom we have heard nothing for a year and a half, since the second entry in the *Diary*. The girl does not realize that the dream is not about him, of course. Now, again, we cannot interpret the dream with any assurance, lacking associations; but as Freud observed, some dreams are so lightly armored that they can be read at sight by a person of experience and some familiarity with the situation of the dreamer, and I think this is such a dream. I would not say that the real subject is Peter Van Daan, as perhaps a hasty impression would suggest. Two passages in the letter of the very next day confirm one's feeling that, as in the case of Lies and her grandmother, we are dealing with *two* screen figures and that the real subject is, naturally, her father: "I am completely upset by the dream. When Daddy kissed me this morning, I could have cried out: 'Oh, if only you were Peter!'" But he *was;* notice that it is otherwise hard or even impossible to account for her being "completely upset" by this very agreeable dream, and for the absence of transition from the first sentence to the second,—her unconscious needed no transition, because the subject had not changed. Needless to say, in view of the well-known slang use of the word "peter," the dream has a phallic as well as a paternal level; as one would expect from the narcissism of the preceding day. The other passage in this: "Once, when we spoke about sex, Daddy told me that I couldn't possibly understand the longing yet; I always knew that I did understand it and now I understand it fully." One of the most interesting and unusual features of this girl's mind—using the term "mind" very broadly—is its astonishing vertical mobility, unconscious and conscious and half-conscious. Three letters later (22 January) she recognizes herself the formative importance of her dream: "It seems as if I've grown up a lot since my dream the other night. I'm much more of an 'independent being.'" The unsuitability of her father as object, like the unsuitability of her mother as model, later, in fact, becomes explicit.

5. This stage, comprising her intense and miserable attempt to create a post-paternal love object out of the unworthy (but solely available) Peter Van Daan, scarcely needs illustration. It fails because she cannot respect him (16 February: "I told him that he certainly had a very strong inferiority complex. He talked about the Jews. He would have found it much easier if he'd been a Christian and if he could be one after the war. I asked if he wanted to be baptized, but that wasn't the case either. Who was to know whether he was a Jew when the war was over? he said. This gave me rather a pang; it seems such a pity that there's always just a tinge of dishonesty about him''); and the girl's independence and moral nature are now such that she cannot love where she does not respect. By the end of this month, February, he is already becoming unreal and shadowy: "Peter Wessel and Peter Van Daan have grown into one Peter, who is beloved and good, and for whom I long desperately." This is hardly a conception to be heard without amazement from anyone in love with another actual human being. But he has *served his purpose,* and it is just two months after the dream, 7 March, that she is able to summarize, with uncanny self-knowledge, the process with which—from our own very different point of view—we have been concerned.

6. "The first half of 1943: my fits of crying, the loneliness, how I slowly began to see all my faults and shortcomings, which are so great and which seemed much greater then. During the day I deliberately talked about anything and everything that was farthest from my thoughts, *tried to draw Pim to me* [my italics]; but couldn't. Alone I had to face the difficult task of changing myself . . . I wanted to change in accordance with my own desires. But *one* thing that struck me even more was when I realized that even Daddy would never become my confidant over everything. I didn't want to trust anyone but myself any more." (pp. 101-03)

There is much more of interest in this long letter, but with a final self-comparison, later this month, to her mother, I think the process that we have been considering may be said to be completed—though what I mean by "completed" will have to have attention later. 17 March: "Although I'm only fourteen, I know quite well what I want, I know who is right and who is wrong, I have my opinions, my own ideas and principles, and although it may sound pretty mad from an adolescent, I feel more of a person than a child, I feel quite independent of anyone.

"I know that I can discuss things and argue better than Mummy, I know I'm not so prejudiced, I don't exaggerate so much, I am more precise and adroit and because of this—you may laugh—I feel superior to her over a great many things. If I love anyone, above all I must have admiration for them, admiration and respect."

In these passages, and particularly with the crushing phrase "more precise and adroit," we are not dealing any longer, surely, with a girl at all but with a woman, and one almost perfectly remarkable. In the sense that *Daniel Deronda* is more "mature" than *Adam Bede,* the process of maturation never ceases in interesting persons so long as they remain interesting. But in the sense—with which, you remember, we began—of the passage from childhood to adulthood, Anne Frank must appear to us here more mature than perhaps most persons ever become.

Our story, of course, can have no happy ending, and so it would be especially agreeable at this point to draw attention to the brilliant *uses* she made of this maturity during the four months of writing life left to her—the comic genius of the dramatization of "the views of the five grownups on the present situation" (14 March 1944), where a description that seemed merely amusing and acute is brought to the level of Molièrean comedy by a piercing conclusion: "I, I, I . . . !"; the powerful account of her despair and ambition dated 4 April; the magnificent page that closes the very long letter of a week later, where in assessing God's responsibility for the doom of the Jews she reaches the most exalted point of the *Diary* and sounds like both spokesman and prophet. I want, indeed, presently to make some use of this last letter. But it is no part of my purpose in the present essay to praise or enjoy Anne Frank. We have been tracing a psychological and moral development to which, if I am right, no close parallel can be found. It took place under very special circumstances, which—let us now conclude, as she concluded—though superficially unfavourable, in fact highly favourable to it; she was *forced* to mature, in order to survive; the hardest challenge, let's say, that a person can face without defeat is the best for him. (pp. 103-04)

It would be easy to draw up a list of the qualities she valued, but it may be more helpful to begin with an odd little remark she once . . . made about her sister. I notice with interest, by the way, that Margot figures hardly at all in the development, and I wonder whether, on this important evidence, the psychologists have not overestimated the role played by sibling rivalry after very early childhood. "Margot is very sweet and would like me to trust her," Anne Frank writes, "but still I can't tell her everything. She's a darling, she's good and pretty, but she lacks the nonchalance for conducting deep discussions . . ." The criticism is given as decisive, and I think it may puzzle the reader until we recall that Socrates' interlocutors were frequently baffled to decide whether he was in earnest or not. She objects, let's say, to an *absence of play of mind*. But I think still further light is thrown on the expression by the formidable self-account that ends the long letter (11 April) I spoke of earlier: "I am becoming still more independent of my parents, young as I am, I face life with more courage than Mummy; my feeling for justice is immovable, and truer than hers. I know what I want, I have a goal, an opinion, I have a religion and love. Let me be myself and then I am satisfied. I know that I'm a woman, a woman with inward strength and plenty of courage."

"If God lets me live, I shall attain more than Mummy ever has done, I shall not remain insignificant, I shall work in the world and for mankind!"

"And now I know that first and foremost I shall require courage and cheerfulness!"

Much of what we need to know of her character is to be found here, and deserves comment, but perhaps it may occasion surprise that among these high ideals should be mentioned as climactic "cheerfulness." I am not sure that its placement should occasion surprise, taken with the remark about her sister. We might seek an analogy, one singular enough, too, in the thought of Whitehead. The philosopher once cast about (the passage can be seen conveniently in Morton White's little anthology *The Age of Anxiety*) in an attempt to decide what few concepts were *indispensable* to the notion of life—not merely our life—any life; and he chose four, and he put "self-enjoyment" first. Now he was writing as a metaphysician, while she writes of course as a moralist. But the congruity seems to me remarkable, and for that matter his other three concepts—self-creation, aim (a negative notion, the rejection of all except what is decided on), creative advance—rank very high also, clearly, in her thought. It will be understood that I am not, with these exalted comparisons, claiming philosophical rank for Anne Frank; I am trying to explain what an extremely thoughtful and serious person she made herself into, and how little conventional.

For the rest, the strongly altruistic character of her immense individual ambition, as well as the scorn for anyone of lesser aim, should perhaps be signalized. And I would say finally that the author of the searching expression "my feeling for justice is immovable" has taken full account of all that which makes human justice so intolerably unattainable that Pascal finally rejected it altogether (Fragment 298) in favour of might.

We began, then, with a certain kind of freedom, which is destroyed; we passed through a long enslavement, to the creation of a new kind of freedom. Then this is destroyed, too, or rather—not so much destroyed—as turned against itself. "Let me be myself and then I am satisfied." But this, of course, was precisely what the world would not do, and in the final letter of the *Diary*, and at the end of its final sentence, we see the self-struggle failing: ". . . finally I twist my heart round again, so that the bad is on the outside and the good is on the inside and keep on trying to find a way of *becoming* what I would so like to be, and what I could be, if . . . there weren't

any other people living in the world." The italics of the lacerating verb are mine, but the desperate recognition that one must advance ("self-creation," in Whitehead's term) and that there are circumstances in which one cannot, and the accusing dots, are hers. She remained able to weep with pity, in Auschwitz, for naked gypsy girls driven past to the crematory, and she died in Belsen. (pp. 104-06)

> *John Berryman, "The Development of Anne Frank,"*
> *in his* The Freedom of the Poet, *Farrar, Straus and*
> *Giroux, Inc., 1976, pp. 91-106.*

GARSON KANIN (essay date 1979)

[Kanin's career as a playwright, director of stage and television productions, novelist, short story writer, and essayist has included the directing of The Diary of Anne Frank, *which won the 1956 Pulitzer Prize in drama. In an unexcerpted portion of this essay, Kanin recounts his introduction to the diary and his involvement as the director of a production of the play, a project which he describes as "not so much a theater job as a rare religious experience." In the following excerpt, Kanin expresses his high regard for Anne Frank as an inspiring individual.]*

On the 12th of June, 1979, Anne Frank would have reached her 50th birthday. To many of us, the fact comes as a jolt. A little girl of 50? Impossible.

She was cheated by life, betrayed by circumstance, murdered by fate, and lived not even sixteen of these 50 years. As we contemplate the waste of her lost time, what lessons are to be learned, what morals drawn, what action taken? Whose imagination is profound enough to encompass the reality of 6 million dead in the Holocaust? And whose is so callous as to remain untouched and unmoved by the story of this bright and wondrous kid? Think of it. By the force of her love of life, she managed to compress a complete personal history into a childhood.

Her father, Otto Frank, enforced a rigid discipline of education during their incarceration, but Anne learned as much from his example as from his books. Remember that he was the man who said, a moment before their inescapable discovery, "For two years we have lived in fear; now we can live in hope."

Anne remains forever adolescent. We look at her famous photograph and see a bright, sweet, smiling little Jewish face—an admixture of humor and tragedy. Like the "Mona Lisa" (which she strangely resembles) her age is a constant. . . . Among other things, the vision of Anne Frank reminds us that the length of a life does not necessarily reflect its quality. (p. 14)

[She] remains for us ever a shining star, a radiant presence who, during her time of terror and humiliation and imprisonment, was able to find it within herself to write in her immortal diary, "In spite of everything, I still believe that people are good at heart."

Thirty-five years of her unlived life challenge humanity to rise to her faith. (p. 15)

> *Garson Kanin, "Anne Frank at 50," in* Newsweek,
> *Vol. XCII, No. 26, June 25, 1979, pp. 14-15.*

STEFAN KANFER (essay date 1984)

[In the following excerpt from a review of Tales from the Secret Annex, *a collection of Anne Frank's stories, fables, essays, and reminiscences, Kanfer notes that these pieces bear testimony to*

the author's raw talent, mature spirit, and unfulfilled potential. For a more comprehensive discussion of Anne Frank's minor works, see the excerpt by G. B. Stern (1962).]

"In spite of everything, I still believe that people are really good at heart." Anne Frank's final words in the play that bears her name seem to belie her fate. She died at 15 in the Bergen-Belsen death camp. Was she merely expressing the naive wishes of a child? What could such an adolescent comprehend of the world?

As her surviving papers prove, the tremulous girl knew all too well the lessons of degradation and inhumanity. But if she was acquainted with the night, she refused to turn her back on the consolations of nature, learning and love. The proof resides in Anne Frank's *Tales from the Secret Annex,* a group of stories, fables, essays and reminiscences that she kept in a private journal. Though some of these works were previously published in her native Dutch, they are making their first appearances in hard cover, sympathetically translated by Ralph Manheim and Michel Mok.

The arrival is long overdue. To be sure, among these entries are minor and childish writings: a recollection of having cheated in a math exam, an unsuccessful attempt at light verse. But most of the 30 pieces show a heartbreaking potential. For Anne, nuances are crucial and all experiences are carefully assayed, even those that come in the Franks' pitiable Amsterdam refuge behind a wall, temporarily safe from the Nazis. Occasionally she succumbs to depression, and a line concentrates the tragedy of her people: "To be interrupted just as you are thinking of a glorious future!" Yet Anne's mind is too agile and her imagination too febrile for enduring self-pity.

In **"Dreams of Movie Stardom"** she constructs a Hollywood that never was, where the '30s stars Lola, Priscilla and Rosemary Lane invite her to join them. Like Kafka's Amerika, Anne's New World is a fanciful arena of high-speed miracles; within days she becomes a photographer's model. . . .

Jack boots sound in the streets, and fear is so palpable it can be tasted in the evening soup, but Anne spends a day worrying about the pathological Dutch dislike of nudity. In **"The Sink of Iniquity"** she protests, "Modesty and prudishness can go too far. Do you put clothes on flowers when you pick them? I don't think we're so very different from nature. Why should we be ashamed of the way nature has dressed us?"

It is in the fables that the young author's gifts are best displayed, as if confinement had forced her to think in brief, ironic parables. In **"Blurry, the Explorer,"** a bear cub ventures into a human city and becomes the intimate—and the quarry—of dogs, cars and people. . . . In **"Eve's Dream,"** plants display a variety of personalities, as they do in the tales of Andersen and Grimm. . . .

There is, of course, no way to determine what kind of writer Anne Frank might have become. Child sacrifice is a tragedy beyond words, and it scarcely matters whether a genius or an ordinary citizen perished in the Holocaust. It is only certain that her final volume is a testimony to a green talent and a mature spirit. Each page refreshingly repeats the invaluable moral lesson of her diary: if it is implausible to bid farewell to anguish, it is impossible to close the book on hope.

Stefan Kanfer, "Child Sacrifice," in Time, *Vol. 123, No. 5, January 30, 1984, p. 77.*

ADDITIONAL BIBLIOGRAPHY

Afterword to *Anne Frank: The Diary of a Young Girl,* by Anne Frank, pp. 245-58. New York: Pocket Books, 1967.
> Provides the historical context of Anne Frank's experiences. Also summarized are her final months in concentration camps, the publication history of the diary, and the phenomenal popularity of the diary and the play.

Brillant, Moshe. "Anne Frank's Friend." *The New York Times* (21 April 1957): 30, 32, 34.
> Describes the close friendship of Anne Frank and Lies Goosens and their sad final reunion at the Bergen-Belsen concentration camp. Goosens's life after her liberation, including her experience of seeing the play based on the diary, is also described.

Frankel, Haskell. "The House of Silence." *Holiday* XLVI, No. 3 (September 1969): 16, 20-1.
> Detailed description of the building in which the Franks and several others hid from the Nazis. Frankel also reports that this site, which was restored by the Anne Frank Foundation, is popular among tourists.

Lewisohn, Ludwig. "A Glory and a Doom." *Saturday Review* XXXV, No. 29 (19 July 1952): 20.
> Cites the sobriety and clarity of Anne Frank's vision as traits which contribute to the poignant quality of her chronicles about the war and about her own personal development. Lewisohn further expresses his hope that the *Diary* will inspire people to an active concern for others who suffer under oppressive governments.

"Germany: The White-Gloved Killers." *Newsweek* LXIX, No. 5 (30 January 1967): 48.
> Describes a then-upcoming trial in which three Nazis were tried for complicity in the murder of thousands of Jews. Otto Frank was one of the plaintiffs in the trial, and the defendants were among the elite group of Nazi organizers, referred to as "desk murderers," who frequently escaped prosecution because they made such favorable impressions on jurors.

Schnabel, Ernst. *Anne Frank: A Portrait in Courage.* Translated by Richard and Clara Winston. New York: Harcourt, Brace and Co., 1958, 192 p.
> A valuable, poignant survey of people and places in Anne Frank's life before and during her last months in concentration camps. Schnabel interviewed forty-two people who describe experiences ranging from brief encounters to long-term relationships with Anne Frank, and their recollections include anecdotes as well as character sketches. These details, facts, and insights provide an informed, sensitive portrait of Anne Frank, her diary, and the play. The book also discusses Nazism, the Dutch underground network of support for the Jews, and the closing months of World War II.

———. *The Footsteps of Anne Frank.* Translated by Richard and Clara Winston. London and New York: Longmans, Green and Co., 1959, 160 p.
> Identical to *Anne Frank: Portrait in Courage,* but does not include illustrations.

Steenmeijer, Anna G., ed., with Frank, Otto, and van Praag, Henri. *A Tribute to Anne Frank.* New York: Doubleday & Co., 1971, 120 p.
> An anthology of historical and biographical material regarding Anne Frank, surveys and critical appraisals of her works, and personal responses to her diary and the play. Many perspectives of Anne Frank, her works, and the influence of her diary and the play are represented in this enlightening, engrossing collection of essays, letters to Otto Frank from young people around the world, poems, photographs, and drawings.

Stevens, George. Preface to *Anne Frank: The Diary of a Young Girl,* by Anne Frank, translated by B. M. Mooyaart-Doubleday, pp. vii-viii. New York: Pocket Books, 1958.
> Focuses on the endurance of the hopes, thoughts, and beliefs of Anne Frank despite the powerful Nazi mission to exterminate the Jews. Stevens points out the irony of the fact that, during the raid

on the secret annex, one of the Green Police—whose mission was to remove the Jews from Holland, loot and plunder, and leave no record or document behind—threw the diary on the floor in his search for valuables, and thus unwittingly left behind a statement to the world about the Nazis' work.

Waggoner, Walter H. "Anne Frank's Home." *The New York Times Magazine* (15 September 1957): 96, 98.

Discusses the Anne Frank Foundation's plans and motivation with regard to restoring the building which contained the secret annex, and establishing it as a place of assembly, thought, and recreation for young people of all nations. Waggoner points out that members of many different political parties and religious faiths comprise the foundation, and that although the victims of nazism were Jews, the pain of nazism is felt by all people of conscience. He also focuses on Otto Frank's life since the end of the war, and on his devotion to his daughter's ideals.

Werner, Alfred. "Germany's New Flagellants." *The American Scholar* XXVII, No. 2 (Spring 1958): 169-81.

States that romantic enthusiasm was a characteristic of fifteenth-century German flagellantism, Nazi anti-Semitism, and the philo-Semitism of the mid-1950's. He examines the aroused German conscience which followed the German stage production of the diary, and analyzes ceremonial and social phenomena that reveal the German people's desire to face responsibility for the Holocaust and atone for their guilt. Werner finds the phenomena at once reassuring and frightening—reassuring after years of denial and repression among the German people, but frightening because of its familiar emotional, romantic, and idealistic charactertistics. Reason, Werner asserts, is essential for clear thinking about issues, and he stresses that both individuals and society as a whole should probe deeply for a true understanding of the past.

Rémy de Gourmont

1858-1915

French critic, essayist, novelist, poet, short story writer, and dramatist.

Gourmont was one of the most renowned scholars and men of letters in late nineteenth- and early twentieth-century French literature. As one of the founders of the Symbolist journal the *Mercure de France,* he became a leader of the French Symbolist movement, and was one of the first critics to clearly articulate the principles of the Symbolist aesthetic. In his *Le livre des masques (The Book of Masks),* an examination of the major Symbolist writers, Gourmont described what later came to be understood and accepted as the defining qualities of Symbolist writing, qualities which were developed by the major Modernist writers of the twentieth century, particularly the experimentation with literary form, extremes of subjectivity, and a concern with the nature of art rather than the issues of life.

The characteristics of Symbolism, as Gourmont outlined them, are perhaps best understood when contrasted with those of Naturalism, another movement of the late nineteenth century. Briefly, Naturalism was allied to the rise of scientism and thus held that the truest manner of presenting human life was in terms of physical and biological forces, which the Naturalists considered the determining factors in shaping individuals and groups. In their fiction, the Naturalists depicted the outward existence of persons from ordinary, often vulgar walks of life, representing these subjects in an uncomplicated, journalistic prose style. To an extent, Symbolism was a reaction against the aims of Naturalism. The Symbolists were for the most part poets rather than fiction writers, and their primary concern was with the expression of their own inward sensations and experiences. The highly individual nature of the Symbolists' material often resulted in works that were harshly criticized as obscure or incomprehensible. Whereas the Naturalists became expert in portraying the lives of such people as businessmen, laborers, and criminals, the Symbolists occupied themselves with the comparatively rare lives of poets, saints, and aristocrats; while the works of the Naturalist were grounded in a philosophy of scientific materialism, the Symbolists followed the teachings of the German idealist philosophers and the mystical philosopher Emanuel Swedenborg. It was this artistic and intellectual milieu which most strongly influenced Gourmont's development both as a poet and a prose writer.

Gourmont was born in Bazoches-en-Houlme, Orne, Normandy. His father was a nobleman and a descendent of Gilles de Gourmont, a famous fifteenth-century printer and engraver. Gourmont's mother, Marie Mathilde de Montfort, was a member of the same family as the sixteenth-century poet François de Malherbe. As a young man, Gourmont was educated at the Lycée at Coutances and at the University of Caen in Normandy. After completing his course at the university in 1883, he went to live in Paris, where he took a job as a librarian at the Bibliothèque Nationale, a position that involved only light responsibilities and allowed him a great deal of time to read and write. It was during this time that Gourmont became acquainted with such figures of the Decadent movement as Joris-Karl Huysmans, whose notorious novel *A rebours (Against the Grain),*

Historical Pictures Services, Chicago

which appeared in 1884, was considered the manifesto of the Decadents. As the immediate predecessor of Symbolism, the Decadent movement of the early 1880s instituted much of what came to be identified with the slightly later and more influential Symbolist movement. Because both literary schools shared a number of common traits, including a world-rejecting escapism, exoticism, and aggressive individualism, many writers—such as Jules Laforgue, Paul Verlaine, and Jean Lorrain—are associated with both movements in literary histories. Through Huysmans, Gourmont met Alfred Vallette and Henri de Régnier, the two young men with whom he collaborated in founding the *Mercure de France* in 1889. Gourmont's essays and criticism soon became regular features in the *Mercure,* and he continued to contribute to every issue of the magazine until his death in 1915. Many of Gourmont's articles were later collected in the fourteen volumes that form the three series *Epilogues, Promenades littéraires,* and *Promenades philosophiques (Philosophical Nights in Paris).* Critics have compared these works to the fifteen-volume *Causeries du lundi* of C. A. Sainte-Beuve, one of the most respected figures in French criticism. The essays in Gourmont's collections cover a wide variety of topics from philosophy, literary criticism, and discussions of grammar to social criticism and discussions of popular issues, reflecting the entire range of Gourmont's interests and the depth of his learning in many areas besides literature.

Despite its later reputation as the premier journal of the Symbolist movement, the *Mercure* was not originally conceived of as a Symbolist publication. Rather, Vallette, Régnier, and Gourmont began the journal as a platform for attacking the intellectual establishment. They published works of all types, including Gourmont's 1891 essay "Le joujou patriotisme," which ridiculed the arbitrary manner in which anti-German sentiment and militarism had become confounded with patriotism in the mind of the French public. Gourmont's article was a plea for international understanding and cooperation, but it was construed by his superiors at the Bibliothèque Nationale as unpatriotic, and he was dismissed. This incident was important to Gourmont's career because the reasons for his dismissal were widely misunderstood and were taken by critics as proof of the negative and corrosive nature of Gourmont's thought; William Aspenwall Bradley, for example, designated him as "perhaps the most corrosive intellectual agent of our time, after Nietzsche." Gourmont was greatly upset by this episode, and thereafter chose to support himself by writing for the *Mercure de France* and other publications in Germany, Austria, France, and North and South America. He became an aloof recluse, avoiding social involvement even with his literary contemporaries. Gourmont's retreat from the world at this time was probably also motivated by his sudden affliction with lupus, a disfiguring variety of facial tuberculosis from which Gourmont suffered for many years. His death in 1915 was the result of a stroke.

Prior to his involvement with the *Mercure de France*, Gourmont published his first novel, *Merlette*. This, as well as such other early works as *Histoires magiques*, *Le pèlerin du silence (The Horses of Diomedes)*, and *Sixtine (A Very Woman)*, was inspired by Gourmont's readings of the works of various Symbolist authors and by his association with Huysmans. While many critics have expressed dislike for the melodramatic plots, frequently bizarre and erotic subject matter, and artificial style of Gourmont's early fiction, others have praised these works for their penetrating psychological analyses of complex mental states. For example, in a recent discussion of Gourmont's novel *A Very Woman* (a work inspired by Gourmont's affair with Berthe de Courrière, the same woman who provided the prototype for Huysman's Mme Chantelouve in his novel *Là-bas*), Peter Fawcett refers to it as "probably the finest Symbolist novel ever written," and one that paved the way "both technically and thematically" for such modern novels as André Gide's *Les faux-monnayeurs*. Nonetheless many critics have argued that Gourmont's manner in most of the works that he wrote prior to *The Book of Masks* was affected and not a reflection of his own tastes, but rather of the pervasive influences of Huysmans. These critics contend that Huysmans's cynical fondness for the bizarre and dislike of commonplace existence were unfortunate influences on the young Gourmont that hindered his intellectual development.

Gourmont's other works from this early period, including the poems in *Litanies de la rose* and his translations and commentaries on medieval Latin poets in *Le latin mystique*, reveal his lifelong attraction to medieval art and the symbols of the Catholic religion. Gourmont often used these traditionally sacred forms to express ideas that were pagan and voluptuous, in the manner of the great French poet Charles Baudelaire. This aspect of Gourmont's technique is most in evidence in his play *Lilith* and in his "philosophical fantasy" *Une nuit au Luxembourg (A Night in the Luxembourg)*. *Lilith*, an exotic "literary" drama based on a story from biblical apocrypha, examines the subject of feminine sexuality. It has never been

performed, and critics agree that, like Gourmont's other dramas from this period, *Le vieux roi* and *Théodat*, its lack of dramatic action and abundance of philosophical discourse make it unsuitable for theatrical presentation. *A Night in the Luxembourg* is a similarly unusual work, as unlike a conventional novel in its static presentation of ideas as Gourmont's dramas are unlike conventional dramas. In it, Gourmont explored the phenomenon of religious revelation from an intellectually detached, epicurean point of view in an effort to discover a connection between the physical passions and the mystic's experience of God, or some other higher reality. *A Night in the Luxembourg* thus reflects Gourmont's concern with the search for beauty, truth, and knowledge, as well as his belief in the preeminence of reason over religious sentiments. Although some critics complain that *A Night in the Luxembourg*, like all of Gourmont's novels, is devoid of warmth and human feeling, most critics have acknowledged that it is an extraordinary work. It does, however, contain an element of cold intellectuality, repellent to some critics, which arises from Gourmont's deterministic belief that all of human behavior has its origin in human biology, and from his conviction that art supercedes life. These qualities in his work are explained by Gourmont's belief that "literature, indeed, is nothing more than the artistic development of the idea, the symbolization of the idea by means of imaginary heroes. Heroes, or men (for every man in his sphere is a hero) are only sketched by life; it is art which perfects them by giving them, in exchange for their poor sick souls, the treasure of an immortal idea, and the humblest, if chosen by a great poet, may be called to this participation."

The appearance of *The Book of Masks* in 1896 marked the beginning of Gourmont's ascendancy to the ranks of the most influential critical minds in Europe. In *The Book of Masks*, Gourmont examined the works of the major Symbolist writers of the era, many of whom, including Paul Verlaine and Stéphane Mallarmé, were made known to a wider public through these critical studies. Gourmont also defined the principles of Symbolist art, noting that Symbolism meant "individualism in literature, liberty in art" and the "abandonment of existing forms," as well as "anti-naturalism" and "a tendency to take only the characteristic detail out of life." In writing *The Book of Masks*, Gourmont sought to establish a philosophical justification for Symbolist art, especially for its frequent obscurity and reliance upon subtle suggestion rather than stylistic clarity. He succeeded not only in promoting a wider understanding of the Symbolist aesthetic, but also in producing one of the most influential critical works of his generation. Some critics contend that Gourmont abandoned Symbolism after writing *The Book of Masks* because in his later critical works, such as *Le problème du style*, he began to advocate modes of expression that were more accessible to the reader and insisted upon the physical act of vision, rather than sensations or intellectual concepts, as the basis of all literary art. Other critics, however, argue that Gourmont was a lifelong supporter of the Symbolist movement. As evidence of this, Amy Lowell cites Gourmont's continuing insistence upon the importance of individualism in art, and Glenn S. Burne notes Gourmont's consistent determination to prove that "individual sensibility is the sole source, and concrete sensation the sole material of the writer—whether he be a poet or a critic." Burne believes that Gourmont found justification for both "the extreme individualism of the Symbolist poet and the extreme subjectivity of the Impressionist critic" in the observations of Charles Darwin and Chevalier de Lamarck on the relationship of the individual to his environment, and in the German philosophy of subjective idealism, which "placed the individual consciousness at the center of every created universe."

Gourmont's critical theories have inspired and influenced many leading twentieth-century writers, including T. S. Eliot and Ezra Pound, both of whom have acknowledged their indebtedness to him for the development of many of their own critical ideas. Eliot, in fact, praised Gourmont as "the critical consciousness of his generation" and as "the perfect critic" for the adroit manner in which he blended subjective impressions with objective, scholarly analysis. Among his critical methods, Gourmont practiced what he called the "dissociation of ideas," a form of thought whereby familiar ideas—such as the idea of liberty or justice—may be abstracted from their conventional meanings and associations. Gourmont believed that this method allowed him to separate sentiment from truth, and enabled him to form new, more useful associations. The Italian critic Giovanni Papini described Gourmont's method of dissociation as the application of the intellect to "the decomposition of thoughts that are apparently simple, to the separation of pairs which had been thought indissoluble, to the reestablishment of harmonies and relationships between ideas which had been regarded as heterogeneous and distant, to the search for bits of truth amid the refuse of prejudice, to the gentle denuding of the most solemn truths, revealing, to startled eyes, the bare bones of contradiction."

While Gourmont's reputation has declined considerably since the height of his influence in the early decades of the twentieth century, many of his writings continue to be regarded as classics of criticism. Although Gourmont never found the same acceptance for his fiction and poetry, critics have praised the technical mastery of his poetry, and recent reissues of such fictional works as *A Very Woman* have attracted favorable critical attention. As a critic, the role for which he is most highly praised, Gourmont gave new direction to modern criticism, and the tributes paid to his work by such contemporaries as Eliot and Pound—themselves among the most influential figures of the age—are testimony to the importance of Gourmont's achievement.

PRINCIPAL WORKS

Merlette (novel) 1886
Sixtine: Roman de la vie cérébrale (novel) 1890
  [*A Very Woman*, 1922]
Le latin mystique (criticism) 1892
Lilith (drama) [first publication] 1892
  [*Lilith* published in the journal *Poet Lore*, 1945]
Litanies de la rose (poetry) 1892
Le fantôme (novel) 1893
Fleurs de jadis (poetry) 1893
Théodat (drama) [first publication] 1893
  [*Théodat, the Old King* published in the journal *Drama*, 1916]
Hiéroglyphes (poetry) 1894
Histoires magiques (short stories) 1894
Proses moroses (short stories) 1894
Le livre des masques (criticism) 1896
  [*The Book of Masks*, 1921]
Le pèlerin du silence (novel) 1897
  [*The Horses of Diomedes*, 1920]
Le vieux roi (drama) [first publication] 1897
Le deuxième livre des masques (criticism) 1898
D'un pays lointain (short stories) 1898
Les saints du paradis (poetry) 1898

Esthétique de la langue française (treatise) 1899
Le songe d'une femme (novel) 1899
  [*The Dream of a Woman*, 1927]
La culture des idées (criticism) 1900
  [*Decadence, and Other Essays on the Culture of Ideas*, 1921]
Oraisons mauvaises (poetry) 1900
Simone (poetry) 1901
Le chemin de velours (criticism) 1902
Le problème du style (criticism) 1902
Epilogues. 4 vols. (essays) 1903-13
Physique de l'amour (treatise) 1903
  [*The Natural Philosphy of Love*, 1931; also published as *The Physiology of Love*, 1932]
Promenades littéraires. 7 vols. (criticism) 1904-27
Dialogues des amateurs (essays) 1907
Promenades philosophiques. 3 vols. (criticism) 1905-09
  [*Philosophical Nights in Paris* (partial translation), 1920]
Une nuit au Luxembourg (novel) 1906
  [*A Night in the Luxembourg*, 1912]
Un coeur virginal (novel) 1907
  [*A Virgin Heart*, 1921]
Couleurs (short stories) 1908
  [*Colors*, 1929]
Nouveaux dialogues des amateurs (essays) 1910
Divertissements (poetry) 1912
Lettres d'un satyre (fictional letters) 1913
  [*Mr. Antiphilos, Satyr*, 1922]
Lettres à l'amazone (letters) 1914
  [*Letters to the Amazon*, 1931]
Pendant l'orage (essays) 1915
Pendant la guerre (letters) 1916
Rémy de Gourmont: Dust for Sparrows (poetry) 1920-21; published in the journal *The Dial*
Lettres à Sixtine (letters) 1921
Epigrams of Rémy de Gourmont (epigrams) 1923
L'ombre d'une femme (drama) [first publication] 1924
Lettres intimes a l'amazone (letters) 1927
Rémy de Gourmont: Selections from All His Works (essays, criticism, short stories, novels, and letters) 1928
Selected Writings (essays and criticism) 1966

*This work contains the essay "La dissociation des idées" ("The Dissociation of Ideas").

Translated selections of Gourmont's poetry have appeared in the following publications: *Six French Poets* and *The Poets of Modern France.*

THE SATURDAY REVIEW, LONDON (essay date 1903)

[*In the following excerpt, the critic provides a general survey of Gourmont's career as well as a review of* Epilogues, *which is described as the "journalism of a philosopher."*]

M. de Gourmont's new volume **Epilogues** is a reprint of the first series of those novel, personal, and surprising "reflections on life" which he has been contributing for the last eight years to each number of the *Mercure de France*. Every month, under the heading "Actualité", one finds a tiny ironical sermon, or some sensation of the day, a new form of crime, religion, morality, or literature, the death of a great or famous personage, the birth of a law or the renewal of an idea. Turning over the pages of this volume at random, one comes upon such titles as : "Une polémique sur les moeurs grecques", "Le Sionisme", "Ibsen et les critiques français", "La Dame au Tzigane", "Le Mysticisme bien tempéré", "Lettre à M. d'Annunzio", "La terreur scientifique", "Diana Vaughan". Here is something, you will say, for all tastes. But no: there is nothing here except for the taste of those who are ready to welcome an imperturbable attempt to see things as they are in themselves, and not as the things wish, or as we wish them, to be. M. de Gourmont appears to have no prejudices, unless a smiling preference or two, and a disdainful rejection or two, can be called prejudices. His mind seems to approach every new fact or idea with an alert, unslackening curiosity; or, rather, may be said to suffer the approach of every new fact or idea. Nothing is too slight or too obvious for his purpose; which is, indeed, a continuous process of thinking, undistracted by what is called the greatness or triviality of the material presented to his thought. Before each question he seems to begin over again at the beginning, without hesitation and without impatience.

This book of *Epilogues* is the journalism of a philosopher, and it marks the height to which journalism can rise. There is not a single section, out of the hundred and twenty-seven, of which the subject has not already supplied many journalists with the material of many columns. Take up an old newspaper, read the leaders which correspond to these *Epilogues,* and then read the *Epilogues,* which were written month by month, often probably with some of the haste of the journalist. These remain; the others have crumbled away with the paper on which they were printed. And it is because these, though written concerning the hour then passing, were not written from the shifting standpoint of that hour. The difference between the two is the whole difference between thought, which is a living thing, and opinion, which is the echo of a beaten drum.

There are few forms of literature in which M. de Gourmont has not at least experimented; it is perhaps as a critic that he is at his best, and there is not in contemporary France a finer, surer, more solid and liberal, critic of literature. In his study of literature he is not concerned only with the art, but, in a very serious and helpful way, with the whole technique of grammar, prosody, language itself. Some of his books are practically books of science: the *Esthétique de la Langue Française,* for instance, and *Le Problème du Style.* In the two volumes of *La Livre des Masques* . . . we have portraits of contemporary writers which are not only fine criticism but themselves literature. An earlier book on *Le Latin Mystique* is a close and learned study of the Latin poetry of the Middle Ages. . . . Always a scholar rather than a creator, yet a creator in his way, through a subtlety and strangeness of analysis which lack only some slight, incalculable thing to become great, M. de Gourmont has elaborated many perverse and fantastic legends, half tradition and half invention; legends of Lilith, of Phocas, of a certain "Château Singulier", of a certain "Princesse Phenissa", sometimes in dialogue, sometimes in vers libres. They are often printed with a not less elaborate art of singularity, sometimes in limited editions, "violet archevêque" and "pourpre cardinalice". In France the writers of books are rarely interested in the form in which their books are to appear, a strange indifference on the part of those who are certainly artists in writing. M. de Gourmont aims at evoking the atmosphere of the imaginary world of which, for the time, he has been an inhabitant, not only through his words, but before a page has been read, or before the book has been opened. (pp. 675-76)

"Rémy de Gourmont," in The Saturday Review, *London, Vol. 96, No. 2509, November 28, 1903, pp. 675-76.*

GIOVANNI PAPINI (essay date 1915)

[*Papini was an Italian novelist, poet, and critic. Early in his career, he became a member of the Futurist movement and helped to found several Futurist reviews, including* Leonardo *and* Lacerba, *both of which he also edited. Papini was an anarchist and an atheist who deliberately courted controversy, and has been described as an Italian H. L. Mencken: violently prejudiced and iconoclastic, polemical, intolerant, and extremely entertaining. Although these qualities limited the value of much of his criticism, they also made him a popular and influential figure in Italian letters. Papini, with others of his generation, put his strong opinions, his flair for brilliant invective, and his profound scholarship to work to purge Italian literature of much that he considered outdated and ridiculous, and to clear the way for a renaissance in Italian culture. Papini's view of Italian life and culture underwent a dramatic change when he converted to Catholicism in 1920. The following year he wrote his* Life of Christ, *a work that brought him world-wide recognition. From thenceforward, Catholicism and patriotism became the touchstones of Papini's philosophy. He became a staunch supporter of fascism, and was the professor of Italian literature at the University of Bologna under the fascist regime. Papini's critics note that his criticism from this later period, although it remained scholarly and eloquent, was often marred by "an hysterical dismissal of intelligence." In the following excerpt from an essay written a few days after Gourmont's death, Papini calls Gourmont "the most intelligent man in France," and "one of the greatest soldiers and heroes of pure thought." Papini praised Gourmont's method of the dissociation of ideas, and states that, despite his great intelligence, Gourmont's talent was not for creating original works of art, but for analyzing and understanding the works of others.*]

[Remy de Gourmont] was the most intelligent man in France, and one of the keenest intellects in the whole world. His brain was an instrument of precision. His thought had the lucidity of distilled alcohol, as clear as water of a mountain spring, yet drawn from purple clusters, and carrying the inebriation, the vertigo, the wild fancy of a year's experience compressed into a single hour. (p. 198)

Remy de Gourmont died too soon. He was only fifty-seven years of age, and he had never swung incense before any fool. Modest and alone in a great dark house full of books—how well I remember a luminous morning in November, 1906, in the Rue des Saints Pères!—he read books, read men and women, read the ancients and the moderns and *les jeunes,* and sought truth, clear French truth, pitiless contemporary European truth. And he set forth that truth ceaselessly, without cosmetics, without reticence or omission. The truth—that hard and unpleasant other side of the shield of illusion. "Je ne ferai que dire la vérité," said Flaubert, "mais elle sera horrible, cruelle et nue" ["I shall only speak the truth; but it will be horrible, cruel, and bare"]. One who takes the vows of obedience to such truth loses all right to earthly beatitude, loses all hope of swift glory, all sympathy. From the days of Socrates to those of Nietzsche, the man who analyzes and dissociates, the man who breaks through the surface of useful and convenient beliefs to reveal the fierce and injurious truths that lie beneath, has been ostracized and condemned as an enemy to the State and to the gods.

Remy de Gourmont was of this ill-regarded family. Less serene and profound than Socrates, less violent and grand than Nietzsche, he resembled more closely the great Frenchmen of the eighteenth century. He had the malice of Voltaire (with Voltaire's apparently innocent narrative simplicity); he had d'Alembert's passion for disinterested exactness; he had the good-natured frivolity of Fontenelle; he had the branching curiosity of Bayle. But the man he most closely resembles is Diderot, who has always seemed to me the most complete and vigorous genius among the Encyclopedists. In Diderot, as in Remy de Gourmont, one may find a natural inclination toward general ideas, an enjoyment of specific facts and scientific theories, a happy, spontaneous interweaving of art and philosophy, of myth and thought, of type and paradox, a common dilettanteism in criticism and in painting.

It goes without saying that Remy de Gourmont was not merely a repetition of Diderot, for no man, least of all a man of genius, is a repetition of a predecessor. Between the one and the other there lies a century of corrective and advancing culture. Romanticism has not been in vain. Stendhal and Taine have left their impress on brains formed after 1870.

The intellectual life of Remy de Gourmont—his only real life—began thirty years ago. His first book, *Merlette,* was published in 1886. That was the time of the beginnings of Symbolism. He was at once convinced of the importance of that movement, which was so long berated by the critics, and is now finding a little affectionate justice. Remy de Gourmont was one of the first of the Symbolist theorists and poets. As artist he worked in the vanguard. Novel, drama, lyric: he set himself free; he sought to find himself.

I do not intend to attempt here an estimate of Gourmont as a creative artist. In *Sixtine* there is new and fine psychology; in *Lilith* there is a harmonious luxury of fancy; in the *Pèlerin du Silence* and in the *Proses Moroses* there are capricious and terrible inventions worthy of Villiers de l'Isle Adam at his best; in the *Divertissements* (in which the *Hieroglyphics,* examples of the most artificial Symbolism, are republished) there is the sensitiveness of a wise spirit bursting at times into poetry. But the greatness of Remy de Gourmont, to my mind, does not lie in these old works of his.

With the keenness of his intelligence and the exquisite refinement of his taste, he succeeded in creating a group of poems which at first sight might be classed with those of Mallarmé. But his creative works will not stand repeated reading. You miss the pulse of life in that magnificent play of words, cleverly sought out and cleverly strung together. In his prose works, even in those of artistic character, the best passages are those in which psychological discoveries or unusual thoughts are stated in surprising form. In view of the wideness of his reading and the aristocracy of his culture, it was easy for him to catch the method of the trade and to give to his bookish imagination a certain electric semblance of life. But his genius did not lie in this field. Art requires intelligence, but it requires something more. Intelligence may discipline and purify inspiration, and it may even imitate it, to the confusion of the incompetent. But it does not suffice for the creation of strong and permanent works.

Remy de Gourmont was born to understand and to enjoy. His famous book on the *Latin Mystique* . . . , almost a masterpiece, revealed his bent for criticism—understood in the broadest sense of the word and of the idea. From then on, while he continued to write stories and poems from time to time, his richest and most important books, the books that perfectly express him, were his books of criticism. One who desires to know and love him should read the two [*Livres des Masques, L'Esthétique de la Langue Française, La Culture des Idées, Le Chemin de Velours, Le Problème du Style*] . . . , and the several volumes in which he collected his extensive contributions to the *Mercure de France;* the *Promenades Littéraires,* the *Prom-*

enades Philosophiques, the *Epilogues,* the *Dialogues des Amateurs.*

Thousands and thousands of pages; hundreds and hundreds of subjects and of thoughts: one motive, one man, with kindly, mobile, piercing eyes.

The dominant principle of Gourmont's great inquiry is to be sought in the essay on the **"Dissociation des idées,"** in the book called *La Culture des idées.*

I do not mean to imply that the whole of Gourmont is to be found in this passionless dismantling and divorcing of ideas. He deals in nuances; he may feign to believe, and to let himself be carried on by the regular and accepted currents. But the secret of his liberating power lies precisely in that delicate virtuosity which applies itself to the decomposition of thoughts that are apparently simple, to the separation of pairs which had been thought indissoluble, to the reëstablishment of harmonies and relationships between ideas which had been regarded as heterogeneous and distant, to the search for bits of truth amid the refuse of prejudice, to the gentle denuding of the most solemn truths, revealing, to startled eyes, the bare bones of contradiction. There is in his work a continual testing and experimenting; a knocking with the knuckles to find out what is empty and what is full; a search this way and that to discover the multiform paths of existence; a sounding of the stagnant wells of life and of the troubled seas of philosophy to find a sunken fragment, a lonely island. There is a turning and tossing on the pillow of doubt; a tenacious and joyous effort toward elemental reality (a reality ignoble, to be sure, but sincere); a polygonal assault upon the strongest fortresses of scientific and moral and metaphysical religion; a mania for examining, elucidating, purifying; and, finally, a delight, at times merely sterile, in giving utterly free play to an intelligence that finds rest and satisfaction only in itself, even though it be on the edge of the abyss.

And there are traces of pleasant dilettanteism, of purposeless irony, of facile journalism, of sportive surface literature. Remy de Gourmont wrote so much—and not always of his own free will or for his own pleasure—that one naturally finds passages which do not rest on thought, improvisations without structure. But if one follows the main line of his thought, even in his fantastic deviations, even in the weary efforts of piece-work, one can trace a penetrating certainty, a thread woven of eagerly disinterested meditation, a sad and personal profundity under a surface so clear that there seems to be no substance beneath, a passionate pursuit of truth amid a nomadism that has the look of vagabondage. And such traits may well lead us to regard Remy de Gourmont as one of the greatest soldiers and heroes of pure thought. (pp. 199-205)

> *Giovanni Papini, "Remy de Gourmont," in his* Four and Twenty Minds, *edited and translated by Ernest Hatch Wilkins, Thomas Y. Crowell Company Publishers, 1922, pp. 198-207.*

AMY LOWELL (essay date 1915)

[*Lowell was the leading proponent of Imagism in American poetry. Like the Symbolists before her, some of whom she examined in* Six French Poets, *Lowell experimented with free verse forms. Under the influence of Ezra Pound, Lowell exhibited in her poetry the new style of Imagism, consisting of clear and precise rhetoric, exact rendering of images, and greater metrical freedom. Although she was popular in her time, standard evaluations of Lowell accord her more importance as a promoter of new artistic ideas than as a poet in her own right. In the following excerpt from* Six French Poets, *Lowell refers to Gourmont as the most influential French writer of his generation. In a discussion of his poetry, she praises him as "the great teacher of certain effects, the instructor in verbal shades." She also praises him for his tireless support of the Symbolist movement, noting that, "individualism, not only in art, but in everything else, has been his creed." In summing up Gourmont's role in literature, Lowell laments the lack of a "singleness of purpose" in his work.]*

[No] one of the later period of French literature has been more prominent than [Remy de Gourmont], and no one has had a greater influence upon the generation of writers that have followed his. He has had this influence directly, through his poems; and indirectly, by his critical writings and philological studies.

As it used to be said that Meredith was the writer's writer, I might say that Gourmont is the poet for poets. He is the great teacher of certain effects, the instructor in verbal shades. No one has studied more carefully than he the sounds of vowels and consonants. Not even from his great teacher, Mallarmé, can more be learnt. As a producer of colour in words, he cedes to no one; his knowledge of the technique of poetry is unsurpassed.

"Poet, critic, dramatist, *savant,* biologist, philosopher, novelist, philologian and grammarian," is the way the editors of *Poètes d'Aujourd'hui* style him. And really, the extent of his literary activity takes one's breath away. Of course, the danger to such a man is in the almost inevitable Jack-of-all-Trades result which such a multitude of avocations trails along with it. It is heresy to whisper such a thing, but it cannot really be denied that in only one of these branches has Gourmont made himself supreme. But in that he has no equal. The aesthetic of the French language (to borrow one of his own titles); there he is on absolutely indisputable ground.

Yet it would not be fair to give you the idea that he has done merely well along his other lines. Can a man so conversant with the art of writing ever write merely well? Gourmont's novels and tales are among the best of the last twenty years, only others have surpassed him; the same is true of his poems. But the way he has written, no one can surpass him there; and we, who try to write, mull over his pages for hours at a time, and endeavour to learn the lesson which he has analyzed and illustrated for us. Along with that is another lesson, written as clearly in his pages, of what not to do, of the necessity for singleness of purpose, of the terrible pitfall looming always before the man who is at once an artist and an insatiably curious person.

Great, excessively great, people can do it. Leonardo da Vinci did it. He pulled the two characters along side by side, to the profit of both. But Remy de Gourmont has not quite done it, and it is natural to suppose that the literary masterpieces he might have made have wasted away while he dabbled in science. *Physique de l'Amour* is a most interesting volume on the sexual instinct in animals. But there are many books on the subject by others more competent for the task. And I cannot help thinking it a little odd that this should be the only purely scientific essay he has written. Interesting though it is, contemplated in its place among Gourmont's work as a whole, should we not consider it as another evidence of that preoccupation with sex which has robbed his books of the large view they might have had? It cannot be denied that a man who plays perpetually upon an instrument of one string is confining himself within a very small musical compass.

Is Gourmont's work so diversified after all? Yes, and no. But let us work up to these considerations gradually, and examine them in their proper place. (pp. 107-10)

[Gourmont's] first book, a novel called *Merlette,* appeared in 1886, and very little of his real originality appeared in it, although it contained pleasant descriptions of Normandy. His next book, *Sixtine,* came out in 1890. Its second title was *Roman de la Vie Cérébrale,* and that might stand as subtitle for all his work. Oh, the delightful book that *Sixtine* is! I remember reading it in a sort of breathless interest. The hero is a writer, and everything that happens to him he translates almost bodily into his work. Two stories are carried on at the same time, the real one and the one he is writing. The chapters follow each other with no regular order, the reader only knows which story is which by the context, and the incidents of the written story are sometimes all he learns of the real story, which is taken up again later at a point farther on.

But what a childish way to tell of a book so full of startling revolutionism! *Sixtine* is indeed a novel of the life of the brain. Gourmont wishes to prove that the world is only a simulacrum, and the perception of it hallucinatory. *Sixtine* is metaphysics masking as a story, and Hubert d'Entrague is the Gourmont of the period, with his knowledge, his curiosity, and, too, his sensual side. But, inconceivable undercurrent though it has, it has an appearance of firm ground. Paris is there, with its *quais,* its Luxembourg, its boulevards, its Museum, its Bibliothèque Nationale; and Normandy is there, with its fields and apple orchards. (pp. 110-11)

In an interview accorded to a representative of the *Écho de Paris,* shortly after the publication of *Sixtine,* Gourmont says, "They tell me that in my recently published novel, *Sixtine,* I have produced *Symbolisme.* Now behold my innocence. I never guessed it. Nevertheless, I learned it without great astonishment: unconsciousness plays so large a part in intellectual operations. I even believe it plays the greatest of all." Certainly, Remy de Gourmont had "produced *Symbolisme,*" as unconsciously as most of the *Symbolistes* produced it at first. "*Symbolisme* is an attitude of mind, not a school," as Tancrède de Visan very well says, in his *L'Attitude du Lyrisme Contemporain,* "a lyric ideal in conformity with other tendencies of modern life." To understand what this lyric ideal was, and how it came about, we must go back a little. No study of Remy de Gourmont can be complete without taking him in connection with the *Symboliste* movement. (pp. 113-14)

Let me quote Gourmont himself, in the "Preface" to the first *Livre des Masques:* "What does *Symbolisme* mean? If one keeps to its narrow and etymological sense, almost nothing; if one goes beyond that, it means: individualism in literature, liberty of art, abandonment of existing forms, a tending toward what is new, strange, and even bizarre; it also may mean idealism, disdain of the social anecdote, anti-naturalism, a tendency to take only the characteristic detail out of life, to pay attention only to the act by which a man distinguishes himself from another man, and to desire only to realize results, essentials; finally, for poets, *Symbolisme* seems associated with *vers libre.*" And farther on in the same "Preface," contradicting Nordau, who believes that only when conforming to existing standards is art sane, Gourmont says: "We differ violently from this opinion. The capital crime for a writer is conformity, imitation, the submission to rules and teaching. The work of a writer should be, not merely the reflection, but the enlarged reflection, of his personality.

"The sole excuse which a man can have for writing is to write down himself, to unveil for others the sort of world which mirrors itself in his individual glass; his only excuse is to be original; he should say things not yet said, and say them in a form not yet formulated. He should create his own aesthetics—and we should admit as many aesthetics as there are original minds, and judge them for what they are and not what they are not. Admit then that *Symbolisme* is, even though excessive, even though tempestuous, even though pretentious, the expression of individualism in art." (pp. 119-20)

Remy de Gourmont is one of the foremost *Symbolistes* then, from every point of view. He has aided the movement and flaunted its banner, first unconsciously, as we have seen, later consciously. Individualism, not only in art, but in everything else, has been his creed. He has welcomed young men of talent, and been their encourager and adviser. For himself, his novels are all "romans de la vie cérébrale," they are pictures of the intimate life of his own brain and personality. He is an intellectual; and his novels, and tales, and poems, are intellectual *tours de force*. (pp. 120-21)

Sixtine was followed, in 1892, by *Le Latin Mystique*, with a preface by J.-K. Huysmans. This book is a study of the Latin writers of the Middle Ages, who greatly attracted Gourmont, as they had Mallarmé and Huysmans. (p. 122)

[In "**Litanies de la Rose**"] the author has given roses of fifty-seven colours. Nowhere else is his wonderful manipulation of words so apparent, and his gift for perceiving and describing colours so displayed. The poem is an astounding profusion of sounds, of pictures, of colours, of smells. It is a mixture of artifice and spontaneity, "of Heaven and Hell," as a critic has said. Each rose is supposed to be a woman, and the kind of women can best be shown by the two lines with which the poem begins:

> Fleur hypocrite,
> Fleur du silence.
>
> ["Hypocritical flower,
> Flower of silence."]

That Gourmont has not much opinion of women, this poem would seem to prove. But that need not matter to us. Some poems are beautiful because of what they say, some because of the way they say it. Gourmont describes these unpleasant women, compounded of lies and deceits, in a way to make one weep with the beauty of the presentation. (p. 126)

An odd pitiful tenderness is here, and an irony as fine and sad as mist.

"**Fleurs de Jadis**" and "**Le Dit des Arbres**," are the two other poems in this pattern. Again they are women, but the bitter jabbing is not here.... Here again Gourmont shows his erudition, his observation, and his love for nature. His flowers are beautiful, believable.... (pp. 127-28)

Undoubtedly these three are Gourmont's finest poems. They, and particularly "**Litanies de la Rose**," are the ones to which Gourmont's admirers chiefly refer. I am an admirer of Gourmont's myself, and I prefer these poems to his others. They contain more of his original and peculiar qualities. But Gourmont has left them out of a collection of his poems called *Divertissements* .... He has underscored this volume *Poèmes en Vers*, which I suppose means poems in regular metres. This is what he says about it in the "Preface:" "In this collection there are very few purely verbal poems, those dominated by

the pleasure of managing the obliging flock of words; it can easily be understood that forcing such obedience has discouraged me in the exact measure that I assured myself of their excessive docility. Perhaps it will be found that I have ended by conceiving the poem under a too despoiled form, but that was perhaps permitted to the author of "**Litanies de la Rose**," which poem has been rejected for a collection that I wished representative of a life of sentiment rather than a life of art." The rest of the sentence we need not quote, it is very sad, and shows Gourmont at fifty-seven considering himself an old man, and rightly so I fear, with waning powers.

What does that mean? That *vers libre*, which he himself considers as one of the most indigenous qualities of the *Symboliste* poet, as we saw in his Preface to the *Livre des Masques*, has been with him not a conviction, but an experiment? Or that this extremely French Frenchman finds himself, now that his energies are weakening, atavistically returning to the traditions of his race? We can only say that whatever his theories, *vers libre* has never seemed an irresistible form with him. (pp. 128-30)

The following years saw the publication of a number of books, all in prose, and his first volume of contemporary criticism, *Le Livre des Masques*. (p. 131)

More novels and tales, a second *Livre des Masques*, and in 1899, another book of poems, *Les Saintes du Paradis*. .... *Les Saintes du Paradis* might have been written by a believer, or by an artist using Catholicism merely as decoration. Gourmont has assured us that with him this latter is the case. With simplicity, with charm, these saints pass before us. Here are nineteen saints stepped out of some old missal, each with her legend carefully detailed, and each painted in the beautiful, bright colours so dear to the mediaeval illuminator. In ... "**Dedication**," they file past us in some country of clear pinks and greens, painted by Fra Angelico. (p. 132)

In 1890, appeared the first of Gourmont's philological works, *Esthétique de la Langue Française*, followed, in 1900, by another, *La Culture des Idées*. Between them was another novel, *Le Songe d'une Femme*, and in 1900, the last of his poems came out. It is entitled, "**Simone, Poème Champêtre**." There is nothing very astounding about "**Simone**," but there is a great deal that is very delightful. Gourmont is doing something more than play with words. Here he makes his words subordinate themselves to feeling, to sentiment. We no longer have the artificial and learned *vers libre* of "**Litanies de la Rose**" and "**Fleurs de Jadis**," nor the long, quiet, uneven lines of *Les Saintes du Paradis*—eleven, thirteen, sometimes nineteen syllables in length. For the first time, Gourmont tries more tripping metres, metres of a sharp, light rhythm. It seems as though a greater interior calm had left him room for simpler, gayer-hearted joys. (pp. 135-36)

Truly, in reading these poems, we go from one pleasant country scene to another, and step from season to season of the bucolic year. Not the least interesting part of them is the new side they show us of Gourmont's complex character. (pp. 140-41)

Following "**Simone**" in *Divertissements*, is a group of poems called *Paysages Spirituels*. [The poem *Chanson de L'Automne*] bears the date 1898, and although it therefore precedes the publication of "**Simone**," it does not really precede it, for "**Simone**" was written in 1892. ... [*Chanson de L'Automne* is almost] a return to the old ballad form. ... So [Gourmont] works out his destiny, at once modern and rooted to the past.

After "Simone" came more philology. *Le Chemin de Velours,* and *Le Problème du Style.* Then his one scientific essay, *Physique de l'Amour,* in which if there were space I could show that he is always a poet, as well in science as in criticism. Then follow the four volumes of literary essays, *Promenades Littéraires,* and the three volumes of *Promenades Philosophiques.* Four volumes of *Épilogues,* which are reflections on current topics, and two more novels, *Une Nuit au Luxembourg* and *Un Coeur Virginal.*

What can one say of such a man? How classify him? How measure the extent of his accomplishment, of his influence? . . . I have only considered him as a poet. And in spite of his tales, his novels, his plays, his criticisms, and his essays, I believe him to be first of all a poet. He has said somewhere, "I write to clarify my ideas." The artist has been crowded out by the thinker, the seeker after truth. Has that been a misfortune? Who knows. (pp. 144-46)

> Amy Lowell, "Remy de Gourmont," in her *Six French Poets: Studies in Contemporary Literature, 1915.* Reprint by Houghton Mifflin Company, 1921, pp. 105-46.

RICHARD ALDINGTON   (essay date 1916)

[*Aldington is perhaps best remembered as the editor of the Imagist periodical* The Egoist *and as an influential member of that movement, which included Hilda Doolittle—who became his first wife in 1913—Ezra Pound, and Amy Lowell, among others. The Imagists viewed themselves as the saviors of a dead language; their major goal was to free poetry from excesive verbiage and vague generalities and to utilize precise imagery. Aldington's work with this group was cut short by his service in World War I, which had a damaging effect on his mental health and his career. It took him years to recover from his experiences, and once he did he virtually gave up writing poetry for prose. However, as a novelist he achieved some success with his angry yet honest attacks on war and on his native England. As a literary critic and biographer, Aldington combined his skills as a poet, his perceptiveness as an extremely sensitive reader, and his personal reminiscences to produce works which are creative as well as informative. In the following excerpt, Aldington offers a general assessment of Gourmont and discusses Gourmont's four plays:* Lilith, Théodat, Le vieux roi, *and* La princesse Phénissa. *Aldington explores the plays' merits as dramatic literature and examines their themes, which he finds include such customary preoccupations of Gourmont's as churchly asceticism, sensuality, and feminine psychology.*]

Remy de Gourmont will never be a popular author—it was the last thing in the world he wanted to be—not even with the finer sort of popularity which men like Robert Browning and Gustave Flaubert have achieved. Browning and Flaubert are typical of the really great author whose work, at first sneered at or ignored, is recognized by all later and less prejudiced generations as being of supreme beauty. (p. 167)

[Remy de Gourmont] was undoubtedly a great master, but he is largely read and appreciated by other authors and artists, not by the generality of mankind. He reflects the influences of his epoch; he did not create one. Like Browning and Flaubert he was at first misunderstood, is still misunderstood, was slow to win appreciation, yet did win it from very many critics of distinction. His name stands for fine work, for a fine standard of literature; he is known to men of letters the world over; but he is not one of the great creators. His work is critical not creative; even in his poems, novels and plays—not the most considerable part of his work—the spirit is largely critical.

Miss Lowell, in her clever essay on Remy de Gourmont [see excerpt dated 1915], hints that she feels his versatility to be the chief cause of his comparative inferiority—an inferiority which places him just below the great creators, though vastly above the horde of imitators. I think she is right: as a poet, Remy de Gourmont beautifully carried out theories which were current in his time; he did not create like Rimbaud or Laforgue, or Mallarmé; as a "cerebral" novelist he has not Huysmans' rasping verve and exasperated precision of epithet; as a sceptic philosopher, he has Anatole France for rival; as a naturalist, as a writer on sex, he has Fabre and Havelock Ellis before him; as a dramatist, he owes a deal to Maeterlinck; even as a prose stylist one hesitates to place him above Henri de Régnier; only as a critic of literature, as an exponent of aesthetic scholarship is he really unrivalled—the two *Livres des Masques,* the five volumes of the *Promenades Littéraires* and *Le Latin Mystique* are marvels of critical insight. He defined and defended Symbolism as no other writer has done or could have done.

All these great names which I have been quoting are of men who were his contemporaries, and whose diverse talents are, as it were, synthesised in the work of one man of their period— Remy de Gourmont. That is what I am trying to get at—he is the synthesis of a great period of intellectual activity (1885-1914), inferior perhaps to some of his contemporaries in their own particular sphere, but superior to them all in the width of his interests and in the diversity of his accomplishments. If he was not supreme in any one branch of literary creation, there exists none in which he has not achieved fine, sometimes magnificent, work.

Subtlety, complexity—an over-subtlety which leads him to paradox, to espouse always the "other side" of a question (against the majority), to prefer an original half-truth to an accepted truism, to abandon the normal for the curious; a complexity which is sometimes impossible to disentangle, a complexity which he sometimes resented himself—these are the two salient characteristics of Remy de Gourmont. To expose all the threads of this multiform personality is perhaps impossible; to gain an adequate notion of his mind from reading one or two of his works is indeed impossible. . . . His four dramas, *Lilith, Théodat, Phénissa,* and *Le Vieux Roi,* are merely part of the output of an immensely active intelligence, constantly preoccupied with reflection and imaginings, but too restless, too complex, to concentrate a life-work on any one subject or branch of literature. (pp. 167-69)

It would be incorrect to represent de Gourmont as a man exclusively or even very deeply preoccupied with drama. But it is also clear that a mind so curious of everything would be certain to experiment in dramatic form. That he wrote four plays proves that his dramatic work was something more than an experiment. He is essentially a literary dramatist, by which I mean that he considered the drama primarily and perhaps wholly as a form of literature and not as an art in itself, as modern critics quite properly insist that it is. One of his plays, *Lilith,* is quite unplayable and was never intended to be played. *Théodat* was played in Paris many years ago, but I cannot find that the other two plays were ever produced. So you will see that as a dramatist, as indeed in almost everything, Remy de Gourmont was rather caviar to the general.

Théodat, the earliest of his plays, is in some ways the best, and is remarkable for the comparative maturity it shows. . . . The tragedy turns about a somewhat out-of-the-ordinary situation, placed in a century (the sixth) which has not been at all over-run by the average novelist and dramatist. In the sixth century the question of the celibacy of the clergy was still a very thorny one in the Western Empire. Popes and Councils had enacted different ordinances on the subject and great confusion prevailed. Apparently—I say apparently for I have no particular knowledge of early church history—clerks were allowed to marry at this time but not bishops, and if a clerk became a bishop it was not uncommon, if he were married, for him to repudiate his wife in order to show his piety. At least that is the situation as I gather it from Remy de Gourmont's play. It is quite certain that he would not have written it unless he had discovered full justification for it in ancient chronicles and church histories. The whole thing is one of those bizarre and curious situations which de Gourmont loved above everything. (The mixture of churchly asceticism and of sensuality is so characteristic of him that someone has described him as a cross between a satyr and a Benedictine monk.) His love of the church, its literature, traditions, and ceremonies was, at any rate partially, derived from his friend, Huysmans, and sex as a motive was one of the strongest features of the Naturalists.

Remy de Gourmont probably did not believe anything; he was interested in everything, and he saw in the church and in church history a source of literature which had been greatly neglected. It is incorrect to represent Remy de Gourmont as wilfully trampling on sacred things; he had more respect for the church than some of its members. But he was an artist primarily and when he wished to work out some situation he did not hesitate to use Christianity for his background and to use it just as it pleased him. "The sins of the flesh," he says in *Le Latin Mystique,* "have been inveighed against by moralists, Christian and non-Christian, in all ages and times; you must not blame me if they are often referred to in these pages." That is his apology and I think a just one. It may not be conventional good morals to show a Catholic bishop seduced from his vow of celibacy by a woman and that woman his own wife (which one would think sufficient excuse), but it is human nature. The contest between the spiritual man and the natural or animal man, is as old as the intellect; in *Théodat* Remy de Gourmont gives a rather special example and gives it well. The play has obvious defects, the chief being the over-duration of the first incident, the too literary talk on heresies and the too "symbolical" enumeration of the properties of the holy vestments. On the other hand the woman's temptation of Théodat is a great deal more human and subtle than, for example, the rather trivial "temptations," of Salomé in Oscar Wilde's play, or even in Flaubert's tale, for that matter. Maximienne is a more or less vital and credible person, for Remy de Gourmont really did know something, even so early as this, of feminine psychology, and later in life his wisdom and tolerance in these matters made one of the amiable sides of his character.

Lilith is simply the Bible story of Adam and Eve retold in dramatic form with great literary skill after a study of mystic or uncanonical works like the Kabbala, the Talmud, and the Apocrypha. It might be briefly described as a mediaeval mystery rewritten and commented on by a sensual sceptic. It is important to admirers of Remy de Gourmont as a turning point in his literary development. It marked a considerable advance in his art, but is most certainly not meat for babes or *jeunes filles* ["young women"]—those chains on free literature whose influence has been analyzed by de Gourmont in one of the most deliciously ironical of his essays.

La Princesse Phénissa and *Le Vieux Roi* fall naturally into another category. There is nothing of the church about them;

they show a more developed, more philosophical mind and a greater mastery of literary technique. There are examples of Symbolisme at its best, and Maeterlinck would not have been ashamed to own them. In each there is a definite philosophical idea worked out originally and skillfully. The *Princesse Phénissa* would be effective, though rather harrowing, if played. It is simply a symbolical working out of the tragedy of youth sacrificed to the selfishness of age. A queen has a lover and a beautiful, young, selfless daughter. The queen makes her lover marry her daughter, the princess. Phénissa then grows jealous, wants her lover back, and persuades him to murder his wife, for if he does, by some mysterious manner he will gain for himself, now growing old, the years which would have been hers and her child's. The poor princess and her unborn child are murdered—it is the past murdering the future; it is a symbol of what Europe is today. People talk about the selfishness of youth; but the selfishness of the aged is infinitely more horrible and more destructive. Remy de Gourmont's *Phénissa* does show under all its pomp and stiff brocades of Symbolisme this eternal struggle. When he wrote it I do not think he was conscious of its full significance, but it has certainly a bitter and obvious interpretation today.

The latest of his plays, *Le Vieux Roi,* was written nearly ten years after the first. He had had plenty of time to increase his knowledge of life and character. Here, as always, he is attracted by the strange and the abnormal. All through the play are veiled or direct references to curious passions; he does not hesitate to reveal thoughts and desires which are most often neglected or shunned by authors. In *Le Vieux Roi* . . . many people will doubtless see a likeness to King Lear, and in a sense de Gourmont has re-written Shakespeare's play from a modern standpoint. It is like the modern Russian novel of "futility"; no one gets what he wants: the Old King dies by accident, Yoland is killed by Gautier, Guislaine kills herself from grief, Floraine loses Yoland, Gautier becomes king but does not get Floraine, and Germaine loses her sister, Guislaine, the person she loved most on earth. It is a sombre little tragedy, with some very beautiful writing in it.

In introducing these plays to English-speaking readers . . . , I feel justified in claiming attention for them first on account of their very real merit and secondly because they are part, and only a small part, of the work of a master in literature. The work of Remy de Gourmont must be studied in its bulk before his real importance emerges. He belonged to a generation which is disappearing, whose influence in literature is declining, but that clear, sceptical, ironic mind can never lose its charm, never lose its real value. The men who direct the political destinies of Europe are uneducated and unintelligent besides a man of his capacity, and it is a melancholy reflection that our age could make so slight a practical use of so magnificent a brain. In one of his little essays Remy de Gourmont says that if all men thought as he the world would be so quiet that even in Paris one would be able to hear the hum of flies; if all men had thought as Remy de Gourmont there would have been no European war. (pp. 178-83)

*Richard Aldington, "Remy de Gourmont," in The
Drama, Vol. VI, No. 22, May, 1916, pp. 167-83.*

JAMES HUNEKER (essay date 1917)

*[Huneker was an American musician and critic. As a critic, he
focused on discovering the best of European music and literature
and introducing them to the American public. Huneker was an*

Holograph copy of a poem by Gourmont. From Rémy de Gourmont: Selections from All His Works, Volume I, *chosen and translated by Richard Aldington. Covici-Friede, Publishers, 1929. Used by permission of Crown Publishers, Inc.*

early advocate of impressionism in literary criticism and, as such, his writings in this genre were characteristically subjective and deeply marked by his often contagious enthusiasm and his love for the voluptuous. His prose style was rich and frequently eloquent. Huneker's critical ideas influenced many young writers of the twenties. Generally, the quality of his critical writings far surpassed the usual journalistic standards of the various periodicals to which he contributed. In the following excerpt from his collection* Unicorns, *Huneker discusses Gourmont's complexity as an artist and a critic. Huneker also argues that, although Gourmont never involved himself in the metaphysical controversy over instinct versus intelligence, those two forces perfectly delineated his personal intellectual dilemma.]*

De Gourmont was incomparable. Thought, not action, was his chosen sphere, but ranging up and down the vague and vast territory of ideas he encountered countless cerebral adventures; the most dangerous of all. An aristocrat born, he was, nevertheless, a convinced democrat. The latch was always lifted on the front door of his ivory tower. He did live in a certain sense a cloistered existence, a Benedictine of arts and letters; but he was not, as has been said, a sour hermit nursing morose fancies in solitude. De Gourmont, true pagan, enjoyed the gifts the gods provide, and had, despite the dualism of his nature, an epicurean soul. But of a complexity. He never sympathised with the disproportionate fuss raised by the metaphysicians about Instinct and Intelligence, yet his own magnificent cerebral apparatus was a battle-field over which swept the opposing hosts of Instinct and Intelligence, and in a half-hundred volumes the history of this conflict is faithfully set down. As personal as Maurice Barrès, without his egoism, as subtle as Anatole France, De Gourmont saw life steadier and broader than either of these two contemporaries. He was one who said "vast things simply." He was the profoundest philosopher of the three, and never, after his beginnings, exhibited a trace of the dilettante. Life soon became something more than a mere spectacle for him. He was a meliorist in theory and practice, though he asserted that Christianity, an Oriental-born religion, has not become spiritually acclimated among Occidental peoples. But he missed its consoling function; religion, the poetry of the poor, never had for him the prime significance that it had for William James; a legend, vague, vast, and delicious.

Old frontiers have disappeared in science and art and literature. We have Maeterlinck, a poet writing of bees, Poincaré, a mathematician opening our eyes to the mystic gulfs of space; solid matters resolved into mist, and the law of gravitation questioned. The new horizons beckon ardent youth bent on conquering the secrets of life. And there are more false beacon-lights than true. But if this is an age of specialists a man occasionally emerges who contradicts the formula. De Gourmont was at base a poet; also a dramatist, novelist, raconteur, man of science, critic, moralist of erudition, and, lastly, a philosopher. Both formidable and bewildering were his accomplishments. (pp. 19-20)

Prodigious incoherence might be reasonably expected from this diversity of interests, yet the result is quite the reverse. The artist in this complicated man banished confusion. He has told us that because of the diversity of his aptitudes man is distinguished from his fellow animals, and the variety in his labours is a proof positive of his superiority to such fellow critics as the mentally constipated Brunetière, the impressionistic Anatole France, the agile and graceful Lemaître, and the pedantic philistine Faguet. But if De Gourmont always attains clarity with no loss of depth, he sometimes mixes his genres; that is, the poet peeps out in his reports of the psychic life of insects, as the philosopher lords it over the pages of his fiction. A mystic betimes, he is a crystal-clear thinker. And consider the catholicity evinced in *Le Livre des Masques*. He wrote of such widely diverging talents as Maeterlinck, Mallarmé, Villiers de l'Isle Adam, and Paul Adam; of Henri de Regnier and Jules Renard; of Huysmans and Jules Laforgue; the mysticism of Francis Poictevin's style and the imagery of Saint-Pol-Roux he defined, and he displays an understanding of the first symbolist poet, Arthur Rimbaud, while disliking the personality of that abnormal youth. Buy why recite this litany of new talent literally made visible and vocal by our critic? It is a pleasure to record the fact that most of his swans remained swans and did not degenerate into tame geese. In this book he shows himself a profound psychologist.

Insatiably curious, he yet contrived to drive his chimeras in double harness and safely. His best fiction is *Sixtine* and *Une Nuit au Luxembourg,* if fiction they may be called. Never will their author be registered among bestsellers. *Sixtine* deals with the adventures of a masculine brain. Ideas are the hero. In *Un Coeur virginal* we touch earth, fleshly and spiritually. This story shocked its readers. It may be considered as a sequel to *Physique de l'Amour*. It shows mankind as a gigantic insect indulging in the same apparently blind pursuit of sex sensation as a beetle, and also shows us the "female of our species" endowed with less capacity for modesty than the lady mole, the most chaste of all animals. Disconcerting, too, is the psychology of the heroine's virginal soul, not, however, cynical; cynicism is the irony of vice, and De Gourmont is never cynical. But a master of irony.

Une Nuit au Luxembourg has been done into English. It handles with delicacy and frankness themes that in the hands of a lesser artist would be banished as brutal and blasphemous. The author knows that all our felicity is founded on a compromise between the dream and reality, and for that reason while he signals the illusion he never mocks it; he is too much an idealist. In the elaborately carved cups of his tales, foaming over with exquisite perfumes and nectar, there lurks the bitter drop of truth. He could never have said with Proudhon that woman is the desolation of the just; for him woman is often an obsession. Yet, captain of his instincts, he sees her justly; he is not subdued by sex. With a gesture he destroys the sentimental scaffolding of the sensualist and marches on to new intellectual conquests.

In *Lilith,* an Adamitic Morality, he reveals his Talmudic lore. The first wife of our common ancestor is a beautiful hell-hag, the accomplice of Satan in the corruption of the human race. Thus mediaeval play is epical in its Rabelaisian plainness of speech. Perhaps the Manichean in De Gourmont fabricated its revolting images. He had traversed the Baudelairian steppes

of blasphemy and black pessimism; Baudelaire, a poet who was a great critic. Odi profanum vulgus! ["I despise the common herd!"] was De Gourmont's motto, but his soul was responsive to so many contacts that he emerged, as Barrès emerged, a citizen of the world. Anarchy as a working philosophy did not long content him, although he never relinquished his detached attitude of proud individualism. He saw through the sentimental equality of J.-J. Rousseau. Rousseau it was who said that thinking man was a depraved animal. Perhaps he was not far from the truth. Man is an affective animal more interested in the immediate testimony of his senses than in his intellectual processes. His metaphysic may be but the reverberation of his sensations on the shore of his subliminal self, the echo of the sounding shell he calls his soul. And our critic had his scientific studies to console him for the inevitable sterility of soul that follows egoism and a barren debauch of the sensations. He did not tarry long in the valley of excess. His artistic sensibility was his saviour.

Without being a dogmatist, De Gourmont was an antagonist of absolutism. A determinist, (which may be dogmatism à rebours), a relativist, he holds that mankind is not a specially favoured species of the animal scale; thought is only an accident, possibly the result of rich nutrition. An automaton, man has no free will, but it is better for him to imagine that he has; it is a sounder working hypothesis for the average human. The universe had no beginning, it will have no end. There is no first link or last in the chain of causality. Everything must submit to the law of causality; to explain a blade of grass we must dismount the stars. Nevertheless, De Gourmont no more than Renan, had the mania of certitude. Humbly he interrogates the sphinx. There are no isolated phenomena in time or space. The mass of matter is eternal. Man is an animal submitting to the same laws that govern crystals or brutes. He is the expression of matter in physique and chemistry. Repetition is the law of life. Thought is a physiological product; intelligence the secretion of matter and is amenable to the law of causality. (This sounds like Taine's famous definition of virtue and vice.) And who shall deny it all in the psychochemical laboratories? It is not the rigid old-fashioned materialism, but a return to the more plastic theories of Lamarck and the transformism of the Dutch botanist, Hugo de Vries. For De Gourmont the Darwinian notion that man is at the topmost notch of creation is as antique and absurd as most cosmogonies; indeed, it is the Asiatic egocentric idea of creation. Jacob's ladder repainted in Darwinian symbols. Voilà l'ennemi! ["Here is the enemy!"] said De Gourmont and put on his controversial armour. What blows, what sudden deadly attacks were his!

Quinton has demonstrated to the satisfaction of many scientists that bird life came later on our globe than the primates from whom we stem. The law of thermal constancy proves it by the interior temperature of birds. Man preceded the carnivorous and ruminating animals, of whom the bodily temperature is lower than that of birds. The ants and bees and beavers are not a whit more automatic than mankind. Automatism, says Ribot, is the rule. Thought is not free, wrote William James, when to it an affirmation is added; then it is but the affirmation of a preference. "L'homme," asserts De Gourmont, "varie à l'infini sa mimique. Sa supériorité, c'est la diversité immense de ses aptitudes." ["Mankind is infinitely various in its gesture of mimicry. Its superiority lies in this immense diversity of aptitudes"]. He welcomed Jules de Gaultier and his theory of Bovaryisme; of the vital lie, because of which we pretend to be what we are not. That way spells security, if not progress. The idea of progress is another necessary illusion, for it provokes a multiplicity of activities. Our so-called free will is naught but the faculty of making a decision determined by a great and varied number of motives. As for morality, it is the outcome of tribal taboos; the insect and animal world shows deepest-dyed immorality, revolting cruelty, and sex perversity. Rabbits and earthworms through no fault of their own suffer from horrible maladies. From all of which our critic deduces his law of intellectual constancy. The human brain since prehistoric times has been neither diminished nor augmented; it has remained like a sponge, which can be dry or saturated, but still remains itself. It is a constant. In a favourable environment it is enriched. The greatest moment in the history of the human family was the discovery of fire by an anthropoid of genius. Prometheus then should be our god. Without him we should have remained more or less simian, and probably of arboreal habits.

A synthetic brain is De Gourmont's, a sower of doubts, though not a No-Sayer to the universe. He delights in challenging accepted "truths." Of all modern thinkers a master of Vues d'ensembles ["general views"], he smiles at the pretensions, usually a mask for poverty of ideas, of so-called "general ideas." He dissociates such conventional grouping of ideas as Glory, Justice, Decadence. The shining ribs of disillusion shine through his psychology; a psychology of nuance and finesse. Disillusioning reflections, these. Not to be put in any philosophical pigeonhole, he is as far removed from the eclecticism of Victor Cousin as from the verbal jugglery and metaphysical murmurings of Henri Bergson. The world is his dream; but it is a tangible dream, charged with meaning, order, logic. The truest reality is thought. Action spoils. (Goethe said: "Thought expands, action narrows.") Our abstract ideas are metaphysical idols, says Jules de Gaultier. The image of the concrete is De Gourmont's touchstone. Théophile Gautier declared that he was a man for whom the visible world existed. He misjudged his capacity for apprehending reality. The human brain, excellent instrument in a priori combinations is inept at perceiving realities. The "Sultan of the Epithet," as De Goncourt nicknamed "le bon Théo," was not the "Emperor of Thought," according to Henry James, and for him it was a romantic fiction spun in the rich web of his fancy. A vaster, greyer world is adumbrated in the books of De Gourmont. He never allowed symbolism to deform his representation of sober, every-day life. He pictured the future domain of art and ideas as a fair and shining landscape no longer a series of little gardens with high walls. A hater of formulas, sects, schools, he teaches that the capital crime of the artist, the writer, the thinker, is conformity. (Yet how serenely this critic swims in classic currents!) The artist's work should reflect his personality, a magnified reflection. He must create his own aesthetic. There are no schools, only individuals. And of consistency he might have said that it is oftener a mule than a jewel.

Sceptical in all matters, though never the fascinating sophist that is Anatole France, De Gourmont criticised the thirty-six dramatic situations, reducing the number to four. Man as centre in relation to himself; in relation to other men; in relation to the other sex; in relation to God, or Nature. His ecclesiastical fond ["foundation"] may be recognised in Le Chemin de Velours with its sympathetic exposition of Jesuit doctrine, and the acuity of its judgments on Pascal and the Jansenists. The latter section is as an illuminating foot-note to the history of Port-Royal by Sainte-Beuve. The younger critic has the supple intellect of the supplest-minded Jesuit. His bias toward the order is unmistakable. There are few books I reread with more

pleasure than this Path of Velvet. Certain passages in it are as silky and sonorous as the sound of Eugène Ysaye's violin.

The colour of De Gourmont's mind is stained by his artistic sensibility. A maker of images, his vocabulary astounding as befits both a poet and philologist, one avid of beautiful words, has variety. The temper of his mind is tolerant, a quality that has informed the finer intellects of France since Montaigne. His literary equipment is unusual. A style as brilliant, sinuous, and personal as his thought; flexible or massive, continent or coloured, he discourses at ease in all the gamuts and modes major, minor, and mixed. A swift, weighty style, the style of a Latinist; a classic, not a romantic style. His formal sense is admirable. The tenderness of Anatole France is absent, except in his verse, which is less spontaneous than volitional. A pioneer in new aesthetic pastures, De Gourmont is a poet for poets. He has virtuosity, though the gift of tears nature—possibly jealous because of her prodigality—has denied him. But in the curves of his overarching intellect there may be found wit, gaiety, humour, the Gallic attributes, allied with poetic fancy, profundity of thought, and a many-sided comprehension of life, art, and letters. He is in the best tradition of French criticism only more versatile than either Sainte-Beuve or Taine; as versatile as Doctor Brandes or Arthur Symons, and that is saying much. With Anatole France he could have exclaimed: "The longer I contemplate human life, the more I believe that we must give it, for witnesses and judges, Irony and Pity. . . ." (pp. 24-32)

James Huneker, "Remy de Gourmont: His Ideas, the Colour of His Mind," in his Unicorns, Charles Scribner's Sons, 1917, pp. 18-32.

EZRA POUND (essay date 1919)

[An American poet and critic, Pound is regarded as one of the most innovative and influential figures in twentieth-century Anglo-American poetry. He was instrumental in editorially and financially aiding T. S. Eliot, Wyndham Lewis, James Joyce, and William Carlos Williams, among others. Pound's Cantos is one of the most ambitious poetic cycles of the century, and his series of satirical poems Hugh Selwyn Mauberley is ranked with Eliot's The Waste Land as a significant attack upon the decadence of modern culture. Pound considered the United States a cultural wasteland, and for that reason, he spent most of his life in Europe. In the following excerpt, which first appeared in the Little Review in 1919, Pound discusses what he calls the "quality" of Gourmont's mind, demonstrating characteristic aspects of Gourmont's approach to art by contrasting his work to that of Henry James. James, Pound contends, was an artist of the circumstantial caught up in describing the "setting, detail, nuance" and "social aroma" of his subjects. In contrast, Pound describes Gourmont as "an artist of the nude" concerned with only the "permanent human elements" of his subjects, and with portraying their "differences of emotional timbre."]

The mind of Rémy de Gourmont was less like the mind of Henry James than any contemporary mind I can think of. James' drawing of moeurs contemporaines ["contemporary manners"] was so circumstantial, so concerned with the setting, with detail, nuance, social aroma, that his transcripts were "out of date" almost before his books had gone into a second edition; out of date that is, in the sense that his interpretations of society could never serve as a guide to such supposititious utilitarian members of the next generation as might so desire to use them.

He has left his scene and his characters, unalterable as the little paper flowers permanently visible inside the lumpy glass paperweights. He was a great man of letters, a great artist in portrayal; he was concerned with mental temperatures, circumvolvulous social pressures, the clash of contending conventions, as Hogarth with the cut of contemporary coats.

On no occasion would any man of my generation have broached an intimate idea to H. J., or to Thomas Hardy, O.M., or, years since, to Swinburne, or even to Mr Yeats with any feeling that the said idea was likely to be received, grasped, comprehended. However much one may have admired Yeats' poetry; however much one may have been admonished by Henry James' prose works, one has never thought of agreeing with either.

You could, on the other hand, have said to Gourmont anything that came into your head; you could have sent him anything you had written with a reasonable assurance that he would have known what you were driving at. If this distinction is purely my own, and subjective, and even if it be wholly untrue, one will be very hard pressed to find any other man born in the "fifties" of whom it is even suggestible.

Gourmont prepared our era; behind him there stretches a limitless darkness; there *was* the counter-reformation, still extant in the English printer; there *was* the restoration of the Inquisition by the Catholic Roman Church, holy and apostolic, in the year of grace 1824; there was the Mephistopheles period, morals of the opera left over from the Spanish seventeenth-century plays of "capa y espada"; Don Juan for subject matter, etc.; there was the period of English Christian bigotry, Saml. Smiles, exhibition of 1851 ("Centennial of 1876"), machine-made building "ornament", etc., enduring in the people who did not read Saml. Butler; there was the Emerson-Tennysonian plus optimism period; there was the "aesthetic" era during which people "wrought" as the impeccable Beerbohm has noted; there was the period of funny symboliste trappings, "sin", satanism, rosy cross, heavy lilies, Jersey Lilies, etc. . . . ; all these periods had mislaid the light of the eighteenth century; though in the symbolistes Gourmont had his beginning.

In contradiction to, in wholly antipodal distinction from, Henry James, Gourmont was an artist of the nude. He was an intelligence almost more than an artist; when he portrays, he is concerned with hardly more than the permanent human elements. His people are only by accident of any particular era. He is poet, more by possessing a certain quality of mind than by virtue of having written fine poems; you could scarcely contend that he was a novelist.

He was intensely aware of the differences of emotional timbre; and as a man's message is precisely his *façon de voir*, his modality of apperception, this particular awareness was his "message".

Where James is concerned with the social tone of his subjects, with their entourage, with their *superstes* of dogmatized "form", ethic, etc., Gourmont is concerned with their modality and resonance in emotion.

Mauve, Fanette, Neobelle, La Vierge aux Plâtres, are all studies in different *permanent* kinds of people; they are not the results of environments or of "social causes", their circumstance is an accident and is on the whole scarcely alluded to. Gourmont differentiates his characters by the modes of their sensibility, not by sub-degrees of their state of civilization.

He recognizes the right of individuals to *feel* differently. Confucian, Epicurean, a considerer and entertainer of ideas, this complicated sensuous wisdom is almost the one ubiquitous

element, the "self" which keeps his superficially heterogeneous work vaguely "unified".

The study of emotion does not follow a set chronological arc; it extends from the *Physique de l'Amour* to *Le Latin Mystique*. . . . (pp. 308-10)

[Gourmont] had passed the point where people take abstract statement of dogma for "enlightenment". An "idea" has little value apart from the modality of the mind which receives it. It is a railway from one state to another, and as dull as steel rails in a desert.

The emotions are equal before the aesthetic judgment. He does not grant the duality of body and soul, or at least suggests that this mediaeval duality is unsatisfactory; there is an interpenetration, an osmosis of body and soul, at least for hypothesis.

> My words are the unspoken words of my body.

And in all his exquisite treatment of all emotion he will satisfy many whom August Strindberg, for egregious example, will not. From the studies of insects to Christine evoked from the thoughts of Diomède, sex is not a monstrosity or an exclusively German study. And the entire race is not bound to the habits of the *mantis* or of other insects equally melodramatic. Sex, in so far as it is not a purely physiological reproductive mechanism, lies in the domain of aesthetics, the junction of tactile and magnetic senses; as some people have accurate ears both for rhythm and for pitch, and as some are tone deaf, some impervious to rhythmic subtlety and variety, so in this other field of the senses some desire the trivial, some the processional, the stately, the master-work.

As some people are good judges of music, and insensible to painting and sculpture, so the fineness of one sense may entail no corresponding fineness in another, or at least no corresponding critical perception of differences.

Emotions to Henry James were more or less things that other people had and that one didn't go into; at any rate not in drawing rooms. The gods had not visited James, and the Muse, whom he so frequently mentions, appeared doubtless in corsage, the narrow waist, the sleeves puffed at the shoulders, *a la mode* 1890-2.

Gourmont is interested in hardly anything save emotions and the ideas that will go into them, or take life in emotional application. (Apperceptive rather than active.)

One reads *Les Chevaux de Diomède* . . . as one would have listened to incense in the old Imperial court. There are many spirits incapable. Gourmont calls it a "romance of possible adventures"; it might be called equally an aroma, the fragrance of roses and poplars, the savour of wisdoms, not part of the canon of literature, a book like *Daphnis and Chloe* or like Marcel Schwob's *Livre de Monelle;* not a solidity like Flaubert; but a pervasion.

> My true life is in the unspoken words of my body.

In *Une Nuit au Luxembourg,* the characters talk at more length, and the movement is less convincing. *Diomède* was Gourmont's own favourite and we may take it as the best of his art, the most complete expression of his particular "façon d'apercevoir"; if, even in it, the characters do little but talk philosophy, or drift into philosophic expression out of a haze of images, they are for all that very real. It is the climax of his method of presenting characters differentiated by emotional timbre, a process which had begun in *Histoires Magiques* . . . ; and in *D'un Pays Lointain*. . . . (pp. 310-12)

But there is nothing more unsatisfactory than saying that Gourmont "had such and such ideas" or held "such and such views", the thing is that he held ideas, intuitions, perceptions in a certain personal exquisite manner. In a criticism of him, "criticism" being an over-violent word, in, let us say, an indication of him, one wants merely to show that one has oneself made certain dissociations; as here, between the aesthetic receptivity of tactile and magnetic values, of the perception of beauty in these relationships, and the conception of love, passion, emotion as an intellectual instigation. (p. 314)

Gourmont's wisdom is not wholly unlike the wisdom which those ignorant of Latin may, if the gods favour their understanding, derive from Golding's *Metamorphoses*.

Barbarian ethics proceed by general taboos. Gourmont's essays collected into various volumes, *Promenades, Epilogues,* etc., are perhaps the best introduction to the ideas of our time that any unfortunate, suddenly emerging from Peru, Peoria, Oshkosh, Iceland, Kochin, or other out-of-the-way lost continent could desire. A set of Landor's collected works will go further towards civilizing a man than any university education now on the market. Montaigne condensed Renaissance awareness. Even so small a collection as Lionel Johnson's *Post Liminium* might save a man from utter barbarity.

But if, for example, a raw graduate were contemplating a burst into intellectual company, he would be less likely to utter unutterable *bêtises, gaffes,* etc., after reading Gourmont than before. One cannot of course create intelligence in a numbskull.

Needless to say, Gourmont's essays are of uneven value as the necessary subject matter is of uneven value. Taken together, proportionately placed in his work, they are a portrait of the civilized mind. I incline to think them the best portrait available, the best record that is, of the civilized mind from 1885-1915.

There are plenty of people who do not know what the civilized mind is like, just as there were plenty of mules in England who did not read Landor contemporaneously, or who did not in his day read Montaigne. Civilization is individual.

Gourmont arouses the senses of the imagination, preparing the mind for receptivities. His wisdom, if not of the senses, is at any rate via the senses. We base our "science" on perceptions, but our ethics have not yet attained this palpable basis. (p. 315)

> Ezra Pound, "Henry James and Rémy de Gourmont," in his Make It New, Scholarly Press, Inc., 1971, pp. 251-333.*

LUDWIG LEWISOHN (essay date 1921)

[*A German-born American novelist and critic, Lewisohn was considered an authority on German literature, and his translations of Gerhart Hauptmann, Rainer Maria Rilke, and Jakob Wassermann are widely respected. In 1919 he became the drama critic for* The Nation, *serving as its associate editor until 1924, when he joined a group of expatriates in Paris. After his return to the United States in 1934, Lewisohn became a prominent sympathizer with the Zionist movement, and served as editor of the Jewish magazine* New Palestine *for five years. Many of his later works reflect his humanistic concern for the plight of the Jewish people. In the following excerpt from his introduction to the 1921 translation of* The Book of Masks, *Lewisohn discusses Gourmont's impressionistic approach to criticism, and praises Gourmont's recognition of the necessity and validity of subjective expression*

in literary criticism. For a contrasting view of Gourmont's subjective approach to literary criticism, see the excerpt by G. D. Klingopulos (1940-41).]

Remy de Gourmont, like all the very great critics—Goethe, Ste. Beuve, Hazlitt, Jules Lemaitre—knew the creative instinct and exercised the creative faculty. Hence he understood, what the mere academician, the mere scholar, can never grasp, that literature is life grown flamelike and articulate; that, therefore, like life itself, it varies in aim and character, in form and color and savor and is the memorable record of and commentary upon each stage in that great process of change that we call the world. To write like the Greeks or the Elizabethans or the French classics is precisely what we must not do. It would be both presumptuous and futile. All that we have to contribute to mankind, what is it but just—our selves? If we were duplicates of our greatgrandfathers we would be littering the narrow earth to no enriching purpose; all we have to contribute to literature is, again, our selves. This moment, this sensation, this pang, this thought—this little that is intimately our own is all we have of the unique and precious and incomparable. Let us express it beautifully, individually, memorably and it is all we can do; it is all that the classics did in their day. To imitate the classics—be one! That is to say, live widely, intensely, unsparingly and record your experience in some timeless form. This, in brief, is the critical theory of Gourmont, this is the background of that startling and yet, upon reflection, so clear and necessary saying of his: "The only excuse a man has for writing is that he express himself, that he reveal to others the kind of world reflected in the mirror of his soul; his only excuse is that he be original."

Gourmont, like the Symbolists whom he describes in this volume, founded his theory of the arts upon a metaphysical speculation. He learned from the German idealists, primarily the Post-Kantians and Schopenhauer, that the world is only our representation, only our individual vision and that, since there is no criterion of the existence or the character of an external reality, that vision is, of course, all we actually have to express in art. But to accept his critical theory it is not necessary to accept his metaphysical views. The variety of human experience remains equally infinite and equally fascinating on account of its very infiniteness, whatever its objective content may or may not be. We can dismiss that antecedent and insoluble question and still agree that the best thing a man can give in art as in life is his own self. What kind of a self? One hears at once the hot and angry question of the conservative critic. A disciplined one, by all means, an infinitely and subtly cultivated one. But not one shaped after some given pattern, not a replica, not a herd-animal, but a human personality. But achieving such personalities, the reply comes, people fall into error. Well, this is an imperfect universe and the world-spirit, as Goethe said, is more tolerant than people think.

It is clear that criticism conceived of in this fashion, can do little with the old methods of harsh valuing and stiff classification. If, as Jules Lemaitre put it, a poem, a play, a novel, "exists" at all, if it has that fundamental veracity of experience and energy of expression which raise it to the level of literary discussion, a critic like Gourmont cannot and will not pass a classifying judgment on it at all. For such judgments involve the assumption that there exists a fixed scale of objective values. And for such a scale we search both the world and the mind in vain. Hence, too—and this is a point of the last importance—we are done with arbitrary exclusions, exclusions by transitory conventions or by tribal habits lifted to the plane of eternal laws. All experience, the whole soul of man—nothing less than that is now our province. And no one has done more to bring us that critical and creative freedom and enlargement of scope than Remy de Gourmont.

In [**"The Book of Masks"**], for instance, he discusses writers of very varied moods and interests. Dr. Samuel Johnson or, for that matter, a modern preceptist critic, speaking of these very poets, would have told us how some of them were noble and some ignoble and certain ones moral and others no better than they should be. And both of these good and learned and arrogant men would have instructed Verlaine in what to conceal, and Gustave Kahn in how to build verses and Regnier in how to enlarge the range of his imagery. Thus they would have missed the special beauty and thrill that each of these poets has brought into the world. For they read—as all their kind reads—not with peace in their hearts but with a bludgeon in their hands. But if we watch Gourmont who had, by the way, an intellect of matchless energy, we find that he read his poets with that wise passiveness which Wordsworth wanted men to cultivate before the stars and hills. He is uniformly sensitive; he lets his poets play upon him; he is the lute upon which their spirits breathe. And then that lute itself begins to sound and to utter a music of its own which swells and interprets and clarifies the music of his poets and brings nearer to us the wisdom and the loveliness which they and he have brought into the world.

Thus it is, first of all, as one of the earliest and finest examples of the New Criticism that . . . the **"Book of Masks"** is to be welcomed. For the New Criticism is the chief phenomenon in that movement toward spiritual and moral tolerance which the world so sorely needs. But the book is also to be welcomed and valued for the sake of its specific subject matter. One movement in the entire range of modern poetry and only one surpasses the movement of the French Symbolists in clearness of beauty, depth of feeling, wealth and variety of music. (pp. ii-vi)

> *Ludwig Lewisohn, in an introduction to* The Book of Masks *by Remy de Gourmont, translated by Jack Lewis, 1921. Reprint by Books for Libraries Press, 1967; distributed by Arno Press, Inc., pp. i-vii.*

RENÉ LALOU (essay date 1922)

[*Lalou was a prominent French essayist and critic and the author of a comprehensive history of modern French literature entitled* La littérature française contemporaine (Contemporary French Literature, *1922; rev. ed. 1941). As a critic, Lalou was noted for his impartiality and frankness (he had no strong ties to any literary movements), for his historical discrimination and perspective, and for the balance and clarity of his critical judgments. Lalou's works include studies of such modern authors as André Gide, Paul Valéry, and Roger Martin du Gard, as well as essays on such classic literary figures as C. A. Sainte-Beuve, Charles Baudelaire, and Gérard de Nerval. In English translation, Lalou's critical works have been credited with introducing the works of leading modern French writers to the English-speaking world. Lalou also helped to make the works of numerous English authors accessible to the French through his translations of the works of Shakespeare, Edgar Allan Poe, and George Meredith, and through critical studies of modern English authors, the best known of which is his* Panorama de la littérature anglaise contemporaine *(1927). In the following excerpt from* Contemporary French Literature, *Lalou discusses Gourmont's approach to criticism and his method of the dissociation of ideas. Lalou explains that Gourmont's "negations drew their force, not from scepticism but from a methodical reclassification of ideas after their dissociation."*]

Criticism seems . . . , with Marcel Schwob, to have been the artist's very intelligent auxiliary. It is rather the reverse that should be said of Remy de Gourmont . . . [who] never renounced the ambitions of the creator: "I am haunted by the technique of the unknown masterpiece," he confesses in the preface to the book in which he recounts the adventures of Antiphilos among men. Now all his imaginative works, from *Sixtine,* a "novel of the cerebral life" and the unactable *Lilith* to the inconceivable *Lettres d'un satyre,* belie this hope of liberation in spontaneous invention. Gourmont's talent remains incontestable but he exceeds his domain. The *Histoires magiques,* the stories in *Un Pays lointain* and *Couleurs* offer us not so much veritable narratives as the delicate fantasies of a writer letting his fancy play about indefinite ideas or sweet past things, already a little faded. *Une nuit au Luxembourg* is only a subtle play upon the strings of curiosity. The allegories of *Le Pèlerin du silence,* the verses of *Le Livre des Litanies,* the poems of *Simone* appear to us to-day very ingenious pastiches of a superannuated art whose cleverness we can admire all the more because it troubles us with no emotion. Even the most successful of these attempts, *Les Chevaux de Diomède,* bears the mark of time. We no longer believe in the superior airs of the hero going through his evolutions in a factitious harem. In the finest chapters of complicated passion (*Les Mains, Les Marronniers*), we are too aware of the intervention of the puppet showman ready to dissect these fictions, to reveal, beneath their passions, the instincts which decoy them. Not that this presence of the ego is odious. It expresses itself sometimes in charming sallies: "Diomède, are you ready to follow your theories to the end?" "To the end? No, not to-day. It is too far"; but verisimilitude suffers from it as does our belief in the reality of the characters. Perhaps the balance between the creator's rights and those of his creations is particularly difficult for so conscious a writer to attain. When Gourmont warns us that "in this book which is a little novel of possible adventures, thought, act, dream, sensuality are exhibited on the same plane and analysed with the same goodwill," he touches the point where the novel is on the eve of becoming an essay. Does he not go beyond it when he adds that "all manifestations of human activity seem quite equivalent," when he writes as a motto for each of the chapters the sentence with which he is most satisfied, when he transforms sensuality into sickly erotomania?

In so subtle a work, interest, however, does not flag. If it turns from the illusory actors, it is to concentrate upon the personality of the author. Gourmont, who entitled his poems *Divertissements,* was too perspicacious not to know that the same title would suit all his imaginative works. Questioning himself he would doubtless have recognized that his desire for artistic creation was only one of the forms of that need for love which obsessed him. The problem of love haunted Remy de Gourmont. On several occasions he sought to solve it. In *La Physique de l'amour,* an "essay on the sexual instinct," he brings a scientific precision to the study of the organs of love and the mechanism of love in animals and in man whom he restores to his place in the scale of creation. The *Lettres à l'amazone* continue the same analysis from another point of view: "To speak of love with a young woman is one of the pleasures of our delicate civilization." He abandons himself to it entirely, speaking at length of chastity, naked love, pleasure, desire. To his erudition he adds the refined art which permits him to say delicate truths brutally and brutal truths delicately. He deploys his coquetry for a friend whose mind he pretends to love no less than her heart. Suddenly he believes himself liberated: "And then, resurrected Amazon, I desire seriously but one thing, to offer you my happy egotism''—a sentiment which, were it true, would be odious; but it too is a snare, and again lassitude returns: ''Then I shall go just like another by the roads and the inns towards the end of the world, which is the nearest shore.'' A drama without conclusion. From *Le Fantôme* and *Les Oraisons mauvaises* where he perversely drowned love in liturgical evocations, to *Un Coeur virginal,* the story of a young girl which, he says in the preface, must certainly be called ''a physiological novel,'' Remy de Gourmont remained haunted by the obsession of love, of its realities, of its depravities, of its simplicity and of its mystery. He explained it to others a hundred times. Did he convince himself? It may be doubted. For, according to his brother's remark, ''nothing entered his intelligence save caressed by his sensibility.'' At least, if this aspiration for unsatisfied voluptuousness paralysed his creative expansion, it sustained in his mind the insatiable curiosity of a lively critic and of a penetrating dissociator of ideas who, in his charming *Lettres à Sixtine,* was at once lover and ''flute-player.''

He has strongly expressed the necessity for this alliance of body and brain in his three essential works, *La Culture des idées, Le Chemin de velours* and *Le Problème du style:* ''We write as we feel, as we think, with our whole body. Intelligence is but a form of sensibility . . . For all is interdependent and intellectual ease is certainly connected with liberty of sensation. He who cannot feel everything cannot understand everything, and not to understand everything is to understand nothing.'' On this point he shows himself unyielding. ''If you do not take, in handling ideas, a physical pleasure akin to caressing a shoulder or a piece of stuff, leave ideas alone.'' Not that he was unaware of the dangers of his method. He knew the seduction of admitted truths, ''commonplaces not yet dissociated,'' of those precise, clear expressions which ''have no meaning, are affirmative gestures suggesting obedience, and that is all.'' He admitted the difficulties of complexity: ''To explain a straw, the whole universe must be taken to pieces.'' He refused to bow before the dogma of the immutability of ideas: ''Believe, and believe also when I tell you the contrary; for it is not necessary always to believe the same thing''; but he rejected the charge of paradox: ''I never made one deliberately. However, I do not claim to dictate judgments upon myself. A mind of some boldness will always seem paradoxical to timid minds. One must accept the rules of the game of thought with all its consequences.'' He was firmly persuaded that the game of thought necessitated this lucid interrogatory of all reality by the whole being, this minute ''dissociation of ideas'' of which he could say: ''It strengthens the muscles, it calms the pulse . . . it is a method of deliverance.''

This anti-bookish, concrete method Gourmont practised for years. Twenty volumes of chronicles *(Epilogues, Promenades littéraires, Promenades philosophiques, Dialogues des amateurs* etc.), vouch for its efficacy. In them Gourmont fully attains his object which is ''to make things known much rather than to appreciate them authoritatively.'' He brings the same competence to the discussion of Quinton's theories or to reconstituting a story of adultery—the same ease in arranging his memories of Symbolism and in defending the services the Jesuits have rendered civilization, in spite of their blemishes. His erudition finds an outlet in connection with Huysmans' *La Cathédrale* or with a thesis on medical psychology. He will show a Swiftian irony in the *Conseils familiers à un jeune écrivain* and a smiling tenderness in speaking of women, from the instant when the ''amphora becomes once more a beautiful young girl with throbbing bosom and anxious eyes.'' He will

show all the wealth of his thought in a fragment like that *Sur la hierarchie intellectuelle.* He will lucidly defend his masters, Villiers and Mallarmé, and will be able, speaking of Verlaine, to maintain an equal distance from idolatry and pedantic vulgarity. An article such as *Psychologie Nouvelle* will show his sympathy for the young writers. Capable of judging his contemporaries with a penetrating gaze in the two *Livres des masques,* it will please him, in the *Dialogues des amateurs,* to comment day by day upon contemporary events in the manner of Anatole France whose learned grace he does not possess but whom he far surpasses in originality and penetrating insight.

One subject in particular held his attention: the life of words, for which his stay at the Bibliothèque Nationale had perhaps increased his love. He believed in their power: ''Pay attention to the words which rise and live, to improvised evocations, to creative incantations, pay attention to the logic of speech. All syllables are not vain.'' In composing articles on linguistics, *Le Latin mystique, L'Esthétique de la langue française, Le Problème du style,* he paid a debt of gratitude: ''Words have perhaps given me more numerous and more decisive joys than ideas''; but there again he kept his independence and, in refuting Albalat's affirmations even to the extent of grammatical subtleties, he declared his aim was ''rather to develop five or six motives for not believing in rhetorical receipts.''

He continued to the end of the task he had assigned himself. His war articles have been collected in *Les idées du jour* and *Pendant l'orage.* He was one of those rare writers not blinded by the catastrophe. He knew that, in the human tragedy, peace was never perhaps more an entr'acte: ''It is so difficult to be a true neutral,'' he added, ''that perhaps it is better to be a belligerent.'' He kept his hope no less high on that account, for ''life is an act of confidence''—a fine reply to those who had not understood that his negations drew their force, not from scepticism but from a methodical reclassification of ideas after their dissociation. Doubtless he had sometimes carried experimentation so far as to ''side with the instinctive creature against the rational creature whose reason is so limited.'' His faith in the law of intellectual and sentimental constancy, based upon Quinton's scientific investigations which he has developed in the *Epilogues,* permitted him to give free play to his intelligence with the tranquil assurance it would not founder and never abdicate. Thereby he lives, even for those whose intellectual development for twenty-five years has not been aided by his chronicles in *Le Mercure,* a great humanist and a very precious thinking-master. (pp. 153-57)

> René Lalou, ''Symbolism,'' *in his* Contemporary French Literature, *translated by William Aspenwall Bradley, Alfred A. Knopf, 1924, pp. 94-158.**

ARTHUR RANSOME   (essay date 1926)

[*Ransome was an English writer, critic, and journalist who is best known as the award-winning author of* Swallows and Amazons *(1931),* Pigeon Post *(1936), and other books for children. In the following excerpt, taken from Ransome's introduction to the English translation of Gourmont's* A Night in the Luxembourg, *Ransome discusses the many controversial aspects of Gourmont's novel. Ransome defends its author's Epicurean treatment of sex and his unsentimental attitude toward religious revelation. He states that, while some may find the work licentious or blasphemous, Gourmont exhibits great piety toward the thing that he most reveres:* ''the purity and the clarity of thought.'']

[*Une Nuit au Luxembourg*], at once criticism and romance, is the best introduction to M. de Gourmont's very various works.

It created a "sensation" in France. I think it may do as much in England, but I am anxious lest this "sensation" should be of a kind honourable neither to us nor to the author of a remarkable book. I do not wish a delicate and subtle artist, a very noble philosopher, noble even if smiling, nobler perhaps because he smiles, to be greeted with accusations of indecency and blasphemy. But I cannot help recognising that in England, as in many other countries, these accusations are often brought against such philosophers as discuss in a manner other than traditional the subjects of God and woman. These two subjects, with many others, are here the motives of a book no less delightful than profound. (pp. 9-10)

There is no ugliness in the frank acceptance of the flesh, that is a motive, one among many, in this book, and perhaps more noticeable by us than the author intended.... We are only fortunate listeners to a monologue, and must not presume upon our position to ask him to remember we are there.

The character of that monologue is such, I think, as to justify me in tampering very little with its design. Not only is *Une Nuit au Luxembourg* not a book for children or young persons—if it were, the question would be altogether different—but it is not a book for fools, or even for quite ordinary people. I think that no reader who can enjoy the philosophical discussion that is its greater part will quarrel with its Epicurean interludes. He will either forgive those passages of which I am speaking as the pardonable idiosyncrasy of a great man, or recognise that they are themselves illustrations of his philosophy, essential to its exposition, and raised by that fact into an intellectual light that justifies their retention.

The prurient minds who might otherwise peer at these passages, and enjoy the caricatures that their own dark lanterns would throw on the muddy wall of their comprehension, will, I think, be repelled by the nobility of the book's philosophy. They will seek their truffles elsewhere, and find plenty.

M. de Gourmont is perhaps more likely to be attacked for blasphemy, but only by those who do not observe his piety towards the thing that he most reverences, the purity and the clarity of thought. He worships in a temple not easy to approach, a temple where the worshippers are few, and the worship difficult. It is impossible not to respect a mind that, in its consuming desire for liberty, strips away not fetters only but supports. Fetters bind at first, but later it is hard to stand without them.

His book is not a polemic against Christianity, in the same sense as Nietzsche's *Anti-Christ*, though it does propose an ethic and an ideal very different from those we have come to consider Christian. When he smiles at the Acts of the Apostles as at a fairy tale, he adds a sentence of incomparable praise and profound criticism: "These men touch God with their hands." It may shock some people to find that the principal speaker in the book is a god who claims to have inspired, not Christ alone, but Pythagoras, Epicurus, Lucretius, St. Paul and Spinoza with the most valuable of their doctrines. It will not, I think, shock any student of comparative religion. He will find it no more than a poet's statement of an idea that has long ceased to disturb the devout, the idea that all religions are the same, or translations of the same religion. We recognise in the sayings of Confucius some of the loveliest of the sayings of Christ, and we find them again in Mohammed. Why not admit that the same voice whispered in their ears, for this, unless we think that the Devil can give advice as good as God's, we cannot help but believe. And that other idea, that the gods die,

though their lives are long, should not shock those who know of Odin, notice the lessening Christian reverence for the Jewish Jehovah, and remember the story, so often and so sweetly told, of the voices on the Grecian coast, with their cry, "Great Pan is dead! Great Pan is dead!"

Turning from particular ideas to the rule of life that the book proposes, we find a crystalline Epicureanism. Virtue is, to be happy; and sin is, where we put it. "Human wisdom is to live as if one were never to die, and to gather the present minute as if it were to be eternal." This is no doctrine that is easy to follow. The god does not offer it to the first comer, but to one who has schooled his mind to see hard things, and, having seen them, to rise above them. M. de Gourmont will tell no lies that he can avoid, especially when speaking to himself, but, if he burn himself, Phoenix-like, in the ashes of a sentimental universe, he has at least the hope of rising from the pyre with stronger wings and more triumphant flight. He will start with no more than the assumption that the universe as we know it is the product of a series of accidents. He will not persuade himself that man is the climax of a carefully planned mechanical process of evolution, nor will he hide his origin in imagery like that of Genesis, or like that which certain modern scientists are quite unable to avoid. He turns science against the scientists with the irrefutable remark that only a change in the temperature saved us from the dominion of ants. Instinct for him is arrested intellect, and he is ready to imagine man in the future doing mechanically what now he does by intention. Such ideas would crush a feeble brain or bind it with despair. They lead him to the Epicureanism that is the only philosophy that they do not overthrow. Our roses and our women make us the equals of the gods, and even envied by them.

All his criticism, not of one or two ideas alone, but of the history of philosophy, the history of woman, the history of man and the history of religion, is made with a mastery so absolute as to dare to be playful. The winter night was changed to a spring morning as the god walked in the Luxembourg, and the wintry cold of nineteenth-century science melts in the warmth of a spring-time no less magical. The book might be grim. It is clear-eyed and sparkling with dew, like a sonnet by Ronsard.... [So] one sees the philosophy of M. de Gourmont, not quarried stone, but a flower, so light, so delicate, as to make us forget the worlds that have been overthrown in its manufacture.

I remember near the end of *The Pilgrim's Progress* there is a passage of dancing. Giant Despair has been killed, and Doubting Castle demolished. The pilgrims were "very jocund and merry." "Now Christiana, if need was, could play upon the viol, and her daughter Mercy upon the lute; so, since they were so merry disposed, she played them a lesson, and Ready-to-halt would dance. So he took Despondency's daughter, Much-afraid, by the hand, and to dancing they went in the road. True, he could not dance without one crutch in his hand; but I promise you he footed it well; also the girl was to be commended, for she answered the music handsomely." Just so, in this book, on a journey no less perilous among ideas, there is an atmosphere of genial entertainment, a delight in the things of the senses illumined by a delight in the things of the mind. And in this there is no irreverence. Only those who have ceased to believe have forgotten how to dance in the presence of their God.

Perhaps the technician alone will observe the skill with which M. de Gourmont has handled the most difficult of literary forms.... [Not] the least pleasure of my intimacy with *Une*

Wood engraving by Gourmont for the cover of an 1895 edition of his short story Phocas.

Nuit au Luxembourg has been to notice the ease and the grace with which its author turns, always at the right moment, from ideas to images, from romance to thought. "The exercise of thought is a game," he says, "but this game must be free and harmonious." And the outward impression given by this subtly constructed book is that of an intellect playing harmoniously with itself in a state of joyful liberty. M. de Gourmont is a master of his moods, knowing how to serve them; and no less admirable than the loftiest moment of the discussion, is the Callot-like grotesque of the three goddesses, seen not as divinities but as sins, or the Virgilian breakfast under the trees.

It is possible that **Une Nuit au Luxembourg** may be for a few in our generation what *Mademoiselle de Maupin* was for a few in the generation of Swinburne, a "golden book of spirit and sense." Ideas are dangerous metal in which to mould romances, because from time to time they tarnish. Voltaire has had his moments of being dull, and Gautier's ideas do not excite us now. M. de Gourmont's may not move us to-morrow. Let us enjoy them to-day, and share the pleasure that the people of the day after to-morrow will certainly not refuse. (pp. 11-18)

> *Arthur Ransome, in a preface to* A Night in the Luxembourg *by Rémy de Gourmont, translated by Arthur Ransome, The Modern Library Publishers, 1926, pp. 9-18.*

JOSEPH WOOD KRUTCH   (essay date 1928)

[*Krutch is widely regarded as one of America's most respected literary and drama critics. Noteworthy among his works are* The American Drama since 1918 *(1939), which analyzes the most important dramas of the 1920s and 1930s, and* "Modernism" in Modern Drama *(1953), in which he stressed the need for twentieth-century playwrights to infuse their works with traditional humanistic values. A conservative and idealistic thinker, he was a consistent proponent of human dignity and the preeminence of literary art. His literary criticism is characterized by such concerns: in* The Modern Temper *(1929) he argued that because scientific thought has denied human worth, tragedy has become obsolete, and in* The Measure of Man *(1954) he attacked modern culture for depriving humanity of the sense of individual responsibility necessary for making important decisions in an increasingly complex age. In the following excerpt, Krutch compares Gourmont with a contemporary in French literature, Anatole France, and states the Gourmont's intellectual skepticism is no longer of interest to a generation concerned with "synthesis" rather than analysis. Krutch's appraisal offers one possible explanation for the dramatic decline of Gourmont's critical reputation.*]

[De Gourmont] deserves a place alongside of Anatole France in the great line of French skeptics, for if he lacked France's felicitous facility, and produced nothing so brilliantly easy as the latter's most popular tales, he had a far wider intellectual curiosity and a more strictly original genius. The two men were alike in cultivating doubt until their skepticism was Pyrrhonically absolute and in professing the most uncompromising Epicurianism in the realm of ethics, but de Gourmont was less often content than was his more popular contemporary merely to ring stylistic changes upon the commonplaces of his sect. France, indeed, seldom wandered far from his few simple themes. He regarded with complete indifference all the fields of human knowledge which have been opened up since the Renaissance and he stated his eternal problems in terms hardly different from those which Lucian employed. De Gourmont was, on the other hand, for all his professed love of paganism, as completely modern as Anatole France was timidly pseudo-classical. Since nothing which could be made the subject of analysis was indifferent to him, he went to science in search of the new weapons which science had forged for the use of the skeptic but which France never attempted to wield, and with them he attacked the faiths of the modern world in the very terms in which those faiths were stated. His central contention that there is no Truth as distinguished from the Truths which various men have variously held was the same as that of France or of any other absolute skeptic, but the route by which he reached it was different and so also is the whole intellectual background against which his mind worked. Unlike France he made full use of the fact that Darwinism gave the satirist's trick of identifying human with animal traits an apparent cogency which it never had before, and when, for example, he dismissed the attempt to presuppose a meaning to existence by asserting that life has no purpose except its own preservation, he was drawing, not upon the speculations of an ancient philosopher, but upon the argument which Schopenhauer documented with facts drawn from the data upon which the theory of natural selection was based.

The difference in temperaments was, moreover, no less marked than the difference between the fields of study which the two men chose. For France, the exquisite voluptuary, intellectual pessimism was the key which made accessible various delicate delights for mind and body. He could cultivate pleasure as the pagans cultivated it and he could achieve something of their lightness of heart. To de Gourmont, on the other hand (as to most nineteenth-century pessimists), loss of faith in any ultimate meaning of existence brought with it a certain depression of animal spirits and made of him a recluse. It would seem, indeed, that while the a priori skepticism of ancient times was joyous, the documented doubt of naturalism is almost inevitably dreary, and de Gourmont, for all his reiterated assertion that the sense of freedom which a profession of nihilism brings is the most precious thing which man can achieve, felt to the full this dreariness of the natural world. "I think," he said, "that we should never hesitate to bring science into literature or literature into science; the age of fine ignorance is gone." And yet the result of his determination to be rational and informed about everything was to destroy the meaning of the very conceptions in which he was most interested. Plagued by the conviction that man is, even at his best, only a rather complicated animal he could, for instance, write:

> Beauty is so certainly sexual that the only undisputed works of art are those which show the human body in its nudity. By its perseverance in remaining purely sexual, Greek sculpture placed itself for all eternity above dispute. It is beautiful because it is a beautiful human body, like that with which every man or every woman would wish to unite to perpetuate themselves according to their race.

And yet he got only a bitter satisfaction out of so absolute a statement, for naturalism, which begins by seeming only an invitation to eat, drink, and be merry, ends by depriving the guest of his appetite. Having committed himself to the exclusive cultivation of rationality, reason itself convinced him that the pleasure which it recognized as the only good was not to be had through the reason and thus he was brought face to face with a dilemma which he never solved: "Man is an animal who has the privilege of watching himself act; and the older he is in civilization, the more cultivated he is, the more delight he takes in watching himself." But "consciousness contaminates the will," and it is the will, not the consciousness, which leads one to do things worth the watching.

Probably no one touched nineteenth-century thought at more of its crucial points than de Gourmont did, and probably no one furnishes a better epitome of its tendency. The name—"dissociation"—which he gave to the object of his favorite intellectual process might, indeed, be used not inappropriately to describe the whole effect of scientific rationalism so far as general social, moral, and aesthetic ideas are concerned. He loved to cut through a whole complex of ethical conviction with a single stroke by remarking, for example, that the major part of the current conception of sexual morality was based upon a merely arbitrary association of the idea of "pleasure" with the idea of "procreation," or through a whole complex of social enthusiasms by pointing out that "political liberty" was generally celebrated by people who associated it quite unjustifiably with "individual freedom." And when he did so he was merely reducing to a formula the most characteristic process of nineteenth-century thought, since, to choose two simple illustrations, the whole task of Nietzsche was to dissociate the idea of "virtue" from the idea of "self-negation" and the whole task of Ibsen to dissociate the idea of "rectitude" from the idea of "respectability."

It is true that when he attempted to assert rather than to deny de Gourmont himself had to depend upon associations no less arbitrary than those which he attacked in others. Distrusting socialism he was capable, for example, of ridiculing a specific proposal of some radical platform of his day ("Suppression of bounties for capability") by assuming that it implied the untenable proposition "one man is as good as another," and he did not stop to consider that his argument was based upon a by no means inevitable association between the idea of "ca-

pacity or virtue" and the idea of "reward or recompense," which he accepted but which his opponents did not. To say this is, however, merely to say that no conviction is possible except upon the basis of some preliminary associations without which every fact and every idea is separate from every other and no thought concerning them possible. It was indeed toward such a completely fragmentary mental world in which no fact had any relation to any other fact and no conclusion could be drawn from any premise that de Gourmont was headed, and with him were going all those who had learned from him, from Nietzsche, or from others the technique by means of which all tablets may be broken.

Doubtless it is the very fact that de Gourmont so adequately represents the tendencies of his time which is responsible for the lack of interest in his work manifested by the present generation. To say that he was, for a brief period, regarded with a superstitious awe like that now accorded in some quarters to Paul Valéry is to suggest how unfashionable his particular kind of thought must have become, since the new watchword "synthesis" is the exact opposite of that "analysis" which de Gourmont sought everywhere to effect. His enthusiasm for doubt and freedom and his hatred of "standards" and absolutes no less than his contempt for "pure" metaphysics and his determination to reduce all aesthetics and all morality to psychological and physiological principles, stand at every point in opposition to the aims and principles of those contemporary intellectuals who are endeavoring to erect structures to replace those which he tore down. In truth one could hardly go much further in his direction. Even skepticism must be supplied with beliefs to dissolve and even the Nihilist must be supplied with affirmations to be denied. Nor is it likely that there will ever be a permanent lack of either. New faiths will be generated, new associations made, and new tablets written. The very fact that his weapons are capable of destroying at least many of them is good reason why no strenuous efforts will be made to keep those weapons from being forgotten. (pp. 357-58)

> *Joseph Wood Krutch, "The Nihilism of Remy de Gourmont," in* The Nation, *Vol. CXXVII, No. 3301, October 10, 1928, pp. 357-58.*

RENÉ TAUPIN   (essay date 1931)

[*In the following excerpt, Taupin discusses the influence of Gourmont upon early twentieth-century American and English writers, and states that while Gourmont is no longer a symbol of "modern sensibility," he continues to interest critics for the "synthesis" of intellect and emotion in his works.*]

Rémy de Gourmont exerted an influence due in part to his personality, to what we may call, if we take pleasure in using words in a vague sense, his temper. He became a powerful, living influence not because he was the centre of a salon and because young men hailed him as master, but rather because his attitudes, the mechanism of his intelligence and the very tone of his voice were bound to please at a certain, particular period.

Thus the *Chevaux de Diomède,* the *Lettres à l'Amazone,* as well as the *Dissociation d'Idées* enjoyed a great vogue, from 1915 to 1920, among certain young Americans; these books were to be found quite as much on the deck-chairs of transatlantic liners as on benches in colleges and university. (p. 615)

The direct influence of de Gourmont, for example that of his tales, is negligible only when it produced a book like Huneker's

Melomaniacs. Nor are the echoes of de Gourmont which we find, at the period of his return in vogue, in the early numbers of the *Dial,* in the prose of Ben Hecht and of Van Wyck Brooks, any more important than the earliest imitations.

It is also partly (and no more than partly) the fact that Rémy de Gourmont was, to some extent, the symbol of his age, which urged certain Englishmen and Americans to turn to him towards 1915. For the rising generation of the time, he represented a liberation from certain highly artificial ways of thought; he was the contrary of the Fabians, say, the Webbists or the Shavians. What is more, he embodied a modern spirit, the beginnings of a new era, a point of departure; and to know him was tantamount to passing from one period of civilization to a far higher stage. He understood, too, that his ideas were not those of a moment, but rather a manner of thinking which was in evolution, which brought sympathy in its baggage and which seemed to exercise a sort of control upon the advancement of the arts. He was interested in young writers and he seemed able, at the same time, to stop them opportunely if their progress appeared to be too rapid.

Some found in him the arch-type of the free spirit. For them he appeared as the man of letters ideally free from all the trammels of false traditions. It is this sort of mind which Aldington admired in de Gourmont in about 1913 and which he still seems to admire to-day: 'I should be as excited', he writes, 'and captured as when I first "discovered" de Gourmont (through F. S. Flint and Ezra Pound). . . . Gourmont is the unfailing champion of individualism.'

Already Huneker had appreciated Rémy de Gourmont's individualism and had made use of his example in his own individualistic propaganda. In 1915, writers saw in de Gourmont a fine mirror of their own aspirations and they were the happier for it because his freedom was in no wise anarchical, because he felt admiration variously for all the periods of our civilization and because he had studied certain literatures in which people were beginning to take interest. 'He has an influence, especially over the younger and more adventuresome spirits, which few writers to-day possess,' Aldington wrote in 1915 in the *Little Review,* at a time when the magazine was very much occupied with Nietzsche. And Aldington's literary activity, his intellect seem certainly to have disciplined themselves upon the activity of de Gourmont. Here we have indeed a good example of the influence of one mind upon another.

Pound, as ever utilitarian, saw in de Gourmont a capital civilizing agent; already jealous of the moral health of his country, he was beginning to use the Frenchman's name as a weapon in his fight against certain germs of ill-health in American civilization. His articles in the *Fortnightly Review,* in the *Little Review* [see excerpt dated 1919] and elsewhere illustrate his intentions very clearly. And again, it is the mind of Rémy de Gourmont rather than the creations of that mind which Pound seeks to set up as an example. 'As you read de Gourmont's work, it is not any particular phrase, poem or essay that holds you so much as a continuing sense of intelligence in the mind of the writer.' Indeed, Pound saw no necessity urging him to speak to a people which lacked any true discipline and which has ever believed in the spirit of 'free discussion' and of free culture as against the catechism and discipline which other nations impose upon themselves. It was, in fact, almost the contrary: de Gourmont had a timely value for he was the first modern writer of his generation, the enemy of the intellectual and emotional haze through which, in France and elsewhere, people moved with such pleasure; de Gourmont was the lo-

gician who loved ideas, who sought a mental equipoise, who strove patiently and accurately to establish the value of things, without ever falling a victim either to anger or to exaggerated enthusiasm.

To what extent Pound's articles made thought popular and to what extent (if a taste for thought really arose) de Gourmont may be deemed responsible are two points difficult to establish. What is absolutely certain, however, is that the interest shown in Rémy de Gourmont's works, in particular his critical works, grew consistently wider after these initial manifestations. Proof of this lies in much activity, from the de Gourmont number of the *Little Review* in 1919 [see Additional Bibliography] down to the translations of the *Promenades Philosophiques* in 1920, of the *Chemin de Velours* in 1921, and the *Physique de L'amour* in 1922. (pp. 615-18)

Is de Gourmont the first modern of his generation? As a fact, this is open to discussion, but not, certainly, as an idea. For therein lies one of the reasons of de Gourmont's influence. But, as T. S. Eliot has shown, de Gourmont is the critical consciousness of his generation. And this brings about a double result. On one hand, any reaction against the symbolist generation must necessarily be a reaction against de Gourmont who expressed it in perfect formulae; but, on the other hand, all the advantage that may be gained from this same generation is to be found in the very work of de Gourmont. Finally, we can follow de Gourmont himself in an anti-symbolist reaction, since he it was, who began it.

The poets of 1914, especially the Imagists, discovered forerunners among the French symbolists and preferred many such a poet to de Gourmont, who, for his part, considered the writing of poetry as but a secondary occupation. His studies on the vers libre, however, are among the most serious works attacking that problem; accordingly they proved of great help to the early English and American vers libristes. These poets themselves have offered sufficient testimony to this fact. Again, certain of Gourmont's poems, being excellent examples of vers libre, couched in powerful and skilful rhythms, such as his *Litanies,* for example, exercised a strong attraction on almost all these poets. It is sufficient to cite merely Pound: 'It seems to me the most valuable contribution since Arnaut Daniel,' and to point to Pound's imitations of de Gourmont in *The Alchemist;* to mention Amy Lowell, who apparently considered him among the six best contemporary French poets and who, in *Lilacs,* draws inspiration from the *Litanies;* and, finally, to show how John Gould Fletcher imitates a poem of *Simone:*

> There is a great mystery, my love
> In the movements of your hands. . . .

as well as the *Litanies* in his *In the City of Night.*

At this period, de Gourmont contributed in giving these poets the idea of the necessity of a strong cadence, well marked by rhythmic elements expressed in cadence from the very outset and repeated in the body of the poem; he proved that rhythm was scansion operated by the respiratory system, itself submitted directly to the emotions. Often, in those days, the name of de Gourmont fell from the lips of these poets; so much so, indeed, that an American parody of modern poetry, *Spectra,* was dedicated to de Gourmont.

But that book of de Gourmont's which most permanently influenced first poetry and next the criticism of poetry, which offered a durable contribution, was undoubtedly his *Problème du Style.* T. E. Hulme would seem to have been the first Englishman to ponder his work. In the pages published by Herbert Read in the *Criterion* in July, 1925, and in *Speculations*, his debt to Rémy de Gourmont is manifest.

We must set aside all the philosophic and artistic critics of the same family, the impressionists or post-impressionists and we must deal with language alone; indeed, it is not a question of reality and images according to Bergson, here, but rather of these same objects according to the *Problème du Style*. Now it is quite certain that Hulme formulated precisely his ideas upon this topic with the aid of this particular work of de Gourmont's. We need but read the chapter on *Romanticism and Classicism* in *Speculations* to be convinced of the truth of this assertion. Style must not evoke, it must present; it can do this only by the use of new images. Originally, the word is nothing else than a picture, de Gourmont said, but since its birth, it has been headed towards abstraction; it loses its picturesque or emotive value and becomes no more than a brass counter. 'Poetry is not a counter language, but a visual, concrete one. It is a compromise for a language of intuition which would hand over sensations bodily . . . it always endeavors to arrest you, to make you continuously see a physical thing, to prevent you gliding through an abstract process. It chooses fresh epithets and fresh metaphors, not so much because they are new, and we are tired of the old, but because the old cease to convey a physical thing and become abstract counters.'

De Gourmont and Hulme were points of departure, educators; they had clearly seen a simple fact, namely that vision is at the very base of all literary art. This truth held good for a rather lengthy period, especially in the form in which Hulme expressed it. It proved to be the most solid support of Imagism and many of Pound's ideas are simply corollaries precisely formulated. The same ideas on style were still valid for T. S. Eliot in 1918; an article published in that year in *The Egoist* proves this.

It was apparently the scientific foundation of de Gourmont's ideas which pleased this new poet; de Gourmont seemed to have studied linguistics and the natural sciences, to have set up his own very simple theories upon these props. It is certain that this book of his was to inspire others; it was not its originality which conferred this importance upon it so much as its exterior charm of striking clarity. Later came the more scholarly works of J. Middleton Murry and I. A. Richards to complement and to correct de Gourmont.

It no longer suffices to state that all thought must be conveyed by an image or an analogy. An anti-Imagist argument lay in the fact that in a language word-images very soon become mere signs, that this is no evil, that the very earliest words could have been no more than signs, and that, if new words are fashioned by images, other words, as in slang, for instance, are fashioned otherwise and enrich the language otherwise and otherwise 'endow the words of the tribe with a very pure sense.'

But the *Problème du Style* was an excellent elementary treatise, which placed the literary problem fitly enough on the basis of style and style on the question of the word. The solution indicated being still valid in 1918, T. S. Eliot reascended this current, and, having passed both style and words, he studied the composition, the architecture of a work. Again, he magnifies certain details of the book which struck him. Thus he goes beyond it and makes the literary work objective, he rids it of that emotional dust which de Gourmont had left upon it. With him, he believes that style is a specialization of sensibility; but he goes further. The artist has an artistic sensitivity and a human sensitivity; the latter is of no interest to us, the more so because it effaces itself in the personality of the author, or else it is of interest to us only in so much as it is transposed in the work. Already de Gourmont had put back psychology into its proper place. Eliot quotes this statement of the Frenchman's: 'The writer with an abstract style is almost always a sentimentalist, or at least a sensitive man. The artistic writer is almost never sentimental and very rarely sensitive.' Here de Gourmont has given Eliot food for thought. 'Any word, any great style corresponds to a vision from the outset.' Eliot is more elaborate: 'The end of the enjoyment of poetry is a pure contemplation from which the accidents of personal emotion are removed; thus we aim to see the object as it really is. . . . And without a labour which is largely a labour of the intelligence, we are able to attain that stage of vision *amor intellectualis Dei*' ['intellectual love of God'].

Further, Eliot, in his development, follows de Gourmont's idea; he takes the same examples of the writer with concrete style and the writer with abstract; again, he adopts ideas upon the function of the unconscious from *La Culture des Idées*. As a result, there appear certain similar methods of criticism which are no longer of yesterday. De Gourmont said: 'The error of Monsieur D—, which is an intellectual one, is that of all literary criticism since Sainte-Beuve and since Taine. He is absolutely determined to find the man in the work, and, as the hazards of literary history have offered him this hero of logic, he makes short shrift of bagging him in his net of reasoning' and again 'A genius is; he is not to be analysed from without and he is to be known only by his results.' The methods which de Gourmont employs in his applied criticism will imply the affirmation of his own personality, and, in order to dominate it, a search for permanent values, the use of tools which may be surely wielded, such as analysis and comparison.

Thus this critic has become, for Eliot, practically an example of the perfect critic. To be sure, we must observe Eliot's indulgence; he absolves Rémy de Gourmont of more than one fault; indeed, he must necessarily absolve him of his *Livres des Masques* and necessarily see in him only the equilibrium established between the dogmatic, the technician, the analyst and the constructive. He does his master a great service, but he must return thanks to de Gourmont for having lived and suffered because of certain prejudices, those of Taine, for instance, those of the Impressionists, which, ultimately, he corrected in himself. This is very clear in the following passage, translated by Aldington in his de Gourmont anthology: 'The critical literature of M. Jules Lemaître has the merits of clarity, acuteness and good sense; we may regret that his has not also, not principles, which it can do very well without, but a direction. Indeed, it moves forward rather at hazard. This witty writer has lacked the possession of a literary faith, even for two or three years. That is the most fortunate of intellectual disciplines. We learn to judge by other motives than our personal taste; we feel the necessity for certain aesthetic sacrifices.'

In effect, de Gourmont became a great critic the day he first felt the need of establishing laws for himself. He always remained free and his taste is truly the basis of his judgments; but this taste was by no means entirely a subjective virtue, since it was the result, not only of the aspirations of his period, but also of a whole past of tradition, of a tradition which he consciously realized, even though he took pleasure in repeating that he was only very loosely bound to it. The ideas expressed upon this point in *Poetry* in July, 1914, had not a little effect upon the young Englishmen and Americans who at the time gathered his ideas. The distinctions he drew between tradition considered as a fact and the tradition which he considered as a choice, the idea that it was a tradition not precisely national but rather European which we needed, tended to clarify their own opinions and to afford them with certainties which they could well afford. Being a Frenchman and having seen the ill effects of servitude to a faulty interpretation of the word tradition, de Gourmont had certainly a right to free himself; the Anglo-Saxons who were seeking a discipline on the contrary owed it to themselves to cling to a tradition; they consequently took what de Gourmont said more seriously than ever he did.

Finally, de Gourmont gave the example of a new critical discipline, and, through his scientific studies, he was preparing himself against the day when he was to make a criticism a perfect instrument of artistic knowledge, a science of art.

De Gourmont gave modern criticism a re-orientation; he was the first to replace critical thought beside intelligence and technique, to free it from the scientific parasitism upon which it lived.

Has Rémy de Gourmont ceased to be the symbol of modern intelligence? He is, of course, no longer that of modern sensibility. We are weary of the too familiar cadence of his sentences, of his elegance, built of irony and doubt. We require something more 'virile'; attempts have actually been made to persuade us that his career was a complete failure. Obviously a man risks failure when he seeks to survive himself and to be the author of more than a single book. In the last analysis, de Gourmont's failure may well be his *raison d'être,* the very thing which continues to hold our interest. His most successful experiments are in no sense those which proved the most important to his contemporaries: we have dissociated few ideas, although we are well aware of the value of this method. And there is but scant heed paid to-day to a law of intellectual constancy. But the works and tests by which de Gourmont reached these theorems are the first acts of a modern intelligence; the problems which he laid down and which he was unable to solve are still the very problems which occupy us to-day. He failed when he determined to extend his subjective individualism into the province of reason; but this was perhaps when he felt that he must find a synthesis elsewhere and that there was a discontinuity to be found between these two provinces. From these initial doubts came other doubts and other problems which he might well have solved with time. After him, a report that took stock of his observations had to be established between life and art, form and essence, the conscious and the unconscious, criticism and philosophy. He would have reached a theoretic synthesis just as he reached one in the practice of his criticism; he came very close indeed to a humanism which took account of all the store of civilization, endowing the speculative spirit with the strengths and virtues of sensitivity, of intuition, of an objective criticism which never lost its subjective antennae, of an aesthetics which would not have violated the laws of psychology. But his intelligence may be considered as the success of this synthesis, by the very great measure in which, in his works, he was able to be both extremely cerebral and extremely emotional, without ever assigning due proportions to these two qualities, but employing them, instead, conjointly or for mutual correction. Anatole France's phrase: 'He is the only one among us who was never wrong' may perhaps be no more than a homage, but it is one which could not be decently paid to any other thinker of his generation. (pp. 618-25)

René Taupin, "The Example of Rémy de Gourmont," in The Criterion, *Vol. X, No. XLI, July, 1931, pp. 614-25.*

HAVELOCK ELLIS   (essay date 1913/1934)

[*Ellis was a pioneering sexual psychologist and a respected English man of letters. His most famous work is his seven-volume* The Psychology of Sex *(1897-1928), a study which contains frankly stated case histories of sex-related psychological abnormalities and which is greatly responsible for changing British and American attitudes toward the hitherto forbidden subject of sexuality. As a critic, according to Desmond MacCarthy, Ellis looked for the individuality of the author under discussion. "The first question he asked himself as a critic," wrote MacCarthy, "was 'What does this writer affirm?' The next, 'How did he come to affirm precisely that?' His statement of a writer's 'message' was always trenchant and clear, his psychological analysis of the man extremely acute, and the estimate of the value of his contribution impartial. What moved him most in literature was the sincere expression of preferences and beliefs, and the energy which springs from sincerity." The following excerpt from Ellis's book* From Rousseau to Proust *originally appeared as two separate essays, the first of which appeared in 1913 and the second in 1934. In these essays Ellis discussed several features of Gourmont's work and style of thought, stressing in particular Gourmont's love of life, his need for intellectual freedom and spiritual independence, and his constant growth as an artist.*]

On one side of his manifold temperament Gourmont is . . . something of a monk; a few centuries earlier he would have added fame to one of the great Benedictine foundations of Normandy. It is notable that his earliest large book was a vividly interesting study of medieval monkish verse, **Le Latin Mystique,** to which Huysmans contributed a Preface. Even his first novel, **Sixtine,** which belongs to the same period as **Le Latin Mystique,** reveals something of the same side of Gourmont's temperament. It is described as '*roman de la vie cérébrale*' ['novel of the cerebral life'], and that description may be applied to the novels and plays that have succeeded it. They are all evocations, phantasmagoric processions called into being by the fiat of a singularly vigorous brain. The fragrance of life, the breath of the actual world, the touch of real warm humanity, though not entirely absent, are rarely felt. Their intellectual insight has in it something of the aloofness of the cloister, and their sensual passion the daring analysis of the early theologians. Even in **A Night in the Luxembourg** this cloistered character remains, although we are here lifted to a height whence the aspirations of religions and philosophies are serenely regarded as harmonious manifestations of a new Trinity: Beauty, Strength, and Intelligence. The procession of variegated imagery that passed before the vision of Saint Anthony in the desert is the symbol of all these achievements in the imaginative field, and Gourmont has himself pointed out that we may regard Anthony's visions as, after all, not the least satisfactory method of experiencing life; at the worst, as a tumultuous passage towards spiritual peace. In the extravagances of the imaginative Gourmont we can find a clue to the clear-eyed sanity of the philosophic Gourmont.

Thus the spirit of the cloister in Remy de Gourmont is not accompanied by any attraction to the religious life. He is constitutionally incapable of that Catholic seduction which finally overcame his early friend Huysmans. His aloofness, indeed, is really an aloofness, not so much from the world as from the prejudices which seem to him to obscure and spoil the world. He is of the school of Goethe and Flaubert. He is a lover of life; intellectual freedom and spiritual independence are to him the prime necessaries of life. The monastery of his heart's desire would be no La Trappe, but rather an Abbey of Thelema. It is thus that he has become a great critic of life, a supreme master and critic of style.

It was less as a moralist than as an inquirer into the aesthetics of language, that Gourmont started on this career. . . . [He] was peculiarly attracted to the art of using words, not only to words as jewels, but still more as the substratum of thought. He recognises that language is a vital growth. 'The beauty of a language is its purity,' but this is to be safeguarded, not by rigid rules, but by good sense, by a fine aesthetic feeling, which watches over growth, not disdaining even slang, but avoiding so far as possible foreign importations and classical neologisms, moulding all in accordance with the genius of the language itself. Such problems as these are discussed in a penetrative and stimulating way in *L'Esthétique de la Langue Française* and elsewhere in Gourmont's work.

The study of words leads on to the study of style, and Gourmont approaches style in the same spirit as words. Style in itself, he argues, is nothing. Whatever is deeply thought is well written; 'the style is the very thought.' In his literary predilections Gourmont may be said to be in the fundamental sense classically French. But for pseudo-classicality he has no taste, and just as little for romanticism; the one seems to him frigid, the other baroque. 'I feel at home,' he remarks, 'before Boileau and after Baudelaire,' though it must be added that his fine literary insight, his sense of justice, do not forsake him even when he is dealing with the pseudo-classical or the romantic period. But this aloofness from each of the opposed extravagancies of the French genius—linking the late nineteenth to the early seventeenth century, Verlaine to Ronsard and Mallarmé to Beroalde de Verville, a continuity of things that are vital, personal, and independent—imparts a rare quality to Gourmont's literary judgments. We feel that we are listening to one who speaks with authority, from the heart of the French genius, which is too alive to be cold, and has too fine a sense of measure to be excessive.

As a critic of literature Gourmont is supreme, and it would be hard to point to any living writer who could produce a volume so decisive and so masterly, so mature in its balanced and mellow judgments, as the latest volume of the *Promenades Littéraires*. If it were necessary to funish any demonstration of this critic's insight into literature, one need only refer to his *Livre des Masques*. Nothing is so difficult as to estimate the literary quality of people the critic himself moves among, still for the most part at the outset of their careers. This is what Gourmont attempted twenty years ago in the brief and firm sketches included in his *Livre des Masques*, and it is doubtful whether a single judgment there recorded needs seriously revising today. Here and throughout his critical work, Gourmont has been aided by his peculiar intellectual aloofness. He can penetrate to the core of the aesthetic product before him unmoved by those secondary considerations which so easily dim the vision of the less unattached critic. The ruthless energy of his criticism may sometimes seem too destructive—as when he declares that of the whole naturalistic period nothing survives but a few stories of Villiers de l'Isle Adam and Guy de Maupassant; but we realise, in the end, that we are in the presence of one who lives habitually with great literature and will tolerate nothing that falls short of perfection. Life is too brief, after all, for the unessential things.

Remy de Gourmont is more than a critic of literature. He is a critic of ideas. He was first led to philosophy and science, he has himself indicated, by the study of words regarded as the substance of thought. But it is clear that, whatever the avenue of approach, his searching and independent spirit was bound, sooner or later, to undertake the task of examining and appraising the current notions of the time. He has devised a doctrine of the dissociation of ideas and what he calls a law of intellectual constancy as clues in these fields, wherein he has approached the most various and the most fundamental problems, not excluding that of sex. In science and in philosophy he is the heroic amateur, lacking in training and in equipment, but never failing in keen penetration. The *Revue des Idées,* of which he is the founder and editor, reflects the extent of his curiosities and the thoroughness of his research.

Above all, Remy de Gourmont is, in the wide and deep sense, a moralist, a great critic of life. A thinker with so powerful an impulse to weigh and to test, to search out the essential things, he could not fail to be profoundly interested in human action. This interest, already pronounced in the **Chemin de Velours,** has steadily developed, growing at the same time more tolerant and many-sided, for he never forgets that 'the true philosopher always smiles.'

Gourmont the moralist may best be studied in the successive volumes of the **Dialogues des Amateurs**. Here questions and incidents of the day, as they occur, are discussed, playfully or gravely, but always with reference to fundamental principles, by the man in the street and the man of the fireside, M. Delarue and M. Desmaisons, who but thinly disguise Gourmont's own attitude. He is a sceptic in the face of social panaceas—'to live,' he says, 'is to grow in wisdom and in scepticism'—but he is always an optimist and on the side of joy in life.

The problem of the supposed antagonism between social organisation and individual liberty has for him no difficulties; his tradition of order, his instinct of freedom, are alike too strong. He values social organisation, but he values it as the guardian of liberty. 'Society is an apparatus to protect the individual.' 'And all progress worthy of the name,' he declares, 'is progress in liberty.' From this standpoint, and with all the resources of his wit and irony and sanely balanced intelligence, he castigates the darling sins of his age, those most deplorable sins of all, which believe themselves to be virtues. In the Latin world Remy de Gourmont thus performs much the same function as our own Bernard Shaw performs in the so-called Anglo-Saxon world, with the inevitable differences involved by the possession of another temperament and the need to react vitally against another group of social prejudices. (pp. 308-12)

· · · · ·

When we look back, less than twenty years after his death, we clearly realise that Remy de Gourmont belongs to an age that is past. That is not by any means to say that he has ceased to possess significance or that his work—his best work—is no longer worth reading. It is, indeed, notable that only since his death have his writings to a considerable extent been rendered available in English. For those who turn to them, there are books of Gourmont's always worth reading; he deals with the essential stuff of life, and he deals with it in the medium of intellect which never dies. But it remains true that, while he appealed sympathetically to the foremost and most daring spirits of his own generation, he answers no pressing questions of the generation of today. Yet that generation is far from having made up its mind about him. He is not placed in any unquestioned niche, for respect or for indifference. Indeed, the extraordinary variety of opinions concerning his place might be held to show that he is still very much alive.

I could quote a great number of variegated and often completely contradictory estimates of Gourmont, put forth since his death. He was 'too vast to weigh or measure,' 'a universal critic,' 'a novelist rather than a critic' (that was Souday, who no doubt regarded him as a dangerous rival in criticism), 'an amiable Benedictine,' 'the author of the Bible of Epicurism' *(A Night in the Luxembourg),* 'a wanderer from the eighteenth century,' 'the representative critic of the immediately pre-war period,' 'still extraordinarily modern.' But Rouveyre, a notable artist who is also a penetrating if capricious critic, and had once bestowed high and subtle praise on Gourmont, comparing him to his advantage with the academic and narrowly classical Anatole France, seemed in 1924 to turn on himself and to render equally subtle dispraise. Gourmont had made the great moral mistake of confusing ethics with aesthetics; he had prettified to infinity the vulgar formula, 'Art is life'; he founded all his personal development on a discredited commonplace, thereby for ever shutting himself out from the company of great thinkers and encountering the fate of Phaeton. And when, a few years ago in Paris, I was discussing the critics of today with one of them—certainly noted for his malicious wit—he dismissed Gourmont as 'esprit de concierge.' I made no comment. But it seemed to me, and still seems, that the thinker who was once considered almost too subversive and dangerous to mention was at the furthest possible remove from the mentality of the porter's lodge.

There has appeared, as I write, another and more balanced estimate of Gourmont, though not notably sympathetic, from a distinguished critic of today, Thibaudet [see excerpt dated 1938]. He denies to Gourmont any large outlook; he was occupied with the trees, not with the forest; he belongs to the nineteenth century, while Gide, who was of the same generation, belongs to the twentieth. But Gourmont remains, Thibaudet adds, 'a Sainte-Beuve of decadence,' the great critic of symbolism. His work has strongly and solidly conquered its place on the shelf of great criticism. It is a too sober estimate, but it touches some actual points.

The reference to Gide recalls to mind that Gide himself—whom I would regard as, like Gourmont, a critic rather than novelist—has criticised Gourmont, a critic rather than novelist—has criticised Gourmont at length even during his lifetime (in *Nouveaux Prétextes,* 1911). Gide as a critic proceeds from a totally different position and approaches life at a totally different angle. It is this that makes his pages on Gourmont illuminating, even when unsympathetic. Not that Gide underrates the power of Gourmont's purely literary criticism; he remarks that he reads the *Promenades Littéraires* (caring less for Gourmont's early work) as he would wish his own books to be read. But: 'Ah! if he only wrote that!' It is in such books as *Dialogues des Amateurs,* where Gourmont goes beyond literature to reflect on life, that Gide becomes devastating. 'If M. de Gourmont pleases me when he is good, he only really excites me when he becomes detestable.' And in approaching this aspect of Gourmont, he applies to him what Carlyle says of Voltaire: that the first question with him always is, not what is true, but what is false, not what is worthy to be loved, but what is to be derided, and pushed with a jest out of the door. Voltaire, in attacking religion, was supported by his age, but Gourmont, by attaching himself on this side to the Encyclopedists, had less excuse today for declaring that 'religious literature is dead' and that 'the word of God is only tolerable in music.' Gide

sarcastically comments: 'What a musician M. de Gourmont must be!' 'Scepticim,' he adds, 'may sometimes perhaps be the beginning of wisdom, but it is often the end of art.' Gide strongly suspects that Gourmont only loves science so much in order the better to hate religion, for there is nothing disinterested in his love; he only seeks in science a provision of arguments, no matter of what sort; even in the most scientific of his books, *Physique de l'Amour,* he is moved by two passionate hatreds, in the first place that of modesty, in the second of Christianity. 'No, no, you know as well as I do, Remy de Gourmont: religions are neither "ugly" nor "foolish"; they are what you make of them.'

But we must supplement this judgment of Gide's by that put forward by Jules de Gaultier, belonging to the same generation and a personal friend, who, if not a critic, is yet a highly distinguished thinker and in touch with the thought of today. In his preface to *Esthétique de la Langue Française* . . . Gaultier claims that Gourmont, too, was a great thinker, a typical representative of *intelligence* in the best sense, and one who successfully followed the difficult path between the superstition of old days and the popular ideologies of our day, which are also superstitions. He might treat dogmas in a frivolous spirit— 'religion is for me a fairyland,' his M. Desmaisons says—but he did not oppose them with the truisms of a crude rationalism; prayer was for him an essentially human fact, and beneath the most naïve fables and beliefs he saw hidden the psychic elements which determine the spontaneous evolution of human life. A great sceptic, Gourmont was completely disinterested and free from all personal ambitions. Gaultier, as we know, defines 'metaphysical sensibility' as the power to enjoy things wihout possessing them, the power of discovering in their mere beauty a source of the highest joy. In this power Gaultier would see the Overman, *homo estheticus.* 'It is possible that the salvation of the world is bound up with the coming of men of this high lineage, that of Intelligence attaining the stage of perfection at which beauty is born. Of this class of men Remy de Gourmont is one of the purest representatives.'

When I turn from these widely divergent and often wildly conflicting views of Gourmont, put forth especially since the Great War, and turn to my own first essay [the first section of the present excerpt], I feel reassured. It had seemed probable to me that my opinions would now need considerable revision. I find certainly that various qualifications are needed. But the miscellaneous estimates of Gourmont more recently put forward seem to furnish no adequate ground for any fundamental modifications.

The changes to be made are in non-essentials. A great critic, but it is true that there were pronounced limitations to the range of his critical powers. He remained always an individualist with his penetrative insight concentrated on individual personalities. So that in spite of his interest in ideas he was not interested in movements. Many-sided, like Voltaire, with whom Gide significantly associated him, he accepted, like Voltaire, his own age and the movement, however narrow, along which he was borne, as a foundation not to be questioned. It is, indeed, interesting to observe Gourmont's attitude to Voltaire. No doubt he was always naturally drawn to *Candide,* but his early attractions to his symbolist contemporaries and friends rendered Voltaire disturbing, if not repulsive. His growing interests in life more and more modified that attitude, and in the end completely reversed it. A year before his death Gourmont wrote: 'After having detested nearly everything of Voltaire's, I now like nearly everything, for I perceive, in reading him, that the man is a great writer, and the very type of the sage. His was the vastest mind I know, and the least superficial. If he spoke of everything, it was because he knew everything.' Gourmont was not the peer of Voltaire; they were both, in the first place, men of the study, but Voltaire was also, almost in the first place, in the full and complete sense a man of the world; one need scarcely say, for instance, how significant for his development was his early visit to England. Gourmont was never in any sense a man of the world, content to spend his whole life in Paris, with occasional visits to his native Normandy; even in Paris he cherished his dislike of society and desired to mix with none but congenial friends with whom he could be almost silent. It was the result of these habits of mind and life that, while Gourmont was from the first completely emancipated from the prejudices of patriotism, his critical skill was never operative outside France. He was interested in some foreign literatures, notably the English and Spanish, as we might indeed anticipate, since England and Spain are in France the traditional lands of individualism and could not but appeal to a professed individualist. But he was never at home in those literatures, and scarcely made even the attempt to approach them as a critic. In this he was true to the French spirit of his day and generation. Nearly every notable French writer of that day was rooted in the Boulevards of Paris. It is almost the last place where one expects to find French writers of the post-war generation, who scatter themselves over the world and seek to absorb the spirit of every land. (pp. 316-21)

Certainly it is necessary in any case to recognise that for the generation of today Gourmont has not the immediate message which he had during his life for his own generation. That is inevitable. Every generation makes its own special demands which are never those of the immediately preceding generation. Gide responds to the needs of today as Gourmont does not, but we cannot be sure that if Gourmont had lived on to the post-war period, like Gide, he would not have been alive to its new needs. A remarkable fact about Gourmont was his constant growth and development, so that, when in 1914 the war broke out, he was really at his best. (p. 321)

Remy de Gourmont is among the great critics of the French nineteenth century. We need not claim for him the miraculous certainty of Baudelaire's occasional eruptions into this field, nor that equable and far-spread, almost impersonal sympathy which (save for his own age) Sainte-Beuve displayed. His reputation need not fear any other competitors. He meant much yesterday: he may mean little today: he will mean more tomorrow. (p. 327)

> Havelock Ellis, "Remy de Gourmont," in his From Rousseau to Proust, *Houghton Mifflin Company, 1935, pp. 307-27.*

ALBERT THIBAUDET   (essay date 1938)

[*Thibaudet was a French critic whose numerous and insightful studies of French authors made him one of the most respected critics of his generation. His criticism is independent of any particular school or stylized doctrine of analysis, and is characterized by its assertiveness, versatility, and insight. In the following excerpt from his* French Literature from 1795 to Our Era *(1938), Thibaudet dismisses Gourmont's dramas and fiction while praising his criticism for its intelligence and analytic force.*]

[Rémy de Gourmont] can be seen in union with an epoch. The immanent genius of French literary geography was just what gave Gourmont the climate of 1889, logically erected him at

the junction of naturalism and symbolism, with Huysmans' *A Rebours* as his place of worship and the Flaubert of *Saint Antoine* and *Bouvard* as an ancestor. He had a very keen nose for stupidity; he sensed stupidity, which attracted him; and he turned beams of cruel light on the conventional, the official, success. But it is precisely the critic in him that is especially interesting as a destroyer and a negater. The creative zest and sympathy of a Diderot are remarkably alien to this spirituals on of the eighteenth century. His two *Livres des masques,* portrait galleries of the symbolist catch-all, of a symbolism in which Philothée O'Neddy would be hung in the same section with Sainte-Beuve and Victor Hugo, testify to his failure in criticism of contemporaries, which here became a clan criticism. No more did he elevate or degrade anyone in the past. His fictional and theatrical works do not count, and it might be said of *Sixtine, roman de la vie cérébrale,* that he was qualified to write it but that he did not really write it. There is another dead side in his books, an arid, overrefined, refrigerated eroticism, the eroticism of the devil at the witches' sabbath. For all that, the fifteen volumes that contain his criticisms, his essays, his thoughts on books and men and his time have held up admirably as a library shelf, held up in the manner of the *Lundis* [of Sainte-Beuve]. They owe this to the almost constant presence of the intelligence, to a gift for analysis and, to use his word, to a dissociation of ideas, a harsh, scornful inspection of accepted ideas, a subtle sense of undersides— the undersides of language, of thought, of literature, of emotions, and of morals. Anatole France and he came to be congenial in the end, and the literature of both is in effect a literature of the full stop, a nutrition of extracts, an experience on the margins. Except that France would have little part in today's dialogue, while Gourmont would still be taking part; France would have nothing to tell us, while the corner of Gourmont's dissociations is still dear to us because it has never been supplanted. (pp. 409-10)

> Albert Thibaudet, "Criticism," in his French Literature from 1795 to Our Era, *translated by Charles Lam Markmann, Funk & Wagnalls, 1967, pp. 400-15.*

MARTIN TURNELL   (essay date 1939)

[*Turnell has written widely on French literature and has published significant translations of the works of Jean-Paul Sartre, Guy de Maupassant, Blaise Pascal, and Paul Valéry. In the following excerpt from an essay originally published in 1939, Turnell discusses Gourmont's impartiality, scientific attitude, elitism, and skepticism, alleging that all of these qualities were at once his greatest critical assets and his worst liabilities.*]

"As I have already explained on several occasions," wrote Remy de Gourmont, "contrary to the opinion generally held, criticism is perhaps the most subjective of all literary forms. It is a perpetual confession on the part of the critic. He may think that he is analysing the works of other people, but it is himself that he is revealing and exposing to the public. This necessity explains very well why criticism is as a rule so mediocre and why the critic seldom manages to hold our attention even when he is dealing with questions in which we are most keenly interested. In order to be a good critic, indeed, one must possess a strong personality. The critic must impose himself on the reader and to this end he must rely not on the choice of subject, but on the quality of his own mind. The subject is of small importance in art, or at any rate it is only one part of art; it is of no more importance in criticism where it is never more than a pretext."

This is not a complete definition of the function of criticism, nor, as we shall see from Gourmont's own work, is it wholly sound; but it draws attention to three points which are seen to be of particular importance when we remember the weaknesses of Sainte-Beuve and Taine. In the first place, it insists on the personal factor in criticism and is therefore a corrective to the attempts of nineteenth century critics to reduce criticism to an exact science. In the second place, although there can be no substitute for personal sensibility, this alone is not enough. Criticism must have behind it the whole force of the critic's personality, the whole force of his powerful, independent mind. In the third place, and perhaps the most important of all, we find a distinguished critic asserting for the first time that criticism is valuable for its own sake and is not (as Taine tried to make it) a branch of some other science.

It was the clarity with which Gourmont grasped this third point that helped to make him one of the most distinguished critics of his time. The *Problème du style* has had, directly and indirectly, a considerable influence on contemporary English criticism. It is one of the finest works of general criticism that has appeared during the past fifty years and though it deals almost exclusively with French writers, it is essentially a European work and should be almost as valuable to the English as to the French specialist. The papers collected in the seven volumes of the *Promenades littéraires* have lost none of their freshness with the passing of time. When they first appeared these brief and eminently readable *chroniques* were something new in literary journalism. They took the place of Sainte-Beuve's elaborate *causeries* with their vast parade of erudition. Gourmont was not only more stimulating, more of a critic than Sainte-Beuve, but in the best of the *Promenades littéraires*—notably in the studies of Renan, Brunetière and Lemaître—he contrived in the space of nine or ten pages to say the essential about his authors. No one who works on the same authors can afford to overlook what Gourmont has said about them; and it is difficult to think of any collection of literary essays to which one returns more often or more profitably.

In spite of his great merits, however, Gourmont's criticism leaves the reader with an ill-defined sense of dissatisfaction. I have sometimes thought that his impression may be due to the economy imposed by the *chronique,* to the fact that it may appear thin when compared with the weighty studies of Gourmont's immediate predecessors; but constant re-reading suggests that Gourmont's particular faults are inseparably connected with his particular virtues and the two can only be discussed together.

"La seule recherche féconde," he wrote in the Preface to the *Problème du style, "est la recherche du non-vrai"* ["The only fertile inquiry is the inquiry into non-truth"]. It is a concise statement not only of his own method, but also of the temper which informed the whole of his writings. He was a sceptic and an amateur of physiology, possibly because physiology seemed to provide the only certain foothold in an age of crumbling systems. His scepticism was complete, but it was a genial scepticism. His criticism is singularly free from the faults which make critics of the same period who wrote in English seem crude and provincial. The fact that he was a Frenchman and his background Catholic enabled him to appreciate the issues better than an Englishman and preserved him from the Nonconformist conscience which has always been one of the greatest enemies of clear thinking. Although he remarked bluntly

in his paper on Renan *"Je n'aime guère le style des écrivains dont je déteste la pensée"* ["I cannot admire the style of a writer whose thought I detest"], his treatment of writers whose beliefs he did not share was often remarkable for its justice and impartiality. (pp. 440-42)

[Gourmont's criticism] marks the end of the method, practised by Sainte-Beuve and Taine, of treating a writer's "style" and his "thought" as though they were in some way separable. . . .

In spite of limitations of which I shall have something to say later, the sceptical approach is impressive in its astringency and up to a point it constitutes a genuine intellectual discipline. Gourmont was one of the first writers who systematically attacked vague romantic appreciation and tried to make criticism not a science, but scientific in a wide sense which was not Taine's sense; and his declaration that "style is a specialisation of sensibility" is a landmark in the history of criticism. The most valuable parts of the *Problème du style* are, indeed, those in which Gourmont sets out to define sensibility. In the well-known passage on Flaubert he wrote:

> Flaubert incorporated his whole sensibility in his works; and by sensibility I mean, here as everywhere, the general power of feeling, as it is unequally developed in each human being. Sensibility comprehends reason itself, which is only crystallized feeling. Outside of his books, into which he decanted himself drop by drop to the dregs, Flaubert is of very little interest; he is nothing but dregs; his intellect disturbs itself, exasperates itself in an incoherent fantasy. . . . Far from his work being impersonal, the rôles here are reversed: it is the man who is vague and woven of incoherences; it is the work which lives, breathes, suffers and smiles nobly.

For Gourmont the great writer is the writer whose work is his life, and the bad writer is the writer who is divided between writing and action. Thus he observes acutely of the solitaries of Port-Royal:

> They wrote in a style wholly external, into which they incorporated hardly a particle of their sensibility, saving it all for their life, for their religious activity.

> (pp. 443-44)

The definition of sensibility is undeniably impressive, but when we find Gourmont writing

> Racine, whose style is so seldom plastic, saves almost all his sensibilities first for his mistresses, then for God. The profound feeling for love which was in him did not enter into the actions of his characters; they express intense passions in an abstract, frigid, and diplomatic style.

it is impossible not to feel disconcerted. There are, I think, two explanations. One is that the definition of sensibility is not as conclusive as it sounds. The other is that like most French critics, Gourmont was more impressive when making general statements of principle than when elucidating a text. They are both worth discussion.

Flaubert was a great novelist, but we may doubt whether he was the perfect writer for which Gourmont took him. Indeed, his admiration appears to be one of the symptoms of the peculiar limitations of his own critical sensibility. His emphasis on the physiological element in sensibility was timely and important, but when he observes

> Style is a physiological product, and one of the most constant, though dependent upon various vital functions.

we may suspect that in practice the definition was narrower than one would expect from the passage on Flaubert given above, that it was reduced to a physiological function in the interests of an inadequate metaphysic. It explains, for example, why Gourmont should admire Flaubert's style, which is rich in the expression of physical sensations, and find Racine's *"abstrait, glacé, et diplomatique"* ["abstract, frigid, and diplomatic"]. The criticism of the style of the *Solitairies* is just, but when Gourmont goes on to assert

> Art is incompatible with a moral or religious preoccupation; beauty leads neither to piety nor to contrition, and the glory of God shines chiefly in works of the humblest intelligence and most mediocre rhetoric.

he imposes a drastic theoretical limitation which he would hardly tolerate in the concrete study of a poet. This view is confirmed by his asides on the nature and value of artistic experience. When he tries to explain why it is valuable, he falls back on generalities:

> Art is that which produces a sensation of beauty and of novelty at the same time, of new beauty; one cannot understand entirely and still be moved.

(pp. 444-45)

Poetry is transformed into a mystery which appears to call not for comprehension, but for adoration. It is a mystery to which only an élite are admitted. *"Car je crois,"* writes Gourmont, *"que l'art est, par essence, absolument inintelligible au peuple"* ["For I believe that art, by its very nature, is absolutely unintelligible to the crowd"].

The language that he uses to describe his favourite writers is not less instructive. He speaks enthusiastically of Mallarmé's *"sonnets les plus délicieusement obscurs"* ["most deliciously obscure sonnets"], and of *"l'art délicat et ingénieux d'aujourd'hui"* ["the delicate and ingenious art of to-day"]. It is to his credit that he was the indefatigable champion of the "advanced" writers of his own time, but Mr. Eliot's description of him as "the critical consciousness of a generation" points to a serious limitation in his criticism. His intense preoccupation with the theories of the Symbolist Movement—a preoccupation that is apparent in his novels and his poetry as well as in his criticism—seems to have turned him into a dilettante who gloried in anything that was recondite and in "novel" and "deliciously obscure" sensations partly because they were inaccessible to other people. The terms that he used to describe poetic experience suggest that his sensibility was distinctly limited. His admiration for *le beau inédit* ["new beauty"] impaired his appreciation of Racine and his emphasis on "the delicate and ingenious art of to-day" accounts, perhaps, for his failure with Rimbaud whom he significantly called *"un crapaud congrument pustuleux"* ["a properly warted toad"]. For an adequate reading of that poet would have needed a range of feeling of which Gourmont was incapable.

It is one of the disadvantages of Gourmont's sceptical approach that he was more effective as a destructive critic and one of the finest papers in the whole of the *Promenades littéraires* is the brilliant attack on Brunetière. But it is symptomatic that his destructive work was limited to academic writers like Brunetière and the unhappy M. Abalat. His attempt to make poetry something for an élite is a sign of the negative attitude he adopted to one of the most pressing problems of his generation, as it is one of the most pressing problems of our own. He does not escape the charge of being the critic of the Ivory Tower whose aim is to take refuge from the barbarism of the outside world.

I have said that Gourmont was more impressive when making general statements of principle than when elucidating a text. It is not without significance that he wrote better about the work of other critics than about poetry. Although he was the official critic of the Symbolist Movement, he never wrote a scarching or substantial book about the *poetry* of the Movement; and compared with his able account of the philosophy of Symbolism in the paper on *Idealism*, his studies of individual writers like Corbière and Laforgue, Verlaine and Mallarmé, are fragmentary and disappointing. For in the last resort he was true to the French approach; he was more interested in the movement of ideas behind the poetry than in the poetry itself. His limitations as a critic sometimes made his discussion of ideas less impressive than it should have been. In his paper on Brunetière he quotes a passage from that critic's book on Balzac:

> "It is not only not true that everything appears differently to different people according to personal idiosyncracies . . . but reality is the same for all intelligences. There is only one point of view from which it is true and 'in conformity with its object,' just as in science there is only one formula that is truly scientific."

With this principle [retorts Gourmont], one ends by denying the legitimacy of all individual activity. Art disappears altogether. . . . Every object, every fact, only permits of one valid representation, which is true; and ideas are necessarily divided into two classes—the true and the false . . .

> Let us remain true to the principles of subjective idealism which are impregnable. The world is my representation of it. It is the only creative principle, the only one which allows the full development and ordering of intelligence and sensibility.

As a criticism of Brunetière this is final; as a statement of the philosophy inherent in the poetry of the period, it is undoubtedly true. But Gourmont was so impressed by idealism as a philosophy, so in love with freedom and individualism, that it did not occur to him to ask whether the influence of this philosophy on poetry was as advantageous as he chose to think. It did not strike him that an extreme individualism was actually having an unfortunate influence on language which was losing its ancient power of translating sensations into words and was already showing signs of developing into the *jeu de mots* ["word play"] which we now know as Surrealism; and the sort of criticism which Rivière made in his fine essay *Reconnaissance à Dada*, was beyond the scope of his method.

Gourmont was a very stimulating and, up to a point, a very able critic; but he seems to me to fall short of greatness. He was endowed in a high degree with the Frenchman's mental alertness and his curiosity about life; but it was precisely an undisciplined curiosity coupled with a fundamental dilettantism which led him into unprofitable ways and detracted from the the critical intensity of his work. His scepticism, which was valuable as a critical approach in his time, had in the long run a disabling effect on his writing and it is impossible not to be struck over and over again with the fundamental poverty of his outlook. (pp. 445-47)

> Martin Turnell, *"Baudelaire, Remy de Gourmont,"* in Critiques and Essays in Criticism, 1920-1948: Representing the Achievement of Modern British and American Critics, *edited by Robert Wooster Stallman, The Ronald Press Company, 1949, pp. 435-48.*

G. D. KLINGOPULOS   (essay date 1940-41)

[*In the following excerpt from an essay originally published in* Scrutiny *in 1940-41, Klingopulos dismisses Gourmont's literary criticism for its subjectivity and lack of intellectual rigor. For a contrasting view of Gourmont's subjective approach to literary criticism, see the excerpt by Ludwig Lewisohn (1921).*]

The best of Gourmont's ideas have been so completely assimilated by later critics that one reads him for the first time either with surprise or disappointment. *La Culture des Idées, Le Chemin de Velours,* and *Le Problème du Style* were written between 1900 and 1902, about twenty years before [T. S. Eliot's] *The Sacred Wood* and [J. M. Murry's] *The Problem of Style.* Particularly memorable are the discussions of decadence, of *cliché,* of imitation, of metaphor, of realism, of plagiarism, pastiche, and sentimentality, which are still lively and more useful than much that has been written, with more show of science, since. Gourmont too had his science. The *cellules nerveuses* ["nervous fibers"] were his most constant "illusions of fact" to which Mr. Eliot refers. The science is not pretentious so much as dogmatic, the dogmatic guess-work of an amateur, frequently impudent. Odds and ends of information from physiology and biology Gourmont put to the same use as Lawrence, with more impudence and less relevance. The simple and comic parallels of Fabre's *Insect Life* excited in him the cynicism of a dilettante. *"Du nouveau, encore du nouveau, toujours du nouveau: voilà le premier principe de l'art"* ["Novelty, again novelty, always novelty: this is the first principle of art"]. [In his *Rémy de Gourmont: Essai de Biographie Intellectuelle*] Dr. Rees leaves unexamined the abstractions in which Gourmont saw the only alternative to Belief—such as Novelty, Beauty, Strength, Intelligence, and devotes space to Gourmont as a philosopher. It is only by a loose application of terms that the title can be extended to him. Gourmont was much more intelligent than Anatole France, but like him *"il n'avait pas de système"* ["he had no system"]. The dissociation of ideas is hardly this, but rather an essayist's formula. His culture of ideas and his scepticism are less important than his reliance on sensibility, on "sensations," which kept him out of aesthetics and gave him his wide range.

Much more could have been made of the *Promenades Littéraires* which illustrate Gourmont's procedure. To call it a method would be misleading, as Gourmont seems to have disdained any show of practical criticism and comparison of authors. He represents good taste rather than practice. His opinions are always suggestive, but cannot be imitated. His indifference to practice meant that his criticism was general and frequently

lacked exactness. He did not care to "understand minutely." Contrast, for instance, his interest in Flaubert with Lawrence's. Flaubert is an excuse for considerations on the ideal artist and *"le but de l'activité propre d'un homme"* ["the aim of activity proper to a man"]. Gourmont's concern with Beauty, Symbols, and the impermanence of feelings should all have been considered together against his *"ériger en lois"* ["to set up as a law"] axiom in the *Lettres à L'Amazone.*

When Gourmont's subject is poetry or art in general, his ideas and the way he expresses them are more delicate and more final than anything in Matthew Arnold. For example:

> ... *Cependant, le vulgaire ressentira plus d'émotion devant la phrase banale que devant la phrase originale; et ce sera la contre-épreuve; au lecteur qui tire son émotion de la substance même de sa lecture s'oppose le lecteur qui ne sent sa lecture qu'autant qu'il peut en faire une application à sa propre vie, à ses chagrins, à ses espérances.*

> ["... However, the vulgar experience more emotion before a banal sentence than before a sentence that is original; and this will be the counterproof; opposed to the reader who derives emotion from the substance of the reading material itself, is the reader who experiences this material only to the extent that he can apply it to his own life, to his sorrows and his hopes"].

But he is inconstant and repetitive, and is distracted by points of philology or other miscellaneous knowledge. Dr. Rees writes, *"Le pouvoir de généraliser semble manquer aux essayistes anglais: ils n'ont pas de facilité pour jouer avec les idées comme des prestidigitateurs"* ["The ability to generalize seems to be absent among English essayists: they do not have the facility to play with ideas like conjurers"]. Pre-eminently Gourmont displays this facility, a facility in being so excited by an idea or theory, becoming so completely a champion, a rebel, or whatever else, that reality is lost and ideas become fantasy. As in his novels and poetry, Gourmont's tendency in criticism is to substitute fantasy for experience and thought. The distinction between fact and fiction, which Eliot desires, is slurred over. The critic becomes an exhibitor of fantasy and a public character. It is here that Gourmont suffers in comparison, again, with Arnold. The Frenchman appears, in his brilliance, less experienced, less fastidious, less wise. (pp. 311-13)

> G. D. Klingopulos, *"Rémy de Gourmont,"* in The Importance of *"Scrutiny"*: Selections from *"Scrutiny: A Quarterly Review"*, 1932-1948, *edited by Eric Bentley, New York University Press, 1964, pp. 311-13.*

DENIS SAURAT   (essay date 1947)

[*Saurat was a French critic whose works include studies of John Milton and William Blake, and the comprehensive* French Literature, 1870-1940 *(1947), which was controversial for its sometimes dogmatic expressions of its author's personal feelings. In the following excerpt from that study, Saurat dismisses Gourmont's literary criticism as flawed by the intrusion of his political beliefs.*]

[Rémy de Gourmont] fails ... for the same reason as Brunetière, although his doctrine is the opposite one. He is such a staunch democrat, or even anarchist, that he cannot see good literature when it comes from the other side. Political passion no doubt perverts literary judgment, and whether you are fanatically royalist or anarchist, Catholic or atheist, makes no difference to your incompetence as a critic. The judgment of literary values must be dissociated from ideas, even from literary theories—how much more dissociated then must it be from political or religious theories.

No doubt writers must have ideas, and critics have a right to ideas, but a critic who cannot judge of the literary values of a work irrespective of both the writer's ideas and the critic's, is simply not a literary critic at all: he is a controversialist. Thus Veuillot is an enemy of Hugo, and quite a good one, but he is not a literary critic of Hugo. An atheist who cannot see the beauty of Bossuet or the depth of Pascal, a Catholic who cannot see the beauty of Hugo or the intelligence of Voltaire, are not literary critics. Rémy de Gourmont invented a good phrase: he said people spoke of association of ideas, but what we needed was dissociation of ideas, since our associations were always wrong. But he failed to carry out his own excellent doctrine. (pp. 66-7)

> Denis Saurat, "Literary Critics," in his Modern French Literature: 1870-1940, 1946. Reprint by Kennikat Press, 1971, pp. 64-71.*

KENNETH BURKE (essay date 1953)

[*In the following excerpt, Burke discusses Gourmont's role as a defender of Symbolism and the doctrine of art for art's sake, as well as his method of the dissociation of ideas. Burke points out that Gourmont's theory is a natural correlative to Symbolism, which relies on the numerous associations surrounding the important words of a poem or fiction for its effects. Burke believes that since such modern writers as James Joyce and Gertrude Stein have chosen to make "dissociative and associative processes a pivotal concern of their works," any technical criticism of these writers must concern itself with theories such as Gourmont's.*]

In his essay on women and language, De Gourmont comments on the tendency of the young males to burn up the race, and adds that certain Asiatic peoples are extinct not on account of their lack of spirit, but because they had too much of it. De Gourmont himself began his career at a time when one of the most feverish attempts in the history of European art was being made to burn up the race. The group of young males that gathered around Mallarmé, with their aesthetic of symbolism, and their philosophy of idealism, were, as De Gourmont proudly showed in one of his early insolent polemics, on the road to intellectual anarchism. If each man was his own world—and surely, there are certain poems of Mallarmé which we can only spy at quizzically, as one might look through a 'scope at Venus under favorable conditions—it was inevitable that each man should have his own idiom. Although the reduction to absurdity of individualism in art is to spend one's life in talking to oneself, they were all too potent, too spirited, to be disturbed by reductions to absurdity. If such was the quintessence of symbolism, there was nothing to do but talk to oneself; the movement *per se* was its justification.

All this fever of innovation was decried under the name of decadence, though De Gourmont shows in his *Mallarmé et l'Idée de Décadence* that the historical concept of *décadisme* referred to times when the creative instinct was at its lowest, not at its suicidally highest.

To be a decadent, by another association of ideas, was to uphold the infamous *L'art-pour-l'art*. De Gourmont always had much too strong a detestation of democratic standards to be anything but a disciple of Art for Art's Sake. In *Une Nuit au Luxembourg* he says:

"The process of thinking is a sport, although this sport must be free and harmonious. The more it is looked upon as useless, the more one feels the need of making it beautiful. Beauty—that is perhaps its only possible value."

And in one of his essays:

"To admit art because it can uplift the masses or the individual, is like admitting the rose because we can extract from roses a medicine for the eyes."

Art was "justified" because art was an appetite—in being desired it found its ample reason for existence. Art did not require defense as an instrument of political or social reform. Art was purely and simply a privilege, to be prized as a cosmic exception. And far from trying to show that art "does good," De Gourmont would find art of primary value even if it "did harm." Art would naturally seem "subversive" if judged by non-art standards. Reversing the customary direction of approach, De Gourmont pointed out that intellectual pursuits alone distinguished man from other organisms—accordingly, instead of appraising these pursuits by their social usefulness, he would appraise our social institutions by their usefulness in making intellectual pursuits possible.

This attitude manifested itself in the experimental nature of both his critical and imaginative writings. His one imperative was to be venturesome. Since art, by becoming an end in itself, became a matter of the individual—or by becoming a matter of the individual, became an end in itself—he was theoretically without external obligations, at liberty to develop his medium as he preferred. And while this theoretical freedom was checked in him, as in every artist, by the desire to communicate, it did contribute to the variability of his work. It is true that he ceased his stylistic development once he had reached a complete lubrication of phrase, but the nature of his books themselves is rarely the same in two successive volumes. Against the opulence of *Sixtine,* with its baggage of erudite irony and rhetorical excursions, is the suave, almost unctuous *Une Nuit au Luxembourg.* There is the nearly conventional novel, *Une Coeur Virginal,* with complications, opportune disclosures, and the like; but there is also *Les Chevaux de Diomède,* "a little novel of possible adventures, with thought, action, dream, and sensuality treated on the same plane and analysed with equal good will." His fantastic stories, written when symbolism was in its first glow, are matched by things like the somewhat nasty *Histoires Magiques.* And scattered among this pliant fiction are his criticisms, grammatical writings, works of scientific research, philosophical essays, notes on contemporary society, discussions of art and literature, and an occasional poem—in all some forty volumes of graceful and intelligent writing. Were they not diffuse, there is no grave objection that could be laid against them. (pp. 15-18)

Super-Copernican, De Gourmont was not content with denying the world as the center of the universe; he also denies man as the center of the world. He found in Darwin "*la pudibonderie religieuse de sa race*" ["the pious prudery of his generation"], and the purely theological tendency, even while endangering the old religion, to place man as the ultimate aim of nature. He insisted that man was neither first nor last upon the earth. The privileges of humanity were hardly more than an accident,

Bust of Gourmont. From Rémy de Gourmont: Selections from All His Works, Volume II, *chosen and translated by Richard Aldington. Covici-Friede, Publishers, 1929. Used by permission of Crown Publishers, Inc.*

these exclusively personal experiences which are important so long as sensation endures. De Gourmont has little time for those perfect systems of government wherein the aggregate of humanity is to be made happy at the expense of each individual. "Let us accept as sufficient this theorem: What is useful to the bee is useful to the hive."

De Gourmont, with his insistence upon the unimportance of humanity and the importance of man, his conception of the intelligence as a disease or an error along with his enthusiasm over the beauty of a perfectly functioning intelligence, his balance of man as an animal over against man as something distinct from all animals, maintained a conflict of attitudes which gives his work considerable liquidity. Such ambivalence was characteristic. Thoroughly godless, for instance, he always manifested a passionate interest in Catholicism. His first important work of erudition, *Le Latin Mystique,* is an anthology, with partial translations and comment, of "the poets of the antiphonary, and Symbolism in the Middle Ages." His *Chemin de Velours* is an analysis of Pascal and the Jesuits. But, as one might expect, his sympathy for Catholicism is hardly likely to earn for him the benediction of Rome. For he admires Catholicism in that it is preserving the rich pagan institutions over against the aridity of Protestantism. Mere matters of creed mean nothing to him; like many of his pious colleagues, he is interested in the Church as a pageant. He observes with regret that before the Reformation the Church was steadily incorporating the elements of paganism; he shows the functions and names of Italian tutelary deities surviving as saints of the calendar; he points out that the Greek god Orpheus, who often figures in early Christian art, was accepted as a prophet by no less an authority than St. Augustine. "A pure Christianity would have rejected the entire Pythagorean system; Catholicism, true to its name, has handed down to us, along with the religion of Christ, nearly all the superstitions and all the theogonies of the Orient." It is not the Protestant Revolution which distresses De Gourmont, but the Catholic Reformation. From then on the existence of beauty in the Church has been precarious; Church art practically ceased; the Church had been Christianized. (pp. 19-21)

As an inevitable corollary to such an attitude towards the Church was De Gourmont's insistence upon the primacy of sex. (Although I do not recall his ever mentioning the name of a psychoanalyst—and he is always frank about his sources—the theories of Freud and his epigons are continually finding expression in his works. The parallelism is natural enough, however—for De Gourmont was the leading apologist of symbolism, and as Charles Baudouin has pointed out, psychoanalysis is the scientific counterpart of symbolist art.) "The mistake of treating man's brain as the absolute centre of the man is both fortunate and commendable, but it is a mistake. The only natural aim of man is that of reproduction." Or from another angle, *"La beauté est si bien sexuelle que les seules oeuvres d'art incontestées sont celles qui montrent tout bonnement le corps humain dans sa nudité"* ["Beauty is so very sexual that the only uncontested works of art are those which very beautifully portray the human body in its nakedness"]. By its insistence on remaining purely sexual, Greek statuary has lifted itself forever above all discussion."

But all this is only one phase of his sympathy with the life of the senses. De Gourmont is even more thoroughly an Epicurean than Anatole France. He says in *Le Chemin de Velours* that "Voluptuosity is a creation of man, a delicate art in which only a few are especially proficient, like music or painting." *Une Nuit au Luxembourg* contains a new apology for Epicurus:

if one could speak of an accident in nature, and this accident might just as well have happened to another species, indeed, may still happen. Intelligence is perhaps an improper functioning of the instincts, or the beginning of instincts which have not yet crystallized—which would mean that the bee or the ant had gone further in evolution than man. In his *Physique de l'Amour,* he says, "Man is not at the pinnacle of nature; he is *in* nature, one of the units of life, and nothing more." The purpose of this book was to "place the sexual life of man in the one and only scheme of universal sexuality." De Gourmont never forgot that a man is of no more importance in relation to the stars than a grasshopper. Nor did he forget that a man in relation to himself is of tremendous importance, *"L'intelligence est un accident; le génie est une catastrophe"* ["Intelligence is an accident; genius is a catastrophe"], he wrote in *Le Succès et l'Idée de Beauté,* and the statement contained his highest possible tribute to intelligence and genius. De Gourmont found delight precisely where his predecessors had found despair.

While emphasizing the futility of the human race as a whole, he affirmed the all-importance of the individual. Descartes' *cogito; ergo sum* ["I think, therefore I am"], he says somewhere, is so simple, so rudimentary, that any savage could probably understand it. Humanity is an abstraction, but the isolated human has cravings to satisfy and pains to avoid; it is

"My friend, for some centuries now the schools have been poisoning your sensibilities and strangling your intelligence by making you believe that the pleasures of Epicurus were exclusively pleasures of the mind. Epicurus was too wise to disdain any sort of pleasure. He wanted to know, and he did know, all the satisfactions which can become the satisfactions of men; he abused nothing, but he used everything, in his life of harmony."

In the closing chapter of his *Physique de l'Amour* he has a long, enthusiastic period: *"Tout n'est que luxure. . . . L'animal ignore la diversité, l'accumulation des aptitudes; l'homme seul est luxurieux"* ["All is lust. . . . The animal is unaware of the diversity, the accumulation of aptitudes; man alone is lustful"]. M. Paul Delior, in his *Remy de Gourmont et Son Oeuvre,* illustrates the attitude of De Gourmont by citing the three souls of Plato: the νους, "mind, intelligence," located in the head; the θυμος, "passions, emotions," located in the breast; the επιθυμητικον, with all the appetites which assure the conservation of the individual and of the race, located in the stomach, and according to Plato a ferocious beast which we should nurture only because it is necessary to existence. De Gourmont not only admired the purest activities of the intellect, and the play of the sensibilities, but also recognized the dignity of the appetites, understood that they are an excellent base on which to erect the superstructure of intelligence and sensibility.

De Gourmont discovered himself for his critics when he used the word "dissociation." He loves to show that a concept which we generally take as a unit can be subdivided. "Man associates his ideas, not in accordance with logic, or verifiable exactitude, but in accordance with his desires and his interests." In his essay, **"La Dissociation des Idées,"** De Gourmont lets himself loose with this method, and produces a type of writing which is delightfully exact. After defining the origin of the commonplace, he gives as an example the association of ideas Byzantium-decadence. He then goes over to the nature of morality, and the reasonable probability that the individual can develop more conveniently in immorality; but morality is the determination to preserve the race at the expense of the individual. From this he comes to the association carnal pleasure-generation, as the foundation of sexual morality. Yet the true association, he holds, is that of intellectuality-infecundity. Christianity, however, did make one remarkable dissociation, that of love and carnal pleasure. Thus was the love of brother and sister made possible. I recall that in his *Octavius,* Minucius Felix found it necessary to refute the Roman scandal about the Christian "brotherly love." De Gourmont, as also Minucius, uses the instance of the Egyptians, who could not understand love without sexual conjunction. He next considers Joan of Arc, and the conflicting associations she brings up in an English and a French mind. Soon he has arrived at the army, showing how at one time the military was associated with high honor; then came scandals, and the mistake was just as radically the other way, the military becoming associated with nothing but complete dishonor. In closing he leaves us a list which he has not troubled to examine, but which seems to fall apart by the mere clarity of juxtaposition: virtue-recompense; wrong-punishment; God-goodness; crime-remorse; duty-happiness; future-progress. It is regrettable that De Gourmont did not carry his dissociative method further into the realm of literary criticism. The method was clearly a companion discovery to symbolism, which sought its effects precisely by utilizing, more programmatically than in any previous movement, the clusters of associations surrounding the important words of a poem or fiction. And such writers as James Joyce and Gertrude Stein are clearly making associative and dissociative processes a pivotal concern of their works. Any technical criticism of our methodological authors of today must concern itself with the further development and schematization of such ideas as De Gourmont was considering.

An author who lives most of his life in his head must perform his transgressions on paper. There was many a wild act more or less definitely spelled out in De Gourmont's ink. In his fiction, the graceful libertinage of the man is perhaps one of his predominant qualities. He seemed to prefer the contemplation of easy conquests, of women that were at once refined and ready of access, and men who were frankly satyrs. "Arise, thy name is Lilith," says Jehovah in creating pre-Eve woman. Lilith, arising, speaks: *"Donne-moi l'homme, Seigneur"* ["Lord, give me Man"]. As a matter of course, Diomedes attains all women except Christine, and she is immune only because she does not exist. True, in *Sixtine,* D'Entragues is baffled, but it is his endless ratiocination that defeats him; and as recompense, this same ratiocination aids him in the last chapter to console himself, and reach *"le repos final"* ["the final repose"], a mock-Victorian "In Conclusion." In *Un Coeur Virginal,* the leading character fails with the heroine because he is dangerously nearing his fifties, and De Gourmont is writing the physiology of virginity; it is part of the physiology that a younger man should win. With this one important exception, as he developed his method De Gourmont seemed to profit more and more by his "illusion of liberty," until in the *Lettres d'un Satyre* we have as hero a complete Olympian, who treats his women as flowers in the earlier Goethe fashion—Röslein, Röslein, Röslein rot!—and plucks them where he will.

Blasphemy is another element which recurs, blasphemy and sacrilege. *Le Fantôme,* for instance, is a perverse account of a courtship which he has enwrapped in mysticism by utilizing the language of the ritual. It is a pagan plot made churchy, with a fictitious mass to celebrate the glory of love. However, in a personality as rich as that of De Gourmont, blasphemy can never be insolence or derision. It is often the expression of the religious inclination in an intelligence which cannot believe. Since it is impossible to praise the divinities with sincerity, there is nothing left but to insult them. Blasphemy is a serious experiment, a transgression by means of the sins of others. To blaspheme is to restore the lost gods by renouncing them; blasphemy is the struggle of an emotional nature, a protest against the intellect which tends to make it sterile of religious ecstasy. Blasphemy is impious, but it is not irreligious.

In his highly pietistic introduction to *Pendant la Guerre,* Jean de Gourmont [Gourmont's younger brother] finds that "in spite of the echo of the battle, and that atmosphere of anguish in which we were all plunged, the writer's hand had not trembled, nor his brain; never perhaps has Remy de Gourmont attained as in these few months such clarity of style and of thought stripped of all vain metaphor, all vain literature."

One was expected to write so during the war, but I doubt if any could still feel that the war had brought De Gourmont a greater "clarity of thought." For here, like poor Diomède of twenty years earlier, De Gourmont had at last slipped against life and been forced to suffer the overbalancing of his intellect by his emotions. A social force had appeared which was strong enough to break through his detachment, and as Diomède finally accepted the ideal of the sluggish Pascase, so De Gourmont half fell in with the universal licking of blood that for five years was supposed to be the purest expression of humanity.

Once he had written, "Detachment is the most aristocratic of all aristocratic attitudes. . . . We should take part in the game, and with pleasure, but not with passion. Passion disqualifies; it is the proof of an elementary organism, without serious coordination. . . ." (pp. 21-6)

And again, in *La Création Subsconciente,* he remarks that a man loses his personality in acting sympathetically with a great number of people. Thus, De Gourmont himself has furnished us with reasons to distrust his blaze of patriotism. And whatever may be said in favor of a blaze of patriotism, we have it on his own authority that it can hardly be admired as an aid to greater clarity of style and thought.

No, De Gourmont was now cast against life for the first time. The war had startled him out of his theory, deprived him of the purity of his Epicureanism. The vigor of his intelligence, it seems, had delayed as far as old age the struggle with vital forces that most of us have experienced before twenty. Until now, he had succeeded in saddling his emotions with ideas; but the war, which was hardly more than an irritation to so many, became to him overwhelming. For the most part, his war books are the magnificent ruins of a great intelligence. Suddenly De Gourmont needed his god; and since the godlessness of his youth was freedom, his god became attachment. He retained his keenness, and in most cases his leisure, but the full force of the war, the threat that France might be destroyed, called for affirmation, for patriotic dogmatizing. De Gourmont, joining the swarm *pour la patrie* ["for the homeland"], trained his learned barrage upon the barbarians. The spirit of irony, of contradiction, of impersonality, that ultimate flavor of his versatility which made him an exquisite writer, had dropped away. As he says of himself, his ideas were mobilized.

But even the ruins of De Gourmont are of no ordinary nature. Never, during the entire war, did he degenerate to the level of a war editorial. He is not among those who would decry Nietzsche, for he recognized that Nietzsche was one of the most important moralists of the time; and further, there is Nietzsche in every sentence he wrote. He admitted the value of German music. He managed to keep reasonably clean of the "regeneration" mud, the thesis which became the reason for existence of half the output of the novel-manufacturing industry of England, the song that the war must create a profound uplift in everyone. But essentially he accepted the formula: that the enemy was *always* wrong. He seemed to have forgotten his own dissociative method, he was so busy helping to nourish the association, enemy-turpitude.

Perhaps De Gourmont could no longer contradict, but he could modify. He recognized that the basis of this war, as of every war, was the pugnacity natural to all individual or collective egos. Even the enemy's "atrocities" he sometimes defended as a corollary of the war-spirit. He blamed the war on militarism, although militarism to De Gourmont was not a term in economics; De Gourmont could always talk more enthusiastically of man in comparison with his analysis of a sea mollusk than he could from consideration of the industrial revolution. Essentially, the present war for him, aside from the painful fact that it was his own personal friends who were dying, was not different from an unwritten event of pre-history, a struggle with clubs.

In *Une Nuit au Luxembourg,* where "Lui" is considering the destruction of the human race, he dismisses the thought of some great cataclysm like an explosion or like collision with a comet, not because it is improbable, but because it is too crude, too broadly theatrical, to interest him. The development of De Gourmont's writing during the war indicates that if he had lived, the war might have suffered the same fate with him. Gradually the brooding quality of his early notes on the war disappears; he becomes more and more discursive, with more emphasis on the theoretical and observational, the essentially egotistic. He is in the war much the way one would be on the sea or in the mountains; since it is the most prevailing fact, he talks about it.

In *La Culture des Idées* he had written, *"La diabolique Intelligence rit des exorcismes, et l'eau bénite de l'Université n'a jamais pu la stériliser, non plus que celle de l'Eglise"* ["The diabolical Intelligence laughs at exorcisms, and the holy water of the University has never been able to sterilize it, no more than that of the Church"]. And he might have added, *"ou de la guerre"* ["or of the war"], for at the time of his death, only a little more than a year after the beginning of hostilities, he was planning *La Physique des Moeurs,* a book entirely free of the war. (pp. 26-8)

Kenneth Burke, "Three Adepts of 'Pure' Literature," in his Counter-Statement, second edition, Hermes Publications, 1953, pp. 1-28.*

MADGE E. COLEMAN BYRNE (essay date 1958)

[*In the following excerpt, Byrne provides a general introduction to Gourmont's theories of aesthetics.*]

[Remy de Gourmont's] work on the problems comprising aesthetics has received little recognition among philosophers. It is my belief that Gourmont's essays in aesthetics deserve more attention than they have hitherto received. . . .

By way of introducing the aesthetic theory of Gourmont, I shall present Gourmont's conception of the poetic genius as an "intelligent sensibility" and his view that the art work is what might be termed an 'objectification' of that sensibility. (p. 299)

The great poet is first of all a man of genius, for only the genius can create new beauty, and this is the only excuse for art. The poet "must say things not yet said and say them in a form not yet formulated." He presents us with a new world, a world ordered by his imagination, shaped by his sensibility.

> . . . The sensibility is rigorously personal. It is what makes individuals, creates differences among humans. Without it, if they had only reason, all men would act and think alike, and that would be very monotonous and completely gray: the sensibility comes to color our activities, our thoughts, and to make of them something unique, something perfectly distinct: the self.

The genius, more than the merely intelligent man, is an individual, a being who perceives the world in a unique way. He perceives fresh significance where others see only the banal because they are blinded, as he is not, by the domination of an intellect dissociated from the sensibility and by an almost ever present concern with the practical. The ordinary man reacts to the world with intensity of awareness only when faced with a problem, and even then his perceptions are limited by the problem and whatever of his preconceptions have not been challenged by the situation. The majority of the time his perception is directed by habits of mind and body. The oft-repeated act and the intellectual abstraction prejudice perception. "It is difficult to see; it is a faculty for the animal, for the human, a gift. Some men see with genius. . . ."

The poetic genius is characterized by a great sensibility and an intelligence closely bound to that sensibility. Freed by its strength from the restrictive forces of the intellect and of habit, his sensibility is open to all possible sensations. The poet sees the world with an "innocent eye." He is, moreover, sensitive to nuances in emotion and feeling as well as to variety in the sensuous texture of experience; he possesses a heightened awareness of the emotive values of each event. He responds to the world presented to his senses, opens himself to human passion, rather than holding himself aloof in analytic calm. He cultivates his sensibility through experience; but this is only to open his eyes and his heart to what is offered, not to seek out the bizarre or perverse.

The poetic genius differs from the ordinary man, not only in his possession of a greater sensibility, but also in having an intellect very adept in the association and dissociation of ideas. This intellectual agility frees the mind from the necessity of following the perceptual paths from one commonplace to another. And the poet's intelligence, while it is not necessarily more agile than that of the scientist, differs from that in another way, in being nonabstractive. The poet's intelligence is rooted in the sensibility. There is, in a manner of speaking, a vital circulation of impulse between the sensibility and the intellect, each responding to the other. Sensation transforms itself to sentiment, and this becomes idea, which, when it has been understood, returns to move the sensibility anew. The poet feels *intellectual emotions;* he experiences a *physical pleasure in intellection.* He is, in short, an *intelligent sensibility,* an intelligence which perceives nature always through the sensibility rather than abstracting from its unique and concrete presentation an impersonal generalization.

There is, of course, no purely intellectual apprehension of nature. Pure intelligence cannot "enter directly into contact with life; all its labor, whatever be the apparent complexity, is limited to eternally taking note of the principle of identity." And in life there are no formal identities; thus, there is no science of man, while there is an art of man. However, both the ordinary intelligence and the theoretical mind tend to think in abstraction from the sensible world, the felt world of individuals; the former operates almost solely in the faded world of clichés and commonplaces, the latter, in the domain of formal constructions. Both tend to a uniformity of perception within their own classes.

The poetic genius, on the contrary, attains to a unique vision or intuition of the world. Unique, original: first, because the poet does not allow his perception to be curtailed or simplified by the practical attitudes or commonplace preconceptions of the busy man; second, because he does not attempt to abstract from his own point of view, to dissociate his intelligence from his sensibility. His intelligence is quick to see symbolic significance *in* the concrete event. He apprehends the universal in the particular without stripping it of particularity. His sensibility mingles with the world and so discovers analogies, correspondences hidden from the unsympathetic eye.

By so maintaining his perception of the world in the sensible mode at the same time that it is informed by his intelligence,

by thinking the universal in the concrete, the poet can, in his work, satisfy both the intellect and the sensibility. He does not comprehend life with his sensibility, since to comprehend is an act of the 'pure' intellect and involves abstraction, but he does know life with his sensibility. He is an intimate of the world—and, happily for us, he keeps no secrets.

Not being a philosopher, the poet, if he is to express his intuition, has "more need of images than of metaphysics." Art must be concrete because only the plastic idea can be assimilated by man—one must touch his sensibility. The poet must give expression to his unique intuition of the world in plastic forms, in images embodying, or objectifying, ideas. To do this, the poet must create a new language. The 'old' or common language is banal, stereotyped: a collection of dead metaphors. As such, it can elicit only notions or abstract ideas. To evoke the concrete, the unique, the poet must create new metaphors, fresh images, and even "within the limits of the genius of the language, his own syntax." Thus each poet speaks his own dialect of the common tongue, or, as it is more often expressed, each has his own style.

In order to create his own language, the poet must have united in his mind two types of memory which are not always found together: sensory memory and verbal memory. There are apparently two species of verbal memory: that of words, and that of groups of words, locutions. "There are men who think with ready-made phrases [clichés] and who make use of them exactly as an original writer makes use of the ready-made words of the dictionary." Whole books are written in clichés and one could not tell who had written them because they give the impression of an "anonymous brain, of perfect intellectual servility." This anonymous brain is characterized by a very extensive memory of the cliché and by an abstractive faculty which is pernicious to the eye of the writer.

The poet, on the other hand, is the very opposite of anonymous—in writing he differentiates himself. His style is the outcome of his unique way of seeing, feeling, thinking. He will have, then, in addition to the special sensibility already described, an extensive vocabulary, but of individual words, rather than clichés. For, while the cliché is rigid, the word has a plasticity, a potential to be realized in construction, which enables the poet to make use of it, to shape the language to his needs. His sensibility makes impossible the use of clichés; and by the same token he is gifted with that other sort of memory first mentioned as necessary to the poet—the sensory. [In a footnote, Byrne explains: *Le Problème du Style* is the primary source for the following discussion, the terms of which are altered slightly from those in which Gourmont expressed his view. Where Gourmont uses the term 'visual memory' or 'visual imagination,' I have substituted 'sensory.' The reason for doing this is obvious—it is too simple to object to the view that the poet is concerned solely with *visual* experience and emotion. The justification for the change will be found in the quotations from Gourmont's work, where it is evident that his concern is not limited to the visual.]

The style of a poet is a manifestation of his intelligent sensibility. There are two broad categories of style, or one might say two general types of sensibility: the *sensoriel* and the *idéo-émotif.* The *sensoriel* is gifted with a vivid memory of sensations—primarily of visual sensations, although some writers have all the senses at their command. "All sensation, present or stored in the brain, is propitious to art." The *sensoriel* will, in remembering an event, have an image, rather precise and complex, present in his imagination:

If, in the place of sensations, of material memories, the brain keeps only the imprint of an emotion, or if the perception of the senses is rapidly transformed into an abstract notion, or an emotive idea, then art is no longer possible, because in art there is only the plastic and the matter has flown, leaving only a trace along the road.

Such is the case of the *idéo-émotif*, the writer who has a strong memory of emotions, but little memory of sensations. Remembering a love affair, he will feel an emotion which he will by an effort be able to exteriorize, that is to contemplate as object. But rather than having present to his mind precise tableaux of the remembered events, images which appear to embody the emotion originally a part of the experience, the *idéo-émotif* thinks an abstract idea of the affair and associates his feeling, his remembered emotion, with the idea. He "cannot translate his ideas, nor the emotions he attaches to them into images. . . ."

What we have called the sensory memory of the *sensoriel* is necessary to the creative mind of the poet. Without this supply of material the imagination cannot make metaphors, turn words into visions. But it is not enough simply to possess the faculty of remembering well what one has seen and felt. Assuming the poet's knowledge of language, his verbal memory, the quality of the poet's style depends on the quality of his eye, his original sensibility to the world, and on the metaphorical faculty, the imaginative power of the poet which, grounded in the sensibility but working in the night of the subconscious intellect, forges new images, symbols expressive of his thought and feeling. With these natural powers, and the craftsmanship which it is necessary for any artist to acquire, the poet creates forms which express emotion by evoking for our imagination a vision of an object, an event, which appears to embody that emotion. He incorporates his sensibility in verbal forms. He expresses his intuition of the world, not by *saying* to us "This is the way the world is," but by making present to our minds and sensibilities that world with all its colors, shapes, and values immediately and concretely given. (pp. 300-04)

> *Madge E. Coleman Byrne, "Introduction to the Aesthetic Theory of Remy de Gourmont," in* Papers of the Michigan Academy of Science, Arts, and Letters, *Vol. XLIII, edited by Sheridan Baker, The University of Michigan Press, 1958, pp. 299-304.*

KARL D. UITTI (essay date 1961)

[*In the following excerpt from his study* The Concept of Self in the Symbolist Novel, *Uitti discusses Gourmont's Symbolist fiction, as well as that of his contemporaries Edouard Dujardin, Jean Lorrain, and Maurice Barrès, as a reaction to the Naturalist movement led by Emile Zola. Uitti concludes that Gourmont's novels, like those of his fellow Symbolists, fail as a result of their distortion of character psychology and their unwillingness to reflect the world around them.*]

During the vehement anti-Naturalist reaction of the 1880's and 1890's certain Symbolists and other writers pointed to the social orientation of "realism" and lamented the despairing determinism of "realist" psychology. . . . Zola's aesthetic, in Gourmont's view, leads to "popular Romanticism", to "democratic symbolism" in turn placed at the service of a rather suspect "signification allégorique". Gourmont objects to the socialization of art and, in so doing, proclaims an irrevocable divorce

between art and the "social anecdote". For Gourmont, the material of art can lie only in the relationship between the individual artist and his perception of reality; it must never attempt to extend beyond this dual *rapport*—except . . . in a very special and new way. If, as he explains in the *Idéalisme* essays . . . , the artist produces works of value, it is because within himself he has at once absorbed and managed to create anew a reality of general scope. The process of absorption is not in itself of the slightest interest (in later years Gourmont will devote much of his critical thinking to this very process). The aesthetic act splits into two factors: creation and pure communication or re-creation through language. Gourmont criticizes the Naturalists for having in effect accepted the tyranny of the external and dealt, at least in their theory, with an isolated reproduction of appearances. For Gourmont and other Symbolist *idéalistes* of the day, the Naturalist aesthetic represented a definite closed circuit leading from a knowable, photographic reality composed of external phenomena to a reader able to understand such phenomena in a manner similar to the way a native speaker understands his tongue. Fidelity to Zola's *réel*, implying as it does a brand of literary etiology, would be tantamount to a heinous betrayal of higher truths. (pp. 19-20)

Having consistently as its subject the definition of possibilities contained within the Self, the *fin de siècle* novel—as do both Symbolist poetry and theater—frequently presents a point of view residing in a kind of interpenetration of author, hero, and reader. This is certainly the case of [Comte de] Villiers' *Axël* (1890), a novelistic drama, Gourmont's *Sixtine,* and many other works. . . . The same triple point of view can also be found in Dujardin's *Les Lauriers sont coupés* where not only all the action is reflected in the mentality of the hero (by means of speech or recorded thought-processes), but also the other characters. The hero's love for Léa makes of her so clearly a creation of his own imagination (or cerebration) that Léa herself tends to fade in and out from the scene, to become focused more or less sharply according to the intensity of Daniel Prince's illusion(?) of love. She is a pretext for his affective experience in much the same way that his experience corresponds to both ours and the author's. Gourmont's *Le Fantôme* . . . carries the same idea to extreme conclusions. Hyacinthe, a delightfully docile prototype of the *jeune fille* appearing in so many twentieth-century French and American novels down to Zazie and Lolita, exists literally only as the object of Damase's affections; when his love fades, she too disappears physically from the scene. Jean Lorrain's *Monsieur de Phocas* (1899-1901) presents in diary form a very similar series of analyses which, in effect, amount to a frustrated quest for liberation more or less parallel to Barrès' relatively more successful *culte du moi* ["cult of self"]. (p. 39)

The ultimate failure of the Symbolist novel must be related to the concept of Self held by the novelists we have mentioned here, and to the intense deformation of reality caused by this concept of Self. The aesthetic-realist dualism . . . typical of the Symbolist novelistic framework is far too fragile to support a structure of fiction. In *Sixtine* Entragues remains a static personality. Consequently the reader feels unable to enter into the makeup of the triple personality so necessary for the comprehension of this type of novel; confronted with Entragues, he has the impression of coming face to face with an enormous (and fascinating) cross-word puzzle and of having but to fill in the empty squares. Entragues has no *history*. Worse, an intellectualized veil of Literature interposes itself between Entragues as impression and Entragues as literature: his artistic value depends to too great an extent upon Gourmont's idealization of "Art". Whereas Proust [in *A la Recherche du Temps Perdu*] unites art and life in a new time, in a kind of "compound tense" as it were, Gourmont, with Entragues, is forced to doubt the very temporal existence of art; an ideal cannot know time. . . . Like M. de Phocas, Entragues, as personality, is created "by contiguity", that is, exclusively literary allusions are made in an effort to "create" Entragues. He reveals *himself* by means of these allusions in his monologues. Located "out of time", the *Divina Commedia* (Gourmont seems to prefer Dante in his literary allusions) possesses a certain ontological existence in the mind of the reader, but twenty *rapprochements*, twenty quotations from Dante cannot make an Entragues. In *Les Chevaux de Diomède* the deformation is even more radical. There Gourmont endeavors to use an "Aesthetic of the possible" in order to reach the purity he sets as his goal. But the protagonist of the novel, Diomède, is no more than "le symbole d'un inconnu et le voile d'un mystère" ["the symbol of an unknown and the veil of a mystery"]; he is a series of psychological analyses given only nominal unity. *Les Chevaux de Diomède* goes against the grain of the novel as a *genre*, because it fails completely to recognize that the novel must be also a "mirror held up to nature". (pp. 63-4)

Karl D. Uitti, in his The Concept of Self in the Symbolist Novel, *Mouton & Co., 1961, 66 p.**

GLENN S. BURNE (essay date 1963)

[*In the following excerpt, Burne argues that Gourmont was not the totally detached critic that he often seemed. Burne maintains that Gourmont was actually committed to the Symbolist aesthetic, and that he saw his mission as a critic as being that of a defender and interpreter of Symbolism. Burne states that while it is sometimes not overtly apparent, much of Gourmont's criticism was aimed at establishing the Symbolist aesthetic on a sound philosophical—or even a "scientific"—basis.*]

To many readers of modern literature the name of Remy de Gourmont is synonymous with "impressionist" criticism. He has been grouped with other "personal" writers such as Anatole France and Jules Lemaître, to whom criticism was the recounting, in France's well-known words, of "the adventures of a soul among masterpieces." This phrase, and all that it suggests in the way of irresponsible subjectivism, might describe some of Gourmont's critical activity, but surely does not apply to his best work; for Gourmont's criticism, after a period of vacillation, ultimately synthesized traditional scholarly criticism and an original sensualist impressionism. He began as a more or less conventional scholar of ideas and ended by developing a method of literary evaluation that not only differed from the method of those very impressionists with whom his name has been linked, but often was sharply critical of them.

Impressionism was already a well-known mode of criticism when Gourmont joined the fray in the early 1890's, and it had been attacked by influential scholars, notably Brunetière. A writer of formidable erudition and thoroughness, Brunetière had stressed what he believed to be the "menace" to scholarly study inherent in a subjective approach to literature, and so it was Brunetière who received the full force of Gourmont's counterattack. But the critical differences between the two men should not obscure fundamental similarities. Gourmont was a match for Brunetière in depth and scope of learning but was reluctant, except in a few cases like *Le Latin mystique*, to risk losing what he felt to be the vital elements of criticism—the

insights of sensibility and intelligence—by submerging them in a mass of scholarly apparatus. Also, both men enlisted the aid of contemporary thought and sought to base their aesthetic doctrines on the findings of natural science. But each asked different questions and received different answers. Brunetière wanted authority, control, scientific classifications, impersonality in criticism, and morality in art. Gourmont wanted individualism, freedom from classification, justification of personality in criticism, and rejection of moral criteria in matters of art. Brunetière's theories brought him to view contemporary literature, by and large, with hostility and contempt, whereas Gourmont's theories brought him to a spirited defense of modern experimental writing. (pp. 76-7)

Gourmont concluded that one must remain firmly with the "unassailable principle" of subjective idealism—"the world is my representation." It is "the only fecund principle, the only one which permits, which demands, the free development of intellects and sensibilities."

The critical theory which Gourmont was eventually to evolve, however, would not have entirely displeased Brunetière. Gourmont was to be commended by T. S. Eliot and others for his erudition, his sense of history and sense of fact, his insistence on sincerity, and his advocacy of analysis and comparison as the bases of a responsible criticism—in other words, attributes and principles favored by Brunetière. Furthermore, an impartial observer would probably grant, in evaluating the two critics' positions, that although Brunetière's methods were unduly doctrinaire and his judgments prejudiced and at times narrowly moral, his insistence on the necessity of studying the influence of works on other works and of seeking in periods of transition the seeds of the art to follow, was a necessary counter-balance to Gourmont's early tendency to over-emphasize the possibility of independent and spontaneous generation in literature. (p. 81)

[For] all his sensuality, Gourmont insisted upon sincerity. To be sure, in the preface to his *Divertissements* he dismissed sincerity as unnecessary to the writing of poetry—which perhaps accounts for the weakness of his own poetic efforts—but elsewhere, and in his literary criticism above all, he saw literary value in terms of honesty of feeling. Art is, or should be, based on concrete sensation, faithfully transcribed by the artist, just as good criticism is dependent upon the sincerity of the critic in explaining his own impressions.

This accounts for the "confessional" quality of Gourmont's work observed by many of his critics. In the preface to his *Livres des Masques,* Gourmont explained this confessional element by claiming it to be the only justification for writing. The only reason a man has for writing, he insisted, is to express himself; the only excuse is to be original. He must create his aesthetic for himself. Seven years later, in 1903, Gourmont expanded this idea, asserting that one always writes of himself in criticism as well as in other genres: "Criticism is perhaps the most subjective of all the literary genres; it is a perpetual confession; while we believe that we are analyzing the works of others, it is ourselves that we are unveiling and exposing to the public."

He believed that this necessity explains why criticism is usually so mediocre and so often fails to hold our attention, even when it deals with questions of vital interest to us: "In fact, in order to be a good critic, a man must have a strong personality; he must be able to impose himself and to rely not on the choice of subjects but on the value of his own mind. In art the subject matters little; at least it is never more than one of the parts of art; the subject is no more important in criticism: it is never anything but a pretext."

This passage is significant, as Martin Turnell points out [see excerpt dated 1939], because it draws attention to three important elements of criticism, usually lacking in the work of Taine and Sainte-Beuve. First, it insists on the personal factor in criticism—a corrective to the nineteenth-century attempt to reduce criticism to an exact science. Second, it shows not only that there is no substitute for personal sensibility but also that this alone is not enough—the force of personality and mind is equally important. Third and most important, in Turnell's estimation, we see "a distinguished critic asserting *for the first time* that criticism is valuable for its own sake and is not (as Taine tried to make it) a branch of some other science." (pp. 83-4)

Gourmont justified his theories of criticism by stressing the reliability of judgment based on a sensibility which is shared by other members of one's generation. Jules Lemaître, on the other hand, defended his Impressionism by pointing out the changeability of all things, both subjective and objective. For this reason, Lemaître believed, literary criticism cannot have a doctrine: the only certainty is the impression of the moment. Tradition is artificial, and the only value of criticism, or of any other genre, is the representation of a personal world. Its destiny is to become merely the art of enjoying books: "Dogmatic at first, [criticism] has become historical and scientific, but it does not seem that its evolution has ended. Vain as doctrine, necessarily incomplete as science, it perhaps tends to become simply the art of enjoying books and through them enriching and improving one's impressions."

Gourmont was in complete agreement with this anti-doctrinaire statement, as far as it goes. In an essay on Jules Lemaître he admitted that his criticism has "the merits of clarity, acuteness and good sense." Gourmont added, however, that "we may regret that it has not also, not principles which it can very well do without, but a direction. It indeed moves forward rather at random." Gourmont believed in the necessity of a "literary faith"; it is the "most fortunate of intellectual disciplines." He explained that thereby we learn "to judge by other motives than our personal taste"; we feel the "necessity for certain aesthetic sacrifices"; we learn that "even in a limited field works may have a social interest independent of their art interest." He summed up by stating that "the great defect of M. Jules Lemaître's criticism is that it had no object; it lacked force, because its author lacked discipline."

This sounds rather strange coming from Gourmont. We are more accustomed to hearing paeans to the virtues of liberty, subjectivism, originality, and so forth. But this essay was written in 1903, by which time Gourmont had somewhat modified his literary anarchism. Furthermore, it is true that this anarchism had been developed and expounded on behalf of a definite movement, Symbolism, which provided the "discipline" that he claimed to be necessary. (pp. 84-5)

Thus we see the protean Gourmont, defending complete freedom of expression when confronted by doctrinaire and traditionalist critics, and then demanding discipline and restraints on judgment by personal taste when confronted by a critic even more independent than himself. This should not be attributed to insincerity, however, for it is not entirely to Gourmont's discredit that he was capable of revising his own arguments and taking the opposite view to one previously held, if the weight of evidence seemed to have shifted. He was far more

afraid of rigidity of mind than of inconsistency. He would have liked Henri Peyre's observation that "the ravage caused by systematic intellects in criticism lies before us. The worst errors of judgment have usually been caused by the critic's obstinate blinkers when he shut himself up in the dungeon of his preordained theory and lost his ability to enjoy new works which did not readily fall into his tyrannical rules or his neat pigeonholes." . . . And Gourmont, however much he insisted that the critic should "remake his aesthetic" for each new work of art while still retaining adherence to a literary faith, never wavered from the central core of his theories: his conviction that the individually cultivated sensibility is the only reliable source of literary judgment. (pp. 85-6)

Gourmont admitted his various contradictions, and he defended them in his preface to *La Culture des Idées* . . . : "I am not one of those who claim to have immutable ideas. Perhaps nobody is more changed than I. That is because successive meditations make me see things from a constantly renewed point of view, and I do not see why I should shut my eyes to those new viewpoints." Surely one must grant the right of a critic to change his mind, to develop and revise. Much of Gourmont's value derives from his capacity to reflect accurately the changes and developments of his time, to become "the critical consciousness of his generation," as Eliot puts it. But the cultivation of contradictions is another matter. . . . Gourmont felt that he "breathed more freely" in an atmosphere of contradiction, for it insured flexibility of mind and resistance to dogmatism. However, his contradictions were often more apparent than real, and when real, he usually applied himself to their resolution, to a new synthesis. But this tendency is unquestionably related to what many critics have singled out as Gourmont's abiding weaknesses: a fundamental dilettantism, a facile skepticism which detracts from the intensity of his work and impoverishes his ideas, and a tendency to repeat himself unduly. It is true that Gourmont echoed himself throughout his numerous articles and thus weakened the value of many of those pieces—perhaps the result of writing too much, too many "feuilletons" dashed off in haste perhaps to meet some deadline. Gourmont's forty-odd published volumes are too many, in view of what he had to say.

Gourmont's essays on individual poets of his time have, however, a lasting value. They contain perceptions and judgments which have lost none of their freshness in the last fifty years. But, because of their brevity, they are often frustrating and disappointing. Gourmont offered us tantalizing fragments, provocative tidbits which he resolutely refused to develop. Although he was an "official" critic of the Symbolist Movement, he never wrote a searching or profound book about the *poetry* of the movement. In his *Livres des Masques* and volume four of *Promenades littéraires* he gave shrewd but often disappointing accounts of individual writers, because he would not dig deeply into his subject. Gourmont is usually more impressive when making statements of principles or dealing in general ideas than when elucidating a single author. In some of his best criticism, the essay on Villiers de l'Isle-Adam, for example, he quickly moves from the text to the philosophy which lies behind it. Turnell is correct when he says that Gourmont wrote better about other critics than about poetry, and that the best essays in the *Promenades* are those concerned with the ideas and practices of Renan, Rivarol, Sainte-Beuve, Brunetière, and Lemaître. For in the last resort, as Turnell says, Gourmont was true to "the French approach"—he was "more interested in the movement of ideas behind the poetry than in the poetry itself." This is especially true of the later Gourmont, who had moved away from the "intoxication of words" to seek out their history and meaning. He became increasingly interested not only in the movement of ideas behind the poetry, but also in the complex relationship between the ideas and the poetry, and in the problems posed by the mysterious process by which sensation and idea become language. Thus, while we may regret Gourmont's failure, or refusal, to discuss specific works with greater thoroughness, it was that very preference for general ideas that gave us his valuable studies of the problems of style. (pp. 90-1)

> *Glenn S. Burne, in his* Remy de Gourmont: His Ideas and Influence in England and America, *Southern Illinois University Press, 1963, 194 p.*

ADDITIONAL BIBLIOGRAPHY

Aldington, Richard. *Rémy de Gourmont: A Modern Man of Letters.* Seattle: University of Washington Book Store, 1928, 41 p.
　　Discussion of Gourmont's mode of thought and the accomplishments and failures of his literary career. Aldington's remarks were reprinted from a lecture that he delivered before the Newcastle Literary and Philosophical Society.

――――. Introduction to *Rémy de Gourmont: Selections from All His Works,* by Rémy de Gourmont, edited and translated by Richard Aldington, pp. 1-33. New York: Covici-Friede, Publishers, 1939.
　　Biographical and critical introduction to Gourmont. Aldington discusses Gourmont's reclusive life, and influence of his highly individualistic and original approach to criticism.

Barnes, H. W. *What Is Pure French?* S.P.E. Tract No. VIII. London: 1922, 11 p.
　　Summary in English of the early chapters of *Esthétique de la langue Française.*

Burke, Kenneth. "Gourmont on Dissociation." In his *A Grammar of Motives and a Grammar of Rhetoric,* pp. 673-77. Cleveland: World Publishing Co., 1962.
　　Discussion of Gourmont's method of dissociation of ideas. Burke describes Gourmont's method as being primarily a useful rhetorical device "for helping the initiate experimentally to break free of all topical assumptions, and thereby to cease to be the victim of his own naive rhetoric."

Burne, Glenn S. "T. S. Eliot and Rémy de Gourmont." *Bucknell Review* VIII, No. 2 (1959): 113-26.*
　　Discussion of Eliot's debt to Gourmont. Burne theorizes that Eliot drew certain critical "principles of order" from Gourmont, using them to strengthen the Imagists' arguments against exhausted language and the lack of concreteness and emotional richness in poetry.

――――. Introduction to *Rémy de Gourmont: Selected Writings,* by Rémy de Gourmont, edited and translated by Glenn S. Burne, pp. 1-8. Ann Arbor: University of Michigan Press, 1966.
　　Discussion of the various phases of Gourmont's literary career. Burne contends that, contrary to some other critics' claims, Gourmont remained interested in the Symbolist movement throughout his life, and that much of his critical work was directed toward establishing a philosophic and scientific basis for Symbolism.

De Casseres, Benjamin. "Rémy de Gourmont: After Man." In his *Forty Immortals,* pp. 118-28. New York: Joseph Lawren, 1926.
　　Discussion of Gourmont as a type of Nietzsche's "After-Man"—that is, the perfect man of thought who has retired from the world to devote himself to contemplation. De Casseres discusses Gourmont's use of skepticism and irony, and his chosen role as a "sower of doubt." De Casseres says of such men that "they affirm nothing. They deny nothing. They menace."

Eliot, T. S. "The Perfect Critic." In his *The Sacred Wood: Essays on Poetry and Criticism,* pp. 1-16. London: Methuen and Co., 1920.
　　Much-discussed essay in which Eliot acknowledges his debt to the critical writings of Gourmont. Eliot says, in praise of Gourmont, that he "had most of the general intelligence of Aristotle," and that "he combined to a remarkable degree sensitiveness, erudition, sense of fact and sense of history, and generalizing power."

Françon, Marcel. "Rémy de Gourmont's *Lilith:* A Critique." *Poet Lore* LI, No. 4 (Winter 1945): 291-98.
　　Discussion of Gourmont and the Symbolist era. Françon notes the romantic and religious roots of the Symbolist movement and identifies the historical and literary sources that Gourmont made use of in writing his play *Lilith.*

Hancher, Michael. "The Adventures of Tiresias: France, Gourmont, Eliot." *The Modern Language Review* 73 (January 1978): 29-37.*
　　Discussion of the influence of the Impressionist style of criticism (as represented by Gourmont and Anatole France) on the critical thought of T. S. Eliot.

Harris, G. W. "Rémy de Gourmont." *The Contemporary Review* 185 (June 1954): 358-61.
　　Discussion of Gourmont's versatility. Harris discusses the enormous variety of topics that Gourmont addressed in his essays, and the many types of writing at which he was adept in an effort to illustrate "the astounding range of Gourmont's vision."

Macy, John. "Rémy de Gourmont." In his *The Critical Game,* pp. 153-62. New York: Boni and Liveright, 1922.
　　Discussion of Gourmont's versatility as a writer, and the daring nature of much of his critical thought.

Pound, Ezra. "Postscript to *The Natural Philosophy of Love* by Rémy de Gourmont." In his *Pavannes and Divagations,* pp. 203-16. Norfolk, Conn.: New Directions, 1958.
　　Humorous essay in which Pound expands upon Gourmont's thesis in *The Natural Philosophy of Love* that there is a correlation between copulation and cerebral development.

Powys, John Cowper. "Rémy de Gourmont." In his *Suspended Judgements: Essays on Books and Sensations,* pp. 225-56. New York: G. Arnold Shaw, 1916.
　　Lengthy discussion in which Powys explains why he believes that the type of disinterestedness and detachment that Gourmont possessed are absolutely necessary if one is to be a first-rate critic.

Rees, T. R. "T. S. Eliot, Rémy de Gourmont, and the Dissociation of Sensibility." In *Studies in Comparative Literature,* edited by Waldo F. McNeir, pp. 186-98. Baton Rouge: Louisiana State University Press, 1962.*
　　Discussion of Eliot's use of the term "sensibility" in his criticism, and the extent to which his definition of the term was influenced by his reading of Gourmont.

Rodker, John. "De Gourmont—Yank." *The Little Review* V, Nos. 10-11 (February-March 1919): 29-32.
　　Discussion of Poe's influence on Gourmont's fiction and poetry.

Sieburth, Richard. *Instigations: Ezra Pound and Rémy de Gourmont.* Cambridge: Harvard University Press, 1978, 197 p.*
　　Examination of Gourmont's influence on the critical ideas and aesthetic philosophy of Ezra Pound.

William Dean Howells

1837-1920

American novelist, critic, essayist, travel writer, short story writer, autobiographer, dramatist, poet, and biographer.

Howells was the chief progenitor of American Realism and the most influential American literary critic during the late nineteenth century. He was the author of nearly three dozen novels which, though neglected for decades, are today the subject of growing interest. He is now recognized as one of the major literary figures of the nineteenth century: he successfully weaned American literature away from the sentimental romanticism of its infancy, earning the popular sobriquet "the Dean of American Letters."

During his youth in Ohio, Howells developed an interest in literature while working in his father's print shop, later serving on the staff of various newspapers in Jefferson and Columbus. Although his first book, *Poems of Two Friends,* received favorable reviews, it was with his second, an 1860 campaign biography of Abraham Lincoln, that Howells attracted national attention. *Lives and Speeches of Abraham Lincoln and Hannibal Hamlin* (the life of Hamlin being written by J. L. Hayes) earned Howells a government appointment to the U.S. consulate in Venice, where he lived during the American Civil War. Howells's impressions of Europe provided him with material for several travel books as well as his first novels.

Howells's long career as a novelist is divided into three overlapping phases. During the earliest, his work paralleled that of Henry James: beginning with *A Foregone Conclusion* in 1875 and ending in 1886 with *Indian Summer,* Howells wrote novels of manners, portraying young, strong-willed American women encountering European culture. The influence of Nathaniel Hawthorne and Ivan Turgenev—both favorites of Howells—is apparent in the work of this period, with each *nouvelle* featuring a small group of characters, intensely examined. Gradually Howells turned to writing novels that focused on social problems. Most of these present provincial characters who are defeated by the corrupt city in their attempts to succeed. This middle phase, which includes *The Undiscovered Country* and *The Minister's Charge; or, The Apprenticeship of Lemuel Barker,* also produced Howells's best-known work, *The Rise of Silas Lapham,* and what the author considered his "strongest" novel, *A Modern Instance.*

Howells's social concerns intensified in his third stage of development. His "economic novels" were the product of his growing awareness of the hardships inflicted upon the poor and working class by the *laissez-faire* capitalist system of the Gilded Age. The popular but unjust persecution of four anarchists convicted of the 1886 bombing of Haymarket Square in Chicago was a major factor in Howells's transition to writing economic novels. As a nationally recognized literary figure, he risked his reputation in pleading for the lives of the Haymarket anarchists. After this incident Howells followed Leo Tolstoy's example and promoted Christian socialism as a just alternative to economic inequalities and injustices, embracing Tolstoy's theory of complicity: the doctrine that each person bears responsibility for the spiritual and physical well-being of all other persons. Included among the economic novels are *The*

The Bettmann Archive, Inc.

World of Chance, the utopian *A Traveler from Altruria,* and *A Hazard of New Fortunes,* which depicts a group of diverse characters working to establish a magazine in New York. Howells considered *A Hazard of New Fortunes* his "most vital" novel and critics generally agree that it marked the peak of his achievement as a novelist.

Rebelling against the popular romantic fiction of his day, Howells sought through Realism, a theory central to his fiction and criticism, to disperse "the conventional acceptations by which men live on easy terms with themselves" that they might "examine the grounds of their social and moral opinions." To accomplish this, according to Howells, the writer must strive to record detailed impressions of everyday life, endowing characters with true-to-life motives and avoiding authorial comment in the narrative. Howells expounded Realism from the "Editor's Study" and "Editor's Easy Chair," monthly columns written during his long tenure as editor of *Harper's Magazine. Criticism and Fiction,* a patchwork of essays from the "Editor's Study," is often considered Howells's manifesto of Realism, although, as René Wellek has noted, the book is actually "only a skirmish in a long campaign for his doctrines."

Throughout his professional life, Howells worked as a literary critic and magazine editor, and his essays appeared in many major periodicals. As editor of *The Atlantic Monthly,* he introduced new features and changes of style which gained the magazine a national readership. He provided a forum for Henry James's short fiction in *The Atlantic*, and, as James's editor and literary agent, played an instrumental role in guiding the younger writer's career. Howells was also the first critic to recognize the satire that underlay much of Mark Twain's work. Twain and Howells were best friends, each offering criticism of the other's works-in-progress. (The popular theory that Howells channeled Twain's work into genteel respectability has been greatly discounted by Twain scholars, most notably by Bernard DeVoto.) In addition to his perceptive criticism of the works of James and Twain, Howells reviewed three generations of international literature, urging Americans to read the works of Emile Zola, Bernard Shaw, Henrik Ibsen, Emily Dickinson, and other important authors.

During his last years, Howells fell into critical disfavor; as he was supplanted by other, more bitter Realists and Naturalists, his work was viewed as prissy, tea-table fare. In a 1915 letter, Howells wrote: "I am comparatively a dead cult with my statues cut down and the grass growing over them in the pale moonlight." His novels were ignored after his death, and have never regained wide popularity, although critics are today gaining increasing respect for his work. *The Rise of Silas Lapham* in particular, according to Edwin H. Cady, "has endured with great vitality the decades of ignorant and often malicious anti-Howells prejudice, and it may be expected to prosper further in readers' attention now that prejudice has begun to subside." Although many of his works are rarely read today, Howells's influence on modern American literature cannot be discounted, for he laid the groundwork for modern literature and helped shape several decades of American fiction.

(See also *TCLC*, Vol. 7; *Contemporary Authors*, Vol. 104; and *Dictionary of Literary Biography*, Vol. 12: *American Realists and Naturalists*.)

PRINCIPAL WORKS

*Lives and Speeches of Abraham Lincoln and Hannibal
    Hamlin* [with J. L. Hayes] (biography) 1860
Poems of Two Friends [with John J. Piatt] (poetry) 1860
Venetian Life (travel sketches) 1866
Their Wedding Journey (novel) 1872
A Foregone Conclusion (novel) 1874
The Lady of the "Aroostook" (novel) 1879
The Undiscovered Country (novel) 1880
Doctor Breen's Practice (novel) 1881
A Modern Instance (novel) 1882
The Rise of Silas Lapham (novel) 1885
The Garroters (drama) 1886
Indian Summer (novel) 1886
*The Minister's Charge: or, The Apprenticeship of Lemuel
    Barker* (novel) 1887
Annie Kilburn (novel) 1889
A Hazard of New Fortunes (novel) 1890
Criticism and Fiction (criticism) 1891
The World of Chance (novel) 1893
A Traveler from Altruria (novel) 1894
Stops of Various Quills (poetry) 1895
The Landlord at Lion's Head (novel) 1897
Literary Friends and Acquaintance (essays) 1900
The Kentons (novel) 1902
The Son of Royal Langbrith (novel) 1904
My Mark Twain (criticism and memoir) 1910
New Leaf Mills (novel) 1913

The Leatherwood God (novel) 1916
Years of My Youth (autobiography) 1916
Mrs. Farrell (novel) 1921
The Complete Plays of W. D. Howells (dramas) 1960
*Mark Twain-Howells Letters: The Correspondence of Samuel
    L. Clemens and William D. Howells, 1872-1910* [with
    Mark Twain] (letters) 1960

KENNETH S. LYNN (essay date 1971)

[*An American literary scholar, Lynn is the general editor of Houghton-Mifflin's "Riverside Literature" series and the author of numerous essays and books on American life and letters. In the following excerpt from his critical biography* William Dean Howells: An American Life, *he favorably appraises Howells's contribution to American letters, debunking the long-held popular conception of Howells as a deservedly forgotten purveyor of genteel optimism.*]

[In 1891] Howells published a book which in the next century would do more to discredit him as a shallow optimist than anything else he would ever write. In the darkening years of the *fin de siécle*, when Howells's foremost literary contemporaries were searching their imaginations for symbols of failure, the author of **Criticism and Fiction** called on American writiers to concern themselves with the "smiling aspects of life"—thereby bringing down upon himself the judgment of many modern critics that any author who could say such a sickly sweet thing at such a sour time must not be worth reading. In the light of his private correspondence, however, we know that **Criticism and Fiction** is an unreliable guide to Howells's state of mind in the nineties. Put out because both publisher and author wanted to make money, the book was hastily assembled out of "The Editor's Study" pieces that Howells had written for *Harper's Monthly* in the previous five years. One of the pieces included was the "Study" column for September 1886, in which Howells had brilliantly commented upon a French translation of Dostoevsky's *Crime and Punishment*. While lavish in his praise of the novel, Howells had oddly insisted that Dostoevsky's vision of life was not relevant to the United States. Even more oddly, he had based his argument on details of Dostoevsky's own life, rather than on the tragic novel he had written. The point Howells was concerned to make was that while Dostoevsky had had the horrifying experience of being sentenced to death and then—following the commutation of the sentence—exiled to Siberia, American writers lived in freedom. "Whatever their deserts, very few American novelists have been led out to be shot, or finally expelled to the rigors of a winter at Duluth. . . . We invite our novelists, therefore, to concern themselves with the more smiling aspects of life, which are the more American. . . ." By way of further justification of his argument, Howells had also pointed out that journeymen carpenters and plumbers in the United States were so far from being oppressed that they were striking for wages of four dollars a day (the outrageous demands of carpenters and plumbers being, of course, lively in the mind of a writer who had built or done over a number of houses); but at the heart of his identification of American with the "smiling aspects of life" he had placed the assertion that the American artist, unlike his Russian counterpart, was not an alien and helpless figure in his society.

As a political comment on the difference between life in czarist Russia and life in democratic America, the assertion is unexceptionable and uninteresting. As a personal comment, however, it is highly interesting. Because only a year and a half before making this denial of social maladjustment, Howells had suffered a nervous breakdown as a direct consequence of his sense of alienation from great issues of the day; and by the time the Dostoevsky review reappeared in book form five years later, he had become overwhelmed by the conviction that "the whole of life" was "unreal" and "unfair." Far from being the hallmark of a stupefying complacency, the phrase about the "smiling aspects" was the fighting slogan of Howells's defiant but doomed effort in the late eighties and early nineties to achieve solidarity with his society and thus to break free of his enveloping sense of isolation and irrelevancy.

Despite what his critics have said about him, Howells was a man of modern sensibility, whose awareness of life was afflicted by a sense of aloneness, emptiness, and the precariousness of his personal being. Although he was not a schizophrenic, he nevertheless experienced, from early childhood onward, a measure of the schizophrenic's tortured and desperate feelings of alienation. The family structure in which he grew up put him under psychic pressures that threatened his identity before it was fully formed, and in his adolescent years in Jefferson, Ohio, he felt trapped by the town as well as by his parents. When the nervous breakdowns of his young manhood began to occur, fear, rage, and despair flooded his soul. It is no wonder that he eventually turned "with the deepest sympathy and interest" to Dostoevsky's "terrible picture of a soul's agony."

Nor is it any wonder that in Howells's early novels he was concerned with personal relationships and problems of self-consciousness—with "the sin and suffering and shame" that flowed "from one to another one, and oftener still from one to one's self." Many of the books he wrote in this period are extraordinarily interesting, and one of them—*A Modern Instance*—bears comparison with the best novels in American writing. But in the climactic psychological breakdown he suffered in the mid-1880s, he was overcome by the feeling that all his life he had been playing roles, and that as an influential man of letters in Boston he was fulfilling an outlander's ferocious ambition at the cost of cutting himself off from his deepest emotional needs. Painfully and haltingly, therefore, he began to try to exhume certain buried feelings for life, and to unite self-consciousness with social consciousness. As he said in his magazine review of *Crime and Punishment,* he admired Dostoevsky not only because he could depict a soul's agony, but because he "teaches in every page patience, merciful judgment, humble helpfulness, and that brotherly responsibility, that duty of man to man, from which not even the Americans are emancipated." Ultimately, Howells failed in his attempt to become the social conscience of his race, but in the process of failing he opened the way to the wider sympathies and broader perspectives of the modern American novel. (pp. 10-13)

Howells wrote no masterpiece that towers over the rest of his work; it is, rather, the collective accomplishment of approximately a dozen books that establishes his claim to our attention. From *A Foregone Conclusion* to *A Modern Instance* to *The Landlord at Lion's Head,* from *A Boy's Town* to *Literary Friends and Acquaintance* to *Years of My Youth,* the Howellsian canon is indeed, as James said, "a great array." Yet half a century after Howells's death the prophecy that he would someday enjoy a "really beautiful time" has become a mockery. Such is the prodigality of our civilization. (p. 325)

Kenneth S. Lynn, in his William Dean Howells: An American Life, *Harcourt Brace Jovanovich, Inc., 1971, 372 p.*

GEORGE N. BENNETT   (essay date 1973)

[*A scholar of Howells's life and works, Bennett is the author of* William Dean Howells *(1959) and* The Realism of William Dean Howells, 1889-1920 *(1973). In the latter work Bennett remarks that he "tried, by drawing freely on Howells's comments on fiction and other matters in the 'Editor's Study' and 'Editor's Easy Chair,' in his letters and elsewhere, to document my understanding of the intellectual, moral, and spiritual context from which his fiction issued." In the following excerpt from a long discussion of* The Landlord at Lion's Head—*a work he deems "one of the finest novels [Howells] ever wrote"—Bennett explores this novel for its pessimistic treatment of the moral "rise" of the individual, examining the traits of each major character to reveal Howells's dark vision of life in turn-of-the-century America.*]

In 1882, Howells confidently believed that Americans were a "thoroughly homogeneous people," believed that there was "such a parity in the experiences of Americans" that the average American was the man who had "risen." Fifteen years later *The Landlord at Lion's Head* showed that his optimism about the common background and the value of "rising" had undergone modification. In 1885, he approved the moral rise of Silas Lapham, one of whose costs was the sacrifice of social ambition. The criticism, however, had been directed against the effects of wealth on Lapham, his swelling pride which sought to feed itself by buying acceptance from Boston society, rather than against the society itself. Howells was aware of the uselessness of a Bromfield Corey, the limitations imposed by mere propriety on a Mrs. Corey. In a Tom Corey, however, he had suggested the hope, if not for a radical reconstruction of society, at least for a revitalization of it through an honorable joining in commercial enterprise and an alliance with Penelope Lapham.

The Landlord at Lion's Head, on the other hand, is a convincing demonstration of the fulfillment of Howells's own prediction that the conditions he was describing in 1882 might, "in another generation or two . . . be wholly different." Now, the society toward which men like Jeff Durgin attempt to rise is more than self-satisfied and punctilious: it is decadent and sick. The infusion of the strength of a Jeff Durgin, directed as it is toward wholly materialistic and selfish ends, will provide no moral restitution. The marriage of a Westover and Cynthia Whitwell is only in a very restricted sense an example of the "simple structure of our society, the free play of our democracy." Even the possibility of a spiritual restoration by a return to the pastoral simplicities (Lapham could go back to Vermont, Lemuel Barker could go back to Willoughby Pastures) is denied. In the first place, Lion's Head represented a life of grinding poverty and intellectual and spiritual impoverishment; in the second, it had now been thoroughly urbanized and commercialized.

The story of Jeff Durgin's climb to material success and a certain amount of social acceptance was no longer the kind of story that could be proudly offered as an example of the American dream. (Indeed, it might be seen as a realist's ironic answer to any of the enormously popular renderings of that myth by Horatio Alger, with whom Howells was contemporaneous for sixty-two years.) Additionally, the fate which the Vostrands suffer in Boston reveals the character of the social conventions which they themselves began by invoking against Jeff.

He is at first treated as an object of social condescension, a jay who can be invited to a second-rate affair and hopefully used in the service of more openly characterized charitable "work at the North End." . . . He contemptuously refuses to allow himself to be used for such purposes, but avails himself of any entree which offers an opportunity of meeting Bessie Lynde. After a time, his "social acceptance" gains "a sudden precipitance; and people who wondered why they met him at other houses began to ask him to their own." . . . Mrs. Vostrand, who had been kind to Westover in Italy, and who has none of the obvious financial and personal disqualifications of Jeff, is briefly launched in Boston through Westover's intervention with friends, but not even Genevieve's "beauty and . . . grace" . . . can make a lasting break in the social hierarchy. It is an interesting complication of theme that it is their common roles as social pariahs that bring Jeff and Genevieve into the intimacy which culminates in his first rejected proposal. Mrs. Vostrand completely accepts the social system, and she fights to win entrance into it through the purchased marriage of Genevieve to an Italian count, the almost continuously absent Mr. Vostrand supplying the money. However, the eventual marriage of Jeff and Genevieve does not furnish, as it might have in an earlier Howells novel, a contrast between American and European arrangements that is favorable to democratic love marriages. Mrs. Vostrand's "mawkish hypocrisy" . . . in furthering this result, and Mr. Vostrand's relieved and long distance approval of Jeff's being a "businessman" . . . like himself, make for little distinction in the two affairs.

It is through the Lyndes, however, that Howells pronounces on an American society which is decadent, useless, and self-protective. The maiden aunt with whom Bessie and Alan live perfectly typifies the impervious complacency of this society. Physically, mentally, spiritually, she is composed entirely of smooth surfaces untouched by the abrasions of life. She has been "stupefied by a life of unalloyed prosperity and propriety." For her, there have been two kinds of people: those like herself, and those not; and she has lived entirely "in the shelter of . . . [the] opinions and ideals" of her own kind. Having little contact with other kinds of people, she is not even forced to scorn them. Her "myopic optimism" . . . has allowed her to believe that Alan's escapades had been sufficiently hushed up (his real guilt results merely in voluntary withdrawal from Harvard, whereas Jeff's circumstantial guilt results in suspension) to satisfy the only public opinion that matters. And though she well understands his present alcoholism with its necessary periodic cures, she can blandly treat it as a problem of physical health. Her slight deafness, which allows her to ignore open quarrels between Alan and Bessie over his drinking and her social freedoms, is a perfect symbol of the means by which she has passed through life without having her Unitarian faith or her trust in the "invulnerable order" . . . of her social arrangements materially discomposed.

Within this protective context, Alan and Bessie practice a social and moral irresponsibility which Howells reveals with such great skill and emotional force that the comparative view jumps all the way to Fitzgerald's *Gatsby* to find suitable parallels. Alan has led a life of "dissolute idleness," . . . devoting himself to his club, to horses, and to drinking. His sister and friends believe that he has great intelligence and "could be anything" . . . he chooses; there is a "distinction" in "even the sinister something" in his appearance, a "style in the signs of [his] dissipation" . . . which compels Jeff's envy. In his drunkenness at elegant social affairs, he either retains enough poise or is so quietly taken care of that no notice need be taken of

his condition. Bessie, as has been shown, has similar qualities: her intelligence and wit have apparently driven off eligible men, she cares nothing for the normal feminine diversions of music or art, she is driven to seek release for her tensions in such "excitements" as her flirting with Jeff, just as Alan turns compulsively to the decanter.

Like the society of which they are representative, they have charm and gaiety and grace. But such qualities are hardly adequate in themselves to give definition to their lives, to establish relationships within an acceptable framework of mutual moral and social responsibility. Daisy and Tom Buchanan retreated behind their money whenever they were faced with responsibility. In much the same way, Bessie and Alan retreat to the impregnable fortress of their social status whenever their peccadilloes demand payment. This position furnishes ready made attitudes which place responsibility squarely on ill-bred pretenders to equality like Jeff. Drunk, Alan can avail himself of Jeff's services in getting home while calling him "a damn jay." . . . Sober, he can rest comfortably in the belief that it was the "gentleman" Westover who performed the service and be protected from the truth by Bessie. . . . She can play with Jeff and judge herself "not despicable" because "the audacity of her behavior with the jay" . . . is not flirting, but can despise the result enough to bring about Jeff's horsewhipping. Nor does Alan's method of assuming the fraternal responsibility he has long neglected make him compare favorably with the jay. From behind, in a horse and buggy, he attacks Jeff, who is on foot, and simply runs away when Jeff attempts to defend himself. Jeff, on the other hand, meets him face to face, announces his intention to kill, does not even use his boxing skill to counter that of his opponent, and desists before carrying out his threat.

The refusal of total revenge by Jeff introduces additional complications of theme which prove how successfully Howells "broke through into the daylight beyond" . . . in probing the dense mass of material he had accumulated in his story. Nick Carraway learned about the brutal stupidity and carelessness concealed beneath the charm of a Tom and Daisy Buchanan. Howells documented a similar perception of the under-lives of the Lyndes. He made use of it, not in the form of a moral pronouncement, but subtly, as a component of Jeff Durgin's pragmatic assessment of society and his relationship to it. Jeff's action in sparing Alan Lynde "was accomplished through his will, and not by it" . . . ; it was apparently the instinctive expression of his past moral and social experience: "He glared down into his enemy's face, and suddenly it looked pitifully little and weak, like a girl's face, a child's." . . . In this compressed and richly suggestive image, Howells completes his indictment of the false American dream of social and material success. American society as represented by the Alan Lyndes was not only brutally stupid and careless, it was weak and pitiful, childishly self-destructive.

The associations are even more complex than this, however. The image of the little girl's face meaningfully connects Jeff's subconscious motivation with the lesson Westover had administered to the boy who was terrifying the Whitwell children. The effect of the association is to suggest that the moral and social values of Westover, which have seemed mostly ineffectual, may at last be making themselves felt. Jeff undergoes no profound spiritual transformation. Yet this rejection of final revenge, together with his capacity to wonder at the goodness that motivated men like his brother and Westover, allow the small hope that his amorality is susceptible, in some degree, at least, to conditioning. That fact was perhaps one of the sources of Howells's liking for him. Such strength and vitality, misdirected by the logical inferences forced upon them by society, but potentially educable, are at least preferable to the self-indulgent decadence of the Lyndes.

That potential, however, is at best embryonic. For another explanation of Jeff's action is simply that he turned away in scorn from Alan Lynde's weakness, turned away with the confidence that it offered no impediment to his goals. As a boy, he had reacted to Westover's rebuke for terrifying the Whitwell children by a different exercise of control over them: "He had begun to convoy parties of children up to see Westover at work . . . and to show the painter off to them as a sort of family property. . . . He seemed on perfect terms with . . . [the young Whitwells] now." . . . The beating of Lynde, like his subsequent pelting of Westover and his canvas with apples, is now enough to dissipate his resentment against a force which no longer has any significant power to affect him. His real answer to the Lyndes is the realization of his material ambitions as proprietor of the hotel and of his social ambitions in his marriage. Implicit in his answer is an ironic comment on the quality of the new American dream to which young men aspire.

To speak of the potentiality of morality in Jeff is to raise the question of Westover's role as a moral positive in **Landlord**. To some extent, Westover's history is also that of a man who has risen. Howells seems to draw on the general outlines of his own past in describing Westover's Wisconsin boyhood, his discovery of his artistic talent, his Italian sojourn to develop it, his return to Boston. The Italian experience provided the basis of two decisions: an acquaintance with Bostonians which convinced Westover that he would like to live among such people; and the opportunity to discover that the conflict of opinion in Milwaukee's view that he was "somebody" and that of New York that he was "nobody" did not really need to be resolved: it was the work that he "was trying to do [that] was the important thing." . . . This attitude, joined with his natural qualities and social graces, allows Westover to be accepted by Boston society, to be in it though he is not of it. In one sense, then, his presumptive marriage to Cynthia will be truly "democratic." As contrasted with Genevieve's arranged foreign alliance and Jeff's valuing of the Vostrands' social position, it will be made without regard for their social difference.

In fact, however, after a visit with Cynthia's father, in which Westover sees that he is "irreparably rustic, that he was and always must be practically a Yankee," a type Westover does "not love or honor," he reacts by thinking Cynthia, too, must grow into such a type "through the lapse from the personal to the ancestral which we all undergo in the process of the years." . . . His proposal comes only after her presence drives away thoughts that the marriage might be "a mistake on the spiritual as well as the worldly side," that it "certainly would not . . . [promote] his career" . . . and might impede it. For her part, Cynthia gives no sign of valuing Westover's social superiority for its own sake, and other factors take away any representative, ideal social significance the match might have. Not only is it true that Westover's social position is not such as to make the marriage an effective comment on false, undemocratic social standards, but, from the other side, Cynthia reduces the social distance between them by being an unusual country girl. Moreover, it is frankly admitted that Westover's ideal of life and marriage is "philistine and bourgeois," and Howells speaks out directly to characterize it as "commonplace

William Dean and Elinor Mead Howells in Venice, shortly after their marriage.

and almost sordid." . . . He intends that it shall be clearly understood that this is an eminently suitable partnership between two generally admirable people. They are no longer, however, the average Americans.

Cynthia's father; Jeff Durgin; the Vostrands; the Lyndes; Mrs. Marven, the patron of Lion's Head who, on a picnic, marked Jeff's inferior social quality by serving him first so that he could go back to his horses; Mrs. Bevidge, Boston society matron and organizer of doubtfully effective charities, who congratulates Bessie Lynde for having "done missionary work" in entertaining Jeff, the Harvard jay, at a tea—these are now, quantitatively at least, the average Americans, confirming the fear expressed by Howells in 1882 that the "parity" of experience might disappear from American life. Some counterweight is represented by Westover, Cynthia and her brother Franky, Mrs. Durgin, and Jackson. However, their special qualities—their preservation of religious and moral values, their humane concern for others, or their devotion to family in a more than social sense—are what now distinguish them from the average. (Jeff, too, is unusual in his self-confident strength and drive for money and power, but those are now the goals, the "ideals" of the average American.) Moreover, even these admirable persons exhibit certain personal inadequacies which limit the degree to which they may be expected to influence the general social order.

Westover's qualities, for example, make him, finally, more neutral than forceful. He is characterized by a "simple-hearted ambition" for a "stated existence, a home where he could work constantly in an air of affection and unselfishly do his part to make his home happy" . . . ; by a lack, apparently, of a sense of continuity from his "emigrant people" whom he left at sixteen; . . . by a tolerant agnosticism, and by a rather timid approach to the emotional commitments of life. His example or his influence may have had a part in causing Jeff to refrain from killing Alan Lynde, but otherwise whatever moral force he represents is ineffectual, not only with Jeff, but with the Vostrands and the Lyndes.

Cynthia, too, has the defects of her virtue: she tends to be "cold," she exhibits little interest in matters outside the area of her personal relations and her immediate family (her intellectual pursuits seem more a part of the contest with Jeff than a disinterested love of knowledge or a concern for a socially useful self-improvement), and she is generally more acted upon than active, more in reaction than action. Franky is a decent, hard-working boy whose decision to study for the Episcopal ministry is commendable, though it also seems to have in it an element of social ambition, a desire to rise above the shiftlessness of his father and the necessity for working at the Durgin hotel. Jackson is a genuinely good and unselfish man, but his physical debilitation is a sign of spiritual ineffectiveness: he exercises no influence in the upbringing of Jeff, and his religious feeling expends itself in the tinkering with the planchette and in speculation about life on Mars.

Mrs. Durgin is by far the most compelling of these figures in her pride, courage, strength, independence, and capacity for honest self-appraisal. Again, however, these qualities are narrowly focused on the preservation of her family and the advancement of its fortunes, and her ambitions for Jeff permit her to be less exacting with him than she is with herself. Right up until her mind becomes confused in her final illness, her tendency is to indulge his selfishness, condone his mischief, and excuse his faults. She is initially disappointed at his choice of Cynthia, for she had thought Harvard would provide him not only a legal education but a society wife. She carefully maintains her personal independence and integrity in her dealings with her summer boarders, and she is a moving embodiment of motherly pride in summarily turning out Mrs. Marven for administering a brutal snub to her son after being the recipient of special kindnesses. Mrs. Durgin is herself capable of recognizing the extravagance of this action, its contradiction of her chosen role as an innkeeper, but she is driven by her own kind of vanity and her ignorance of the social conditions into which she is trying to force Jeff. She is a magnificent individual portrait because Howells does equal justice to her shortcomings and her strengths. Both, however, are of a kind to disqualify her from any representative role.

It may be an appropriate final comment on the controlled richness of this novel to note that such characterizations in combination with the general picture of rural life eliminate the possibility of an oversimplified opposition between country and city. It does not celebrate pastoral virtue over urban sophistication. Village insularity exacts a cultural levy: Jackson's manipulation of the planchette establishes the level of metaphysical inquiry; Whitwell's inchoate reflections, the philosophical; various comments on Westover's lack of representational skill, and the successful transformation of Lion's Head Inn into a "tasteless and characterless" . . . mass under Jackson's management and into "runnaysonce" . . . under Jeff's, the aes-

thetic. If there is a bias in favor of the country, it expresses itself, not through picturing the inherent superiority of the people found there (who include Jeff and Whitwell and, in the past, Mrs. Durgin's father), but through the more uniformly critical picture of the Boston society Howells chose to include in *The Landlord at Lion's Head*. (pp. 144-53)

> *George N. Bennett, in his* The Realism of William Dean Howells: 1889-1920, *Vanderbilt University Press, 1973, 254 p.*

EDWIN H. CADY (essay date 1973)

[*Cady is an American educator and prolific literary scholar who is the editor-in-chief of the distinguished periodical* American Literature. *He has written extensively on Howells's works, authoring* The Road to Realism: The Early Years, 1837-1885, *of* William Dean Howells *(1956) and* The Realist at War: The Mature Years, 1886-1920, *of William Dean Howells (1958), editing* The War of the Critics over William Dean Howells *(1962), and serving for two years as general editor of the Indiana University Press's "Selected Edition" of Howells's novels. In the following excerpt from his introduction to* W. D. Howells as Critic, *Cady discusses Howells's importance as a literary critic and offers a glossary of Howells's key critical terms.*]

Howells achieved criticism in what might have been reviewing or fluffy gossip because he cared for theory and consciously admired the serious critic. Frequently tendentious, sometimes polemic, he meant always to accomplish something worthy, was therefore tactical and upsetting to readers, and has been often misunderstood, even misrepresented to this day. Only the reading of his criticism, however, not scholarly argument, can lead to understanding of Howells as critic. . . . (p. 1)

It is fair to say of Howells that he thought criticism should be above all serviceable, functional. Though there are many modes, manners, methods, styles, tools, and techniques of criticism, it justifies itself in two goals, both of which help readers, the consumers of literary art. Criticism helps us to read more accurately, more completely. It helps us judge literature, to estimate its worth or importance, more truly. To be serviceable the critic ought, Howells believed, to be essentially taxonomic: skilled but humble, engaging but accurate, broadly informed but personally unobtrusive. But the serious critic must also be morally concerned and responsible. Ideally, in the last analysis, Howells believed in the culture critic, the man of letters intent upon elevating the customs, refining the language, clarifying the motives, helping to raise the quality of the life of the people.

Perhaps the oddest misapprehension current about Howells is that which supposes him narrow, superficial, and in effect ignorant. He was in fact almost incredibly informed, sophisticated, and many-minded; in his time an absolute insider, an old professional, long a standard-bearer of the *avant garde,* the friend and ally of the great, the sponsor and patron of the gifted young and friendless, the despair of the entrenched and ancient. As critic he enjoyed the advantages of living at the heart of three worlds. Creatively he had tried or was about to try almost everything literary and he lived in close contact with the world of his peers; he knew art and its life at daily firsthand. Critically he worked in the craft, and multilingually, a long time; and most of his best work he wrote between the ages of fifty and seventy. Commercially, he was in the business of authorship not only as author but as editor, consultant, friend of the great, and a treasured name—he was 'in the know' for half a century.

Howells's sophistication as critic was technical, too. He mastered the modes, knew what each could accomplish, and could wield each to exact, conscious effect. It is always a mistake in a reader to suppose that he is cleverer than Howells. It was also, however, true that Howells as critic was sophisticated in the commercial way. He wrote to be paid by journals which maintained theories of their readership and expected him to appeal to their subscribers. As a professional, Howells obliged. Almost all his criticism, then, like almost all serious criticism—which is nothing if not professional—he shaped to its outlet. His modern reader must attend to this factor in his subtly-adapted, varying styles.

Howells may sometimes seem not at all to be—to the stuffy, portentous, modern sense—a serious critic. Though he maintained the surface of a strolling, personal commentator, of a man of letters *en passant,* his surfaces were protective. They protected the professional in his business relations with outlets. They also, as a necessary, invaluable screen, protected the creative artist. Introducing the Library Edition reprint of essays called *Literature and Life,* Howells noted

> the wide, the wild, variety of my literary production in time and space. From the beginning the journalist's independence of the scholar's solitude and seclusion has remained with me, and though I am fond enough of a bookish *entourage,* of the serried volumes of the library shelves, and the inviting breadth of the library table, I am not disabled by the hard conditions of a bedroom in a summer hotel, or the narrow possibilities of a candle-stand, without a dictionary in the whole house, or a book of reference even in the running brooks outside.

I am sure the picture is true, but the comment is uncannily beguiling and self-protective.

As quite another aspect of his sophistication, in fact, what Howells brought with him to the narrow possibilities of that summery 'candle-stand' was broad, exact, international multilingual learning. He never really went to school, but he read literature in English from Chaucer through Robert Frost and often knew it, as he told one challenging friend, '*au fond.*' He knew Italian and its literature pretty well from Dante through D'Annunzio and seems to have read literary Spanish, French, and German easily and accurately. At the same time, however, he remained not only an American but, as it was then called, a Westerner, with deep concerns for the development of literature and culture in the United States. For that above all he served as a critic. And the thing which interested him most, as it had Jefferson, Emerson, and Whitman, was contemporaneity, culture now and the quality of culture to come.

Though it took Howells almost thirty years to assimilate Emerson to himself, his posture as critic proved much the same. Emerson urged on the young men of America a first-hand, an 'original relation.' So did Howells. The hard thing was that their grounds quarreled. The essence of Howells's contemporaneity was to be agnostic and realistic in reductive revolt against the Emersonian faith in ideality. As critic, then, Howells, achieved a stance of considerable originality. He became the chief molder and champion of realism and a realistic movement in his country. And the resultant fights, the American aspects of the great Realism War in Western culture at large, turned Howells militant.

In every major critic, as I see him, aesthetics become ethics, then politics, then metaphysics. Howells's ultimate distinction as critic is to have made that major passage under the power of his own vision, sensibility, and imagination, his own theory and his own faith in realism. (pp. 2-3)

The most spectacular feature of Howells's realism was its condemnation—frank, serious, contemptuous—of a false but popular romanticism. People were told, with a force that employed every device from homily to derision to strike home, that the clap-trap they consumed by the car-load was vicious. If they resented that, or, more to the point, if the producers and purveyors of a bad romanticism resented Howells, very well. He then had the positive ideal of a sane and beautiful art to substitute for the false and bad.

To the charge that he was reductive, Howells cheerfully pleaded guilty. His principles of reality were humane, this-worldly, and tough-minded. But the imputation of pessimism he denied. After the fashion of his mind, he could take to himself Emersons's famous defiance of mere rationalism, 'I am always insincere, as always knowing there are other moods.' Like any alert, responsive man, Howells changed his moods with the logic of life and events. No sentimental Pollyanna, he not infrequently felt Jeffersonian—on the whole sanguine about the world's chances. No defeatist, he sometimes felt a Franklinian if not a Swiftian disgust at the obdurate idiocies of humankind. His criticism reflects both polar moods together with the more constant mixed mood, the mood he trusted most.

Agnostically without the Jeffersonian faith in reason, in revolt against all Platonisms, very doubtful about the presence of Jehovah, the realistic sensibility kept a stubborn, desperate, even Hebraic faith in the value and ultimacy of personhood. Howells's realist believed in persons in defiance of monism, whether monism lost men and women in soaring abstraction, the minuet of bloodless categories; or whether it lost them in vortices of blind force and chance. This humanism might be more desperate than that of the Psalmist:

> O Lord my God, I cried unto thee and thou has healed me.
> O Lord, thou has brought up my soul from the grave; thou has kept me alive, that I should not go down to the pit. . . .
> What profit is there in my blood, when I go down to the pit? Shall the dust praise thee? shall it declare thy truth?

The realist was more desperate but no less humane. He was more desperate because his assurance, if he had any, of the intervening Hand was dim and far indeed, but his faith in personhood stubbornly remained.

For criticism all this issued into a set of terms by which Howells undertook to communicate new ideas, concerns, and attitudes. They nearly set out a paradigm of his criticism, and some are worth adding to anyone's critical vocabulary. Aside from the then conventional terms of literary criticism which Howells used rather conventionally, a glossary of his then special terms would list:

academic	devoted to dead convention.
Altruria	futuristic Utopia where 'synthetized sympathies' replace egotism.
commonplace, the	essence of reality, the one uncommon subject of art

confidential atti-tude	habitual intrusion by an authorial persona upon the integrity of fictional illusion.
democracy	political *equality*, a principle of the imagination essential to *realism*.
distinction	vestigial remnant of feudalism, now a *neo-romantic* egotism.
effectism	sacrifice of aesthetic and ethical integrity to induce intense, irresponsible emotions.
equality	cognate with reality, the common and *democracy*—all essential ingredients of the best art.
genius	a delusion.
humanism	ultimate moral, aesthetic concern for common persons.
literosity	self-conscious attention to literary precedent and convention, an imitative yen to appear literary.
neo-romantic	seeking romantic emotional effects in the cynical absence of romantic belief.
photographic	what *realism* is not because realism is not mechanical or cartographic but an art like painting.
realism	the heart of the matter, great imaginative art (too many definitions to quote).
romanticistic, the	see *neo-romantic*.

Howells felt and in some meaningful sense was contemporaneous with the four generations of British authors from the Early Victorians through the Edwardians. With a few notable exceptions, most lamentably Melville, he knew, often intimately, the American authors from long-lived Bryant through the New Poets of 1912. And he was vitally concerned with the coeval Italian, French, Norwegian, Russian, Spanish, and German writers: altogether, 'literary generations' too numerous to list. He introduced to the general literary audience of the English-speaking world a great number of important authors: one set to the Americans, including their own; a variant set, of course, to British readers (including those in the world-wide imperial dependencies). He stood among the pioneer critics introducing, sponsoring, and elucidating Björnson, Cahan, Chesnutt, Clemens, Stephen Crane, Dickinson, Dostoevski, Frederic, Garland, Gorky, Hardy, Harrigan, Herne, Ibsen, Henry and William James, Frank Norris, Tolstoi, Turgenev, Palacio Valdés, Veblen, Verga, and Zola, among others.

The importance of Howells to his large audiences is obvious. It is obvious, that is, that a major influence emanated from Howells for not less than four crucial decades. While certain facts are patent, nobody has systematically studied the reputation or the influence. Several significant books will be written before we can really know how and how much Howells was influential and can understand what the facts mean. In what we now know about the general influence there is no way to discriminate the impact of the fiction from that of the criticism.

There lie certain frontiers of knowledge in literary history, and the trails run abruptly into tangles.

We know that Clemens thought his friend the national court of last resort in criticism. We know that James deplored 'The Editor's Study' but regularly sought and got Howells's support. It is no surprise to learn that Crane thought him 'our first critic of course.' But one was not prepared to hear Cable respond to the quarrel over 'Henry James, Jr.' in the spirit of an old Confederate trooper, praising 'the emphatic truth of what you say about the mighty men of a school that would not do for today. Hold that ground. Hold hard.' What does it mean that George Ade, Henry Seidel Canby, Richard Harding Davis, Clyde Fitch, Alice French (Octave Thanet), Lafcadio Hearn, Henry Cabot Lodge, Stuart Merrill, Booth Tarkington, William Allen White—a very mixed bag—paid eager tribute to Howells? What shall we make of the protestations of debt made by Grant Allen, Leonard Merrick, Edward Garnett, and Kipling, as well as Arnold Bennett?

Howells appears to have sensed the meaning of this century to literature, that it would decline as a medium of entertainment but that decline would open the way for 'the serious artist' to aim for the heights. We have still some way to go before we sense the whole meaning of Howells. (pp. 4-6)

> Edwin H. Cady, "What Kind of Critic Was Howells?", in W. D. Howells as Critic, by W. D. Howells, edited by Edwin H. Cady, Routledge & Kegan Paul, 1973, pp. 1-6.

S. FOSTER (essay date 1978)

[*In the following excerpt, Foster closely examines Howells's best-known novel,* The Rise of Silas Lapham, *finding it a work that clearly demonstrates the motivation and nature of the author's realism.*]

[W. D. Howells] has been called the founder of and spokesman for the Realist school of fiction in America—a claim which, though somewhat sweeping, rightly draws attention to his life-long interest in Realism as a literary development, and to his earnest efforts to promote what increasingly seemed to him the only artistically valid mode of writing. . . . For Howells, the flowering of Realism was not merely a passing phenomenon, but a major cultural advance which, he felt, demanded his personal championship as well as emulation. (pp. 149-50)

The Rise of Silas Lapham, perhaps Howells's best-known novel, demonstrates most clearly the connection between his practical and his theoretical realism, and the nature of the literary motivation behind them. Published in book form in 1885 (it was previously serialized in the *Century Magazine* beginning in November 1884), the work was produced at a time when Howells's demands for Realism were becoming noticeably more direct and pronounced in his criticism. Two years before, his controversial essay **'Henry James, Jr.'**, in the *Century* of November 1882, which had praised the new and 'finer art' of fiction exemplified by James—the analysis of character rather than mere story, artistic impartiality instead of overt commentary, and the engagement of sympathy through depth of detail, not insinuation—had helped to set off lengthy discussion about the novelist's art, especially its relationship to the romance. Now his novel could take its part in the debate, both as an exemplum and as a commentary on the principles and techniques of earlier European Realists which Howells had had time to absorb and develop in his own writing.

Howells did not conceive of his propagandist intention as in any way undermining the supreme need of truth to life, but it involved the conscious exploitation of certain realistic devices in order to express his call for literary reform and innovation. Without violating his own belief in authorial impersonality, Howells permits his views to enter the book in various ways. Firstly, several of the characters make references to other fiction, real and imaginary, which point either directly or implicitly to the criteria which Howells himself seeks to uphold. Tom Corey, discussing *Middlemarch,* remarks that George Eliot seems too hard on those characters she dislikes; and Penelope Lapham complains that this novelist is too evidently in control: '''I wish she would let you find out a little about the people for yourself'''. . . . Both comments clearly reflect Howells's own reservations about George Eliot's direct intrusions into her story and her obvious preferences for certain characters, and show his commitment to authorial impersonality. (pp. 155-56)

More importantly, the main sub-plot of the novel, the Tom/Irene/Penelope triangle, serves primarily to illustrate the substance of a literary argument. At the Coreys' dinner-party, one of the guests mentions a novel she has been reading, called *Tears, Idle Tears,* which she finds '''perfectly heartbreaking''' . . . since its heroine sacrifices herself for her ideal of love. Another guest, Mr. Sewell, the minister who later acts as adviser to the Laphams, expresses his objection to such works, and suggests that:

> The novelists might be the greatest possible help to us if they painted life as it is, and human feelings in their true proportion and relation, but for the most part they have been and are altogether noxious . . . The whole business of love, and lovemaking and marrying is painted by the novelists in a monstrous disproportion to the other relations of life. . . .

The spectacle of romantic self-sacrifice is, he claims, '''wholly immoral'''. . . . We do not need the evidence of Howells's own disapproval of the emphasis on false duty and sacrifice in novels, expressed in several of his *Harper's* 'Editor's Study' columns, to recognize that Sewell is here speaking for his creator. Words alone, however, do not point the message strongly enough. His remarks are made to prove prophetically relevant, for when Penelope, the elder Lapham daughter, discovers that Tom Corey loves her, and not, as all had supposed, her sister Irene, her response is both exaggerated and foolish; although she, like Mr. Sewell, agrees that in *Tears, Idle Tears* the heroine's action of giving up the man she loves to another woman just because this 'other' loved him first, is '''silly . . . wicked''', . . . in her own case reason fails her, and by indulging in misplaced heroism she makes herself a burden and causes unhappiness to all concerned.

Thus, despite Howells's dislike of plot contrivance, he has here created and implemented an incident purposely to demonstrate a literary thesis. This seems to be the most valid way of regarding the sub-plot. Howells is making the point that even an intelligent and perceptive girl like Penelope has become so imbued with the standards of the novels she has read that she acts out the very principles which she theoretically despised. To view it in any other way is to see Howells as muddled and confused, on the one hand allowing Sewell to speak for him, and on the other presenting a story which appears to support those attitudes which Sewell is opposing. As has been suggested, this kind of propaganda does not preclude realistic

presentation. But the thematic framework of literary reference in the novel implies the extent to which Howells's Realism was not only the exemplification of a mode, but also an obvious and conscious protest.

The main plot of *The Rise of Silas Lapham* is less patently illustrative, and is, furthermore, not specifically concerned with literary issues. But here, too, Howells is concerned with opposing the sentimentalist approach. He puts forward his 'anti-romantic' views by deliberately denying the expectations which would result from an addiction to sentimental novels. The book has the form and pattern of much romance fiction: the hero, risen from obscurity and become highly successful, has to endure suffering and disappointment before finally discovering his true self in spiritual re-birth; the love-affair, having passed through a series of vicissitudes and misunderstandings, ends happily with the 'right' people marrying each other. Within this pattern, however, Howells carefully puts to work his belief that fiction must 'portray men and women as they are, actuated by the motives and the passions in the measure we all know'. In the first place, the central character is very different from 'the stock hero' of romance. Silas Lapham, a native Yankee, is a hard-headed, successful businessman, who has made his money through paint, and whose lowly antecedents are still only too obvious in his lapses of grammar, his vulgarity, and his social ineptitude; he is boastful, stubborn, and self-engrossed, and has execrable aesthetic tastes. The revelation of his faults is part of the author's scheme of portraying imperfect humanity; whenever Lapham seems limited or ridiculous, this is an intentional effect, and not because he is the absurd embodiment of a romantic concept. Silas's good qualities are inextricably mixed with his bad ones. He is not inhumane (he maintains the wife and daughter of the man who saved his life, for instance), but he reveals sad deficiences of tact and sympathy in his personal relationships; his pride distorts his concern for his daughters' welfare; his good business sense is marred by a weakness for speculation and display; his moral awareness is often blurred or muddled.

Catastrophe, too—the overwhelming tragedy of melodramatic fiction—is qualified according to normal experience. As in many of the other Realist novels, misfortune seems here merely a part of the cycle of life, temporarily crippling for certain people, but without a sense of utter and irremediable disaster. Even at the lowest depths of his fortunes, caught between conflicting impulses and desires, Lapham's mood fluctuates between optimism and gloom, and the process of his financial disintegration is

> like the course of some chronic disorder which has fastened itself upon the constitution, but advances with continual reliefs, with apparent amelioration, and at times seems not to advance at all, when it gives hope of final recovery not only to the sufferer, but to the eye of science itself. . . .

(pp. 156-58)

The achievement of personal happiness through love is not presented as an absolute in the novel, either. The affection between the two young people does not have to go to the extreme expedient of defending itself against parental opposition. When Tom Corey announces his intention of marrying one of the Lapham girls, his father (as the older man himself jokingly remarks) acts quite unconventionally in accepting the fact instead of cutting him off with a shilling in paternal fury. Moreover, though Penelope and Tom love each other, when the marriage takes place it is not the instrument of general reconciliation so dear to romance writers. The disparity in social status, experience, and ideals between the Coreys and the Laphams remains ineffaceable, and even if Tom's career in Laphams' paint firm represents a potentially healthy business alliance between aristocratic culture and proletarian shrewdness, his union with Penelope in no way draws together the two families. (p. 159)

The Rise of Silas Lapham also seems to be countering another tendency which Howells disliked in sentimental fiction—the superimposition, through a contrived plot, of a rigid and artificial pattern upon life. The novel is not unstructured, and is in fact built around four main climaxes: the 'revelation' in the Penelope/Irene/Tom triangle, the burning of the house, the affair of the mills, and the financial disaster which overtakes Lapham's business, all of which are stages in Lapham's progress towards humility and self-knowledge. But Howells manages to incorporate them within his overall scheme of showing life as a natural and recognizable process. Firstly, like many of the other Realists, Howells accepts a connection between chance and causality, and so although there is a sense of 'necessity' in his novel, it is what Lukács has called a 'poetic necessity' and not an obviously contrived fatality. Thus the stages of disaster have been prepared for and are accountable for in terms of character and circumstance, while at the same time they are illustrative of the 'bad luck' which can happen to any individual. . . . Tom's preference for the witty and amusing Penelope, instead of for the lovely but somewhat insipid Irene, is perfectly credible, and the revelation seems an incomprehensible blow to all concerned only because they have been viewing the affair according to preconceived assumptions. The burning of the house (a week after the insurance has run out), perhaps the nearest Howells comes to obvious manipulation of plot for ethical purposes, is the direct result of Lapham's carelessness, and even though the element of chance is closely involved, the 'accident' is appropriate to character and situation. Similarly, the series of financial disasters which overtake Lapham are related both to his personal irresponsibility (his initial treatment of Rogers and his material over-ambition) and to natural contingencies which include the discovery of gas in West Virginia and a fall in the demand for paint. Secondly, the misfortunes create a pattern only in as far as they contribute to a general downward trend in Lapham's career; they are not linked according to an obviously super-imposed plan. The distress caused by the unexpected love-affair contributes to the family's suffering but is not connected with the final disaster, and the house-burning and the sale of the mills are separate elements in the gradual collapse which leads to the crash. Howells has sought to replace the artificiality of romance with the arbitrariness of real life.

In suggesting that Howells's Realism was to a considerable extent inspired by literary protest, I have indicated what seems the particular purpose of some of the thematic and structural elements of the novel. Examination of the work in more general terms reveals that despite Howells's urge to propagandize he implements his aim largely in accordance with the principles established by the writers he so much admired. To reiterate an earlier point, his desire to combat tendencies which he considered inimical to true art may have led him into a kind of 'telling', but it did not alter his firm intention to make his work practically illustrate the required standards. Even though parts of the book may have a slightly literary flavour—some of the exchanges between Mr. and Mrs. Corey, and the incident of the mistaken suitor, for instance, have a certain affinity with

the novel of manners as represented by Jane Austen—as a whole it reveals the author's commitment to a new mode of writing. So as well as seeing *The Rise of Silas Lapham* as a deliberate 'anti-romance', we must recognize it as an accomplished example of nineteenth-century Realism, in an American setting. One of its most noticeable features is its truth to life, revealed firstly in its fidelity to place. Centred almost entirely on Boston, the novel, like James's *The Bostonians* (published the following year), gives a convincing picture of the city with its narrow streets, its thronging crowds, and its splendid views across Back Bay to the spires and roofs of Cambridge 'in a black outline, as if they were objects in a landscape of the French school'. . . . It also pays careful attention to the physical appearance of buildings; the contrasting details of the Laphams' house with its mixtures of wall colourings, its chandeliers of 'massive imitation bronze' and its carpets 'of a small pattern in crude green', . . . and the Coreys' house with its classic proportions, its 'slim and fluted' columns, and its staircase climbing 'in a graceful, easy curve from the tesselated pavement' especially reminds us of Flaubert's painstakingly specific descriptions of domestic interiors. Howells further seeks to render reality accurately by reproducing the peculiarities of individual speech: the Laphams' provinciality is revealed by their use of colloquialisms and their grammatical lapses, while the Coreys' refinement and education is revealed in their more measured, formal language.

The Rise of Silas Lapham illustrates the Realist's aim for 'truthfulness' in a historical sense, too. . . . Howells is concerned with a specific period as well as an actual place, and with the representative qualities of his characters and circumstances within this period. In his dual concern with both the human and the historical significance of his protagonists he fulfils Lukács's criterion that the truly great realists were those who recognized the organic and indissoluble connection between man as a private individual and man as a social being, thus synthesizing the particular and the general. (pp. 159-62)

Lapham himself is not only an individual linked to 'real life' by his similarity to his creator (Howells was of humble origins, though he came from Ohio, not Vermont, and his family was considerably more cultured than the Laphams; he, too, bought a house 'on the water side of Beacon Street', and in fact jokingly told James that the proceeds of the novel might pay for it); he is also 'typical'. It is significant that we first see him as a subject for the 'Solid Men of Boston' series in a local newspaper, since this in many ways establishes him as one of a species or group. Like another self-made man, Verga's Gesualdo, in whom, as a new capitalist motivated by the principle of material self-interest, a whole historic process is typified, Lapham is a representative figure. In his rise from lowly beginnings, through a mixture of good luck and hard work, to commercial success, he is reminiscent of the great millionaires of this era such as Rockefeller and Vanderbilt, even if his achievements are not so spectacular as theirs. This kind of representativeness was clearly foremost in Howells's mind, for as early as 1869, he wrote that 'the history of a man's rise from poverty and obscurity to distinction' is a 'perpetual romance' which 'delights and touches all, for in this nation it is in some degree the story of every man's life or the vision of his desires'. Lapham's succumbing to the business ethics of the age is further indicative of a general trend. The relationship between the Laphams and the Coreys also has a representative significance: the awkwardness and misunderstandings which never completely disappear on a personal level illustrate the conflict between the older Boston aristocratic society and the new brash world of business which demands acknowledgement from it.

None of the characters, however, embodies a single aspect of the social reality with which Howells is concerned. All are 'real' in the way that Howells found so admirable in Galdós's work, where the people are 'typical of a certain side of human nature . . . but not exclusively of this side or that. They are . . . of mixed motives, mixed qualities'. (pp. 162-63)

If the Laphams are vulgar, materialistic, and muddled, they are also energetic, resourceful, and refreshingly frank; if the Coreys are elegant and cultured, they are also snobbish and cruel. We are given in the novel a clear-eyed, though not unsympathetic, view of an imperfect world in which our attitudes towards humanity have continually to be revised.

Another essential element of Howells's artistic credo, which is closely linked to his ideal of truthfulness, is objectivity of narration. He felt that it is neither possible nor desirable totally to exclude the writer's personal vision, but that the author must not be in evidence 'to moralize openly and badly . . . to "sympathize" with certain of his people, and to point out others for the abhorrence of his readers'. (p. 164)

Objectivity is clearly a predominant aim in *The Rise of Silas Lapham*, even if it is not wholly consistent in practice. Howells does not in fact entirely abandon the use of direct authorial commentary, but, as I shall show later, his remarks tend to be reflective and speculative, directing attention from the specific to the more universal aspects of human experience, rather than narrowly prescriptive or moralistic. For the most part he is the conventional narrator who tells the story, but he often assumes an ironic tone which distances him from the action. He frequently disclaims omniscience about characters' motivation or intentions by using words and phrases such as 'perhaps', 'maybe', or 'it may have been' to describe their actions. Information about his protagonists is often conveyed from within the story itself, instead of by the more obvious method of straightforward narrative. The opening of the novel is a good example of this: Silas Lapham is being interviewed by Bartley Hubbard, a Boston journalist, who interrogates him about his career and business achievements. This question-and-answer device not only introduces us to Lapham without any explicit 'telling' from the author himself, but it also presents us with a double viewpoint: Hubbard's cynical and unscrupulous reporter's eye seizes on Lapham's naïvety, his sentimentality, and his tasteless self-assertion, but it also indirectly reveals his idealism, his openness, and his magnanimity. Later in the book, other characters comment on Lapham, thus building up a composite picture. (p. 165)

The extensive use of conversation in the novel, enabling people both to reveal themselves and to cast light on their fellows, helps to create the sense of Howells's essentially free and impartial view of his characters. Penelope Lapham, for instance, is variously referred to by others as a pert young thing, a wise and witty observer, and an ideal partner in marriage, and the reader must assimilate and distinguish between all these ways of regarding her. Conversations between groups of characters, too, show up contrasts and similarities in particular situations. The discussions between Mr. and Mrs. Lapham, and between Mr. and Mrs. Corey about their children's matrimonial plans are structurally paralleled and provide a dramatic way of suggesting a mutual concern for filial welfare, despite differences of emphasis and expression.

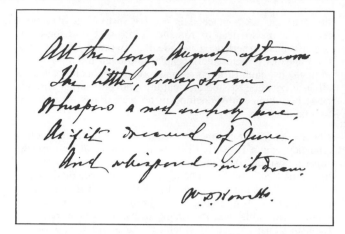

Holograph copy of a poem by Howells. Miscellaneous Manuscripts, The Newberry Library.

Howells sometimes combines an apparently impartial presentation of his protagonists and their attitudes with an ironic gloss on them, thus managing to reconcile a sense of distinctions with objectivity of method. Though by no means as skilful or consistent in this as James, he seems to be experimenting with the Jamesian 'point of view' technique, which allows the author to make or suggest evaluations without directly inserting his own opinions, while giving the illusion that his characters are free agents. In the following passage, we are shown the Coreys' reluctant acknowledgement that they owe some kind of 'return' to the Laphams for their kindness in helping the sick Mrs. Corey the previous summer.

> [Mrs. Corey] opened the matter with some trepidation to her daughters, but neither of them opposed her; they rather looked at the scheme from her own point of view, and agreed with her that nothing had really yet been done to wipe out the obligation to the Laphams helplessly contracted the summer before, and strengthened by that ill-advised application to Mrs. Lapham for charity. Not only the principle of their debt of gratitude remained, but the accruing interest. . . .

This is a fine example of the Realist's method of refusing to comment overtly on his characters, yet at the same time drawing attention to certain aspects of their behaviour. The passage seems on the surface a simple description of the Coreys' attitudes, using reportage instead of direct speech, and with no evident authorial evaluation. But by suggesting that they look on 'their debt of gratitude' in essentially financial and calculating terms, and by the use of words such as 'helplessly' and 'ill-advised' (which represent the Coreys' reactions, not the author's), Howells makes us see not only the Coreys' snobbish regret at forming such an unfortunate acquaintance, but also their desire to conclude it as quickly and conclusively as respectability and self-esteem will allow. (pp. 165-67)

Howells's ideal of objectivity included stress on the dramatic mode. By this he seems to have meant the rejection of verbose and elaborate description, the direct presentation of character, and an 'organic' plot depending on a natural and unheralded progression of events. . . . 'Drama' in his novels . . . usually consists of placing characters in certain scenes and allowing them freely and directly to express themselves through their subsequent behaviour, giving the illusion that they are acting independently and not according to the author's intentions towards them. One of the best illustrations of this in *The Rise of Silas Lapham* is the Coreys' dinner party. This occasion, during which the Laphams feel themselves at a strong social and cultural disadvantage, contrasts effectively with the previous confrontation between members of the two families—Broomfield Corey's visit to Lapham's office—when Lapham, feeling himself in the secure position of employer and successful businessman, assures Corey with embarrassingly patronising condescension that all are not fortunate enough to have an aptitude for business and that '"The idea is to make the most of what we *have* got'''. . . . At the dinner-party these roles are reversed. The Laphams are hopelessly inept: Mrs. Lapham announces bluntly and unexpectedly that Penelope is not coming after all, and Silas, worried about social proprieties and uncomfortably conscious of his large hands which 'looked, in the saffron tint which the shop girl said his gloves should be of, like canvassed hams, . . . fiddles with the glasses at table, talks with his cigar in his mouth, and drinks too much. He ends the evening by boasting wildly, treating all the other guests (the Boston élite) like old friends whom he can help to better things, and taking leave of all 'with patronising affection'. . . . The scene is finely executed, and Howells's skill is evident in the manner in which not only do we see the pitiable gulf between the Laphams and these 'old Bostonians', but we also recognize the complacent superiority and clannishness of the Coreys and their ilk, as they debate aesthetic questions and make sweeping assumptions about social hierarchies. This is truly dramatic presentation, character unfolding itself in action. As with the other instances of Howells's objectivity, the reader is not required to do more than observe, but finds himself becoming involved, paradoxically because of the lack of imposed authorial judgements.

The Rise of Silas Lapham, then, sets out to focus on the Reverend Sewell's objections that '"those novels with old-fashioned heroes and heroines in them . . . are ruinous"', . . . and by direct polemic and exemplification of the anti-romantic position to reinforce Howells's plea for fiction which paints life as it really is. Using many of the techniques of other nineteenth-century Realist novels, it strives to show the strength of accurate and uncontrived presentation of familiar material. But when we consider the novel as an example of Howells's Realism, we are inevitably made aware of the ambiguities or conflicts intrinsic in the genre, not only in his explicit promotion of it as a literary method, but also in the nature of the book as a whole. If the work of the other Realists demonstrates the impossibility of 'pure' realism, Howells's fiction is no exception; like theirs, his novel is inevitably coloured and shaped by his own vision of the world and his sense of its significance. (pp. 167-68)

The Rise of Silas Lapham clearly shows the result of Howells's growing commitment to the idea of conscience and ethical clarification, both in its themes and its structure. Its critical or evaluative emphasis in the social sphere—its portrayal of the changing values of a materialistic age in which the lure of money and the desire for upward social mobility are pervasive, and the individual is caught up in the temptations and corruptions of a capitalist society—has already been suggested. But there is more than this: we are not only made to realize the particular significance of the central character in this general theme, we have also to regard his involvement to a considerable extent in ethical terms. Although Howells is not directly didactic, by giving his novel a traditionally Christian frame-

work—a pattern of sin, guilt, retribution, and regeneration—he compels us to recognize a moral relationship between cause and effect, and a difference between 'good' and 'bad' behaviour, even while he implies that these are relative distinctions. 'What is' in the novel is accompanied by a definite suggestion of 'what should be'. (pp. 169-70)

The central moral idea of the novel seems to be that by wronging a fellow man an individual will himself suffer spiritual injury, which must be atoned for before health can be restored. At the beginning of the story, we are told that Lapham has acted badly towards his former partner, Rogers, in forcing him out of the business when it was prosperous and he no longer needed him. . . . To repair this wrong, Lapham lends Rogers some of the money which he was going to spend on the new house, and we are obviously meant to see this both as an admirable act of conscience and an appropriate way for Lapham to assuage his wife's long-standing unease about the affair. From this point on, however, the moral focus becomes less clear. On the one hand, we see that Lapham is by no means free of blame for what subsequently happens to him—he speculates in the financial world, he is eager to promote the marriage between Tom and Irene because it will offer him social advancement, and he is proud and boastful—and that therefore to some extent the code of guilt and expiation, stressed by his wife, is applicable to him. On the other hand, Howells makes it quite evident that Mrs. Lapham has serious limitations as a moral guide: though she often keeps her husband straight by her shrewd common sense, she is helpless and confused when the trouble over Tom and her daughters arises, and she continues to view Lapham's relationship with Rogers in terms of sin and atonement even after reparation has been made. In fact Howells strongly suggests that her need to attribute blame and to find a discernible cause for misfortune and pain are not to be taken as unqualified wisdom, and that crime, punishment, and re-birth are not simple concepts but need modification according to individual circumstances.

At the end of the novel, Lapham is presented with what seems an intolerable choice: he can either sell the mills and save Rogers from financial ruin, or act with uncompromising uprightness and forgo the deal. Mrs. Lapham, who originally saw the potential dishonesty in the proposed sale, now fails him at this crisis, and he is left to make the decision on his own. Though he has been tempted to do business with the Englishmen, and though he himself is aware of the ostensible absurdity of his scruples, his actual choice (and even though the letter from the G.L. & P. comes before he has spoken to Rogers, we know which way he is drawn) has to be seen as an act of absolute moral value. We recognize this as the climax of his moral 'rise' (as spelt out in the title), an indication that through suffering he has reached a state of spiritual health; and his honourable refusals—to sell the mills either directly to the Englishmen or via Rogers, since he knows the purchase will be worthless, or to accept help for his business without telling the prospective investor about the West Virginia company—clearly have authorial approval. (pp. 171-72)

We have here, then, the apparent anomaly of the Realist who wants to portray life in all its natural and normal aspects imposing a pattern of moral imperatives on his work. The appeal to such imperatives need not, of course, be at odds with the Realist's aims—after all, virtuous behaviour is as much a part of 'real' life as weakness and vice—but *The Rise of Silas Lapham* seems a less than satisfactory fusion of Realism and morality because of the way in which the ethical elements are introduced. It would be simple to argue that the ambivalence created by the contrasting moral viewpoints in the novel represents the Realist's refusal to acknowledge ethical absolutes, were it not for the fact that at the end, despite Sewell's uncertainty about the operation of evil in the spiritual world, a definitive moral statement does seem to have been made. This statement affects the book in three main ways. Firstly, the resolution seems both socially and psychologically unconvincing. It not only asserts Howells's positive faith in the spiritual integrity of the American businessman, by asking us to accept that Lapham, as a representative of his class and kind, in an age of compromised values, would pass up an opportunity to avert financial ruin when no law-breaking is involved, and this surely in the face of much contemporary evidence to the contrary, but it is also inadequate in terms of character and motivation. Given that Lapham was behaving 'normally' (that is, according to his natural impulses) in his initial treatment of Rogers, and given the view we have of him for much of the novel, with his moral uncertainties and his shifting attitudes, it is hard to see why he should be so virtuous at the end. The progress of his growth to this position is not shown clearly enough, and his final declaration that '"... it seems to me I done wrong about Rogers in the first place; that the whole trouble came from that"', and his feeling that if '"the thing [the refusal to sell] was to do over again, right in the same way, I guess I should have to do it"', ... seem scarcely commensurate with his character as it has been drawn.

Secondly, the moral emphasis affects the novel's structural significance. Though earlier it was suggested that the major crises of the book are essentially in accordance with 'natural' chance—apparently random and fortuitous circumstances which are yet probable because of the nature of the people and situations concerned—they must also be seen as stages in the hero's spiritual development. Hence, they may seem somewhat contrived, 'message pointers' rather than merely steps to financial ruin, and standing out from the general naturalistic quality of the plot. Thirdly, the pattern of guilt/atonement/regeneration, with the hero attaining moral victory and with character ultimately defined and evaluated by a kind of ethical idealism, gives the novel something of the flavour of the very genre which Howells was trying to counteract—the romance. As in the case of the almost impossibly virtuous Tom Corey, the essentially romantic vision tends to undercut the other successful elements of Realism in the work. (pp. 172-74)

In his determination to examine the moral implications of man's behaviour, then, Howells perhaps comes closest to the appearance of didacticism. But we cannot say that this nullifies the achievement of the novel as a whole. Its portrayal of its chosen world is well-detailed, perceptive, and sympathetic, and by making us understand human nature, Howells gives us a sense of values without demanding our allegiance to one particular interpretation of the world. Such an approach ... is both honest and enlightening. ... Though, to some extent, *The Rise of Silas Lapham* looks back to the tradition of didactic and romantic literature, in many ways it represents reform and innovation. Adapting the interests and techniques of European Realism to the native American material which Howells grew to believe was the only material for the novelists of his country, it is an excellent example of the move towards a new kind of writing in the United States. Despite the fact that Howells was regarded by later and more revolutionary Realists as outmoded, tame, and prudish, it is undeniable that without his lead the development of Realist American fiction would have been far less rapid and self-confident. (p. 176)

S. Foster, "W. D. Howells: 'The Rise of Silas Lapham' (1885)," in The Monster in the Mirror: Studies in Nineteenth-Century Realism, edited by D. A. Williams, Oxford University Press, Oxford, 1978, pp. 149-78.

HENRY NASH SMITH   (essay date 1981)

[*Smith is an American educator who has written extensively on the works of American novelists, particularly the works of Mark Twain. He is currently serving on an editorial committee at work on* The Mark Twain Papers, *which will be published in fifteen volumes by the University of California Press. In the following excerpt, Smith closely examines* Their Wedding Journey, *arguing that Howells's commitment to American middle-class values and perspectives impeded his success in creating truly modern fiction.*]

In 1871 [Howells] wrote his father (with whom he discussed all his literary plans) that he had in mind a book based on a summer trip he and his wife had taken down the St. Lawrence River. He said the new work would differ from standard travel books in having "the form of fiction so far as the characters are concerned," but apparently it was not to be exactly a novel. He continued: "If I succeed in this—and I believe I shall—I see clear before me a path in literature which no one else has tried, and which I believe I can make most distinctly and entirely my own." Later he declared, "The thing is quite a new species of fiction," being not at all "dependent on plot," but relying on "the interest of character ... and some notable places."

The book that carries out this experimental program, entitled *Their Wedding Journey*, appeared serially in the *Atlantic Monthly* in 1872. In it Howells scrupulously avoids such melodramatic features as suspense, "big" scenes, and exalted language, relying instead on his powers of observation in describing "notable places," on deftness of style, and on humor. But his self-confidence was not misplaced: no less a critic than Henry Adams, writing for the *North American Review*, found in *Their Wedding Journey* an "extreme and almost photographic truth to nature, and remarkable delicacy and lightness of touch" [see *TCLC*, Vol. 7]. It is true that Howells does not avoid fictional convention altogether, for Basil and Isabel March, the pair of newlyweds (closely resembling the writer and his wife) whose journey provides the book's only structure, enact to some extent the role ordinarily assigned in novels to the two lovers. But most of the time Howells' handling of the Marches avoids the beaten track of sentimental practice, and he often has them converse about topics that would never find a place in the usual fictional courtship. For example, he introduces a discussion of the technical problems he faced in writing the book, assigning to Isabel the role of a partisan of established aesthetic doctrine and causing Basil to deliver little lectures for her benefit in which he expounds the new ideas that Howells was incubating.

We Americans, Basil tells Isabel, "shall never have a poetry of our own til ... we make the ideal embrace and include the real...." The notion of the "ideal," although difficult to define, was thoroughly familiar. The meaning of "the real," on the other hand, was elusive. Adams implied a definition in his remark that Howells had undertaken "the idealization of the commonplace." (p. 44)

The standard sentimental novel had striven to depict the ideal by choosing characters of high social status and exquisite sensibilities, by focusing on a love story, and by excluding every "low." This formula, however, was evidently worn out. The task of the new generation of writers was to discover a new way of revealing ideal values in the novelist's materials. When Howells wrote *Their Wedding Journey,* he had solved only half the problem. Although he had found in the narrative of travel a tolerable framework for a long prose narrative, he had not found a satisfactory way to elevate it above the level of observed fact. I shall examine a few passages from the book in order to illustrate the various ways in which Howells tried to carry out the program set forth by Basil.

What is most striking about these early fumblings is the extraordinary effort required to reach the ultimate goal. Howells' procedure is instructive because it reveals clearly what factors entered into the solution he would eventually find. That solution was nothing less than his highly individualized conception of realism—which can be recognized as the ultimate development of Basil's formula of a synthesis of the ideal and the real. The reality was of course the novelist's inevitable subject matter—the society to which Howells was exposed in his own daily life in Cambridge and New York. What was original in his theory was the notion of the ideal that he considered to be latent in that commonplace material. This was simply the spirit of democracy, which was for him identical with equality. (p. 45)

Howells was firmly convinced that the primary obstacle to truthful representation in fiction was the persistence of outworn literary conventions. Looking back a hundred years later, however, we can see that the most serious distortion of his vision was caused by his uncritical acceptance of the standard American ideology. In all good faith he took it for granted that his own social class (represented for example by Basil and Isabel March) made up the bulk of the American people. To depict this class in fiction, he thought, was to demonstrate the novel. Moreover, he believed that the "honest" portrayal of such characters would necessarily reveal moral principles or laws operating in society. Thus although Howells recognized that realism as a literary mode had originated in Europe, and praised many continental European writers for their achievements in it—Turgenev, Dostoevsky, Tolstoy, Valdés, in certain moods even Flaubert and Zola—he believed the American novelist had a great advantage over his transatlantic rivals because in this country the writer need do nothing more than tell the truth about society in order to illustrate the ideal of democracy and equality. After Howells' conception reached its full development he tended to repudiate even the great Victorian novelists on the ground that English fiction and criticism expressed "class interests," grew out of "class education," and admitted "only class claims to the finer regard and respect of readers," whereas the American novel was characteristically in "sympathy with race interests"—that is, the interests of all mankind. He claimed for "the American novelist" the "inherent, if not instinctive perception of equality: equality running through motive, passion, principle, incident, character, and commanding with the same force his interest in the meanest and the noblest, through the mere virtue of their humanity."

In following the development of Howells' theory of realism I have moved chronologically far beyond the date of composition of *Their Wedding Journey.* Let me now return to that work and consider some passages from it within the conceptual framework I have established. The debates between Isabel and Basil March show that Howells had not yet clearly defined the relation between ideal and real in his own mind. In the first passage I shall quote, the oversimplified dyadic contrast tends to force Isabel into an indiscriminate partisanship for the ideal

that is not far from mere snobbishness, whereas Basil is forced into defending folklore and vernacular humor simply because they embody a characteristic American reality. But he is not fully convinced that an ideal value is immanent in these elements of popular culture, with the result that his defense is rather lame, and he soon abandons it.

The Marches are viewing the Genesee Falls near Rochester from a high bluff. Basil points out to his bride

> the table-rock in the middle of the fall, from which Sam Patch had made his fatal leap; but Isabel refused to admit that tragical figure to the honors of her emotions. "I don't care for him!" she said fiercely. "Patch! What a name to be linked in our thoughts with this superb cataract." . . .

Basil has previously explained to Isabel that Sam Patch "invented the saying, 'Some things can be done as well as others,' and proved it by jumping over Niagara Falls twice," but when he attempted "the leap of the Genesee Falls," he was killed. . . . The name in fact had great resonance in the masculine world of barbershops and popular theaters. In addition to Patch's significance as stunt man and exemplar of the "Go Ahead" spirit of the mid-nineteenth century, he represented native American humor. Although he had been an actual person, his position in popular culture resembled that of the fictitious Mose, the Bowery B'hoy, protagonist of Ned Buntline's novel *The Mysteries and Miseries of New York* (1848) and of several plays starring Francis S. Chanfrau in the 1850s. . . . In mentioning Patch, Basil means to remind Isabel that they have spent much time along the way exchanging reminiscences of European travel, taking it for granted that the United States is in comparison a cultural desert. And he speaks for Howells the apprentice writer in finding serious implications in Isabel's scorn for the name of Sam Patch.

> "Well, Isabel [Basil replies], I think you are very unjust. It is as good a name as Leander, to my thinking, and it was immortalized in support of a great idea—the feasibility of all things; while Leander's has come down to us as that of the weak victim of a passion." . . .

I must interrupt Basil here to supply a gloss. Patch's remark that "Some things can be done as well as others" is strikingly similar in spirit to the observation of the Stranger in Angel's Camp concerning Jim Smiley's celebrated jumping frog, Daniel Webster: "I don't see no p'ints about that frog that's better'n any other frog." In other words, Howells has arrived at a point in his narrative where he has an opportunity to exploit the kind of native American humor that Mark Twain would show to be so rich a vein of literary ore. (pp. 46-8)

What Howells does is to modulate rather awkwardly toward a quite different subject. He has Basil notice that he and Isabel are standing outside a German beer hall. Though Basil's tone is jocose, Howells uses him as a mouthpiece to make a serious point:

> "The Germans are braver than we, and in them you find facts and dreams continually blended and confronted. Here is a fortunate illustration. The people we met coming out of this pavilion were lovers, and they had been here sentimentalizing on this superb cataract, as you call it, with which my heroic Patch is not worthy to

be named. No doubt they had been quoting
Uhland or some other of their romantic poets,
perhaps singing some of their tender German
love-songs, the tenderest, unearthliest love-songs
of the world. At the same time they did not
disdain the matter-of-fact corporeity in which
their sentiment was enshrined; they fed it heartily and abundantly with the banquet whose relics we see here.''

On a table before them stood a pair of beer-
glasses, in the bottoms of which lurked scarce
the foam of the generous liquor lately brimming
them; some shreds of sausage, some rinds of
Swiss cheese, bits of cold ham, crusts of bread,
and the ashes of a pipe. . . .

Howells' difficulty in defining the contrast between the ideal
and the real is shown by the images he chooses to represent
commonplace experience in the two passages I have quoted:
first Sam Patch, redolent of vernacular humor and the popular
theater, and then an empty beer glass, scraps of cheese and
sausage, the ashes from a pipe. The emblems of the ideal are
a waterfall seen by moonlight and German love-songs. In yet
another passage exploiting the same contrast Howells comes
nearer representing an actual synthesis of outer and inner worlds,
although the result still falls short of revealing the immanence
of the ideal realm in the actual: the significant transaction takes
place entirely in the mind of the observer. Sitting alone at
daybreak on the deck of a Hudson River steamer, Basil observes ''a fisherman drawing his nets, and bending from his
boat, there near Albany, N.Y., in the picturesque immortal
attitudes of Raphael's Galilean fisherman.'' . . . In producing
the association with Raphael's painting, Basil is linking ordinary American life with an image that belongs to the ideal
realm on four counts: it relates to the remote past; it is European
(and therefore exotic); it concerns one of the fine arts; and it
alludes to the New Testament. Yet the total effect of the passage
is to isolate Basil in his function as registering consciousness
from the commonplace average of humanity. An observer who
is reminded of Raphael by a Hudson River fisherman is obviously cultivated; he has traveled abroad and has stored his
mind with memories of the paintings of old Masters. The unnecessary initials ''N.Y.,'' suggesting the address of a business
letter, convey a mild astonishment that so prosaic a place can
have any relation to so exalted an image. And there is a further
overtone in the Biblical allusion: not only does the physical
posture of the fisherman recall a certain painting, but also the
scriptural story sanctifies the humble labors of daily life everywhere—a suggestion certainly intended by Raphael. But the
difference between Howells' effort to make the ideal include
the real and the true consummation of the synthesis becomes
obvious if we place this passage beside Whitman's references
[in ''Song of Myself''] to the ''mechanic's wife with her babe
at her nipple interceding for every person born'' and ''the snag-
tooth'd hostler with red hair redeeming sins past and to come.''

Having entered upon Basil's reverie, Howells makes a rather
arbitrary transition to the recollection of a collision with another
vessel during the previous night in which a sailor was badly
scalded. The link, by way of heat, is awkward:

. . . and now a flush mounted the pale face of
the east, and through the dewy coolness of the
dawn there came, more to the sight than to any
other sense, a vague menace of heat. But as
yet the air was deliciously fresh and sweet, and

Basil bathed in his weariness in it, thinking with
a certain luxurious compassion of the scalded
man . . .

Although the phrase ''luxurious compassion'' places Basil for
a moment at an ironic distance from the narrative voice, Howells abandons this perspective at once and develops Basil's
reverie quite seriously. The language grows correspondingly
abstract and conventional:

He bade his soul remember that, in the security
of sleep, Death had passed them both [i.e.,
Isabel and himself] so close that his presence
might well have chilled their dreams. . . . But . . .
sense and spirit alike put aside the burden that
he would have laid upon them; his revery reflected with delicious caprice the looks, the
tones, the movements that he loved, and bore
him far away from the sad images that he had
invited to mirror themselves in it. . . .

In contrast with the linkage between the fisherman on the Hudson and Raphael's painting, which at least places an ideal image
beside the commonplace scene, the allusions here to Basil's
soul, to Death as an allegorical entity, and to a carefully bowd-
lerized lover's reverie drop all connection with actual experience and thus surrender all claim to novelty in narrative technique. Basil's feeling for Isabel is particularly conventional; it
has only a remote basis in conceivable psychological fact. Thus
the passage does not make ''the ideal embrace and include the
real'' because it captures almost no reality.

A more important shortcoming of this way of linking the two
realms of experience, from the standpoint of Howells' ultimate
goal, is that there is little if any democracy about it. Basil feels
no human tie with the fisherman; he might be an eighteenth-
century aristocrat noting an example of the picturesque. In
Howells' own terminology, the ideal coloring here is merely
aesthetic; it has no moral or political significance. (pp. 48-50)

In order to illustrate Howells' long but on the whole unsuccessful struggle to find a way of affirming the democratic ideal
in fiction, let me consider another passage from *Their Wedding
Journey*. Leaving their steamboat at Albany, the Marches take
a train for Buffalo and Niagara Falls. At the outset the first-
person narrator intrudes for some two pages to describe his
own response to a landscape that he loves ''for its mild beauty
and tranquil picturesqueness.'' As these epithets suggest, he
is elaborately literary. While the animistic train ''strives furiously onward,'' he fancies himself loitering and sauntering
''up and down the landscape,'' pausing for a cup of buttermilk
served him by ''old Dutch ladies . . . with decent caps upon
their gray hair,'' or ''some red-cheeked, comely young girl,
out of Washington Irving's pages, with no cap on her golden
braids . . .'' . . . Or again, he says: ''I walk unmolested through
the farmer's tall grass . . . and learn . . . that his family has
owned that farm ever since the days of the Patroon; which I
dare say is not true.'' . . . (The skepticism must represent a
hint of self-consciousness in a writer who suspects that this
mood of nostalgia is too fragile for post-Civil War America.)
After a few more fantasies, the narrator turns the responsibility
for producing associations over to the ''wedding-journeyers.''
But they in turn are treated with apologetic irony. ''They cast
an absurd poetry over the landscape,'' he says; ''they invited
themselves to be reminded of passages of European travel by
it; and they placed villas and castles and palaces upon all the
eligible building-sites.'' When this amusement palls, Basil

"patriotically tried to reconstruct the Dutch and Indian past of the Mohawk Valley...." But his effort is frustrated by Isabel's absolute ignorance of American history (a subject that is less essential to general cultivation than is European history)....

Wearied by their failure to "extract any sentiment from the scenes without," Basil and Isabel turn instead to look about them for amusement within the railway car. The narrator approves of the decision on ideological grounds: it is merely "an ordinary carful of human beings" and "perhaps the more worthy to be studied on that account." For "the sincere observer of man will not desire to look upon his heroic or occasional phrases, but will seek him in his habitual moods of vacancy and tiresomeness." Howells probably believed he was turning here from an outmoded sentimental exercise in the ideal (extracting sentiment from the landscape) to a more profound undertaking, that in fact of the realistic novelist. For this reason, the narrator's comment is worth quoting at greater length. Man in his vacant and tedious phases, he goes on to say, is

> very precious; and I never perceive him to be so much a man and a brother as when I feel the pressure of his vast, natural, unaffected dulness. Then I am able to enter confidently into his life and inhabit there, to think his shallow and feeble thoughts, to be moved by his dumb, stupid desires, to be dimly illuminated by his stinted inspirations, to share his foolish prejudices, to practise his obtuse selfishness....

Howells presumably thinks that the superciliousness of this comment is offset by the narrator's declaration that he himself enters into the dullness and stupidity of common humanity. This, one supposes, would represent the democracy that is expressed in realism. Thus the Marches take an important step in the right direction by turning their attention to the interior of the railway car and observing their fellow passengers. But the tone seems patronizing nevertheless. Basil and Isabel, we are told, "had deliberately rejected the notion of a drawing-room car as affording a less varied prospect of humanity, and as being less in the spirit of ordinary American travel."... Now they "were very willing to be entertained." "They delighted" in some of the passengers, "they were interested in" others, they "found diversion" in yet others. The Marches invent elaborate and sympathetic biographies for several characters, but Isabel is outraged by the indecent behavior of "tender couples" who "reclined upon each other's shoulders and slept," and she is disgusted by having to overhear a detailed account of a case of typhoid fever. Presently she is punished for her censoriousness by falling asleep herself with her head on Basil's shoulder.... He consoles her for her embarrassment with an amused irony that would often serve Howells in future novels as a device for ending scenes that seemed on the point of placing his protagonists in awkward situations.

Thus the implied challenge to Isabel's right to sit in judgment—which threatened to raise questions about class feeling and perspectives—has been turned into a stock joke about the inconsequence of women. Yet the issue is a real one. What is the basis for Basil's and Isabel's assumed superiority to their fellow passengers? Their status is a residue from conventional fiction that Howells has not looked at closely enough. They occupy a position equivalent to that of the genteel hero and heroine in the traditional narrative structure. Even though the narrator occasionally backs away from them with ironic comments showing that he judges them in turn, they share with him the innate sensibilities and acquired cultivation which in

this fictive world confer on a character the capacity for transcendence. That is to say, both the Marches and the narrator have access to the mental processes of the people they observe and can evaluate them by reference to absolute moral and esthetic principles, whereas the other characters remain sealed within their limited horizons. The Marches and the narrator are free because they are in contact with the ideal; the other characters are not free. The ideal is still made to embrace the real only within the consciousness of privileged observers, the implied author or his surrogates.

What, in fact, has Howells accomplished in *Their Wedding Journey* toward creating a new species of fiction? In cutting himself loose from plot as conventionally conceived he has eliminated the standard devices of the sensation novel: mysteries, ghosts, gothic wickedness, disguises, long-lost heirs, physical combat, and so on. In choosing the Marches as hero and heroine he has avoided such absurdities as perfect lovers and superhuman renunciations as well as fiends in human form. He has made a perceptible effort to get rid of the stylized motivations and melodramatic moral contrasts of popular fiction. But he has not completely freed himself from outworn fictional conventions. Although using a husband and wife—even a recently married pair—as the lovers is mildly innovative, what tangible plot the story has is after all still centered on the relation of a man and a woman; and this relation, like the characters of the two protagonists, retains important vestiges of ideality: they are very genteel lovers. The Marches' status is not technically aristocratic, but it is functionally so: they consider themselves and the author considers them to be equal or superior in intellect, taste, and cultivation to anyone they encounter.

The systematic blindness, or perhaps one should say "tunnel vision," that prevented Howells from recognizing the contradiction between his doctrine of equality and his failure to recognize the existence of a hierarchy of classes in American society based on differences in wealth and cultivation is the characteristic effect of any ideology that is firmly held by the observer and reinforced by being generally accepted throughout his own social class. Howells cherished an almost subliminal belief that the settlement of North America by English-speaking colonists had set in motion a providentially ordered historical scheme which would lead, indeed was already leading, toward a millennial consummation. For him, the United States had a meaning not available to empirical observation: it was destined to bring freedom and democracy to the world, and he was convinced that the facts of American society, as contrasted with those of European societies, demonstrated the operation of the process. I think this ideologically determined belief proved to be an insurmountable obstacle to Howells' full development as a novelist. The social reality of urban industrial America refused to yield the ideal truth and beauty that his theory of realism claimed would be revealed by an honest examination of it. Yet he was unable to conceive of any other fresh and interesting approach to the material. (pp. 51-4)

> *Henry Nash Smith, "Fiction and the American Ideology: The Genesis of Howells' Early Realism," in* The American Self: Myth, Ideology, and Popular Culture, *edited by Sam B. Girgus, University of New Mexico Press, 1981, pp. 43-57.*

ALFRED HABEGGER (essay date 1982)

[*In the following excerpt, Habegger discusses Howells and Henry James as writers who first began to define themselves and their literary direction during the 1850s, "the one decade in American history in which women wrote practically* all *the popular books." The critic posits that Howells and James "were born to, and then established themselves against, the maternal tradition of Anglo-American women's fiction."*]

Given the prevailing literary and social conditions in the post-Civil War period, our first good realistic novelists *had* to be fugitives from the rough masculine world—a world that was a lot rougher in a day when boys routinely owned firearms, scores of people were killed in accidents every Fourth of July, fighting if not dueling was still common, politics was intimately associated with saloon cliques, and business was apparently more of a free-for-all than today. Only a couple of rather effeminate men—in sympathy with the best feminine values but still in a position to criticize women's sphere from the outside—were able to understand and fictionalize the crazy quilt of American life. Essentially, Howells and James seized a popular women's literary genre, entered deeply into the feminine aspirations it articulated, yet brought to bear on them the critical sense of reality that was at that time basically masculine. Only a couple of sissies, so to speak, could perform such a balancing act.

Sissy! Baby! Crybaby! These taunting insults, so inadmissable in civilized life, are the key to many aspects of masculine American culture. They are the key because they name the fear that is one of the chief operative causes of the classic forms of masculinity. (p. 56)

The feminine traits that are stigmatized by the word *sissy* are the traits developed by boys excluded from the most active and turbulent masculine clique within a given cohort. It is because femininity is often the shadow of masculinity that a sissy is an effeminate boy, one who is too timid, careful, considerate, polite, or unwilling to join the rough play of other boys. He is thus seen by them as a weak male unable to earn the accolade theoretically open to any male—manhood—and for that reason he is scorned. Chances are, he is more closely bound to his mother than are other boys and more sympathetic to her way of seeing things. Thus, he is dismissed as a mama's boy and the insults applied to him—such as *pantywaist*—derive from characteristically feminine articles of clothing.

Howells and James became sissies partly because they were born into loving families rather different from the norm.... Significantly, both fathers were Swedenborgians who disapproved of "egotism" and associated it with capitalistic enterprise. Both men had a theoretical commitment to socialism, James adopting an eccentric form of Fourier's utopianism. Howells Sr. actually spent a year in a family milling commune with his brothers at a time when Will was thirteen years old. In his son's fictionalization of this quixotic venture, *New Leaf Mills*, the mother has the practical mind, while the father, a dreamer, philosopher, and ideologue, is always full of hope and speaks in a mild and lofty tone reminiscent of Bronson Alcott. His wife keeps him going: "She had always had to fortify him for his encounters with the world, and she understood how in this retreat from it he had felt a safety and peace that he had never felt in its presence." It is striking that the fathers of our first important realists both deviated in the same significant way from masculine norms. Appropriately, one of the basic issues in their sons' fiction would be the legitimacy of selfish desire. (pp. 57-8)

The aspect of James's and Howells's fiction that made them famous, tagging them with their public image in the late seventies and early eighties, was their meticulous study of American girls. James's one hit was "Daisy Miller." His first consciously "big" book was *The Portrait of a Lady*, the American edition of which had a tasteful arrangement of flowers in gold and brown embossed on the cover.... Howells also became known as a writer who wrote about women. In 1883 Ambrose Bierce called him and James "two eminent triflers and cameo-cutters-in-chief to Her Littleness the Bostonese small virgin." Howells' 1870 novels hinged on delicate social embarrassments—a girl's accidentally taking a strange man's arm in *A Chance Acquaintance*; another girl's isolation among a boatful of men in *The Lady of the Aroostook*, an Austrian officer's unauthorized courtship of Lily Mayhew in *A Fearful Responsibility*. Like "Daisy Miller," these works all dealt with a young woman's unintentional violation of the code. In this early fiction, as one reviewer noted, "there is the more than masculine, almost feminine, touch to be found." After reading one of Howells's plays, Charles Dudley Warner wrote: "You must have been a woman yourself in some previous state, to so know how it is yourself. You are a dangerous person. Heaven grant you no such insight into us men folk." A hostile male critic wrote, "Mr. Howells is never exciting; the most nervous old lady can read him without fear."

The man who wrote this didn't see that many ladies, old or young, disliked Howells. In the early eighties, he moved be-

Cartoon from Tid-Bits, *May 1, 1885, captioned "Men of the Day—W. D. Howells: Demonstrator of the American Girl."*

yond decorum into a sustained critical analysis of American femininity. (pp. 60-1)

The powerful literary ambition that drove both writers from adolescence on is evidence, I believe, that the idea of becoming a great man of letters was attractive partly because it offered them an escape from both the threat of feminization and the pressures of normal masculinity. Passing through adolescence in the "feminine fifties," as Fred Lewis Pattee named the decade, Howells and James knew all the time that they would have to live a man's life. The solution was to enter literature, which promised to be at one and the same time a pleasant feminine pursuit and a public career.

James's death-bed dictation would disclose his Napoleonic fantasies, the megalomania fermenting inside the creator of Roderick Hudson, Christopher Newman (*the* American), and Adam Verver (founder of American City). Also, both writers undoubtedly responded to the great male dream of power and conquest, a dream which became far more compelling in an age of rapid industrial expansion and incredible opportunities. Howells, thinking of himself, well understood the compulsion, the desperation, young men felt to "get ahead.":

> Throughout his later boyhood and into his earlier manhood the youth is always striving away from his home and the things of it. With whatever pain he suffers through the longing for them, he must deny them; he must cleave to the world and the things of it; that is his fate, that is the condition of all achievement and advancement for him. He will be many times ridiculous and sometimes contemptible, he will be mean and selfish upon occasion; but he can scarcely otherwise be a man, the great matter for him is to keep some place in his soul where he shall be ashamed. . . . No man, unless he puts on the mask of fiction, can show his real face or the will behind it.

This remarkable passage says that a boy *must* abandon and violate his home in order to make his way in the world, but that if he is good he will always be ashamed of himself. Meanness, shame, guilt, an inner lack of integrity or simplicity—all of these belong, unavoidably, to the masculine condition. Here one sees the terrible split in Howells, who as a youth experienced both homesickness and ambition and as a man was torn between his parents' altruistic values and the necessary egotism of man's world. The young man couldn't respect himself unless he joined in the "blind struggle" for a place in the world, but the old man found that he couldn't respect himself for having succeeded.

The split in Howells was the condition that made it possible for him to become a realist. He was painfully double, both male and female, and his sexual doubleness gave him an objective perspective on the undeclared war between the sexes, the vast impasse between two opposed systems. At the same time his duplicity was a source of real uncertainty and wavering, and it often made him hypocritical, two-faced, or compromising. It is fitting that he chose the odd word *complicity* as the base of his ethics in the late 1880s.

James, though also trapped between man's world and women's sphere, was different. He never succeeded, as did Howells, in winning manhood as it was understood in the United States. Of course he supported himself, by writing fiction, but he was fired by the New York *Tribune* in his only salaried job; he

never had an editorial position or worked for an organization of any kind; he never married or entered into any kind of stable domestic living arrangements with anybody outside his family, aside from servants; he left his native country; and late in life he admitted to a friend that "the port from which I set out was, I think, that of the essential loneliness of my life."

In spite of all differences, Howells and James were alike in their deep opposition to their culture's central gender roles. Their uncompromisingly competitive, hard-driving men—Caspar Goodwood, Basil Ransom, Bartley Hubbard, Royal Langbrith—are never seen sympathetically. Their idealistic women—Isabel Archer, Olive Chancellor, Florida Vervain, Grace Breen—are apt to be misguided and occasionally destructive. And both writers would be obsessed most of all with the sensitive outsider, male or female, who cannot find a satisfying niche in the social order—Fleda Vetch, Maisie Farange, Lambert Strether, Helen Harkness, Annie Kilburn, Theodore Colville, Lemuel Barker. Howells and James were odd men out, and their realism arose in part from a passionate desire to grasp the system that had excluded them. That is why they became our first critical realists. (pp. 62-4)

After Howells and James exhausted their American material in the 1880s and early 90s, having explored the noble and self-sacrificing woman and the powerful American man to the best of their ability, they were succeeded by a group of writers (superficially called naturalists) who pushed the exploration of American masculinity much farther. Dreiser, Norris, Garland, London, Stephen Crane, Richard Harding Davis, and David Graham Phillips were interested most of all in depicting men under conditions of intense struggle, whether in war, in the capitalist economic system, on the frontier, or anywhere else away from the constraints of female civilization. With these writers, the enormous rift that had opened up in the heart of American life in the early 1800s—the split that made the novel far more feminine than it had ever been before and in effect banished our rough American masculinity from polite fiction—began to close. Women's fiction led to James's and Howells's realism (and in another direction, to the triumphs of local color), and realism led to "naturalism." The split in gender roles had banished the American man from the parlor; two or three generations later, he would be allowed back in. Howells and James, two distinctly unmasculine figures, were the crucial middle men—and the best writers—in this large historical movement. (p. 65)

Alfred Habegger, "Henry James and W. D. Howells as Sissies," in his Gender, Fantasy, and Realism in American Literature, *Columbia University Press, 1982, pp. 56-65.**

KENNETH E. EBLE (essay date 1982)

[*Eble is an American educator who has written several critical works on American literature and edited* Howells: A Century of Criticism *(1962; see Additional Bibliography). In the following excerpt from a recent book-length study of Howells's life and work, he surveys Howells's career, addresses the question of the author's decline in reputation since his death, and assesses his importance to American literature.*]

The loss of wide reader interest in Howells's work after his death and the confinement of his reputation to scholars today is not because he did or did not work in [what he termed] "the right American stuff" or because he wrought in "common, crude material" [see *TCLC*, Vol. 7]. It is more the lack of what James calls "a really *grasping* imagination." James put the matter metaphorically in his preface to *The American:*

> The balloon of experience is in fact of course tied to the earth, and under the necessity we swing, thanks to a rope of remarkable length, in the more or less commodious car of the imagination; but it is by the rope we know where we are, and from the moment that cable is cut we are at large and unrelated; we only swing apart from the globe—though remaining as exhilarated, naturally, as we like, especially when all goes well. The art of the romancer is, "for the fun of it," insidiously to cut the cable, to cut it without our detecting him.

Every reader of James must make the adjustment which goes with relinquishing his grasp on this world and entering into James's special realm. The realm of Howells is earthbound; his fiction seldom soars, and when the reader becomes impatient with finding out what life was like then, he is also likely to become impatient with the questions of personal and social values which are, for Howells and ourselves, a novelist's proper, even primary, concern.

The art of fiction, James wrote, "lives upon exercise, and the very meaning of exercise is freedom. The only obligation to which in advance we may hold a novel, without incurring the accusation of being arbitrary, is that it be interesting." He did not excuse Howells or himself or other realists from this fundamental obligation. "The ways in which it is at liberty to accomplish this result (of interesting us)," he went on, "strike me as innumerable, and such as can only suffer from being marked out or fenced in by prescription." Realism was for Howells something of a prescription, and his novels took on more life and interest in the mid-1880s when social and economic conditions so pressed upon him that he fully enlisted his imagination in peopling a larger canvas to address these issues of conscience and social reality. Howells describes the what and how of writing *A Hazard of New Fortunes,* "the most vital of my fictions," in a preface written twenty years after: "incidents, interests, individualities," got into the novel "which I had not known lay near. . . . the story began to find its way to issues nobler and larger than those of the love-affairs common to fiction. . . . the action passed as nearly without my conscious agency as I ever allow myself to think such things happen." The bulk of Howells's fiction, however, creates the kind of judgment made by a sympathetic critic, Oscar Firkins, and without detecting its implied dispraise: "To write six novels like *The Lady of the Aroostook* was admirable; to have written thirty would have been effeminate."

It is easy to say that Howells's loss of reputation was a result of changes in manners and morals as well as in attitudes toward art taking place in the early twentieth century. Yet his two great American counterparts, James and Twain, did not experience a similar drop from favor, even though each may have retained his hold on a different audience. Howells was very much the man in the middle; to be admired personally because he was able to maintain such a close relationship with two such different literary men; to be thought less of as a writer because, for all his literary presence, his body of fiction did not have the distinctive excellence of either.

Today Howells's work seldom arouses the intemperate responses of earlier critics. It has been given an increasingly respectful attention from academic scholars, and a handful of his novels are being kept before a wider audience in cheap reprints, largely, I suspect, read by college students in American literature classes. Out of the scholarly work devoted to Howells in the last fifty years have come some valuable recognitions: that the transition from nineteenth-century sentimentalism to the modern novel was affected by and revealed in the work of Howells; that Howells's many works accurately disclose much about American manners, tastes, morals, and values in his time and which have not been entirely disavowed by the twentieth century; and that Howells, as limited as he may appear to be, judged by some of his fiction, was an admirable and less narrow man than his earlier critics perceived.

Though it is not often remarked, Howells's reputation may suffer because of the very volume and diversity of his work which resists careful examination except by literary scholars. It can also be observed that the style that Howells's contemporaries found so admirable became more and more distant from modern American prose style. Unlike Mark Twain, he did not arrive at a vernacular which anticipated the great change which separates twentieth-century style from that of the nineteenth. Instead, he continued to write, to some degree, in the literary style of English and American predecessors who first established his sense of fitting literary expression.

As a novelist, Howells wrote at least a half-dozen novels that deserve continuing general readership: *A Modern Instance, The Rise of Silas Lapham, Indian Summer, A Hazard of New Fortunes, The Landlord at Lion's Head,* and *The Leatherwood God.* Other critics might add to or substitute in this list *The Undiscovered Country, Annie Kilburn, The Quality of Mercy,* or *The Son of Royal Langbrith.* The more one extends the list, however, the more one includes novels, like *The Undiscovered Country,* which are only in part successful. If one expands the list, the obvious way is toward including novels *of a kind,* novels that illustrate specific intentions on Howells's part and which are the best representatives of other similar novels. *The Lady of the Aroostook* is such a book, illustrative of the early novels of courting and marriage, as *The Shadow of a Dream* is illustrative of Howells's interest in the psychological novel; *New Leaf Mills* is representative of works which transmute personal experience into fiction.

The distance between Howells's best novels and his poorest is great. Most of the latter were written to meet contractual obligations and most rely upon some kind of innocuous love story. Yet he is not merely the writer of one stunning work, but of a sufficient variety of estimable works to mark him as a major novelist. Clearly, he is to be recognized for his contributions to the novel of manners. Moreover, he is the most prolific and forceful American novelist of the nineteenth century to turn the novel toward the examination of social and economic issues. In addition, he manifests an interest second only to that of Henry James in developing the novel in technical ways. Though he does not dwell upon theories of fiction in his criticism, it is clear from his work that he helped move the novel in at least three directions: one, from the small, focused character study to novels embracing a variety of representative types perceived within a complex social milieu; two, away from the dominance of an authorial voice toward the presentation of a story in an objective manner through adopting various devices of point of view; and three, away from the conventions of accepted behavior toward an examination of individual motivation and choice characterized by the psychological novel.

As a critic, Howells had more influence on American readers than any other person of his time, and this despite his avowed disaffection for criticism. Cady adds up his contributions to criticism: publication in sixty-four periodicals and nineteen newspapers; eight periodical columns, mainly literary reviews and commentary; seven volumes of criticism; and more than forty prefaces to other authors' books; altogether "substantially more than one, perhaps as much as two million of words in reviews and literary comment—virtually all of it, as was his habit, somehow contributions to criticism." Cady affirms . . . the immense knowledge of language and literature that Howells brought to his criticism. By virtue of that knowledge, he helped sophisticate both the practices of writers and the responses of readers. Though the succeeding generation saw Howells as a defender of outmoded conventions and values, his position as critic in his own time was firmly with those who rejected not only romantic sentimentality but the Emersonian idealism which embodied a moralism more constricting by far than Howells's own moral bent. Currently, Howells may be at more odds with criticism than at any other time, for his criticism was never narrowly literary nor highly theoretical. As Cady has put it: "Howells believed in the culture critic, the man of letters intent upon elevating the customs, refining the language, clarifying the motives, helping to raise the quality of the life of the people" [see excerpt dated 1973].

Many American writers have been good travel writers, whether describing the American scene or places abroad. Howells deserves a high place among them. His travel volumes, like his criticism, had the purpose of widening his audience's acquaintance with European as well as American culture. *Venetian Life* and *Tuscan Cities,* for all that they were early works and are now over a century old, are still useful and pleasing literary works: Although none of his works on England is as original a work as Emerson's *English Traits,* all are more than the conventional travel book.

As for Howells as a writer of poetry and short fiction, little can be said. [There is evidenced] a growth in his poetry, both in technique and in substance, but it is growth still within the conventions of nineteenth-century poetry and within what might be expected of one growing older. Most of Howells's short fiction was written after 1895, and probably he found the one-act farce a more congenial form of short work. (His only collection of early short fiction is *A Fearful Responsibility and Other Stories* . . . ; the two other stories are **"Tonelli's Marriage,"** written during his Venetian years, and **"At the Sign of the Savage,"** first published in 1877.) His short fiction of his later years does reflect some of his more serious concerns, though it does not show much greater mastery of technique. No one could collect a volume of Howells's short stories or his poetry and present it as a distinguished example of the form. (pp. 181-85)

To the number and variety of plays Howells wrote should be added the many essays which show his continuing interest in drama, playwrights, and the theater. **"Recent Italian Comedy,"** in 1864, helped establish him as a critic, and his defense of Ibsen and his pointing out that "Mr. Shaw is the comic analogue of the tragic Ibsen," are discerning acts of criticism at a later period. Nevertheless, his playwriting and criticism are minor achievements, even in an age that provided little support for serious American drama. The short comic plays that Howells fashioned were virtually limited to private theatricals.

When all allowances are made, and for all his sustained interest in drama, Howells cannot be brought forth as a dramatist of great skill. Walter Meserve's guarded praise says about as

much as can be said: that his successes in the theater were few, that he had definite limitations as a dramatist, and that his plays only become significant in the rise of realism and in the development of American social comedy [see *TCLC,* Vol. 7].

The variety of writing Howells accomplished year by year would, in itself, earn him the title "man of letters," but his reviews and essays show a variety of interests beyond the literary. Picking at random a two-year span of writing in "The Editor's Study," 1885 to 1887, I find him touching upon Louis Agassiz, Napoleon, the Crusades, Japanese homes, Berlioz, Arctic exploration, history of California and Norway, English aristocracy, Dolly Madison, Socrates, tramps, the Russian church, and Horatio Greenough. To be sure, a reviewer faces possibilities of this sort with every week's crop of books, but few reviewers embrace such a wide selection. (pp. 186-87)

The range of Howells's immense productivity and the influence it exercised are reason enough for continuing to recognize his importance. Until the 1960s, social realism as advocated and practised by Howells was the prevailing mode in American fiction. Even such an idiosyncratic novelist as Faulkner pursued that course within his preferred locale of Yoknapatawpha county. Faulkner's work is as critical of the social order of the South as Howells's was of Boston, and the moral concerns which underlay Howells's social criticism are present, and of the same kind, in Faulkner. Moreover, the fact that Howells's writing life stretched over the period between the Civil War and World War I makes his work, fiction and nonfiction, essential to an understanding of American literature and the culture from which it came during this long period.

Howells is likely to retain his curious standing in American and English literary scholarship. Within American literature, he is to be regarded as a major author, though not as likely to be read as James, Twain, Hawthorne, or Melville, to mention our chief nineteenth-century fiction writers. Within the larger body of literature in English, he probably occupies a lesser position than that of George Eliot, perhaps somewhat higher than that of Trollope. (pp. 187-88)

New writers replace old writers, and though old writers do not altogether disappear, they survive, if they survive at all, by the presence of works which somehow transcend the time in which they were written. The greatest of writers become part of a culture, and even defy American culture's ability to wear everything out at an increasing rate or to discard it for temporary or permanent oblivion. Howells's works, though some will continue to be read, are not likely to become a common cultural possession. (p. 190)

Howells's general recognition today comes in part because of his identity with Mark Twain and Henry James, and it comes in part from a vague recognition that there was such a writer as Howells who wrote a great many books and who was a literary figure of some importance back then. As that importance can be defined, it probably gets defined in terms of some kind of fussy morality, concern for the common folk, and a strange fear of sex. Though Howells scholars are prone to resent such simple and inaccurate identifications, they might better be grateful for them, for it is in such peculiarities that Howells may continue to exist at all as a literary figure. The nineteenth century cannot be quite detached from the twentieth, though it seems to be even more remote from twentieth-century consciousness than the pre-Civil War decades or even the age of the American revolution. We may, symbolically and actually, find our grandparents more interesting, certainly more benevolent and understanding, than our parents. We find our great-great relatives sufficiently mysterious to arouse curiosity that leads to finding out about them. And though Howells by now, measured by the actual time of generations, is more than a grandfather, he still, it seems to me, is close enough to us to be father of us all. Though we grant him the importance necessary to that which produced us, we are yet reserved in both the respect and the understanding given him. (p. 192)

> *Kenneth E. Eble, in his* William Dean Howells, *second edition, Twayne Publishers, 1982, 225 p.*

GORE VIDAL (essay date 1983)

[*The author of such works as* Visit to a Small Planet *(1956),* Myra Breckenridge *(1968),* Burr *(1973), and* Lincoln *(1984), Vidal is an American novelist, short story writer, dramatist, and essayist. He is particularly noted for his historical novels and his iconoclastic essays. In his work Vidal examines the plight of modern humanity as it exists in a valueless world and amid the world's corrupt institutions. Vidal's work in all genres is marked by his urbane wit and brilliant technique. He has written: "I have been a student of Petronius and Apuleius, Peacock and Meredith, as well as that grand but unpopular line which amuses itself with ideas and wit, with an irreverence for whatever 'truths and verities' are currently regnant. I detest dogma. I believe it possible, mandatory, to function without absolutes: to realize simultaneously that though life is human relationships, splendid in human terms, all our games, nonetheless, are essentially irrelevant. I suspect it is this double sense which I have tried most to communicate: the 'yes' at the center of the 'no'." In the following excerpt, Vidal discusses* A Foregone Conclusion, A Modern Instance, The Rise of Silas Lapham, *and* Indian Summer: *four novels collected in The Library of America's edition of Howells's most notable work,* Novels, 1875-1886.]

Howells, a master of irony, would no doubt have found ironic in the extreme his subsequent reputation as a synonym for middlebrow pusillanimity. After all, it was he who was the spiritual father of Dreiser (whom he did nothing for, curiously enough) and of Stephen Crane and Harold Frederic and Frank Norris, for whom he did a very great deal. He managed to be the friend and confidant of both Henry James and Mark Twain, quite a trick. He himself wrote a half-dozen of the Republic's best novels. He was learned, witty, and generous.

Howells lived far too long. Not long before his death at the age of eighty-four, he wrote his old friend Henry James: "I am comparatively a dead cult with my statues cut down and the grass growing over me in the pale moonlight." By then he had been dismissed by the likes of Sinclair Lewis as a dully beaming happy writer [see *TCLC,* Vol. 7]. But then Lewis knew as little of American literary near-past as today's writers know, say, of Lewis. If Lewis had read Howells at all, he would have detected in the work of this American realist a darkness sufficiently sable for even the most lost-and-found of literary generations or, as Howells wrote James two years after the Haymarket Square riots: "After fifty years of optimistic content with 'civilization' and its ability to come out all right in the end, I now abhor it, and feel that it is coming out all wrong in the end unless it bases itself on a real equality." What that last phrase means is anyone's guess. He is a spiritual rather than a practical socialist. It is interesting that the letter was written in the same year that Bellamy's *Looking Backward* was published. The ideas of Robert Owen that Howells had absorbed from his father (later a Swedenborgian like Henry James, Sr.) were now commingled with the theories of Henry George, the tracts of William Morris, and, always, Tolstoy.

Howells thought that there must be a path through the political jungle of a republic that had just hanged four men for their opinions; he never found it. But as a novelist he was making a path for himself and for others, and he called it realism. (p. 46)

The Library of America now brings us four of Howells's novels written between 1875 and 1886. . . .

Of the books written before *A Foregone Conclusion* (the first of the four now reissued [in *Novels, 1875-1886*]), the ever-polite but never fraudulent Turgenev wrote Howells in 1874:

> Accept my best thanks for the gracious gift of your delightful book *Their Wedding Journey,* which I have read with the same pleasure experienced before in reading *A Chance Acquaintance* and *Venetian Life.* Your literary physiognomy is a most sympathetic one; it is natural, simple and clear—and in the same time—it is full of unobtrusive poetry and fine humor. Then—I feel the peculiar American stamp on it—and that is not one of the least causes of my relishing so much your works. . . .

Unfortunately, Turgenev never lived to read the later books. It would be interesting to see what he might have made of *A Modern Instance,* a book as dark and, at times, as melodramatic as a novel by Zola, whose *L'Assommoir* Turgenev disliked. (p. 50)

[*A Foregone Conclusion*] has, as protagonist, the . . . American consul at Venice. The consul is a painter (young writers almost always make their protagonists artists who practice the one art that they themselves know nothing about: It's the light, you see, in Cimabue). The consul attracts a young priest, Don Ippolito, who wants to emigrate to America and become an inventor. It is no accident that practically the first building in Washington to be completed in imperial marble splendor was the Patent Office. Don Ippolito is a sort of Italian Major Hoople. The inventions don't really work but he keeps on because "Heaven only knows what kind of inventor's Utopia our poor, patent-ridden country appeared to him in those dreams of his, and I can but dimly figure it to myself." Here the auctorial "I" masquerades as the "I" of the consul, Ferris, who is otherwise presented in the objective third person. Howells has not entirely learned Turgenev's lesson: stay out of the narrative. Let the characters move the narration and the reader. Howells's native American garrulousness—and tendentiousness—occasionally breaks in.

Enter, inexorably, middle-aged American lady and daughter—Mrs. Vervain and Florida. This was four years before Howells's friend sicked *Daisy Miller* onto a ravished world. But then The American Girl was to be a Howells theme, just as it was to be James's and, later, and in a much tougher way, Mrs. Wharton's. As every writer then knew, the readers of novels were mostly women; and they liked to read about the vicissitudes of young women, preferably ladies. But while James would eventually transmute his American girls into something that Euripides himself might find homely (e.g., Maggie Verver), Howells tends, gently, to mock. Incidentally, I do not believe that it has ever before been noted that the portrait of Florida is uncannily like Kate Chase.

It is a foregone conclusion that American girl and American mother ("the most extraordinary combination of perfect fool and perfect lady, I ever saw") will miss the point to Don

Ippolito and Venice and Europe, and that he will miss the point to them. Don Ippolito falls in love with Florida. The Americans are horrified. How can a priest sworn to celibacy. . .? Since they are Protestants, the enormity of his fall from Roman Catholic grace is all the greater. Although Don Ippolito is perfectly happy to give up the church, they will not let him. Mother and daughter flee. As for Ferris, he has misunderstood not only Don Ippolito but Florida's response to him. Don Ippolito dies—with the comment to Ferris, "You would never see me as I was."

The consul goes home to the States and joins the army. Like so many other characters in the works of those writers who managed to stay out of the Civil War, Ferris has a splendid war: "Ferris's regiment was sent to a part of the southwest where he saw a good deal of fighting and fever and ague" (probably a lot easier than trying to get a job at the *Atlantic*). "At the end of two years, spent alternately in the field and the hospital, he was riding out near the camp one morning in unusual spirits, when two men in butternut fired at him: one had the mortification to miss him; the bullet of the other struck him in the arm. There was talk of amputation at first. . . ." Pre-dictaphone and word processor, it was every writer's nightmare that he lose his writing arm. But, worse, Ferris is a painter: *he can never crosshatch again.* Broke, at a loose end, he shows an old picture at an exhibition. Florida sees the picture. They are reunited. Mrs. Vervain is dead. Florida is rich. Ferris is poor. What is to be done?

It is here that the avant-garde realism of Howells shoves forward the whole art of the popular American novel: "It was fortunate for Ferris, since he could not work, that she had money; in exalted moments he had thought this a barrier to their marriage; yet he could not recall anyone who had refused the hand of a beautiful girl because of the accident of her wealth, and in the end, he silenced his scruples." This is highly satisfying.

Then Howells, perhaps a bit nervous at just how far he has gone in the direction of realism, tosses a bone of, as it were, marzipan to the lady-reader: "It might be said that in many other ways he was not her equal; but one ought to reflect how very few men are worthy of their wives in any sense." Sighs of relief from many a hammock and boudoir! How well he knows the human heart.

Howells smiles at the end; but the smile is aslant, while the point to the tragedy (not Ferris's, for he had none, but that of Don Ippolito) is that, during the subsequent years of Ferris's marriage, Don Ippolito "has at last ceased to be even the memory of a man with a passionate love and a mortal sorrow. Perhaps this final effect in the mind of him who has realized the happiness of which the poor priest vainly dreamed is not the least tragic phase of the tragedy of Don Ippolito."

This coda is unexpectedly harsh: and not at all smiling. A priest ought not to fall in love. It is a foregone conclusion that if you violate the rules governing sexuality, society will get you, as Mrs. Wharton would demonstrate so much more subtly in *The Age of Innocence;* and Henry James would subtly deny since he knew, in a way that Howells did not, that the forbidden cake could be both safely eaten and kept. It is an odd irony that the donnée on which James based *The Ambassadors* was a remark that the fifty-seven-year-old Howells made to a friend in Paris: No matter what, one ought to have one's life; that it was too late for him, personally, but for someone young. . . . "Don't, at any rate, make *my* mistake," Howells said. "Live!"

Kenneth S. Lynn has put the case, persuasively to my mind, that the "happy endings" of so many of Howells's novels are deliberately "hollow" or ironic. After all, it was Howells who had fashioned the, to Edith Wharton, "lapidary phrase": Americans want tragedies with happy endings. There are times when Howells's conclusions—let's end with a marriage and live happily ever after—carry more formidable weight than the sometimes too-lacquered tragic codas of James: "We shall never be again as we were." The fact is that people are almost always exactly as they were; and they will be so again and again, given half a chance.

At forty-four, the highly experienced man of letters began his most ambitious novel, *A Modern Instance.* Although the story starts in a New England village, the drama is acted out in the Boston of Howells's professional life, and the very unusual protagonist is a newspaperman on the make who charms everyone and hoodwinks a few; he also puts on too much weight, steals another man's story, makes suffer the innocent young village heiress whom he marries. In a sense, Howells is sending himself up; or some dark side of himself. Although Bartley Hubbard is nowhere in Howells's class as a writer, much less standard-bearer for Western civilization, he is a man who gets what he wants through personal charm, hard work, and the ability to write recklessly and scandalously for newspapers in a way that the young William Randolph Hearst would capitalize

Howells and his close friend, Samuel L. Clemens (Mark Twain), 1909.

on at century's end, thus making possible today's antipodean "popular" press, currently best exemplified by London's giggly newspapers.

Unlike Howells, or the Howells that we think we know, Bartley is sexually active; he is not about to make the Howells-Strether mistake. He *lives;* until he is murdered by a man whom he may have libeled in a western newspaper. It would have been more convincing if an angry husband had been responsible for doing him in, but there were conventions that Howells felt obliged to observe, as his detractors, among them Leslie Fiedler, like to remind us. (pp. 50-2)

Whatever our romantic critics may say, Bartley Hubbard is an archetypal American figure, caught for the first time by Howells: the amiable, easygoing bastard, who thinks nothing of taking what belongs to another. Certainly Mark Twain experienced the shock of recognition when he read the book: "You didn't intend Bartley for me but he *is* me just the same. . . ." James, more literary, thought the character derived from Tito, in the one (to me) close-to-bad novel of George Eliot, *Romola.* In later years Howells said that he himself was the model. Who was what makes no difference. There is only one Bartley Hubbard, and he appears for the first time in the pages of a remarkable novel that opened the way to Dreiser and to all those other realists who were to see the United States plain. The fact that there are no overt sexual scenes in Howells ("no palpitating divans," as he put it) does not mean that sexual passion is not a powerful motor to many of the situations, as in life. On the other hand, the fact that there are other motors—ambition, greed, love of power, simply extend the author's range and make him more interesting to read than most writers.

In this novel, Howells is interesting on the rise of journalism as a "serious" occupation. "There had not yet begun to be that talk of journalism as a profession which has since prevailed with our collegians. . . ." There is also a crucial drunk scene in which Bartley blots his copybook with Boston; not to mention with his wife. It is curious how often Howells shows a protagonist who gets disastrously drunk, and starts then to fall. Mark Twain had a dark suspicion that Howells always had *him* in mind when he wrote these scenes. But for Mr. Fiedler, "drunkenness is used as a chief symbol for the husband's betrayal of the wife." Arguably, it would have been better (and certainly more manly) if Bartley had corn-holed the Irish maid in full view of wife and child, but would a scene so powerful, even *existential,* add in any way to the delicate moral balances that Howells is trying to make?

After all, Howells is illuminating a new character in American fiction, if not life, who, as "he wrote more than ever in the paper, . . . discovered in himself that dual life, of which every one who sins or sorrows is sooner or later aware: that strange separation of the intellectual activity from the suffering of the soul, by which the mind toils on in a sort of ironical indifference to the pangs that wring the heart; the realization that in some ways his brain can get on perfectly well without his conscience." This is worthy of the author of *The Sentimental Education*; it is also the kind of insight about post-Christian man that Flaubert so often adverted to, indirectly, in his own novels and head-on in his letters. (pp. 52-3)

[*The Rise of Silas Lapham*] begins with Bartley Hubbard brought back to life. It is, obviously, some years earlier than the end of *A Modern Instance.* Bartley is interviewing a self-made man called Silas Lapham who has made a fortune out of paint. Lapham is the familiar diamond in the rough, New England

Jonathan-style. He has two pretty daughters, a sensible wife, a comfortable house; and a growing fortune, faced with all the usual hazards. Howells makes the paint business quite as interesting as Balzac made paper making. This is not entirely a full-hearted compliment to either; nevertheless, each is a novelist fascinated by the way the real world works; and each makes it interesting to read about.

In a sense, Silas Lapham's rise is not unlike that of William Dean Howells: from a small town to Boston back street to Beacon Street on the Back Bay. But en route to the great address there are many lesser houses and Howells is at his best when he goes house hunting—and building. In fact, one suspects that, like Edith Wharton later, he would have made a splendid architect and interior decorator. In a fine comic scene, a tactful architect (plainly the author himself) guides Lapham to Good Taste. "'Of course,' resumed the architect, 'I know there has been a great craze for black walnut. But it's an ugly wood. . . .'" All over the United States there must have been feminine gasps as stricken eyes were raised from the page to focus on the middle distance where quantities of once-beauteous black shone dully by gaslight; but worse was to come: ". . . and for a drawing room there is really nothing like white paint. We should want to introduce a little gold here and there. Perhaps we might run a painted frieze round under the cornice—garlands of roses on a gold ground; it would tell wonderfully in a white room." From that moment on, no more was black walnut seen again in the parlors of the Republic, while the sale of white soared; gold, too.

The rise of Lapham's house on Beacon Hill is, in a sense, the plot of the book, as well as the obvious symbol of worldly success. Howells makes us see and feel and smell the house as it slowly takes shape. Simultaneously, a young man called Tom Corey wants to work for Lapham. Since Corey belongs to the old patriciate, Lapham finds it hard to believe Corey is serious. But the young man is sincere; he really likes the old man. He must also work to live. There are romantic exchanges between him and the two daughters; there is an amiable mix-up. Finally, Tom says that it is Penelope not her sister whom he wants to marry. Mr. and Mrs. Lapham are bemused. In the world of the Coreys they are a proto-Maggie and Jiggs couple.

Corey takes Lapham to a grand dinner party where the old man gets drunk and chats rather too much. It is the same scene, in a sense, as Bartley's fall in the earlier novel but where Bartley could not have minded less the impression he made, Lapham is deeply humiliated; and the fall begins. He loses his money; the new house burns down; by then, the house is an even more poignant character than Lapham, and the reader mourns the white and gold drawing room gone to ash. But there is a happy enough ending. Maggie and Jiggs go back to the Vermont village of their origin (which they should never have left?) while Corey marries Penelope. . . . The young couple move from Boston.

Then Howells shifts from the specific to the general:

> It is certain that our manners and customs go for more in life than our qualities. The price that we pay for civilization is the fine yet impassable differentiation of these. Perhaps we pay too much; but it will not be possible to persuade those who have the difference in their favor that this is so. They may be right; and at any rate the blank misgiving, the recurring sense of disappointment to which the young people's

departure left the Coreys is to be considered. That was the end of their son and brother for them; they felt that; and they were not mean or unamiable people.

This strikes me as a subtle and wise reading of the world— no, not *a* world but *the* world; and quite the equal of James or Hardy. (p. 53)

Civilization was very much on Howells's mind when he came to write *Indian Summer*. . . . He deals, once more, with Americans in Italy. But this time there are no Don Ippolitos. The principals are all Americans in Florence. A middle-aged man, Theodore Colville, meets, again, Mrs. Bowen, a lady who once did not marry him when he wanted to marry her. She married a congressman. She has a young daughter, Effie. She is a widow. (p. 54)

Mrs. Bowen has a beautiful young friend named Imogene. Colville decides that he is in love with Imogene; and they drift toward marriage. There are numerous misunderstandings. Finally, it is Mrs. Bowen not Imogene who is in love with Colville. The drama of the three of them (a shadowy young clergyman named Morton is an undelineated fourth) is rendered beautifully. There are many unanticipated turns to what could easily have been a simple-minded romantic novella.

When Colville is confronted with the thought of his own great age (forty-one), he is told by a very old American expatriate:

> At forty, one has still a great part of youth before him—perhaps the richest and sweetest part. By that time the turmoil of ideas and sensations is over; we see clearly and feel consciously. We are in a sort of quiet in which we peacefully enjoy. We have enlarged our perspective sufficiently to perceive things in their true proportion and relation; we are no longer tormented with the lurking fear of death, which darkens and imbitters our earlier years; we have got into the habit of life; we have often been ailing and we have not died. . . .

Finally, "we are put into the world to be of it." Thus, Howells strikes the Tolstoyan note. Yes, he is also smiling. But even as *Indian Summer* was being published, its author was attacking the state of Illinois for the murder of four workmen. He also sends himself up in the pages of his own novel. A Mrs. Amsden finds Colville and Imogene and Effie together after an emotional storm. Mrs. Amsden remarks that they form an interesting, even dramatic group:

> "Oh, call us a passage from a modern novel," suggested Colville, "if you're in a romantic mood. One of Mr. James's."
>
> "Don't you think we ought to be rather more of the great world for that? I hardly feel up to Mr. James. I should have said Mr. Howells. Only nothing happens in that case."

For this beguiling modesty Howells no doubt dug even deeper the grave for his reputation. How can an American novelist who is ironic about himself ever be great? In a nation that has developed to a high art advertising, the creator who refuses to advertise himself is immediately suspected of having no product worth selling. Actually, Howells is fascinated with the interior drama of his characters, and quite a lot happens—to

the reader as well as to the characters who are, finally, suitably paired: Imogene and Mr. Morton, Colville and Mrs. Bowen.

The Library of America has served William Dean Howells well. (pp. 54-5)

For those who are obliged for career reasons to read Howells, this is a useful book. For those who are still able to read novels for pleasure, this is a marvelous book. (p. 55)

Gore Vidal, "'The Peculiar American Stamp'," in The New York Review of Books, Vol. XXX, No. 16, October 27, 1983, pp. 45-7, 50-5.

ELLEN F. WRIGHT (essay date 1983)

[*In the following excerpt, Wright examines a number of Howells's novels to uncover the author's frequent sympathetic portrayal of such "irrational" qualities as sentimentality, impulsiveness, and romantic reverie, a sympathy that many early twentieth-century critics failed to perceive in a writer they had labeled unimaginative and dull.*]

The generally prevailing view of Howells as a complacent writer devoted to the ordered and boringly reasonable has of late increasingly come under critical fire. More and more scholars, taking issue with the accepted view, have noted that Howells exhibits a strong, albeit sporadic, interest in the darkly mysterious or irrational side of human nature. They have pointed to characters who suffer psychological or sexual turmoil, show signs of an almost modernist angst or alienation, become involved with the disquietingly spiritualistic, or demonstrate either demonic or mythic dimensions. I would like to add to this body of criticism by calling attention to Howells's emphasis on a different kind of human irrationality, an irrationality which, if less dramatic, is perhaps more pervasive. This is the irrationality which Howells repeatedly describes in his ordinary characters, his normal, nonmythic, nonalienated, nonpsychologically tortured characters. It is an irrationality which has to do with sentiment, with impulsiveness, with whimsy, and with poetry. Not only does Howells focus on these qualities, but he seems to do so in order to approve of them, in order to argue that this kind of gentle irrationality is an essential and desirable part of the human personality. A sensitivity to this approval of the irrational can allow us to evaluate better the artistry of some of Howells's novels, as well as to provide support for the growing consensus that Howells was by no means simply an apologist for the tediously commonsensical.

From the start of his career, Howells praised sentiment in his characters. As they travel in *Their Wedding Journey*, Isabel and Basil March continually sentimentalize the places and the people they encounter. So, for example, they imaginatively construct "villas and castles and palaces upon all . . . eligible building sites," they turn a man with a sensitive face into the author of a rejected manuscript, and they speculate dreamily on the histories, personalities, and motivations of the early inhabitants of a Canadian convent. The narrator's attitude to all this is accepting: "I do not defend the feeble sentimentality,—call it wickedness if you like,—but I understand it, and I forgive it from my soul." . . . Kitty Ellison in *A Chance Acquaintance* is another character who has this faculty of imagining other people's lives and of using real life as the starting point for the whimsical construction of elaborate romantic stories. It is, in fact, partially on the basis of her lively imagination that readers judge her to be so much more appealing than her suitor, the stiff Bostonian Miles Arbuton.

These, of course, are early novels, but in his later works Howells continues to praise the sentimental and "unreasonable." . . . A philosophical conversation in another late work, *The Vacation of the Kelwyns*, focuses explicitly on the matter. Professor Kelwyn says: "I suppose we should agree that sentimentality is always to be avoided." But his friend does not agree—"Why, I'm not sure—yet." The debate seems to reverberate throughout the novel. The sentimentality can be associated with what is continually termed the characters' "impulsiveness." This impulsiveness leads to acts which are generally regarded by the perpetrators as regrettable failures of control. But by Howells, by other characters in the novel, and by the reader they are regarded as spontaneous effusions of good nature breaking through the constricting rules of our overrational civilization. So, for instance, we come to regard as endearing, if sentimental, Elihu Emerance's outburst in the schoolroom and Parthenope Brook's reckless efforts to help an ailing trained bear.

The Marches and Kitty, as well as the characters in *The Vacation of the Kelwyns*, indulge in their whimsical romanticizations and actions more or less knowingly. This irrationality is but one facet of their personalities; if necessary it could be controlled. But Howells also creates other characters who are less balanced, who exist almost solely as representations of irrational traits. And, once more, he is surprisingly appreciative of these characters. (Again, I am speaking not of the almost mythic characters, the Dylkses of *The Leatherwood God* and the Jeff Durgins of *The Landlord at Lion's Head*, but of less violently dramatic characters and character types.) For instance, *New Leaf Mills*, an autobiographical novel, features a hopelessly idealistic father (a man similar to Howells's own father). But though this man is responsible for the precariousness of his family's existence, the novel concludes by affirming him. He is important to the community because, by remaining true to his ideals, he manages to keep his neighbors from taking the law into their own hands. And he is important to his family because, as the reader becomes increasingly aware, he contributes to the marriage a poetry and a love of the spiritual which enhance the lives of all the family members.

An even more problematic parent is the irresponsible mother of *The World of Chance*. But she too escapes Howells's condemnation. Mrs. Denton is frivolous, as the hero of the novel admits, but there is something delightful in her frivolity. Her father concurs to the extent of favoring her over his other daughter, who is far more noble and virtuous. A similar judgment about a character whom we might be inclined to malign is made in the novel *Mrs. Farrell*. The titular heroine has gone through the novel practicing deception after deception to attract and manipulate her admirers. At the conclusion, as so often happens in Howells, a married couple comments on the action. Mrs. Gilbert remarks of Mrs. Farrell that "a whole lifetime would not be enough to atone for what she's done." But Mr. Gilbert disagrees: "you have to make some allowances for human nature. I had no idea she was so charming."

It does not make sense that the poetic thinking of an impractical husband, the frivolity of a Mrs. Denton, and the charm of a Mrs. Farrell should add so much to life. But Howells realizes that they do. The most obvious irrationality in life which should not make sense but does, however, is that element of the romance or romantic novel that is acknowledged by the use of the word "romance" to describe a love affair. Romance in that sense is the topic which Howells deals with repeatedly. And what he stresses repeatedly is the irrationality of love.

There is something which pulls lovers together: Louise Maxwell in *The Story of a Play* calls it "volition."

Perhaps Howells's fullest exposition of the irrationality, inevitability, and desirability of romance occurs in the Isabel and Basil March novels. The Marches at the beginning of their marriage, meditate on their relationship:

> So the old marvel was wondered over anew, till it filled the world in which there was room for nothing but the strangeness that they should have loved each other so long and not made it known, that they should ever have uttered it, and that, being uttered, it should be so much more and better than ever could have been dreamed. The broken engagement was a fable of disaster that only made their present fortune more prosperous. The city ceased about them, and they walked on up the street, the first man and first woman in the garden of the new-made earth.

The Marches are older in *An Open-Eyed Conspiracy* and more sophisticated. But romance is still important to them. As Basil observes of their interest in young lovers: "It is curious . . . how we let this idiotic love-passion absorb us to the very last. It is wholly unimportant who marries who, or whether anybody marries at all. And yet we no sooner have the making of a love-affair within reach than we revert to the folly of our own youth, and abandon ourselves to it as if it were one of the great interests of life." In *Their Silver Wedding Journey*, after Basil makes similar sardonic remarks, the Marches laugh together "and then they laugh again to perceive that they were walking arm in arm too, like the lovers, whom they were insensibly following." Romance wins. Though older and wiser, the Marches are following and duplicating the young lovers' movements (the "idiotic love-passion," the "folly"), not only physically but also emotionally.

Two critical commonplaces—that Howells firmly condemned the sentimental self-sacrifice and the romantic revery—might seem to argue against this picture of Howells as a proponent of the irrational. Careful examination of these motifs in several of the novels, however, suggests that this is perhaps not so, that the critical commonplaces may themselves need modifying.

Self-sacrifice in Howells is especially complicated. Critics have noted that Howells does not automatically surround self-sacrifice with its traditional aura of affirmation. Indeed, he often shows acts of renunciation as quixotic and impractical. But we should not, I would caution, necessarily conclude that Howells disapproves of these sacrifices or the impulses which prompt them. For example, in *The Quality of Mercy* Sue Northwick sells her house to pay back the company from which her father has embezzled money, even though there is no legal compulsion to do so. In *A Woman's Reason* Helen Harkness makes a similar magnanimous gesture, and then rejects dependency on her wealthy friends for a life of hard work and ill health, but financial self-sufficiency, among the lower classes. Though the sacrifices of the heroines may be quixotic, they are also clearly noble; the women are praised by the other characters for their actions. Helen's self-sacrifice is elevated further by its association with the unquestionably heroic sacrifice her lover is making at the same time.

With some novels we can tell that Howells approves of the self-sacrifice because it becomes an integral part of the thematic statement. In *The Minister's Charge*, for instance, Lemuel Barker, fresh from the country, has become heavily involved with a girl, Statira Dudley, who is beneath him in intellectual capabilities and aspirations. He then meets and falls in love with the elegant, artistic Miss Carver. The minister of the title, the Reverend David Sewell, advises Lemuel against sacrificing himself and Miss Carver for a union with Statira, a union that would probably eventually make everyone unhappy. But Lemuel rejects Sewell's reasonable, pragmatic advice. And we applaud both his and Miss Carver's decisions to think of something besides their own private happiness. What we are approving, of course, is the sacrificing lovers' realization of the major theme running throughout the novel, Howells's doctrine of complicity, the idea that each individual's actions have an effect on society as a whole.

So, though self-sacrifice in Howells may seem to be irrational and sentimental, as often as not it works to gain sympathy and respect for the sacrificers. And while Howells's critical writings contain passages condemning egocentric self-sacrifice, they also contain passages explicitly praising altruistic self-sacrifice. For example, Howells heartily commends one author for "establish[ing] his system of ethics on the grounds of self-sacrifice." He extols another for teaching "self-renunciation, so hard to learn, so insistent in the human heart, so cogent in the human reason, the only sufficient and final and eternal answer to fate."

The situation with regard to the revery is somewhat similar. A number of critics have argued that Howells is suspicious of, if not downright hostile to, his characters' daydreaming. It is true that some of these reveries, like the adolescent Boyne Kenton's fantasy of a relationship with the Queen of Holland (*The Kentons*), lead to comic or not so comic disasters and arguably need to be expunged by heavy doses of reality. But again that is not the whole story of revery in Howells.

Some reveries, for example, definitely help the characters. In *A Woman's Reason*, Helen, impoverished and left alone after her lover is lost at sea, has the strength to live on because she has reveries of triumphing in each of the professions she takes up to support herself. In *A Modern Instance*, Marcia Hubbard has the will to survive the first months after Bartley's desertion because she so intensely believes in her ridiculous theories about his disappearance. And when *Ragged Lady's* Clementina Claxon is languishing for lack of word from her lover, "her fond reveries," Howells tells us, "helped her to bear her suspense; they helped to make the days go by, to ease the doubt with which she lay down at night, and the heartsick hope with which she rose up in the morning."

Other reveries, while having no such practical effect on the characters' histories, have the tone of Howells's approval, since their main function appears to be to make some of his outwardly sterner characters seem more vulnerable, more appealing. For example, Ellen Kenton possesses such a "morbid" sense of duty that she is, as her sister says, something of a "crank." But when she falls in love with the fine young man Hugh Breckon, she has charmingly poignant reveries about his possible reactions should he learn of her past connection with the ignoble Clarence Bittridge: "Sometimes [Breckon] mournfully left her . . . , left her forever, and sometimes he . . . remained with her in a sublime kindness, a noble amity, lofty and serene, which did not seek to become anything else." In *Dr. Breen's Practice*, Grace Breen has a "proud soul" and a "severe morality." But she also has reveries as touching as Ellen Kenton's. And Howells apparently condones them when he remarks that

"she was behaving as wisely as a young physician of the other sex would have done in the circumstances." (Indeed, Howells's "young physician of the other sex" in *An Imperative Duty* has the same sort of reveries.) These lovers' reveries result in no particular good nor in any permanent harm. But the characters gain sympathy because the reveries reveal a romantic, emotional side to their personalities. In *Annie Kilburn*, the Reverend Julius W. Peck is criticized for being "a man without an illusion, without an emotion."

Howells, incidentally, admits to indulging in revery himself. He speaks of the time when he was a young boy working as a compositor: "A definite literary ambition grew up in me, and in the long reveries of the afternoon, when I was distributing my case, I fashioned a future of overpowering magnificence and undying celebrity. I should be ashamed to say what literary triumphs I achieved in those preposterous deliriums." Ashamed because it is polite to say so, perhaps, but Howells does not in fact sound very ashamed of these youthful fantasies, and he did scale some rather impressive heights, an achievement which may have been possible only because of the "preposterous deliriums." When he was well beyond the compositor stage, Howells was still having reveries. Just after the completion of *The Parlor Car,* for instance, he wrote to a friend, "Managers are already (in my imagination) competing for it."

In short, there is considerable evidence that Howells approves of his characters' imaginative reveries and of their desires for idealistic self-sacrifice. This approval together with Howells's condoning attitudes toward sentiment, impulsiveness, frivolity, and romance suggest that he is much more appreciative of the irrational and illogical than has been generally recognized. (pp. 304-12)

When evaluating literature, according to Howells, one should ask: "Is it true?—true to the motives, the impulses, the principles that shape the life of actual men and women?" What I have been suggesting here is that in emphasizing Howells's sanity and commonsense we may have been neglecting to see to what extent Howells recognizes the irrational and sentimental as "impulses . . . which shape the life of actual men and women." He not only recognizes these impulses but, more importantly, he approves of them. Louise [in *The Story of a Play*] is more attractive because she is passionate, Cornelia [in *The Coast of Bohemia*] more interesting because she shares Charmian's romanticism, and Penelope and Silas [in *The Rise of Silas Lapham*] nobler because the are motivated by "foolish," "irrational" ideals. Furthermore, art must reflect this irrationality to be true, to be realistic. Miss Pettrell's second performance of Salome is more successful because it reveals a more passionate heroine. The paintings which reflect nature are superior to those which simply reflect training. Even a *Tears, Idle Tears* may have some merit because its sacrifices are so "wildly unsatisfactory."

If we go back to Howells's frequent use of the revery, we can see that it has another function: it validates the irrational on a philosophical level. For the reveries in the novels always point out the unpredictability of life. Ellen Kenton does not know (nor do we) what Breckon's reaction to her confession will be. The untrained Helen of *A Woman's Reason* will not actually become a highly successful ceramic decorator or actress, but the reveries themselves reinforce the sense of not knowing what *will* happen to her. Percy Bysshe Shelley Ray, the hero of *The World of Chance,* an aspiring novelist, has fantasies similar to Helen's dreams of glory, one in which he is hailed as the heir to Hawthorne, another in which he becomes the owner of a newspaper. Both scenarios seem wildly improbable, but the final outcome, his eventual success, is in fact no more predictable. And if life can be unpredictable, unfathomable by the normal processes of reasoning, there is no particular brief for people who are always reasonable or choose the illogical course of action, even supposing that such behavior were possible.

It is primarily Howells's subject matter which has damned him, made him seem irrelevant to this age. To join with the revisionist critics who emphasize his interest in the irrational is, of course, to join in connecting Howells with the prevailing temper of the twentieth century. But a good part of his potential attraction for twentieth-century readers may well lie not so much in his focus on the irrational per se as in his philosophical and artistic complexity. With an expanded view of what constitutes the irrational in Howells, with a recognition of the importance of his approval of frivolity, sentiment, and "foolish" self-sacrifice, we can, I think, develop a stronger feeling for this complexity: we can better appreciate the sensitivity with which he looks at life, and we can also better understand the artistic sophistication with which he constructs his novels. (pp. 322-23)

> Ellen F. Wright, "William Dean Howells and the Irrational," in Nineteenth-Century Fiction, Vol. 38, No. 3, December, 1983, pp. 304-23.

MICHAEL SPINDLER   (essay date 1983)

[*In the following excerpt, Spindler closely examines* A Hazard of New Fortunes *as a novel that reveals an imperfectly reconciled division in Howells's outlook: between the pro-socialist sympathizer with the common laborer in industrial America, and the comfortable, upper middle-class writer whose wealth depended on the support of the well-to-do book-buying public.*]

William Dean Howells had, until the writing of *The Rise of Silas Lapham,* been confident that the American social system was fundamentally right and that it bestowed a general benefaction upon all its citizens. However, while he was writing that novel in his new Beacon Street home in Boston, he became increasingly aware of the disparities of wealth which gave the lie to that egalitarianism upon which his confidence was based. Simply to be alone in the relative comfort of his huge empty house on the water's edge in the heat of August made him feel guilty.... His social conscience was further sensitised first by what he regarded as a disturbing miscarriage of justice—the trial and execution in an atmosphere of hate and hysteria and on the basis of spurious evidence of some anarchists for their alleged part in the Haymarket Riot of 1886 in Chicago, and secondly, by his first-hand acquaintance with industrial conditions when in February 1887 he visited factories in Lowell, Massachusetts. He was shocked by what he saw there and used the experience in *Annie Kilburn,* ... in which he condemned labouring conditions and false, middle-class philanthropy. (p. 76)

Increasingly, his intimate correspondence became loaded with the problem of contemporary American society and expressive of a critical attitude. 'I should hardly like to trust pen and ink with all the audacity of my social ideas', he announced to Henry James, 'but after fifty years of optimistic content with "civilisation" and its ability to come out all right in the end, I now abhor it, and feel that it is coming out all wrong in the end, unless it bases itself anew on a real equality. Meantime, I wear a fur-lined overcoat and live in all the luxury my money can buy.' He thus found himself caught in the contradictions of the humane liberal who, though he might feel sympathy for

the poor, could never express solidarity with them since his own financial and class position by no means coincided with theirs. Howells was both Ohio democrat and dean of American letters and the egalitarian thrust of his social thought coexisted uneasily with the income and social success that he enjoyed. So hand in hand with his moral indignation at poverty there walked a guilty acknowledgement of his egotistic indulgence. These ambivalences of social life, these contradictions which contemporary circumstances forced upon the humane, middle-class liberal and the weak compromises that usually resulted, are dramatised and explored in *A Hazard of New Fortunes*.

In 1888 Howells moved from Boston to New York and he begins the novel with a similar migration on the part of the Marches. They leave the comparatively protected milieu of the older cultural centre for the teeming heterogeneity of the economic capital and through their reactions of bewilderment and disillusion Howells was able to present his own sense of social change and class conflict. New York better represented the new social and ethical context created by industrialisation and urbanisation, and Howells, both fascinated and repelled by the city, could draw upon his own fresh experience for striking realistic detail and perceptive psychological response. The Marches' middle-class sentiments, then, provide the novel's controlling perspective, but they are brought into relief, redefined and measured, against several other ideological standpoints embodied in appropriately conceived characters. (pp. 76-7)

[Jacob Dryfoos] totally accepts the 'dog eat dog' basis of *laissez-faire* economics and has nothing but contempt for the poor. Fulkerson is a more humane but nevertheless complacent apologist for the status quo. 'One of those Americans', Howells tells us, jibing at the shallow optimism which he had found inadequate, 'whose habitual conception of life is unalloyed prosperity.' Ranged as a battery of representative critical viewpoints upon the condition of the working class are the Christian Socialism of Conrad Dryfoos, who prefers the rigours of charity work amongst the poor to the luxurious entertainments of his class; the patriarchalism of Colonel Woodburn, who compares the cash-nexus callousness of the industrialised North unfavourably with the feudal relations of a romanticised antebellum South; and the materialistic socialism of the old German, Lindau, who in the most cogent critique presented in the novel points to capitalism and big business as the real cause of mass poverty and the corruption of the ideals contained in the Declaration of Independence: 'Dere *iss* no Ameriga any more: You start here free and brafe, and you glaim for efery man de righdt to life, liperty, and de bursuit of habbiness. And where haf you entedt? No man that vorks with his handts among you hass the liperty to bursue his habbiness. He iss the slafe of some richer man, some gompany, some gorporation, dat crindts him down to the least he can lif on, and that rops him of the marchin of his earnings that he might pe habby on'. The republic, he says, is 'bought oap by monobolies, and ron by drusts and gompanies, and railroadts andt oil gompanies'.

Edwin H. Cady interprets the old German as a fanatic and idealist committed to an 'irrational philosophy of violence', but such a view, heavily ideological in itself, distorts Howells's presentation. Nowhere in the novel, through either direct or reported speech, does Howells show Lindau advocating the destruction of life or property or calling for violent revolution. It is only the *tone* of his arguments which is violent, not their content. (pp. 77-8)

Howells's solitary stand in defence of the Chicago anarchists had taught him that the conservative prejudices of a large section of the American public, including his friends, required undermining and not reinforcement. In the light of the Haymarket affair any characterisation of a left-wing opponent of *laissez-faire* capitalism as a bomb-throwing hothead would have seemed reprehensible to Howells since it was upon such vicious caricature that a conscienceless repression had based itself. Consequently, Howells takes pains to portray Lindau as a highly cultured, patriotic (he is an injured veteran of the American Civil War), compassionate and justly embittered man. However, he was also aware of the limitations of his audience, and he knew that such socialistic views could not be put forward in the novel unless they were at least formally, if not polemically, countered. The process of emasculating Lindau's subversive critique is accomplished first by the careful rendering of the German accent, which emphasises his foreignness, and secondly, by the Marches' evasion or complacent rejection of his arguments.

The Marches represent the liberal centre, half-way between the callous Social Darwinism of Dryfoos senior and the uncompromising socialism of Lindau. Basil March, humane, observant, critical, is, in the Jamesian phrase, 'the centre of revelation' of the novel, and the story charts his deepening unease as his traditional ideology of Jeffersonian individualism and egalitarianism is forced to come to terms with the brute realities and inequalities of urban-industrial America. On his arrival, New York seems a personal, hospitable place. The familiar hotels and restaurants welcome him and his wife and reception clerks and waiters remember their names. Their initial image of the city is thus inevitably coloured by their financial and class security, and they do not suffer the dispiriting anonymity which is often the fate of the newcomer to the metropolis. Although the city is teeming with thousands of immigrants, these do not threaten the Bostonian Marches with 'dispossession' of their Americanness as they would with Henry James. Rather, the Marches take pleasure in the impression that Southern Europe has been transported across the Atlantic and, like tourists in their own city, they relish the sights and sounds of the ethnically diverse neighbourhoods. To them the immigrants are so 'picturesque' and 'gay', an exclusively aesthetic appreciation that denies the human reality of poverty. 'I don't find so much misery in New York', Basil announces complacently to his wife. Gradually, Howells displaces this bland view of the city as colourful spectacle by showing how a growing acquaintance with the suffering of the poor deepens and humanises the Marches' response.

To appreciate fully the mild, and probably self-deprecatory, irony with which Howells depicts the Marches' accommodation to an uncomfortable social awareness we must recall a telling sociological detail. Howells informs us several times over that the Marches receive an unearned income of 2000 dollars from stocks together with an unspecified rent from their house in Boston. . . . [The] average working wage at this time was one dollar fifteen cents a day, or about 400 dollars annually, assuming a full year's work. Howells, therefore, means us to recognise that the Marches are comparatively well-off and that they belong in a moderate way to the propertied class. As sensitive, humane people they may come to have sympathy for the poor, but they could never, as Lindau does, express solidarity with them since to do so would clash with their own class and material interests. This tension between altruism and egoism in which the Marches are caught and the shifts they

adopt in order to resolve or evade its contradictions provide the novel's central ideological issues.

The Marches, as relatively prosperous citizens of the republic, are convinced of the essential rightness of the American social system and, as members of the petty bourgeoisie, they cling to its ideology of individualism and egalitarianism. Lindau tries to expose that ideology to them as false consciousness in the light of contemporary conditions, but they resist his criticisms, preferring the security of their reassuring middle-class values. It alarmed Mrs March 'to hear American democracy denounced as a shuffling evasion' and to be told that 'there was not equality of opportunity in America', and Basil dismisses Lindau's ideas as 'false' even though he himself recognises the loss of the old egalitarian society and the rise of an aristocracy in fact if not in name. It is part of Howells's irony that despite March's growing perception of the arrogance of the *nouveaux riches* and the undeserved suffering of the urban poor, he does not shift his ideological stance until his own material prospects and middle-class lifestyle are threatened by the collapse of the journal. The sudden possibility of having to struggle himself in a hostile social world inclines him to a much more cynical view of American civilisation: 'Some one always has you by the throat, unless you have some one else in *your* grip.' He has arrived at Jacob Dryfoos's conception of society as Darwinian struggle, but unlike Dryfoos he finds such a state of affairs reprehensible for the individual corruption it entails: 'So we go on, pushing and pulling, climbing and crawling, thrusting aside and trampling underfoot; lying, cheating, stealing; and when we get to the end, covered with blood and dirt and sin and shame, and look back over the way we've come . . . I don't think the retrospect can be pleasing.'

March, Howells's liberal representative, tends to think of society largely in moral categories and sees capitalists and entrepreneurs naively in individual, ethical terms as men of ill will or good will. He criticises Jacob Dryfoos for his moral decay but not for his social parasitism as a speculator on Wall Street, and he seems unable to see (as Howells seems unable) that membership of the property-owning class inevitably involved the selfishness of living off the work of others. Yet in the compromises of viewpoint Basil is forced into, Howells does present a half-hearted adoption of social determinism.

In the moralist-individualist perspective derived from Protestantism the blame for conditions lies not with the social structure but with personal character. Mrs March propounds this view, but her husband, while partly agreeing, also significantly qualifies it: 'We can't put it all on the conditions; we must put some of the blame on character. But conditions *make* character; and people are greedy and foolish, and wish to have and to shine, because having and shining are held up to them by civilisation as the chief good of life.' This mild determinism with its insight into the conditioning to which individual values and behaviour are subject represents the farthest point of the Marches' education into the nature of the new socio-economic order. Towards the close of the novel there is a retreat from the understanding gained and the book's conclusion is marked by a conservative reassertion of the continuing reality of American democracy and egalitarianism as Lindau's views are finally dismissed as 'wrong'. *A Hazard of New Fortunes* then, like *The Rise of Silas Lapham*, represents the testing of a traditional ideology against a complex contemporary situation and the eventual validation of that ideology. Unconvincingly, Christian moralism and middle-class values (and middle-class income!) are left secure at the end so that the novel's departing note is one of comfort and reassurance. It is to the climactic strike scene that we have to look for any audacity in Howells's presentation of social conflict.

In the year he moved to New York Howells came face to face with the war between capital and labour when a serious traction strike was called. The dispute lasted for months and erupted into violence when the company brought in strike-breakers and every car had to be guarded by police. Howells uses this strike to bring his plot to a dramatic head and to provide a focal event around which the contrasting social perspectives of the main characters are brought into relief. Basil March, petty-bourgeois intellectual, decides to stand on the side-lines and be a 'philosophical observer' of the struggle between the workers and owners; Jacob Dryfoos, millionaire speculator, is not so detached, regarding the strikers as a 'pack of dirty, worthless whelps' who deserve to be shot; and Conrad, his Christian Socialist son, believes they have 'a righteous cause, though they go the wrong way to help themselves.' Even this gentle assertion of support is too much for the speculator embittered at his son's class betrayal and he hits him, causing a wound on the temple. Subsequently, Conrad comes upon a violent scene in which strikers are being attacked by the police and there sees Lindau taunting the lawmen and about to be clubbed to the ground. As he moves to the old man's rescue he is shot through the heart, and Basil March (by one of those strained coincidences Howells occasionally resorts to in the novel) finds the two bodies of Conrad and Lindau lying together on the pavement. It is an intense and emotive passage of social drama and a close reading reveals how Howells uses certain details

---

A HAZARD OF NEW FORTUNES

A Novel

BY

WILLIAM DEAN HOWELLS

AUTHOR OF

"APRIL HOPES" "ANNIE KILBURN" "MODERN ITALIAN POETS" ETC.

ILLUSTRATED

NEW YORK

HARPER & BROTHERS, FRANKLIN SQUARE

1890

Title page of A Hazard of New Fortunes.

---

to manipulate our feelings against the police and, by implication, in favour of Lindau and the strikers.

He emphasises the brutality of the police; when they attack the strikers, 'Conrad could see how they struck them under the rims of their hats; the blows on their skulls sounded as if they had fallen on stone.' He reminds us of Lindau's age and patriarchal dignity just before the old German becomes a target, and of his infirmity and self-sacrifice during the Civil War when he throws up his arm to protect himself and Conrad sees 'the empty sleeve dangle in the air, over the stump of his wrist.' Conrad, it seems, is shot by a policeman. This is left unclear, but since the bullet came from the tramcar which had police guards it is a plausible deduction. The specific and general culpability of the police is further indicated by Conrad's perception on immediately being shot of the policeman who is clubbing Lindau. His face 'was not bad, nor cruel; it was like the face of a statue, fixed, perdurable; a mere image of irresponsible and involuntary authority'. In one remarkable moment of insight Howells succinctly conveys the petrifaction of the human responses and the abdication of moral responsibility—the pejorative tone of that 'irresponsible' is forceful—the dehumanisation in short that the policeman has undergone during his metamorphosis from individual to 'authority'.

Howells thus makes it plain that Conrad and Lindau are both victims of police repression, a repression that is associated in two ways with the ruling class. Before being clubbed into silence, the indomitable old socialist accuses the police of being the partisan agents of the bosses and physical violence as an aspect of authority is embodied directly before the strike passage in Jacob Dryfoos, arrogant millionaire. Why does Howells have Dryfoos hit his son? It seems unlikely that a writer of his mature artistry would have engineered the incident solely to exploit some coffin-side sentimentality later. The wounding is surely intended to prefigure the mortal wounding by the police and the blow of the authoritarian father against the son's opposition is the dramatic equivalent of the violence of the ruling class against those who, however slightly, threatened its domination. That Dryfoos is himself an indirect victim of that violence is, of course, an irony calculated to enforce the pacifist point that those who advocate the use of brute force against others may themselves come to suffer by it. 'I should hardly like to trust pen and ink with all the audacity of my social ideas', Howells wrote, and he seems to be conveying dramatically here what he dare not have made explicit. Interpreted in this way, *A Hazard of New Fortunes* reveals more tensions in its attitudes than are superficially apparent, and it shows how bravely, if finally inadequately, Howells came to grips in literary terms with the problems posed for traditional American values by society's polarisation into rich and poor. (pp. 78-83)

Michael Spindler, "The Condition of the Poor in the Work of Howells, Dreiser and Sinclair," in his American Literature and Social Change: William Dean Howells to Arthur Miller, *Indiana University Press, 1983, pp. 74-93.**

ELIZABETH STEVENS PRIOLEAU (essay date 1983)

[*Prioleau is an American critic who has published articles on nineteenth-century English and American literature in the journals* Twentieth Century Literature *and* Victorian Poetry, *and in* The American Journal of Dermatopathology, *for which she is a literary consultant. In her study* The Circle of Eros: Sexuality in the Work of William Dean Howells *(1983), she offers a predominantly Freudian examination of Howells's novels, focusing on their re-*

flection of the author's personal background. "A strangely fearful child who suffered phobias and nightmares," she writes, "Howells endured three psychological collapses during his adolescence and early youth. Thereafter and to progressively lesser degrees, he was plagued by various neurotic ailments." From this starting point, Prioleau chronicles the psychological development of Howells, who "began as a priggish young editor of the Atlantic Monthly, *with an early neurotic terror of sexuality, and ended as one of the leading exponents of frankness in literature. He grew lenient to the point of advocating 'scandalous' reforms like divorce and trial marriages, and his fiction moved from filigree indirection to bold erotic allegory." In the following excerpt, Prioleau examines* A Modern Instance *as a work in which the conflicting forces of Howells's sexual psyche—uninhibited passion and puritanical restraint—reach an impasse, with sexual license inevitably leading to death, as does chaste morality.*]

There was a tone of crisis about sexuality during the late seventies and early eighties that was almost without parallel in America. Advice books warned of the doom and corruption in indulgence, and the *Atlantic* ran an article advancing the Schopenhaueresque thesis that the sexual will led to "final and total destruction." An ultrarestrictive puritanism accompanied this cataclysmic fear. . . . Prudery became brittle and anemic; repression, fanatical.

The literary movement that captured this mood and dominated the intellectual world during the late nineteenth century was naturalism. Zola's "realism" (as it was then called) filled the journals of the day, setting off a tidal wave of controversy. His work dramatized the national sexual tenor. His protagonists, left to the free expression of their passions, end exactly where [Anthony] Comstock's followers promised—in corruption, death, and sterility. And, like them, Zola was fiercely prudish. His influence on Howells during these years was immediate and profound. Zola supplied an artistic framework for the dark sexual truths he wanted to treat "seriously" and "tragically," and corroborated the fears he was exploring. At the same time, the very extremism of Zola's prudery helped direct his imaginative sympathies away from the official ethic. (p. 54)

Zola's effect on his erotic art was revolutionary. The subjects he had concealed in fine print and comedy he learned to handle boldly, profoundly, and panoramically. "Every literary theory of mine was contrary to him when I took up *L'Assommoir,*" he admitted and added that Zola gave him the courage "not to shrink from the things of dirt and clay." By nineteenth-century standards, *A Modern Instance* was filled with "dirt"— scandalously so. Even after Howells had diluted the original version for *Century* magazine, an outraged reader complained: "[T]he whole thing from beginning to end is revolting." He had dealt directly with such tabooed themes as sadomasochism, narcissism, and promiscuity and—even more incriminating— divorce.

Not only did Zola and his contemporaries encourage Howells to face these topics directly; they showed him powerful means of rendering them. The French "realists," first of all, reinforced the direction he was already pursuing. Their use of dramatic method, circumstantial detail, the physical surroundings to convey sexual passion, paralleled Howells's own practices of the past eight years. Beyond strengthening his approach, though, they—particularly Zola—taught him abundant methods of encoding sexuality and eliciting its power. The epic scale Zola employed to duplicate the magnitude of desire was one of Howells's most significant borrowings. For Marcia's and Bartley's tempestuous appetites, he utilized a canvas as large as *Nana's* and symbols as all-encompassing. Thus, an-

imality, heat, food, horses, and clothes became central motifs in *A Modern Instance*, spanning the whole drama. Zola's erotic vocabulary was equally valuable. Howells not only found such euphemisms as "kiss" handled explicitly (with *baiser* as the French pun for intercourse) but found images that had special significance for his autobiography—alcohol, heat, dizziness, and suffocation. Through the continental novelists he was put in touch with an eroto-literary tradition of the highest sophistication. (pp. 54-5)

Just as Mrs. Farrell [of *Private Theatrical*] springs out of the erotic wasteland of West Pekin, Marcia and Bartley arise in a town bled dry by neopuritanism. Surrounded by "iron-grey crags" and "arctic quiet," . . . the inhabitants live in houses that smell of decayed rats and peer through "funereal" . . . blinds for signs of excitement. Marcia's parents are grim examples of sexual desolation in Equity. Locked up in their silent house together, estranged, and dressed in permanent black, the Gaylords are caricatures of marital death. The Squire, with his "hawk-like profile" and "harsh rings of black hair," . . . reigns over his wife like a Plutonian deity, and she sits embalmed in her rocker, listening to the clock tick. Her calcified and anemic puritanism and his skeptical negations have leeched their lives completely of Eros.

Marcia and Bartley enter this blasted landscape with the same show of life and brilliance as Mrs. Farrell. The connection, though, between Mrs. Farrell's deadliness and her apparent vitality is underscored from the beginning with the two lovers. Their first entrance foreshadows a fate for their undiscipline that is just as lethal as the Gaylords'. They dash into the dark, lifeless town in Bartley's redlined, "musically clashing" . . . cutter behind a colt who is sure to "be the death" . . . of them. Illustrating Darwin's two savage types, the possessive monogamist and expansive polygamist, they steadily substantiate every tooth-and-claw axiom of the age. Egged on by a corrupt purity cult, they regress into the sort of "fools" the Victorians most dreaded: bankrupt children who end in the "house of death."

Their opening scene together—one of the steamiest in Howells's fiction—is freighted with portents of their ruin. As always, Marcia's and Bartley's appearance is revelatory. Marcia resembles a Southern beauty with the low forehead of "savage" races, who blushes and blanches, and dresses in red or black as her untamed appetites swing from ecstasy to deadly despair. The blond, debonair Bartley cuts an unbashedly sensual figure. He has long-lashed eyes that cast "deliberate look[s]," . . . a "rich, caressing voice," . . . and an appetite that equals Mrs. Farrell's. Signifying special gratification for Howells, his mustache sweeps up "like a bird's wing" . . . and his manner is casual, bohemian, and jocular. Yet his eyes are "clouded gray," . . . the chin beneath his mustache recedes weakly, and he indulges his gluttony in "choking air" . . . and gets sick afterwards.

During the midnight rendezvous with Marcia that initiates their courtship, the sinister side of his easygoing charm insinuates itself into his love-making. As their excitement rises before a smouldering fire (reminiscent of the laundry seduction in *L'Assommoir*), Bartley ominously threatens to strangle Marcia with his stylish coat; then forces her, in an adumbration of the sadistic power he will wield over her, to write Y-E-S on an imaginary note. In the context of their humid tête-tête, the "yes" comes with the force of Molly Bloom's "yes" in *Ulysses*. The culmination of their interview confirms this sense of the word. Her brain filled "like wine" by Bartley's advances,

Marcia reels "dizzily" . . . into his embrace and kisses him (with clear sexual implications to Victorian readers) at the door. Afterwards, in a phallically loaded gesture, she kisses the doorknob behind him.

Similar omens surround their engagement. When Bartley's dyspepsia and egotistic self-pity prompt his love declaration, Marcia abandons herself to her passion in ways that are bitterly prophetic. Indulging her feeling of "foolishness," she playfully regresses to an infantility she will experience through her marriage. "There is something about this that lets me be as silly as I like," she exclaims, and begins to talk baby talk to Bartley. But her child's play grows inadvertently portentous. Her fevered caresses garrote Bartley, and she cries with delight, "You may kiss me—you may *kill* me, now!" . . . Prefiguring that very fate, Bartley seizes her when he leaves and pinions her arms against her sides until she is "helpless": "I knew you were dead in love with me," he exults.

Their engagement celebration and marriage further elucidate their contrasting savage dispositions and predict their doom. After they have committed themselves to each other, they drive off in Bartley's cutter on a joyride that symbolizes the course of their romance. In an image of their runaway libido, they let the colt "open up" on a country road until they enter a forest which bears the same relation to their passion as Mrs. Farrell's primeval dell to hers. There, in the "wild and lonesome" . . . woods, the Darwinian compulsions in their free sexuality come forward. As the colt picks up faster and faster speed, they run into another sled carrying the town spitfire. Bartley promptly engages in a torrid *à deux* with her, while Marcia watches "*almost killed*" . . . from the sidelines. Afterwards, she clutches "herself tighter to him" . . . and sobs, to Bartley's uncontrollable laughter.

Their wedding is an equally inauspicious occasion. Preceded by a quarrel and separation over Bartley's polygamous adventures, it takes place impulsively under dubious circumstances. With the undisciplined possessiveness that characterizes her, Marcia pursues Bartley on his flight out of town and captures him "at the touch." . . . A five-dollar bribe buys their illegal license and their aphrodisiacal wedding supper of oysters and coffee is part of the same fraudulent deal. Later they consummate their union under a cloud of death imagery. They see "The Coleen Bawn," a melodrama about marital murder, which Marcia watches like a "savage" . . . who witnesses her own execution. Bartley, in turn, roars with laughter, and cracks a joke as he turns off the bedroom light that changes the plot so that the protagonists are "both found suffocated in the morning." . . .

In fact, they both suffer genuine and slow death as their marriage and personalities dissolve bit by bit. Rather than regulating their unbridled appetites, marriage only encourages darker, crueler, more pathologic expresions of them. When the charm of novelty wears off, they submit to the laws of their mutually incompatible primitive personalities. Bartley's libido expands outward in direct ratio to Marcia's tightening grip, until they propel themselves into a death-in-life entrapment. As Bartley's flesh swells on beer and oysters and his extramarital reveries with it, Marcia contracts into a mute, frigid recluse whose slammed door—earlier kissed—resounds fatally through their marriage. In their downward spiral, the negative powers of Eros have full vent. Bartley's egotistic sadism grows with the increase of Marcia's masochism and jealousy, and they both drift into the incoherence and amoral instinctuality of childhood. At last, like Mrs. Farrell, they lose their inner vitality

with their outer sexual failure. With her disintegration, Marcia faces the "deadly unsympathetic stillness" . . . of psychic emptiness. Bartley's robbery, similarly, is only visible manifestation of what he has stolen from himself. Each layer of fat sinks him further into animal apathy, regression, and *néant*. Thus, amid Marcia's sobs and Bartley's laughter, they circle down to a pure center of death that is both internal and external. And in an elaboration of Mrs. Farrell's self-destruction, theirs infects and poisons the whole community. (pp. 55-8)

[At] the divorce trial, the two negative principles of their tragedy reach a fatal juncture. The death wielding powers of orthodox repression collide head-on with the murderous influence of uncontrolled Eros. When Marcia walks into the courtroom, she looks like an allegorical representation of death. She is "heavily veiled in black," . . . and Bartley appears just as reft of life. Paradoxically, he has regressed to a corpse-like infancy. Three chins descend to his chest and his complexion has turned a baby's 'tender pink" beneath a white mustache. The sight of his father-in-law brings a "tallowy pallor" . . . to his face and he wanes into progressive inanimateness as the Squire's accusation proceeds.

In his rigid, fierce indictment of Bartley, the Squire represents the collective force of the official morality. Looming over the courtroom in his black frock coat, he, too, embodies Thanatos. He distills the deadliness of suprarepression with his inhuman vengeance, and epitomizes its sensationalistic infirmity through his rhetoric. . . . While Marcia and Bartley sink under this harangue into deeper insentience, he reinflicts on them what they have already visited upon themselves. In a perfect illustration of Marcuse's theory of "surplus repression," he pronounces the lifeless Bartley "dead to honor; dead to duty, dead to her [Marcia] . . . [and] dead to the universal frame of things." . . . When he tried to double lock them into the death-in-life imprisonment by calling for Bartley's incarceration, the two lethal forces meet and implode in a slaughterous dénouement. Marcia flings herself at her father with stifled sobs and renounces her vengeance—her last remaining vital sign. He, in turn, falls victim to the Hubbards' very fate. He "fetche[s] his breath in convulsive gasps," and collapses into a state of paralysis, infantilism, and imminent death. Bartley escapes in the fracas to a dark, airless room and the "long, frightened wail of a child" . . . sounds the requiescat to his and Marcia's tragedy.

On this note of helpless pathos, they go to their deaths. "I am very sorry," Howells told his editor, R. W. Gilder, "that I can't leave out the last chapter." It is one of his most chilling endings. Marcia and Bartley fall to their dooms in diametrically opposite ways, the society sinks lower in credibility, and the ambivalence leaves the conclusion caught on the horns of contradiction. Bartley lights out once more for the West where he dies in a gunfight in Whited Sepulchre, Arizona, over a sexual scandal. Marcia withdraws to Equity and buries herself in her parents' empty house—becoming "dry, cold, and uncommunicative," . . . and growing queerer, more infantile with age. (pp. 65-6)

The concluding mood is that of the nihilistic, melancholy Jacques [of William Shakespeare's *As You Like It*] who lambasts wellfed prigs like [the lawyer] Atherton with their "wise saws and modern instances" and sees all lovers as "fools." Howells had inadvertently backed into the "impenetrable darkness" of pure tragedy—the realm, he later said, where man "cannot lift or shift or move." He had wedged himself between two withering negations: the deadliness of uncontrolled Eros and the deadliness of the official ethic. "Divorce" became a larger theme than he realized. Besides the separation of men and women, he found a separation of mind and body in a critically strained culture. A ferocious sexuality had proved resistant to morality; and spirituality seemed leagued with another death through oversuppression. (pp. 66-7)

Worn out and "thoroughly broken up about [his] work," Howells wrote John Hay at the end of *A Modern Instance*: "I do work hard, and I know that I *aim* at the highest mark, morally and artistically." Harder work still awaited him as his sexual theme expanded outward into a broadened concept of complicity and turned inward to the psychological mysteries. Yet, to reach his high "mark," this tragic low point of his career had been necessary. It became a major turning point of his quest for a positive Eros. Without the defenses of comedy, without the surreptitious arts of the miniature painter, he had brought his and his era's excessive sexual fears forward, had discredited the cult of repression, forged further into the domain of pleasure. That the terms were heightened and extreme only forced him with greater urgency to the next plateau of his erotic quest. Despite the pain and difficulty it caused him, Howells continued to call *A Modern Instance* his favorite book until the mid-nineties. If the chief function of the novel, as he claimed, was to "adjust the proportions" this may have been his reason. The exaggerated doom Marcia and Bartley drew down on themselves through their undiscipline, the exaggerated cultural controls against it, and the crisis pitch of sexual conflict may have shown him the depth of the need for proportion and erotic adjustment, both personally and creatively. Though he sank into the most "wholly tragic" mire of his literature and lost his "moral" and "distinct" meaning, he may have gained a vision of the "highest mark" as a consequence—the aureole of light around the windmill, the ideal of an associated sexuality—and pledged himself to strive for it. (pp. 68-9)

> *Elizabeth Stevens Prioleau, in her* The Circle of Eros. Sexuality in the Work of William Dean Howells, *Duke University Press, 1983, 226 p.*

ALFRED KAZIN (essay date 1984)

[*A highly respected American literary critic, Kazin is best known for his essay collections* The Inmost Leaf *(1955) and* Contemporaries *(1962), and particularly for* On Native Grounds *(1942), a study of American prose writing since the era of William Dean Howells. Having studied the works of "the critics who were the best writers—from Sainte-Beuve and Matthew Arnold to Edmund Wilson and Van Wyck Brooks" as an aid to his own critical understanding, Kazin has found that "criticism focussed many—if by no means all—of my own urges as a writer: to show literature as a deed in human history, and to find in each writer the uniqueness of the gift, of the essential vision, through which I hoped to penetrate into the mystery and sacredness of the individual soul." In the following excerpt, Kazin summarizes Howells's career, depicting him as a writer of polite, bland novels of manners that were based on mere reportage of the ordinary.*]

During his prime years Howells made the current equivalent of $150,000 a year. His literary tone of voice satisfied—though a shade of irony proclaimed his intellectual independence—the conscious propriety of Beacon Hill. Always working up social topics (the businessman, the police station, divorce), Howells managed to retain the benevolence of the Brahmins, to inform and edify the largely feminine reading audience, to earn the plaudits of Mark Twain, who obviously found him harmless ("you are my only novelist"), and the polite interest

of Henry James. (Howells was James's loyal admirer. His admission that he had "never lived" led to the character of Lambert Strether in *The Ambassadors*.) Howells, though he soon bored the elite like Henry Adams and exasperated the socially pretentious by his insistence on the ordinary ("that is the right American stuff"), managed dangerous topics as he managed his relations with publishers, the reading audience, and society in Boston. He was a friend to both Mark Twain and Henry James, and who else could have managed that?

In the early nineties Howells, outraged by the legal lynching of some immigrant anarchists in the Haymarket affair and the increasingly brutal influence of American business, rebelled against the self-satisfaction of Boston, moved to New York, and for a time regarded himself as a socialist and wrote with more bite. But "the question of the opportunities," as Henry James liked to put it, was always on Howells's mind. One feels about Howells that he trained himself to become a novelist at a time when the novel had become synonymous with magazines as a way of disseminating to the new middle class information about itself. If Howells had been brought up in the eighteenth century, he would have been a party pamphleteer in America, in Europe a librettist for Mozart's operas. He was a literary jack-of-all-trades who before the Civil War wrote imitations of Heine and after it social novels based on reportage—he had come to Boston in 1860 as a reporter investigating the shoe trade. He was a literary factotum who knew he could pass muster at every kind of writing. Thanks to his being in Europe during the Civil War, he was able to launch the novel of manners in America.

Howells's concern with the strategy of success would not have been possible without his "literary passions." He was crazy about writers as well as about books. James always buttered Howells up with faint praise. He appreciated what Howells had done for this newfangled business of describing "society" for itself alone, what Howells's vogue had opened up for James himself, and how much and in the end how little all this had done for Howells himself. With his head always turned to Europe, James of course thought Howells suburban. As he said in reviewing a routine Howells production, *A Foregone Conclusion*, ... "Civilization with us is monotonous, and in the way of contrasts, of salient points, of chiaroscuro, we have to take what we can get."

Howells's characters come out of the same American pot. They are essentially mild civil beings, even genuinely resemble one another in their American good faith—a recipe not likely to make for excitement. (pp. 220-21)

> *Alfred Kazin, "The James Country," in his* An American Procession, *Alfred A. Knopf, 1984, pp. 211-34.*

ADDITIONAL BIBLIOGRAPHY

Alexander, William. "Howells, Eliot, and the Humanized Reader." In *The Interpretation of Narrative: Theory and Practice,* edited by Morton W. Bloomfield, pp. 149-70. Harvard English Studies, Vol. 1. Cambridge: Harvard University Press, 1970.*
> Compares and contrasts the techniques of Howells and George Eliot, exploring their similar humanistic visions of literature as an "instrument of moral good."

Baxter, Annette K. "Archetypes of American Innocence: Lydia Blood and Daisy Miller." In *The American Experience: Approaches to the*

Study of the United States, edited by Hennig Cohen, pp. 148-56. Boston: Houghton Mifflin Co., 1968.*

Closely compares and contrasts the principal characters of *The Lady of the "Aroostook"* and Henry James's *Daisy Miller.*

Bennett, George N. *William Dean Howells: The Development of a Novelist.* Norman: University of Oklahoma Press, 1959, 220 p.

A valuable biographical and critical work.

Brooks, Van Wyck. *Howells: His Life and Work.* New York: E. P. Dutton & Co., 1959, 296 p.

An excellent biography.

Brown, Maurice F. "The Rise of Lapham: The Fall of Howells." *Journal of American Culture* No. 2 (Summer 1983): 39-43.

Finds *The Rise of Silas Lapham* to be a "seriously flawed novel" in which "Howells, the committed realist, carefully details an action which his moral vision and artistic skill cannot master."

Budd, Louis J. "William Dean Howells' Debt to Tolstoy." *The American Slavic and East European Review* IX, No. 4 (December 1950): 292-301.

Outlines the Christian ideals that Howells learned from the works of Leo Tolstoy.

Cady, Edwin H., and Frazier, David L., eds. *The War of the Critics over William Dean Howells.* Evanston, Ill.: Row, Peterson and Co., 1962, 244 p.

A festschrift of criticism on Howells's works, including essays by Henry Van Dyke, Owen Wister, Ernest Boyd, and many others.

Carrington, George C., Jr. *The Immense Complex Drama: The World and the Art of the Howells Novel.* Columbus: Ohio State University Press, 1966, 245 p.

An excellent examination of the relationships of form, subject, theme, and technique in Howells's novels.

Carter, Everett. Introduction to *A Hazard of New Fortunes,* by W. D. Howells, pp. xi-xxix. Bloomington: Indiana University Press, 1976.

Ties the themes of *A Hazard of New Fortunes* to various crises that faced Howells at the time of writing.

Cooke, Delmar Gross. *William Dean Howells: A Critical Study.* New York: E. P. Dutton & Co., 1923, 279 p.

An able examination of Howells's work by genre.

Crowley, John W. "Howells and the Sins of the Father: *The Son of Royal Langbrith.*" *Old Northwest* 7, No. 2 (Summer 1981): 79-94.

Close reading of *The Son of Royal Langbrith,* which Crowley deems "one of the finest expressions of Howell's psychological realism."

————. "Howellsian Realism: A Psychological Juggle." *Studies in the Literary Imagination* XVI, No. 2 (Fall 1983): 45-55.

Seeks to understand Howells's commitment to realism through examining the relationship between his various neuroses and the form of his fiction as it developed throughout his career.

Eble, Kenneth E., ed. *Howells: A Century of Criticism.* Dallas: Southern Methodist University Press, 1962, 247 p.

A collection of critical essays by Henry James, C. Hartley Grattan, Edwin H. Cady, and many others.

Elliott, Gary D. "Howells' Ideal Man: Theme in *The Rise of Silas Lapham.*" *Wascana Review* 16, No. 2 (Fall 1981): 80-6.

A reading of *The Rise of Silas Lapham* that interprets Lapham, Bromfield Corey, and Tom Corey as equally significant characters in the work.

Eschholz, Paul A., ed. *Critics on William Dean Howells.* Coral Gables: University of Miami Press, 1975, 128 p.

Collected retrospective of criticism on Howells's works.

Ewell, Barbara C. "Parodic Echoes of *The Portrait of a Lady* in Howells's *Indian Summer.*" *Tulane Studies in English* 22 (1977): 117-31.

Compares and contrasts *Indian Summer* with Henry James's *The Portrait of a Lady,* and seeks to demonstrate that Howells's novel is a parody of James's.

Feigenoff, Charles. "'His Apparition': The Howells No One Believes In." *American Literary Realism: 1870-1910* 13, No. 1 (Spring 1980): 85-9.

Examines the story "His Apparition," finding Howells's unique use of the ghost-story format a shrewd means by which the author explores psychological and spiritual issues without violating the conventions of realism.

Garland, Hamlin. "Howells." In *American Writers on American Literature by Thirty-Seven Contemporary Writers,* edited by John Macy, pp. 285-97. London: Horace Liveright, 1931.

A defense of the nature of the characters in Howells's novels. Garland cites Howells's interest in the average individual as the reason for his frequent depictions of imperfect and occasionally unpleasant characters.

Garlin, Sender. *William Dean Howells and the Haymarket Era.* Occasional Papers Series, No. 33. New York: American Institute for Marxist Studies, 1979, 54 p.

Extensively quotes from Howells's letters and articles of the mid-1880s to demonstrate the depth of his radical social concern, debunking the popular image of Howells as a program of genteel respectability in American letters.

Hough, Robert L. *The Quiet Rebel: William Dean Howells as Social Commentator.* Lincoln: University of Nebraska Press, 1959, 137 p.

A study of Howells's role in promoting such liberal causes as women's suffrage and labor reform, emphasizing the author's faith in his writings as agents of change.

Kirk, Clara M., and Kirk, Rudolph. *William Dean Howells.* New York: Twayne Publishers, 1962, 223 p.

A useful biographical and critical study.

Maffi, Mario. "Architecture in the City, Architecture in the Novel: William Dean Howells's *A Hazard of New Fortunes.*" *Studies in the Literary Imagination* XVI, No. 2 (Fall 1983): 35-43.

Discusses *A Hazard of New Fortunes* as "one of the first American novels of the second half of the nineteenth century to make extensive use of an urban architectural imagery."

Marston, Jane. "Evolution and Howellsian Realism in *The Undiscovered Country,*" *American Literary Realism: 1870-1910* XIV, No. 2 (Autumn 1981): 231-41.

Study of *The Undiscovered Country* as the work in which Howells's interest in evolution first found significant expression.

Modern Fiction Studies: William Dean Howells Number XVI, No. 3 (Autumn 1970): 271-419.

Collection of essays by James W. Tuttleton, Marion W. Cumpiano, and others. A helpful bibliography of criticism of Howells's work is included.

Payne, James Robert. "Psychological and Supernatural Theme in Howells's *The Flight of Pony Baker.*" *The Markham Review* 9 (Spring 1980): 52-6.

Examination of the "boy-book" *The Flight of Pony Baker* as a novel that "has an interest for the reader today that goes well beyond children's literature, specifically in its strongly developed psychological theme, its imaginative projection of supernatural and psychic material, and its startling imagery of tragic potentialities of life."

Reeves, John K. "The Limited Realism of Howells's *Their Wedding Journey.*" *PMLA* 77, No. 5 (December 1962): 617-28.

Finds, from examining the author's manuscript, that Howells softened some potentially offensive passages of *Their Wedding Journey.*

Tarkington, Booth. Introduction to *The Rise of Silas Lapham,* by William Dean Howells, pp. xiii-xxi. Boston: Houghton Mifflin Co., 1937.

Praises Howells as one of America's literary giants, who, with Mark Twain and Henry James, stood as nineteenth-century America's answer to England's Joseph Conrad and George Meredith.

Trilling, Lionel. "William Dean Howells and the Roots of Modern Taste." In his *The Opposing Self: Nine Essays in Criticism,* pp. 76-103. New York: Viking Press, 1955.
  Examines the causes of Howells's unpopularity with twentieth-century readers.

Vanderbilt, Kermit. *The Achievement of William Dean Howells: A Reinterpretation.* Princeton: Princeton University Press, 1968, 226 p.
  Interprets four of Howells's novels in light of concurrent biographical events.

Van Nostrand, Albert D. "Fiction's Flagging Man of Commerce." *The English Journal* XLVIII, No. 1 (January 1959): 1-11.
  Contrasts *The Rise of Silas Lapham* with John P. Marquand's *Point of No Return* as novels concerned with American businessmen.

Wagenknecht, Edward. *William Dean Howells: The Friendly Eye.* New York: Oxford University Press, 1969, 340 p.
  A psychological interpretation of Howells's life and work.

Wright, Ellen F. "Given Bartley, Given Marcia: A Reconsideration of Howells' *A Modern Instance.*" *Texas Studies in Literature and Language* 23, No. 2 (Summer 1981): 214-31.
  Interprets *A Modern Instance* as primarily a study of character rather than of American institutions, as most critics have hitherto seen it. "Howells seems *not* to say that all American institutions are bad, that there has been a deterioration in American life, or that America can produce only young people like the Hubbards," concludes Wright. "Rather he seems simply to say that personalities such as Bartley's and Marcia's can occur, and if they do, they are unlikely to combine well in marriage."

(Joseph) Rudyard Kipling

1865-1936

English short story writer, poet, novelist, essayist, and auto-biographer.

Kipling is one of the most popular authors of all time and one of the finest short story writers in world literature. His critical reputation, however, has suffered because attention has often been paid not to his frequently flawless technique, but to the jingoistic political beliefs expressed in his work. After Kipling's death a major reassessment of his talents has led to his recognition as a masterful storyteller who possessed profound insights into the role of "beneficent imperialism," even if these insights were often clouded by a chauvinistic patriotism.

Born in Bombay, India, to English parents, Kipling was sent to school in England at the age of six. At first he lived with harsh and unsympathetic relatives, an unhappy experience he later wrote about in "Baa Baa, Black Sheep" and *The Light That Failed*. At twelve he went to the second-rate boarding school described, and somewhat embellished, in *Stalky and Co*. Just before his seventeenth birthday Kipling returned to India to work as a journalist on the Lahore *Civil and Military Gazette* and the Allahabad *Pioneer*. The verses and short stories he wrote as filler for these two newspapers were eventually published in books, and the successful sales of *Departmental Ditties* and *Plain Tales from the Hills* enabled Kipling to spend three years traveling. He married an American woman, Caroline Balestier, the sister of his one-time collaborator Wolcott Balestier, and lived on her family's estate in Vermont for four years. During this time, Kipling wrote some of his best children's stories, including the two *Jungle Books,* and began work on *Kim,* which is considered his finest work. A lawsuit brought by another of his wife's brothers, and an attack of influenza which struck the entire family and caused his elder daughter's death, left Kipling disenchanted with life in the United States. In 1896 he returned to England and settled in the Sussex countryside, which figures prominently as the setting for many of his subsequent works. He was awarded the Nobel Prize in literature in 1907, the first English author to be so honored, and at his death in 1936 he was buried in the Poet's Corner of Westminster Abbey.

Kipling was an admirer of the French *conte,* and he brought this finely crafted short story form to English literature. He frequently narrated the action of his early stories in a tone of cynical worldliness which prompted J. M. Barrie's often-quoted remark that Kipling "must have been born blasé." These stories, brief, concise, and vigorous, display little depth of characterization, but are remarkable for their innovative plots and deceptively simple structure. Kipling's tendency to concision is sometimes overdone in his later stories. "Mrs. Bathurst," for example, is so compressed and elliptical that many critics admit they cannot discern what happens in the narrative. Kipling's stories for children are perhaps the most widely known and read of his works. Kipling had a gift for anthropomorphism, and he presented his animal characters, in works like the *Jungle Books,* with simplicity, humor, and dignity, marred only occasionally by a sense of patronizing cuteness. Kipling also tended to anthropomorphize machinery. This tendency, to-

The Bettmann Archive, Inc.

gether with his overuse of technical jargon, flaws such works as ".007" and "The Ship That Found Herself."

Of Kipling's four novel-length works, only *Kim* was critically well-received. Critics attributed the poor plotting and weak characterization of his first novel, *The Light That Failed,* to his youth and inexperience. His second novel, *The Naulahka,* written with Wolcott Balestier, exhibits the same shortcomings. In his last two novels, *Captains Courageous* and *Kim,* these weaknesses were turned to Kipling's advantage, for both share an essentially plotless, picaresque structure that contributed to their effect. Both are also his most popular novels with modern readers, although *Captains Courageous* is now read primarily by children. Called "the finest story about India in English," *Kim* is also considered a revealing self-portrait of its author. Through his young protagonist, Kipling explored the duality of his emotional committment to both British imperialism and Eastern philosophy and values. While some critics contend that a lack of introspection on the part of the protagonist of *Kim* forms the primary fault in a potentially great work, others hold that Kipling's penetrating scrutiny of his dual attachments, as well as his sympathetic depiction of the Indian people, place this novel among the masterpieces of English literature.

In his poetry Kipling broke new ground by taking as subject matter the life of the common soldier and sailor in such off-duty activities as drinking, looting, and brawling. Most critical comment centered at first on Kipling's ignominious choice of topics for his verses and on his insistent, often-times offensive, imperialism. Then, in 1942, T. S. Eliot prefaced a new collection of Kipling's poetry and verse with a lengthy, and favorable, reassessment of Kipling as a poet. Eliot's study has been the starting point of many subsequent analyses of Kipling's poetic accomplishment, which is still in contention.

Although he is generally accepted as one of the masters of the short story form, Kipling's literary stature is still in flux. "During the later years of his life and even at the time of his death, the logic of his artistic development attracted no intelligent notice," Edmund Wilson noted. Some critics, perhaps most especially Eliot, have made the mistake "of defending him where he is not defensible," as George Orwell said. However, a considerable number of critics argue that attempts to define Kipling's stature in terms of such categories as "major or minor" and "poet or verse writer" are irrelevant. As James Harrison has remarked: "To have reached, as no English author since Dickens had done, a world-wide readership of immense size and the widest possible intellectual and social range, and to be quoted scores of times a day by people who have no idea whom they are quoting, is to be honored in a way many authors of the front rank might envy."

(See also *TCLC*, Vol. 8; *Contemporary Authors*, Vol. 105; *Dictionary of Literary Biography*, Vol. 19: *British Poets, 1880-1914;* and *Dictionary of Literary Biography*, Vol. 34: *British Novelists, 1890-1929: Traditionalists.*)

PRINCIPAL WORKS

Schoolboy Lyrics (poetry) 1881
Departmental Ditties (poetry) 1886
In Black and White (short stories) 1888
The Phantom 'Rickshaw (short stories) 1888
Plain Tales from the Hills (short stories) 1888
Soldiers Three (short stories) 1888
The Story of the Gadsbys (short stories) 1888
Under the Deodars (short stories) 1888
Wee Willie Winkie (short stories) 1888
The Courting of Dinah Shadd (short stories) 1890
The Light That Failed (novel) 1890
Life's Handicap (short stories) 1891
Barrack-Room Ballads (poetry) 1892
The Naulahka [with Wolcott Balestier] (novel) 1892
Many Inventions (short stories) 1893
The Jungle Book (short stories and poetry) 1894
The Second Jungle Book (short stories and poetry) 1895
The Seven Seas (poetry) 1896
Captains Courageous (novel) 1897
The Day's Work (short stories) 1898
From Sea to Sea. 2 vols. (sketches) 1899
Stalky and Co. (short stories) 1899
Kim (novel) 1901
Just-So Stories (short stories and poetry) 1902
The Five Nations (poetry) 1903
Traffics and Discoveries (short stories and poetry) 1904
Puck of Pook's Hill (short stories and poetry) 1906
Abaft the Funnel (short stories) 1909
Actions and Reactions (short stories and poetry) 1909
Rewards and Fairies (short stories and poetry) 1910
Songs from Books (poetry) 1912
A Diversity of Creatures (short stories and poetry) 1917
The Years Between (poetry) 1919

Letters of Travel, 1892-1913 (sketches) 1920
Debits and Credits (short stories and poetry) 1926
A Book of Words (speeches) 1928
Thy Servant a Dog (short stories) 1930
Limits and Renewals (short stories and poetry) 1932
Souvenirs of France (essays) 1933
Complete Works. 35 vols. (short stories, poetry, novels, essays, sketches, speeches, and unfinished autobiography) 1937-39
Something of Myself (unfinished autobiography) 1937

CHARLES WILLIAMS (essay date 1930)

[*Williams was a writer of supernatural fiction, a poet whose best works treat the legends of Logres (Arthurian Britain), and one of the central figures among the literary group known as the Oxford Christians, or "Inklings." The religious, the magical, and the mythical are recurrent concerns in his works, reflecting his devout Anglicanism and lifelong interest in all aspects of the preternatural. Although his works are not today as well known as those of his fellow-Inklings C. S. Lewis and J.R.R. Tolkien, Williams was an important source of encouragement and influence among the group. In the following excerpt from his book* Poetry at Present, *Williams debates Kipling's status as a distinguished poet by considering specific strengths and weaknesses of his verse, such as his moralizing stance, his traditional, unvarying rhythm and diction, his two dimensional vision, and his ingenuity at expressing universal emotions.*]

Almost all the poets considered in this book [among them, Thomas Hardy, W. B. Yeats, Lascelles Abercrombie, and T. S. Eliot] have some sort of relation in their work to our general methods of existence. Some of them, and those among the most important, have adopted an hypothesis on which they base a decision on life, a judgement or criticism of it as a whole. Mr. Kipling is apparently an exception. It is not that he fails to instruct us how to live; he does that oftener than more metaphysical poets. He is our great moralist. His verses, 'embellished with the *argot* of the Upper Fourth Remove', preach the doctrines of that inarticulate Upper Fourth to the rest of society. Is this an enlargement of English verse? Did the Muse of Tourneur and Marvell and Johnson and Landor— to say nothing of greater poets—need to know this other language also? And can there be any valuable meaning of which it is the foreordained expression? At first thought, it would seem not.

Yet, as much as with any other of these poets, lines and stanzas of his remain in the memory when the book is closed. Sometimes pleasing, sometimes irritating, they pursue us with a fantastic recurrence. But this is the kind of thing that only happens with distinguished poets. Is Mr. Kipling, then, a distinguished poet?

It seems as if the answer to both these questions must be a combination of two. Our verse had needed Mr. Kipling and yet he is not a distinguished poet; or alternatively we had not needed him and yet he is. The populace know him, and so (sometimes in spite of themselves) do the intelligentsia. It is not enough to say that he sometimes writes badly; all poets do that—except Mr. Housman.... Even Mr. Yeats, even Mr. Abercrombie, occasionally shoot an arrow awry. But Mr. Kipling seems to be writing best when he is writing worst, which is why he leaves us in confusion, and why the *bourgeoisie* of verse cannot deal with him. He cannot be forgotten and yet he cannot be endured. The Muse corrects with him her own conventions. For even the English Muse, with Keats and Coleridge in her train, has to remind herself that

> There are nine-and-sixty ways of constructing
> tribal lays,
> And every single one of them is right.

'Tribal lays' is of course capable of two meanings: it may mean lays after the manner of the tribe or lays in praise or exhortation of the tribe. Of the second Mr. Kipling has been justly accused often enough. He will talk of England in a way that destroys all England's greatness, and makes her seem always what she has only sometimes been—one of a horde of semi-barbarians fighting for the richest pasture. But it is difficult to read him without feeling that he also is part of the greatness he has forgotten. For the poems in which England is booted to her place among the nations are interspersed with others in which man becomes more important even than an Englishman. Mr. Max Beerbohm created a marvellous cartoon of 'Mr. Rudyard Kipling takes 'is gal Britannia out'. But on other evenings, when Britannia is engaged and Mr. Kipling is alone, he remembers the East and all the myriad generations, and speaks of them simply and poignantly. . . . The English country is then no longer a place through which Britannia and Mr. Kipling can triumphantly tramp, but rather of continuity, memory, and present satisfaction. Under the trouble of an exile which is a greater burden than the official White Man's, the ends of the Empire remember the real English flowers. Against 'the old trail, our own trail, the out trail' lies 'the way through the woods'. (pp. 40-3)

Most poets have considered a little the desire for joy and peace that seems natural to man. But, though Mr. Kipling may at times allude to them, there is never the sense of joy or peace in his verse. Partly perhaps this is the fault of his rhythm and diction, both of which tend to be common, and by mere repetition to become commonplace. Partly it is due to an apparent lack of philosophical perspective; this poetry moves always in the foreground of the mind. His poems, intellectually speaking, are often two-dimensional, and it is for this reason that the climax in some of them merely does not happen. This is so with nearly all the controversial verses—those on Ireland, on Pacificism, on the attitude of the Holy See during the War, on the cause of the Boer War, and so on. It is not that Mr. Kipling is necessarily wrong; it is that he gives us no idea of his opponents' having a case at all. His question in effect is always quite simply: 'My God, man, how can you be such a swine?' And, curiously enough, the 'My God' is not a mere oath; it is a quite sincere prayer—so much so that a more accurate implicit reading would be: 'My God, how can this man be such a swine?' Mr. Chesterton is occasionally casual enough in his controversies, but Mr. Kipling, in his annoyed disgust, merely abolishes the controversy. It creates exactly the same effect as that sentence which haunts more than one modern novelist—'He was the kind of man who called a napkin a serviette'; the unfortunate creature is left to 'the Wind that blows between the worlds' (which is presumably, though Mr. Kipling does not say so, the Wind of the Holy Ghost that blew on Pentecost), and we are left face to face with snobbishness.

But if Mr. Kipling has no use for the man who disagrees with him, he has certainly no more use for the inefficient man who agrees with him. (pp. 44-5)

If the rulers of England and Mr. Kipling's Empire were corrupt, if justice were sold or the seats of justice defiled, and he knew

it, it is certain that his voice would be the loudest in protest. It is very likely that he would not know it; but there is a poem called 'Gehazi,' dated 1915, apparently on some appointment to the Justiciary, which has something of this anger. . . .

> Well done, well done, Gehazi!
>   Stretch forth thy ready hand,
> Thou barely 'scaped from judgement,
>   Take oath to judge the land
> Unswayed by gift of money
>   Or privy bribe, more base,
> Of knowledge which is profit
>   In any market-place . . .
>   Stand up, stand up, Gehazi!
>   Draw close thy robe and go,
>   Gehazi, Judge in Israel,
>   A leper white as snow.

But the difficulty with this poem and with others is their topicality. They are, in that sense, journalistic. Dates are already needed for many of them, and are already useless for many. 'We forget so soon', as another doctrinal poet has said; and if there is no greatness of style to help us keep the poems, and therefore their occasions, in memory, what is to become of Mr. Kipling's reputation?

The answer is in the second of those ancient landmarks, and this time it is an outstanding one. It is, quite simply, death. But this landmark is set up, not so much in the poems that call attention to it—the 'Hymn before Action,' for example—as in the narratives. And the narratives are some of Mr. Kipling's best work.

For one thing, the efficiency which he has praised befriends him; for another, he has no opponents; for another, his metres are as straightforward as, and therefore of use to, his stories; for another, his choice of words is equally simple and direct; for another, the very 'imperialism' which may, for some readers, destroy the effectiveness of his hortatory or comminatory poems, is here of use. (pp. 46-7)

These advantages make admirable things of the tales—'The Ballad of the King's Mercy,' 'The Ballad of the King's Jest,' 'With Scindia to Delhi,' 'The Ballad of East and West,' 'Shiv and the Grasshopper,' 'Tomlinson,' and the rest. But most of them, and nearly all of the best, are sharpened to a point of death or the nearness of death. In that point it is only honour or the lack of honour that is felt, whenever there is anything beyond the mere story to be felt at all. And this honour is also, in a sense, efficiency. As a man's ability for his job should be clean and sure, so should his soul be able to meet the extreme of Fate unterrified, and it is Fate that he has to meet—Fate and no other kind of god, though in some of his lesser poems Mr. Kipling gives it divine names, 'Jehovah of the Thunders' and so on. There are even one or two poems in which the persons of the Christian myth are introduced: the Child Jesus, and an occasional Madonna. But they are not very convincing. The real force which appears, aboriginal and almost irresistible, is not the energy of those mortal and deific figures. Another religion has captured Mr. Kipling; he is the nearest to a Mahommedan poet that the English have produced. It is not only the poems in which he borrows the phraseology of Islam that make one say so; the name Allah in 'The Answer' or in 'The Legend of Mirth', or (from the last) such lines as

> the shining Courts were void
> Save for one Seraph whom no charge employed,

With folden wings and slumber-threatened brow,
To whom The Word: 'Beloved, what dost thou?'
'By the Permission', came the answer soft,
'Little I do nor do that little oft.
As is The Will in Heaven so on earth
Where by The Will I strive to make men mirth.'

More strongly this Force is felt in the tempest at sea and the famine on land, the desert and the pestilence, the natural forces against which his chosen heroes conduct their successful or unsuccessful war, and combined with these the mere law of cause and effect which he proclaims so often, the fact that inefficiency produces disaster. No excuse however good, no reason however weighty, can turn aside the Law, and Mr. Kipling is passionately in love with that Law. Even more than he dislikes his intellectual opponents he despises those who try to avoid it or are surprised at the results of its existence.... (pp. 48-9)

It may be because of this that his sea poems are so good, because the sea is the best image of that element in life which cannot be persuaded or overcome, but with which every fight must be a drawn battle; and because of this that his high figures are great in death, because death comes to all and the Law wins in the end. (p. 49)

But the Law is found in yet another place, in machinery. In **'M' Andrew's Hymn'** a Scotch engineer compares the working of the engines of the ship to Calvinism, and indeed Calvinism, like Islam, found the secret of the universe in the unchanging Will. So in many poems, and by many ways, we come back to the same central idea. Nor is it the idea only that relates machinery to Mr. Kipling's verse. To say it is machine-made would be silly. But so many of the poems do seem to jingle—now and then deliberately, as in the light verse on the 'jingling tonga-bar', but generally because obviously he thinks and feels in that way. It is machinery—these rhythms and rhymes—but it is conscious machinery. They are machine-emotions, machine-thoughts (or, in another simile, herd-emotions and herd-thoughts). But they know that they are so, and have so chosen to be—their nature being also their choice—and therefore they are in the end saved from the dreadful curse of nonentity. They are machinery, but they are. The rattle and clang are tiring sometimes and sometimes irritating, but they are not negligible. It has been said that nearly all Mr. Kipling's verse would be poetry, if only a poet had written it; it would be truer to say that most of his verse is not poetry though a poet has written it. But if it persuades us that he is a poet, whereas the verse of other more solemn and humane and high-principled writers does not, it has at least achieved a not insignificant result.

The best-known part of his work is the poems of life in the army; the **Barrack Room Ballads** and their like. But if they are important, it is not because they show us the modern soldier, or tell us of his hardships or heroism—that might make them valuable for sociology or ethics, but not for poetry. It is because with them a new and peculiar sound entered English verse. Universal emotions were expressed in a new technique. Taken as a whole, it might be doubted whether any poems, for all their Cockney slang, were less like the English soldier. They may express him or not; none but he (and of course there is no such being) could possibly say. But they have a high, feverish, bitter, unhappy note, which is quite unparalleled. This fever and unhappiness are not the speculations of the study; they arise from mists endured and wounds suffered and vigils kept. (pp. 49-51)

'The Passing of Danny Deever' might rank with Wilde's *Ballad of Reading Gaol*. In these moments there is vocalized, sometimes in a thin shriek, sometimes in a note of deeper endurance, the loneliness of the soul. And the answer comes in the poems of a passionate brotherhood. Wars and controversies and the tumults of a day have caused Mr. Kipling to shrill out his curses against the enemies of a day; the cloud that ascends from them has perhaps blinded his sight and certainly hidden from us his high concern. The Upper Fourth Remove, the barrackroom Cockneys, are followers of chivalry and Romance. In two poems Mr. Kipling has spoken of that Romance. The first is called **'The King,'** and describes how every age sees Romance in a by-gone period and not in its own, as ours does. But

His hand was on the lever laid,
　His oil-can soothed the worrying cranks,
His whistle waked the snowbound grade,
　His fog-horn cut the reeking Banks;
By dock and deep and mine and mill
The Boy-god reckless laboured still.

This is the lesser romance, efficiency and order and achievement. But there is another, since every god known to man has a greater deity in its nature of which we only dream; and this is the **'True Romance.'**

Thy face is far from this our war,
　Our call and counter-cry;
I shall not find Thee quick and kind,
　Nor know Thee till I die.
Enough for me in dreams to see
　And touch Thy garments' hem:
Thy feet have trod so near to God
　I may not follow them.

This is the Romance to which man looks for salvation 'in the hour of death and in the day of judgement', the spirit of an inner virginity which should accompany and produce the outer efficiency. It is in the ritual where the praise of both is mingled that Mr. Kipling has sung his part. (pp. 53-4)

> *Charles Williams, "Rudyard Kipling," in his* Poetry at Present, *Oxford at the Clarendon Press, Oxford, 1930, pp. 40-55.*

GEORGE ORWELL　(essay date 1942)

[*An English novelist and essayist, Orwell is significant for his unwavering commitment, both as a man and an artist, to personal freedom and social justice. His unpretentious self-examination and his ability to perceive the social effects of political theories inspired Irving Howe to call him "the greatest moral force in English letters during the last several decades." Throughout his career Orwell attacked exploitation of the weak by the powerful, whether in a modern democracy or a totalitarian state. He was particularly attuned to the confining effects of class and social standing in modern life. Foremost among Orwell's work is his novel* Nineteen Eighty-Four (1949), *one of the most influential books of the century. An attack on totalitarianism, it warns that absolute power in the hands of any government can deprive a people of all basic freedoms. Orwell's prose style, especially that of his essays, has become a model for its precision, clarity, and vividness. Many of his essays, which combine observation and reminiscence with literary and social criticism, are considered modern masterpieces. In the following excerpt, originally published in* Horizon *in February, 1942, Orwell discusses Kipling's conservative political beliefs and attempts to dispel allegations that he was fascistic by arguing that he was a staunch supporter*] *of typically Romantic nineteenth-century values. He also examines the merits and defects of Kipling's poetry and offers an explanation for its popularity.*]

It was a pity that Mr Eliot should be so much on the defensive in the long essay with which he prefaces this selection of Kipling's poetry [see *TCLC*, Vol. 4], but it was not to be avoided, because before one can even speak about Kipling one has to clear away a legend that has been created by two sets of people who have not read his works. Kipling is in the peculiar position of having been a byword for fifty years. During five literary generations every enlightened person has despised him, and at the end of that time nine-tenths of those enlightened persons are forgotten and Kipling is in some sense still there. Mr Eliot never satisfactorily explains this fact, because in answering the shallow and familiar charge that Kipling is a "Fascist," he falls into the opposite error of defending him where he is not defensible. It is no use pretending that Kipling's view of life, as a whole, can be accepted or even forgiven by any civilised person. It is no use claiming, for instance, that when Kipling describes a British soldier beating a "nigger" with a cleaning rod in order to get money out of him, he is acting merely as a reporter and does not necessarily approve what he describes. There is not the slightest sign anywhere in Kipling's work that he disapproves of that kind of conduct—on the contrary, there is a definite strain of sadism in him, over and above the brutality which a writer of that type has to have. Kipling *is* a jingo imperialist, he *is* morally insensitive and aesthetically disgusting. It is better to start by admitting that, and then to try to find out why it is that he survives while the refined people who have sniggered at him seem to wear so badly.

And yet the "Fascist" charge has to be answered, because the first clue to any understanding of Kipling, morally or politically, is the fact that he was *not* a Fascist. He was further from being one than the most humane or the most "progressive" person is able to be nowadays. An interesting instance of the way in which quotations are parroted to and fro without any attempt to look up their context or discover their meaning is the line from **"Recessional,"** "Lesser breeds without the Law". This line is always good for a snigger in pansy-left circles. It is assumed as a matter of course that the "lesser breeds" are "natives," and a mental picture is called up of some *pukka sahib* in a pith helmet kicking a coolie. In its context the sense of the line is almost the exact opposite of this. The phrase "lesser breeds" refers almost certainly to the Germans, and especially the pan-German writers, who are "without the Law" in the sense of being lawless, not in the sense of being powerless. The whole poem, conventionally thought of as an orgy of boasting, is a denunciation of power politics, British as well as German. Two stanzas are worth quoting (I am quoting this as politics, not as poetry):

> If, drunk with sight of power, we loose
>   Wild tongues that have not Thee in awe,
> Such boastings as the Gentiles use,
>   Or lesser breeds without the Law—
> Lord God of Hosts, be with us yet,
> Lest we forget—lest we forget!
>
> For heathen heart that puts her trust
>   In reeking tube and iron shard,
> All valiant dust that builds on dust,
>   And guarding, calls not Thee to guard,
> For frantic boast and foolish word—
> Thy mercy on Thy people, Lord!

Much of Kipling's phraseology is taken from the Bible, and no doubt in the second stanza he had in mind the text from Psalm cxxvii: "Except the Lord build the house, they labour in vain that build it; except the Lord keep the city, the watchman waketh but in vain." It is not a text that makes much impression on the post-Hitler mind. No one, in our time, believes in any sanction greater than military power; no one believes that it is possible to overcome force except by greater force. There is no "law," there is only power. I am not saying that that is a true belief, merely that it is the belief which all modern men do actually hold. . . . Kipling's outlook is pre-Fascist. He still believes that pride comes before a fall and that the gods punish *hubris*. He does not foresee the tank, the bombing plane, the radio and the secret police, or their psychological results.

But in saying this, does not one unsay what I said above about Kipling's jingoism and brutality? No, one is merely saying that the nineteenth-century imperialist outlook and the modern gangster outlook are two different things. Kipling belongs very definitely to the period 1885-1902. The Great War and its aftermath embittered him, but he shows little sign of having learned anything from any event later than the Boer War. He was the prophet of British Imperialism in its expansionist phase (even more than his poems, his solitary novel, *The Light that Failed*, gives you the atmosphere of that time) and also the unofficial historian of the British Army, the old mercenary army which began to change its shape in 1914. All his confidence, his bouncing vulgar vitality, sprang out of limitations which no Fascist or near-Fascist shares.

Kipling spent the later part of his life in sulking, and no doubt it was political disappointment rather than literary vanity that accounted for this. Somehow history had not gone according to plan. After the greatest victory she had ever known, Britain was a lesser world power than before, and Kipling was quite acute enough to see this. The virtue had gone out of the classes he idealised, the young were hedonistic or disaffected, the desire to paint the map red had evaporated. He could not understand what was happening, because he had never had any grasp of the economic forces underlying imperial expansion. It is notable that Kipling does not seem to realise, any more than the average soldier or colonial administrator, that an empire is primarily a money-making concern. Imperialism as he sees it is a sort of forcible evangelising. You turn a Gatling gun on a mob of unarmed "natives," and then you establish "the Law," which includes roads, railways and a court-house. He could not foresee, therefore, that the same motives which brought the Empire into existence would end by destroying it. . . . His outlook, allowing for the fact that after all he was an artist, was that of the salaried bureaucrat who despises the "box wallah" and often lives a lifetime without realising that the "box wallah" calls the tune.

But because he identifies himself with the official class, he does possess one thing which "enlightened" people seldom or never possess, and that is a sense of responsibility. The middle-class Left hate him for this quite as much as for his cruelty and vulgarity. All left-wing parties in the highly industrialised countries are at bottom a sham, because they make it their business to fight against something which they do not really wish to destroy. They have internationalist aims, and at the same time they struggle to keep up a standard of life with which those aims are incompatible. . . . A humanitarian is always a hypocrite, and Kipling's understanding of this is perhaps the central secret of his power to create telling phrases. It would be difficult to hit off the one-eyed pacifism of the

The Light that failed

Chapter V.
How goods were bought cheap and sold dear and who profited
by the Bargain.

I have a thousand men, said he
To wait upon my will
And towers nine upon the Tyne
And three upon the Till

And what care I for your men, said she
Or towers from Tyne to Till
Sith you must go with me, she said
To wait upon my will.
                    Sir Hoggie and the Fairies

Next morning Torpenhow found Dick sunk in deepest repose
of tobacco.
"Well you madman. How d'you feel. What made you go to bed last night."
"I don't know. I'm trying to find out."
"You had much better do some work."
Maybe, but I'm in no hurry. I've made a discovery Torp,
there's too much Ego in my Cosmos.
"Not really. Is this revelation due to my lectures on the Nilgheris?"
"No it came to me. Suddenly, all on my own account much
too much ego; and now I'm going to work."
He turned over a few half-finished sketches, drummed on a
new canvas, cleaned three brushes, set Binkie to bite the
tail of the lay-figure, rattled through his collection of arms
and accoutrements and then went out abruptly, declaring
that he had done enough for the day.
"This is positively indecent" Said Torpenhow. and the first time
that Dick has ever broken up a light morning. Perhaps
he had found out that he had a soul or an artistic temperament. or something equally valuable. That comes of
leaving him alone for a month. Perhaps he has been
going out of evenings I must look to this." He rang for
the bald-headed old housekeeper whom nothing could
astonish or annoy.

A portion from the manuscript of The Light that Failed.

English in fewer words than in the phrase, "making mock of uniforms that guard you while you sleep." It is true that Kipling does not understand the economic aspect of the relationship between the highbrow and the blimp. He does not see that the map is painted red chiefly in order that the coolie may be exploited. Instead of the coolie he sees the Indian Civil Servant; but even on that plane his grasp of function, of who protects whom, is very sound. He sees clearly that men can only be highly civilised while other men, inevitably less civilised, are there to guard and feed them.

How far does Kipling really identify himself with the administrators, soldiers and engineers whose praises he sings? Not so completely as is sometimes assumed. He had travelled very widely while he was still a young man, he had grown up with a brilliant mind in mainly philistine surroundings, and some streak in him that may have been partly neurotic led him to prefer the active man to the sensitive man. The nineteenth-century Anglo-Indians, to name the least sympathetic of his idols, were at any rate people who did things. It may be that all that they did was evil, but they changed the face of the earth (it is instructive to look at a map of Asia and compare the railway system of India with that of the surrounding coun-tries), whereas they could have achieved nothing, could not have maintained themselves in power for a single week, if the normal Anglo-Indian outlook had been that of, say, E. M. Forster. Tawdry and shallow though it is, Kipling's is the only literary picture that we possess of nineteenth-century Anglo-India, and he could only make it because he was just coarse enough to be able to exist and keep his mouth shut in clubs and regimental messes. But he did not greatly resemble the people he admired. I know from several private sources that many of the Anglo-Indians who were Kipling's contemporaries did not like or approve of him. They said, no doubt truly, that he knew nothing about India, and on the other hand, he was from their point of view too much of a highbrow. While in India he tended to mix with "the wrong" people, and because of his dark complexion he was wrongly suspected of having a streak of Asiatic blood. Much in his development is traceable to his having been born in India and having left school early. With a slightly different background he might have been a good novelist or a superlative writer of music-hall songs. But how true is it that he was a vulgar flag-waver, a sort of publicity agent for Cecil Rhodes? It is true, but it is not true that he was a yes-man or a time-server. After his early days, if then, he never courted public opinion. Mr Eliot says that what is held against him is that he expressed unpopular views in a popular style. This narrows the issue by assuming that "unpopular" means unpopular with the intelligentsia, but it is a fact that Kipling's "message" was one that the big public did not want, and, indeed, has never accepted. The mass of the people, in the 'nineties as now, were anti-militarist, bored by the Empire and only unconsciously patriotic. Kipling's official admirers are and were the "service" middle class, the people who read *Blackwood's*. In the stupid early years of this century, the blimps, having at last discovered someone who could be called a poet and who was on their side, set Kipling on a pedestal, and some of his more sententious poems, such as **"If,"** were given almost Biblical status. But it is doubtful whether the blimps have ever read him with attention, any more than they have read the Bible. Much of what he says they could not possibly approve. Few people who have criticised England from the inside have said bitterer things about her than this gutter patriot. As a rule it is the British working class that he is attacking, but not always. That phrase about "the flannelled fools at the wicket and the muddied oafs at the goal" sticks like an arrow to this day, and it is aimed at the Eton and Harrow match as well as the Cup-Tie Final. (pp. 100-05)

Kipling's romantic ideas about England and the Empire might not have mattered if he could have held them without having the class-prejudices which at that time went with them. If one examines his best and most representative work, his soldier poems, especially **Barrack-Room Ballads,** one notices that what more than anything else spoils them is an underlying air of patronage. Kipling idealises the army officer, especially the junior officer, and that to an idiotic extent, but the private soldier, though lovable and romantic, has to be a comic. He is always made to speak in a sort of stylised Cockney, not very broad but with all the aitches and final "g's" carefully omitted. Very often the result is as embarrassing as the humorous recitation at a church social. And this accounts for the curious fact that one can often improve Kipling's poems, make them less facetious and less blatant by simply going through them and transplanting them from Cockney into standard speech. (p. 105)

Can one imagine any private soldier, in the 'nineties or now, reading **Barrack-Room Ballads** and feeling that here was a writer who spoke for him? It is very hard to do so. Any soldier capable of reading a book of verse would notice at once that Kipling is almost unconscious of the class war that goes on in an army as much as elsewhere. It is not only that he thinks the soldier comic, but that he thinks him patriotic, feudal, a ready admirer of his officers, and proud to be a soldier of the Queen. Of course that is partly true, or battles could not be fought, but "What have I done for thee, England, my England?" is essentially a middle-class query. Almost any working man would follow it up immediately with "What has England done for me?" In so far as Kipling grasps this, he simply sets it down to "the intense selfishness of the lower classes" (his own phrase). When he is writing not of British but of "loyal" Indians he carries the "Salaam, sahib" *motif* to sometimes disgusting lengths. Yet it remains true that he has far more interest in the common soldier, far more anxiety that he shall get a fair deal, than most of the "liberals" of his day or our own. He sees that the soldier is neglected, meanly underpaid, and hypocritically despised by the people whose incomes he safeguards. "I came to realise," he says in his posthumous memoirs, "the bare horrors of the private's life, and the unnecessary torments he endured." He is accused of glorifying war, and perhaps he does so, but not in the usual manner, by

pretending that war is a sort of football match. Like most people capable of writing battle poetry, Kipling had never been in battle, but his vision of war is realistic. . . . If anything, Kipling overdoes the horrors, for the wars of his youth were hardly wars at all by our standards. Perhaps that is due to the neurotic strain in him, the hunger for cruelty. But at least he knows that men ordered to attack impossible objectives *are* dismayed, and also that fourpence a day is not a generous pension.

How complete or truthful a picture has Kipling left us of the long-service, mercenary army of the late nineteenth century? One must say of this, as of what Kipling wrote about nineteenth-century Anglo-India, that it is not only the best but almost the only literary picture we have. He has put on record an immense amount of stuff that one could otherwise only gather from verbal tradition or from unreadable regimental histories. Perhaps his picture of army life seems fuller and more accurate than it is because any middle-class English person is likely to know enough to fill up the gaps. At any rate, reading the essay on Kipling that Mr Edmund Wilson has just published or is just about to publish, I was struck by the number of things that are boringly familiar to us and seem to be barely intelligible to an American. But from the body of Kipling's early work there does seem to emerge a vivid and not seriously misleading picture of the old pre-machine-gun army—the sweltering barracks in Gibraltar or Lucknow, the red coats, the pipeclayed belts and the pillbox hats, the beer, the fights, the floggings, hangings and crucifixions, the bugle-calls, the smell of oats and horse-piss, the bellowing sergeants with foot-long moustaches, the bloody skirmishes, invariably mismanaged, the crowded troopships, the cholera-stricken camps, the "native" concubines, the ultimate death in the workhouse. It is a crude, vulgar picture in which a patriotic music-hall turn seems to have got mixed up with one of Zola's gorier passages, but from it future generations will be able to gather some idea of what a long-term volunteer army was like. On about the same level they will be able to learn something of British India in the days when motor-cars and refrigerators were unheard of. It is an error to imagine that we might have had better books on these subjects if, for example, George Moore, or Gissing, or Thomas Hardy, had had Kipling's opportunities. That is the kind of accident that cannot happen. It was not possible that nineteenth-century England should produce a book like *War and Peace*, or like Tolstoy's minor stories of army life, such as "Sebastopol" or "The Cossacks," not because the talent was necessarily lacking but because no one with sufficient sensitiveness to write such books would ever have made the appropriate contacts. Tolstoy lived in a great military empire in which it seemed natural for almost any young man of family to spend a few years in the army, whereas the British Empire was and still is demilitarised to a degree which Continental observers find almost incredible. (pp. 106-08)

Kipling is the only English writer of our time who has added phrases to the language. The phrases and neologisms which we take over and use without remembering their origin do not always come from writers we admire. It is strange, for instance, to hear the Nazi broadcasters referring to the Russian soldiers as "robots," thus unconsciously borrowing a word from a Czech democrat whom they would have killed if they could have laid hands on him. Here are half a dozen phrases coined by Kipling which one sees quoted in leaderettes in the gutter Press or overhears in saloon bars from people who have barely heard his name. It will be seen that they all have a certain characteristic in common:

East is East, and West is West.

The white man's burden.

What do they know of England who only England know?

The female of the species is more deadly than the male.

Somewhere East of Suez.

Paying the Dane-geld.

There are various others, including some that have outlived their context by many years. The phrase "killing Kruger with your mouth," for instance, was current till very recently. It is also possible that it was Kipling who first let loose the use of the word "Huns" for Germans; at any rate he began using it as soon as the guns opened fire in 1914. But what the phrases I have listed above have in common is that they are all of them phrases which one utters semi-derisively . . . , but which one is bound to make use of sooner or later. Nothing could exceed the contempt of the *New Statesman*, for instance, for Kipling, but how many times during the Munich period did the *New Statesman* find itself quoting that phrase about paying the Dane-geld? The fact is that Kipling, apart from his snack-bar wisdom and his gift for packing much cheap picturesqueness into a few words ("Palm and Pine"—"East of Suez"—"The Road to Mandalay"), is generally talking about things that are of urgent interest. It does not matter, from this point of view, that thinking and decent people generally find themselves on the other side of the fence from him. "White man's burden" instantly conjures up a real problem, even if one feels that it ought to be altered to "black man's burden." One may disagree to the middle of one's bones with the political attitude implied in **"The Islanders,"** but one cannot say that it is a frivolous attitude. Kipling deals in thoughts which are both vulgar and permanent. This raises the question of his special status as a poet, or verse-writer.

Mr Eliot describes Kipling's metrical work as "verse" and not "poetry," but adds that it is "*great* verse," and further qualifies this by saying that a writer can only be described as a "great verse-writer" if there is some of his work "of which we cannot say whether it is verse or poetry" [see *TCLC*, Vol. 8]. Apparently Kipling was a versifier who occasionally wrote poems, in which case it was a pity that Mr Eliot did not specify these poems by name. The trouble is that whenever an aesthetic judgment on Kipling's work seems to be called for, Mr Eliot is too much on the defensive to be able to speak plainly. What he does not say, and what I think one ought to start by saying in any discussion of Kipling, is that most of Kipling's verse is so horribly vulgar that it gives one the same sensation as one gets from watching a third-rate music-hall performer recite "The Pigtail of Wu Fang Fu" with the purple limelight on his face, *and yet* there is much of it that is capable of giving pleasure to people who know what poetry means. At his worst, and also his most vital, in poems like **"Gunga Din"** or **"Danny Deever,"** Kipling is almost a shameful pleasure, like the taste for cheap sweets that some people secretly carry into middle life. But even with his best passages one has the same sense of being seduced by something spurious, and yet unquestionably seduced. Unless one is merely a snob and a liar it is impossible to say that no one who cares for poetry could get any pleasure out of such lines as:

> For the wind is in the palm-trees, and the temple-bells they say: "Come you back, you British soldier; come you back to Mandalay!"

and yet those lines are not poetry in the same sense as "Felix Randal" or "When icicles hang by the wall" are poetry. One can, perhaps, place Kipling more satisfactorily than by juggling with the words "verse" and "poetry," if one describes him simply as a good bad poet. He is as a poet what Harriet Beecher Stowe was as a novelist. And the mere existence of work of this kind, which is perceived by generation after generation to be vulgar and yet goes on being read, tells one something about the age we live in. (pp. 109-11)

In so far as a writer of verse can be popular, Kipling has been and probably still is popular. In his own lifetime some of his poems travelled far beyond the bounds of the reading public, beyond the world of school prize-days, Boy Scout singsongs, limp-leather editions, poker-work and calendars, and out into the yet vaster world of the music halls. Nevertheless, Mr Eliot thinks it worth while to edit him, thus confessing to a taste which others share but are not always honest enough to mention. The fact that such a thing as good bad poetry can exist is a sign of the emotional overlap between the intellectual and the ordinary man. The intellectual *is* different from the ordinary man, but only in certain sections of his personality, and even then not all the time. But what is the peculiarity of a good bad poem? A good bad poem is a graceful monument to the obvious. It records in memorable form—for verse is a mnemonic device, among other things—some emotion which very nearly every human being can share. . . . Such poems are a kind of rhyming proverb, and it is a fact that definitely popular poetry is usually gnomic or sententious. One example from Kipling will do:

> White hands cling to the tightened rein,
>   Slipping the spur from the booted heel,
> Tenderest voices cry, "Turn again!"
>   Red lips tarnish the scabbarded steel. . . .
>
> Down to Gehenna or up to the Throne,
> He travels the fastest who travels alone.

There is a vulgar thought vigorously expressed. It may not be true, but at any rate it is a thought that everyone thinks. Sooner or later you will have occasion to feel that he travels the fastest who travels alone, and there the thought is, ready made and, as it were, waiting for you. So the chances are that, having once heard this line, you will remember it.

One reason for Kipling's power as a good bad poet I have already suggested—his sense of responsibility, which made it possible for him to have a world-view, even though it happened to be a false one. Although he had no direct connexion with any political party, Kipling was a Conservative, a thing that does not exist nowadays. Those who now call themselves Conservatives are either Liberals, Fascists or the accomplices of Fascists. He identified himself with the ruling power and not with the opposition. In a gifted writer this seems to us strange and even disgusting, but it did have the advantage of giving Kipling a certain grip on reality. The ruling power is always faced with the question, "In such and such circumstances, what would you *do*?," whereas the opposition is not obliged to take responsibility or make any real decisions. Where it is a permanent and pensioned opposition, as in England, the quality of its thought deteriorates accordingly. Moreover, anyone who starts out with a pessimistic, reactionary view of life tends to be justified by events, for Utopia never arrives and "the gods of the copybook headings," as Kipling himself put it, always return. Kipling sold out to the British governing class, not financially but emotionally. This warped his political judgment, for the British ruling class were not what he imagined, and it led him into abysses of folly and snobbery, but he gained a corresponding advantage from having at least tried to imagine what action and responsibility are like. It is a great thing in his favour that he is not witty, not ''daring,'' has no wish to *épater les bourgeois*. He dealt largely in platitudes, and since we live in a world of platitudes, much of what he said sticks. Even his worst follies seem less shallow and less irritating than the ''enlightened'' utterances of the same period, such as Wilde's epigrams or the collection of cracker-mottoes at the end of *Man and Superman*. (pp. 112-13)

> George Orwell, ''Rudyard Kipling,'' in his Critical
> *Essays, Secker and Warburg, 1946, pp. 100-13.*

JONAH RASKIN   (essay date 1971)

[*Raskin is an American critic, fiction writer, and educator whose special interest is the subject of imperialism in English fiction. In the following excerpt he examines the broad areas of duality and contrast in Kipling's fiction—geographic, cultural, social, and racial—and maintains that unity in his works comes through a denial of any serious conflict in these areas of difference and an enforced loyalty to the imperial hierarchy.*]

In poem after poem, story after story and novel after novel Kipling repeatedly and untiringly carved out sharp, broad areas of contrast. Kipling insists on the distinctions between man and beast, the primitive and the civilized, the insider and the outsider, the patrician and the plebian, East and West, England and India, black and white, heaven and hell. There is the possibility for violent antagonism here but it doesn't develop in Kipling's world, even though his characters are often bloody and scarred. In his earliest work—*Plain Tales from the Hills, Life's Handicap* and *The Phantom Rickshaw*—he contrasts the plain with the extraordinary, phantoms with realities, the handicapped with the potent; he contrasts provincial Anglo-India with England, comfortable society with the anarchic forces beneath its surface and beyond its frontiers. . . . He compares the world of respectability, love and marriage with passion, sex and the disreputable. He contrasts the demands of art with the necessities of action. In *The Jungle Book* he compares the tribe with the outsider, the village of man with the confederation of beasts, law with anarchy.

The contrasts are firmly established but the dramatic situations are terminated without rigorous struggle. They do not precipitate dialectical conflicts. Kipling's heroes stand in a world which is divided between East and West, Black and white, rich and poor. They are composed of atomic particles which pull them toward the East and then back toward the West, toward the Brown man and then back to the white man. But there is little pull or push. The particles do not collide to produce new particles or antiparticles. Kipling keeps the opposing impulses in his heroes and the rival armies in society under control. He is the master at the machine, pulling levers and pushing buttons. Kipling's contrasts are immutable; he catalogs and compartmentalizes his characters. He allows his men time to wander on the leash, but demands of them that they remain close to home. They inevitably do. Hell, the East, the Jungle—these worlds are seen and explored by his heroes, but they are seen in concave or convex mirrors and they are scouted rather than explored. The under- and the outer worlds are rejected. Kipling's characters scurry back to heaven, the West and civilization. Early in the game the outcome of the foraging expeditions is clear. (pp. 37-8)

Kipling describes the organization man in isolation, the puritan in Bohemia, the white man among Brown men. His men are defined, their minds made flexible, their muscles made taut, through contact with their opposing types. They watch the moves of their adversaries in a magical mirror and adjust their own selves accordingly. There is rarely open conflict between Kipling's characters. In *Captains Courageous* there is no conflict between workers and bosses. In the tales of Anglo-India there is no dialectical relationship between East and West, Black and white. Kipling creates harmony between classes and cultures. On his ladder there is movement in only one direction: the puritan moves down among the bohemians, but the bohemian cannot move up among the puritans; the white man lives among Brown men, but the Brown man cannot live among whites. The rich boy plays poor boy, but the poor boy cannot play rich boy. (p. 39)

Mowgli is the prototype of all Kipling's heroes. He defines his own predicament when during a jungle ritual after the hunt he chants:

> I dance on the hide of Shere Khan, but my heart is very heavy. My mouth is cut and wounded with the stones from the village, but my heart is very light because I have come back to the jungle. Why? These two things fight together in me as the snakes fight in the spring. The water comes out of my eyes; yet I laugh while it falls. Why? I am two Mowglis . . .

Mowgli the son of man is an alien in the jungle, and Mowgli a brother of the jungle tribe is an outcast among men. He has parents in both the Indian village and the Indian jungle. He is manchild in the jungle. Kipling creates a contrast between man and beast, but it is diversionary. The vital contrast in *The Jungle Books* is not between man and beast but between law and anarchy, the empire and the Indians. When Mowgli chooses sides he leaves the beasts to join the world of men; but the men are white men, not Brown men. He exchanges the yoke of jungle law for the yoke of empire; he rejects the lawless rabble and embraces the stern officials. Mowgli leaves the beasts' world to become a man, but he mounts a rung at the bottom of the imperial ladder in the Department of Woods, exchanging a tribe for a bureaucracy. Kipling's contrasts give the appearance of objectivity, but no stories are more partisan. Behind the cunningly arranged contrasts lie the values of an authoritarian.

The first story Kipling wrote about Mowgli, ''In the Rukh,'' describes the last incident chronologically in his saga—his coming of age. His hero is married to an Indian woman and appointed to a post in the empire. From the start Mowgli is respectable. In the stories that followed, Kipling retraced his earlier career; he described the boy Mowgli. But Kipling does not reject the British Empire, as one might expect, when he describes Mowgli's youth. He celebrates law, hierarchy and empire in different ways. At the conclusion of *The Jungle Book* Kipling's spokesman says:

> Mule, horse, elephant, or bullock, he obeys his driver, and the driver his sergeant, and the sergeant his lieutenant, and the lieutenant his captain, and the captain his major, and the major his colonel, and the colonel his brigadier commanding three regiments, and the brigadier his general, who obeys the Viceroy, who is the servant of the Empress.

The tales about men and beasts offer a message: the empire. *The Jungle Book* culminates in a vision of the imperial hierarchy. The little world of the jungle forms a small circle within other circles within the circle of empire. Kipling's circle of empire contains all. In *The Naulahka, Captains Courageous* and *Plain Tales from the Hills,* contrasts are sustained and differences are tolerated because all individuals, classes, races and groups are incorporated under the empire or into the imperial hierarchy. In Kipling's model society the bear, the wolf, the snake, accept the law. In the Anglo-Indian society of his day men pledged their allegiance to Victoria, Empress of India. Each species is different from the next, each man is distinct from his fellow-man, but they are all contained in an overarching structure. Divisions in the hero are subsumed under his one patriotic self. (pp. 39-41)

Kipling's theme is simultaneously the separation of races, classes and lands, and the links between two men of opposite places of origin. The societies are opposed, but the individual men are together. Kipling writes of diversity in unity and unity in diversity. Rich and poor are different, but Harvey Cheene and Dan Troop are comrades; man and beast are different, but Mowgli is a friend of the wolf and the bear. The contrast at the core of Kipling's work is between cultures which are at opposite ends of the spectrum and individuals from those cultures who stand side by side. Kipling's classic statement of the theme is from **"The Ballad of East and West"**:

> Oh, East is East and West is West, and never the twain
> shall meet,
> Till Earth and Sky stand presently at God's great
> judgment Seat,
> But there is neither East nor West, Border nor Breed
> nor Birth,
> When two strong men stand face to face though they
> come from the ends of the earth!

Kipling is concerned equally with the irreconcilable hemispheres and the reconciled men. He is the poet of inequality who simultaneously celebrates the friendship between the Brown man and the white man, the rich man and the poor man. The poet of inequality deceives us; he appears in the guise of the poet of democracy and lauds Black men, Brown men, poor men. In Kipling's work the common soldier loves his officer and praises the colonial people. "The finest man I knew," says the cockney soldier in one of Kipling's best-known poems, "was our regimental bhisti Gunga Din." But when two strong men from the ends of the earth come face-to-face and embrace in Kipling's world, it is not a celebration of human fraternity. The friendships between the rich and the poor, Black and white, the tribe and the alien, in *Captains Courageous, The Jungle Book,* "The Ballad of East and West" and "Gunga Din" are unlike the genuine moments of humanity reflected in literature. When Melville describes Ishmael and Queequeg locked in each other's arms, he presents an ideal of human fraternity in a world of violent hatred. When Tolstoi depicts an old Russian peasant sharing bread with Levin, he offers a utopian vision in a world where masters and peasants are in conflict. At first glance Kipling's scenes have the look of these situations in Tolstoi and Melville. But unlike Melville and Tolstoi, Kipling neglects the real conflicts between rich and poor, Black and white. Kipling is out to co-opt us. He wants us to remember the friendship between Kim and the lama, Cheene and Troop, and forget about the exploitation of Black by white, the oppressed by their oppressors. . . . Kipling's images of unity define oppositions and contrasts. The exception proves the rule.

His characters offer fellowship to each other because they know their places, they accept the social hierarchy. There is only fraternity between unequal partners in Kipling's world, and that is no fraternity at all. (pp. 41-3)

Kipling's contrasts, his celebrations of individual customs and traits, are incorporated into a world of masters and slaves, rich and poor, victimizers and victims. The fear of miscegenation, rebellion and social upheaval struck deep into the core of his being. In his nightmares he envisioned the overthrow of white by Black, West by East. Those nightmares were warnings to him that the things which he loved, things as they were and as he hoped they would continue to be, were threatened. He believed in the necessity of racial separation, class lines, law, social hierarchy; but he was captivated by the things he feared most. Kipling defended the establishment, the West, the white man, the rich, and was fascinated by the world outside and beyond those limits—by the poor, the East, the Black man. His fascination for the latter does not call into question or negate his commitment to the former. Kipling stands for order, empire and white men, and he stands for them precisely by going beyond them to describe disorder, Black men, loneliness and horror. Kipling creates his contrasts—sits in heaven as opposed to hell, with the white as opposed to the Black, with the philistines as opposed to the bohemians, with the tribe as opposed to the alien—but he descends into the regions he fears. When he describes his expeditions into the world beyond and below, his vision is more significant than when he describes the protected, secure world. When he stops seeing the jungle as the law, as he does in *The Jungle Books,* and begins to see it as a threat, when he describes white men as estranged from white society and fearful of Black men and hostile nature, he reveals himself, the white man, and offers work of importance. His intention was usually to strengthen the law and the imperial hierarchy through making the descent into hell, but apart from his conscious aim the sense of contrast which results from the descent is important. When he writes that "When a man is absolutely alone in a Station he runs a certain risk of falling into evil ways," when he notes that "Few people can afford to play Robinson Crusoe anywhere—least of all in India," there is the sound of truth. This Kipling encircled the core of reality that Conrad probed in *Heart of Darkness.* While he did not confront loneliness as Conrad did, he offers more meaningful and vital material when he presents horrors and terrors than when he hides the facts and retreats into his luxurious, exotic and nostalgic worlds. (pp. 44-5)

Jonah Raskin, "Kipling's Contrasts," in his The Mythology of Imperialism: Rudyard Kipling, Joseph Conrad, E. M. Forster, D. H. Lawrence, and Joyce Cary, *Random House, 1971, pp. 37-45.*

JOHN A. McCLURE   (essay date 1981)

[*McClure is an American critic and educator specializing in English literature. In the following excerpt he examines Kipling's depiction of English imperialism in India.*]

In his fiction, Kipling presents a number of heroes—the common soldier, the freebooter, and the imperial officer. He celebrates the virtues and indicates the weaknesses of each, always from an authoritarian perspective. But the group to which he is most committed, whose values and aspirations he most fully shares, is that of the imperial service elite, the field officers—civil and military—of the Raj.

The Kipling hero lowest on the social and psychological ladder of power is the common British soldier. Kipling portrays the soldier as an essential component in the machinery of domination and as a figure motivated by the urge to destroy. "Speaking roughly," he writes in **"The Drums of the Fore and Aft"** . . . , "you must employ either blackguards or gentlemen, or, best of all, blackguards commanded by gentlemen, to do butcher's work with efficiency and despatch." Kipling sees the soldier's work as necessary, then. But he also finds it appealing, for soldiers act out the common authoritarian dream of total destructiveness, in which the dark undercurrents of hostility fed by years of impotent rage are allowed to surface, control the personality, and express themselves in acts of untempered aggression.

Because Kipling himself dreams of the perverse catharsis his soldier heroes actually achieve, he presents them realistically and sympathetically: "Mulvaney, Ortheris and Learoyd are Privates in B Company of a Line Regiment, and personal friends of mine. Collectively I think . . . they are the worst men in the regiment as far as genial blackguardism goes." The three characters' geniality resides solely in such qualities as kindliness to harmless children, obedience to powerful superiors, and a penchant for rather comic acts of deception and manipulation. For the rest, they are men whose greatest pleasure in life is killing, and whose pastimes are brawling, drinking, thieving, and looting. Yet Kipling so successfully communicates his enjoyment of the three that it is difficult to describe them for what they are without losing completely the tone of many of the stories in which they appear.

Several stories collected in *Soldiers Three* provide real insights into the life of the common soldier of the day. **"With the Main Guard"** . . . , for instance, conveys a vivid sense both of bloody battle and of the dreadful monotony of garrison life in India. **"On Greenhow Hill"** . . . shows how deeply Kipling understood the process by which the urge to destroy was instilled in the common soldier. The three privates are waiting in ambush for an Indian deserter who has been sniping at them for several nights. As they wait, Learoyd recalls his adolescent love for an English girl, and wonders for a moment if the deserter hasn't left his regiment because of a woman. Mulvaney checks him for "suggestin' invidious excuses for the man Stanley's goin' to kill," but encourages him to tell his story. Learoyd proceeds; the burden of his tale is that for a time in England his sense of love and community drew him toward positive feelings and actions, but that the fatal illness of his fiancée and the hostile indifference of English society destroyed his hope. His narrative clearly indicates that the thwarting of love on a human and social level induces a love of destruction, and this vital insight is reinforced throughout the story. In the final paragraphs, for instance, Learoyd's bitter bereavement at the death of his beloved is juxtaposed with Ortheris's deeply sensual murder of the deserter.

Kipling is clearly aware that libidinal forces can become destructive. Throughout the story he describes Ortheris's commitment to killing in phallic terms: "He jerked the cartridge out of the breech-block into the palm of his hand. ''Ere's my chaplin,' he said, and made the venomous black-headed bullet bow like a marionette. ''E's goin' to teach a man all about which is which, an' wot's true, after all, before sundown'." . . . The particular ferocity of Ortheris's hatred is due, the story suggests, to the fact that he has enjoyed even less nurturing than his companions. . . . With no experience of love to give him a sense of his own and other people's worth, and

with a deep fund of bitterness at having been so deprived, Ortheris uses a rifle to establish a place for himself in the community. A mere cipher, unwanted, inessential, and powerless, he proves by killing that he does exist, that his existence makes a difference to others, and that his power is in some ways at least absolute. He establishes, too, a terrible negative community, based on acts of murder rather than on support. Kipling dramatizes, with brilliant lucidity, Erich Fromm's insight into the source of authoritarian destructiveness: "The more the drive toward life is thwarted, the stronger is the drive toward the destruction . . . *Destructiveness is the outcome of unlived life.*"

Kipling's insights into the dynamics of this process and his sympathy for its victims are impressive, but he shows sympathy as well for their twisted values and deeds. The last words of **"On Greenhow Hill,"** with their identification of the artist and the sniper, of creation and destruction, suggest the degree to which Kipling shares the traits of his characters: "He was staring across the valley [at the dead man], with the smile of the artist who looks on the completed work." . . . In fact, dreams of destruction are the implicit source of many of Kipling's fictional creations; they are also the legacy of his own abandonment to a hostile world.

Kipling licenses his soldiers not only to kill but also to torture and rob their victims. (pp. 18-20)

The only limitation that Kipling places on his soldiers' licensed excesses is that they take place within a larger context of absolute loyalty to military authority. Mulvaney, the most accomplished rogue of the group, is also the most untiring defender of his officers' superiority. He never sides with the men against their commanders, and is always willing, as in **"The Big Drunk Draf'"** . . . , to suggest extra-legal methods of keeping unruly troops in line. Like the three schoolboy heroes of *Stalky and Co.*, the grown-up children of *Soldiers Three* only appear to be rebels. In fact they are dedicated defenders of their masters' authority. As licensed outlaws, they boast of their defiance and take privileges denied to their more authentically rebellious comrades, while still enjoying the security of their larger submission. In the end, however, Kipling demonstrates that the privileges granted to the common soldier, no matter how crafty he may be in exploiting them, by no means make up for his exclusion from the larger possibilities of life. Even in authoritarian terms, destructiveness is an unsatisfying way of dealing with a sense of isolation and sterility. Unlike domination, it leaves the individual alone, without living servants or accumulated wealth to attest to his superiority.

Kipling's second imperial hero, the freebooting gentleman-rover, does without official license and support, and so can take even more liberties with conventional codes of conduct than the soldier. A member of a "wholly unauthorized horde," he disdains the dependency of his brothers in government and the military. The freebooters of **"The Lost Legion"** . . . boast:

> Our fathers they left us their blessing—
>   They taught us, and groomed us, and crammed;
> But we've shaken the Clubs and the Messes
>   To go and find out and be damned.

Having "shaken" the fear of exposure which binds his fellow imperialists to the club and the mess, the freebooter can pursue his goals of domination and wealth without any of the restraints imposed by social custom or the unsympathetic restrictions of a central government.

Nor is he deterred by any internalized ethical standards. Nick Tarvin, the American hero of *The Naulahka* . . . , having come to India in search of loot, pursues his goal without compunction. He observes of his fiancée that "she could not know, and probably could not have imagined, how little his own sense of the square thing had to do with any system of morality." Kipling clearly admires Tarvin's utter lack of scruples and the spurious freedom it confers. (pp. 21-2)

Kipling's freebooters, like his other imperial heroes, are firmly rooted in historical reality. In Kipling's time, personal kingdoms were still being carved out of Africa and the Far East by men like the second Rajah Brooke of Sarawak and Cecil Rhodes of South Africa. Company agents, often with their own private armies, were penetrating ever deeper into unexplored and unexploited regions. And gradually the direct rule of the British was beginning to appear unnecessarily cumbersome in the light of less formal types of largely economic domination. *The Naulahka* anticipates the transfer of power from the Empire-weary British government to eager European and American neocolonialists. But it is perhaps a distortion on Kipling's part to describe his freebooters as wholly unauthorized and totally independent. In many cases they worked not as mere individuals, but as the representatives of capital, the lieutenants of industry. (p. 22)

Unlicensed but also unbound, the freebooter would seem to be the ideal authoritarian hero; yet Kipling depicts him only occasionally. Perhaps the very autonomy of the freebooter made it hard for Kipling, so concerned with domination in a social sense, so dependent on external reinforcement for his own security, to identify with him. Inclusion in a large and powerful community is important to Kipling; although he denies the freebooter his place in the official community, he gives him a community of his own, portraying him as part of a "wholly unauthorized horde," a "Lost Legion."

Unlike soldiers and freebooters, the members of the imperial service elite are both licensed and relatively unrepressed. Kipling was bound by birth and education to this caste; only his vocation as journalist kept him at its periphery, for its members were mainly district officers, military men, engineers, or field officers in some other branch of the government. Kipling sometimes describes these men in terms of Victorian ideals of service and self-sacrifice, but his more convincing stories illuminate them with a less flattering light. In these, the colonial official appears as a genial but unscrupulous despot gratifying at once his urge to dominate and the Indian's need for domination.

Kipling never questions the latter need. He accepts and reiterates the commonplace identification of the Indians with children who must remain under protective custody: "Never forget that unless the outward and visible signs of Our Authority are always before a native he is as incapable as a child of understanding what authority means, or where is the danger of disobeying it." Kipling's own work could easily be introduced to challenge this assertion, for in several stories he portrays Indians who act with great restraint and assume important responsibilities. But such a challenge misses the point. Statements like the one above are not primarily generalizations based on experience, but ideological weapons in the imperialist's struggle for legitimation. Having labeled the Indian a child, the imperialist can argue that any rebellion stems not from rational political grievances, but from irrational impulses. He can argue, too, that his use of force to maintain control is necessary, since children are not rational creatures.

So labeled, the colonized are caught in a double bind. If they obey, they prove the contention that they need and want to be dominated. If they rebel, they prove only that domination is necessary. Moreover, some members of the colonized community, awed by the superior power of the imperialist forces, may actually come to believe that they are intrinsically inferior creatures. Trapped by being defined as children, demoralized by their sense of inferiority, they will be hard put to recover any self-confidence.

Nor does the imperialist desire any such recovery. His aim, as Kipling makes clear time and again, is to perpetuate the myth of intrinsic inferiority both in the colonies and at home. In fact, as Kipling argues in **"The Man Who Would Be King"** . . . , the imperialist's life depends on the maintenance of this illusion; the man who would be king must convince his subjects that he is not just accidentally and temporarily but fundamentally and permanently their superior. Once he has enchained them with this illusion, they will no longer pose a constant threat. (pp. 23-4)

But to justify permanent imperial domination the metaphorical definition of the Indian as child must be qualified. Children grow up; their inferiority is only provisional. But the Indian, Kipling and his fellow imperialists claim, is a peculiar kind of child, one who will "never stand alone." In **"The Head of the District,"** Kipling's dying district officer is bidding farewell to his escort of native soldiers:

> "I do not know who takes my place. I speak now true talk, for I am as it were already dead, my children,—for though ye be strong men, ye are children."
>
> "And thou art our father and our mother," broke in Khoda Dad Khan with an oath. "What shall we do, now there is no one to speak for us, or to teach us to go wisely!"
>
> "There remains Tallantire Sahib. Go to him; he knows your talk and your heart. Keep the young men quiet, listen to the old men, and obey."

Such conversations undoubtedly occurred; such bonds were formed. But Kipling's heroic district officer deliberately maintains his identity as father to the Indian's child. Even on his death bed, he utters not "true talk" but an enslaving lie. Or, more correctly, he utters a lie that has become, for his servants at least, an enslaving truth.

The district officer's interests, his desire to establish himself as an autocratic ruler, lead to his alliance with the most reactionary forces in Indian society. Kipling illuminates and endorses this alliance in **"The Judgment of Dungara."** . . . The hero of the story, a young district officer, rules his territory with the help of the high priest of the local religion, Athon Dazé. Everything is running smoothly until two missionaries arrive on the scene; then both the Englishman and his pagan cohort feel threatened.

Why should the district officer see Christian missionaries as potential enemies? We are used to thinking of them as an imperial fifth column dividing once stable communities, obscuring the exploitative motives of European incursions, and providing pretexts for intervention. Missionaries have indeed served all these functions, but they have also provided colonized peoples with the knowledge and faith to begin overthrowing their masters. It is in this role that the missionaries of **"The**

Judgment of Dungara'' are cast. They serve a Christian ''God of Things as They Should Be'' who threatens not only Dazé's pagan ''God of Things as They Are'' but also the security of the district officer, who has a large psychological stake in maintaining the status quo. The district officer realizes this, and although he promises the missionaries ''all the assistance in my power'' he actually abandons them to the mercies of the local priesthood.

The young Englishman's secret enjoyment of Dazé's offensive reveals the substratum of anarchy in his own apparently ''civilized'' personality. As is often the case, Kipling disguises the cruelty of his hero's acts by presenting them in comic form. When the well-dressed converts line up to welcome the British Collector to the thriving mission, they are suddenly overwhelmed by burning pains and break into a chaotic rabble. They interpret their agonies as the revenge of Dungara, their traditional god, but in fact the burning is caused by the juice of the plant fiber from which their clothes have been made, fiber provided by Athon Dazé. Dazé's plot succeeds, and the story ends with an image of triumphant disintegration: ''the chapel and school have long since fallen back into jungle.'' . . . Both Kipling and his hero approve the rout of knowledge and hope; watched over by the God of Things as They Are and the Empire, the Indians will remain in intellectual and political bondage.

What is it that the district officer gains from such a crippling of his subjects? What qualities make him heroic in Kipling's eyes? The description of the hero of **''The Judgment of Dungara''** provides the answer: he is ''a knockkneed, shambling young man, naturally devoid of creed or reverence, with a longing for absolute power which his undesirable district gratified.'' . . . Unburdened by internal checks, licensed by his government as a despot, and able to operate without the immediate support of an external framework, the ideal district officer is able to gratify the need for absolute power that has been instilled in him during childhood. His escape from self-doubt and fear is the most satisfying one imaginable.

But the district officer of **''The Judgment of Dungara''** is only an ideal. Kipling recognized that most of his fellows in the imperial service had no such chance to achieve the gratifications of despotic autonomy, gratifications that, he thought, were their due. Instead they had to take what satisfaction they could from their role as servants of a powerful master. In **''The Galley-Slave,''** . . . he illuminates the situation of these men.

The poem, a dramatic monologue, unfolds as an extraordinary allegory of the psychological dynamics of the imperial servant. The speaker is a slave who has just been retired after years of service as an oarsman. The slave admits that his experience on the ship, which represents the British Raj, ''broke'' his ''manhood,'' but he insists that he has gained a more heroic masculinity through his servitude: ''If they wore us down like cattle, faith, we fought and loved like men.'' His reductive definition of manhood, however, only confirms his subjugation, for he has accepted his owners' limitations on what he can be. His description of life aboard the galley shows, furthermore, that he fights and loves not like a man but like an animal, with neither insight nor compassion. This conduct serves his masters' interests, too, for it makes him a willing oppressor of the other slaves in the galley, the ''niggers'' in the deepest hold who are threatening rebellion.

The slave takes his sense of masculinity from another source as well. Robbed of power himself, he identifies with the powerful ship. As a result, he comes to fear liberation, to serve willingly, and to respond to any threat to the institution by which he is enslaved as if it were a threat against himself. Bitter at his retirement, he takes pride in the badges of his servitude and curses his freedom:

> By the brand upon my shoulder, by the gall of clinging steel,
> By the welt the whips have left me, by the scars that never heal;
> By eyes grown old with staring through the sun-wash on the brine,
> I am paid in full for service—would that service still were mine!

It is difficult to imagine any of Kipling's fellow imperial servants actually making such a statement, but not hard at all, considering the educational program in which they were raised, to imagine them feeling this way. The poem offers a tragically perceptive picture of the process by which the sons of the English ruling class were reconciled to their roles as upper servants in the house of Empire.

Does Kipling actually wish to affirm the world the galley-slave presents—the submission, the reduction of potential, the displaced hostility, the masochistic pride in bondage? On one level, I believe, the answer is yes, for all of these are conditions with which he has cause to identify. Kipling is suggesting here, it seems to me, that although imperial servants are indeed slaves, their slavery is more satisfying than impotent isolation. But he is also acknowledging, if only implicitly, the disparity between the ideal self-image of the imperial service elite as a fellowship of lords and the reality of their status as privileged slaves. (pp. 24-8)

This disparity seems to have been widely felt, for the local administrators of Kipling's time were engaged in a struggle both to hold off the imperial bureaucracy and to consolidate their status as heirs of a perpetual despotism.

In the Punjab, where Kipling lived and worked, British local administrators had been encouraged for years to act as virtual despots, guiding affairs in their districts on the basis of their own decisions. In the last decades of the century, however, this practice of direct rule was under attack on two fronts. The central bureaucracy, aided by improved communications and inspired by the theories of despotic utilitarianism, was tightening its control over officers in the field. At the same time, Indians educated in Western ideals of the government of law were calling for the end of arbitrary personal rule. (p. 28)

The district officers of Kipling's time responded to these two threats by supporting the tradition of direct rule and by modifying it somewhat. The modifications were offered by a loosely organized group of British administrators called the Orientalists, who defended personal rule but argued in addition that this rule, to be effective, should be expressed in terms of Indian customs and traditions. These were the only terms, the Orientalists argued, that the fundamentally benighted natives could understand. Since the Indians had proven themselves hopelessly incapable of appreciating Western values, they must be ruled in accordance with their own.

This argument was an extremely convenient one. It arose at exactly the time when Indians were proving themselves embarrassingly adept at using Western ideals to criticize British rule, and it provided an ideological rationale for the suppression both of these ideals and of the new class that was espousing them. As can be seen in Kipling's own stories, the Indian traditions to which the Orientalists appealed were the authoritarian ones of the old ruling class, the landowners and the priesthood. . . . In the name of sympathetic rule, then, the Orientalists sought to realize the authoritarian ideal of absolute, autonomous power.

Kipling's vision in the imperial fiction of the eighties and nineties is that of the Orientalists. These were the men with whom he had grown up; he shared their fears, their values, and their aspirations. But he recognized their weaknesses as well. His stories and novels illuminate the source of these weaknesses, argue that they constitute a threat to imperial security, and offer a program for their eradication. Kipling's insights are frequently brilliant, his stories compelling. But his own authoritarian qualities, instilled during childhood, keep him from imagining morally palatable solutions to the problems he confronts. (pp. 28-9)

> *John A. McClure, "Kipling's Empire," in his* Kipling & Conrad: The Colonial Fiction, *Cambridge, Mass.: Harvard University Press, 1981, pp. 9-29.*

JAMES HARRISON (essay date 1982)

[*Harrison is a Canadian poet, educator, and critic specializing in Victorian literature. In the following excerpt he summarizes the outstanding features of Kipling's work, such as his wide variety of subject matter and narrative techniques, and his skillful use of speech and dialect to develop characterization. Harrison also compares Kipling to his contemporaries, Joseph Conrad and E. M. Forster, but hesitates to label him a greater or lesser artist than either of the two.*]

Probably the main obstacle to be overcome in trying to sum up Kipling is the sheer range and diversity of his work, as well as the wide readership to which he appeals. There is, in the first place, the fact that he appears as ambidextrously at home in verse as in prose. We may clearly value his prose more than his verse, and there is some internal evidence that Kipling himself came to do so. Yet all his life he continued to write both with equal freedom, and to link them to an increasing extent, deliberately using the one to complement or act as a foil to the other. Confusingly, however, he often seems to have employed verse in a more essentially prosaic manner than he did prose.

Turning to the subject matter of his stories, we find a bewildering variety. There are tales set in India, America, Africa, Germany, France, England, and on the high seas, as well as in prehistoric, Roman, medieval, and Renaissance times, to say nothing of the eighteenth, nineteenth, twentieth, and twenty-first centuries. There are accounts of battles, of supernatural encounters, and of the inner spiritual struggles of holy men; there are descriptions of the varying skills of bridge-builders, ships' engineers, soldiers, journalists, administrators, doctors, priests, and artists; there are stories whose protagonists range from commanding officers to private soldiers, from cabinet ministers and the Chairman of A.B.C. to cook-housekeepers and farm laborers, not to mention children, animals, locomotives, the parts of a ship and the very winds and waves. The mere fact that Kipling remained so faithful to the short story rather than the novel, moreover, is evidence of his need just as much as his aptitude for such a form, as one permitting him this kind of range and variety.

As for the styles and approaches Kipling uses, here too all seems to be variety. In the greater part of what he writes he

The first-edition covers of several of Kipling's books. Grenville Taylor Collection.

clearly relies on realism, both of incident and speech. Yet in an unusually high proportion of his stories he is equally clearly addicted to fable, parable, and allegory. As in the case of his prose and verse, moreover, the former is more often open-ended and suggestive, the latter more precise and didactic. In the Pyecroft and Mulvaney stories above all, but over and over again elsewhere also, Kipling patently feels a need for the release of tension supplied by comedy. Yet in **"Without Benefit of Clergy"** and **"The Wish House"** he comes as close to tragedy as is possible in twenty-five pages or so, and achieves varying degrees of pathos in many other stories. In his prose style he can be as stark and direct as in **"The Story of Muhammad Din"** and **"Little Tobrah,"** as archaically embellished as in **"The Enemies to Each Other,"** as richly tapestried as in **"The Eye of Allah,"** or as flamboyant and idiosyncratic as in the speaking voices of Mulvaney and Pyecroft. And in his mode of narration he can be as economic as in **"Beyond the Pale," "My Sunday at Home,"** and **"The Gardener,"** as convoluted as in **"The Bonds of Discipline,"** as enigmatic as in **"Mrs. Bathurst,"** or as dramatically ironic as in **"Marklake Witches"** and **"A Doctor of Medicine."**

There is even variety in Kipling's frequent use of a narrator. Within such variety, however, there is a polarizing dichotomy which, paradoxically, may help us find the overall pattern or unity amid the diversity. Sometimes, as in the case of **"A Sahibs' War,"** the narration is a pure dramatic monologue with an implied listener. Elsewhere, as in most of *Plain Tales from the Hills,* we are told the tale by a fairly opinionated "I" narrator who presumably witnessed or was himself told about the events he describes, but who played no part in them. Most often, one (or more) of the characters relates certain events in which he (or they) played a major or minor role. One of the listeners is a secondary narrator or scribe, and he in turn transmits the whole, frame and yarn alike, to the reader, much as the narrator-scribe records Conrad's Marlow stories for us. One function of such a format is to provide continuity between groups of stories with the same distinctive narrator. Another, as in "Black Jack," and "The Man Who Would Be King," is to provide the narrative with a frame which in some way sets it off. But in most cases this technique owes most to Kipling's love affair with the spoken word.

It has often been remarked that Kipling conveys the sensuous ambience of the events he describes with peculiar vividness. And of nothing is this more true than the speaking voices of his characters. Indeed, speech is Kipling's principal method of characterization. One thinks of the clipped, throw-away self-deprecation of all those subalterns, the bureaucratese of the Archangel of the English, the self-indulgence of grown men reverting to being schoolboys in "Slaves of the Lamp," or the color and pungency of Mahbub Ali's speech in Kim, by contrast with the way Huree Babu interlaces his way of saying things with incongruous idioms picked up from his English contacts. And where a single narrator tells all or most of a story, whether "A Conference of the Powers," "Dray Wara Yow Dee," or "On Greenhow Hill," he lends character to the whole narrative. The overall effect of this is to create still more variety, since Kipling's ear was attuned to a wide range of voices and accents, and he clearly enjoyed exercising his virtuoso skill at reproducing them on paper. Louis Cornell, writing of the gift Kipling showed even in his schoolboy verse for imitation and parody, states:

> A skilful parodist at eighteen, Kipling never lost his ability to imitate the mannerisms of other authors, but he never fully developed the gift of assimilation: unlike Joyce and Eliot and Pound, he never learned to use the work of earlier writers in such a way as to make it his own.

And what is true of the writers Kipling imitates is equally true of the speakers whose intonations he captures. For instance, apart from indicating that their common author enjoyed reproducing the spoken word and had a certain talent for it, the conversations recorded in the three sea stories, Captains Courageous, "Their Lawful Occasions," and "The Manner of Men," give us little sense of the essential Kipling quality they share. Each new set of cadences, and therefore each new story, seems a fresh start.

On the other hand, there are those other narrators, or narrator-scribes, all of them to a greater or lesser extent Kipling in disguise. Admittedly, it has been argued that the "I" of Plain Tales from the Hills is not to be identified with Kipling. Yet unless the two could often be mistaken for one another, any ironic distancing Kipling achieves would lose its subtlety and point. And clearly it is the same commentator ubiquitously pontificating in all the stories and lending a quasi-didactic unity to the whole collection. Similarly, the recurring Kipling-like narrator of the late Masonic stories links them by means of a shared set of values and a common tone. (pp. 149-52)

Thus the presence of a narrator in such a high proportion of Kipling's stories serves two seemingly opposed ends. Used in

one way, it ensures a wide range of narrative tone, and adds to the overall variety of his work. Used in another, it allows him to impose a recurring and often somewhat didactic tone, not far removed from his own. Kipling yearns equally, it seems, for the negative capability of the chameleon and the pulpit privileges of the egotistical sublime. . . . Yet a balance or bargain between such opposing tendencies is merely that which must always be struck, in each and every creative act, between the chaotic richness of life and the exigencies of artistic form. All that is unusual, in Kipling's case, is that the contrast between these two sides to his head seems particularly acute. Few authors can rival the immediacy with which he creates the whole diverse world of the five senses—indeed, a whole series of such worlds. Yet few are more committed than Kipling to using their writing to point the moral, underline the message, spread the gospel.

The gospel of what? Above all, clearly, that of law and order, of discipline, of hard work, of respect for skill and know-how and efficiency, of the wisdom of experience rather than mere book learning. Yet, in a dichotomy of content paralleling those of style noted above, this emphasis on a highly controlled quality to life must be set against Kipling's love of laughter and of almost anarchical farce. The wisdom of age, moreover, is so often to be found in alliance with the enthusiasm and the vitality of youth, whether in the persons of Baloo and Mowgli, the Lama and Kim, Sergius and Valens, or the commanding officers and subalterns who populate such stories as "The Tomb of His Ancestors" and "Only a Subaltern." Most insistently of all, as we have noted of "On the City Wall," "Without Benefit of Clergy," "The Bridge-Builders," and above all of Kim, the need for law and order as represented by the British is counterbalanced by the Lalun-like attractions of India's corrupt and chaotic variety. The same antagonism is apparent, moreover, between the forces contending for the soul of Mulvaney, with neither Kipling nor his readers wanting to see absolute victory for either side.

Many people's hostility to Kipling is the result, one suspects, of their not sensing his saving ambivalences, and taking him at his word when he is sounding off about law and order and the faults of democracy. . . . Kipling the artist is far wiser than this, and knows that complete victory for the forces of law and order would be as disastrous as the triumph of chaos. He acknowledges as much, clearly if almost sadly, in "As Easy as A.B.C." Some sort of precarious equilibrium, as achieved at the end of Kim, and as advocated so far as the artist is concerned in "The Bull that Thought," is the best man can hope for.

Kipling is not an easy author to place among his contemporaries, but a brief comparison with E. M. Forster and Joseph Conrad, one somewhat younger, the other a little older than he was, may help us to see him in a clearer perspective.

At first sight Kipling and Forster have nothing in common other than their differences on the subject of India. Yet Forster's constant quest is best summarized in the epigraph to Howards End: "Only Connect." And in A Passage to India, despite his satire of the Sahibs, and more particularly of the Memsahibs, he explores and attempts to bridge the chasm that yawns between the races. (pp. 152-54)

Kipling, as we have seen, does connect. He is not, as Forster is, the self-sufficient, disinterested onlooker, attempting to interpret the rest of us to each other. The connections he works out are connections within his own polarized self. Forster attempts to transmit to his readers a deeper understanding of

Hinduism than they are in all likelihood capable of grasping in the first place, and fails—though we must salute the failure. Kipling, on the other hand, attempts to capture as much of the Lama's philosophy as is already intuitively a part of his own makeup (though a small part, perhaps), and to reconcile it with all the other seeming irreconcilables of which he is composed. And he makes his connections, builds his bridges, not so much through rational explanation or analysis as by an unconscious balancing of opposing tendencies within the very texture of his writing. Kipling may not introspect, or have his characters do so, with any great success. But he does seem to be able to externalize, to project or act out his internal contradictions in the themes and forms of his stories. Or rather, this is what happens when Kipling achieves his effects least overtly. As we have seen, however, he sometimes, indeed he too often short circuits the process and imposes on the narrative a political or social doctrine as to the way individuals and societies should relate to each other, instead of allowing resolutions to emerge from the creative act itself.

That this is something Conrad avoids is best illustrated by his use of symbol. Take, for instance, Stein's collection of lepidoptera in *Lord Jim*. All Conrad has him say of them is: "Look! The beauty—but that is nothing—look at the accuracy, the harmony. And so fragile! And so strong!" To which the reader cannot help but add: "And formerly so wayward and free! And now so pinned down and categorized and imprisoned!" All these characteristics are doubly present, moreover, in the prize specimen captured as a direct result of Stein's being lured into, and escaping, an ambush. There is almost nothing these creatures could not symbolize, we feel; their relevance to the story seems both precise and open-ended. Forster's wasp, by contrast, is less a symbol than a peg from which to hang an idea. And Kipling's **"Butterflies"** makes explicit, through its allegory, what the preceding story, **"Wireless,"** merely implies. Indeed most of Kipling's symbols, whether a wound in the foot in **"The Tender Achilles,"** the Wall in Parnesius's Roman stories, or the road, the wheel, and the mountains (to which the Lama must not lift up his eyes) in *Kim*, are half way to allegory, just as his allegories or parables or fables are often more than half way to propaganda.

On the surface, Conrad and Kipling are remarkably alike. Both write of the East and of Africa and use such locales as in some sense metaphors for the human condition, as well as making extensive use of other symbols. Both write, as no other modern author of comparable standing except perhaps Hemingway has done, about men of action. Both use the short story extensively. And both favor the device of a narrator. Yet in *The Heart of Darkness* Conrad uses Africa, in *Lord Jim* he uses a life of action and moments of paralysis (and butterflies), and in *Nostromo* he uses buried treasure, in each case as a compellingly suggestive image seeming to arise out of the characters' own efforts to arrive at a clearer understanding of the nature of their lives, rather than as a symbol whose meaning is imposed by the author. This in turn creates a sense of unity in Conrad's work—a sense that, like his characters, he is engaged in a constant search of this kind instead of, as is sometimes true in Kipling, presenting the reader with some hand-me-down vision of life. Similarly, so many of Conrad's novels began as short stories, and so many of his short stories might equally well have grown into novels, that any work of his seems to have the potential to become a major work, partly at least because it is integral to a larger unity. Finally, for Conrad to develop a constant though developing relationship between himself and a single recurring narrator not only makes for an interesting

kind of stereoscopic vision, but implies a similar overall unity. (pp. 154-56)

To argue in this way that Conrad is a greater artist than Kipling because of the greater consistency, almost the remorselessness with which he explores, confronts, and compels us to confront his vision of the human condition, might seem to contradict what was said earlier about the unity to be found in the apparent diversity of Kipling's *oeuvre*. And indeed, if mere variety of subject matter and technique were all that detracted from the coherence and integrity of Kipling's output, he might well survive the comparison relatively unscathed. There is a unity to Kipling's work when he is functioning wholly as an artist. But he does not seem to trust his art sufficiently to say all that must be said. And this results in a fatal inconsistency to his work which is far more damaging than mere variety, arising as it does from a readiness to use his art to serve those social and political beliefs which are so often at odds with his deeper wisdom as an artist. This is what leads to the crudely simplistic polemics of **"A Walking Delegate"** and **"The Mother Hive,"** to the complacent exchange of inner-circle prejudices in **"A Deal in Cotton"** and **"The Honours of War,"** or to the enthusiastic and ingeniously didactic absurdities of **".007"** and **"The Ship that Found Herself."** It is in the main because of this kind of unevenness in his work that Kipling relegates himself to minor status when compared with Conrad or James or Lawrence.

As Angus Wilson has argued, however, it is given to far fewer writers to achieve the multiplicity and variety of Kipling's output than to attain a more single-minded greatness. To have reached, as no English author since Dickens had done, a worldwide readership of immense size and the widest possible intellectual and social range, and to be quoted scores of times a day by people who have no idea whom they are quoting, is to be honored in a way many authors of the front rank might well envy. Moreover, to have written at the same time one of the world's most engaging novels of childhood, perhaps eight or ten of the hundred best short stories in the language, and a number of very fine poems, is arguably to redefine "major" and "minor" in a way that makes nonsense of all such classifications. (pp. 157-58)

James Harrison, in his Rudyard Kipling, *Twayne Publishers, 1982, 173 p.*

ROBERT F. MOSS   (essay date 1982)

[*Moss is an American educator, critic, and novelist. In the following excerpt he discusses the fiction Kipling wrote between 1888 and 1901, focusing on the ways in which the adolescent perceptions and behavior of the male protagonists gradually develops into a mature recognition and acceptance of the world.*]

[The works Kipling produced between 1888 and 1901] can be studied very advantageously as an organic phase in Kipling's career; indeed, there are compelling reasons for doing so. Not only do these works share an abundance of common attitudes, characterizations and motifs, but they are further linked by a discernible, though uneven, maturational process in which Kipling's command of his materials, initially shaky and unsatisfying, grew impressively, reaching a distinct pinnacle in *Kim*. (p. xiv)

Soldiers Three, examined in retrospect, reveals the crude beginnings of the most important creative period in Kipling's life and of Kipling's most characteristic subject-matter. The reader who moves chronologically through Kipling's tales, even if he is wholly ignorant of the later, explicitly adolescent stories, is apt to regard the adventurous trio of *Soldiers Three* as boys in men's garb. Their behaviour—the *ipso facto* rebelliousness against authority, the boisterous swagger, the passion for excitement, the frequent fits of hysterical giggling—correspond to a generally accepted view of adolescence, one which is substantiated by scientific treatises on the subject. It is clear that the soldiers have also passed through a rigidly prescribed process of acculturation which has its less rigid analogue in the lives of most adolescents. One facet of this acculturation is simply the training the soldiers undergo in order to become first-class fighting men; the other is the confusion of selfhood they experience, the conflict between the two vastly different cultures to which they belong simultaneously—the civilian realm back home and the military world that they presently inhabit. Kipling, however, devotes little space and less energy to developing this conflict and though in the end he puts his soldiers back in mufti, there is no suggestion that any greater maturity has been gained in the process; rather, Mulvaney, the leader of the clique, is seen wallowing in sentimental longing for the good old military days—a mood that Kipling seems to approve of.

The Light That Failed offers another unintentionally adolescent hero, Dick Heldar, whose conduct and values are strikingly similar to that of the soldiers. The same immature traits are prominent in his activities. In other respects, though, *Light* is an advance over *Soldiers:* the learning process is given greater emphasis, as is the identity quest. The two worlds that Dick must choose between—East and West—are a principal source of tension in the book. It is not difficult to isolate the personal forces in Kipling's life that lifted this dichotomy from its peripheral status in *Soldiers* to its primacy in *Light*. The psychological turbulence of Kipling's two years in London, characterized by piercing conflicts, left him with an artistic vision that was conceived in dualities. In *Light* the polarities are athrob with authentic, if unbalanced, emotion. As in *Soldiers,* however, these antitheses lack intellectual interest and offer only intermittent dramatic power because the conflict is weighted too strongly in favour of the East, with its martial romantic ideals, rather than the West, home of the peaceful and the mundane. Dick's flamboyant death, fully endorsed by Kipling, is a refusal to leave boyhood. Still, it is evident from the fuller attention Kipling devoted to acculturation in *Light,* as compared to *Soldiers,* that he was moving towards an intentional rather than an unwitting treatment of adolescence.

He reached this more artistically rewarding stage in the Mowgli stories, where his hero—who exhibited many of the same qualities as Dick and Mulvaney—was finally a boy in name as well as in spirit. Moreover, Kipling brought the same intensity to the acculturation theme that he had in *Light,* while refining it in certain ways. Examining his own mixed cultural heritage in the serenity and objectivity of Vermont, Kipling achieved a measure of detachment he only infrequently attained in his work. Then, too, nostalgia over his lost boyhood in Bombay imbued the tales with a wistful charm and mythic otherworldliness that nullified any questions of psychological or social validity.

Like Dick, Mowgli suffers considerable emotional stress over his divided loyalties—to the jungle, on the one hand; to the man pack, on the other. When he is at last compelled to rejoin the human community we are conscious not only of a racial philosophy that is inevitable in Kipling ("East is East," etc.)

but also of a maturation process that has brought Mowgli to the gates of manhood. Although the clash between alien cultures is as simplistic here as in *Light* and *Soldiers,* it is defensible on two grounds—(1) the mythic, fairy-tale atmosphere of the jungle, which permits a relaxation of the standards of realistic fiction, and (2) the fact that this time the hero's choice is specifically related to his maturation and that the world he opts for, though drab and offensive in many ways, is, in the context of the stories, a necessary concomitant of growing up. This way lies maturity, Mowgli realizes.

Captains Courageous, the product of Kipling's American experience, continued most of the patterns Kipling had been working with since *Soldiers;* it also presented another boy hero, Harvey, and perpetuated as well the general adolescent pattern that reached back to *Soldiers.* Harvey's boyish behaviour and brutal education are the logical descendants of similar elements in Kipling's earlier efforts. In *Captains,* however, he concentrated on broadening and deepening one aspect of the adolescent paradigm—the hero's antinomic worlds. The two societies of *Captains* (again East and West, but this time Eastern and Western America) are handled with greater sophistication than Kipling had evinced previously. The New England fishing culture, with its noble, weather-beaten virtues, is presented eulogistically and warmly, without any sign of ambivalence or irony. The American West, on the other hand, has three separate layers apparently: the pampered, effete world of Mrs Cheyne and the unconverted Harvey; the rugged, self-reliant professionalism of Cheyne, Sr (in many respects a mirror image of the Gloucester society); the free-wheeling expansionism and robust spirit of the West, which Kipling admires. The relationship between the ostensibly antipodal cultures of *Captains* is explored with a complexity that is missing from the other works we have looked at. The book is Kipling's ode to America, while he was still tucked away snugly in the hills around Brattleboro; soon the ode would be transformed into a hate-drenched philippic. Unfortunately, even at this stage Kipling's depiction of the American scene is expressed in sociological rather than literary terms. Unlike Mowgli, Harvey experiences very little internal confusion or turmoil over conflicting societal claims. He is instantly converted to life on the *We're Here* and then instantly severed from it at the end. In between, his mind, when we are allowed to look into it at all, is mostly occupied with the intricacies of cod-fishing. Harvey is perhaps the least dynamic of all Kipling's adolescent heroes.

Stalky & Co., though lively and enjoyable, brought nothing new to Kipling's rapidly growing conception of boyhood. The stories, mostly written in the last year or two of the nineteenth century, provide an excellent compendium of the various traits Kipling assigned to adolescents. Stalky and his friends scheme against the adult establishment, play pranks, forge an impenetrable clique, create a private language, seek out excitement and adventure and reveal a mixture of overt cynicism and covert idealism. Moreover, the education, official and unofficial, that they receive at the College is yet another variant of the training process that is crucial to adolescence in Kipling's other studies of the subject. Yet in *Stalky* Kipling ignores completely the search for identity that is so integral to *Captains,* the Mowgli stories and *Light* and peripherally important to *Soldiers.* The explanation is simple enough. Kipling had set himself the task of celebrating a kind of boyhood—life at his alma mater, the militarily oriented United Services College—whose single-mindedness of training and direction allowed for no uncertainty of self, no divided loyalties. His own recollections of schoolboy days were joyful, misty-eyed, idealized; he looked back on a homogeneous environment with no serious divisions of temperament, culture or outlook. With *Stalky* Kipling moved neither forward nor backward; he merely held his ground.

Two years after the publication of *Stalky & Co.,* however, Kipling's myth of boyhood arrived at its culmination. Reunited with his parents and finding at last a permanent home in the English countryside, Kipling was able to create a final, splendid testament to the India of his youth. In *Kim,* the adolescent strain, cultivated from Mulvaney and his friends through *Stalky & Co.,* reached its most dramatically successful form. More than any of Kipling's other boys—certainly more than his adolescent men—Kim comes across as he was intended. Kim's instinct for where adventure is to be found, his gift for self-preservation in the midst of adversity, his game-playing, his love of professionalism—all these are superbly rendered. He receives his education in the streets of India, in an Anglo-Indian school, in the secret training grounds of the Great Game. Fundamentally, it is the same education that Kipling's other heroes receive, but here there is less emphasis on brutalization of the learner and more on the joy of learning. In addition, Kim is the only one of Kipling's heroes who is educated both indirectly, through sink-or-swim immersion in reality (like Dick and Cheyne, Sr) and directly, through formalized pedagogy (like Mowgli, Stalky and the soldiers). But the real profundity of *Kim* lies in Kipling's handling of the search for identity. Always uncertain as to his real destiny, Kim's odysseys are all, in some sense, a quest to find his true self, an attempt to assess the conflicting demands of two radically different ways of life. In the first two-thirds of the book, the clash Kim feels is between his Western heritage and his Eastern upbringing. In the latter portion of the novel, however, the conflict alters considerably; it is no longer a choice between East and West, but between the Game, which is both Eastern and Western in nature, and the Search, which is exclusively Eastern. At virtually all points in *Kim* the conflicts are viewed through the hero's troubled soul; never are they merely painted backdrops.

There is no doubt that *Kim* is the most intimate revelation of Kipling's inner self, as much a spiritual autobiography as Wordsworth's "Prelude"; the book is an attempt to seize all the jagged, confusing, remarkable fragments of his psychic life and incorporate them into a great fictional kaleidoscope. But the brilliance of the novel may have more to do with its depth than its breadth, with the excavations Kipling was able to make into his own soul. There he examined the warring forces of his personality with the longest, most penetrating scrutiny he ever gave them. Through Kim, he probed his dual attachments to the life of action and the life of art; to progress and permanence; to Eastern mysticism and Western pragmatism; to sensuality and asceticism; to the hard-nosed Yorkshire naturalism of his father and the leaping Celtic poetry of his mother.

Yielding himself up fully to his art at last, Kipling succeeded in combining the cultural complexity of *Captains* with the psychological depth of the Mowgli stories. His achievement was further enhanced by the sympathetic, loving picture of the Indians in *Kim,* proof against the blanket accusations of racism that his works have always had to face. Though Kipling went on to create other magnificent works in various modes ("**Dayspring Mishandled**" and "**The Gardener**", for example), *Kim* marks the end of the most fruitful and best remembered phase of his career, a journey toward artistic fulfilment that began with the inauspicious *Soldiers Three* and ended with this remarkable novel. (pp. 142-47).

> *Robert F. Moss, in his* Rudyard Kipling and the Fiction of Adolescence, *St. Martin's Press, 1982, 165 p.*

Kipling as a young boy.

ELOISE KNAPP HAY (essay date 1984)

[*Hay is an American critic and educator specializing in English literature. In the following excerpt, she outlines an approach to a dual critical biography of Kipling and E. M. Forster, showing the ways in which the values conveyed in their fiction are complementary.*]

No one has yet successfully combined criticism and biography for either Rudyard Kipling or E. M. Forster. It seems that their life stories interpose obstacles which positively distort our readings of their works. As Edmund Wilson says of Kipling, he was "the man nobody read" because his personal politics were so outrageous to the critical establishment that they virtually blocked him out. In Forster's case the issue of his homosexuality intruded, blocking his own impulse to square with his readers. (p. 123)

My imagined symbiography might begin with showing that both writers modeled their prose on the pure well of English undefiled they found in Jane Austen. They both disliked the non-English arbiters of prose fiction so praised in their time, whether Flaubertian, Jamesian, Conradian, or Joycean. Kipling's story on the "Janeites" and Forster's tribute to Jane Austen in *Abinger Harvest* would here be a starting point. Their narrative point of view, like hers, is knowingly in cahoots with the reader, yet inseparable from their tale. The prose styles of Kipling and Forster—for all their differences of tone—are like

Austen's in being spare, epigrammatic, deceptively simple, and deceptively relaxed. Both Kipling and Forster have been accused of using shock tactics to cover up a poverty of narrative invention. But then Jane Austen's breadth has also been called in question.

Starting from this point of agreement between Kipling and Forster, one would then have to note the opposing faces presented in their art and their biographies, particularly their attitudes to politics, to war, to heroism, and to mass psychology. Neither of them sympathized with the English mania for sports in their lifetimes, symbolized in "the playing fields of Eton" as builders of character; but Kipling wanted war games to replace cricket and football, as he showed in his story **"The Army of a Dream"** and his poem **"The Islanders."** He naively believed that man has a natural instinct for battle, "a desire for slaughter," which he said makes men yearn for their officers to sound the bugle whenever the nation requires defense. Forster never wrote a war story. Indeed he played advocate for pacifism in spirit if not in fact.... [When] the First World War broke out, Forster could "think of nothing but young men killing one another while old men praised them." Kipling at the time was England's chief eulogist for young fighting men, even inspiring his seventeen-year-old son John to join the army, despite disqualifyingly poor vision. When John was killed in France within two years, Kipling's praises for such men remained as strong as ever. He never would have sanctioned Forster's view that "hero worship is a dangerous vice." The symbiographer would note that Forster's fiction is as empty of heroes and heroines as it is empty of battles. Forster gave democracy a cheer because instead of producing great men, it produces "different kinds of small men."

The kinds of "small men" who figure in Forster's life and fiction would also make an instructive comparison with Kipling's characters. Forster's chief characters are often wistful because they are not simpler and poorer. Their education and class consciousness weigh heavily on them. They long to be simply creative, whether in marriage, in discovering a new idea, or in spiritual expansion. And they are as repelled by superiority as Kipling's small people (the children in the Puck stories, for instance) are exhilarated by the roles played in history by great craftsmen, great military men, and kings.

In the field of science, too, Kipling's heroic vision carries over. The invention of the motor car and airplane seemed like time machines to Kipling, linking past and future, even linking the living with the dead in the story **"They."** These machines terrified and depressed Forster, as we see in his story **"The Machine Stops."** The dual biographer would show in Kipling and Forster the two faces of science fiction in England at the time—the utopian and dystopian. (pp. 126-28)

A similar antithesis emerges in their opposite views of high social organization in modern life. Kipling never ceased to believe—even when repelled by Russian Communism and German Fascism—that "the strength of the Pack is the Wolf, and the strength of the Wolf is the Pack," as in **"The Law of the Jungle."** Forster's longing for connectedness failed when it came to the Pack mentality, and all his fiction proclaims it. In "What I Believe" he said, "The more highly public life is organized, the lower does its mentality sink." Mankind has never yet found a way "by which private decencies can be transmitted to public affairs."

Little as the two men resemble each other in these ways, my fancied symbiography would show surprising accord between

them in others, revising our view of Kipling's chauvinism and much-derided vulgarity on one side and revising our view of Forster's genial tolerance and sophistication on the other. We should see that Forster held many of the same prejudices as Kipling, suggesting that English blood is stronger than the milk of human kindness. Forster shared Kipling's respect for the superiority of English character, over the Irish for instance. (p. 128)

In view of such parallels and intersecting lines, our understanding of both writers and their work could go deeper. For brevity's sake, let me look closely at two scenes that speak to each other in their writing—the scene Kipling paints in his **"Ballad of East and West"** and Forster's last scene in *A Passage to India*. In both episodes, a man of the West rides forth into an allegorical Indian landscape with a fellow horseman, a man of the East. Kipling's two warriors, the Afghan chief Kamal and the English Colonel's son, begin as deadly rivals. Forster's two, the Afghan-descended doctor Aziz and the English educator Fielding, ride out together as friends. But in Kipling's episode the Muslim wins the contest and holds the Englishman's life in his hands (as earlier in *A Passage to India* the English held the Muslim's life in their hands). What turns the tide in Kipling's narrative is the Muslim Kamal's recognition of a no-win situation—the blood-for-blood feud that will follow if he kills the Colonel's son. Kamal's admiration for the English youth's unexampled bravery in riding into the Afghan's territory also determines the happy end. In tribute to the Englishman's character, Kamal not only spares his life but sends his own son back with him, to guard him and to stay in the English camp, helping keep peace on the border between their two peoples. "For there is neither East nor West, Border, nor Breed, nor Birth, / When two strong men stand face to face, tho' they come from the ends of the earth!"

In Forster's novel the case is similar but reversed. All the enmities in the novel appear at first more broadly humane: there are no blood feuds or heroics; instead we find social quarreling, sexual misalliances, and cultural misunderstanding. Just before the last scene, all hostilities have been resolved, not through the Muslim's wisdom and generosity (as in Kipling) but through the English Mrs. Moore's despairing insight into the nature of matter and spirit. Communicating this dark knowledge first to the non-religious Adela Quested, Mrs. Moore finally transmits her vision mysteriously to Aziz and the whole Muslim community. Insofar as heroism exists in Forster's novel, it flows only from the English intruders in India, ending with restored legality as well as a heightened awareness of political justice and personal honesty. Forster has none of Kipling's exhilarating wonder at Oriental prowess and spiritual superiority (if we remember the lama in *Kim* and the hero in **"The Miracle of Purun Baghat"**). Forster's equivalent to Kipling's Purun Baghat is the bungling Brahmin Godbole, who turns away from both the cave mysteries and Dr. Aziz in his hour of need. Unlike Kipling's spiritual seekers, both Eastern and Western, Godbole prays to a god who does not come, except in the form of an old English woman (Mrs. Moore) and the wasp she mysteriously loved. For unlike Godbole, Mrs. Moore submitted herself to the alien earth and took the consequences in despair, disorientation and torment. Just before the last scene I wish to consider in Forster's novel, his English visitors and Aziz are reunited—but only momentarily—during a Hindu festival. When their boats accidentally collide, over-turning them in ceremonial waters, they feel a resurgence of affection—not through any Kiplingesque testing of their mettles but through passive surrender to ritual immersion into the nature of things.

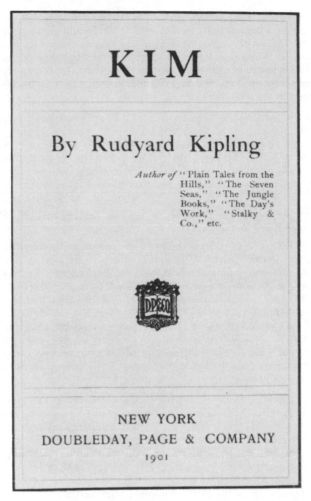

The title page of the first edition of Kim.

Then comes the last episode I have compared to Kipling's scene. Fielding and the Muslim Aziz go on a long horseback ride to celebrate their reconciliation. They begin to quarrel again; then answering an impulse to confirm their friendship forever, they reach out to embrace each other. But a group of rocks suddenly rears up—similar to those which bring Kipling's men of East and West together. The rocks interrupt their embrace, and Forster ends: "the horses didn't want it, sending up rocks through which the riders must pass single file." All the features of India's life and landscape seem to cry out against the union of East and West—saying "in their hundred voices, 'No, not yet.'" And the sky tells them, "No, not there."

The dual biography I visualize would ask: why is it that Kipling's two men can shake hands finally while Forster's cannot? We must go deeper than the obvious answer that in 1889, when Kipling published the Ballad, there was still hope that England would retain her empire, whereas in 1924, Forster's novel reflected the end of that possibility. In fact, Forster denied that he was writing about the incompatibility of East and West, saying "he was really concerned about the difficulty of living in the universe." Forster's novel makes clear that he was writing about human failure on many levels, including the great unresolved and perhaps unresolvable questions of sexual disorientation. As Furbank's biography suggests, Forster's sexual agony was a continuous preoccupation. Under its stress, he rejected the Judeo-Christian tradition and much else that glued

together the social structures of his world. For Kipling, whatever pessimism he felt, the earth itself was never alien, as it is in this last of Forster's major scenes. For Kipling, the earth waits, as in Genesis I and Isaiah, to have man's dominion harmoniously established. Kipling's Mowgli grows up very like the little child who will lead the leopard and wolf in Isaiah's peaceable kingdom, though Mowgli must first learn the law of the jungle. The great Kipling hymns, so dear to the English nation (though they frightened liberals like Forster), are squarely in the English tradition of biblical struggle and renewal. By contrast, the earth so powerfully imaged in Forster's fiction, whether in the caves of India or the earthquake at Colonus, is fundamentally alien to mankind and is likely to become increasingly so. There is no original innocence in Forster and therefore no second innocence. Beneath Forster's gentle humanism lies a darkness that looks like despair even beside Kipling's darkest tales. It affected Forster's creative energy, accounting for his few volumes of fiction beside Kipling's prodigal outpourings even in the worst of his troubles. Furbank associates Forster's "writer's block" with Freud's theory on those who are "wrecked by success." But combining Forster's biography with Kipling's, we see that both men had the same early success and the same "superstitious fears" connected with it. (pp. 129-31)

We can hardly say that Kipling's super-masculinity insured his creative flow if we recall Hemingway and his creative block late in life. But Kipling's late fiction shows a source of energy and optimism that Hemingway and Forster both lacked. Stories like **"The Gardener," "The Manner of Men,"** and **"The Church at Antioch"** accent the biblical tradition underlying Kipling's art. His original law-givers were Moses and St. Paul, whom Forster explicitly rejected, saying "my lawgivers are Erasmus and Montaigne." (p. 131)

Not only Forster's two best novels, *Howards End* and *A Passage to India,* but all his best critical works suggest that he identified himself strongly with the non-rational, relational, and intuitive powers of the "soul" that Jung saw embodied in the anima. Jung believed such identification to be fairly common among male artists and homosexuals, who identify less than other men with the "animus" in themselves—with the law finding, law making, scientific, and rational impulses that assert themselves in emphatically male artists like Kipling. Jung notes that such an "identity with the anima" as we may find in Forster is too common to be considered "a pathological perversion" and "should not be adjudged negative in all circumstances, in so far as it preserves the archetype of the Original Man, which a one-sided sexual being has, up to a point, lost." In this light one could say that Forster's dissatisfaction with marriage, as with other kinds of union in our modern context, reflected a profound discontent with the dichotomies he saw projected in "normal" life and sexuality. By contrast, Kipling's art thrived on these divisions, both in his early work, where a "one-sided" masculinity runs rampant, and in his late work, where an equally one-sided femininity often has its day.

Kipling's projections of the Jungian animus in his male-dominated fiction and poetry seem to reflect the "loss of the anima" that Jung says is necessary at one stage of a man's growth. After writing his children's books, however, Kipling focused increasingly on a whole range of women—from the mothering Demeter types found in *Kim*'s Kula woman and the more erotic Woman of Shamlegh to the Hecate figures in **"Mary Postgate"** and **"The Gardener,"** who savagely suffer, possess, and protect their men, even breaking fundamental human and divine laws in the process. Jung might say that Kipling saved himself in late life from that "loss of the anima" which results in "a diminution of vitality, of flexibility, and of humane kindness." (pp. 131-32)

Forster's pessimistic views of political, scientific, and religious "order" ... left him convinced, like Mrs. Moore, that no union of races or bodies or even hearts is likely to be achieved ever, on earth ("not there"). *A Passage to India* will not allow that the stone barriers between hearts and spirits are ever to be rolled away, as they are rolled away in both **"The Ballad of East and West"** and **"The Gardener"** of Kipling. Which, then, was the more just—Forster's philosophical anarchism or Kipling's religious optimism? Today, when the strong men of East and West do indeed "stand face to face," with the borders between them as adamantine as ever, Forster's pessimism may appear more justified than Kipling's sanguine optimism. At the same time we must not forget how well Kipling's art reflected the best of each world. (pp. 132-33)

> Eloise Knapp Hay, *"Kipling and Forster: A Case for Dual Biography,"* in *Biography, Vol. 7, No. 2, Spring, 1984, pp. 123-33.**

ZOHREH T. SULLIVAN   (essay date 1984)

[*Sullivan is an American critic and educator specializing in modern British fiction. In the following excerpt, she examines the dual worlds of dreaming and waking in the short story "The Brushwood Boy" in order to discuss the pervading sense of psychological repression in Kipling's fiction and autobiographical writings.*]

Increasingly, critics from Edmund Wilson to Randall Jarrell, and most recently John A. McClure, have drawn attention to Kipling's psychological complexity, his sense of terrifying powerlessness and isolation in a hostile world, his fear of "a certain darkness into which the soul of the young man sometimes descends—a horror of desolation, abandonment, and realised worthlessness, which is one of the most real of the hells in which we are compelled to walk." Kipling's life project was an attempt to negotiate descents into uncontrollable elements—darkness, water, and the unconscious itself.

As a study in such psychological negotiations, Kipling's most compelling and curiously neglected story is **"The Brushwood Boy."** Somerset Maugham in his Introduction to a few of the tales concludes that, though the dreams in **"The Brushwood Boy"** are fascinating, the outer story is dull, and one must finally look upon it "not as a tale that has any relation to real life, but as much of a fairy story as The Sleeping Beauty or Cinderella." And Angus Wilson in his splendid biography dismisses **"The Brushwood Boy"** as one of the dream stories whose "vision is flawed with whimsy or self-pity." Although it is indeed a highly charged fantasy, the story is neither whimsical nor trivial. Rather, it is Kipling's fullest, most explicit dream story that taps his most personal core of recurring fears, fantasies, and myths. What I hope to establish in this reading is that the thematic, psychological, and structural principles at work in this story resonate through Kipling's fiction and his autobiography, that the dream life of the brushwood boy mirrors not only what George Cottar represses but all Kipling journeys that take their protagonists over much threatening landscape only to teach them how *not* to immerse themselves in its destructive elements. As a significant example of a paradigmatic Kipling story, its action involves the protagonist in a descent into unconscious material that conforms to, rather

than transcends, the values of his waking life. Yet, as this essay will demonstrate, in both autobiography and fiction nightwalking is a persistent theme that held special charms for Kipling. It signaled a delicate encounter with the repressed that always threatened to return, and thereby offered the protagonist yet another test and a chance for mastery over the unconscious and the uncontrollable.

On its simplest waking level, **"The Brushwood Boy"** is an initiation story about the typical training of a colonialist, George Cottar (the brushwood boy), from childhood to maturity. We follow his rise in the ranks and his public successes through school, Sandhurst, and India, after which he returns to his parental home in England to receive his final reward: marriage to the princess of his dream life, who turns out to have been systematically dreaming the same series of dreams as George all these many years.

The dream story reflects the more dangerous underside of his lyrical journey through life and involves a series of journeys into and over progressively threatening landscapes. The basic configuration of the dreamscape includes entrance through a safe outer region guarded by a pile of brushwood and by a street lamp crowning a ridge of high ground, a middle region of valleys and a Sea of Dreams, and a still more dangerous interior with mysterious strangers eating amid roses and gardens in a railway station, and, finally, the mysterious end of the journey—a huge house containing, in its deepest recesses, a Sick Thing.

The entrance to the delightful secret world where "anything was possible" ... is guarded by two recurring signs—a pile of brushwood and a lamppost, clearly differentiated emblems of femininity and masculinity that mark the boundaries of a day world of recognizable sexual differentiation.... Beyond these signposts lie worlds of "incommunicable delight ... glorious, for he felt he was exploring great matters." ... His unpredictable night world confronts him with a road "eaten away in places" that spans ravines, runs along the edge of precipices, and tunnels its way through endless mountains. The sea, sometimes a lyrical sea of dreams, is often a black and angry sea that rages under a full moon and lashes at him "black, foamless tongues of smooth and glossy rollers." ... Although he loses himself on unknown seas and slips and slides across many-colored islands, rescue always appears in the form of his brushwood girl, a figure who first comes to life out of an illustrated edition of *Grimm's Fairy Tales*, then takes on the form of a real girl he meets in an Oxford pantomime theater. In the dreams the girl evolves from a childhood fairy tale princess, into his boyhood's AnnieanLouise, then into his young brushwood companion. (pp. 218-20)

The waking world, then, is one in which Kipling's protagonist realizes all his fantasies and desires and acquires that ultimate object of desire—Miriam.... Miriam is class, money, and legitimate aristocracy. Miriam, with her ailing mother, is fatherless, and, by marrying her, George will inherit not only her wealth, but the parental role that would be forbidden to him were her parents active participants in society. Marriage will therefore resolve social and familial contradictions: the son will become the father, and the working soldier will become the aristocrat. This simple and mythic outer story with its light and whimsical tone is meant to compensate for the disturbingly incomplete inner metaphoric journey into the house of the Sick Thing. The inner story also subverts the expectations raised by its form. Twin journeys embedded with a dream story might lead the reader to expect, in the protagonist, changes in perception, self-awareness, or wisdom. But our George learns primarily how to defend himself against external threat without gaining any significant insight into the nature of his hidden fears.

As in the stories of Kipling's own life (**"Baa, Baa, Black Sheep"** and his autobiography), this story also begins with images of society's natural victim—the child. Part of the intention of this study is to see how that victimization is resolved in another curiously absent theater—India. On the level of dream, we watch the child explore increasingly threatening geographical areas that he attempts at first to control by naming, miniaturizing (Hong Kong and Java become tiny lilies, stepping stones in his path), defining, and displacing, but that grow increasingly uncontrollable. On the waking level, however, we see the boy's encounters with a series of microsocieties in which the disempowered and marginalized child-protagonist gradually assumes a position of centrality and power.

The story begins, "A child of three sat up in his crib and screamed at the top of his voice, his fists clenched and his eyes full of terror." . . . His helplessness is exacerbated by the geographic isolation of his nursery—in the west wing where no one could hear him. . . . When the housekeeper, whose special pet he is, tries to soothe him by asking what it was that frightened him, the boy answers that a policeman came into the house. The dream by itself does not appear fearful: it is a dream of intrusion by public authority into a private, intimate space; it has its real-life source in an actual meeting with policeman Tisdall on Dowhead that morning. But the original manuscript and typescript of the story suggest that the author edited that which might have been most fearsome to the child. In that unrevised version the child says, "'It was—it was a policeman. He came in froo the window an' ate the rug! I saw him do it!'" To which the nurse replies, "'Nonsense Master George. Policemen never come through windows. They live in the Garden just like Ponto. Go to sleep'." . . . That added detail of intrusion through a forbidden entrance—the window—to eat forbidden contents—the rug—suggests why the child might wake up terrified: the next object for consumption on the policeman's menu might be the child. That first dream of a boundaryless appetite and of intrusion into a forbidden space will later be displaced or, as Edward Said might put it, "Orientalized." India will become the place of excess undermining the rational control of the Englishman, who will in turn test his manhood, his character, and his rationality by repeatedly intruding into threatening territory that he will decode, tame, and circumscribe within manageable domains. And within his sequential dream story, he and the brushwood girl will intrude into the house of the Sick Thing "It," whose distant bedroom surrounded by gardens must be a late displacement of his own early geographically remote nursery—and on one level (as in Kafka's dream story "The Country Doctor") he is the sick thing who fears anatomical loss. Only now, that distant marginal room is the central nightmare region of the dream. And on this level the bedroom is both the beginning and the end of one of his many journeys.

When we next see the boy as a child of six, we see how he has learned in part to conquer his three-year-old fear of the night world. He has turned his ability to dream into a "new power . . . a secret," . . . by transposing an unfinished bedtime story told by his mother into a dream in which he becomes the prince, the pasha, and the giant-killer. Rather than fear intrusion, as he did in his first dream, he becomes the intruder entering the forbidden dreamscape through a safe outer region

guarded by a pile of brushwood stacked somewhere near a beach. It is a territory casually divided between land and sea, so casually that "ships ran high up the dry land and opened into cardboard boxes; or gilt and green iron railings that surrounded beautiful gardens turned all soft and could be walked through and overthrown so long as he remembered it was only a dream." . . . And because he is in control, he can choose not to be alone in his dreamscape as he had been in his nursery. He peoples it with playing children, and in particular with a brushwood girl whom he names AnnieanLouise, whose magic words "'Ha! Ha!' said the duck, laughing" . . . rescue the boy from drowning by raising the bottom of the deep as he wades out with a twelve-inch flowerpot on each foot. The boy has acquired the early power to domesticate and control even the depths of the sea. (pp. 220-22)

The next three phases of his life—ten years at an English public-school, Sandhurst, and India—lead to a restructuring of his private inner emotional life that must be subordinated to the public and external world of school and games. Now, Home becomes "a far-away country, full of ponies and fishing and shooting, and men-visitors who interfered with one's plans; but school was the real world. . . . And Georgie was glad to be back in authority when the holidays ended." . . . We are also told that school defines for the boy certain boundaries between that which is discouraged (dreaming and emotions) and that which is encouraged (precision, accuracy, strength). It is during this third stage then that we see the boy defining a hierarchy of values to be measured against that which was most "real"—his school. And it is here that the outer world encroaches upon, contests, and begins its triumph against the claims of his inner life—a triumph that materializes when George returns to England to discover that his dream brushwood girl is the real-life Miriam whom he is destined to marry, thereby renouncing any need for an inner dream life. It is at this stage that we see the evolution of the Kipling ideal—discipline, sexual innocence, self-control, the value of the "school mask," and the upholding of public official policy. If part of the conscious meaning of the story is that "England's wars are won on the playing fields of Eton," then George's school must take credit for his triumphs on the battlefield of Empire.

In India he is the most loved, most sought after, most quoted barrack authority. In spite of all the designing ladies, George keeps free from the intrigues of the Indian outpost and from sex. . . . His seniors worry about his turning into a "regular 'Auntie Fuss' of an Adjutant" . . . but fate proves him a man by sending him to fight a "real" war. . . . (p. 223)

What is singularly minimized during his heroic combat is India and Indians. We are told, probably concerning the Second Afghan War of 1881, that "fate sent the change that was needed, in the shape of a little winter campaign on the border, which, after the manner of little campaigns, flashed out into a very ugly war; and Cottar's regiment was chosen among the first." . . . George's distance from the reality of war and India (and from the events of his own life) are reflected not only in the increasingly coy use of the third-person omniscient narrator whose voice seems only accidentally related to a boy encountering death and India, but in the curious language exemplified in the passage above. The angle from which the event is perceived is so distant that the horror of war is miniaturized into a "little" campaign, and its only significance seems to be contained within the context of sports—Cottar's regiment was chosen among the first. Those who are to be warred against, subdued, defeated, killed are neither named nor romanticized.

They are simply and significantly absent. And India is an empty space, an absence, that serves as a means for progressing from school to life, from the playing fields of Eton to Home, Marriage, and Empire. The war therefore is an excuse to glorify and fortify the men into manliness. . . . The experience in India allows George to construct a code of personal behavior and leadership based on public school codes that results in the nonsexual commitment to the brotherhood of Empire, in the infantilization of his men into "good children" and a "football fifteen," of a war into a "little" campaign, and of India into an absence. . . . Maturity and character are gained by a colonization of the self—by denial, repression, and mechanization. But once this stage is accomplished, a limited intimacy is allowed:

> "There's no place like England—when you've done your work."

> "That's the proper way to look at it, my son."

But as other Kipling stories have demonstrated, outward success is no guarantee for survival in India; midway through Cottar's phenomenal successes with subordinates, superiors, and women in the army, a major prophesies: "but, then, that's the kind that generally goes the worst mucker in the end." . . . The fear of going "the worst mucker," of disintegrating irrationally and publicly, of being invaded, engulfed, or petrified by threatening others results in the elaborate development of denial and repression in the real world, and a night world haunted with a sexually charged dreamscape whose action mirrors his deepest anxieties.

Those anxieties are provoked by areas of his waking life over which he has no control: home, England, and sex. If school, Sandhurst, and India do not consciously threaten George (as they did Kipling), it is partly because they obey the rules of his defense system and partly because he has displaced onto the language of his dreams that which is most fearsome about them. As opposed to the "real" world of games and war, home is soft, unreal, dreamlike, and relatively scary. If the only way to reconcile these two opposing worlds is through marriage to Miriam, then the main threat to that ultimate reward of union is illicit maternal love. All through his years in India, he is, unknown to himself, threatened with motherly sex—from Mrs. Elery, who complains to a Commander that he is "workin' my nice new boy too hard," to Mrs. Morrison, who admits "*I* want to kiss him. Some day I think I will. Heigh-ho! she'll be a lucky woman that gets Young Innocence," . . . to the designing Mrs. Zuleika, to his actual mother back home. (pp. 224-25)

The sexual anxiety at the heart of this story repeats itself in the recurring flight of the boy from exposure, vulnerability, and danger to a sheltered place of total security, away from the threats of forbidden, motherly relationships toward a safe, mature sexuality. The defense system he establishes against his dangerous fantasy is careful self-control under the magical protection of an internalized fantasy girl, who in his dreams keeps changing ages to remain as remote from the mother as possible. The entire journey carries an implicit Kipling theme: that we mature by escaping maternal love and being "manly" until we find a suitable love object free of material associations, after our colonial characters are built and tested. And someone back home is always watching, censoring, controlling our most dangerous actions, and we must trust that silent watcher in the night as we must our Empire: so later, Miriam admits to dreaming of "another woman—out there on the sea. I saw her." . . .

Kipling in his study. Courtesy of Prints and Photographs Division, Library of Congress.

The ordinary adventure story holds its tension and the reader's interest because of the potential threat in store for the protagonist as he encounters his next major test in the real world. Here, however, the boy's triumphs in encountering worldly tests are tediously predictable. The question that remains problematic is if he can cope with and survive the threats of his unconscious life.

This private obsession with the unconscious as a source of terror and fascination lies at the heart of the Kipling myth and informs all his tales. Consequently, almost all his stories involve night journeys into alien realms. But what makes these journeys so idiosyncratic, so typical of Kipling (rather than Conrad or Lawrence), is their timid and guarded nature, their sense of forced continuity and cohesion that constantly represses and conceals elements of disturbance in the text. The outer journey of the wooden, predictable protagonist from England to India and back at first jars against the inner unpredictable dream life—but only for a while. The deus ex machina at the end gives the reader a sense of an ending in narrative and in history that is radiant with confidence. Always in Kipling, tranquility and order will be restored if necessary through a hysterical insistence on forced closure. In this story the closure is charming, the brushwood boy will be saved, rescued from the dangers of his own unconscious, even from his own self—and he will be rescued by a member of the ruling class: a princess. What the story leaves incomplete is the inner journey that simply stops without allowing the boy a final confrontation with the beast in the jungles of his unconscious—the Sick Thing. (pp. 225-26)

The dream journey also reflects Kipling's characteristic ways of dealing with what R. D. Laing has called the "three forms of anxiety encountered by the ontologically insecure person: engulfment, implosion, petrification." He deals with the fear of engulfment (whose signs are the enclosed, stifling garden and house) by taking along a talisman, a guide, and a legitimate sexual companion; he deals with implosion, or the terrifying sense that at any moment the world might "crash in and obliterate all identity" . . . , through control and retreat, by always reminding himself in mid-dream "that he would be safe if he could reach the down with the lamp on it" . . . ; and he deals with the fear of petrification, of being turned into stone or dying, by projecting that anxiety onto others, by turning the threatening mother into a thing, by turning his elders into nameless, depersonalized "They" and "Them." Within the larger polarization between his waking world guarded by Policeman Day and his nightworld of dreams exist many other oppositions, the most significant between "They" and "Us." This defining of boundaries and defenses against intrusion by others serves to insulate the Kipling protagonist against "unknown continents" within and without. "Them," "They," "It," and "the mob of stony white people" are all dream objects of petrification caused by the dreamer's need to dehumanize, simplify, and classify Others into stony anonymity in order to control them. George's dream journey might involve perilous crossings over ferocious seas, stony ravines, and sandy deserts, but even then he is sure that there was less danger from the real elements than "from 'Them' whoever 'They' were." . . . The division between Us and Them is also a wish-fulfilling inner division between desire and fear, between the realm of possibilities allowed the boy and the girl when they are a self-contained secret unit, and the restricted realm allowed by the larger world that contains Others.

This division haunts the story on levels of form, imagery, actions, and ideology. The schizophrenic fragmentation of this text into the non-sexual world of action, war, colonial discipline, and empire and the sexual world of dream, desire, freedom, and fear is repeated in both the form and the ideological content of the story. Quite simply, the work of empire is daytime work and therefore incompatible with objects of nighttime desire. Once that fundamental division is accepted and assumed on a private level, then its social implications can be expected to follow. The story of George Cottar, like that of other Kipling protagonists, is that of a young man who has gone through an exemplary Kiplingesque regime of repression, control, and denial in India and can now return to England and its release from discipline, armed against its dangers with "character." In the real world it will allow him to enter threatening colonized spaces like India to test this resistance against immersion in the destructive elements of desire or empathy for the alien Other. His reward for such personal and ideological schizophrenia will be social reconciliation (return to the parental English home, smoking in the garden with father, parties) and union with a significant Other (marriage with the heiress who has appropriately aristocratic English lineage). (pp. 227-28)

In his autobiography Kipling refers several times to Browning's Fra Lippo Lippi as a "not too remote ancestor" . . . , to "young Lippo, whose child I was" . . . , and prefaces his third chapter, "Seven Years Hard," with the words:

> I am poor Brother Lippo by your leave.
> You need not clap your torches to my face.

It is not difficult to see Kipling's kinship with Lippi as analogous to his kinship with his fictional dream self, the brushwood boy. Brother Lippi also led a life divided between his daytime identity as a life-denying monk cloistered within his monastic cell and his nighttime identity as a street urchin and artist of the profane. Doomed to an eternally divided life, Lippi tries in his art to reconcile his conflicts between the earthly and the divine. And so his *Coronation of the Virgin* includes not only portraits of real mistresses of Priors but also, as a daring self-referring finale, a portrait of himself—"I, caught up with my monk's things by mistake"—violating the "pure company" with yet another reminder of the disturbed connections between life and art, flesh and spirit, the profane and the sacred. Kipling saw in Lippi yet another divided nightwalker who, no more than Kipling, could succeed in reconciling, through art, a divided consciousness. (pp. 234-35)

> *Zohreh T. Sullivan, "Kipling the Nightwalker," in Modern Fiction Studies, Vol. 30, No. 2, Summer, 1984, pp. 217-35.*

ADDITIONAL BIBLIOGRAPHY

A. E. "Ulster." In his *Imaginations and Reveries*, pp. 80-85. London: Maunsel & Co., 1915.
  Harshly criticizes Kipling for publishing what A. E. considered a slanderous attack on the character of Catholics in Ulster.

Amis, Kingsley. *Rudyard Kipling and His World.* New York: Charles Scribner's Sons, 1975, 128 p.
  Concise biography and critical study containing many photographs and illustrations.

Bennett, Arnold. "Rudyard Kipling." In his *Books and Persons: Being Comments on a Past Epoch, 1908-1911*, pp. 160-66. New York: George H. Doran Co., 1917.
  Discusses *Actions and Reactions* and the ways in which Kipling's social and political opinions intruded upon and weakened the quality of his work.

Birkenhead, Lord. *Rudyard Kipling.* New York: Random House, 1978, 421 p.
  Critical biography, making extensive use of previously unpublished material, including letters, diaries, and dictated memoirs.

Braddy, Nella. *Rudyard Kipling: Son of Empire.* New York: Julian Messner, 1941, 278 p.
  Anecdotal biography.

Braybrooke, Patrick. *Kipling and His Soldiers.* Philadelphia: J. B. Lippincott Co., 1926, 180 p.
  Study of Kipling's stories and poems about soldiers and war. Braybrooke states that "Kipling has drawn a picture of the British soldier with an accuracy that can only come from a perfect combination of knowledge and sympathy."

Brooks, Cleanth, Jr., and Warren, Robert Penn. "'The Man Who Would Be King,' Rudyard Kipling." In their *Understanding Fiction*, pp. 28-64. New York: F. S. Crofts & Co., 1943.*
  Provides an interpretation of Kipling's short story and some suggestions for class discussion.

Brown, Hilton. *Rudyard Kipling.* New York: Harper & Brothers Publishers, 1945, 237 p.
  Study of Kipling's life and work. Brown devotes the first half of his book to biographical facts, and the second half to critical comment on Kipling's work.

Chevrillon, André. "Rudyard Kipling's Poetry." In his *Three Studies in English Literature: Kipling, Galsworthy, Shakespeare,* translated by Florence Simmonds, pp. 1-152. London: William Heinemann, 1923.
    Study of Kipling's critical reception in France.

Cook, Richard. "Rudyard Kipling and George Orwell." *Modern Fiction Studies* VII, No. 2 (Summer 1961): 125-35.*
    Discusses the similarities in the lives and philosophies of Kipling and Orwell.

Cornell, Louis L. *Kipling in India.* New York: St. Martin's Press, 1966, 224 p.
    Study of Kipling's literary apprenticeship, his early years of journalistic work in India, and the subsequent effect of this work on his later writing.

Croft-Cook, Rupert. *Rudyard Kipling.* Denver: Allan Swallow, 1948, 107 p.
    Critical study of Kipling's works, with introductory and concluding chapters summarizing his life.

Fido, Martin. *Rudyard Kipling.* New York: The Viking Press, 1974, 144 p.
    Profusely illustrated biography.

Ford, Boris. "A Case of Kipling?" In *The Importance of "Scrutiny,"* edited by Eric Bentley, pp. 324-37. New York: New York University Press, 1964.*
    Questions T. S. Eliot's enthusiastic defense of Kipling. Ford contends that aspects of Kipling's work are tinged with an "atrophy of feeling."

Gilbert, Elliot L. *The Good Kipling: Studies in the Short Story.* Oberlin: Ohio University Press, 1970, 216 p.
    Analysis of Kipling's approach to the short story.

Green, R. Lancelyn. *Kipling and the Children.* London: Elek Books, 1965, 240 p.
    Examines the fiction which Kipling wrote for and about children, with particular attention given to Kipling's own childhood years.

Griswold, Hattie Tyng. "Rudyard Kipling." In her *Personal Sketches of Recent Authors,* pp. 266-80. Chicago: A. C. McClurg and Co., 1899.
    Early biographical sketch in which the critic predicts that "it is as a storyteller, and not as a poet, that Kipling is best known, and probably will be in the future."

Gross, John, ed. *The Age of Kipling.* New York: Simon and Schuster, 1972, 178 p.
    Collection of essays about Kipling's life and art by Leon Edel, Roger Lancelyn Green, Bernard Bergonzi, J.I.M. Stewart, and others, including many illustrations and photographs.

Harris, Frank. "Rudyard Kipling." In his *Contemporary Portraits,* pp. 44-63. New York: Privately printed, 1919.*
    Author recalls his relationship with Kipling and also appraises the strengths and weaknesses of his work.

Harris, Joel Chandler. "Another Jungle Book." *The Book Buyer* XII, No. 10 (November 1895): 656-57.
    A favorable review of *The Second Jungle Book* which assesses it as being "a feast for those who admire literature that is vital" and holding "the truth that is naked to life and experience."

[Henley, W. E.] "The New Writer." *The Scots Observer* III, No. 76 (3 May 1890): 662-63.
    Favorably reviews three works by Kipling: *Soldiers Three, Plain Tales from the Hills,* and *Departmental Ditties.* Henley especially praises Kipling's gifts of using dialect and developing fully realized characters.

Henn, T. R. *Kipling.* London: Oliver and Boyd, 1967, 141 p.
    Critical study of Kipling's short stories, poems, novels, travel literature, and literary criticism. An extensive bibliography is included.

Hinchcliffe, Peter. "Coming to Terms with Kipling: *Puck of Pook's Hill, Rewards and Fairies,* and the Shape of Kipling's Imagination." *University of Toronto Quarterly* XLV, No. 1 (Fall 1975): 75-90.
    Examines the ways in which Kipling's notion of history affected his narrative form.

MacInnes, Colin. "A Disconcerting Gift." *New Statesman* LXVI, No. 1698 (27 September 1963): 402-03, 406.
    Addresses, then dismisses, T. S. Eliot's attempt to define Kipling as a writer of verse rather than of poetry, and maintains that "with the exception of *Kim,* and a few final stories, the prose cannot, in bulk, stand up in quality to the poetry."

Matthews, Brander. "Cervantes, Zola, Kipling & Co." In his *Aspects of Fiction and Other Ventures in Criticism,* pp. 162-81. New York: Harper & Brothers Publishers, 1896.*
    Contrasts *Don Quixote, Le Débâcle,* and *The Naulahka.*

McLuhan, Herbert Marshall. "Kipling and Forster." *The Sewanee Review* LII, No. 1 (Winter 1944): 332-43.*
    Compares the "two world" view of British India as presented in the works of Kipling and E. M. Forster.

Mencken, H. L. "George Bernard Shaw as a Hero." *The Smart Set* XXX, No. 1 (January 1910): 153-60.*
    A positive review of *Actions and Reactions* and *Abaft the Funnel.*

Meyers, Jeffrey. "The Idea of Moral Authority in 'The Man Who Would Be King'." *Studies in English Literature 1500-1900* VII, No. 4 (Autumn 1968): 711-23.
    Examines the thematic development of Kipling's short story and concludes that it fails to maintain a "consistent moral perspective."

Norris, Faith G. "Rudyard Kipling." In *British Winners of the Nobel Literary Prize,* edited by Walter E. Kidd, pp. 14-43. Norman: University of Oklahoma Press, 1973.
    Discusses the reasons for the choice of Kipling as the recipient of the 1907 Nobel Prize in literature. The critic also examines all of Kipling's work published prior to this date.

Pritchett, V. S. "Kipling's Short Stories." In his *The Living Novel and Later Appreciations,* pp. 175-82. New York: Random House, 1964.
    Characterizes Kipling as "the only considerable English writer of fiction to have been popular in the most popular sense and to excite the claim to genius."

Rao, K. Bhaskara. *Rudyard Kipling's India.* Norman: University of Oklahoma Press, 1967, 190 p.
    Reevaluation of Kipling's stature as a writer about India. Rao concludes that "Kipling managed successfully to create the illusion that he knew and understood India."

Rutherford, Andrew, ed. *Kipling's Mind and Art: Selected Critical Essays.* Stanford: Stanford University Press, 1964, 278 p.
    Includes essays on Kipling by Rutherford, Lionel Trilling, Alan Sandison, and others.

Shahane, Vasant A. *Rudyard Kipling: Activist and Artist.* Carbondale: Southern Illinois University Press, 1973, 157 p.
    A study by an Indian critic which is aimed at "detailed textual analyses and explication" of Kipling's fiction. Shahane focuses particular attention on *Kim,* which he considers Kipling's masterpiece.

Shanks, Edward. "Mr. Rudyard Kipling." *The London Mercury* VII, No. 39 (January 1923): 273-84.
    Brief critical overview of Kipling's career. Shanks concludes, "It does not happen very often in English literature that the political opinions of a writer interfere with critical judgement of his work," but such is the case with Kipling.

————. ''Rudyard Kipling'' *A Study in Literature and Political Ideas*. New York: Doubleday, Doran & Co., 1940, 267 p.

    A discussion of Kipling's political philosophy as revealed in his fiction which contends that Kipling ''is an historical force which we ought to endeavor to evaluate in all its aspects.''

''Rudyard Kipling's Place in English Literature.'' *The Times Literary Supplement* No. 1773 (25 January 1936): 65-6.

    An anonymous obituary article which labels Kipling a ''national institution'' who ''will live and be admired as one of the most virile and skilful of English masters of the short story.''

Tompkins, J.M.S. *The Art of Rudyard Kipling*. London: Methuen & Co., 1959, 277 p.

    Study of Kipling's major themes.

(Nicholas) Vachel Lindsay

1879-1931

American poet and essayist.

Lindsay was a popular American poet of the early twentieth century who is remembered as a celebrant of small-town Midwestern populism and the creator of strongly rhythmic poetry designed to be chanted aloud. He is widely known for his often-anthologized poems "General William Booth Enters into Heaven" and "The Congo," which are notable for their vividness, vigor, and popularity with lecture audiences. While these poems secured recognition for Lindsay during his lifetime, and while they typify the characteristics with which the poet's work is associated, their reception imposed limitations on his career and established a precedent from which public acclaim and favorable criticism would not permit him to deviate.

Lindsay was born in Springfield, Illinois, in a house designed by the architect of Abraham Lincoln's home, and in a room said to have been one in which Lincoln himself had slept. In this milieu, Lindsay developed a deep-rooted and abiding respect for Lincoln's love of the common people, which later directed the course of his artistic career. Lindsay's father, a struggling physician who fully expected his son to assume the duties of his practice, was not unkind, but was humorless and a strict disciplinarian. Lindsay's mother, regarded by her neighbors variously as a social climber and an eccentric, was active in the local Campbellite church and in Springfield literary circles. She undertook her children's education until they were old enough to attend public school, introducing Lindsay and his two sisters to the fine arts, to classic English and Latin authors, and to a wealth of Greek, Roman, and Nordic legends. It was his mother who encouraged Lindsay in his early artistic pursuits, and to whom he turned for approval and support throughout much of his career. While Lindsay wrote poetry as early as childhood, art was his primary passion. Lindsay's mother, an artist herself, encouraged his artistic pursuits; however, she also supported her husband's insistence that Lindsay become established in a more secure occupation.

In 1897 Lindsay attended Hiram College, a small sectarian school in Ohio, where he showed little aptitude for medical studies, largely neglecting them for personal reading and writing. Despite his parents' advice that he persevere, the poet abandoned his medical education and, in 1901, enrolled at the Art Institute in Chicago, where the regimen of technical and anatomical studies made him equally unhappy. Lindsay discovered that while drawing gave him pleasure, a structured learning environment did not; he found, furthermore, that his actual artistic abilities, at least within such an environment, were minimal. Convinced that he would progress more rapidly at the New York School of Art, Lindsay enrolled there in 1903 to study painting with William Merritt Chase and his associate, Robert Henri. When approached by Lindsay to appraise one of his illustrated manuscripts, Henri, who both respected Lindsay and applauded his determination to succeed at painting as much as he doubted the likelihood of its occurring, candidly advised Lindsay to concentrate instead on writing poems, which he found more impressive than Lindsay's art. After following Henri's advice, Lindsay took his poetry to the New York streets

The Bettmann Archive, Inc.

in 1905, distributing copies of his verse among merchants and passersby for a nominal sum. A year later, Lindsay left the city for what was to be one of several tramping expeditions across the country, offering a sheet of his verses extolling beauty and democratic ideals in exchange for bed and board. Enamored as he was of America's heroic figures—such as John Chapman (Johnny Appleseed) and populist statesman William Jennings Bryan—who had lived and worked for the common people, and eager to imbue every American with his own sense of beauty and goodness, Lindsay was drawn irresistibly to the open road which, though arduous, invigorated and inspired him.

While Lindsay spent the summer of 1912 on the road, Harriet Monroe, a Chicago poet who was in the process of launching the periodical *Poetry* after recognizing the urgent need for an American journal devoted to poetry, published "General William Booth Enters into Heaven." The poem received wide attention and much praise from readers and critics alike, some of whom had before summarily rejected Lindsay's work. A collection of Lindsay's poetry, headed by "Booth," was published in 1913; and another collection which included "The Congo," a poem inspired both by the poet's fascination for Africa's spiritualism and Joseph Conrad's *Heart of Darkness*, was published the following year. In *General William Booth Enters into Heaven, and Other Poems,* and *The Congo, and*

Other Poems Lindsay, in an attempt to reach a less educated and less culturally sophisticated audience than that addressed by other contemporary poets, insisted that poetry is most effective when recited, and many of his selections were accompanied by marginal notations governing the specific volume and tone of voice to be used, among other directives. It had also occurred to Lindsay, in observing the overwhelming popularity of vaudeville, that despite his own reservations regarding this form of entertainment, certain of its elements might be employed to capture an audience's attention. Lindsay devised pieces referred to as "poem games," which were ritualistic enactments involving dancing and chanting, and which required the participation of an audience as well as specific players. In addition to these performances of "higher vaudeville," an exhausting schedule of popular and lucrative public readings was adhered to by Lindsay. Although at first encouraged by the enthusiastic response of his audiences and by their eager participation in his "poem games," Lindsay soon wearied of incessant public demand to hear "Booth" and "The Congo" to the exclusion of his other work. It also exasperated Lindsay that those dramatic elements employed to entice an audience succeeded, as well, in overshadowing the idealistic visions of beauty and democratic virtue underlying his art.

After the appearance of his first three volumes, Lindsay was both acclaimed as the people's poet and caricatured as a vagabond American minstrel whose resounding phrases were shouted to the clouds and stars as he strode across the Midwestern plains. Painfully aware of the frustrating limitations inherent in such a publicly allocated role, and conscious, too, of the dangers of fulfilling this caricature, Lindsay nevertheless found it impossible to give up the lucrative entertainer's circuit. Although he constantly had ideas for new works, his exacting schedule did not permit him to pursue most of these. While inwardly distressed over the shape his career was assuming, and while not a wealthy man, Lindsay did enjoy moderate success for several years. By the early 1920s, however, Lindsay's popularity began to wane as widespread, optimistic faith in America's future was supplanted by pessimism bred of World War I and as traditional small-town and rural values were pilloried by more worldly cosmopolitans. Disparagement of Lindsay's work became widespread, shaking the poet's faith in himself. H. L. Mencken mockingly wrote of Lindsay that "what was new in him, at the start, was an echo of the barbaric rhythms of the Jubilee songs. But very soon the thing ceased to be a marvel, and of late his elephantine college yells have ceased to be amusing." In the last years of his life, Lindsay, who had married at forty-five and now had two children, experienced crushing debts, deteriorating health, and periods of unreasoning rage and paranoia which were directed, by turns, at his family, supporters, and a world he perceived as too urbane to embrace his unsophisticated and now unfashionable philosophies. In 1931, bitter and disappointed, Lindsay poisoned himself. He announced to those attendant on his deathbed: "They tried to get me; I got them first."

The fervent rhythms of Lindsay's poetry are based on those of the Protestant camp meeting, and his tireless patriotism and love of democracy are linked closely to the concept of Christians of all social stations as a spiritual family, of which the camp meeting is symbolic. Imbued with faith in the inherent goodness and efficacy of common people united in a democratic cause, Lindsay's poems encourage the continued efforts of people to better and beautify their lives and environments, as well as celebrating both their realized and untapped abilities to do so. Many of his works also extol nature and a life lived close to the soil, and nearly all affirm God's immanence when they do not directly invoke His powers. While most of Lindsay's works were much more accomplished than were the better-known early poems, critics conclude that the selections that have endured clearly evidence the strongest of the poet's descriptive and exhortative powers. Although some denigrate his ideals and unsophisticated style, many commentators agree that Lindsay's best efforts are found in his verses commemorating such little-known heroes as William Booth and John Chapman, whose lives evoked from Lindsay vivid portraits largely unmarred by the prosy moralization and commonplace thought found in many of his works. "General William Booth Enters into Heaven," for example, is a colorful, teeming panorama which escapes the tribute's customary restrictions; critics have noted that Booth, whose life of sacrifice and charitable labor admits him into heaven, is as vigorously and interestingly portrayed as are the unwashed and unwanted to whom he ministered. Critics have also found that Lindsay's fictionalized account in "Johnny Appleseed" of John Chapman, whose solitary odyssey to sow for the enrichment of future generations perhaps inspired the poet's own expeditions, is, like his other portrayals, made vivid by Lindsay's fusion of fact with myth. Lindsay embellished history with his own imaginative additions in these portraits to arouse the ambition of Americans to live up to the nation's heritage; his widely anthologized "Abraham Lincoln Walks at Midnight," for instance, departs from a staid representation or rigid documentary style to present a great leader who cannot rest peacefully in his grave because of worldwide strife and injustice.

Although Lindsay's work is no longer widely read, most commentators find his contribution to American poetry valuable because of his colorful depiction of American ideals and idealists, and his attempt to address certain sectors of society ignored by other artists. Like the figures he immortalized, Lindsay refused either to surrender his ideals to modern exigencies, or, in their preservation, to divorce them from the world. Rather, he perceived pursuits of democratic and aesthetic goals to be integral to life and, accordingly, took them to street corners, farmhouses, and rural meeting places. While not of the highest rank, Lindsay's poetic legacy is valued for its vivid presentation of distinctly American characters and ideals.

(See also *Contemporary Authors,* Vol. 114.)

PRINCIPAL WORKS

Rhymes to Be Traded for Bread (poetry) 1912
General William Booth Enters into Heaven, and Other Poems (poetry) 1913
Adventures While Preaching the Gospel of Beauty (poetry) 1914
The Congo, and Other Poems (poetry) 1914
The Art of the Moving Picture (criticism) 1915; also published as *The Art of the Moving Picture* [revised edition], 1922
A Handy Guide for Beggars (poetry) 1916
The Chinese Nightingale, and Other Poems (poetry) 1917
The Golden Whales of California (poetry) 1920
Johnny Appleseed, and Other Poems (poetry) 1928
Selected Poems of Vachel Lindsay (poetry) 1963
Springfield Town Is Butterfly Town, and Other Poems for Children (poetry) 1969)
Letters of Vachel Lindsay (letters) 1979

R.S.B. [RANDOLPH S. BOURNE]   (essay date 1914)

[*An American essayist who wrote during the years of World War I, Bourne is recognized as one of the most astute critics of American life and letters of his era. During his short life, he contributed numerous articles to national magazines and became known as a champion of progressive education and pacifism, as well as a fierce opponent of sentimentality in literature. Bourne was on the original staff of* The New Republic *and was also a contributing editor of* The Dial *and* The Seven Arts, *until the latter was officially supressed during the war for its pacifist position. In a tribute published in* The New Republic, *Floyd Dell listed the characteristics of Bourne's mind as "restless and relentless curiosity, undeterred by sentiment and never recoiling in cynicism; the mood of perpetual inquiry, and the courage to go down unfamiliar ways in search of truth." In the following excerpt from a review of Lindsay's first three major volumes of poetry, Bourne affirms the existence of powerful originality in Lindsay's poems, finding the progression of Lindsay's career to be marked by the poet's discovery of his own sincerity.*]

You must hear Mr. Lindsay recite his own **"Congo,"** his body tense and swaying, his hands keeping time like an orchestral leader to his own rhythms, his tone changing color in response to noise and savage imagery of the lines, the riotous picture of the negro mind set against the weird background of the primitive Congo, the "futurist" phrases crashing through the scene like a glorious college yell,—you must hear this yourself, and learn what an arresting, exciting person this new indigenous Illinois poet is. He has a theory of his work, which Miss Monroe has supported in "Poetry," that he is carrying back the half-spoken, half-chanted singing of the American vaudeville stage to its old Greek precedent of the rhapsodist's lyric, where the poet was composer and reciter in one. After hearing the now so well-known **"General Booth Enters Into Heaven,"** and the **"Santa-Fé Trail,"** and **"The Firemen's Ball,"** one's imagination begins to run away with the idea of this Greek rhapsodist-vaudeville stage, where one could get the color and the smash of American life interpreted on a higher and somewhat more versatile plane than is now presented. One finds one's self beginning irresistibly, "Fat black bucks in a wine-barrel room," or "Booth led boldly with his big bass drum," and whirling along to rhapsodic improvisation of one's own. The explicitly poetical stage directions which accompany these poems "to be read aloud or chanted," initiate the reader at once into the art, and rather spoil him for the tame business of reading. One hopes that these verses must have come in sweeps of improvisation as the poet swung along on one of his vagabond walks through the interminable prairies of the West. They sound as if they had been shouted to the winds and the clouds, their gaudy rhythms marking time for the slow roll of the sun over the blistering sky.

These later poems [in *The Congo, and Other Poems* and *General William Booth Enters Into Heaven, and Other Poems*] represent Mr. Lindsay's finding of his own sincerity. Like most undistinguished and unendowed young Americans of talent, born into an atmosphere without taste and without appreciations, he had to flounder in a tangled maze of "trial and error" before he could even touch his own quality. . . . With almost too facile a fluency of rhyme and metre, Mr. Lindsay has tried every variety of verse from children's poems to political and up-to-date war poems. The "other poems" of the two volumes suggest that he has seized and developed every ingenious idea that came to him, pleasantly regardless of its reconciliation with the rest, or of its relation to any deep-lying philosophy of life. He has reminiscences of every kind of poetic diction and philosophy and creed and moral attitude. One poem stamps him

Christian, the next agnostic, the next Socialist, the next aesthete or rapt vulgarian at the "movies." It is all tumbled in with an astonishing insensitiveness to what is banal and what is strong.

After reading the adventures, one doubts a little whether the "Gospel of Beauty" was anything more than a stage on the road to sincerity, one of those ideas we Americans like to play with when we are young. Mr. Lindsay is concentratedly American, and his work and career are an illumination of the American soul. If that American soul had ever had any genuine hunger for the beauty of town and countryside which Europe clothes itself in, it would long ago have created that beauty, and not left itself to starve in shabbiness. The poet on his walk seems not to have found natural American beauty down through that long stretch of Missouri and Kansas, nor does he seem to have been saddened at its absence. One thinks of the visual richness of English vagabonds like Borrow and Jefferies, and is amazed at the thinness and poverty of these impressions. A few flowers along the railroad track, plenty of queer people, wheat interminable, but little hint of the quality of the life lived and the high-hearted scenery. Perhaps it is because Mr. Lindsay is too much of a poet not to require verse, for several of his Kansas poems do send long vistas down the mind that has never seen the West, and one still feels through these lines the torturing violence of a nature amost too big for man. The powerful originality of all this later work means the hope that he will leave other apprenticing with ideas alone forever, and enter at last into his sincerity. (pp. 26-7)

> *R.S.B. [Randolph S. Bourne], "Sincerity in the Making," in* The New Republic, *Vol. I, No. 5, December 5, 1914, pp. 26-7.*

W. D. HOWELLS   (essay date 1915)

[*Howells was the chief progenitor of American realism and the most influential American literary critic during the late nineteenth century. He was the author of nearly three dozen novels which, though neglected for decades, are today the subject of growing interest. He is recognized today as one of the major literary figures of the nineteenth century: he successfully weaned American literature away from the sentimental romanticism of its infancy, earning the popular sobriquet "the Dean of American Letters." Through realism, a theory central to his fiction and criticism, Howells sought to disperse "the conventional acceptations by which men live on easy terms with themselves" that they might "examine the grounds of their social and moral opinions." To accomplish this, according to Howells, the writer must strive to record detailed impressions of everyday life, endowing characters with true-to-life motives and avoiding authorial comment in the narrative.* Criticism and Fiction (1891), *a patchwork of essays from* Harper's Magazine, *is often considered Howells's manifesto of realism, although, as René Wellek has noted, the book is actually "only a skirmish in a long campaign for his doctrines." In addition to his perceptive criticism of the works of his friends Mark Twain and Henry James, Howells reviewed three generations of international literature, urging Americans to read the works of Emile Zola, Bernard Shaw, Henrik Ibsen, Emily Dickinson, and other important authors. In the following excerpt, Howells turns from a review of James Oppenheim's* Songs for the New Age *to examine Lindsay's* General William Booth Enters into Heaven, and Other Poems *and* Adventures While Preaching the Gospel of Beauty, *welcoming in Lindsay's poetry a harmonious blend of thought and aesthetic sensibility.*]

It is a sensible relief to turn from our uncertainty about the *Songs for the New Age,* which do not sing, but can possibly be chanted, to Mr. Nicholas Vachel Lindsay's book [*General William Booth Enters into Heaven, and other Poems*], where

GENERAL WILLIAM BOOTH
ENTERS INTO HEAVEN AND
OTHER POEMS BY

NICHOLAS VACHEL LINDSAY

NEW YORK • MITCHELL KENNERLEY 1913

Title page of the first edition of General William Booth
Enters into Heaven, and Other Poems.

the songs begin their music with the cymbal clash and bass-drum boom of the fine brave poem, **"General William Booth Enters into Heaven."** That makes the heart leap; and the little volume abounds in meters and rhymes that thrill and gladden one. Here is no shredding of prose, but much of oaten stop and pastoral song, such as rises amid the hum of the Kansas harvest fields and fills the empyrean from the expanses of the whole Great West. There is also song of solemn things everywhere, civic things, social things, and all of it, so far as we know, good. There are two books of it, and in the one we have not named—namely, *Adventures While Preaching the Gospel of Beauty*—there is such novelty as you may find in Heine's *Reisebilder*—the old, old novelty of beautiful thought and thinking emotion, but with a conscience and a pathos which the novelty of Heine did not always know. That is Mr. Lindsay's contribution to the American poetry which has felt itself new from the beginning, whether it spoke with the voice of Bryant, or Longfellow, or Whittier, or Emerson, or Lowell, and did not prefer the ground-gripping shoes of prose to the singing robes of rhyme. As in the *Reisebilder*, there is quick transition from prose to verse and back from verse to prose, but the prose does not put on the form of verse.

> *W. D. Howells, in a review of "General William
> Booth Enters into Heaven, and Other Poems" and
> "Adventures while Preaching the Gospel of Beauty,"*
in Harper's Monthly Magazine, *Vol. CXXXI, No.
DCCLXXXIV, September, 1915, p. 636.*

LOUIS UNTERMEYER   (essay date 1919)

[*A poet during his early career, Untermeyer is better known as an anthologist of poetry and short fiction, an editor, and a master parodist. Horace Gregory and Marya Zaturenska have noted that Untermeyer was "the first to recognize the importance of the anthology in voicing a critical survey of his chosen field." Notable among his anthologies are* Modern American Poetry *(1919),* The Book of Living Verse *(1931),* New Modern American and British Poetry *(1950), and* A Treasury of Laughter *(1946). Untermeyer was a contributing editor to* The Liberator *and* The Seven Arts, *and served as poetry editor of* The American Mercury *from 1934 to 1937. In the following excerpt, Untermeyer pronounces Lindsay's flamboyant technique daring and innovative, despite other critics' contentions that he is not a serious artist. Untermeyer admits, however, that Lindsay's verse is weakened both by doggerel and careless word choices resulting from the poet's haste to deliver his message.*]

Striking as are the differences between Frost and Oppenheim, the diversity of our new American poets is even more emphasized by the contrasting work of Vachel Lindsay. His background, like Frost's, is definitely local; his impulse, like Oppenheim's, indefinitely religious. But his blend of these forces is peculiarly individualized and peculiarly national. A pagan by intention and a puritan by intuition. He is, as I think he desires to be, the minstrel turned missionary; a corn-fed Apollo singing to convert the heathen. This *flair* for reformation exhibits itself in many ways. It includes a rhymed explanation as to why Lindsay voted the socialist ticket, exhortative verses pleading for Prohibition, a Salvation Army tribute (with all the drums and tambourines) to General Booth Entering Heaven, and a jeremiad (running to the other extreme) addressed bluntly "to the United States Senate." But his first and most enduring concern is doubtless embodied in the doctrine which he has called "The New Localism," which is explained in his prose volume *Adventures While Preaching the Gospel of Beauty,* a thesis that will be found amplified and applied in his forthcoming *The Golden Book of Springfield*. I doubt if there is any man in America who has laboured longer and more earnestly than Lindsay to encourage the half-hearted beauty that hides and fears to declare itself in our dull and complacent villages and townships. His gay, intrepid spirit, his racy little prose pamphlets, his tramping journeys on which the sixteen-page *Rhymes to be Traded for Bread* (printed and distributed by himself) were given for a meal or a night's lodging—these, in themselves, compose a gospel of beauty more persuasive and potent than a hundred sermons. (pp. 65-6)

There is something curious, almost contradictory about a man leaving his home town to tell men they should return to their birthplaces. But this is precisely what Lindsay preached and did. One should know the earth but one should not be a gypsy forever. The vagabond, he insisted, should taste the scattered largesse of the world. But he should return home. And having returned, he should plant the seeds he had gathered abroad. (pp. 70-1)

With an appreciation of these matters, one approaches his first important volume of poetry, *General William Booth Enters into Heaven and Other Poems* . . . , with sympathetic understanding. Here one immediately encounters the curious blend of athletic exuberance, community pride and evangelism. Consider the first poem, which gives the book its title. Here is the apotheosis of a great social-religious movement; but it is not so much a tribute to the Salvation Army as it is a glorification of a spirit greater and far beyond it. From a technical standpoint, Lindsay's attempt to blend noise, novelty and an old ecstasy is highly successful—and almost fortuitous. The experiment of setting lofty lines and reverential sentiment to cheap and brassy music is daring and splendid; especially since, in its very tawdriness, the music of the verse gives back the flavor of those earnest and blatant gatherings. It is, in a more definitely revivalistic spirit, the first of those characteristic chants (with the germs of the ''higher vaudeville'') which Lindsay lifted to so individual a plane. . . . No more colorful and solemn noise has yet been heard in our living song.

> The banjos rattled, and the tambourines
> Jing-jing-jingled in the hands of Queens!

Such a scrap is as orchestral as a dozen pages of elaborate instrumentation. It is, in its brazen directness, another phase not only of the new spirit that has enlivened American poetry but of America itself.

It would be too much to expect the rest of the volume to live up to this amazing piece of work, and it does not. Lindsay the man is always a poet, but Lindsay the poet does not always write poetry. When he errs it is not, as one critic has pointed out, ''on the side of the time-spirit''; when he fails it is not because he tries to express his age but because he expresses it badly. Frequently his verse rises from nothing more carefully constructed than a conviction, an anger, a crusade against the white-slave traffic or the corner saloon. Here his voice gets beyond his control; in his haste to deliver his message, he has no time to choose sharp and living words; he takes what comes first to hand—good, bad, indifferent—and hurries on, blurring the firm outline, losing the sense of leashed power without which no art-work can be ennobled. His aim is commendable but his volleys are erratic. In his anxiety to bang the bell, he sometimes shoots not only the target but the background to pieces. Such an effect is **''The Trap,''** with its glib didacticism and its stock-worn phrases. Such a poem also is the polemic **''To the United States Senate''** and one or two more. But these things are the poet in his dullest periods even though they be the propagandist in his most fiery moments. The excellent blend of both of them is achieved otherwise, notably in the dignified and sonorous [poem **''The Eagle That Is Forgotten''**]. (pp. 72-5)

This fused quality is to be seen, in a lighter vein, in **''Upon Returning to the Country Road,''** in **''Where is David, the Next King of Israel?''** and **''A Net to Snare the Moonlight.''** In these we note the growth of fantasy and whimsical extravagance which, in the ensuing volumes, come to play so great a part in Lindsay's work. Touched with an elfin charm that is both good-humored and grotesque, they reach their highest pitch in **''The Light o' the Moon,''** a series in which different people and animals look upon the moon and each creature finds in it his own mood and disposition. (pp. 76-7)

This series is continued and amplified in the succeeding volume. (p. 78)

[*The Congo and Other Poems*] gives us Lindsay's mixture of rhymes, rag-time and religion in his best blend. Here the rubberstamp idioms, the trade jargons of poetry, are lost in a sudden sweep of infectious and impulsive rhythms. These chants which form the larger part of the volume may not be the most powerful poetry that Lindsay has written, but they are undoubtedly the most popular; they give people that primitive joy

in syncopated sound that thrills them far more than critical didacticism or an ingenious theory of aesthetics. These verses demand to be read aloud; they are fresh evidence of the fact that poetry is fundamentally an oral art, an art appealing to the ear rather than to the eye. And it is an experiment in widening the borders of this song-art that they must be regarded. In pleading for a consideration of the possibilities of its development, Lindsay calls attention (*via* Professor Edward Bliss Reed's volume *The English Lyric*) to the Greek lyrists who, accompanying themselves, composed their own accompaniments. ''Here,'' he says, ''is pictured a type of Greek work which survives in American vaudeville, where every line may be two-thirds spoken and one-third sung; the entire rendering, musical and elocutionary, depending upon the improvising power and sure instinct of the performer. . . . I respectfully submit these poems,'' continued Lindsay, ''as experiments in which I endeavor to carry this vaudeville form back towards the old Greek precedent of the half-chanted lyric. In this case the one-third of music must be added by the instinct of the reader. He must be Iophon. And he can easily be Iophon if he brings to bear upon the piece what might be called the Higher Vaudeville imagination.''

It must be admitted that, to bring out their full surge and swing, it is not only necessary to hear these poems chanted, but to hear them chanted by Lindsay himself. Once having heard his highly original declamations, it is impossible for any one to forget the tunes and *tempi*. Without this variation of manner and melody—the rich unction of certain phrases contrasting sharply with the metallic *staccato* of others, the abrupt changes from a slow, deliberate *andante* to the briskest and most burly of *allegros*—much of the verse is merely rumbling and repetitive. Lindsay does his best to help his readers by means of a running fire of stage-directions along the edge of each page. But it is difficult, for any but a trained musician, to achieve half the effects he calls for. In the speed and clatter of the verses, Lindsay's admonishing voice, coaching, as it were, from the side-lines, is often lost.

For all this, the title-poem is a complete success, even on the printed page. The same flaming sincerity that kindled **''General Booth Enters into Heaven''** turns what is noisy or extravagant in these lines to eloquence. The cold type warms with a savage, insistent beat; the roll and sweep, even without Lindsay's sonorous baritone, quicken passages prosy and almost perfunctory by themselves. (pp. 79-81)

''The Sante Fé Trail,'' which follows this poem, is the most daring experiment in the volume, and there are about a dozen excellent aesthetic reasons why it should be a complete failure. Strangely enough, it is a complete success. This delicate and light-hearted humoresque is sung to an orchestral accompaniment of race-horns, klaxons, trumpets, thundering motors, the mad tympani of open mufflers, and a list of cities blared through the megaphone or shouted ''like a train caller in a Union depot.'' And all this uproar whirls around fairy interludes and scraps of fancy which somehow are not drowned in the shrieking maelstrom. So strikingly does each contrast set off the other, that the effect of the whole is startling in loveliness no less than speed.

It is in the third poem (**''The Firemen's Ball''**) that Lindsay unconsciously reveals how this very power, when pushed beyond its limits, fails; how, as in this instance, it often falls into dogma and doggerel. The musical content shows this poet at his worst (although it is still a far cry from the futurism of Marinetti and the typographical tricks of his followers like

Apollinaire and others); it is seven parts unlovely noise and three parts uninspired nonsense. This very increase of clangor defeats itself. Poe, many years ago, accomplished the magic of mere sound; but he did it by bringing to such poor rhymes as "Ulalume" and "The Bells," a subtle music that rang new changes under the insistent reiteration.

To return to **"The Firemen's Ball,"** its philosophy is even more questionable than the melody. It is its own amazing contradiction. From a roaring picture of a burning building, which is meant to symbolize the holocaust of life, Lindsay turns to the horrible (to him) glimpse of the firemen making love to their sweethearts (the baleful fires of passion mingling with the "lustful, insinuating music") and, as a grand finale, he gives us a rumbling, vague and negative Buddhistic sermon, quoting approvingly from a section of the Mahavagga that ends, "By absence of passion he is made free." The contradiction is in Lindsay's very treatment; he cannot get his spirit to believe in his theme. Even while he writes:

> Life is a flame:—
> Be cold as the dew
> Would you win at the game,

his lines refuse to obey him and go leaping along. Lindsay in this, as well as in some of the other poems, is like a man dancing gaily on the top of a windy mountain, his eyes blazing, his whole body kindled with the energy of living—and shouting all the while, "We must abolish passion! Down with Life!"

It is hard to understand this unwillingness on Lindsay's part to understand passion. It is harder to understand why he misrepresents and misinterprets it. And it is all the more strange since this passionate *élan* is his most valuable possession. The passion for making drab villages beautiful (*vide* **"The Soul of the City," "I Heard Immanuel Singing"** and his early broadsides); the passion for peace, as evinced in the somewhat rhetorical but none the less earnest war poems at the end of *The Congo;* the passion for righting hideous wrongs—these are some of the passions that burn through Lindsay's work and illuminate his lines with their quickening flame. There are many times, indeed, when he reminds one of the revivalist turned socialist; he has the strangely mingled passions of both. (pp. 83-5)

I pass hurriedly over the unaccountable stupidities which have been injected into the volume: The mawkish tributes to the doll-like Mary Pickford, the flashing Blanche Sweet *et al*, the 'comic'-supplement humor of **"When Gassy Thompson Struck It Rich"**—and proceed to Lindsay's most recent volume. Here (*The Chinese Nightingale . . .*) we have a similar mixture of high-flying fantasy and dogged fact, of primitive emotionalism and evangelistic propaganda. The two volumes give the weird effect of Buddha dancing to a jazz band; of the doxology performed on a steam calliope; of the Twentieth Century Express running lightly over a child's flower garden; of The Reverend William Sunday and Bert Williams reciting the Beatitudes. The latter effect is particularly evoked by **"The Booker Washington Trilogy,"** most strikingly in the poem **"Simon Legree."** It would be interesting to see what genuine negro composers like Will Marion Cook, Rosamund Johnson or H. T. Burleigh could do with this poem. Or with the **"The Congo,"** using it as a symphony for full orchestra, reinforced by banjos, bones, marimbas, xylophones and a dark baritone solo. Or **"King Solomon and the Queen of Sheba"** as the libretto for an opulent, afro-oriental cantata. Here again one wishes for Lindsay's vocal delivery in order to receive the full flavor of

these lines. But the person who can read them without feeling a good part of their racy imagery, vigor and humor, is dead not alone to poetry but to persuasion. No one can fail to enjoy the spectacle of the white poet speaking through the confused oratory of the old negro preacher, working up his audience and himself, and making desirable the very thing he set out to make horrible—Simon Legree being described, with loving envy, in a hell that sounds suspiciously like a poor slave's paradise. (pp. 86-7)

It is these original chants that have made many critics exaggerate Lindsay's standing as a bizarre innovator and minimize his importance as a serious creator. Most of his deprecators insist on discussing only the twenty per cent of his art that they think is the novelty. But even here, they are mistaken. They have taken a journalistic, almost a jejune attitude toward his work; and they fail to realize that when they assume he is lost in technical mazes (he has even been grouped, by two cataloguing critics, with the Imagists) he is distracted little by method and not at all by form. Technical discussions rage, he surmises, because most poets are twenty-five, which is the technical age. It is therefore somewhat distressing to an artist who has reached the maturity of thirty-nine years, to have his detractors protest at violations that he never committed. These critics assume that **"The Congo,"** for instance, is a new form. It is not. It is, as Lindsay has retorted, one of the oldest, most orthodox, most over-conventionalized forms in the English language:—the Ode. It is a form which, says Lindsay, has been worn out and practically dropped because it degenerated into false and pompous apostrophes. One can doubtless find precedents for every line of **"The Congo"** in a long array of odes in English, which have not failed to be in print simply because they were originally intended to be sung. Many times the most successful odes are not specifically so labeled and this adds to the critics' confusion. It seems probable that Lanier thought he was inventing a new form when he wrote "The Marshes of Glynn" and that Coleridge was laboring under a similar delusion when he began "Kubla Khan" and "Christabel." Lindsay is not so self-deceived and it seems an ironic injustice that he should be accused of doing or, what is still more ludicrous, failing to do the very thing he has carefully avoided even trying to do.

The defects in this volume are of an entirely different caliber. He has, in a commendable effort to extend the borders of the ode, gone a few steps farther and (taking his cue, I suspect, from Dryden's "Alexander's Feast") has expanded the chant into what he calls "Poem-Games," which add an undercurrent of alien music and the services of a dancer to the elocutionist's art. "In the 'Poem-Games,'" the author writes in an introductory note, "the English word is still first in importance, the dancer comes second, the chanter third." But in order to keep the chanter from getting too far ahead of the dancer, the poet has been compelled to repeat insignificant and fugitive phrases, until the English word loses not only its importance but its import. For instance, observe how the rich and simple music of **"King Solomon"** has been attenuated and dragged out into tiresome commonplaces by the dull and devasting repetitions. Or see how so slight a piece of fooling as **"The Potatoes' Dance"** has been lengthened far beyond the poem's limits and the reader's interest. The opening lines will explain:

> "Down cellar," said the cricket,
> "Down cellar," said the cricket,
> "Down cellar," said the cricket, . . .

(pp. 87-9)

Compare this doggerel to the amazing **"John Brown,"** which, lacking these verbal impediments, begins with a childlike catalog and runs through negro pomposity to a picturesque and powerful close.

But Lindsay is not only the lyric interpreter of the dark race. He can play on other instruments as well as the bones and calliope. In fact, some of his strummings on the lute are even more potent though less dynamic than his improvisations for brass band. Turn to the title poem and see how lightly the music evokes new hints of the ancient East. Forgetting programs or pronunciamentoes, Lindsay has let his whimsical mind loose among singing idols, "golden junks in a laughing river," rainbow fishes, explanatory nightingales, river-pirates, windbells, affable dragons, peacock landscapes and ghostly suggestions of a culture that was old when the Ming dynasty was young.

Elsewhere the mixture is less enticing. The evangelist seems to be in the ascendancy and the verse suffers in consequence. The war has undoubtedly brought out in Lindsay the usual religious reaction, but it is a somewhat ministerial fervor. Compared to the cosmic religion celebrated by James Oppenhiem, it has a prim and parochial tang; it sounds frequently less like a surge of song than a Sunday sermon. The Chatauqua platform performer is a rôle to which Lindsay seems to be growing increasingly partial. This shifting of artistic bases recalls how difficult a position Lindsay maintained in his other volumes; how dexterously he balanced himself in a devotion to a liberal socialism on one hand and a strict prohibition on the other. So in this collection. Pulled one way as a poet by the imperious demands of Beauty and another way, as propagandist, by the moral dictates of the Uplift crusade; he shows a vacillation, almost pathetic, between a universal compulsion and, to be literal, local option. Any admirer of Lindsay will observe with distrust the growing emphasis on the sermonizing features of his work. Even his Heaven is uninviting; a Nirvana of communal kitchens, daily parades and a Beauty scrubbed and worshiped with prescribed regularity. In **"The Eagle That is Forgotten,"** **"Sunshine"** and others of the poems already mentioned, there was a successful mingling of poet and pamphleteer. But in the present volume it is somewhat disturbing to witness Lindsay hitching his clipped Pegasus in front of the meeting-house, mounting the worn-out steps and going into the pulpit to deliver himself of such orotund banalities as **"God Send the Regicide,"** **"Where is the Real Non-Resistant?"** and the still flatter wordiness of rhymes like:

> When Bryan speaks, the sky is ours,
> The wheat, the forests, and the flowers.
> And who is here to say us nay?
> Fled are the ancient tyrant powers.
>
> When Bryan speaks, then I rejoice.
> His is the strange composite voice
> Of many million singing souls
> Who make world-brotherhood their choice

When he forgets to preach, or when the preachment takes on a less predetermined and more unconscious tone (as in the highly-colored **"Tale of the Tiger Tree"** and the brightly ironic **"Here's to the Mice"**), he regains his power—a power with an artistic dignity that his revivalistic gusto scarcely reaches. It is a relief to turn to those poems in which Lindsay's native fancy is given full swing. To **"The Ghosts of the Buffaloes,"** where he takes the reader on a midnight scamper with nothing more purposeful than the driving power of the imagination. Or

to the **"The Prairie Battlements."** Here again he is not trying to prove anything or convince any one; he is concerned only with trying to snare a glimmering and elusive loveliness. No village improvement societies will embroider this on their banners; no anti-vice crusaders will take it up as a slogan. And yet I like to feel that the real Lindsay is in these unofficial and merely beautiful poems. Or witness these lines, a part of **"The Broncho That Would Not Be Broken":** ...

> "Nobody cares for you," rattled the crows,
> As you dragged the whole reaper, next day, down the
>   rows.
> The three mules held back, yet you danced on your toes.
> You pulled like a racer, and kept the mules chasing.
> You tangled the harness with bright eyes side-glancing,
> While the drunk driver bled you—a pole for a lance—
> And the giant mules bit at you—keeping their places,
> O broncho that would not be broken of dancing.

It is in this homely fantasy, this natural extravagance that Lindsay excels. It runs through things as delicate as the moon poems and as burly as **"Simon Legree"** with its fallacious moral and its rollicking high spirits. And it is this last quality which will keep Lindsay from accumulating too fat a churchliness. It is the whimsical buoyancy, the side-spring, the gay appraisal of beauty as he finds it in people, places and art (as he hopes to find it even in politics) that will keep Lindsay the missionary from superseding Lindsay the minstrel. A careless singer of democracy, he goes adventuring with one hand on his lyre and the other on his sword. And the tune that he whistles is *"Gaily the Troubadour—"*. (pp. 89-93)

Louis Untermeyer, "Vachel Lindsay," in his The New Era in American Poetry, *1919. Reprint by Scholarly Press, 1970, pp. 65-93.*

AMY LOWELL   (essay date 1920)

[*Lowell was the leading proponent of Imagism in American poetry. Like the Symbolists before her, some of whom she examined in* Six French Poets, *Lowell experimented with free verse forms. Under the influence of Ezra Pound, Lowell's poetry exhibited the new style of Imagism, consisting of clear and precise rhetoric, exact rendering of images, and greater metrical freedom. Although she was popular in her time, standard evaluations of Lowell accord her more importance as a promoter of new artistic ideas than as a poet in her own right. In the following excerpt from a review of* The Golden Whales of California, *Lowell contends that Lindsay's best work, which is characterized by a blend of grotesque and lyric elements, is accomplished when the poet does not subordinate verbal and rhythmic images to his often commonplace thought.*]

Mr. Lindsay speaks authentically for a certain body of people in America, strenuously as they would probably deny it. He is of them through and through, even if in many ways he is their apotheosis. His greatness lies in his being so firmly one of a group, his weakness is just in the fact that when we expect him to rise above the group-consciousness by the strength of individual genius he so often falls heavily back upon it. (p. 251)

There has always been a suggestion of the Sunday school orator about Mr. Lindsay. Preaching and he are old comrades, but we felt also something else, a strong imagination carrying him forward, and we did not realize at first how much this imagination was merely the product of words and a remarkable facility for rhyme. What are Mr. Lindsay's poems about, what is the thought in them? Quite commonplace usually, it must be admitted, except—and this is the great exception—when he gives free opening to his talent for the grotesque. When there is no thought required, when the verbal and rhythmic magic are all, Mr. Lindsay transcends himself, he forgets the good little girls in starched pinafores of the Sunday school picnic and becomes the artist for whom one dares predict a successful future. Unhappily the word "dares" seems to have taken on a past tense in this latest volume. We dared indeed predict in *General Booth,* we more than dared in *The Congo,* we rejoiced in the heightened lyric beauty and changing rhythms of "**The Chinese Nightingale**" and forgot the rest of the volume (with the exception of "**Niagara**" and "**The Broncho That Would Not Be Broken**" in our belief. If we shivered at the jingoism of "**When Bryan Speaks**" and the Jane Addams poems, and regretted the triteness of the poem games, still we knew from proof that Mr. Lindsay was a poet. He would learn, he must learn, the critical faculty would wake in time to save him.

With the publication of "**General Booth,**" it was quite evident that here was a poet who could use the grotesque to illuminate high truth. He was powerful, original, fearless. *The Congo* strengthened his position enormously, he leaped at a bound to the forefront of contemporary poetry. "**The Congo**" itself must always be considered one of the most remarkable poems which the new movement has produced; it is astounding. In "**The Santa Fé Trail**" there was rather more buffoonery and rather less depth, but Mr. Lindsay kept his inspiration well in hand, as the charming refrain of "**Far Away the Rachel-Jane**" &c., showed. "**The Firemen's Ball**" ran away with him, but that was a matter of small account considering the two poems which preceded it, and the Moon Poems in the fourth section were altogether delightful.

With the publication of "**The Chinese Nightingale**" three years later, Mr. Lindsay gave us what I personally think is his best poem. It is grotesque, serious, lyric and beautiful. It shows great technical mastery over his own best qualities. One may read the poem again and again, it never grows stale, but becomes always more satisfying like a well-loved tune. Now comes *The Golden Whales of California,* and one asks what has happened. The book, taken by and large, might be a parody on Mr. Lindsay, all the Mr. Lindsays. What has happened, indeed? And yet one knows very well what has happened. The superstition has got him, the group-consciousness has sucked him down. The old fallacy has him by the teeth, that the poet is born complete, that God sits in the poet's heaven and requires no effort on the part of that much-pampered individual. This is a very old superstition and comes near to ruining all of our present output in the world of letters.

Only a most tenacious superstition could have nailed these blind glasses to our eyes. There are books to read which might prove to us how much man makes himself upon the frame his god has provided for him. There never was a great poet who had not a hand in his own destiny. In *The Chinese Nightingale* Mr. Lindsay seemed to be learning his art sanely and soberly; in *The Golden Whales* volume, he snaps his fingers at all restraint. Such an attitude is suicidal, but I believe the reason for it lies in another group trait—ignorance, the pathetic belief that what many people say must be true. Mr. Lindsay has listened too readily to his kind public, his critical faculty, never strong, has been smoked and blurred by incense. Not that one would wish to curb the splendid and intended exaggeration of Mr. Lindsay's manner; he has made exaggeration his most personal vehicle, and where such exaggeration leads to a balanced end, where it is a calculated effect admirably serving the author's

needs, is excellent. But when Mr. Lindsay loses control of his own method and merely babbles words beause they tickle the tympanum of his ear with a jingle rhyme or some other pleasantness, he does himself a gross injustice.

Of course, there are fine lines in the book; unfortunately they are, for the most part, merely lines. "**The Golden Whales**" itself is a rollicking allegory of the kind which Mr. Lindsay did so well a few years ago. But often in it his taste deserts him as it did not in those days. "Thunderclouds of grapes hang on the mountains" is a fine, imaginative line, but "Bears in the meadows pitch and fight" drops the quatrain to inanity. Mr. Lindsay has permitted his flair for the grotesque to degenerate into bombast. The frain in "**Shantung,**"

> Now let the generations pass—
> Like sand through Heaven's blue
> hour-glass,

is beautiful, but the poem itself is weak. "**The Blacksmith's Serenade**" would be good if Mr. Lindsay were not a poet, but a versifier. There is a sort of cheap morality in "**John L. Sullivan**" and "**Bryan, Bryan, Bryan, Bryan.**" It is quite possible that those persons who care more for local color than for anything else in a work of art may find these poems valuable. They certainly give the attitude of a certain person in a certain place at a certain time perfectly. In fiction, such faithful reproduction is in order, but a poem must be poetry (odd, but true), it must differentiate itself from prose in one of three ways—either by subject, presentation, or point of view. It may be a poem in all three ways or in one alone, but with none it is a mere jingled statement. These poems may be interesting to the psychologist or the student of manners; to the lover of poetry they are dead things. "**A Rhyme for all Zionists**" gives the Sunday school orator undisputed floor, and in quieter poems like "**The Spacious Days of Roosevelt,**" Mr. Lindsay is merely commonplace; also, why must he ape Ralph Hodgson in "**The Lame Boy and the Fairy,**" when he has shown in his other books how well he can write child poems without incurring debts to anybody?

It is a rough business, counting the lapses in a body of work one admires. This is an off book, that is all; a little attention and Mr. Lindsay will pick up the threads and go on. (p. 251, 253, 255)

"**My Fathers Came from Kentucky**" is a splendid poem and in Mr. Lindsay's best and most personal manner, and so is "**Written in a Year When Many of My People Died.**" Here is sincere feeling quietly and yet most originally expressed. Mr. Lindsay misunderstands himself if he feels obliged to bang the big drum almost to breaking to be heard, and yet one can understand his fear, for sometimes he is betrayed into a painful usualness of presentation as, for instance, in "**Rameses II.**" The war poems are inadequate; war is out of Mr. Lindsay's consciousness; he cannot conceive it enough even to hate it vigorously in poetry.

The poem-games are an idiosyncrasy of Mr. Lindsay's. I might almost call them a phobia, along with his idealization of the movies. It is a sort of new pathetic fallacy to believe that the vulgar and the thin can be ennobled by simply willing to believe that they are noble. Mr. Lindsay loses his way in this again and again. He seems hypnotized by the jazz. I suppose he thinks it American. Well, so it is, but America has other music as well. This is what I mean by saying that Mr. Lindsay is not leading his group, not transcending it; on the contrary, he frequently drops to its level. Take, for an example, this very

A MAP OF THE UNIVERSE ISSUED IN 1909.
THIS MAP IS ONE BEGINNING OF THE
GOLDEN BOOK OF SPRINGFIELD.

Lindsay's "Map of the Universe," drawn in 1904.

question of the jazz: a musician can work certain of its effects into a score and yet keep the score at the height of serious music, as Debussy has done with ragtime in "Minstrels," for instance. If he merely writes another jazz he is no better than the man who wrote the first one. In **"The Congo"** Mr. Lindsay was the guide of his subject and its prophet; it was nigger-minstrels, if you like, but it was also the pathos of the jungle savage ground by a ghastly fear. But in what way can Mr. Lindsay be said to have treated his subject in **"The Apple Blossom Snow Blues"**? He is level with it, is he not? That being level is growing on the poet. He should beware. But I think all this starts from a mistake, the fear of losing that group-consciousness which he feels, and quite rightly, is his *raison d'être* as a poet. Now, that is a groundless apprehension I am certain; he could no more lose his group than he could lose his finger; he may very well lay his preoccupation with it aside for a time while he brings his critical faculty up abreast with it. Only then can he speak adequately for it, being at once a great poet and the authentic voice of a section of the people. Mr. Lindsay need not hurry. He can afford to wait, to make haste slowly, for the result would appear to be entirely in his own hands. (p. 255)

Amy Lowell, "Mr. Lindsay's Latest Venture," in The New York Times Book Review, May 16, 1920, pp. 251, 253, 255.

MARIANNE MOORE (essay date 1923)

[*Moore was an American poet, translator, essayist, and editor whose poetry is characterized by the technical and linguistic precision with which she reveals her acute observations of human character. In the following excerpt, she commends Lindsay's vigor and preoccupation with humanitarianism, but criticizes his lack of aesthetic discipline, which is evidenced in irregular versification, choppy enunciation, and repetitions which serve no artistic purpose.*]

The outstanding impression made by Mr Lindsay's collected poems is that the author pities the fallen, deplores misunderstandings, and is saddened that the spirit should so often be at the mercy of the body. One cannot but revere his instinctive charity and determination to make a benevolent ordering of the universe possible. . . . It is a fine courage that enables a writer to let himself loose in the religious revival sense of the term at the risk of being thought an unintentional clown. It is impossible not to respect Mr Lindsay's preoccupation with humanitarianism, but at the same time to deplore his lack of aesthetic rigour. In a lover of the chant, one expects a metronomelike exactness of ear; it is the exception, however, when the concluding lines of Mr Lindsay's stanzas are not like a top which totters, or a hoop which rolls crazily before it finally stops. We have:

> Murdered in filth in a day,
> Somehow by the merchant gay! . . .

It is difficult to enunciate the words in such lines as:

> With my two bosomed blossoms gay

> Like rivers sweet and steep,
> Deep rock-clefts before my feet

> You were a girl-child slight.

One is disaffected even in the mood of informal discursiveness by adjacent terminal words such as calculation, Appalachian; whole, jowl; ore, floor; trial, vile; fire, the higher; and

> Join hands,
> Poets,
> Companions

is a metrical barbarism. Why, in a **"Dirge for a Righteous Kitten,"** "His shirt was always laundried well"? What of the prose lines, "A special tang for those who are tasty"? And in the phrase, "when the statue of Andrew Jackson . . . is removed," we have that popular weak misuse of the present tense which we have in such an expression as "I hope he gets there." There is a lack of neat thinking in such phrases as "Lining his shelves with books from everywhere" and "All in the name of this or that grim flag." There is inexactness of meaning in

> The long handclasp you gave
> Still shakes upon my hands.

(pp. 498-99)

As a visionary, as an interpreter of America, and as a modern primitive—in what are regarded as the three provinces of his power, Mr Lindsay is hampered to the point of self-destruction by his imperviousness to the need for aesthetic self-discipline. Many poets have thoughts that are similar, in which case, only heedlessness prevents the author of the less perfect product from giving place to the author of the stronger, and much of Mr Lindsay's collected work is unfortunate in thus provoking comparison with attested greatness. Unfortunate also, is the conscious altering of great familiar expressions:

> The times are out of joint! O cursed spite!
> The noble jester Yorick comes no more. . . .
>
> (p. 500)

Although it was not intended that the poems should be read to oneself, they will, on occasion, be so read, and so surely as they are it is inevitable that the author will in certain respects be presented amiss. Certain repetitions suggest the pleonasm of the illiterate preacher who repeats a phrase in order to get time to formulate another:

> Love is not velvet, not all of it velvet

> When a million million years were done
> And a million million years beside,

We have not that reinforcing of sentiment which we have in reiteration by Yeats:

> She pulled the thread and bit the thread,
> And made a golden gown.

In his essay on "Poetic Diction," Robert Bridges says, "the higher the poet's command of diction, the wider may be the field of his Properties; . . . and this is a very practical point, if a writer with no command of imaginative diction, should use such Properties as are difficult of harmonization, he will discredit both the Properties and the Diction." Despite the fact that Mr Lindsay's properties are abundant and often harmonious as in the fantasy of the gipsies:

> Dressed, as of old, like turkey-cocks and zebras,
> Like tiger-lilies and chameleons,

the grouping is often conspicuously self-destructive. One feels that

> Percival and Bedivere
> And Nogi side by side

distracted from the poet's meaning as do the statesmen, artists, and sages, in **"The Litany of the Heroes"**: Amenophis Fourth—Hamlet and Keats "in one"—Moses, Confucious, Alexander, Caesar, St Paul, "Augustine," Mohammed, St Francis, Dante, Columbus, Titian, Michael Angelo, Shakespeare, Milton, Napoleon, Darwin, Lincoln, Emerson, Roosevelt, Woodrow Wilson, Socrates. Like paintings in public buildings of the world's cultural and scientific progress, such groups sacrifice impact to inclusiveness. **"Johnny Appleseed"** is marred, one feels, by such phrases as "the bouncing moon," and

> He laid him down sweetly, . . .
> Like a bump on a log, like a stone washed white.

We rejoice in the resilience of imagination in the idea of a grasshopper as "the Brownies' racehorse," "the fairies' Kangaroo"; and in **"The Golden Whales of California,"** there is controlled extravagance in the enumeration of "the swine with velvet ears," "the sacred raisins," "the trees which climb so high the crows are dizzy," "the snake fried in the desert," but "the biggest ocean in the world," and the whales "whooping that their souls are free," suggest the tired European's idea of America. . . . (pp. 501-02)

Objecting further, it is impossible not to say that Mr Lindsay's phrases of negro dialect are a deep disappointment. A familiarity with negros and the fact that the adaptations are intentional cannot absolve such Aryan doggerel as:

> And we fell by the altar
> And we fell by the aisle,
> And found our Savior
> In just a little while.

Such lines are startlingly at variance with real negro parallelism as we have it in:

> Oh, Hell am deep 'n Hell am wide
> an' you can't touch bottom on either side

and are incompatible with that perfect fragment of negro cadence which Mr Lindsay has combined with it, "Every time I hear the spirit moving in my heart I'll pray." A stentorianly emphatic combining of the elements of the black genius and the white, but emphasizes their incompatability. . . . In stage directions, the most expert craftsmen such as Shaw and Yeats barely escape pedantry and one feels that however necessary to Mr Lindsay's conception of the spoken word particular information may be, when he asks us "to keep as lightfooted as possible," to read "orotund fashion," "with heavy buzzing bass," et cetera, one can but feel, unfairly or not, that he is subordinating a poorly endowed audience to wit which he proposes to furnish.

Some of Mr Lindsay's work would lead one to infer that "a man is out on three wide balls but walks on four good strikes." The literary reader tends not to be compensated by moral fervour for technical misapprehensions, but there is life in any kind of beauty and in these poems avoidance of grossness and the entirely vengeful, is fortifying. **"Why I Voted the Socialist Ticket"** is full of contagious vigour . . . but in his **"Curse for Kings,"** Mr Lindsay gives the effect of an emotional pacifism which is incompatible with earnestness.

"This whole book is a weapon in a strenuous battlefield," Mr Lindsay says; "practically every copy will be first opened on the lap of some person . . . trying to follow me as I recite as one follows the translation of the opera libretto." He is not to be refuted. There is a perhaps not very exact analogy between him in his *rôle* of undismayed, national interpreter, and a certain young eagle conveyed by American naval officers to the Philippines, styled "an American rooster," and pitted invariably with mortal consequence against Philippine gamecocks.

If a reader felt no responsibility for a writer, and were merely culling felicities, certain of Mr Lindsay's poems would undoubtedly give complete pleasure; disregarding as a whole the poem, **"How a Little Girl Danced,"** there is a fine accuracy in the lines:

> With foot like the snow, and with step like the rain.

There is suggested fragility in the poem game of yellow butterflies:

> They shiver by the shallow pools. . . .
> They drink and drink. A frail pretense!

There is beauty in **"The Dandelion"**; especially also, in **"The Flower of Mending"**:

> When moths have marred the overcoat
> Of tender Mr Mouse.

And the lines:

> Factory windows are always broken.
> Somebody's always throwing bricks,

are expertly captivating. Lincoln is not added to, but he is not travestied in **"Abraham Lincoln Walks at Midnight"**; there is glory in the conception of Alexander Campbell stepping "from out the Brush Run Meeting House": and reality in **"Bryan"**:

> With my necktie by my ear, I was stepping on my
> dear. . . .
> The earth rocked like the ocean, the sidewalk was a
> deck.
> The houses for the moment were lost in the wide
> wreck.

We have in this poem, some of Gertrude Stein's power of "telling what you are being while you are doing what you are doing," and there is "blood within the rhyme" in:

> The banjos rattled and the tamborines
> Jing-jing-jingled in the hands of Queens.

> (pp. 502-05)

Marianne Moore, "An Eagle in the Ring," in The Dial, *Vol. LXXV, No. 5, November, 1923, pp. 498-505.*

HARRIET MONROE (essay date 1924)

[*As the founder and editor of* Poetry, *Monroe was a key figure in the American "poetry renaissance" which took place in the early twentieth century.* Poetry *was the first periodical devoted primarily to the works of new poets and to poetry criticism, and from 1912 until her death Monroe maintained an editorial policy of printing "the best English verse which is being written today, regardless of where, by whom, or under what theory of art it is written." Monroe played a major role in bringing Lindsay's poetry to a wide audience, printing much of his early work in* Poetry. *In the following excerpt from an essay originallly published in* Poetry *in 1924, she finds Lindsay to be a modern knight-errant battling an unromantic age with childlike wisdom, wistful humor, and frequently astonishing insight.*]

Lindsay is a modern knight-errant, the Don Quixote of our so-called unbelieving, unromantic age. To say this is not scorn but praise, for Don Quixote's figure looms heroically tall in perspective, and his quests, however immediately futile, become triumphant in the final account. Lindsay's whimsical imagination, even as the madder fancy of Cervantes' hero, cuts the light into seven colors like a prism, so that facts become glamorous before our eyes. Booth strides, full-haloed, into a Salvation Army heaven; fat black bucks of South State Street dance along a mystical glorified Congo; motor-cars on a Kansas road are chariots from now to forever; Bryan "sketches a silver Zion"; Johnny Appleseed is a wandering god of the soil, as mythical as Ceres; our yellow neighbor the Chinese laundryman is a son of Confucius, and his nightingale utters deathless beauty. Lindsay links up the electric sign with the stars:

> The signs in the street and the signs in the skies
> Shall make a new Zodiac, guiding the wise.

and sometimes, not always, he does this so effectively that we believe him. For his art, at its best, is adequate; Rosinante becomes Pegasus and soars beyond the moon.

It is appropriate that the American sense of humor should be, in this poet's mind, the law of perspective which ensures sanity. Looking over a Sunday comic supplement the other day, I felt that it is in such laughter that hate dies among us. The neighborhood rages of Europe break into absurdity against it; if not the fire under the melting-pot, it is at least the crackling gas

in the fuel. If Europe could only laugh as universally, as nonsensically, the heroic pose of war would become as impossible among her quarreling nations as among our forty-eight widely differing states.

Lindsay's sense of humor is true to type in its extreme variety; a faint and wistful smile, yearning for elusive and everlasting beauty, in **"The Chinese Nightingale,"** it becomes a sly grin in **"So Much the Worse for Boston,"** a tenderly sympathetic laugh in **"Bryan, Bryan,"** a louder laugh in **"The Santa Fe Trail"** or **"The Kallyope Yell,"** and a real guffaw in **"Samson."** But the laugh, whether whispered or loud, is always genial, is never a satiric cackle. Often there is a wistful pathos in it, the trace of those tears which spring from the same bubbling fountain of human sympathy. Like the Chinese philosopher squinting at the cataract, Lindsay feels the tragedy—he is aware of the littleness of man. And to know man's littleness is to know also his greatness, for the point of the cosmic joke lies in the contrast. One finds man's greatness implied throughout the four hundred pages of Mr. Lindsay's volume, and expressed without even the reservation of a smile in such triumphant or tragic poems as **"General Booth," "John Brown," "Eagle Forgotten,"** and **"Abraham Lincoln Walks at Midnight."**

James Stephens, the Irish poet and teller of tales, praises **"The Chinese Nightingale"** as one of two masterpieces in the poetry of these prolific fifteen years—"a great poem on the one subject which poetry has any true concern with, the soul of man and its meaning and destiny." It is characteristic of Lindsay, poet that he is, that he states nothing in this poem, but disguises "the one subject" in imagery—in the quaint and almost humorous phantasy of oriental costume and magic. (p. 24-5)

The poem flows along like a river, iridescent with light, melodious with sound, bearing its cargoes gaily to the deep seas. There are lines which entrap the imagination with their beauty. . . . (p. 26)

One would like to quote a number of poems to show forth Mr. Lindsay in his various moods: **"The Righteous Kitten"** for pure nonsense; **"The Kallyope Yell"** for utter flamboyance; **"The Congo"** or **"Samson"** for, not the Negro himself, but a sublimated expression of his meaning, his relation to our civilization; **"The Leaden-eyed"** for aphoristic wisdom; **"Lincoln Walks at Midnight,"** or **"Eagle Forgotten"** for tragic beauty. And still others, if one were to give a fair hint of his extraordinary range.

If this poet was born into a rather thin and bloodless strain of puritan thought, his instinct for beauty led him early into richer regions. He has loved the mediaeval lily and the oriental lotus, even the scarlet African orchid; and has given us, if not their precise form and color, at least something of their several perfumes. Mr. Lindsay's mind, while child-like in certain aspects, is surprisingly sagacious in others. If one finds his thinking trivial at times, all of a sudden one may be astonished by such an evidence of searching critical insight as his article on Whitman in the *New Republic*. He is full of profound intuitions, and if he gropes among them sometimes, it is because his own awkward slow-moving self gets in his way and keeps him from turning on the light. But the light is there.

Lindsay imparts a new flare of whimsical and colorful beauty to this American scene, and presents its extraordinary variety of emotion and mood. It is a generous gift—it makes us aware of ourselves in the true tradition of authentic art the world over.

And the gift is not likely to diminish seriously in value under the chemical tests of time. (pp. 27-8)

Harriet Monroe, "Vachel Lindsay," in her Poets and Their Art, *revised edition, Macmillan Publishing Company, 1932, pp. 21-8.*

CARL VAN DOREN   (essay date 1924)

[*Van Doren is considered one of the most perceptive critics of the first half of the twentieth century. He worked for many years as a professor of English at Columbia University and served as literary editor and critic of* The Nation *and* The Century *during the 1920s. A founder of the Literary Guild and author or editor of several American literary histories, Van Doren was also a critically acclaimed historian and biographer. Howard Moss wrote of him: "His virtues, honesty, clarity and tolerance are rare. His vices, occasional dullness and a somewhat monotonous rhetoric, are merely, in most places, the reverse coin of his excellence." In the following excerpt from an overview of Lindsay's career, Van Doren declares Lindsay a crusader who is at his best when mythologizing neglected heroes rather than when voicing the poetic prophecies that frequently engaged him. Van Doren notes and then dismisses as relatively unimportant Lindsay's inattention to refinement of phrase, his limited range, and even specific poetic failures in weighing these against his crusade for mass appeal.*]

If Mr. Lindsay's poetry is more original than his philosophy, so is it more valuable. Like all crusaders, he has difficulty in looking ahead to the end of the bright path he follows with such rapture. *The Golden Book of Springfield,* in which he sets forth his notion of what his native town may have become by 2018, is a Utopia of Katzenjammer. History serves him better than prophecy, as when he celebrates the fame of that John Chapman who as Johnny Appleseed is remembered for his gift of orchards to the Middle West. Indeed, Mr. Lindsay is at his best when he is engaged in promoting to poetry some figure or group of figures heretofore neglected by the poets: the Salvation Army, the motorists of the Santa Fe trail, the Springfield blacks, Alexander Campbell, John Chapman, John L. Sullivan, John P. Altgeld, the Bryan of 1896.

On these occasions the poet is not content to write history merely; he makes myths. His Alexander Campbell still rides his circuit, announcing the millennium and snatching back renegade souls to the faith; his John Chapman still roams the great valley, a backwoods St. Francis, with the seeds of civilization in his wallet. During the war, in **"Abraham Lincoln Walks at Midnight,"** Mr. Lindsay thus poetically brought to life the greatest of all Springfield's citizens, to move restlessly through the streets.

Yea, when the sick world cries, how can he sleep?

Poetry, in a conception like this, joins hands with religion, keeping the heroes and the saints and the gods alive because those who depend upon them will not believe that they have died. In a fashion like this patriotism grows up, knitting many hearts together by giving them common memories and common hopes.

And yet Vachel Lindsay is not the personage he was when he published *The Congo* in the same year with *Spoon River Anthology.* Both he and Edgar Lee Masters were deliberately going back to Greek models, the one to the chanted lyric, the other to the ironical epigram. Irony, however, won the day, helped by the presence in the times of a tumult through which nothing less cutting than the voice of irony could reach; and in the eight years since the appearance of the two books the tendency of American literature has been steadily toward irony, satire, criticism. To the drive for the new localism there has succeeded a revolt from the village, turning to ridicule the eloquence of the local patriot and laughing at the manners of the small community. To the confidence that much might be made for literature out of the noisier, rougher elements of the national life by the process of lifting them to richer, surer rhythms and giving them a sounder language, has succeeded the feeling, best voiced by H. L. Mencken, that such elements are menace, nuisance, or nonsense, and that the cause of the higher vaudeville, to be based upon them, is not worth fighting for. Some sense of this shift in the current literary mood must have been responsible, at least in part, for the loss by Mr. Lindsay of the full vigor with which he sang in those first hopeful days; for his inclination to turn away from creation to criticism and scholarship, from poetry to design.

The crusader cannot be a connoisseur. He must meet the masses of men something like halfway. Nor can it be merely in the matter of language that he meets them. He must share as well a fair number of their enthusiasms and antipathies. He must have gusto, temper, rhetoric; must apply them to topics which are not too much refined by nice distinctions. These qualities Mr. Lindsay has, and he lets them range over a wide area of life, delighting in more things than his reason could defend. He rejoices, too, in more things than his imagination can assimilate. For Mr. Lindsay's poetical range is not very great. His eye is bigger than his appetite. That eye embraces the Anti-Saloon League and the sons of Roosevelt and Comrade Kerensky and dozens of such morsels; he gulps them down, but no digestion follows. He is a reformer, an evangelist. He lifts his standard for all who will gather round it; he spreads his arms to all who will come to them. His business is not, as that of a different poet might be, to find only the purest gold or the clearest gems. It is rather to spade up new sod and see what unexpected flowers will spring from it; to peer into dusky corners and see that nothing precious has been hidden there; to explore the outer boundaries of the regions of poetry and see if they cannot be extended to include virgin territories hitherto unoccupied. No wonder he has made as many poetic failures as any poet of his rank.

But besides his failures, there are his successes. To appreciate them it is necessary to have heard him read his own verse. His reading is almost singing; it is certainly acting. The rhythms of the camp-meeting, of the cake-walk, of the stump-speech, of the chantey, of the soldiers' march, of patriotic songs, of childish games, throb through him and are from him communicated to the most difficult audience. His singsong is as contagious as that of any revivalist who ever exhorted; his oratory rings. The pulse of human life has beat upon him till he has left its rhythm and meter; simplifying them by his art, he turns and plays with them upon his hearers till they, too, throb in excited unison. Noise by itself, when orderly, has some poetical elements; rhythm, without tune or words, may be thrilling. The potency of Mr. Lindsay's verse, however, shows how far he goes beyond mere noise and rhythm. He has pungent phrases, clinging cadences, dramatic energy, comic thrust, lyric seriousness, tragic intensity. Though he may sprawl and slip and though a large portion of his work is simply sound without importance, he is at bottom both a person and a poet. He is, after all, like none else. Something in him which was better than his conscious aims has taught him, however much he might borrow from the circuit-rider, the crusader, the booster, that true eloquence comes from the individual, not from the mass; that true poetry is actually lived, not merely shared or argued. (pp 161-66)

Carl Van Doren, "Salvation with Jazz: Vachel Lindsay," in his Many Minds, Alfred A. Knopf, 1924, pp. 151-66.

ALBERT EDMUND TROMBLY (essay date 1929)

[Trombly was the author of the first book-length study of Lindsay's life and work. In the following excerpt, he depicts Lindsay as a poet whose lyrical genius is too often impeded by triviality, sermonizing, and, above all, the absence of a self-critical faculty.]

[Mr. Lindsay] is the victim of faith in inspiration. Everything that enters his head he puts down on paper; and he lacks the self-criticism necessary to see in his inspiration nothing but a starting-point.

His genius is lyrical, and, if not oratorical, certainly verbose. It is not without significance that one of the poets who have meant most to him is Swinburne. His longer poems, even those of which the core is narrative, are rhapsodically constructed. To the lyrical impulse he adds a quaint and richly pictorial imagination, large sympathies, and a certain intellectual independence. His weakness appears in frequent triviality, in sermonizing, in diffuseness and over-emphasis. The didactic is never long away; and in so recent an utterance as the last imprint of the *Village Magazine* he urges those readers who would know his present-day *opinions* to read his new *poems*. (pp. 152-53)

There has been nothing precocious in his development. The earliest of his meritorious poems were done when he was already well launched in his twenties. Intellectually he is never profound, and emotionally only rarely. He remains well within the mean of the great masses whose voice he is. Except in his very best poems he falls below many of his fellow-poets in workmanship and inspiration. In his latest, to be found in what I [call] the picture books, there is a noticeable gain in concision and in the direction of a personal lyric cadence. We do not know, to be sure, what lies ahead of him, though we may feel that while a meditative poet only ripens with the years, to a rhapsodical one like Mr. Lindsay youth is necessary. Be that as it may, what he has already done is a contribution to be reckoned with; and while he may add to it, nothing which he will do can destroy it. (pp. 154-55)

His present reputation, which rests so much on his forensic powers, will not stand. To his own generation he is primarily the interpreter of his poems. When we think of the *Congo,* our ears still ring with his over-emphatic presentation of it. This will not be true of another generation. The poet will be appraised ultimately from the printed page, and never can black and white make of the *Congo* what his voice and gesture have made of it. And while I believe that his delivery has obscured the beauty of much of his poetry, I am far from thinking that his poems will fall. I believe that they will have a meaning for our children, a different and perhaps a better one; and I think that what the poet sang of the steam-organ will be true of him.

Prophet singers will arise,
Prophets coming after me,
Sing my song in softer guise
With more delicate surprise;

I am but the pioneer
Voice of the democracy.

(pp. 155-56)

Albert Edmund Trombly, in his Vachel Lindsay, Adventurer, Lucas Brothers, 1929, 164 p.

G. K. CHESTERTON (essay date 1932)

[Regarded as one of England's premier men of letters during the first half of the twentieth century, Chesterton is best known today as a colorful bon vivant, a witty essayist, and creator of the Father Brown mysteries and the fantasy The Man Who Was Thursday (1908). Much of Chesterton's work reveals his child-like joie de vivre and reflects his pronounced Anglican and, later, Roman Catholic beliefs. His essays are characterized by their humor, frequent use of paradox, and chatty, rambling style. In the following excerpt from an essay originally published in 1932, Chesterton juxtaposes Walt Whitman's paganism with Lindsay's traditionalist frame of reference.]

Vachel Lindsay was a Puritan in the personal sense; one might almost say in the political sense. He was even a Prohibitionist, and it is only fair to say that his orgiastic verse does demonstrate how very drunk a man can be without wine when he drinks the American air. Occasionally, even, a critic might be tempted to call it the American hot-air. For though Vachel Lindsay was a natural artist, and went right by the clue of the imagination, there are passages of his finest writing which would have been finer still if he had not lived in the land of the megaphone rather than the ivory horn; or if his traditions had not given him the choice of two trumpets—the brazen trumpet of publicity as well as the golden trumpet of poetry. He was himself a wholly simple, sincere, and therefore humble man; but the people around him did not believe in humility; no, not even when they practised it. But they did believe in go and gusto and the big noise; and to a certain extent Vachel Lindsay even at his best did practise that. I have myself a huge sympathy with his special gift for describing men banging their gongs to the glory of their gods; but it were vain to deny that in some ways their gods were not our gods. (pp. 38-9)

Vachel Lindsay was something more than an American; he was (wildly as the term would be misunderstood) a Spanish-American. He was, spiritually speaking, a Californian. He did not get drunk only on the American air; he drank the air of a strange paradise, which is in some way set apart and unlike anything in the New World or the Old; a fairy sea, calmed as by a spell, that stretches far away into fantastical China and of which even the nearer coast is ruled by ghosts rather than by its modern rulers. For there is spread all along that Pacific Coast, in some fashion too vivid for definition, the presence and the pressure and the splendour of Spain. It was something in this rich sunset air that got into the verse of a Puritan like Vachel Lindsay, and made it so much more instinctively ornate and gorgeous than that of a mere Pagan like Walt Whitman. Whitman was a great man; but he was a man of the Eastern States and of the Northern sun, and therefore his passion was colourless even when it was not cold. The Puritanism of Lindsay was more glowing than the Paganism of Whitman. And the reason was, I think, this unconscious influence which possesses all the West of America, as the old Celtic romance possesses all the West of England. The poetry of Vachel Lindsay proves, in every sort of broken and unconscious fashion, how much he was haunted by this presence; how much he felt under his feet this Spanish subsoil of American States. It was, to quote the words of his own vision, the Wrecks of the Galleons of Spain that towered and swelled above him in a sort of glowing monstrosity, and gave their real symbolic outline to the **Golden Whales of California.** (pp. 39-40)

> *G. K. Chesterton, "On Vachel Lindsay," in his* All I Survey: A Book of Essays, *Books for Libraries Press, 1967; distributed by Arno Press, Inc., pp. 37-42.*

SHERWOOD ANDERSON (essay date 1935)

[Anderson was one of the most original and influential early twentieth-century American authors. A writer of brooding, introspective works, he was among the first American authors to explore the effects of the unconscious upon human life. Anderson's "hunger to see beneath the surface of lives" was best expressed in the collection of bittersweet short stories which form the classic Winesburg, Ohio *(1919). This, his most important book, exhibits the author's characteristically simple, unornamented prose style and his personal vision, which combined a sense of wonder at the potential beauty of life with despair over its tragic aspects. Anderson's style and outlook were influential in shaping the writings of Ernest Hemingway, William Faulkner, Thomas Wolfe, John Steinbeck, and many other American authors. In the following excerpt Anderson depicts Lindsay as a poet of heroic proportions, who considered his task as nothing less than an attempt to lay the foundation for a new American culture.]*

There is the Lindsay house in Springfield, Illinois, Lincoln's home town, town of the struggles of the great and forgotten Altgeld, town to which the beaten and defeated Grant went to make a new start, town in the midst of the fat rich Illinois country, land of corn, of corn like forest trees. There is a picture of the house opposite page 28 in [Edgar Lee Masters's book "Vachel Lindsay"]. I think Edward Hopper should go to Springfield some day and make a painting of that house . . . house full of haunts it would be for the poet born into it. There are not many houses in the Middle Western corn country in which one family has lived so long. It was the house in which Lindsay was born. He died there. That was good. (p. 194)

The great broad sweet land that Lindsay did love, that he sang of, often with such glowing gusto . . . with such clear sweetness often enough. . . .

Trying, in his flaming days, always to lay the foundation for an American culture. What matter if he sometimes went religiously fantod? Johnny Appleseed, Boone, Jefferson, Altgeld, John L. Sullivan, Bryan in his good days before they got him into the money racket . . . Lindsay trying to set up in America a nest of heroes, to do for American life what Greek heroes once did for Greek life.

The man Lindsay doing this most of his life, in a kind of religious ecstasy . . . tramping . . . strange enough figure, God knows . . . through the streets of cities . . . the long walk South, from New York to Florida . . . North again, then later West, toward the Pacific . . . Talking, talking, talking . . . singing sometimes . . . shouting sometimes . . . land-love, town-love, city-love. . . .

Garages, livery stables . . . I dare say factory doors where workers pour out, drug stores, hardware stores, doors of farmhouses . . . shoes often enough worn-out, clothes worn-out . . . "I had an apple and a can of beans, bought at a store, yesterday. I walked fourteen miles."

Then sudden fame, as it would come to such a man here . . . his queerness, strangeness, helping a lot to bring it on. Bang! Bang! Bang! Here comes General Booth on his way to heaven.

Lindsay reciting one of his poems, 1928. Courtesy of Charles Scribner's Sons.

If it were to be a Lindsay heaven it would be a strange enough place. It, that is to say fame, was no heaven for Lindsay. They do it to you if you let them.

The usual story. They took him, I think, most of all, for a kind of freak . . . this sugar-lame boy who couldn't grow into something. It might be what manhood is, the thing we must grow to. Call it sophistication. It's being on to the racket.

They petted him for a time, made much of him—I dare say spoiled him a lot—and then forgot him. They found someone else to entertain them, be freak for them. Wear-your-hair-long boys. Parade for them.

Then for Lindsay, lecture touring for the women. That will finish a man O. K.; it's almost as sure as going to Hollywood. The Hollywood boys get more dough. His spirit strength ebbing away, the realization coming of what he was doing to himself, knowing his power to see going, to feel going, to love going. Then the Lysol. It's a disinfectant, isn't it? . . .

And I dare say that if painters do go some day to Springfield, to paint the house Lindsay lived and died in, they'll find it has become a museum. We do very well by our poets here, when they are dead. (p. 195)

> *Sherwood Anderson, "Lindsay and Masters," in* The New Republic, *Vol. LXXXV, No. 1099, December 25, 1935, pp. 194-95.**

ALICE McGUFFEY RUGGLES (essay date 1940)

[In the following excerpt Ruggles links Lindsay, William Blake, and D. H. Lawrence together as prophets and rebels who opposed the respective social orders in which they lived.]

Vachel Lindsay's devotions were legion but his literary passions varied with his moods. In 1921 he wrote that Poe had been the dominant influence in his life; three years later he declared it had been Milton. The mixture of Puritanism and aestheticism in Milton attracted Lindsay strongly. But it is with other Englishmen that I see him finally grouped. One of them, William Blake, Lindsay admired and studied in his college days. The other, David Herbert Lawrence, probably meant nothing to him and at first glance their figures seem far apart.

Of the obvious relationship with Blake, Lindsay's official biographer, Edgar Lee Masters, makes little. Yet Blake's favorite doctrine that the true power of society depends on its recognition of the arts, was what Lindsay preached, in season and out; and Blake's dictum "Giving form is eternal existence," might have been the motto of Lindsay's life.

Both men were romantic, simple, and pious in the deepest natural sense. In their early work, one need only place their poems and drawings side by side to be struck by an affinity of spirit, though in that stage of development Blake's art was superior to Lindsay's. Lindsay's illustrations, which are as closely related to his poetry as Blake's, have been curiously neglected; it may be that he will have to wait as many years for his drawings to be seriously considered as Blake waited for his poems to get into the anthologies. (p. 88)

As with Blake, the artistic instinct in Lindsay was attracted first by the pictorial element of an idea and with both men it was difficult for them to tell when the poem came into being as a picture and when the picture suggested the poem. The technique of Lindsay's later, and greatly improved, drawing is reminiscent of Egyptian, East Indian, and Japanese art. Yet always his individual touch is there; and always his otherworldliness is that of the Christian mystic, which in spirit keeps him at one with Blake.

Where then does the path of D. H. Lawrence approach the ladders to heaven on which these other two went up and down? Lawrence, who is popularly supposed to tread the earthiest of earth? (p. 89)

Lawrence, like Blake and Lindsay, was a prophet and rebel against the social order in which he lived. Blake was gentle in his revolt, for that was his nature in all things. Lindsay was wistful and hopeful, at first; towards the end, disheartened and sad. Lawrence was bitter and violent. But each longed in his heart, and worked with his pen, for a new dispensation of freedom, beauty, and brotherhood.

All three men possessed in common those which H. G. Wells calls the greatest human qualities, childishness and courage. They dared in all simplicity to live their lives and say their say. (p. 90)

Blake, in an earlier and less complex era, Lindsay and Lawrence, contemporary but separate in their lives and ways, spent themselves in the same quest, haunted by the same gleam. Blake gazed at the sunset and saw supernatural wonders. Lindsay speaks of having "visions in cataracts." Lawrence, wherever he might be, brooded; darkly inspired to set down endlessly, effortlessly, his magic words. The fertility, the gorgeous plenty of pure genius, belong to them all. And that further

mark of authenticity—conviction in the truth of their own insight.

Finally, the trait that links the three is their *tenderness* of spirit. Through all their art and thought recurs a preoccupation with God and death and man's relation to eternal things. But there is a characteristic quality in their attitude that sets them apart from their spiritual kin. Their feeling for their fellow man is closer and warmer in its embrace than Milton's; their sense of brotherhood less cosmic than Shelley's or Whitman's.

Blake's tender nature shines through all his work. Lindsay's **"Heart of God"** and a hundred less familiar poems breathe a glowing love. Lawrence thought of naming his last novel *Tenderness*, and given the clue, one discovers beneath all his writing the thwarted and torturing tenderness of his soul. Perhaps he, no less than Lindsay, died because he could not endure the cruelty of life.

Lindsay has the sweeter nature, but the spirit that goaded Lawrence to his harsh utterances is akin to that which produced Lindsay's humble prayers—the old Christian striving for perfection, what Lawrence's Miriam calls his struggle between dark and light. Lawrence would have vehemently denied that he had never freed himself from his early evangelical background but as a matter of fact he never did. Lindsay, for his part, was never apologetic for the old Puritan influence, though his biographer is for him. (pp. 91-2)

Alice McGuffey Ruggles, "The Kinship of Blake, Vachel Lindsay, and D. H. Lawrence," in Poet Lore, *Vol. XLVI, No. 1, Spring, 1940, pp. 88-92.**

H. L. MENCKEN (essay date 1947)

[From the era of World War I until the early years of the Great Depression, Mencken was one of the most influential figures in American letters. His strongly individualistic, irreverent outlook on life and his vigorous, invective-charged writing style helped establish the iconoclastic spirit of the Jazz Age and significantly shaped the direction of American literature. As a social and literary critic—the roles for which he is best known—Mencken was the scourge of evangelical Christianity, public service organizations, literary censorship, boosterism, provincialism, democracy, all advocates of personal or social improvement, and every other facet of American life that he perceived as humbug. In his literary criticism, Mencken encouraged American writers to shun the anglophilic, moralistic bent of the nineteenth century and to practice realism, an artistic call-to-arms that is most fully developed in his essay "Puritanism as a Literary Force," one of the seminal essays in modern literary criticism. Another important polemic, "The Sahara of the Bozart"—considered a powerful catalyst in spurring realism in Southern literature—attacked the paucity of beaux arts in Southern culture as well as the tendency in the region's literature toward romanticizing the Old South as a land of latter-day knights and fair ladies. A man who was widely renowned or feared during his lifetime as a would-be destroyer of established American values, Mencken once wrote: "All of my work, barring a few obvious burlesques, is based upon three fundamental ideas. 1. That knowledge is better than ignorance; 2. That it is better to tell the truth than to lie; and 3. That it is better to be free than to be a slave." In the following excerpt from an essay originally published in 1947, Mencken proclaims Lindsay a representative voice of Middle America, and the only poet since Walt Whitman to display any notable originality.]

Of Vachel Lindsay's lasting importance there can be no doubt. He was the only poet since Walt Whitman to strike a really original note in American poetry, and though his direct imitators were as few as Whitman's, his influence will probably be as lasting. As Dr. Hazelton Spencer has well said, he was a genuine bard, and not a mere versifier. That is to say, he was a poet who felt his poems profoundly, and really lived them. They were not pretty things fashioned at a desk; they were passionate realities that he had genuinely experienced. I well remember sitting with him one day while **"The Trial of the Dead Cleopatra"** had possession of him. To me it was a piece of relatively small interest, and I believe that most critics acquiesce in that judgment of it, but to Lindsay, as it took form in his mind, it was overwhelming. He marched up and down chanting it in the manner of a man moved by some tremendous discovery. It was, to him at least, less a conscious work of art than a spontaneous reaction to a vast and baffling series of natural phenomena.

Such emotions, of course, were bound to wear out. He outgrew them inevitably. Thus such things as **"The Congo"** lost their power to move him—that is, their first power, their full and irresistible power. But the needs of his daily life obliged him to keep on mouthing them. (p. 15)

The professional tasters of poetry have treated him a bit patronizingly. They prefer more intellectual poets, which is to say, poets who are more decorous and timorous. Their predecessors of two generations ago took the same attitude toward Whitman. He was cried down for many years, and such elegant fellows as James Russell Lowell were cried up. But Whitman is alive today and Lowell is dead. I believe that Lindsay will live longer than any of his contemporaries, save maybe the Edgar Lee Masters of the *Spoon River Anthology*. There was an immense sincerity in him. He could write pretty stuff too, but he did very little of it. In the main he fetched his dithyrambs out of the very depths of his being. He was, in more than one way, the true voice of Middle America. He will be remembered. (p. 16)

H. L. Mencken, "Vachel Lindsay: The True Voice of Middle America," in The Courier, *Vol. II, No. 4, December, 1962, pp. 13-16.*

EDWIN H. CADY (essay date 1960)

[*Cady is an American educator and prolific literary scholar who is the editor-in-chief of the distinguished periodical* American Literature. *He has written extensively on the works of William Dean Howells and other major American authors. In the following excerpt Cady suggests that Lindsay's works, particularly his heroic depictions of select American figures, nurture the imagination and remain valuable to modern audiences.*]

If you grew up in the 1930's, you ran across Vachel Lindsay if you cared anything about poetry at all. You knew about Lincoln in Springfield and General Booth in Heaven, you had boom-lay'd **"The Congo"** and, if you were lucky, had discovered **"Simon Legree"** in an anthology. . . . [At] that moment, in spite of the dominance of Eliotian, metaphysical poetry and the burgeoning New Criticism to enforce it, the vision of Lindsay at his best seemed somehow precious. The bardic voices in which he sang that vision seemed, again at his best, appropriate if not inevitable. In short, twenty years ago Lindsay could seem a true poet.

But the two decades since 1940 have almost wholly neglected him. Out of fashion, scornfully ignored by "Criticism," his poetry has been apparently dead. Still worse, there stands a chasm of terrible events between us now and him, possibly far less passable than barriers of time and fashion. After Dachau and Warsaw, Bataan and Hiroshima, Czechoslovkia, Korea,

Hungary, and all the chilling rest, can a Lindsay be supposed poetically audible? Cartoons and editorials on the Congo's time of troubles showed that newspaper people think allusions to **"The Congo"** will ring a bell with the public—that Lindsay's word and mood-magic still live for the popular imagination. But might he be taken as in any sense now a serious poet? (pp. 5-6)

To that end, Lindsay's poetic program as public poet was devoted. The potential value of preserving his dream must not, of course, beguile us into begging the question of the intrinsic value of the poetry. Only faithful reading and criticism can decide that value. (p. 8)

One difficulty for the post-metaphysical taste is the unabashed theatricality of Lindsay's verse. Yet after one has finished wincing at the bass drums and calliopes, he is invited to second thoughts. Even in the study, the stage directions can add effectively to the inward ear's sense of an intricate phonetics. And publicly it was, as it doubtless now could be, good theatre. Some 4,000,000 people paid admissions to be caught up in Lindsay's bardic net, to be engaged actively with the poet in performing his art. It was fun and entertainment, but it was also a socially shared and therefore culturally overt kind of poetry. That would not be at all a bad thing to have alive in our culture to reinforce the covert poetries. And as for TV, Lindsay, thou shouldst be with us at this hour!

Performance, of course, is notoriously ephemeral; and lyricism only cloys. Does Lindsay have anything seriously to give us beyond them? Perhaps he does as a moralist (**"The Leaden-Eyed"**), though one would have to study the question out carefully to be sure that Lindsay's ideas are not as dated as those of his contemporary and fellow progressive Midwesterner, the great historian Parrington. Like Parrington, however, Lindsay lives as a notable satisfier of a major need of the American imagination. (It almost goes without saying that as lyricist, imagist, and impressionist Lindsay was incomparably the finer artist.) He fulfilled his roles as bard and public poet by convincing American historical experience into myth.

By "myth," I must say, I mean nothing more than a technique of meaning. The picture of a major symbolic act performed by some larger-than-life figure permits us to cluster our ideas around it, fuse them with our emotions, and translate the whole into that experience through the imagination which is one of the deepest forms of human meaning. Precisely that is what happens when **"General William Booth Enters Into Heaven"** is read with full realization of the effects of the words of the poem. Subject to all intensities of color and music, whether one "believes" or not he registers the emotional life of Booth's movement, the sense of a simple but most vivid supernaturalism, and the full metaphysical pathos of evangelical fundamentalism. The meaning here is the experience of registering, and it is communicated through the myth. Of Lindsay's treatment of the Negro, I do not feel competent to judge. It was obviously sympathetic, obviously romantic, obviously patronizing: how accurately interpretive was it? But these are not altogether the questions one asks of myths. The Negroes of **"The Congo"** and of several **"Sermons"** have great human and imaginative vitality. So also Lindsay's Lincoln and Johnny Appleseed, in his multiple approaches to them. Less so, his John Brown. The power of myth is clearly the source of the success of **"Bryan Bryan Bryan Bryan," "The Eagle That Is Forgotten,"** and **"The Flower-Fed Buffaloes,"** to name a few.

The plea here is for reconsideration of Lindsay. And the only basis of such a plea must be his best verse and thought. His work was often marred by naivete, confusion, vulgarity, even hypocrisy. His life ended in suicide. Some of the poems are more or less feeble or shallow or merely failures. But any poet is valuable only as of his best. It is glory to have written one enduring poem. Across the chasm, Lindsay might be taken simply as a potent symbol of the loss of American Innocence. Perhaps he was, with Sandburg, the last of the Whitmanian dreamers, or finally an index to the death of the innocent side—the side polar to Nazism—of romanticism, the last of the Shelleyans. Maybe we shall conclude that something like this is it and we must read the best of Lindsay with the full sympathy of the historical imagination. But it could be that he is at his best currently viable. If so, he might be really important. We need to reach across the chasm to him and consider Vachel Lindsay again and find him out. (pp. 9-11)

> Edwin H. Cady, "Vachel Lindsay across the Chasm," in The Indiana University Bookman, No. 5, December, 1960, pp. 5-11.

ANN MASSA (essay date 1968)

[In the following excerpt, Massa explores the relationship between Lindsay's artistic awareness and his social conscience.]

Lindsay was convinced of the existence of a national *malaise;* and it was this conviction which diverted his artistic conscience into social channels. He was worried about amorality, conspicuous consumption, and urban eyesores. He was horrified by the perversion of electoral processes at city level, and by scandals at Federal Government level. Darwinistic indifference to social and financial inequalities appalled him; so did the jungle that awaited immigrants. Dedicated materialism was gaining adherence, while traditional standards of religion and morality, to which he subscribed, were slipping.

He determined to stir up awareness of these alarming tendencies; and in the *War Bulletins* of 1909 (his privately printed monthly journal, which only ran to five issues) and in **'The Golden Whales of California'** . . . he fulminated against the almighty dollar. To counteract American 'deviationism' he put together his gospel of (oecumenical) Religion, (moral) Beauty, and (socialist) Equality; and through a series of poems on American history and myth—**'Our Mother Pocahontas', 'In Praise of Johnny Appleseed', 'Old, Old, Old Andrew Jackson', 'Abraham Lincoln Walks at Midnight', 'Bryan, Bryan, Bryan, Bryan', 'The Eagle That Is Forgotten'** (John Peter Altgeld), and **'Roosevelt'**—he tried to establish an American entity. It is in such social contexts that the bulk of Lindsay's writings become comprehensible. (p. 241)

Lindsay moved in the theological milieu of the reform impulse of the first two decades of the twentieth century. He had points of contact with the political theories of Herbert Croly, the economic panaceas of Henry George, the Social Gospel of Walter Rauschenbusch, and the muckraking activities of Henry Demarest Lloyd. But his diagnosis of the national *malaise* was too grim for him to affiliate himself with men whose vision of a root evil, and whose advocacy of one-stroke remedies—the readjustment of constitutional checks and balances, a Single Tax, the municipal ownership of utilities, trustbusting—sprang from basic confidence in a just off-course, easily righted America. Lindsay was not so sanguine. He considered America's problems were as much the formidable problems of mentality as the soluble ones of institutional defects. For him the American Dream had become 'a middle-class aspiration built on a bog of toil-sodden minds'.

In the 1920s his brand of pessimistic realism made him an even more alien figure. 'Arm yourself against the worst so that disappointment in humanity is impossible' he had noted in his diary; and he had too few expectations to be disillusioned by the 1914-18 war, or by the Peace of Versailles (in his eyes it was a step forward that the idea of international government had been given top-level airing). As an internationalist he found it hard to condone American isolationism and crudely domestic Presidential criteria; as a conscientious practitioner of the kind of Christian morality that was preached in the Mid-west bible belt he could not come to terms with the decade's frenetic relaxation of taboos and its cultivation of materialism for its own sake.

But it was not solely in his capacity as an American citizen that Lindsay took it upon himself to criticize and protest; if the national need arose, the artist, as an individual with exceptional talents of perception and expression, had a duty to practise remedial art. Lindsay thus had a writer's concern with style and form; but the nature of his concern was idiosyncratic. He believed that a writer's duty was not to himself, but to his audience, which should be all-class and nation-wide. His artistic conscience told him to put matter and mass appeal before self-expression and aesthetics. Form was to follow the function of social utility.

In 1915 in *The Art of the Moving Picture,* and again in the 1922 edition, Lindsay hailed the motion picture as the most important artistic event of his lifetime. Not only could it lure people in

Illustration by Vachel Lindsay from his Going to the Sun. *D. Appleton and Company, 1923. Copyright, 1923, by D. Appleton and Company. Renewed 1951 by Elizabeth C. Lindsay. Reprinted by permission of the publisher, E. P. Dutton, Inc.*

for entertainment, and proceed to please whilst insidiously educating; it was an art form, with an art form's power to regenerate and refine. He tried to imitate it by making his writing a deceptive art for the people.

This stance was as extreme as art for art's sake, and as open to disputation. The logic of Lindsay's theory placed severe limitations on subtleties of construction and vocabulary; obliqueness was at a premium when the common man was the envisaged audience. For, while Lindsay believed in a dormant equality of taste, the American masses he was writing for were at the stage when 'they love best neither the words that explain, nor the fancies that are fine, nor the voice that is articulate with well-chosen speech'. They only responded to emotional, raucous modes of expression, and 'words must be chosen accordingly'.

It could be argued that Lindsay's disregard for traditional refinements of style, and for the Imagist experiments of the New Poetry, was less revolutionary and independent than it seemed. One of his talents was for the production of large, generous, rumbustious verse, which flowed along in spite of its imperfections, and without a great deal of stylistic reworking. A poet of emotion rather than one of intellectual discipline, he had a voracious appetite for recitation, both professionally (from 1913 to 1931) and in his leisure time at home. His conscientious response to duty, in fact, came easily, fulfilled his dramatic dimension, and involved genuine pleasure.

But talent and enjoyment did not guide his conscience; on the contrary, he almost failed to make the connexion. The national literary circuit acclaimed the choruses in **'The Congo'** of 'Boomlay, boomlay, boomlay, Boom', and 'Mumbo-Jumbo will hoo-doo you'; but Lindsay wondered whether he was writing poetry. After all, he admitted, 'one composes it not by listening to the inner voice and following the gleam, but pounding the table and looking out of the window at electric signs'. Even a prize from *Poetry* in 1913 for **'General William Booth** . . . ' did not still his doubts; it took the approval of William Butler Yeats to do that.

Lindsay and Yeats met at a dinner party given by Harriet Monroe for Yeats in Chicago in March 1914. Lindsay's recitation of **'The Congo'** was the sensation of the evening, and impressed Yeats. In after-dinner conversation with Lindsay he preached the virtues of folk-culture, and told Lindsay that all that survived in America of the much-to-be-desired 'primitive singing of poetry' and the Greek lyric chant was American vaudeville and Vachel Lindsay. The *imprimatur* reconciled Lindsay to his achievement; a man whose artistic conscience was avowedly a social conscience was bound to develop what he came to call 'The Higher Vaudeville'. (pp. 242-44)

To emphasize that his aim was more serious than vaudeville's, and to counteract its slapstick and revue connotations, Lindsay coined the phrase 'The Higher Vaudeville' to describe the poems he wrote in 'a sort of ragtime manner that deceives them [the American masses] into thinking they are at the vaudeville'. In spite of the rag-time manner he was 'trying to keep it to an art': it was a refined vaudeville, which sprang from his sensitive, critical response to American society, and his awareness of 'democracy [which] is itself a paradox'. Any beauty the Higher Vaudeville might describe or create was as paradoxical as democracy. . . .

One might usefully coin a . . . term, Higher Chautauqua, to convey what Lindsay was trying to achieve in the Higher Vaudeville, and throughout his writings. The Chautauqua

movement (1875-*c*. 1925), which carried on the popular educational traditions of the lyceums with correspondence courses and tours of eminent speakers ranging from Phineas Taylor Barnum to William Rainey Harper, was a uniquely effective way of communicating with the adult population. Chautauqua's aim was mass morality and mass education, McGuffey-style; and Chautauqua's realistic and successful technique was to insert entertainments—minstrels, opera singers, circus acts—among its educational items, or even to disguise education as entertainment. (p. 246)

The Higher Vaudeville coincided with the pre-war heyday of Imagism, a movement which reflected precisely that dedication to form for form's sake, to the intrinsic worth of beautifully constructed, but comparatively unread and unheard poems, which Lindsay opposed. He scornfully called the imagists 'the Aesthetic Aristocracy', who 'were singing on an island to one another while the people perish'. Ezra Pound, *imagiste*, spoke for this school when he gleefully noted in July 1918 about the fourth volume of *The Little Review:* 'The response has been oligarchic; the plain man, in his gum overshoes, with his touching belief in W. J. Bryan, is not with us.' In the September issue, Lindsay was stung into an equally exaggerated, but telling response: 'I write for the good-hearted People of the Great Pure Republic.

He might be writing for the people; but was he reaching them? Lindsay found himself in a quandary. He had the message—but had he found the medium? Higher Vaudeville recitations brought in a large audience, and reached a new set of hearers (and sometimes readers): the American *bourgeoisie*. But Lindsay gradually realized that audiences enjoyed and remembered **'The Kallyope Yell'**, for instance, because that poem revived memories of steam and circus, and not because he had made the calliope an image of bathetic democracy in the lines

> I am but the pioneer
> Voice of the Democracy;
> I am the gutter dream
> I am the golden dream
> Singing science, singing steam. . . .

As well as becoming dissatisfied with audience responses, Lindsay came to feel the difficulty of tying the Higher Vaudeville, a natural 'fun' medium, to serious topics; and he began to think of other media and other audiences. He was learning the hard way what Albert McLean noted about vaudeville, that 'cause and effect relationships were completely bypassed, the question of ultimate ends was never raised, and the problem of higher values could be submerged in waves of pathos and humor'. But up to 1920 he continued to operate within the limitations of his audiences; the acclaim he received from 1913 to 1920, however narrowly based, was exhilarating, and must have seemed to him to augur well for the popularization of his ideas through literature. However, in 1920 the tide swung against him. The Higher Vaudeville was no longer a novelty, and his unfashionable artistic conscience would not allow him to project universal dilemmas in personal terms, as Hemingway and Fitzgerald did so successfully. And in 1920 his message in its most studied form, *The Golden Book of Springfield,* flopped. Ironically, its failure was partly due to the logic of Higher Chautauqua. Lindsay was still orienting himself to an all-class audience, and tempered his discussion of social and political trends with a linking fantasy-cum-story. The end-product was an incongruous mixture of the sane and the silly, which irritated serious readers, and bored the rest. Stylistically, the sentiment and rhetoric which he could control in poetry ran away with him in prose. Digressions and exaggerations spilled over one another. But what uncomfortably persistent critique would have been acceptable in 1920, except Mencken's unique brand? Lindsay had picked the wrong moment to be preoccupied with what Americans ought to be: hedonism was about to set in. Today, the sombre fascination of Lindsay's perceptions redeems the book; an ironic reversal of the stylistic success of the Higher Vaudeville. In neither case was the medium the message.

Lindsay hung on to his belief in equality of taste; but he concluded that mass potential was more deeply buried than he had imagined, and mass crassness more deeply rooted. He decided to concentrate on élite audiences, who might read his books, and respond to his schemes: on teachers, students, journalists, businessmen and local dignitaries. Higher Chautauqua techniques were not applicable to these audiences; and he approached them differently. He prepared the ground by sending out a circular letter, 'The kind of visit I like to make'. The letter adjured journalists to teach his verses 'by running them in the newspaper with paraphrases and local applications by the editor'; and made it clear that Lindsay expected the English teachers to have his books 'in the school library or the public library the month beforehand. I mean nothing whatever to an audience unfamiliar with my work . . . I want every member of my audience to have at least some knowledge of these books. When he lectured on one particular book, 'Dear reader, either bring the book or stay away!' . . . At one time he made the half-serious suggestion that only those who could pass an examination on his books should be admitted to his recital/lectures.

Lindsay's attitude to his audience was barely recognizable as that of a creative writer seeking a hearing. He had come to think of himself as a teacher, and of his writings as textbooks. He had obviously become irritated and impatient, for he believed, however mistakenly, that he was offering a vital service to a public which would not avail itself of the service. An element of compensatory, personal arrogance was involved; but so was a generic, artistic arrogance. . . . (pp. 247-49)

To his contemporaries Lindsay's work seemed stagnant and retrospective, though in content, if not in style, it was naggingly valid. In one sense, however, he was an anachronism: he was a precursor and practitioner of present-day 'pop art'. He affirmed that popular taste—'the human soul in action'—was a neo-artistic perception; and he, as an artist, by acts of will, representation and reproduction, made this perception total art. Mass consensus had made Mary Pickford a folk-culture queen; and Lindsay repeatedly celebrated her national visual impact in a way comparable to Andy Warhol's statement-painting 'Marilyn Monroe', which consists of repeated rows of her face. The American collage of popcorn and yellow cabs, 'Arrow-collar heroes' and the Star Spangled Banner preoccupied him as realistically and sentimentally as it does many pop artists. And, just as pop artists let others finish their creations, and have them mass-produced, Lindsay, with the same mixture of arrogance and humility, urged other people to adapt and rewrite his work—though he was too far ahead of his times to be taken at his word.

Lindsay diverged from the main stream of pop art in that his aim was propaganda; pop artists tend to draw the line at comment. He was as much concerned to create as to accept popular culture, and he was interested in new media for the specific purposes of uplifting and educating the masses. Yet his enthusiastic support of the motion picture bears comparison with the pop-art theory of the interchangeability of words and pictures, and the communication potential of a nationally recognized alphabet of images. 'Edison is the new Gutenberg. He has invented the new printing', Lindsay wrote; and he went so far as to try his own hand at a new word/picture art which he called 'hieroglyphics': an entirely public art, an easily identified currency of national symbols. His nearest approximation of a successful hieroglyphic was the drawing of a lotus/rose . . . to celebrate the East/West symbolism of the Panama Canal; a pacific symbolism that would have found one American dissenter in T. R.! Motion pictures were hieroglyphics of a more complex sort. They were sculpture-in-motion, painting-in-motion, architecture-in-motion and furniture-in-motion; they were the American people in its envisaged likeness; they were the pop artist's multi-evocative images.

H. L. Mencken wrote of Lindsay's career that 'the yokels welcomed him, not because they were interested in his poetry, but because it struck them as an amazing and perhaps even a fascinatingly obscene thing for a sane man to go about the country on such bizarre and undemocratic business'. As usual, Mencken had a point amidst his hyperbole. Lindsay was implying not only mass deprivation, but temporary mass inferiority. He thus showed a certain lack of tact; and also, in failing to follow up the implications of the theory his conscience made him formulate, a lack of rationality. For instance, was abstract art necessarily selfish art? Did social insight always accompany creative ability? Was equality of taste desirable? Could any writer, without being an ideological weather-vane, consistently appeal to mass audiences which changed their tastes and *mores* in less than a generation?

Lindsay's failure to answer, perhaps even to pose, such questions made him react irrationally to his popularity with an audience which licked off the sugar coating, but left the rest of the pill. He had wanted to be like William Jennings Bryan—but resented being gaped at like a 'Bryan sensation' or 'like Tagore in his nightgown'. He felt he was being 'speculated in like pork'—but wasn't he himself pushing a commodity—his gospel and his urban blueprint—and making certain assumptions about the market? He was paying the penalty of his illogic; he was reacting with heart rather than mind. But his confusion and irateness were measures of his ambitious, earnest socioartistic conscience; and they were telling comments on his organization of himself as a writer. (pp. 250-52)

Ann Massa, "The Artistic Conscience of Vachel Lindsay," in Journal of American Studies, *Vol. 2, No. 2, October, 1968, pp. 239-52.*

GRANVILLE HICKS   (essay date 1968)

[*Hicks was an American literary critic whose famous study* The Great Tradition: An Interpretation of American Literature since the Civil War *(1933) established him as the foremost advocate of Marxist critical thought in Depression-era America. Throughout the 1930s, he argued for a more socially engaged brand of literature and severely criticized such writers as Henry James, Mark Twain, and Edith Wharton, who he believed failed to confront the realities of their society and, instead, took refuge in their own work. Hicks was shocked by the effects of the Great Depression and believed that events demanded a new commitment on the part of writers to clearly understand and express their times. In Marxist terms this meant that all American artists should comprehend the growth of capitalism and its negative side effects, such as war, periodic depressions, and the exploitation and alienation of the working class. Thus the question Hicks posed was always the same: to what degree did an artist come to terms with the economic condition of the time and the social consequences of those conditions? What he sought from American literature was an extremely critical examination of the capitalist system itself and what he considered its inherently repressive nature. After 1939, Hicks sharply denounced communist ideology, which he called a "hopelessly narrow way of judging literature," and in his later years adopted a less ideological posture in critical matters. In the following excerpt, while acknowledging the reign of such modernist poets as W. B. Yeats and Ezra Pound, he anticipates a possible revival of interest in Lindsay's popularism, particularly among young readers of the late 1960s, many of whom rejected conventional craftsmanship for spontaneous expression and perceived, as did Lindsay, the necessity for social reform.]*

In his introductory essay [to *Adventures, Rhymes & Designs,*] Robert F. Sayre comments on the decline of Lindsay's reputation, speaking particularly of the way in which Ezra Pound, after cautiously praising Lindsay's poetry, repudiated him altogether. ("Lindsay," he wrote in 1915, " . . . Oh gawd!!!") "Lindsay," Sayre writes, "turned to the then bright prospect of a broad, popular movement in twentieth-century art while Pound grouped his forces and eliminated quantity in favor of critical intelligence, and quality." As everyone knows, Pound's modernism triumphed over Lindsay's populism. "Recently, however," Sayre continues, "in numerous younger poets, among the new folk singers, and in many parts of the New Left, populism has shown important signs of life, a surge of liberality and hope missing from the established modernism."

It would be amusing if there should be a Lindsay revival, and of course there might be. All we know for sure about literary taste is that it is constantly changing, and there is no reason to believe that the reign of Yeats, Eliot, and Pound will last forever. As Sayre says, some of the young have rejected the uptight craftsmanship of the modernist establishment in favor of expansiveness and spontaneity, and persist in being hopeful even when the grounds for hope are not apparent. As Mark Harris points out in his introduction to *Selected Poems of Vachel Lindsay,* the poet began "with the intention of doing nothing less than rehabilitating—absolutely reforming—a gross and greedy civilization." A certain number of young today share that intention, and, unlike most of the young of the past twenty-five years, they believe that the sorry scheme of things can be remolded.

Lindsay was part of the amorphous but powerful movement of revolt that developed in the years before the First World War. He was much concerned with the evils of industrialism, and he denounced the values of a business civilization. The gospel of beauty, which he preached on his several walking trips, was aimed against the gospel of success. He said later on: "The reason my beggar days started talk was that each time I broke loose, and went on the road, in the spring, after a winter of Art lecturing, it was definitely an act of protest against the United States commercial standard, a protest against the type of life set forth for all time in two books of Sinclair Lewis: *Babbitt* and *Main Street.*"

In his objections to businessmen and their values and the way they ran the country, he was typical of the revolt, but in other respects he dissented from the dissenters. In 1921 Carl Van Doren described what he called "the revolt against the village," mentioning Masters's *Spoon River Anthology,* Anderson's *Wineburg, Ohio,* and *Main Street* as examples. Far from revolting against the village, Lindsay held it up as his ideal; he wanted to improve the villages, of course, but he saw them as centers of a new and higher culture. Most of the rebels prided themselves on being sophisticated, whereas he was os-

tentatiously naïve. They were hard-boiled, and he was romantic. If he grew away from his mother's piety, he was as evangelistic as his sister, who spent many years as a missionary in China. As a young man he lectured for temperance societies, and in the Twenties—paradox of paradoxes—he was a prohibitionist as well as a poet. He once said that he was as much opposed to the ideas of H. L. Mencken as he was to those of George Horace Lorimer, whose *Saturday Evening Post* was the laughing stock of the intelligentsia.

Lindsay took walking tours in 1906 and 1908, and in 1912 he made the trip from Illinois to New Mexico that is described in *Adventures While Preaching the Gospel of Beauty.* His program on all these expeditions was to avoid cities, railroads, money, and baggage, to present his ideas on life to individuals and groups as opportunity offered, and to give his little pamphlet, *Rhymes to Be Traded for Bread,* in exchange for food and lodging.

Without having seen *Adventures While Preaching,* I had an idea that it was probably a pretentious book, whimsical and full of attitudinizing. It isn't at all. It's a simple, straightforward, almost commonplace book, based on letters that he sent home to family and friends. His account of the country through which he passed is not particularly vivid, though there are colorful touches here and there. There is a smattering of humor, usually at his own expense: "I still maintain that the auto is a carnal institution, to be shunned by the truly spiritual, but there are times when I, for one, get tired of being spiritual." He describes the migrant workers moving from harvest to harvest, without minimizing either their hardships or their vices. They were not likely converts to the gospel of beauty, but they seem to have borne with him. What must they have thought if they read in his little book or heard him say, "Go to the fields, O city laborers, till your wounds are healed." They would have thought, of course, that he was a nut, and in a way he was, but a useful nut to have around in his time and perhaps in ours.

"It is simply astounding," Harris wrote in the introduction to *Selected Poems* in 1963, "how the poetry of Vachel Lindsay has improved since 1945." (That was when he began work on his book about Lindsay, *City of Discontent.*) Looking through the selection again, I am inclined to agree. The picture of Lindsay reciting **"The Congo"** in what appeared to be a trance but probably was a kind of self-hypnosis induced by weariness, is fading, and some of the poetry seems fresh and pertinent. I don't really believe that the young will make him one of their heroes, but they could do worse.

> *Granville Hicks, in a review of "Adventures, Rhymes & Designs," in* Saturday Review, *Vol. LI, No. 49, December 7, 1968, p. 41.*

PIERRE DUSSERT   (essay date 1969)

[In the following excerpt, Dussert discusses the verses Lindsay wrote for children, placing particular emphasis on the poet's attempt to infuse a young audience with his own sense of beauty and artistic delight.]

As a poet for children, Vachel Lindsay is known mainly for his "poem-games" (as he called them) and for his poems written to the glory of heroes, particularly American heroes. Poem-games were long poems intended to be chanted by the narrator and danced. The most famous one, perhaps, is **"The Potatoes' Dance."** Among the poems celebrating American heroes, **"Johnny Appleseed"** is certainly known of many children.

To understand the real intention of Lindsay when he wrote poem-games and semi-epics, it must be remembered that he was dreaming of a new America, where all citizens would love beauty and democracy—two words which, in Lindsay's eyes, could not be separated. The building of the Ideal City was the aim of his life, and *The Golden Book of Springfield,* which Lindsay published in 1921, was his most serious attempt to realize his dream. Several years before, he had already proclaimed the gospel of a social religion which embraced both politics and arts in three poems assembled under the common title of **"Gospel of Beauty": "The Proud Farmer," "The Illinois Village,"** and **"On the Building of Springfield."** In children, Lindsay saw possible disciples who might become the citizens of the ideal society he was dreaming of. (pp. 5-6)

Therefore, when he wrote poem-games, when he chanted them to children, when he made young girls and boys dance to their rhythms, Lindsay aimed at giving them a sense of beauty, a feeling of artistic delight. And when he wrote such poems as **"Johnny Appleseed,"** or **"The Statue of Old Andrew Jackson,"** his purpose was to praise champions of democracy, in order to urge children to follow their example.

There is no poem-game in [*Springfield Town Is Butterfly Town, and Other Poems for Children*], and no poem to the glory of some American hero. However, we still find Lindsay the preacher, teaching children how to find and to love Beauty. . . .

Lindsay felt a messianic impulse to conquer all ugliness. In his **"Village Magazine,"** the banners of the Village Improvement parade proclaimed that "a bad designer is to that extent a bad citizen," that "Fair streets are better than silver" and that "bad public taste is mob law." He was a crusader who hoped that children would follow him. (p. 7)

In the poem **"On the Building of Springfield,"** Lindsay was inviting all children to help him in the accomplishment of his mission. In the poem **"Springfield Town is Butterfly Town,"** he urges them to fulfill his dearest wish: "Rebuild our Springfield Town," says the Butterfly Pegasus, "with halls all flowers and wings." We feel, however, that Lindsay sometimes wonders if it is not too late. Perhaps the ugliness of our mechanical world has already conquered all beauty, and nothing can be done about it. This doubt is apparent in the poem **"The Warning,"** and in the **"Cat Pegasus."**

In many other poems, we find a wholly different Lindsay, a Lindsay who no longer speaks to the children of America in general, thinking of them as future citizens, but to a more restricted audience. These poems were written by a father for his own children. Vachel Lindsay married Elizabeth Conner in 1925. He was forty-six years old. They had a daughter, Susan, and a son, Nicholas. These three brought a complete change in the poet's life, and, subsequently, regenerated his inspiration. . . . Now he had a new audience, his wife and his children; and, to Stephen Graham, who was complimenting him for these poems, he replied: "Well, I shall be content to start at the foot of the Parnassus and climb it again in the steps of my children."

In several poems, Lindsay, as any father would do, warns his children against the perils of life. Here we find a good deal of bitter realism. Lindsay was no advocate of milk-and-water poetry for children. (pp. 8-9)

Vachel Lindsay's rendering of "the Unicorn-No-Storm-Can-Tame" from his Going to the Sun. *D. Appleton and Company, 1923. Copyright, 1923, by D. Appleton and Company. Renewed 1951 by Elizabeth C. Lindsay. Reprinted by permission of the publisher, E. P. Dutton, Inc.*

Although he speaks to children, he does not speak of trifles. We are reminded of what La Fontaine said in the preface to his *Fables:* "The form is childish, I admit it, but this childishness serves as an envelope for important truths." Like La Fontaine, Lindsay teaches children what they ought to know about life, and often does it in a very realistic way. Take the poem **"The Butterflies Showing Off,"** for instance: the story Lindsay tells us in this poem happens every day, cruel as may be. This poem is the reverse of La Fontaine's fable "The Hare and the Tortoise," but quite as realistic in its way. Several poems in this book remind us of La Fontaine's fables, if only by the choice of animals for characters. But the major difference between the two poets is that La Fontaine formulates a moral at the end of each fable, and Lindsay does not. It will, however, be easy for any child to find out the moral of each poem. From the poem **"The Orchid,"** he will learn that beauty may hide cruelty. The poem **"A Meritorious Villainous Bakerman"** will teach him that people cannot be judged from appearances. Or he will learn that he who thinks much of himself will always meet his master: the mountain-goat that boasts of butting better than a ram is devoured by a puma (**"One Boaster"**) and the ram that boasts of butting better than a goat is shorn naked (**"Another Boaster"**). It will not be difficult to draw a conclusion from poems like **"A Big-eared Rat," "Cork-Bird Picture,"** or **"Mud-Hen."**

In some of his purely humorous poems, it would be difficult or pretentious to find any message or philosophy at all. The poet just winks at children; and, more often than in other poems, we can feel how much he liked them. **"The Illinois State Mews," "Playing Cards Drawing," and "Buzz-saws"** were written just for the sake of making children smile. Lindsay loved to romp with children. A lot of anecdotes attest to the deep understanding that always existed between children and him. . . . Just open the *Handy Guide for Beggars,* and read the Gretchen-Cecilia story. You will see how easily, how spontaneously Lindsay could strike up a friendship with a child.

Knowing children as he did, Lindsay could not resist the temptation of writing a few poems full of mystery. All children love mystery; it suits their imagination, and Lindsay knew this. In his **"Sixty-first on the Moon,"** he tells us about a little boy who is going to ride on a cloud to the moon, which is not, as his gray-haired father thinks, "a little planet with a hundred dried-up seas," but a "big brass door" he will "open wide" to "look into the nursery, and see what's on the floor." In the poem **"Adventures with the Eldest Daughter Eight Years Old"** which announces all the other poems—the poet says:

> Then we will ride on tremendous clouds
> To nowhere,
> Thus we will ride
> Where the ride is the whole adventure.

And he keeps his promise. He carried children away in a world of mystery and fancy, where things remain unexplained, as in a dream. What are these strange creatures riding and whipping salamanders? Where is the **"Independent Thomas"** coming from? Where is he going? In the poem **"Fairy Land,"** who is this proud lady named Jane? Who are the giants of **"The Unexpected Door?"** Each child will find his own answer to these questions.

Lindsay the poet-prophet, the preacher, the hero-worshipper, has always appealed to children, even in poems that were not written for them. . . . But in the poems he wrote for them in particular, there is an ingenuousness to be found nowhere else in his work. This is why Edgar Lee Masters refers to them as Lindsay's "songs of innocence." Nevertheless, this book is for adults, too. Many books have delighted both children and grown-ups. When Saint-Exupery wrote *Le Petit Prince*, he dedicated the book to an adult, but to children he said: "I dedicate this book to the child this adult was once. All adults have been children." (pp. 9-12)

> *Pierre Dussert, in a foreword to* Springfield Town
> Is Butterfly Town and Other Poems for Children *by*
> *Vachel Lindsay, The Kent State University Press,*
> *1969, pp. 4-12.*

PETER VIERECK (essay date 1976)

[*Viereck is a Pulitzer Prize-winning American poet, novelist, critic, and essayist. His poetry is considered conservative in form, witty, intelligent, and analytical. In the following excerpt, Viereck links Lindsay with Dante as poets representative of their respective religious communities. The critic also discusses literary techniques that Lindsay employed which repelled rather than won him audiences.*]

The end of an outer material frontier to explore in the west and midwest has helped cause the increasing inner explorations of the spirit. Vachel Lindsay represents a transition: apparently still an outer explorer, an evoker of picturesque place-names and loud American voices in the fashion of an older school; yet in reality an inward voyager of the religious imagination and the aesthetic imagination. Lindsay remains the finest religious poet produced by America's most local native roots. He is the Dante of the Fundamentalists (A Yankee Doodle Dante).

The comparison of Lindsay with Dante is intended not in terms of greatness, whether of poetry or thought, but in terms of voicing one's roots. In their respective religious communities, each was the poet who best voiced his particular heritage. The contrasting views of man in those two heritages will broaden the second part of this discussion from Lindsay to American culture as a whole.

Lindsay is the Dante of America's only indigenous church: Fundamentalist Bible-belt revivalism. For that church he wrote major poetry of mystical vision, as well as the jingly junk (boom-lay-boom) for which he is better known. Carrying further, church for church and relic for relic, the analogy with the Florentine poet of Catholicism, we may summarize: Lindsay's Rome was Springfield, Illinois; his Holy Roman Emperor was the specter of Abe Lincoln; his Virgil-guide was Johnny Appleseed. His Beatrice was **"A Golden-Haired Girl in a Louisiana Town"**: "You are my love / If your heart is as kind / As your eyes are now." His martyred Saint Sebastian was Governor Altgeld (persecuted for saving the Haymarket anarchists from lynching). His angel hosts were the Anti-Saloon League and the Salvation Army, lovingly washing in the "blood of the lamb" the stenos and garage mechanics of Chicago.

To continue the analogy: Lindsay's version of the Deadly Sins, as a middleclass Fundamentalist schoolma'am might see them, were the beguiling depravities of "matching pennies and shooting craps," "playing poker and taking naps." These two lines are from **"Simon Legree,"** a combination of a Negro spiritual with a Calvinistic morality; the result of that combination can only be called: intoxicated with sobriety. Dante's medieval heretics partly corresponded to what Lindsay called "the renegade Campbellites," a Fundamentalist splinter group secession:

> O prodigal son, O recreant daughter,
> When broken by the death of a child,
> You called for the graybeard Campbellite elder,
> Who spoke as of old in the wild . . .
> An American Millennium . . .
> When Campbell arose,
> A pillar of fire,
> The great high priest of the spring . . .

But then, in the same poem, comes the sudden self-mockery of:

> And millennial trumpets poised, half-lifted,
> Millennial trumpets that wait. . . .

Here the verb "wait," mocking the ever-unfulfilled prophecies of Fundamentalist revivalism, is the kind of slip that occurs accidentally-on-purpose. Such frequent semi-conscious slips represent Lindsay's protest against his self-imposed, self-deceiving role of trying to be more Fundamentalist than any Fundamentalist and more folkish than the real folk.

That self-imposed role, which ultimately became his shirt-of-Nessus, may have resulted from two tacit postulates. First, that poetry readers have no more right to laugh at the homespun Fundamentalist theology of the old American west than at the subtler but perhaps no more pious-hearted theology of Dante's day. Second, that the American small-town carnival deserved as much respect as Dante's medieval pageants; it was as fitting a literary theme; it was no less capable of combining the divine with the humdrum.

Once you concede these two postulates to Lindsay, all the rest seems to follow, including such lofty Lindsay invocations as: "Love-town, Troy-town Kalamazoo" and "Hail, all hail the popcorn stand." It follows that the Fundamentalist prophet, Alexander Campbell, should debate with the devil upon none other than "a picnic ground." It follows that real, tangible angels jostle Lindsay's circus-barkers and salesmen of soda pop. And certainly Lindsay has as much aesthetic right to stage a modern Trojan war, over love, between Osh Kosh and Kalamazoo as Homer between Greeks and Trojans. So far so good. But Lindsay often absurdly overstrains this aesthetic right, these old-world analogies. For example, he hails not an easily-hailed American *objet* like, say, Washington's monument but the popcorn stand.

Lindsay's motive for choosing the popcorn stand is not unconscious crudeness but conscious provocation. In effect he is saying: "By broadening the boundaries of aestheticism to include such hitherto-inacceptable Americana, my poetry is deliberately provoking, and thereby re-educating, all you supercilious eastern-seaboard-conditioned readers or Europe-conditioned readers."

But at the same time there is a suppressed saboteur within Lindsay, as within every exaggerated nationalist. That underground saboteur infiltrates Lindsay's poems via the most awkward-looking, absurdity-connoting letter in our alphabet, the letter "K." For whatever psychological reasons many Americans go into convulsions of laughter over the names of foreign towns like Omsk, Tomsk, Minsk, Pinsk, and nearer home, Hoboken, Yonkers, Keokuk, Sauk Center, not to mention those two Lindsay favorites, Osh Kosh and Kalamazoo. The core of each of those place-names is a throaty, explosive "K." (pp. 124-26)

Of course, no such deliberate linguistic analysis determined Lindsay's obsessive use of awkward town-names with "K." Rather, his use was determined by a blind instinct—a shrewdly blind instinct—for catching the very soul of spoken Americana. No one has ever equalled Lindsay's genius for manipulating the unconscious connotations of the colloquial, even though he perversely misused those connotations for the self-torturing purpose of provoking and then staring-down the ridicule of sophisticated audiences.

That willingness to provoke ridicule may produce his worst poems. Yet it is also the root of the moral courage producing his best poems, such as his elegy for Governor Altgeld of Illinois. Altgeld had defied a nineteenth-century kind of "McCarthyism" by his idealistic defense of slandered minorities. Political poetry, even courageous political poetry, is by itself merely a rhymed editorial, better written in prose, unless universalized beyond journalism and arid ideologies into the non-political realm of artistic beauty. Lindsay's Altgeld poem remains one of the great American elegies because it does achieve this humanizing process, transfiguring courage into lyric tenderness. . . . (p. 128)

However, more frequently the heroes Lindsay's poetry presents as the American equivalent of old-world Galahads are not exactly Altgelds. For example, the subtitle of his actual poem **"Galahad"** reads: "Dedicated to all Crusaders against the International and Interstate Traffic in Young Girls." The subtitle

of his poem **"King Arthur's Men Have Come Again"** was equally earnest and uplifting, namely: "Written while a field-worker in the Anti-Saloon League of Illinois." Of course, the moral heritage of rural Fundamentalism particularly objects to alcohol, along with "playing poker and taking naps."

These twin odes to the Anti-Vice Squad and the Anti-Saloon League are bad poems not because the evil they denounce is unserious but because their treatment of that evil sounds like a mock-heroic parody. To explain such bad writing in so good a poet, let us suggest the hypothesis that Lindsay's mentality included a demon of self-destruction, forever turning the preacher into the clown. This compulsion forced Lindsay, again and again in his verse, to strip himself in public of every shred of what he most prized: human dignity. Perhaps this inner demon was related to the compulsion that finally made Lindsay choose not just any method of suicide but the most horribly painful method imaginable: swallowing a bottle of searing acid.

When a poet consistently exalts whatever heroes, place-names, and occupations sound most ludicrous to his modern poetry audience (for example, Lindsay was an avid exalter of college cheerleaders), it may be either because he has no ear for poetry or because he has an excellent ear knowingly misused. The first explanation is easily ruled out by the beauty of the above Altgeld elegy. Aside from the self-destructive aspect, there is an important messianic-pedagogic aspect making the second explanation the more plausible one. For example, by inserting the pedantic adjective "interstate" in front of "traffic in young girls" and thereby incongruously juxtaposing the prosaic Mann Act law with the poetic word "Galahad," Lindsay says in effect:

> If you accept my hick-fundamentalist approach to morality, which I happen to consider the only true and autochthonous American religion, then you must also accept its humorless terminology, its ridicule-provoking bigotries. What is more, you must accept them with a religious spirit exactly as earnest as that with which Homer and Dante accepted their own autochthonous religious traditions.

Thus considered, Lindsay's poetry is not mere clowning, whether intentional or unintentional, but—in his own revealing phrase—"the higher vaudeville." The adjective "higher" makes all the difference; it means a medieval vaudeville, a messianic circus, a homespun midwest equivalent of the medieval fool-in-Christ.

In refusing to be apologetic toward the old world about America's own kind of creativity, Lindsay does have a valid point. In refusing to allow European legends, heroes, place-names a greater claim on glamor than American ones, he again does have a valid point. Likewise when he establishes the American gift for finding loveliness in the exaggerated, the grotesque. But the self-sabotaging demon within him tends to push these valid points to extremes that strain even the most willing "suspension of disbelief."

When Lindsay fails to make us suspend our disbelief, the reason often is this: he is trying to link not two compatibles, such as prosaic object with prosaic rhetoric or fabulous object with fabulous rhetoric, but prosaic object with fabulous rhetoric. Modern university-trained readers of poetry react unsolemnly to: "Hail, all hail the popcorn stand." Why? Because of a gap I would define as: the Lindsay disproportion. The Lindsay disproportion is the gap between the heroic tone of the invocation and the smallness of the invoked object. But Lindsay's aim, rarely understood by modern readers, was to overcome that disproportion between tone and object by conjuring up a mystic grandeur to sanctify the smallness of American trivia. That mystic grandeur derived from his dream of America as a new world free from old-world frailty, free from original sin. His dream-America was infinitely perfectable, whatever its present faults. Even its most trivial objects were sacred because incarnating the old Rousseauistic dream of natural goodness of man and eternal progress.

Lindsay believed, or felt he ought to believe, in the impossible America invented by the French poet Chateaubriand and other European romantics. Later, much later (nature imitating art) that invented America was sung by Americans themselves, by Emerson and Whitman. In poetry this utopian American myth culminated in Lindsay's *Golden Book of Springfield* and Hart Crane's *The Bridge*; in politics it culminated in the Populist and Progressive movements of the west. (pp. 128-31)

Instead of pouncing with shoddy glee on the absurd aspects of the Lindsay disproportion between tone and object, let us re-examine more rigorously the Chateaubriand-style dream of America behind those absurd aspects. That American myth is part of a romantic, optimistic philosophy seriously maintained, whatever one may think of it, by great or almost-great minds like Rousseau and Emerson. Therefore, it is unjust to dismiss that same philosophy contemptuously in Lindsay merely because his name has less prestige than theirs. What is wrong-headed in him, is wrong-headed in his preceptors also. He and they dreamed of a new world miraculously reborn without the burden of past history. That unhistorical myth of America distinguishes Whitman and Lindsay from Hawthorne and Faulkner in literature. It distinguishes Jefferson from John Adams in political philosophy. It distinguishes Fundamentalist revivalism, with its millennium just around the corner, and the hope of quick redemption that Lindsay's poetry hailed in the Salvation Army, from Niebuhrian pessimism within the American Protestant religion. While Lindsay is the Dante of the Fundamentalists, he differs from the old-world Catholic Dante by substituting a romantic, optimistic view of man for the tragic view held by traditional Christianity as well as by Greek classicism.

On this issue American literature has two conflicting traditions, the first romantic and progressive, the second classical and conservative. The first heartily affirms American folklore, American democratic and material progress. That Whitman-Emerson literary tradition cracked up in Vachel Lindsay and Hart Crane. It cracked up not merely in their personal breakdowns and final suicides—let us not overstress mere biography—but in the aesthetic breakdown of the myth-making part of their poetry. The non-mythic part of their poetry, its pure lyricism, never did break down and in part remains lastingly beautiful.

A second American tradition is that of the literary pessimists, a new-world continuation of the great Christian pessimists of the old world, from Saint Augustine to Kierkegaard and Cardinal Newman. In America the second literary tradition is just as authentically American as the first one but has never received the same popular recognition, being less comforting. The most influential literary voices of our second tradition are Melville, Hawthorne, Henry Adams, William Faulkner. Its greatest political heritage comes from the Federalist papers and from the actual anti-Jeffersonian party of the Federalists, with their partly European source not in Rousseau but in Burke. Its most influ-

ential theological voices in America today are Paul Tillich and Reinhold Niebuhr. Note that all these literary, political, and theological voices are characterized by skepticism about man and mass and by awareness of the deep sadness of history. Therefore, their bulwark against man and mass and against the precariousnes of progress is some relatively conservative framework of traditional continuity, whether in culture, literature, politics, or religion. (pp. 131-33)

The optimistic progress-affirming and folklore-affirming voices of Emerson and Whitman cracked up in their disciples Lindsay and Crane when the crushing of the individual in modern mechanization became simply too unbearable to affirm. The modern poet of progress may try to keep up his optimistic grin for his readers while the custard pie of "higher vaudeville" drips down his face. But past a certain point, he can no longer keep up the grin, whether psychologically in his private life or aesthetically in his public poetry. Our overadjusted standardization becomes just one custard pie too many for the unadjusted poet to affirm, no matter how desperately he tries to outshout his inner tragic insight by shouting (in Lindsay's case) "Hail, all hail the popcorn stand" and by hailing (in Crane's case) the Brooklyn Bridge as "the myth whereof I sing." Lindsay and Crane committed suicide in 1931 and 1932 respectively, in both cases in that depression era which seemed temporarily to end the boundless optimism of American material progress. (p. 134)

What is shoddy in the American myth is not affirmation itself; classic tragedy affirms ("Gaiety transfiguring all that dread"). What is shoddy is not the hard-won affirmation that follows tragic insight but the facile unearned optimism that leads only to disillusionment. Here is a prose example of how Lindsay's valid crusade against the adjective "standardized" collapses suddenly into a too-easy optimism:

> I have been looking out of standardized windows of "The Flat-Wheeled Pullman car." I have been living in standardized hotels, have been eating jazzed meals as impersonal as patent breakfast-food. . . . The unstandardized thing is the overwhelming flame of youth . . . an audience of one thousand different dazzling hieroglyphics of flame. . . . My mystic Springfield is here, also, in its fashion . . . a Springfield torn down and rebuilt from the very foundations, according to visions that might appear to an Egyptian . . . or any one else whose secret movie-soul was a part of the great spiritual movie. . . .

Note the typical Lindsay disproportion by which this moving passage ends with an appalling anticlimax, equating Hollywood's facile commercialized "visions" with the tragically-earned classic ones. Yet his best and worst writing are so intertwined that this "movie soul" gush is immediately followed by one of his finest prose passages about American democracy at its noblest:

> I believe that civic ectasy can be so splendid, so unutterably afire, continuing and increasing with such apocalyptic zeal, that the whole visible fabric of the world can be changed. . . . And I say: change not the mass, but change the fabric of your own soul and your own visions, and you change all. . . .

(p. 139)

Lindsay's authentic western Americana were never presented for their own sake, never merely as quaint antiques for the tourist trade. Rather, they were presented for the more serious purposes of either his Whitman-messianic aspect or his Ruskin-aesthetic aspect. . . . (pp. 140-41)

Part of Lindsay's aesthetic compulsion, giving him the uniqueness only possessed by major poets, lies in his juxtaposition of the delicate and the grotesque: for example, in his phrase "the flower-fed buffaloes of the spring," subject of one of his purest lyrics. Running through his diversities of titles and subject matter, note also the delicate and the grotesque color-juxtapositions of "the king of yellow butterflies" with "the golden whales of California" and the semantic juxtaposition of "harps in heaven" with "the sins of Kalamazoo." Such gargoyle tenderness is a genre of sensibility explored by few other poets beside Beddoes and Rimbaud, the poets with whom Lindsay's unfulfilled genius, beneath its tough loud disguises, properly belongs. (p. 141)

Delicacy is not a noun most modern readers associate with Lindsay. Yet his sense of cadence was so very delicate that it disguised itself defensively, his time and place being what they were, beneath ear-splitting auditory signposts. His signposts deliberately pointed in the wrong direction, the loud indelicate direction. Living where he did and believing the myth he believed, he needed to conceal his bitter, introverted sensitivity beneath the extroverted optimism of American folklore. That is, beneath a tone deliberately coarse, chummy, whooping, the whiz-bang claptrap of poems like **"The Kallyope Yell."** In such curiosities of our literature, no poet was ever more perversely skilful at sounding embarrassingly unskilful. No poet was ever more dexterous at sounding gauche. . . .

Consequently Lindsay's poetry is often defined as mere oratory, to be shouted aloud by a mob chorus. Part of him wanted this view to be held. Another part of him lamented: "I have paid too great a penalty for having a few rhymed orations. All I write is assumed to be loose oratory or even jazz, though I have never used the word 'jazz' except in irony." His best work, often his least known work, was produced by the part of him that once confessed: "All my poetry marked to be read aloud should be whispered . . . for the inner ear . . . whispering in solitude." (p. 142)

Like Yeats, Lindsay transforms sentimentality into true art by means of the accompanying anti-sentimentality of nervously sinewy rhythms. Note, for example, the craftsmanship with which the lean rhythmic rightness of these two Lindsay quatrains redeems their otherwise sentimental rhetoric:

> Why do I faint with love
> Till the prairies dip and reel?
> My heart is a kicking horse
> Shod with Kentucky steel.
>
> No drop of my blood from north
> Of Mason and Dixon's line
> And this racer in my breast
> Tears my ribs for a sign. . . .
>
> (p. 144)

Let us consider that extraordinary Bryan poem first aesthetically, then politically. Note the sensuous concreteness of imagery. Instead of characterizing Bryan's enemies with the abstract, unlyrical word "the rich," Lindsay says concretely: "Victory of letter files / And plutocrats in miles / With dollar signs upon their coats." His self-mocking sense of humor, the

subtlely of his pseudo-crudity, explains the surrealist fantasy of pretending, with wonderful preposterousness, that plutocrats literally wear dollar signs on their coats. (p. 145)

In Lindsay's day, the midwest dream of messianic "civic ecstasy" in politics (really, Fundamentalist revivalism secularized) still had a touching youthful innocence; his Bryan poem, despite its doctrinaire social message, could still succeed in being movingly lyrical; American optimism was cracking but not yet cracked up. In contrast, the neo-Populist nationalism of our own day can find no voice, whether poetic or social-reformist, of Lindsay's cultural or moral stature. For meanwhile American standardization plus Ortega's "revolt of the masses" have transformed salvation-via-mob from innocent dream to sordid nightmare. And from genuine economic needs (such as Populist farmers exploited by railroads) to economic hypochondria. (p. 146)

From this salvation-via-mob dilemma, with its false choice between leftist and rightist mob-hatreds, Lindsay himself pointed the way out. The way out was love; not that philistine-humanitarian love of progress (so aptly refuted by Edmund Burke and Irving Babbitt) whose hug squashes individuals into an impersonal mass; but the creative lyric love that flows healingly from the inner integrity—the holy imagination—of great art. In short, when Lindsay did voice deeply enough the roots of the human condition, he became a fundamental poet, rather than merely the poet of the Fundamentalists. His poem **"The Leaden-Eyed"** describes perfectly the human price paid for unimaginative standardization and at the same time, through the very act of being lyrical, demands the rehumanizing of the machine age:

> Not that they starve, but starve so dreamlessly,
> Not that they sow, but that they seldom reap,
> Not that they serve, but have no gods to serve,
> Not that they die but that they die like sheep. . . .

Such a rehumanizing-through-creativity as Lindsay achieved at his best, seems the only way out from our age of the three impersonal M's: masses, machines, and mediocrity. This great, absurd, and holy poet of America's native religious roots merits the adjective "God-intoxicated" because he found the redeeming religious imagination everywhere, everywhere—in the absurd as well as in the high. . . . (p. 147)

> *Peter Viereck, "Vachel Lindsay: The Dante of the Fundamentalists," in* A Question of Quality: Popularity and Value in Modern Creative Writing, *edited by Louis Filler, Bowling Green University Popular Press, 1976, pp. 124-47.*

BLAIR WHITNEY (essay date 1976)

[*In the following excerpt, Whitney compares and contrasts the portrayal of Illinois as a Garden of Eden in the work of three Illinois poets—Lindsay, Edgar Lee Masters, and Carl Sandburg.*]

Three Illinois poets, Vachel Lindsay, Edgar Lee Masters, and Carl Sandburg, write of their native place as if it were an Eden. To them the prairies and small towns of central Illinois are places equal to man's "capacity for wonder," and their poems are often versions of the myth of America as Promised Land. In this Eden, natural beauty, human goodness, liberal politics, and the fine arts combine to fulfill America's best possibilities. Lindsay believes this ideal may be realized in the future, and he devotes much of his work to preaching a Gospel of Beauty that imagines it. Masters, on the other hand, writes of a former paradise that has disappeared. Sandburg is neither as optimistic as Lindsay nor as pessimistic as Masters. His poems provide glimpses of the good life in the present.

All three poets know the beauty of central Illinois. The landscape here is not spectacular—no mountains, waterfalls, or oceans—but gentle, peaceful (although powerful, like the sea), fertile, green. . . . The powerful life force of these prairies, as well as their beauty, serves as solace to people and as a source of their strength. This is a theme in several poems by these three men. (p. 17)

These prairies, however, are not merely picturesque and fertile. They are the true heartland of America, its vital center. "Heartland of America" is not a cliche to the three poets. They believe that the prairies of Illinois are invested with a special significance because of their location and history. Masters explains this in the opening pages of his Lindsay biography. La Salle saw this land; Marquette and Joliet canoed down its rivers; George Rogers Clark saved it in the Revolution. To these prairies, Masters writes, came men from Kentucky who brought with them the pioneer virtues and a rich store of folklore. . . .

These strong-willed Kentuckians, according to Masters, "made a garden of Illinois and Indiana," but they did more than just turn the thick sod and clear the timber. They brought to Illinois the best American ideals and values. (p. 18)

[The] view of the Illinois farmer as Adamic child of nature is, of course, a literary invention, since the average Illinois farmer of Sandburg's time was capitalist whose hands probably dreamed not of Illinois corn but of the steering wheel of his tractor. Yet this myth is one of the most powerful in American intellectual and literary history, finding believers from Hector St. Jean de Crèvecoeur and Thomas Jefferson to the intellectual farmers of today's rural communes.

Masters believes that the day of the pioneer farmer is over, that the present generation is no longer capable of living a true, free life, close to the soil, out in the clear, fresh air. . . . Lindsay, however, still believed in the possibility of a Jeffersonian agrarian ideal. In **"The Virginians Are Coming Again,"** he imagines a new generation of long-legged pioneers that will replace the degenerate Babbitts of the 1920's. These Virginians are true Americans who have absorbed the wisdom of Washington, Jefferson, and (an aboriginal American) Powhatan and will bring back "the old grand manner" of the pioneers. Masters looks backward, Lindsay forward. Sandburg sees in present-day Americans a strength born of the land. (p. 19)

Out of the prairie towns, out the frontier came Abraham Lincoln. To Lindsay, Sandburg, and (in his early poems) Masters, Lincoln represents all their ideals made flesh. He is the historical proof of their thesis, the rich harvest of the garden of Illinois. (p. 21)

Lindsay's Lincoln is also a suffering humanitarian. He imagines him come back to life, walking the streets of Springfield during World War I. "The prairie-lawyer, master of us all" cannot sleep because of the war. "Too many peasants fight, they know not why, / Too many homesteads in black terror weep." Lincoln, the idealist, waits for a "spirit-dawn" that will bring peace, justice, and equality to "Cornland, Alp, and Sea." . . . In other poems and in his prose, Lindsay longs for a generation of "Lincoln-hearted men" to create a utopia in Springfield, Illinois by following Lincoln's example. (p. 22)

Those who have corrupted the garden of Illinois come mostly from the East, especially from New England. These children

of the Puritans lack the natural vigor and rich understanding of Virginians and Kentuckians. Instead their only interest is money. Wealth does not come for the soil, these men believe. It comes from factories, mills, banks, railroads, and coal mines ripped out of the garden. Swollen by financial and industrial power, the village ruled by farmers becomes the city ruled by lawyers. Honesty, humility, and charity are replaced by duplicity, greed, and hypocrisy. (pp. 22-3)

The best poetic treatment of this theme is Lindsay's **"Bryan, Bryan, Bryan, Bryan"** . . . written in 1919 when Lindsay was at the height of his poetic power and still optimistic about the future. In this poem, he describes Bryan's visit to Springfield during the 1896 campaign. Lindsay, Sandburg, and Masters all admired Bryan—at least until he turned "down and theological," as Masters put it—because Bryan was one of them, born in Illinois, a son of the prairie, a fighter for the poor farmer, an enemy of the moneyed East. He was a Lincoln-hearted man who if elected might restore the old pioneer spirit. Also, he was young, vigorous, and a mighty orator in the best American tradition. All of Lindsay's idealistic notions and all his hopes for the future are expressed in **"Bryan"** in a joyous, extravagant lyricism that gives the poem life long after Bryan's death. This excellent poem presents both the dream of an American garden on the prairie and the reasons why that dream is unrealistic, perhaps even foolish, yet still wonderful. (p. 23)

Even more serious than the growth of industrialism and the supremacy of Eastern financial power over Western farmers was the threat of war. All three poets were opposed, in varying degrees, to World War I—Sandburg ultimately decided that America's entry was necessary—and all wrote anti-war poems. They agreed with young critic Randolph Bourne's statement, "The war—or American promise: one must choose. One cannot be interested in both. (p. 25)

As they watched the machine dig deeper into their rich prairie soil with each year, as they saw their idealistic dreams for a Jeffersonian America disappear along with the Populist party and the Illinois village, Lindsay and Masters grew increasingly bitter and strident in their attacks on the enemy. Although in his public appearances Lindsay kept on reciting his optimistic poems, and although he preached his old-fashioned Gospel of Beauty to the generation of flivvers and flaming youth, he worried about his fading popularity. His utopian books and magazines did not sell well, and by 1931 he was virtually bankrupt. The world did not live up to his vision of it. (p. 26)

Masters, Sandburg, and Lindsay imagined the garden of Illinois as a place where America's promises might be fulfilled. In this garden, men and women could live the good life in beautiful surroundings. Whether such an Eden really existed on New Salem Hill in the 1830's or whether it could have been established in Springfield, Galesburg, Petersburg, or Chicago just before World War I is not important now. What is important are the poems in which the ideals of the poets are made real. (p. 27)

> *Blair Whitney, "The Garden of Illinois," in* The Vision of This Land: Studies of Vachel Lindsay, Edgar Lee Masters, and Carl Sandburg, *edited by John E. Hallwas and Dennis J. Reader, Western Illinois University, 1976, pp. 17-28.*

JAMES DICKEY   (essay date 1979)

[*Dickey, an American poet, novelist, and critic, is considered one of America's foremost contemporary poets. He is also the author of the bestselling novel* Deliverance *(1970). In the following excerpt, Dickey argues for a reappraisal of Lindsay's works, discovering in the poet's career a unique and total commitment to the powers of invention achieved by few American poets before him.*]

Though the small Midwestern towns of the early part of the century did not, for Sherwood Anderson's Hugh McVey in "Poor White," "burn and change in the light," they strangely and confidently did for Nicholas Vachel Lindsay . . . ; in fact, they were the light, glowing with every imaginable color, giving off the odd-angled and essential glimmers of New World "promise" from a smoldering bedrock communality, a combustion always latent, and always—especially under Lindsay's own ministrations—capable of leaping into full, vital flame, warming, entertaining and explaining us all. His birthplace, Springfield, Ill., was for him this quintessential town, the rapt, chanting keeper of the Christian-Populist flame, undevious and irresistible, in whose light all things look and sound as they are: obvious, clumsy, crazy, good-hearted, vigorous, outgoing and, above all, loud. Lindsay's **"Golden Book of Springfield"** is the Book of Books of this ideal, its Platonic frame and firecave.

Have we really buried foolish, half-talented, half-cracked Lindsay in the textbooks—the very oldest and most mistaken ones—of literary history? Have we settled him in the dust of provincial libraries, in the unimaginable oblivion of metropolitan bookvaults? Was there ever anything, really, in all his wandering, his "gospel of beauty," his "higher vaudeville"? In those forgotten audiences hungering for him and his readings, providing thunderous response to his poems? Or in his curious, exasperating, self-enchanted, canny, bulldozing and somehow devilish innocence? Can any of him be saved, or is it better to move on? (pp. 9, 17)

It seems to me . . . that Lindsay's career and example raise some interesting—if not exactly crucial—questions about the relation between the poet and his audience, and also about the desirability and danger of self-delusion in the artist. I have always felt that Lindsay provided a kind of focus by means of which we might, if we so choose, gauge such questions and to some extent resolve them, each privately. But beyond a few superficial assumptions gleaned from the author notes of anthologies, I have never, before reading [**"Letters of Vachel Lindsay"**], known much of what sort of man Lindsay actually was, or how he lived and worked, that he had studied medicine and trained as an artist before devoting himself mainly to poetry.

I use the word *worked* advisedly, for Lindsay was very consciously a *worker* in the cause of his version of poetry, and of some mysterious entity he and his Campbellite mother called "art": for example, his accounts of the means he used to get his poems and graphics—his "Christian cartoons"—before a public are not only enthralling in themselves but show a kind of crank ingenuity that is quite impressive and even heartening in its singlemindedness. One would like to have the guts, the *chutzpah*, to do some of the things he did to reach people, and these not in isolated instances but as a mere matter of course. (p. 17)

The letters after [the] early ones are an erratic reverse "Pilgrim's Progress" through successive states of eroding self-delusion, a raw account of the manner in which a man of compassion and of odd-ball, shamanistic insight was fashioned into a freak—or, better still, into a carnival geek. For Lindsay, what seemed at first to be the incredibly fecund native ground

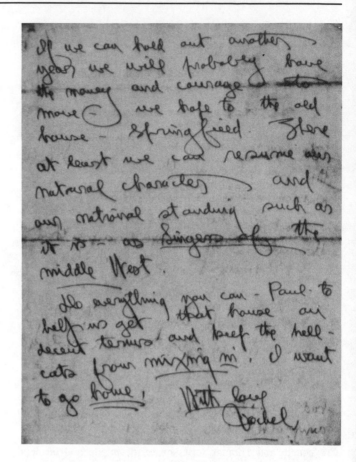

Portion of a letter from Lindsay to Paul Wakefield written May 2, 1928. Catharine Wakefield Ward.

of the American village turned into a tangled, sterile wilderness of hamlet-studded, boob-haunted railroad track, once the mere novelty of his personal presence and his "message" had been worn off by over-exposure; just before his suicide at 52 in the house of his birth in "golden" Springfield, he confessed that both he and his "dream" had failed utterly, that he had wasted himself, and spoke of "my best years . . . simply used up in shouting."

If I had the power, I should like very much to save Lindsay, to hold on to at least some aspects of him, if for only one reason. He lived naturally in a condition that many greater poets never had, or if they had it, were embarrassed or diffident about it: a total commitment to his own powers of invention, a complete loss of himself in his materials. To his fantasies, to the absurd figures he made—not a whit more convincing than Disney's—by trying to mythologize American history and legend, he gave himself in unthinking abandon: He invited and gloried in seizure, and as a result was totally immersed in his creative element, no matter what might be the end result. Perhaps that is not much, but perhaps it is more than we think. The best of Lindsay's poetry seems to me unique, its innocence not only real but unified and valuable. The letters, too, make available the same kind of right-or-wrong totality, the hell-with-it and go-with-it. (pp. 17-18)

James Dickey, "The Geek of Poetry," in The New York Times Book Review, *December 23, 1979, pp. 9, 17-18.*

DONALD WESLING (essay date 1982)

[*In the following excerpt, Wesling distinguishes Lindsay's as an overtly moral, spirited type of verse which is currently excluded from the living American poetic canon because of its epic elements*]

The poetic canon as it has evolved in America in the Twentieth Century is a genteel canon, and it associates heavily marked predictable rhythms and repeated lines with defects of learning and ear, defects of thinking. However the reasons, rhythmic and ideological, why Lindsay is now excluded are the same reasons why this hebraist, mystic, and profound Jeffersonian democrat could burst with such success into a literary scene whose representatives are Moody, Markham, Stoddard, Aldrich, and Stedman.

In 1913, the strutting and flailing, barking and whispering of Lindsay's selfstyled Higher Vaudeville were emergent and unincorporated, and to some extent (as I shall argue) his bardic virtues still challenge the exclusions of the American canon. But round about 1922, year of *The Waste Land* by that one of Harriet Monroe's newer protégés who had publicly called Lindsay "impossible," the Higher Vaudeville had been, in canonic terms, eclipsed through the achievements of fierce high Modernism. Like William Carlos Williams, Lindsay must have felt Eliot's poem to be a "bullet" to his own hopes for an American poetry, but he had none of Williams' resources to go on and regenerate his career. Unquestionably he understood what was happening. "They tried to get me; I got them first" [Lindsay's announcement before he died] is to be read, with pity and respect, as his reply to the exclusions of the canon. (p. 480)

Looking back, we judge poems to be failures with the help of the canon acting as selective tradition. However the canon may also be observed, to some extent I believe, from the prospective point of view of the writer. I think Lindsay was so tangled in his family romance, a warring with the Campbellite religious and moral influences of his own mother and father, that he could not conduct a satisfactory struggle with the mighty literary dead. As a consequence, it wasn't his fault but his fate to undervalue the role of educational ideals in producing canons of authority. No doubt Williams, Eliot, and Wallace Stevens were deformed as well as formed at their Eastern universities, but all three learned some things a writer needs to know from and about a literary canon. Poetry, Stevens said, is the scholar's art. Every innovative or canon-changing poet was first a canonically-informed reader.

I'm not saying that Lindsay should have gone to Harvard, but rather that his limitation derives from not being able to validate his own selective tradition. How that validation happens, as for instance with Eliot and his Donne, Dryden, and Laforgue, is not my brief to describe. The fact that Lindsay does not validate his chosen, mainly nonliterary precursor figures. His Johnny Appleseed, Williams Jennings Bryan, and John P. Altgeld are genial and not antithetical. In some other treatment perhaps they could be made to yield more heroism. The same is true of the verbal sources Lindsay lifts into literature, the anecdote, the fairytale, the sermon, the hymn, the college yell and jazz lyric, all these promising for a poetry from and about the American people. Lindsay wanted a great poem about the common man which would also be read by that common man: that is why the Higher Vaudeville stays close to speech and popular song in its flagrant attempt to be anti-literary, and that is why Lindsay nevertheless always wanted audiences to bring their books and follow along with his oral performances. The reading tours themselves, Gospel by Pullman, were his way

to bring poetry back to the people from whom it came. It did seem to work for a while, till the inadequacy of the prosodic, literary, imaginative, and historical basis of it all became evident even to Lindsay himself. (pp. 481-82)

If there is such a thing as American Bardic, an overtly moral, declaratory, expansive writing, the line of transmission runs through Lindsay. He was oversold in the thirties, and the reaction that set in against him between 1940-1960 was devastating; then with the rise of Ginsberg and Olson in the sixties the bardic-epic mode was more permissible and Lindsay returned in a small way as a subject of scholarly investigation. Out he went in the seventies, when the epic gesture came once again to seem an absurdity and the pricking of bardic balloons became a canonical method in poets like John Ashbery. We are now in the privileged moment of his and American Bardic's near-total obliteration, and this has occurred in strict adherence to Ernst Curtius's axiom of literary systematics, "the selection of authors presupposes a classification of genres. The hierarchy of genres, however constituted, wants to suppress American Bardic from its pantheons and pléiades, and must continuously find that this is an unkillable genre.

Lindsay's permanent value, then, goes some distance beyond what he actually achieved as a poet. He is what the canon excludes; his American Bardic is an indictment of the canon. It is an act of contestation to bring him forward, if only sadly. He is thus a reminder of certain other exclusions which can only be mentioned: the canon, however constituted and by whom, excludes eighteenth century thinkers like Jonathan Edwards and Thomas Jefferson; Blacks and Chicanos and Indians and West Coast Orientals; women and homosexuals; American writers in other languages than English; writers in other genres than fiction and poetry; writers extreme in brevity or gigantism or difficulty. (p. 483)

> *Donald Wesling, "What the Canon Excludes: Lindsay and American Bardic," in* Michigan Quarterly Review, *Vol. XXI, No. 3, Summer, 1982, pp. 479-85.*

TERENCE DIGGORY (essay date 1983)

[*In the following excerpt, Diggory examines the influence of W. B. Yeats on Lindsay.*]

[When he spoke in Chicago at a banquet organized in his honor by *Poetry* William Butler Yeats] described the struggle in which he and his fellow members in the Rhymers' Club had engaged to free their verse of rhetoric, and he expressed disappointment at opening an American magazine and finding all that the Rhymers had struggled against. Yet, at the same banquet, Yeats acknowledged the help of an American, Ezra Pound, as a symbol of Yeats's intention to go even farther in removing rhetoric from his verse. . . .

The meaning of rhetoric for Yeats is thrown into some doubt by his praise at the *Poetry* banquet for another American, Vachel Lindsay, whose poetry seems often deliberately rhetorical in the conventional sense of being florid in imagery or diction. Lindsay was present at the banquet to read his new poem **"The Congo"** after Yeats's talk, and Harriet Monroe had made sure that Yeats was acquainted with **"General William Booth Enters into Heaven,"** which had appeared in *Poetry* in January 1913 and as the title poem in Lindsay's first book. To some degree, then, Yeats could hardly avoid paying Lindsay a compliment. Yet the phrase Yeats chose when he described **"William Booth"** as "stripped bare of ornament" . . . comes too close to a principal area of his concern to be dismissed as mere courtesy. A phrase Yeats used immediately after the one about ornament helps to make his meaning clearer. There was "an earnest simplicity" in **"General Booth,"** Yeats found. In other words, the poem seemed sincere.

A poet's sincerity was an ambiguous issue for anyone who placed as much value in posing as Yeats did, but a poem might be judged sincere if the speaker, to return to Ezra Pound's formulation, was felt to be real. Rhetoric, for Yeats, was a function not of a poem's diction but of its *persona*. If the sentiment expressed in a poem, no matter how simply, seemed to have descended from social opinion rather than having arisen from individual experience, the poem would be rhetorical. On the other hand, any words, no matter how extravagant, would have the ring of sincerity if the poem suggested an individual character who might plausibly speak them. The conventions underlying Lindsay's poems immediately establish such a character because they derive from an oral tradition, that of soapbox oratory and the sidewalk sermon, rather than the printed page. The evocation of revival meetings supplies a mundane base for the most visionary imagery in **"The Congo":** "And some had visions, as they stood on chairs, / And sang of Jacob, and the golden stairs." . . . Such curious mixtures of the real and the visionary help the poet to establish his own singularity, the goal of "the American orator-poet," according to Harold Bloom, who gives Emerson that title. A similar goal led Yeats to admire "fine oratory" . . . as opposed to rhetoric, and to commend Lindsay for, in effect, achieving natural speech.

Ideally, oratory would incorporate another of Yeats's concerns that might seem to conflict with the goal of natural speech, that is, the goal of bringing out the music in poetry. That he saw no contradiction in his aims is indicated by his belief that he had found the two combined in Pound, whose verse was "definitely music" yet "effective speech." . . . Lindsay's verse seemed to promise a similar combination. After praising Lindsay for stripping away ornament, Yeats asked him privately, "What are we going to do to restore the primitive singing of poetry?" which Lindsay took to refer to "the old Greek precedent of the half-chanted lyric." Yeats's chants had been accompanied by the psaltery, whereas Lindsay called for bass drum and banjo in performance of **"General Booth"** and **"The Congo."** Yet each man recognized the initial impulse that united them. Lindsay's recognition had come long before the *Poetry* banquet, at least as early as 1906, when he chose Yeats's poems as suitable for recitation on the first of his celebrated tramps through America.

For his third tramp, in 1912, Lindsay prepared a pamphlet of his own poems, *Rhymes to Be Traded for Bread*, which included a poem that he came to regard as a prophecy of his meeting with Yeats. Entitled **"The Perilous Road,"** the poem recalls Browning's mechanical rhyme and metrics in "Love Among the Ruins," but the situation is similar to that of Yeats's "The Blessed" (1897). A youth approaches a hermit for instruction: "Teach me, the while I kneel, a curious prayer / To rule the air." Such an attitude of reverent discipleship ensured that Lindsay, after his meeting with Yeats, would dutifully carry out his master's instructions. Specifically, Yeats advised Lindsay to modulate the tone of his chanting, advice Lindsay first applied in **"The Santa Fé Trail,"** a poem written shortly after his meeting with Yeats.

While writing **"The Santa Fé Trail,"** Lindsay told Harriet Monroe, "I have tried hard to take Yeats' advice and put something *under* it—and have over-tones and minor strains and

whispers." Another reader entered Lindsay's thoughts, however. The poet Sara Teasdale, with whom Lindsay was in love, had been an admirer of Yeats from her youth, and Lindsay promised her that, for her sake, his poem would include "tiny flutes and fairy whispers and Yeatsy quietnesses and twilights." The fairy whispers are audible at the end of the poem: "Listen . . . to . . . the . . . whisper . . . / Of . . . the . . . prairie . . . fairies." . . . But the result of Yeats's advice is most fully displayed in the structure of the poem as a whole, which contrasts the opposing tones of nature and machines. One turning point in particular illustrates Lindsay's inability to manage contrast with Yeats's adeptness:

> But I would not walk alone till I die
> Without some life-drunk horns going by.
> And up round this apple-earth they come
> Blasting the whispers of the morning dumb.

Yeats usually managed to keep one term implicit when he made its opposite explicit, but Lindsay opposes terms only to annihilate one of them. (pp. 61-4)

By 1917, with Yeats still to be heard from, Lindsay was bitterly convinced that Yeats's praise had been little more than "polite taffy," as he told Harriet Monroe. In the same letter he decided it was more important to have the esteem of Monroe and her circle "than that I should have been praised on one evening by a mysterious stranger who has since disappeared."

Although Lindsay felt personally estranged from Yeats, he retained a fondness for Yeats's poetry. In his home town of Springfield, Illinois, he would read poems such as "Red Hanrahan's Song About Ireland" . . . and "He Wishes for the Cloths of Heaven" . . . to the young people who gathered around him. (pp. 64-5)

In December 1931, two months after writing to Yeats, Lindsay committed suicide. Although his estrangement from Yeats could not have been nearly as painful as the fear of failure that led Lindsay to take his life, the two problems can be traced to the same root. As **"The Perilous Road"** indicates, Lindsay desperately wanted to have a master and thought for a time that Yeats would be willing to play the role, but Yeats's long silence proved otherwise. The desire to claim a master was a desire to be one of a company, to be part of a tradition, to be read in a context within which one's work might be understood. Lack of understanding was the greatest cause of Lindsay's despair as well as the reason behind his attempt to assimilate popular tradition along with the literary tradition represented by Yeats. Neither tradition proved open to Lindsay as a poet, however. He found himself facing the task that American poets inevitably face, not that of inventing new things to say in an inherited language, but rather that of inventing the language itself. (p. 65)

Yeats had read "September 1913" (1913), proclaiming that "Romantic Ireland's dead and gone." He had always known that Ireland's past was "gone," but now he feared that it was "dead" in the sense of having no meaning to Irishmen of the present, even if past forms were revived. The impulse for survival that Yeats had once felt correspondingly waned, and the movement he had built around that impulse left him behind in an isolation that called for a considerable readjustment in his outlook. Faced with a similar isolation after the *Poetry* movement had lost its initial energy, Vachel Lindsay was unable to adjust. One explanation may lie in the difference between the elegiac mode, which allowed Yeats to write after hope was lost, and the prophetic mode, on which Lindsay's hope depended. More important, Yeats looked to himself; Lindsay looked to others, as he looked to Yeats. Ironically, Yeats was better prepared than Lindsay to endure the extreme of individualism that Alice Corbin Henderson described as uniquely American. (p. 66)

> *Terence Diggory, "Natural Speech: The Nineteen-Tens," in his* Yeats & American Poetry: The Tradition of the Self, *Princeton University Press, 1983, pp. 59-86.**

ADDITIONAL BIBLIOGRAPHY

Enkvist, Nils Erik. "The Folk Elements in Vachel Lindsay's Poetry." *English Studies* 32, Nos. 1-6 (1951): 241-49.
> Examines the sources and treatment of American folklore, Negro history, and American Indian legend in Lindsay's work.

Massa, Ann. *Vachel Lindsay: Fieldworker for the American Dream.* Bloomington: Indiana University Press, 1970, 310 p.
> Biography that sympathetically details Lindsay's life and explores *The Golden Book of Springfield* at length.

Masters, Edgar Lee. *Vachel Lindsay: A Poet in America.* New York: Charles Scribner's Sons, 1935, 392 p.
> Biography that includes lengthy excerpts from Lindsay's journals and offers Masters's own insights on the poet's life and career.

[Woolf, Virginia.] "An American Poet." *The Times Literary Supplement,* No. 941 (29 January 1920): 64.
> Favorably reviews *General William Booth Enters into Heaven, and Other Poems* for its exuberance, but expresses reservations regarding Lindsay's need for aesthetic tempering and discipline.

George Meredith

1828-1909

English novelist, essayist, poet, and short story writer.

Meredith was a major Victorian novelist whose career developed in conjunction with an era of great change in English literature during the second half of the nineteenth century. While his early novels largely conformed to Victorian literary conventions, his later novels demonstrated a concern with character psychology, modern social problems, and the development of the novel form that has led to his being considered an important precursor of English Modernist novels. In particular, Meredith is noted as one of the earliest English psychological novelists and as an important experimenter with narrative told from a variety of shifting, unreliable perspectives, reflecting a modern perception of the uncertain nature of both personal motivation and of social or historical events.

Meredith was born in Portsmouth, England. His father inherited a seemingly prosperous Portsmouth naval outfitters and tailor shop from his own father, but soon discovered that one reason for the shop's popularity with customers was that delinquent bills were rarely pursued. He ran the failing business at a loss for several years while the family lived extravagantly on the dowry that Meredith's mother had brought into the marriage. Considering themselves superior to ordinary tradespeople, the Merediths unsuccessfully attempted to establish themselves as the social equals of the elegant patrons of the tailor shop. Meredith was sent to private schools and quickly learned to say nothing of his family's position, instead encouraging the assumption that he was of the gentry. Meredith remained secretive about his origins all his life, and much is unknown about his childhood because of his unwillingness to disclose details of this period.

When Meredith was five his mother died, leaving her money in a trust for her son's education. Lacking access to these funds for his business, Meredith's father was forced into bankruptcy. The boy was sent to boarding schools and had very little contact with his father thereafter. At fourteen Meredith was sent to school in Neuwied, Germany, where he remained for two years, leaving with a love of German culture, especially music, that lasted the rest of his life. Upon Meredith's return to England, his father wanted to apprentice him to a bookseller and publisher, but Meredith, disinclined to follow the advice of a man he considered "a muddler and a fool," found a post for himself assisting an attorney, for whom he worked for five years.

As he entered his early twenties, Meredith began writing poetry, influenced in particular by John Keats and Lord Tennyson. He became acquainted with Edward Gryffydh Peacock and Mary Nicolls, the son and widowed daughter of the satirist Thomas Love Peacock, a man he admired. With the younger Peacock he collaborated on the publication of a privately circulated literary magazine, *The Monthly Observer,* to which he submitted his own poetry and critical essays. A tempestuous relationship with Nicolls culminated in their marriage in 1849, but the marriage was neither a happy nor a lasting one, in part due to Meredith's precarious financial situation. Although his father-in-law offered to secure him an office position, Meredith preferred to try to make his living by his pen. However, his

first book, *Poems,* a volume published at his own expense, attracted little notice and never recouped printing costs. During the first years of their marriage Nicolls suffered several miscarriages and stillbirths, while Meredith developed nervous and digestive disorders that led him to demand a highly specialized diet. Nicolls turned this to financial advantage by writing and publishing, with her father's help, a successful cookbook. In 1853, with Nicolls again pregnant, the couple's financial difficulties forced them to move in with Thomas Love Peacock. Peacock could not adjust to the disruption of his household, which was exacerbated by the birth of the Meredith's son Arthur later that year, and he eventually quit his own house to take rooms elsewhere.

By 1856 Meredith and his wife were living apart, and in 1858 she left for Italy with another man, leaving Meredith alone with five-year-old Arthur. When she returned to England years later, alone and seriously ill, Meredith refused to let her see their son until shortly before her death. Meredith's lifetime of reticence about his early years carried over into a stolid refusal to discuss his first marriage, though critics maintain that the sonnet cycle *Modern Love,* which painstakingly details the dissolution of a marriage, actually chronicles that event. Meredith's subsequent relationships with women proved for some time unsatisfactory. He fell in love with a much younger woman whose socially prominent parents cultivated the rising novelist as a valuable social asset, but refused to consider him a suitable match for their daughter. Meredith lived alone or with male friends for years, traveling extensively in Switzerland, France, and Italy. In London he shared a house briefly with Dante Gabriel Rossetti and Algernon Charles Swinburne, but, unprepared for their unconventional way of life, soon took single lodgings. Upon his second marriage in 1864, Meredith settled at Box Hill, Surrey, where he lived the rest of his life.

During the 1850s Meredith began to receive an income from magazine writing and was thus encouraged to attempt a longer prose work. His first work of fiction, *The Shaving of Shagpat: An Arabian Entertainment*, is a lighthearted fantasy that contains a number of themes that recur throughout Meredith's career, including ridicule of social conventions and disdain for social climbers, and features as a central character a young man whose growth to maturity is aided by a woman. The favorable reception of *Shagpat* inspired Meredith to write a serious novel, *The Ordeal of Richard Feverel: A History of Father and Son*. In this partially autobiographical work, a man is abandoned with an infant son by his wife and brings up the child according to a strict scientific system designed to insure that the boy will accept his father's social, political, and ideological beliefs, and will ultimately select an ideal mate who will prove faithful. However, the son eventually rebels against the debilitating and stifling environment created by his father and marries a woman of the lower classes. The novel contained a great deal of irony at the expense of both the characters and the conventions of Victorian society and created a stir due to its sarcastic tone and freethinking atheism. Moreover, many reviewers misread the work as an attack on science or scientific systems in general, despite Meredith's claim that "the moral is that no System of any sort succeeds with human nature, unless the originator has conceived it purely independent of personal passion." The novel also lost many readers when Mudie's lending library refused to circulate it because it depicted extramarital sex. Thus, after promising early sales, the novel fell both in critical and public regard.

Following the failure of *The Ordeal of Richard Feverel*, Meredith entered into a complex relationship with his readers, attempting, according to Ioan Williams, "to reconcile his artistic purpose with the demands of the reading public." Most critics agree that during the period from 1860 to 1875, Meredith was very responsive to the desires of the book-buying public. Several critics have theorized that Meredith tried in each new novel to correct the faults that had been criticized in the last, and to incorporate elements that would appeal to Victorian readers. As a part-time reader for Chapman and Hall publishers, Meredith was able to observe literary trends and to employ them in his early novels. In *Emilia in England* and its sequel *Vittoria*, for example, Meredith was inspired by the current interest in local-color fiction to give the heroine a vividly realized Italian background and to introduce historical figures and events into the story. Despite the introduction of fictional devices and elements that had proved successful for many other writers of the time, Meredith was unable to attract either readers or favorable critical notice. Some critics contend that Meredith's attempts to craft his books to the public taste by utilizing literary conventions was a calculated attempt on his part to couch his radical ideas concerning the impermanent nature of human values and the inconstancy of human nature in a form that would be acceptable to his readers. It is now commonly accepted by critics that Meredith possessed what Judith Wilt has called a "sensitive and aggressive awareness of the presence, at the heart of his creative art, of the reader." This assumption contradicts the formerly widely-held belief that he wrote in lofty disregard of his readers out of a single-minded dedication to his own artistic values. This estimation was reached by some commentators when Meredith, after years of courting a broad readership, professed his contempt for readers in occasional angry statements that his books were ignored by an unworthy and hypocritical public. Once he despaired of reaching a large audience, Meredith began to write primarily to please himself and the small circle of admirers who had defended and praised his works from the first. It was then that he found his works more popular than at any other time in his career.

Meredith's early novels share a number of characteristics of plot and style. Walter F. Wright has written that "without being autobiography, Meredith's creative work manifests the qualities revealed in his own life," and this is most noticeable in the novels written before 1876. The novels often open with a single father, abandoned by his wife or widowed, raising a son alone. The son's growth to young manhood and experiences with first love—often ending in tragedy—occupy many of the early novels. Many of them portray the marriage of an upper-class man with a woman of the lower classes, and the antagonisms resulting from differences between the classes is a recurring subject. These early novels contain Meredith's nascent attempts at psychological portraiture, and are typically concerned with demonstrating the instability of human nature as they satirically attack egoism, pretense, snobbery, and false values.

Meredith's most critically acclaimed work is the 1877 lecture *On the Idea of Comedy and the Uses of the Comic Spirit*, printed in the *New Quarterly Magazine* and published separately twenty years later. In this essay, which Arthur Symons called "his most brilliant piece of sustained writing," Meredith did not discuss comedy in general terms, but rather expounded on the comic approach that characterized his own fiction. Meredith contended that great comedy rectifies the excesses of human behavior by permitting audiences to laugh at their own foibles, depicting, according to Joseph Warren Beach, "the discrepancy between the real and the supposed motive" for human actions. True comedy thus has a beneficial social effect. For that reason Meredith asserted that true comedy is both "impersonal" and "thoughtful" and can only appear in a civilized nation. The novel *The Egoist*, written immediately after the essay on comedy, is the most successful example of his comic method and remains his most critically praised novel. In this comedy of manners, Meredith attacked a widely embraced element in the thought of John Stuart Mill, who held that individuals could think and do as they wished provided that they did no harm to others. Meredith demonstrated through the character of Sir Willoughby Patterne that such a belief was both alienating and harmful in that it ultimately denied the legitimacy of other opinions through the domination of egoistic individuals. Critical consensus is that with this work Meredith most successfully combined his theory of comedy, writing style, and thematic concerns. With *The Egoist*, Meredith finally achieved popular success and his popularity grew with subsequent novels.

Following *The Egoist*, Meredith was most concerned with writing psychological novels that portrayed the tangled motivations of individuals and explored the disparity between the public and private aspects of self. These later novels demonstrate a heightened social awareness, a more tolerant view of human folly, and a corresponding softening of the satiric and ironic portraits of individuals. In these works there is no clear explanation of individual behavior, but rather an examination of the various ways that individuals and their actions are perceived. Often it is unclear what actually happens in the novels, and the reader is forced to extract the truth from the gossip, half-truths, and misdirection arising from the different characters' perceptions; in many cases Meredith gave several versions of the same event through the eyes of several characters. Critics contend that in Meredith's experiments with the novel form and with complex characterizations can be seen the germ of the modern psychological novel. Throughout these works Meredith sought to demonstrate that most human motivations are concealed and that, while much in life is relative, including morality, actions are not: once something has happened, it is unchangable and often irredeemable.

The most popular and artistically successful of Meredith's later works was *Diana of the Crossways*, a novel inspired by a scandal involving an adulterous married woman accused of selling a state secret. It has been theorized that readers were attracted by the belief that in this novel Meredith was revealing some inside information about this widely discussed affair; in fact, so many readers assumed that the novel reflected the facts of the scandal that later editions contained disclaimers disallowing any connection between Meredith's creation and the affair. The character of Diana, who leaves her husband to pursue a writing career, became a favorite with feminists and the prototype of many subsequent novel heroines who, misunderstood and unappreciated, strike out boldly on their own. Throughout his career Meredith had explored the circumscribed role of women in society, a topic known in his day as "the woman question," and had long contended that civilization can only flourish when men and women are equal. It was in *Diana* that his didactic intentions, novelistic devices, and analysis of character achieved their greatest unity.

Critics have been united in comparing Meredith with Thomas Hardy as a "poet-novelist" who considered poetry his true literary vocation but turned to writing novels for financial reasons. Meredith's poetry has received increasing attention in recent years and critics have noted that it follows the same course of development as his novels, moving from early examinations of the self in society to a later concern with broader social issues and defiance of the conventions of the form. In particular, Meredith explored new meters and stanzaic forms and experimented dramatically with syntax and grammar. Critics characterize his poetry as verbally dense, allusive, and metaphorical, and in many ways reflective of the late nineteenth-century inclination toward aesthetic artifice. Although *Modern Love* is considered his most important poetic achievement, several of his late poems provide important perspectives on his fiction, particularly a series of odes on the purpose of literature and the nature of the historical process. In these works, as well as in his novels, Meredith demonstrated his desire to challenge and overcome what he perceived as narrow and constrictive world views.

At the time of his death Meredith was considered one of England's premier men of letters. In the years since, his critical reputation has undergone several reassessments, although he has never enjoyed the resurgence in general popularity enjoyed by such Victorian novelists as Charles Dickens and Anthony Trollope. Several reasons have been cited for this. Meredith's novels feature very little action, relying instead on dialogue, or what Meredith called "action of the mind," to advance the story. This resulted in a popular perception of his novels as static and "talky." However, Meredith's prose is most often identified as the barrier that makes his works inaccessible to readers. Meredith's narrative style, making extensive use of metaphor, allusion, and aphorism, has been described by his admirers and detractors alike as so difficult that close rereadings of passages are frequently necessary to extract the meaning. Some critics contend that Meredith became so enamored of his mannered style that style itself became the end of his work and not the means to tell a story. His supporters, however, praise the poetic quality of Meredith's prose, maintaining that each line of Meredith's work is written in the allusive, rich language usually reserved for poetry. Although Meredith's career has undergone several reappraisals as new generations of critics rediscover his works, the difficulties presented by his narrative style have been cited as the factor that has discouraged a resurgence of widespread interest. However, as has been true throughout the history of commentary on Meredith, there remains a dedicated group of admirers who contend, with J. B. Priestley, that Meredith's difficult style, requiring as it does the full and undivided attention of the reader, paved the way for the public acceptance of much subsequent serious fiction, helping to shape "the modern attitude towards fiction and the modern novel itself."

(See also *Dictionary of Literary Biography*, Vol. 18: *Victorian Novelists After 1885*; and Vol. 35: *Victorian Poets After 1850*.)

PRINCIPAL WORKS

Poems (poetry) 1851
The Shaving of Shagpat: An Arabian Entertainment (fiction) 1856
The Ordeal of Richard Feverel: A History of Father and Son (novel) 1859
Evan Harrington; or, He Would Be a Gentleman (novel) 1861
Modern Love, and Poems of the English Roadside, with Poems and Ballads (poetry) 1862
Emilia in England (novel) 1864; also published as *Sandra Belloni*, 1886
Rhoda Fleming (novel) 1865
Vittoria (novel) 1867
The Adventures of Harry Richmond (novel) 1871
Beauchamp's Career (novel) 1876
On the Idea of Comedy and the Uses of the Comic Spirit (essay) 1877; published in journal *New Quarterly Magazine*
The Ordeal of Richard Feverel: A History of Father and Son [revised edition] (novel) 1878
The Egoist: A Comedy in Narrative (novel) 1879
The Tragic Comedians: A Study in a Well-Known Story (novel) 1880
Diana of the Crossways (novel) 1885
The Adventures of Harry Richmond [revised edition] (novel) 1886
Ballads and Poems of Tragic Life (poetry) 1887
One of Our Conquerors (novel) 1891
Poems. The Empty Purse. With Odes to the Comic Spirit, to Youth in Memory, and Verses (poetry) 1892
Lord Ormont and His Aminta (novel) 1894
The Amazing Marriage (novel) 1895
Last Poems (poetry) 1909
The Works of George Meredith. 27 vols. (novels, short stories, essays, and poetry) 1909-1911
Celt and Saxon (unfinished novel) 1910

W. M. R[OSSETTI]   (essay date 1851)

[*English art and literary critic Rossetti, the younger brother of noted poet Christina Rossetti and painter Dante Gabriel Rossetti, was a part of the English pre-Raphaelite movement established by Dante Gabriel in 1848. Revering pre-Renaissance artistic qualities of religious symbolism, lavish pictorialism, and natural sensuousness, the pre-Raphaelites cultivated a sense of mystery and melancholy that influenced later writers associated with the Symbolist and Decadent movements. In the following excerpt, Rossetti compares Meredith's poetry extensively with that of Keats. Although he and Meredith were not acquainted at the time Rossetti wrote this review, Meredith later became an intimate of the Rossettis and their circle, for a time joining in a communal household arrangement that included Dante Gabriel Rossetti and Algernon Charles Swinburne.*]

Mr. Meredith seems to us a kind of limited Keats. He is scarcely a perceptive, but rather a seeing or sensuous poet. He does not love nature in a wide sense as Keats did; but nature delights and appeals closely to him. In proportion, however, as his sympathies are less vivid, excitable, and diffusive, he concentrates them the more. He appropriates a section of nature, as it were; and the love which he bears to it partakes more of affection. Viewing Mr. Meredith as a Keatsian, and allowing for (what we need not stop to assert), the entire superiority of the dead poet,—we think it is in this point that the most essential phase of difference will be found between the two: and it is one which, were the resemblance in other respects more marked and more unmixed than it is, would suffice to divide Mr. Meredith from the imitating class. The love of Keats for nature was not an *affectionate* love: it was minute, searching, and ardent; but hardly personal. He does not lose himself in nature, but contemplates her and utters her forth to the delight of all ages. Indeed, if we read his record aright, he was not, either in thought or in feeling, a strongly affectionate man; and the passion which ate into him at the last was a mania and infatuation, raging like disease, a symptom and a part of it. It is otherwise with Mr. Meredith. In his best moments he seems to sing, because it comes naturally to him, and silence would be restraint, not through exuberance or inspiration, but in simple contentedness, or throbbing of heart. There is an amiable and engaging quality in the poems of Mr. Meredith, a human companionship and openness, which make the reader feel his friend.

But, perhaps, it is chiefly in the impressions of love that our new poet's likeness and unlikeness at once to the author of *Endymion* and *Lamia* are to be recognised. We are told that women felt pique at Keats for treating them in his verses scarcely otherwise than flowers or perfumes; as beautifiers and the object of tender and pleasurable emotion,—a charm of life. They missed the language of individual love, dignified and equal. . . .

Surely, it may be said, there is passion enough . . . [in Meredith's **"Love in the Valley"**], and of a sufficiently personal kind. True, indeed: this is not a devotion which sins through lukewarmth, and roams uncertain of an object. It will not fail to obtain an answer, through dubiousness of quest: and if it shocks at all, it shocks the delicacy, not the *amour-propre.* But its characteristics are, in fact, the same as those at which exception was taken in the case of Keats. The flame burns here, which there only played, darting its thin quick tongue from point to point: but the difference is of concentration only. The impressionable is changed for the strongly impressed—the influence being similar. Here again the love, like our poet's love of nature, has the distinct tone of *affection*. It is purely and unaffectedly sensuous, and in its utterance as genuine a

thing as can be. We hear a clear voice of nature, with no falsetto notes at all; as spontaneous and intelligible as the wooing of a bird, and equally a matter of course.

The main quality of Mr. Meredith's poems is warmth—warmth of emotion, and, to a certain extent, of imagination, like the rich mantling blush on a beautiful face, or a breath glowing upon your cheek. That he is young will be as unmistakably apparent to the reader as to ourself; on which score various shortcomings and crudities, not less than some excess of this attribute, claim indulgence. (p. 539)

> W. M. R[ossetti], in a review of "Poems," in The
> Critic, London, Vol. X, No. 255, November 15, 1851,
> pp. 539-40.

[R. H. HUTTON]   (essay date 1862)

[*Hutton and Meredith Townsend were coeditors of* The Spectator *following their acquisition of this journal from Stephen Rintoul in 1861. Hutton subsequently provided literary reviews concerned primarily with the moral content of a work of literature, such as the following excerpt, which includes the well-known and much-quoted contention that Meredith's sonnet cycle* Modern Love *would be more accurately titled "Modern Lust." This review elicited an angry response from Algernon Charles Swinburne (1862).*]

Clever bold men with any literary capacity are always tempted to write verse, as they can say so much under its artistic cover which in common prose they could not say at all. It is a false impulse, however, for unless the form of verse is really that in which it is most natural for them to write, the effect of adopting it is to make the sharp hits which would be natural in prose, look out of place—lugged in by head and shoulders—and the audacity exceedingly repellent. This is certainly the effect upon us of [*Modern Love, and Other Poems*]. Mr. George Meredith is a clever man, without literary genius, taste, or judgment, and apparently aims at that sort of union of point, passion, and pictorial audacity which Byron attained in "Don Juan." There is, however, no kind of harmonious concord between his ideas and his expressions; when he is *smart,* as he is habitually, the form of versification makes the smartness look still more vulgar, and the jocularity jar far more than it would in prose. On the whole the effect of the book on us is that of clever, meretricious, turbid pictures, by a man of some vigour, jaunty manners, quick observation, and some pictorial skill, who likes writing about naked human passions, but does not bring either original imaginative power or true sentiment to the task. The chief composition in the book, absurdly called **"Modern Love,"** is a series of sonnets intended to versify the leading conception of Goethe's "elective affinities." Mr. Meredith effects this with occasional vigour, but without any vestige of original thought or purpose which could excuse so unpleasant a subject, and intersperses it, moreover, with sardonic grins that have all the effect of an intentional affectation of cynicism. This is not quite always the case, however, or we should soon throw the book contemptuously aside; for the jocularities are intolerably feeble and vulgar. . . . Mr. George Meredith has a sense of what is graphic, but he never makes an excursion beyond that into what he intends for poetry without falling into some trick of false ornamentation. (p. 580)

The thing has no kind of right to the title **"Modern Love:"** "Modern Lust" would be certainly a more accurate though not a true title, there is something of real love, but more of the other embodied in the sonnets.

In the verses which do not hinge on this sort of subject, there is the same confusion between a 'fast' taste and what Mr. Meredith mistakes for courageous realism—poetic pre-Raphaelitism. For instance, Mr. Meredith has, in some verses on a scene in the Alps, given us a vision of the spirit of Beauty, whom he proposes in a vehement kind of half-and-half enthusiasm, one half sentiment the other half beer, to introduce to a London cabman. . . . This is not intellectual courage, nor buoyancy of spirit, nor anything but a spasmodic ostentation of fast writing. There are moods in which a man of high animal spirits is apt to think that any nonsense which amuses himself in an irrational moment is good enough to amuse the world; and because Mr. George Meredith was amused for the moment with the incongruity of fancying a greasy-coated cabman with his arm round Calliope, and with his own poor pun on that person's "driving the world," he thought it, we suppose, a mark of intellectual pluck to print it. It really is only noisy vulgarity, which, in so clever a man—for he is clever and graphic in his way—is exceedingly unworthy. There is a deep vein of muddy sentiment in most men, but they should let the mud settle, and not boast of it to the world. Mr. Meredith evidently thinks mud picturesque, as, indeed, it may be, but all picturesqueness is not poetry. One gains a graphic picture of a good deal of interior mental mud without verse to help us. Mr. Meredith thinks we do not get enough, and the solution given here is sometimes a very thick one indeed. The best thing in the book is "**Juggling Jerry**," which is not vulgar nor tawdry, as so much of the volume is. (p. 581)

> [*R. H. Hutton*], "*Mr George Meredith's 'Modern Love*'," *in* The Spectator, *Vol. XXXV, No. 1769, May 24, 1862, pp. 580-81.*

A[LGERNON] C[HARLES] SWINBURNE (letter date 1862)

[*Swinburne, an English poet renowned during his lifetime for the skill and technical mastery of his lyric poetry, is remembered today as a preeminent symbol of rebellion against the Victorian age. The explicitly handled sensual themes in his* Poems and Ballads *delighted some, shocked many, and led Robert Buchanan to mention Swinburne in his 1866 condemnation of Charles Baudelaire and "the fleshly school of poetry." To focus on what is sensational in Swinburne, however, is to miss the assertion, implicit in his poetry and explicit in his critical writings, that in a time when poets were expected to reflect and uphold contemporary morality, Swinburne's only vocation was to express beauty. In an explanation of his aestheticism, he stated: "Art is not like fire or water, a good servant and a bad master; rather the reverse. . . . Handmaid of religion, exponent of duty, servant of fact, pioneer of morality, she cannot in any way become. . . . Her business is not to do good on other grounds, but do good on her own: all is well with her while she sticks fast to that." In the following letter to the editor of* The Spectator, *Swinburne protests that* Modern Love, *an accomplished and technically skilled work of poetry by an established author, deserves careful consideration of its literary qualities and not of its moral content, a direct attack upon R. H. Hutton's review in* The Spectator (*see excerpt dated 1862.*]

Sir

I cannot resist asking the favour of admission for my protest against the article on Mr. Meredith's last volume of poems [*Modern Love, and Other Poems*] in the *Spectator* of May 24th [see excerpt by R. H. Hutton dated 1862]. That I personally have for the writings, whether verse or prose, of Mr. Meredith a most sincere and deep admiration is no doubt a matter of

infinitely small moment. I wish only, in default of a better, to appeal seriously on general grounds against this sort of criticism as applied to one of the leaders of English literature. To any fair attack Mr. Meredith's books of course lie as much open as another man's; indeed, standing where he does, the very eminence of his post makes him perhaps more liable than a man of less well-earned fame to the periodical slings and arrows of publicity. Against such criticism no one would have a right to appeal, whether for his own work or for another's. But the writer of the article in question blinks at stating the fact that he is dealing with no unfledged pretender. Any work of a man who has won his spurs, and fought his way to a foremost place among the men of his time, must claim at least a grave consideration and respect. (p. 632)

But even if the case were different, and the author were now at his starting-point, such a review of such a book is surely out of date. Praise or blame should be thoughtful, serious, careful, when applied to a work of such subtle strength, such depth of delicate power, such passionate and various beauty, as the leading poem of Mr. Meredith's volume: in some points, as it seems to me (and in this opinion I know that I have weightier judgments than my own to back me) a poem above the aim and beyond the reach of any but its author. Mr. Meredith is one of the three or four poets now alive whose work, perfect or imperfect, is always as noble in design as it is often faultless in result. The present critic falls foul of him for dealing with "a deep and painful subject on which he has no conviction to express." There are pulpits enough for all preachers in prose; the business of verse-writing is hardly to express convictions; and if some poetry, not without merit of its kind, has at times dealt in dogmatic morality, it is all the worse and all the weaker for that. As to subject, it is too much to expect that all schools of poetry are to be for ever subordinate to the one just now so much in request with us, whose scope of sight is bounded by the nursery walls. . . . We have not too many writers capable of duly handling a subject worth the serious interest of men. As to execution, take almost any sonnet at random out of the series, and let any man qualified to judge for himself of metre, choice of expression, and splendid language, decide on its claims. And, after all, the test will be unfair, except as regards metrical or pictorial merit; every section of this great progressive poem being connected with the other by links of the finest and most studied workmanship (pp. 632-33)

Of the shorter poems which give character to the book I have not space to speak here; and as the critic has omitted noticing the most valuable and important (such as the "**Beggar's Soliloquy**," and the "**Old Chartist**," equal to Béranger for completeness of effect and exquisite justice of style, but noticeable for a thorough dramatic insight, which Béranger missed through his personal passions and partialities), there is no present need to go into the matter. I ask you to admit this protest simply out of justice to the book in hand, believing as I do that it expresses the deliberate unbiassed opinion of a sufficient number of readers to warrant the insertion of it, and leaving to your consideration rather their claims to a fair hearing than those of the book's author to a revised judgment. A poet of Mr. Meredith's rank can no more be profited by the advocacy of his admirers than injured by the rash or partial attack of his critics. (p. 633)

> *A[lgernon] C[harles] Swinburne, in a letter to R. H. Hutton, in* The Spectator, *Vol. XXXV, No. 1771, June 7, 1862, pp. 632-33.*

THE SPECTATOR (essay date 1879)

[In the following excerpt, an anonymous reviewer of The Egoist *makes one of the most usual and persistent criticisms of Meredith's writing: that his extravagantly witty and epigrammatic style often becomes more important than the subject of his writing.]*

We have been amused, impressed, bored, and filled with admiration and disappointment by Mr. George Meredith's new story [*The Egoist: A Comedy in Narrative*]. Of Sir Willoughby Patterne, the typical egoist and the hero of the comedy, Mrs. Mountstuart Jenkinson observed at his coming of age, "You see he has a leg." The word is mystic, and of various interpretation; it characterises him from that time forth. Mrs. Mountstuart, we may remark, is a fatal coiner of epithets. She hits off all her acquaintance with a good-natured, but appalling accuracy, and thereby saves Mr. Meredith the necessity of too often blushing at his own cleverness. He naïvely admires her wit as much as we do. . . . We are the more grateful to Mrs. Mountstuart for . . . [her] luminous hints concerning the people with whom we are brought in contact, because after Mr. Meredith has done his best, he does not succeed in teaching us much more about them. We get plenty of elaboration, but little further practical insight. . . .

Mr. Meredith's reputation is high, and there is no doubt about his ability. Now, it is conceivable, but not inevitable, that a man of ability should be able to write a good novel, or even comedy in narrative; and there are few more agreeable sensations for a reviewer than to open a virgin volume with the assurance that he will find it full of good literature,—as good ten years hence as now. It was with an assurance, or at least with an anticipation, of this sort that we applied our paper-knife to the *Egoist*. The first effect was vigorous, and not unpromising. The writer has an individuality; he is a humourist. . . . His thought moves in images, sometimes felicitous, but as often grotesque or obscure. An inability to fall into conventional modes of expression is characteristic of humourists, but then the unconventionality should throw fresh light upon the subject-matter, should explain it, not disorganise it merely. Mr. Meredith's eccentricity is like that of a "left-handed" snail-shell; he must curl the wrong way, or the genius of his eccentricity is lost. The humourist, being himself a person, and generally the most conspicuous person in his book, he should be careful always to be captivating, otherwise his reader is liable to reject all he brings in rejecting him. Mr. Meredith is frequently captivating, but he does not know when to stop. We are compelled to question whether he is humorously affected, or only affectedly humorous. He is a sort of modern hermetic philosopher of drawing-rooms; there is too often more novelty in his way of saying a thing than in the thing he says; and although Mr. Meredith is ordinarily very circumspect, this is a fault which is quite as apt to mislead the writer as the reader. It is occasionally best and wisest to be straightforward and simple; there are times when wit will not do the work of strength. Such times are perilous to Mr. Meredith. Once more, he does not know when, or he is unable, to stop; and we find him lavishing much delicate fancy and brisk ingenuity upon matters in themselves unimportant; as if a man were to spend his life carving out of a perishable melon-rind, a work of art that he might just as easily have wrought in everlasting ivory. The links in his chain of argument are elaborated in such cunning open-work of verbal filagree, that the argument is no longer a chain, but a curiosity; it must be supported, it will support nothing. Again, his subtlety in the matter of adverbs and adjectives—the latter especially—is astonishing; but qualification is not invariably insight, and we are driven to ask whether the writer, who knows so well what a thing looks like, knows equally well what it is? He can always say a good thing, when he gives his mind to it; but now and then he is absentminded, and then he is prone to parody himself; his pen, left to its own devices, and still conscious whom it belongs to, perpetrates an empty quip, that has the form, but not the substance, of its owner. Upon the whole, as we turn page after page, our expectations are continually whetted, because of the difficulty of believing that so much promising material shall not fulfil its promise; but we are constrained to say, at the end, that it does not. The story, such as it is, would be better plainly dressed; its clothes are too good for it. (p. 1383)

Mr. Meredith knows many clever tricks of narrative. For example, he will reproduce, at an interval of several pages or chapters, a particular, marked phrase or conceit, which, carrying the mind back to the previous utterance of it, causes all that lies between to appear parenthetical, and thus gives an appearance of rapidity and homogeneity to the whole. Again, in the midst of much logical incoherence, he will observe a thread of humorous coherency, like a juggler who pretends to make a mistake with what we afterwards discover to have been his best skill. In his moralising moments he does not proffer you the naked truth, but gives you the conventional lie, robed in the ridiculous splendour of a monkey on a hand-organ, thus revealing its ugliness better than actual revelation could do. Of dialogue he is prodigal; but it is not characteristic dialogue, or rather it is characteristic of nobody but Mr. Meredith. The speeches chime with the context, but not with the people who are made to utter them. Precious human nature is pulled out of shape, in order that the author may not lose the credit of his own epigrams; and sometimes the ear catches in these utterances the fatal lilt of blank verse. But his people are altogether Mr. Meredith's weak point; he can see them, he can "hit them off," but he cannot enter into them and sympathise with them as individualities. What they are made to say and think is what they really might have said and thought,—presented through the refracting medium of the thoughts and sayings of Mr. Meredith. . . . [Mr. Meredith] describes his characters admirably, piecemeal; when it comes to the putting of them together, he does it coldly. After closing the book, we feel, in the retrospect, that the style is the most memorable thing about it. It is like a wayward wind blowing against the current of the story, and raising little humourous waves and eddies which both look pretty, and prevent our getting a clear view of what lies underneath. The whole work (to use another simile, for which Mr. Meredith must excuse us, since a prolonged and not unprofitable indulgence in his society is answerable for it) reminds us of one of those picture-puzzles that are given to children, to find out the figure or the significance which is hidden from the first view. The result of our inspection of Mr. Meredith's puzzle resolves itself into the single word,—"Clever." (p. 1384)

> *"Mr. George Meredith's New Novel," in* The Spectator, *Vol. LII, No. 2679, November 1, 1879, pp. 1383-84.*

MARK PATTISON (essay date 1883)

[In the following excerpt, Pattison reviews Poems and Lyrics of the Joy of Earth, *Meredith's first volume of poetry in the twenty years since* Modern Love. *Noting that Meredith is best known as a novelist, Pattison praises the poetic nature of Meredith's prose and names* "The Woods of Westermain" *as his finest poetic*

creation, but criticizes several unpoetic or awkward tendencies in the poems of the volume.]

[*Poems and Lyrics of the Joy of Earth*] is one of the most remarkable, perhaps the most remarkable, of the volumes of verse which have been put out during the last few years. But, indeed, the name of the author is a sufficient guarantee that so it would be; Mr. George Meredith is known to be little given to offering his readers that which is common.

Mr. Meredith is well known, by name, to the widest circle of readers—the novel-readers. By name, because his name is a label warning them not to touch. They know that in volumes which carry that mark they will not find the comfortable conventionalities and paste diamonds which make up their ideal of "life." Worse than this, Mr. Meredith's prose requires attention—an impertinent requirement on the part of a novelist. Everybody knows that we go to a novel in order that we may occupy a vacant mind without giving attention.

To a higher, and vastly smaller, circle of readers, Mr. Meredith's stories—*The Ordeal of Richard Feverel, Emilia in England, Vittoria, The Egoist*—are known as creations, singular without being eccentric, but whose singularity is marked by an imaginative presentment rather than by any special attraction of the characters and events presented. There is an atmosphere of poetry about the doings of his personages which gives us a happy fairy-land sensation, even when, as is often the case, we do not much care for the doings themselves. The circle (a select one) of the readers of these novels, know that Mr. Meredith is a poet—in prose. Perhaps some of them may not know that he is a poet in the more usual acceptation of the term. . . .

It is . . . no disparagement to say of the poems in the present volume that they are unequal in poetic merit. They all have the Meredithian quality, but in varying degrees of perfection. They are all out of the same vineyard, but of different vintages. To come to details. "**Love in the Valley**," *e.g.*, does not rise in general conception and design above the average level of the "minor poet" as we know him. For this reason it will probably be one of the most popular. It has also the ordinary fault of the modern English poetry—diffuseness, the beating out of a small particle of metal into too thin foil. Yet "**Love in the Valley**" is redeemed from commonness by single strokes which are not within the reach of everyday, as well as by a vigour of language which is Mr. Meredith's own property among all his competitors. (p. 37)

The piece which gives its character to the volume, and raises the whole above the average of the reproductions of Rossetti with which we are familiar, is the first, which is entitled "**The Woods of Westermain.**" This piece seizes the imagination with a power which the vague and rather featureless "**Daughter of Hades**" does not possess. Many poets have signalled the romance that lies in forest depths, "the calling shapes and beckoning shadows." No poetical forest has surpassed in wealth of suggestion "the woods of Westermain." In these woods is no wizardry; no supernatural agents are at work. But if you enter them with a poet's eye and a poet's sensibility you may see and hear that natural magic which surpasses all the fictitious tales of sorcerers, witches, wood gods, of Fauns and Dryads. The poem teaches, not didactically—for nothing is farther from its form or its thought than the inculcation of doctrine—how what we see depends upon what we are; how transcendent influences are only to be approached through the real. . . . The doctrine is old enough; the psychology of religion and that of poetry agree in it. Keats's Endymion, baffled in the search of

the ideal, learns to find it in the real. In "the woods of Westermain"—ordinary woods, peopled only by the squirrel and the snake, the green woodpecker and the night-jar—you may read the whole history of the origin and development of things. . . . In contrast with the pessimistic tone and despairing notes of the modern school, Mr. Meredith offers "a song of gladness," and smiles with Shakspere at a generation "ranked in gloomy noddings over life."

Such seems to be the drift of this remarkable lyric, remarkable rather for its expression than for its contents. Unfortunately, Mr. Meredith's healthy wisdom is veiled in the obscurity of a peculiar language which makes even his general drift doubtful, and the meaning of many score lines absolute darkness. Some writers, whom it is a fashion to admire, are obscure by twisting plain things into words that are not plain. They make platitudes into verbal puzzles. Mr. Meredith's obscurity proceeds from a better motive. He knows that poetry can only suggest, and destroys itself if it affirms. And as the moods he desires to suggest are remote from common experience, so also must the suggestive imagery be. Even the English language is inadequate to his requirements, and he tries to eke it out by daring compounds. The same resource tried long ago by Aeschylus was found to degenerate into bombast in a language which lends itself more readily to compounds than ours does. In Mr. Meredith's lines these compounds have seldom the merit of being happily formed or of condensing expression. If we allow that their use originated in the poverty of the existing language, the habit of employing them constantly and upon all occasions grows up from their trouble-saving convenience. They are stopgaps, and fill the place when the sense cannot be moulded into words proper without an expenditure of time which no modern writer will give. That the habit has settled itself upon Mr. Meredith's pen the following sample, taken from a very few pages, will show. We have—poppy-droop; bronze-orange; swan-wave; shore-bubble; rock-sourced; lost-to-light; instant-glancing; iron-resounding; spear-fitted; fool-flushed; ripple-feathered; dew-delighted; fountain-showers; stripe-shadowed; treasure-armful; circle-windsails; bully-drawlers; and so on without stint or limit. How many in the above collection, gathered at random, can be said to recommend themselves by their own elegance, or to be indispensable to the sense required, which most do but feebly express? (pp. 37-8)

Mark Pattison, in a review of "Poems and Lyrics of the Joy of Earth," in The Academy, *No. 585, July 21, 1883, pp. 37-8.*

ARTHUR SYMONS   (essay date 1885)

[*While Symons initially gained notoriety as an English decadent of the 1890s, he eventually established himself as one of the most important critics of the modern era. As a member of the iconoclastic generation of fin de siècle aesthetes that included Aubrey Beardsley and Oscar Wilde, Symons wholeheartedly assumed the role of the world-weary cosmopolite and sensation hunter, composing verses in which he attempted to depict the bohemian world of the modern artist. He was also a gifted linguist whose sensitive translations from Paul Verlaine and Stéphane Mallarmé provided English poets with an introduction to the poetry of the French Symbolists. However, it was as a critic that Symons made his most important contribution to literature. His The Symbolist Movement in Literature (1899) provided his English contemporaries with an appropriate vocabulary with which to define their new aesthetic—one that communicated their concern with dreamlike states, imagination, and a reality that exists beyond the boundaries of the senses. Symons also discerned that the concept of the symbol as a vehicle by which a "hitherto unknown reality was suddenly revealed" could become the basis for the entire modern aesthetic. A proper use of the symbol "would flash upon you the soul of that which can be apprehended only by the soul—the finer sense of things unseen, the deeper meaning of things evident." This anticipated and influenced James Joyce's concept of an artistic "epiphany," T. S. Eliot's "moment in time," and laid the foundation for much of modern poetic theory. In the following excerpt, Symons reviews* Diana of the Crossways, *calling the lack of a wide circle of Meredith admirers as acute a satire on public taste as any novel that Meredith ever wrote. Symons maintains that Meredith's call for "philosophy in fiction" intimidates the reading public, while his difficult style is a further barrier to a wide popularity. Charlotte M. Yonge, referred to in the excerpt, was a prolific and popular novelist who infused her work with lofty Anglican spiritual sentiments.]*

Mr. Meredith's latest novel [*Diana of the Crossways*] is the event of the day to a small, but very select and very devoted, circle of admirers. That it should be this, and little more than this, is a practical satire on contemporary taste more convincingly bitter than the sharpest of Mr. Meredith's purposed epigrams. Is the general public then truly given over to its "rose-pink" and "dirty drab," its rose-pink of sentimentalism, its dirty drab of so-called realism? Certainly when Charlotte M. Yonge is openly adored, and Emile Zola sneakingly relished, it looks like it. To read, without the trouble of a thought, to read with lazy acquiescence, with agreeable sensations of relish, softly charmed by the mild radiance of the rose-pink, shrewdly appealed to by the strong savour of the dirty drab; that seems to be the ideal of the novel reader. And of course he gets what he wants. Union is strength, and the novel readers are a strong band, firmly formed against the foe, shoulder to shoulder. "Everybody knows," says Mark Pattison, "that we go to a novel in order that we may occupy a vacant mind without giving attention"; and he remarks it in explanation of Mr. Meredith's unpopularity [see excerpt dated 1883]. "Mr. Meredith's prose requires attention—an impertinent requirement on the part of a novelist." As a consequence—I still quote Pattison—his name is a label warning novel readers not to touch.

To reflect on it makes one feel sermonic. Here is a man who for a quarter of a century has been producing a series of the most brilliant novels, written in English, since the death of Thackeray; a man whom Swinburne and Myers name in the same breath with George Eliot; and for the general public, for the public that buys up editions and makes what is called a "success," he is still only a name, and a name of terror. (p. 632)

Let us look at a few of his leading characteristics, and see if they seem very likely to harmonise with the public taste. In the first place, Mr. Meredith conceives that the novelist's prime study is human nature, his first duty to be true to it. Moreover, being an artist, he is not content with simple observations; there must be creation, the imaginative fusion of the mass of observed fact. And it should be noticed that to Mr. Meredith, human nature does not begin and end in those surface traits which we carelessly seem to know our friends by, and which can be cunningly selected and joined together without difficulty by any clever story-teller. It is needful to say it, because this operation is often considered very profound, and the result a wonderful triumph of psychology, human nature in photograph almost. To Mr. Meredith the conditions of truth seem harder; and I suppose they seem very hard indeed to the reader.

Philosophy in fiction; that is Mr. Meredith's demand in the introduction to *Diana of the Crossways*, and it is for philosophy

in fiction that he has been battling all his days. Do not ask if this is the road to popularity; the very word is ominous to the reader of novels. Philosophy in fiction! Double notes of exclamation cannot convey the emphasis with which I hear it shrilled in chorus. . . . An obtuse public requires a revelation of human nature in a series of explosions, galvanically directed acts, with little expressed connection, cause, or likelihood; only startling. Above all, there must be those "set scenes of catching pathos and humour," which Mr. Meredith declines to supply. Why? He declines to supply them, he consciously, purposely loses what are called "good points," because it is not in nature to run to a crisis at every action. When they come, in the course of things, he rises to them, and treats them grandly, as he alone can; but he does not strain for them, nor break the right development of events for a sensation's sake. With a reliance profoundly true and artistic he subordinates incident and character, working everywhere under the lead of philosophy in fiction.

This philosophy of his seeking is only another name for intuition, analysis, imaginative insight. It can subsist, I suppose, without creation. It should presuppose this, as in Mr. Meredith it does. He has comprehension of a character from height to depth through that "eye of steady flame," which he attributes to Shakespeare, and which may be defined in every great artist. He sees it, he beholds a complete nature, at once and in entirety. His task is to make others see what he sees. But this cannot be done at a stroke. It must be done little by little, touch upon touch, light upon shade, shade upon light. The completeness, as seen by the seer or creator—the term is the same—must be microscopically investigated, divided into its component parts, produced piece by piece, and connected visibly. It is this that is meant when we talk of analysis; and the antithesis between analysis and creation is hardly so sheer as it seems. Partly through a selection of appropriate action, partly though the revealing casual speech, the imagined character takes palpable form; finally it does, or it should, live and breathe before the reader with some likeness of the hue and breath of actual life. Here it would seem we must stop, to judge by the conduct of most of our esteemed writers. But there is a step farther, and it is this step that Mr. Meredith is strenuous to take. You have the flesh, animate it with spirit, with soul. Here is the task for the creator. If his eye be not of steady flame, if it falter here, he is lost. But seeing with the perfect completeness of that vision, it is possible, step by step, with a trained multitude of the keenest words of our speech, to make plain, though in our groping twilight, the incredible acts of the soul. If this is an unworthy aim, contemn Shakespeare. This is Mr. Meredith's, and it is this and no other consummation that he prays for in demanding philosophy in fiction. As to the chances of popularity with our public, I have not observed that our present "favourite novelists" aspire to philosophy in fiction.

Then again, Mr. Meredith's style is a singular one. His swift-glancing wit is very trying to the general reader, his irony is terrible in its subtle unexpectedness. The public loves an easy style; a style that it considers direct, not trifling. Mr. Meredith's style is confessedly not easy; but the difficulty in it is due very much to a careful attempt at that very directness and veracity which men ignorantly worship. . . . The main peculiarity of Mr. Meredith's style is this: he thinks, to begin with, before writing—a singular thing, one may observe, in the present day. Then, having certain definite thoughts to express, and thoughts frequently of a difficult remoteness, he is careful to employ words of a rich and fruitful significance, made richer and more fruitful by a studied and uncommon arrangement. His sentences are architectural, and every word is a plain or an adorned piece of masonry fitting into the general structure. It is natural that in reading him you are inclined to cry out at the strangeness; perhaps you will add, the affectation. It is not affectation, but a rarely-revealed nature, such as we usually expect in poets, but are not thankful for in prose writers. The poet's cunning use of words in another than the common way; his art in surcharging them with a wealth of spiritual meaning. This is a commonplace of our criticism, and is accepted in the poet. Why not then in the man of prose? Mr. Meredith, who is likewise so fine a poet in the actual metre, is, in this sense, as well as in others, a poet in prose.

But I have mentioned his wit. Everybody acknowledges the wit. Wit surely is popular! Then why not Mr. Meredith's? It is not popular, in the first place, because it is too dazzling for weak eyes; because it is too fantastical, too learned, remote, allusive; very much because it is subtly ironical; perhaps most of all because it is shrewdly stinging to our prejudices. What is known as "social satire" is very taking; the more rabid the better. But it is so by compromise. The satirist must chuckle behind the sneer, must wink in token of concealed amity behind the mask of the professional Diogenes, and the public will be ready in return to smile a pleasant enjoyment. But if the satirist is very much in earnest, and terribly bitter, and terribly true, it is another matter. Like the greatest of his fellows, Mr. Meredith is not a story-teller merely, he is a spiritual fighter. His shafts are deadly to the dull, the sham, the conventional; the cruelty of the world, its folly, tyranny, and panics, its ancestral treatment of women—a pet topic, and a dangerous. . . . This satire is too quiet, too clinging, too pervasive and incontestable, to be taking. The *sauce piquante* to the British palate is a lighter condiment than this, which is prepared from a recipe not in its cookery books.

Thus much of Mr. Meredith's present chances of popularity beyond that small circle to which I referred; the circle of persons who think. (pp. 633-35)

Arthur Symons, "Mr. Meredith's Latest Novel," in Time, *London, n.s. Vol. XII, No. 5, May, 1885, pp. 632-36.*

WILLIAM WATSON (essay date 1889)

[*Watson was an English poet and critic who maintained that a writer should be an integral part of the social and intellectual life of an era and contribute to decisions of public policy. One of his primary aims as a poet was to elucidate current affairs; for that reason, he wrote much occasional poetry. He was alien to the aesthetic temper of his era—the 1890s—and in fact held more imaginative realms of poetry to be the province of the second-rate. Selected to compose the official elegy for Tennyson, "Lacrimae Musarum" (1892), he appeared to be Tennyson's successor to the position of poet laureate. However, Watson's strong anti-imperialist views, expressed in particular in* The Purple East *(1889) and his numerous denunciations of the Boer War were probably responsible for his being passed over for that position. Although knighted in 1917, Watson died an impoverished and embittered man. In the following excerpt Watson attacks Meredith's fiction as "anaemic," lacking in skillful plot and believable characterization, and further marred by an obscure style. Richard Le Gallienne (1890) responded to Watson's article with a defense of Meredith as a novelist.*]

Mr. George Meredith was in the field long before Mr. Howells or Mr. James, but although he has been writing for upwards of a quarter of a century, the credit of discovering his tran-

scendent greatness has apparently been reserved for the crescent generation. On the whole, the lateness of the discovery may well give us pause in our acceptance of it as a genuine "find." A poet may have, and frequently has, his due recognition by the public unjustly and cruelly retarded, but such a fate is hardly possible to the novelist, and it may be questioned whether a single decisive instance of it can be pointed to in the whole record of English literature. . . . [There] is a novel-reading public which is not only large but may really be said to be always on tiptoe so see and applaud everything first-rate in fiction— a public actively bent upon allowing nothing good in that kind to escape it. It is a vigilant public, a hungry public, a public of gourmands, ever avid for some new dish, and interested even in a new sauce. . . . Now Mr. George Meredith always had *some* readers, at least enough to form the requisite nucleus for a novelist's public. How comes it that this public held off so long? Why, until the other day, was this all-capacious epicure so loth to be feasted?

One can hear an admirer replying that although Mr. Meredith is one of the master minds of the age, who has chosen the novel as the medium through which to utter his burden, this selection of a vehicle has been in a sense accidental, and the so-called novel-reading public are not precisely the people at whom he aims, or whose intellectual jurisdiction he acknowledges. This is much as if one should write stage-plays, and use means to get them acted, at the same time disclaiming any ambition of pleasing a theatrical audience. If a man has a burden to utter, why select for his expressional medium the one form in favour with that one class whose ears and whose suffrages he neither expects nor desires to gain?. . . Dickens, Thackeray, George Eliot—surely Mr. Meredith's peers—had confidence that a fair verdict could be obtained from a representative jury of novel-readers; and if a novelist carries his appeal to some other court, even though a higher court—denying the authority of the one tribunal which his fellows submit to as decisive— it is because he is not essentially and primarily a novelist at all. Yet the claim which Mr. Meredith's admirers put forward on his behalf is that he is the greatest novelist of the age.

Now it is easy, and it is also unfair, to quarrel with anything because it is not something else. We have no right to anathematise a still wine because it does not sparkle, or a white one because it is not red. Besides, real greatness can afford to have plenty of very real faults. . . . But when greatness is claimed for a novelist, there are certain broad and obvious tests which it is both pertinent and natural to apply, and by which he must submit to stand or fall. Is he great at construction? Is he great as a master of narrative? Is he great as an artist in dialogue? Is he great as a creator of character? It is perhaps conceivable that a novelist may be found wanting in one or more of these cardinal virtues, and yet be able to make good his claim to a somewhat unbalanced and maimed greatness; but this much at least is certain, that if he staggers equally under the application of all these tests, the validity of his title to greatness is irreversibly disproved.

Criticism in superlatives is so much the habit of the day that no one perhaps attaches much importance, or even meaning, to announcements like Mr. Louis Stevenson's that **Rhoda Fleming** is "the strongest thing in English letters since Shakespeare died." Such utterances are scarcely taken seriously, and it is hard to believe that they are even meant seriously. As a matter of fact, **Rhoda Fleming** is not even Mr. Meredith's own "strongest thing." Like most of his books, it is an ill-constructed and very unequally written story, having some fine scenes and clever, if unattractive, character studies. If only an author could live by virtue of sporadic good things! But a novelist, at all events, cannot. . . . It may be much to a reader's discredit that he is forced to confess ignorance or uncertainty on . . . vital points [of plot], but the incidents are so confused, the story in places is such a jungle, and the task of "thridding the sombre boskage" of this thicket of narrative is so laborious and cheerless, that even a fairly vigilant reader is often finding himself at fault in this way. And the obscurity which frequently hangs about Mr. Meredith's narrative has no such excuse as a canvas crowded with figures, or an elaborately complex structure of incidents might supply. In the way of story he has not very much to tell, and he is obscure simply because he has not an aptitude for telling it. There is literally no construction, but a certain not too great abundance of material lying loose about in various stages of disorder.

In such a book as *Diana of the Crossways,* the thinness of the subject-matter may be forgiven in consideration of the frequently glittering dialogue, and the brilliance of the author's asides. But in *Rhoda Fleming* we have nothing of that; the people are mostly humble country-folk, or are supposed to be, for to tell the truth Mr. Meredith is not at home with them, and makes them talk neither like country-folk nor any other well-defined class of whom one has experience. Rhoda herself, it must be owned, says extremely little throughout the whole story, and is to be congratulated on her attainments in silence, seeing that her father, whom the author depicts as a plain, rough, bluff, matter-of-fact, everyday English yeoman, is made to talk in this imaginative fashion—"That letter sticks to my skull as though it meant to say, 'You've not understood me yet.' . . . In any case, Robert, you'll feel for me as a father. I'm shut in a dark room, with a candle blown out. I've heard of a sort of fear you have in that dilemmer, lest you should lay your fingers on edges of sharp knives, and if I think a step—if I go thinking a step, and feel my way, I do cut myself, and I bleed, I do."

In this book, Edward Blancove's brother, Algernon, is a clever and faithful, but uninteresting and profitless study of the heartless and brainless young man of the upper classes. What impels Mr. Meredith to produce such careful photographs of this dreary type of humanity it is not easy to see. The limited truth of photography is there certainly, together with its unlimited hardness; but that is all.

Mr. Meredith's real powers are much better shown in such a book as *Diana of the Crossways.* He is essentially an artifical writer, and when he tries to move freely and look at his ease among simple folk he fails. If one may so put it, naturalness is not natural to him; but when he is frankly artificial, he is then himself, and may be expected, at least intermittently, to coruscate. In *Diana* he is frankly artificial, and produces a clever and entertaining book. Twice, indeed, the interest in the mere story rises high, making us regret all the more that the author usually thinks it good form to have so little to tell. Elsewhere the story is attenuated enough, and the interest mostly centres in the brilliancy of the casual comment on society. This is often sparkling and keen. The account of Diana Warwick's peculiar position and social arts is about as good as anything of the kind could be. (pp. 170-75)

Occasionally an aphorism as concise as true falls from his pen, as when he finely says, "Observation is the most enduring of the pleasures of life." But, speaking generally, Mr. Meredith's admirers exaggerate his epigrammatic talent, real and considerable as it is, and overlook the fact that the epigrams, even when good, are often in the way. The hard staccato movement, and brittle snip-snap of conversations literally carried on in epigrams, tires the reader. It is not dialogue, but a series of mental percussions. . . . Mr. Meredith is a wit: thus much may be conceded. But a great wit he is not, and his *esprit,* such as it is, exhibited in season and out of season, plays him in an ill turn almost as often as it does him real service. It is a fine keen rapier blade, but you cannot plough a field with it. Or it is an amusing companion in whose society Mr. Meredith neglects his business. And this liability to be diverted from the main matter in hand is too apt to infect his whole method of work. With conscientious art and with a vigorous hand he sketches some minor and unimportant figure, while he leaves his chief personages half-defined. (p. 176)

Mr. Meredith really pays scant courtesy to an average reader's intelligence. . . . But, in truth, orderly and natural evolution of incident is one of the things Mr. Meredith hardly ever has at his command; and such a deficiency, needless to say, is more than a mere surface-flaw in a novelist; it is a vital and radical defect, and inevitably relegates him to an inferior rank among imaginative creators. Nay, more, it proves his essential unfitness for the novelist's task—an unfitness which may, of course, co-exist, as in him it undoubtedly does co-exist, with many extraneous gifts and graces. Is it extravagant to surmise that Mr. Meredith's early adventure in a quite different field, that of arabesque romance—has left a fatal mark upon all his subsequent and quite dissimilar work? Absence of logical progression, of natural outgrowth and sequence—a glaring want of organic evolution in narrative—this is what vitiates his stories, destroying them as works of art. In profuse but disorderly brilliance he can heap together blocks of porphyry and chalcedony and jasper: he cannot build. In that astonishing feat of unbridled fancy *The Shaving of Shagpat,* such a defect is scarce distinguishable from a virtue. There we are delighted with the mere reign of lawlessness, the riot and anarchy of invention, the magnificent irresponsibility and libertinism of a dream. There we are content to wander through gorgeous palaces of enchantment, without requiring that they shall have any foundation more solid than a cloud or a sunbow. But something of this unchecked, self-chartered freedom seems to appertain to Mr. Meredith's literary methods in departments of imagination where it is wholly out of place, with the result that his leading incidents often lack not only moral inevitableness but artistic cohesion. It is not thus that masters of fiction weave their web of human lives and fates. (p. 178)

"But *The Egoist,*" one hears some disciple of Mr. Meredith asking; "what of that unique masterpiece, *The Egoist*?" For that is the novel which seems to call forth more unlimited enthusiasm among the members of a certain esoteric cult than any other of our author's works. That is pre-eminently the sacred book by which the faithful swear. (p. 179)

Well, it is only fair to avow that I distrust myself to speak of *The Egoist.* A critic can only record his own impressions, always taking care to test and revise them by such light as his own private study of the principles of literary art may lend him; and speaking in sober literalness, with due attention to the force and value of words, my impression of the *The Egoist* is that it is the most entirely wearisome book purporting to be a novel that I ever toiled through in my life. . . . Opinions and tastes may be questioned; delight in a thing cannot be argued with. Although Sir Willoughby Patterne, his insufferable selfishness, his colossal puppyism, his stilted phraseology, and his endless triflings with the hearts of the very unrealisable women who revolve around him, are to me simply soporific in their monotony and inanity, it is none the less clear that the book has qualities which fascinate some superior minds, and a reader who cannot enjoy them will do best to recognize the fact that he is not one of Mr. Meredith's elect, acknowledge his own limitedness, and say no more about it. On the subject, however, of literary style, even a person not preordained from the beginning of things to appreciate Mr. Meredith's peculiar intellectuality, may venture to say a word. In all this author's books one is apt to be irritated by occasional verbal extravagances usually taking the form of a perverse reluctance to say a plain thing in a plain way. "Hippias perspired conviction." Somebody "infrigidated a congenial atmosphere by an overflow of exclamatory wonderment." "Her head performed the negative." "His novel assimilation to the rat-rabble of amatory intriguers tapped him on the shoulder unpleasantly," and so forth. But what is at worst a rather too frequent indulgence elsewhere, becomes in *The Egoist* a habitual vice. Hardly a page but is disfigured by some fantastic foppery of expression. . . . "A strong smell of something left out struck Dr. Corney." (This gentleman says to a boy, "You are worthy of a gratuitous breakfast in the front parlour of the best hotel of the place they call Arcadia.") "Clara swam to meet them." "The celestial irony suffused her, and she bathed and swam on it." "She swam for a brilliant instant on tears." "Mrs. Mountstuart swam upon Willoughby." (All the people in Mr. Meredith's novels swim a great deal in conversation, besides frequently "pouncing" and "plumping" upon one another.) "De Craye shadowed a deep droop on the bend of his head before Clara." (This means he bowed to her.) . . . What kind of English is the following—"This petrifation of egoism would from amazedly to austerely refuse the petition.". . . . (pp. 180-81)

No milder word than detestable can be applied to the preposterous style of which the foregoing sentences are examples, and vile as it is, it is surpassed in extremity of insufferableness by the—what shall we call it? Intellectual coxcombry seems a blunt phrase, but is any courteous phrase available that will adequately describe the airs of superiority, the affectations of originality, the sham profundities, the counterfeit subtleties, the pseudo-oracularisms of this book? "The poet is at once the spectre of the kitchen-midden and our ripest issue." "The Egoist is the Son of Himself: he is also the Father." Pretentious verbiage like this, spread over three volumes, which contain no more solid substance in the shape of actual story than might have been fitly compressed into three chapters, becomes, to a common-sense reader, simply nauseating. As for the meagre and bloodless puppets that jibber and posture before us in lieu of credible human figures, Mr. Meredith himself has unintentionally described them by anticipation long ago in *The Ordeal of Richard Feverel*. Honest Farmer Blaize is looking at the coloured prints in a book of feminine fashions, and is requested to admire the attitudes. "Attitoods!" he exclaims. "Why, they're all attitood! They're nothing but attitood!"

To be the idol of the aesthetes, the darling of the superior people, is perhaps a hard fate, but no one can be held accountable for the antics of his own admirers. Rather is he to be condoled with on the folly of his friends, the friends from whom, perhaps, he deserves to be saved. Severe criticism will not necessarily kill even the worst and most meretricious writer, but such a one cannot long survive deification. We see hurry, strain, fatigue, written even upon Mr. Meredith's best work; what true service is rendered him by pitting him against the easeful, victorious masters?. . . We have many delightful novelists still amongst us, and their charm is usually strongest

when they seem freest from any supposed obligation to be great, from any tendency to assume that greatness is expected of them. They are the men—and women—who have gauged their own powers, recognized their own limits; who know what they can do, and do it quietly. Mr. Meredith is not one of them. He tries to do something more, and a look of defeat, of frustration, of perplexity, hangs about his partial achievement. It is painfully reflected in his style, which suggests a perpetual craning forward to snatch something that swings out of reach. Now, mere ease of style often gets more credit than is its due. It is ease with power, or ease with splendour, that is the valuable thing. Anybody can be at ease in a shooting-jacket and knickerbockers. To look comfortable in court-dress is distinction. Either costume has its recommendations; but Mr. Meredith seems to fancy himself in combination of the two, and the effect is not happy. It is not a sartorial triumph. A style that seems at once stiff without dignity and lax without ease; a style that attempts rapidity, to achieve fuss; a style aggressively marked and mannered, an intractable style that takes the initiative, leads the way, dominates the situation, when it should be (as style should always be in prose fiction) simply an obedient instrument, a blade to carve with, not to be flashed in our eyes; the possession of such a style may not seem to argue a high degree of fitness for any line of literary effort, but it does assuredly indicate a special degree of unfitness for the task of telling a story. And in truth Mr. Meredith can at all events do anything else better than he can tell a story. Without constructive ability, without power to conceive and fashion forth realisable human creatures, without aptitude for natural evolution of incident, without the *raconteur's* instinct for knowing what will keep his company awake, he has yet many endowments. He is an epigrammatist, with scintillations of steely-cold wit; he is a poet, with glimpses of beauty; he is a social essayist, with acute observation and suggestive criticism of human conditions and conventions. He is all these excellent things, and more; and the fault is nature's rather than his, that he is not a novelist. (pp. 181-83)

William Watson, "Fiction—Plethoric and Anaemic," in The National Review, *London, Vol. XIV, No. 80, October, 1889, pp. 167-83.**

RICHARD LE GALLIENNE (essay date 1890)

[*Le Gallienne was an English poet, essayist, and novelist who was associated early in his career with the fin de siècle movement of literary aestheticism that is commonly referred to as the Decadent movement. The literature of the Decadents, which grew out of French aestheticism, displays a fascination with perverse and morbid states; a search for novelty and sensation (the frisson nouveau, or "new thrill"); a preoccupation with both mysticism and nihilism; and the assertion of an essential enmity between art and life implicit in the "art for art's sake" doctrine. In their writings the Decadents routinely violated accepted moral and ethical standards, often for shock value alone. Most of Le Gallienne's poetry appeared in the journal* The Yellow Book, *the primary organ of the English Decadents, and he was a cofounder of the Rhymers' Club, an informal group of poets associated with Decadence that included Dowson and W. B. Yeats. In the following excerpt, Le Gallienne responds to William Watson's negative assessment of Meredith's achievement as a novelist (see excerpt dated 1889), calling it representative of the opinion the general public holds of Meredith as a "novelist's novelist" whom it is difficult to appreciate.*]

How horrific . . . is the title of Mr. William Watson's article [see excerpt dated 1889]. He calls Mr. George Meredith's work "anaemic," and if "anaemic" will not frighten his admirers, are they not bold indeed? It is ill disturbing the happily-buried, and I but resurrect Mr. Watson's article on "Fiction—Plethoric and Anaemic"—of which three pages deal with Mr. Robert Buchanan, and fourteen with Mr. George Meredith—that it may serve as a text. For it is interesting, not so much as serious criticism, but as the British Public's long insensitive disregard of Mr. Meredith finding voice, and endeavouring to justify itself, graceless and unrepentant. It is also curious as being one more proof of that futility of criticism which we all hold as a creed—and follow as a creed. Indeed, Meredith "literature," even within the camp, has already most abundantly illustrated that. For example—almost every novel of Mr. Meredith's in succession has by one or another critic been declared his masterpiece. (pp. 307-08)

"Mr. Meredith writes such English as is within the reach of no other living man," says a critic, in *The Daily News*. "His style," says James Thomson, "is very various and flexible, flowing freely in whatever measures the subject and mood may dictate. At its best it is so beautiful in simple Saxon, so majestic in rhythm, so noble with noble imagery, so pregnant with meaning, so vital and intense, that it must be ranked among the supreme achievements of our literature." . . . [Yet] Mr. Watson, (though not wishing to be thought rude) holds that "no milder word than detestable can be applied to" (that "supreme achievement of our literature,") "the preposterous style.". . . And so on *ad infinitum*, till the brain fairly reels with contradiction, and in agony of soul, one calls again, "what, indeed, *is* the use of criticism?" Is it any use? Waiting for a clearer mood wherein to answer the question, when our eyes have grown a little accustomed to these mists of confusion, we may come to see some solid ground whereon to stand. After all, these contradictory figures have a common denominator, and by that may be illustrated what is to my mind the one yet very notable service of criticism. Whatever else is to be proven, one thing is certain, that George Meredith is a centre of power, of whatever nature, in whatever degree, no matter. So much have we learnt by being thus sent, as we say, "from pillar to post."

And that, indeed, is all that criticism should say with any tone of finality—here is a notable figure, consider him! . . . It is not impossible that after all this wrangling about Mr. Meredith's novels, posterity in its quiet way will go up to the shelf and lay its hand on *Modern Love*. Who knows? (pp. 308-10)

[As] to the objection against Mr. Meredith's dialogue, that all his characters talk Meredith, that never man spake like this man, and so on, does not the same apply to Shakspere and Mr. Browning? Yet I don't think Hamlet or Lippo Lippi are less alive to us for that. Literalness is not the essential of dialogue, truth to the spirit of the speaker is. There are many instances when the letter would distort the whole significance of a character—indeed, it is oftener so than not. If the novelist *is* to use dialogue, why should he be refused the same freedom with it as the dramatist or the poet? But, indeed, only one of Mr. Watson's provisions is fundamental—that the novelist should be able to tell a story. What story and how he tells it is his business, not ours. Dialogue or disquisition matters not, so that the end is reached; the end of presenting to us a living thing, for in Art the end does justify the means. Character-drawing is really included in that fundamental power, for unless we have a living sense of the *dramatis personae*, the story is not really told at all. A chronicle of what happened to lay-figure M or N may be interesting, but till we know who or

what either was it is not a story. Events have no significance of themselves—except to schoolboys, who get over the difficulty by appropriating them, through their imaginations, to themselves. (p. 313)

To show how any being or fact is alive is the end of all Art, and especially of the novelist's. If he can do that for half-a-dozen he has succeeded. Why should "the million" or the average intelligence be the test of Art? Fame, either present or posthumous, is no test. It may be (as it would seem to be in Mr. Meredith's case) that the novelist's methods of presentation are eccentric and difficult, that his particular story needs a new technology, like science. (pp. 313-14)

There is no reason why he should do his work in the British vernacular. It is time the superstition of "good plain Saxon" was exploded. To do much with little is a fine quality, but to *do* is the essential, and once done, neither number and variety of tools nor prodigality of material can depreciate perfection.

That Mr. Meredith does not write the vernacular, at least in that of his work which is most really his own, that which we can find nowhere else, does not really so much matter as may at first sight appear; for, supposing it imaginable as having been written in any other style, in their own Saxon, would *The Egoist* have had any stronger appeal to "the general" than it has at present? I think not, for though to some of us, there is there an unmistakably living man (and the greatest masters cannot do more than make his creations alive), and a story as much tragedy as "a comedy in narrative;" he is a man who, if they could be made to understand him, could not possibly interest them, and it is a tragedy which they could not appreciate, for there are not four deaths in the fifth act—only the marriage of a girl whose soul has been slowly atrophied with a man who has come to be but the corpse of her god. You cannot really appeal to the heart (by which one means the elemental centre within us) without first appealing to the brain, and the average brain is still busy with the obvious. In this respect Mr. Meredith is really in the position of a poet's poet—one might call him the novelist's novelist. Indeed, it is a question for thought, it seems to me, if that is not always the position of every great artist. It is a commonplace to say that he is always in advance of his age, but does posterity ever catch up with him? There is a great deal more cant than truth in the chatter about the universal appeal of Shakspere, and who is it that reads Dante? The fact is, that posterity is as much in the dark as their own age was, but a few dead critics have made a noise about them, so it tries to get over the difficulty by unintelligently making a superstition of them. Was it Thoreau who said that the great artists have really been taken by the world on the faith of a few critics? That was certainly a fine saying of his—"The great poets have never yet been read by mankind, for only great poets can read them." And yet, at the same time, there are at least two of Mr. Meredith's books that should make that "universal appeal," one thinks, dealing with interests near home, and written mainly in the vernacular. Surely there is plenty of "human interest" and ruddy enough humour in *Evan Harrington*, and I cannot imagine a public taking *Adam Bede*, and finding nothing in *Rhoda Fleming*. *Richard Feverel* is largely on another plane and makes a subtler appeal, but if it gave one critic (I forget where I read his words) the idea that Mr. Meredith should be able to write a good boys' book, there must be much in it to suit the public, for, after all, "boy's books" are really what the public want. (pp. 314-15)

But while it is really Mr. Meredith's stories for which his critics have no taste, it is about his style that they make the great fuss—it is even a stumbling-block to the wise, at times. . . . Everybody agrees in quoting the Ferdinand and Miranda passage in **Richard Feverel** as perfection, everybody quotes it in small type. . . . But his phrase-making! It seems hopeless to expect agreement upon that. With Mr. Watson it stands for nothing but "intellectual coxcombry.". . . (p. 315)

Every artistic message needs a new medium for its expression peculiar to itself, as surely as each new soul finds a new body; and to me it seems impossible to imagine, vain to hope for, a style more adapted for the work which it is called on to do than Mr. Meredith's.

His power of metaphor is certainly unequalled by any English contemporary known to me, and to me it seems that not since Shakspere has there been a handling of imaginative phrase more truly masculine. The manner in which continually a vivid word comes like a flash of lightning and lights up some hidden track of thought, some inaccessible lair of sensation, fairly takes one's breath at times. It hardly seems to be metaphor at all, but the very process of thought and feeling literally described.

The distinction between objective and subjective is overleaped, and we seem to see matters of spirit and nerve with our very physical eyes. Indeed, that is just what such art as Mr. Meredith's must do; for in proportion as it is art, will the relevancy of that distinction diminish, if it is true, as surely it is, that the subjective once embodied in art really becomes objective. It is this very realistic closeness to the fact, I am persuaded, that has misled many, unfamiliar with the *nuances* of experience with which it deals, to charge Mr. Meredith with fantasticality. His fancy is prolific and delightful indeed, or we must have missed **Shagpat** from our shelves, but the metaphor I speak of comes of a higher power with which Mr. Meredith is no less richly endowed—imagination. His images have roots, they are there for another service than fancies. Moreover, he has apparently discovered the secret of a mental process which operates more or less with us all, but of which we are only occasionally, some perhaps never, conscious; for, is it not true that all impressions come to the most unimaginative through a medium of imagination more or less fantastic in its influence, and that thus the most commonplace occurrence often assumes the quaintest guise? Through the subtlety of his imagination Mr. Meredith has come into possession of this distorting glass, and it is either because we have never realised the process in ourselves, or are unable to recognise it again in his characters that he may sometimes seem puzzling or overstrained. In short, Mr. Meredith's imagination is subtle enough to embody the workings of imagination. (pp. 315-16)

I am convinced that the majority of Mr. Meredith's so-called fantasticalities have such true imaginative basis, and that if the reader cannot realise it, the fault is certainly his own. Not that I would say that Mr. Meredith never misses. Like everyone else, he has "the defects of his qualities," and it would not be difficult to place one's finger on images that seem the result of his employing his method in uninspired moments—a certain bewildering and unbeautiful personification of old Time, for instance, on an early page of **The Tragic Comedians**—but such are quite inconsiderable set against page after page of brilliant success. (p. 317)

I do not feel the superior person that Mr. William Watson says the admirer of Mr. Meredith always does feel. Moreover, though I know a great many admirers of Mr. Meredith, as yet I have not found in them either that peculiar conceit. Really, I think Mr. Watson must have made a mistake, or maybe he has been

amongst some of those people who turn every new faith into a cant before it is a week old. There are such in town. If so, I sincerely sympathise with him. (p. 318)

Richard Le Gallienne, "The Meredithyramb and Its Critics," in Time, *London, March, 1890, pp. 307-19.*

WILLIAM CRARY BROWNELL (essay date 1901)

[*Brownell was an American literary critic who preceded the New Humanist movement in letters and philosophy and is often associated with it. New Humanism was a critical movement which subscribed to the belief that the aesthetic qualities of any literary work must be subordinated to its moral and ethical purpose. The New Humanists, led by Irving Babbitt and Paul Elmer More, have often been perceived as following in the footsteps of Brownell, who in his* Victorian Prose Masters *(1901),* American Prose Masters *(1909),* Criticism *(1914), and* Standards *(1917), took just such an approach to literary criticism. Central to Brownell's critical method is his belief that a critic's analysis of a given work should be founded on a thorough knowledge of art, culture, and ideas. Traditional moral and artistic standards assimilated by the critic could then be applied to particular works, yielding critical judgments based on the objective criteria of a culture rather than the subjective preferences of the critic. In his criticism, Brownell also sought to articulate "the abstract qualities informing the concrete expression of the artist," believing that the essential task of criticism is "the pertinent characterization of great writers, in the mind and art of whom their works are co-ordinated with an explicitness and effectiveness not to be attained by any detailed and objective analysis of the works themselves." In the following excerpt, Brownell discusses Meredith's skillful portrayal of female characters, noting that Meredith stressed in his fiction that women are as psychologically, morally, and ethically complex as men.*]

[A] considerable part of Mr. Meredith's vogue is probably due to his treatment of women, which is very special, and for that reason no doubt has especially won the suffrages of "the sex," as he is fond of calling it. . . . It can hardly have escaped observers of such phenomena that it is as a sex that, currently, women particularly appreciate being treated as individuals. The more marked such treatment is, the more justice they feel is done to the sex. Mr. Meredith's treatment of them is in this respect very marked. . . . With his women readers he has accordingly been, perhaps, particularly successful. He makes it unmistakably clear that women are psychologically worth while, complex, intricate and multifarious in mind as well as complicated in nature. He makes a point of this and underscores it, in a way that produces a certain effect of novelty by the stress he lays on it. The justice so fully rendered is given the fillip of seeming tardy justice, and therefore an element of Mr. Meredith's originality among writers of fiction. This is a good deal, but I think it is witness of a still greater originality in him that he goes still further. He lays even greater stress upon the fact that the being thus intricately interesting and worthy of scrutiny from the constitution of her individual personality is also that most interesting of all personalities, a feminine one. He adds the requisite touch of chivalry. He is, after all, a true *aficionado* of "the sex." He can be trusted to understand, not to be too literal, not to forget that the singularization implied in apotheosis is a very different thing from that involved in limitation. Women are to be discriminated as individuals, like men, but the fact that they possess in common and as women a certain distinctive quality is, above all, not to be lost sight of. This is the permanent, the *ewig* ["eternal"], fact about them. Only it is to be taken as a crown, not as a mere label.

Having thus won their confidence, he may say what he chooses without risk, of misinterpretation at their hands. . . . He runs no risk of being thought to have "a contempt for women," of being thought superficial, that is to say. His talk about women is really as clever as that. A celebrated novelist of the present day is said to have remarked that he had reached a point finally when he could say anything he liked. Mr. Meredith has always been able to do that in the, for fiction, immense field concerned with women. It is—may one say?—almost touching to note the success with which by the simple means of compensatory magnification he contrives to be most uncompromising in his treatment of their defects. They have waited so long, some of them doubtless think, to be taken seriously in just this way and to just this extent!

One of his notable contentions, which he thus sets forth in security, is that women are morally quite as complex as men, and in virtue of an equally developed organization rather than of a contradictory and capricious nature. This is one of his main themes. The sexes have their differences, as he frequently points out, but he finds an exact equivalence here. And the idea is, in the prominence that it receives from him, probably a genuine contribution to fiction. Other writers, notably Shakespeare (but one can hardly be theoretic without differing from Shakespeare), depict the moral side of women as both simpler and more closely allied with the entire nature. (pp. xxviii-xxx)

With Mr. Meredith all this is changed by endowing women with an organization morally equivalent—and perhaps one may even say ethically identical—with that of men. He considers their responsibility the same, and, as a consequence, neither enjoys, in virtue of any singularity of native constitution, an immunity denied to the other. He permits himself to exercise the same freedom in his treatment of his women that he indulges in dealing with his men, and makes them do anything he chooses to have them in order to illustrate any point he wishes to make, exactly as if their moral actions were as unpredictable, as facultative with him, as those of even his adventurers and feather-headed enthusiasts of the opposite sex. They are played upon by an equally wide range of conflicting emotions, desires, temptations, and their errors are quite as much due to their baser selves. When they succumb, they fall no lower, having suffered no perversion of their higher nature; and on the other hand, no complementary exaltation results from what is often exhibited by other artists as an uncontrollable deflection of this same higher nature. Diana Warwick is an instance of the former; and, among others, Lord Ormont's Aminta is a striking one of the latter, her infidelity needing to be explained and minimized by an amount of philistine machinery which makes her out rather an unfeeling creature at bottom and makes one long for a touch of human nature—like George Sand's. (p. xxx)

No writer has a more abiding sense of the charm of women, that charm which is so peculiar to them that when it is possessed by men it is only characterizable as feminine charm. He is haunted by it, as evinced in their physique, their manner, their movements. Diana "swims to the tea-table"—all his heroines "swim" in walking. He lingers over minute, caressing descriptions of their beauty—at somewhat confusing length over Clara Middleton's features, for example, though he is quite aware, as he says elsewhere, that a minute description of a face precludes a definite impression. But charm in his women is never incompatible with a kind of knowingness that makes innocence, strictly so-called, as little a characteristic of them as it is of the opposite sex. They have a great deal of self-reliance, of independence, of clairvoyance, such as even in men, one would say, is usually the fruit of experience. (p. xxxi)

Diana is the book in which his ideal of the equivalence—as distinguished from the mere interdependence—of the sexes is most explicitly exposed, though everywhere in his novels one finds evidence of it, and, as an important deduction in detail from this general proposition, the according to women of a sentimental freedom corresponding to the grosser liberty condoned in men. The unworthiness of the old pursuer-and-pursued sex-division yields to the justice of permitting woman the same spontaneous interest in the other sex that is allowed to man, instead of confining such interest to reciprocation; and the further step is, perhaps regularities upon the same plane with his excesses. (pp. xxxi-xxxii)

At all events, innocence in the sense of simplicity is rather pointedly excluded from Mr. Meredith's feminine ideal. And it follows naturally, perhaps, that, having set up "the sex" in a more elaborate spiritual organization than is usually conceded to it by those who affirm it to be nearer to nature than the other, he should exalt its claims to standards of its own. This is the other main proposition that he is fond of enforcing—or rather, considering his inveterate elusiveness, of allowing it to be divined that he advocates. Women have been long enough what men like them to be, what men make them. It is time that they imposed their own ideal and became a little more exacting. Let them study their own independence as the one priceless possession, exalt their dignity as women and extort from masculine fairness conformity to *their* order of aspiration. Let man, on the other hand, learn that woman is never so admirable as when she substitutes for the motive of pleasing him the nobler one of realizing her own destiny and following her own star, developing to its highest potency her own individuality.

Some such view as this I gather, at all events, is the basis of Mr. Meredith's infinite talk about "the sex," and of his various incarnations of what to him is the *ewig weibliche* ["eternal feminine"]. It is doubtless an inspiring view, though, as I have intimated, its novelty, perhaps, consists largely in its emphasis. (pp. xxxii-xxxiii)

Mr. Meredith's treatment of women is distinctly an imaginative treatment and reminds us that one of his chief titles to his high rank as a novelist is an extraordinary imagination. (p. xxxv)

William Crary Brownell, "George Meredith," in The Egoist: A Comedy in Narrative *by George Meredith, Charles Scribner's Sons, 1901, pp. vii-xli.*

G. K. CHESTERTON (essay date 1909)

[*Regarded as one of England's premier men of letters during the first half of the twentieth century, Chesterton is best known today as a colorful bon vivant, a witty essayist, and creator of the Father Brown mysteries and the fantasy* The Man Who Was Thursday *(1908). Much of Chesterton's work reveals his childlike joie de vivre and reflects his pronounced Anglican and, later, Roman Catholic beliefs. His essays are characterized by their humor, frequent use of paradox, and chatty, rambling style. In the following excerpt, Chesterton characterizes Meredith as the last exemplar of nineteenth-century literature, whose death in 1909 marks the real end of the nineteenth century. In contrast, Arnold Bennett (1909) proclaims Meredith the first truly modern novelist.*]

The death of George Meredith was the real end of the Nineteenth Century, not that empty date that came at the close of 1899. The last bond was broken between us and the pride and peace of the Victorian age. Our fathers were all dead. We were suddenly orphans: we all felt strangely and sadly young. A cold, enormous dawn opened in front of us; we had to go on to tasks which our fathers, fine as they were, did not know, and our first sensation was that of cold and undefended youth. Swinburne was the penultimate, Meredith the ultimate end.

It is not a phrase to call him the last of the Victorians: he really is the last. No doubt this final phrase has been used about each of the great Victorians one after another from Matthew Arnold and Browning to Swinburne and Meredith. No doubt the public has grown a little tired of the positively last appearance of the Nineteenth Century. But the end of George Meredith really was the end of that great epoch. No great man now alive has its peculiar powers or its peculiar limits. (p. 30)

Of the men left alive there are many who can be admired beyond expression; but none who can be admired in this way. The name of that powerful writer, Mr. Thomas Hardy, was often mentioned in company with that of Meredith; but the coupling of the two names is a philosophical and chronological mistake. Mr. Hardy is wholly of our own generation, which is a very unpleasant thing to be. He is shrill and not mellow. He does not worship the unknown God: he knows the God (or thinks he knows the God), and dislikes Him. He is not a

pantheist: he is a pandiabolist. The great agnostics of the Victorian age said there was no purpose in Nature. Mr. Hardy is a mystic; he says there is an evil purpose. All this is as far as possible from the plenitude and rational optimism of Meredith. And when we have disposed of Mr. Hardy, what other name is there that can even pretend to recall the heroic Victorian age? The Roman curse lies upon Meredith like a blessing: "Ultimus suorum moriatur"—he has died the last of his own.

The greatness of George Meredith exhibits the same paradox or difficulty as the greatness of Browning; the fact that simplicity was the centre, while the utmost luxuriance and complexity was the expression. He was as human as Shakespeare, and also as affected as Shakespeare. It may generally be remarked (I do not know the cause of it) that the men who have an odd or mad point of view express it in plain or bald language. The men who have a genial and everyday point of view express it in ornate and complicated language. Swinburne and Thomas Hardy talk almost in words of one syllable; but the philosophical upshot can be expressed in the most famous of all words of one syllable—damn. Their words are common words; but their view (thank God) is not a common view. They denounce in the style of a spelling-book; while people like Meredith are unpopular through the very richness of their popular sympathies. (pp. 31-2)

[The] glory of George Meredith is that he combined subtlety with primal energy: he criticized life without losing his appetite for it. In him alone, being a man of the world did not mean being a man disgusted with the world. As a rule, there is no difference between the critic and ascetic except that the ascetic sorrows with a hope and the critic without a hope. But George Meredith loved straightness even when he praised it crookedly: he adored innocence even when he analysed it tortuously: he cared only for unconsciousness, even when he was unduly conscious of it. He was never so good as he was about virgins and schoolboys. In one curious poem, containing many fine lines, he actually rebukes people for being quaint or eccentric, and rebukes them quaintly and eccentrically. . . . That is the mark of the truly great man: that he sees the common man afar off, and worships him. The great man tries to be ordinary, and becomes extraordinary in the process. But the small man tries to be mysterious, and becomes lucid in an awful sense—for we can all see through him. (p. 33)

> *G. K. Chesterton, "George Meredith," in his* The Uses of Diversity: A Book of Essays, *fifth edition, Methuen & Co. Ltd., 1927, pp. 30-3.*

ARNOLD BENNETT   (essay date 1909)

[*Bennett was an Edwardian novelist who is credited with bringing techniques of European Naturalism to the English novel. His reputation rests almost exclusively on* The Old Wives' Tale *(1908) and the Clayhanger trilogy (1910-16), novels which are set in the manufacturing district of Bennett's native Staffordshire and which tell of the thwarted ambitions of those who endure a dull, provincial existence. The following excerpt is taken from an essay that originally appeared in the periodical* New Age *under the pseudonym Jacob Tonson. In contrast with Chesterton's claim that Meredith's death marked the true end of the nineteenth century, (see excerpt dated 1909), Bennett pronounces Meredith not the last of the Victorians, but rather the first truly modern novelist, an assessment that is echoed by Stuart P. Sherman (1909) and J. B. Priestley (1926).*]

The death of George Meredith removes, not the last of the Victorian novelists, but the first of the modern school. He was

Meredith's first wife, Mary Ellen Nicolls, in 1858.

almost the first English novelist whose work reflected an in- telligent interest in the art which he practised; and he was certainly the first since Scott who was really a literary man. . . . Between Fielding and Meredith no entirely honest novel was written by anybody in England. The fear of the public, the lust of popularity, feminine prudery, sentimentalism, Victorian niceness,—one or other of these things prevented honesty.

In *Richard Feverel,* what a loosening of the bonds! What a renaissance! Nobody since Fielding would have ventured to write the Star and Garter chapter in *Richard Feverel.* It was the announcer of a sort of dawn. But there are fearful faults in *Richard Feverel.* The book is sicklied o'er with the pale cast of the excellent Charlotte M. Yonge. The large constructional lines of it are bad. The separation of Lucy and Richard is never explained, and cannot be explained. The whole business of Sir Julius is grotesque. And the conclusion is quite arbitrary. It is a weak book, full of episodic power and overloaded with wit. *Diana of the Crossways* is even worse. I am still awaiting from some ardent Meredithian an explanation of Diana's marriage that does not insult my intelligence. Nor is *One of our Con- querors* very good. I read it again recently, and was sad. In my view, *The Egoist* and *Rhoda Fleming* are the best of the novels, and I don't know that I prefer one to the other. The later ought to have been called *Dahlia Fleming,* and not *Rhoda.* When one thinks of the rich colour, the variety, the breadth, the constant intellectual distinction, the sheer brilliant power of novels such as these, one perceives that a "great Victorian" could only have succeeded in an age when all the arts were at their lowest ebb in England, and the most middling of the middle-classes ruled with the Bible in one hand and the Riot Act in the other.

Meredith was an uncompromizing Radical, and—what is sin- gular—he remained so in his old age. . . . No wonder this temperament had to wait for recognition. Well, Meredith has never had proper recognition; and won't have yet. To be ap- preciated by a handful of writers, gushed over by a little crowd of thoughtful young women, and kept on a shelf uncut by ten thousand persons determined to be in the movement—that is not appreciation. (pp. 134-37)

> *Arnold Bennett, "Meredith," in his* Books and Per- sons: Being Comments on a Past Epoch, 1908-1911, *George H. Doran Company, 1917, pp. 134-39.*

STUART P. SHERMAN (essay date 1909)

[*Sherman was, for many years, considered one of America's most conservative literary critics. During the early twentieth century, he was influenced by the New Humanism, a critical movement which subscribed to the belief that the aesthetic quality of any literary work must be subordinate to its support of traditional moral values. During ten years of service as a literary critic at* The Nation, *Sherman established himself as a champion of the long-entrenched Anglo-Saxon, genteel tradition in American let- ters and as a bitter enemy of literary Naturalism and its propo- nents. Theodore Dreiser and his chief defender, H. L. Mencken, were Sherman's special targets during the World War I era, as Sherman perceived the Naturalism they espoused to be a life- denying cultural product of America's enemy, Germany. During the 1920s, Sherman became the editor of the* New York Herald Tribune *book review section, a move that coincided with a distinct liberalization of his hitherto staunch critical tastes; in the last years of his life, he even praised his old enemies Dreiser and Mencken. In the following excerpt, Sherman identifies Meredith as a thoroughly modern writer who addressed the problems of twentieth century literature "half a century before it existed."*]

[Meredith] wanted art no less as a story-teller than as a stylist. It is true that he undertook a very difficult task. He desired to represent men and women dramatically, revealing the secret springs of their characters in their speech and acts. But for fatally long periods in many of his novels he would allow them neither to speak nor to act. Sometimes, like the messenger of the Senecan tragedy, he reported the great things that were going on behind the scenes. Sometimes with a kind of choric fury he drowned the voices of the actors and assaulted the ears of the audience with a prolonged and often partly enigmatic commentary. Sometimes he translated whole conversations into telegraphic Meredithese. These methods of telling a story are inartistic, because they deprive the auditor of the legitimate and expected pleasure of hearing the *ipsissima verba* in the critical moment, and the spectator of seeing the decisive gesture with his own eyes. Defenders of Meredith will say that he was bent on our perceiving the finer meanings of act and speech, and that he could be sure of his purpose by no other method. That is to confess again that he wanted the skill of the supreme literary artist, that his intention was greater than his power. He had himself a subtle sense of the deeper implications of speech, but he did not possess steadily that master instinct which finds a single word to tell all. . . . Shakespeare's plays are sown with such volume-speaking words; in Meredith's nov- els I do not know where you will find anything approaching it.

But if Meredith was not a first-rate literary artist, is it possible that he was a first-rate literary genius; or are the two things inseparable? It would be gratifying to find some substantial ground for the apparently extravagant claims of his friends. (p. 554)

[If] Meredith is "built for immortality," he will survive not merely as an epigrammatist, or as a subtle poet, or as a psy- chologizing novelist, but as a man with a mine of vital ideas, a constructive critic of life, if not an artist, at any rate a genius, one of the spokesmen and master spirits of his time.

Herein lies one of his most indubitable claims to genius—he solved the problems of our contemporary literature half a cen- tury before it existed. Though his exposition was unequal to his insight, and his own coevals missed his points, such of our authors to-day as face the future smiling have found him out. The problems of contemporary literature are manifold in ap- pearance, but in essence single: How to present a view of life both wise and brave, answering to experience as well as to desire, serviceable in art or the daily walk? Single in essence, in appearance they are manifold: How to give pleasure without corrupting the heart, and how to give wisdom without chilling it? How to bring into play the great passions of men without unchaining the beast? How to believe in Darwin and the dignity of man? How to believe in the nerves without paralyzing the nerve of action? How to recognize the weakness of man, and not forget his heroism? How to see his acts, and believe in his intentions? How to renounce his superstitions, and retain his faith? How to rebuke without despising him? How to reform society without rebelling against it? How to smile at its follies without contempt? How to believe that pain is invincible, and that joy is invincible, too? How to believe that evil is fleeing forever before good, but will never be overtaken and slain? How to look back upon a thousand defeats, and yet cling to the fighting hope? If you go through this list of questions, you will not find one which Meredith did not answer. Long before Mr. Shaw broke into mock Mephistophelean laughter, and Mr. Chesterton discovered his loyalty to the universe, when they—

if one can conceive such a thing—were quietly sleeping in their cradles, George Meredith had already bottled their thunder.

"Richard Feverel," published in 1859 with "The Virginians," "Adam Bede," "The Tale of Two Cities," and "The Origin of Species," was a repudiation and a prophecy, but was recognized as neither. . . . [Not until] he published the **"Idea of Comedy,"** did he finally make clear his message. From that time it began slowly to be evident that he had made his novels, after all, but the vehicles of an impassioned conviction. He, like so many earnest men of his century, had sought a way of salvation from skepticism, melancholy, *ennui*, and despair; and he had found a way. Other men had other remedies. . . . To those who have read intelligently Meredith's **"Idea of Comedy"** I do not think it will seem an anti-climax to say that he believed the one thing needful, synthesis of all needs, was to instruct men in the proper uses of the comic spirit that they might laugh and be laughed at unto their souls' salvation. For to him the comic spirit is a fine celestial sunlight in the mind, answering to the theological grace of God in the heart, which preserves those into whom it passes from a very evil thing. It is not hostile to prayer, nor to labor, nor to logic, nor to truth, nor to grandeur, but very friendly to them all. It keeps prayer sweet, labor cheerful, logic sane, truth serviceable, and grandeur human. But over every form of animalism, egotism, sentimentalism, cowardice, and unreason, "it will look humanely malign, and cast an oblique light on them, followed by showers of silvery laughter." . . .

Once grasp that idea of comedy and you suddenly find yourself at the centre of a coherent critical system. You open his works anywhere and you find yourself at home in an ordered world. You perceive why the younger generation is turning toward him, and you see the relation in which he stood to his fellows in fiction fifty years ago. The definitions by which in the essay the comic spirit is isolated furnish a complete critical arsenal. (p. 555)

To his view, life is neither wholly comedy nor wholly tragedy, but both at once. In order to distinguish either element one must be able to distinguish both; the comic spirit, one may almost say, is that which perceives the tragic fault. In order to represent life bravely and wisely, one must see it steadily, and see it whole. . . . [To] represent the whole course of the struggle is to write tragi-comedy.

Tragi-comedy as the position of equipoise in life and art—that, in Meredith's time, was a notable discovery. When we attempt to measure his achievement we should not lose sight of the originality, the scope, and the difficulty of his design. He planned to produce thoughtful laughter, an aim which demanded that the characters in his novels, as well as in his audience, should possess some of the culture of the drawing-room. But he planned at the same time to move the great passions which are generally attenuated under intensive cultivation. . . . To his fellows in fiction Meredith owed very little. On his serious side nearest akin to George Eliot, he preceded her into the field. Carlyle and Browning and Wordsworth were all his natural allies, but his master was Shakespeare. From him he learned to choose out for the favorite theatre of his play a country-house, where, as in a court, were assembled enough actors of civilized life to be visible against the scenery. From him he learned to let poor clowns play humble parts, and if anyone had to be sent out on a barren heath to send a king who even in madness was a match for the storm. From him he learned to line the back and sides of his stage with gray and middle ages of wisdom, pedantry, sanctity, craft, and cynicism;

and then to release in the foreground young Romeo and Juliet, or Perdita and Florizel, or Ferdinand and Miranda to discover the brave new world under a stinging rain of comment from prudent or disillusioned antiquity; and then, at last, whether to youth and beauty the vista of days opened smiling, or whether some dire mischance closed their fond eyes forever, to intimate that to youth belong the untrodden ways.

Meredith's life began and closed on that note. In an age when a general disintegration of ideas was taking place, he showed an extremely keen sense of what was permanent and what transitory. He woke early to the necessity and the possibility of a new organic synthesis. Though his creative power and craftsmanship were inferior to his critical faculty, they worked harmoniously, and, therefore, effectively. Several of his contemporaries possessed separately in a higher degree the intellectual or emotional powers with which he was gifted; but no one of them fused within himself so many and so diverse powers. (p. 556)

Few, indeed, are the writers of fiction who have striven so steadily to seize and conserve for posterity all the sound ideas afloat in their time. (p. 557)

> *Stuart P. Sherman, "George Meredith," in* The Nation, *Vol. LXXXVIII, No. 2292, June 3, 1909, pp. 554-57.*

JOSEPH WARREN BEACH   (essay date 1911)

[*Beach was a professor of English at the University of Minnesota for many years and a lecturer at Johns Hopkins University. As a literary critic, Beach specialized in the study of American literature, and is the author of the studies* The Twentieth-Century Novel *(1932) and* American Fiction 1920-1941 *(1941), as well as major studies of Henry James and W. H. Auden. Beach's* The Comic Spirit in George Meredith *traces in Meredith's novels the theme that the central function of comedy was to induce thought, not laughter. Meredith presented a type of comedy derived not from ludicrous situations but from "the discrepancy between the real and the supposed motive" for the action of the characters.*]

My aim . . . is to trace in Meredith's novels the comic spirit that makes their chief distinction. This aspect of his work has been much ignored by the critics. . . . This is the more surprising in view of the many passages in which the author discusses the nature of comedy, and the frequency with which he applies the term to his own novels. Not only does he describe three of the novels explicitly as comedies, and designate as "tragic comedians" the leading characters of another book. But, aside from frequent allusions throughout the novels and poems, Meredith has a set treatise on comedy in the prelude to the *Egoist;* and he has published both a lecture on **"Comedy"** and an **"Ode to the Comic Spirit."** No writer since Ben Jonson has given plainer advertisement of what he was about. And yet the comic method of Meredith was in some ways so new, and he used the word comedy in a sense so unfamiliar to contemporary English readers, that they have not understood his intention. It has not often occurred to the critics to extend the application of the word comedy beyond *Evan Harrington* and the *Egoist.* Outside these novels, they find the comic merely in such drolls as Mrs. Chump and Master Gammon. I believe that, in Meredith's own view, the comic spirit has just as striking manifestations in such a serious character as Victor Radnor; that no novel of Meredith is quite free from it; and that most of them it pervades like an atmosphere.

In his famous "Essay," Meredith was not so much reviewing the practice of the comic art as attempting to shadow forth the method on which he was at work himself. . . . He would have been more intelligible had he drawn his illustrations from his own novels. He must have been sore tempted to do so. One might suppose that the *Egoist,* which appeared two years after the lecture was delivered, was offered to show what he had in mind.

Taking humor as an inclusive term for all varieties of the ludicrous, we may distinguish two functions of humor. The primary function is to make one laugh, the secondary function is to make one think. With most English humorists, the primary function has prevailed, largely to the exclusion of the secondary. With Meredith the secondary function is all-important. He would make us laugh to make us think. Or rather, he would make us smile, and that not always with the muscles of eye and mouth, but inwardly. Meredith would reserve the terms comic and comedy for humor that is addressed to the mind. He would not apply them to those works of humor which are controlled by feeling, whether the bitter feeling of the satirist or the rosily genial sentiment of the humorist proper. . . . His comedy is "humor of the mind."

His comedy is hard to define. . . . It is humor divested of those appurtenances of the sensuous, of sentimentality, of naturalistic detail, of material accident, of waggish impertinent wit, that make so fat and succulent the work of most English humorists. I do not mean that Meredith is wanting either in wit or in human sympathy. He is a famous master of epigram, and commands a most frolicsome fancy, fertile in all manner of drolleries. But, save in his earliest works, these are instruments under strict control of the comic idea, and they are not indulged wantonly for their own sake. As for humanity, the characters upon whom he turns the most searching light of ridicule are shown the gentle indulgence of one who has taken a wide survey of human nature, and who feels the force of that saying, *"que tout comprendre c'est tout pardonner"* ["to understand all is to forgive all"]. And nothing equals the tender sweetness with which he treats his Richards and Lucys, his Emilias and Carinthias. But this is very different from the familiar and "larmoyant geniality" in which the humorist wades, and which has no purpose beyond the sensation of the moment. Meredith has ever in mind the more thoughtful and fruitful method of comedy, whose aim is the correction of folly. (pp. 1-7)

Meredith is not concerned with those lower strata of society in which vice and suffering have so debased as to make unrecognizable the divine features of man. Debased humanity has nothing to teach us. Disease and crime are for the doctor. Intelligent, clean, respectable men are the subject of comedy. . . . Among the best lies the hope for mankind, and it is there one finds the foibles and cunning vices that are at once most diverting and most instructive.

Meredith's characters are chiefly drawn, moreover, from the higher degrees of social rank, and represent high life in the special sense. His comic figures in particular are prone to flourish titles. From the entrance of the Countess de Saldar to the retirement of the Earl of Fleetwood, we find ourselves in distinguished company. This is not, I think, a betrayal of aristocratic tastes on the part of the Radical author, a desire to adorn his pages with titles that should bestow an artificial lustre. Comedy makes choice of persons wealthy and high in rank because here the comic traits of character have freest play. It would be hard to find in a society not aristocratic an intelligent and witty person in whom vanity and egoism had a chance to develop so freely as in Sir Willoughby Patterne. Richmond Roy and Victor Radnor could not have indulged their foolish ambitions without command of large sums of money. The comic spirit gives them rope.

But, we must observe, true comedy does not consist in the exploitation of originals. . . . [The] oddity of an eccentric is no lesson to men in society. There is no significance in Captain Cuttle's hook or Admiral Trunnion's patch. These appeal to the eye for laughter; they have no message to the mind.

Meredith is in contrast with the humorists in this respect, that his more humorous characters are not those he is hunting. It is the serious characters that are comic. Sterne and Dickens summon us to the enjoyment of persons whom we cannot conceive as related to ourselves, though we recognize in them an amplification of universal human traits. We might take them, like Don Quixote, for comic symbols of humanity. We can afford to welcome and caress them. Whimsical, good-hearted fellows appeal to us for laughter at their odd and captivating ways. Nick Bottom and Justice Shallow we relish hugely, looking down upon them. In the company of Dickens and Smollett, we have the pleasure of laughing to scorn the hypocrite, the uncharitable, the grossly affected among us. Meredith invites us to the anatomy of ourselves.

Not even the author's favorites are wholly exempt from the comic inquisition. The comic spirit is an atmosphere, completely enveloping the group in view. It is possessed of chemical properties, and infallibly attacks any soluble matter with which it comes in contact. Thus we find it at work upon certain weak spots in the character of young Evan Harrington. Evan Harrington is inevitably associated with Meredith himself: son of a tailor, but endowed with the instincts of a gentleman. Oneself is the last person upon whom one turns the light of comedy. In the *Egoist* our sympathy is chiefly solicited for Clara Middleton and Vernon Whitford; but we read one chapter in which "the comic muse has an eye on" these "two good souls." And the most favored of all the author's heroines are often conducted on the way with some touch of sympathetic but mildly patronizing drollery. (pp. 7-11)

Meredith is not concerned with saints and sinners, but with the natural and the unnatural, the honest and the dishonest, those who know their own minds and the victims of delusion. His appeal is not so much to the conscience as to the judgment. He asks for an exercise of imagination in the discovery of our own folly. (p. 12)

It is the discrepancy between the real and the supposed motive that makes the comedy; the game of bluff played by the actor against himself, his complacent self-deception, his mock sublimity.

This is the heart of Meredith's comic method, what distinguishes him among comic writers. The incongruity that is the basis of the ludicrous in general is here found within a man's very soul. Meredith is not content to make laughter from the exhibition of those obvious discrepancies between character and profession, those glaring vanities, simplicities and hypocrisies that have occupied a Fielding and a Thackeray. He insists on sounding the depths for comedy. . . . Meredith deals with persons not comic on the surface, and shows them to be comic by the exhibition of their inner life. One character is comic because of the discrepancy between the passion on which he prides himself and the factitious sentiment he harbors. One, upon investigation, proves to be the primitive egoist mistaking himself for a social being.

Thus we are taught to recognize ourselves. . . . [We] learn that our most cherished ideals are often based upon false estimates of value; that our very refinement has sometimes carried us beyond the reach of common sense.

The mere presentation of comic types is not comedy. This art requires that a character should be presented in its social relations. (pp. 13-14)

A comedy does not mean with Meredith, any more than with Shakespeare, a story in which all the characters are ridiculous. For one egoist in Sir Willoughby, we have a Clara, a Laetitia, a Vernon Whitford. It is the humorist and the satirist that offer a whole gallery of originals. The comic artist puts on the boards an actual group of human beings, among whom the real and the unreal cast reflections on one another. Both parties gain by the exchange. The complete natural simplicity of a Sandra or a Carinthia is the best foil for the fantastic excrescency of a Wilfrid or a Fleetwood.

Meredith's comedy is not even incompatible with a tragic outcome for the stories. In the case of the "tragic comedians," he undertakes to show "how the comic in their nature led by interplay to the tragic issue." Meredith does not write tragedy. Tragedy celebrates the magnificence of heroic criminals, and the sunset splendors of star-crossed unfortunates. She chisels beauty out of the stern granite of fate. She is on the watch for grandeur. Comedy is content with less distinguished actors. Not crime but folly is her concern; and of fate she knows less than nothing. (pp. 18-19)

We must not suppose that Meredith put forward the comic as a special type of novel, offering the word as a label for the critic's application, like realist and romantic; that he wished to establish a new school of fiction, and compel all men to write comedy. "Life, we know too well," he says, "is not a Comedy, but something strangely mixed." He did not intend, himself, the writing of works that might be labelled comedy to the exclusion of romantic elements. He repudiates neither realism nor romance. Romance is the quality that gives lift and inspiration. It is the chiming of overtones with the single note struck by the musician. If we let romance go, "we exchange a sky for a ceiling." Even a credible realism cannot be had without an element of the romantic; it would be to leave out human nature. But neither romance nor realism can dispense with the critical spirit of comedy.

Comedy Meredith proposed as a corrective, a disinfectant, a leaven. In launching his masterpiece, he indicates the two extremes of naturalism and sentimentalism as in need of comic discipline. Here he deplores in particular the dull prolixity of that philistine, "the realistic method of a conscientious transcription of all the visible, and a repetition of all the audible." Art is the specific he recommends for the disease of sameness; and he has in mind the art of the comic writer. What the naturalist lacks is not so much a sense of decency as a sense of humor. (pp. 19-20)

The comic spirit . . . is foe alike to the sentimental and the naturalistic style in fiction. The one is too fastidious to touch the material fact; the other will touch nothing else. There is in both cases a divorce of body and soul. (p. 22)

The comic essence closes round and proves each character, dissolving what is soft in each, but leaving in beautiful entirety such as are entire. The result is far from merely laugh-compelling; far likewise from the depressing effect of merely negative criticism. There is entertainment and edification to be had from the exhibition of folly. Edifying and inspiring is the portrayal of fair and noble character.

It is clear the laugh is an incidental consideration in Meredith's comedy. His aim is to make us think. (pp. 23-4)

Joseph Warren Beach, in his The Comic Spirit in George Meredith: An Interpretation, *1911. Reprint by Russell & Russell, 1963, 230 p.*

J. B. PRIESTLEY   (essay date 1926)

[*A highly prolific English man of letters, Priestley is the author of numerous popular novels that depict the world of everyday, middle-class England. In this respect, Priestley has often been likened to Charles Dickens, a critical comparison that he dislikes. His most notable critical work is* Literature and Western Man *(1960), a survey of Western literature from the invention of movable type through the mid-twentieth century. In the following excerpt, Priestley discusses some general characteristics of Meredith's novels, maintaining that Meredith excelled in those areas of fiction writing that are the most difficult, such as "the creation of a real heroine, the subtle exhibition of character dramatically, the handling of highly poetic moments," while the novelist's most basic task—the straightforward telling of a story—was beyond him. Nevertheless, Priestley considers Meredith an artistic genius and* The Egoist *one of the greatest novels in English literature.*]

There is much to be said for the practice, now out of favour in criticism, of dealing systematically with a novelist, totalling his faults on one side and his virtues on the other, giving him good or bad marks, as it were, for construction, creation of character, wit and humour, descriptive power, and so forth. The weakness of this formal method is that after all its labour it frequently fails to give us the essential character of a writer. . . . Its advantage is that it does succeed in clearing ground woefully cumbered with vague and unsystematic praise and detraction; it does tell us what goods our author has brought to market. And as Meredith is a novelist who has been almost buried under such vague and unsystematic praise and detraction, whose goods, stored away in an unusual bulk of complicated work, are therefore all the more difficult to weigh, measure, and value, there is a great deal to be said in favour of reviving the method and applying it to him. . . . Unfortunately it is not possible to do this. The peculiar character of Meredith's fiction prevents our formally tabulating its strength and weakness because its virtues and faults do not naturally group themselves as those of many authors do. He is pre-eminently a writer who has the virtues of his defects and the defects of his virtues. They follow closely on one another's heels. . . . And into whatever compartment we should follow him, those compartments beloved of formal criticism, such as characterisation, descriptive power, wit and humour, style, and so on, we should find this contradictory double character, this opposing strength and weakness.

He is an extremely faulty story-teller and yet contrives to enlarge the whole scope of the art. The bulk of his characters, that is practically all the secondary figures, are not created nor even constructed; they are mere names and dialogue and nothing more, without any hold upon our imagination; and yet he who has given us so many of these creatures of straw has also given us some of the greatest figures in fiction, some heroines inferior to none but Shakespeare's. His style is such that it cannot always cope with the expository and other matter that forms the ground level of fiction, the kind of matter that presents no difficulty to the ordinary novelist; and yet it shows itself capable of handling the heightened moments, the great scenes, in a fashion that lifts such passages far beyond the reach of any but the great masters of the Novel. It is this odd combination of weakness and strength that makes Meredith a unique figure in the history of English fiction. . . . The very things that have always been recognised as the most difficult things to do in prose fiction, such as the creation of a real heroine, the subtle exhibition of character dramatically, the handling of highly poetic moments, he can do magnificently and with apparent ease. What he cannot do successfully are the very things that we find done to perfection in the ordinary intelligent novel, the very commonplaces of fiction. This is in part due to the fact that his pride forbade him to take any interest in the commonplaces, in what any Tom, Dick, or Harry could do fairly well. He was always too self-conscious on this score to be a really great artist, for the really great artist, forgetful of everything but the work in hand, does not wonder whether he is being original or merely commonplace and platitudinous, does not try to be different from other people, but merely does the work as well as it possibly can be done.

A great many of his defects proceed from this self-consciousness. His later novels are almost ruined by the writer's obvious desire to avoid the commonplace. As he grew older he coddled himself and frankly abandoned himself to his pet mannerisms. His pride would not allow him to state a plain fact in a plain way. In much of this work he was compelled to appear somewhat obscure simply because he was trying to express really subtle and difficult impressions and states of mind. But by the time he came to write *One of our Conquerors, Lord Ormont and his Aminta,* and *The Amazing Marriage,* he had to give an appearance of subtlety and difficulty whether there happened to be anything subtle and difficult to express or not. His style had mastered him, and the reason why it was allowed to master him was that his genuine artistic impulse was by this time weak, whereas his pride, his self-consciousness, his desire not merely to be ''different'' but to be increasingly more ''different'', to be more and more the Meredith whom the public had neglected and his friends had adored, were stronger than ever. It is generally supposed that these later novels of his are more subtle and complicated than the earlier ones, but actually they are nothing of the kind. They are not more but less complicated than *Richard Feverel, Sandra Belloni, Beauchamp's Career,* and *The Egoist;* they are far simpler in conception, the action is less involved, the thought and feeling less subtle, and therefore they demanded simpler treatment. But this is just what Meredith would not or could not give them. Either he was by this time the slave of his own mannerisms, or he deliberately covered up this interior simplicity with a surface complexity, determined that it should not be said that George Meredith was at last coming to terms with his hostile critics and the public.

But while many of his defects proceed from this self-consciousness in the man himself, not a few of his weaknesses appear to be the result of a lack of self-consciousness, a want of it not in the man but in the artist. . . . There is about him not a little of that casual air which is typical of so many of the greater novelists of his century. A touch of that almost reverent deliberation which we find in Flaubert and Henry James would have left his work vastly improved. Remembering what he did with the form, we cannot say that he did not take his fiction seriously, but we can say that if he had treated it with even a little more respect than he did, most of its minor faults would have disappeared. It may be, of course, that the root cause is to be found in the very shape and nature of his mind, for the same faults appear in his poetry, which lay next to his heart, and it would seem that Meredith, for all his amazing powers,

had little or no instinctive sense of form. Thus, many of those minor faults in his fiction are the result of the writer's faulty sense of proportion.

Time after time in the novels he irritates the most admiring reader by throwing a disproportionate emphasis upon relatively unimportant characters, situations, and topics. He could detach himself sufficiently to lay down the general lines of construction, but having done that, he could not resist the temptation to make his novel reflect his interests of the moment even if it meant that the narrative would be knocked out of shape, its progress held up, its appeal considerably weakened. As time went on, he made less and less effort to resist this temptation, with the inevitable result that not only are his novels badly proportioned, but that, ironically enough, he himself, this hyper-sensitive chronicler of a hyper-sensitive social life, becomes at times that thing he most dreaded, a bore. (pp. 167-71)

All his most memorable figures, his heroines apart, are alike in this, that though they may be there to be satirised, to be whipped with laughter, there is certainly not a little of George Meredith himself in them. He may have thrown off any allegiance to their ideas, but he could enter fully into their lives and minds; and while his intellect was preparing to chastise them, his imagination was enjoying them. The two noteworthy exceptions would seem to be Squire Beltham in *Harry Richmond,* and Everard Romfrey in *Beauchamp's Career.* These two hard-bitten, plain-speaking, fox-hunting squires of the old school are magnificently alive. Every word they speak positively rings with truth. Yet there can have been little of Meredith himself (except his sharp dogmatic temper) in them, and they must be considered, at least on the masculine side, the best examples he has of close observation. But the others who stand out, the selfish wits, snobs, and egoists, owe their extraordinary vitality to this secret imaginative sympathy. It is the characters of this type who, at first standing on one side, become more and more the centre of the Comedy. . . . (p. 176)

[Meredith's] greatest triumphs in the creation of the character are, by common consent, his heroines. . . . His are the most enchanting ladies that fiction, of this or any other literature, can show us. . . . Meredith's heroines have a double function, just as he himself appears, in his fiction, in a double capacity. The poet in him sees in them glowing images of health and beauty, the fruits of right living, lovely and loving symbols of Earth. The critic in him uses them as a kind of test. This gives them a very strong position, quite different from that they occupy in most fiction. We . . . ask what it is that makes his heroines so infinitely superior to those of previous writers. The secret lies, of course, in his manner of presentation. Earlier novelists were convinced that if their readers *saw* their heroines clearly, it would not be necessary to *know* them; if every detail of the lovely face were described, then the character of the lady could be left misty and vague. Meredith simply reverses the process. He presents his women as definite individualities, clearly marked characters, and takes the greatest care to show us the springs of their action, to examine their motives. At the same time, having described the character, he leaves the lovely face and figure, as they should be left, misty and vague. He gives them a kind of aura, makes them move in a golden mist, shows us shining figures in which every man sees his own Helen of Troy. The poet in him, contenting himself with hinting at this and that touch of beauty, but too wise to build up one of those elaborate portraits so familiar and so fatal in the Novel, bathes his women in glamour. If this poetic glamour is effective—and it is effective—then the psychologist can set to work with the knowledge that every stroke will only strengthen the appeal of the character.

It is this combination of definite individuality with poetic glamour that is the secret of Meredith's heroines. Shakespeare's, with whom they have often been compared, have precisely the same appeal. Cleopatra, Rosalind, Imogen, and the others are distinct characters whose beauty and witchery are, as it were, created by our imaginations, as we read, simply out of the atmosphere surrounding them. And all Meredith's psychological richness and acuteness would be of little avail if he too had not been able to create this atmosphere, to bathe his women in light and make them move to music. His task is to obliterate the old easy sentimentalities of the sexual relation, to approach it intellectually and make of it something finer and more honest, to compel us to think and not merely to feel about it; but in order to do this with any success, it is necessary for him to raise the power of the relation all round, to compensate us for the loss of those easy sentimentalities by emphasising the poetic enchantment of sex, otherwise we lose sight, amid all this intellectual analysis, of the driving force behind it all. So while he gives us more intellect in the matter, he also gives us more poetry, and nothing is lost but the whole is raised to a higher power. Had he been less of a poet, less able, in some curious fashion, to suggest sheer lyrical ecstasy in the middle of his analysis of motive and action, his heroines would have been little more than factors in an intellectual problem. But they walk in light and music and loveliness. (pp. 180-82)

Mention of wit brings us inevitably to some consideration of Meredith's manner and style, round which so many battles have raged. To say, as some critics have said, that he is too witty is a curious grumble. There is not so much wit in the world that we can afford to accuse a writer of giving us too much of it. If Meredith were frequently witty when wit was not demanded, there might be some justice in the charge.... But Meredith practically always changes his manner, heightening his prose until it becomes almost a poetical instrument, for the more emotional moments. It is not that he gives us too much wit, too many epigrams, but that, particularly in his later work, he will keep up an apparently witty and epigrammatic manner that prevents him from making a plain statement but does not compensate us by giving us any actual wit, any real epigrams. He is too frequently occupied in providing us with a Barmecide feast of wit and profound comment; we note the elaborate gestures, but nothing arrives for the mind to feed on. Once more we see how he contrives to do the difficult thing and fails to do the easy one. Nobody has excelled him in witty and really subtle comment or in bursts of really brilliant dialogue, just as no novelist has given us more gorgeous and memorable poetic moments. But his manner and style, especially in the later novels, refuse to undertake what might be called the donkey-work of narration. He will go miles out of his way, giving us pages of what can only be considered sheer bad writing, in order to avoid making a few plain statements of fact, necessary for the conduct of the narrative. (pp. 186-87)

No other writer of anything like his genius, so crowded with ideas and the master of such a massive vocabulary, has ever indulged in such pieces of cheap verbal affectation. Practically all his bad passages, from those in which a genuine thought is almost buried under an elaboration of imagery, to those that are simply fancies tortured out of all recognition, cruel Euphuism, are clearly the result of an impatience with ordinary methods of statement. That such ordinary methods would not always serve his turn, that he was compelled to be different

by the very nature of what he frequently had to communicate, is true enough, but it does not clear him from the charge of sheer bad affectation. He frequently wished to be different when there was no necessity to be different. If he has not a happy image on hand (and imagery at once daring and felicitous is the mark of his style at its best), he will press into service any metaphors that occur to him and swell them out monstrously. If the matter looks like being commonplace, then the manner is rushed into fantastic fancy dress.... We are prepared to overlook those single sentences and phrases that have drawn down upon themselves the wrath of so many critics, phrases like "feeling a rotifer astir in the curative compartment of a homeopathic globule" and "a fantastical planguncula enlivened by the wanton tempers of a nursery chit", because they may be accepted as Meredith's "fun", a verbal spree. But [some of Meredith's passages] are rank bad writing. Nor do they strike one as being the exuberant freaks of a prose master, larking with his instrument. If we met them for the first time, we should set their author down as some pretentious novice trying to write "above himself". And in most of these passages that is what Meredith is trying to do, for there being no Meredithian marble on hand, he is giving us super-Meredithian stucco instead, preferring to parody himself rather than lapse into plain speech.

But when all such criticisms have been made, what treasures of witty comment remain. Poetry, humour, subtle psychology, all crammed into a phrase, and he gives us hundreds and hundreds of such phrases, illuminating a character, a situation, like flashes of lightning. Open the novels anywhere and they meet the eye.... What most intelligent novelists would regard as a somewhat exhausting excursion into the witty epigrammatic is merely the ordinary level of these novels of Meredith's, the common stuff of the narrative. If his Comedy had no significance whatever, if there blew through his work no great wind of poetry and romance, to read the greater part of it would still be an intellectual delight as we leaped from crag to crag with our athletic and agile narrator.

It is not difficult to say many hard things about his prose style, which bears a close relation to his poetical one.... But his aim and method in fiction demanded such a style and could not have been achieved without it. Undoubtedly it is far more deliberate than most critics would seem to imagine.... He... worked to produce [an] electrical agitation in the mind. He wished to disintegrate the ordinary prose mass, having much that was new to express, and then recombine the elements in his own way, making it far more elastic. His style might be compared to that of the artists who paint only in little spots of colour, thereby creating an unusual impression of vividness and vitality. His aim is always to present only the essentials of a scene and situation, what is obvious being ruthlessly cut away; and his actual style closely follows his manner of observation, for it gives us a succession of rapid direct statements that are entirely disconnected and without the usual links and logical forms. The reader is pelted with impressions and observations that he must synthesise himself. If he is lazy, unresponsive to that electrical agitation, he will make little or nothing of the matter before him; but if he is keeping pace with the author, he will be constantly and delightfully thrilled. He will live, to the fullest extent of his capacity, with the actors in the scene, and yet, as we have seen before, will be able to see them against the novelist's background.

This disintegrating process in the prose of fiction, keeping step with an ever-increasing subjectivity, has gone much farther in our time than ever Meredith took it or would have liked to have taken it. The poet and romancer never died in him, and he took care never to let his prose lose all semblance of a fabric, never let it crumble into fine dust. Thus he could always raise it for the moments that demanded a fuller sweep, a larger compass in the instrument. At such times the staccato drumming of his short and swift statements will ebb out and music and colour will come flowing into the prose. (pp. 187-92)

Throughout his fiction, as we have seen, he was apt to do the easy thing, the journeyman's work, badly, and for this, however great our enthusiasm for the man and his work, he must be blamed, judged to be the faulty artist. But the difficult thing, approached with dread by most novelists, he did not only well but, in many instances, incomparably, scaling heights that have yet to be overtopped. That is why he is such a simple target for adverse criticism. Any reader who is acquainted with a few competent pieces of fiction can remark the faults in Meredith, for they sprawl at length, inviting comment. But a reader who can go no farther dubs himself incompetent. To go farther is to encounter Meredith's undeniably great, perhaps unique, virtues, and these cannot be estimated and appreciated as we run. Appreciative criticism finds in him a very full subject. The more often we read this fiction as a whole, faulty though it may be, the more we are astonished at its richness and virility. Dropping all talk of comedy and romance and subjectivism and narrative and what not, we may say that these novels, whatever else they may be, are a literary feast, crammed with good things, the largesse of a marvellously rich and generous personality, in whose house of letters it snows meat and drink. We rise from a reading of this fiction at once more critical, more sensitive, and more in love with life than ever, braced and blessed, because it is the testament of a rich and glowing experience, of a personality that never relaxed its strong grasp upon life and lived intensely all its eighty crowded years. (pp. 193-94)

The direct literary influence of Meredith is difficult to assess, but, perhaps owing to the peculiar character of his genius, it does not seem to have been very extensive, certainly less than that of such later novelists as Hardy, Henry James, and Conrad. But the indirect influence of Meredith has been enormous. As we have seen, he enlarged the scope of fiction, gave it new matter and a new manner, and when the history of the Modern English Novel comes to be written, he should be given a prominent place in it, not only as an original genius but also as a highly important innovator, a man who added a whole new octave to the instrument of prose fiction. The modern novel begins with him.... So far small justice has been done to Meredith as an innovator. Nor must it be forgotten that the Novel itself and the intelligent novelists who came after him owe him a debt of gratitude, because he did much to raise the status of the form and the persons who made use of it. He may not have approached the Novel with the prayers and fasting of a Flaubert or a James, but he did treat it seriously and made it the receptacle of so much "brain-stuff" that all manner of persons, previously accustomed to relaxing their minds over a novel, were also compelled to treat it seriously. No longer could they use merely one quarter of their brains in reading fiction, which became something more than an aid to digestion or a prelude to a nap. In order to be read at all, the Meredith novel asked for the full and undivided attention demanded by other forms of literature, and thereby smoothed the way for other serious fiction. Meredith paid heavily for his pioneering, and novelists and critics of to-day, however irritating they may find his occasional antics and touches of sheer perversity, will

Meredith's second wife, Marie Vulliamy, in 1864.

do well to bear in mind that even those antics were not without their influence in making possible the modern attitude towards fiction and the modern novel itself.

Whatever may happen to his name and fame, he cannot but remain a splendid flashing figure in our literature. Those who can see nothing but his faults—and he had many faults as a man and an artist—declare themselves blind to genius, and even prodigal genius. That he was not a genius of the highest order goes without saying. His work is obviously without that universality, that appeal on many different levels, which mark that of a Homer, a Cervantes, a Shakespeare, or, in their own fashion, a Dickens, a Molière. It is not merely that his work does not reach perfection, for the work of greater men is equally faulty, but that in spite of its richness, its breadth and depth, it lacks, just as he himself lacked, that four-square humanity which we expect from the supreme masters. He will never be everybody's man. A whole range of emotions never seems to have found its way into his work, which wants that charity, that brooding tenderness for man as man, which would endear it to whole populations as yet unborn. But, when all is said and done, he remains a giant, even though a giant somehow so twisted by pride and wilfulness that he appears of lesser stature. He touches greatness at an extraordinary number of points. No English writer of his century cast a wider net; he is a philosopher, poet, and novelist; he challenges Thackeray and James on the one side of his work just as he challenges Browning and Swinburne on the other; and whatever he touches he makes his own; his thought is his own, so is his poetry, and as for his fiction, it is original in every particular, in scope, form, matter, manner and style. His blend of philosophy and poetry, wit and rhapsody, comedy and romance, is unique, and there are moments when, overpowered by his breadth and force, we see in him the only writer of the last two centuries who can be placed by the side of Shakespeare. But then there comes home to us his plain lack of the Shakespearean broad humanity, the unfailing sense of form and rightness of touch, and his uneasy self-consciousness, afraid of simplicity even when simplicity is demanded, taking refuge in a hard brilliance. Yet the fact that this comparison with Shakespeare should even be entertained for a moment, and it has been actually boarded and lodged by some writers of note, gives us some measure of the man's stature. An undeniably great but puzzling figure; a genuine poet and philosopher, on the heroic plan, who can dwindle at times into a mere fop; a rich genius in whom there is some curious streak of the shoddy adventurer; a man of Shakespearean mould crossed with the strain of a Beau Brummell; and withal the author of an astonishingly full, brilliant, and varied canon in prose and verse, and of at least one novel, *The Egoist,* that takes its place among the six best pieces of fiction in the language; whose splendid figure gives colour and light to his century as it flashes down the years; who will brighten the wits and lift up the hearts of innumerable choice spirits when we, who have been taking our foot-rule round him, are all dead and forgotten. (pp. 197-200)

> *J. B. Priestley, in his* George Meredith, *The Macmillan Company, 1926, 204 p.*

HARRIET MONROE (essay date 1928)

[*As the founder and editor of* Poetry, *Monroe was a key figure in the American "poetry renaissance" that took place in the early twentieth century.* Poetry *was the first periodical devoted primarily to the works of new poets and to poetry criticism, and from 1912 until her death Monroe maintained an editorial policy of printing "the best English verse which is being written today, regardless of where, by whom, or under what theory of art it is written." In the following excerpt, Monroe praises the sonnet cycle* Modern Love *for uniquely developing the themes of a novel in verse form and contends that the work may eventually be considered Meredith's artistic masterpiece.*]

When the centenary of George Meredith's birth swung around in February, there were tributes and revaluations from many critics. His novels were dusted off and psycho-analyzed, and put in their proper place, mostly on the shelf; and the name which had sprung to life so suddenly back in the eighties and had reëchoed for two or three decades among the great ones of the century, seemed to give forth, strangely enough, a slightly hollow sound. Apparently this novelist had tried too hard and too self-consciously; he had written each tale from too definite a thesis. And so they ranked not among the great books, the ever-memorable, but among the near-great, the half-remembered. And the laurel wreath brought to his tomb by the so swiftly passing world seemed already turning from green to brown.

But, in the articles I happened to see, very little was said about George Meredith's poetry; so perhaps it is not too late to pause over the beauty of certain poems, and to note, more specifically, his interesting experiments with four-time measures. It may be that in the ultimate analysis the sonnet-sequence *Modern Love,* done in fifty sixteen-line sonnets, will outrank any of his novels as an artistic achievement. Here the form compelled condensation; the subtle tragedy of emotional clash and strain between two high-strung characters in marriage had to

be stripped bare of all excess and carried without pause to the woeful passion of its climax and the dark beauty of its end. *Modern Love* is not only its author's finest poem, it is one of the finest poems of the nineteenth century, and the precursor of a number of twentieth-century narratives of passionate clash and strain—Robinson's, for example, and Leonard's. (pp. 210-11)

[*Modern Love*] was his first and last attempt to present a novel-theme in verse; thereafter he availed himself of the greater freedom and expansiveness to be found in prose. Yet, like Thomas Hardy, he preferred his poetry to all the novels. (p. 211)

Of the poems later than *Modern Love,* probably only a few will arrest the obliterating hand of time. (p. 214)

A few beautiful poems, among them one masterpiece—that is Meredith's achievement as a poet. And the masterpiece, antedating Freud and the other psychologists by a half-century, is yet intensely modern, a searching study of modern agonies of perishing love in marriage. (p. 216)

> *Harriet Monroe, "Meredith as a Poet," in* Poetry, *Vol. XXXII, No. IV, July, 1928, pp. 210-16.*

VIRGINIA WOOLF (essay date 1928)

[*Woolf is considered one of the most prominent literary figures of twentieth-century English literature. Like her contemporary James Joyce, with whom she is often compared, Woolf is remembered as one of the most innovative of the stream of consciousness novelists. Concerned primarily with depicting the life of the mind, she revolted against traditional narrative techniques and developed her own highly individualized style. Woolf's works, noted for their subjective explorations of characters' inner lives and their delicate poetic quality, have had a lasting effect on the art of the novel. A discerning and influential critic and essayist as well as a novelist, Woolf began writing reviews for* The Times Literary Supplement *at an early age. Her critical essays, which cover almost the entire range of English literature, contain some of her finest prose and are praised for their insight. Along with Lytton Strachey, Roger Fry, Clive Bell, and several others, Woolf and her husband Leonard formed the literary coterie known as the "Bloomsbury Group." In the following excerpt, published in the* Times Literary Supplement *in 1928, Woolf summarizes Meredith's development as a novelist, concluding that while greatly skilled, he often settled for second-rate literary effects. Nevertheless, Woolf believes that this combination of strength and weakness in Meredith's novels makes him one of the great eccentrics of English literature whose works will be alternately forgotten and discovered as long as English fiction is read.*]

Twenty years ago the reputation of George Meredith was at its height. His novels had won their way to celebrity through all sorts of difficulties, and their fame was all the brighter and the more singular for what it had subdued. (p. 245)

But that is twenty years ago. . . . On none of his successors is his influence now marked. When one of them whose own work has given him the right to be heard with respect chances to speak his mind on the subject, it is not flattering. . . . No, the general conclusion would seem to be, Meredith has not worn well. But the value of centenaries lies in the occasion they offer us for solidifying such airy impressions. Talk, mixed with half-rubbed-out memories, forms a mist by degrees through which we scarcely see plain. To open the books again, to try to read them as if for the first time, to try to free them from the rubbish of reputation and accident—that, perhaps, is the most acceptable present we can offer to a writer on his hundredth birthday.

And since the first novel is always apt to be an unguarded one, where the author displays his gifts without knowing how to dispose of them to the best advantage, we may do well to open *Richard Feverel* first. It needs no great sagacity to see that the writer is a novice at his task. The style is extremely uneven. Now he twists himself into iron knots; now he lies flat as a pancake. He seems to be of two minds as to his intention. Ironic comment alternates with long-winded narrative. He vacillates from one attitude to another. Indeed, the whole fabric seems to rock a little insecurely. The baronet wrapped in a cloak; the country family; the ancestral home; the uncles mouthing epigrams in the dining-room; the great ladies flaunting and swimming; the jolly farmers slapping their thighs: all liberally if spasmodically sprinkled with dried aphorisms from a pepperpot called the Pilgrim's Scrip—what an odd conglomeration it is! But the oddity is not on the surface; it is not merely that whiskers and bonnets have gone out of fashion: it lies deeper, in Meredith's intention, in what he wishes to bring to pass. He has been, it is plain, at great pains to destroy the conventional form of the novel. He makes no attempt to preserve the sober reality of Trollope and Jane Austen; he has destroyed all the usual staircases by which we have learnt to climb. And what is done so deliberately is done with a purpose. This defiance of the ordinary, these airs and graces, the formality of the dialogue with its Sirs and Madams are all there to create an atmosphere that is unlike that of daily life, to prepare the way for a new and an original sense of the human scene. Peacock, from whom Meredith learnt so much, is equally arbitrary, but the virtue of the assumptions he asks us to make is proved by the fact that we accept Mr. Skionar and the rest with natural delight. Meredith's characters in *Richard Feverel*, on the other hand, are at odds with their surroundings. We at once exclaim how unreal they are, how artificial, how impossible. The baronet and the butler, the hero and the heroine, the good woman and the bad woman are mere types of baronets and butler, good women and bad. For what reason, then, has he sacrificed the substantial advantages of realistic common sense—the staircase and the stucco? Because, it becomes clear as we read, he possessed a keen sense not of the complexity of character, but of the splendour of a scene. One after another in this first book he creates a scene to which we can attach abstract names—Youth, The Birth of Love, The Power of Nature. We are galloped to them over every obstacle on the pounding hoofs of rhapsodical prose. (pp. 246-48)

The writer is a rhapsodist, a poet then; but we have not yet exhausted all the elements in this first novel. We have to reckon with the author himself. He has a mind stuffed with ideas, hungry for argument. His boys and girls may spend their time picking daisies in the meadows, but they breathe, however unconsciously, an air bristling with intellectual question and comment. On a dozen occasions these incongruous elements strain and threaten to break apart. The book is cracked through and through with those fissures which come when the author seems to be of twenty minds at the same time. Yet it succeeds in holding miraculously together, not certainly by the depths and originality of its character drawing but by the vigour of its intellectual power and by its lyrical intensity.

We are left, then, with our curiosity aroused. Let him write another book or two; get into his stride; control his crudities: and we will open *Harry Richmond* and see what has happened now. Of all the things that might have happened this surely is the strangest. All trace of immaturity is gone; but with it every trace of the uneasy adventurous mind has gone too. The story bowls smoothly along the road which Dickens has already

trodden of autobiographical narrative. It is a boy speaking, a boy thinking, a boy adventuring. For that reason, no doubt, the author has curbed his redundance and pruned his speech. The style is the most rapid possible. It runs smooth, without a kink in it. Stevenson, one feels, must have learnt much from this supple narrative, with its precise adroit phrases, its exact quick glance at visible things.

It goes gallantly, but a little self-consciously. He hears himself talking. Doubts begin to rise and hover and settle at last (as in *Richard Feverel*) upon the human figures. These boys are no more real boys than the sample apple which is laid on top of the basket is a real apple. They are too simple, too gallant, too adventurous to be of the same unequal breed as David Copperfield, for example. They are sample boys, novelist's specimens; and again we encounter the extreme conventionality of Meredith's mind where we found it, to our surprise, before. With all his boldness (and there is no risk that he will not run with probability) there are a dozen occasions on which a reach-me-down character will satisfy him well enough. But just as we are thinking that the young gentlemen are altogether too pat, and the adventures which befall them altogether too slick, the shallow bath of illusion closes over our heads and we sink with Richmond Roy and the Princess Ottilia into the world of fantasy and romance, where all holds together and we are able to put our imagination at the writer's service without reserve. . . . That Meredith can induce such moments proves him possessed of an extraordinary power. Yet it is a capricious power and highly intermittent. For pages all is effort and agony; phrase after phrase is struck and no light comes. Then, just as we are about to drop the book, the rocket roars into the air; the whole scene flashes into light; and the book, years after, is recalled by that sudden splendour.

If, then, this intermittent brilliancy is Meredith's characteristic excellence it is worth while to look into it more closely. And perhaps the first thing that we shall discover is that the scenes which catch the eye and remain in memory are static; they are illuminations, not discoveries; they do not improve our knowledge of the characters. It is significant that Richard and Lucy, Harry and Ottilia, Clara and Vernon, Beauchamp and Renée are presented in carefully appropriate surroundings—on board a yacht, under a flowering cherry tree, upon some river-bank, so that the landscape always makes part of the emotion. The sea or the sky or the wood is brought forward to symbolise what the human beings are feeling or looking. (pp. 248-51)

Meredith . . . is not among the great psychologists who feel their way, anonymously and patiently, in and out of the fibres of the mind and make one character differ minutely and completely from another. He is among the poets who identify the character with the passion or with the idea; who symbolise and make abstract. And yet—here lay his difficulty perhaps—he was not a poet-novelist wholly and completely as Emily Brontë was a poet-novelist. He did not steep the world in one mood. His mind was too self-conscious, and too sophisticated to remain lyrical for long. He does not sing only; he dissects. Even in his most lyrical scenes a sneer curls its lash round the phrases and laughs at their extravagance. And as we read on, we shall find that the comic spirit, when it is allowed to dominate the scene, licked the world to a very different shape. *The Egoist* at once modifies our theory that Meredith is pre-eminently the master of great scenes. Here there is none of that precipitate hurry that has rushed us over obstacles to the summit of one emotional peak after another. The case is one that needs argument; argument needs logic; Sir Willoughby, "our original male in giant form'', is turned slowly round before a steady fire of scrutiny and criticism which allows no twitch on the victim's part to escape it. That the victim is a wax model and not entirely living flesh and blood is perhaps true. At the same time Meredith pays us a supreme compliment to which as novel-readers we are little accustomed. We are civilised people, he seems to say, watching the comedy of human relations together. Human relations are of profound interest.... He imagines us capable of disinterested curiosity in the behaviour of our kind. This is so rare a complement from a novelist to his reader that we are at first bewildered and then delighted. Indeed his comic spirit is a far more penetrating goddess than his lyrical. It is she who cuts a clear path through the brambles of his manner; she who surprises us again and again by the depth of her observations; she who creates the dignity, the seriousness, and the vitality of Meredith's world. Had Meredith, one is tempted to reflect, lived in an age or in a country where comedy was the rule, he might never have contracted those airs of intellectual superiority, that manner of oracular solemnity which it is, as he points out, the use of the comic spirit to correct.

But in many ways the age—if we can judge so amorphous a shape—was hostile to Meredith, or, to speak more accurately, was hostile to his success with the age we now live in—the year 1928. His teaching seems now too strident and too optimistic and too shallow. It obtrudes; and when philosophy is not consumed in a novel, when we can underline this phrase with a pencil, and cut out that exhortation with a pair of scissors and paste the whole into a system, it is safe to say that there is something wrong with the philosophy or with the novel or with both. Above all, his teaching is too insistent. He cannot, even to hear the profoundest secret, suppress his own opinion. And there is nothing that characters in fiction resent more. If, they seem to argue, we have been called into existence merely to express Mr. Meredith's views upon the universe, we would rather not exist at all. Thereupon they die; and a novel that is full of dead characters, even though it is also full of profound wisdom and exalted teaching, is not achieving its aim as a novel. But here we reach another point upon which the present age may be inclined to have more sympathy with Meredith. When he wrote, in the seventies and eighties of the last century, the novel had reached a stage where it could only exist by moving onward. It is a possible contention that after those two perfect novels, *Pride and Prejudice* and *The Small House at Allington,* English fiction had to escape from the dominion of that perfection, as English poetry had to escape from the perfection of Tennyson. George Eliot, Meredith, and Hardy were all imperfect novelists largely because they insisted upon introducing qualities, of thought and of poetry, that are perhaps incompatible with fiction at its most perfect. On the other hand, if fiction had remained what it was to Jane Austen and Trollope, fiction would by this time be dead. Thus Meredith deserves our gratitude and excites our interest as a great innovator. Many of our doubts about him and much of our inability to frame any definite opinion of his work comes from the fact that it is experimental and thus contains elements that do not fuse harmoniously—the qualities are at odds: the one quality which binds and concentrates has been omitted. To read Meredith, then, to our greatest advantage we must make certain allowances and relax certain standards. We must not expect the perfect quietude of a traditional style nor the triumphs of a patient and pedestrian psychology. On the other hand, his claim, ''My method has been to prepare my readers for a crucial exhibition of the personae, and then to give the scene in the fullest of their blood and brain under stress of a fierce situa-

tion'', is frequently justified. Scene after scene rises on the mind's eye with a flare of fiery intensity. If we are irritated by the dancing-master dandyism which made him write ''gave his lungs full play'' instead of laughed, or ''tasted the swift intricacies of the needle'' instead of sewed, we must remember that such phrases prepare the way for the ''fierce situations''. Meredith is creating the atmosphere from which we shall pass naturally into a highly pitched state of emotion. Where the realistic novelist, like Trollope, lapses into flatness and dullness, the lyrical novelist, like Meredith, becomes meritricious and false; and such falsity is, of course, not only much more glaring than flatness, but it is a greater crime against the phlegmatic nature of prose fiction. Perhaps Meredith had been well advised if he had abjured the novel altogether and kept himself wholly to poetry. Yet we have to remind ourselves that the fault may be ours. Our prolonged diet upon Russian fiction, rendered neutral and negative in translation, our absorption in the convolutions of psychological Frenchmen, may have led us to forget that the English language is naturally exuberant, and the English character full of humours and eccentricities. Meredith's flamboyancy has a great ancestry behind it; we cannot avoid all memory of Shakespeare. (pp. 252-53)

[To] read Meredith is to be conscious of a packed and muscular mind; of a voice booming and reverberating with its own unmistakable accent even though the partition between us is too thick for us to hear what he says distinctly. Still, as we read we feel that we are in the presence of a Greek god though he is surrounded by the innumerable ornaments of a suburban drawing-room; who talks brilliantly, even if he is deaf to the lower tones of the human voice; who, if he is rigid and immobile, is yet marvellously alive and on the alert. This brilliant and uneasy figure has his place with the great eccentrics rather than with the great masters. He will be read, one may guess, by fits and starts; he will be forgotten and discovered and again discovered and forgotten like Donne, and Peacock, and Gerard Hopkins. But if English fiction continues to be read, the novels of Meredith must inevitably rise from time to time into view; his work must inevitably be disputed and discussed. (p. 256)

> *Virginia Woolf, ''The Novels of George Meredith,''*
> *in her* The Second Common Reader, *Harcourt Brace*
> *Jovanovich, 1932, pp. 245-56.*

EDWARD WAGENKNECHT   (essay date 1943)

[*Wagenknecht is an American biographer and critic. His works include critical surveys of the English and American novel and studies of Charles Dickens, Mark Twain, and Henry James, among many others. His studies of Dickens and Twain employ the biographical technique of ''psychography,'' derived from American biographer Gamaliel Bradford, who writes of this method: ''Out of the perpetual flux of actions and circumstances that constitutes a man's whole life, it seeks to extract what is essential, what is permanent and so vitally characteristic.'' In later works Wagenknecht has focused more on the literary than biographical aspects of his subjects, though he states: ''I have no theories about writing except that I think people should write about what they care for.'' In the following excerpt, Wagenknecht characterizes Meredith as a thoroughly modern novelist whose works address many of the central concerns of twentieth century life, but whose writing style was so obscure that only the most dedicated readers have discovered his works.*]

With Meredith the ''new'' novel is upon us with a vengeance— obliqueness, indirectness, elaborate psychological analysis, sustained intellectuality, and all the rest of it. It will be interesting to compare him at the outset both with George Eliot and with Thomas Hardy.

Meredith's first novel, *The Ordeal of Richard Feverel,* came out the same year as *Adam Bede.* . . .

Both Meredith and George Eliot were tremendously interested in the problems of human conduct, and both found the root of our difficulties in the same fault—selfishness. (p. 336)

The differences between the two writers, however, are even more striking than their resemblances. George Eliot worked through tragedy, Meredith through comedy. So completely was he committed to the comic standpoint that he saw even the woeful story of Ferdinand Lassalle and Helena von Dönniges as the history of a pair of "tragic comedians." George Eliot wrote verses but Meredith was a poet, and, profoundly ethical though he was, his approach to fiction, unlike hers, was less a moralist's than a poet's. He was, too, a far more original, though a far less systematic, thinker than she. George Eliot identified religion so completely with the dogmas she discarded that, having lost the dogmas, she never found religious certitude again. Meredith, on the other hand, worked out a philosophy of life which, whether he was right or wrong, completely satisfied his conscious needs. Finally, George Eliot, though she rearranged her material to suit her thesis, still attempted a realistic representation of life. Meredith's picture of life, on the other hand, can be called realistic only if God is a Meredithian.

Meredith and Hardy both accepted the teachings of modern science, but so far as human life was concerned they deduced diametrically opposed conclusions. In Hardy nature is coldly indifferent to man when she is not actively malevolent. Egdon Heath is the real hero of *The Return of the Native;* the human characters can find peace only as they submit themselves to it; whoever resists is crushed. How different is Richard Feverel's experience when he goes out walking in the rain on the darkest night of his life! (p. 337)

Meredith himself had much to say to men to strengthen their courage for life; Hardy's is often interpreted as a voice of despair. Yet because Hardy's novels are easy, delightful reading they are a living force in men's lives today, while, thanks to the difficulties of their style, Meredith's too often stand, a set of books, in quiet dignity upon the shelf. (p. 338)

Meredith's novels were the result of his philosophy of life and of his philosophy of fiction. First, we must consider his philosophy of life.

Basically, he was a nature-worshiper, deriving ultimately from Wordsworth. His later views were modified by his study of Darwin, who seems to have helped him to retain his optimism by making it possible for him to think of struggle and death as simply part of a vast cosmic process whose ultimate development should be perfection.

This is Meredith's new romanticism, a romanticism based on science and therefore not open to the objections which have been justly urged against the old evasive romanticism of the past. (pp. 340-41)

Though Meredith was an evolutionist, he did not share the easy faith in automatic progress which comforted such men as Macaulay and Herbert Spencer. He goes far deeper than they do. It is true that the evolutionary process has operated unconsciously in the past. But it is also true that on that basis it has produced an "all but sensational world." Now that the process

has achieved a directive intelligence in the minds of purposeful men, better things are in prospect. Only, to serve the needs of life, man must get rid of self. (p. 341)

From Meredith's attitude toward nature follows inevitably his attitude toward love. He rejects asceticism; he will not disown his mother; the tree can grow only when it is "planted in good gross earth." A man who hates women hates nature, and men who hate nature are insane. . . . Meredith perceived that even the male demand for "purity" in women is often merely a means of feeding the male ego. (pp. 341-42)

But though the tree is "planted in good gross earth," it does not blossom there. Meredith was not interested in sex; he was interested in love. This does not mean that he shies from sex. He defends sex wholeheartedly against the Puritan, but that is because the Puritan attitude toward sex, as he sees it, is an impure attitude. His real interest is in something far transcending any physical relationship. . . .

Hating sensuality, Meredith hates sentimentalism also, for sentimentalism is a kind of ingrown sensuality. Sentimental people "fiddle harmonics on the strings of sensualism." Indeed sentimentalism is more dangerous than sensuality, for the very reason that its true character is disguised. (p. 342)

It is a mistake to suppose that Meredith knew no influence from his predecessors. Shakespeare's influence appears in more than the "Ferdinand and Miranda" chapter of *Feverel.* Meredith admired Fielding. His early books are full of Dickensian grotesques, generally badly handled. Both *Clarissa* and *The Mill on the Floss* are reflected in *Rhoda Fleming.* . . . More important than any of these was Meredith's father-in-law, Thomas Love Peacock, who anticipated a number of his themes and specific convictions.

Yet he was one of the most original of writers. What he did was done deliberately. . . . He is as much interested in the thoughts of his characters as in their emotions, but he insists on presenting them in action rather than in repose. (pp. 346-47)

The difficulty is that sometimes he does not prepare. He longed for an audience which would "feel the winds of March when they do not blow," which is perhaps not quite a reasonable demand. As a narrator he stands, among English novelists, at the opposite end of the scale from Defoe. If it be a pardonable exaggeration to say that Defoe is all narrative, then one may also say of Meredith that he has no interest in narrative and no gift for it. This is what that often surprisingly just and acute critic, Oscar Wilde, had in mind when he remarked that Meredith could do everything except tell a story.

As a narrator he never seems to know what to "develop." He may labor an unimportant point through pages and pages, and then pass over a vital crisis with a phrase. The central situation in *Rhoda Fleming* is poignant but it fails to move us as it should because, for fatally long periods, the author keeps the principals out of sight, while the foreground is occupied with minor characters like Algernon Blancove and Mrs. Lovell. Elaborate preparations are made in this novel for the meeting between Rhoda and her sister Dahlia. When at last it occurs, it takes place between chapters!

We follow Emilia through two long novels to find out whether she will wed Merthyr Powys or not, but when the last page of *Vittoria* has been turned, we still do not know. Much of *Beauchamp's Career* is given over to the hero's attempt to force his uncle to apologize to Dr. Shrapnel for having beaten him— which is surely a minor incident either in Beauchamp's "career'' or in his life—while his marriage and death, for no particular reason, by drowning, are both crowded into the last two chapters.

Perhaps the real difficulty in such instances is not that Meredith goes too far but that he does not go far enough. Possibly, having broken away from so many elements in the Victorian novel, he ought to have broken away from one more—the plot. His plots have the unbelievable complexity of a Congreve comedy; and they are no easier to follow because, unlike Congreve, he presents them indirectly. As J. B. Priestley points out, there is no "middle distance" in his fiction. "Either we see his people as little puppets illuminated by lightning flashes of wit, or we are almost inside their minds, swayed hither and thither by their lightest emotions." At times they really are puppets, for Meredith is not incapable of violating the integrity of a characterization to serve the needs of a "theme" or a plot. Few readers are convinced that Richard Feverel really would have stayed away from Lucy . . . and few are convinced that Diana would have sold the secret.

The difficulties of Meredith's narrative art are only reinforced by the difficulties of his style. (pp. 347-48)

There are times when Meredith as a stylist seems to have taken the advice of the Countess de Saldar: "Yes, dear Van!" she told her brother, "that is how you should behave. Imply things." (p. 348)

Sometimes, to be sure, Meredith only makes us the dupes of our own stupidity, and then we have no right to complain. The following passage from *Beauchamp's Career* is often cited as an example of his implicational style; all the essential clues are there:

> Captain Baskelett requested the favor of five minutes of conversation with Miss Halkett before he followed Mr. Austin on his way to Steynham. She returned from the colloquy to her father and Mr. Tuckham. The colonel looked straight in her face, with an elevation of the brows. To these points of interrogation she answered with a placid fall of her eyelids. He sounded a note of approbation in his throat.

We are to understand that Captain Baskelett has proposed marriage, has been rejected, and that the colonel approves.

But Meredith is not always as clear as this. And there are passages which are ineffective not because they are obscure but because they are affected and absurd. His women never walk; they swim; Diana swims to the tea-tray. The Countess de Saldar "rambles concentrically." Dahlia "eyes" Edward a "faint sweetness." (pp. 348-49)

It was a tragedy—for Meredith and for his readers. Here is one of the finest minds that ever devoted itself to English fiction. Here is a writer who, in his fashion, achieved a solution of half the problems which beset the modern mind before very many people knew that they existed. Here is a thinker who, whether one accepts all the implications of his philosophy or not, did have something to say to his age in terms which that age ought to have been able to understand; yet because he was unable or unwilling to make himself clear to his contemporaries, he has never reached—and he never will reach—more than a fraction of his potential audience. (p. 349)

Meredith seems to have been a man who could not bear to say even obvious things in an obvious manner; a visitor at Box Hill has recorded being invited to "lave" his hands before lunch. Unfortunately one cannot write a novel without saying a good many obvious things. And when they are not said obviously they are said badly.

It is impossible to read Meredith without noticing these things, but it would be a mistake to blame him for them. With him, as with all great writers, the style is the man. Katherine Mansfield was perfectly correct when she perceived that she must change her Self before she could change her work. But Meredith lacked Katherine Mansfield's divine humility. (pp. 349-50)

There is an element of self-castigation in his fiction. Sir Austin Feverel fails with his wife and child in something the manner that Meredith himself failed; and at the very time he was concealing the facts of his origin he revealed them as fiction in *Evan Harrington,* and in such detail that he made all his relatives squirm. If Thackeray, historian of snobbery, was himself a snob, why could not Meredith, authority on egoism, be an egoist himself? Especially since he himself declared that Willoughby was all of us?

Take such a man, with a natural dislike of banality and a natural tendency toward indirection . . . ; subject him for years to consistent neglect as a writer (and we have positive evidence that Meredith smarted under that neglect and actively resented it); then bring him, in his later years, into widespread fame; and it is inevitable that he should indulge himself somewhat. (pp. 350-51)

It is too bad that he was not able to rise above all this, but we who are human will understand only too well why he did not. And however he may try our patience, we can neglect him only at our peril. He was no poseur. Even those who are most annoyed by his idiosyncrasies find his work persistently coming back to them, long after they had imagined they were done with him. He has vitality despite all his indirection; a profound sincerity underlies his innumerable flourishes. In some inexplicable way, his pages seem curiously flooded with light. (p. 351)

> Edward Wagenknecht, "The Poetic Comedy of George Meredith," in his Cavalcade of the English Novel, 1943. Reprint by Henry Holt and Company, 1954, pp. 336-51.

WALTER F. WRIGHT   (essay date 1953)

[In the following excerpt, Wright discusses the philosophical and psychological theories that are developed in Meredith's novels.]

When Meredith published *The Ordeal of Richard Feverel,* in 1859, literature was still in the main dominated by what is vaguely termed classical psychology, with its emphasis on the importance of the will. Before his death, as students of the novel are aware, many writers had come to stress the role of the subconscious, to explore the obscure emotional impulses which often shape a man's life unrecognized by his conscious mind. With the new field of exploration there came, too, much experimentation in narrative method. Though Meredith began writing when Dickens and Thackeray were popular, with their traditional straightforward plots and their tendency to hold the individual consciously responsible for his actions, and though he continued into the era of Proust, his literary career does not represent a steady progression from the old to the new. Rather, his early fiction anticipates the new and his late work still has much of the old. In *The Ordeal* appeared subtle illuminations of the subconscious; and *One of Our Conquerors,* published thirty-one years later, differs only in exploring what for Meredith were yet unscanned recesses of the mind. At the same time, he did not waver from his initial appeal to the conscious mind, and he invariably judged man's darkest actions in the daylight that permits conscious choice.

Meredith was also from the beginning given to experiment, trying to bend the narrative form to his wish, whether to include a chapter of lyric prose-poetry or to indulge in a leisurely character or philosophic analysis; in fact, he rarely thought of plot as having a tight dramatic sequence or a uniform epic perspective. Yet he did not use several of the techniques which by 1900 were replacing chronological order with that of psychological awareness, as in Conrad's *Lord Jim.* Though interested in the mental turmoil of his characters, he continued to resort to dots to indicate that a mind had deserted the realm of articulate thought and entered that of the loose association of images—an area which Henry James and others were beginning to open as a rich field for the artist to explore. Some of his most effective scenes are ultratraditional, indeed closely reminiscent of his favorite comic dramatists—Menander, Terence, and Molière—in their brilliant dramatic clash of ideas and types of character; and in such traditional scenes the reader finds both novelty and subtlety. On the other hand, some of his shrewdest character analyses helped in the growth of the psychological novel.

The transitional position of Meredith is amusingly revealed in the history of his reputation among journalistic reviewers and literary critics. His first books were disturbing to conventional reviewers because they did not conform to established patterns. . . . Today . . . the general narrative patterns of his fiction are safely within the limits of current practice and so present no obvious newness to the casual reader, and his interpretations of life are in danger of being insufficiently appreciated because they have lost not their depth but their novelty. Actually, Meredith was an experimentalist well grounded in tradition. (pp. 2-4)

Like Sir Philip Sidney, Meredith held that literature must unite precept and example. Again and again he wrote, often within a novel itself, that fiction must present ideas; and his Pilgrim's Scrip, Book of Maxims, Philosopher, and other choral commentaries are devices to introduce informal discussion of ideas. Stressing the need of philosophy, he would have all character analysis and all romance philosophic. Poetry, however—and by implication prose fiction—he once wrote, was superior to philosophy by itself in that it wedded ideas and emotions. In short, it presented both ideas and the emotional involvements which arise as soon as the ideas find a home in a human mind. The major province of the novelist, as illustrated in Meredith's own fiction, was the dramatic turmoil within the mind when, having but imperfectly understood the ideas, the mind could not easily resolve apparent conflicts between them or, more often, between the emotions which accompanied them. The resolution of these conflicts for a character or the analysis of the cause of his failure to resolve them made the principal action of a novel. (p. 5)

Underlying Meredith's literary theory are his concepts of the world of nature, of the intellectual and emotional structure of human beings, and of the social order in which the mind can best develop. His own perception of nature allowed him to recognize the ruthlessness in animal and plant struggle for survival; and he considered the life of the savage, that is, the life which adapted itself least from primitive nature, to be uniformly deplorable. Savagery, of course, was not a matter

of living in wattled huts; it was a submission to animal standards of culture and, under a veneer of politeness, could dominate an industrial society. To achieve self-discipline man must accept the stern fact that nature destroys the spiritually passive mind. . . . (pp. 5-6)

Like the Romantics, Meredith found in nature immediate spiritual inspiration. *Love in the Valley,* the well known Ferdinand and Miranda scene in *The Ordeal of Richard Feverel,* and lines in "**Meditation under Stars**" typify the exaltation brought by natural scenery; and elsewhere, as in Richard's walk in the German forest, Meredith can speak of the healing and purifying which nature brings. (p. 6)

An evolutionist, Meredith believed the "Spirit of Life" to be forever unfolding itself within man and nature, with man contributing to the progress. Here in accord with the Positivists, he nevertheless preferred artistic insight to scientific inquiry in identifying man's part in the universal growth. He did not speculate on abstract concepts of ultimate causes, but, both in his poetry and his novels, he was, like George Eliot, preoccupied with the capacities of the human mind. He felt that a man could be held personally responsible for contributing to the spirituality of the universe.

Meredith's favorite trinity, given always in ascending order—blood, brain, spirit—assumes the latent existence of animal joy, reason, and the capacity for aspiring to beauty and goodness. . . . Ideally, blood was not to be suppressed, but, on the contrary, strengthened and at the same time disciplined by brain to contribute to spirit. (p. 7)

Stress on this point is necessary because, though there was ample authority in the tradition of Chaucer, Shakespeare, and Fielding for the frank acceptance of man's animal nature, the novelist believed that his own age in its determination to be civilized was setting up a foolish conflict by repression and under a refined and polished exterior was really perpetuating animality in its rawest form. With the attack by the clergy upon *The Ordeal of Richard Feverel* as an immoral book, he had full justification for reasserting his trinity and for repeating his objections to the artificial education which would build spirit with disregard for nature as expressed in blood. (pp. 7-8)

It was a major fault of the sentimentalists of the time that they glossed over egoism as a maladjustment easily overcome. Meredith accepted it as an inevitable condition of human nature. Though he gave no specific illustration, he admitted in the introductory chapter to *The Egoist* that in the youth of a nation the aggressive assertion of the ego could be harmless and might accompany action of benefit to the race. When the ego ceased, however, to exert itself in the mastery of nature and the building of a social order and began instead to resist social change from fear of loss of self-importance, it became defensive and abnormal. Only then should it be castigated and corrected. The instinct would remain, as it was inseparable from the urge to survive; its negative expression as defensive resistance must be destroyed if brain were to develop spirit and evolution were to be a process of spiritual improvement.

Of the seriousness of the perversion of egoism Meredith could find sufficient evidence in literature. . . . In nineteenth-century England itself Meredith could discover almost unlimited evidence of man's fear of change. The resistance to the idea of evolution by those who could not see that it expanded the boundaries of a human mind and saw instead only a shunting of themselves from the center to the periphery was a gigantic defensive assertion of the ego against aggressive new ideas.

Though he did not specifically attack anti-evolutionists, Meredith made very clear in his novels that he felt that the clergy were generally among those who resisted philosophic change and who looked upon the soul not as an agent fighting its way upward in a limitless spiritual world, but rather as a precious static entity to be protected from external struggle.

Actually Meredith more directly reprimanded the scientists, including the evolutionists; indeed the reason why he is perenially alive is that he never accepted a significant view or a mode of conduct without looking at once for its possible absurdities and laughing heartily at them. Scientists he found too willing to make science an explanation for everything and so to defend the limited faculty of reason against the encroachment of the poetic imagination. It should at once be pointed out that in neither instance, whether in satirizing the clergy or the scientists, was Meredith passing judgment on religion or on science as they could be understood by the well-rounded philosophical thinker. He was concerned with the popular inertia in religion which retarded change and with a popular inertia no less serious which would make knowledge of scientific fact a protective shell in which the mind of a Sir Willoughby Patterne, for example, could take egoistic refuge against the complexities in the world of the artistic imagination. Putting man in some outer region of the spiritual universe or making him a deterministic creature was contradictory to Meredith's belief in the significance of individual spirituality. At the same time, he believed that the individual mind reached its highest form only when in intimate concord with nature and when self-forgetfully participating in a community of ideas. It was a function of literature to illustrate this truth and to show how affinity of human minds was to be achieved.

In political and social life Meredith found egocentric assumptions almost proportionate to the seriousness of one's convictions. The obstinacy of the political traditionalist is nicely epitomized by Tory Squire Beltham's comment, in *The Adventures of Harry Richmond:* "It's Scripture says we're going from better to worse, and that's Tory doctrine." It is reflected by Everard Romfrey, in *Beauchamp's Career,* by Sir Willoughby, and by the dozen or more others who insist on living in a past age and opposing democratic change. But the radicals, among whom Meredith classed himself, could be equally intolerant and defensive in their determination to twist the world to their views instead of adapting themselves—witness the comic inconsistencies of the radical Beauchamp. Here was a fertile area for literature comic in method but profoundly serious in intent; for as Meredith insisted, we need the mental stimulation provided by society, and yet as soon as we take part in it we lose our detached acceptance of ideals and become the self-conscious defenders of ourselves as the possessors of the ideals. The clash of idea with idea could be examined in a speculative treatise in philosophy, but literature gave the ideas a lively and complex psychological significance by making them struggle for survival in a conflict of instinct and emotion within intricate and humanly inconsistent minds.

Of all the manifestations of egocentricity the relation of the sexes was, Meredith maintained, the most striking and persistent. In novel after novel he gave delightful variations on the theme laid down in *The Egoist* that "the love-season is the carnival of egoism, and it brings the touchstone to our natures." The comic paradox resided in the fact that, though the typical lover, as the novelist saw him, began by worshiping his beloved because she was a goddess, he never thought of following her to Olympus, but at once started plotting to entrap her in his own little windowless hut on the plain. Having glimpsed a new region of crystal atmosphere, he returned defensively to his own dusty haze. . . . The pattern of the lover's conquest, identified closely with man's erratic voyaging between the rock of asceticism and the whirlpool of sensuality, was, like it, deeply serious in import yet comic in its incongruous shiftings of course and in the contrast between pretense and reality.

From the egoism of the individual, as Meredith stressed, rose the colossal coral fabric of conventions and mores, built by a multitude of egoists down through history and extended as devotedly by women, the persons who suffered most, as by men. Courtly polish, protective chivalry, the development of a cult of worship of woman might mitigate the crudeness of the act, but they were sometimes actually the devices for the marital rape of her body and the enslavement of her mind. Of crude sexual passion Meredith wrote only briefly and never in detail. Undesirable as such passion might be, it was not likely to be correctible through literature, least of all through literature requiring superior intelligence to comprehend. But the masqueraded form protected by convention might be found in highly intellectual persons, and it was a province of literature to strip away the mask to reveal the crass brutality beneath. At a time when the John Stuart Mills were pointing out the glaring legal injustices to women and later when the advocates of women's rights were demanding specific social changes, Meredith was a steady proponent of revision of the marriage laws, and he once went so far as to approve of trial marriage. Though in his novels he did not propagandize for legal reforms, he repeatedly exposed the actual relation of the sexes to make his readers see that marriage as the possession and control of one mind by another was unpardonable folly. In stressing the mental tyranny involved in the relationship of the sexes, as in each of his other attempts to correct man's egocentric bias, the novelist was concerned with expanding his reader's imagination, an essential, indeed primary, function of the literary artist. (pp. 9-13)

In a general way Meredith's theory would apply to the works of a diverse group of novelists, including the most objective writers as well as many who have been preoccupied with tracing the vagaries of the subconscious. In actual practice it meant for Meredith strong emphasis on the theme of a novel and a tendency to make his characters symbolize the values which he was contrasting. The conflict within his stories is always of a type that would have pleased Aristotle; the character is at fault, either in having an unsound sense of values or in letting passion destroy his judgment. Though at times the novelist inconsistently turned a scene over to comic eccentrics who contributed little to the progress of his narrative and though he sometimes made obvious, even tedious interpretations of the action which he had objectively presented, the best of his novels have a symmetry based on the weaving throughout of a dominant theme, with variations and with contrasts to heighten its significance. (pp. 13-14)

Meredith himself sought to keep in close touch with actuality to the extent of sometimes using actual persons and incidents in his stories. But he interpreted them in reference to what he understood of psychological principles, and he chose them initially because he believed that they exemplified themes. When successful, as in *The Tragic Comedians,* he gave to the actual historical persons motives for their actions where the memoirs were scant and ambiguous. When he fumbled in *Diana of the Crossways,* it turned out that the historical incident which he believed had occurred—the betrayal of a state secret—had actually not taken place, but the weakness of the novel was in the author's inability to bring to his own incident the motivation to make it plausible. Realism . . . is what gives verisimilitude to his scenes, as in the excellent sketches of London; and it is sometimes the lack of it that leaves his minor characters uninteresting abstractions. But it is idealism which makes his best-drawn characters symbolize truths. When tracing the shoddy parasitism of Algernon Blancove in *Rhoda Fleming,* Meredith supplied extensive realistic details on his gambling and his hand-to-mouth struggle to survive, but he had first of all in his mind the ideal concept of a man with the survival-of-the-fittest amorality of the beast. The external phenomena were subordinate to the novelist's use of Algernon in the interpretation of his theme.

Though he wrote little about his methods of composition, a letter to [G. P.] Baker, July 22, 1887, reveals his emphasis on character and scene—with no mention of articulation of plot—and his defense of his highly intricate style of expression:

> My method has been to prepare my readers for a crucial exhibition of the personae, and then to give the scene in the fullest of their blood and brain under stress of a fiery situation.
>
> Concerning style, thought is tough, and dealing with thought produces toughness. . . .
>
> In the Comedies and here and there where a concentrated presentment is in design, you will find a 'pitch' considerably above our common human; and purposely, for only in such a manner could so much be shown. Those high notes and condensings are abandoned when the strong human call is heard—I beg you to understand merely that such was my intention.

Clearly the novelist considered his fiction to be at its best a thoughtful, indeed philosophic, distillation of life and at the same time a conscious work of art fusing idealism and romance in its tone and pattern.

Humanly inconsistent, Meredith often fell short of his own ideals of composition. Blaming Hugo for working too much with black and white characters, he made his own Vernon Whitford, Redworth, and Matey Weyburn paragons of good sense, learning, and virtue. Protesting, too, in *Sandra Belloni* that readers wanted to read about puppets and that he would at least put noses on those he gave them, he could still imitate Dickens' eccentrics, sometimes with only one distinguishing feature. . . . Despite the shortcomings, however, in such unrealistic sketches—the novelist himself trimmed away some in revision—his novels at their best approach his ideals. It is when his dramatic representation of complex motives begins that idealism and realism work together to create not only noses but subtle indentations in the folds of the brain. It is then that comedy, by laying bare feelings and ideas, performs its function of stripping romance of tinseled illusion and tragedy of the taint of unreflecting sentimentality. Then the world in which the characters and we, the readers, move is revealed to be not an artificial realm, with its dinner parties, *fêtes champêtres,* and witty conversation, but the composite of a multitude of human minds, each a veritable world within itself, yet each possessing spiritual affinities with others to make broad symmetric patterns and reveal general truths. (pp. 15-17)

> *Walter F. Wright, in his* Art and Substance in George Meredith: A Study in Narrative, *University of Nebraska Press, 1953, 211 p.*

I. M. WILLIAMS (essay date 1967)

[*In the following excerpt Williams examines the comic structure of* The Ordeal of Richard Feverel, *finding that in Meredith's works comedy develops not from comical action but from the motivation of the characters.*]

Richard Feverel is the history of a Father and a Son—and both are comic. Meredith's definition of Comedy relates not to the pattern of action, but to the motivation of characters. Thus, the crucial scene which describes Sir Austin's reception of the news of his son's marriage is comic. . . . Sir Austin is not comic because of his System, but because of the attitude to life which he masks with the System. Meredith takes care to point out that the System is successful up to the point when Richard chooses Lucy, and he makes it clear in this chapter, 'Nursing the Devil', that Sir Austin was abandoning the System in fact, though attempting to appear as if he were carrying it on. . . . This is a time when he could have acted the part of the protective father with advantage. Instead, he withdraws behind his mask and nurses the devil of his own pride. This stamps him as a comic character, whatever the consequences of his action for himself.

Richard also bears the responsibility for his own actions. Meredith takes care to point out that he is in persistent danger of falling into the heroic pose. At first his doing so is entirely a result of his upbringing. It is as the son of his father's System that he seizes Lucy in London. The chapter headings make Meredith's attitude to him plain at this point: 'In which the Hero Takes a Step'; and 'Records the Rapid Development of the Hero'. It is as the hero that he sets out to save his cousin Clare, and to redeem Mrs. Mount—in both cases with disastrous consequences. With the same chivalric motive he sets out to 'rescue' his mother from Diaper Sandoe and Meredith's treatment of the scene reveals a ludicrous disparity between the heroism of the object and the bathos of the reality. This impulsive behaviour eventually brings him to his ruin. After his seduction by Bella Mount and his reading of Clare's Diary he had sufficient evidence as to the danger inherent in the heroic mode to enable him to come to terms with reality. In Germany under the influence of his discovery that he is a father and after the immediate contact with Nature which comes in the storm, he is brought to his senses. But then, when he reads Mrs. Mount's letter to him in London, he turns again into the course of sentimental chivalry and insists on fighting a stupid and pointless duel. Meredith makes it plain that Richard's motivation is wrong. . . . The responsibility for the circumstances which bring about the death of Lucy is his. On the other hand, Lucy's death cannot be said to be his fault. Meredith's treatment of this event is carefully managed so as to prevent too easy a distribution of blame. We do not hear about Lucy's death direct from the narrator, but in a letter from Lady Blandish to Austin Wentworth. It is plain that the direct cause of the catastrophe is the joint decision of the men of Science, Sir Austin and the doctors, that Lucy should be kept away from her husband. But our attitude to the death is conditioned by the fact that we learn about it from someone who admits to being biased against Sir Austin. . . . In their different ways Sir Austin and Richard had done the same thing. Sir Austin would not face the reality of his own motivation; later, he failed to realize that he was no longer in control. . . . Richard himself was going to a scene which should have been ample warning to him as to the consequences of treating life as if it were a heroic romance. He failed to learn the lesson and so fell.

Yet this is merely to say that *The Ordeal of Richard Feverel* is comic according to the author's definition of Comedy. One cannot excuse the fact that so many readers have felt that the end of the novel is not justified by the form, by saying that such a shock was part of the author's intention. (pp. 17-21)

The end of the novel remains painful, however the novel is read, but it is well prepared for. . . . [Meredith] does not lead the reader on in ignorance of the eventual end of the action. . . . What Meredith actually does is to take the 'well-established literary convention', establish it at an early stage in the action and then give us adequate warning that the successful conclusion of the action from that point on, after the pattern had been disturbed, depends on the fulfilment of certain conditions which all the characters are bent on ignoring. He built his novel around a close and meaningful contrast between the earlier comedy and the later, making it clear in the chapter headings that the two comedies were related. In the heading of the wedding-chapter he tells us directly what he is doing and what the relationship between the two Comedies is. He manipulated the 'normal' concept of Comedy in order to stress the fact that according to his view of life, Comedy depended not on the pattern of action, but on the motivation of the characters. The terrible catastrophe does not alter the fact that the father and the son are comic characters; the catastrophe grows out of the circumstances which they make for themselves and the purpose of the novel is to show the way in which they made them.

If there is a basic flaw in *The Ordeal of Richard Feverel* it is not the result of a structural failure, but exists rather in the tension between contradictory elements within it. Meredith seems to have been uncertain as to how he wanted us to feel about his central characters. We are quite clear about what we should *think* about them, but they are referred to in terms which create a degree of uncertainty as to how we should react emotionally. There is on the one hand, a series of references to them which is clearly comic, and on the other, a series which is quite clearly not comic. Thus Richard is referred to as a mock hero and his heroism is as much a matter of Comedy as the masks of Sir Austin. Meredith even adopts at times a traditionally mock-heroic style. . . . (pp. 25-6)

Another source of difficulty is the series of metaphors for Richard. He is several times referred to either as an arrow drawn to the head, or as gunpowder. Both these metaphors tend to reduce our awareness of the fact that Richard is responsible for his own actions. This awareness is further reduced by the references to him as a seed-bed for good and evil principles; a flower; a weed; and a tree; all of which tend to increase our feeling that Richard is helpless to change himself. This situation is not made more simple by the opposition which is made between father and son in terms of Nature and Science. Whenever reference is made to this opposition it is evident where the narrator's sympathies lie—and those of the reader naturally follow them. The result is that it is difficult to achieve a sufficiently objective view of Richard to be able to make the correct assessment of his behaviour.

Yet perhaps the most important source of tension in the novel is the presence of the element of romance. It is significant that the passages describing the early courtship of Richard and Lucy have been popular anthology pieces. . . . The predominant tone of the scenes which describe the meeting and the courtship of Richard and Lucy is one of straightforward romance. The incident is deliberately withdrawn from life by the references to Richard as Ferdinand and Lucy as Miranda. The whole episode is closely related to Nature and set aside from the material world. . . . (pp. 27-8)

Richard and Lucy are only partially comic; so is Sir Austin, but those parts of his character to which the reader gives his admiration and sympathy do not interfere with his finding him comic, in the Meredithean sense. Traditional Comedy can allow and often encourages us to regard the characters with entire sympathy, but Meredithean Comedy, being entirely dependent on character and existing regardless of the nature of the action, cannot allow a conflict between different elements in the reader's attitude to the comic characters. *The Ordeal of Richard Feverel* does contain such a conflict. Meredith makes us feel very strongly for Richard and Lucy and, at the same time that he is insisting that Richard bears comic responsibility for his own actions, he is drawing out the elements of innocence and unconsciousness in his hero which make us see what happens to him as tragic in the strict sense. Consequently the ending of the novel arouses mixed emotions in the reader.

The end of *Rhoda Fleming* is similar to that of *The Ordeal of Richard Feverel* in that Dahlia dies as innocently as Lucy, and Edward lives on without a sense of purpose. Yet the later novel has none of the uncertainty that marks the ending of the earlier; and this is because the way in which Meredith presented Dahlia and Edward was relatively simple. This uncertainty is not the result of any failure in the novel's structure—the novel is built around the basic contrast between the two major episodes and the relationship between them is made plain. Furthermore, the inversion of the 'normal' comic pattern which governs that

Meredith, age 34, with his son Arthur.

relationship underlines the new idea of Comedy which the author is putting forward in the novel. The point at which the novel is unsatisfactory is in the attitude of the narrator to his main characters—and particularly to Richard Feverel himself. Meredith actually portrayed a hero who is more than comic and for whom the reader is forced to feel a sympathy which takes him too close to the character to leave him free at the end of the novel to make the objective estimate which is necessary to the author's comic purpose. This was a mistake which Meredith never made again; and yet it was a mistake which gave the book that degree of attractiveness which has made it one of the most popular novels that he wrote. As his career developed, so did the degree of formal certainty in his novels. But it is doubtful whether he ever wrote better than he did in *The Ordeal of Richard Feverel,* or if any of his later novels are as moving as his first. (pp. 28-9)

> I. M. Williams, "The Organic Structure of 'The Ordeal of Richard Feverel'," in The Review of English Studies, n.s. Vol. XVIII, No. 69, February, 1967, pp. 16-29.

GEORGE WOODCOCK (essay date 1968)

[Woodcock is an author, editor, and currently a professor of English at the University of British Columbia. He is best known for his literary criticism and for his biographies of George Orwell and Thomas Merton. Woodcock also founded Canada's most important literary journal, Canadian Literature, and has published widely on the literature of Canada. In the following excerpt, Woodcock discusses the structure, characterization, and themes of The Egoist.]

The Egoist is George Meredith's most self-consistent and characteristic novel. It is the work in which he makes the least concession to the ways of Victorian novelists and to the predilections of Victorian readers; in which he reveals most openly the tensions between his own nature and his philosophy of living; in which he exposes with the most accurate and merciless of laughter the distortions of feeling which a society of self-seekers imposes on its devotees.

The Egoist was not the most popular of Meredith's novels among his contemporaries; that distinction was reserved for *Diana of the Crossways,* a much weaker book, in which he compromised notably with the sentimentality he himself always denounced. (p. 9)

Yet *The Egoist* is the book for which Meredith is most regarded at that crucial period in a writer's fame, the second half-century after his death; today it is probably more read and certainly more discussed than any of his other novels. Like Congreve's *The Way of The World,* which Meredith regarded highly, and Wilde's *Importance of Being Earnest,* which as far as I know he never even mentioned, it is among those *jeux d'esprit* in which art and intellect dance together in forms that are literature's nearest effective approach to abstraction. In Meredith's other works his mannerisms and artifices perplex and annoy; in *The Egoist,* for once, they are entirely appropriate, entirely absorbed into a carefully integrated structure of speech and thought.

The thought is important, for Meredith's intent in writing *The Egoist* was far from that of producing a work of art for art's sake. Wilde's occasional propagandizing for a hedonistic libertarianism may perhaps be dismissed as a lapse of aestheticist consistency; Meredith never ceased to be—in his own way—a self-consciously didactic writer, and even *The Egoist* reflects

his didacticism. He had definite and detailed views on the need to live naturally. In his novels the physical exertions in which he rather loudly indulged in daily life were transferred to the positive characters, and in such a context became the symbols of a healthy attitude to existence. He had, moreover, strong opinions on that malignant sickness of Victorian England, the class system, and the agonies of snobbery and social pride which he suffered within himself were transformed into fiction so that they might be observed and analysed with exemplary effect. (pp. 9-10)

The peculiar flavour of *The Egoist* comes largely from this fact that it is a study of social pretensions within a stable situation. Its characters are limited deliberately to a group of people close enough in terms of class to come together naturally in an extended house party; no major character is socially insecure, ascending or descending the ladder of class.

Thus *The Egoist* in fact differs from the earlier novels not only in the elimination of the more flamboyantly heroic aspects of the struggle against social conventions, but also in abandoning, as fictional mechanisms, acute class differences and extreme snobbery; both exist in the world of *The Egoist,* but they seldom surface, to make a telling point, as in Sir Willoughby's treatment of his distant relative, Lieutenant Patterne.

By contrast, Meredith's first novel, *The Ordeal of Richard Feverel,* introduces class in a very direct way through Richard's marriage to a girl of lower status, which leads to his later troubles. . . . (p. 12)

In Meredith's novels, sexual passion is never in fact so important as sexual domination, which may often be a matter of the coldest calculation. . . . Yet the outspoken feminism of Meredith's later years was a by-product rather than a cause of the sexual conflicts represented in his novels. A didactic writer, in that he recognized and sought to use the power of comedy in affecting the outlooks and hence the actions of men, Meredith was not a reforming propagandist. Here there was a sharp distinction between him and a writer like Bernard Shaw, who criticized him from the Fabian point of view. Shaw would use a play quite deliberately to discuss an immediate social problem and to implant in the minds of his audience the idea of a concrete remedy. The problems that concerned Meredith were not so easily solved; placed in an unavoidable social setting, they were essentially problems of personal awareness. The therapy of comedy was not expected to reform societies; it was expected to cure individuals of certain malformations of feeling. (pp. 17-18)

It is when we touch this sensitive problem of the materials out of which Meredith fabricated his novels, and particularly *The Egoist,* that we come near the roots of his view on the war of the sexes. His relationship with the Peacock family, in particular, is central to any consideration of his characteristic moral preoccupations, of the content of his novels, and even in his ways of writing. (p. 18)

Meredith's marriage [to Peacock's daughter Mary Ellen] brought him close to Thomas Love Peacock, particularly when the financial difficulties of the young couple made them accept his temporary hospitality. . . .

Peacock's literary outlook impressed itself strongly on Meredith at this formative stage in his development as a writer. (p. 19)

It is in *The Egoist* that the Peacockian dialogue is most effectively naturalized into an instrument of Meredithian analysis.

Meredith's dialogue is not necessarily more realistic in its texture than Peacock's. One cannot imagine any two living creatures conversing as Sir Willoughby and Laetitia Dale do at their most sententious. But it does chart the emotional lives of those strange beings of Meredith's imagination in such a way that we are aware not of mere intellectual crotchets, but also of genuine feelings, of worthy and unworthy calculations, of cracks in the carapace of affectation through which we can feel a beating of human blood. In fact, it is one of Meredith's great originalities that he can give a highly poised and intellectualized dialogue such transparency that in the end it becomes more revealing of the inner motives of the speakers than a deliberately realistic conversation would be. (p. 20)

The formal elaboration of *The Egoist,* paralleling the elaboration of conventions within which the appropriately named Patterne dances his pompous minuet of life, is characterized by the triangular grouping of characters: Willoughby–Clara–Laetitia; Willoughby–Clara–Vernon; Clara–Vernon–Horace; Willougby–Mrs Jenkinson–Clara. The shifting relations within and between such triangles are the choreography of the work as a whole. Most interesting of all the triangles is that of Willoughby–Clara–Dr Middleton, the triad which provides the clues to the genesis of *The Egoist.*

In this key triad Dr Middleton alone is immediately recognizable as a character rather faithfully derived from a model in real life. Willoughby and Clara have gone through many rebirths before they are incarnated in *The Egoist,* but their beginnings are to be found in Meredith's own past, in the early triangle of Peacock–Mary Ellen–Meredith. (pp. 20-1)

Neither Mary Ellen's departure nor her death was for Meredith the end of the relationship. It dominated the rest of his life, haunting him with the images of her misery and his inflexibility, but as the years went on these twin spectres underwent curious transformations. The most literal rendering of the lost marriage was Meredith's long poem, *Modern Love.* (p. 21)

Meredith's view of the relationship of the sexes, as symbolic of the wider relationship between freedom and the tyranny of custom, led him far from the real-life origin of his preoccupations. Dr Middleton, an essentially minor character, could safely be modelled on Peacock. But Clara Middleton had grown as far from Mary Ellen Nicoll as Meredith's views on the fate of women had changed since the agony he exorcized in *Modern Love.*

The Egoist, in its construction, has the kind of economy which is more usual in drama than in fiction. It is true that like almost every book that Meredith wrote, its entrance is protected by a rather fearsome *chevaux-de-frise* in the form of a preface on comedy, heavy with elaborate parody, and an introductory chapter on Sir Willoughby's youth and his celebrated leg, which appears excessively precious until one realizes how surely it sets the artificial tone of the world in which Willoughby poses for the edification of his admirers, the formidable Mrs Mountstuart Jenkinson (surely a lineal ancestress of Wilde's dowagers) and the languid and brainy Laetitia, that personification of the feminine mind made sterile by enslavement to convention. But once the reader has undergone the preliminary tests which Meredith expects of him, the course is clear and the action follows in a brisk series of dramatic episodes, each fulfilling a triple purpose of enlightening us a shade more on Sir Willoughby's nature, of developing the resistance of the other characters to his insolent expectations, and of building the tension that rises steadily in this close circle of emotionally

involved people like the heightening atmosphere before a thunderstorm. Apart from any of its other virtues, it is a fine work of suspense, paced on by witty conversation, economical in introspection and narrative, and, from the moment when Clara begins to detect the real and detestable Sir Willoughby, making the reader a fascinated observer of the shifts by which her feminine cunning surmounts the obstacles successively falling in her path. There are aspects of *The Egoist* which are madly improbable. Could Dr Middleton really betray his beloved daughter for a diet of old port? Was Willoughby's only way of living down his rejection by Clara really to marry a Laetitia who had learnt to despise him? Such an ending is indeed not consonant with realism but it is with poetic justice, and that is what Meredith seeks. For *The Egoist* is after all a comedy, and, just as Meredith observes the unity of place and—within reasonable limits—the unity of time, so he ensures that the good—Clara and Vernon—shall get their reward, and the villain shall live to digest his suitably dusty answer.

All this gains in meaning when we remember that *The Egoist* is the extreme expression of Meredith's recurrent drama of the defeat of Egoism by the power of Comedy. (pp. 23-5)

It is the sign of Sir Willoughby's complexity [as a fictional character] . . . that he is not guilty of a single affectation, of one glaring manifestation of vanity or hypocrisy, but that all the sins against common sense which Meredith details can be brought against him. Nor does the complexity lie merely in the many-sidedness of his folly. It lies also in the method of representation. . . . [In] the case of Sir Willoughby we have not merely the external witness; we see the process at work within him and realize, in the depth of his thoughts, the extent to which natural impulse has been replaced by artificial calculation, in the same way as the living substance of some perished animal is replaced by the fossil's hard stone. This probing complexity gives Meredith's comic art an analytic quality, which, before him, was almost unknown among the writers of comedy. Their approach tended to be the descriptive one of the old-fashioned natural historian; to observe, and represent, and wonder at man's folly. Meredith's is the diagnostic approach, seeking the pathology of vanity and its ultimate causes. Once we know those causes, he suggests, we may not suddenly cure a patient so chronic as Sir Willoughby, but we shall cease to become enslaved by his pretensions and, in ceasing to do so, we may—as Meredith suggests that Laetitia will do—begin his liberation.

But, though Meredith undoubtedly intended this lesson to be understood by those who read *The Egoist,* to end on the didactic note would be to leave a wrong impression of his actual achievement. It is as a consummate portrait of vanity and egoism that *The Egoist* succeeds; Sir Willoughby reformed would be Sir Willoughby destroyed, and in the wisdom of his art Meredith did no more than hint at the possibility. Here his obedience to the rigid laws of classical drama stood him in good stead; no novel benefits more from its observance of the unities. This is the story of the exposure and the defeat of Egoism; the transformation of Egoism would be another story, and Meredith was too much Sir Willoughby and too sensible an artist, to attempt it. (pp. 28-9)

George Woodcock, in an introduction to The Egoist *by George Meredith, edited by George Woodcock, Penguin Books, 1968, pp. 9-29.*

V. S. PRITCHETT   (lecture date 1969)

[*Pritchett is a highly esteemed English novelist, short story writer, and critic. Considered one of the modern masters of the short story, he is also considered one of the world's most respected and well-read literary critics. Pritchett writes in the conversational tone of the familiar essay, a method by which he approaches literature from the viewpoint of a lettered but not overly scholarly reader. A twentieth-century successor to such early nineteenth-century essayist-critics as William Hazlitt and Charles Lamb, Pritchett employs much the same critical method: his own experience, judgment, and sense of literary art are emphasized, rather than a codified critical doctrine derived from a school of psychological or philosophical speculation. His criticism is often described as fair, reliable, and insightful. In the following excerpt, Pritchett discusses some of the difficulties faced by the reader who approaches Meredith's novels, noting especially the intrusiveness of the author's personality in his works, the essentially poetic nature of his prose, and the complexity of his theories of comedy.*]

It is because we learn so much from the writers who have either got into difficulties or who have a certain vanity in creating them, that I have chosen Meredith as my subject. He is pretty well as vain of his messes as he is of his accepted achievements. He consciously created many obstacles for himself: to take one example, the Idea—and everything was Idea to him—that there was such a thing as absolute Comedy. He had theories about Comedy. He was not thinking of comic relief, humourous observation, farce or satirical orgy. He allowed Laughter as a healthy exercise but Comedy was a rather chaste Platonic Idea. Now the comic tradition in the English novel is a powerful one; it is an alternative to the Puritan tradition; it inspects as it alleviates or makes finer the demands of moral seriousness. Meredith who was a great adapter from the past can tell us a good deal about our comic tradition. What he was trying to do was to conceptualise—which is not a common English habit; and he was conceptualising a dominant tradition of the English novel. In comic irony our novelists have been pre-eminent. It is their most militant and most graceful gift. It has moderated or refined their didactic habit and drawn them closer to nature.

There is a serious initial difficulty in dealing with Meredith now. At any time during the last forty years it has been pretty safe to put on superior and evasive airs and to say that "no one reads him". Just as "no one" reads Scott or Thackeray. We can easily add to the list of such complacencies and they change from generation to generation. But there is no doubt that Meredith not only is but always *was* a difficult case. His small number of distinguished admirers were intense in their delight in him; but his many detractors ended with exasperation. (pp. 10-11)

Meredith's difficulties, his chosen obstacles, I think, are the following:

First there is Meredith himself. He is a persistently, blatantly, intrusive person. He must be in the centre of the stage. In a famous poem Auden suggested that the novelist is a non-person who becomes other people. Meredith is *all* person. Other people become *him*. As a narrator he is always before our eyes, often sign-posting. The English novelist—Henry James complained—again and again ruin their tales by such personal intervention. But Meredith's novels *are* the intervention. He far outdoes Thackeray who skilfully played the role of master of ceremonies. Meredith acts *his* people off the stage. One has to look to Carlyle and Browning for anything like Meredith's intrusion.... (p. 23)

The second stimulating difficulty for Meredith is that he is a poet. I am not going to discuss Meredith's poetry.... I find it thin. The intrusive person diminishes into an almost furtively biographical figure in many of the verses. He was capable of rhapsody—rather over-exercised rhapsody to my ear—in *Love in the Valley*, but one can see the bearing of this poem on the summer love scene in *Richard Feverel*. The sonnet sequence in *Modern Love* is another matter. Here he comes out with something that he cannot say outright in any of the novels. He spoke out about "modern love" before any of his contemporaries. A genuine Meredith, dispersed by no trick of evasion, has crystallised. One can complain of the occasional romantic cliché, but (in general) the images are hard and clear, the statement is laconic, the scenes are sharp, the whole is concentrated and compressed. It is a paradox, but Meredith, the interminable talker, was made interminable by his passion for compressing, for crystallising, for the economy of telescoping his ideas, and for the abrupt transition from image to image. He was totally fitted to write another great narrative poem like *The Ring and the Book* and one could argue that the literary conventions of his time, the need to earn his living and an intellectual laziness made him choose a stultifying form when he wrote novels. But, from the critic's point of view, the poet in Meredith made him concentrate on intensity, economy and the image in his prose.

The third difficulty for him is that being a poet he was led on to Romance. Romance would allow the rhapsodic; it would suggest either the epic or the tale. It would enable him to put a distance between himself and industrial or commercial England.... But Meredith went further than Romance towards a genre he calls Poetic Romance and treated as High or Artificial Comedy. His people had to be Great People; and his difficulty was to juggle Great People into a contemporary scene which was neither epic nor great. For us the difficulty is to believe in the extraordinary aristocracy he created; the question was and is, could he bounce us into suspending our unbelief? And whether we can regard his scene as anything but Ruritanian? The hopeful answer was that Meredith was a writer of enormous ingenuity and that it would all be a question of making his disparate indeed conflicting gifts come to a single coherent point. Would his feeling be strong enough; would his moral sense be deep enough to bind all together? He could be brilliant but would brilliance be enough?

The binding element was to be what he called the Comic Spirit. What did he have to say about it in his two well-known lectures? ... The lectures were, naturally, a dazzling performance by a considerable actor and mellifluous talker and wit, but one is never quite sure (outside of one or two eloquent passages), what he is saying half the time. He is clearly a romantic idealist. Comedy must be pure comedy, and outside of the ancients, outside of Molière and Congreve, he sees little that is pure. He has a low opinion of the Restoration drama, partly because of its realism, its hoydens and its knockabout morals. He is too much a Victorian to take Charles Lamb's point of defence. He found the people low. The interesting thing is that Meredith concentrates on the theatre, and although he has some general praise for the English novelists, he has little to say in detail. There is not even a quotation. This casual treatment of the novelists is important to our understanding of Meredith's comedy: it is, at heart, conceived of as theatre. His novels will not only be poetic romantic comedies, they will be staged. Comedy, for him, required an aura of court life.... Comedy appeals to the head rather than to the heart; it is the enemy of the sentimental—that, for him, means the earnest, bemusing, over-bosomed feelings that cheat the Life Force and distract us from our sensual well-being. Comedy is "the fountain of sound sense". Sound sense is a good deal pagan. (pp. 23-6)

Meredith is, as I have said, giving us theatre. But there is an earlier point which is more precise and more suggestive. I refer to his belief that comedy cannot exist without equality of the sexes. There must be cultivated women who can give as good as they get. Meredith is a feminist and often drew women well—in a different way, almost as well as Gissing drew women. But for Meredith, the equality of the sexes meant the contest of the sexes: the sex-battle in Molière's *Le Misanthrope* or in *The Way of the World,* is fundamental to these two comedies. We can see now where his interest lies: it is in the conflict, in the militancy. We shall find these quicken all his novels and that the campaign is (for him) basic and the sign of vitality— the human species shows its vitality by a war-like sorting out, with its brains, of the fittest to survive. (pp. 27-8)

There is something in criticism called the biographical fallacy which we are told the critic ought to avoid. I am not going to avoid it. In Meredith we are faced with the biographical necessity if we are to get to the heart of his very intrusive manner. Meredith is not the novelist as conceived by Auden—the man who is a non-person who finds his life in other people. Meredith is enraptured by the question of persona; he is personal to the point of ornament. (p. 33)

It has been said that Meredith was ashamed of his tailoring forbears. He hated being the son of a "snip"—tailors being thought more ridiculous than any other class of shop-keeper; and that he became a preposterous snob who never referred to his embarrassing family, except to a few friends, in later life. His mannered prose is sometimes thought of as a product of this shame. Now, it is possible that the very young Meredith was a romantic snob; it is natural to be snobbish when one is young; but he publicly proclaimed the low comedy of his origins in his early, closely autobiographical novel, *Evan Harrington.* He did not even bother to change the names of some of his relatives. When we come to his first important novel, *The Ordeal of Richard Feverel,* another autobiographical element is explicit. There is a close connection, in the plot, between Meredith's life as a son and his life as the father of a son—a father, moreover, deserted by his wife as Meredith himself was deserted. An egoist, he was unforgiving, and in a later novel (*The Egoist*) the psychological meaning of this very personal imbroglio is examined. It is solipsistic:

> Consider him indulgently: the Egoist is the Son
> of Himself. He is likewise the Father. And the
> son loves the father, the father the son. . . .
> Absorbed in their great example of devotion,
> they do not think of you. They are beautiful.

This is a central theme of his work.

Meredith is very much a tailor-novelist with a large wardrobe who is always trying on new jackets in front of the reader and the new jacket is for himself (and for his characters) a new persona. (pp. 33-4)

The effect of a foreign experience like Meredith's [German education] is to stimulate the romantic idea; one becomes the more English and the more foreign for it, for distance gives enchantment to both views; but it also gives one a disturbed and penetrating view of one's own country. . . . Meredith is the only English novelist of the nineteenth century to see that rich England was overfed and gluttonous to the point of stupor. . . . The England Meredith saw was unlike the England of all our Victorian novelists, except two, and their minds had the foreign touch also: Disraeli the Jew and Gissing, a sort of Orwell who had been down and out in Manchester and Chicago.

Disraeli saw English politics operatically; Gissing, with something like the eye of an outcast emigrant. (p. 36)

But what sets Meredith apart is the effect of his education in Germany. Several of his novels are really *educations sentimentales.* Foreign education must have freed him (just because he *was* abroad) from defensiveness or aggressiveness about his inferior social position; he could assume any role he wished and if he was caught in the English class system, he could elect himself to membership of a private aristocracy. (p. 37)

[In Meredith's novels] the important ordeal is spiritual. The soul has to pass through fire. And what has to be burned away? Pride above all and self-delusion. The business of comedy is ruthlessly to expose the false emotions and the false image of oneself and the purpose of comedy is to establish sanity. This is the theme that dominates all Meredith's novels; it is his only important theme. His hero should emerge at the end, fitted at last to face life. By nature his heroes are honourable but wilful extremists. They live in the imagination, which gives them a tremendous energy.

The intensity which Meredith brought to his theme is personal and bitter. (p. 59)

The important thing for us is that it was in the year of his wife's flight that Meredith wrote his second ordeal story, *The Ordeal of Richard Feverel.* It was published in 1859, the year of Darwin's *Origin of Species* and of *Adam Bede,* George Eliot's first full length novel that was to become the lengthiest best-selling novel since *Waverley.* Meredith hoped for an equal success. He did not get it. . . . Among the novels that attacked the Victorian father, and in spite of being broken-backed, it has lasted. *Richard Feverel* is an extremist's book—the extremism is intellectual and poetic—and extremists are apt to exhaust themselves when they get to the critical point of a work of art. They are apt, as Meredith always is, to become perverse and at the very point where they are masters.

Once the rope is cut *The Ordeal of Richard Feverel* floats free as a bold and believable psychological novel. The world of Romance is established first by making the hero and his father enormously rich and handsome; by the invention of Sir Austin Feverel's preposterous yet idealistic System; by exposing it to idyllic pagan love and by establishing Richard as the ideal Youth, dedicated to virginity. This will lead to disaster. For the poetic part Meredith went to Shakespeare in the story of Romeo and Juliet; but the tragedy unfolds in the setting of comic irony. Sir Austin is a monomaniac; he hopes by his educational system to conduct his son, with a father's love, through the stages of growing up, which he calls Simple Boyhood, the Blossoming Season, the Magnetic Age, the period of Probation. He will enter a Manhood worthy of Paradise— in other words he will inherit the father's great estate, conduct it honourably, marry a carefuly selected wife of the right social class, and produce the children that guarantee the immortality of a superb social order. The System ends by turning a pleasant boy into a man almost as maniacal and masked as the father. For the flaw is that Sir Austin has become a *scientific* systematiser—Meredith hates science—because he is a misogynist whose pride has been injured by an unfaithful wife. Woman is the serpent—the image of Woman as serpent recurs continually in Meredith's accounts of passion. (pp. 60-1)

[A] weakness for complicating his narrative . . . , once the dénouement is reached, is chronic in Meredith's novels and no doubt part of his morbidity. Perhaps he realised he was a static novelist of set scenes and thought he was adding the action and suspense that were expected by the reader of the padded-out three volume novel. But he was really a contriver I think because he lacked calm and large powers of invention. He was certainly indulging the love of his own cleverness. Yet even when he is going to pieces Meredith can write a fine scene that will restore the shape and symbolism of the tale. (p. 64)

Meredith is above all a novelist of youth and growth; for he accepts with pleasure the conceit, the severity, the aggressiveness and self-encumberedness of young men and women, the uncritical impulses and solemn ambitions. Their follies are undertaken with passionate single-mindedness. To my mind only Tolstoy and Stendhal really succeed in portraying young men because they understand and admire egotism; that is Meredith's interest, too, and it gives his young men something in common with Stendhal heroes above all. (p. 66)

The Ordeal of Richard Feverel shows henceforth what Meredith will contain and the methods he will use. First, the novel will have an essay-like frame, enclosing set scenes. The essay will carry the narrative forward. Obviously Peacock must have taught him something here. The essay-like form will help him in his greatest difficulty as a writer: how to pull together his conflicting interests. He is a poet, a symbolist who must be lyrical; lyrical, he must also be comic, moving from the comedy of manners to the grotesque; there is the social satirist; there is the man of fantasy; there is the realist. And there is the man who has ideas about the state of England; there is the wit and artist who feeling deeply for Nature as a headlong Force yet identifies it with the sanity Comedy teaches us—a not impossible but very difficult conjunction of ideas. As he sees it, the extraordinary mixture can be made to look coherent by the skilful use of styles and by a new view of narrative. Narrative can no longer be a straightforward, chronological arrangement of stirring events in an exciting plot. It must first be oblique. The exciting *scène à faire* need not be faced. It can be foreshadowed, rumoured, evaded, commented on by the guesses of several different witnesses afterwards. Climax may be conversation. No one will quite know what happened and though the reader may be maddened the suspense is thereby increased. And anyway it is like life. Time is open, as it was to become for novelists like Proust, Virginia Woolf and Ford Madox Ford. . . . As he said in *Modern Love* "passions spin the plot". That is to say plot is a *web* and not a mechanism. (pp. 66-8)

The weakness of intensely personal novels is that they do not wholly transfigure the personal experience. It is well-known that *The Ordeal of Richard Feverel* is very much an autobiographical novel. It was inspired, as I said earlier, by two fathers—his own and by himself as a father. He wrote it in the bitter period when, deserted by his wife for another man, he poured an overwhelming amount of love upon the son he was left to bring up. As shadows, his wife and her lover appear in the novel; so that we are blatantly invited to see that under the comedy there is an unresolved torture and that real life is grimacing unassimilated. It is as though here the actor forgot to put on his paint.

Like all novelists, Meredith drew his characters from life, but the general practice is to mix oneself, one's idea, with the portrayed person; and after starting off, the novelist is almost certain to combine several models in one. . . . Meredith, in his egotistical way, was apt not only to take characters from real life, but often read his accounts of them to the models who approved or criticised. This does not necessarily show great delicacy or discretion; rather it seems to indicate that as far as

the romantic egoist was nonchalantly concerned, they were not real people to begin with. Only *he* was real. (pp. 71-2)

V. S. Pritchett, in his George Meredith and English Comedy: The Clark Lectures for 1969, *Random House, 1970, 123 p.*

GILLIAN BEER   (essay date 1970)

[*In the following excerpt Beer provides a thematic survey of Meredith's career, discussing in particular his examinations of egoism and sexuality, his concern with portraying the inner lives of his characters, his theories of comedy and tragedy, and the use of ornamentation in his literary style.*]

Meredith's work has always aroused strong antipathy and admiration. From the first, hostile critics have seen him as merely obscure and pretentious. Yet his admirers in his own time greeted him as a writer whose intensity of insight and expressiveness made him something more than a literary figure—something closer to a prophetic consciousness. (p. 1)

Through his exploration of the possibilities of the novel as a form Meredith discovered new channels for consciousness to flow in. He was a consciously experimental writer; his technical innovations pushed the novel almost as far as it would go towards the compression and ellipsis of poetry. His work is not only interesting in itself but crucial to an understanding of the way the English novel developed towards the end of the nineteenth century. He was the first to express a major shift of sensibility, registered in the increasing introspection, lyricism, psychological analysis and symbolistic organisation of the novel in the ensuing period.

For any sympathetic modern reader of Meredith's novels antipathy and admiration are likely to alternate. Some of his views must now seem remote, even naive: his assurance that man is evolving towards perfection; his belief in the inevitably healing power of laughter; his assertion that mental and physical punishment brace a man. Yet the exploring intelligence which informs his writing should make us wary of dismissing what is alien as meaningless for us. His novels never sacrifice insight to dogma: they work through a process of testing and scrutiny. The free play of his emotions and intelligence involves him in constant reappraisal. He is sensitive to the way a change of perspective can alter the nature of experience.

No novelist has ever been more conscious of the closeness to each other of comedy and tragedy. His nervous, even hectic, awareness of the other face of either experience leaves him only at rare moments of intense lyricism. (pp. 1-2)

Part of the modern rejection of Meredith seems to me to be based on misreading—where it is not simply received opinion. He is commonly referred to as a precious writer, intent on his own wit. He *is* a witty writer and like Joyce, who felt a strong kinship with him, he is part of that other tradition of the English novel which moves through Lyly and Sterne: dramatic plot is abandoned, ornamentation flourishes, and brilliance is an end in itself as well as an instrument of exploration. But Meredith's intensely experimental approach to the novel is always a part of his moral concern with human personality. By the method of fiction he makes many of the discoveries that Freud was making, but he uses them to reach absolute moral judgments: 'These are the ways egoism works and this is what is wrong with it', rather than 'These are the ways the ego has been observed to work'. Meredith tries to combine the roles of sage and explorer, bard and craftsman.

He is interested above all in the inner life of his characters and particularly in those levels which are beneath conscious control. The novel, as a form, is particularly appropriate to the exploration of the 'submerged self' [the term is from *Sandra Belloni*]. The process of silent reading approximates to the life of thought and feeling rather than to speech and action; the novel becomes a prolonged, intermittent part of the reader's unspoken daily life. But Meredith is not simply a novelist of sensibility: he recognises that personality is most vividly focussed in action and that drama can be the most economical means of expressing what a character cannot acknowledge about himself. In his attempt to be faithful to his material he is forced to find new ways of relating plot and character. Equally, he tries to evolve a style capable of dramatising the characters' *unformulated* impulses and perceptions. (pp. 2-3)

Meredith's kinship of methods and perceptions often seems to be with twentieth-century writers rather than with his own earlier contemporaries. The fragmented chronology, the refracted experience, the dense flux of symbol and metaphor in his novels, all link him with later writers. Without refashioning him into a modern novelist, it may be possible for readers now to approach him more directly than at any time since the eighteen-nineties. (p. 5)

In the course of his long creative life Meredith completed thirteen full-length novels: the first, *The Ordeal of Richard Feverel,* was published in 1859, in the same year as George Eliot's first full-length novel, *Adam Bede*. The last, *The Amazing Marriage,* appeared in 1895, alongside H. G. Wells's *The Time Machine*. The novels share certain insistent themes, the most pervasive of which is the power of unconscious egoism. In some ways Meredith's ideas seem extraordinarily set: observations and situations recur throughout his work. But they recur with the energy and inventiveness of obsession rather than with monolithic assurance. The manifestations of egoism are so devious that this one theme alone can include the whole variety of social being. And although many of Meredith's preoccupations remain constant, the novels themselves are remarkably diverse. He usually rejects his last piece of work completely—and often seems to set out to write its opposite. (p. 6)

Throughout his work Meredith draws attention to his use of the modes of comedy and tragedy and insists on their interpenetration. The effectiveness of the novel as a form lies in large measure in its power to mingle the comic and tragic and to demonstrate to us the inextricably mixed quality of life. As Meredith said in the *Essay on Comedy:* 'Life we know too well is not a comedy, but something strangely mixed. Nor is comedy a vile mask'. Meredith's mastery of high comedy, with its surface tension of words remaining smooth above the forceful currents of man's animal nature, has led some critics to treat him as essentially a precious writer, an ironist in the tradition of his father-in-law, Peacock, in whose work men exist only as the sum total of their views. None of Meredith's books however offers an impervious comic completeness. . . . (p. 108)

A writer with so powerful a belief in individual identity and free-will might well be expected to find the sustaining of a single mode particularly unattractive ('But I do not make a plot. If my characters, as I have them at heart, before I begin on them, were boxed in a plot, they would soon lose the lines of their features.') The gratification we are permitted is rarely that of the perfect cadence; it is rather a sense of the new range of possibility discovered by modulation. Meredith's belief in the individual's responsibility for his fate is an element in this

attitude. Plot conventions are akin to fatalism; once the reader has recognised the pattern he is absolved from responsibility—this may be true also of the characters, who in their suffering are passive instruments of something preordained. When Meredith takes a traditional story, such as the happy marriage against odds in *Richard Feverel,* he subjects it to fierce pressures instead of allowing it to be its own justification.

Meredith attempts to combine the free flow of experience with scenes which probe and epitomise personality under stress. Mrs Mountstuart in *The Egoist* . . . says 'I suppose there are clever people who do see deep into the breast while dialogue is in progress. One reads of them.' Despite his concern for what is 'deep in the breast', Meredith recognises that analysis and action tend to be disjoined in human behaviour: we recognise ourselves and others *in retrospect*. He tries to demonstrate this through the form of his novels and he shows in the body of the work how far this disjunction is the spring of comedy and of tragedy. (pp. 108-09)

Meredith did not have the integral vision needed to sustain and fulfil tragedy in the novel. George Eliot's stable concern for her characters allows her to use the novel as a tragic form. Hardy's indeflectible calm, which makes coincidence part of a larger determinism, could not be encompassed by Meredith's febrile and kaleidoscopic method. Meredith's relationship to his characters works by appropriation and rejection, so that he moves between lyricism and irony. The tragic episodes in his novels are the appalled reversal of comedy. . . . Richard Feverel goes to his death in a duel, abandoning his wife and child, because the woman who seduced him writes that Lord Mountfalcon has attempted to seduce his wife. Beauchamp loses his life in a heroic act, 'an insignificant bit of mudbank life remaining in this world in the place of him'. Alvan, in *The Tragic Comedians* . . . , makes tragedy inevitable by handing Clotilde back to her mother with a theatrical smile instead of recognising that her flight to him has used up the last ounce of her courage.

The tragic hero who stalks the books is Othello: a man bereft and fooled, ruined by something akin to the comedy of errors in which characters not only lack self-knowledge but also crucial information. In *The Tragic Comedians* Meredith overtly uses the parallels between his hero and Othello: the special pain of both works comes from the reader's knowledge and impotence. Meredith responded to Othello's personality and situation as to an idealised version of his own character and early experience. In his approach to tragedy there is always a sense of the radical concurrence of comedy and tragedy. (p. 110)

The late *One of Our Conquerors* . . . is the novel closest to sustained tragedy. The hero is ruined and elevated by suffering—but here again Meredith uses the *methods* of comedy for his tragic purposes. In his youth Victor Radnor has married an elderly widow, Mrs Burman, and run away with her young companion, Nataly. Their love is faithfully sustained but their relationship is constantly under strain, because of their fear that Mrs Burman will expose the irregularity of their union and so harm their daughter, Nesta (as well as undermining Victor's social supremacy). By the end of the book Mrs Burman is dead, Natalie is dead, Victor is mad, and Nesta has survived a broken engagement and gone forward into a happy marriage. The tragic essence of the work lies in the deeply intimate married relationship which is both intensified and diminished by fear. Meredith attempts to combine this theme with mordant comedy concerning society, the cash-nexus, flaccid imperialism, and attitudes to class and religion. The meeting point of social and private concerns is in Victor's unreflective sensibility. (p. 111)

All Meredith's novels expressly exploit the relativity of comedy and tragedy. He sees them—as in the scene just analysed—not as dealing with different *orders* of experience but as representing different *attitudes* towards it. He connects these attitudes to the different levels of personality in his characters: his recurrent image of the 'two men' within us does not set man's spiritual against his animal nature. It expresses the conflict between a man's rationalised image of himself and his self in action. . . . Meredith shows that the failure to recognise the disparity between these two selves is the source of that confusion which can, equally, produce comic and tragic results. He identifies the comic attitude with reason's control and hence with retrospection; the tragic attitude with involvement and action and hence with the continuous present. The two attitudes are shown jarring against each other and it is their friction, rather than any reconciliation betweeen them, which generates the energy of his novels.

Meredith presents the habitually irreconcilable views of experience: that of those who have undergone it and know its confusion and agony and patternlessness, and that of those who look on, to whom the experience seems limpidly and satisfyingly diagrammatic. One of the most peculiar features of his approach is his way of presenting an incident concurrently as fully comic and fully tragic. Willoughby's jealous torment in *The Egoist* is presented in language whose intensity is not destroyed by the sharp wit of the narrator's comments. Victor Radnor's disintegration is dogged by his fruitless attempt to recapture the 'Idea' (which momentarily illuminated him when he slipped on a banana skin). The effect is not one of irony, for this implies equilibrium. Meredith veers disquietingly between two poles, avoiding either tragedy's commitment to experience or the 'point fixe' of comedy. The reader is forced to undertake simultaneously two contradictory roles: that of living through the experience and that of analysing it dispassionately.

Throughout his creative life Meredith recognised (at times unwillingly) how narrow is the sphere of reason within human personality. Constantly in his later novels his characters are confronted with the limits of their reason and control. Comedy, which in his work yokes together analysis and action, is Meredith's method of instruction. . . . The method is, strictly, antirealistic. Within the novels he shows how difficult it is for men to recognise the nature of their actions; he forces on the reader-as-character (though not always on the character) the act of recognition.

In the late eighteen-seventies Meredith explored the idea of comedy in a variety of works—short stories (**'The House on the Beach'** and **'The Case of General Ople and Lady Camper'**), an unpublished drama, 'The Satirist', the *Essay* and two novels, ***The Egoist*** and ***The Tragic Comedians***. Through these works he elucidated his own vision of comedy and defined its limits. In ***The Tragic Comedians*** he wrote a work which annihilated comedy. 'Comedians' is the detached general description of the characters, 'Tragic' the adjectival particular. Never again after 1880 did he write a novel in which the comic was the controlling ethos.

On 1 February 1877 Meredith delivered a lecture which later became known as ***An Essay on Comedy and the Uses of the Comic Spirit***. . . . [Its] composition was artistically crucial for Meredith himself. Meredith's own avowed favourite among his novels, ***Beauchamp's Career***, was written during the pre-

ceding years, and ***The Egoist***, which immediately succeeds the *Essay*, is often taken to be his masterpiece.

Many of the effects in *The Egoist* can be traced directly to Meredith's theories on comedy, and its introductory chapter presents an epitome of the main ideas of the *Essay*. (pp. 112-15)

Meredith's description of the comic spirit [in the *Essay*] sheds light on his attitude as narrator in *The Egoist*, his 'comedy in narrative' as he sub-titled it. *The Egoist* was his first full-length novel after writing the *Essay*. (p. 122)

In *The Egoist* he examines many of the epitomised observations of the *Essay* against the shifting world of human personalities and relationships. The book is his only attempt to write a sustained 'comedy' invoking the conventions of the stage, and particularly of Molière's comedies, the source of whose wit, Meredith says, is pure reason. (p. 123)

The comedy he most often cites in the *Essay* is [Molière's] *Le Misanthrope*, and this has some obvious plot connections with *The Egoist*: it is about an unfulfilled engagement, and one in which the hero, although a good man, makes demands upon the heroine which it is impossible for her to fulfil without running counter to her nature. Just as the first cause of the dissension between Sir Willoughby and Clara is his wish to banish the world, so that between Alceste and Célimène is his wish to retire into a deserted countryside far from the corruptions of the court. Just as Sir Willoughby offers his hand to Laetitia, so Alceste attempts at one point to revenge himself on Célimène by proposing marriage to her cousin, who is devoted to him. Here however the resemblance ends. Alceste is shown as truly (and unreasonably) in love with Célimène, whereas we see nothing of the relationship of the lovers in *The Egoist* until Clara's withdrawal has begun. The suggestion is that there has never been any relationship. The attitude of the two writers to their characters has less in common than might at first appear: Molière is the more truly reasonable because more truly charitable. Alceste is endearing as well as infuriating, whereas there is a coldness in Sir Willoughby and in Meredith's treatment of him which creates an effect of cruelty. Meredith gives himself the position of comic spirit—detached, disengaged; but he uses it in a way that sometimes seems self-flagellatory and reminds us that Sir Willoughby represents much that Meredith wants to drive out of himself as well as others.

The effect of near-hysteria in parts of *The Egoist* does not, of course, derive always from autobiographical pressures; it is also a dramatisation of Clara's state of mind. Meredith's apparent detachment from the characters in *The Egoist* (he is even at a distance from the comic imps) helps him to keep the control which he admired in Molière. . . . (pp. 123-24)

Its power derives from a sense of barely, exquisitely, contained emotion.

The Egoist becomes an exploration of the boundaries beyond which comedy cannot venture. 'Life, we know too well, is not a Comedy, but something strangely mixed', he wrote in the *Essay; The Egoist* ranges beyond what Meredith had earlier declared to be the province of comedy: social follies rather than man's inescapable nature. 'Do not offend reason', enjoin *Essay* and Prelude—but as soon as Meredith is dealing with human figures he shows a heightened consciousness of how narrow is reason's power in human conduct: and he sees further that since the flouting of reason is the root of comedy, comedy may have a tragic issue in the lives of human beings. . . . The entirely reasonable man is quite as likely to be a cold self-seeker, like Cecil Baskelett in *Beauchamp's Career* who can only see *through* men, as he is to be a self-abnegating rational lover, like Vernon Whitford in *The Egoist*. Although tragedy is not in question, the special emotional edge of *The Egoist* comes from a sense of poignancy held at bay.

The narrative language represents the characters' active inner life and sets it off against their elaborately controlled dialogue exchanges. (pp. 124-25)

Meredith says in the *Essay* that comedy does not deal with 'periods of fervour' but in the novel both Clara and Willoughby are in a state of ferment, swelling beneath the glossy surface of polite interchange in which a raised eyebrow is the only possible representation of rage. The basis of the novel is the struggle between the instinctual demands of a man or woman's nature and the social forms they adopt by demand or as disguise. The struggle is not judged easily: Meredith believes in civilisation and evolution. What he shows is that a man like Willoughby may use the forms of civilisation to disguise from himself an uncontained and animal voraciousness, and that the same civilised forms may prevent a woman like Clara from responding in her own full identity because they present her with a model of what a lady should feel and be—a model which is static and anti-evolutionary.

The clash takes its crucial form in the disparity between the pre-ordained conventional patterns of fiction and actual existential feeling. Sir Willoughby Patterne is a 'model' gentleman ('He has a leg', as Mrs Mountstuart cryptically observes). He is the ideal hero of popular Victorian fiction—handsome, intelligent, wealthy, generous, and admired by all about him. Clara, the girl to whom he is engaged, seems to have all the qualities of a typical novel heroine: she is pretty, absolutely 'pure' and inexperienced sexually, with means of her own and the only daughter of an elderly scholar-gentleman. Everyone is preparing for a conventional courtship and wedding. But this is an anti-conventional novel which takes the easy expectations of society and the plot judgments of fiction and turns them askew. Thus, Clara who has been swept off her feet by Willoughby's romantic whirlwind courtship begins to realise that whirlwind courtships may be a form of aggression and a prelude to annihilation. She comes to understand (all unwillingly) that Sir Willoughby's ideal of marriage is not partnership but absorption. . . . Clara's growing dislike of Willoughby's possessiveness develops into a sullen physical antagonism. She cannot bear him to kiss her.

> The gulf of a caress hove in view like an enormous billow hollowing under the curled ridge.
>
> She stooped to a buttercup; the monster swept by. . . .

These passages show the range of strategies by which the reader is led to judge Sir Willoughby; the representation of his consciousness in which his thoughts and the narrator's overlap; direct speech; motives imputed to him by an epitomising commentator; mock-heroic aggrandising metaphor. Willoughby is indeed pursued.

Meredith does not entirely avoid rousing our sympathy for Sir Willoughby by the end of the book. . . . What makes us stand apart from Sir Willoughby . . . is that the last thing he himself wants is to rouse pity. Most of his activity in the second half of the book is part of the effort to save face, to allow the world no opportunity to pity him. Meredith denies him tragic stature by allowing him to be successful in his efforts. The book ends

with him handing Clara over to the cousin whom he still sees as inferior to himself, discomfiting his friend De Craye who has tried to get Clara, and presenting Laetitia to a not entirely sceptical world as his inescapable destiny. He remains much the same man at the end as he was at the beginning. The Comedy has corrected but not reclaimed him. Although the function of comedy is 'to teach the world what ails it', it never really teaches Sir Willoughby.

If the reader's role is to be primarily that of judge, it is necessary that our detachment should be sustained. Meredith's usual method of rousing and flouting our expectations has to be modified. Elsewhere he emphasises the devious flow of life, the often undynamic nature of significant emotion, the pressure of free will on circumstances and of circumstances on individuality, and in his later works he begins to abandon belief in congruity of character. In some of his novels where he claims to be writing internal history, such as *Sandra Belloni,* recognisable plot patterns are more or less obliterated, while in others he uses patterns the reader will recognise but which give only a deliberately limited insight into the conduct of the action. Only in *The Egoist* does he use reassuring analogues within the work whose promise is fulfilled: our concern for Clara is tempered because we have been told at the outset that the book is 'a comedy in narrative': because Sir Willoughby's previous, ironically-named fiancée, Constantia, escaped, and because we know that he is selfish before Clara does. (pp. 127-30)

[Although] our sympathy is in the main invited for Clara, Meredith is too subtle an observer to refuse a measure of fellow-feeling to Willoughby or to suggest that he has a monopoly of egoism. . . . Meredith is showing the workings of egoism in *all* his characters and particularly in Clara, and in this way he suggests that egoism is common to us all. Nor does he suggest that egoism is *necessarily* destructive. In the youthful Cross-jaye, egotism is part of a sturdy, growing identity and the other characters are judged by their response to his demands. Vernon wants to send him to train in London at his own expense because it is best for the boy; Laetitia behaves like an anxious, upright mother towards him; Willoughby spoils him but is ready to abandon him if he goes against his wishes (as he has done the wretched Flitch and will do Vernon if he leaves); Clara delights him and uses him in her escape. She forgets him (having bound him to wait for her by a childish obsessional promise) and she plays on his awakening sexuality.

Laetitia's declaration at the end of the book, 'I am an Egoist', is a declaration of growth as well as of hardening. Her timid self-abnegation has given way to independence. Clara's egotism is inextricable from her discovery of her self, which includes her sexual self—and *The Egoist* is exceptional among Victorian novels in the closeness and intensity with which it suggests sexual revulsion (just as *The Tragic Comedians* is exceptional in the ferocity with which it depicts sexual obsession). (pp. 132-33)

The book is an intricate account of the duel between Willoughby and Clara: neither of them is a particularly scrupulous fighter. Both are fighting defensively to preserve the same thing: their identity. Willoughby *cannot* release Clara from her engagement because his love for her is intimately entangled with his assurance of his own worth—if she goes he will no longer be Sir Willoughby Patterne, cynosure of the county, but a twice-jilted man. Clara *cannot* marry Willoughby to be absorbed by his voracious love. Although the original cause of his dispute with Clara is his vaunted wish to 'banish the world' and live in total absorbed intimacy with her, he is really entirely dependent on the world's estimate of him. He exists to himself only through the mirror image it reflects of him, and his relationship with Clara was to have been a rosy and enlarging mirror—extending his image beyond death. (pp. 133-34)

The book is long (about 600 pages): it may seem an excessive length for the breaking of an engagement—even so solemn a betrothal as Willoughby has enforced. Until two-thirds of the way through there is little physical action. . . . The length of the book corresponds to the density of the emotional life described: it is swift, not leisurely. . . . The claustrophobia of the relationship between Willoughby and Clara, which is the cause of its dissolution, also makes it almost impossible to dissolve.

In order to underline the claustrophobic effect Meredith follows a form of three unities: the action is continuous, in one place, and never moves out of its narrow range of emotions, chief among which is frustration (Laetitia, Vernon, Clara and Willoughby are all frustrated). He adds the further, fictive, unity that the book is seen largely from a single point of view, that of Clara. He does, however, allow us to know Sir Willoughby's thoughts: he transcribes them apparently quite straightforwardly and often without commentary. But the mind of the reader scrutinises them. In this way he allows us to make the same discoveries about Sir Willoughby as Clara does, by a means additional to, and to some extent independent of, hers. At times it seems scarcely believable that Sir Willoughby should fail to recognise his motives for what they are, so clearly does he state grossly selfish ideas to himself; but it is precisely the failure to take that final step to self-consciousness which involves self-criticism which makes Sir Willoughby what he is. By making us share Sir Willoughby's stream-of-consciousness, Meredith further suggests that we all think, quite lucidly, many more thoughts than we dare scrutinise.

His observation of the two principal characters is scrupulously exact. (pp. 134-35)

The delight of the book's conclusion (as well as its drop in intensity) comes because the solutions imposed derive from a more familiar literary world. Willoughby has been made to look ridiculous (to the reader, but not entirely to the other characters). His victories may be hollow, but they clothe his nakedness—and for him this preserves his identity, which is vested in appearances. (His favourite image of himself is as *le roi soleil*.) Clara has won her battle—but at the end of the book is a little withdrawn, so that she seems again just an ordinary young woman.

The sense of comic release at the end of the novel is in part a sense of release from the stringency of Meredith's comic vision. He said himself that the book contained 'only half myself'; the tart rationality of the scrutinising Comic Spirit cannot fully contain the emotional force of the characters. The comic imps are not our representatives. They come from a different world. They inhibit our involvement with the characters, but we are not like them. It is a situation akin to the fourth book of *Gulliver's Travels:* we cannot comfortably identify ourselves with either group. Comic imps and Houhyhynyms, however admirable, are ineffacably different from us. At times the primness of the narrative insistence on folly seems limited in the face of the characters' suffering, whether or not the suffering is self-imposed. We are not kept at the 'point fixe' of comedy: we move into the characters, then very far away, to where they seem like comic china ornaments caught in grotesque attitudes. The emotional energy of the book is such that at times the rigid comic form is almost shattered. (pp. 136-37)

The Egoist is high comedy of the kind which 'refines even to pain'. Despite his belief in the power of reason, Meredith's own creative sympathy is usually given to passionate feeling. Clara is justified by her passionate revulsion against Sir Willoughby in which both mind and instincts play a part. The characters speak with grace and wit; they are allusive, urbane, epigrammatic, apparently articulate—but what they say nearly always serves as a foil to their urgent, often ugly feelings. Meredith sets up a fruitful tension between the poise of high comedy and the primitive emotions with which the characters are grappling. It is the abrasion between comedy and passion which makes the book both witty and poignant. (p. 139)

Meredith never thoroughly trusted his readers. Despite the growing critical enthusiasm for his work his sense of being at odds with the reading public intensified in the later years of his career. . . .

There are a number of reasons for Meredith's radical, and perhaps exaggerated, mistrust of the reading public. His forty years as publisher's reader for Chapman and Hall meant that he had to spend a good deal of his time reading manuscripts by writers with 'ability below the level of a commonplace theme'. Though he was occasionally able to encourage high talent, such as that of Hardy and Gissing, most of the time he was reading great numbers of inferior manuscripts, feebly treating well worn themes of the day. (p. 182)

The attacks on the 'low ethical tone' of *Richard Feverel* and *Modern Love* at the beginning of his career, and [the lending

Portrait of Meredith by John Singer Sargent.

library] Mudie's refusal to circulate the novel, also had repercussions for many years in Meredith's art. It was not until the eighteen-eighties that he turned anew to the theme of marriage; by then he had created a subtle network of sexual metaphor which went beyond the double-entendre of . . . *Sandra Belloni.*

His sense of isolation never left him and he attributed it to the neglect he had suffered in the earlier part of his career. (p. 184)

[In his novels Meredith] struggled to avoid the merely familiar. He attempted to build up language from perceptions afresh and oblige the reader to act out for himself the thing described rather than accept it as something foreknown. The narrative rhetoric of the books does not suggest the speaking voice— the sound of conversation or monologue—as in Dickens's novels, where repetition, exclamation and a syntactical piling of phrase on phrase reach their full expressiveness only when read aloud. Meredith's work, by contrast, supposes a silent reader, the sentence structures moving in the mind and becoming assimilated to one's own processes of consciousness. Contrasted rhythmical movements convey the characters' feelings and modes of thought as surely as do imagery and analysis. Grammar and syntax have a heightened role, constantly shifting us in and out of twisting consciousnesses and epigrammatic formulations. (pp. 186-87)

Meredith mistrusted his reader partly because he gave him so vital a part to play in the re-creation of the novel's experience. Sometimes the quiddities of his writing become mere ornamentation and the thronging pages submerge the sustained narrative meaning. . . . Meredith makes at times almost unconscionable demands on our activity as readers (as in his disordering of chronology and suppression of connections). . . . Meredith turns away from conventional plot so far that he rarely shows us the momentary crisis of external action. Yet it is also true that his novels in memory resolve themselves into remarkably vivid 'scenes'. The same thing happens with the novels of Samuel Richardson and Virginia Woolf. This is surely because the method of these three closely-related writers is to engage us in the flux of experience in a manner parallel to the processes of life. (pp. 187-88)

Meredith was learning 'the novelist's lesson' throughout his creative life. His repudiation of box-like plot meant that he was obliged to find alternative ordering processes for his novels. He shaped his books primarily by varying the tempo at which action is recorded. Events rarely reach us intact; they come refracted through the wishes and dreads of the characters. He fused the narrator's commentary with the character's stream-of-consciousness; this creates a fluid form for our experience as readers but it does not absolve us from the need to judge. Indeed the most arresting of his organising techniques is his way of forcing on the reader a variety of conflicting roles within the novel. In some ways the organisation of Meredith's novels *depends* upon conflict between author and reader. Moreover Meredith seems to have needed to sense a hostile public in order to give form (and limits) to his experiments. The vivid achievement of the novels is inhibited by Meredith's uneasiness about the implications of his perceptions.

The range and power of his novels, their interpenetration of lyricism and comedy, their fierce mining for the sources of human personality, their richness of invention and perception, tempt me to praise them even beyond their achievement. Historically, they are close to the source of much that has been most fruitful in the twentieth-century novel in English. But they are limited by a final timidity in Meredith's artistic per-

sonality: a refusal to be committed to his perceptions, a tendency to grimace belligerently at his reader. (pp. 188-89)

Meredith's defence of the marriage of realism and idealism [persisted], but his championship of one or the other varies at different periods of his career. In the eighteen-fifties and sixties writers such as Stendhal and Flaubert were little appreciated in England and the tendency was (as in Ruskin) to insist on observation finally as a way of interpreting the parable of the universe rather than for its own sake. At that time Meredith emphasised the importance of scrutinising our emotions, of avoiding the transcendental, of recognising the devious and the complicated. *Richard Feverel* and *Sandra Belloni* are in their different ways both attacks on sentimental idealism. In the eighteen-seventies when Meredith was much involved with the *Fortnightly*, its editor Morley, and liberal thinking generally, he again reacted against his environment and scrutinised the rationalism by which he was surrounded, emphasising the unaccommodated role of fantasy in our lives *(The Adventures of Harry Richmond)* or the temperamental sources of political thought *(Beauchamp's Career)*. In the eighteen-eighties and nineties when fashion favoured French writers such as Mendès who 'monsterised' Zola with their 'cataturient' realism, he moved to defend the sense of the ideal within us, couching it in terms of aspiration, albeit thwarted, or romance. *Lord Ormont and His Aminta,* one of the few novels with a 'happy' ending shows the unmarried lovers Weyburn and Aminta escaping from her husband Lord Ormont and running a progressive school in Switzerland. This socially conscious conclusion is possible only because of the erotic scene in which Weyburn and Aminta first discover and express their love through swimming together out at sea. The novel is one of Meredith's most forthright though least profound attempts to combine the ideal and the real in the form of freedom and duty.

Meredith's effect on the writers of his own time and the generation which followed establishes him as an artist who 'strikes his impress right and left around him'. Gissing and Hardy both acknowledged the practical encouragement that Meredith had given them early in their careers. Robert Louis Stevenson considered him 'out and away the greatest force in English letters'. (pp. 191-92)

Meredith . . . delighted in brilliance and expected his readers to share his delight. If at times the prodigal energy with which he strives to be memorable produces simply an effect of strain, at other times a single image or the whole retrospect of a scene can open up for us new areas of imaginative comprehension. He works not by accretion but by variety. The total effect is of unrest, excitement, growth. Meredith demands of the reader a pitch of receptiveness and of participation more commonly granted to poetry than to the novel. He rewards him with an experience complex, peculiar and vivid. (p. 194)

Gillian Beer, in her Meredith, a Change of Masks: A Study of the Novels, *The Athlone Press, 1970, 214 p.*

BARBARA HARDY (essay date 1971)

[*Hardy is the author and editor of numerous studies of the novels of George Eliot and of the moral and narrative aspects of form in the novel, in particular* The Appropriate Form: An Essay on the Novel (1964). *In the following excerpt, she examines* Lord Ormont and His Aminta *and* The Amazing Marriage *as two typical examples of "the Meredith novel," the first demonstrating the artificiality and sentimentality that she dislikes in Meredith, the second revealing the complexity, continuity, and sophisticated development of ideas and values that are representative of Meredith at his best.*]

I want to look at these two late novels [*Lord Ormont and his Aminta* and *The Amazing Marriage*] together, at the risk of doing less than justice to *Lord Ormont and his Aminta,* because they have made plain to me what I find good and bad in Meredith. Their chronological neighbourhood and their strong affinities of story and theme throw their difference in fictional quality into strong relief.

I think it is necessary to say something about the quality of Meredith's achievement. As with other very mannered artists, critics are either too totally repelled to say much of interest or too totally won over and absorbed in the mannerism to see anything wrong in it. The polarity of hostility and admiration tends to be self-perpetuating: the more rudely Meredith is excluded from the Great Tradition without much in the way of argument, the more passionately his admirers protest. The protest is very understandable. Even to read one novel properly (with the possible exception of the very accessible *Harry Richmond*) involves considerable investment of time and mental energy which naturally direct us towards justification by profits. And as with other cases of mannerism, the slow and patient reading that his obscure narrative and clotted prose demand tend to over-acclimatize us to the mannerism. This can happen with Henry James, George Moore, or Ronald Firbank, but in Meredith it is almost guaranteed by the combination of artificiality with difficulty, and in a fairly even spread throughout the novels. With James, for instance, the habituation to mannerism can happen gradually. . . . But Meredith's mannerism and obscurity are present from the beginning, and though I would not want to suggest that they do not vary from novel to novel, in form and degree, there is no slow development which habituates us gradually or alienates us at certain points. Meredith criticism does tend to fall apart into all-or-nothing judgments. I think this is a pity, not because I am particularly interested in the sport of submitting literature to competitive and carefully graded examinations, but because I am interested in the imagination and values of Meredith, and believe that his admirers can afford (and need) to become tougher with their author and themselves.

Lord Ormont and his Aminta is a more readable and simple version of 'the Meredith novel' than *The Amazing Marriage,* but it is also, in my opinion, a novel which shows him at his most sentimental, and where the famous artificiality serves the interests of the sentimentality. *The Amazing Marriage* has that particularity and continuity which *Lord Ormont* lacks, and expresses and explores the same ideas and values with complexity and completeness, justifying the mannerism which postures vapidly, like Sir Willoughby Patterne, in *Lord Ormont.*

Perhaps one reason why Meredith appeals to some of us is his apparent worldliness, his refreshing difference, in candour and toughness about love, marriage, egoism, women, religion—so many of the mid-Victorian sacred cows. . . . Meredith comes late enough to break down these walls, and we tend to find his sheer extension of subject and lack of moral and religious cant refreshing and exciting.

In practice I suspect that we like Meredith not because he is really less sentimental about faith and ethics and social convention than Dickens and George Eliot, but because he is sentimental about different things. His is the sentimentality of the 1890s, which still has a certain appealing, if diminishing, affinity with our own: it tends to be strongly affirmative about youth rather than babies, about sex rather than true love, about the right relationship rather than the perfect marriage, about nature rather than God, feminism rather than womanliness, discovery of identity rather than the moral change of heart. We might want to say that Meredith's beliefs are progressive, or *avant-garde* in the double sense that implies both courage and progress, but his ninetyish *avant-garde* sentimentality is still sentimentality. He can become as ludicrously ecstatic, soft and blurred on the subjects of feminism, England and co-education as Dickens could on the subjects of womanly virtue, religion and child-death. It is this sentimentality which marks Meredith at his worst, and whose triumphant absence marks him at his best. It has also, I suggest, an interesting relation to his mannerism and his obscurity. When Meredith is flaccidly and pompously directing our sympathies, his artifical style and elliptical manner can work in the interests of evasion and open invitation to the feelings. But artificiality and obscurity are still present when his values and ideas are more thoroughly and toughly analysed. There is no simple one-to-one relation.

Lord Ormont and his Aminta was published in 1894, *The Amazing Marriage* in 1895. The chronological relation was more complicated than these dates suggest, for he had been working on *The Amazing Marriage,* on and off, since finishing *The Egoist* in 1879. (pp. 295-97)

There is no simple and straightforward relation between his own broken marriage and his discussion in the novels. **'Modern Love'** retold his own story with the painful eloquence and valuable reticence of poetry, and may perhaps have freed him for more impartial (or effectively disguised) contemplation of the difficulties and disadvantages of this *bourgeois* institution. In many of his novels he attacks marriage as a typically possessive and proprietorial relation, and I believe that his last novel, *The Amazing Marriage,* is the most effective mythological attack and the best novel. Perhaps it is no accident that its title comes closest to a generalized proclamation of theme, and that the framework of the novel is an argument and a struggle between a modern realistic novelist and a myth-making Dame Gossip. It has the kind of complex success that suggests that the qualities of good myth and good psychological fiction are not, after all, in opposition to each other.

The married woman was for Meredith as blatant a case of social oppression and unfair possession as the child was for Dickens or the working man for Mrs Gaskell. . . . Whatever his personal discontent, the amazing marriage was a social fact. And it is as social fact that Meredith treats it, not attacking its permanence, its fragility, or its relation to other ties, but bringing out, in particularly plain cases of marriage between aristocrat and commoner, wealth and poverty, the acquisitive typicality of the institution. He brings this out—very noticeably in comparison with Dickens and George Eliot—not by describing the extremes of marital suffering in incompatibility, but, with increasing emphasis, in the ties and torments of reasonable, decent, complex and even compatible human beings. If we trace the subject through, especially from *The Egoist* to *The Amazing Marriage,* this kind of candour, completeness and complexity seems to grow. (p. 297-99)

Lord Ormont and Lord Fleetwood are both aristocrats, of old family, great landed possessions and immense wealth. Their wives, Aminta and Carinthia, are commoners and very poor. In each novel it is as if Meredith wants to emphasize the psychic and sexual oppressiveness he analysed in *The Egoist* with a much clearer and fiercer attack on the institution. *The Egoist* and *Diana* were implicit attacks on *bourgeois* marriage, but their central and explicit concerns were broader. In his last novels Meredith narrows down his action and his theme. He narrowed it excessively in *Lord Ormont,* and he found the right form in *The Amazing Marriage.* In both novels he sorts out what he thinks about individual men and women getting married, getting unmarried, and finding alternatives, but the sorting out involved sentimental loss of control and distortion in the one, and very effective control in the other.

There are several ways in which both novels show an advance in identifying the subject. First, Meredith needs to show the difficulty even in a marriage of strong attachment. We never really see Diana's first marriage, but are shown its motivation, the rude assaults and assumptions surrounding a single woman: the marriage is simply written in as a hasty solution to economic need and isolation. We are told—and lengthily—that Clara has believed herself attached to Sir Willoughby Patterne, but what is dramatized is the slow and very difficult process of disentanglement. In the last two novels Meredith seems to be realizing that hard cases make bad myths: the January and May story, found in other Victorian novelists like Dickens, George Eliot and George Gissing, must not be told too allegorically or it will lack the particularity of a novel (obviously) and the typicality of the myth (perhaps a little less obviously). . . . Although Carinthia's is an amazing marriage, it is, in extravagant form, the story of recognizable affinity, passion and loss. Although there is too much ellipsis in *Lord Ormont,* we are both shown and told enough of Aminta's hero-worshipping and her aunt's mercenary and snobbish social climbing. Meredith is looking both at the social and economic reasons for marriage and the social and economic structure, even of marriages of feeling. It is, after all, self-evident that loveless and incompatible marriages are wrong, but all we can really learn from the stories of total incompatibility or abject impotence is that *bourgeois* society can make marriages, despite an absolute lack of relationship. Meredith also wants to say that *bourgeois* marriage, even based on feeling and compatibility, is a difficult and dangerous enterprise. He is letting himself in for an analysis that needs to be social and psychological. And he is making a much more fundamental criticism of the institution of marriage.

Both husbands marry 'beneath' them. Meredith's emphasis on Lord Ormont's disgust with his class and his country, and Lord Fleetwood's more intuitive version of the same feeling, excellently shifts the emphasis from the wives (both poor and both commoners) who marry high rank and great wealth. It is important not just that the women should marry out of strong feeling (though in each case there is an economic motive, most delicately handled) but that they should be seen as victims. Meredith emphasizes the purchasing-power of Ormont and Fleetwood, but he wants us to be less impressed by the actual purchase of the woman than by the power both rank and money exercise after the marriage. Aminta is deprived of social reputation, Carinthia of reputation, freedom, and security. The eventual release has great momentum, though very much more in *The Amazing Marriage,* where the relationships are much more intricate and held in suspense, and where the woman is subjected to very much greater, and very much less justified, restriction and pain. Both novels are feminist novels, and at the point of release or rescue Meredith makes this clear by forcing a large breach of convention. Lady Ormont not only leaves her 'tyrant' but goes off to live with an unconventional schoolmaster who has refused the obvious professions in favour of starting an international co-educational school. (The point is weakened when Lord Ormont dies and leaves the free lovers free to marry.) Carinthia not only leaves Fleetwood, but is

willing to leave her child and to go off to the wars in Spain with her brother. (The point is weakened when this plan is frustrated and when Meredith marries her off to Owain Wythan.) He takes each action to the point of dismissing marriage as the vocation for woman, but can't quite make it.

Perhaps this is expecting too much of the liberalism of the 1890s, at least in public and moral art. But the woman is also presented in pastoral terms. As Empson would say, she is the 'swain' of Meredith's fiction. Here we find the first instance of the superiority of *The Amazing Marriage.* In *Lord Ormont* the pastoral theme is only slightly present, and made rather arch, hearty, and slightly ridiculous by associations with athletics, fresh air, and hygiene. Woman is shown as debarred from the free and healthy life, and, unable to play cricket or join in snowball fights. Aminta turns passionately to the hero-worship of a great general. Later a small girl rescues another child from drowning, helped, but from the rear, by her elder brother. Later still the declaration of love between Matey Weyburn and Brownie (Lady Ormont) is expressed and ritualized in the famous swimming scene. Last we see the free and healthy life in the progressive school in Switzerland. There is nothing wrong with these values: it was hard on girls to wear long skirts and not throw snowballs, a sea scene has great erotic potential, and there is nothing wrong with co-educational schools in healthy spots, with open windows and good food. . . . But Meredith makes his pastoral small and rather ridiculous in such symbols, and, moreover, gushes over their value. . . . The open-air cult is understandable enough, both as an educational value and as a glance at the restricted female life—'the thought of the difference betweeen themselves and the boys must have been something like the tight band—call it corset—over the chest'—but its expression tends to be arch and its instances humourlessly domestic—the white ducks, 'The Jolly Cricketers', the heroine's love of long walks. It is perhaps a Surrey Nature cult which has suffered even further from week-ends and country tramps and food fads—all excellent enough in their way, but not grand enough for the real pastoral stuff.

There is nothing of the week-end pastoral about *The Amazing Marriage.* Something of the slightly ludicrous fad may cling to Carinthia's ideas about child-rearing—weaning at nine months, breathing through the nose, and sleeping in the open air. But the central symbols have a real enough ring of grandeur, with the beginning in the German mountains, with the brother and sister going out to call the dawn and walk through the forests. . . . (pp. 299-303)

I can only refer readers to each novel, and suggest that *The Amazing Marriage* establishes a real pastoral, as Wordsworth does in *The Prelude,* by three chief means: by building up, particularly, actively and variously, the landscape of the novel, especially of Germany and Wales; of creating the characters' relation with that Nature, through their sensuous and symbol-making reactions; and of extending and developing the symbols in metaphor. In *Lord Ormont* the pastoral is stagey or sentimental because Meredith has not established a Nature; it exists only in a few shorthand versions and stimuli, which will not do. In *The Amazing Marriage* we feel that Carinthia is swain, earth goddess, or whatever, because she is seen as growing with Nature, as breathing in its air, climbing its rocks, having some affinity with the austerity and grandeur which justifies the Gorgon image. In comparison, Brownie (like her name) seems a little vulgar, especially when she is watching the cricket or going for a swim. The potentially ridiculous side of Carinthia—the childrearing fads and love of walks—is realized by the sensuous particularity which *Lord Ormont* lacks. Meredith had a real pagan feeling for Nature, but it got into one novel adequately and into the other in a tame, arch, and domesticated form. In *The Amazing Marriage* there is also the distancing effect of the two cultists, the Old Buccaneer who has taught his children how to jump with knees bent, etc., and Gower Woodseer, the pastoral and Stevensonian figure, who . . . is no less effective for being slightly ludicrous. There is no such evidence in *Lord Ormont* that there was anything ridiculous in making such a business of the open-air-life, long tramps and outdoor girls.

It is sensuously realized, but it is also poeticized. This happens in *Lord Ormont,* too . . . ; the swimming metaphors, as in *Beauchamp's Career* and *Harry Richmond,* are pervasive. They are very neatly used, appearing conspicuous because having no real matrix in solidly particularized Nature, and simply diagrammatically traced. *The Amazing Marriage* shows signs of more imaginative and less schematic image-patterns, which perhaps may have come from its longer history in Meredith's mind: its characteristic pattern is that of transfer from the literal to the metaphorical, to be found elsewhere, and particularly in *Harry Richmond.* Here, as in the earlier novel, it gives us a rich and casual texture, though the clarity remains. Thus, when Carinthia is described in terms of height, air, hardness, rock, we have seen all this in action, they are earned and substantial images, looked at one way, seen in the process of image-making, looked at in another. Meredith often shares his authorial images with his characters, and does this with the image he uses for Fleetwood, prisoner of his wishes, which he allows Henrietta to use 'independently' in a letter. The image of the Gorgon, and the mad dog, and the fire also shift in this way, and sometimes the metaphor precedes the large symbolic or even literal action.

It is the integrity rather than the blurring of the symbols which I want to stress. Fleetwood is a prisoner of his will, and the image of imprisonment is a pervasive one, belonging to the pastoral treatment of marriage. As it is, in the central case and all others, it is an urban restriction, a bond and pattern imposed by civilization on Nature (a metaphor with its own good logic, by the way). In *Lord Ormont* the pastoral values are assumed; in *The Amazing Marriage* Meredith defines the pastoral nature of action and character much more profoundly—and the second novel has profundities to be defined which the first lacks. Thus, Carinthia's actual imprisonments become more important than the pastoral symbol and cut across it, so that the mean, stifling and dirty street in Whitechapel, which began as a terrible restriction for her, ends by being the city pastoralized, as at times in the London scenes of *The Prelude,* by the values of 'natural' (i.e. spontaneous, generous, uncommercial, unsnobbish, class-free) human love. But the actual pastoral movement is very important.

The rescue into freedom and love is marked by Nature imagery and felt as the return to Nature after constraint. But this is not confined to Carinthia's imprisonment and release. The criticism of society involves a complex contrast between the pastoral outsider, Carinthia, and the urban hero, Fleetwood. This is a less schematic and much more rich and complex version of the diagram of *Lord Ormont.* Lord Ormont, however, is also seen as an outsider, though what he is 'outside' is an establishment which is attacked less for its values than for giving him and his military schemes insufficient recognition and for placing England in a weak position. Neither husband-figure, it is important to see, represents the establishment in the very simple

and direct way that Casaubon or Sir Clifford Chatterley represent authority, money, intellectual sterility, impotence, the older order in Church and State. The complexity of Lord Ormont is a bit of a muddle: we are likely to sympathize with him only up to a point, and then sympathy will probably be deflected by his military values and his eventual capitulation. The complexity of Fleetwood strikes me as entirely successful.

Here it is necessary to stress the common properties, and not the differences, of the novels. In showing the husband-authority figures much more complexly, Meredith is not just making the novel more 'realistic', as we say, in the usual assumptions about complex verisimilitude, but is making a much more devastating and profound criticism of Victorian England. Lord Ormont and—very strongly—Lord Fleetwood, have something of the pastoral outsider in their make-up which reveals the destructive power of money and rank, and money—and rank-dominated relationships. The difference is that between the simple and the complex antithesis. The simple antithesis between George Eliot's Casaubon and Ladislaw, or between Lawrence's Sir Clifford Chatterley and Mellors, dramatizes and presents a conflict of values. The complex antithesis, like that between Fleetwood and Carinthia, or between Lawrence's Gerald and Birkin, refuses to mythologize by abstracting qualities and mythologizes the more effectively for showing the processes of social conditioning at work within the complete individual. So the destructive power of rank and money and all the unnatural sports of the sweet life which they command are not defined as 'that which is in opposition to Nature', far removed from the life of instinct, entirely role-determined and so on, but as 'that which can tame, corrupt and constrict even the impulsive and imaginative man'. This corruption is analysed in both novels, and it enlarges the themes of marriage and feminism, but it only gets fully, persuasively and toughly into action, language and character in *The Amazing Marriage. Lord Ormont*'s greater sentimentality, ellipsis and confusion help us to see more clearly that Meredith is doing something of great importance to all novelists—getting his ideas clearer and in the process increasing, and not diminishing, the psychological interest.

In *Lord Ormont* we have the ageing general married to the young and beautiful woman who hero-worshipped him. Betrayed by the country he has served, he is obsessed by her military weakness and by his own sense of outraged honour. He is both of, and not of, the establishment values, essentially an authority figure, deeply traditional and conventional, but driven to deny his strongest allegiances, refusing to move in respectable society, refusing to live in his family seat, refusing to have his wife presented at court. Most of these refusals make admirable plot levers, and make his motives crystal clear. But this very clarity damages the presentation of his Aminta. It is really not at all clear why she fails to see what the reader sees, possessing as she does the double advantage of long, intimate knowledge and a strong sympathy for her husband's unpopular position. Part of the obscurity may come from Meredith's reticence about the sexual history of the marriage. Aminta seems to look back to a passionate honeymoon, but it is not very clear whether a certain coolness and separateness is cause or effect of her resentment at her social position. The implications seem to be those of the January and May pattern, with some deviation. Meredith adds the sinister and fascinating touch about the possibility (but rareness and difficulty) of inflicting sexual refusal on a husband who is apparently not completely impotent, but certainly getting on. If this part of the history were clearer, Aminta might be more thoroughly placed. As it is, we are left wondering why she plays with fire with Morsfield, why she attaches such importance to living at Steignton and being presented at court, since she is carefully shown as so spirited, natural and drawn to Matey's pastoral virtues. It may be that Meredith is compressing some suggestion of change here: the second stage of her acquaintance with Matey disabuses her of some conventional notions about a gentleman's career, and she develops in 'naturalness'—if this is possible—throughout the novel. Even so, Carinthia would plainly snap her fingers at the presentation at court, so it isn't a matter of the novel having dated. Perhaps Meredith contracted Carinthia's changes in drawing Aminta. Carinthia is shown as spontaneous, unschooled, in some ways (though less naïve than ignorant) naïve, and such qualities are important in the novel's scheme of values as well as in the motivation of her amazing marriage. She is shown, most subtly, as growing in all the externals of civilization—speech, manners, deportment—and much of this change is drawn by the language which Meredith shows very naturally and very pointedly as a growth in the accomplished knowledge and use of English. But she does not grow an inch in the disapproved 'internals' of civilization. . . . Carinthia seems to me to acquire the analytic mode without losing anything of instinctive strength. By the time she comes to refuse her bed— 'I guard my rooms'—to Fleetwood, she has learnt not to react instinctively and spontaneously, but to analyse, judge and defend herself by the use of her considerable intelligence. I do not see her as a large simple nature, but as very like Fleetwood, only on the right—that is the other—side of civilization.

I stress this reading because it seems to me characteristic of the novel that it avoids antithesis where *Lord Ormont* is drawn towards it. *The Amazing Marriage* invites us to dismiss the tension we often set up between ideological clarity and complex realism, for in it Meredith's fundamental social sight about the possessive marriage is inseparable from his profound rendering of the human hearts.

Meredith shows in very great detail how painful the marriage was for Carinthia and for Fleetwood—in his imprisonment by his word, in her imprisonment in ignorance, in his and her love, in her maternity coming out of rape, in his gradual realization of the meaning of the furtive memory and its enlargement in his consciousness (this instance of Meredith's obscurity seems to be an excellent instance of inattentiveness on the part of his readers). He shows them both driven by outside manipulation—in the form of the unscrupulous Henrietta and Chillon and the miserly Lord Levellier—as well as by the corruptions within Fleetwood. Fleetwood is a brilliant instance of the *droit de seigneur*—passion, imagination, energy, courage, and generosity corrupted. His affinity with both Carinthia and Woodseer (the name-overlap is important and links them all with Carinthia's forests) is immensely important. Meredith shows the terrible conditioning power of money, possession, and the roles and relations they determine, because his central case, Fleetwood, is a creature of heart. His pride, passion and imagination are ironically betrayed by the natural man—drawn to the beautiful Gorgon in the rocks—but betrayed more profoundly by civilized society. He feels wildness, impulse, solitude, integrity, courage, unconventionality, and the stroke that makes this a great love-story is his deep and long-denied recognition that all these things are to be found in Carinthia.

What is right as social fable and as human observation is his inability to forget his jealous desire to buy Henrietta: he is kept goadingly reminded of her and her husband through Carinthia, so that what should take him away from the old love keeps it

painfully in his mind, what should free him from money-determined acts make him insist on them. If he can't buy Henrietta, or if he hasn't been able to buy her yet, he will keep money away from Chillon by denying it to Carinthia. (pp. 303-09)

[Fleetwood] needs those values expressed by and in Carinthia, Woodseer (in a more literary, doctrinaire, and comic-Meredithean or Stevensonian fashion) and in the landscape of forest and mountain, in Wales and Germany. The scenes and characters which present the pastoral have a deep appeal—not as unacknowledged as all that, even early on—to Fleetwood. He shares Woodseer's desire for solitude, freedom, hardness and grandeur, and has a contempt for what he knows and is and follows: the depths below the heights, the fouler air, money, gambling, sexual sport, fashion, culture which is bought and sold. His not very attractive contempt for his parasites and for Livia, as well as his feeling for Catholicism, must all be understood in terms of this need. The tragic aspect of the novel lies in the missed affinities. Fleetwood's case is put in reverse, for elucidation and stress: Woodseer's purity is tested and fails when he succumbs to Livia and gives her the letter that might help Carinthia, and he too gambles, and even buys new clothes out of social shame. The only one who does not succumb is Carinthia, but the hardness which is both her protection and her guarantee of integrity has to turn against Fleetwood at the end. He is right after all to see the Gorgon quality at the beginning, or to seize on it in Woodseer's vision. Their relationship is shown in fine and consistent detail. It is there in the rape, which she comes only slowly (I think) to see for what it is, just as she comes to understand the wild ride and the prize-fight; and which becomes for him the cherished sexual evidence of that charm he had first felt—the proof of the subliminal wisdom. It is revealed too in his finely defined passion for Henrietta, which combines desire, contempt, self-contempt, and a jealous desire to have her and be done with her. The sexual detail which is cloudy in *Lord Ormont* is significantly clear in *The Amazing Marriage*. Its presentation is decorous: a shameful furtive act, hardly to be mentioned, it comes in hurried glimpses and is eventually given more space in his reverie as he comes to dwell on it, from shame and new desire. (pp. 309-10)

Meredith creates a major feminist triumph, but it has its sadness. The fable is made possible by the brilliant analysis which the Novelist in the novel has to keep defending. He shows the importance of exhaustion and timing in the sex-war: Carinthia is in fact not unforgiving, and might have forgiven, but the last revelation of Fleetwood's attempt to seduce Henrietta comes at the wrong moment. It is no use 'coming round' or 'being converted' because, unfortunately but definitely, people come round at different stages, and Fleetwood's repentance is badly timed. Carinthia's capacity to endure is limited. What she cannot finally accept happened in the past, is only one more thing, smaller than others, but her feeling has worn out. When George Eliot's Dorothea finds that it is really love that she feels for Ladislaw, there he is waiting for her—there is a slight suggestion that it might have been too late, for George Eliot did know about these things—but the novel resolutely curves back into the conventional moral pattern. In *The Amazing Marriage* Carinthia is nearly but not totally a patient Griselda. It is a book where really creative and strongly affined people tear each other to bits, commit rape, are cold, are deeply revengeful, just give up. Something like an elective affinity is demonstrated and shown not as strong, but as fragile, as subject to change, wars, desperate men, social role, class, status and possessions.

One man blows his brains out, another dies, and the fable and the psychic history reinforce each other's clarity and power. And I would say that this is why the Novelist and Dame Gossip have to struggle. Their conflict makes a good joke and just the kind of joke Meredith loved, at once boastful and self-depre- catory. But their joint presence helps to remind us that *The Amazing Marriage* is both realistic and fabulous. (pp. 311-12)

> Barbara Hardy, "'Lord Ormont and His Aminta' and 'The Amazing Marriage'," in Meredith Now: Some Critical Essays, edited by Ian Fletcher, Barnes & Noble, Publishers, 1971, pp. 295-312.

JUDITH WILT   (essay date 1975)

[*Wilt's* The Readable People of George Meredith, *from which the following excerpt is taken, explores the relationship between Mer- edith and the readers of his novels. Wilt maintains that all of Meredith's works demonstrate a sensitive and creative awareness of the reader, in contradiction of the popular legend that Meredith wrote always in "lofty disregard" of a readership.*]

How might a revaluation and rereading of this late Victorian novelist be a proper product of this decade of the twentieth century? Well, to some readers even the "flaws" first pinned down in the counterreaction of early twentieth-century critics are beginning to look good; [Meredith's] so-called intellec- tuality, the knotty, mind-disciplining complexity of his lan- guage, the healthy sanity of his balanced optimism. (p. 3)

George Meredith was obsessed with the real and the fictional Reader. [The critic adds in a footnote that: "I am attempting to use the words reader and writer, or author, in several ways. . . , both to draw attention to the qualities of Reader and Writer when they approach the status of fictional characters and to refer to the living persons involved. My tendency has been to capitalize as sparely as possible, after the distinctions are ini- tially established, and leave to the reader the necessary dis- criminations. The same principle holds for major Meredithian concepts, like Egoism, which are occasionally capitalized by Meredith to strengthen a rhetorical point."] Writing at perhaps the most self-conscious and self-questioning period in the his- tory of the novel, he made his obsession one of the foundations of his style and his ambivalence part of the material of his fictions. Driven by the diverse and contradictory aspects of his genius to try to integrate into the novel such alien elements as poetry, philosophy, and verbal "play," Meredith is a reader's novelist, not least because he had the reputation of being "un- readable." Concern with the real and the fictional reader is a living principle in work after work of his, growing as the whole matrix of his aesthetic grows. The struggle to define, distin- guish, understand, and finally to shape and change the reader becomes in various subtle, often exciting—sometimes dam- aging ways—the very core and content of his novels.

Meredith's aesthetic has its psychological roots in the profound ambivalence that the man Meredith felt about being "ac- cepted" in the England he loved and hated not like a son but like a foreigner turned Anglophile, as one critic phrased it. He craved public acceptance, but not from the public as he knew it—divided, contradictory, whimsical, petulant, gifted, stray- ing child that he saw it to be. The public, of course, returned the compliment. So extravagantly praised and condemned was Meredith by his contemporary readers that his work was held by one critic to demonstrate the very "futility of criticism," so utterly contradictory were the responses even to the same passages in Meredith novels.

Meredith came to expect, even to invite, such responses. He even depended on them, making them part of the content of his novels. His stories in a crucial sense are always stories in which different readers are pitted against each other. . . . Again and again, by every device of tone and style, structure and rhythm, by every trick of metaphor and turn of narrative per- sona, Meredith demonstrates his sensitive and aggressive awareness of the presence at the heart of his creative act of the reader—that formidable, inert piece of wayward human individuality who must be shaped, animated, "ensouled" by the novel.

It is crucial to point out Meredith's creative attention to the reader in his novels because such attention contradicts part of the Meredith Legend, which holds that he despaired of his contemporary readers and proceeded according to his ideal of his art, in lofty disregard of criticism. Meredith did often talk of such despair and such disregard, especially toward the end of his career. . . . And yet the implied author of Meredith's novels is so clearly in the presence of his recalcitrant, aggra- vating, mysterious, and powerfully important reader that one is reminded of Sartre's mystical picture of the reader as the true Creator of the artwork. . . . Meredith's frequent rages at the lack of attention and the lack of "real" criticism of his novels are clearly traceable to a kind of artistic despair and fury that nothing has been accomplished, that the critic has declined the difficult role of reader and so the book has fallen dead, out of Being entirely. On the other hand, while Mere- dith's reader is certainly invited and meant to work as hard as Sartre's, awakening the words, Meredith does absolutely give his literary object *in* language, testing and twisting that lan-

Meredith, crippled by a spinal condition, being taken for a ride in a donkey cart, circa 1907.

guage mercilessly and deliberately to challenge the reader. And he gives his reader not silence in which to place the language of the book, but sound argument, conflict. For he assumes that the implied author and many of the kinds of readers in his prose audience are in serious conflict over how to regard the literary object.

In the dramatization, the admitting and welcoming of this conflict, Meredith parts from Fielding and others of the English comic tradition of the characterized reader. Fielding, too, interposes that extra action, that attention to the fictional reader and writer, between the man reading and the experiences portrayed, depriving the reader of that silence in which, Sartre says, the reader can really encounter the story. But Fielding seems quite certain what sort of people he means the fictional writer and reader to be, how they are made that way, and why it is a good thing to be a certain sort of Writer and Reader. . . . By Meredith's time many of Fielding's human and artistic certainties were fading, and the very act of writing a novel, or of reading one, was becoming an existentially vulnerable, perhaps even morally questionable, act.

It is this latter quality of exhilarated, fascinated, horrified exploration of the crimes and triumphs of being a writer and a reader that is partly responsible for the renewal of the tradition of the characterized reader in contemporary literature. Writers like Barth and Nabokov use it, I think, in a sort of hilarious and grumpy surrender to the convolutions of self-awareness that edify and cripple contemporary man. Meredith could never make such a surrender openly, let alone joyfully. He was, after all, the self-proclaimed champion and fountainhead of "Philosphy in fiction"; his liberal and comic aesthetic called for a writer and a reader to get on top of life, to marshal awareness and self-awareness in orderly patterns, to see life as a whole organism with unity, system, and direction. But this very stance is undercut in several crucial ways in Meredith's novels by portraits of philosophers whom philosophy has made less than human. There was in Meredith a tendency toward the seemingly irresponsible ellipticism of a Barthelme, the sly sleight of personality of a Nabokov, the open play with literary and real worlds of a Borges. I see this tendency—one of the first and most significant appearances of the contemporary "comic" stance—working itself out in Meredith's continuing wrestle with the fictional reader and the philosopher in his novels. This conflict, it is crucial to say, is evident on two levels of his fiction, the level of story and theme and that of "reader-making," the activity of the subplot.

On the level of story, it seems clear that Meredith's fictions were from start to finish governed by a fascination with three ideas or processes (or rather an interlocking matrix of ideas or processes) which he called sentimentalism, egoism, and civilization. All these ideas are evident in each of these novels, but *Sandra Belloni* makes a direct effort to deal with the human consequences of sentimentalism, *The Egoist* with those of egoism, and *One of Our Conquerors* with the philosophical basis of, and flaws in, the idea of civilization. I therefore want to single these novels out for special attention.

Sentimentalism and egoism are Meredith's names for diseases of the human spirit which promote isolation, solitariness. Sentimentalism is man in pleased contemplation of his own states of feeling, and egoism is man bemused by the fact of his own individual being. Both states are unhealthy first because they are unreal, and then because, being unreal, they are destructive. Reality, "comic" reality, is connection, the impingement of one being upon another, the flow of one man's feeling toward

another for the sake of the other's response. Denial of this reality on anyone's part brings him destruction by chaining him firmly to abstraction; it also spreads destruction through the whole situation he inhabits, as far as his being impinges, as widely as his feelings touch others. Steps in the direction of abstract idealization (of oneself or of another, it is the same sentimentalism) or of abstract contempt (here again, as demonstrated powerfully in the story of Willoughby Patterne, contempt for others is contempt for oneself) are for Meredith the source of human distress. Since for Meredith reality is connection, integration, since for him the evolutionarian civilization is an organism maturing as its intradependent elements grow and change, this concession to unreality at the individual level is felt as civil and social distress too. Civilization is distorted by sentimentalism and egoism; and then the social distress feeds and confirms unreality back on the personal level.

Meredith has a prescient sense of the inevitability of these temptations into the unreality of overvaluing one's individual states. In fact, he shows a profound insight into the source of the energies drawing man into the unreal. Man, he feels, at his earliest primitive vulnerable stages needed all the dark brutality of egoism, all the blinding brilliance of sentimental, even superstitious, ideal feeling to jolt himself into the long slow journey toward the state of civilization. But the task is different now. Reality itself has changed, become community, civilization, and the self survives or is destroyed now according to the nourishment it receives and gives to others in that context. Men and societies are all still in a semiprimitive state, Meredith observes, and men and societies may both be counted on to move tentatively back and forth to sentimentality or egoism. There are tolerable and intolerable, culpable and nonculpable, surrenders to these unrealities in Meredith's world, and the explorations of sentimentalism in *Sandra Belloni,* of egoism in *The Egoist,* and of civilization in *One of Our Conquerors* show that keen eye for "moral distinctness" that Meredith says distinguishes the comic writer from the satirist.

What is most interesting about these novels for my purpose, however, is that the author plays in the subplot with the temptation that the characters feel in the plot, so that the reader is made to feel these temptations too [the critic earlier gave Wayne Booth's definition of "subplot" as "the interpolated world between the story and the man reading the story"]. For the kinds of sentimentalism and egoism Meredith explores are exactly those subtle kinds of hypnotized self-worship that the civilized sensitive man is prey to and that he may conceal behind the facade of the "philosophic" outlook. In each of these novels the narrative strategy can be seen as a game in which the author and reader meet the same sort of temptation as the characters to "unreality," self-worship, idealization, and contempt. Each time Meredith draws back from the temptation, leaving the civilized reader to find his own way either deeper into unreality, abstraction, superiority, dissociation, or back again to community and comedy—the "centre of the world," as Meredith calls it in *One of Our Conquerors.*

The form of this author-reader game is interestingly different in each of these three novels, which is another reason for their being chosen for study. In *Sandra Belloni* the narrative voice is openly split between two narrative characters who struggle to control the story and the reader's attitude toward it. In *The Egoist* there is one narrative voice, but it creates several sorts of reader attitudes, "looks" on life, characterized as the Comic Spirit, the Comic Muse, the Satiric Imps, and the tone of the book varies among these attitudes. In *One of Our Conquerors* a striking proto-stream-of-consciousness narrative technique enables the narrator's voice to diffuse itself convincingly through many of the characters' looks on life, and allows Meredith to reconcile inside his diffused, enlarged, compassionate implied author the problem of **Richard Feverel**'s Adrian Harley, here restructured, matured, and rounded into the character of the satirist cynic, Colney Durance.

Meredith's last published novel, **The Amazing Marriage,** is at once a summing up and a bursting asunder of Meredith's philosophy, and makes an indispensable final chapter for any study of the artist. In it he returns to the shadowboxing with fever, fate, and philosophy that marked **Richard Feverel,** to the open narrative dualism he experimented with in **Sandra Belloni,** to the examination of the peculiar flaws of the civilized reader, sentimentalism and egoism, to the psychoses, the internal detachments and deaths that are charted in **Sandra Belloni, The Egoist,** and **One of Our Conquerors**. In this novel more than any, on the levels both of story and subplot, he finally dramatizes his agonizing conclusion that the shadow, the sickness, the very principle of duality and disintegration is somehow inherent in, coherent with, the truly human integrationist philosophy of fiction and life. (pp. 3-10)

[My] first assumption . . . is that the anticipated community of *homo legens* ["reading men"] represents to authors a wholly new and welcome, if not fully predictable, civilization. The second is that this civilization is anticipated to consist of minds quite different in value orientation but similar in that stance that we have seen the novel creating, a stance whose qualities are capaciousness born of distance, sympathy born of analysis, skepticism born of the experience of the malleability of reality, the story, the intuition, the Book. This is the mind that Meredith calls philosophic, and of which he asserts in **Diana of the Crossways:** "The forecast may be hazarded that if we do not speedily embrace Philosophy in Fiction, the art is doomed to extinction." . . . My third assumption, crucial in practical criticism, is that the subplots of novels, especially of novels with as complex a narrative strategy as Meredith's always are, will yield interesting dramas of the making of the new civilization and its minds, and that these dramas are always necessary to the understanding of the whole work. They support or expand the plot, so-called, and may in fact hold the real key to the single work, or even to a large body of an author's whole work.

Meredith is an author whose work embodies these assumptions. . . . I find that in Meredith [the plot and the subplot] are usually directly related. They are related in the self-conscious attention to the evolution of civilization and the novel's production of the civilized reader that I have seen operating in the plots and subplots of pivotal novels in the comic tradition. Meredith sees "making philosophers" through the act of writing-reading and reading-writing as the business of fiction as well as of life. His wrestle with the dark side of that activity, with the hidden dragons of contempt and moral paralysis that wait to tempt the civilized reader, is the source of my fascination with him. . . . (p. 50)

> *Judith Wilt, in her* The Readable People of George Meredith, *Princeton University Press, 1975, 253 p.*

ADDITIONAL BIBLIOGRAPHY

Auchincloss, Louis. "Meredith Reassailed." In his *Reflections of a Jacobite*, pp. 85-94. Boston: Houghton Mifflin, 1961.

Expresses surprise that Meredith's long and productive career resulted in only two "perfect" novels, *Diana of the Crossways* and *The Egoist*.

Bogner, Delmar. "The Sexual Side of Meredith's Poetry." *Victorian Poetry* VIII, No. 2 (Summer 1970): 107-25.
Demonstrates with numerous examples the ways that Meredith implicitly and explicitly depicted sex in his poetry. Bogner finds that this aspect of Meredith's poetry has been overlooked by earlier critics.

Chesterton, G. K. "About Meredith." In his *As I Was Saying: A Book of Essays*, pp. 98-103. London: Methuen & Co., 1936.
Calls the popular and critical disregard of Meredith extraordinary, both because of the high regard in which Meredith was once held, and because his works presaged so many modern attitudes.

Crees, J. H. E. *George Meredith: A Study of his Works and Personality*. Oxford: B. H. Blackwell, 1918, 237 p.
Favorable, biographically oriented appraisal of Meredith's works.

Doyle, A. Conan. "Mr. Stevenson's Methods in Fiction." *The National Review* XIV, No. 3 (January 1890): 646-57.*
Considers Meredith a distinct literary influence on Robert Louis Stevenson, further anticipating that Meredith will have an enduring influence on modern literature.

Dunsany, Lord. "George Meredith." *The Nineteenth Century and After* CXXXIX, No. dcccxxxvii (January 1946): 32-35.
Argues that modern readers are unwilling to devote the time necessary to fully appreciate and understand Meredith's works.

———. Introduction to *The Egoist*, by George Meredith, pp. v-ix. London: Oxford University Press, 1946.
Praises Meredith's skillful characterizations and depictions of mood, which Dunsany believes are enhanced by the poetic quality of Meredith's prose.

[Eliot, George.] Review of *The Shaving of Shagpat, An Arabian Entertainment*, by George Meredith. *The Westminister Review* LXV, No. cxxvii (April 1856): 350.
Praises the imaginative qualities of Meredith's first book of fiction.

Fletcher, Ian, ed. *Meredith Now: Some Critical Essays*. New York: Barnes & Noble, 1971, 317 p.
Compilation of admittedly modest scope, intended not to provide a revaluation of Meredith's critical standing but to closely address specific issues. Included are essays by John Lucas on "Meredith's Reputation" and "Meredith as Poet," and studies of individual works by Margaret Tarratt, Ioan Williams, Arnold Kettle, Gillian Beer, and others.

Forster, E. M. "The Plot." In his *Aspects of the Novel*, pp. 134-40. New York: Harcourt, Brace and Co., 1927.*
Notes that in the typical Meredith novel, the plots consists not of a closely woven pattern of events, as is usual, but rather of a seemingly unconnected "series of contrivances" arising out of the personalities of the characters.

Gide, André. Journal entry for 23 November 1928. In his *The Journal of André Gide, Volume III: 1928-1939*, translated by Justin O'Brien, p. 29. New York: Alfred Knopf, 1949.
Criticizes Meredith's tendency to summarize important scenes, particularly those involving significant dialogue.

Granville-Barker, Harley. "Tennyson, Swinburne, Meredith—and the Theatre." In *The Eighteen-Seventies: Essays by Fellows of the Royal Society of Literature*, edited by Harley Granville-Barker, pp. 164-95. New York: The Macmillan Co., 1929.*
Considers Meredith, Tennyson, and Swinburne nineteenth-century writers whose creative impulses were inclined toward the drama. Granville-Barker also discusses the fragments of several discarded dramas that were found among Meredith's posthumous papers.

Handwerk, Gary J. "Linguistic Blindness and Ironic Vision in *The Egoist*." *Nineteenth-Century Fiction* 39, No. 2 (September 1984): 163-85.
　　Discusses *The Egoist* as a striking example of Meredith's ironic view of human relationships.

Hardy, Thomas. "G. M.: A Reminiscence." *The Nineteenth Century and After* CIII, No. dcxii (February 1928): 145-48.
　　Reminiscence written on Meredith's centenary, shortly before Hardy's death. Hardy characterizes Meredith's literary achievement as individualistic and brilliant, and recalls a meeting with him nearly sixty years earlier when Meredith, as a reader for Chapman & Hall publishers, cautioned Hardy against devoting his life to writing.

Hearn, Lafcadio. "The Poetry of George Meredith." In his *Pre-Raphaelite and Other Poets: Lectures by Lafcadio Hearn*, edited by John Erskine, pp. 311-73. London: William Heinemann, 1923.*
　　Fulsome praise of Meredith's poetry, characterizing Meredith as a "test-poet" and maintaining that the reader's own level of culture and capacity to think and feel is tested by her or his ability to enjoy the works of Meredith.

[Henley, W. E.] Review of *The Egoist*, by George Meredith. *The Athenaeum*, No. 2714 (1 November 1879): 555-56.
　　Offers such a mixed reaction to Meredith's novels that Meredith said of this review that Henley "put a laurel on my head and then gave me a buffet in the stomach."

[Howells, William Dean.] Review of *Beauchamp's Career*, by George Meredith. *Harper's New Monthly Magazine* LXXVII, No. cdlxviii (May 1889): 984.
　　Contends that *Beauchamp's Career* demonstrates an ethical attitude that allies Meredith with such great masters of fiction as Tolstoy.

Kelvin, Norman. *A Troubled Eden: Nature and Society in the Works of George Meredith*. Stanford, Calif.: Stanford University Press, 1961, 250 p.
　　Examines the ways that Meredith explored the concepts of nature and society in his major narrative works, concluding that Meredith viewed nature as a beneficent force while his attitude toward society shifted from staunchly conservative views to a belief in liberal reforms of social problems.

Korg, Jacob. "Expressive Styles in *The Ordeal of Richard Feverel*." *Nineteenth-Century Fiction* 27, No. 2 (December 1972): 253-67.
　　Discussion of the functions fulfilled by the variety of narrative styles in *Richard Feverel*.

Le Gallienne, Richard. *George Meredith: Some Characteristics*. London: John Lane, 1905, 200 p.
　　Approbatory overview of Meredith's works based on the premise that Meredith is a much-favored author of genius.

Lewis, C. S. Letter to Arthur Greeves. In his *They Stand Together: The Letters of C. S. Lewis to Arthur Greeves (1914-1963)*, edited by Walter Hooper, pp. 230-31. New York: Macmillan Publishing Co., 1979.*
　　Rejects a suggestion that he reread Meredith's works, writing that "there is so much good stuff to read that it is wasteful to spend time on affectations."

Lindsay, Jack. *George Meredith: His Life and Work*. London: The Bodley Head, 1956, 420 p.
　　Biographical and critical study with an emphasis on the political nature of Meredith's works.

MacCarthy, Desmond. "George Meredith." In his *Portraits*, pp. 170-86. London: Douglas Saunders, 1955.
　　Reminiscence of a meeting with Meredith late in his life, followed by a discussion of Meredith's works. MacCarthy characterizes Meredith as a "poet-novelist"—a writer who is a poet first and novelist second, maintaining that it is Meredith's poetic power of expression that is the strongest element of his prose fiction.

Meynell, Alice. "George Meredith." In her *The Second Person Singular, and Other Essays*, pp. 117-21. London: Oxford University Press, 1922.
　　Credits Meredith with having raised the novel to its high position in current literature.

Miller, J. Hillis. "'Herself Against Herself': The Clarification of Clara Middleton." In *The Representation of Women in Fiction*, edited by Carolyn G. Heilbrun and Margaret R. Higonnet, pp. 98-123. Baltimore: Johns Hopkins University Press, 1981.
　　Close examination of the character of Clara Middleton from *The Egoist*.

Moses, Joseph. *The Novelist as Comedian: George Meredith and the Ironic Sensibility*. New York: Schocken Books, 1983, 265 p.
　　Reassessment of Meredith's contribution to literature, placing him in the ranks of James Joyce, André Gide, and Virginia Woolf as a modernist who established irony as a comic device in the twentieth-century novel.

Noyes, Alfred. "Meredith." In his *Pageant of Letters*, pp. 290-96. 1940. Reprint. Freeport, N.Y.: Books for Libraries Press, 1968.
　　Notes the waning of interest in Meredith, who according to Noyes does not deserve a place among the great Victorian authors because of the faults of his novels, but will be remembered for the poem "Love in the Valley," which Noyes ranks among the greatest love poems ever written.

Sassoon, Siegfried. *Meredith*. New York: Viking Press, 1948, 269 p.
　　Biography with extensive critical comment on Meredith's major works of fiction and poetry.

Shaheen, Mohammed. *George Meredith: A Reappraisal of the Novels*. London: The Macmillan Press, 1981, 150 p.
　　Maintains that a chronological examination of Meredith's novels reveals a clear pattern of development that is overlooked by most critics.

Shaw, Bernard. "Meredith on Comedy." *The Saturday Review (London)* 83, No. 2161 (27 March 1897): 314-16.
　　Praises Meredith's *An Essay on Comedy* but questions the value of reprinting this perceptive study at a time when comedic works are seldom presented and little appreciated.

Shaw, Flora L. "George Meredith." *The New Princeton Review* III, No. 2 (March 1887): 220-29.
　　First essay on Meredith published in the United States, based largely on personal interviews. Shaw suggests that *The Ordeal of Richard Feverel*, *Emilia in England*, *Vittoria*, and *Diana of the Crossways*—Meredith's favorites among his works—are his finest novels.

Simpson, Arthur L. "Meredith's Alien Vision: 'In the Woods'." *Victorian Poetry* 20, No. 2 (Summer 1982): 113-23.
　　Asserts that Meredith's often overlooked poetry of the period 1860-1880 (especially the long narrative poem "In the Woods") are essential to an understanding of Meredith's poetic development.

Stevenson, Lionel. *The Ordeal of George Meredith: A Biography*. New York: Charles Scribner's Sons, 1953, 368 p.
　　Standard biography. Extremely thorough examination of Meredith's life, employing passages from letters to and from Meredith as well as lengthy descriptions of the circumstances surrounding the writing of the major works. Stevenson also provides summaries of the critical reception of Meredith's works.

Stevenson, Robert Louis, "Books Which Have Influenced Me." In his *Essays in the Art of Writing*, pp. 75-90. London: Chatto & Windus, 1919.*
　　Considers *The Egoist* a satire of singularly high quality that shows each reader her or his own faults.

Watt, Stephen. "Neurotic Responses to a Failed Marriage: George Meredith's *Modern Love*." *Mosaic* XVII, No. 1 (Winter 1984): 49-63.

Applies psychoanalyst Karen Horney's study of neuroses and neurotic character formation to the narrator's conflicts in the sonnet cycle *Modern Love*.

Wharton, Edith. "London, 'Qu'Acre' and 'Lamb'." In her *A Backward Glance*, pp. 213-56. New York: D. Appleton Century Co., 1934.*

Reminiscence recounting a tirade by Henry James against the obscure nature of Meredith's writing style.

Woolf, Virginia. "On Rereading Meredith." In her *Granite and Rainbow*, pp. 48-52. New York: Harcourt, Brace, & World, 1958.

Review of J. H. E. Crees's *George Meredith: A Study of his Works and Personality*, reprinted from the *Times Literary Supplement*, 25 July 1918. Woolf hails Crees's book as an aid to establishing Meredith's final place in English literature, and calls Meredith a great writer.

Jules Renard

1864-1910

French diarist, novelist, short story writer, and poet.

Renard is celebrated as the author of the five-volume *Journal inédit* (*The Journal of Jules Renard*), which is considered one of the most prominent works of modern autobiographical writing. The *Journal* illuminates the time in which Renard lived as well as revealing facts about his personal life that are important to the understanding of his other works. With the posthumous publication of his *Journal,* Renard's novel *Poil de Carotte* could be clearly viewed as an autobiographical novel based on its author's childhood, and other works by Renard gained a new interest when read in the light of the mordant and often unhappy personality revealed in the *Journal*. Obsessively concerned with ascertaining the truth in both the trivial and the crucial events of life, Renard wrote in a style marked by vivid, succinct language and ironic humor, qualities which critics find save his works from being overwhelmed by their often tragic themes.

The youngest of three children, Renard was raised in the isolated Burgundy village of Chitry-les-Mines. He was an unwanted child who was treated with mocking cruelty by his mother and ignored by his father. Renard responded to this mistreatment with acts of sadism toward animals and a crafty vengefulness toward others, later recreating this period of his life in his most famous novel, *Poil de Carotte*. After he began his education in Chitry-les-Mines, Renard was sent to boarding school in Nevers, which he considered a relief from his life at home. He did well in school and planned to follow a career in teaching, attending the Lycée Charlemagne in Paris and afterward the École Normale Supérieure. Renard's interest in becoming a teacher was supplanted, however, by growing attraction to writing, which he had enjoyed since early adolescence. But after receiving his baccalaureate in 1883, his attempts to earn a living as a writer were largely unsuccessful. Following a year spent in the military, Renard took a job with a real estate firm whose owner was so impressed with his intelligence and learning that he hired him to tutor his three sons. This association gained Renard access to social gatherings of cultured and influential people, and he soon began an affair with the actress who later served as the model for the title characters of the novella *La maîtresse* and the drama *Le plaisir de rompre*. This woman was also the mistress of a wealthy man, and her influence gained Renard entrance into library salons where he read his poetry; she also used money from her rich lover to finance the publication of Renard's early poetry collection *Les roses, les bulles de sang*. In 1887 Renard married the daughter of a prosperous businessman, a union which eventually enabled him to pursue a literary career without having to depend on his writing for an income. Entries in his *Journal* make it clear, however, that despite the expediency of this marriage, Renard was a loving and devoted husband who held his wife in high regard.

Settling in Paris, Renard wrote essays and short stories for humorous periodicals and influential newspapers, and his name became well known through his frequent contributions to the *Mercure de France,* a distinguished journal he helped found and edit. Welcomed into Parisian literary circles, he became

Mary Evans Picture Library

aquainted with Anatole France, André Gide, Edmond de Goncourt, Edmond Rostand, Alphonse Daudet, and other prominent figures of the time. But Renard's jealousy and quick temper alienated many of his friends, and in his *Journal* he made revealing statements on his relationships to many of his more famous contemporaries. In one instance he remarked: "The success of others irks me, but less than if it were deserved." Renard's own success was established with the publication in 1894 of *Poil de Carotte,* and continued with the publication of his subsequent works of fiction and the performance of his dramas. For the remainder of his life Renard divided his time between Paris and his farm in Chaumot, near Chitry-les-Mines. He died at age forty-six as a result of arteriosclerosis.

During his lifetime Renard's literary reputation rested on both his prose works and his dramas, all of which had as their basis the life and character of their author. While such works as *Poil de Carotte, L'écornifleur* (*The Sponger*), and *La maîtresse* were presumed to be autobiographically inspired, the posthumous publication of Renard's *Journal* proved the extent to which the works were faithfully rendered recollections of actual experience. Indeed, in the *Journal* Renard wrote: "I have put too much of my life into my books. Now I am nothing but a gnawed bone." The most familiar characters in his works are the Lepics, a family modelled on Renard's own and introduced in numerous sketches collected as *Sourires pincés.* In *Poil de*

Carotte the family is characterized as ignorant, hypocritical, and chaotic, with a cruel and peculiar mother at the source of much of the suffering endured by the child protagonist. This work challenged the accepted nineteenth-century image of sensitive parents and happy children, but was saved from the sentimentalism of a tale of child-martyrdom by the candid presentation of the child as, in Renard's word's, "a little animal which throws its claws into anything tender that comes its way." A plotless work written in what Robert Phelps has called "swift, elliptical sketches, ink-washes, really," *Poil de Carotte* displays a clarity and concision of language that brought Renard the admiration of his contemporaries. The pathos and tragedy of the story are relieved by irony and comic strokes that lend the work an artistic balance.

Renard's most important dramas are adaptations of his fictional works or treatments of themes similar to those found in these works. A heavy dependence upon dialogue to move forward the action of his novels, which are primarily concerned with human relationships, made adaptation for the stage highly appropriate; however, Renard's obsession with capturing life on stage caused him to reject many theatrical conventions, and his succinctness did not easily lend itself to the development of three-act plays then in demand. Although they enjoyed varying degrees of critical and popular success, Renard's plays were not as well received as his fiction, with the exception of the dramatic adaptation of *Poil de Carotte*. Among Renard's other works is the bestiary *Histoires naturelles* (*Natural Histories*). In this work, critical observations of human life are presented through vivid descriptions of animals and plants. Concerning this traditional literary form and Renard's use of it, Richard Howard has stated: "Writers have always turned to animal fables when the truth was too much for them, too much for their society to face out of the mouths of men. Jules Renard crystallizes this tendency, keeping his eyes sharp, his mind free, his ears and nostrils wide, and thereby produces a kind of quintessence of all the fabulists."

During the second half of his short life, Renard kept a journal which spans a twenty-three year period from 1887 until his death. Published fifteen years after his death, the *Journal* provides details about Renard's childhood and the bizarre relationship between him and his parents, as well as reflections about nature, the peasants of his village, and the fashionable social and literary circles of Paris. Renard's characterizations of peasants have earned him praise for his ability to capture their uniqueness while still presenting them as individuals rather than as exotic caricatures. The often harsh analyses of human character which also pervade the *Journal* are considered by critics as neither sentimental nor grotesque because Renard's keen insights are tempered with detached sympathy and warmth. Perhaps the most characteristic feature of the *Journal* is Renard's concern with avoiding conventional ideas of truth. Religion, politics, patriotism, and other topics are treated with equal skepticism, displaying, in the words of Louise Bogan, "mockery of the false, the half-observed, and the grandiose."

In a clear and simple style employed to reflect life faithfully, Renard candidly recorded his perceptions of himself and the world around him. Despite their often disillusioning honesty, his works are regarded as neither bitter nor pessimistic because, as Phelps has noted, "he does not hate or fear the created world. On the contrary, he reveres it, the proof being that he accepts it so entirely as it is. Renard is what we ought to mean when we use the word 'realist'."

PRINCIPAL WORKS

Les roses, les bulles de sang   (poetry)   1886
Crime de village   (short stories)   1888
Sourires pincés   (sketches)   1890
L'écornifleur   (novel)   1892
   [*The Sponger*, 1957]
Poil de Carotte   (novel)   1894
   [*Poil de Carotte*, 1967]
Le vigneron dans sa vigne   (sketches)   1894
Histoires naturelles   (prose)   1896
   [*Hunting with the Fox*, 1948; also published as *Natural History*, 1960; and *Natural Histories*, 1966]
La maîtresse   (novella)   1896
Le plaisir de rompre   (drama)   1897
   [*Good bye!*, 1916; also published as *The Pleasure of Parting* in *Poil de Carotte, and Other Plays*, 1977]
Bucoliques   (drama)   1898
Le pain de ménage   (drama)   1899
   [*Homemade Bread*, 1917; also published as *Household Bread* in *Poil de Carotte, and Other Plays*, 1977]
Poil de Carotte   (drama)   1900
   [*Carrots*, 1904; also published as *Poil de Carotte* in *Poil de Carotte, and Other Plays*, 1977]
Monsieur Vernet   (drama)   1903
Les cloportes   (novel)   1919
Journal inédit. 5 vols.   (journal)   1925-1927
   [*The Journal of Jules Renard* (partial translation), 1964]
Oeuvres complètes. 17 vols.   (journal, letters, essays, poetry, dramas, sketches, short stories, and novels) 1925-1927
Lettres inédites   (letters)   1957

RÉMY DE GOURMONT   (essay date 1896)

[*Gourmont was a prominent man of letters in late nineteenth- and early twentieth-century French literature. One of the founders of* Le Mercure de France, *which for a time served as a forum for the Symbolist writers of the period, Gourmont was a prolific novelist, short story writer, dramatist, and poet. His creative works, however, were never as highly regarded or influential as his literary criticism. These works, particularly* Les livre des masques (1896; The Book of Masks, 1921), *are important for Gourmont's sensitive examinations of the Symbolists and for his adherence to a critical style that made him a significant influence on modern English and American poetry and which led T. S. Eliot to call him "the perfect critic." As Glen B. Burne explains: "Symbolism meant for [Gourmont] the absolute freedom of the artist to follow and express the impulses of his individual sensibility." Gourmont's criticism also follows this criterion of subjectivity, reflecting in his case a sensibility that combined a keen artistic intuition with a background of scientific learning. Both were employed throughout the body of his literary and philosophical writings. His most esteemed intellectual achievement was in articulating the concept of the "dissociation of sensibility," a method of thought whereby familiar ideas—such as the idea of liberty or justice—could be abstracted from their conventional meanings and associations, chiefly in order to separate sentiment from truth. This type of intellectual discipline, along with a mystical temperament which he shared with the Symbolists of his generation, make clear Richard Aldington's description of Gourmont as "a mixture of a Romantic artist—poet and novelist—and an eighteenth-century philosophe." In the following excerpt from*]

The Book of Masks, *Gourmont praises Renard's literary style,
particularly his use of imagery.*]

Jules Renard has given himself this name: the hunter of images.
He is a singularly fortunate and privileged hunter, for alone
among his colleagues, he only captures, beasts or little creatures, unpublished prey. He scorns the known, or knows it not;
his collection is only of the rare and even unique heads, but
which he is in no trouble to put under lock, for they belong
to him in such wise that a thief would purloin them in vain.
So penetrating and attested a personality has something disconcerting, irritating and, according to some envious persons,
extravagant. "Do then as we do, take the old accumulated
metaphors from the common treasury; we go swiftly and it is
very convenient." But Jules Renard disbelieves in going swiftly.
Though unusually industrious, he produces little, and especially little at a time, like those patient engravers who carve
steel with geologic slowness. (pp.109-10)

To be begotten quite alone, to owe his mind only to himself,
to write (since it is a question of writing) with the certitude of
achieving the true new wine, of an unexpected, original and
inimitable flavor, that is what must be, to the author of *l'E-
cornifleur* a legitimate motive of joy and a very weighty reason
for being less troubled than others about posthumous reputation. Already, his *Poil-de-Carotte,* that so curious type of the
intelligent, artful, fatalistic child, has entered into the very
form of speech. The "Poil-de-Carotte, you must shut the hens
in each evening" equals the most famous words of the celebrated comedies in burlesque truth, and he is at once Cyrano
and Molière and will not be robbed of this claim.

Originality being undeniably established, other merits of Jules
Renard are distinctness, precision, freshness; his pictures of
life, Parisian or rural, have the appearance of dry-point work,
occasionally a little thin, but well circumscribed, clear and
alive. Certain fragments, more shaded off and ample, are marvels of art, as for instance, *Une Famille d' Arbres.* (pp. 111-12)

> Remy de Gourmont, *"Renard," in his* The Book of
> Masks, *translated by Jack Lewis, 1921. Reprint by
> Books for Libraries Press, 1967; distributed by Arno
> Press, Inc., pp. 109-13.*

MARCEL PROUST   (essay date 1919?)

[*Proust was a French novelist and essayist best known for his
seven-volume novel* A la recherche du temps perdu *(1913-27), an
artistic masterpiece that combines a precise portrait of turn-of-
the-century Parisian society with reflections on the nature of time
and consciousness and psychological portraits of a diverse group
of personalities. In the following excerpt, Proust discusses Renard's examination of psychological depth in his works, as well
as his occasional failure to pursue what Proust terms "hidden
truth."*]

I admire [Jules Renard] because he does not look for means
of escape—contrary to almost all those who, unable to fathom
what they feel, instead of persisting in the attempt to discover
what there is in it, give up, glide on to something else, fail to
get any deeper into that and scrabbling here, scrabbling there,
end by covering a vast amount of ground, and believe that this
will result in pleasing more readers than at some one point
having persevered and dug right down. Renard does fathom a
sensation, and seizes on its hidden truth. The whole truth?—
No. He too, but not, after all, until he has already got down
to a certain depth, has his little means of escape—or rather,
he has two different kinds of base metal with which he com-

pletes the body of his little poem, which without this addition
could not be coined into truth. And these two other things
which qualify the absolute truth of the poem, and on which,
when he feels truth running short, he pounces so that he may
make the poem all the same and preserve the truth which
without this alloy would be infinitesimal, are Drollery and the
Conceit. (The Peahen: "Because of her hump, she dreams only
of sores; and on the ground, she wallows like a humpback."
The Hen: "She never lays golden eggs." The Butterfly: "This
love-letter folded in half is looking for a flower's address.")

Note that the drollery is nearly always a Conceit—that is, a
drawn-out image (like the Peahen quoted above). And that the
conceit is sometimes the truth. For instance, the butterfly
"looking for a flower's address" is not merely a conceit: that
is, when one has run out of truth, going on with the image
which turns into a play on works and supplies an ending which
has only a verbal connection with the truth. But the butterfly
"looking for a flower's address" is true because of the way
the butterfly flits tentatively from flower to flower, and en-
quires, and must have been mistaken since it goes on to another
flower.

> Marcel Proust, *"Jules Renard," in his* Marcel Proust
> on Art and Literature 1896-1919, *translated by Sylvia
> Townsend Warner, Meridian Books, 1958, pp. 382-83.*

RENÉ LALOU   (essay date 1922)

[*Lalou was a prominent French essayist and critic, and the author
of* La littérature française contemporaine *(1922, rev. ed., 1941),
a comprehensive history of modern French literature. As a critic
who had no strong ties to any literary movement, Lalou was noted
for his impartiality and frankness, his historical discrimination
and perspective, and for the balance and clarity of his critical
judgments. His critical works in English translation have been
credited with the introduction and interpretation of the leading
modern French writers for English-speaking readers. Lalou also
helped make the works of numerous English authors accessible
to his own countrymen through his translations of the works of
Shakespeare, Edgar Allan Poe, and George Meredith, and his
critical studies of modern English authors which include the well-
known* Panorama de la littérature anglaise contemporaine *(1927).
In the following excerpt, Lalou provides a brief survey of Renard's
career, assessing the influences of both Romanticism and Naturalism on his works.*]

Naturalism always ends in escape from Naturalism. From the
crude painting of the naked truth the Goncourts escaped by
their impressionistic mobility, Daudet by the freshness of his
Provencal fantasy, Zola by his lyrical imagination, Maupassant
by psychology and the fantastic, Huysmans by an art in which
the "writing" was infinitely more important than the "subject." This demonstration could not be better completed than
by studying the epigrammatic Naturalism of Jules Renard.

The quality whereby Jules Renard first of all holds our attention
is loyalty. This conscientious virtue has a double aspect, positive and negative. It explains the form adopted by him, his
regard for finish. It also explains his refusal to generalize any
experience, his resolve, in portraying peasants, never to go
beyond what he had seen, simply "to reproduce a few traits
of that fierce, primitive figure, only a shade sad and rather
reassuring." His known work is fairly brief. What he published
of it was even less. He did not give the public his first novel,
Les Cloportes, which is already the book of his village, attesting
his hatred of romantic plots and his desire to refine the Goncourts' *écriture artiste* to the point of perfection. (pp. 45-6)

There still remains a trace of the Romantic in Jules Renard, if we are to consider as a mark of the Romantic the incapacity to accept life simply and without adopting towards it a pre-concerted attitude. This appears already in *L'Ecornifleur* where the narrative carries the assumption of haughty detachment to the point of improbability. The clearsightedness with regard to himself turns to sourness. This pretended confession becomes a pessimistic anatomical chart. The hero, a false man of letters, a false friend, a false lover, remains throughout an *écornifleur;* but is it quite natural that he should thus reveal his parasitic quality? Doubly ironical expressions like ''the bourgeois is the person who has not my ideas'' or ''have I held up my end? I do not remember having fallen below my level'' are rather out of keeping in the mouth of so sorry an individual.

The secondary characters appear truer: M. Vernet who is perhaps merely a Lepic grown rich and stupid; Mme. Vernet, a sentimental *bourgeoise;* their niece, Marguerite, who develops so curiously; but however skilful the description of the little Norman watering-place, this book, though short, is not exempt from tedious passages. Above all it is too visibly an exercise, a construction of the literary theme furnished by the Goncourts: ''To let, a second-hand parasite.'' (pp. 46-7)

In *Poil de Carotte,* which so quickly became popular, Jules Renard has drawn the portrait of the miserable, clumsy child oppressed, in varying degrees, by a shrewish mother, a selfish father and a profiteering brother and sister. The picture might easily have become conventional. It remains admirably true because, as a counterpoise, it implies, on the part of Poil de Carotte, a series of sly revenges. The victim of his family, he is not a child-martyr idealized in literary fashion. He is sly, fearful, as cruel towards animals as are his parents towards him. The drama remains latent, the pessimism inexpressed, the comic reestablishing a welcome balance. Not that analysis ever abdicates. With just a touch of caricatural exaggeration, Mme. Lepic is terribly true. . . . The most detailed, the most original character in the book, M. Lepic, is not an enigma for his son alone. In him, as in *Poil de Carotte,* stir strange, confused things they will never succeed in becoming aware of; but beneath the ridiculous phrases pronounced by them this lends their talk a sort of rudimentary poetry which occasionally stirs the emotions.

This poetry peculiar to Jules Renard—poetry inverted like his delicacy—reappears in a work which presents united the diverse aspects of his talent, *Le Vigneron dans sa vigne.* Here he confesses his personal beliefs, his sincere love of the peasantry which does not blind him however to the differences between them and himself. *Les Tablettes d'Eloi* contains the most vigorous arraignment of the hypocrisies of modern life and preaches, by example, the necessity for a pitiless self-examination. . . .

[*Histoires naturelles*] is the author's most perfect achievement, the logical outcome of his literary ideal. Indeed Jules Renard, like the Goncourts' whom he admired, devoted himself wholly to the sevice of his art. Not that he saw in it, after the fashion of the Romantics, a priesthood; but he found a beauty and a grandeur on these virtues of conscientiousness and of discipline which the title of writer exacts of an honest man: ''Yes, man of letters,'' he wrote in *Le Vigneron;* ''I shall be one to the day of my death . . . and if, by chance, I am immortal, I shall devote myself, throughout eternity, to literature. And never do I tire of writing, and I write eternally, and I don't give a damn for the rest, like the vine-grower treading his wine-press.''

The very subject of *Les Histoires naturelles* confines the writer within the exact limits which Jules Renard desired: to observe

Title page illustration by Henri de Toulouse-Lautrec for Histoires Naturelles.

an object and portray it—the art of the painter, if you will, but of the literary painter who must evoke rather than represent. Jules Renard's entire work tends towards this simplification because he aims at this simplicity: to offer, of nature and of mankind, something like instantaneous photographs expressing at once the object and the mind's reaction. The simplest method is that which adds a literal image to the description: ''This evening the setting sun is a dirty yellow. One would say it had eaten an egg.'' Another step and the comparison will widen out: ''The green of these gardens rejoices my eye like a display of cutlery. Let us strive to cast rings on these points.'' Advancing still further, Jules Renard suppresses all the relationships underlying two ideas: ''Ah! I can breathe here! Yes, it is the favourite climate of the scrofulous.'' Finally, supreme refinement, the intellectual idea takes concrete form: ''I write only from life and I wipe my pens on a living poodle.'' The success of this epigrammatic realism is the impossibility for the reader to decide where the thought ends and the image begins, so intimately are they involved in each other.

It is easy to conceive that the animal portraits offered an adequate matter for all his gifts of humour, of fancy, of precision and of patience. For this illusion of the instantaneous is the reward of a long subconscious gestation and of a methodical labour. Picturesqueness and poetry are the two qualities of *Les Histoires naturelles* and Maurice Ravel was not mistaken when he saw in these pieces of highly wrought prose a certain degree of musical suggestion. On an instrument which might have been believed monotonous, Jules Renard plays subtly varied airs. . . . When he attains . . . perfection, Jules Renard's art evokes the memory of Japanese prints in which an animal, a tree or a branch makes the whole picture, filling the spirit with a mysterious joy. The Goncourts' influence aiding the natural bend of his genius, Jules Renard avoided Zola's naturalism to arrive at the realism of Hokusaï. (pp. 47-9)

> René Lalou, "Realism," in his Contemporary French Literature, *translated by William Aspenwall Bradley, Alfred A. Knopf, 1924, pp. 28-51.*

ARTHUR J. KNODEL   (essay date 1951)

[*In the following excerpt from his* Jules Renard as Critic, *Knodel examines the critical temperament that lay behind Renard's works. Although he finds elements suggestive of various critical doctrines, Knodel considers Renard's critical and creative theories so individualized that he should be considered an artist isolated from French literary movements.*]

[In] spite of a deep dislike for professional criticism, Renard could not help being a critic. . . . [It] is time to explain just why that was so and what significance the fact has.

Such an explanation entails a brief consideration of the way Renard set about writing his books. His creative method involved two processes which may be designated respectively as watchful waiting and critical selection. The process of watchful waiting is most picturesquely described in the opening pages of *Bucoliques,* but the principle had already been formulated more than a decade before the publication of that book. . . .

The unwilled, spontaneous, and fragmentary character of his "raw material" was the only guarantee of its artistic authenticity which Renard would accept. After all, there is no reason why a larger work in which "the whole mind must submit to the requirements of a subject that it has imposed on itself" should not be as genuine and unforced as a smaller and more discontinuous piece of writing. Renard, however, keenly critical from the outset, perhaps even overcritical, saw that his gifts did not lie in the field of the architectonic, methodically constructed novel or play. Nor does he seem to have had the slightest conception of the kind of literary composition, in which purely external technical problems are often the mechanism that "induce" a whole work to take shape, was completely foreign to Renard. But if the method of watchful waiting narrowed down Renard's field of creation to extreme limits, it was generally successful in assuring the artistic authenticity of what he did actually produce.

But Renard went even further than observing [an] act of pious presence. Had he completely discarded the validity of criticism, he might have bent over backward to the point of seeking some mechanism whereby the spontaneous flow of artistic *données* might be provoked. But even that sort of provocation was scorned. In short, Renard never dreamed of the devices later used by surrealists to tap the reservoir of the unconscious. Then, going still one step further, Renard would not even accept the unsolicited gifts of his consciousness at their face value.

But here it is necessary to emphasize that the process of watchful waiting is not the simple equivalent of "inspiration." For Renard, inspiration was almost synonymous with genius. "I can achieve nothing through genius, by inspiration," he writes. For him, inspiration meant a state of being so much possessed

and dominated by one's materials that elaboration and arrangement become almost automatic and inevitable. Inspiration, in short, meant Lamartine, Balzac, Hugo. Nothing was more foreign to Renard; for even during the process of watchful waiting the writer must at no time let himself be "possessed" by the materials that present themselves to him. Throughout, the critical spirit must remain wide awake, accepting, modifying, or rejecting even what has come to one unsolicited.

Watchful waiting is, therefore, neither idle revery nor semicomatose supineness. It is, rather, what Renard called "the restless but clairvoyant, i.e., active and healthy, state of mind of the man who doesn't work." Criticism thus becomes an integral part of creation. "you have far more talent than I; but I, much more than you, have the sense of what must be done and what must not be done, " says Renard to an imaginary interlocutor. If I may borrow and amplify a metaphor which Thibaudet used in connection with Renard—under the extreme and relentless pressure of his critical spirit, Renard transformed the exiguous and unpromising raw materials of his art into a substance of remarkable properties, much as the thin and ordinary air that surrounds us is transformed into a liquid of amazing properties when that air is subjected to extreme pressures.

Critical revision and readjustment were so important to Renard that he literally never completed any of his books. The novel of *Poil de Carotte* was modified at each successive appearance; the *Histoires naturelles* were constantly being revised as each new edition appeared; *Ragotte* is the last reworking of sketches about the Philippe household that had appeared in earlier books. Renard was never wholly satisfied. And at the same time, he was painfully aware of the dangers of his creative methods. He wrote at an early date, probably in a fit of depression, "I'll never be anything but a miserable literary note-taker." But the statement foreshadows the more sober judgments of four years later: "Sometimes what I write strikes me as *ferret* literature," and, "When I reread at random a page of what I have written up to now, it strikes me as somewhat desiccated in spite of everything." And in the year of his first great literary success, 1900, he notes: "I have a mania for little things." Renard's severest critics have seldom been more merciless.

It is clear that creation and criticism were inseparable for Renard and that, hence, his criticism of others is of a piece with the rest of his writing. And conversely, his creative method represents a very special application of his wider critical principles. It is true that the limitations of his creative gifts are reflected in his criticism; yet his fundamental credo was general enough to permit transcendence of these limitations. Looking back over . . . his critical opinion, it is possible to indicate where Renard did and did not successfully achieve this transcendence.

One very obvious flaw runs through both his creative writing and his criticism, and that is his inability to resist metaphor, especially the witty metaphor, at any cost. Just as many of the images of the *Histoires naturelles* lapse into mawkishness or even impose a barrier between the reader and the apprehended reality, in the same way many of Renard's capsule judgments fail to convey any real meaning. But the flaw here proceeds not so much from Renard's critical reactions as from faulty expression. And the examples of the failing are not too numerous. Many of his condensed criticisms are brilliant and valid.

More fundamental and serious are those flaws in criticism which are à direct reflection of his limitations as a creator. His obsession with the fragmentary and the discontinuous and his concomitant distrust of all "constructed" works hampered his understanding of the kind of imagination possessed by the true novelist. Even then, however, he had a surprising catholicity of taste in fiction. Furthermore, one feels that this shortcoming in his criticism of the novel reflects a real and unavoidable incapacity. Much more serious is the element of *willed* incomprehension in his judgments of poetry. Nowhere else did he violate his principle of availability more seriously. In his theatrical criticism, however, he avoided both sorts of the shortcoming.

A defect of a different order resulted from Renard's inadequate intellectual underpinnings and from the exclusively literary character of his preoccupations. Renard had no well-defined esthetic system. He likewise had no general historical or philosophical approach—for his rather blandly accepted Tainean positivism remained quite apart from his artistic attitudes. It is true that in Renard's day the varied dogmatisms—whether of a Taine, a Brunetière, or a Maurras—had done much to deform and spoil criticism. Yet the various methods of these dogmatists, no matter how faulty, were so well adapted to the understanding of certain phases of literature or of certain particular works that they all produced occasional insights that surpass almost anything one finds in Renard. Moreover, today it is difficult for us to conceive of a critic in exclusively literary terms. The current controversy over "engaged" literature has thrown into bold relief the dependent position of literature in relation to other human activities. Yet, although he held them in a sort of intellectual vacuum, Renard did have critical principles—even though they did not make up a true esthetic system—and these principles were flexible enough to embrace most significant literature. Renard tried to apply them conscientiously, and, within the historical framework of his epoch, he succeeded very well. Thanks to his credo, he was able to avoid the more glaring blunders of the pure impressionists, even though he was temperamentally closest to them. He supplemented his own impressionist tendencies, not only with this credo, but with a firm faith in the French classical tradition. And this faith compensated somewhat for his lack of a reasoned esthetic theory and for his failure to integrate his artistic activities with wider concepts. The final result was that Renard avoided the twin shoals of extreme dogmatism and complete subjectivism.

He likewise appears as that most valuable thing, a nonacademic and nonpolitical defender of tradition. At a time when most French writers outside the Sorbonne and the Academy were going far afield in time and space for their inspiration, Renard upheld a living tradition which he saw continue all through the nineteenth century. And as a corollary to this position, Renard appears as the embodiment of artistic integrity and artistic sanity at a time when, on the one hand, "slick" writing was the order of the day among financially successful writers while, on the other hand, the literary vanguard went in for cults of inspired insanity and willful obscurity.

Yet sanity, balance, and traditionalism have their price. It should be clear from . . . his critical opinions that Renard did not anticipate any of the significant postwar movements and was even largely out of touch with those prewar currents that were to emerge in full force after 1918. Perhaps the most significant result of the study of Renard's criticism is the added weight it brings to the view of Renard as a terminal figure in French letters. (pp. 210-14)

Sartre is [near] the truth when he says that Renard "is the tail end of that great literary movement that goes from Flaubert to Maupassant, passing through the Goncourt brothers and Zola." Renard's simplicity is a by-product of the last and most desperately artistic phase of the naturalist tradition, in which documentation has been abandoned in favor of the "refelt" sensation. Like most last scions, Renard is isolated and lonely. Sartre, however, is quite wrong when he sees in Renard faint prefigurings of the "antiliterary" movements that flourished after both World War I and World War II. What Sartre takes for intimations of the fundamentally nauseous quality of nature in Renard's *Journal* are merely a few very self-conscious images in willful bad taste, reflecting the prevailing tone of the *fin de siècle* groups that frequented such haunts as the Chat Noir. Renard, on the contrary, found nature in no way fundamentally nauseating. The indispensable *goût de fumier* did not disgust him. True peasant that he was, the odor was welcome to his nostrils. Thus, I would go further than Sartre and say that Renard represents an almost complete terminus in French letters.

If any modern trend is prefigured in Renard, it is to be found in the "peasant" writings of such authors as Renard's disciple Henri Bachelin and so-called regionalists like Chamson, Giono, and Ramuz. But even this affirmation must be made with caution, for the peasants of a Giono and a Ramuz are miles from those of Renard. Renard's peasants, in spite of their extraordinary vitality and convincingness, are almost classic in their generality. Although it is known that Ragotte and Philippe and Barnave were Nivernais peasants who lived close to Renard, one thinks of them primarily as French peasants, not as Nivernais peasants. Thus, in the main, Renard stands as a kind of literary exile. He belonged neither with the fashionable successful writers of his day such as Capus, Bernard, and Rostand, nor with the vanguard groups, whether symbolist, postsymbolist, or otherwise. Renard occupies a place apart as a sort of lonely latter-day La Bruyère. (pp. 215-16)

> *Arthur J. Knodel, in a conclusion to his* Jules Renard
> as Critic, *University of California Publications in*
> *Modern Philology, No. 3, University of California*
> *Press, 1951, pp. 210-16.*

LOUISE BOGAN (essay date 1964)

[*Bogan was a distinguished American poet whose work is noted for its subtlety and restraint, evidencing her debt to the English metaphysical poets. She served for many years as the poetry critic at* The New Yorker *and is the author of* Achievement in American Poetry: 1900-1950, *a respected volume of criticism. In the following excerpt from her preface to* The Journal of Jules Renard, *Bogan examines the stylistic exactness and passion for truth which account for much of the substance and subject matter of the* Journal.]

The keeping of a journal may become a futile and time-wasting occupation for a writer. Temptations toward the inconsequential detail, the vaporous idea and the self-regarding emotion are always present and can become overwhelming. Renard's *Journal,* from its beginning, shows a young writer who is consciously moving away from early mistakes, whose goal is cleanness of style and precision of language. We do not see him as an innovator, but as one who made restitution of certain classically severe effects which the French Romantics in their exuberance, and the Symbolists in their search for the extremes of musicality, had overlooked or ignored. It is possible, in the pages of the *Journal,* to watch Renard training himself, "independent of schools . . . how to reproduce in compressed and resistant [prose] life completely pure and completely simple''—his life and the life of others.

The atmosphere of the period was hardly propitious for this sort of truth-telling, or this sort of style. The great days of Symbolism were over—Mallarmé had died in 1898—and the central figures of the modern revolt in all the arts were still too young to have made their mark. A tired exoticism afflicted academic and ''official'' art, and poetry (no matter how feeble)—not prose—gave entrance to the *salons*. Renard's early apprenticeship writing reflects this atmosphere. But by 1890, when he was twenty-six, he had begun to put his youthful affectations and artificialities behind him for good; the *Journal,* from its first pages, abounds in mockery of the false, the half-observed, and the grandiose.

Renard's passion for factual truth and stylistic exactitude, once formed, remained central to his work throughout his career. This preoccupation never hardened into obsession; one of the great pleasures of reading Renard is the certainty, soon felt by the reader, that nothing is being put down in meanness or malice. The shadow of the small boy who had suffered bitterly because of the obsessions of his parents—his father's mutism, his mother's hypocrisy—always falls across the page. But Renard, in speaking difficult and shocking truths concerning Mme. Lepic (the name given to the mother of *Poil de Carotte* was carried over, in the *Journal,* to denote his own mother), does not hesitate to tell equally shocking truths about her red-headed son. Hard facts concerning family relationships were not usual in end-of-the-century writing. And Renard, in the *Journal,* presents the erotic elements in the son-mother relationship with extraordinary frankness—a frankness he shares with Stendhal (in *Henri Brulard*) before him, and with the Proust who is to come.

Truth about life, in Renard's view, had been distorted by literature. He applied himself to correct that distortion, not by the crass realism of Zola, but by an analysis based on sympathy, warmth and tenderness. The peasants of his countryside were as important to him as his Parisian colleagues; they were his friends and his neighbors; even the dullest of his servants was not separated from his affection and attention. Animals were his familiars; he visited the Paris zoo regularly with enthusiastic interest, and he knew and felt for the wild and tame creatures of field and barnyard. The *Journal* celebrates the mystery, strangeness and beauty of bird and beast, seen without romantic coloring within their natural scene.

The final impression received from the *Journal* is one of delicacy backed up by power—power of character and power of intellect. Again and again those moments of insight appear which can only stem from absolute honesty of perception added to complete largeness of spirit. At these moments we understand why Renard's compatriots have not hesitated, some fifty years after his death, to name him among the masters. (pp. 6-7)

There are, always, the single descriptive phrases, usually centered around an image that is at once poetic and piercingly exact; the insights into people and situations; the sketches of ''his country'' (one wishes he had done the same for Paris); the literary comment. Among the ''threads'' that run through the years we see the life of the writer as a man of letters, both in what it meant to him personally and in its aspect of worldly success—the *gloire* he always longed for but never quite achieved. We have his family life, especially the strange in-

terrelations of his parents and himself; we have the Paris friends, the big names—Sarah Bernhardt, Edmond Rostand, Lucien Guitry; and the country people to whom he always returned. As Léon Guichard wrote: ''The *Journal* is a mine of inexhaustible riches.'' (pp. 7-8)

Louise Bogan, in a preface to The Journal of Jules Renard *by Jules Renard, edited and translated by Louise Bogan and Elizabeth Roget, George Braziller, 1964, pp. 5-8.*

GERMAINE BRÉE (essay date 1964)

[*Brée is a French-born American critic and translator. Her critical works are devoted to modern French literature and include* Marcel Proust and Deliverance from Time *(rev. ed. 1969),* Gide *(1953), and* The French Novel from Gide to Camus *(1964). Concerning her work as a critic, Brée has written: ''I do not consider myself a writer and should probably be classed among the 'academic' critics . . . I have no particular critical method and am, in fact, an eclectic. Each writer seems himself to suggest to me the method of approach I should use as I attempt to elucidate the kind of book he has written. . . . I attempt, with a good deal of difficulty, to communicate what seems to me essential about each, rather than to prove, attack, or praise.'' In the following excerpt Brée likens Renard to other French journal writers, whom she regards as somewhat removed from their contemporaries and the works of their era. She contends that such a detachment in Renard can be observed in the narrowness of his subjects and settings, which are primarily limited to his family and his village.*]

Among French authors, the journal-writers from Stendhal to our time (in which, one can surmise, dozens of journals are being written) have been infinitely diverse: the Goncourt brothers, Amiel, Renard, Gide, Julian Green, to name only the best known. But they all have a family likeness: they seem to feel somewhat removed from their contemporaries and from their own work. A Balzac or a Proust does not keep journals.

Although he was a relatively successful writer and the mayor of his small town, Jules Renard was, in some ways, a man as removed as it is possible to be from the literary and artistic world around him. At a time when Paris was seething with new ideas he stayed on the sidelines—closed to the Impressionists, scornful of Mallarmé, ridiculing Cézanne. But at least he did not pretend. He remained tied to his own world—family and village—and to the countryside he loved. ''Complete fidelity to self'' would be an apt subtitle for his *Journal.*

Renard's journal covers almost a quarter of a century of his short life, from 1887, when he was twenty-three, to his death in 1910 at forty-six. . . .

As in the journal of any writer, we may glean from his pages unorthodox and not always impartial views of literary mores and personalities: Sarah Bernhardt, Duse, Rostand, Guitry, Daudet, Edmond de Goncourt. Yet perhaps the deepest pleasure Renard affords us we owe to a quality that gives the best journals their appeal: the sense we have of watching a mind at work, day by day, on the raw materials of a specific experience, shaping them subtly, inclining them, slowly drawing a true self-portrait out of what one might call an approximate sincerity. Of all diarists Jules Renard is surely the one who comes closest to absolute sincerity—truthful sometimes to the point of silence or banality, at others unflinching in his description of just what he saw and felt, however intimately, as in his unvarnished account of his reactions to the ill-assorted and rather terrifying parents he had already depicted in *Poil de Carotte;* truthful, too, in the delight he felt at rendering in words certain impressions of light, season, and atmosphere, at coining the aphorisms in which he liked to clothe his thought. (p. 38)

[The] quality of his language and its precision meant so much to Renard. Only the discipline of expression, one feels, made it possible for him, endowed as he was with an abnormally retractive though intense sensitivity, to face up to the harsh realities he observed.

Renard's journal elicited one of Sartre's sweeping paradoxes: "Directly or indirectly, Renard is at the origin of contemporary literature." Sartre no doubt meant that Renard, like most French writers today, faced the insoluble paradoxes involved in the act of writing itself. "I know," he wrote lucidly, "the exact point at which literature loses its footing and no longer is in touch with life." To keep literature as closely in touch with life as possible and still keep writing was his ambition, and it was accompanied by a wry irony: "Here's a page of description that is well worth another," he could write, with a somewhat devastating detachment, of a piece of his own work.

Renard was blessed with an acute sense of what we have since smothered under a thick blanket of rhetoric, the sense of the inexplicable, of the "absurd" nature of all things. But he also enjoyed a sense of the wholeness of the world of nature and felt a deep though tacit compassion for human beings, a compassion he often stifled and held in check, not in his actions but in his writing, so scrupulous was he in his use of words, so uneasily sensitive to any distortion, sentimentality, or wordiness. Impressions of the countryside he loved; aphorisms, ironical, witty, deflationary and yet not bitter; starkly realistic sketches of peasants; transcriptions, verbatim one feels, of current conversations in all their inanity; a real underlying compassion—these are the varied facets that give his *Journal* a multidimensional quality. (pp. 38, 43)

> *Germaine Brée, "Between Silence and Rhetoric,"*
> in Saturday Review, *Vol. XLVII, No. 45, November 7, 1964, pp. 38, 43.*

JOHN WEIGHTMAN   (essay date 1964)

[*Weightman, an English journalist, translator, and educator, has written widely on French literature and history, English literature, and sociology. In the following excerpt he provides a sketch of Renard's career, examines his strengths and weaknesses as a writer, and criticizes both the selection and imprecision of the English translation of the* Journal; *for a contrasting opinion of the Journal, see the excerpt by Naomi Bliven (1965). Weightman concludes that Renard was a minor writer, but that his* Journal *and the sketches collected as* Poil de Carotte *are small classics.*]

Jules Renard, who died in 1910 at the age of forty-six, had his moment of fame at the turn of the century with his collection of autobiographical sketches called *Poil de Carotte,* the basis of which is an Oedipal hate-relationship between mother and son. His output of short prose studies and of plays was quite meager, but he left behind him a *Journal,* which has become sufficiently well-known to run into at least three major editions.... There are grounds, then, for considering it as a classic, and it seems natural enough that Renard should be brought to the notice of the English-speaking public.

However, [*The Journal of Jules Renard*] hardly represents a satisfactory way of carrying out the operation. The text, as Louise Bogan explains in her Introduction, is only a selection from the original. When a Journal consists entirely of aphorisms and very short reflections or descriptions, the effect is

achieved by the mass of tiny impressions; to trim the mass is to risk producing an effect of thinness or bowdlerization. I notice that some of the more disagreeable or indecent jottings have been left out and other entries have actually been shortened by the translator. Renard, who was not blessed with a lavish literary nature, does not gain by being truncated....

Then, the translation is often unidiomatic and at times frankly incorrect, which is a serious matter in the case of so painstaking a writer as Renard. For instance, we do not say "to have something in the belly" *(avoir quelque chose dans le ventre)* but "to have something in him," "to have something to say," "to have talent," etc. Nor is the following description of Verlaine an acceptable English sentence: "Above clothes in ruins— a yellow tie, an overcoat that must stick to his flesh in several places—a head out of building stone in process of demolition."

But the main defect is that Louise Bogan's Introduction [see excerpt dated 1964] consists of indiscriminate praise, makes no attempt to put Renard into any critical perspective, and includes a number of doubtful statements: e.g., "Hard facts concerning family relationships were not usual in end-of-the-century writing." A final, meretricious touch is that a quotation from Sartre is used for publicity purposes on the dust-jacket: "Directly or indirectly, Renard is at the origin of contemporary literature." It is nowhere explained that the sentence is drawn from the brilliant, but ferociously hostile, essay on Renard's

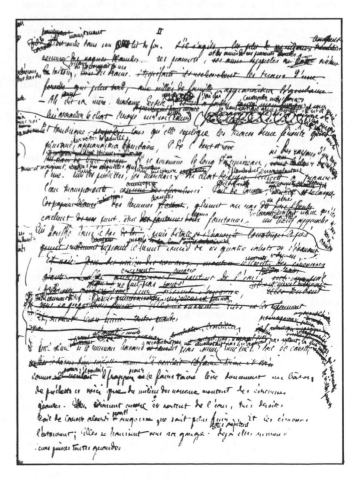

Holograph copy of manuscript by Renard. Courtesy of Libraire A-G Nizet Sari.

Journal in *Situations I* and that Sartre accuses Renard of being responsible for negative tendencies in modern literature.

Louise Bogan writes of Renard's "steadily augmented" reputation in France since his death in 1910. I have noticed no signs of this augmentation; it seems to me, rather, that Renard, from the start, fitted into a little niche and is destined to stay there for all time. He is an excellent subject for disquisitions on literary impotence, realism, preciosity, and the conflict between vanity and talent; he is a good minor writer, whose *Journal* is at best a nostalgic, puzzled meditation on the fact that he is not a great writer. (p. 14)

The first entries in his *Journal,* which he began in 1887 at the age of twenty-three, show that he was aware of being no torrential Zola. After a false start in poetry and failing to find a satisfactory and lasting bread-and-butter job, he made the acquaintance of a girl of seventeen with a house in Paris and a small fortune. He married her when he was twenty-four, through affection, certainly, but perhaps also partly through interest. His basic livelihood was thus ensured and his subsequent earnings from literature, journalism, and the theater were extras that bolstered up his middle-class standard of living. For the rest of his life he divided his time between literary circles in Paris and his house in the country, where he lived as a small gentleman-farmer with two or three servants.

Perhaps Renard's retreat into security through marriage was a mistake which cushioned him off from the strains and stresses that would have broadened his talent. His *Journal* shows that he was never really satisfied, and was always reproaching himself with laziness and a feeling of unfulfillment. On the other hand, had he not taken refuge in middle-class comfort, he might have written nothing at all, especially since he had been permanently affected by an unhappy childhood. It could be argued that he had only one vital subject—his mother whom he hated—and that since she lived until the last year of his own life, he was never able to get her fully into perspective and to exorcise her by devoting a whole book to her, as he had intended.

His best work seems to me to be undoubtedly the one that made him famous, *Poil de Carotte,* a collection of short sketches in which he enshrined the mute hostility between his father and mother, his mother's vicious persecution of himself and an old maid-servant, the complexities of his own sadistic, boyish nature, and all the inarticulate uneasiness of family life, as seen from the angle of the child. The book, although so short, is a minor classic, vibrating with discreet intensity.

Its quality is due to his temperament, no doubt, but Renard was also writing at the end of the "Realist" and "Naturalist" period and, being a literal-minded person, he took Realism seriously as an ideal of truth, which he contrasted with the distortions of the Romantic imagination. We can see from the *Journal* that he never got his attitude on this score quite straight; he keeps talking about the need to put down the "truth," yet he also shows a recurrent taste for preciosity, and the contemporary he seems to have most admired was Edmond Rostand, whose neo-Romantic flamboyance is now generally considered to be hollow. For the most part, however, Renard was determined to set down the truth as he saw it, and the more deflating and unpalatable it was, the greater the likelihood of its genuineness. In debunking family affection and sexual love, he remains short-winded; he refused to give sordidness and disillusion that imaginatively splendid arrangement that was Zola's distinctive form of art. The small scope of *Poil de Carotte* does not matter, since the book expresses a child's view of the world, which is by definition limited and fragmentary. In the later works, the narrowness of vision seems to be a deliberate restricting of a talent for writing to minor subjects, or more precisely, to the minor treatment of a few subjects which, in other hands, could have been dealt with quite differently.

Some critics have spoken very highly of *L'Ecornifleur,* a short novel, based apparently on Renard's own experiences, before his marriage, as a "sponger" on credulous bourgeois culture-snobs. It is a sweetly acid little story about an impoverished pseudo-poet who is kept for a few months by a middle-class couple and half seduces the wife and a niece. Although it is delicately written and contains, in a diffused form, the uneasy melancholy of someone who does not know what to do with life, it cannot be seriously classed among the outstanding novels of the nineteenth century. The figure of the bourgeois, M. Vernet, is just another, mild version of the conventional Philistine lambasted by so many Romantic and post-Romantic writers. The "sponger" is a failed artist with a wry smile; he does not bear comparison with the other great failures in the literature of the century, because he is incapable of deep concern about other people or of any general artistic or social ambition; he has committed spiritual suicide, as it were, before the story begins, and everything that happens to him has a dim, posthumous flavor.

In his other short sketches, of which he published a few collections, Renard falls back on rural subjects, that is, on descriptions of landscapes, birds, and animals, or anecdotes about peasants, and in particular about the old countryman and his wife who worked for the Renard household. He keeps repeating that most writers have romanticized the peasant and the country and that he, who has known both from childhood, will describe things as they really are. Certainly, he produces some vivid little pictures in a plain, meticulous style which makes them obvious anthology pieces for primary schools. But I do not think he altogether avoids the pitfalls of sentimentality, because he frequently personalizes the landscape and, while debunking the poetic myth of some animals in a rather obvious way (e.g., the swan), he gives others the pretty, varnished appearance they might have in an old-fashioned children's story-book. He has sometimes been compared to La Fontaine, but one cannot feel behind his prose that consistent hardness which makes the seventeenth-century fabulist so diamantine a poet.

I may appear to have said comparatively little, so far, about the *Journal* itself. The reason is that it is hardly comprehensible without a knowledge of Renard's background and literary works. The larger part of it consists of jottings about his family that might have gone into a sequel to *Poil de Carotte,* or about the Parisian milieu touched on in *L'Ecornifleur,* or about the countryside described in *Histoires naturelles* or other collections of sketches. It is essentially the sort of notebook a writer keeps to soothe his conscience when he is not building up his impressions and insights into an extended work of art. Some such notebooks, in their very fragmentariness, have a suggestive power that surpasses the organized effect of a finished work. . . . Renard's *Journal* makes him a rather bigger man than one might expect from any of his finished works, except *Poil de Carotte.* It shows him aware of, and puzzled by, the contradictions in his character; wondering, for instance, why he should be so pleased to receive the ribbon of the Legion of Honor or to be elected to the Académie Goncourt when, in other moods, he had the typically nineteenth-century artist's disdain for collective approval. It is also a touching document about the mind of a minor writer who is straining to understand why his inspiration is so weak and fitful, why he cannot get through to himself: "Between my brain and me, there is always a layer I cannot penetrate." (pp. 15-16)

In the last resort, his *Journal* boils down to a collection of desolate aphorisms:—"Imagine life without death. Every day, you would try to kill yourself out of despair"; "Truth on earth is to falsehood what a pin's head is to the earth"; "Let us not forget that the world makes no sense." Some people may think that such maxims put him into the ranks of the great French pessimists; I doubt it, however, because pessimism is only tolerable and interesting when tensed against vitality, and in Renard's case, this only occurs in *Poil de Carotte.* (p. 16)

> *John Weightman, "The Bound Man," in* The New York Review of Books, *Vol. 111, No. 7, November 19, 1964, pp. 14-16.*

NAOMI BLIVEN (essay date 1965)

[*Bliven is an American editor and book reviewer who has contributed to such periodicals as* The New Republic *and* The New Yorker. *In the following excerpt she praises the faithfulness of the English translation of Renard's* Journal, *in contrast to the opinion of John Weightman (1964). Bliven also discusses the various subjects treated in Renard's* Journal, *particularly his portrayal of provincial life*]

During his lifetime . . . the French writer Jules Renard saw his fiction published and his plays produced with considerable popular and critical success. In France, the esteem he won has lasted, but in England and the United States, readers are scarcely aware of his work. . . . Luckily, an enticing and generous sample of Renard's work is now offered us by Louise Bogan and Elizabeth Roget, who have produced an excellent translation of **"The Journal of Jules Renard."** . . . I can't help regretting the abridgment they have made, though I appreciate the practical reasons for it. The uncut work, the product of nearly all Renard's writing life, is huge, and would doubtless have been exhausting to translate and much too expensive to print. Renard began it in 1887 and kept at it until a few weeks before his death. Abridged or no, the book is a collection of treasures. His style, which the translators have reproduced marvellously, is crisp, witty, and shrewd. His matter is as rich as life, and though he takes life seriously, he also finds it funny. For the length of the **"Journal,"** at least, Renard's readers will agree with him that "we are in the world to laugh." . . .

[He] wanted a place to put down his musings about writers and writing—about living writers he knew or had met, and about dead writers he was only reading—and to note what he could use of their work or learn from their lives. He was still reading, musing, using, and learning in the last year of his life. His remarks are more interesting than most criticism, for he writes about writing with the keenness of any man discussing his own business. After a while, the **"Journal"** also begins to keep track of Renard's family life: the relation between his parents, who did not converse for thirty years, and his own marriage, which, in defiance of the decree of psychology that children of unhappy marriages contract unhappy marriages, was very happy. "At a sign from Sarah Bernhardt," he wrote, "I would follow her to the ends of the earth, with my wife." He had two children, and his **"Journal"** records the pleasure of parenthood and its anxieties: "Today the word 'croup' was uttered by a celebrity with a pince-nez, who charges 40 francs a visit." The assorted Renard family illnesses brought several eminent physicians into the **"Journal."** No matter where lit-

erary historians will place Renard himself, his pompous doctors all descend directly from Molière's. Renard notes, after a consultation, "Their adverbs: 'bacteriologically.'" (p. 153)

His **"Journal"** has many sketches of celebrated people in characteristic and/or revealing attitudes. More interesting still, it contains something special—the life of his native Burgundy countryside, where he spent a good part of every year and took a hand in local affairs. . . . His involvement with his particular bit of France was all to please himself and was not affected by his wish to cut a worldly figure. He never wearied in his determination to get his land and its laborers on paper. His many passages about the Burgundy peasants are among the best in the **"Journal."** Renard shows them as a group apart but also as individuals. His peasants are not a bit like his readers, but they are not beasts in a fable—excuses for his readers to think of something else, as is the case with the peasant in Markham's "The Man with the Hoe" and the Millet painting that inspired the poem; these works assume, mistakenly, that a wretched man is no longer a personality. Renard does not. His peasants are themselves, like Philippe, who "had tears in his eyes only once in his life: he was watching the hail come down."

What Renard tried to do was to tell the truth. The problem of "truth" recurs throughout his **"Journal":** "Every moment my pen drops because I tell myself: 'What I am writing here is not true,'" or, more optimistically, "I always stop at the brink of what will not be true," or, despairingly, "Truth exists only in the imagination." Despite such alternations of self-assurance and self-doubt, he convinces us that he is telling the truth, though it is no easier to determine the realiability of a writer than it is to determine the realiability of a candidate on television or of a defendant on the stand. . . . Philosophers have tended to rely on God to guarantee that human perceptions and ideas generally correspond with reality, but Renard, as a Republican of the Third Republic and a passionate anticlerical, was not exactly overflowing with religious certitudes. Nor with any other certitudes, for he did not replace prayers with politics or nationalism. His references to God, to socialism, and to his country are alike in their unaggressive skepticism. . . . (pp. 153-54)

[It] is not—or not primarily—his unique style that makes Renard so convincing. His language does bear some of the marks we associate with truthtelling; it is, for instance, simple and concrete. But a simple, concrete style may be used sentimentally, as Hemingway used it, and an elaborate style, like Proust's, is also compatible with veracity. Renard's **"Journal"** seems truthful because it is full of other people—and animals and plants, too—who are not reflections of Renard. They are not metaphors for his moods. They are not steps in his argument. They are as close as he can come to describing being someone or something not Renard. . . . Renard's truthfulness is the truthfulness of a scrupulous, disinterested witness. You trust him as you trust a Quaker, who doesn't swear on a Holy Book, either. (p. 155)

> *Naomi Bliven, "Renard the Fox," in* The New Yorker, *Vol. XLI, No. 17, June 12, 1965, pp. 153-55.*

RICHARD HOWARD (essay date 1966)

[*Howard is an American poet and critic who won the 1970 Pulitzer Prize for poetry for* Untitled Subjects. *However, he is perhaps best known as the preeminent contemporary translator of French literature into English and the person most responsible for intro-*

ducing many significant contemporary French authors to American readers. In the following excerpt from his introduction to Natural Histories, *Howard discusses Renard's intimate renderings of animals as autobiographical reflections of himself. Noting Renard's fidelity to truth, Howard observes that in order to make certain truths palatable, Renard used the traditional fabulist's convention of disguising human traits with animal corollaries.*]

In the mid-eighteenth century, Buffon published his massive *Histoire Naturelle,* which in its sober, enlightened style describes—quite monolithically, when we compare his observations with those of La Fontaine, so evidently drawn *sur le vif*—nothing less than the life of nature on earth, if not always, like the classical fabulist, the nature of life. The man who said "style is the man" accounted, heroically, humorlessly, for the races of animals and birds, working for the most part from stuffed specimens, skins and sketches. His enterprise was preeminently mental, rationalizing, deductive...; and the pre-Darwinian intuition of evolution is a characteristic note sounded by this master of the Age des Lumières, with his ordering, unifying, generalizing impulse toward enclosing structures.

And such a notion of the life of beasts was to stand—illustrated, most recently, by Picasso—as the representative work in the genre until the very end of the nineteenth century, when—in 1896—it was not so much supplanted as disputed by Jules Renard's *Histoires Naturelles,* eventually illustrated by Toulouse-Lautrec and Bonnard. The singular thing about Renard's work from the very start is the plural in the title: there is nothing structural, nothing unifying, nothing monolithic here, but instead a delight taken, an elation shown in the various, the complex, the manifold. Indeed Renard is not concerned to describe or classify at all, but rather to dramatize, to embody, to make exceptional the very characteristics of life it is usually a matter of systematizing in "natural history"; for Renard, in other words, an animal is real when there is no other like it; for Buffon, say, an animal is real because it is so painstakingly coherent and lifelike—i.e., dead.

Yet Renard differs just as sharply from later nature-writers like Colette and D. H. Lawrence, whose method is to identify themselves with the animal life being observed and described, to become Other by stripping themselves of their own specifically human styles. Instead, Renard, whose voice is one of extreme concision, proceeds to identify the animals with *himself*—the characteristic nineteenth-century touch, I think—so that the ox or the kingfisher speaks as if, for one lucky moment, it *were* Jules Renard, though no less ox or kingfisher for all that. What saves such work from being merely cute or curious is the *intimacy,* the combination of intense observation and ruthless honesty, in Renard's undertaking.

In manuals of French literature, Jules Renard, the author of a number of plays, three novels and an enormous journal, is often referred to as a writer of "autobiographical tendency," and for once the manuals are correct: even these "natural histories," accounts of the animals, the birds, the insects, even a few trees and flowers at a single, incised moment of their being, are the accounts of the toad-*as*-Jules Renard, of the guinea-hen-*as*-Jules Renard, and so on. These creatures are moments in the writer's biography.

Renard spent a lifetime devising a way of telling the truth which would be acceptable, even palatable (as so much of his *Journal* is not): it was not surprising that he should have turned to nature and set it speaking—with all possible charm, condensation and wit—in his own voice. For in the history of literature, writers have always turned to animal fables when

Title page by Pierre Bonnard for Histoires Naturelles.

the truth was too much for them, too much for their society to face out of the mouths of men. Jules Renard crystallizes this tendency, keeping his eyes sharp, his mind free, his ears and nostrils wide, and thereby produces a kind of quintessence of all the fabulists: the world of nature through the sense-assigning lens of one man's senses. (pp. 7-9)

> *Richard Howard, in an introduction to* Natural Histories *by Jules Renard, translated by Richard Howard, Horizon Press, 1966, pp. 7-9.*

MELVIN MADDOCKS   (essay date 1966)

[*In the following excerpt Maddocks discusses Renard's* Natural Histories, *concluding that these are witty portraits of human conceits in animal guise.*]

The bestiary—that verbal zoo celebrating the particularity of animals, birds, and insects—is one of the most charming of literary traditions. Despite its deceptively impromptu look it is also one of the most demanding.

The bestiarian must combine a number of not especially congruous abilities. He should possess the knowledge of a good amateur naturalist. He needs to have the tart bite of a not overly fierce satirist and the dry lyricism of a not overly mellow nature poet. And he cannot do without a certain subversive reverence that links the post-Darwin bestiarian, almost against his will, to the original tradition of those medieval monks painstakingly composing their "naturalists' scrap-books" as psalms to their creator.

Jules Renard, that curious figure of the 1890's—so remote despite his lengthy *Journal*—has all these rarely matched qualities [in *Natural Histories*], plus an approach that is pure Renard. Richard Howard has put his finger on Renard's uniqueness in his introduction . . . [see excerpt dated 1966]: "These 'natural histories,' accounts of the animals, the birds, the insects, even a few trees and flowers at a single, incised moment of their being, are the accounts of the toad-*as*-Jules Renard, of the guinea-hen-*as*-Jules Renard, and so on. These creatures are moments in the writer's biography.". . .

Renard's genius is that he achieves his projections without making his animals one whit less four-footed. When he writes, for instance, that the delivery man's donkey walks with "the quick, sharp little step of a government clerk," the reader must ask himself: Does this witty image tell more about donkeys or about government clerks? Every second of hesitation is a tribute to Renard's mastery.

Like a madcap sorcerer, Renard plants personality not only in animals but in caterpillars, bees ("Everybody says I'm a good worker. By the end of the month I should be promoted to department head."), and even watering cans:

> Flowers: Will it be sunny today?
>
> Sunflower: Yes, if I want it to be.
>
> Watering Can: Excuse me, if I want, it will rain, and if I remove my nozzle, it will rain in torrents.

One should be diffident about belaboring so delightful a dialogue as this, or another in the same series ("In the Garden")

> Onion: My! What an awful smell!
>
> Garlic: I bet it's that carnation again.

But the fact is, here Renard has gone beyond mere fairy-tale personification into a kind of playful metaphysics. He is not writing about flowers or vegetables or watering cans but about the self-conceits and delusions of human will.

One begins by thinking that as a bestiarian Renard must do less than fable writers: he draws a portrait, they draw conclusions. But it turns out otherwise. The fabulist is tied down to earth by obligations to common sense and everyday moralizing. The bestiarian, with no copybook destiny to plod toward, can soar as far as imagination can lead the kite-string of observation. . . .

> Melvin Maddocks, "Who's Who in Renard's Zoo," in The Christian Science Monitor, *December 8, 1966, p. 18.*

FRANKLIN RUSSELL (essay date 1967)

[*Russell is a New Zealand writer specializing in studies of animal behavior, history, and the ocean who has also written several nature books for juveniles. In the following excerpt, he compares the merits of two English translations of* Natural Histories *and characterizes the sense of despair and vulnerability that lies behind Renard's witty animal portraits.*]

When two translations of Jules Renard's *Natural Histories* are published simultaneously, it is a collision between six people—three artists, two translators, and the author. The translators and the artists have such a fine time dashing around the world of natural history that at times poor old Jules Renard gets lost in the scuffle. Richard Howard, in a brilliant translation, . . . masters the subtleties of the work. He changes walnut trees into willows for euphony but he does not bend the facts of natural history. He is supremely confident, rejects "**Merle**" as a poor English title for one of Renard's vignettes, and changes it to "**The Language of Trees.**"

Miss Elizabeth Roget is more literal, but dead unlucky to be appearing with Richard Howard. She stumbles, both in understanding Renard and on natural history. She turns *merle* into *grackle*, a straight dictionary translation which misses a Renard joke. She turns *pinsons* (finches) into canaries, which do not occur wild in Europe, and has goldfinches eating worms (*chenilles*, actually caterpillars), which they don't eat. She also slips a new English word past her editors—*beakfuls*. All the same, her translation is a fairly satisfactory pocket bestiary. . . . The [Howard translation], however, is a careful and fascinating penetration of the work of the artist. . . .

[In this work Renard] darts about, ironic, witty, to catch the creatures, trees, and flowers, as Howard notes, "at a single incised moment of their being" [see excerpt dated 1966]. A wooden weather-vane cockerel is knocked from his perch by a metal upstart and is immolated (in a burning nest) clear into heaven. A real rooster crows himself hoarse trying to blast the metal interloper off his perch. The peacock screams uselessly for a non-existent mate. Travel does not broaden the tiny brains of pigeons. . . .

Frogs "rise like sighs" out of the mud and a caterpillar wanders, lost, in a gardener's footprint. Dragonflies fly by electricity. A partridge sternly tells an ant that the days of La Fontaine are long since past. A scallion and a garlic smell an awful stench. It must be one of those carnations again. Renard makes what is perhaps history's most involuted pun when a blackbird *(turdus merula),* sits in a dying tree and cries out the one French word that "sounds right": *Merle!*

This is all very jolly. What sophisticated fellows these French are! But it doesn't seem to add up to very much. Then the reader remembers Howard's "Quintessence of all the fabulists" and turns the pages back. The clues are there: the bitter ascetic adult, the ill-remembered past. The author feeds seeds to his pet thrush which, for a European thrush, is about as useless as trying to feed a cat on bananas. Like Thoreau, he is a watcher who does not always see. His view of nature is a view of himself. It is a journey through the ignorance of childhood. Each vignette is a progression of childish awareness, from the tumbling, naive imagery of a toddler venturing into the farmyard where its huge animals astound him, to the child, older and stronger, who walks in the fields, is taken to the zoo, begins to see birds and, finally, enters the world of the hunter and sees trees.

This had seemed a fun world (toads with British accents) but now, the child beside us, it is a bitter world. The plow furrows are dark refuges for the hunted. The veterinarian is incompetent. Animals die in agony. Parents are cruel. Little boys are lonely and desperately unhappy. Father is a fool. At the end, only the trees are consolatory. They do not die easily. They take care of their families. They are steadfast.

> Franklin Russell, "A Quintessential Fabulist," in Book Week—World Journal Tribune, *March 12, 1967, p. 12.*

ROBERT PHELPS (essay date 1967)

[*Phelps is an American novelist, editor, and widely published reviewer. As founder of* The Grove Press, *he has contributed greatly to the introduction of European avante-garde literature to American readers. In the following excerpt Phelps examines the difficulties that arise in trying to classify* Poil de Carotte, *and praises Renard's ability to depict, without sentimentality or bitterness, an abused youth.*]

In 1890, [Renard] published nine autobiographical short stories about a tough little provincial boy with carrot-red hair. They were included in a book characteristically called **"Sourires Pincés"** (**"Pinched Smiles"**) and they attracted so much attention that, by 1894, Renard had added another 30 and gathered them all into a book, **"Poil de Carotte."** It became popular at once. In 1900, the year of the Paris Exposition, he adapted **"Poil"** for the stage. Along with Colette's **"Claudine à l'Ecole,"** it became the talk of the town and Poil de Carotte himself has remained a household word in France ever since. . . .

In the lower-middle-class family to which he belongs, Poil is the youngest. There are also an older brother and sister; a taciturn father who works as an inspector of public roads; and a malevolent mother, Madame Lepic, who is as complex a villainess as any in literature. Intelligent, sly, despised by her husband, she in turn loathes her last child and finds every possible way to inflict suffering on him.

There is rarely any "story"; only character in action. Poil wets the bed because there is no chamber pot. Madame Lepic lies, claiming there was one, and shames him. Poil is goaded into going out in the dark to close the henhouse door; he is given oatmeal mixed with his own urine. But he is tough. He can keep his own counsel. Vindictive as Madame Lepic is, he can survive her. Nor is he anything like a saint. He can be vindictive himself. When one of his boarding-school teachers kisses another boy too often, too tenderly, it is Poil who gets him fired. It is also Poil who can kill birds without batting an eyelash, and who can be sycophantic and false when survival requires it.

A progressive psychologist would blame the mother, the father, the economy, the society. But Renard is not progressive. He is simply perennial. He accepts. He is more interested in how human beings *are* than in how they should be. Therefore he assents, without editorials, to all the unpleasant truths: that we really love anything but ourselves; that good acts or evil acts are usually no more than strategies for getting through a particular situation; that human relations are mostly a matter of imposing one's own self on others, or of failing to do this.

At the same time, Renard is not at all bitter or dismayed. He is not that romantic; he is simply unflinching in his watchfulness, never inclined to see the apple without the worm. (When Cocteau read his **"Journal,"** he cried, "At last the frogs have found their king!") The satisfaction Renard gives is cold but healthy. Life is not at all terrible. It is just *not* roseate, nor good, nor evil. It is not even trivial, as it so often seems. It is simply consistent: self-interest, self-survival are its essence.

If you have ever lived in France, you will find some of this view, this inveterate aplomb, this stoic assumptiveness, in the concierge of your hotel, in the lady who collects your ticket in the Métro, in the young apprentice in a blue *salopette* who bicycles to his job very early every morning. It is not the view of the French which has been sold to tourists all these years: haute cuisine, cancan girls, ciel-de-Paris, castles-on-the-Loire. It is closer to the view Frenchmen have of themselves: unde-

luded, self-sufficing, able to live on very little, unsentimentally efficient about gustatory and sexual satisfaction, firm about property values, keen at survival, and taking profound pride in this.

For Frenchmen, then, **"Poil de Carotte"** was and remains a mirror. For the non-French, especially for sheltered Americans, he may seem sad, pathetic, abrasively unpleasant.

Nor will the form in which he is presented—swift, elliptical sketches, ink-washes, really, with no over-all story line or any proper ending—be much of an encouragement. An American reader might almost regard this book as the material out of which, now, the author should make a normal novel. Perhaps this is the reason why (as far as I can ascertain) there has been no American edition until now. . . .

[Renard's] prose is faultless, perfectly embodying Baudelaire's ideal of *la littérature sévère et soignée.* I have never found a sentence of his which I could budge. Every work, every rhythm is absolutely, joyously right. For another, he does not hate or fear the created world. On the contrary, he reveres it, the proof being that he accepts it so entirely as it is. Renard is what we ought to mean when we use the word "realist."

Robert Phelps, "Very, Very French," *in* The New York Times Book Review, *October 1, 1967, p. 4.*

HENRI PEYRE (essay date 1967)

[*Peyre is a French-born critic who has lived and taught in the United States for most of his career. One of the foremost American critics of French literature, he has written extensively on modern French literature in works that blend superb scholarship with a clear style accessible to the non-specialist reader, most notably in* French Novelists of Today *(rev. ed. 1967). Peyre is a staunch defender of traditional forms of literature that examine the meaning of life in modern society and the role of individual destiny in an indifferent universe; he dislikes experimentalism for its own sake, noting that "many experimenters are the martyrs of a lost cause." Peyre particularly disagrees with critical trends that attempt to subsume literary analysis under the doctrines of restrictive theories, such as those of structuralism. Regarding his critical stance, Peyre has written that "there is no single approach that is infallible or systematically to be preferred when dealing with literature. Pluralism seems to me to be a far more fruitful attitude. . . . Any dogmatism, while it may provide the lover of systems with a cheaply acquired consistency and unity of point of view, soon proves detrimental to the most varied of human pursuits—the pursuit of beauty, truth, and 'greatness' in works of art. Fiction . . . sets everything in motion in us: our senses. . . , our sensibility, our intellect, our religious, philosophical, and social views, our esthetic joys, our desire to know ourselves better and to penetrate other lives. Any approach to the novel, therefore, that is honest and intelligently sustained is valid if it draws us nearer to the work of art or its creator." For these reasons, Peyre has utilized several different approaches in his criticism—aesthetic, biographical, philosophical, political, and social. In the following excerpt he discusses French ideals of childhood and the destruction of those ideals through the character of Poil de Carotte.*]

The French have seldom given a favorable view of themselves in their literature. Even more than the nineteenth-century Russians or the Americans of today, they seem to have been fiercely intent on projecting the selfishness of their aristocrats, the corruption of their rich, the greed and philistinism of their bourgeois, the brutality and beastliness of their peasants.

One subject, however, had long remained untouched by French writers: childhood. For centuries children rarely appeared in their literature. When they did they were scarcely moving. . . . But the fiction was usually maintained that children were surrounded with affection; that no mother could ever be a ruthless tormentor against whom sons and daughters might nurture a lifelong grudge. . . .

Among the wreckers of the myth of happy childhood (they included Balzac, Jules Vallès, and Maupassant) Jules Renard remains supreme. His *Poil de Carotte,* a cold, pungent minor classic, masterfully written . . . , appeared in 1894, just as the author was getting to know Toulouse-Lautrec, Forain, and the playwright Courteline, all masters of sarcasm and anti-Romanticism. Soon after this Renard turned his collection of wry and dry vignettes into a play, which was staged with great success. . . .

The period during which Renard wrote is often dubbed Symbolist. But that movement's esoteric allusions, dreams, vagueness, idealization of women, and longing for the lost purity of childhood never touched the down-to-earth peasant Renard. He could only sneer at those who waxed ecstatic over the mysterious soul of the *jeune fille.* He denied profundity to women. Long before the Freudians discovered the interesting ''polymorphous perverseness'' of children, Renard called the child ''a little animal which throws its claws into anything tender that comes its way.''

Poil de Carotte (''Carrot Top''), a freckled, red-haired boy with an older brother and a sly older sister, had probably come into the world unwanted. He is the butt of his family's contempt and persecution. But he is in no way sentimentalized by Renard into a saintly little martyr. Incessant harrassment has forced him to be ugly, vicious, and devious merely in order to survive in a household that never shows him any affection. (p. 32)

The book is a series of sketches, of sparse, bitterly ironic dialogues, of touches added one to another in pointillist fashion. Renard is primarily a great stylist, ''a termite of genius,'' as he has been called. To Paul Morand, to Giraudoux, even to Gide he offered lessons in spare form, relentless clarity, worship of *le mot juste.*

The reader soon realizes that Jules Renard felt compelled to write this little masterpiece in order to settle an old account with life. We know from his *Journal,* one of the most cynical but also one of the most entertaining in French, that *Poil de Carotte* was derived from experience. Like Madame Lepic, Renard's own mother was constantly nagging and complaining, quarrelling with her husband, finding fault with her son and punishing him sadistically. She so exasperated Renard *père* that he spent as much time as he could out shooting and hunting. At home, he never said a word to his wife, but wrote on a slate with chalk the few things he had to communicate to her.

Renard, the objective and sarcastic disciple of the Naturalists, poured out his inner self in his few writings, just like any Romantic. He jotted down in his *Journal:* ''I have put too much of my life into my books. Now I am nothing but a gnawed bone.'' (pp. 32-3)

　　　　　Henri Peyre, ''A Hand-Me-Down Life,'' in Saturday Review, *Vol. L, No. 48, December 2, 1967, pp. 32-3.*

STANLEY HOCHMAN (essay date 1977)

[*Hochman is an American journalist and critic who has written extensively on American film and American history. He has also*

translated a volume of Renard's plays, and the following excerpt is taken from the introduction to that work. In his essay, Hochman credits Renard for countering the Victorian myth of the harmonious family headed by sensitive parents, and for presenting a portrait of the child as one who responds in kind to the treatment he receives. In addition, Hochman examines the artistic changes Renard employed in adapting the prose work for the stage.]

''I have everything that should contribute to my happiness—wife, child, success, and an independent fortune. Nevertheless, my life is like a long desolation. I am very unhappy.''

Jean Giraudoux, to whom these remarks were made, was stupefied. Before him sat Jules Renard (1864-1910), one of the best writers of that happy time known as *la belle époque.* He had set all Paris laughing, albeit with ''pinched smiles,'' and his 1900 play, *Poil de Carotte* (literally, ''carrot bristles''), had been the talk of the Paris Exposition. He numbered among his friends and acquaintances . . . all the other luminaries of the capital's literary and theatrical world. A loving and ''good'' marriage had left him free to follow his genius. How could such a man be unhappy? (p. 9)

The reasons were not hard to find. They had been set down with acerbic wit and icy-eyed clarity in the novel on which the enormously successful play had been based. In it Renard had deftly punctured the Victorian myth of the joys of family life. He offered instead a portrait of adult cruelty and insensitivity, and a vision of the child as a fierce little animal—wanting love, capable of cruelty, and determined to survive on its own terms.

And Poil de Carotte, the book's ''hero,'' was, of course, none other than the red-haired Jules Renard himself, of whom critic André Billy later wrote: ''An unhappy child will almost fatally become a disenchanted man.'' In replying to those who called him an enemy of the family, Renard once noted that on the contrary he felt that happiness could only be obtained within the family. The problem was that while a family might not be difficult to plant it was difficult to cultivate.

Poil de Carotte is unique in the literature of adolescence. With the possible exception of our own marvelous *Huckleberry Finn*—published almost a decade earlier—there is no more complex portrait of the child, no truer tale of his uneven struggle against adult hypocrisy and cant. Like *Huckleberry Finn,* it is in fact too strong for many tastes, and for a long time it was thought that like certain French wines it would not ''travel well.'' (pp. 9-10)

When he came to write the dramatic version for the *Théâtre Libre* of the famous naturalistic director Antoine—who played the role of Monsieur Lepic—Renard was in a somewhat mellower mood. Perhaps inner necessity required that here at least he grant himself a moment of understanding between the son and the father—François Renard, who has been described as ''a rough man, distant, brutal, sarcastic, a peasant, and the son of a peasant.'' Or perhaps it was only dramatic necessity, as he noted in a talk given in 1904, that made him ''bend to the famous classical law of the three unities'' by providing for a novel ''written in gusts'' a central incident on which the action could focus. (Renard had originally planned to write a three-act play, but he quickly realized that given the diffuse nature of the original work ''a *Poil de Carotte* in three acts, or even in two, would have been intolerable on the stage.'')

How was he to create the atmosphere of the book in the theater? He decided to put on stage the courtyard of the Lepic house, the courtyard in which Poil de Carotte found moments of peace near his rabbits and chickens and ''at a respectable distance

Jean-Paul Roussillon as Poil de Carotte in the 1960 Co-médie-Française production that marked the fiftieth anni-versary of the play's first performance. Courtesy of the Cultural Service of the French Embassy.

from his family.'' Sister Ernestine (based on Renard's own sister, Amélie) was eliminated from the action; Brother Félix (in real life Maurice Renard, the author's brother) is only mentioned. The focus is on Poil de Carotte, Monsieur Lepic, and the terrible Madame Lepic—a close portrait of Renard's mother, to whom he nearly always referred in his famous *Journal* as Madame Lepic. As a catalyst to the action he introduced Annette, a newly arrived servant who causes what Poil de Carotte originally fears is a catastrophe, but who actually brings about the conditions for his possible salvation.

When the play was first produced, Antoine's naturalistic predilections originally made him consider putting real earth on the stage and populating the courtyard with live rabbits, but Renard feared that a rabbit wiggling its ears at the wrong moment could destroy the drama. Interestingly enough, in spite of this naturalistic bent, Antoine chose a young actress, Suzanne Desprès, for the title role. This tradition continued for some time, even after the play entered the repertoire of the Comédie-Française in 1912. (pp. 10-11)

How did Renard ultimately feel about his mother, whom he had made famous—infamous?—as Madame Lepic? In 1909, shortly before her death, he recorded in his journal:

> "Forgive me! Forgive me!" maman says to me.

She holds out her arms and draws me to her. She falls at the feet of Marinette [Renard's wife], whom she had not appreciated; she throws herself at the feet of Amélie, of *her* two daughters.

To these "Forgive me! Forgive me!"'s, all I can find as a reply is, "I'll come back tomorrow."

Afterwards, she gives herself violent blows on the head with her fist.

(p. 12)

> *Stanley Hochman, in an introduction to* Poil de Carotte, and Other Plays *by Jules Renard, translated by Stanley Hochman, Frederick Ungar Publishing Co., 1977, pp. 9-13.*

RITA S. MALL   (essay date 1980)

[*In the following excerpt Mall examines the ambiguity of Renard's attitude toward the drama, and its importance to the poetic, true art he sought to create. Observing that on the surface the privacy of the journal and public nature of the drama appear to be extremely disparate forms of expression, Mall notes the importance of the two forms in Renard's concept of art as a reflection of truth.*]

Jules Renard was for a long time considered little more than an excellent minor artist, known chiefly for his impeccable style and his insistence on brevity and clarity in a period dominated by long-winded naturalism and often obscurantist symbolism. The posthumous publication of his *Journal* in 1925 made it clear that he was not so simple. In fact, he was tormented by what he saw as a polarity between truth, conceived of as austere, and art, or poetic richness of expression. Some of the important implications of this polarity were brought to light by Sartre's provocative essay, "L'Homme ligoté," in *Situations I,* which showed Renard to be a problematic figure, a man shackled by his adherence to a positivistic world view that had lost its validity. For Sartre, Renard remains incapable of penetrating to the heart of reality, victim to a myth, caught between passivity and control, structure and chaos, truth and art. Sartre's analysis proved that Renard was to be seen as something more than a cutely self-conscious stylist, but its perspective is almost entirely negative, pointing to the contradictions as evidence of failure. I believe, however, there is an underlying unity to Renard's work that emerges from the ambiguities themselves. These, elucidated primarily in and by the *Journal,* are also revealed strikingly in an important aspect of Renard's work the implications of which have been neglected by critics: the theater.

While it is true that Renard revealed the best and worst of himself and his art in the *Journal,* the most private of forms, it is also true that the solitary journal writer continued to be absorbed in the most public of forms, the theater. The split is an intriguing one; but the poles of the paradox are not so clear-cut, for the *Journal* and theater illuminate each other and what is at base a dualistic esthetic. Renard's plays themselves, admittedly short and simple, are nonetheless richer than they seem and are interesting for what they suggest of Renard's most persistently held ideas about art. Moreover, the ambivalence that permeates the *Journal* is reflected and heightened in his ambivalent feelings *about* the theater, expressed in comments in the *Journal* and elsewhere. An examination of his plays and of his attitudes toward theater may serve to clarify and even to resolve some of the paradoxes implicit in his esthetic.

Renard was quite successful as a playwright, having created at least two minor masterpieces and one character that has become a classic. He attended the theater assiduously, wrote drama criticism regularly, and contributed to the literature of the time with eight plays, one written in collaboration and another never performed. Not an abundant offering, perhaps, but for a writer as unprolific as Renard, it represents a sizeable fraction of his work.... Renard at once loved and despised the theater, and despised himself somewhat for loving it. He sometimes feels a need to excuse his attraction to it, as when he says: "Ce qui n'est pas du théâtre m'ennuie, mais ce qui est du théâtre m'ennuie aussi."... (pp. 270-71)

The contradiction seems simple enough on the surface; after all, perhaps Renard was never really a man of the theater, but only used it for what it could offer him: money, success, glory, and never stopped thinking of it with contempt. But this view ignores the genuine values, other than material, of the theater for him. A more valid position is the one Pierre Nardin adopts, that Renard's style is naturally suited to the theater, that in fact he was a born playwright who had only to transfer his natural prose style to the stage. But Nardin deals here exclusively with questions of style and does not touch on the inescapable fact of Renard's objections to the genre, which cannot be dismissed. Of course Renard was not alone in objecting to the excesses of many contemporary plays; the disgust with the well-made play predominant at the time was fairly widespread. Indeed some critics feel that Renard's most virulent attacks were directed only against the plays of the period, and do not represent "une mise en accusation du théâtre en soi." Personal antagonism, jealousy and the like *were* involved in some of Renard's remarks, but it is impossible not to see in his statements something more than annoyance with particular plays. Renard may not have entertained notions of a modern anti-theater, but he mistrusts theater *as* form even as he makes that form his own.

If he seems to suspect theater even more than other "false" forms of art, it is in large part because it is linked inextricably in his mind to the "cuisine" of Paris, to greed, corruption, ephemeral fashion. This relationship to the city and what it stands for is too often underestimated. There is a significant dualism in Renard that is rarely emphasized, the alternance in his inner space-time clock between his own "deux côtés": the fragmentation and instability of Paris, and the solidity and continuity of the Nivernais countryside. The theater, belonging as it does to the former, remains ineradicably tainted. It is caught up in the fickle atmosphere of fashion—styles change, and the shifting tastes of the public must be reckoned with.

The direct contact with the public may be viewed positively, as it permits the clarity Renard cherishes. But here too we are confronted with a paradox, for this contact also renders impossible or at least difficult nuances of character and relationships that are important to him. The actual coming to life of a play must take place in an inescapable *presence:* the inexorable immediacy of clock time, and the immediate existence of the audience. In a sense, perhaps the theater is too real not to appear false. The presence of the audience suggests a further problem, for Renard seems to have contempt for the theater-going public.... [His] deprecation of the spectator goes beyond mere impatience with an audience's poor taste or its inability to appreciate true beauty. His distaste is borne out in some of his comments on his desire to avoid contact, to be able to write without a public in mind: "N'écris ni pour le peuple, ni pour l'élite: pour moi."... Most revealing is his unsent answer to an inquiry by Jules Huret: "Je donerais vo-lontiers ma pièce à un théâtre vide, sans directeur, sans acteur, sans public, et sans presse."... (pp. 272-73)

These comments point to an understandable disgust with the machinery of the theater, the indifferent public, recalcitrant actors, unjust critics. But they, and indeed the very writing of the *Journal,* suggest an additional and perhaps more significant concern: the very presence of others becomes itself a kind of falsification. Somehow the presence of the spectator, because it implies a certain intent with regard to him, is connected with lying.... [There] is a feeling that the purity of the work is violated. This reinforces the polarity between the work as spectacle and as solitude, between the theater and the *Journal.*

Yet, if Renard objects strenuously to theater's artifices, nonetheless it is precisely theater's need for constraints that may *seem* artificial which represents one of its chief attractions for him. It demands the attitudes and techniques that are already part of his values system, and that he uses everywhere as guarantees of authenticity, because they seem closest to his ideal of transparency and free the work from the pitfalls of excessive stylization. His constricted goal of "subject, verb, attribute"... finds a curious echo in his notion that the theater *demands* that kind of reduction; "Au théâtre, le sujet, le verbe et l'attribut suffisent: plus, c'est trop."... Further, "Le théâtre est très bon parce qu'on ne peut pas s'y servir de phrases dites 'psychologiques' pour préparer des états d'âme." ... Thus what may appear fetters to some become comfortable shackles to Renard. Nardin and others amply demonstrate how the theater answers many of Renard's stylistic needs; what is insufficiently stressed is this "negative" value of theater. Condensation, directness, reduction, all are exigencies Renard extends to all forms, and so theater's limits become a literary value.

Even his disgust with theater becomes a positive catalyst for a work that strives to free itself of artifice. Renard typically finds negative inspiration in the faults of other writers, and this is particularly true in the theater. In fact, one of the latter's most important negative values is that it allows Renard, as drama critic and as playwright, to develop his critical faculties. Criticism becomes for him an integral part of creation; the constant presence in him of a lucid and demanding judge suggests the duality of the passive man who watches and waits, and the active creator. In this sense, his entire work becomes a kind of theater, in which Renard is at once spectator and actor. (pp. 273-74)

The theater ... takes on particular ambiguity for Renard, and seems to reveal especially well his persistent ambivalence about authenticity and falseness in art; it is itself the most natural, because the most immediately present, of forms, and yet the most contrived. Also, each side of the love-hate polarity is seen to be complex: his negative attitude implies something more than mere irritation with specific works, as his abiding interest in the theater suggests more than the simple enjoyment of the production itself. We are left less with clear-cut contradictions than with coalescing polarities that work together dialectically to create the value and meaning of his best plays.

To the reader familiar with Renard's other works, the plays give a sharp sense of *déjà lu:* themes, characters, whole works are adapted for the stage. This sort of repetition is characteristic of Renard, and reflects his limitation of subject and ideas, which limitation, as often as it is a cause for torment, is also for Renard a gauge of authenticity; the writer must write "himself," and not fabricate a world of events and feelings he knows nothing about. A summary of the "action" of his plays would give no hint of their subtleties nor of the interest the nuances take on for the reader aware of Renard's ideas and goals. . . . Renard's plays do not simply resemble his other works, as adaptations must: they epitomize the paradox of artifice and naturalness, since it is in the *plays* that we see most clearly the rejection of drama in the usual sense, a rejection which Renard's protagonists share with their creator.

One result of this rejection is that the denial of a fundamental theatrical quality, dramatic action, carries further an essentially dramatic, if not necessarily theatrical, element: language *as* action. Renard's dualistic view of language, ideally balanced between expressiveness—"art"—and simplicity—"nature" or "truth"—produces a tension which is a precondition of the works and is itself dramatic. It is finally, as Renard himself suggests. . . , language and not physical adventure which uncovers human relationships and constitutes the dramatic confrontation of individuals with themselves and with each other. Let us consider briefly how Renard handles these anti-theatrical elements in his theater by looking at three "typical" plays: *Le Pain de ménage, Poil de Carotte*, and *Monsieur Vernet*.

The first of the three represents the zenith of Renard's playwriting art. Pierre and Marthe, each contentedly married to someone else, sitting alone together in a country parlor, reflect on their marriages and on their philosophies of life. They are attracted to each other, have always been; each recognizes that the other represents the world of beauty, mystery, excitement, a world denied by the banal contentment they have found with their respective mates. (pp. 275-76)

The essential relationship between the two, and indeed their whole attraction for each other, is verbal. It is Pierre's witty and poetic use of language that delights Marthe, wed to a prosaic and uncommunicative man who loves her, she says, without ever speaking to her of love. . . . Just as Alfred would never remember a certain madly flattering hat Marthe wore last season, so Berthe would be totally uncomprehending if Pierre yielded to the temptation to pour out the words of love flowering within him. He must be allowed to use his gifts on Marthe. . . . Pierre is something of a poet, and the poet needs an audience. This play may really be seen as a statement about art, or at least about a certain attitude toward art. The poet's romantic nature needs to find expression in language, which in a play is action too. He wants to translate the dream into reality, but reality overpowers the dream, and he and Marthe will be satisfied simply to talk about the quasi-drama on whose brink they stood for a dangerous moment. Much of the dialogue has an aphoristic, highly stylized quality. The play is not a slice of life in a crudely realistic sense, but, with irony and suggestiveness, it reaches, by means of language akin to what Renard admired in Marivaux's "phrases pures comme du cristal," . . . a psychological truth: that it is sometimes better to keep the dream alive than to succumb to it, to see the possibility of "drama" without clutching at it and thereby reducing it also to triviality. Pierre will go on making pretty speeches, just as Renard will continue to write charming things for the public. Art is special, for it can portray the dream while it finds its source in life, it can reject theater while creating it. We can see how close to Renard's own concerns this play is.

When we move . . . into the world of *Poil de Carotte* and its depiction of village life, the poetic quality of the language becomes somewhat less brilliant. Poil de Carotte is a very untheatrical character in that he is not an instigator of action: as child-man, he is a passive observer of the complex life about him, forced to submit to others' desires and demands. One can

clearly see the future Renard in him. Yet his situation is dramatic, for he will be led, through the necessary intervention of the "outsider," the new maid Annette, to reveal his plight to his father and thereby to change their relationship with each other. When Annette appears and questions him about the Lepic family and her duties, he gives her information that is on the surface very simple and straightforward, but the audience is aware of the import behind his words. The "drama" is again almost entirely verbal: the contrast between his efforts to make his family life sound perfectly normal, without actually lying about it, and the truth, which is the same but somehow different, suggested without really being stated. Mme. Lepic is the theatrical focus, just as she is in the novel; it is her character which establishes the situation, she disrupts plans, eavesdrops, appears suddenly to spoil things. She is the loudest one of all, and her sudden "crise" is a real *coup de théâtre*, as M. Lepic makes haste to point out; it is only a game, he says to Annette, he has been through this before, and when the frightened girl says she will follow Madame, who is in such a state, the taciturn man delivers himself of one remark: "Comédie!" (This suggests the ironic consciousness Renard's characters frequently have of being themselves participants in a drama with its own rules of discourse; this is particularly clear in *Le Plaisir de rompre*, where the analogy between the protagonists' position and literature itself is heightened by the central "action" of the play, the reading aloud of an emotion-charged letter.)

Poil de Carotte's most fervent desire is to leave home for good; it is the man's need, expressed after the child's yearning to go hunting is thwarted. But the real resolution of the play is, again, the decision to stay, in his case to comfort his father. . . . [He] has rejected the dramatic leave-taking in favor of the status quo, but the real drama is the new-found relationship with his father. This kind of dramatic subtlety is echoed in the language, in which there are certain nuances that one would probably not notice in the theater, and that are perhaps more the mark of a man of letters than of a man of the theater.

Critics agree that *Monsieur Vernet* represents a greater deformation of its source than do the other plays; the subject is basically the same as that of the novel on which it is based (*L'Ecornifleur*), the rejection of the false literature of illusion, and of life as it is affected by this perversion of true values. But the play reveals a great change from the earlier Renard, a mellowing of attitude, a closer identification of himself with the gentle bourgeois of the play's title than with the parasitic littérateur of the novel's; more, I think that there is a significant development, or rather, clarification, of Renard's notion of poetry, of the authentic in art. In a brief scene at the end of the first act, Renard himself hints at the idea of the separation between "true" and "false" art: M. Vernet is astonished to learn that Henri has never seen the sea; he has the maid call his wife to inform her of this incredible fact.

> Vernet: Et je offrais ce voyage comme une petite promenade de rien du tout; ce sera un événement!
>
> Mme V.: La mer ne lui fera peut-être aucune impression.
>
> Vernet: Nous serions alors plus poètes que lui?
>
> Mme V.: Je commence à le croire.

The novel was a biting indictment of life falsified by a romantic conception of literature; but only in the play, where M. Vernet takes on more importance than Henri, does Renard suggest that perhaps the tender, ignorant husband is the truer *poet* than the would-be lover. Moreover, the same sentimental M. Vernet is also the demythifier; he admires Henri and all men of letters, but he wishes to save his marriage from the dangers of illusory romance. The necessary exposure of Henri is partially achieved through the device of dialogue within dialogue, as when Vernet tells his wife of his growing friendship with the young man and of what they say to each other. Vernet, in his naive admiration for the writer, says to praise him: "On croirait qu'il prépare tout ce qu'il dit avant de venir," which piques Henri, who answers huffily: "Je vous assure que c'est naturel." The irony of this being said in a play, where indeed the words *have* been prepared in advance, is a characteristic Renardian touch. In a sense, language, which is Henri's stock in trade, turns on him, because he allows it to speak for factitious emotions, whereas M. Vernet unwittingly achieves the kind of unselfconscious conjunction of feeling and expression that is the province of simple souls, in Renard's view, and which he values above all.

On the whole, Renard succeeded in his theater in eliminating those elements to which he so vigorously objected in others' plays: false eloquence, the mechanical predictability of the well-made play, the extension of a minor idea into a four or five-act play, and so on. His theater seems to recapitulate the whole drama, if I may use that term, of his esthetic, the continual movement from complexity to simplicity, from action to language, from "empty" language to the kind of "full" silence of which Pierre Schneider speaks. . . . (pp. 276-80)

[The] poles we have been discussing seem essential paradoxes in a dialectic rather than sharp contradictions. Even the seeming separation between the *Journal* writer and the playwright is a kind of resolution of certain problems. The theater is not problematical from one point of view, because it is so clearly artificial, and, from another point of view, neither is a journal which does not really pretend to be "art." But there is a fundamental overlapping; the plays, within the artificial form, will strive for truth; the *Journal*, the freest of genres, will be written with style.

The fact that the theater in itself cannot be the ideal form for Renard as wholly as Nardin suggests in no way negates the extreme value of the dramatic for his art and vision. It is a vital stepping-stone for Renard in his continued search for what he chose to call the "poetic," the "true" art he so longed to create. But I have tried to show that neither can his suspicion of theater be dismissed. In this sense, too, his criticism of the theater is a microcosm of his fundamental mistrust of art itself, as his persistence in writing for it is a sign of his continued need to *be* an artist, to find, even in an apparently inauthentic form, a vehicle for poetic truth. The way to that truth is through artifice, as the way to silence is through language. It is, finally, the movement *towards* that counts—not eliminating the polarities but using time to create meaning.

Thus the theater, in its virtues and flaws, seems to epitomize much of the struggle within Renard. His attitude remains ambiguous, but the problems are generally worked out in his favor *in* the plays. As we have seen, it is precisely the ambiguity which gives his theater its impact, and, in a larger sense, which underlies the connection between it and his work as a whole. (pp. 280-81)

> *Rita S. Mall, "False Theater and Dramatic Truth: Jules Renard and the Theater," in* Nineteenth-Century French Studies, *Vol. VIII, Nos. 3 & 4, Spring & Summer, 1980, pp. 270-82.*

ADDITIONAL BIBLIOGRAPHY

Coulter, Helen Brewster. *The Prose Works of Jules Renard.* Washington, D.C.: Privately printed, 1935, 195 p.
  First full-length biographical and critical study in English. Coulter, in a work written as a doctoral dissertation, examines Renard's style and influences.

Malcolm, Janet. Review of *Poil de Carotte*, by Jules Renard, translated by Ralph Manheim. *The New Yorker* XLII, No. 43 (16 December 1967): 169-72.
  Discussion of *Poil de Carotte* as a painful illustration of cruelty against children.

Maugham, W. Somerset. "Three Journalists." In his *Points of View*, pp. 189-255. London: Heinemann, 1958.*
  Biographical essay that relates Renard's works to incidents in his life. In an essay that examines the journals of Edmond and Jules de Goncourt, Paul Leautaud, and Renard, Maugham characterizes Renard as a writer with remarkable talent who lacked creativity.

Thatcher, Nicole. "Plot, Time and Space in Jules Renard's Novels." *Nottingham French Studies* 21, No. 1 (May 1982): 26-36.
  Examines the ambiguity of form in Renard's prose works that are loosely classified as novels. Thatcher contends that in *Les Cloportes, L'écornifleur, Poil de Carotte*, and *Nos freres farouches*, Renard blends elements of symbolism with realism and humor in a manner that transforms or destroys traditional conceptions of the novel.

Wescott, Glenway. "Le Carrot-Top: Renard's Rich, Dense Record of Everyday Life Remains Unsurpassed." *Book Week* (27 December 1964): 1, 6.
  High praise for Renard's *Journal* and the English translation by Louise Bogan and Elizabeth Roget. Wescott discusses Renard's background, his philosophy of literature, and the style and themes of his *Journal* entries.

O(le) E(dvart) Rölvaag

1876-1931

(Also Rølvaag and Roelvaag; also wrote under pseudonym of Paal Mörck) Norwegian-born American novelist, short story writer, essayist, lexicographer, and poet.

Rölvaag is recognized as one of the most important writers to chronicle pioneer life in America. His *Giants in the Earth* trilogy, a panoramic portrayal of the conquest of the South Dakota prairie by Norwegian immigrants, is praised for its epic power and unsparing realism. Contrary to previous chroniclers such as Hamlin Garland and Willa Cather, who depicted the rustic glamour of frontier life, Rölvaag exposed the physical, psychological, and social dangers inherent in adapting to life on the western prairies. For that reason he is credited with producing a tragic saga of enduring artistic and historical importance.

Rölvaag was born in northern Norway in a fishing hamlet on Dönna Island, where he spent the first twenty years of his life. Although considered a slow learner by his teachers and family, Rölvaag was a voracious reader. He greatly enjoyed the classics of Norwegian literature by Björnstjerne Björnson and Jonas Lie, as well as those of world literature by such writers as Charles Dickens, William Shakespeare, and Alexandre Dumas. But one novel, James Fenimore Cooper's *The Last of the Mohicans,* he particularly cherished as a work that inspired his interest in America. Rölvaag remained happily attached to the rugged life on Dönna Island throughout his childhood and it was not until 1893, following a near-fatal encounter with a squall while at sea learning the cod fishing trade, that he considered leaving his homeland. Convinced that remaining on Dönna meant resigning himself to the perilous, desolate life of a North Atlantic fisherman, Rölvaag wrote to his uncle, an immigrant farmer in Elk Point, South Dakota, expressing his desire to join him in America. After three years of waiting, he finally received a letter from his uncle that contained a ticket for the crossing. Once settled in Elk Point, Rölvaag gained work as a farmhand, but after laboring for two years he again sensed that he would soon be bound to another unpromising trade. Encouraged by a pastor in the community, he enrolled at nearby Augustana Academy to further his education. Following his graduation—at which time he delivered an address on the topic of cultural development within a multicultural nation that foreshadowed a recurrent concern of his fiction—Rölvaag obtained admission to St. Olaf, a prominent Norwegian-Lutheran college located in Northfield, Minnesota. There, he quickly distinguished himself as a skilled debater, entertaining storyteller, and enthusiastic member of the campus Norwegian Club. During this time, Rölvaag first displayed a desire to become a writer. After publishing several stories and poems in the college newspaper, he began a novel, *Nils og Astri,* during his junior year. Discouraged by the lack of interest of Norwegian publishers in this love story set within a rural immigrant community, Rölvaag gave up writing for a time, and the novel remained unpublished.

Rölvaag's display of academic and leadership abilities in the classroom assured him of a teaching position at St. Olaf upon his graduation and, after spending a year of post-graduate study at the University of Oslo, Rölvaag returned in 1906 to assume

The Bettmann Archive, Inc.

it. Successfully lecturing in a variety of subjects during his first years, Rölvaag earned particular renown from administrators, faculty, and especially students for his lectures on the life and work of Henrik Ibsen and on the history of Norwegian immigration to America. Rölvaag's deep-felt, lifelong regard for his people and their shared heritage led to his publication in 1909 of a Norwegian-English dictionary. His first fictional work, *Amerika-breve* (which can be translated as "Letters from America"), appeared three years later. The autobiographical, epistolary novel was well received by reviewers in Norwegian-American literary journals but, despite its realistic account of a Norwegian's first encounters with a new society, remained untranslated until its appearance as *The Third Life of Per Smevik* in 1971. Rölvaag's second novel was *Paa glemte veie,* an artistically unsuccessful work that is nonetheless deemed noteworthy for its anticipation of themes and characters developed more effectively in *Giants in the Earth.* In the six years between *Paa glemte veie* and his next novel, *To tullinger* (*Pure Gold*), Rölvaag greatly expanded his extraliterary activities, assuming the chair of the Department of Norwegian at St. Olaf, fulfilling lecture and organizational responsibilities for various cultural groups, and participating in meetings concerning the future of the Norwegian Lutheran Church in America. In addition, Rölvaag produced a handbook of Norwegian orthography and pronunciation and began, in conjunction with a department colleague, a three-volume series of Norwegian readers for elementary, secondary, and college students. When *Pure Gold* appeared, Rölvaag again captured the attention of America's Scandinavian literary community, which perceived obvious talent in his forceful portrayal of an immigrant couple overcome with pathological greed. The novel was soon followed by *Laengselens Baat* (*The Boat of Longing*), considered a near-masterpiece for its fusion of myth and reality in the evocation of the profound emotional loss experienced by a Norwegian youth who leaves his family and homeland to further his musical interests in America. *The Boat of Longing* is also praised as a demonstration of Rölvaag's ability to invoke the mystique of his native country through extended lyrical description.

The pivotal point in Rölvaag's literary life came in 1923, when he discovered that the Norwegian novelist Johan Bojer planned to write an epic novel of Norwegian immigrant life to coincide with the centenary of Norse immigration two years later. Convinced he was better qualified than Bojer to complete such a work, Rölvaag requested a sabbatical from teaching and left with his family for their lake cottage in northern Minnesota, where he could work in seclusion. Although he had managed to meet and discuss with Bojer their respective approaches to the subject and discovered that his distinguished rival possessed an entirely Norwegian perspective, therefore posing little serious competition to the bicultural Rölvaag, he nevertheless intended to complete his novel before Bojer in order to avoid possible charges of plagiarism. By early 1924 the first part of *I de dage* (which can be translated as "In Those Days") appeared in his native country, instantly winning widespread critical and popular acclaim. Retitled *Giants in the Earth* for an American audience, the novel was the first of Rölvaag's to be translated into English, and in 1927 he received national recognition as a unique American realist. Although in his last years he spent an enormous amount of time as archivist and secretary to the Norwegian-American Historical Association, an organization he helped found, Rölvaag completed his immigrant saga with the publication of his last two novels, *Peder Seier* (*Peder Victorious*) and *Den signede dag* (*Their Fathers' God*). Suffering from heart disease throughout this period, Rölvaag died in Northfield in 1931.

In his most critically discussed novel, *Giants in the Earth*, Rölvaag constructed a tale of mythic proportions, replete with Norse legends and biblical allusions, tracing a Norwegian couple's trek across the American prairie of the 1870s to a homestead in South Dakota. The husband, Per Hansa, represents an incarnation of the fabled Nordic *askeladd*—a courageous, indomitable young man who performs great feats and eventually receives the hand of a princess and her father's kingdom as his reward. The progressive conquest of the midwestern prairie, in Per's case, becomes both his enormous feat and earned reward. Beret, the antithesis of her husband, is a gravely religious woman plagued with the knowledge that the pioneers, Per included, have forsaken the faith and traditions of their ancestors and recklessly presumed to control their own destinies, thus incurring the wrath of God. Although her dread of the New World and all it portends borders on the psychotic, many critics contend that she assumes the role of spokesperson for Rölvaag, himself a devoted Lutheran who believed that individuals could freely seek salvation through adherence to a God-directed existence. This doctrine of free will, derived from Danish theologian Sören Kierkegaard's *Enten-Eller* (*Either/Or*) and Ibsen's drama *Brand*, underscores all of Rölvaag's novels. For example, Per, the archetypal pioneer, maintains his vision of a bright, self-directed future in an outspoken disregard of

God's help and so ultimately meets with tragic death in a raging snowstorm. With ironic symbolism, Rölvaag presents the frozen, contented Per propped against a barn and facing westward, incorrigibly optimistic but, Rölvaag submits, misguided. For this reason, modern critics agree that the trilogy's true hero is Beret, for she is the character whose spiritual integrity is maintained and whose mental outlook, albeit perpetually dark since her arrival in America, is eventually renewed through the aid of a minister following the death of Per. Her presence in *Peder Victorious* and *Their Fathers' God*, during which the succeeding generation of immigrants are faced with the many problems of acculturation, further testifies to her role as an inspired advocate of pious conduct and ethnic preservation in a complex, predominantly secular society.

A powerful representation of the consequences inherent in adapting to a new land and a new way of life, *Giants in the Earth*, critics agree, overshadows its sequel novels in dramatic power and grandeur. As Rölvaag focussed more on the sociopolitical aspects of cultural assimilation and the corresponding evils of materialism and corruption in *Peder Victorious* and *Their Fathers' God*, the personified natural force of a once bloodthirsty but now subdued prairie steadily faded. The central obstacle with which the new generation of Norwegian-Americans is faced becomes American society itself—the difficulty of choosing between the traditions of their own ethnic community and that of the larger, integrated community outside. Despite a pessimistic conclusion to the trilogy, critics stress Rölvaag's success, through all three novels, of demonstrating the fallacy of manifest destiny while affirming the need for retaining established ethnic customs and values within a mixed society so that a high moral and ideological foundation might be preserved within individual cultures.

Although Rölvaag is primarily remembered for a single novel, that novel is one of the most realistic and compelling documents of the settling of the western prairies. Heavily influenced by the work of Ibsen, Björnson, and Knut Hamsun, Rölvaag nonetheless dealt with predominantly American subjects and settings which he founded upon themes of universal interest. Historians and critics agree that *Giants in the Earth*, for its comprehensive, artistic portrayal of the pioneering era and its examination of the psychology of an immigrant people, is a significant work of American literature.

(See also *Dictionary of Literary Biography*, Vol. 9: *American Novelists, 1910-1945*.)

PRINCIPAL WORKS

Amerika-breve fra P.A. Smevik til hans far og bror i Norge
    [as Paal Mörck] (novel) 1912
    [*The Third Life of Per Smevik*, 1971]
Paa glemte veie [as Paal Mörck] (novel) 1914
To tullinger: Et billede fra ida (novel) 1920
    [*Pure Gold*, 1930]
Længselens baat (novel) 1921
    [*The Boat of Longing*, 1933]
Omkring fædrearven (essays) 1922
*I de dage—: Fortælling om Norske nykommere i Amerika
    (novel) 1924
*I de dage—: Riket grundlaegges (novel) 1925
Peder Seier (novel) 1928
    [*Peder Victorious: A Tale of the Pioneers Twenty Years Later*, 1929]

Den signede dag   (novel)   1931
   [*Their Fathers' God*, 1931]
Fortællinger og skildringer   (short stories)   1932
   [*When the Wind Is in the South, and Other Stories* (partial
   translation), 1984]
The Romance of a Life   (unfinished autobiography)   1936;
   published in journal *American Prefaces*

*These works were translated and published as *Giants in the Earth:
A Saga of the Prairie* in 1927.

JULIUS E. OLSON   (essay date 1926)

[*In the following excerpt Olson stresses that the favorable reception of* I de dage *by Norwegian critics attests to Rölvaag's mastery
of his native language. Olson also praises Rölvaag's ability to
create a remarkable saga of Norwegian pioneer life.*]

The purpose of this paper is to call the attention of our members
not of Norwegian blood, to a Norwegian-American novelist—
a member of our Society—who has recently won recognition
and distinction at the hands of keen critics in the mother country. He is proclaimed by them as a competent portrayer of
Norwegian pioneer life in the Dakotas. Possibly these critics
may not be in a position to speak of the competency of an
author to handle the life and scenes of a region with which
they have but slight acquaintance. But they surely are competent to pass judgment on his ability to write a novel in modern
Norwegian. This they have done. And it is a fact for con-
gratulation among us. For it surely is a matter of significance
in the history of our intellectual and artistic development, if
we have really produced an adequate portrayer in fiction of
any phase or phases of our life as pioneers in this country.
(p. 45)

In a paper on "Literature and the Press" among our Norwegian
people, published some time ago, I said that the chief literary
form among the descendants of the pioneers will doubtless be
the novel, though verse at first prevailed. Several important
novels, among them Martha Ostenso's, have appeared since
to strengthen that opinion. The paper said of Professor Rölvaag:
"He knows Norway, Norwegian history and literature, has
experienced the heart-aches and hardships of pioneer life on
the prairies, is familiar as both student and professor with
college life and the life of the church, is in close contact with
the press, and has solid qualifications for taking a leading part
in the new literary movement. He knows what the Norwegian
pioneer has done for America, and the price he has paid in
doing it. He understands the possibilities of this land of opportunity for the grandchildren of the pioneer—and the tragedies that have made these opportunities possible. This author
has already won distinct favor, *and much is expected of him.*"
This was my opinion in 1921.

It is a pleasure to note that that expectation has been realized
through the publication of his double novel of Norwegian pioneer life in the Dakotas. The first part is entitled *"I de dage"*
(**"In Those Days"**). . . . The second part bears the sub-title of
"Riket grundlægges," (**"Founding the Kingdom"**). . . . (pp.
46-7)

The significant thing in Rölvaag's case is that his book has
passed muster with Norwegian critics and Norwegian readers
in the homeland. (p. 47)

[Rölvaag's] novels, and particularly the one under consideration, bear the distinct impress of the great Norwegian novelists,
with such limitations as his experience and Norwegian-American environment impose. In his last novels, the careful reader
will find, I think, reflections, if not echoes, of the early idyllic
romanticism of Björnson's peasant novels, both linguistic and
artistic, as well as suggestions of the rugged style and a faint,
though hazardous, suggestion of the blunt speech of his realistic
pen. I know well enough that it is usually most difficult to
trace the influences that an author has been under. It is something to be felt, and cannot always be satisfactorily demonstrated. It surely is significant that Norwegian critics and the
press have treated Rölvaag as generously as if he were a successful novelist of their own. And that means that he is not a
crude beginner, but a mature artist. That is highly compli-
mentary. And it means, furthermore, that his Norwegian language seemingly presents no offensive dissonances to their
sensitive ears. That is remarkable. (p. 48)

Rölvaag's novel has made a satisfying beginning of a saga of
Norwegian pioneers who have transformed the prairies of the
Dakotas into a region fit for human habitation—which it hardly
seemed to be when the pioneers first came. For to some of
them the spirit of the prairies seemed a monster, ready to devour
them. Rölvaag has seen and felt the tragic aspects of this epoch.
He personally experienced it. He knows that immigration is
always tragic. It is the price the pioneer pays for the future
welfare of his children. And hence his story is impressively
tragic—more tragic than if it had dealt with the early Norwegian
settlements in Illinois or Wisconsin, although these settlements,
too, had their tragedies,—cholera and the Civil War.

But despite the tragic phases of this pioneer life, Rölvaag's
books are not gloomy. The pages fairly scintillate with humor
and kindliness.

The story of the first volume is a very simple one, and tells
the trials and tribulations, and the simple joys and victories of
a small group of settlers—eight adults, and four children. (p. 49)

Now a large part of this first volume is devoted to a detailed
and realistic account of the everyday life of this small group
of Nordland stock,—their solidarity in days of loneliness and
uncertainty, their courage, their kindness, and helpfulness in
the struggle for very existence.

It would be a difficult task to give an epitome of these daily
struggles, and it would be unnecessary, for most of us know
from experience or from oft-told tales something of the pioneer
life on the prairies. These details are presumably meant primarily for readers in the homeland, that they may get an impressive and convincing picture of pioneer life in the great
Northwest,—a picture that surely will teach respect for the
brave souls of Norwegian blood who helped to conquer the
prairies, and forced them into the service of humanity.

That great conquest and achievement have cost human lives—
human tragedies. Both the conquest and the tragic cost of it
are typified in the lives of Per Hansa and his wife Béret. Despite
their great love for each other, they cannot agree on the important question of attempting so rash a thing as the conquest
of the prairies.

Per Hansa is a fine pioneer. He plows and sows, reaps and
builds with the ardor of a hopeful lover. He worships the latent
mysteries of the prairie soil. His toil is an adventure. It has all
the elements of romance. He rejoices in it and waxes strong.
But it takes a heart of oak and sinews of steel to cope with the

moods and forces of nature that surround him. But he glories in the combat.

There are those, however, who cannot stand the strain. Where there is play and clash of mighty forces, the weak will cower and falter. And for those who lack nerves of steel, and who have come from the land of fjords and mountains, the change to the prairies—the land of great open spaces and of brooding silence—tragedy is ever a menace.

Per Hansa's wife is the one in the story who is not so constituted and equipped as to stand the strain of such things. She typifies the hopeless struggle of the weak with the spirit of the prairie, not only in its angry moods, but also in its immensity, its boundlessness, and its great silences. These things appall her, unnerve her, crush her courage, and derange her mind. Here lies Per Hansa's greatest problem. Her fate hovers before the reader throughout the whole story; and even at the end of the second book we are left in uncertainty, though we learn, at the very end, of the tragic fate of her husband, Per Hansa, whom, in her insane insistence, she drives out into a fierce snow storm to fetch a minister, not a doctor, for a dying neighbor, Per Hansa's friend, Hans Olsa.

The first volume, too, seemed likely to end in dire tragedy, with the wife as a central figure. The Christmas of the first year on the prairies was drawing near. The wife was an expectant mother, and all manner of gloomy thoughts had filled her mind for months. She had forebodings of certain death. She had even planned to be buried in the old Norwegian chest, as there was no lumber for a coffin.

But the author ingeniously turns the advent of the child on Christmas morning into a source of rejoicing and merry-making for the whole little band of pioneers, who had all been wrought up to a high pitch of anxiety over the distraught mother. Two warm-hearted and capable women of the little colony, however, snatch both mother and child from the clutches of death.

Rölvaag's handling of this episode in the life of Per Hansa and wife Béret, reveals his ability as a novelist, his powers of characterization, his dramatic instinct, his sense of artistic values, his storytelling qualifications; and they also reveal the author's all-embracing human sympathy. This scene will make an appeal to any heart that has not been seared and blighted by human wickedness and degradation.

The second volume has much more to tell of the wife Béret, and the reader hopes that the Christmas child will prove an anodyne to her troubled soul; but it is not until an itinerant minister appears on the scene that any betterment comes. Informed by the anxious husband as to her state of mind, the kindly minister is able to raise her out of her gloom. But then follows a fanatical mood of religious brooding, which, as already indicated, causes the death of the husband. (pp. 50-2)

In regard to the further content of this second volume, reference should be made two episodes: the blizzard of the early 80's, which is most vividly, realistically, and effectively described. It is an account of an expedition made by three of the men to a settlement a few miles farther east for fuel.

Equally effective is an account of the coming of the grasshoppers, which caused such devastation during several years in the 70's.

In both of these episodes, Rölvaag, in my opinion, shows real power. In effectively handling these tremendous catastrophes he proves himself a master. (pp. 52-3)

Julius E. Olson, "Rolvaag's Novels of Norwegian Pioneer Life in the Dakotas," in Scandinavian Studies and Notes, *Vol. IX, No. 3, August, 1926, pp. 45-55.*

LINCOLN COLCORD (essay date 1927)

[*An American novelist, poet, journalist, and nautical authority, Colcord aided Rölvaag in securing an American publisher to print an English version of the two-part novel* I de dage. *With the sizable role Colcord played in the ensuing translation of the novel, a close friendship developed between the two writers. In the following excerpt from his introduction to* Giants in the Earth, *Colcord notes Rölvaag's fusion of a European literary style with predominantly American subject matter.*]

It is a unique experience, all things considered, to have this novel by O. E. Rölvaag, so palpably European in its art and atmosphere, so distinctly American in everything it deals with. Translations from European authors have always been received with serious consideration in the United States; in Rölvaag we have a European author of our own—one who writes in America, about America, whose only aim is to tell of the contributions of his people to American life; and who yet must be translated for us out of a foreign tongue. I think I am right in stating that this is the first instance of the kind in the history of American letters.

There are certain points of technique and construction which show at a glance that the author of this book is not a native American. Rölvaag is primarily interested in psychology, in the unfolding of character; the native American writer is primarily interested in plot and incident. Rölvaag is preoccupied with the human cost of empire building, rather than with its glamour and romance. His chief character, Beret, is a failure in terms of pioneer life; he aims to reveal a deeper side of the problem, by showing the distress of one who could not take root in new soil. Beret's homesickness is the dominant *motif* of the tale. Even Per Hansa, the natural-born pioneer, must give his life before the spirit of the prairie is appeased. This treatment reflects something of the gloomy fatalism of the Norse mind; but it also runs close to the grim reality of pioneering, a place the bravest art would want to occupy. *Giants in the Earth* never turns aside from the march of its sustained and inevitable tragedy. The story is told almost baldly at times, but with an unerring choice of simple human detail. When we lay it down we have gained a new insight into the founding of America. (pp. xi-xii)

Does Rölvaag's work belong legitimately to Norwegian or to American literature? The problem has unusual and interesting features. The volume before us deals with American life, and with one of the most characteristically American episodes in our history. It opens on the western plains; its material is altogether American. Yet it was written in Norwegian, and gained its first recognition in Norway. Whatever we may decide, it has already become a part of Norwegian literature. Rölvaag's art seems mainly European; Rölvaag himself, as I have said, is typically American. His life and future are bound up in the New World; yet he will continue to write in a foreign language. Had he been born in America, would his art have been the same? It seems unlikely. On the other hand, had he remained in Norway—had he accepted the boat that fine, clear day in Nordland—how would his art have fared?

But such speculation, after all, is merely idle; these things do not matter. It has not yet been determined, even, what America is, or whether she herself is strictly American. And any sincere art is international. Given the artist, our chief interest lies in trying to fathom the sources of his art, and to recognize its sustaining impulses. What were the forces which have now projected into American letters a realist of the first quality writing in a foreign language a new tale of the founding of America? It is obvious that these forces must have been highly complex and that they will continue to be so throughout his working life; but beyond that we cannot safely go. The rest is a matter of opinion. When I have asked Rölvaag the simple question, Did Norway or America teach you to write? he has invariably thrown up his hands. (pp. xx-xxi)

> Lincoln Colcord, in an introduction to Giants in the Earth: A Saga of the Prairie by O. E. Rölvaag, translated by Lincoln Colcord and O. E. Rölvaag, Harper & Row, Publishers, 1927, pp. xi-xxii.

HENRY COMMAGER   (essay date 1927)

[Commager is a renowned scholar of American history and the author of several important studies, including the standard text The Growth of the American Republic (1931). In the following excerpt he declares Rölvaag the first novelist to adequately document the immense psychological toll that frontier life had upon the pioneers.]

The same year which has witnessed America's coming of age in the profound historical and critical studies [The Golden Day: A Study in American Experience and Culture; Main Currents of American Thought: An Interpretation of American Literature from the Beginnings to 1920; and The Rise of American Civilization, written by Lewis Mumford, Vernon L. Parrington, and Charles A. Beard respectively], has witnessed, with singular appropriateness, the appearance of the most penetrating and mature depictment of the westward movement in our literature. It is O. E. Rölvaag's Giants in the Earth, and it inspires this encomium because it chronicles as no other volume has that combination of physical and spiritual experience which is the very warp and woof of American history. It indicates in the realm of fiction the same attitude which has already expressed itself in criticism and in history—that the story of America is not the story of physical and material development and expansion to the utter exclusion of the spiritual or psychological. The westward movement ceases to be the victim of romance and becomes a great physical and spiritual adventure. It ceases to be the proud epic of man's conquest of earth and becomes the tragedy of earth's humbling of man. (p. 319)

The appearance of the volumes of Mumford, Parrington, and Beard seems to mark the beginning of a new era in American historiography—the "sober second thought" of the historian, the intellectual maturity of the critic. The emphasis in these studies is on the cultural and psychological aspects of American history rather than on the economic, though Beard's volumes may be something of an exception to this generalization. . . . From the economic point of view that phenomenon was an epic. From the psychological point of view it was a tragedy. (p. 324)

It is fitting and not altogether without significance that this new attitude in history should find concomitant literary expression. It is for this reason that we can hail Giants in the Earth as a milestone in American literature. It is not only that it portrays more completely than any other novel the synthesis of what Schlesinger has happily termed the "two grand themes of American history"—the westward movement and immi-

gration. It is rather because for the first time, adequately, in the literature of the middle border the primary concern is not economic but psychological; the main interest of the story centers not on the taking up of the land but on the effect of that experience upon the characters. For the first time a novelist has measured the westward movement with a psychological yardstick and found it wanting.

We do not necessarily imply that Rölvaag is either the first or the only author to call attention to the psychological aspects of the westward movement. Neither [Hamlin] Garland nor [Edward W.] Howe, nor their numerous successors, have ignored this element. Willa Cather, indeed, in her remarkable O Pioneers! and My Ántonia, has dwelt intelligently and sympathetically upon the problem. To a certain extent she may be said to anticipate Rölvaag and some passages from her volumes might serve as a text for Giants in the Earth. . . . But, withal, Miss Cather records the triumph of Alexandra and of Ántonia over their grim environment, and her novels are panels rather than murals.

Hamlin Garland has furnished us, perhaps, with the explanation of the partial failure of the novelists of the middle border to penetrate the spiritual life of the frontier. He was looking back upon his first courageous efforts, when he said, "I intend to tell the whole truth." He confesses, however: "But I didn't! Even my youthful zeal faltered in the midst of a revelation of the lives led by the women on the farms of the middle border. Before the tragic futility of their suffering, my pen refused to shed its ink. Over the hidden chamber of their maternal agonies I drew the veil." Rölvaag is not less tender, but he is inexorable. The even tenor of his tale nowhere falters, nor does he choose to draw the veil of silence over the "tragic futility" of the women's suffering, over the "hidden chamber of their maternal agonies." Indeed, it might be said that his volume is primarily concerned with the "futility of their suffering," and the emphasis is not so much on suffering as on futility. Of all tragedies the most poignant is that of futility. Not to have suffered, but to have suffered in vain, ah, there's the rub!

And futility is the moral of Giants in the Earth. Of what avail is the conquest of the soil by man; the scars which man inflicts upon the virgin earth are as nothing to the scars which nature inflicts upon the souls of men. . . . And what indeed shall it profit a man that he gain the world if he lose his soul? The life is more than the living, and living could be achieved only at the cost of life itself.

This literary diagnosis of the spiritual realities of pioneer life harmonizes strikingly with the critical interpretation of Mumford; the narrative and the interpretation are complementary, and passages from the latter merely point the moral and adorn the tale.

> The vast gap between the hope of the Romantic Movement and the reality of the pioneer period is one of the most sardonic jests of history. On one side, the bucolic innocence of the Eighteenth Century, its belief in a fresh start, and its attempt to achieve a new culture. And over against it, the epic march of the covered wagon, leaving behind it deserted villages, bleak cities, depleted soils, and the sick and exhausted souls that engraved their epitaphs in Mr. Masters' Spoon River Anthology. . . .
>
> The truth is that the life of the pioneer was bare and insufficient: he did not really face Nature,

he merely evaded society. Divorced from its social context, his experience became meaningless.

Per Hansa, buoyant, vital, lovable, with his hand to the plow and his eyes fixed hopefully upon a golden future, and Beret, his wife, disconsolate and sick at heart, physically, mentally, spiritually stricken by her cruel experience—these are Rölvaag's symbols for the hope of the romantic movement and the reality of the pioneer West. The symbolism is sustained and terribly convincing. It is Beret, at first a tragic figure in the background, who gradually dominates the scene, just as spiritual tragedy overwhelms physical phenomena. Her experience, subtly and profoundly described by Rölvaag, loses its immediate application and becomes as universal as that of Goethe's Margarete. It is this ability to universalize, to translate the experience of his characters into spiritual values of catholic and transcendent significance, that stamps *Giants in the Earth* as a work of genius.

The "two grand themes of American history" Rölvaag has infused with a profound psychological significance. Immigration ceases to become the story of Americanization and becomes the problem of spiritual adaptation and acclimatization. The westward movement is metamorphized from an economic enterprise or a romantic epic and becomes a struggle against the "power of evil in high places." The characters of this drama are not hailing "fair freedom's star," but "facing the great desolation." Not for them the triumphant song of "Pioneers! O pioneers," but the silence "on the border of utter darkness."

It is upon the eternal verities that Rölvaag concentrates—on birth and death and suffering—and he recites them with a profound understanding and a tender sympathy and yet without sentimentality. The birth of Peter Victorious is the focal fact of the book; he is for Per Hansa a symbol of victory, for Beret a symbol of sin. Over him this strangely and beautifully mated pair wage their silent battle for life and salvation, and when Per Hansa wins and the child is restored to grace and the mother to sanity, it is by a religion which is the harbinger of death. It is the "eternal yea" and the "eternal nay" echoed here on the western plains, but Per Hansa's magnificent "yea" was to be choked out by the icy hand of death. "The Great Plain drinks the blood of Christian men"—it is the handwriting on the wall of Amerian history. (pp. 324-28)

> *Henry Commager, "The Literature of the Pioneer West," in* Minnesota History, *Vol. VIII, No. 4, December, 1927, pp. 319-28.*

CLIFTON P. FADIMAN (essay date 1929)

[*Fadiman became one of the most prominent American literary critics during the 1930s with his insightful and often caustic book reviews for* The Nation *and* The New Yorker *magazines. He also reached a sizable audience through his work as a radio talk-show host from 1938 to 1948. In the following excerpt Fadiman finds* Peder Victorious, *which is concerned with the socialization process of the Norwegian immigrant, to be inevitably less captivating than the epic, panoramic vision of* Giants in the Earth. *For a similar assessment of the novel* Their Fathers' God, *see the excerpt from the* New York Times Book Review *(1931).*]

Always interesting and intelligent, often beautiful, the tale of the second generation of Norwegian pioneers [*Peder Victorious*] nevertheless fails to grip the reader as intensely as Mr. Rolvaag's splendid first novel. But that the sequel to *Giants in the*

Earth should be less moving than its predecessor was inevitable. The difficulty lies in the step down from a theme of universal import, surrounded with honest glamour, to one which is not so much a theme as a problem. In *Giants in the Earth* the conflict was a primordial one—man's lone struggle with the land. In *Peder Victorious,* which deals with the boyhood of the son of Per and Beret Hansa, the land has already ceased to function as a labor for giants, with the result that the giants are gone and with them some of the epic quality that filled the first book. Instead of the struggle of Titans we must now be content with a very sensitive portrayal of the rather familiar conflict between the strong, dominating mother and the rebellious, burgeoning son. With the Norwegian pioneers the acceptance of America was a profound necessity, but subconsciously apprehended; with the sons and daughters of the pioneers it has already become a "problem." The talk is now of "assimilation"; mother and son take up their inevitable positions as antagonists in the language controversy. The rounded Hamsun note, holding within it an accent to the eternal, has begun to die out, and the first faint whine of the problem novelist is heard. Consequently, there is a general lowering of emotional tone.

But, as has been said, this was inevitable; for it is dependent on the historical evolution of the Norwegian immigrants within their given territory. (p. xx)

Peder Victorious, then, was bound to be a less inspiring and satisfactory work than *Giants in the Earth*; but it is not without its extraordinary excellences. Particularly admirable, for example, is the slow care with which the unique Lutheran morality of the Norwegians is illuminated and the perception which enables Rolvaag to distinguish it from the more customary forms of American Puritanism. Rolvaag's ethnic sensitivity is as delicate as a seismograph; his older generation, at least, is completely and recognizably Norwegian. Never could it be confused with a nineteenth century native American farming population. His people form that most admirable thing, a genuine free-born peasantry. They are a peasantry, not a yokelry, possessing an indigenous culture and a definite code of morality which may be narrow and is often terrifying, but which is never the expression of brutality or ignorance. It is this community, so lovingly portrayed with not even a hint of sentimentality, and not the central characters, which one remembers long after the last page of this fine book has been closed. (p. xxii)

> *Clifton P. Fadiman, "Diminished Giants," in* Forum, *Vol. LXXXI, No. 3, March, 1929, pp. xx, xxii.*

PERCY H. BOYNTON (essay date 1929)

[*An American literary scholar and critic whose writings are often cited for their wit and engaging interest, Boynton, in the following excerpt, analyzes* Giants in the Earth *and* Peder Victorious *as chronicles of the immigrant community's successive adaptation to the physical and social environment of the American prairie.*]

Although Ole Edvaard Rölvaag deserves all the acclaims with which his two novels, *Giants in the Earth* and *Peder Victorious,* have been received in the United States, he is fortunate in the moment of his entrance on the stage. He has been prepared for, like any prima donna, by the accumulating literature on the frontier; and his first harbinger was F. J. Turner as far back as 1893. The Turnerian thesis of the frontier, none too rapid in spreading among the historians themselves, was slower still in penetrating the thickish skins of the literarians. We had enjoyed long training in overlooking implications and ignoring geniuses. But time and fate provided a Rusk and a Dondore and a Hazard; and now those of us who have caught up belatedly with Hearn and Bierce and Melville, and who are not exhausted in our attempts to cope with the riotously competing forms of literary modernism, and who are unseduced by the biographical theory of the Freudulent complex or the permanently catastrophic influence experienced at the age of eighteen months— we are somewhat breathlessly plodding along after the covered wagon in the pursuit of frontier trails. (p. 535)

In [Rölvaag's] two consecutive chronicles the non-English-speaking immigrant is confronted by the double ordeal of a new land and a new speech. To the first he can physically move; the second, except in rarest instances, he can never fully master. And in a new country anything less than the mastery which makes the new language a medium for emotional expression prevents the newcomer from ever becoming completely at home.

It is the tragedy inherent in this situation that brings us at last to the conquest of the pioneer—to Turner's brief statement that "the wilderness masters the colonist." As I see it in the broad, the immigrant pioneer is confronted by peril on peril: first, of physical defeat, even while he and his kind are achieving the conquest of the soil; then as the community closes around him, of social submergence without social inner adjustment; finally, if he have the capacity for making a new soul which is forever beyond the power of the average man, of ostracism that follows independence, or the surrender of soul to Mammon that follows material success in the midst of small-town philistinism. Let us see how far such catastrophes befall the chief figures in the Rölvaag chronicle, for it is one long chronicle and still far from completed.

Taken in their present temporary entirety *Giants in the Earth* and *Peder Victorious*, the natural division falls not between the covers of the two books but in the middle of the first volume with the end of the part called "The Land Taking." This is a tale of primitive life which can be discussed and interpreted wholly in folk terms. Per Hans, the hero, is the incarnation of primitive strength; he builds largest, plows longest, sows earliest, laughs loudest, rages most wildly, forgives most quickly. He is pre-eminent in all performance. His wife Beret is primitive fear. Her man has overwhelmed her in love and marriage; the prairie overwhelms her as she faces its vast reach and ominous silence. And the prairie is primitive nature—the earth spirit as known to a people who have always had to contend with it—no south-European Ceres. So Per Hans confronts the plains. (pp. 537-38)

For a while Per Hans, apparent conqueror of the plain, lacks the strength to contend with the foreboding of Beret, but the great joy that comes with the birth of Peder restores him. Immediate and overwhelming disaster is averted. Over Per Hans and his generation the monster of the plains "might have had her way; but the newcomer made a breach in her plans— a vital breach!" Beret's primitive fear drives Per Hans out into the blizzard from which he never returns, but not until her own sanity has been restored to her by the last folk element to enter the tale—the primitive faith embodied in the parson, the spokesman of God in whose voice could be heard the reassurance of the intercessor. She is reserved for a less elemental chapter in the story and for a less elemental, though no less complete, defeat.

Analysis expresses itself in abstract terms; art with the concrete. Critical analysis is bound, therefore, for the moment, to do

Holograph copy of manuscript of I de dage, *the Norwegian version of* Giants in the Earth. *Courtesy of The Norwegian-American Historical Association, St. Olaf College.*

violence to the object of its attention. Yet the harsh process must be followed a step farther in a word of summary: *Giants in the Earth* is presented in two parts. I have tried to suggest the essentials of the former in terms of primitive ethnology: man and nature in their eternal conflict; man as part of the tide of human life inexorably certain of success; man, the individual, ephemeral as the grass of the field. In "The Land Taking" the conflict is presented, the sentence is pronounced alike on human strength and human weakness, but Peder Victorious is born. Man falls in the taking of the land, but his seed survives for the founding of the kingdom.

This second part, then, becomes a more complicated and sophisticated tale of community life, not to be interpreted in the same terms; no longer primarily a conflict with nature or with primitive fears, sooner or later destined to success, but concerned with the later problem of how man, who in some degree can subdue the prairie, can subdue his own nature to a life of social adjustments. (p. 539-40)

The concluding picture in *Giants in the Earth* is of Per Hans in the horrid dissolution of death, struck down by the Monster of the Plain. The concluding scene in *Peder Victorious* is of mother Beret bending to the inevitable. Her son, promise of the future, is advancing to meet it, speaking the alien tongue of a new land, marrying an alien immigrant from another land, their son to be American-born of American-born. For her it is either estrangement or surrender, and the final choice is inevitable. Once more and in another way the pioneer is overcome, even while in the act of creating a new America.

And now the problem arises as to what will happen to Peder and his like. What does happen to them? They are the new Americans. They have sloughed off the traditions of Europe. Their own are in the making. . . . (p. 540)

So, for such a truth-teller as Rölvaag, I see only two dominant possibilities for the remaining chronicles of Peder. The soil is subdued, relatively speaking; a truce has been declared between himself and his mother, the immigrant pioneer and her offspring. The perils he faces are in the people who surround him with their lust for small prosperity and petty comfort. The monster of the plains no longer intimidates them. For them the seventh and successive deadly sins are to disburb the market, or the sanctity of the Republican party, to tamper with a vague and unknown something they call the Constitution, to depart from a literal interpretation of the early chapters of the book of Genesis, or to grant others the slightest indulgence in any of these bolshevisms or blasphemies. If Peder stands for the magnanimities and sees life in the large, he will be ground between the upper and nether millstones that smug conservatism substitutes for the mills of the gods. He may save his soul, but he will be an outcast. Or, on the other hand, if he adjusts himself to his barns and silos and barbed wire and windmill and tractors, avoids conflict, and makes his little fortune, he will make it at the price of his soul. So the tragedy of Peder, in the evolving American community, is quite as devastating as the tragedy of Per Hans or the tragedy of Beret. It is the inevitable consequence of draughting the energies of a whole community during a whole generation for the promotion of material ends. There must be some valid relationship between this and the fact that the country has been spun on a pivot so that the erstwhile wild and woolly West has become the unimpregnable fortress of tidy conservatism.

But this is literary criticism and not a stump speech. If I may not resist the temptation to speak in prophetic terms I may at least resort to a familiar document of 1782—*Crevecoeur's Letters from an American Farmer*—to the third essay therein, which he entitled, "What is an American?" It is a rhapsody; it is a prophecy unfulfilled; "He is an American, who, leaving behind him all his ancient prejudices and manners, receives new ones from the new mode of life he has embraced, the new government he obeys, and the new rank he holds. . . . Here individuals of all nations are melted in a new race of men, whose labours and posterity will one day cause great changes in the world."

Maybe so. The fusing process is still on. A crucible is hardly a bed of roses. And that is why the honest teller of frontier tales—who undertakes neither to idealize nor to prophesy, but simply to portray—is bound to be a somber recorder of the successive conquests of the pioneer. (pp. 541-42)

> *Percy H. Boynton, "O. E. Rölvaag and the Conquest of the Pioneer," in* English Journal, *Vol. XVIII, No. 7, September, 1929, pp. 535-42.*

THE NEW YORK TIMES BOOK REVIEW (essay date 1931)

[*In the following excerpt the critic regards* Their Fathers' God *as a less "glamorous" study of Norwegian immigrant life than* Giants in the Earth, *but one that nevertheless emerges as a powerful conclusion to Rölvaag's trilogy. See the excerpt by Clifton P. Fadiman (1929) for a similarly qualified appraisal of the intervening novel,* Peder Victorious.]

In the fact that ["**Their Fathers' God**"] is a translated novel one should not lose sight of the added fact that it is also a novel of America. . . . "**Their Fathers' God**" is a continuation of the theme (and the family) in "**Giants in the Earth.**" This sweeping narrative of our Northwest had to do with the struggles of Norwegian pioneers; the next book concerned itself with the children of that generation, and the present narrative revolves around the third generation.

In "**Their Fathers' God,**" with no little of that high resolve which animated his pioneer settlers, Mr. Rölvaag attacks the forbidding problem of a mixed marriage. Those who read "**Peder Victorious**" will recall that Peder marries Susie Doheny, for the Scandinavians were not the only people to settle on the prairie and suffer and subdue. . . .

If it is perhaps unfortunate that Mr. Rölvaag is of the nationality of one of his two central figures, it must be conceded he does not unduly side with Peder or coddle him. This portrait of the stalwart Norwegian lad striving to understand a point of view utterly alien to him, surrounded by people of his own race who, because they hold so tenaciously to tradition, are blind to his excellencies and strive only to hinder him, casts a white light on certain aspects of the evolution through which America is passing and must pass. If Rölvaag is right—and he convinces one that he is—then that fond dream of the "melting pot" went into the discard during the very years when it was most vigorously being talked.

In narrowing himself down to an ethnical and ethical study Rölvaag has of necessity forbidden his story any such sweep of canvas as made "**Giants in the Earth**" an oustanding novel. "**Their Fathers' God**" is not, however, anticlimactic in consequence. The seeds of the intellectual anguish of the third novel were sown in the hopeful enthusiasms of the first. There is no more of an anticlimax here, because the story has turned inward, than there is in the history of the country itself, with intensive development and searching taking the place of national expansion and extensive development. But the glamour has gone. However, Rölvaag is not unmindful of such dramatic setting as the new era permits; a blizzard could not have for Peder the terrors it held for his grandfather, but the sizzling, endless drought with which the novel starts is scarcely less terrible or less-capable of dealing ultimate death.

The present novel, although the close of a trilogy, is complete in itself and can be read without reference to what has gone before. But it is illuminated and clarified by the previous books. . . . "**Their Fathers' God**" is a commentary, human and sincere, a commentary set forth in terms of dramatic narrative. Those interested in American evolution will find much to ponder in this frank study.

> *"Racial Conflict," in* The New York Times Book Review, *November 1, 1931, p. 6.*

GEORGE LEROY WHITE, JR. (essay date 1937)

[*In the following excerpt White discusses Rölvaag's thematic treatment of destiny as well as his masterful depiction of the struggles of Norwegian immigrants with a new society and the natural world in the* Giants in the Earth *trilogy.*]

The magnus opus about the Scandinavian settlement in America came in 1927 with the translation into English of O. E. Rölvaag's *Giants in the Earth.* Out of confusion he formed the master picture of the settlement. All the themes which the early novelists, Irving, Paulding, and Sawyer, all the more complex discussions of Boyesen, Stump, Cather, Glassmire, Lewis, and others, became clarified and unified in his writing. . . . The individual is, of necessity, a character in his novels, but it is the settlement and its struggles that provoked him to record and interpret in literature the facts of its origin and development.

Back of a changing world there is a horizon that changes little; back of days of prose there are days of poetry; back of passing events there are people. To reach the infinite is a worthy aim. To write of man, not only as he lives but as he thinks, and feels, and dreams, makes literature. Rölvaag in *Giants in the Earth* does this and the secret of its literary merit is that aiming high it did not fall far short.

Anyone who has stood upon a rising mound of ground and looked out over an expanse of prairie which lies beyond the vision of the strongest eye has felt that there is a strange power there that only the most sensitive of heart can feel in all its magnitude. There are evenings on this vastness, "magic, still evenings, surpassing in beauty the most fantastic dreams of childhood! Out to the westward—so surprisingly near—a blazing countenance sank to rest on a white couch—set it afire . . . kindles a radiance . . . a golden flame that flowed in many streams from horizon to horizon; the light played on the hundreds and thousands and millions of diamonds and turned them into glittering points of yellow and red, green and blue fire. Such evenings were dangerous for all life. To the strong they brought reckless laughter for who had ever seen such moon-nights? . . . To the weak they brought tears, hopeless tears. This was not life, but eternity itself. . . . "

This is the first quality that lifts Rölvaag above the mere writer of prairie novels—description of nature. Colors appeal to his eye and whether he writes of the glaring October skies to which no twilight brought even the witch's veil of a cloud, or whether he pictures the lazy spring, drinking in the moisture of the day, there is complete abandon to all of nature's moods. But this is not enough. Countless authors have seen the descriptive value of prairie winters, prairies in spring, fathomless expanses. There must be something more if we would remember. There is something more, and it seems to be the heritage of the Scandinavian to express it. Long communion with the soil has given to that people an ability to personify every changing of the face of nature. It is present in Selma Lagerlöf's trilogy, *The Ring of the Lowenskolds;* Sigrid Undset has it in *Kristin Lavransdatter;* Knut Hamsun catches a wisp of it in *Growth of the Soil,* and Rölvaag writes it into his South Dakota trilogy. In Rölvaag, particularly, it becomes an atmosphere as well as a force. It becomes oppressive; you feel that you must put the book down, you are so tired. The closer the peasant life identifies itself with the soil, the more oppressive is this atmosphere. The more powerful the novelist, the more powerfully moving the atmosphere. It is this quality that is first noticed in *Giants in the Earth, Peder Victorious,* and *Their Fathers' God.* It is this force that sweeps over Per, Beret, Tonseten, Kjersti, all, like wind-waves over lily-pads. Call it what you will: the eternal varieties, fate, the Norms, the infinite power of nature, anything; it is undeniable and at times it becomes greater than the characters. It is this ability to grasp at the incomprehensible that raises Rölvaag above most of his contemporaries. (pp. 97-9)

Now in regard to characters, there is this to say. The characters are, paradoxical as it may seem, both types and individuals in the novels of Rölvaag. As types they are used as symbols to express one of the main themes of the novel. For example, Per is the full embodiment of the spirit of adventure. He has deliberately chosen to come to the west to wrestle a living from

nature. The elements are strong against him, the loneliness of the country sinks into his soul, discouragements array themselves before him, but he is possessed of that spirit which dares and fights to the end. (p. 100)

Beret symbolizes the conservative, introspective type of mind. She is Rölvaag's most completely portrayed character. The first volume, *Giants in the Earth,* shows Beret to be a woman possessed of a poetic quality all her own. She is not a chronic fault-finder. Her trouble goes much deeper than the irritations of the skin. She first of all does not love pioneering. She has torn the home-ties from her heart solely because she loved Per more than anything else. She has followed him to America, looked for the last time upon a Norway, dear to her, passed through many towns of the new world, seen countless dwelling places vanish behind her as she pushed her sun-burnt face westward, all because she loved this foolish man. This love, with the few times she has been able to catch a little of the magic of Per's dream, has been the only thing that has sustained her. Here in early America where stars are prying eyes, and a small hill a silent sentinel; here where nothing breaks the expanse of blue by day and black by night; here where people ride for miles to see a strange face, Beret loses her mind—a victim of the small things of life that prey upon her: the loneliness of their place; the taking of new names; the naming of the boy Peder Victorious; the stake incident; the fear of Indians, and the fear of the stars. In her reaction to these things does Beret become human, a symbol humanized.

The change from a symbol to a human being is demanded of Beret; it is not demanded of Per, for this reason. There is no place for Per in *Peder Victorious.* As a moving spirit, yes, but as a person, no. He must die at the close of the first volume, because it is then that the early pioneer spirit dies. His death is not only characteristic of him: going for the minister for his dear friend Hans, and dying out in the snow with his face turned toward the west, toward the new country, but it is symbolic of the death of the early spirit, dying to give birth to new ideas and new methods that will bring about the glorious future. It is Beret, the rebellious, who must carry on the work of Per. It is for her to guide the life of Peder Victorious who is to be the link between the old and the new. In Peder there is a combination of the supreme individualism of Per and the sensitiveness of Beret. Beret must keep before Peder the vision of his father. The change in her is significant. Under the stress and strain of having to run the farm herself, she emerges a true character. Gone is her desire to return to Norway, gone much of her restlessness. The completion of the windmill and the barn—visions that Per had—cut her free of her past. She had now helped to make Per's dream a reality. She even thought she might be going beyond the dreams of Per in completing the windmill. At the end of the second volume, therefore, Beret has become in a measure Per—a conservative and tradition-loving Per—but the possessor of his spirit. In the volume, *Their Fathers' God,* Beret mellows into old age. The fearful, almost to sensitive Beret, who had become the masterful, forceful, farm woman, now becomes the quiet, modest grandmother who wishes all well. She is lovable, rich in years, and her work is done. Her character is complete. (pp. 101-02)

Undoubtedly these three volumes are the most artistic document on the Norwegian settler (1873-1894-20th century) in American literature. As record of the hopes and strivings of a people, they are packed with scholarship, selectiveness, and interpretation of fact. As a history of the problems the Norwegian-Americans faced as a group and as individuals, they are revealing and invaluable for future use. But it is as literature, as novels, that these documents will live. It is for their contribution to the American novel that they are significant. (pp. 103-04)

When dealing with the forces of nature that work upon the settlement Rölvaag lets himelf go. His poetic expression, evidenced in his description of nature, fits itself to the mood of nature as he pictures it. In the first novel, *Giants in the Earth,* as has already been noted, the vigor and wildness of nature is matched by a similar style of expression. Take this sentence: "That night the great Prairie stretched herself voluptuously, giant-like and full of cunning. She laughed softly into the reddish moon. Now we will see what human might may avail against us." In *Peder Victorious* there is a note of hesitancy in the descriptions of nature. The seasons are not so independent, they are becoming somewhat obedient to the will of man. Hence the figures, the descriptions of that type of nature, are full of alternating flaring-up and cooling-off. Most characteristic of this change in nature is this passage from *Peder Victorious:* "From eternity the prairie had lain here lapping sun and drinking moisture and had peered up into an endless blue sky, brimful to running over. At evening it had listened to strange tales told by the twilight breeze. But now other concerns had come to occupy the thoughts of the great plains, giving it not so much as a moment of rest. . . . Even the elements had to learn the power of man had to be respected, especially when energized by a great joy." And then you have nature almost completely tamed as in *Their Fathers' God.* Here the rain-maker defies the natural elements and his defiance and the people's prayers bring nature to task. This is nature's last stand. Her position is usurped by the interests of man. Only now and then does Peder go out into the fields and feel the pulse of nature beat in the spring time. Politics, love, the life of the farm, children, all these have taken nature's place, and so the poetry of description is taken from nature and given to them. (pp. 105-06)

Two very noticeable influences are present in Rölvaag's work and life. The first of these is the Bible. Rölvaag's style, his phraseology, his poetry and much of his method of presenting his ideas he took from the Old Testament. The Scandinavian migration brought to his mind, steeped as it was in Biblical lore, the migration of the tribe of Israel into the promised land, and he worked out the parallel in idea and language. From Ibsen he secured his philosophy of the divine call. This call comes to every man, Rölvaag believed, and "woe to him who fails to listen." With such a conception, therefore, of what a man should attempt to accomplish, and such a heritage behind him, it is no wonder that Rölvaag was able, in the brief span of years allotted to him, to make his name felt among Norwegian circles and to leave an imperishable record to American literature. In conclusion, there is no finer picture of a Scandinavian settlement in American fiction than his famous trilogy. It presents a consummate literary artist dealing with material he knew personally and fired with a zeal to show his people their virtues and their faults. Of the four things that are never satisfied: "the grave; and the barren womb; the earth that is not filled with water; and the fire that saith not, it is enough", Rölvaag has them all in his novels. (p. 108)

> George Leroy White, Jr., *"The Scandinavian Settlement in American Fiction,"* in his Scandinavian Themes in American Fiction, *University of Pennsylvania Press, 1937, pp. 69-108.**

THEODORE JORGENSON AND **NORA O. SOLUM**   (essay date **1939**)

[*Jorgenson, who knew Rölvaag while himself a professor at St. Olaf College, and Solum, also a St. Olaf colleague of Rölvaag who aided him in the translation of* Peder Victorious *and independently translated* The Boat of Longing, *published the first and most extensive biography in English of the novelist. In the following excerpt from that work, they discuss religious, cultural, and social themes in the* Giants in the Earth *trilogy, noting in particular evidence of the stylistic and philosophical influence of Norwegian dramatist Henrik Ibsen.*]

If an estimate were to be made concerning what literary influences are most apparent in the epic of Per Hansa and his wife [Rölvaag's *Giants in the Earth*] it would have to include Ibsen, the Old Norse sagas, the Norwegian fairy tales, and the Nordland dialect and folk memories.

Henrik Ibsen is most clearly present in the vivid scenes by means of which the six "acts" [or sections in Volume I] are constructed. The style is at times so near the terseness of the sagas that whole sentences might easily be transferred from Rölvaag's work into the ancient narratives, or vice versa, without the least disturbance. And as long as Per Hansa is the major figure in the drama, the fairy-tale influence is manifest and palpable. He is the Askeladd through and through; has all the hidden inventiveness, the joy of doing things, the upward drive, the ambition expressed in the terms "the princess and half the kingdom," the unassuming naturalness, the genuine humanity, the gambling instinct, and the inexhaustible resourcefulness of the fairy-tale hero, whom Rölvaag thought of as a projection of the deepest aspirations in the national mind, and whom he also recognized as his fellow traveler in life. But all this is cast in the Nordland mold. It is beyond a doubt true that the fresh originality of Rölvaag's style, as to both choice of words and turn of phrase, is attributable to his command of a native dialect. (p. 344)

The second "act" of the drama, which is called "Home-Founding," deepens the contrast already apparent between Per Hansa and his wife. In the technique of development, Ibsen has taught Rölvaag a great deal. Like the great dramatist, he strikes the keynote firmly at the very start: the conflict between man and wife, not because of any external coldness or lack of devotion, but because of inherently different natures. Even in the make-up of these characters, it is possible to detect Ibsenian traits, although the author himself was probably entirely unconscious of the similarity. The robust conscience is an element of character that Ibsen used time and again. The vikings are said to be blessed with it. They plundered their enemies, captured their beautiful women, and—made these women love them. They swept away opposition, worrying only about fairness and bravery and manliness. They never seemed to regret their deeds, were never inclined to be morbid.

Modern psychology has called these people extroverts. Per Hansa is one of them in a whole-souled way. But Ibsen also sets before us a type he calls the tender or sickly conscience. They are introverts. Their peace of mind is eaten away by an ever-present sense of guilt. In the works of the Norwegian dramatist, the explanation of these phenomena is frequently sought in the mysterious workings of hereditary forces. In our day, much of it would be ascribed to faulty education, or, in a broad sense, to social inheritance. Beret was definitely a psychological introvert by nature; yet this conscience was not altogether native to her. She had been taught certain authoritarian religious dogmas and had made her God an incarnation of law. The living God of Per Hansa she hardly knew except when the great moments of love came to her, and when she cared, in unconscious devotion, for her children. Her God was not the God of life, but the God of law. A morbid, doleful theology had been taught her from childhood. It had warped her mind almost beyond recognition, for she must have been very gentle and radiant and true during her childhood years. Rölvaag remarked of his own father that his religion had warped him. The legalism and the occultism of it had taken the living God from its heart and given the human soul over to the dominion of fear. The same is eminently true of Beret. She had been brought up in a system of doctrine and belief that had warped her mind, and made her sensitive nature still more ineffective than nature had designed her to be.

If Per Hansa is the viking of the prairie, it may be argued that, like the ancient vikings, he came to exploit rather than to build and perpetuate a civilization. The entire group of pioneers is subject to the charge of exploitation. Yet it is not easy to think of Per Hansa in that way. His object was not to *win* the kingdom but to *make* it. He was positively a creator, eager to establish contact with creative life. Nevertheless, it is true that Beret represents cultural values of a more enduring kind than her husband's physical achievements. Not all her values are genuinely fine and salutary. One can sympathize with her morbidity, her sense of guilt, and her rigid moral demands, but he is loath to see them overtake the freer life that pulsates in Per Hansa and in Store-Hans. (pp. 344-46)

A book in which Per Hansa is the leading character and in which the Norwegian Askeladd motif is basic in the story, must of necessity be romantic both in tone and in idea. With a few exceptions, notably the struggle with his wife's illness and the final tragic issue of that struggle, this empire builder of the prairie is the typical child of fortune. He might almost have come directly from the Aladdin of Oehlenschlaeger or be the Haakon of Ibsen's *The Pretenders* if he had not been the true Askeladd himself. (p. 347)

Beret, on the other hand, is far from being a romantic character. She is partly realistic, partly naturalistic. In so far as her bringing up is largely to blame for her warped religious attitudes, she is a tragic victim of prudery. In *Ghosts* Henrik Ibsen coined the phrase "the joy of life." Mrs. Alving is, in reality, the victim of a social philosophy and a religious dogma calculated to suppress the natural human urges and their resulting joy. She and her husband and her son go down to the same defeat, and they are brought into the jaws of hell by the prim society whose laws they have followed. Beret is in their class. It is only incidental that she is on the prairie of South Dakota. Her mind would certainly have been affected by loneliness even if she had been a fisherman's wife in Nordland. But the crucial difference is to be found in the sense of kinship she might have enjoyed there. With true artistic intuition, the author gives her recourse to the old family chest, and in it she hides from the ghastly eyes of a demon prairie. In so far as she is the product of hereditary and environmental forces minutely portrayed in their human consequences, the tragic Beret is also a naturalistic character in literature. (pp. 347-48)

The disordered condition of Beret's mind is temporarily relieved through the salutary influence of the pastor. In her seriously split personality a measure of stability is gained from the thought that God approved of her son Peder Victorious. But she is not released from the effects of her misguided upbringing. She becomes even more rigid in her dogmatic views. Her consciousness of guilt stands firmly on its extremely le-

galistic basis. In fact, the change within her is in the nature of a rebound; Peder, whom she had regarded as the captive of the devil, is now to become a minister of the church. Naturally, a good deal of her antagonism toward the immigrant community is dispelled when it becomes apparent that Spring Creek will have its church and its social institutions in keeping with her own traditions. But the *fear-full* attitude toward life—the groundwork of authoritarian discipline laid in her childhood—is as firm as ever, and it permeates in a smaller measure all these pioneers.

On the one hand, the book deals with the courageous labors, the manly fortitude, and the buoyant optimism of the early settlers. On the other, it is a realistic study of the effects seen to issue from basically wrong educational principles in the home and in the common schools. There are two demons in the novel: the evil monster of the plain and the more insidious demon of man-instilled fear. Both demand blood. In the Norwegian fairy tale, the troll drinks the blood of Christian men; nothing less will satisfy it. Rölvaag has used the idea as a caption for the closing section of the book. In the tale of the prairie, the monster of the plain also drinks the blood of Hans Olsa and of Per Hansa, but the religion of fear drives Beret to send her husband into the jaws of a certain death. Per Hansa understands the folly of it all, but he is caught in an inescapable dilemma, a psychology more dreadful than the plain. Like Socrates of old, he accepts the hemlock from the hands of his own blinded people.

Rölvaag as a student in 1906.

But his viking heart is in this book; there it will beat through the ages. (pp. 350-1)

Rölvaag said frankly that he was not seriously concerned with plot as an element in his stories, contending that if he could portray life vividly it would be impressive art and it would live. Nevertheless, he was concerned with structure and was fully aware of the problems of technique in which his purposes in this particular novel involved him. Whether he solved it adequately is problematic, as many reviewers have pointed out. Certainly there is no question that the reader of **Giants** asks with greater concern than the one regarding Beret and the home she was destined to lead and manage. It might, therefore, have been an improvement to have begun the sequel with the story of Beret during the winter months following the catastrophe. One senses Rölvaag's objection to a structure of that sort, namely, that it would make Beret the main character. It seems, however, that unity would not necessarily have been jeopardized by it, especially if the book is considered as a part of the larger series. From Per Hansa to Beret to Peder was a straight road.

In a letter to Mr. Colcord written January 2, 1929, just when **Peder Victorious** appeared, Rölvaag stated some of the leading ideas he himself had in mind while laboring on the novel. He says: "The theme of **Peder** is revolt. Beret had to come into the picture to the extent she did in order to bring out the theme clearer. He, like all the others of his class, had to revolt in order to gain foothold in American life. (p. 382)

A story of adolescent psychology must naturally have a flavor different from that of Per Hansa's magnificent saga. In **Peder** there is but one actual scene reminiscent of the rollicking merriment of sodhouse days. That instance is Tönseten's moistening of the ridge pole, when the large new Holm barn was being built. Very little, if any, swearing occurs in the sequel. The language in the Norwegian version is heavier, keeps closer to the Nordland dialect, and nearer the up-country vernacular of Norway than to the prevailing Oslo norm. The reader of the Norwegian is conscious of a definite effort to choose rare terms, with the evident intention of gaining strength and color. And beyond doubt the book exhibits increasing mastery along these very lines. Conscious power and certainty breathe through the paragraphs—but with rather less of the exciting joy that comes when confidence battles doubt in regard to a work that is to make or break its author. (p. 386)

[The conclusion to Rölvaag's trilogy, **Their Fathers' God,**] is built around a deep human conflict, Ibsenian in character. The triad set up in Peder-Susie-Beret. It would not have done to let the pioneer son issue forth as a harmonious continuation of his parents' life and nature. Peder is drawn from the very beginning as a fine intelligence, a person who in time will be imbued with the sense of a significant destiny. His rebellion against the parents as well as against the Lutheranism he found in the Spring Creek churches is in every way natural. It is only intensified because the American system refuses to him, as the son of non-English-speaking pioneers, a proper relation to the mind of his own kin. Tom Paine, liberal political idealism, and American scientific thought hold the main ground in the soul of Per Hansa's heir.

Contrariwise, it would not do to make Susie Doheny [Peder's wife-to-be] intellectual. She is luxuriantly fertile, a brimming cup of surging life. Her home is, strictly speaking, a matriarchate. Her being closes tightly and warmly around the child. The father is present mainly as a biological and economic factor. And because Susie is love and motherhood, she is instinctively religious. Her Catholicism is naïve, but it is as genuine as her own nature. (pp. 415-16)

Even a cursory study of the book is enough to impress upon the reader the great similarity between the technique of the Ibsenian drama and this final work of Ole Edvart Rölvaag. It is built not upon a plot but upon a conflict resulting from a tragic situation. What happens as the days and the weeks pass is of little significance to the life pattern drawn. It merely serves to reveal more and more convincingly the inner chasm that cannot be bridged. And as people are made to look into their own selves, life is intensified. As in the plays of Ibsen, there is an intense inner activity for which the outer events are little more than tokens. The author has lived, in his thought, with meanings and values and deeply human problems until a rational world has been set up within his own mind. This rational world is from time to time perceived back of the actual happenings of the novel. The effect is that of meanings behind meanings; suggestions and venturesome probings make the novel stimulating rather than delightful. (p. 417)

Rölvaag had learned from Ibsen to fuse his story with an inner thought element, which from time to time gives the impression that the characters are in the hands of relentless fate. Some readers—especially those who are not favorably disposed toward the novel—will say that the dice were loaded, that Peder and Susie might with some mutual good will have made their union a real marriage. It is likely that such readers have had little direct experience in matters of this kind. And certainly the loaded dice bring us a consciousness of natural law, against which human beings cannot sin with impunity. That is precisely the goal the author labored toward. **Their Fathers' God** is his most courageous as well as his most prophetic work. It speaks a solemn warning about shoals ahead, with possible disaster to the individual, to the fundamental institutions of our social order, and to the whole empire founded by the American pioneers.

All these considerations are brought to a climax in the fourth section of the book, "On the Way to Golgotha." This road to the hill of sacrifice and suffering has nothing to do, by way of analogy, with the atonement of Christ. The author had grown accustomed to using the Bible much as he used other literature. The allusions he drew from it are to be regarded from the standpoint of their inherent power and suggestiveness rather than as the basis of dogma. The road which Peder has to walk is the road of atonement only in the sense that he must suffer for the sin he has committed in establishing a home that cannot, in the long run, be the path of a creative God. (p. 420)

The high point, the Golgotha of the book, is reached when the pioneer mother, Beret, dies, and Susie, because of the terror that she undergoes, has a miscarriage. It should always be kept in mind that Peder's Irish wife is forced into a struggle as bitter as Peder's own. The circumstances of Beret's passing were ghastly to the simple mind brought up in an altogether different world. On the sickbed of her untimely motherhood, she hovered between life and death. Kind and devoted as her husband was to her, the whole confinement must have seemed a nightmare indeed. And Peder, still in his early twenties, discovered gray hair above his temples.

The middle sections of the book show us Rölvaag at the height of his interpretative power. A smaller man would have brought in Nikoline Johansen as Peder's true love and would have made him come into a self-examination ending in the conclusion that he did not love Susie at all and that the marriage was a direct error. Life is seldom like that. The author of *Their Fathers' God* knew that there are many kinds of love. Psychologically, it was indeed more than natural that Susie and her husband should have moments of great joy. Biologically they were properly mated. Had they lived more constantly on the purely racial plane, they might have experienced very little difficulty. The great calamity that finally overtook them issued from another realm of existence, namely, that of cultural creativity. In that realm Peder had a mission to fulfill; and in proportion as that mission gripped his faculties until he sensed it as a life calling, in that proportion he pulled away, up and beyond. Susie's temperament made it impossible for her to follow and in the realm of the mind they had nothing in common. (p. 423)

The concluding section of the book is scarcely as powerful as the one on Golgotha. Beret's death is among the finest and the most elevated literature that Rölvaag ever produced. Nevertheless, the ground for the denouement is well chosen. Peder is starting out upon the high road of life. As long as he stayed at home and kept his manhood's goal in a cloudland of dreams, he was able to delay the ultimate crisis. But when he finally arrived at the point where he stood face to face with an implacable enemy and then realized that this enemy might be the friend of his own wife, his volcanic nature erupted and swept the whole structure of his home into a heap of miserable ruins.

Although *Their Fathers' God* cannot boast of the magnificent surge and the godlike lift that are the glory of *Giants,* it may be said unequivocally that the author's last volume is artistically his surest product. On earlier occasions critics had pointed to a good deal of amateurish talk in his novels. Perhaps their boyishness is, in reality, their great strength. But it is plain that Rölvaag strove for the terseness and the calm elevation of the Old Norse sagas. The story of Beret's death is, indeed, classic-saga style, a pure and vivid account that might have been written by an actual observer. Noble expression and a vocabulary greatly enriched by his own melodious Nordland dialect constitute the stylistic splendor of the work. An artist sure of his powers, yet struggling on toward greater heights, finished the third volume of a mighty pioneer drama.

In a sense, Rölvaag made his American saga complete when he finished *Their Fathers' God.* Those among the readers who demand an ending that leaves few questions to be asked will, of course, say that final artistic unity has not been achieved. But the books do, in fact, take us to the point where America stands at the present time. The future is a question mark. The author of *Giants* knew that a kingdom had been founded, but he was not certain that it was being creatively advanced toward high, purposive cultural achievement. He threw out a warning, earnest and solemn in its message. (pp. 424-25)

> *Theodore Jorgenson and Nora O. Solum, in their* Ole Edvart Rölvaag: A Biography, *Harper & Brothers Publishers, 1939, 446 p.*

JOSEPH E. BAKER (essay date 1942)

[*In the following excerpt Baker notes that he perceives in* Giants in the Earth, *particularly in the character of Per Hansa, an affirmation of the Western conception of a rational humanity possessing free will rather than the Eastern, deterministic outlook upheld by such American romantic writers as Ralph Waldo Emerson. For an interpretation that limits Per's role as hero and spokesman for Rölvaag's values, see the excerpt by Paul A. Olson (1981), who regards Beret Hansa, for her adherence to a traditional Norwegian-Lutheran outlook, as the actual protagonist*

of the novel; also see the excerpt by Harold P. Simonson (1977), who discusses Beret's high spiritual consciousness but arrives at no conclusion on the issue of Beret's absolute heroism.]

Rölvaag's *Giants in the Earth* is a vision of human life rich in its implications. Here the pioneer struggle with the untamed universe may serve as a symbol for the condition of man himself against inhuman Destiny. The hero, Per Hansa, is a typical man of the West, both in the regional sense that he represents our pioneer background and in the universal human sense that he embodies the independent spirit, the rationalism, and what has often been condemned as the utilitarianism of Western civilization—European mankind's determination to cherish human values against the brute force of Fate. (p. 19)

This conception is developed most fully in the great tragic dramas of European literatures, but we find a similar respect for man at the very dawn of our civilization in the first Western author, Homer. His men are "like gods"; indeed, sometimes they are better and wiser than the supernatural forces and divine giants they come in contact with. Before the Heroic Age, mankind was sunk in an Age of Terror, given over to the superstition that the world is ruled by forces which can be dealt with only by magical rites—a view that still survives in Per Hansa's wife Beret. But with Homer, man emerges into the epic stage of human consciousness, with its great admiration for men of ability. Rölvaag's *Giants in the Earth* is a modern epic of Western man.

In this novel, as in Homer, or, for that matter, in *Beowulf,* there is the heartiest gusto and admiration for human achievement—sophisticates would say a naïve delight in the simplest things: "Wonder of wonders!" What had Per Hansa brought back with him? "It was a bird cage, made of thin slats; and inside lay a rooster and two hens!" . . . Nobody but Homer and Rölvaag can get us so excited over merely economic prosperity, man's achievement in acquiring fine things for his own use. One of the high dramatic points in the novel is the discovery that, after all, the wheat has come up! This sort of thing means life or death; and the preservation of human life, or the evaluation of things according to the pleasure they can give to individual men, is the very opposite of submission to material forces.

> Hans Olsa was cutting hay; his new machine hummed lustily over the prairie, shearing the grass so evenly and so close to the ground that his heart leaped with joy to behold the sight. What a difference, this, from pounding away with an old scythe, on steep, stony hillsides! All the men had gathered round to see him start. . . .

That sounds like a passage from the *Odyssey.* And the central figure in the novel is an epic hero. Like Odysseus, Per Hansa is "never at a loss." Hans Olsa says to him, "No matter how hard you're put to it, you always give a good account of yourself!" . . . This might be used to translate one of Athena's remarks to Odysseus. Or one may think of Virgil. Here are some of the phrases that make the novel seem epic: "[They talked] of land and crops, and of the new kingdom which they were about to found. . . . Now they had gone back to the very beginning of things." . . . This comes in the earliest pages of the book; while the last chapter states their attitude thus: "There was no such thing as the Impossible any more. The human race has not known such faith and such self-confidence since history began"—one ought to say, since the Homeric Greeks. But in the translation of this novel from Norwegian into English, made by a New Englander, there has been added, out of respect for our Atlantic seaboard, "so had been the Spirit since the day the first settlers landed on the eastern shores." . . . Thus the novel, especially in the English translation, brings out what America meant to mankind. "He felt profoundly that the greatest moment of his life had come. Now he was about to sow wheat on his own ground!" . . . This is exactly what Jefferson wanted America to be. And as the Middle West became the most complete type of democratic civilization that the world has ever known, our leaders have fought many battles, in politics and war, to enable the ordinary hard-working farmer to sow his wheat on his own ground.

America at its most American, this is embodied in Per Hansa, who "never liked to follow an old path while there was still unexplored land left around him." . . . That is the spirit of the West against the East, of America against Europe, of Europe against Asia. It is not that the amenities of life are undervalued; even Per Hansa is working to achieve a civilized life. But the amenities are less exciting than the achieving. . . . The conquest of material nature has been superciliously criticized by comfortable New Englanders from Emerson to Irving Babbitt (both guilty of an undue respect for oriental passivity) as a case of forgetting the distinction between the "law for man and law for thing," meaning by the "law for thing" not material force but human mastery. It "builds town and fleet," says Emerson; by it the forest is felled, the orchard planted, the prairie tilled, the steamer built. But it seems to me that human triumph over matter is a genuine practical humanism, and that this is the true spirit of the West; that in Bacon's phrase, knowledge may well be used for "the relief of man's estate." Emerson was closer to the spirit of the pioneers when he said, in "The Young American":

> Any relation to the land, the habit of tilling it, or mining it, or even hunting on it, generates the feeling of patriotism. He who keeps shop on it, or he who merely uses it as a support to his desk . . . or . . . manufactory, values it less. . . . We in the Atlantic states, by position, have been commercial, and have . . . imbibed easily an European culture. Luckily for us . . . the nervous, rocky West is intruding a new and continental element into the national mind, and we shall yet have an American genius.

And he calls it a "false state of things" that "our people have their intellectual culture from one country and their duties from another." But happily "America is beginning to assert herself to the senses and to the imagination of her children." If this be true—and I must confess that it seems rather extreme doctrine even to a middle western regionalist like myself—then Rölvaag, born in Europe, is more American than some of our authors of old New England stock. All Emerson's "Representative Men" were Europeans. It was not until the Middle West came into literature that we get an epic and broadly democratic spirit in works never to be mistaken for the products of modern Europe. Emerson recognized this in Lincoln; at last he admired a representative man who came from the West. And middle western leadership in American literature, begun with Lincoln's prose, established beyond a doubt by Mark Twain, was confirmed in our day by Rölvaag. (pp. 19-22)

Thoreau said: "I love the wild not less than the good," but his Walden was within suburban distance of the cultural center and the financial center of the New World. Rölvaag had known Nature as the sea from which, as a Norwegian fisherman, he must wring his living. In 1893 a storm at sea drowned many of his companions; and this, he says, caused him "to question the romantic notion of nature's purposeful benevolence." So in this novel there are giants in the earth. On the prairie, "Man's strength availed but little out here."

> That night the Great Prairie stretched herself voluptuously; giantlike and full of cunning, she laughed softly into the reddish moon. "Now we will see what human might may avail against us! . . . Now we'll see!" And now had begun a seemingly endless struggle between man's fortitude in adversity, on the one hand, and power of evil in high places. . . .

"The Power of Evil in High Places" is the title of the chapter, which includes a plague of locusts and also the terrible insanity of Per Hansa's wife. That is what we really find to be the method of Nature. For by this term Rölvaag, of course, does not merely mean scenery. He means the whole created universe that man is up against and the blind inhuman force or might that moves it. Sometimes he calls it Destiny, as in speaking of the murderous storm of 1893: "That storm changed my nature. As the seas broke over us and I believed that death was inescapable, I felt a resentment against Destiny." Twenty-seven years later another even more bitter tragedy occurred to impress Rölvaag with the murderousness of Nature: His five-year-old son Gunnar was drowned, under terrible circumstances. He writes that this tragedy changed his view of life. Previously he "had looked upon God as a logical mind in Whom the least happening" was planned and willed. Now he saw that much is "due to chance and to lawbound nature." In this novel, written later, it should be noticed that Per Hansa's wife Beret, especially when she is insane, continues Rölvaag's older view, blaming God for all miseries as if he had planned all. She broods that "beyond a doubt, it was Destiny that had brought her thither. Destiny, the inexorable law of life, which the Lord God from eternity had laid down for every human being, according to the path He knew would be taken. . . . Destiny had so arranged everything." . . . Another poor miserable woman in this novel, her husband receiving his death blow from a cruel Nature, has this same dark pagan view: "Now the worst had happened and there was nothing to do about it, for Fate is inexorable." . . . This is a continuation of the deadliest oriental fatalism, always current in misconceptions of Christianity, though actually it is just this which it has been the function of Christian philosophy and Western humanism to cast out, to exorcise in rationalizing man's relation to the universe. . . . So, Beret does not believe they should try to conquer the prairie; she feels that it is sinful to undergo the conditions of pioneer life; she is "ashamed" that they have to put up with poor food. "Couldn't he understand that if the Lord God had intended these infinities to be peopled, He would not have left them desolate down through the ages?" . . .

But her husband, Per Hansa, is a man of the West; he glories in the fact that he is an American free-willer, self-asserting. He rebels against Destiny and tries to master Nature. . . . It should be noticed that Per Hansa, though a rationalist, is also a Christian; so the author designates him in the title of the last chapter, "The Great Plain Drinks the Blood of Christian Men." Per is defending a higher conception of God. When Hans Olsa, dying, quotes "It is terrible to fall into the hands of the living God," Per says, "Hush, now, man! Don't talk blasphemy!" . . . Rölvaag is aware of the divine gentleness of Christianity; the words of the minister "flowed on . . . softly and sweetly, like the warm rain of a summer evening'' . . . in a tender scene which suggests ''Suffer little children to come unto me.'' This is in a chapter entitled ''The Glory of the Lord''—for it is a clergyman who ministers to the ''mind diseased'' of Beret and brings her out of her ''utter darkness'' in a passage that may be considered the greatest yet written in American fiction. What is implied in this novel becomes explicit in the sequel, *Peder Victorious,* where the first chapter is concerned with the religious musing of Per's fatherless son Peder. At one point he feels a difference between a Western as opposed to an Eastern or Old World conception of God and concludes that ''no one could make him believe that a really American God would go about killing people with snowstorms and the like.'' But more significant is the account, in this sequel, of what the minister said to Beret after she had driven her husband out into the fatal snowstorm to satisfy her superstitious reverence for rites:

> You have permitted a great sin to blind your sight; you have forgotten that it is God who causes all life to flower and who has put both good and evil into the hearts of men. I don't think I have known two better men than your husband and the friend he gave his life for . . . your worst sin . . . lies in your discontent with . . . your fellow men.

Surely, whatever Rölvaag's religious affiliations may have been, this is the expression of a Christian humanism. From this point of view it is far from true to say that American literature has sunk down in two or three generations from the high wisdom of Emerson to the degradation of the ''naturalistic'' novel. *Giants in the Earth* is a step in the right direction, abandoning the romantic idolatry that worshipped a Destiny in Nature and believed ''the central intention of Nature to be harmony and joy.'' ''Let us build altars to the Beautiful Necessity''—as Emerson puts it in his ''Fate''—''Why should we be afraid of Nature, which is no other than 'philosophy and theology embodied?''' This sentiment can be found repeated in many forms throughout the rhapsodies of the ''prophets'' of our ''Golden Day.'' I, for one, am rather tired of the glorification of these false prophets, and I am glad that American literature has outgrown their enthusiasms, so lacking in a sense for the genuine dignity of man. Wisdom was not monopolized by the stretch of earth's surface from a little north of Boston to a little south of Brooklyn Ferry. Another passage from ''The Young American'' could bring home to us the repulsive inhumanity of Emerson's conception of God. Enumerating the suffering and miseries of man's lot, how individuals are crushed and ''find it so hard to live,'' Emerson blandly tells us this is the

> sublime and friendly Destiny by which the human race is guided . . . the individual[s] never spared . . . Genius or Destiny . . . is not discovered in their calculated and voluntary activity, but in what befalls, with or without their design. . . . That Genius has infused itself into nature. . . . For Nature is the noblest engineer.

In opposition to this deadly submission to cruel natural force, I contend that Western civilization was built by innumerable details of calculated and voluntary activity, that the Christian God is a God concerned not with race but with individuals according to their moral worth, and that in the tragic event which befalls Per Hansa in this novel, without his design, we do *not* witness a God infused into Nature. (pp. 23-6)

Joseph E. Baker, ''Western Man Against Nature: 'Giants in the Earth','' in College English, Vol. 4, No. 1, October, 1942, pp. 19-26.

CHARLES BOEWE (essay date 1957)

[*In the following excerpt Boewe discusses Rölvaag's fiction, particularly the* Giants in the Earth *trilogy, as the artistic embodiment of the author's critical attitude toward American culture and similarly strong desire to preserve Norwegian traditions and values.*]

The social thought of the novelist Ole Edvart Rölvaag . . . has an unusual critical importance. As an immigrant, he was able to make comparisons denied American writers. He gives us a glimpse of ourselves through discerning alien eyes. (p. 3)

The mind and heart of the immigrant became Rölvaag's lifelong study. His fiction is of course the fruit of that study, yet his basic conclusions were mostly elaborated before he began writing the novels that were to make him famous. In 1920, in a lecture on Norwegian immigrant history—a subject that he introduced at St. Olaf College—he discussed the seven causes which he believed had brought Norwegians to America. Perhaps the motivations for emigration have been explored more thoroughly since, but Rölvaag's conclusions are significant as a basis for his own views on the position of the immigrant in American society.

Rölvaag never denied the primacy of the economic motive; as the first of a series of causes for emigration, he asserted that ''it was the hope of a better and easier livelihood that made most of our fathers emigrate.'' Yet he was careful to point out that it was not always the poorest people who were most eager to take so drastic an action to better their economic condition. He noted that often the ambition to acquire wealth was not matched by economic resources in the old countries which made wealth possible; thus, in reality, immigration often acted as a sieve to screen out for America the more ambitious members of a nation, the less adventurous having to stay home and be content with their lot in life. Two of the causes for emigration were specifics underlying this first reason; namely, the Norwegian law of primogeniture which tended to cut the younger sons loose from home ties, and the difficulties both the cottager and business classes of nineteenth-century Norway found in recovering from debts. As a fourth reason, unrequited love made what may be called a ''migratory situation.'' The seductive advertisements plastered across Europe by the great steamship lines were a fifth impetus. The glowing letters from previous immigrants who had succeeded or still hoped to succeed were a sixth.

His seventh and final reason was a poetic idea that likely had much to do with Rölvaag's own decision to emigrate. ''There is a young good-for-nothing fellow, a sort of Askeladd [in Norwegian folklore, the undiscovered genius, the male Cinderella],'' he said. ''He comes to America. Here he wakes up, because he has the choice of either doing that or starve.'' Nils by the Sea, in *The Boat of Longing,* is a kind of Askeladd. He dreams of a great fulfillment that cannot take place in the cramped confines of Norway; he must come to America where, he thinks, dreams become reality. There are touches of the Askeladd, too, in the character of Per Hansa in *Giants in the Earth;* for he almost miraculously escapes the hardships of his neighbors; when the plague of locusts comes his wheat is spared, the claim jumpers do not try to steal his land, he triumphs over the prairie, and even in death his eyes are set prophetically toward the West. (pp. 3-4)

But . . . Rölvaag could see only too well that the pattern of the Askeladd was not the only one the immigrant might follow in America. In the same year that he laid down his reasons for the impulse to emigrate, he published *To Tullinger* (*Two Fools*), a novel which appeared in an English version ten years later under the title *Pure Gold*. *Pure Gold* is one of the most devastating attacks on cupidity ever written in America. Its two chief characters, Lars and Lisbet, are second generation Norwegians who have cut themselves off entirely from the old-world culture and have acquired little of value from the new. At the beginning of the novel both are likable people. Lars, though somewhat slow of thought and speech, is strong and manly, with an admirable ambition to rise in the world solely by his own effort. Lisbet has aspirations of achieving what is to her a measure of intellectual advancement by going to business college, though her father frustrates her plans because he cannot see the need of such education for women. After Lars and Lisbet marry, Lisbet is caught up in all the unwholesome aspects of Americanization. She renounces her Norwegian heritage; she changes her name to Lizzie, and insists that Lars be called Louis; and she drives them both with an insatiable desire to pile up thousand-dollar bills and gold coins. Their love for money becomes physical; they play with it, fondle it, kiss it, talk to it, and call their thousand-dollar bills their babies. In order to have their money ever near their persons they reduce all their assets to large-denomination bills which they can carry next to their skins in money belts. They end their tawdry lives in two unheated rooms, frozen to death because they refuse to spend money for fuel. And the money they have drudged a lifetime to acquire is at last only a wisp of smoke when the undertaker, to prevent the spread of contagion, cuts off their stinking clothes and burns them along with the unnoticed money belts.

These two early works prefigure Rölvaag's major concerns in his three better known pioneer novels. Nils by the Sea, in *The Boat of Longing*, with his firm identification with the culture of Norway, his poetic yearnings, his artistic competence on the violin, his appreciation of literature and especially of poetry, represents the positive side of Rölvaag's analysis: the ideal. That Nils does not realize the fulfillment of his dream in America and is driven to an essentially tragic end when he is unable to keep his promise to watch over his friend Per Syv is only Rölvaag's realistic recognition that dreams usually do not come true. In the main, he implies, this is the expected outcome of idealism. Nevertheless, failure does not mean that the ideal should be abandoned, for the idealistic failures bring about whatever graciousness obtains in the world. When Nils cries to the Stril, a man who has spent his life confronting the vagaries of the sea, that there *must* be happiness, that it cannot be otherwise, he is reminded of the unpleasant facts of existence. . . . (pp. 5-6)

Obviously, all is not well in a society that fosters people like Lizzie and Louis and frustrates people like Nils. In an articulated philosophy of culture, Rölvaag elaborated a program to guide the immigrant toward a positive contribution to American society. (p. 6)

In his catalogue of the traits of the Norwegians, whom he considered a race, he unblushingly listed nearly all of the cardinal virtues. The Norwegians are marked, he said, by a "reverence for law and order; a deeply poetic appreciation of nature; a great hunger for knowledge; hospitality; emotional reserve; deep religiousness; integrity; and creative activity in art and letters." (Rölvaag did not, however, claim that these virtues

were the result of an immutable heredity; rather, he said, racial differences are the result of "environment and teaching and training for many centuries," and "suffering and conditions of servitude have placed them there.") If the Norwegians submerged themselves in American culture, what positive virtues their own culture possessed would be lost, and little if anything would be gained in return. His condemnation of the shallowness of American culture which threatened to engulf the Norwegians was expressed in a speech, **"American Social Conditions,"** which he delivered in Norway in 1906 after he had completed his studies in Oslo. . . . It is especially . . . [a] loss of richness and variety that worried Rölvaag about the immigrants' hell-for-leather stampede to become Americanized. Besides his concern over the purely aesthetic side of the question, he doubted that a people could suddenly change its "racial" character without doing violence to itself. The attempt to blot out all distinguishing traits, he said, "is tantamount to national suicide."

How then is a people to maintain its national identity? For Rölvaag as professor of Norwegian language and literature there was but one answer. Language is the enduring foundation of culture; as long as the native language exists as a living language—not in the pale half life of language courses but as the language men speak and in which they think—as long as the Norwegian language lives the Norwegian culture will live, and no longer. In a Seventeenth of May address delivered at St. Olaf after his return from Oslo, Rölvaag gave the finest expression of his cultural nationalism and of his conception of the intimate relationship between culture and language. "What in reality is culture?" he began by asking.

> I may say briefly that the person who is rich in ideas, who has true depth of emotion, whose will is firm and has great projecting power, that person is cultured. . . . Now, the soul grows and unfolds like a flower; even as the flower it must be nourished. And the nourishment which our spirit particularly needs is to be found in thoughts, feelings, and in the exercise of the will. But neither the thoughts nor the feelings come to us immediately; they do not drop as it were from the empty sky into our minds. They come to us through language. . . .
>
> If a man is to realize in full measure the potentialities of his being, he must first of all learn to know the people of his own kin. He must discover the peculiar situation and the special talents of his own race. He must also learn its weaknesses. . . . Through its language he learns to know his own people's history and literature. This knowledge is of supreme importance to our cultural development. It constitutes our cultural roots. Without it, we become drifting vagrants, scrubs or tramps, culturally speaking.

The three novels of Rölvaag's pioneer saga—*Giants in the Earth, Peder Victorious*, and *Their Fathers' God*—are the artistic expression of this philosophy of culture. While they are devoid of explicit moralizing—for in the early 'twenties Rölvaag became a convert to realism—nevertheless they show what Rölvaag thought Norwegian culture might have accomplished in America, and more especially they show how little he thought it did accomplish. *Giants in the Earth,* concerned with the land-taking in the 1870's and therefore based on secondhand knowledge, is the most aesthetically satisfying of the three but at the same time the poorest history. The other two novels, which deal with second-generation immigrants and consequently were written out of their author's own experience, are better history, and indeed can almost be read as social chronicles of South Dakota in the 'eighties and 'nineties.

Most critics have considered *Giants in the Earth* as Beret's story exclusively. It is true, of course, that Beret's loneliness makes a more lasting impression on one than her husband Per Hansa's heroic vitality and exuberance. But in the light of Rölvaag's other writing, it is clear that *Giants in the Earth* is not merely the story of two individuals, however epic their story may be. The novel is as much a part of Rölvaag's philosophy of culture as any of his speeches; it is in fact an object lesson in the paucity of culture on the frontier.

Both Beret and Per Hansa retain the old culture so far as they are able; yet Beret becomes insane and Per Hansa is driven like a tragic hero to a fated death. Rölvaag's indictment of America is this: physical conquest is not enough for the sensitive souls of the world like Beret. "I'm so afraid out here," she says to her husband, early in the novel. "It's all so big and open—so empty—Oh, Per! Not another human being from here to the end of the world!" The Dakota prairie lacked the nuance, the perspective, the contrast that make life endurable; and while such conditions could be forgiven a frontier settlement, the point was that the prairie never developed nuance, perspective, and contrast. As time went on, people forgot the mellowness of the old country and came to glory in the rawness and brashness of the new. Beret remembered, and she became insane (though she was eventually restored to sanity through the saving influence of religious self-abnegation); but what of the second generation which accepted what it found—was it insane without knowing it? Per Hansa was saved because he was not continually confined to the drab sod house; he could always find an excuse for a week's journey to town or a fishing trip. Besides, he had the heroic task of carving his kingdom out of the primeval prairie and was buoyed up by a superhuman joy of life not shared by ordinary mortals like Beret. Had Per Hansa lived to see all his land under cultivation, and had he been compelled to settle down to the dull routine of farming, how then would he have fared?

Even in *Giants in the Earth,* then, the breakup of the old cultural solidarity begins; it accelerates as Rölvaag follows the career of Per Hansa's son, Peder Victorious, through the other two novels. In these novels Rölvaag's condemnation of hybrid immigrant culture becomes increasingly emphatic. Yet again the criticism is wholly implied, not stated, for Rölvaag is always a conscious artist, and he makes the characters who represent views different from his own speak almost as convincingly as his spokesmen.

The spiritual unrest of Beret in *Giants in the Earth,* which has presaged the crumbling of the old culture, continues to expand in ever-widening circles in the immigrant community portrayed in *Peder Victorious.* (pp. 6-9)

The last volume of the Trilogy, *Their Fathers' God,* is the account of how poorly this mixed culture could succeed in marriage. Physically and temperamentally, Peder and Susie are suited to each other; but in their disparate outlook on life, especially as regards religion, they are hopelessly mismatched. Susie, reverent, eager to follow explicitly the friendly advice of Father Williams, cannot understand Peder's intellectual self-reliance when he flares out at her, "What do I care about your apostolic succession? The Bible is as much mine as it is any

priest's. . . . My people have been reading and studying it for hundreds of years." But Peder himself is a member of the new generation for whom the old certainties are no longer certain; his defense of his right to interpret the Bible his own way is fundamentally a defense of his right to disbelieve it. It is his mother who truly believes; and when Susie becomes a mother, Beret has the child secretly baptized in the Lutheran faith, sure that by so doing she has saved its soul from the Catholics.

Rölvaag, who had once thought of the ministry for himself, who taught at a church college, and who had been a professor of Biblical history, always made the church the cornerstone of his program of cultural conservation. Many of its leaders he thought had failed in their duty, had too glibly accepted the generalities of the melting-pot theory; and he did not fail to castigate them for their shortcomings. It is significant that in this final novel of his trilogy he has a minister, the Rev. Mr. Kaldahl, deliver an Isaiah-like adjuration to the people—the sort of speech, Rölvaag would urge, that should be more often on the lips of the Norwegians' spiritual leaders. "There is nothing in all history comparable to the deeds of our viking ancestors," says the preacher at a Christmas gathering in a Norwegian home. "You have been entrusted with a rich inheritance built up through the ages. How much of it, what portion, are you trying to get? Isn't it your irrevocable duty to see how much of it you can preserve and hand down to those coming after you? *A people that has lost its traditions is doomed!"* Though the Norwegians pride themselves on what they have done in this country, really it is pitiably little, says Mr. Kaldahl, when compared to what their ancestors did in the ninth and tenth centuries. Then Norwegians were leaders; now they follow a blazed trail. If they are to accomplish anything in the future it will be only by maintaining their cultural integrity. (pp. 10-11)

It can hardly be said that Rölvaag's crusade for the conservation of Norwegian culture in America was successful. Yet if his desire to perpetuate the culture which he thought could add richness to American life did nothing more than provoke his novels, he at least achieved a personal triumph, and America in the long run was also a gainer. Aside from the substantial literary worth of Rölvaag's fiction, his criticism of a thin, money-grubbing society, which he found the United States to be, and his positive program of cultural pluralism based on the integrity of language and religion entitle him to a respectful hearing and place him among the significant social critics of America. (p. 12)

Charles Boewe, "Rölvaag's America: An Immigrant Novelist's Views," in Western Humanities Review, *Vol. XI, No. 1, Winter, 1957, pp. 3-12.*

HAROLD P. SIMONSON (essay date 1977)

[*In the following excerpt, Simonson, a distinguished American scholar and literary critic, analyzes the influence of Danish philosopher Søren Kierkegaard's philosophies of religious faith, free will, and identity on Rölvaag's* Giants in the Earth *trilogy. Consequently, Simonson considers the key underlying theme of the prairie saga to be the attainment of personal salvation—a spiritual level denied Per Hansa due to his disavowal of allegiance to God and immodest pride in himself. For a similar discussion of Beret as the true hero of Rölvaag's saga, see the excerpt by Paul A. Olson (1981); for a contrasting interpretation of the importance of Per Hansa and his success as an embodiment of Rölvaag's ideals, see the excerpt by Joseph E. Baker (1942).*]

Critics of Ole Rølvaag's fiction have emphasized his great themes of immigration and the westward movement as well as ancillary themes related to American realism, tragedy, fate, myth, etc. One topic that teases and tempts but has not yet received sustained attention pertains to something Rølvaag's biographers, Theodore Jorgenson and Nora O. Solum, note with only the briefest mention [see excerpt dated 1937]: "it is tempting to believe," they say, "that he may have been under the influence of the Danish philosopher, Søren Kierkegaard." They add: "Rølvaag read Kierkegaard, presumably quite early in life and with greater diligence after he had begun to specialize in Norwegian literature." Beyond noting that Rølvaag could hardly have studied and taught Henrik Ibsen without knowing "Ibsen's spiritual kinsman in Denmark," Jorgenson and Solum say little else, except to point out that Rølvaag's use of the diary as a literary device in *Letters from America* . . . resembled Kierkegaard's same technique in *Either/Or.* (p. 67)

That Rølvaag came under the influence of the great Danish thinker is reasonable to assume. Common to both men was not only a Scandinavian culture but also a certain system of regulative ideas that shaped their lives. Moreover, a profoundly religious spirit as well as a deep restlessness intensified the paradoxes they found in life. Hating what was trivial and passionless, both men probed into the depths of existence and dared to contemplate divine meanings. Furthermore, a spiritual grandeur coupled with a brooding darkness mark Rølvaag's *Giants in the Earth,* as these same qualities distinguish the vast themes in Kierkegaard's *Either/Or, Fear and Trembling, The Sickness Unto Death, The Concept of Dread*—the very titles evoking a sense of awe. More specifically, both men equated the matter of choice with what it means to be human: to choose is to acquire self-hood. Kierkegaard explained that "choice itself is decisive for the content of personality." Not only does he immerse himself in the thing chosen, but in the act of choosing or in what Kierkegaard calls "choosing to will," a person chooses to be. To avoid choosing, to deliberate, to postpone is to fall short of real personhood.

These were some of the ideas Rølvaag encountered in Kierkegaard's *Either/Or.* In varying degrees these same ideas inform other Ibsen plays and, especially, *Brand,* in which the clarion theme of All or Nothing is surpassed only by the imperative of choice itself. About the play, set in Norway's forbidding mountains, Rølvaag said it chilled him to the marrow of his bones. "But that chill did something for me. It made me run on and on and on." In his lecture notes about Ibsen's plays Rølvaag wrote: "We fairly reel as we peer into the depths that he opens. . . . He seems to wage the despairing struggle of a strong soul against the riddles of eternity, which he feels that no soul can solve. His [Brand's] is a Prometheus-like combat . . . a Titan's heaven-storming struggle to find light." Affirming his own oneness with the spirit of Brand, Rølvaag continues: "Of his motto 'All or Nothing' I have nothing but good to say. . . . The motto is in perfect harmony with the teachings of Christ." Determined to pursue this theme, Rølvaag, as it were, set his own face to go up to Jerusalem. (pp. 67-8)

Existence in terms of either/or was Kiekegaard's answer to Hegel's idea of "synthesis" which includes and also reconciles the contradictory ideas of "thesis" and "antithesis." This notion of mediation was as abhorrent to Kiekegaard as was the timorous postponement of choice itself. To Kierkegaard mediation meant compromise. Whereas the concept of either/or is "the pass which admits to the absolute" and "the key of heaven," the concept of both/and, Kierkegaard said, is "the

way to hell." With equal fervor Ibsen's Brand declares, "Compromise is the way of Satan." The devil that Brand saw was the spirit of moderation, luxury, ease, and moral laziness among the dull and cloddish townspeople. As for Rølvaag's Per Hansa, a heroic superiority shines forth in his great decision to face the unknown west. In his choosing to will, a choice which lifts his existence into the ethical, he finds his selfhood. That his son Peder Victorious embodies compromise suggests something of a diminished if not withered sense of being.

Heroic in his choosing, Per Hansa is fallen in his choice. This is the paradox informing great tragedy. Choice and the dreadful possibility of damnation are inseparable. Moreover, if choice bespeaks the freedom to choose, then even the most heroic self-attainment is doomed. Grand as Per Hansa was in choosing to build a "new kingdom," as equally darksome was his pride and, in Christian terms, his sin for presupposing total human initiative. His choice in the end did not lie merely between two cultures or between tradition and freedom but between human initiative and divine imperative. What Per Hansa never came to realize was that the problem of life was not the discovery of an ideal or the power of will whereby to achieve it but rather the redirection of the will away from self and toward the ruling sovereignty of God. Ultimately, choice must give way to faith, which is not a matter of will but of grace.

Giants in the Earth is far more than a national epic of immigration and the westward movement. Its underlying issue is salvation, and Per Hansa is as far from it at the end of the novel as he was at the beginning. That he achieved Kierkegaard's ethical level of choice raises him to the stature of a tragic hero. But of Kierkegaard's religious level of faith he knows nothing. At the heart of the matter is the question of will, basic in Pauline and Reformed theology and best spoken of in America by Jonathan Edwards. Will is as its strongest motive is. Prior to will by which a person chooses is a more fundamental cause identified as motive. According to one's motive, so he chooses; as he chooses, so he acts. But again the paradox arises: the free act of choice is already determined by a prior motive which among the unregenerate is always that of self-love. The credo of natural man is always not Thy will but mine be done. Per Hansa leaves no doubt as to whose will is sovereign for him and whose kingdom he seeks. (pp. 68-70)

In [Kierkegaard's] *Fear and Trembling,* he re-told the story of Abraham and Isaac in order to contrast the ethical world view of either/or with the religious imperatives that take priority over all ethical principles. On the abstract and ethical level of right or wrong Abraham's sacrifice of Isaac was patently and universally wrong; but God's sovereign commands, not bound by any set of principles or laws, were made singularly to Abraham and required of him the suspension of the ethical in favor of the teleological—because the *telos* involved was God. According to Kierkegaard, it was not that Abraham balanced the claims of ethical principles against the claims of God and then chose the latter, but rather that as between the two Abraham believed in the latter. With purity of heart he took the leap of faith. In *Fear and Trembling* Kierkegaard presented a Lutheran denunciation of ethical moralism which had substituted abstract principles for God's authority. The faith of Luther, Kierkegaard, and finally that of Rølvaag's Beret in *Giants in the Earth* ruled out both a moralistic interpretation of God's action and a self-willed choice as the way of human response. God's design was clearly more than a system of ethical ideas requiring choice on the part of His people. Instead, His was a glory requiring faith through grace.

Throughout Rølvaag's novel the tension between Per Hansa and Beret corresponds to these two Kierkegaardian levels of existence. We notice that despite Per Hansa's "indomitable, conquering mood" and what at times appear to be his super-human achievements against the elemental forces of earth and sky, a note of apprehensiveness like some dimly minor key surfaces repeatedly in Beret's moods and words. This presence, of course, has psychological causes related to her loneliness on the desolate prairie, her deep need for tradition, and her guilt for pregnancy out of wedlock. But Rølvaag intends something more in the spiritual desolation Beret feels as she joins Per Hansa in his work and vision. As the farms all around get finer and the barns bigger, the certainty of divine judgment overwhelms her. To Beret the psychological cost in leaving their fathers' homeland is nothing when compared with the spiritual cost in forsaking their fathers' God. In Per Hansa's pride she has a terrible sense of God's condemnation. (pp. 71-72)

The real dilemma Rølvaag sets before Per Hansa and Beret is not that of Norwegian versus American claims but that of culture *per se* on the one hand and an existential religious consciousness on the other. As between All or Nothing, Per Hansa's cultural All becomes Beret's Nothing, just as her religious All was his Nothing.

Yet why does Rølvaag stress with such compulsion the need for the immigrants to retain their Norwegian traditions? Jorgenson and Solum provide abundant evidence that in his St. Olaf College lectures and his many speeches and sermons in the community Rølvaag argued for the continued nurture of

Rølvaag's revised typescript of Giants in the Earth. *Courtesy of The Norwegian-American Historical Association, St. Olaf College.*

these roots, especially those of language, the Lutheran church, and what he considered the personal traits of Scandinavians as a people. Perhaps reasons can be found in Rølvaag's deep loyalty to his own Norwegian roots which he traumatically severed when he first came to America at the age of twenty. The pain and guilt he suffered in leaving his parents shook him again and again. Nevertheless, despite his persistent call for cultural continuities including institutional Lutheranism, this call has a penultimate emphasis at best, and the essential point finally has to do with religious claims. In spite of Beret's indomitable effort to preserve her Norwegian ways, her greater strivings concern a transcendent faith.

How to handle the religious level of experience in art has tortured many creative persons, including Kierkegaard who lived to aver the ultimate discontinuity between art and religion, imagination and faith. Rølvaag never thought of himself as one to grapple with these theological subtleties, though from his early years he was interested in such speculation and, as a student at St. Olaf College, thought seriously of entering the ministry. That he chose to be a teacher and novelist did not diminish this seriousness. When he came to write his second novel, *On Forgotten Paths* . . . , he was actuated partly by a desire to prove that religious experience could in fact be made the central element in a secular novel. And when he started *Giants in the Earth* in the autumn of 1923 his own religious consciousness had conceived of God as a being "Who is searching and pressing and pushing even as life itself is." Rølvaag's matrix, however, serves only to point in the direction of Beret's religious experience in the novel. This experience is best seen in the tension, already discussed, between the Kierkegaardian levels exemplified by Per Hansa and herself. These ethical and religious levels serve to structure the novel, with Per Hansa dominating three-fourths of the narrative but giving way in the last portion to Beret. (pp. 72-73)

The authenticity given to Beret's religious experience comes in the way she resembles Kierkegaard's knight of faith who finds strength that is impotence, wisdom that is foolishness, hope that is madness, and love that is hatred of self. The knight of faith in Kierkegaard's *Fear and Trembling* discovers joy in the absurd and, like Abraham, believes "by virtue of the absurd." The absurd is the paradox without which faith becomes only an extension of ethical choice. Kierkegaard rejected any concept of faith not based upon the radical distinction between religious faith and ethical choice. For Rølvaag's Beret the paradox of believing by virtue of the absurd meant that all motives and all achievements were challenged, including those of her husband and the whole immigrant community. In the challenge, moreover, was a singular and terrifying self-with-God relationship that required the particular to be higher than the universal and that left Beret separated from the rest, face to face with her destiny, with God Himself who had singled her out. (p. 76)

From the regulative view of Per Hansa's world, the divine imperatives Beret obeys are an outrage and affront. They are an offense. In Per Hansa's totally human scheme Hans Olsa's avowal is even blasphemous. At issue is the ground of being itself. When the authority of God-fearingness collides with that of human initiative, hard work, fortitude, and imagination; when God's order contradicts human expectations; when, in Kierkegaard's terms, the particular contravenes the universal, or when a transcendent kingdom challenges the new American one, the result is an offense to those persons committed in each case to the latter and to those whose foundations of self-reliance have been truly shaken. (p. 77)

That Per Hansa yields to Beret at the cost of his life does not point to the direction future Americans would take. Rølvaag's next two novels [*Peder Victorious* and *Their Father's God*] make this point emphatic enough. Americans would tolerate no such taunting and accept no such condemnation. Their kingdom would need no reliance upon divine initiative, and it would harbor no concern for any so-called "offense." Yet we have Beret's judgment and her vision.

This is not to say that Rølvaag stands unequivocally with Beret. He admired Per Hansa's barn-building; indeed he transformed this immigrant Norwegian into a giant whose heroic will enabled him to bear any load. Yet for all his strength, Per Hansa refuses the one burden the minister calls him to take up. No, says the giant of the earth, "We find other things to do out here than to carry crosses!" . . . Rølvaag has struck here his profoundest level of irony, its antithesis reflected in Beret's strength of spirit.

That Rølvaag stands closer to Beret than to Per Hansa remains intriguing speculation. Perhaps the more cautious estimate is that he stands closer to Beret than has been generally assumed. What seems clear, however, is that Kierkegaard's ideas never stopped simmering, and that the distinction he drew between the tragic hero who exists on the ethical level and the knight of faith who exists on the religious level informed Rølvaag's major writing. To Rølvaag the demands of great art exceeded even the question of All or Nothing; to him art demanded nothing less than the impossible. A clue to what Rølvaag meant comes in his analysis of Ibsen's *Peer Gynt*, first on the level of aesthetics, then on that of ethics, and finally on that of religion. It is on this level, he said, that Ibsen's play "glorifies the efficacy of unselfish sacrifice. We might state the ideal thus: 'Take up your cross and follow me!'" Per Hansa might be a great American, but Beret is a truer Christian. And Rølvaag knew the difference. (pp. 78-9)

> *Harold P. Simonson, "Rølvaag and Kierkegaard,"*
> in Scandinavian Studies, *Vol. 49, No. 1, Winter,*
> *1977, pp. 67-80.**

STEVE HAHN (essay date 1979)

[*In the following excerpt, Hahn explores Rølvaag's use of Norse mythology and Christian faith to portray the spiritual and physical isolation of the protagonists of* Giants in the Earth.]

Ole E. Rølvaag intended *Giants in the Earth* to be more than just a novel about pioneer life on the Great Plains frontier. . . . [His] interest in the human drama of self takes precedence over the physical drama inherent in the novel. In this he was following the lead of perhaps his greatest influence, Henrik Ibsen, whose concern with the human psyche transcended the physical environment of his characters. Ibsen believed that "to be of more than local or trivial appeal a historical drama must also be a psychological drama." Rølvaag's intense portrayals of Beret and Per Hansa confirm his adherence to this dictum. Lincoln Colcord's introduction to the English edition of *Giants in the Earth* states, "It is a unique experience . . . to have this novel . . . so palpably European in its art and atmosphere, so distinctly American in everything it deals with" [see excerpt dated 1927]. Upon examination of the novel, however, it may be seen that not everything dealt with is "distinctly American." The major psychological themes in *Giants in the Earth*, though of universal application, are pointedly Norwegian in composition. What we have, then, is a novel with a tense dichotomy of structure: the physical world of the Great Plains, and a reality which is envisioned in terms of Norwegian religious and cultural structures.

The purely physical theme of *Giants,* the settling of the American frontier, is "distinctly American," of course. Even this historically American event has an explicitly Norse flavor, however, judging from the title of Book I in both the Norwegian and English editions. The original "Landnam" in *I de dage* and "The Landtaking" in *Giants* recall the Norse *Landnámmabópk* ("The Book of the Land-taking"), the account of Norse colonization in Iceland. Rølvaag's association of the Norwegian settlers with their Norse pioneering ancestors is no shallow allusion. By doing so, he equates the South Dakota narrative to the Iceland folk settlement, and associates it, therefore, with epic saga literature. Apart from historical implications, the identification with the saga helps to create much of the psychological tension in the novel, for the ways in which Beret and Per Hansa interpret their experiences are based on old "pagan" Norse belief as well as Christian viewpoints.

Rølvaag's vision of the Norwegian settlers in *Giants* is that of a people who cannot escape their heritage; they are part and parcel of Norwegian culture, displaced though they may be. The land itself is not Norwegian; it does, however, possess qualities which the settlers perceive as being Norwegian. The land perception of the Norwegians is a device constantly used by Rølvaag to portray their alienation from their homeland, their separation from a spiritual knowledge of the world, and their inability to impose a traditional sense of order on the new landscape. This perception is first delineated in Nordic, rather than Christian terms. (pp. 85-6)

The Plains setting presents a duality of meaning in . . . [the] first scenes of *Giants*. On the one hand, in its reality, it is simply a "wilderness"; on the other, the plains have acquired an added supernatural dimension in the minds of Per Hansa and, especially, Beret. They immediately apply to the Plains their own sense of cosmological structure, a reflection of Norse as well as Christian belief. The land is seen in a physical sense, but it also projects a non-human dimension, like the habitation of trolls and giants in Utgard, the third ring and Outer World in the Norse cosmology. The human world, or Midgard, of this structure, is reduced to the knowable self and has no physical realm. This estrangement from the land is vital in interpreting the perceptions of Beret and Per Hansa. (p. 87)

Per Hansa's physical existence is one entirely different from his mental state. He plows and plants like any homesteader; however, these actions are, on another level, deeds he must do to gain his kingdom from the trolls. The land, then, presents two faces to Per Hansa. At its physical level, it is the makings of his real life, his farm; on the visionary level, the land is the makings of a kingdom, controlled by forces he must defeat. To explain this characterization, one must consider factors other than the Old Norse influence on Rølvaag. His familiarity with the folk figure of the *Askeladd* (ash-boy) is certainly evident in this dual perception of Per Hansa's. The *Askeladd*, the Norwegian equivalent of English-world "Cinderella" stories and the Germanic figure "*Aschenputtel*", is, in its simplest form, a story of triumph over adversity; Bruno Bettelheim also notes that the form stresses the importance of being oneself. It would also do well, in the interpretation of Per Hansa's dual perception of both himself and the land, to recall Rølvaag's familiarity with Pietism on his native Dønna and his admiration of Ibsen's *Brand*, whose protagonist was based partially on the Pietistic clergyman Lammers. Ibsen, in turn, developed Kierkegaardian traits in Brand, although Kierkegaard's direct influence on the playwright is an obscure subject. Per Hansa's dual perception can be taken as an example of Kierkegaard's concept of the aesthetic (passion) and the ethical (reason). Kierkegaard writes, "... he who lives aesthetically seeks as far as possible to be absorbed in mood, he seeks to hide himself entirely in it, so that there remains nothing in him which cannot be inflected into it." Per Hansa the aesthetic man sees his homesteading in mythological terms of hero (himself) and monster (his demonic perception of the land). The ethical man, however, "... being endowed with reason, can apprehend God directly as Idea and Law, transcend his finite bodily passions, and become like God." So Per Hansa the ethical man exults in his creativity as a sower and the builder of a perfect world. . . .

Beret's psychology assumes a new character in the wake of her discovery of the tampered land-stakes. . . . Her response to her situation turns from a vague fear to an inward resignation and moralism. She is vocal in her condemnation of Per Hansa's actions; prior to this, there had been little basis for an outright Christian condemnation of her husband. The removal of land markers, however, is a grave sin against both God and fellow humans. It moves her to remark upon what she sees as their chief danger out on the Plains, the loss of their religion: "Remember what the Book says: 'Cursed be he that removeth his neighbour's landmarks! And all the people shall say, Amen.' . . . words like these we used to heed . . . In my opinion, we'd better take care lest we all turn into beasts and savages out here!'" . . . Beret's Norse perceptions are not evident here; the image of the Plains as Utgard is being supplanted by a Christian concept of evil. Her pietistic development becomes more pronounced: "Beret had grown more sober as the autumn came, more locked up within herself; a heavy heart lay all the time in her bosom." . . . Resigned to a life which she regards as sinful, her obedience to a divine will becomes fully developed during this chapter, "Facing the Great Desolation." (pp. 90-1)

Rølvaag's Norwegian motifs are constructed, in Book I, of three parts: Norse, folk (fairy tale), and Christian. As we have seen, it is Beret who provides the Norse-Christian tension; Per Hansa expresses the folk motif as well. These three themes are used throughout Book II; it is the Christian theme which dominates the remaining narrative, however, for the question of self is Rølvaag's prime concern. Though the Norse and folk backgrounds of Per Hansa and Beret continue to express themselves, it is their Christianity which will determine the survival of their physical and spiritual worlds. (p. 94)

The coming of the Norwegian pastor to Spring Creek produces change in the lives of both Per Hansa and Beret. He serves, for each, as an organizer of their power to love in the Christian sense. Beret's life on the Plains has been one of "negative" Christianity; not able to live by a doctrine of grace, which she sees as absent on the Plains, she has resorted to a doctrine of a wrathful God. Beret's transformation is slow in coming; she is distrustful of the pastor at first, reflecting perhaps the Haugean disdain for the church hierarchy: "'He is playing us false . . . he will lead us to something that is not good'." . . . This distrust deepens to fear; the pastor becomes another instrument of the devil, and she tries to prevent the baptism of Peder Victorious. . . . At the same time, Per Hansa is not ready to yield to a will other than his own, rejecting the pastor's suggestion that his self-pride and his will have led him into sin: "'We find other things to do out here than carry crosses!'." . . . The pastor, however, is able to renew Per Hansa's faith in himself: "... he experienced a blessing descending

upon him, and his burden grew lighter." . . . The kingdom fantasy has been tempered by Per Hansa's recognition of a will greater than his own. . . . (p. 97)

[But it] is Beret who emerges as the survivor of this story, for she retains the means to order her life, to create a knowable world for herself. Per Hansa cannot accept the concept of love which the pastor has shown him; it would require him to recognize not only a will, but a love, greater than his own. The final scenes are ironic in that it is Beret, through what she sees as the will of God, who forces Per Hansa out "into the jaws of death." . . . Here we have the ultimate drama of self in the novel: will versus duty. It is not that Beret's sense of duty toward God and her fellow Christians triumphs over Per Hansa's sense of will, for Per Hansa's journey into the blizzard is his last great battle against the trolls, a final quest for the Soria Moria of self. If he is, as Jorgenson and Solum write, "a symbol of the entire westward movement," then that movement was one of courageous but foolish Romanticism, devoid of the means which were needed to establish valid cultural and spiritual structures. Having cut himself off from the Norwegian quarries of culture, Per Hansa has little with which to build on the barren Plains. For Beret, the important direction is east, back across the ocean to Norway; only through the means of the knowable is she able to survive in the strange land of the Great Plains. (p. 98)

Steve Hahn, "Vision and Reality in 'Giants in the Earth'," in The South Dakota Review, *Vol. 17, No. 1, Spring, 1979, pp. 85-100.*

KRISTOFFER PAULSON (essay date 1980)

[*In the following excerpt Paulson explores themes of loss in* The Boat of Longing, *a novel he regards as the quintessential expression of Rølvaag's lifelong concern with the cultural and psychological disruption caused by emigration.*]

In Ole Rølvaag's first published book [*Amerika-breve*], a series of "Letters from America," the immigrant Per Smevik in South Dakota writes to a brother in Norway answering his questions about what he could eventually gain by coming to America. Per's answer is to ask, "Why don't you turn the question around and ask what you would lose?" He continues by saying that "Last year at a Fourth of July celebration . . . I heard a speech on the theme: 'What is gained and what is lost, upon exchanging the Fatherland for the new land.'" The climactic 4th of July speech in this book, *The Third Life of Per Smevik,* shows a paradoxical balance sheet for Norwegian emigration, with the final entries on the loss side of the ledger: "First they tried to become Americans, but found they couldn't; then they wanted to become Norwegians again, but found that to be equally impossible. Herein lies the tragedy of emigration."

All of Rølvaag's novels follow a tragic pattern, inevitably ending in catastrophe. However romantic, buoyant and optimistic his characters appear to be during the course of the drama, tragedy awaits them at the end. In *The Boat of Longing,* . . . Rølvaag gives this tragic vision his most personal, intimate, and moving treatment. Referring to *The Boat of Longing,* Rølvaag frequently stated that he had put more of himself "into that book than into any other."

The opening sentence of *The Boat of Longing* leads to the quintessential center of Rølvaag's art, and everything in Rølvaag works out from the center. He opens by saying that the place, a point of land with one fisherman's home on it, lay far out to sea: "The place lay on the sea, as far out as the coast dared push itself, and extremely far north, so far, in fact, that it penetrated the termless solitudes where utmost Light and utmost Dark hold tryst." . . . Central to this passage and to the artistry of Rølvaag's novels is the tension of opposites, the clash of extremes. All of Rølvaag's works may be seen in microcosm within this single sentence, moving out from it in an ever widening whorl caused by the clash of eternal opposites, dominated first by one and then another extreme, never static but constantly shifting, rising and falling like the sea, the season, the day and life itself. One need only think of *Giants in the Earth* and the tension of wills characterizing Per Hansa and Beret and their reactions to emigration, to the prairie, and to the temporal and spiritual kingdoms they wish to build on the South Dakota prairie.

The clashes between realism and romance create the power and tension within Rølvaag's *The Boat of Longing*. Rølvaag plays realism off against romance to create his action, his characters, his philosophy, his symbols and his themes. On a realistic level Nils Vaag, sensitive and only son of Jo and Anna, lives on this point of land—so far out and so far north. On a fishing trip he discovers a shipwrecked girl, Zalma, and his family befriends her. She responds to Nils's love when he plays haunting melodies on the violin. His father, Jo by the Sea, fearing the developing relationship between his Norwegian son and this foreign and different girl, arranges to have her sent away while Nils is off on a fishing trip. This act of exclusion and disappearance sets the stage for the repeated images of disappearance throughout the novel. Unable to face his familiar surroundings without Zalma, Nils makes the choice to emigrate to America to find his future.

On the romantic level Rølvaag models Nils Vaag on the Askeladden, the hero of Norwegian fairy tales. In the fairy tale the Askeladden finds the path, kills the troll, frees the princess and succeeds to the inheritance of Soria Moria, the golden castle and kingdom, which lies east of the sun and "way to the west of the moon." . . . Soria Moria is symbolic of success and fulfillment: love, wealth, fame, and the highest endeavors of artistic and spiritual aspiration. For Rølvaag the character of the Askeladden was both "a projection of the deepest aspirations in the national mind, and . . . [also] a fellow traveler in life." Nils's dream of America corresponds to the Askeladden's dream of Soria Moria, but in *The Boat of Longing* Nils's quest remains unfulfilled. His dream of fulfillment in the promised land of America darkens and then vanishes, just like the "boat" in the folklore of Nordland.

The boat of *The Boat of Longing* is the phantom ship that appears on the western horizon along the northern coast of Norway. It appears to those about to die, to those who have lost lovers, and to those who search for Soria Moria, that is, to those who would attempt the highest endeavors of artistic and spiritual aspiration. . . . (pp. 51-2)

Shortly after Zalma is secretly sent away, Nils and his family see the boat on the western horizon "right in the sun, where the eye would have difficulty in capturing it." . . . Ignoring the terrified warnings of his parents Nils rows out to reach it: "Straight on the Boat, discernible through the evening dimness, Nils seemed to hold his course." . . . He continues rowing through the twilight night of the midnight sun, indifferent to everything except the "only one thought dominating him: 'I must see that Boat.' Goal other than those sails floating out there on the sea rim he did not have." . . . As he seems to

come closer he hears a "tone" emanating from the boat: "Not song. Nor yet the tone of an instrument. An interweaving rather of song and violin." . . . But at dawn, just as he seems to have gained his goal, he "was brought to his senses by a deafening roar [and] the sea in every direction fairly boiled with fish." . . . Interrupted in his pursuit of the phantom boat, he starts the trawling lines and begins to haul in one huge black cod after another: "Yet in the midst of the wild joy of battle the consciousness of his goal stood clearly before him: he was heading straight for the Boat." . . . But a moment later the boat has disappeared and he "abandoned himself wholly to the mad joy of the fight." . . .

That scene dramatically renders the Kierkegaardian existential choice of "*Either/Or*." At the crucial point of existential choice, Nils falters in his quest for the unknowable, and allows his singleness of will to become double-minded. At the point of the final leap of faith Nils chooses "Both/And" rather than holding to the singleness of will demanded by the existential choice of "Either/Or." Rølvaag was familiar with Søren Kierkegaard's work, *Either/Or* and very familiar with *Purity of Heart Is to Will One Thing*, the first of Kierkegaard's *Edifying Discourses*, 1847. Rølvaag delivered a sermon, "What Is It to Will One Thing?" to the St. Olaf College Luther League on March 18, 1907, a point by point rendering of Kierkegaard's first "Discourse." Rølvaag's sermon stresses that "there is only one thing between heaven and earth which in its essence is one, and that is the good." He goes on to say that "If you are going to in truth will only one thing, then you must will the good. Anything else is not one, and if you want the other you are double-minded." Because double-mindedness is worldly, for Rølvaag, and for Kierkegaard, to will one thing in worldly terms is impossible: "neither pleasure, nor wealth, nor power, nor honor is one in its essence."

Note that Nils is indifferent to everything except that "only one thought" of reaching the boat, but he is brought back to his "senses" by the "deafening roar" of the rising black cod, a roar which overwhelms the mystical "tone" coming from the boat. (p. 53)

This scene calls forth the clash of extremes and the tension of opposites: the boat is romantically and philosophically symbolic, but the quest is specifically realistic. In this scene Rølvaag fuses thought and emotion. He has "the power of impregnating thought with emotion" and "making psychological analysis palpitate with dramatic interest." . . .

The second section, "In Foreign Waters," dramatizes Nils's experiences as a young Norwegian newcomer to Minneapolis about 1910. (p. 54)

On a Sunday night walk Nils hears a man haranguing a crowd on a downtown street corner. Nils's English is not good enough to understand the speech, but he repeatedly hears the word "injustice," and later asks his friend Weisman the meaning of the word:

> "*Injustice?*" The Poet blew his nose with a deafening crack as he reiterated the word. "*Injustice?* That's what I've suffered from my people. . . .
>
> "Can you imagine a person," he continued, "who walks about among fellow beings and is not seen by them? He meets one, stops and talks to him. He whom he addresses passes by

in care-free complacency. He has not heard him, not seen him? . . .

> "The lone one moves on. He encounters thousands, hails them, calls with might and main— only to find that not one among the thousand is even aware of his presence?" . . .

Observe the startling similarity in both theme and imagery of this passage from Rølvaag's *The Boat of Longing* with those of Ralph Ellison's *Invisible Man*. Ellison opens his odyssey with a metaphor of invisibility, a metaphor which controls the entire novel: "I am an invisible man. . . . I am invisible, understand, simply because people refuse to see me. . . . When they approach me they see only my surrounding, themselves, or figments of their imagination—indeed everything and anything except me."

The metaphor of invisibility is obviously unique neither to Black literature nor to immigrant literature, but appears in both. These two authors, Rølvaag, a Norwegian-American, and Ellison, a Black-American, come from widely divergent backgrounds and yet both disclose strikingly correspondent attitudes toward the American experience. In Rølvaag's works the impossibility of the immigrant to enter the promised land of America without losing his soul and his identity becomes in Ellison the Black's loss of identity through his repeated expulsions from American society to a world of second-class citizenship.

The Boat of Longing is Rølvaag's most powerful and extended treatment of this vision of the immigrants' existential hell, their complete loss of identity, their invisibility within American society. The repeated image of immigrant invisibility is Rølvaag's main point. He specifically and continually repeats his image of disappearance without a trace, like mirrors within mirrors, or the Russian doll which contains another and then another doll within it. (pp. 54-5)

The final section, "Hearts That Ache," has Jo by the Sea, Nils's father, finally going to America in search of both boys. When he arrives at Ellis Island, however, he learns that because he is more than sixty years old and has no guaranteed support during his stay, he cannot enter. He is literally excluded from the promised land.

Jo is forced to remain on Ellis Island until the ship on which he came is ready to return to Norway. On this return voyage he is able to convince himself that Nils now lives in a castle in Minneapolis. The day Jo returns home he repeats to his wife, Anna, his fantasy which had taken on "the strange spell of a fairy tale." . . . The scene is one of dramatic irony and pain, for the reader knows the truth of Jo's fruitless journey to America and that Nils has not found Soria Moria, has not won the inheritance. And that evening Jo by the Sea takes out his boat, ostensibly to fish, but in fact to follow a golden cloud on the western horizon, which he envisions as the Soria Moria Castle, "where dwelt his boy." . . . Just as Nils's vision of the unblessed chasm destroys his dream of Soria Moria, so the reality of the final paragraph in the novel destroys Jo's fantasy of finding Nils in the Soria Moria Castle of his dreams:

> Jo by the Sea was seen no more. Folk thought it strange that they didn't find the boat, though the search was both long and thorough. No one could explain it. For it had been a still night. An off-wind had, to be sure, set in in the course of the morning; but even so it should have been possible to find the boat. But there was never so much as a sliver seen of it. . . .

Some readers might consider this concluding section of the novel unsatisfactory. None of the reader's natural questions about what happened to Nils are ever answered. But the reality of Nils's disappearance into the void, the reality of his becoming invisible, the reality that "not one among the thousand is even aware of his presence," is the controlling metaphor and thematic point of the novel. Rølvaag knew exactly what he was doing. (pp. 57-8)

In the tension of opposites, the clash of extremes that hold tryst in Rølvaag's novels, the realistic, the tragic, and the Dark, invariably overwhelm the romantic, the comic and the Light. . . . (p. 58)

The Boat of Longing is Rølvaag's attempt to give artistic expression to this feeling—to dramatize and clarify the inexpressible. Rølvaag does hope for some kind of redemption, but his comments projecting realizable hopes of redemption are general and occur outside his novels, outside the artistic integrity of the novels themselves. In his subsequent novels, that hope inevitably leads to even darker layers of the tragedy of the immigrant American tempted farther and farther on as the mirage of promise recedes even farther away toward the horizon, like the Boat of Longing itself, until it finally vanishes and becomes invisible. (pp. 58-9)

> *Kristoffer Paulson, "What Was Lost: Ole Rølvaag's 'The Boat of Longing'," in MELUS, Vol. 7, No. 1, Spring, 1980, pp. 51-60.*

PATRICK D. MORROW (essay date 1980)

[*In the following excerpt Morrow discusses Rølvaag's utilization of and departure from tragic conventions in* Giants in the Earth, *a novel he ranks alongside the great American tragedies* A Farewell to Arms, The Sound and the Fury, *and* The Red Badge of Courage. *Morrow finds earlier critical interpretations of the characters Per and Beret Hansa incomplete, for he believes previous critics neglected to fully address the tragic nature of each. For further discussion of the importance of these characters, see the excerpts by Joseph E. Baker (1942), Harold P. Simonson (1977), and Paul A. Olson (1981).*]

> It's nothing but a common, ordinary romantic lie that we are 'captains of our own souls'! Nothing but one of those damned poetic phrases. Just look back over your own life and see how much you have captained!

This statement by Ole Rølvaag, less about fate than the human error of false pride, points us in a rewarding direction for an interpretation of *Giants in the Earth*. Concerned with *hamartia*, irreconcilable values, and dramatically rising to state man's universal predicament, Rølvaag's masterpiece is fundamentally a tragedy. Henry Steel Commager [see excerpt dated 1927] and Vernon Louis Parrington suggested this possibility in 1927, shortly after the book's publication. But neither Commager nor Parrington shed much light on Rølvaag's methods for establishing *Giants* as a tragedy. Since those early days, the considerable scholarship on this important writer has pretty much moved to do battle on other fronts. Yet, by understanding *Giants* as a tragedy, I believe we can resolve much critical debate over the novel, especially about Beret and Per Hansa; perceive the book's real form, motivations, and complex thematic unity; and finally, appreciate Rølvaag's intention and considerable accomplishments as an artist.

Rølvaag develops *Giants in the Earth* as a tragedy by several methods. . . . In terms of genre, tragedy becomes established with a process of definition by negation. Rølvaag includes many aspects and conventions of both saga and epic, but then undercuts both by parodying them, and by having the tragic aspects increasingly dominate as his novel progresses. In terms of form, *Giants* has ten chapters of five well-defined acts, adhering to the tragic rhythm of exposition, conflict, crisis, and catastrophe. Unities of time and place appear with the predictable seasons, tragic winter being dominant, and almost all action takes place within the Norwegian prairie settlements. Imitations of Ibsen's dramas and Shakespearian tragedy abound, hardly surprising since from early youth Ole Rølvaag had been an avid reader of great literature. . . . Finally, for the key issue of tragic recognition, Rølvaag fashions out of his Norwegian milieu and literary consciousness, a particularly American awareness. (pp. 83-4)

It seems widely agreed that tragedy emphasizes free will and individual responsibility, rather than inevitability and an external determinism, so happy in the saga or epic, but so dismal in naturalism. A tragic work typically presents a chain of events leading to catastrophe, often depicting a fall from high or successful station because of the hero's pride or *hybris,* an apt description of Per Hansa's life journey and fate. Some kind of chorus or community voice may function as spokesman for society's viewpoint and values. In *Giants in the Earth* the chorus not only advises but judges. As a community, they support Per; but later, as a congregation, they start to rally behind Beret.

Giants also has a tragic rhythm—nothing so episodic as scenes constructed and then struck, but a thematic movement of wax and wane. The exposition, the establishment of this Norwegian colony on the far edge of the prairie, is long, almost three and a half chapters. About midway in Chapter IV, "What the Waving Grass Revealed," Beret's disaffiliation and conflict with Per begins to become the book's dominant issue. Beret's withdrawal and conflict become deeper, even shocking, until a crisis is reached in Chapter VIII, "The Power of Evil in High Places." After a chapter of reprieve or counter-action, the catastrophe is consummated in the final chapter with its outrageous title. Before we can understand the recognition phase, the final tragic aspect in this book, we must see the terms of this tragedy.

Professor Harold Simonson has suggested [in a paper read before the Western Literature Association on October 7, 1977] that *Giants in the Earth* presents two intersecting but irreconcilable dimensions, Time (Beret) and Space (Per). Simonson is concerned with the opposition between traditional Lutheran faith and the frontier ethic in *Giants,* but if expanded, this notion can also clarify the tragic character conflict in this novel. Forceful, physically powerful and handsome, skillful and even lucky, Per Hansa is a great natural leader. He loves the frontier because it is so expansive, a fitting, infinite surface on which to move his will, enact his own destiny and that of his people. Per attempts to change the prairie, or conquer time, by establishing a kind of immortality with his pioneer kingdom. Per's will and ego fill all space. Morally, he is a pragmatic teleologist who first ignores then hates the past. In the tradition of American Romanticism, he sees himself motivated by a dream of absolute good and right. Per fears rejection by those whom he leads far more than he fears impending failure because of the overwhelmingly hostile Dakota environment with its blizzards, floods, wind, clay soil, and grasshopper plagues. Per Hansa has confused his dream with reality.

As Per acts in terms of his vision, Beret acts in terms of consequences. Beret is the party of time; she wants to find her place in history, not escape it. Beret is defined and informed by what has already been created, and thus she is drawn to the old Norwegian culture, the Lutheran religion, and such other institutions as education, motherhood, and being a wife. Within an established community, institutions have been developed to deal with time, ritualizing the cycle of birth, growth, and death. But the prairie is infinity, as Rølvaag relentlessly reminds us throughout *Giants,* the zone where space cancels time, making the individual reach an absolutely Kirkegaardian state of being forever alone. . . . From this beginning, then, Beret is literally and figuratively "spaced-out."

Nevertheless, as critic Barbara Meldrum [see Gerald Thorson entry in Additional Bibliography] has established, Beret can control her disorientation and depression until she comes to feel that Per Hansa has rejected her. Like Hester in *The Scarlet Letter,* Beret is no witch, but a passionate woman. She does feel guilt for her productive passion with Per, but her love for him continues to increase. Out on the prairie, she loses all sense of purpose with the realization that it is his dream, not Beret, which Per loves more than life. Beret comes to see Per as a person without fear, totally, blindly committed to his vision through his all-consuming pride. Per is thus daemonic, and the consequences for following this evil course shall most certainly be destruction. Beret must bear this burden alone. She has reached a Cassandra-like impasse—doomed to knowledge, but never to be believed because he who hears her cries heeds only his own voice.

In terms of Per's dream and the ideal goals of the community, Beret does indeed lose her sanity. But in Beret's terms, her bizzare behavior—having tea with her absent mother, sleeping in her hope chest, ceasing her household chores, and attacking Per for godless megalomania—ritualizes punishment for worshipping Per, the false god, her punishment for sins against time. Beret is not, as Lloyd Hustvedt once half-seriously proffered, "a party pooper out on the prairie." Nor is she a pietistic, guilt-ridden fanatic bent on precipitating Per Hansa's early death. Nor is she the opposing view, Kirkegaard's "Knight of Faith" following God's divine imperative [see excerpt by Harold P. Simonson dated 1977]. However critically misunderstood, Beret remains a very human character, very hurt, and very much alone, pursuing a direction out of her moral and emotional wilderness by the only way she trusts. (pp. 85-7)

That *Giants in the Earth* is a tragedy of two characters frozen in their irreconcilable dimensions may now seem evident, but where is that tragic recognition scene that changes and enlightens the protagonist? Since, as Maynard Mack reminds us, "tragic drama is in one way or other, a record of man's affair with transcendence," where might this transcendence be found? Nowhere in the novel. Playing his trump card of dramatic irony, of making his characters realize less about themselves than the audience understands, Rølvaag throws not only the burden of interpretation but the responsibility of awareness squarely on his readers. Far from undercutting tragic conventions, by this strategy Rølvaag expands *Giants* into relevance, into our own dimension and consciousness.

Four key scenes in *Giants,* all revealing to the audience rather than to the characters, establish our participatory role in this tragic novel. The first is that opening scene of the prairie as mystical infinity, a landscape more formidable and incomprehensible than any of the characters. The second scene is the visitation of the grief-stricken and insane Kari, her husband Jakob, and their children. This episode forms a kind of play-within-a-play, a dumbshow or mirroring device for the relationship between Per and Beret. Kari's hysteria is Beret's largely self-contained depression put into action, and Jakob surely must be enacting a Per Hansa fantasy by roping Kari down in the wagon and saying: "Physically she seems as well as ever. . . . She certainly hasn't overworked since we've been travelling." . . . The third scene is the christening of Peder Victorius, where the Per-Beret schism becomes public, but here too, actions are taken and positions are stated without any understanding by the characters. This pattern continues into the last scene. Per departs for his death with an almost spitefully disconnected calm, while Beret broods, paralyzed by guilt and doubt, wondering how history and the community will judge her.

Dramatically, then, Rølvaag opposes his audience's recognition against his character's actions. But beyond dramaturgy, Rølvaag limits his characters' awareness by significantly limiting their language. Typically a tragic hero defines himself by overstatement, using hyperbole and metaphor to establish a momentum towards change and understanding. But Beret moves in circles inside the soddie, while Per Hansa moves in circles outside the house. Never soliloquizing, Beret conducts a long series of spinning monologues, usually in the form of unanswered questions in the conditional voice. Per Hansa, as suspicious of words as he is of emotions, wanders a path around the community, seeking tasks and deeds that will establish his goodness. Per and Beret are not fools blindly driven by some all-powerful malignant force. Perhaps the novel's greatest tragedy is that it centers on two very human characters who cannot understand their own tragedy. We can.

In the establishment of *Giants in the Earth* as a tragedy, Rølvaag owes a particular debt to two sources, Ibsen and Shakespeare. From Ibsen, whom Rølvaag intensely studied and taught for many years, he adopts a tone of pervasive overcast along with the thematic emphasis of self-deception as a psychological prison. Thus, Per Hansa is a synthesis of Brand and Peer Gynt, Brand predominating. Surely Beret's character has been filtered through the apprehension of Nora and Hedda Gabler. Ibsen's celebrated and tragically overwhelming momentum of cause and effect gives the pattern for the plot of *Giants.* As Rølvaag once concluded in a potent lecture on Ibsen: ". . . the free exercise of will in the dramas results in disaster. . . . Life is tragic."

Shakespeare's *Macbeth* provides an analogue if not a source for the characterization and context in *Giants.* Both Lady Macbeth and Beret act with a sane and visionary madness, reflecting on all that has happened before and its consequencs. Like Macbeth, Per Hansa just gives up. Certainly the eerie atmosphere of *Macbeth* exists out on the prairie, but, like the knocking at the gate in *Macbeth, Giants* also has its moments of saving humor. Maynard Mack notes an aspect of Shakespeare's later tragedies particularly appropriate to the tragic movement of *Giants in the Earth:*

> Whatever the themes of individual plays . . .
> the one pervasive Jacobean theme tends to be
> the undertaking and working out of acts of will,
> and especially (in that strongly Calvinistic age)
> of acts of self-will.

Tragedy provides neither eternal answers nor temporal game plans, but heightens our awareness, our realization of the hu-

Rølvaag in 1927. Photo courtesy of St. Olaf College News Service.

man condition. This is Rolvaag's mission with **Giants in the Earth.**

Giants in the Earth, then, is not a saga or epic about Norwegian settlements and triumphs in the Land of Goshen. This tragic novel is an amalgamation of Norwegian culture and concerns turned to a pioneer experience, set on the most extreme American frontier. As John R. Milton has noted, **Giants** is the premier account of "how people remember the Dakotas or learn about them." As such, especially with Rølvaag forcing the tragic realization upon his audience, **Giants** is squarely in the tradition of American tragic realism, in the company of such works as *The Red Badge of Courage, A Farewell to Arms, The Sound and the Fury,* and even *One Flew Over the Cuckoo's Nest.* In the manner of Ibsen and Shakespeare, Rølvaag's masterpiece transcends time and space to make a dramatic and universal statement about the meaning of life. (pp. 88-90)

> Patrick D. Morrow, "Rølvaag's 'Giants in the Earth' as Tragedy," in North Dakota Quarterly, Vol. 48, No. 4, Autumn, 1980, pp. 83-90.

PAUL A. OLSON   (essay date 1981)

[*In the following excerpt Olson explains Rölvaag's diminution of the traditional epic hero, Per Hansa, in* Giants in the Earth, *concurring with Steve Hahn (1979) that Beret and not Per is the truly heroic figure of the tragedy. For further discussion of the spiritual superiority of Beret, see the excerpt by Harold P. Simonson (1977); for a contrasting discussion of the superiority of Per Hansa, see the excerpt by Joseph E. Baker (1942).*]

Rølvaag's use of the Germanic epic mode has already been explained by Steven Hahn [see excerpt dated 1979]. In his eyes, Per Hansa is a combination of the Germanic *askaladd*, the Ibsenian or existentialist hero of Ibsen's early lyrical-drama period (*Brand* and *Peer Gynt*), and the saga hero—the conqueror of new lands and the slayer of dragons. As Hahn argues, the plains sunset in his world is a Ragnarock; the plains themselves are trolls, the kin of Cain, the "giants of the earth" which also appear in Beowulf. The structure of the book is also very closely related to the structure of early Germanic epics in that the hero begins with a conquest over a series of physical threats and ends with defeat before some spiritual ones. Per Hansa has come to the world of the Great Plains in the name of a progress which will place him beyond conventional peasant morality and the acquisition of material wealth which is cast in his imagination as the gaining of a fairy-tale castle and garden. He means to be Beowulf to the plains: to kill the monsters of the physical vastness and menace of the plains and overcome the spiritual isolation of modern man from God and community with sheer autonomous high-heartedness.

As in the sagas and in *Beowulf,* the early physical struggle with the external monsters appears easy enough to the confident hero; among the immigrants, he plants first and builds best; he handles the mysteries of tractless snowstorms and intricate fur trades, of duck trapping and prairie fishing, of early planting and locust plague, with a combination of ingenuity, arrogance, and dumb luck (or providential protection) which also characterizes the saga hero in his early feats. Per Hansa conquers the Irish stake setters who would rival his Norse dominion of his island in a sea of prairie, even as the ancient Norse conquered the Irish. But conventionally the hero of the saga, having conquered all of the "external" world, succumbs to the effects of evils within, which destroy him and very nearly the kingdom or cultures which he has begun to create. Beowulf is destroyed by the avarice of his old age which awakens the dragon; Sigurd by his own deception of Brynhild; Njal and Grettir experience similar problems. What is interesting about Rølvaag's book is that Per Hansa, as epic hero, symbol of autonomy and western materialistic progress, destroys himself at first in a series of acts of neglect of love directed toward wife and community and finally in a gesture of heroic self-justification at the end of the book: the journey into the snowstorm to prove to Beret that he can do what she says—not out of piety but out of pique.

Interestingly, the survivor in the book and to my mind the strong person is Beret, who is at the antipodes from Per spiritually—a woman who has made a kind of Kierkegaardian descent into religious madness and is willing, like Abraham, to sacrifice child, husband, anything at the behest of the transcendent voices which she hears, a figure surrounded like Kierkegaard's Abraham with a sort of *horror religiosus*. She *knows* that she is abandoned and sees herself, perhaps accurately, in the metaphor of the preacher, the metaphor of a child pulled by the leash of God through the streets of a life which she cannot understand. (pp. 269-70)

Beret's people, to her perception, leave Norway (or "Egypt") to find plagues of locusts in the new world; Zion becomes Goshen when they arrive; they forget their rules and their purpose with the land taking. Though the pastor in *Giants* can declare the journey to the new land a journey to Zion and can declare the struggle grand, he knows that his metaphor does not work and turns to the more personalistic metaphor of the rope of God tied to the individual. The journey to America's holy city is fully pronounced a failure by the pastor who acts as the normative figure in the third book of the series, *Their Father's God*. . . . (p. 271)

What Rølvaag does in *Giants* is to display heroic accomplishments of the old saga variety as impossible on the frontier because its competitive ethos of individual prosperity, fairy palaces, and super-whitewashed walls separate the hero from his community and make of the heroic an expression of a private autonomous self tied to no community and directed by no divinity. Heroic accomplishment becomes an Old Norse brag and no more. The price of the settlement is the transformation of epic hero into Faustian man. Because Rølvaag finds that man ultimately so empty and self-destructive, he complements him with a heroic woman who can survive and find meaning in the circumstances of mobile autonomous life. She is also without a country, a community, or even a family which is close to her, and is not heroic in the way the *Beowulf* is, accomplishing great deeds and reminding her audience that God gave her arms and strength. She does almost nothing in the book but listen to the voices and do what they tell her, accepting the leash of God when it is thrown to her. Her heroism is the tragic heroism of Lear, or Kierkegaard's Abraham or Job. This, I think, is because Rølvaag realized that heroic accomplishment in a society beset by anomie, loss of sense of community, and loss of the sense of transcendence, could not begin where it began for the saga heroes—with large physical feats attributed to the hero *and* God, but had to begin with the finding of reason for accomplishing which had to be felt by human beings as more than a self-centered private fantasy. Interestingly, the heroic vision and inaction which is sanitive—if that be what Beret's is—is located in a woman. (pp. 271-72)

> *Paul A. Olson, "The Epic and Great Plains Literature: Rølvaag, Cather, and Neidhardt," in* Prairie Schooner, *Vol. 55, No. 182, Spring-Summer, 1981, pp. 263-85.**

EINAR HAUGEN   (essay date 1983)

[*In the following excerpt Haugen, a former student of Rølvaag's and a specialist in Scandinavian languages and literature, provides a survey of Rølvaag's career.*]

In Rölvaag's day, the term *ethnic* was not yet applied to American immigrant or racial groups, and the term *ethnicity* had not even been invented. Like *sibling,* it began as a bit of sociological jargon that became popular because it filled a hole in the English language. Before the 1950s, such words as *nationality* or *race* had been used. But a term was needed that would neither emphasize biological differences, like *race,* nor suggest conflicting political allegiance, like *nationality,* and that would not be pejorative. (p. 23)

However vague the term, it can usefully be projected backward to Rölvaag's thinking. When he spoke of his "people" *(vårt folk)* or his "kin" *(vår ætt),* he meant his ethnic group in America, and when he spoke of its "ancestral heritage" *(fædrearven),* he meant its Norwegian "ethnicity." To him the preservation of that ethnicity as intact as possible and its infusion into the developing American culture was an ethical duty laid down by divine fiat in every ethnic group. It was implied by the commandment to "honor thy father and thy mother that thy days may be long upon the land." This is why we may call it an "ethnic imperative."

We shall now review his first published novel, *Amerika-Breve* [which can be translated as *Letters from America,* but was published as *The Third Life of Per Smevik*] . . . and see how he embodied this idea in the story. (pp. 23-4)

The epistolary form was suggested to Rölvaag by a now forgotten novel, which caused him to say to his wife, "If I couldn't do better than that, I wouldn't even try." The form is of course as old as the novel itself: we think of Samuel Richardson's epoch-making *Pamela* (1740) and *Clarissa* (1748). Travelers' books about America were often cast in letter form, from the Frenchman Crèvecoeur's *Letters of an American Farmer* (1782) to the Swedish Fredrika Bremer's *Homes of the New World* (1853).

If *Amerika-Breve* is a novel at all, it comes close to the format of a *Bildungsroman* à la *Wilhelm Meisters Lehrjahre* (1796) by Goethe. The form is defined by Burgess as being "about the processes by which a sensitive soul discovers its identity and its role in the big world." Per Smevik grows from naiveté to maturity in the New World and finds himself a place within it. The climax comes when he tears himself loose from parental domination and goes off to school. The style is carefully differentiated according to recipient: with his father he is more formal and distant, with his brother, more spontaneous and humorous. (One wonders why he never addresses a letter to his mother in view of his frequently expressed love for her; can she be thought of as illiterate?) The language is enlivened from time to time by dialect words that express intimacy and, as time goes on, English words that reflect a growing distance.

If not a masterpiece, it is respectable and can still be enjoyed for its vignettes of immigrant farm life and its portrayal of the Americanization of a bright, if naive immigrant youth. Most readers are likely to find that the overly lengthy Fourth of July speech, however eloquent, is a static passage. Here the author steps into the action and preaches over the head of his hero. (pp. 30-1)

Rölvaag's second published novel, *Paa Glemte Veie* . . . , is his most neglected in the critical literature, in part because it has never appeared in English. But in Rölvaag's own development as a novelist, it is an important milepost. Contrary to "the easiest possible task" (as his brother Johan put it) that he had set himself in *Amerika-Breve,* he now tackled the problem of creating a plot with plausible characters and a significant message. He returned to the scene of his earlier book, but now reached down into deeper layers of immigrant psychology. Against a background of rural Norwegian South Dakota, he created a story exploring the interplay of love and religion, themes that were conspicuously absent in *Amerika-Breve.* Per Smevik tried to explain to his relatives the religious conditions among his countrymen, but dwelt mostly on the controversies and their disastrous effect. This time he hit upon themes that point forward very clearly to *Giants in the Earth.* (p. 33)

This tale can be read as an exegesis on what Rölvaag meant in 1901 when he listed the "Faith of the Forefathers" as the third and climactic aspect of his ethnic heritage. In spite of his overall loyalty to the church and its institutions, he clearly did not equate mere membership with faith. Lutheranism was (and is) a house of many mansions. Thanks to its status in each European country as a state church, it became more ethnic in America than most other immigrant churches. As Rölvaag knew it, its spiritual jurisdiction was coequal with the political boundaries of Norway. Every Norwegian who did not expressly and formally repudiate it was a member from birth. (p. 38)

In the state churches of Europe were housed a great store of conflicting views, which in America could and usually did result in lengthy and bitter doctrinal disputes as well as in the establishment of different churches on both the local and national levels (where they came to called synods).

What had been one religion in Norway thus turned into a *smörgåsbord* of Lutheran synods, large and small, in America. We need not consider the factors of social class, local tradition, or psychological stance that led to individual choices and organizational membership. Suffice it to say that there was among Norwegians a strong strain of lay evangelism associated with the name of Hans Nielsen Hauge, a strain that Rölvaag stood very near. This exhibited an "inwardness" which emphasized personal faith and conversion, a mystic experience of God, often leading to condemnation not only of all "worldly" delights but also of the "dead" faith of their fellow members. In its extreme form, it could cause the condemnation by lay preachers of their ordained brethren, thereby reversing the situation in the early 1800s, when laymen like Hauge were quite simply thrown in jail.

Two other names that were influential in the Norwegian religious scene, without ever achieving the status of Hauge, were the Danish leaders N.F.S. Grundtvig (1783-1872), founder of the Folk High School, and Sören Kierkegaard (1813-55), philosopher of the absolute ideal. In Norway, ideas from both were fused in the life and work of Christopher Bruun (1839-1920), whose book *Folkelige Grundtanker* (1872) was a strong influence on Rölvaag. He met some of the same thinking in Ibsen's play *Brand* (1866). It is generally recognized that Brand's motto of "All or Nothing" is closely connected with Kierkegaard's "Either-Or." The central feature of this peculiarly Scandinavian religious asceticism is its emphasis on the irrevocable choice, just such a choice as Mabel is faced with time and again, when she is tempted to stray from the "call" that has become her mission in life. (pp. 39-40)

Suffice it to say that *Paa Glemte Veie* is Rölvaag's attempt to portray a life in which these uncompromising ideas are put into practice on the South Dakota prairies. That the attempt was a literary failure is less important than the fact that it was tried. . . .

Unfortunately Rölvaag still lacked the skill to create a literary fusion of faith and art, which few if any moderns have managed since Kierkegaard. Large parts of this book sound like a Christian tract. Mabel, who presumably represents Rölvaag's ideal, is priggish and opinionated. Her father, the frustrated pioneer, is more humanly understandable, interesting in all his perverted and almost comical attempts to keep Mabel enslaved. The major problem is of course that a Kierkegaardian attempt to portray the struggle of God and Satan in the human soul (in this case Mabel's, since Chris struggles only in his dying moments) can lead only to a tragic conclusion. Kierkegaard rejected Hegel's notion of synthesis of opposites, leaving no alternative but death, as in Ibsen's play. But Rölvaag provides his Mabel with a deus ex machina who not only permits her to lay down her cross but foreshadows a life of happiness in marriage. As in any good Christian tract, what started out to be a tragedy, is capped by a sentimental conclusion. (p. 40)

Six years were to pass between the appearance of *Paa Glemte Veie* and Rölvaag's next novel, *To Tullinger,* which we shall here refer to either by this title or its literal translation, **"Two Fools."**

These were years of hard work, but also of sore travail and maturation. (p. 43)

In addition to . . . disillusionment with the cautious and even negative views of his church friends came the personal tragedies within his own family. His favorite brother Johan died in 1913, his mother in 1915; his oldest son died in the same year, six years old; and his youngest in 1920 by drowning, five years old.

The book that gave vent to his accumulated bitterness and despondency was "**Two Fools**"; but it also proved to be the best he had so far written, with a tense plot and an entirely new concentration that fell on his Norwegian-American world like a bombshell. (p. 44)

It is significant that this book appeared in the same year as Sinclair Lewis's *Main Street,* the scene of which is also Minnesota. "**Two Fools**" is a Norwegian-American satire in a vein not unlike Lewis's. The latter's scorn of the dull pretentiousness of small-town America is matched by Rölvaag's evocation of miserliness in the Norwegian-American rural population. (p. 48)

The story moves briskly from episode to episode without digressive descriptions or discussions. The dialogue is spare and lively, with much humor. Its realism is enhanced by the author's liberal use of Americanized Norwegian, drawn from his own experience of immigrant speech. . . .

Perhaps the greatest weakness of *To Tullinger,* among many good qualities, is the lack of any character with whom we can identify. Louis is weak and stupid, and Lizzie becomes so predictable that one turns from her in disgust. As a psychopathic case, she is more petty than powerful. (p. 49)

After Rölvaag had made a name for himself in the English-speaking world with *Giants* and its sequel *Peder Victorious,* he was eager that his earlier novels should also be known. He retitled the book *Pure Gold,* all reviewers having agreed that *To Tullinger* was a poor title. (p. 50)

The text itself has been so thoroughly revised that one can almost speak of a new book. Descriptive passages are expanded in the manner of *Giants.* The opening scene in *To Tullinger* only says: "It was a beautiful autumn day. The air was quiet, a clear sky above." . . . In *Pure Gold* this has become: "It was already late afternoon; the day beautiful; the loveliest autumn weather imaginable; clear skies—the whole firmament only lazy, indolent blueness domed over a drowsing earth." . . . Passages that had been little more than stage directions have now become part of the story. The characters are more human, and even Lizzie is given a paragraph containing some insight into her psychology. The mixed American-Norwegian is in part replaced by giving Louis a rather more colorful speech with abundant expletives. . . .

One can understand Rölvaag's efforts to adapt the book to American taste, while regretting some of the lost terseness and authenticity. (p. 51)

In 1921, within the year after *To Tullinger,* readers were surprised to receive a new book from Rölvaag's pen, *Længselens Baat.* They were even more surprised by the difference in tone: after the harsh, tightly structured study of warped minds came an episodic, romantic novel. Here Rölvaag spanned a young immigrant's life in Norway and in Minneapolis. . . .

The book is noteworthy, as one American reviewer remarked, for its combination of two widely dissimilar strains, "the mystical folktale and the realistic novel." Its four sections are neatly balanced between the two, with the first and last taking place in Norway, which embodies the mystical, emotional part, the middle two in Minneapolis, where Rölvaag's special brand of realism prevails. (p. 53)

The lack of a well-wrought plot line and the many "caprices" (as Ibsen called the digressions in his *Peer Gynt*) make this one of Rölvaag's richest but also most frustrating books. The flyleaf tells us that it is about the immigrant's soul. The Poet enunciates the moral of the Ashlad's quest for Soria Maria: "Simply stated, it means that he gained his own soul, his own Self. That's the most which any human being can win!" Implied in this statement is the biblical injunction: "What is a man profited, if he shall gain the whole world, and lose his own soul?" It is hard to know just how to take theology coming from the lips of the derelict Poet. He modifies the concept of "soul" by adding "his own Self," which suggests the theme of *Peer Gynt.* Rölvaag saw *Peer Gynt* as a Christian allegory of salvation, with Peer finding his own "self" at the end of the play on Solveig's bosom.

Whatever the "self" that Nils is seeking, it is not the wealth that America represented to most immigrants. The Poet drily declares, "So far no Norwegian has come to America without looking for gold." But when the fellow with the scythe catches up with him and asks for his soul, "he hunts and digs in every nook and cranny; but he can't find what the Lean One is asking for. No, not a shred of soul." Nils has brought his soul with him intact from Norway, but he finds little nourishment for it in Minneapolis. He sees his calling in music, but at least as far as Rölvaag completed the book, he finds no opportunity to carry it out. The Ashlad "saw his own potentialities . . . God's serious intent with him. And when it says that after unbelievable battles he really arrived at the castle and won the princess, this is the folk imagination's poetic way of expressing this ethical truth." This interpretation of the Ashlad's aspirations is hardly the usual one, that the Ashlad was looking for wealth and power, which to most people represents happiness. But Rölvaag is specifically denying these values: happiness lies in finding your own self, the soul that God has entrusted to each person to discover and develop. (pp. 58-9)

It is one of the theses of this study that the success as well as the inner significance of *Giants in the Earth* can be grasped only against Rölvaag's background and his most firmly held convictions. One cannot, as some have done, separate his work as a writer from his work for his ethnic heritage. There is less overt propaganda in this book than in most of his others, but the situation, the characters, and the plot not only illustrate his basic idea but embody it in innumerable allusions. His faith in creative aspiration is present in his characters, and the work itself is a creative presentation of his and their potentialities. (p. 75)

Even in this first book, it is clear that Rölvaag has succeeded in giving his theme a wider perspective than any of his predecessors in novels of the westward movement. By themselves, the events are simple and everyday, such as might have occurred to anyone. But the framework into which he has placed them deserves to be called epic. (pp. 80-1)

Giants reached its tragic but esthetically satisfying ending with the death of Per Hansa. But the climactic emphasis given to the birth of Peder, Per's only American-born child, with his ambitious byname of "Victorious," inevitably called for a continuation. As the representative of a new generation, he is expected to fulfill the first generation's dream of building a new kingdom.

Both sequels are novels of conflict, but no longer of man against nature, with its glamor of myth and folktale. These characters are locked in conflict, social and psychological, within a rural immigrant community that is trying to define new norms and find its American identity. In *Peder* we see Peder's maturation in a conflict with his mother that gradually weakens his bond with the Norwegian past. In *Their Fathers' God,* the conflict is with his Irish wife Susie, whose resistance brings out the obstacles to their harmonious union that rise from his lingering Norwegian ethnicity. Neither conflict is so much resolved as severed like Gordian knots by the author's fiat. (p. 98)

There are many excellently conceived scenes in [*Peder*]. We might mention the tragic "churching" of Oline Tuftan; Beret's speech at the church meeting; Peder's thoughts after his first contact with Susie; Beret's vision of herself sitting on a rock back home in Nordland and watching a bird hacking corpses in the sea; the thatching party with Tönseten's usual bottle; the Fourth of July celebration; and Beret's vision of Per Hansa. There is also a vigorous effort to promote realism of speech in an intensified use of dialect and of English loanwords in the dialogue. These nuances are of course lost in the translation. The Norwegian publishers felt obliged to annotate some of the Americanisms for Norwegian readers, mislabeling them as "vulgarisms." Such words as *fila* ("the field"), *krua* ("the crew"), or *miden* ("meeting") were part of the everyday, unconscious speech of all rural Norwegian-Americans.

Yet it is true, as Rölvaag himself wrote to Colcord while working on the novel, that "it won't have the sweep, the vastness, and the lift" of *Giants,* "because the theme is so entirely different." (p. 102)

Peder is a young man in revolt, not only against his mother's dominance, but also against her ethnicity, her language, and her church. To Rölvaag, these were indissolubly connected: reject one and you reject all. (p. 103)

The pictures of church strife and religious intolerance are understandable in terms of Rölvaag's feeling about the ministry in this period of his life, but are something less than fair-minded or adequate portrayals. they are calculated to account for Peder's revolt and his inner development. In spite of the title, this is not so much Peder's book as it is Beret's. For all her unreasonableness, she is still Rölvaag's love.

Peder is twenty-one when [the] . . . last of Rölvaag's novels [*Their Fathers' God*] opens. Susie and he have been married for six months, she is pregnant, and they are living on Beret's farm. It would seem to be the dawn of a "blessed day," as in the pentecostal hymn by Grundtvig after which the Norwegian original is named. But the English title *Their Fathers' God* comes closer to identifying the central theme, although the problems of this mixed marriage have less to do with God than with temperaments and ways of life. (pp. 103-04)

Rölvaag's work has been called an "anomaly" in American literature, because he wrote about his new life in Norwegian: as if all American literature had to be in English! In our day it has been recognized that America has a "multiethnic" literature, much of it written in languages other than English. In a recent study, Rölvaag was described as "a writer between two countries," but I would amend that to read "a writer *with* two countries," both of which he loved as a man can love both mother and wife. . . .

On both sides of the Atlantic, he fought his gallant battle to promote understanding. He may have lost most of the skirmishes, but by his lifework he still won the war. His writings held up a mirror to the life of Norwegian-America, illuminating its reality for the enjoyment and understanding both of Norwegians "back East" and Americans "out West." (p. 121)

Einar Haugen, in his Ole Edvart Rölvaag, *Twayne Publishers, 1983, 164 p.*

SOLVEIG ZEMPEL (essay date 1984)

[*An assistant professor of Norwegian at St. Olaf College and a granddaughter of Rölvaag, Zempel has selected and translated into English six of Rölvaag's short stories that first appeared in Norwegian periodicals or children's readers. In the following excerpt from her introduction to this collection, Zempel contends that Rölvaag's short fictions are accomplished works that often approach the same high level of stylistic and thematic maturity displayed in his longer fiction.*]

Although Rølvaag first gained nationwide recognition as a writer when *Giants in the Earth* came out in English, he had been a leader in the Norwegian-American community for many years. He was known not only for his novels, but also for the many short stories which had appeared in Christmas annuals, newspapers, and other Norwegian-American periodicals.

Rølvaag's experiences during his early years contributed to his deep love for the Norwegian-American people and to his desire that they should make a worthwhile contribution to their adopted land. This he firmly believed could only be done by preserving the best in their own cultural traditions. "A people that has lost its traditions is doomed," says the minister in *Their Father's God.* Rølvaag's vision of immigration is essentially tragic, his immigrants characterized by rootlessness. "We have become strangers; strangers to those we left and strangers to those we came to," he writes in *The Third Life of Per Smevik.* According to this vision, the immigrant remained forever a stranger drifting without anchor or rudder. Throughout his life, with ever increasing skill and sensitivity, Rølvaag focused on these two intertwined themes, the rootlessness of the immigrant and the importance of preserving cultural traditions. (pp. 9-10)

[His masterpiece, *Giants in the Earth,*] is epic in scope, depicting both the promise and the cost of the great westward movement. Rølvaag shows the prairie as the great enemy, yet he is ever mindful of its beauty and richness, and some passages read like prose poems in praise of nature. Rølvaag's fiction can be characterized as a psychological interpretation of the pioneer and immigrant experience. (p. 10)

[His] artistic vision presents us not only with a great epic of the American frontier, but also with a penetrating insight into the universal human condition.

Before writing his masterpiece, *Giants in the Earth,* O. E. Rølvaag served a lengthy apprenticeship. Not only had he published four novels, he had also written a number of short stories, poems, articles, textbooks, readers, and hundreds of letters. The early stories were his apprentice pieces, and, as such, are worthy of attention. They show how he was developing his ideas and learning to express them in his own personal style. These shorter pieces are little known, having appeared only in Norwegian-American periodicals or long out-of-print textbooks. (pp. 11-12)

Rølvaag's short stories can be divided into three broad categories, with the understanding that there is much overlap in style and content. The majority may be classified as humorous sketches, in which he pokes fun at the foibles of humanity, and particularly at the weaknesses of Norwegian-Americans. The characters in some cases become almost cartoon figures, caricatures which exaggerate and emphasize certain aspects of personality or experience. Other stories are more didactic in nature, still focusing on Rølvaag's perception of human flaws, but without the laughter. Rølvaag's role as teacher and preacher of values to his fellow Norwegian-Americans comes out most clearly in these stories. Finally, some of his short works can hardly be called stories at all; they are "mood" pieces, prose poems perhaps, lyrical descriptions of nature without plot or character, except to the extent that nature personified becomes a character or the changing of the seasons can be regarded as forward movement of plot.

In all of his writing, Rølvaag circles around the same themes, constantly moving towards a deeper understanding, and refining his skills in expressing his ideas in words. As well as developing theme and character in these early stories, Rølvaag is also clearly practicing and moving toward his own personal and highly effective style. He uses many of the same stylistic devices as in his later novels, though somewhat more clumsily. Nature personified often becomes a secondary character in his stories, or functions symbolically. The lyrical descriptions of nature are reminiscent of the scenes in *Giants in the Earth.* Influence from the style of Old Norse Sagas may be seen in his use of a mixture of direct and indirect quotation. Norwegian folk literature has also clearly left its mark on Rølvaag's writing in theme and characterization, as well as in turn of phrase. He uses, and sometimes overuses, dashes to indicate thoughts and speech. Sentences tend to be long and run-on, and in some cases the punctuation and division into paragraphs show that he was rushed for time or perhaps not yet quite skilled enough as a writer. In addition, Norwegian-American writers lacked good editors and critics, something which Rølvaag gained when his books were published by major Norwegian and American firms.

"When the Wind is in the South," the first story in this collection, was originally published in *Jul i vesterheimen 1921* under the title **"Klare morgen og vaate kveld"** (Clear Morning and Wet Evening). (pp. 12-13)

This charming story is surely based on a true incident; the "I" of the story is Rølvaag himself, "Erik," his next door neighbor Erik Hetle, and "Halvor," their fishing companion Halvor Oakland, who was also a neighbor. It shows Rølvaag at his most humorous, poking fun at himself and investing the most trivial incident with hilarity. In some ways, it could be said to be atypical of Rølvaag, in that it does not deal with his central theme of Norwegian-American traditions and culture but is simply an amusing tale of one of Rølvaag's favorite pastimes. It is also a relatively late story, and the style is more polished than in the earlier stories. Certain stylistic features characteristic of Rølvaag's writing appear here, for example, the way in which he described nature, and his use of a mixture of direct and indirect quotation in the dialog (which can sometimes be difficult to translate adequately).

"Whitebear and Graybear," which Rølvaag cast in the form of an Indian legend, is clearly an allegory based on what happens to Norwegian-Americans, and indeed to all "hyphenated Americans," when they try to deny their own cultural heritage. He makes no claims for the superiority of one culture or tradition over another; rather, he shows the foolishness of attempting to imitate another's lifestyle. This was a message which permeated his whole life as both teacher and author; that a people must remain true to its own culture identity, and must

strive to retain that which is of value in its own traditions. (pp. 13-14)

Comedy and tragedy are masterfully blended in **"Molla's Heart Attack."** . . . Rølvaag shows great perception and insight in his characterization of Molla, the young woman who, because of her size and lack of physical beauty, becomes the butt of community jokes and has no prospects for marriage, but is left with only "vague, sweet longings." In **"Molla's Heart Attack,"** as in many of his stories, he uses colorful seafaring expressions for humor in these tales of the land-locked Upper Midwest. The sea was a powerful influence in Rølvaag's life, and he often compares the endlessness of the prairie to the ocean.

"The Boy Who Had No Jackknife," one of Rølvaag's stories for children, appeared in several places in slightly different versions. . . . The depiction of Henry's mother and his family situation suffers from the sentimentality which so plagued Norwegian-American writers; however, Rølvaag's understanding of the psychology of childhood lifts the story up from the mundane. The thoughts and feelings of the young boy, his ambivalence and guilt, his longing for the unobtainable jackknife, temptation and self-justification are all embodied in Henry. This could be called a "trial run" for Rølvaag's much longer, deeper, and fuller description of the youth and adolescence of Peder Victorious.

"The Butter War in Greenfield" appeared first in Norway in 1925 in the Christmas annual *Julen* under the title **"De Kloke Jomfruer"** (The Wise Virgins). . . . In it, Rølvaag shows the weakness of humans whose pride is masked by false generosity and points out the trivialities which can tear a congregation apart. Presented as an amusing anecdote, there is an underlying tragedy in this story. Although the ending trails off somewhat unsatisfactorily, the implication is clear that an innocent person's career has been destroyed. No one single character dominates this story; instead, Rølvaag presents the reader with an entire gallery of distinct personalities skillfully delineated in very few words. (pp. 14-15)

The characters of Anna Katrina and Simeon [in **"The Christmas Offering"**] have parallels in Chris Larson of *Paa glemte Veie,* and, perhaps more obviously, in Lars and Lizzie in *Pure Gold.* In this story Anna Katrina develops the strength to overcome circumstances which have kept her at a disadvantage. Both Anna Katrina and Molla in **"Molla's Heart Attack,"** demonstrate Rølvaag's ability to create strong female characters, as he does with Beret in *Giants in the Earth.*

These stories were originally written for a Norwegian-speaking audience, and have become inaccessible as knowledge of Norwegian has died out in the Norwegian-American community. With the revival of interest in ethnic identity and cultural diversity, this literature has a renewed relevance. Though these shorter pieces may lack the maturity and breadth of *Giants in the Earth,* they are by no means insignificant literary works. They offer to the reader insight into the universal human condition, as well as into individual personalities set in a particular time and place. The humor, the characterization, and the deft stylistic touch of these stories have as much appeal today as when they were first published. (pp. 15-16)

Solveig Zempel, in an introduction to When the Wind Is in the South and Other Stories *by O.E. Rølvaag, edited and translated by Solveig Zempel, Center for Western Studies, 1984, pp. 7-16.*

ADDITIONAL BIBLIOGRAPHY

American Prefaces 1, No. 7 (April 1936): 98-112.
Entire issue devoted to Rölvaag, including a commemorative poem written by Paul Engle, four prose works written by Rölvaag (including an excerpt from his unfinished autobiography), and an essay containing reminiscences by the author's daughter.

Bjørk, Kenneth. "The Unknown Rølvaag: Secretary in the Norwegian-American Historical Association." *Norwegian-American Studies and Records* XL (1940): 114-49.
Biographical study detailing Rölvaag's importance to the Norwegian-American Historical Association.

Blegen, Theodore C. *Grass Roots History*, pp. 6ff. Port Washington, New York: Kennikat Press, 1969.
Several brief references to Rölvaag's depiction of Norwegian immigrants' acculturation in America. Blegen believes that the author's entire literary output "assumes increasing significance with the passing years, and the reason is plain. For in the sweep of his entire work, with deeper insight and greater power than almost any other writer, he recorded and interpreted the American transition of the immigrants who made their way to the Western World."

Colcord, Lincoln. "Rölvaag the Fisherman Shook his Fist at Fate." *The American Magazine* CV, No. 3 (March 1928): 36-7, 188-9, 192.
Contains Rölvaag's conversations with Colcord recounting his decision to emigrate to America, his eventual rise to chair of the department of Norwegian at St. Olaf College, and the writing of *Giants in the Earth.*

Eckstein, Neil T. "The Social Criticism of Ole Edvart Rølvaag." In *Norwegian-American Studies, Vol. 24,* edited by Kenneth O. Bjork, pp. 112-36. Northfield, Minnesota: Norwegian-American Historical Association, 1970.
Biographical and interpretive study of Rölvaag's works focussing on the treatment of family, religion, and ethnicity in his novels. Eckstein believes Rölvaag's primary concern as a social critic was for "the ethnocultural solidarity of the [Norwegian] immigrants."

Flanagan, John T. "The Middle Western Farm Novel." *Minnesota History* 23, No. 2 (June 1942): 113-25.*
Presents a general overview of the American farm novel and ranks Rölvaag's *Giants in the Earth* as the greatest artistic achievement in the genre.

De Grazia, Emilio. "The Great Plain: Rölvaag's New World Sea." *South Dakota Review* 20, No. 3 (Autumn 1982): 35-49.
Examines sea motifs, particularly as they relate to themes of loss and alienation, in Rölvaag's fiction.

Grider, Sylvia. "Madness and Personification in *Giants in the Earth.*" In *Women, Women Writers, and the West,* edited by L. L. Lee and Merrill Lewis, pp. 111-17. Troy, New York: Whitson Publishing Co., 1979.
Character study of Beret Hansa. Grider regards Beret as a traditional Norwegian woman who undergoes a profound mental breakdown following her emigration to America and then recovers, ironically, to blindly conspire with the forces of nature and effect the death of her husband.

Haugen, Einar I. "O. E. Rölvaag: Norwegian-American." *Norwegian American Studies and Records* VII (1933): 53-73.
Biographical and thematic study. Haugen emphasizes Rölvaag's "dominant passion"—"his attachment to race. Everything of consequence that he wrote was either a loving delineation or a bitter scourging of his Norwegian people in America."

Haugrud, Raychel A. "Rølvaag's Search for Soria Moria." In *Norwegian-American Studies, Vol. 26,* edited by Kenneth O. Bjork, pp. 103-17. New York: Twayne Publishers, 1974.
A biographical portrait and thematic study of Rölvaag's work which regards the search for ultimate happiness—symbolized in Norse myth as the castle of Soria Moria—as the novelist's major concern.

Heitmann, John. "Ole Edvart Rølvaag." In *Norwegian-American Studies and Records, Vol. XII,* edited by Theodore C. Blegen, pp. 144-66. Northfield, Minnesota: Norwegian-American Historical Association, 1941.
Reminiscences by one of Rölvaag's childhood friends.

Hutchinson, Percy. "Norwegian-Americans in the Northwest." *The New York Times Book Review* (9 February 1930): 9.
Favorable appraisal of *Pure Gold* and high assessment of Rölvaag's importance to the Norwegian novel.

Jordahl, Owen. "Folkloristic Influences upon Rölvaag's Youth." *Western Folklore* XXXIV, No. 1 (January 1975): 1-15.
Discusses Rölvaag's knowledge of Norwegian folk tales, figures, and motifs, and examines *The Romance of a Life,* Rolvaag's unpublished biographical manuscript in which he himself explains and recounts these early influences.

Laverty, Carroll D. "Rölvaag's Creation of the Sense of Doom in *Giants in the Earth.*" *The South Central Bulletin* XXVII, No. 4 (Winter 1967): 45-50.
Emphasizes Rölvaag's literary artistry through an analysis of fear and isolation motifs found in *Giants in the Earth.*

Meyer, Roy W. "The Pioneering Venture: The Farm Novelist as Historian." In his *The Middle Western Farm Novel in the Twentieth Century,* pp. 35-78.* Lincoln: University of Nebraska Press, 1965.
Declares *Giants in the Earth* the most comprehensive as well as artistically perfect treatment of pioneering in the literature of the Midwest.

Reigstad, Paul M. "Journey to Rölvaag: A Visit to the Birthplace of the Famous Norwegian-American Author." *The Norseman,* No. 3 (1967): 56-9.
Recounts the journey to Dønna Island that Reigstad took in preparation for writing his study of Rölvaag. Reigstad affirms the strong autobiographical element in Rölvaag's work and maintains that portions of *The Boat of Longing,* arguably the author's most personal novel, rank among the finest fiction that Rölvaag ever produced.

———. *Rölvaag: His Life and Art.* Lincoln: University of Nebraska Press, 1972, 160 p.
General introduction to Rölvaag and his novels.

———. "Mythic Aspects of *Giants in the Earth.*" In *Vision and Refuge: Essays on the Literature of the Great Plains,* edited by Virginia Faulkner and Frederick C. Luebke, pp. 64-70. Lincoln: University of Nebraska Press, 1982.
Discusses Rölvaag's presentation of myth and mythical figures, particularly trolls, in *Giants.* Reigstad concludes that these aspects lend considerable symbolic force to Rölvaag's frontier tragedy.

Ruud, Curtis D. "Beret and the Prairie in *Giants in the Earth.*" In *Norwegian-American Studies, Vol. 28,* edited by Kenneth O. Bjork, pp. 217-44. Northfield, Minnesota: Norwegian-American Historical Association, 1979.
Character study of Beret Hansa, whom Ruud regards as a significant figure in continual struggle with the prairie.

Sandburg, Carl. Review of *Giants in the Earth,* by Ole Rölvaag. *The Chicago Daily News* (11 February 1928): 9.
Declares: "If we should be asked to name the six most important and fascinating American novels past and present, *Giants in the Earth* would be one of them. It is so tender and simple. It is so terrible and panoramic, piling up its facts with incessantly subtle intimations, that it belongs among the books to be kept and cherished."

Simonson, Harold P. "The Tragic Trilogy of Ole Rölvaag." In his *The Closed Frontier: Studies in American Literary Tragedy,* pp. 77-97. New York: Holt, Rinehart and Winston, 1970.
Examines the trilogy *Giants in the Earth, Peder Victorious,* and *Their Fathers' God* and concludes that it is one of the most sustained frontier tragedies in American literature.

Thorson, Gerald, ed. *Ole Rølvaag: Artist and Cultural Leader.* Northfield, Minnesota: St. Olaf College Press, 1975, 74 p.

A collection of eight papers presented at the Rölvaag Symposium held by St. Olaf College, October 28-9, 1974. Among the topics considered are ''The Fictional Heart of the Country: From Rølvaag to Gass'' by Robert Scholes, ''*Pure Gold:* An Appreciation'' by Robert L. Stevens, and ''Fate, Sex, and Naturalism in Rølvaag's Trilogy'' by Barbara Meldrum.

Van Doren, Carl. ''Revolt from the Village.'' In his *The American Novel, 1789-1939*, pp. 294-302. New York: Macmillan Co., 1940.
Labels *Giants in the Earth* ''the best of all immigrant novels in the United States'' for its ''profound realism'' and ''magical'' style.

Vogdes, Walter. ''Hamsun's Rival.'' *The Nation* CXXV, No. 3236 (13 July 1927): 41-2.
A highly favorable review of *Giants in the Earth*. Vogdes writes, ''We may wish desperately that Rölvaag could have ended his tale in triumph and satisfaction, as Hamsun ended *Growth of the Soil*. But no, Rölvaag had to stand close to the facts and the truth. It is another story.''

Pedro Salinas

1891-1951

Spanish poet, novelist, short story writer, dramatist, essayist, critic, and translator.

Salinas is recognized as one of Spain's outstanding twentieth-century poets. Although he associated for nearly a decade with an influential group of Madridian poets known as the Generation of 1927, his work is not usually considered representative of any particular poetic movement or school. The dominant themes of Salinas's work reflect the conflicts between being and nothingness and between internal and external reality. All phases of Salinas's diversified career have received high critical acclaim: from his technically-varied early poetry, to his essays and literary criticism, to his late experiments with drama and the short story. However, his finest achievements are considered to be his long sequences of love poetry, which many critics regard as some of the most beautiful meditations on the theme of love written in any language.

Salinas was born in Madrid and lived there until he was a young man. As a youth he developed a deep love for the city, for its local color, and for Spanish tradition and culture. Although Salinas entered the University of Madrid intending to study law, his love of literature and growing enthusiasm for poetry caused him to change his original plans, and he graduated with a Licentiate in Letters degree in 1913. The following year he accepted a lectureship at the Sorbonne and moved to Paris, where he lived for the next three years. During this time he married Spanish-born Margarita Bonmatí and completed his doctoral dissertation. While in Paris he also immersed himself in French culture and made numerous acquaintances in various artistic and literary circles.

Salinas returned to Spain in 1917 and was offered a professorship at the University of Seville the following year. The city of Seville fascinated Salinas, and many of his early poems were inspired by its exotic beauty and vitality. Salinas also became increasingly active in the literary life of Madrid, contributing poems to several prestigious literary journals, and associating with a group of poets that eventually became known as the Generation of 1927. Salinas was the oldest member of the group, which included Jorge Guillén, Luis Cernuda, Dámaso Alonso, Rafael Alberti, Vincente Aleixandre, and Federico García Lorca. These writers were interested in restoring traditional elements to modern Spanish poetry and were particularly inspired by folk songs, ballads, epic verse, and the work of a little-known Spanish Renaissance poet, Luis de Góngora. The group was also intrigued by the radical modes of aesthetic experimentation that had been flourishing in Europe since World War I, such as Cubism, Futurism, and, specific to Spanish art, Ultraism, all of which generally championed the dissociation of art from immediate reality, scorned sentimentality, and demonstrated ambivalence toward the emerging technological age. The Generation advocated poetry as a means to discover and explore the relationship between external reality and the poet's internal world, and, while they rejected sentimentality, love was a dominant theme in the group's work. During his years of association with the Generation, Salinas wrote and published five volumes of his most important poetry. When the Spanish Civil War broke out in 1936, the group,

Courtesy of Ediciones Alfaguara

which held strong but unmilitant anti-Fascist sentiments, disbanded and all but three of the group's members, including Salinas, went into exile.

Salinas emigrated to the United States and accepted a visiting professorship at Wellesley College in Massachusetts. He had not intended that his exile would be permanent, but he spent the last fifteen years of his life in North America, teaching at several universities. Between 1942 and 1945, Salinas taught at the University of Puerto Rico, where he was exhilarated by the abundance of Spanish culture and the opportunity to speak his native language freely. Here he wrote a volume of poetry entitled *El contemplado (Sea of San Juan: A Contemplation)* which was largely inspired by the warmth and beauty of the island and is considered by critics to be his most serenely reflective work. During the last few years of his life Salinas traveled extensively in South America and Europe, with the exclusion of Spain. This contact with the Old World cheered him and renewed his conviction in the importance of tradition, but also kindled nostalgic longing for his homeland. All who have written of Salinas at this period in his life indicate that his state was one of wistful homesickness and fond reminiscence which remained untinged with the common bitterness of exile. He died of cancer in 1951.

In his first two volumes, *Presagios* and *Seguro azar*, Salinas established the themes and central concerns of his poetry: the function of poetry, the ambiguous nature of reality, and the ways by which the poetic process attempts to bridge the gap between external reality and the poet's internal reality. *Presagios* is frequently considered the most technically traditional of Salinas's works, demonstrating as it does the influence of Renaissance ballads and sonnet forms as well as Góngora's verse. In this work Salinas also begins to examine the theme of love—specifically, the difficulties in perceiving the reality of love and acquiring knowledge of the beloved, both considerations which pervade much of his later work. Salinas's second book, *Seguro azar,* shows the strongest evidence of the Ultraist tendencies held by the Generation of 1927. It contains a significant number of poems inspired by modern inventions, and it is written in a sparse, dissociative style devoid of most connective words. The overall tone of the work is one of curiosity, optimism, and naïve perception.

According to poet Jorge Guillén, "Salinas's poetry . . . reached its highest point with the theme of love." Most critics share this opinion. His great love poetry is contained in two sequences, *La voz a ti debida* and *Razón de amor,* the first of which is divided into seventy untitled segments and is over two thousand lines long. Because Salinas neither titled nor numbered the segments, *La voz a ti debida* is generally considered as a single continuous meditation on the loved one which begins with the discovery of love, moves through the fullness, then loss, of love, and ends with hope for its rediscovery. Some critics believe that Salinas's love poetry exhibits extreme self-absorption on the part of the poet, and that the verse is too intellectual and remote to be considered a celebration and lamentation of an earthly love affair. In the words of the philologist Leo Spitzer, Salinas's friend and colleague, "I am acquainted with no love poetry in which the two lovers are so completely reduced to the poet's own ego, in which the beloved woman lives only as a function of the man's mind and is no more than a phenomenon of his consciousness." This, however, is the less popular view of *La voz a ti debida.* While most critics acknowledge the highly contemplative nature of the work, they cite Salinas's concrete imagery as evidence of his concern with love between two sentient individuals. In *Razón de amor* the redemptive nature of love is emphasized, and the vision of the world is more expansive than that of the "universe of two" created in *La voz a ti debida.* According to John Crispin, in *Razón de amor* "Salinas progressively acquired a new vital perspective, a sense of purpose, and accrued faith in the importance of his poetic mission. Until then, his poetry shows that he had been unable to find in the material world the measure of permanence which might help to give it meaning."

During his exile Salinas wrote two volumes of poetry and began to experiment with other genres as well. The poetry contained in *Sea of San Juan* and *Todo más claro* is thought to be his most spiritually ambitious and his most foreboding. In these works the poet expresses a desire to unite with a reality greater than himself, while at the same time he senses the imminent doom of humanity. This late poetry virtually advocates rejection of and escape from the material world through contemplation of spiritual ideals. The long poem "Cero," ("Zero"), which concludes *Todo más claro,* was originally written in 1944 and is considered prophetic of the atomic holocaust that occurred at Hiroshima only months later. In keeping with his growing concern over the outcome of rapid technological advances and the development of the atomic bomb, Salinas wrote a novel entitled *La bomba increíble* in which he portrayed the sterility of a futuristic society whose lack of regard for hu-

manistic values nearly brings about its destruction. In the short stories and plays Salinas wrote near the end of his career, he returned to his concern with the disparity between appearance and reality, but used it to examine the flaws of modern society, rather than love, particularly what he saw as a growing devaluation of individuality and human rights.

Although critics express consistent admiration for the remarkable degree of precision, flexibility, and universality in all aspects of Salinas's work, it is primarily on the basis of his tremendous achievement in poetry that he is remembered and regarded as one of the most important contributors to modern Spanish literature.

PRINCIPAL WORKS

Presagios (poetry) 1923
Seguro azar (poetry) 1929
Fábula y signo (poetry) 1931
Amor en vilo (poetry) 1933
La voz a ti debida (poetry) 1933
Razón de amor (poetry) 1936
Lost Angel, and Other Poems (poetry) 1938
Reality and the Poet in Spanish Poetry (lectures) 1940
Truth of Two, and Other Poems (poetry) 1941
El contemplado (poetry) 1946
 [*Sea of San Juan: A Contemplation,* 1950]
Zero (poetry) 1947
El defensor (essays) 1948
Todo más claro y otros poemas (poetry) 1949
La bomba increíble (novel) 1950
El desnudo impecable y otras narraciones (short stories) 1951
Poemas escogidos (poetry) 1953
Confianza (poetry) 1957
Teatro completo (dramas) 1957
Volverse sombra y otros poemas (poetry) 1957
Poesías completas (poetry) 1971

Translations of Salinas's poetry have appeared in the following anthologies: *The Bread Loaf Anthology; Contemporary Spanish Poetry: Selections from Ten Poets; The European Caravan; The Poem Itself; Roots and Wings: Poetry from Spain 1900-1975;* and *Translations from Hispanic Poets.*

PEDRO SALINAS (essay date 1938)

[*In the following excerpt from his preface to* Lost Angel, and Other Poems, *Salinas discusses the reasons why poetry attracts a much smaller audience than do other literary genres.*]

Upon the appearance of some of my poems in English, . . . an inevitable question comes to my mind. Is there a public for these poems? Who will this public be? What will it be like?

Once more I am confronted with a puzzling subject upon which to ponder: the problem of the "public for poetry." It is without doubt the hardest public to capture by vision or imagination, the one most difficult for us to visualize. It is a very world of phantoms.

The writer of plays has the privilege, if it is a privilege, of seeing his public with his own eyes. There it is before him, shut up for some hours within the walls of the theatre. He may run his eyes over the thousand various faces which make up his public, take apart that complex and indistinct whole, as he would take apart a watch in minute bits, and examine one by one the makeup of the whole. For him it is possible to say: "The public is that blonde young woman with her fiancé, that corpulent, somewhat sleeply gentleman, that lanky, melancholy youth." And thus going over the whole theatre, the public materializes for the playwright, in an almost brutal manner, into the concrete, the definite.

The novelist, for his part, cannot assemble his readers in a definite place, nor scrutinize their individual faces, as the dramatic writer can. Nevertheless he can have an idea of his public. How? From the very beginning, the novel was a type of entertainment. In the Middle Ages, the knights had enemies of flesh and blood to kill. What greater amusement than that, a sort of human chase! But the ladies in their castles were facing a dread foe, one which they had to fight in their own homes, in a daily warfare: time. It was necessary to employ their idle moments, their leisure, they had to kill time. The novel was a marvellous expedient discovered for this need of conquering the hours. In spite of all that has been added to the large pattern of the novel, that form still preserves its character of pastime, entertainment. And for that reason the public for the novel is more easily found. It is to be supposed that behind each novel-reader is a person who seeks entertainment; therefore the novel-reading public is very large: nearly every one to-day seeks entertainment, and in consequence the public for the novel is made up of almost the whole world.

Novels and plays have one point in common. They aspire to distract, to take us out of ourselves, to make us live outside that reality which we call our "ego," in actions and personages invented by the author. . . . We stop living in our individual feelings, we live in the feelings of a neighbor that the author invented to distract us, to bear us off to where we forget ourselves and take pleasure in the delight of being a spectator.

But poetry, does it distract? It is very doubtful. Because, instead of dis-tracting, or at-tracting us to another place, it makes us turn in upon ourselves, invites us to an inner activity, to something like a reproduction within ourselves of the feelings of the poet. A poem, although primarily it may be something experienced in the spiritual life of the poet, is experienced over again in the soul of the reader, if it is deeply read. It brings us face to face with ourselves, not with a person in a book or a character in a play. It reaches to the deep waters of the inner being and touches them or moves them, but always breaking their tranquillity. Like persons who make themselves loved by simply existing, because of their mere presence, a true poem at its approach calls to our deepest interest, makes us take part in its life, makes us wish to live in it. Only a certain class of frigid professors or students can be spectators of poetry, for, like love, it either conquers or does not exist. For that reason poetry inspires a certain fear. Because instead of dis-tracting us it re-tracts, withdraws, us into ourselves. And what most persons wish to-day is to go out of themselves, not to enter into themselves. The great infirmity of the modern being is his

incompatibility with his own deepest and most mysterious self, it inspires him with fear, he feels an unconscious anxiety to avoid it. Therefore he gives himself up to all sorts of escapes to the external, or distractions that the world of to-day provides for him on a great scale: dancing, sports, superficial society. And so we limit a little more our possible public for poetry. It will be made up of separate beings who row against the current, who wish to re-tract, withdraw, into themselves, not dis-tract themselves, to look within and not at exterior circumstances. Poetry demands intense collaboration, not simple reading. How then could there be many readers of poetry in a world tired of work as this is to-day? Humanity is accustomed to look for chances to rest and not to collaborate, as one does always who reads a poem. Therefore we infer that the poetic public is rare and distinguished. It is composed of individuals scattered here and there. If a public is an assemblage, a gathering of people, a crowd, then poetry has no public. (pp. vii-xi)

I believe that no matter how much the literary public in general increases, the poetry-loving public will not grow proportionately. America, for example, is the most extraordinary case that the history of "publics" has known. The numbers of editions and sales are astonishing. They inspire me with as much wonder, bordering on terror, as the towers of Babylon must have caused. They are one of the most prodigious signs of the imperial magnitude of the United States. But can it be thought that that multiplication of the reader, the most fabulous arithmetical proposition of all times, evident in this country, has also reached the reader of poetry? I do not believe it. Some poets complain of this; I find it excellent. Except for the books of eloquent or narrative poets, or poets of a nationalistic type, like Kipling, the book of poems is of small mercantile value, in spite of the efforts at propaganda and advertisement. It is impossible to popularize poetry, for the mere reason that it is not an article in common use. That is proved by this simple argument: that few persons of a certain class can live for a year without reading a novel or going to the theatre, while millions of beings of the same social class live all their lives without reading a book of verse. Not by election or caprice of the poets, but on account of its intrinsic nature, poetry is not for everyone. And what I say should not be taken as a vain affirmation of aristocracy: it is on the contrary a recognition of a human truth, of a reality. It is not that poets wish to write for the few, no: it is that poetry *is* for the few. All intent to popularize it, to make it reach further than its natural limits, I suspect, is false and artificial. Poetry has always been surrounded by an atmosphere of wonderment, and in this resides its great strength. Nothing protects it more than its quality of being a thing of exceptional value and luxury, a useless thing. How delightfully moving and ironical, at the same time, the daily appearance of that poetry in the New York Times! It is one of the most delicate things that can be pointed out to a stranger, in that city of implacable geometry. . . . This very faithful and modest corner of the Times is the best witness to the fact that it considers poetry invincible, precisely because it needs scarcely any material space for existence. And the daily delicate and inevitable presence of a poem in the secret shelter of that enormous periodical, is for me a perfect symbol of the place which poetry occupies and should occupy, scarcely visible, either subterranean or celestial, but always in the centre of the confusion of fugitive signs and shadows, called daily "news," which surround it. Poetry, when we think of the aims of life, as conceived by the immense majority of people to-day, is useless. It does not serve either to teach or to distract. Hence its position, every day more puzzling, and more assured at the same time, in the modern world. We find our world possessed by an insane desire for utility and efficiency. Men have peopled the earth with images of gods, made in the semblance of their desires and dreams: machines. And poetry is transformed, in a manufacturing and functional world, into something inexplicable, without an appropriate place in the picture of normal utilitarian activities. Poetry is superfluous, not wanted, because for the great mass of people it contributes to no form of practical or visible service.

Here is the reason why in the present state of civilization, of technical ability, of social and economical science, of statistics, poetry finds even less justification with people than palmistry or reading of the future in crystal balls. Poetry to-day is in the air. It has no other place. And happily, because the air is its proper and natural element. Like the bird, it lives by liberty and discovery. It is useless to wish to convert it into a domesticated fowl, subdued, confined, ready at any moment to be useful, transforming it into familiar every day fare on the family table. It does not accept cages or poultry yards. And when the world appears to turn towards forms of life which resemble cages or barnyards more than anything else, the fate of poetry appears to us, at first sight, as if more in danger than ever. But I do not think so. Its salvation is in its strength of resistance to utility. Its most sure place is in the air. In that element it will live always while people work, calculate or amuse themselves.

This is why I was wondering where the public for poetry could be found. Perhaps the answer is that that public is, like poetry, in the air, that is, everywhere and not in any determined spot, a vast, countless, illusive public, but existent nevertheless, though like poetry, inexplicable.

To you, American readers of poetry, to you who are neither here nor there, to you who are invisible and inexplicable, I submit these poems—as a throw of dice: to try my luck, if by chance you exist—to those hands which still, in addition to their function of work and usefulness, know how to hold before the eyes, under a lamp, all alone, or in a street-car or train, among many others, a book of verses. (pp. xi-xv)

> *Pedro Salinas, in a preface to his* Lost Angel, and Other Poems, *translated by Eleanor L. Turnbull, The Johns Hopkins University Press, 1938, pp. vii-xv.*

ROBERT P. TRISTRAM COFFIN (essay date 1941)

[*In the following review of* Truth of Two, and Other Poems, *Coffin praises Salinas's ability to render vast, spiritual contemplation with simple, exacting language.*]

Love used to be the morning or evening star of most lyric poets. Today, it has shrunk to the magnitude of an asteroid, and you will look long and in vain for morning or evening light from it. In other times than ours, mysticism was a fire at which poets warmed their long hands and wide hearts. Now it is a rare and vanishing spark whirling in the vast dark which astrophysics has made of our universe. Hence it is an event to find both mysticism and love as major concerns to a man of our time who is young and vigorous as a man and as a poet.

Pedro Salinas is all these—a man of vigor, a poet, and a man of these days, and he is, through the tragedy of the collapse of European civilization, no longer a resident of Spain but a resident of the United States. It is one of the great indictments of fascism that the two greatest modern Spanish poets have been driven out of Spain: Salinas into the hemisphere of the democracies; Lorca to his death. Here Salinas is still very much

alive and writing still in his native language and is, through the happiest of accidents, becoming known to an enlarging circle of readers in English translation.

Modern as a marconigram, Salinas finds his poetry in the midst of movies, telegraph wires, and the nervous weariness of life rendered safe and sterile by scientific improvements. But he has no sterility or weariness in him, for he believes in love, and he believes loving is a mystery and an infinity.

At first sight, the Spanish writer seems poor among the poets, especially among the rich old poets. He has no machinery or romances. He has no gules or azure of the churchly science of the mystical approach to God. Almost, it seems, he is skeptic enough to have no God. No God but this tremendous vibration that he feels for one other human being.

Salinas builds a small house carefully. It is neat, compact; there are no wasted phrases or ideas. His carpentry is exact. His words a child could use. And yet he achieves vastness. . . .

Other mystics have started with the palms of lovers and ended up with the law of love holding all creation in place. But this Spanish lover starts with the hand of his beloved and remains there, heaping into it all motions, all matter, all the toys of time, all warmth, all light, the urge to be and continue being, eternity. His hand is a large one. It holds the universe. His house is a mansion where all proper names are submerged and lost in the personal pronoun *you*, all time runs down to *now*, all created matter is turned back to its dewy origins. Salinas desires, like all mystics, to drown himself in the One, in the light. But his light is one woman. He reads her primeval beauty in the alphabets of foam on the sea, the clover blossoms, and the dome of the stars. Time rolls up as he reads, and he is at the infancy of the world, at the center, and very wise:

> It seemed that we were living on
>   the eve of the world,
> Nothing had been created.
> Neither matter, nor numbers,
> Nor stars, nor centuries, nothing,
> Coal was not black
> Nor the rose tender.
> Nothing was nothing still.

In a day of the statistics of the power of facts and their material splendors, it is our great fortune to have such fierceness of faith in things of the spirit, to have a man who can put his faith in the passion that merges all patterns of the spirit into such sharp, plain words—words we mouth every hour without knowing what flames and arrows we are mouthing—that the simplest and most direct minds can comprehend.

> *Robert P. Tristram Coffin, "Not Spanish but Heaven,"* in New York Herald Tribune Books, *March 23, 1941, p. 25.*

JOSE GARCIA VILLA (essay date 1950)

[*Philippine-born Villa is an award-winning poet, short story writer, critic, and educator living in the United States. Considered a highly talented and innovative writer, Villa has stated that he is "not at all interested in description or outward appearance, nor in the contemporary scene, but in essence. A single motive underlies all my work and defines my intention as a serious artist: the search for the metaphysical meaning of man's life in the Universe. . . ." Critics have praised Villa's verbal skill as well as the passionate intensity of his poetry. Both his poetry and prose have been published in numerous collections and his work has*

been widely anthologized. In the following excerpt, Villa reviews
Sea of San Juan *and praises the overall quality of Salinas's poetry,
saying that he is a finer poet than Federico García Lorca.*]

Pedro Salinas is possibly the finest living Spanish poet. . . . In
this reviewer's opinion, Salinas' work excels the better known
Federico Garcia Lorca's in many ways: Lorca's is an almost
elementary though genuine poetry; Salinas' poems are rich,
complex and full of reverberations—a finer, more cultivated
instrument.

While Lorca is a poet of the people (his simplicities are easily
absorbed) Salinas is a poet of great culture—and, therefore,
much more difficult. His work is always a gentle, modulated
poetry, but it is rich with metaphysical subtleties. Usually the
poems take the form of dramatic meditations, as in [*Sea of San
Juan*] . . ., where the poet contemplates the sea, but these
contemplations do not remain mere sea-meditations but spiral
upward to higher involvements.

A poet of superb and delicate craft, and a poet of fine themes—
this is not the little poetry that abounds everywhere; this is that
rare poetry of final essences. If a fault is to be found it is that
a certain haze results from the poet's revolvement of his themes—
but even then the effect is more that of an aura than of unclarity.

> *José Garcia Villa, "Rich with Reverberations," in*
> The New York Times, *December 3, 1950, p. 44.*

JULIAN PALLEY (essay date 1957)

[*Palley is an American critic, translator, and educator who spe-
cializes in Spanish literature. He has written extensively on Salinas and other twentieth-century Spanish poets. In the following
excerpt, he traces the development of Salinas's prominent theme
of the struggle between love and nothingness (nada), in "La voz
a ti debida."*]

La voz a ti debida by Pedro Salinas is a long meditation on the
reality of the beloved. It is a hymn in praise of the beloved.
It is the victory of love—Being—over the Nada, Non-Being.
It is perhaps the final and most consummate expression of those
themes which were repeated—with infinite variation—in his
three earlier books: the search for the reality of the beloved,
the struggle against nothingness. The book is meant to be one
long paean of love, of affirmation; and no subject unrelated to
the beloved enters here. This is why the poet chose to leave
the poems unnumbered and untitled: so they might be read as
a whole, rather than as single units. But though the book's
thematic unity justifies this approach, the poems tend to emerge
as self-enclosed units, as in the earlier works.

The first poem announces the praise of the beloved which will
be sustained through most of the work: . . .

> [You live always in your actions.
> With the tips of your fingers
> you touch the world lightly, and draw
> from it dawns, triumphs, colors
> and joys, for it is your music,
> and life is what you play upon.
> (Translated by Eleanor L. Turnbull)]

But in the midst of this wonderment at the miracle of the
beloved, her beauty, vital force and magic, *una sombra* ["a

shadow"] is cast, and the shadow is himself, the artist, the
mind examining itself: . . .

> [And you never made a mistake,
> save one time only, one night when
> you fell in love with a shadow
> —the only one that has pleased you—.
> A shadow appeared.
> And you wished to embrace it.
> And I was the shadow.
> (Translated by Eleanor L. Turnbull)]

Y la quisiste abrazar ["And you wished to embrace it"]: always in Salinas the hand which reaches and never finds, the
elusive and deceptive nature of reality, the *peau de chagrin*
which shrivels up as its owner is on the verge of achieving his
desire. And the search goes on, the eyes pierce deeper and
deeper in their quest for the beloved: . . .

> [Yes, back of all other people
> I seek you.
> Not in your name, if they speak it,
> not in your likeness, if they paint it.
> Back, further back, back of all.
> (Translated by Eleanor L. Turnbull)]

And suddenly, reminiscences of San Juan de la Cruz, of Santa
Teresa: the conceptual mysticism of the sixteenth century: . . .

> [And in order to find you,
> I would give up living in you,
> in me, and in others.
> I would live back, back of all,
> on the other side behind all
> —in order to find you—
> as if I were dying.
> (Translated by Eleanor L. Turnbull)]

The annihilation of self to achieve the *Amado;* the poet's profound kinship with the Castilian mystics is here delineated in
precise terms. (p. 450)

As the mystics used profane analogies to define divine experience, so Salinas used divine analogies to define profane experience. But, unlike Calisto, he never commits blasphemy.
Though the deity is never mentioned, Salinas, a true mystic,
walks the narrow line between the profane and the divine. In
this book he is addressing a woman, let there be no doubt about
that; but this woman, like Dante's Beatrice, has, in a sense,
become the symbol of the unknowable. . . .

> [If you should call me, yes,
> if you should call me!
> I would leave all for you,
> I would fling away all:
> prices and catalogues,
> and the blue of ocean on the maps,
> the days and the nights . . .
> (Translated by Eleanor L. Turnbull)]

(Again the search: for the beloved, God, reality, the unknown?
In this poem the woman of flesh and blood fades away, and
there is left only the cry of the mystic.) Then again, love as
the reply to the Nada: . . .

> ["To-morrow." The word had
> no meaning, it hung empty
> and weightless in the air,
> so without soul and body,
> so without color and kiss . . .
> (Translated by Eleanor L. Turnbull)]

(*Ingrávida* ["weightless"]: a favorite word of Salinas. So often, as if haunted by nothingness, the Real becomes weightless, diaphanous, elusive.) . . .

> [But suddenly you spoke:
> "I, to-morrow . . ."
> And all was provided
> with flesh and with banners.
> (Translated by Eleanor L. Turnbull)]

The presence, the act of the beloved, was all that was needed to give form and weight to the chaos. . . .

> [How many lost things there were
> that were never lost!
> (Translated by Eleanor L. Turnbull)]

begins one poem; and he lists, in poetic enumeration, the things that were lost and then recovered by the *amada:* . . .

> [If they had escaped from me,
> it was not to die, to fade
> into nothingness.
> In you they kept living on.
> That which I called oblivion
> was you.
> (Translated by Eleanor L. Turnbull)]

The beloved once again has saved him from the Nada, *olvido.* In the following poem he states that the beloved cannot be known by outward signs and words spoken: . . .

> [He who seeks you in the life
> you are living, knows nothing
> more than suggestions of you,
> pretences where you hide yourself.
> (Translated by Eleanor L. Turnbull)]

He who would know her inner self must rely on revelation: . . .

> [I knew you in a flash,
> in that brutal rending
> of darkness and light,
> where is revealed the background
> which escapes the day and the night.
> (Translated by Eleanor L. Turnbull)]

and, finally, he lives in his beloved as the mystics lived in God: . . .

> [I have known you for such a time,
> that I close my eyes in your love,
> and I walk without swerving,
> blindly in the dark, asking nothing
> of that slow and certain light
> with which we recognize letters
> and forms or make up accounts.
> Yet they think that they see
> who you are, my invisible one.
> (Translated by Eleanor L. Turnbull)]

Never in Spanish lyrics, since San Juan de la Cruz, have poetry and mysticism been so perfectly united.

In this book as in no other his poetry has been reduced to the *pronominal dimension:* all objects of sense perception have faded into the background, and what remains is the interplay, the interpenetration, the mutual seeking, the struggle against the Nada of *tú* and *yo.* . . . (pp. 450-51)

The struggle between the *nada,* nothingness, on the one hand, and love, Being, on the other, is a central preoccupation of the poetry of Salinas. In this poem the Nada, the primordial chaos, is, however, deeply desired by the nihilistic lover, in order to return, through love, to some absolute beginning: . . .

> [Let all things collapse! . . .
> And as I embrace you,
> the touch of your delicate skin
> takes me back to the very first
> heart throb, without light, without form,
> before the beginning of the world,
> when there was only chaos.
> (Translated by Eleanor L. Turnbull)] . . .

But the almost perfect joy in the beloved is dominant in this book, and offers its reply to previous doubts: . . .

> [What a joy it is to live
> feeling myself lived by another!
> To give myself up humbly
> to the great certainty
> that another being outside myself, far away,
> is living for me.
> (Translated by Eleanor L. Turnbull)]

This is a joy which is tempered by the mystical belief in the identification of the lover with the beloved: . . .

> [And all enraptured, my body will be able
> to rest, quiet, already dead. Dying
> in the high confidence
> that this living of mine was not my living alone,
> it was ours. And that there lives for me
> another being beyond all possible death.
> (Translated by Eleanor L. Turnbull)]

The oriental mystic, on dying, unites with the continuum, the Absolute; the Christian mystic is united with God. The beloved of Salinas partakes of some of the qualities of both. The lovely poem which begins: . . .

> [I cannot give you more.
> I am not more than I am.
> (Translated by Eleanor L. Turnbull)]

is a supreme expression of human love, a love whose intensity and purity are so great that any further refinement is difficult to conceive. It combines an Arabic sensualism . . . with a very Castilian conceptualism: . . .

> [And how I should like to be
> a joy above all others,
> one alone, the rapture
> with which you rejoice your soul!
> A love, one love alone:
>
> the love which you wind round your heart!
> (Translated by Eleanor L. Turnbull)]

And the praise of the beloved continues in its mystic intensity: . . .

> [The only fault of the light is
> that it does not come from you.
> That it comes from suns,
> and from rivers, from the olive tree.
> But I love your darkness more.
> (Translated by Eleanor L. Turnbull)]

Quiero más tu oscuridad ["But I love your darkness more"]: once again, echoes of the great Carmelite: "oh noche amable más que el alborada:" and the fascination with the mystery of the void. One would have to hark back to the Provençal lyrics to find parallels for the absolute devotion to another human being which is manifest in this next poem: . . .

> [When you close your eyes
> your eyelids are as the wind.
> They sweep me off
> to go with you, within.
>
> When you open your eyes
> once more, I return again
> outside, blinded now,
> and stumbling also,
> without seeing here either.
> (Translated by Eleanor L. Turnbull)]

He lives within her when she closes her eyes; in a new, hidden world which requires new senses to perceive. When she opens her eyes, he returns to a world no longer his, and, *inútil, desvalido,* he wanders back and forth between the real, but bleak, world of the outside, and the unknown world which is created at the whim of the beloved. Such is the new courtly and mystical love of Pedro Salinas; but in place of the troubadour's submission to an artificial tradition, we have the simplicity and sincerity which characterize this poet's best work.

The immense love of Salinas, expressed in countless variations of emotion and intellect, of being and absence, in the infinite modulations that lie between joy and despair, wavers always between the sense world and the unknown. . . . The poetry of Wallace Stevens gives rise to one assured interpretation: that the ideal world of art was, for him, more real than the world of the senses. We are tempted to make a similar statement about Salinas, but the Spanish poet is far more elusive, far less malleable to the critic's tools, far less reducible to dogma than most of our American poets. It is part of the Spanish genius to seek truth through paradox and contradiction; Unamuno is our most obvious example. Salinas is, at times, a platonic idealist, and at times he is a mystic, and at times (less often) a sensualist untroubled by the unknown. Because he is a man; because that's what a man is, all these things and many more.

Positive, affirmative as is the major note of this book, the Nada is always present in its multiple disguises. It becomes stronger toward the middle of the volume, and by the end it is once again an overwhelming threat, as if the joy of his love, great as it was, were not vigorous enough to suppress, through this rather long book of verses, the invading and undermining force of nothingness.

Sometimes it is the metaphysical, Mallarmean play of presence and absence, brought to new extremes of subtlety: . . .

> [No longer can I find you
> there in that distant place, with its special name,
> where you used to be absent.
> To come in quest of me
> you have already left it. You came forth from your
>   absence,
> and still I do not see you, nor do I know where you
>   are.
> (Translated by Eleanor L. Turnbull)]

The poem that begins *La frente es más segura . . .* ["The forehead is more assured"] . . . is existentialist in the strict sense; because here there is a kind of hope founded on the most absolute despair, there is a new kind of hope (that of Sartre and Samuel Beckett) that one may build on the frankest acceptance of philosophical desolation. Here life and love are

reduced to its absolute minimum, bone. . . . "After death all that will remain of our love, our kiss, will be the bone—your forehead." But this also is a kind of salvation. . . . In this next poem the beloved has saved him—at least for a while—from the Nada: . . .

> [When your choice fell on me
> —it was love that chose—
> I came out from the great
> unnamed crowd, out from nothing.
> (Translated by Eleanor L. Trumbull)]

But when she leaves—as she will—he will return to the *osario inmenso* ["vast charnel house"]: . . .

> [Back to the vast charnel house
> of those who have not died,
> and to whom no more is left
> than to die while still living.
> (Translated by Eleanor L. Turnbull)]

The tone is more and more one of despair as we approach the final pages of the book. (pp. 451-54)

The book's final poem is a magnificent resumé of the poet's struggle against the Nada. He would endow with corporality the shadows created by his love: . . .

> [Do you not hear how they ask for reality,
> these, the dishevelled ones, these, the untamed ones,
> the shadows we invent, you and I,
> on this immense plain of distances?
> Weary now of the infinite, weary
> of time without measure, of namelessness,
> and sick with longing for the material,
> they ask for boundaries, days and names.
> No longer
> can they live like this: they are on the border
> of the death of shadows, which is nothingness.
> (Translated by Eleanor L. Turnbull)]

This is his endeavor: to defeat the Nada by forging—with his art—an unquestionable reality of their love. (This is the endeavor of every artist: to create a reality where there was none before.) . . .

> [Come with me to the rescue.
> Stretch out your hands to them, offer your body.
> Together we shall seek for them
> a color, a time, a breast, a sun.
>
> And their eager wistful dream
> of shadows, once more, shall be the return
> to this mortal existence of roseate flesh
> where love invents its infinity.
> (Translated by Eleanor L. Turnbull)]

After the joy, the despair, the doubts and hope, the book ends, then, with the affirmation that love (and art) can overcome the Nada, can create its own reality, its own *infinito* ["infinity"]. (pp. 454-55)

> *Julian Palley, "'La Voz a ti Debida': An Appreci-*
> *ation," in* Hispania, *Vol. XL, No. 4, December, 1957,*
> *pp. 450-55 [the translated excerpts of Pedro Sali-*
> *nas's poetry used here were originally published in*
> *his* Truth of Two, and Other Poems, *translated by*
> *Eleanor L. Turnbull, The Johns Hopkins University*
> *Press, 1940].*

JULIAN PALLEY   (essay date 1959)

[In the following excerpt, Palley discusses the poems in Todo más claro, *which he believes express Salinas's darkest vision regarding the future of the technological age.]*

Pedro Salinas was for fifteen years a grateful resident of the United States, an admirer of our democratic forms and a celebrator of the conveniences of modern technology. Those who heard him lecture will recall his fascination with modern artifacts, how, for example, he baptized with the name of *el buzón de los ángeles* that perpendicular mail chute which reaches to the summit of our skyscrapers. But eventually he had to react, as the poet he was, to the harsh and foreboding aspects of our materialism and technological proficiency. His book *Todo más claro,* which appeared in 1949, contains what is probably his most significant poetry written in this country during the years of exile before his death. His books of verse composed in Spain, from *Presagios* through *Razón de amor,* were concerned with universal, rather than contemporary problems: love, death and the sense of nothingness. The Spanish Civil War and the years spent in America awakened him brutally to the realities of the technological forces which are most significant for our life in the twentieth century. The amatory, two-dimensional dialogues ended with *Razón de amor;* and human love is generally absent from the works that follow. *Todo más claro* is the most anguished of his books. It is the poet, the pure and limpid thinker and artist that was Pedro Salinas, face to face with the horrors and the promise of the technological revolution which is everywhere and inescapably occuring. As his residence was in our industrial East, he could not fail to be impressed by the bleakness and the crushing of the spirit which technology often effects in that region. In this book the sense of nothingness, which runs as a threat to Being and love, as an agonistic undercurrent through most of his work, is carried to its most anguished conclusion. Despair could not reach, in Salinas, a greater synthesis, and his posthumously published work, the poems of *Confianza,* are of a serene and lyrical optimism.

Why the title, *Todo más claro,* for a book full of inquietude and dark foreboding? The poet tells us about the content of the book in the prologue:

> ... Conozco la gran paradoja: que en los cubículos de los laboratorios, celebrados templos de progreso, se elabora del modo más racional la técnica del más definitivo regreso del ser humano: la vuelta del ser al no ser. Sobre mi alma llevo, de todo esto, la parte que me toca; como hombre que soy, como europeo que me siento, como americano de vivienda, como español que nací y me afirmo. Porque las angustias arremeten por muchos lados. Y ahí están las mías, en este librito....

> [... I know the great paradox: that in the cubicles of the laboratories, the celebrated temples of progress, the most rational technique of the most definitive return to being human is elaborated: the turn from being to not being. Deep in my soul, I carry all of this, the part that touches me; like the man I am, like the European I feel myself to be, like the American by residence, like the Spaniard I was born and still consider myself. Because the anxieties at-

tack from many directions. And there, in this little book, are mine. ...]

Why then the title?

> ... la poesía siempre es obra de caridad y de claridad. De amor, aunque gotee angustias y se busque la solitaria desesperación. De esclarecimiento, aunque necesite los arrebozos de lo oscuro y se nos presente como bulto indiscernible, a primeras. Eche por donde eche, vía de San Francisco o vía de Baudelaire, *Fioretti* o *Fleurs du mal,* todo poema digno acaba en iluminaciones. Hasta la más enredada poesía suelta enigmas. En lengua española resplandecen, sobre todo, esos pocos poemas en donde se encuentra al clarísimo a través de las tinieblas....

> [... Poetry is always the work of charity and of clarity. Of love, although it would drip anxieties and would seek for the solitary desperation. Of enlightenment, although it requires the scarves of the dark and is presented to us as indiscernible bulk, at first. Whether it follows Saint Francis or Baudelaire, the *Fioretti* or the *Flowers of Evil,* every worthy poem worthy of the name achieves illumination. Even the most entangled poetry untangles enigmas. In the Spanish language there shine, over everything, those few poems in which can be found utter clarity shining through the darkness. ...]

Here then is a creed for students and practitioners of modern poetry. The book's title comes from the first poem, which is a description of the act of creation. At the beginning there is only the chaos and multiplicity of reality. ... The poet only knows that he must create. He has the impulse, but there is no certainty about the source or the time; the word will materialize only when it is ready. ... Chance always has the last word in poetry, logic never; this is the key to the excitement of the most difficult and most common of the arts. The [middle] section of the poem deals with the poet's materials, words, *santas palabras,* the hoard of centuries. ... He goes on to speak of *aquel doncel de Toledo,* and of *aquel monje de la oscura / noche del alma,* as well as *el que inventó a Dulcinea:* the masters of the language. ... In the last section the poet is face to face with his creation, in the serenity which follows the struggles of birth. ... (pp. 336-37)

"Hombre en la orilla" opens with a description of what is doubtless the flow of traffic in a large American city. The poet compares the flux to a river. ... A river without water, foam, pebbles, grass, poplars: only wheels. And then the refrain, which could be the cry of Kierkegaard on his mountain:

> El hombre en la orilla, tiembla.

> [The man on the sidewalk trembles.]

At the vision of this frenetic and senseless activity, a man, watching from the sidewalk, trembles. Then there is an abrupt change of style, and Salinas uses for the first time that mixture of realism and symbolism which, since Eliot, has characterized much American poetry:

> Mrs. Dorothy Morrison, rodando.
> Va rodando, a este viernes, y a las cuatro.
> Sus años treinta y siete, y su belleza. ...

[Mrs. Dorothy Morrison, rolling.
Rolling along, on this Friday, and at four o'clock.
Her thirty-seven years, and her beauty. . . .]

"Mrs. Morrison" is going to a beauty parlor. The second *ruedas* is a business man going to sign an important contract, and the third is a student going home from school. . . . And the "man on the shore"—the observer—trembles at this march toward nothingness as at the terror of the jungle. . . . This is the most clearly existentialist of Salinas' poems. . . . But this poem, an attempt at synthesis of the chaos that Salinas felt in industrial America, does not supersede that chaos to achieve a higher order, the essence of the poetic method. The poem conveys only the anguish and frustration which the poet felt on writing it, and for this reason it is only partially successful.

"**Nocturno de los avisos**" is beyond doubt the poet's reaction to New York, especially to Times Square. Whoever has not stood in this place and watched incredulously the enormous, meretricious, offensive advertisements that crowd one against another like so many demons, Cerberus and Geryon, from the *Inferno,* will not understand the horror of this poem. It opens with a vision of the skyscrapers. . . . He contemplates the skyscrapers until night comes on, and the electric signs emerge with their insistent repetitions. . . . The poet becomes more and more bewildered by the profusion of signs, often in themselves contradictory. . . . Finally, exhausted and benumbed by the hucksters' supreme victory over taste and sensibility, he sits down to await the appearance of the sky's older lights, the "publicity of God". . . . (pp. 337-38)

"**Angel extraviado**" . . . is a poem of internal conflict—the familiar forces of good and evil, of Being and Non-Being—resolved hopefully by the strength of love. . . . The poet is on the verge of destroying himself and all that he loves best. . . . Then he is saved by the intervention of the *ángel extraviado.* Although at first sight this poem seems to fit into the traditional Christian pattern of salvation through divine intervention, a closer examination reveals that the force behind the *ángel extraviado* is not the anthropomorphic Judaeo-Christian divinity, but rather a symbol of the force of love, both the love of one being for another and the love of all beings for each other, leading us therefore to a kind of pantheism which is close to Spinoza. (pp. 338-39)

"**Error de cálculo**" forms part of a group called "Entretiempo romántico." Two of the three poems describe a hopeless love in the atmosphere of a large American city. "**Error de cálculo**" describes, simply, the conversation of a man and woman in a crowded and fashionable bar. . . . They begin to calculate, in terms of an affective mathematics, the future of their love. . . . The poem continues with a surrealistic juxtaposition of the ideal and the real. Nothing is decided. . . . Finally a miracle occurs. An angel enters the bar, and there ensues a scene strongly reminiscent of medieval Spain:

> Un ángel entra por la puerta rotatoria
> todo enredado con sus propias alas,
> y rompiéndose plumas, torpemente.
> Angel de anunciación. Lo incalculable
> se nos pasa en las frentes y nosotros
> lo recibimos, mano en mano, de rodillas.

[An angel enters through the revolving door
entangled in his own wings,
and clumsily tearing up his feathers.
Angel of annunciation. The incalculable
passes before our faces and we
receive it, hand in hand, kneeling.]

There is no need for further conversation. The decision is left to *lo incalculable, seguro azar*. On leaving the bar they take a taxi which quietly traverses the night, transporting them to *una alcoba*. . . . In this poem, as in many in this book, the sense of nothingness appears in strong relief against a background of modern urban civilization.

"**Cero**," the final poem of *Todo más claro,* offers the poet's last and most anguished presentation of the idea of nothingness. That its theme is the modern nuclear weapon is stated unequivocally in the book's introduction. After describing the weapons being manufactured in the *cubículos de los laboratorios,* he offers this book as an expression of his *angustia*. . . . (p. 339)

"**Cero**" is the most ambitious poem in this collection. Its imagery, though enigmatic, is powerfully suggestive; its lyrical intensity is maintained throughout. It requires perhaps a half dozen readings to perceive the unity which is achieved over the four hundred lines. Its theme is the possibility of total destruction which the atom bomb has made feasible. . . . It concludes with the agonized cry of man on his spiritual desert, alienated as never before from God, endowed as never before with the power of his own destruction. . . . The *obra del hombre* becomes a zero only when it explodes. There follows a description of an atomic explosion, perhaps in the American Southwest, perhaps Hiroshima, perhaps in some cataclysmic future. . . . And, the poet goes on to say, who feels pity for a distant map? For a bubble that bursts, for a snail crushed underfoot—what is immediately perceived—one may feel pity, but not for this abstract configuration separated from the observer by a thousand layers of transparent air. . . . In the middle part of the poem, the Greek column becomes the symbol of the works of man which, after centuries of slow and painstaking development, are threatened by destruction. . . . Besides the *obras,* the *horas*—the joys of daily simple living—are also threatened by the *cero*. . . . Finally, the works—products of centuries of endeavor—and the hours—our quiet joy in the privilege of life—are alike threatened by nothingness. . . . There follows a vision of the ruins of civilization which calls to mind the canvases of Bosch. The poet envisions these ruins not as merely stones and images, but as *tercos defensores de sus sueños*. . . . The poem ends with an agonized portrayal of man alone in the rubbish heap that threatens his civilization. . . . It may be justifiably argued that the poem suffers from a diffuseness and a tendency toward prolixity. Perhaps a greater conciseness of expression would have been desirable, but evidently such a revision would have been false to the foreboding, prophetic message the poet wanted to convey, in this final effort in the poet's battle against nothingness. (pp. 339-40)

> *Julian Palley, "'Todo más claro': Salinas and the United States," in* Hispania, *Vol. XLII, No. 3, September, 1959, pp. 336-40.*

JORGE GUILLÉN (essay date 1966)

[Guillén is a well-known Spanish poet, critic, translator, and educator who has lectured widely in North America. He was a member of the group of Spanish poets known as "The Generation of 1927," which included Federico García Lorca, Pedro Salinas, Dámaso Alonso, Vincente Aleixandre, and Emilio Prados. The Generation of 1927, whose name derives from the approximate date of many of their first or most significant publications, combined techniques of classical Spanish poetry with many of the experimental techniques that flourished in European poetry after World War I. In this way they created one of the most original

and significant forms of poetry to emerge during the era of European Modernism. With the outbreak of the Spanish Civil War in 1936, the group, which held strong anti-Franco sentiments, was forced to disband. Most of its members, including Guillén, went into exile, and its most famous member, Lorca, was executed by Franco's nationalist army. Although deeply affected by the political conditions in Spain, Guillén's poetry is more generally concerned with life-affirming, spiritual values. His early poems in Cántico *(1928) are considered his best. In the following excerpt, Guillén divides Salinas's career into three periods and discusses the salient features of his work from each period. In Guillén's opinion, the finest examples of Salinas's poetry can be found in the love sequences ''La voz a ti debida'' and ''Razón de amor,'' in which Guillén finds Salinas's most exceptional descriptions of the total fulfillment of love.]*

The sixty years of [Salinas's] life constituted one single line of development. Thirty years of preparation. Thirty years of production. After the withdrawn boy, the reserved adolescent, the poet who wrote little and published less, there appears—beginning in 1923, the date of his first book, *Presagios*—a man of great complexity, an active personality, reaching full maturity during his last years. . . . (p. ix)

His poetic work consists of nine books, which may be grouped into three periods. The early period, from 1923 to 1931, includes *Presagios, Seguro azar,* and *Fábula y signo.* The second period, strictly speaking, constitutes a cycle: from 1933 to 1938 his great theme develops in *La voz a ti debida, Razón de amor,* and finally, a volume as yet largely unpublished, *Largo lamento.* With this cycle our author's activity reaches its highest point. But this metaphor is not intended to reduce the early period to a mere preliminary tryout, nor the later poems to a mere epilogue. Salinas is Salinas throughout his entire career; each volume contributes to defining the whole, and the whole is the most important aspect of a great poet's work. So the three volumes of the forties are also essential: *El contemplado, Todo más claro,* and the posthumous *Confianza.* (This final collection had no name; its general title is taken from that of one of the poems and is appropriate to Salinas' final style.)

The beginnings were slow. The youthful apprentice made great demands upon himself. *Presagios (Presciences),* a word which the poet told me occurred to him as he was walking through the Puerta del Sol in Madrid, a word here used in its etymological sense, this word reveals a soul. And soul . . . is the key term of that poetry, a soul always in contact with the Other and the others. Inner life alone? A soul turned in upon itself? Not at all. The spiritual quality which is so evident in the whole work does not imply any solipsism, not even within the cloistered walls which are sometimes raised by love. Salinas is always involved in relationships of love or friendship with things and people, always ready to discover in them their value, their transcendence, their inner meaning. This vital meaning is understood and felt only when it is well fixed and rooted in a concrete particular.

From *Presagios* to *Confianza (Confidence)* we find a voice that delicately but firmly intensifies more and more this bringing to life of the world. That it has a soul is not a legend or a false ornamentation, but the deepest truth. Great poetry does not deceive itself, much less tell lies. Our poet knew what he was saying: *Fábula y signo.* All of his poems, not merely those belonging to the volume with this title, move from the fable to the sign: bringing an object to life reveals its transcendent meaning. Salinas' theme is, then, the conversion of the outer world into its inner soul, by means of friendship and love. *Todo más claro:* everything brighter. In his preface to this

Federico García Lorca, Salinas, and Rafael Alberti in 1927. From García Lorca: Biografías Illustradas. *Ediciones Destino, 1962. Reproduced by permission of the publisher.*

volume Salinas explains: ''Whether it follows Saint Francis or Baudelaire, the *Fioretti* or the *Fleurs du Mal,* every poem worthy of the name achieves illumination.'' A completely human illumination, of course, without mystical implications. A ''passion d'absolu'' has been seen in Salinas by Elsa Dehennin, the intelligent and enthusiastic Hispanist of Belgium. The absolute is a very human goal. Salinas is always faithful to his vocation as a humanist. (pp. xxii-xxiv)

Vision is our poet's primary faculty. One desires what is real. And in order to convert it into spirit, one must go deep into matter. Not the orange, an easy solution, but its secret: the juice, an internal reality. . . . Of course the external world is not self-sufficient, for in order to reach its fullness, it needs its complement. On a beautiful afternoon, blueness is not enough, ''nor that singing repetition of the wave,'' nor the seashells as iridescent as clouds. All of those details are summed up, comprehended, and transcended by the spectator; it is he who brings the beautiful afternoon to its perfection. But this does not mean mere impressionism, a pleasant dissolving of the landscape into the sensations of an artist. The landscape is brought into relationship with an ideal significance. Nor is the sea during a summer's hour reduced to an ''impression'' of that hour. For him who contemplates it from this shore—''**Orilla**'' is the title of a poem in *Seguro azar*—the sea throbs like an organic living animal, with a will of its own. . . .

If it were not for the fragile
rose of whitest foam
invented by the distant sea,
who would have thought
that its breast moved
with breathing, or that it's alive,
that it's impetuous inside,
that it wants the whole earth,
the blue, quiet sea of July?

The words could not be more delicate, but they do not dissolve into a pictorial blob. The Mediterranean, viewed probably from a beach near Alicante, is transmuted, by grace of a metaphor, into a vision: the sea as a breast, the waves as the movement of one who breathes, breath as impetuosity or the will to power. And the foam, by an incidental metaphor, is converted into an "invented" rose: an ingenious stroke, offset by the very colloquial, and here very expressive, phrase, "¿quién me iba a decir a mí?" From this shore, in sum, everything does look brighter, and its reality is made completely human: fable and sign. Does all this have anything at all to do with the "dehumanization" which was being talked about at the time?

The poet takes delight in the innumerable variety of things, and he does not exclude even the most recent things, from the automobile to the typewriter, those technical inventions which the "futurists" had already proclaimed. But innovations do not conceal the permanence of Nature. There is a "joyful knowledge"—that which is learned by contemplating natural life—which makes us able to endure the tribulations of historical life: Nature is our salvation. With what leisurely enjoyment he composes the poems of *El contemplado (The Contemplated Sea)* and *Confianza*! One must apply oneself lovingly to what one sees in order to reach what is not seen: the whole and its meaning. For, he tells us, "everything is on purpose, the world is headed somewhere." Everything is ordered and reaches a conclusion in meaningful action. That is how we perceive the total unity of the earth, which has, in fact, the perfection of the circle. . . .

A world turns peacefully
What a perfect roundness!

Also, he tells us, "light is said to be round." This assertion could not be proved by science. Nevertheless, from the point of view of the soul's light, that other material light does appear as something round and surrounding. What re-creative power, piercing through everything with rays of the human mind!

Pedro Salinas' poetry, we know, reached its highest point with the theme of love. "Since Espronceda and Bécquer," as I have said on another occasion, "since the former's *Canto a Teresa* and the latter's *Rimas,* has there been anything more important written in Spain than *La voz a ti debida* and *Razón de amor*?" The lovers live by themselves, seeking and finding one another, happy and yet concerned, in their own insular world. That is the way it always happens. Can there ever be lovers who are not, or do not try to be, the sole inhabitants of an island which is closed off from the rest of the world? For they are a world in themselves. Salinas' love poetry does not give us a strange, eccentric love, but one which is perfectly normal, a love story which is fulfilled in a normal way. The story itself amounts to no more than a series of situations involving sentiment, situations which never degenerate into sentimentalism, although they always retain their warmth. These situations are developed and analyzed under a profound drive full of thought and feeling. Thought, passion, tenderness, and sensuality are fully fused in this poetry which is made up exclusively of intense words. The voice owed to love, "la voz a ti debida," is impassioned throughout all its yearning researches. Where does so constant a yearning come from? There is no social conflict. Society then does not exist. Is there an internal conflict? No. The lover uses the love which he has attained as his point of departure and pursues the beloved, the most perfect beloved possible: the woman that love continues to discover and create, at the same time that it discovers and creates the lover. An ever new "I" eagerly pursues an ever new "you." I, you: that is all. The poet sums it up wittily: "It is the highest joy, simply to live in pronouns!" It is the "you and I" of all lovers which here acquires an extraordinary height and depth. Salinas pushes this basic situation to an extreme point of intensity and sublimation, without however destroying its naturalness. With regard to this we should recall Max Scheler, who has been referred to by several critics who have seen a relationship between his philosophy and Salinas' poetry. "Love only exists," we read in *Wesen und Formen der Sympathie,* "when in addition to the value already made real in love, there is the further movement or impulse toward further possible higher values. Precisely in the fact that love is motion in the direction of the highest level of value, precisely in this lies the creative significance of love." This is what Scheler says. And Salinas says to his beloved: "What I want to do is to draw out of you your best self." Thus the beloved, now nameless, is transformed into a You which hints at its own Beyond. Love must be sought and striven after, as it were, by fighting, and not against the beloved, but rather on her behalf, by striving in the direction of the best beloved possible.

Hence we find it incredible that Spitzer, the great philogian, Salinas' friend and colleague at . . . Johns Hopkins University, should have asserted: "It is a curious thing that even the beloved woman is negated by our poet; I am acquainted with no love poetry in which the two lovers are so completely reduced to the poet's own ego, in which the beloved woman lives only as a function of the man's mind and is no more than a phenomenon of his consciousness." What a monstrous conclusion! For once the great Spitzer made a mistake. There was every reason why Salinas, as he confessed to me here in Baltimore, should have been unable ever to read that essay, even though it is important in other respects. It is impossible that Salinas' love poems should have been merely "the metaphysical speculations of the poet by himself," that "the beloved is a purely abstract concept." Such are the extreme conclusions that a rigid intellectual formula can lead to, in this case the concept of "Spanish *conceptismo.*"

As a matter of fact the poet pursues and encounters . . .

This mortal, roselike corporeality
where love invents its infinite.

An infinite that would be nothing at all without its adorable "locus": "your sweet body in my thought." How could that thought ever have been born without the sweetness of that actual body? These images all tend to transport us to a planet which is governed by the law of gravitation. . . .

Look for weights,
the deepest ones, in yourself, and let them drag you
down to that great center where I wait for you.
Total love, the mutual attraction of masses.

The last line is quite clear, and its tone is emphatic. Totality, masses: total love, which extends from the presentiment to the fulfillment of love, almost from the very beginning, as is more solemnly declared in the longer poems of *Razón de amor (Love's Reason)*. Pedro Salinas already occupies a place which is very much his own, and very eminent, in the history of the love poetry of all times. (pp. xxiv-xxx)

> *Jorge Guillén, "Introduction: Pedro Salinas," translated by Elias L. Rivers, in* Reality and the Poet in Spanish Poetry *by Pedro Salinas, translated by Edith Fishtine Helman, The Johns Hopkins University Press, 1966, pp. ix-xxx.*

C. B. MORRIS (essay date 1969)

[*In the following excerpt, Morris examines Salinas's love poetry, noting that Salinas was not concerned with portraying the physical and sensual aspects of love, but rather sought to explore the effects of love on his sensibilities.*]

The freedom Salinas declared when he stated in *Presagios* that 'No hay nada afuera que me ponga linde' ['There is nothing outside me that restricts me'] . . . was not a passport to a world of uninhibited fantasy but a permit to drill his mental agility, which after the tension, litheness and coherence of *La voz a ti debida* stiffened into the automatic manoeuvres of *Razón de amor*. In his eagerness to censure 'the glacial psycho-technical madrigals' of *La voz a ti debida*, Domenchina forgot that, although Salinas's intelligence was animated and sharpened by love, the love about which he rhapsodized in his poems found its stimulus in a woman's body, which he commemorated in his voluptuous references to its lips and voice, to its 'carne tibia' ['warm flesh'] . . . and 'tierno cuerpo rosado' ['tender pink body']. . . . That the woman's body was the foundation of the elaborate verbal structure Salinas built around love is clear from the closing lines of *La voz a ti debida*, where he predicted that the shadows which are the only possible offspring of separation will have to return for regeneration.

> a esta corporcidad mortal y rosa
> donde el amor inventa su infinito.
>
> ['to this pink and mortal body
> where love invents its infinite']. . . .
>
> (pp. 163-64)

Despite his lingering memories of the pink body, it was with the *infinito* that Salinas was more concerned. His definition of happiness in *Presagios* as an 'alma sin cuerpo' [a 'body without soul'] . . . and his description of the body in *Seguro azar* as 'sombra, engaño' ['shadow, illusion'] . . . anticipated the mental surgery of *La voz a ti debida*, where, as he explained in characteristically deliberate lines, he methodically amputated the woman's lips, destroyed her complexion and stilled her arms and voice in order to live and love in a world free from the exciting but troublesome presence of the flesh. . . . (p. 164)

Salinas's neat admission in *La voz a ti debida* that he was 'sin ganas de ganar' ['without wishing to win'] . . . and his equally pert accusation in *Presagios* that 'Cierro brazos, tú los abres' ['I close my arms, you open them'] . . . illustrate his belief that to win a woman's body would end the timeless pleasures generated by her form but sustained by his mind. His decision to 'vivirlo dentro' ['live within'] . . . forced him further and further away from his sensual recollection, repeated as if in disbelief, that

> Ayer te besé en los labios.
> Te besé en los labios

['Yesterday I kissed you on the lips.
I kissed you on the lips'] . . .

until he found himself alone firstly 'kissing a kiss', and finally, as he precisely explained to himself, kissing his memory of a kiss. . . . (pp. 164-65)

When Salinas stated that 'por detrás de las gentes / te busco' ['I seek you behind people'] . . . , he pointed to his search outside reality for a private identity unseen by other people. His insistence that

> También detrás, más atrás
> de mí te busco. No eres
> lo que yo siento de ti
>
> ['I also seek you behind me,
> way behind me. You are not
> what my senses tell me you are'] . . .

reveals his clear distinction between the woman who inspired his love and his love for her, suspended in a timeless, unmarked plane which he imagined in lines reminiscent of Quevedo as a living death. . . .

To possess his *amada* would thwart Salinas's ambition to live perpetually cocooned within a love from which he excluded the banal data of time, place and circumstance. Rejecting the normal senses in favour of new ones like the 'luz del tacto' ['light of touch'] . . . and the 'luz del oír' ['light of hearing'] . . . , he detached himself from reality and particularly from his ubiquitous *amada*, who is so fully a creature of the physical world that she appears unpredictably

> . . . en los alfabetos,
> en las auroras, en los labios.
>
> ['in alphabets,
> in daybreaks, in lips'.]
>
> (p. 165)

Hostile to the roofs which weigh on him as heavily as they did on Altolaguirre, Salinas took himself in his fantasy to 'cielos intemporales' ['timeless heavens'] . . . , where he and his *amada* drift as 'nadadores celestes' ['celestial swimmers'] . . . in a rarefied atmosphere. His neat opposition of where he lived and where he refused to live, together with his precisely qualified specification of his chosen milieu, made his lines more reasoned and controlled than Prados's, more taut than Altolaguirre's plain statement that 'mi vida vuela celeste' ['my life flies celestial'] . . . :

> No en palacios de mármol,
> no en meses, no, ni en cifras,
> nunca pisando el suelo:
> en leves mundos frágiles
> hemos vivido juntos.
>
> Nos cobijaban techos,
> menos que techos, nubes;
> menos que nubes, cielos;
> aun menos, aire, nada.
>
> ['Not in marble palaces,
> not in months, no, nor in numbers,
> never treading the earth:
> in light and fragile worlds
> have we lived together.

We were sheltered by roofs,
less than roofs, clouds,
less than clouds, skies,
even less, air, nothing'.] . . .

Determined to savour the 'delicia lenta / de gozar, de amar, sin nombre' ['slow delight / of enjoying, of loving, without a name'] . . ., Salinas opted for an existence kept pure, remote and impersonal by a screen of pronouns, summarized neatly in the phrase 'Yo te quiero, soy yo' ['I love you, it is I']. . . . To use a name, which he imagined melodramatically as a dagger thrust into a pure breast . . ., would destroy the freedom of anonymity, which he celebrated in a joyful chant:

> Para vivir no quiero
> islas, palacios, torres.
> ¡Qué alegría mas alta:
> vivir en los pronombres!
>
> ['In order to live I do not want
> islands, palaces, towers.
> What sublime joy:
> to live in pronouns!'] . . .

His declarations that

> Entre figuraciones
> vivo, de ti, sin ti
>
> ['Without you
> I live among outlines of you'] . . .

and:

> Nosotros, sí, nosotros,
> amando, los amantes
>
> ['We, yes, we,
> the lovers loving'] . . .

outlined a simple situation which, although highly personal, was sterilized by anonymity and by the distance he maintained between her and himself. Clearly agreeing with Proust that 'as soon as one loves one no longer loves anyone', Salinas stilled and silenced the woman while he hymned the love which she had stimulated. Love was not something he was prepared to share with a woman, whom he needed in order to begin loving but whom he purged from his thoughts in order to keep loving; his tribute to her was not the conventional praise of beauty, figure or elegance, but an epitaph to the separation which he enforced and maintained. . . . (pp. 166-67)

Love gave meaning to Salinas's life and coherence to *La voz a ti debida*, which, unimpeded by numbers or titles, moves with irresistible fluency as his thoughts revolve around love. Sharing Shelley's view of love as 'Thou Wonder, and thou Beauty, and thou Terror' . . ., Salinas was more interested in probing and weighing its effects on his sensibility than in imagining what it could look like. His perfunctory description of falling in love as lightning . . . is buried in lines that lack colour and image but are tense with precise and balanced arguments, whose movements hinge on such words as *sí, no, quizá, porque, por qué?* and *si*, in which he posed in frequent questions like:

> ¿Abrazarme? ¿Con quién?
> ¿Seguir? ¿A quién?
>
> ['Embrace? With whom?
> Follow? Whom?'] . . .
>
> (p. 167)

Salinas's exclamation in *Seguro azar* that loving his *amada* was

> . . . ir y venir
> a ti misma de ti misma!
>
> ['coming and going
> to yourself from yourself!'] . . .

placed her at the centre of his world and at the axis of his thoughts; all haphazard movements are futile. In *La voz a ti debida* his precisely balanced formula and his solemn litany of disparate sites emphasize that she was the fixed point to which he was chained. . . . When in his play *La bella durmiente* Soledad exalted anonymity and enjoyed 'being unknown, escaping from the image which others have of one', she expresses Salinas's contempt for the public identity adopted by his *amada* as she moves by instinct through a cautiously charted life of predictable acts and physical sensations. . . . (p. 168)

Piercing the public image of a person whom other people expect to be gay, Salinas refused to be dazed and deflected by her capricious gyrations, breathlessly captured in his indiscriminately sweeping censure of

> tus rostros, tus caprichos y tus besos
> tus delicias volubles, tus contactos
> rápidos con el mundo
>
> ['your faces, your whims and your kisses,
> your voluble delights, your rapid
> contacts with the world'.] . . .

and went straight 'a lo desnudo y a lo perdurable' ['to the bare and the lasting'] . . ., which he defined elsewhere in the work in phrases composed of pronouns and inelegant but emphatic adjectives as 'la irrefutable tú' ['the irrefutable you'] . . . and 'pura libre, / irreductible: tú'['pure, free, irreducible: you']. . . .

Because Salinas observed the principle established by Proust that 'each one needs to find reasons for his passion', *Razón de amor* suffered from what Ángel del Río properly diagnosed as 'a drop in poetic tension'. Salinas seemed unable to recognize and therefore remedy the monotony caused by the impasse in his thoughts, in which the *amada* still occupied a central position as the immobile figure whose body he ignored in his pursuit of fleshless purity. Although he insisted in lines that echo the conclusion of *La voz a ti debida* that

> . . . un sueño sólo es sueño
> verdadero
> cuando en materia mortal
> se desensueña y se encarna,
>
> ['a dream is only a real dream
> when it shakes off its dream
> and embodies itself in mortal matter',] . . .

he maintained his stubborn opposition to 'estas formas cansadas de este mundo' ['these weary forms of this world'] . . . in order to undertake a flight from life which he defined in the crisp title **'Suicidio hacia arriba'**. Suspended in the heavens, the two lovers drift so freely that Salinas pitied those who are oppressed by roofs and choked by cobwebs,

> los que viven aún bajo techado,
> donde telas de araña se entretejen
> para cazar, para agostar los sueños . . .

['those who still live beneath a roof,
where cobwebs entwine
to hunt, to wither dreams'.] . . .

(pp. 168-69)

Eager to remain enclosed within a capsule where all that mattered to him was love and his thoughts about love, Salinas seemed to clench his teeth, steel his nerves and utter a challenge to himself as he expressed his determination to love and keep on loving:

> hay que querer sin dejarlo,
> querer y seguir queriendo.

> ['one must love without let,
> love and carry on loving'.] . . .

But when he insisted in '**Suicido hacia arriba**'

> que nosotros estamos
> contentos, sí, contentos
> del cielo alto, de sus variaciones,

> ['that we are
> contented, yes, contented
> with the lofty heavens, with its variations',] . . .

he appeared to feel the need to convince us by repetition of his contentment, to combat the tiredness caused by his conscious efforts to defy the stiffening of his thoughts, to keep the past alive and to maintain the tension and fluidity of *La voz a ti debida.*

The energetic delight in the 'trajín, ir, venir' ['bustle, coming and going'] which animated *La voz a ti debida* . . . evaporated in *Razón de amor* into a weariness with 'este vaivén, / este ir y venir' ['this fluctuation, this coming and going'] and a subdued search for 'un quererse quieto, quieto' ['a still, still love']. . . . Unable to sustain in *Razón de amor* the elan of *La voz a ti debida*, Salinas composed a work at once discursive, emotionally inconsistent and structurally loose, in which digressions on water . . . and '**Una lágrima en mayo**' . . . coexist with the vigorous affirmations of '**Suicidio hacia arriba**' and '**Destino alegre**'.

Love's search in *Razón de amor* for

> un más detrás de un más,
> otro cielo en su cielo

> ['something more behind something more,
> another heaven in its heaven'] . . .

signalled the determined pursuit of a private goal undertaken in their writings by Altolaguirre, Cernuda, Prados and Salinas. When they disengaged themselves from the outside world and focused on themselves, their pose of inactivity and their chants of isolation should have led them ideally to compensate for their narrow range of theme with emotional intensity, imaginative power and verbal energy, for a hermit has to create interest in a narrative of solitude, a recital of his meditations and an exposure of his spiritual condition. Lacking intense feelings and an active fantasy, Altolaguirre, who was a competent and lucid manipulator of words, made a virtue out of sober dignity and staid, uncoloured precision. Feeling deeply and writing tensely, Prados appealed to the reader's stamina as he charted in his taut, nervous and spasmodic lines a mind caught in trance-like communion with itself. Salinas's disdain of direct contacts and direct sensations detached him consistently from reality and particularly his *amada;* accomplished by his intelligence when his emotions were tranquillized and

his senses dormant, Salinas's graph of love's effects on him was a closely reasoned exercise in eloquence, dense and controlled in *La voz a ti debida,* loose and predictable in *Razón de amor.* (pp. 170-71)

> *C. B. Morris, "The Closed Door," in his* A Generation of Spanish Poets 1920-1936, *Cambridge University Press, 1969, pp. 143-71.**

JOHN CRISPIN (essay date 1974)

[*Crispin is an American educator and translator specializing in Spanish literature. In the following excerpt he examines Salinas's poetry and discusses the salient themes and techniques used in each of his most significant poetic works.*]

Salinas' poetry can be divided into three phases of thematic and stylistic development. The first phase, his period of experimentation, includes three books of poetry, written between 1918 and 1931: *Presagios (Presages),* 1923, *Seguro azar (Steadfast Chance),* 1929, and *Fábula y signo (Fable and Sign),* 1931. The two books which follow, *La voz a ti debida (The Voice Owed to You),* 1933, and *Razón de amor (Love's Reason),* 1936, form a continuous cycle of love poetry, corresponding to Salinas' second phase. Many critics consider this cycle to be Salinas' best, or at any rate the most representative of his mature technique and personality. The last phase includes all the poetry written during Salinas' years of residence in the United States and Puerto Rico. Two books, *El contemplado (The Contemplated Sea),* 1946, and *Todo más claro (All Things Made Clearer),* 1949, were published during Salinas' lifetime, while *Confianza (Confidence),* 1954, is a posthumous collection of poems which Salinas had written some ten years previously but never quite readied for publication, although he clearly viewed them as forming one volume. The last phase shows divergent moods, ranging from anguish, in parts of *All Things Made Clearer,* to optimistic praise of life in *Confidence* and near mystic exaltation in *The Contemplated Sea.* In spite of these differences, all the poetry included in these last three books reflects a new, mature outlook on life, within which all the conflicts evident up to *Love's Reason* are ultimately resolved.

Salinas' first three books of verse form a unit because they represent three progressive steps in formulating his basic position, as man and as poet, toward reality, and in dealing with the related question of the proper function of poetry. . . . As we shall see, each book shows a conflict between a basic skepticism, which encourages Salinas to withdraw from the external world, and an irrepressible love of life which constantly brings him back to it.

The title of each volume indicates a step in the poetic process. The word "Presages" (which Salinas understood in its etymological meaning: *prae-sagire,* or "before perception") is an allusion to the first affective contact with reality and a foreboding of deeper meanings behind surface appearance. *Steadfast Chance* refers to the significant moment in which the encounter of external reality with the poet's memory may result in a chance discovery or a fresh insight into reality. *Fable and Sign* distinguishes between the two aspects of reality, before and after its poetic transformation. External reality is the point of departure (or "sign") which is necessary to set the poetic process in motion. The choice of the word "Fable" in reference to the end result implies that the poet seeks to rise above an objective vision by creating new myths.

None of the three books is rigidly structured, although there are significant clusters of obviously related poems in each. (pp. 39-40)

Presages is Salinas' most varied book as far as technique is concerned. Some poems are based on literary reminiscences from Golden Age poets. . . . Influences of Bécquer and Juan Ramón Jiménez . . . are also easily traceable. Save for one or two exceptions, these classical and modern sources are not as immediately apparent in later works, though, as we shall see, stylistic features inspired by the poetry of Fray Luis will later become distinctive traits of Salinian technique. Another feature present in *Presages* which will completely disappear later is the use of popular sayings, as in No. 43, *El río va a su negocio / corre que te correrás* . . . (The river goes about its business / flowing as it will . . .), or of a colloquial and sometimes flippant style reminiscent of Antonio Machado's *Proverbios y cantares*. . . . (p. 41)

The first five poems of *Presages,* including a five-verse introductory epigraph, can be seen as forming a kind of initial aesthetic creed. The five introductory verses underline the poet's awareness of his temporal and spatial circumstances, seen not as limitations, but as forming the necessary concrete starting point of all poetry:

> Forjé un eslabón un día
> otro día forjé otro
> y otro.
> De pronto se me juntaron
> —era la cadena—todos.
>
> (I fashioned a chainlink one day
> On the next day I forged another
> and another.
> Soon I found them all joined together
> and between them they formed the chain.)

The chain of life is made up of each momentary contact with the material world, and poetry, ideally, joins these moments in a creative whole. (pp. 41-2)

Poems 2 and 3 pursue the meditation on the nature of Poetry. No. 2 is a warning about what poetry should not try to do: deal in abstract speculations. The poem, set in the form of a dialogue with a swiftly flowing stream, expresses the timeless metaphysical problem concerning what forms the essential, as opposed to the accidental aspects of a thing. . . . Poetic intuition which may result in a direct insight into reality at any given moment: *beso te doy* cannot easily translate that particular moment. The dilemma of poetic expression lies in the attempt to preserve in timeless form an experience which is perceived in the flux of existence. (pp. 42-3)

In the final poem of this series an implied comparison is made between the poet and his infant daughter who greets every new sensation with exuberant enthusiasm, but can express her feelings with only two incomprehensible words: Tatá, Dadá, so that she is unable to communicate anything more precise than her spontaneous joy:

> "Todo lo confunde," dijo
> su madre. Y era verdad
> Porque cuando yo la oía
> decir "Tatá, Dadá,"
> veía la bola del mundo
> rodar, rodar.

> ("She confuses everything," said
> her mother. And it was true
> Because as I heard her
> say "Tata, Dada,"
> I could see the ball of the world
> roll and roll.) . . .

(p. 44)

The five opening poems of *Presages* thus complete each other and summarize the general feelings expressed in the book. Its characteristic trait, says Angel del Río, is the position of the poet always situating himself on the edge between reality and inner life . . . because all the material world seems to him an illusion, despite its exact appearance. (p. 45)

Steadfast Chance marks Salinas' full adherence to the spirit of Ultraism as it was first assimilated by the Generation of 1927. In fact, both in spirit and in style, the book (written between 1924 and 1928) could well be chosen as a prototype of the group's initial period.

The predominant attitude is now one of marvelling discovery of the everyday world. The mood is generally optimistic, and several poems recall, both in tone and technique, the exuberant praise of life of Guillén's *Cántico* . . . . Salinas seeks to show harmony and almost geometric perfection in each apprehended moment. As in Cubist painting, objects are often reduced to their essential lines, and Salinas strives for a concise, almost telegraphic, style by eliminating connecting words such as articles and conjunctions. Verbs are used very sparingly, especially those which suggest movement. To further underline this static quality, Salinas prefers to use an infinitive or gerund where one would normally expect a conjugated verb. . . . Finally, Salinas makes frequent use of very concentrated metaphors, based either on remote visual approximations, or, more often, on mental play on words in the *conceptista* tradition. (pp. 48-9)

Many poems of *Steadfast Chance* are inspired by those modern inventions which have revolutionized man's perception of time and distance, and have created a new life-rhythm. In No. 10, **"Navacerrada, abril"** (**"Navacerrada, April"**), the first of Salinas' Futuristic poems, the automobile becomes a partner to the poet's discovery. . . . (p. 49)

Nine poems of *Steadfast Chance* deal with the equivocal nature of reality, and twelve love poems also repeat previous attitudes. Such conflicting stands show only that when Salinas gives in to spontaneous reactions, his irrepressible love of life, in all its excitement and variety, can temporarily overcome a skepticism which is born of reflection. But sooner or later, Salinas always returns to his search for a deeper and more lasting reality and to his defense of poetry's role in revealing *la trasrrealidad*.

The poems of *Steadfast Chance* which deal with Salinas' aesthetics no longer center, as did those in *Presages*, around the initial impact of an object's discovery, but rather on the process of its transformation by means of intuitive associations. (p. 51)

The nature of a constant interchange between outer and inner worlds is thus ultimately defined in *Steadfast Chance*. The poet interprets reality and re-creates it in a poem. But the poem will do more than just communicate a certain world-vision through a special perspective; it will also create a new myth, which will render life as less conventionally precise, richer in imaginative overtones, and therefore more acceptable in the face of disillusion. This is the implied message contained in Salinas' third book of verse, *Fable and Sign.*

In this book, Salinas does not introduce any theme or technique not already present in his earlier poetry. The fascination with technical progress and big-city life is still evident—though to a lesser degree—in poems such as **"Underwood Girls,"** No. 28, in praise of the typewriter as "partner" in the act of creation, or in the evocation of a permanent ideal Spring in a Paris shop window, in No. 7: **"Paris, abril, modelo" ("Paris, April, Model").** In No. 9, **"Amsterdam,"** the city is described solely in terms of neon signs flashing in the night: *verdes, rojos, azules, rapidísimas / luces extrañas por los ojos / [. . .] anuncios luminosos de la vida* (green, red, blue, swiftest / lights dazzling to the eye / . . . luminous signs of life). These city lights are, for the moment, still regarded as elements of beauty and throbbing excitement. As we shall see later, they will be evoked in *All Things Made Clearer* to symbolize a civilization tied to artificial and dehumanizing values.

Already in *Fable and Sign* there is a noticeable change in the poet's appraisal of the material world. The prevailing mood is no longer one of carefree enjoyment of the here and now. Salinas still praises life, but he does so rather stoically, with the full realization that all human and material existence is engaged in a frenetic race with death. (pp. 52-3)

Throughout *Fable and Sign,* the least permanent elements are material objects, and their only hope for survival is the succession of viewers capable of endowing them with a new life, a new soul. (p. 54)

The theme of love is of greater importance than ever before in *Fable and Sign.* Of the various attitudes already discussed in connection with *Presages,* skepticism and disillusionment now prevail. Only three of the book's twelve poems on this theme can be said to show love as a fulfilling and satisfactory experience. More abundant are poems which deal with separation or estrangement. . . . **"Ruptura sin palabras" ("A Wordless Breaking-off"),** No. 21, is one of Salinas' most poignant poems about a moment of total incomprehension very close to hate. The poem begins with the description of a landscape which seems to embody the antagonism of the two lovers. . . . (p. 56)

The poem's ending is a nostalgic lament for a happiness already irrevocably passing. (p. 57)

When, in 1933, Salinas published *The Voice Owed to You,* the poetry of the Generation of 1927 had already undergone the noticeable change of mood which marked the beginning of its second period. As the carefree optimism of the 1920's ended abruptly, around the beginning of the new decade, it was followed for many by emotional crisis and a feeling of alienation in a now hostile modern world. The attitude of some of the best-known members of the group became akin to what Salinas would later describe as the Romantic revolt against reality.

Apart from this general attitude, a more definite factor which has enabled critics to refer to the Generation of 1927's second period as a neo-Romantic revival was the strong resurgence of the theme of Love viewed as the unattainable ideal, or ultimately as man's supreme illusion. For poets such as Cernuda and Alberti, the betrayal implied in the loss of this love ideal became a broad symbol for the frustrated human condition. Love was evoked in the image of a lost paradise, or as a happiness that never really existed except as a dream. . . . Aleixandre's poetry in *Espadas como labios (Swords Like Lips),* 1932, and *La destrucción o el amor (Destruction Equals Love),* 1934, presents love as a clashing and frustrated encounter. It adds the concept, also Romantic in origin, of sexual passion as a terrifying force underlying the perpetual cosmic cycle of creation and destruction.

At first glance, there would seem to be little similarity between the luminous verses of Salinas' great love cycle and the agitated near-Surrealistic imagery used by Alberti, Cernuda, or Aleixandre in the same period. Yet, though the means of expression were different, Salinas echoed similar conflicts, received the same Romantic influences, and made use of parallel allusions to love as biblical paradise or cosmic force. Salinas differed, however, in that he saw love not merely as an illusion or dream wished for, but as an idyllic reality whose fragility and ultimate loss was due only to its temporal limitations.

The main conflict in Salinas' love poetry arises in attempting to transcend these limitations. The problem is stated in Part One of the cycle, *The Voice Owed to You,* which describes a private love paradise, first discovered then lost. In the course of Part Two, *Love's Reason,* Salinas resolves the conflicts caused by the loss of this particular love to his satisfaction. Love for him becomes an eternal cyclic force, which, if properly understood and accepted, should give sufficient justification to all human existence. On the basis of this rediscovery of love, Salinas holds the promise of a new paradise, forever recaptured.

Though most critics agree that the poetry collected in these two books is probably Salinas' best, or at any rate his first truly mature verses, they hold basically divergent views concerning both the structure and meaning of the cycle. Questions arise about whether to consider the two books as one continuous poem, as two poems, or merely as a series of variations connected only by their common love theme. *The Voice Owed to You* bears the generic subtitle of *poema,* which suggests some structural unity. Yet, the first edition divided the 2462 verses into seventy clearly independent segments or "poems," each beginning on a fresh page, with no overlapping permitted. It is soon apparent that each section was conceived and must be read on two levels, both as an entity complete in itself and as a part of the entire poem. Similarly, *Love's Reason* is subtitled *poesía,* but is divided into two parts. The first 1930 verses are separated into forty-two segments, following the method of the preceding book, while eight titled poems—a total of 839 verses—make up Part II.

Faced with this paradox, most critics have chosen to minimize the importance of the subtitles and to see the book as collections of "variations" or "meditations" on the theme of love. Stephen Gilman suggests that formal ambiguity—poem or poems, whole or parts—was perhaps intentional, at least in the case of *The Voice Owed to You.* The same critic briefly considers, and rejects as overly Romantic, the possibility of a unity based on a narrative sequel: the story of a single love from beginning to end. Joaquín González Muela was the first to point out that there is at least some validity to this interpretation, since the text of *The Voice Owed to You* begins with verbs in the present and future tenses—corresponding to an incipient love affair—whereas from a point which he indicates as verse 986, a progressive separation of the two lovers is evidenced in the use of past tenses.

In general, critics have been puzzled by this long love poem, which, as its title indicates, seems to be addressed to a real woman, though she remains unnamed, and who is described only in the vaguest terms. As her feelings are never expressed, and the entire love experience is seen solely through its effects on the poet-protagonist, she seems almost totally absent. Thus, although in both books the beloved is addressed as *Tú*, the poem might give the impression of being more a self-searching monologue than a true dialogue.

Such is the ultimate opinion of an important group of mostly early critics. They conclude that the poem has no biographical basis and that, possibly, it does not even really deal with love. Leo Spitzer ends a lengthy and often-quoted article by saying that the poem is really "the lament of a soul who, lacking faith in God, seeks fulfillment in self-knowledge." The same critic adds: "I am acquainted with no love poetry in which the two lovers are so completely reduced to the poet's own ego. . . . This poet is really a Narcissus who knows no one outside himself." (pp. 59-61)

More recently, C. B. Morris still viewed the poem as pure mental speculation, and although he does not deny the existence of a real woman, he minimizes her importance: ". . . to possess his *amada* would thwart Salinas' ambition to live perpetually cocooned within a love from which he excluded the banal data of time, place, and circumstance. . . . Salinas was more interested in probing and weighing [love]'s effects on his sensibility than in imagining what it could look like" [see excerpt dated 1969]. It is, of course, statements such as these which have gained Salinas a controversial reputation as an unfeeling and cerebral poet.

The opinion of the opposing group of critics can best be summed up in the following statement by Jorge Guillén. "Salinas' love poetry does not give us a strange, eccentric love, but one which is perfectly normal, a love story which is fulfilled in a normal way. The story itself amounts to no more than a series of situations involving sentiment, situations which never degenerate into sentimentalism, although they always retain their warmth" [see excerpt dated 1966].

Such divergences concerning the basic meaning and composition of a poet suggest that there may be more than one level of interpretation intended. Salinas first published an important fragment of *The Voice Owed to You* under another title: *Amor en vilo (Love Unbound)*. The same year, he adopted the more personal title, borrowed from a verse from the sixteenth-century poet Garcilaso de la Vega, for the definitive edition. The difference between the two titles points to the dual nature of the book. On one level it is a volume of sentimental memoirs from which Salinas has discreetly eliminated all personal allusions (except for two references to the young woman's age: twenty). Discretion is one reason, but a more compelling one is the wish to make the poem transcend his individual experience as a general statement on the paradoxical nature of love. This is indicated in Salinas' choice as his book's epigraph, of a verse from Shelley's *Epipsychidon:* "Thou Wonder, and Thou Beauty, and Thou Terror." . . . [The] poem is also developed on a symbolic level, based on the story of Genesis; and on the Christian concept of man's fall and salvation. (pp. 62-3)

The Voice Owed to You follows a circular narrative plan going from the discovery of love (a new reality), to plenitude of love (the creation of an earthly paradise), lost love (Paradise Lost), until the very last poem, which anticipates a recovery of lost happiness. Within this plan, the book could be divided into an Introduction and four parts. (p. 63)

Bearing in mind this organization, one can agree with J. Palley's statement on the poem's three basic directions: "*La voz a tí debida* is a long meditation on the reality of the beloved. It is a hymn in praise of the beloved. It is the victory of love—Being—over the Nada, Non-Being" [see excerpt dated 1957].

Although the poem deals only with love, we shall see that Salinas' previous themes—poetry as discovery, the deceitfulness of appearances, inner vs. outer reality—also come into play.

The first motif is introduced in the "proem," where the woman's personality and her dominant role are established. . . . (p. 64)

What is immediately apparent in this young woman's nature is her boundless vitality, her self-sufficiency in creating her own circumstances, and her capacity not only for looking beyond ordinary reality, but for transforming it, "playing" on the world as if it were a musical instrument of unexpected melodious quality: *La vida es lo que tú tocas* ["Life is everything that you touch."] . . . By life, Salinas means of course existence already transformed by the imagination, discoverer of *"trasrrealidad."* The *amada*'s life is, so to speak, a continuous poem. (p. 65)

Salinas' beloved is also "poetry," but she does not lead him outside this world. The material world is the only reality on which she operates. C. Feal Deibe has pointed out that the three most important senses, touch, sight, hearing, come into play in the initial description of her, making her a very tangible being who enjoys life to its fullest, in marked contrast with the poet himself who appears as a "shadow," still buried in a moribund routine world.

The initiation into love begins with a depurative process, at first slow and hesitating, one by which the poet must learn to abandon his predefined and conventional view of reality and direct himself to its rediscovery with the *amada* as a guide, conscious and fearful of his own limitations. Above all, he fears that the promised happiness will be only temporary and all the more deceitful if then lost. . . . There is briefly a temptation to abandon the promise of a real happiness and to take refuge in an inner world of dreams which, though a pale shadow of this new Spring, would at least be permanent. . . . Soon, the poet abandons this cautious stand. Beginning with the seventh poem [which marks the beginning of Part II] his verses reflect a steadily rising enthusiasm for a world now seen through a sensibility transformed by love and the beloved's contagious vitality. . . . (pp. 65-6)

At this point, the plenitude of love is only a promise: "tomorrow." The first necessary transformation will be the shedding of circumstantial limitations. The very name of things must be forgotten. Even the name of love, since it is so often associated with too trivial sentiments, stands as a barrier to the full play of the deep poetic and emotional experience on which the poet is about to embark. . . . (p. 67)

In this newly found bliss, with the *amada* to lead him, the poet first begins to free himself of the limitations of time, anticipating a world where present, past, and future will be abolished, or at least forgotten. The first quality of this new world will be its immutability, the eternal quality and instantaneous perfection of each moment. . . .

At the same time, love and beloved are confused in this world where all sensations are accumulated, preserved, and directed toward ever greater perfection. . . . (p. 68)

Part II of *The Voice Owed to You* is the proclamation of faith in life transformed by poetry and spontaneous feeling, which we have seen as the driving force behind Salinas' poetry since *Presages*. The message is always the same: keep your eyes wide open to the marvels of the world, and be prepared to embark without question in the adventure of each new day. . . . (p. 72)

[Part II] contains some of the most beautiful love poetry ever written, but Part III is the most moving, as we witness the poet's desperate attempts to uphold this perfection, and to convince himself that it still exists, even when it is obvious that the lovers have already begun to drift apart. The poet can no longer maintain in his verses the intensity which characterized Part II. Instead, there is a constant movement between Love's presence, still sung in rapturous praise . . . , and love's absence: love in the form of memories, dream, or illusion.

The beloved's self-reliance and her constantly changing perspectives on the world, which the poet can no longer share, are now seen as signs of frivolity. She is still the "pure living impulse," but she does not always live up to her fullest promise, and needs the poet to hold her to her "true" self. (p. 73)

It is in this context that the poet once again becomes skeptical of reality, including that of the beloved. Even as she stands before him, he may feel so completely estranged from her that she might as well be a mirror reflection. . . . (p. 75)

The logical reaction is, as before, to take refuge in an inner world of dreams, more stable than reality. This is expressed in the verses which so disturbed many critics and prompted C. B. Morris to write that: "[Salinas] methodically amputated the woman's lips, destroyed her complexion . . . to live and love in a world free from the exciting but troublesome presence of the flesh" [see excerpt dated 1969]. . . . (p. 76)

We have to understand these verses in the poet's present frame of mind, reflecting his loss and his sense of frustration at having been deceived, not as reflecting the mood of the entire poem. No. 63 shows the poet's desperate clinging to memories, even to pain, as the last vestige of his lost love:

No quiero que te vayas,
dolor, última forma
de amar. Me estoy sintiendo
vivir cuando me dueles [. . .]

tú me serás, dolor, [. . .]

La gran prueba, a lo lejos,
de que existió, que existe,
de que me quiso, sí
de que aún la estoy queriendo.

(I don't want you to leave me,
sorrow, ultimate form
of love. I feel that I am
alive only when you hurt me . . .

for me—O sorrow—you will be

The ultimate and distant proof
that she existed, and still exists,
that she loved me, yes,
and that I still love her.)

It is no wonder that as his book contains poems of such emotional depth, Salinas himself should have been shocked—as J. Guillén tells us—by Spitzer's interpretation of *The Voice Owed to You* as dry conceptualization [see excerpt dated 1966].

Only six poems remain, forming the fourth and final "act" of *The Voice Owed to You.* In a sense, we may consider Part IV as a prelude to *Love's Reason.* These poems are meditations on the nature of love once the actual experience has ended, as most of the next book also will be.

Although *Love's Reason* was published three years after *The Voice Owed to You,* it cannot be regarded as a totally new book, and it would be difficult to understand its meaning and imagery fully without the preparation which occurred in the first part of the cycle.

On the narrative level, the book makes allusions to the love experience now totally ended, and which the poet strives to justify and recapture, not in real life—where it could again be lost—but in a more durable and meaningful realm. What he attains in the end is both a personal solution and the basis for a whole philosophy of life founded on love. For this reason, the title of the book should perhaps more aptly be translated as *Love's Purpose.* On the symbolic level, some of the motifs introduced in *The Voice Owed to You* are continued and ultimately resolved in the new book.

The overall plan of *Love's Reason* is less apparent than that of *The Voice Owed to You.* Salinas indicated two parts and chose to give titles to the eight poems which make up Part II. These poems thus stand out more. They are also considerably longer than any previously included in either book, yet they contain no new theme or motif. Part II could be viewed as a final summary of arguments put forth in defense or justification of love.

Part I might further be divided into two sections. The first . . . connects clearly with *The Voice Owed to You,* elaborating further on the myth of the Garden of Eden, now closed to the lovers . . . , and introducing with more insistence the possibility of a "redemption." . . . In this section, a positive view of love alternates with a sense of nostalgia and loss. For example, the first poem is in praise of love as creator of light, but the second proclaims that from its first moment of inception love was already an inevitable parting. Numbers 3 and 4 are "positive" poems. The first offers the consolation that even if paradise is negated, life will be made richer in its search; the second again praises the beloved as "tamer of miracles" and as guide, even in absence. But in No. 5 (p. 344), we have again a "negative" view. Love is an obscure force desperately seeking new incarnations and being offered only dreams to satiate its desires.

This opening section of *Love's Reason* also contains some rather mediocre poems [e.g., No. 14; No. 16] . . . and some so involved in conceptual subtleties as to obscure feeling (No. 12, . . . especially the first two verses). However . . . , the text regains an intensity matching that of *The Voice Owed to You.* New imagery is introduced, based on the symbolism of water and the sea, and surrounding the motif of salvation or "paradise regained." (pp. 76-9)

The first lasting value of love, as is to be expected with Salinas, is the new "perspective" that it has given him on the world. Even though the *amada* is no longer with him, the poet will never be alone because she has taught him to see the world through her eyes. The *amada* now appears as the "soul" of all things, present in all things. (p. 79)

The poet no longer lives in the world, but in her *traspresencia,* or *trasrrealidad:* the new associations with which she has imbued even the most trivial things. . . .

In turn, the world, and all things in the world, reinterpreted through poetry will forever be the irrefutable proof of his great love for her. . . . (p. 80)

The first victory of love, then, is to have brought the poet out of himself and into contact with another sensibility, widening his experience in so doing. In turn, the lovers have acquired a collective "Truth of Two" . . . , a unique perspective which is theirs alone but which will be assimilated by future generations of lovers, presumably through poetry. For love is an eternal cyclic force, always repeated and yet never reincarnated in exactly the same way. This idea gives love the eternal quality which Salinas previously sought in vain, and, at the same time, it gives lovers immortality and a justification on the basis of each individual experience. . . . (p. 81)

The paradise which is regained is not a private world as before, but the great sum of love experiences, past and future, adequately symbolized by the sea: *el gran querer callado, mar total* (the great silent love, the total sea). . . . The sea is complete in itself and immutable, always repeated in the eternal joining and parting of waves, yet never the same. The sea collects the waters of all rivers. Therefore, if the sea represents the ultimate and unchanging perfection, the river, and in general flowing water, stands for a future promise: the movement of all lives and of Nature toward their harmonious fulfillment in the sea. (p. 82)

[The] last poem, **"La felicidad imminente" ("Imminent Happiness")** . . . is Salinas' personal proclamation of faith in life, containing much the same message as *"Cara a Cara,"* the last poem of Guillén's *Cántico*. Happiness is fullness of life and acceptance of reality regardless of what may come, joy or sorrow. . . . (p. 86)

Such is the conclusion drawn from Salinas' great love cycle. It is not that of an abstract idealist, an existentialist, or a Neoplatonist, but of a man very much of this world, accepting its imperfections, and optimistically making the best of his earthbound condition.

By the time he wrote *The Voice Owed to You,* Salinas had left behind the experimentations of the Vanguardist years and adopted a style which we now recognize as unmistakably his own. I have mentioned in passing some of the stylistic peculiarities of each of the first three books, but in the light of the poetry just discussed I can now point out some of the more permanent characteristics which contribute to Salinas' originality and poetic greatness. As with all the members of his literary generation, we will see that this style makes use of both traditional and very modern features.

Although *The Voice Owed to You* and *Love's Reason* are composed entirely of unrhymed verses, and often combine short and long meters in a single poem, they are not written in what is generally referred to as free verse. Anyone familiar with Spanish versification will recognize that Salinas used only traditional meters, and that even the combinations are not new.

Up to *The Voice Owed to You,* the favorite medium is the eight-syllable, very symetrically accented verse predominant in Spanish popular poetry and in the ballads, but from which Salinas has eliminated all but vague echoes of assonantal rhymes (and even these used only rarely). Octosyllabic verses are still very much in evidence in *The Voice Owed to You,* and even more in *Love's Reason,* especially in meditative poems for which its regular cadence is particularly suited. In *The Voice Owed to You,* however, Salinas mostly uses the Renaissance seven-syllabled verse, either alone or in combination with verses of eleven, or less frequently nine, syllables, and with *enjambements* of three to five syllables. (pp. 87-8)

Also very much in evidence in *The Voice Owed to You* is the whole Petrarchian tradition of love poetry, especially in the use of parallel constructions and images, and antagonistic elements. But, as in the case of popular tradition, Salinas adopted classical models while disregarding rhyme schemes entirely. He did not want to call attention to the music of rhymes, but to a more subtle internal cadence. Salinas is indeed a modern poet, and a characteristic which J. Maritain points out as one of the main innovations of the poetry of our time is strikingly evident with Salinas:

> . . . Modern poetry had to dispense . . . with the necessity of rhyme and the other requirements of classical prosody. Modern poetry is bound to obey more exacting laws and rules, for they are free and contingent rules, depending at each moment on the correctness of the ear, and on the fact of each and every word, measure and period in the poem being exactly in tune with the soundless music stirred by poetic intuition within the soul.

What particularly distinguishes Salinas from his models, then, is the free displacement of accents within each verse, to create this internal rhythm, paralleling emotional surges within the poem, and reinforced by a very particular use of *enjambement*.

After *Fable and Sign,* Salinas seldom used complicated metaphors. In *The Voice Owed to You,* his images are mostly tied to a symbolic structure, such as the love-paradise or world-woman motifs. Single images tend not to be visual—as, for example, those of Lorca are—but conceptual, dealing with a reality of the mind rather than that of the world outside. Frequently, Salinas "concretizes" abstractions. (pp. 88-9)

In *Love's Reason* we have seen that Salinas progressively acquired a new vital perspective, a sense of purpose, and accrued faith in the importance of his poetic mission. Until then, his poetry shows that he had been unable to find in the material world the measure of permanence which might help to give it meaning. If all things with which man came in contact were irrevocably doomed to destruction, and with individual existence necessarily rooted in the irreversible flux of time with death as its ending, life, however beautiful and enjoyable, could have no ultimate meaning; it was no better than a cruel illusion. We have seen that this conclusion is implicit throughout Salinas' first period. There is little evidence that he ever had a strong religious faith or any belief in values outside the material world of which he felt himself to be an intrinsic part. Therefore, his metaphysical skepticism should logically have led him to despair or to rebellion. But we have also seen that such an attitude was contrary to his basically optimistic inclination. (p. 96)

In stage three, the definition of a collective reality and a collective, as opposed to individual, fulfillment at the end of the love cycle became from then on Salinas' unwavering preoccupation, as reflected at least in all the poetry written after 1939. (p. 97)

El contemplado (The Contemplated Sea), 1946, is a song of near-mystic union with nature symbolized by the Caribbean Sea. It was written during two particularly happy years which Salinas spent as a visiting professor at the University of Puerto Rico (1943-1945). (pp. 97-8)

Todo más claro (All Things Made Clearer), 1949, on the other hand, is closely associated with Salinas' residence on the U.S. mainland, and particularly with urban life in the megalopolis of the upper eastern seaboard. At the request of his Argentine editor, Salinas wrote a short preface for this book, in which he partially clarifies its narrative context. This poetry was written in the United States between 1937 and 1947. Salinas points out [in his preface to the work] the paradox involved in the choice of a title which hardly seems appropriate for a book speaking mainly of the anguish of man in modern times. He states his intention of presenting the vision of a science-fiction mechanistic world surpassing even the chaotic nightmares painted by Hieronymus Bosch or Goya. He adds that this nightmare has been created by modern science which, in the name of progress, is preparing man's total destruction, both spiritually and literally, in warfare.

Having raised the question of the curious title, Salinas gives an evasive aesthetic reason for his choice. Clearly, a promise of some form of salvation is implied in the title, and Salinas' drawing attention to it is his warning to the reader that he should not interpret this book as a totally despairing view of the future. The clue to the title's choice lies in the book's structure. . . . Taken out of context, several poems might be interpreted as totally defeatist. Considering the book as a whole, however, we shall see that its message is, conditionally, one of hope; substantially the same message as that expressed in *The Contemplated Sea.*

The same can be said for the posthumous *Confianza (Confidence)*, written between 1942 and 1944 and published posthumously. . . . In this last book, it is impossible to rely on structure for the corroboration of theme, since Salinas himself did not arrange the poems in their final order. The text, as it appears in the first edition, was compiled by [his son-in-law and editor] Juan Marichal, with the advice of Salinas' lifelong friend, Jorge Guillén. The title was borrowed from the last poem which seems to epitomize the mood of the book and could be interpreted as Salinas' ultimate profession of faith.

From the dates given above, it is apparent that the three books overlap chronologically. It is entirely possible that Salinas wrote poems included later in *All Things Made Clearer* at approximately the same time that he was writing others destined to find their place in *Confidence* or *The Contemplated Sea.* This is all the more reason to see all this poetry as intimately related. *The Contemplated Sea* is made up of an initial poem entitled "**Tema,**" followed by fourteen titled "**Variations.**" . . . The entire book is a sustained dialogue of the poet with the sea, object of this contemplation. Gustavo Correa has noted that ["Tema"] operates on four levels. The first is simply the description and praise of the beauty of nature—seascape, sky, clouds, beaches, and islets—all joined in cosmic harmony in the island paradise of Puerto Rico. This reality immediately perceived, as always with Salinas, is then given poetic meaning, and the process of recreation from a real to a poetically meaningful world—the poetic process as theme—is the second level of meaning. The third and fourth levels are intimately related on metaphysical and symbolic planes equivalent to the second and third stages of spiritual perfection according to Teilhard de Chardin's theories. The poet finds personal justification and fulfillment in a spiritual communion with a Being greater than himself.

As in *Love's Reason,* the sea emerges as the symbol of an essential reality, eternal, immutable and complete in itself, yet constantly recreating itself in an endless dynamic cycle. Correa also notes that the dominant motif in the entire poem is the image of the sea as an orchard or as a garden in spring, fecundated by light, and giving forth a daily harvest of flowers and fruit. In short, the motif of the sea as Edenic Paradise, already introduced in *Love's Reason,* is completed in this poem. (pp. 98-100)

The message of *The Contemplated Sea* can be summarized as follows: The sea is a symbol for life itself, both the permanent human feelings and the beauties of nature as contemplated by generations since the creation of man.

It is enough for Salinas to know that even though he must die one day, the beauty he perceived in the sea is permanent. It is no longer reality which is illusory, but each viewer whose life time destroys. Salinas' previous conflicts are resolved when he ceases to attach value to the realization of his individual self (important only in so far as he is able to assimilate and communicate beauty to others). The poet is only one link in the chain; the chain is the important thing. Salinas thus has traded individual happiness for a greater happiness of sharing and feeling a common bond with all humanity. (p. 105)

The Contemplated Sea expresses with the greatest clarity Salinas' new philosophy of life, and in this respect is probably his most significant book. Yet, it never quite attains the lyrical level of the love cycle or the intensity of feeling of *All Things Made Clearer,* which is perhaps the book with which the contemporary reader can best identify. No one can fail to empathize with the poet's desperate struggle to preserve his faith in the future of humanity while at the same time facing squarely the inherent dangers of its destruction through the misuse of technology.

By the time *All Things Made Clearer* was completed, in 1947, Salinas had been the recent witness to nine consecutive years of armed conflict. Modern warfare seemed to him the one real threat to culture, and he became obsessed with the fear of total destruction. His long poem "**Cero**" ("**Zero**"), first published individually in a Spanish-English bilingual edition, then added as the last poem of *All Things Made Clearer* . . . , was written in 1944 and has seemed to many an uncanny prophecy of the Hiroshima holocaust which was to take place only a few months later. The protest against war is also a dominant theme of Salinas' novel, *La bomba increíble (The Incredible Bomb).* . . . (p. 106)

The change in the level of language between the poetry of the Love Cycle and that of *The Contemplated Sea,* on the one hand, and that of *All Things Made Clearer* on the other, should be apparent to any reader even without much analysis. In *The Voice Owed to You* and *Love's Reason,* we were accustomed to an elegant, at times "precious," style, and to the harmonious cadences inspired in the Renaissance models of Garcilaso and Fray Luis. Similarly, the style of *The Contemplated Sea* has been compared with that of the Golden Age mystic, San Juan de la Cruz. In all three books, Salinas' verses seek to appease and to reflect the order and beauty of an harmonious vision.

In *All Things Made Clearer,* particularly in the poems which are an indictment of modern life, Salinas often attempts to shock his reader. . . . In this book, he generally speaks in plain everyday language, and through symbolic levels of meaning less remote and esoteric than in previous books. The immediate relationship between a world of real, clearly identifiable objects, and their poetic equivalents, is also much more apparent than before.

Yet, Salinas' language is never commonplace. It remains "learned," chiefly through the use of many mythological or cultural-literary allusions (and an occasional conceptual metaphor) which at first might seem out of place in a description of contemporary reality. (pp. 120-21)

The last known poem written by Salinas, in the midst of great physical suffering from the disease which was to take his life two months later, still expresses the same unwavering faith. The poem, dated September 28, 1951, is entitled "**Futuros**"

("**Futures**"), and its last stanza is very much in the spirit of *Confidence:*

> En la cima del pasado
> cantando el futuro está.
> Calla y óyele: ya es tuyo.
> Porque todo acaba en *a.* . . .
>
> (In the past's crest one can hear
> the future already singing.
> Be silent, and listen: it is yours.
> Because everything ends in *a.*)

(p. 132)

John Crispin, in his Pedro Salinas, *Twayne Publishers, Inc., 1974, 180 p.*

ADDITIONAL BIBLIOGRAPHY

De Torre, Guillermo. "Contemporary Spanish Poetry." *Texas Quarterly* IV (1961): 55-78.*
  General discussion of the evolution of Spanish poetry in the twentieth century which mentions Salinas's connection with the "Generation of 1927."

Dunham, Lowell. "Not in the Reviews." *Books Abroad* XXVI, No. 2 (Spring 1952): 155-56.
  Eulogy containing the writer's memories of Salinas.

Gilman, Stephen. "The Proem to 'La voz a ti debida.'" *Modern Language Quarterly* XXIII, No. 4 (December 1962): 353-59.
  Detailed discussion of Salinas's famous love sequence with particular attention given to the ambiguous identity of the second person in the poem.

Helman, Edith. "A Way of Seeing: 'Nube en la mano' by Pedro Salinas." *Hispanic Review* XXXXV, No. 4 (Autumn 1977): 359-84.
  Detailed discussion of the opening poem of Salinas's posthumous collection *Poemas escogidos.*

Hispania: Salinas Number XXXV, No. 2 (May 1952): 131-60*.
  Memorial issue devoted to Salinas that contains brief reminiscences of him by American and Spanish writers and critics, including Vincente Aleixandre, Stephen Gilman, Jorge Guillén, and Edith Helman.

House, Roy Temple. Review of *La bomba increíble,* by Pedro Salinas. *Books Abroad* XXVI, No. 1 (Winter 1952): 39-40.
  Favorable review of Salinas's "quasi-scientific" novel that addresses the threat of nuclear war.

Morris, C. B. "Visión and Mirada in the Poetry of Salinas, Guillén and Dámaso Alonso." *Bulletin of Hispanic Studies* XXXVIII (1961): 103-12.*
  Discusses the importance of poetic vision and image in Salinas's work and in the work of two of his contemporaries.

———. "Pedro Salinas and Marcel Proust." *Revue de littérature comparée* XXXXIV (1970): 195-214.*
  Examines the ways in which Proust's work influenced Salinas's love poetry.

Newman, Jean Cross. "Salinas Remembered and Remembering." *Revista Canadiense de Estudios Hispánicos* I, No. 3 (1977): 307-15.
  Discusses Salinas's early life in Spain and his yearning for his homeland during the last years of his life in the United States.

Spitzer, Leo. "El conceptismo interior de Pedro Salinas." *Revista Híspanica Moderna* VII (1941): 33-69.
  First important study of Salinas's poetry. Written in Spanish.

(Count) Leo (Lev Nikolaevich) Tolstoy

1828-1910

(Also transliterated as Lyof; also Nikolayevich, also Tolstoi, Tolstoj, and Tolstoĭ) Russian novelist, short story writer, essayist, dramatist, and critic.

The following entry presents criticism of Tolstoy's novel *Anna Karenina*. For a complete discussion of Tolstoy's career, see *TCLC*, Volumes 4 and 11.

Tolstoy's literary stature rests largely on two monumental works: *Voina i mir* (*War and Peace*) and *Anna Karenina*. Although both of these rank among the classics of world literature, many critics considers *Anna Karenina* superior to the earlier *War and Peace* due to its greater artistic focus, the subtle brilliance of its structure, and the mature psychological insights that Tolstoy offers into the actions of his characters. In many ways, *Anna Karenina* is unique among Tolstoy's works. It has none of the self-assured moral didacticism of Tolstoy's later writings, and although it resembles *War and Peace* in its epic proportions, critics agree that *War and Peace* is essentially optimistic, while *Anna Karenina* is pervaded with a sense of tragedy. Traditionally considered the ultimate achievement in nineteenth century realism, *Anna Karenina* also contains elements that critics now recognize as innovations foreshadowing the development of the twentieth-century psychological novel.

Tolstoy began writing *Anna Karenina* in the spring of 1873, shortly after abandoning work on a novel about Peter the Great which he had unsuccessfully begun seventeen times. The year before he had attended the inquest of his neighbor's mistress, a woman named Anna Pirogova, who had thrown herself under a train in a fit of jealousy. This incident, according to biographers, linked the idea of romantic passion with violent death in Tolstoy's mind. Tolstoy's original idea was to discuss the issue of women's rights in a story about a "disgusting" adulterous woman who ruins both her husband and her lover, with the men portrayed as sympathetic figures. Boris Eikhenbaum, an important Russian critic and the author of several biographical and critical works on Tolstoy, points out that Tolstoy did write a work with this theme many years later when he completed his *Kreitserova sonata* (*The Kreutzer Sonata*). However, Tolstoy's plan for *Anna Karenina* changed drastically during the years he worked on the novel, with Anna ultimately emerging as a sympathetic figure. Critics offer various explanations for the transformation of Tolstoy's conception of Anna. Eikhenbaum, for example, attributes this change to Tolstoy's desire to develop the theme of the superiority of country life to city life through the character of Constantine Levin. Eikhenbaum explains that Levin's role as the representative of ideal agrarian community made it necessary for Anna's husband Karenin to become the representative of corrupt St. Petersburg society, and that this, in turn, led Tolstoy to portray Anna more sympathetically. Another explanation is proffered by Henri Troyat, author of a major biography of Tolstoy, who contends that Tolstoy was seduced by his own creation—that he fell in love with Anna and that her role in the novel changed accordingly. This topic has received a great deal of attention from critics because *Anna Karenina* was written at a pivotal period in Tolstoy's life, shortly before the spiritual crisis that led him to dramatically alter his ideas on the meaning of life,

Reproduced by permission of APN, Novosti Press Agency

embrace a radical form of Christianity, and abandon the creation of realistic fiction. Many critics believe that his complex attitude toward Anna and the sense of moral irresolution that pervades the novel, as well as the distaste that Tolstoy frequently expressed for the work during its composition, all reflect the spiritual torment and subconscious conflicts that led directly to his spiritual crisis.

Writing *Anna Karenina* was an enormous struggle for Tolstoy. In 1894, after he had nearly completed the novel, he abandoned the work on the grounds that he found it "terribly disgusting and nasty." According to Eikhenbaum, he might never have returned to it at all had he not found himself in need of ten thousand rubles for the purchase of a piece of land. In November of 1874 he began negotiating with the magazine *Russky vestnik* (*The Russian Messenger*) for rights to publish *Anna Karenina* in serial form. The price that was agreed upon was twenty-thousand rubles—an immense sum for serialization rights. Following these negotiations Tolstoy began rewriting and revising *Anna* for publication, a task that occupied him through the spring of 1877, for he abandoned the work several times in depression and disgust, delaying the appearance of the installments. Although the novel was an immediate popular success, it received a mixed critical reception, with Russian critics applauding or condemning the novel primarily in response to Tolstoy's criticism of Russian society. In particular, the pacifist ideas expressed in the novel antagonized the editor of the *Russian Messenger,* who refused to publish the novel's final chapters, which include Levin's disparaging remarks on the Russo-Turkish War then being waged, because he found the implied condemnation of that conflict unpatriotic. In consequence, Tolstoy was obliged to publish the final part of the novel himself in pamphlet form in order to satisfy the curiosity of the many readers who had followed the story from the beginning. *Anna Karenina* was subsequently published in book form in 1878. The first English translation appeared in 1886.

In *Anna Karenina* Tolstoy explored themes that were of central concern to him during the period of his life that immediately preceded his spiritual crisis, later described in the 1882 essay *Ispoved* (*A Confession*). These themes were the importance of family life, the role of social institutions in the life of the individual, and the destructive force inherent in the passion of love. They are developed in the novel through the subtle interplay of events in the lives of four couples: Stiva and Dolly Oblonsky, Anna's casually adulterous brother and his wife; Dolly's young sister Kitty and her husband Constantine Levin; Anna and her husband; and Anna and her lover Vronsky. Anna's relationship with her husband reveals the unattractive nature of her social and moral obligations. Of the others, the novel is most concerned with Levin and Kitty, and Anna and Vronsky. Those critics who interpret the novel in light of Tolstoy's often-stated fondness for Jean-Jacques Rousseau's theories about the superiority of the man of nature over the man of society generally conclude that Levin's and Kitty's relationship, with their active and useful life in the country, represents goodness, while Anna's and Vronsky's immoral liaison represents evil. It is this evil, they believe, that brings about their doom. However, other critics find that the interrelationships between Tolstoy's characters and the moral questions raised in the novel are considerably more complex and subtle than such a reading suggests. Anna, for example, is widely regarded as one of the most attractive heroines in world literature. Her presence dominates the novel, and the other characters admire her for her goodness and her vitality as well as for her beauty; her love for Vronsky is genuine and overwhelming, and she sacrifices everything for it. Similarly, once committed to his relationship with Anna, Vronsky sacrifices a promising military career for her, loves her faithfully, and tries to satisfy the ever-increasing demands of Anna's obsessive jealousy. Corresponding to this sympathetic view of Anna and Vronsky is a more complex understanding of Levin, the character whom critics consider Tolstoy's alter ego in the novel. While Levin is a good man, much concerned with spiritual fulfillment and with discovering the meaning of life, he is often rude and self-centered, and, like Anna, tempted by self-destruction. Moreover, many critics look askance at the spiritual peace that Levin seems to have achieved at the end of the novel, noting that many of his problems remain unresolved. Recent critics of *Anna Karenina* recognize that neither couple is intrinsically good nor evil and that Levin and Kitty survive problems similar to those that destroy Anna and Vronsky because their alliance is socially sanctioned, they are committed to spiritual values, and they are able to contain their passion within the limits imposed by family life and society.

Tolstoy's portrayal of this society is rife with ironies. Its hypocrisy and superficiality are relentlessly exposed in his treatment of many of the novel's minor characters, most notably in his portrayal of Princess Betsy Tservaya. Stiva's and Dolly's story also emphasizes the bitter irony of Anna's fate. Like Anna, Stiva commits adultery, and from far less compelling

motives, yet he escapes unpunished. Most critics now point out that Tolstoy offers no final judgments in *Anna Karenina*: despite his conservatism, personal dislike of the women's rights movement, and the morbidity of his views on sex, in *Anna Karenina* his artistic integrity prevailed over the didactic tendencies that so often marred his later fiction. In *Anna Karenina* Tolstoy did not preach universal solutions, but depicted instead life's often insoluble complexities, or, as Tolstoy's contemporary Anton Chekhov observed, he contented himself with the "correct presentation of the problem." As a result, he set a standard of excellence for the realistic novel that many critics believe has never been surpassed. In *Anna Karenina,* the ambiguities and confusion that so often blur moral vision are reproduced so fully that most critics now believe that even the novel's biblical epigraph—"Vengeance is mine. I will repay," which at first glance seems a harsh reminder that sins such as Anna's must inevitably invoke God's punishment, is more likely a warning to society not to arrogate to itself a power that belongs only to God.

The potential destructiveness of sexual passion is also a major theme in *Anna Karenina.* Tolstoy's ambivalence toward women has been well documented by his critics and biographers, and, as he grew older, he himself often stated his distaste for passionate love and his conviction that it was most often a destructive and evil force. Many critics believe that this conviction lies behind the consequences of passion in *Anna Karenina.* In his analysis of *Anna Karenina* the noted novelist and critic Vladimir Nabokov has explained that there can be little doubt that Tolstoy intended Anna's death under the wheels of the train to serve as a final outward manifestation of the sin of excessive sexual passion that was "battering and destroying" her soul. However, although Tolstoy's views on love and sex were eccentric and extreme, most critics accept that Anna's death is both symbolically and psychologically justified within the context of the novel, however much Tolstoy's own personal views may have influenced him to conclude Anna's story in violence.

Tolstoy's narrative technique in *Anna Karenina* was essentially realistic, with critics frequently remarking upon the author's extraordinary eye for everyday details and his talent for revealing character through precise physical descriptions. As Tolstoy himself explained: "No detail must be neglected in art, for a button half-undone may explain a whole side of a person's character. It is absolutely necessary to mention that button. But it has to be described in terms of that person's inner life, and attention must not be diverted from important things to focus on accessories and trivia." Tolstoy also believed that it was essential for a novelist to fully and accurately portray the milieu in which his characters function. For this reason he provided an extensive cast of carefully described minor characters, and included scenes that critics note are entirely superfluous to the progress of the story, but which assist in establishing a strong sense of the time and the place in which the story unfolds. However, there are elements of *Anna Karenina* that extend beyond realism. The influence of the German philosopher Arthur Schopenhauer's work "On Seeing Ghosts," which Tolstoy read, and of Tolstoy's friend, the poet Afanasy Fet, apparently awakened Tolstoy to the possibility that his work might profit from the use of such poetic techniques as symbolism and allegory. Thus, in *Anna Karenina* Tolstoy made extensive use of symbols for the first time in any of his fiction. Some of the elements which have a symbolic function within the novel include the snowstorm in which Anna returns to St. Petersburg, the recurring motif of the railroad, and the flickering candle by which Anna reads a book. In addition, the fall of Vronsky's mare Frou-Frou and Anna's recurring dream of a dirty peasant beating on iron are commonly interpreted by critics as allegories representing respectively Anna's own fall and the sin that is disfiguring her soul, though the precise meaning of the latter image remains the subject of much critical debate.

Following the completion of *Anna Karenina*, Tolstoy turned his attention to numerous nonliterary projects, including the composition of a reader for Russian school children based on his own educational theories. Then, with the culmination of his spiritual crisis in the early 1880s, Tolstoy renounced representational art in favor of didactic fiction. In the fictional works that date from this later period, such as the *Kreutzer Sonata* and *Voskresenie (Resurrection)*, critics agree that the artist in Tolstoy was nearly always handicapped by the philosopher and the moral pedant. *Anna Karenina* thus not only represents Tolstoy's finest artistic achievement, it holds a special fascination for critics hoping to perceive the roots of the spiritual crisis that divided Tolstoy's career.

(See also *Contemporary Authors*, Vol. 104 and *Something about the Author*, Vol. 26.)

IVAN TURGENEV (letter date 1875)

[*Turgenev was a major novelist in nineteenth-century Russian literature. In the following excerpt, he discusses his dislike of* Anna Karenina *for its "society" setting and what he regards as its Slavophile tendencies. In another letter, written to A. S. Suvorin in April, 1875, Turgenev noted that Tolstoy "is remarkably talented, but in* Anna Karenina *he has, as people here would say, 'lost his way' [original in French]: the influence of Moscow, the Slavophile gentry, Orthodox old maids, his own seclusion and the absence of real artistic freedom! The second part is simply tedious and shallow, that's the real shame!"*]

We've received a copy of Rubinstein's *Demon* arranged for the piano and have looked it over attentively. We are convinced it's extremely worthy, but tedious and unoriginal. We were even more disappointed (because our expectations were higher) with Tolstoy's novel [*Anna Karenina*]. With all his talent and then to wander off into that high-society bog and mark time there and to treat all that nonsense not humorously but with pathos is, seriously, no trifling matter! Moscow has ruined him; he's not the first, nor will he be the last, but I'm more sorry for him than for all the others. (p. 213)

Ivan Turgenev, in a letter to A[lexander] V[asilyevich] Toporov on April 1, 1875, in his Turgenev's Letters, *edited and translated by A. V. Knowles, Charles Scribner's Sons, 1983, pp. 212-13.*

V. V. CHUYKO (essay date 1875)

[*Chuyko was a Russian critic of art and literature, and an anglophile whose 1889 study of Shakespeare was one of the most important works on the Elizabethan dramatist to appear in Russia up to that time. In the following excerpt taken from two articles that appered in the liberal paper* Voice *in 1875, Chuyko, like other liberal critics of the time, attacks* Anna Karenina *on the grounds that the affairs of aristocratic characters are necessarily devoid of interest. However, Chuyko was more insightful and generous in his attitudes than most of his fellow liberals in that*

he perceived the irony in Tolstoy's attitude toward the society he portrayed in Anna Karenina, *and conceded that perhaps the choice of a milieu in which social problems had no part in anyone's life was wise insofar as it enabled Tolstoy to concentrate exclusively on examining problematical psychological situations.*]

This is but the beginning of [*Anna Karenina*] and all is not yet clear. The drama lies ahead, and drama there will be if the beginning is anything to go by. So far only the background has been sketched in and a few characters drawn. Kitty is certainly a re-working of the wonderful portrait of Natasha in *War and Peace*; we can already see the same general characteristics, the same springs of spiritual life and the same sort of spiritual organism. Some of the other characters are already fully drawn and this is where Count Tolstoy's pre-eminence lies. I think that several of the characters in the new novel are better, are drawn in greater relief, than in his previous works; there is nothing incomplete in them, nothing left unsaid, nothing illogical; all of them are well constructed and integral; characteristic flows from characteristic naturally and logically; they have none of the hazy outlines, none of the posing and flabbiness of Pierre in *War and Peace*. In that novel Count Tolstoy was paradoxical to a marked degree, but here there is no paradox; the author is the same investigator of the varieties of humanity and not so much the investigator of types as the analyst of various psychological moments in a man's development. (pp. 233-34)

The February number of the 'Russian Messenger' contains the continuation of Count Tolstoy's novel *Anna Karenina*. This continuation produces a less charming impression than the beginning; it is, if one can so express it, paler, although still interesting. The novel still revolves around high society which in itself provides little of interest for the artist. Levin leaves for the country in despair after Kitty has refused his hand and his heart, Anna departs for Petersburg and her husband; Vronsky who is in love with her also sets out for the capital. Little by little they draw nearer each other.

All in all we have had more than one hundred and sixty pages, and the novel's two main characters, Count Vronsky and Anna Karenina, are still not fully developed and it is still unknown what will become of them. Surely such a leisurely development of the action and the characters is a mistake and is harmful to the interest in the novel? Furthermore the action takes place in high society circles and the leading characters are from this society and neither these people nor this society can form the basis of strong drama, even in the realm of personal relationships. Count Tolstoy is a talented artist and, because of the nature of his talent, a realist. He does not endow the thoughts and feelings of these people with any independence because on account of their upbringing and social position they could not possess it. He does not belong to the number of those of our writers who endow the puppets of their imagination with the title of Count or Prince and fill them with unheard-of virtue and, copying the habit of several French novelists, fill the boredom and emptiness of their lives with a spurious drama.

Count Tolstoy is a true realist in the broadest and most exact sense of the word and consequently one does not meet any sort of idealization in his works; he is the enemy of everything affected, everything artificial, everything false and therefore the pictures he paints, while not being simple photographs, present life in all its hard and sometimes bitter truth; nor is there any hidden plan to paint one phenomenon to the detriment of any other or to present in an unfavourable light a fact which he himself possibly does not like. This trait is especially clearly seen in *War and Peace* where Count Tolstoy set himself the task of showing the utter inability of the upper classes to help during the national disaster of 1812. Count Tolstoy generally likes to remove from people and phenomena everything done for effect or obviously theatrical and more often than not looks on life with an ironic smile. Such irony shines through *War and Peace* and a similar pitiless and caustic irony is to be seen in *Anna Karenina* too, in relation to the same high society which apparently comprises the novel's main subject matter.

· · · · ·

Something strange has been noticed both by society and critics concerning Count Tolstoy's novel *Anna Karenina*. Before the appearance of the first chapters everyone awaited the novel with the greatest impatience and eagerly anticipated the same aesthetic and intellectual pleasure which they had received from *War and Peace*. Consequently a number of prejudices about the novel developed from which the majority of the reading public have not yet managed to free themselves. The first chapters were found disappointing. It appeared that the idea behind the novel was not as well thought out as that behind *War and Peace*. Instead of the history of a whole period of Russian society, *Anna Karenina* presents the intimate story of several individuals almost without reference to the collective life of society; however at the beginning the reader was struck by the masterly style, the subtly depicted characters and the clear and interesting exposition of the plot. The second series of chapters further disappointed the reader; many saw that there were no particular types, the external interest was somewhat weak and that although the characters were consistent in themselves their psychological aspects were poorly delineated and were even occasionally self-contradictory. Then the March number of the 'Russian Messenger' completely depressed the reading public. It turned out that from past custom and the pattern he had earlier established people were expecting precisely what Count Tolstoy had no intention of giving them and that the belletristic side of the novel was decidedly unsatisfactory and it was the general opinion that for the author of *War and Peace* the latest work was extremely poor and did not possess even any general interest. It is my opinion that just as the expectations for the novel were unjustified so are the attacks upon it now that we know what it is. I think that Count Tolstoy has been found lacking in any aesthetic view about Russian society but that the demands of this society will not in themselves stand up to even the most modest criticism. Our babbling critics repeated the hesitations of public opinion and presented in their writings a series of contradictory and clumsy conclusions about the novel: some were dissatisfied because *Anna Karenina* was not *War and Peace*, or because it did not display sufficient Slavophile tendencies; others that the author seemed to be too *pochvennik* or Slavophile; or lastly those—the most persistent and at the same time most ridiculous—who considered that it was not worth the trouble to comment on the novel and that besides obscenity and disgraceful goings-on there was nothing in it, and then in all due seriousness explained this as a sign of the decline and fall of society. But one also heard some rather more weighty criticisms.

The first of these concerned the fact that Count Tolstoy had narrowed down all the interest in contemporary Russian society to that embodied in the so-called 'upper' class. In the Russia of today are there really no more interesting products of life than these which would give the author of *Childhood* and *Boyhood* interesting and original material for psychological comment? Is it really worth studying this high society which has

been exhausted by our so-called upper-class authors and which Count Tolstoy himself does not regard at all favourably? An upper-class dandy, be he even as well-behaved and intelligent a young man as Count Vronsky, is but a faded flower of a former society and the circles in which he exists have destroyed in him any original or individual characteristics and left only specific traces of a certain nature. (pp. 237-38).

A good education should have certainly opened up for Vronsky wider ideals and ambitions in life and his talents should have opened up for him a wider field of activity. And to what, by the way, have his talents led him? Besides his activities in the army and society he does have one other interest—horses, for which he has an immense enthusiasm. If we add to this his love for Anna Karenina then it would seem that Vronsky is seized by two passions; but these two passions do not get in each other's way although he looks upon them both from the same point of view; in other words for him love for a woman is in no way different in kind from love for a horse. Such is Vronsky. His society friends are no better—nor, we might add, any worse. Yashin, for example, is a gambler and hard drinker; far from being a man who lives without principles, he is drawn by Count Tolstoy as living by immoral ones. Yashin was Vronsky's best friend in the regiment. Vronsky liked him both for his unusual physical strength which was expressed for the most part in the fact that he could drink like a fish, go without sleep and show no ill effects and also for his great moral strength which he displayed to his superiors and his friends attracting both fear and respect, and also at cards when he would lay tens of thousands but always, in spite of the vast amounts of wine he had drunk, carefully and deliberately, so that he was looked upon as the leading player in the English Club.

Such is the psychological material which the author has found in high society. It is unattractive and by no means interesting; but Count Tolstoy did not intend to portray contemporary heroes and if I were forced to comment on the choice of milieu for the novel then I would say without fear of erring greatly that he chose this one precisely because it is not characteristic and does not present any remarkable traits of its own. With no attempt at presenting the history of social ideas or of the morals of contemporary society and restricting himself to a specific circle of psychological observations, the author evidently chose such a milieu which in the realm of ideas contains absolutely nothing and in that of morals has to such a degree surrounded itself with certain rules and forms and has to such a degree become petrified within them that it gives the very best conditions for psychological observations. When he concerns himself with such a milieu the writer is not obliged to anticipate, to evade, to explain or even to comment upon the course of social ideas inasmuch as these ideas are reflected in that milieu—in high society there are no ideas to be reflected; he is not obliged to paint the morals of this milieu and consequently he can devote himself exclusively to the history of psychic movements because in Yashin and even in Vronsky there do exist such psychic processes. I think this is the best excuse for Count Tolstoy, especially as he is not at all drawn to that society and sometimes, albeit rarely and in passing, as it were, paints it in such a way that it could only bring a blush of shame to the face.

In the novel therefore the whole matter centres of psychological analysis. In this connection there is a further point of a more serious nature. Many people have noticed inconsistency and illogicality in the actions of Levin, who lives on his estates in the country. A man who is clearly passionate and deeply sincere, Levin falls in love with Kitty. He is completely absorbed in his love and has arrived in Moscow with the determination (which has cost him so much) to offer Kitty his hand and his heart; he is agitated and ill at ease and the empty chat of Oblonsky produces upon him a sharp and unpleasant dissonance. When Kitty refuses him he recognizes that she is attracted to Vronsky. In despair he immediately returns to the country and although deeply depressed begins to plan his future; despite his despair he listens with the greatest interest to his steward who tells him that one of his cows has just given birth and sets off with the passionate love of the estate owner and country dweller to look over his land and forgets for a time his shattered hopes and ruined life. It is said that there is something lacking in Levin and that because of excessive originality the author has made him a lifeless character. I think that Levin is a remarkably alive person; there is not only nothing lacking in him but on the contrary something too much, namely that Great Russian lymph, a scrofulous passion and an absence of impulse or irritability. This trait marks both Levin's character and his actions. A Russian who has suffered since his childhood from scrofula and in whom both the drab natural surroundings and the dark grey sky and the whole sum of social and historical life have caused a huge amount of lymph just cannot act as a vivacious Italian or an impressionable Frenchman. An Italian would never settle for such an outcome of his love; he would either put a bullet through his head like Jacopo Ortis or take his revenge like Iago; a Frenchman would probably soon forget the object of his passion but then at the first opportunity perpetrate a multitude of stupidities; but Levin as a lymphatic Russian could not act in either fashion. Thanks to his lymph his spiritual processes are much slower and as it were blunter. The passion wanders darkly and sombrely through his soul, his enthusiasms lack lustre and his habit of eternal mental reflection (also the result of the influence of his social milieu and his lymph) leads him not to any great spiritual outburst but to a more or less dim analysis, to a fruitless mental vicious circle and not to the very process of life but rather to a re-living of the reflection. Levin is an extraordinarily well-described Russian in whom is seen immensely clearly the whole complicated influence of climate and social organism, a climate which oppresses the nervous passion of a tender man living under a clear sky and the warm sun, and a social organism which gives no opportunity of developing the instincts of the community and which in the absence of any live activity nips many talents in the bud and allows only one characteristic to develop: a fruitless theoretical philosophizing which lies like a black spot upon the Russians.

Certainly *Anna Karenina* presents no history of social ideas but because of this it presents far more. It presents foreshortened and unusually clearly, profoundly and with great talent, what the greatest European writers present to their readers: an ethnographic and spiritual history of Russian man, not as an individual or as an exception who has arisen because of this or that social phenomenon but as the representative of a certain nation or race. O'Connell and a whole school of contemporary European critics have shown that Shakespeare did essentially the same thing and his basic worth lies precisely in this and is proof of his unusual genius. To achieve the same objective Count Tolstoy did not, of course, need to be such a genius, for science has considerably eased his path, but nevertheless in Shakespeare's time it was but an accidental result of his genius when then, as now, everything was striving to solve the problem, and this is why in *Anna Karenina* Count Tolstoy shows himself to be far more contemporary a writer than many of those who depict contemporary heroes, make huge efforts

to write a history of social ideas, concern themselves with the propagation of unusual humaneness or unusual progressive trends and forget that before ideas there exists life itself and in the present case Russian life, with its dull skies, its dull ideas and its even duller spiritual processes.

The supporters of contemporary writing are dissatisfied with Count Tolstoy for his apparent paradoxes in consequence of which Anna Karenina is some incomprehensible moral monster. She is an intelligent and good woman, she loves her son passionately, she is well disposed towards her husband, and, moreover, once she has fallen in love with Vronsky, she gives herself to him after some initial hesitation without the slightest spiritual suffering, without the slightest torment, and only after her so-called fall as it were comes to herself and begins to realize the consequences of her actions. On this basis Count Tolstoy has been accused of a psychological paradox and even of negligence towards the main character in his novel. Of course the majority of contemporary Russian novels are guilty of the same thing: they concentrate as we all know on so-called psychological analysis; the author will carefully and in detail describe all the processes of spiritual alarms, torments and pangs of conscience and will note all shades of feeling and every doubt. This is all done in the most banal manner which explains nothing yet at the same time fills dozens of pages. . . . Naturally Count Tolstoy is not responsible for this banal ideal in modern writers and in *Anna Karenina* he shows that without turning to trite descriptions of spiritual processes one can nevertheless write a great page from the history of the human soul.

Discarding the dubious and essentially ridiculous descriptions of pseudo-psychological processes he seizes the spiritual life of man taken from the very facts of life; he does not tell us that Anna Karenina is suffering from this or that or that certain thoughts occurred to her—he only tells us what Anna did, and this is quite sufficient to explain her fully. And here we have one of Count Tolstoy's particular facets as a psychologist: he suggests that man's spiritual processes are for the most part unconscious and that in the majority of cases we are controlled not so much by ideas as by words; the simple fact is often of no great significance but when this fact is given a code name in which is hidden a certain conventional concept the fact immediately is turned into consciousness and immediately is seen in all its striking nakedness. The author has noticed something similar in Anna. The very fact of her love for Vronsky, although it had radically affected the happiness of her husband and son, destroyed her family and ruined Kitty's happiness appeared to her as neither unfitting nor immoral; on the contrary it all seemed natural, simple; she gave herself over to the feeling unreasoningly, submitting herself to the impulsiveness of her nature. But as soon as *her fall* has been accomplished, when the rude fact appeared before her eyes in all its clarity and logicality, she realized the meaning of the fact for her life and the lives of those near her; she gave the fact a name which explained to her all its true meaning. This is unusually accurate: words are as it were the receptacle of ideas where our impressions and convictions slowly and imperceptibly accumulate; words are like mathematical formulae which for the most part and in the normal run of things have little significance but which contain within themselves the sum total of our experience and our convictions.

Precisely in the character of Anna Karenina Count Tolstoy has revealed a rare talent for subtle and vivid observation. The psychological law, so deftly caught by the author, finds its application mainly in that sphere to which Anna belongs by her birth, upbringing and habits. In this milieu more than any-where else people are governed by words which encapsulate concepts and form an unchanging moral code. Words them-selves in this milieu are confined in a certain legitimized frame-work and thus rules for all the trivia of life are worked out. Anna's behaviour in this milieu is up to a point not out of the ordinary and is in itself no way immoral or beyond the bounds of propriety: consequently Anna submits to the emotions of a new love with such ease and with the complete absence of any inner struggle. It appears to her that with the observance of certain external conventions her new feelings are as much of the accepted order of things as her former behaviour towards her husband; it further appears to her that in this milieu such a complication in her feelings and passions would lead to no complications in life because in essence there occurred there neither sincere liaisons nor deep passions but only a certain form and caprice both vindicated by the code of behaviour of this society. Unfortunately Anna Karenina is not fully a society lady; her passion and enthusiasm for it are deeper and when she finds herself face to face with the rough fact of life, when all her past life and her peace of mind are staked on this one fact there then wells up within her that vulgar struggle of a bifurcated and ruined life which is experienced by all mere mortals who do not belong to the upper class and consequently do not have the slightest idea of its moral code.

Finally one must understand that Count Tolstoy is an artist who does not follow the beaten track but who attempts to seek out new paths and new vantage points. He is no routine copyist, taking ready-made paths and taking on trust familiar conclu-sions. In the main he is a lively observer bringing to his almost scientific researches the peculiarities of his nature and the turn of his mind. Realist by nature and fatalist by general outlook, he looks at man's psychological mechanism from this dual point of view. However great his errors might be, however terrible his apparent paradoxes might seem, both these errors and paradoxes are far more valuable and important than the current and recognized truths and banalities of the majority of our writers. (pp. 239-44)

> *V. V. Chuyko, in an excerpt from two articles in "Voice," translated by A. V. Knowles, in* Tolstoy: The Critical Heritage, *edited by A. V. Knowles, Rout-ledge & Kegan Paul, 1978, pp. 233-44.*

LEO TOLSTOY (letter date 1876)

[*In the following excerpt from Tolstoy's often-quoted letter to his friend N. N. Strakhov, he defends the "scenic" technique he employed in* Anna Karenina *from some critics's allegations that it represented only a shallow depiction of externals. For further discussion of the narrative structure of Anna Karenina, see the excerpts by Tolstoy (1878), Percy Lubbock (1921), Louis Au-chincloss (1961), Elizabeth Stenbock-Fermor (1975) and Vladimir Nabokov (1958).*]

[If] I were to try to say in words everything that I intended to express in my novel [*Anna Karenina*], I would have to write the same novel I wrote from the beginning. And if short-sighted critics think that I only wanted to describe the things that I like, what Oblonsky has for dinner or what Karenina's shoul-ders are like, they are mistaken. In everything, or nearly ev-erything I have written, I have been guided by the need to gather together ideas which for the purpose of self-expression were interconnected; but every idea expressed separately in words loses its meaning and is terribly impoverished when taken by itself out of the connection in which it occurs. The

connection itself is made up, I think, not by the idea, but by something else, and it is impossible to express the basis of this connection directly in words. It can only be expressed indi-rectly—by words describing characters, actions and situations.

You know all this better than I do, but it has been occupying my attention recently. For me, one of the most manifest proofs of this was Vronsky's suicide which you liked. This had never been so clear to me before. The chapter about how Vronsky accepted his role after meeting the husband had been written by me a long time ago. I began to correct it, and quite un-expectedly for me, but unmistakably, Vronsky went and shot himself. And now it turns out that this was organically nec-essary for what comes afterwards. (pp. 296-97)

It's true that if there were no criticism at all, then . . . you who understand art would be redundant. But now indeed when 9/10 of everything printed is criticism, people are needed for the criticism of art who can show the pointlessness of looking for ideas in a work of art and can steadfastly guide readers through that endless labyrinth of connections which is the essence of art, and towards those laws that serve as the basis of these connections.

And if critics already understand and can express in a news-paper article what I wanted to say, I congratulate them and can boldly assure them qu'ils en savent plus long que moi ["that they know more about it than I do"]. (p. 297)

> *Leo Tolstoy, in a letter to N. N. Strakhov on April 23, 1876, in his* Tolstoy's Letters: 1828-1879, *Vol. I, edited and translated by R. F. Christian, Charles Scribner's Sons, 1978, pp. 296-97.*

A. S. SUVORIN? (essay date 1876)

[*Suvorin was a Russian dramatist, critic, and the founder and editor of the conservative newspaper* New Time. *In the following excerpt from an 1876 review believed to be the work of Suvorin, the critic praises Tolstoy for his astute psychological insights in* Anna Karenina. *He also maintains that, although the novel is lacking in social significance, and therefore represents a waste of Tolstoy's talents on trivial subject matter, its psychology is so penetrating that the reader cannot help but admire the work.*]

The long-awaited continuation of Count Tolstoy's novel *Anna Karenina* appeared at last in the January number of the 'Russian Messenger'. In reading it, one becomes again convinced of the justice of the regret expressed by the majority of critics that such a great talent is being wasted on absolutely insignificant subject-matter such as the depiction of empty lives, foolish concepts and petty interests. Indeed, is it possible to interest oneself in the life, thoughts, ambitions and spiritual suffering of, for example, a character like the novel's hero, Vronsky? . . . (p. 282)

The brilliant qualities, however, of Count Tolstoy's talent are well enough known to everyone. The most outstanding of these qualities and the one which contains the very essence of his genius is that striking knowledge of the process which governs the life of feelings and his ability to draw down to the finest detail all their nuances—of age, sex, social position, education and so on. Count Tolstoy's works form a kind of discourse on experimental psychology; take, for example, Karenin's thought processes when his wife tells him of her relations with Vronsky. With what a wonderful clarity the inner workings of the si-multaneous confluence of various feelings and sensations are here depicted! The quantitative influence of each and every one of them leads Karenin to decide to keep her with him in his home and hide from the public gaze what had taken place and take all necessary measures to put an end to the relationship and most importantly, which he did not admit to himself, to punish her.

What knowledge of the human heart! How wonderfully expressed the ability of a man to adapt the demands of religion and moral duty to his own egotistic interests and personal advantages! Furthermore man not only has the tendency and the ability to find in religion and moral dictates some justification for his own selfish inclinations, but in following them he is quite sincerely convinced that he is sacrificing his own interests to those of others.

Look also at the scene of Anna's meeting with Vronsky when she announces to him that she has told her husband everything. What a subtle analysis of minute and quickly changing impressions and sensations! In half a dozen words, uttered by the characters with the smallest change of expression on their faces which the ordinary observer would not even notice, you immediately see the complex psychic processes which the characters themselves would like to conceal and which to describe would normally take many pages. To quote this passage or even to relate the contents of the novel or its best sections we consider quite unnecessary, for there must be very few people who are not reading *Anna Karenina* for themselves. (pp. 282-83)

> *A. S. Suvorin? in an excerpt from "Russian News," translated by A. V. Knowles, in* Tolstoy: The Critical Heritage, *edited by A. V. Knowles, Routledge & Kegan Paul, 1978, pp. 282-83.*

LEO TOLSTOY   (letter date 1878)

[*In the following excerpt Tolstoy explains the structure of* Anna Karenina *in terms of the "internal linkings" that hold its various sections together.*]

Your opinion about *Anna Karenina* seems to me wrong. On the contrary, I'm proud of the architecture—the arches have been constructed in such a way that it is impossible to see where the keystone is. And that is what I was striving for most of all. The structural link is not the plot or the relationships (friendships) between the characters, but an inner link. Believe me, this is not unwillingness to accept criticism—especially from you whose opinion is always too indulgent; but I'm afraid that in skimming through the novel you didn't notice its inner content. . . . [If] you wish to speak about the lack of a link, then I can't help saying—you are probably looking for it in the wrong place, or we understand the word 'link' differently; but what I understand by link—the very thing that made the work important for me—this link is there—look for it and you will find it. (p. 311)

> *Leo Tolstoy, in a letter to S. A. Rachinsky on January 27, 1878, in his* Tolstoy's Letters: 1828-1879, Vol. I, *edited and translated by R. F. Christian, Charles Scribner's Sons, 1978, pp. 311-12.*

S. E. SHEVITCH   (essay date 1879)

[*In the following excerpt from an essay discussing the works of Tolstoy and Ivan Turgenev, Shevitch views Tolstoy's portrayal of the Russian aristocracy in* Anna Karenina *as shallow and indulgent of the abuses of this class of Russian society. For a contrasting reading of* Anna Karenina, *see the excerpt by S. P. Bychkov (1965).*]

The first of Tolstoy's works, which appeared shortly before the Crimean war, *Childhood and Youth,* marked the place its author was to occupy in Russian fiction. This strange book, which can scarcely be termed "a novel," contains a full and eminently poetic account of the education, moral and intellectual development of a young Russian nobleman. The first part of it, "Childhood," is a poem of Russian domestic life, of wonderful beauty and purity. The author dwells with fond tenderness on every petty incident in the early life of his hero, Prince Nechludoff. With a masterly art and a profound knowledge of those mysterious laws by which from a series of early impressions the nature and character of man are gradually shaped, the author shows us how the idle and monotonous country life in Russia, devoid of intellectual interests, works on the mind and imagination of a naturally clever, impressible boy. Nechludoff becomes a dreamer, utterly detached from the realities of every-day life, thirsting for higher, metaphysical science. The studies in abstract philosophy which he pursues at the university with indefatigable ardor give a new direction to his morbid mind; he becomes a skeptic, an infidel, and thence rushes headlong into the coarsest form of sensualism, into a life of dissipation and debauchery of every kind, which ultimately leads him through a series of the bitterest deceptions to—suicide.

This type of the Russian nobleman, created by Tolstoy, a type we meet with in almost every one of his novels, and his method of treating it, might lead to the conclusion that Tolstoy, as a portrayer of Russian society, is still more negative, still more disconsolate than [Ivan] Turgenieff. Yet it is not so. While the latter finds in the Russian aristocracy nothing but an artificial graft on the nation's body, rotten to the core, and past any attempt at regeneration, the former, on the contrary, though perfectly aware of the vices and foibles of the class he describes, seeks to revive it by an ideal born out of its own life, by a philosophy corresponding to all its peculiar characteristics.

This ideal is the family with all the feelings, duties, and pleasures it engenders, and severed, in order to preserve its entire purity, from all interests and passions of public life. (pp. 331-32)

An illustration of Tolstoy's ideal of family life, which he but slightly touches in *War and Peace,* we find in his last novel, finished a year ago, *Anna Karenina.* As a true and artistic picture of "high life" this novel is a masterpiece without an equal, perhaps, in any literature. In one frame the author has combined two love-stories—the one pure and quiet, the other passionate and criminal. The latter, the love between the heroine, Anna, and the brilliant aide-de-camp, Prince Vronsky, is conducted by Tolstoy step by step to its tragical end with a pitiless logic, and a profound knowledge of all the subtle instincts of the human heart, of all the innumerable prejudices and peculiarities of Russian aristocratic life. The scene of the heroine's suicide, which she commits by throwing herself under the wheels of a railway-train, is in its tragical grandeur one of the most remarkable dramatic effects in modern literature. Beside these two rebel hearts, who seek their own way to love and happiness in open defiance of the decrees of society, the author has placed another pair—the plain, unsophisticated country gentleman Levin and the young girl who ultimately becomes his wife. Their romance, disturbed for a moment by the interference of the disorderly element in the person of Vronsky, flows on quietly and peacefully. The young Mrs. Levin becomes an utterly prosaic and even somewhat slovenly *mater-familias* ["mother of a family"]; her husband remains what he always had been, a quiet country gentleman, ignoring entirely all manner of social "problems" or political "questions," raising his corn and potatoes with the persistency, if not with the civic courage, of a Cincinnatus. And at the close of the book we seem to hear the author exclaiming, "Go and do likewise!"

Such is the moral and social creed of this great poet of Russian aristocracy. The reader will not be slow in detecting all its shallowness. An author who says to the class he represents: "You are estranged from the rest of the people—you are by nature lazy and indolent, that is true, but no matter; be still more indolent, retire once for all from public life, bury yourselves in your families, on your estates, and you shall be saved!"—such an author is unconsciously writing a bitterer satire on that class than any of its most implacable enemies could have done.

Thus the two greatest novelists of modern Russia, both born and bred in that class of Russian society which has until now held undisputed the scepter of intellectual and political power—both, the one with a set purpose, the other unconsciously, pass a death-warrant against the present social organization of their country. (pp. 332-33)

> S. E. Shevitch, "Russian Novels and Novelists of the Day," in The North American Review, Vol. CXXVIII, No. CCLXVIII, March, 1879, pp. 326-34.*

KONSTANTIN LEONTIEV   (essay date 1890)

[*Leontiev was a Russian novelist and critic whose critical philosophy combined a thoroughgoing aestheticism with reactionary political and religious views. He was also a zealous representative of the Slavophile movement in nineteenth-century Russia, believing that Russia's hope of cultural progress lay in keeping itself untainted by the influence of the "declining" countries of the West. Leontiev's The Novels of Count L. N. Tolstoy (1890) is regarded as his most important contribution to literature and a masterpiece of critical analysis. In the following excerpt from that work, Leontiev compares* War and Peace *and* Anna Karenina. *Finding the later work superior in terms of realism and psychological insight, he examines several episodes in the novel which display Tolstoy's powers of realistic character portrayal and psychological analysis. For further comparisons of* Anna Karenina *and* War and Peace, *see the excerpts by Henri Troyat (1965) and Elizabeth Gunn (1971). For further discussion of Tolstoy's psychological portraiture in* Anna Karenina, *see the excerpts by Leon Edel (1961) and Edward Wasiolek (1978).*]

Count Tolstoy's two chief works, *Anna Karenina* and *War and Peace* not only can but should be compared. In comparing their particularities and giving preference in such a detailed examination, first to one and then to the other, we must admit that the sum of their merits is equal.

In *War and Peace* the task is more noble and the choice more gratifying; but, for the very reason that in *Anna Karenina* the author was to a greater extent left to his own resources and no longer aided by the historic grandeur of events provided from without, and so had to choose something for himself from the motley of events flashing by in the contemporary stream and "fix" what he had chosen with a "lasting idea," one wants to give preference to the author of *Karenina* instead of the author of the national epic.

It goes without saying that *War and Peace* contains more tragedy and more stunning scenes. Moreover, the very nature of the tragedy is better. In the epic, people are fighting for their native land (this is true on both sides, for the French are waging

offensive wars for the predominance of France, for the benefit of their native land). In the contemporary novel, the warfare of the Russian "volunteers" on the side of Serbia takes place only in the distance and is unconditionally condemned by the author. There are two attempts at suicide (successful and unsuccessful), and there are thoughts of suicide on the part of Levin. It is incomparably more somber, and even more vulgar; however, Count Tolstoy is not to blame here, but contemporary life. This, too, was provided from without, just as the conflagration of Moscow and the Battle of Borodino were provided from without in *War and Peace.* It is even difficult to write a long, truthful, and interesting novel about contemporary Russian life without including in it at least some thoughts of suicide, so common has it unfortunately become in our life.

At any rate, the great merit of *War and Peace* is the fact that its tragedy is sober and healthy, not ugly, as in the case of so many of our other writers. (pp. 240-41)

And even in *Anna Karenina* Vronsky's attempted suicide and Anna's real one drown in such an abundance of health, strength, physical beauty, luster, peace, and mirth that they cannot too deeply offend the heart and taste of the normal reader.

In both novels, the incredible subtlety of Tolstoy's mind could not kill his sense of the healthy, or, let us say, his "flair." (p. 242)

[If] I turn . . . to both of Tolstoy's outstanding novels, I shall find, despite the great merits of *War and Peace,* that *Anna Karenina* has its advantages, precisely from the standpoint of good and healthy realism.

If I ask myself: "Is the outer work in *War and Peace* as pure as that in *Anna Karenina*?"

I want to say: "No, it is not as pure."

"Is the psychological analysis as precise and mature in the semiepic, semichronicle *War and Peace* as it is in the contemporary novel?"

"No, it is not as precise and mature."

"Is the general atmosphere of *War and Peace* as true to the style and spirit of the life of 1812 as the atmosphere of *Anna Karenina* is true to the style and spirit of our time?"

"It seems to me that it isn't."

And finally:

"Can one say of *War and Peace* what the Russian connoisseur, whose words I quoted above, said of *Anna Karenina:* namely, that from the second novel, 'One can study life itself'?"

I think not.

First about analysis.

When it was necessary in *Anna Karenina* to make Vronsky—that proud, stable, and calmly self-assured man, who is endowed with all the blessings of this world—suddenly attempt suicide, Count Tolstoy realized that Vronsky's passion for Anna and certain external obstacles were not enough. First it was necessary to humiliate him in his own eyes, at least slightly. But how to achieve this? Another man would not be able to humiliate him deliberately; Vronsky would kill him, or would himself be killed in the fight, but he would never let himself be humiliated in his own eyes by an adversary, as almost all Turgenev's weak-willed heroes are humiliated, or as Tolstoy's energetic and brave, but tactless, shy, and socially awkward

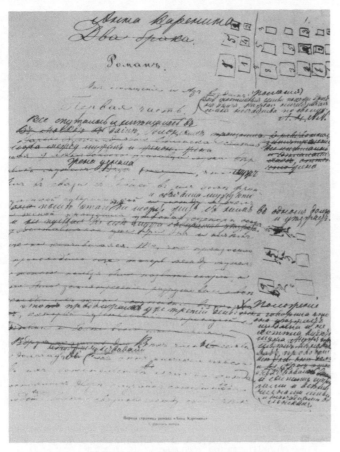

Holograph copy of a manuscript page of Anna Karenina.
Reproduced by permission of APN, Novosti Press Agency.

Levin is frequently, if not humiliated, at least thrown into confusion. Vronsky is not like that. How then to overcome him? Into what unusual, but at the same time natural, circumstances could he be placed so as to lose his "moral balance"? Count Tolstoy found those circumstances. Vronsky's loved one, as she is supposedly dying, humiliates him before the ugly, old, and prosaic Karenin. Let us also recall that a short time earlier, as if on purpose, Vronsky had misgivings about himself for the first time in his life. He felt a dislike for himself as a result of his acquaintance with a foreign prince. The prince had annoyed him with his subtle and profound arrogance, and in the unpleasant features of this high-ranking foreigner, Vronsky saw, as if through a magnifying glass, his own features, and exclaimed: "The stupid ox! Is it possible that I'm like that?"

And then when Anna subsequently makes him ask Karenin's forgiveness, he shoots himself with no great struggle. "For about two minutes he stood motionless with the revolver in his hands, with lowered head and an expression of a strained effort of thought. 'Of course,' he said to himself," et cetera.

What truth! Vronsky was so unaccustomed to humiliation and self-criticism that even this was enough for him.

Everyone knows that people who are accustomed to insults and sorrow do not attempt suicide as readily as those who are unaccustomed to such things. For example, the young (at least in our time) decide on suicide more often than the old. Even

in newspaper accounts, one frequently finds great surprise expressed over the fact that "as it was, the suicide was old."

This particular kind of psychological preparation for Vronsky's attempt at suicide is so astonishingly true, and at the same time it is original. It is such a true tour de force of talent that one can perhaps regard it as being of purely scientific value. (pp. 256-58)

To the number of such surprisingly beautiful, subtle, and true observations, by the way, also belongs the passage where Vronsky, as he pensively and distractedly gets into his carriage to go to the races, momentarily admires some "whirling columns of gnats."

Let us recall that at this time he is both happy and agitated. Anna has just told him that she is carrying his child. For the first time, a much more serious, perhaps even tragic element, or at any rate a vague fear of something severe and dangerous, has been added to their love and passion, which hitherto was only pleasant.

Energetic people, when carried away by passion, if they are not yet wearied by the life struggle, are not frightened by such a serious tinge in their emotions or by such hints by life at the possiblity of tragedy; they are only more greatly aroused and are inclined to even greater firmness and determination. But no matter how firm and calm a person may outwardly be (that is, in his meetings and dealings with other people), this agitation does not appear in him for nothing; in such moments, every person inwardly, when alone with himself, is not exactly the same as he usually is. Vronsky is by no means a dreamer; he is not in the least inclined to ponder over anything for very long, to let himself be distracted, et cetera. Moreover, he is hurrying to the races. And suddenly, instead of simply getting into the carriage, he stares at "gnats swarming in the sun." I must admit that on reading this for the first time I thought it was one of Tolstoy's descriptive remarks that lead to nothing—analysis for analysis' sake, an observation for observation's sake. "It sometimes happens that a person suddenly stares in wonderment at gnats." But on reading farther, I soon repented and honored the author with the sincerest enthusiasm possible. I shan't dwell here on the superb description of the officers' races; I hope that everyone very well remembers how many factors converged at that one time to destroy in Vronsky's soul precisely the composure which, according to the English trainer, he needed to defeat Makhotin: the news of Anna's pregnancy, the presence of the Sovereign and the entire court, the presence of Anna and her husband, the unpleasant remarks of his brother, his sportsman's feelings in themselves, and, at the very bottom of his heart, a certain tendency to unaccustomed contemplation, to fanciful distraction, a tendency at not quite an opportune moment to stare at gnats. And then Vronsky, again in a moment of distraction, through a false and clumsy movement, breaks the back of his favorite horse!

When I reached the point where Frou-Frou falls, I understood the full significance of those "gnats in the sun." Precisely for Vronsky. I might also note in connection with these same gnats, another profound touch, another subtle but very strong connection: Vronsky is something of a painter by nature, and when in Italy, he even tries, although unsuccessfully, to engage in serious painting.

In Anna's preparations for suicide, which, on the whole, are superbly depicted, there are also two particularly significant details that determine everything that happens later. One is the opinion loudly expressed in the railway carriage, in Anna's presence, by an unknown lady (a lady whose person, let us note, Anna found very unpleasant): "Man has been given reason to rid himself of what bothers him." The other is the fact that Anna quickly and irrevocably decides on suicide only when a peasant working near the tracks reminds her momentarily of the entire past, beginning with the workman who was crushed on the rails during her first meeting with Vronsky.

Prior to the unpleasant lady's remark and prior to the moment she saw the workman, Anna herself probably did not know what she would do.

Of course, Anna had often heard the opinion that "reason will provide a way out"; but it is a common psychological law that a most infallible and ancient idea, or, on the contrary, a most clever and recent idea, has a strong effect on us and influences our actions only when we are prepared by our emotions for its perception.

Our emotions are prepared; another person's idea has a strong effect on us, and our will carries this idea out.

The hackneyed idea expressed by chance, but at an opportune moment, by the unpleasant lady had an intellectual or rational, so to say, influence on Anna's decision, which was prepared by her emotions. The sight of the worker later on acted instantaneously, almost like something mystical, on her imagination and will.

It is amazing!

In Anna's preliminary deliberations, there is still another very touching and true observation: She sees a sign: *"Tyut'kin coiffeur. Je me fais coiffer par Tyut'kin."*

"'I'll tell him about that,' and she smiled; but at that very moment she recalled that now she had no one to whom she could tell something funny."

A momentary flash of something funny, cheerful, and good-natured in the midst of all the horrors of mental confusion. That often happens, particularly with people of a lively disposition. In the most brutal moments of life, there comes to mind some amusing and cheerful bit of nonsense. But this true and subtle observation has no connection with any future action. And I intentionally introduced it here for contrast only, in order better to explain my views on the different kinds of analysis in Tolstoy and their relative merit.

It is also interesting to compare both preparations for suicide: those of Vronsky and those of Anna.

Both these people have, of course, been led to this act by a whole series of inner processes and outer stimuli. But, nevertheless, there is a great difference. Vronsky is stronger of will and firmer. He knows in advance what he wants. Anna is more impressionable, active, and timid; up to the last minute before her encounter with the workman, she does not yet know what she will do. Vronsky's decision depends primarily on his own careful and ponderous reasoning; he thinks his decision over alone in his room. There are no outer stimuli, no outside opinions, no chance or decisive meetings. He thinks it over; he says to himself: "Of course!"—and he fires the shot.

Anna leaves the house without any plan or decision; her decision is made almost instinctively, under the influence of chance impressions. "And suddenly, as she recalled the man who was crushed on the day of her first meeting with Vronsky, she realized what she must do."

I do not know in which other writer or where else we can find personal variations on one and the same psychological theme which are so strikingly true to life.

It seems in no other writer in the world. (pp. 259-62)

> Konstantin Leontiev, *"The Novels of Count L. N. Tolstoy: Analysis, Style, and Atmosphere,"* in Essays in Russian Literature, the Conservative View: Leontiev, Rosznov, Shestov, *edited and translated by Spencer E. Roberts, Ohio University Press, 1968, pp. 225-356.*

PRINCE KROPOTKIN   (lecture date 1901)

[Kropotkin was a geographer, political theorist, and critic. He left Russia in 1876 after escaping from prison in the Peter and Paul fortress in St. Petersburg, and remained in exile in England until after the February Revolution of 1917. He was the leading theorist of communist anarchism, and wrote many works advancing his political theories. He is also the author of an autobiography entitled Memoirs of a Revolutionist *(1899-1906) and the critical study* Russian Literature: Ideals and Realities *(1905), originally delivered as a series of lectures in 1901. In the following excerpt from the latter work, Kropotkin discusses attitudes toward marriage and divorce in Russian society, and explains that no educated, sensitive person in Russia would believe that Anna Karenina morally deserved the tragedy that befell her. For further discussion of the presentation of moral problems in* Anna Karenina, *see the excerpts by Boris Eikhenbaum (1959), J. P. Stern (1964), R. F. Christian (1969), Angus Calder (1976), and Vladimir Nabokov (1958).]*

Of all the Tolstóy's novels, **Anna Karénina** is the one which has been the most widely read in all languages. As a work of art it is a master-piece. From the very first appearance of the heroine, you feel that this woman must bring with her a drama; from the very outset her tragical end is as inevitable as it is in a drama of Shakespeare. In that sense the novel is true to life throughout. It is a corner of real life that we have before us. As a rule, Tolstóy is not at his best in picturing women—with the exception of very young girls—and I don't think that Anna Karénina herself is as deep, as psychologiclly complete, and as living a creation as she might have been; but the more ordinary woman, Dolly, is simply teeming with life. As to the various scenes of the novel—the ball scenes, the races of the officers, the inner family life of Dolly, the country scenes on Lévin's estate, the death of his brother, and so on—all these are depicted in such a way that for its artistic qualities **Anna Karénina** stands foremost even amongst the many beautiful things Tolstóy has written.

And yet, notwithstanding all that, the novel produced in Russia a decidedly unfavourable impression, which brought to Tolstóy congratulations from the reactionary camp and a very cool reception from the advanced portion of society. The fact is, that the question of marriage and of an eventual separation between husband and wife had been most earnestly debated in Russia by the best men and women, both in literature and in life. It is self-evident that such indifferent levity towards marriage as is continually unveiled before the Courts in "Society" divorce cases was absolutely and unconditionally condemned; and that any form of deceit, such as makes the subject of countless French novels and dramas, was ruled out of question in any honest discussion of the matter. But after the above levity and deceit had been severely branded, the rights of a new love, serious and deep, appearing after years of happy married life, had only been the more seriously analysed. Tchernyshévsky's novel, *What is to be done,* can be taken as the best expression of the opinions upon marriage which had become current amongst the better portion of the young generation. Once you are married, it was said, don't take lightly to love affairs, or so-called flirtation. Every fit of passion does not deserve the name of a new love; and what is sometimes described as love is in a very great number of cases nothing but temporary desire. Even if it were real love, before a real and deep love has grown up, there is in most cases a period when one has time to reflect upon the consequences that would follow if the beginnings of his or her new sympathy should attain the depth of such a love. But, with all that, there are cases when a new love does come, and there are cases when such an event must happen almost fatally, when, for instance, a girl has been married almost against her will, under the continued insistence of her lover, or when the two have married without properly understanding each other, or when one of the two has continued to progress in his or her development towards a higher ideal, while the other, after having worn for some time the mask of idealism, falls into the Philistine happiness of warmed slippers. In such cases separation not only becomes inevitable, but it often is to the interest of both. It would be much better for both to live through the sufferings which a separation would involve (honest natures are by such sufferings made better) than to spoil the entire subsequent existence of the one—in most cases, of both—and to face moreover the fatal results that living together under such circumstances would necessarily mean for the children. This was, at least, the conclusion to which both Russian literature and the best all-round portion of our society had come.

And now came Tolstóy with *Anna Karénina,* which bears the menacing biblical epigraph: "Vengeance is mine, and I will repay it," and in which the biblical revenge falls upon the unfortunate Karénina, who puts an end by suicide to her sufferings after her separation from her husband. Russian critics evidently could not accept Tolstóy's views. The case of Karénina was one of those where there could be no question of "vengeance." She was married as a young girl to an old and unattractive man. At that time she did not know exactly what she was doing, and nobody had explained it to her. She had never known love, and learned it for the first time when she saw Vrónskiy. Deceit, for her, was absolutely out of the question; and to keep up a merely conventional marriage would have been a sacrifice which would not have made her husband and child any happier. Separation, and a new life with Vrónskiy, who seriously loved her, was the only possible outcome. At any rate, if the story of Anna Karénina had to end in tragedy, it was not in the least in consequence of an act of supreme justice. As always, the honest artistic genius of Tolstóy had itself indicated another cause—the real one. It was the inconsistency of Vrónskiy and Karénina. After having separated from her husband and defied "public opinion"—that is, the opinion of women who, as Tolstóy shows it himself, were not honest enough to be allowed any voice in the matter—neither she nor Vrónskiy had the courage of breaking entirely with that society, the futility of which Tolstóy knows and describes so exquisitely. Instead of that, when Anna returned with Vrónskiy to St. Petersburg, her own and Vrónskiy's chief preoccupation was—How Betsey and other such women would receive her, if she made her appearance among them. And it was the opinion of the Betseys—surely not Superhuman Justice—which brought Karénina to suicide. (pp. 126-28)

Prince Kropotkin, "Turguéneff; Tolstóy," in his Ideals and Realities in Russian Literature, *Alfred A. Knopf, 1915, pp. 88-150.**

MAXIM GORKY (essay date 1920)

[*A Russian novelist and critic, Gorky is recognized as one of the earliest and foremost exponents of socialist realism in literature. From 1920 until his death in 1936 he was considered Russia's greatest living writer and the literary mouthpiece of the Soviet proletariat. In the following excerpt, Gorky briefly comments on his sense of Tolstoy's hostility toward women as exemplified in* Anna Karenina.]

[Tolstoy] talks most of God, of peasants, and of woman. Of literature rarely and little, as though literature were something alien to him. Woman, in my opinion, he regards with implacable hostility and loves to punish her, unless she be a Kittie or Natasha Rostov, i.e , a creature not too narrow. It is the hostility of the male who has not succeeded in getting all the pleasure he could, or it is the hostility of spirit against "the degrading impulses of the flesh." But it is hostility, and cold as in *Anna Karenina.* (p. 15)

Maxim Gorky, "Reminiscences of Leo Tolstoy," translated by S. S. Koteliansky and Leonard Woolf, in his Reminiscences, Dover Publications, 1946, pp. 4-70.

PERCY LUBBOCK (essay date 1921)

[*Lubbock's literary criticism was greatly influenced by Henry James. Like James, he believed that the novel was meant to be, above all else, a realistic portrait of a portion of life. Also like James, Lubbock considered dramatic presentation, rather than authorial narration and description, as the best means of narrative expression. However, Lubbock disagreed with his mentor on a number of points, most significantly the correspondence of form and content. In this matter he considered the "sense of life" presented more important than formal symmetry, though when combined with the latter the former becomes much more effective. In general, Lubbock saw the history of the novel as a matter of evolution. Fiction progressed from the mere telling of tales to the intricate use of dramatic presentation and irony evidenced best in the work of Henry James. In the following excerpt Lubbock contends that Tolstoy's "scenic" or dramatic approach to his story in* Anna Karenina *"damaged a magnificent book." Lubbock argues that, by failing to provide the reader with a general view of Anna's background and history, and opting instead for an episodic approach to her story, Tolstoy made it impossible for the reader to fully appreciate who Anna is, or to sympathize with her actions. For further discussion of the narrative structure of* Anna Karenina, *see the excerpts by Tolstoy (1876 and 1878), Louis Auchincloss (1961), and Elizabeth Stenbock-Fermor (1975) and Vladimir Nabokov (1958).*]

I turn to [*Anna Karenina*] now, not for its beauty and harmony, not because it is one of the most exquisitely toned, shaded, gradated pieces of portraiture in fiction, but because it happens to show very clearly how an effect may be lost for want of timely precaution. Tolstoy undoubtedly damaged a magnificent book by his refusal to linger over any kind of pictorial introduction. There is none in this story, the reader will remember. The whole of the book, very nearly, is scenic, from the opening page to the last; it is a chain of particular occasions, acted out, talked out, by the crowd of people concerned. Each of these scenes is outspread before the spectator, who watches the characters and listens to their dialogue; there is next to no generalization of the story at any point. On every page, I think, certainly on all but a very few of the many hundred pages, the hour and the place are exactly defined. Something is happening there, or something is being discussed; at any rate it is an episode singled out for direct vision.

Tolstoy and Maxim Gorky in 1901.

The plan of the book, in fact, is strictly dramatic; it allows no such freedom as Balzac uses, freedom of exposition and retrospect. Tolstoy never draws back from the immediate scene, to picture the manner of life that his people led or to give a foreshortened impression of their history. He unrolls it as it occurs, illustrating everything in action. It is an extraordinary feat, considering the amount of experience he undertakes to display, with an interweaving of so many lives and fortunes. And it is still more extraordinary, considering the nature of the story, which is not really dramatic at all, but a pictorial contrast, Anna and her affair on one side of it, Levin and his on the other. The contrast is gradually extended and deepened through the book; but it leads to no clash between the two, no opposition, no drama. It is an effect of slow and inevitable change, drawn out in minute detail through two lives, with all the others that cluster round each—exactly the kind of matter that nobody but Tolstoy, with his huge hand, would think of trying to treat scenically. Tolstoy so treats it, however, and apparently never feels any desire to break away from the march of his episodes or to fuse his swarming detail into a general view. It means that he must write a very long book, with scores and scores of scenes, but he has no objection to that.

It is only in its plan, of course, that *Anna Karenina* is strictly dramatic; its method of execution is much looser, and there indeed Tolstoy allows himself as much freedom as he pleases. In the novel of pure drama the point of view is that of the reader alone, as we saw; there is no "going behind" the characters, no direct revelation of their thought. Such consistency is out of the question, however, even for Tolstoy, on the great scale of his book; and he never hesitates to lay bare the mind of any of his people, at any moment, if it seems to help the force or the lucidity of the scene. And so we speedily grow familiar with the consciousness of many of them, for Tolstoy's hand is always as light and quick as it is broad. He catches the passing thought that is in a man's mind as he speaks; and though it may be no more than a vague doubt or an idle fancy, it is somehow a note of the man himself, a sign of his being, an echo of his inner tone. From Anna and the other figures of the forefront, down to the least of the population of the background, I could almost say to the wonderful little red baby that in one of the last chapters is disclosed to Levin by the trimphant nurse—each of them is a centre of vision, each of them looks out on a world that is not like the world of the rest, and we know it. Without any elaborate research Tolstoy expresses the nature of all their experience; he reveals the dull weight of it in one man's life or its vibrating interest in another's; he shows how for one it stirs and opens, with troubling enlargement, how for another it remains blank and inert. He does so unconsciously, it might seem, not seeking to construct the world as it appears to Anna or her husband or her lover, but simply glancing now and then into their mood of the moment, and indicating what he happens to find there. Yet it is enough, and each of them is soon a human being whose privacy we share. They are actors moving upon a visible scene, watched from the reader's point of view; but they are also sentient lives, understood from within.

Here, then, is a mixed method which enables Tolstoy to deal with his immense subject on the lines of drama. He can follow its chronology step by step, at an even pace throughout, without ever interrupting the rhythm for that shift of the point of view—away from the immediate scene to a more commanding height—which another writer would certainly have found to be necessary sooner or later. He can create a character in so few words—he can make the manner of a man's or a woman's thought so quickly intelligible—that even though his story is crowded and overcrowded with people he can render them all, so to speak, by the way, give them all their due without any study of them outside the passing episode. So he can, at least, in general; for in *Anna Karenina,* as I said, his method seems to break down very conspicuously at a certain juncture. But before I come to that, I would dwell further upon this peculiar skill of Tolstoy's, this facility which explains, I think, the curious flaw in his beautiful novel. He would appear to have trusted his method too far, trusted it not only to carry him through the development and the climax of his story, but also to constitute his *donnée,* his prime situation in the beginning. This was to throw too much upon it, and it is critically of high interest to see where it failed, and why. The miscalculations of a great genius are enlightening; here, in *Anna Karenina,* is one that calls attention to Tolstoy's characteristic fashion of telling a story, and declares its remarkable qualities.

The story of Anna, I suggested, is not essentially dramatic. Like the story of Emma Bovary or of Eugénie Grandet, it is a picture outspread, an impression of life, rather than an action. Anna at first has a life that rests on many supports, with her husband and her child and her social possessions; it is broadly based and its stability is assured, if she chooses to rely on it. But her husband is a dull and pedantic soul, and before long she chooses to exchange her assured life for another that rests on one support only, a romantic passion. Her life with Vronsky has no other security, and in process of time it fails. Its gradual failure is her story—the losing battle of a woman who has thrown away more resources than she could afford. But the point and reason of the book is not in the dramatic question—what will happen, will Anna lose or win? It is in the picture of her gathering and deepening difficulties, difficulties that arise out of her position and her mood, difficulties of which the only solution is at last her death. And this story, with the contrasted picture of Levin's domesticity that completes it, is laid out exactly as Balzac did *not* lay out his story of Eugénie; it is all presented as action, because Tolstoy's eye was infallibly drawn, whenever he wrote, to the instant aspect of his matter, the play itself. He could not generalize it, and on the whole there was no need for him to do so; for there was nothing, not the last stir of motive or character, that could not be expressed in the movement of the play as he handled it. Scene is laid to scene, therefore, as many as he requires; he had no thought of stinting himself in that respect. And within the limit of the scene he was always ready to vary his method, to enter the consciousness of any or all of the characters at will, without troubling himself about the possible confusion of effect which this might entail. He could afford the liberty, because the main lines of his structure were so simple and clear; the inconsistencies of his method are dominated by the broad scenic regularity of his plan.

Balzac had not the master-hand of Tolstoy in the management of a dramatic scene, an episode. When it comes to rendering a piece of action Balzac's art is not particularly felicitous, and if we only became acquainted with his people while they are talking and acting, I think they might often seem rather heavy and wooden, harsh of speech and gesture. Balzac's *general* knowledge of them, and his power of offering an impression of what he knows—these are so great that his people are alive before they begin to act, alive with an energy that is all-sufficient. Tolstoy's grasp of a human being's whole existence, of everything that goes to make it, is not as capacious as Balzac's; but on the other hand he can create a living scene, exquisitely and easily expressive, out of anything whatever, the lightest trifle of an incident. If he describes how a child lingered at the foot of the stairs, teasing an old servant, or how a peasant-woman stood in a doorway, laughing and calling to the men at work in the farmyard, the thing becomes a poetic event; in half a page he makes an unforgetable scene. It suddenly glows and flushes, and its effect in the story is profound. A passing glimpse of this kind is caught, say, by Anna in her hungry desperation, by Levin as he wanders and speculates; and immediately their experience is the fuller by an eloquent memory. The vividness of the small scene becomes a part of them, for us who read; it is something added to our impression of their reality. And so the half-page is not a diversion or an interlude; it speeds the story by augmenting the tone and the value of the lives that we are watching. It happens again and again; that is Tolstoy's way of creating a life, of raising it to its full power by a gradual process of enrichment, till Anna or Levin is at length a complete being, intimately understood, ready for the climax of the tale.

But of course it takes time, and it chanced that this deliberation made a special difficulty in the case of Anna's story. As for Levin, it was easy to give him ample play; he could be left to emerge and to assume his place in the book by leisurely degrees, for it is not until much has passed that his full power is needed. Meanwhile he is a figure in the crowd, a shy and disappointed suitor, unobtrusively sympathetic, and there are long opportunities of seeing more of him in his country solitude. Later on, when his fortunes come to the front with his marriage, he has shown what he is; he steps fully fashioned into the drama. With Anna it is very different; her story allows no such pause, for a growing knowledge of the manner of woman she may be. She is at once to the front of the book; the situation out of which the whole novel develops is made by a particular crisis in her life. She meets and falls in love with Vronsky—that is the crisis from which the rest of her story proceeds; it is the beginning of the action, the subject of the earliest chapters. And the difficulty lies in this, that she must be represented upon such a critical height of emotion before there is time, by Tolstoy's method, to create the right effect for her and to make her impulse really intelligible. For the reader it is all too abrupt, the step by which she abandons her past and flings herself upon her tragic adventure. It is impossible to measure her passion and her resolution, because she herself is still incompletely rendered. She has appeared in a few charming scenes, a finished and graceful figure, but that is not enough. If she is so soon to be seen at this pitch of exaltation, it is essential that her life should be fully shared by the onlooker; but as Tolstoy has told the story, Anna is in the midst of her crisis and has passed it before it is possible to know her life clearly from within. Alive and beautiful she is from the very first moment of her appearance; Tolstoy's art is much too sure to miss the right effect, so far as it goes. And if her story were such that it involved her in no great adventure at the start—if she could pass from scene to scene, like Levin, quietly revealing herself—Tolstoy's method would be perfect. But as it is, there is no adequate preparation; Anna is made to act as a deeply stirred and agitated woman before she has the *value* for such emotions. She has not yet become a presence familiar enough, and there is no means of gauging the force of the storm that is seen to shake her.

It is a flaw in the book which has often been noticed, and it is a flaw whch Tolstoy could hardly have avoided, if he was deetermined to hold to his scenic plan. Given his reluctance to leave the actually present occasion, from the first page onwards, from the moment Anna's erring brother wakes to his own domestic troubles at the opening of the book, there is not room for the due creation of Anna's life. Her turning-point must be reached without delay, it cannot be deferred, for it is there that the development of the book begins. All that precedes her union with Vronsky is nothing but the opening stage, the matter that must be displayed before the story can begin to expand. The story, as we have seen, is in the picture of Anna's life *after* her critical choice, so that the first part of the book, the account of the given situation, cannot extend its limits. If, therefore, the situation is to be really made and constituted, the space it may cover must be tightly ·packed; the method should be that which most condenses and concentrates the representation. A great deal is to be expressed at once, all Anna's past and present, the kind of experience that has made her and that has brought her to the point she now touches. Without this her action is arbitrary and meaningless; it is vain to say that she acted thus and thus unless we perfectly understand what she was, what she had, what was around her, in the face of her predicament. Obviously there is no space to lose; and it is enough to look at Tolstoy's use of it, and then to see how Balzac makes the situation that *he* requires—the contrast shows exactly where Tolstoy's method could not help him. His refusal to shape his story, or any considerable part of it, as a pictorial impression, his desire to keep it all in immediate action, prevents him from making the most of the space at his command; the situation is bound to suffer in consequence.

For suppose that Balzac had had to deal with the life of Anna. He would certainly have been in no hurry to plunge into the action, he would have felt that there was much to treat before the scene was ready to open. All the initial episodes of Tolstoy's book, from Anna's first appearance until she drops into Vronsky's arms, Balzac might well have ignored entirely. He would have been too busy with his prodigious summary of the history and household of the Karenins to permit himself a glance in the direction of any particular moment, until the story could unfold from a situation thoroughly prepared. If Tolstoy had followed this course we should have lost some enchanting glimpses, but Balzac would have left not a shadow of uncertainty in the matter of Anna's disastrous passion. He would have shown precisely how she was placed in the conditions of her past, how she was exposed to this new incursion from without, and how it broke up a life which had satisfied her till then. He would have started his action in due time with his whole preliminary effect completely rendered; there would be no more question of it, no possibility that it would prove inadequate for the sequel. And all this he would have managed, no doubt, in fewer pages than Tolstoy needs for the beautiful scenes of his earlier chapters, scenes which make a perfect impression of Anna and her circle as an onlooker might happen to see them, but which fail to give the onlooker the kind of intimacy that is needed. Later on, indeed, her life is penetrated

to the depths; but then it is too late to save the effect of the beginning. To the very end Anna is a wonderful woman whose early history has never been fully explained. The facts are clear, of course, and there is nothing impossible about them; but her passion for this man, the grand event of her life, has to be assumed in the word of the author. All that he really showed, to start with, was a slight, swift love-story, which might have ended as easily as it began.

The method of the book, in short, does not arise out of the subject; in treating it Tolstoy simply used the method that was congenial to him, without regarding the story that he had to tell. He began it as though Anna's break with her past was the climax to which the story was to mount, whereas it is really the point from which the story sets out for its true climax in her final catastrophe. And so the first part of the book is neither one thing nor the other; it is not an independent drama, for it cannot reach its height through all the necessary sweep of development; and on the other hand it is not a sufficient preparation for the great picture of inevitable disaster which is to follow. Tolstoy doubtless counted on his power—and not without reason, for it is amazing—to call people into life by means of a few luminous episodes; he knew he could make a living creature of Anna by bringing her into view in half a dozen scenes. She descends, accordingly, upon her brother's agitated household like a beneficent angel, she shines resplendent at some social function, she meets Vronsky, she talks to her husband; and Tolstoy is right, she becomes a real and exquisite being forthwith. But he did not see how much more was needed than a simple personal impression of her, in view of all that is to come. Not she only, but her world, the world as she sees it, her past as it affects her—this too is demanded, and for this he makes no provision. It is never really shown how she was placed in her life, and what it meant to her; and her flare of passion has consequently no importance, no fateful bigness. There is not enough of her, as yet, for such a crisis.

It is not because Vronsky seems an inadequate object of her passion; though it is true that with the figure of Vronsky Tolstoy was curiously unsuccesful. Vronsky was his one failure—there is surely no other in all his gallery to match it. The spoilt child of the world, but a friendly soul, and a romantic and a patient lover—and a type fashioned by conditions that Tolstoy, of course, knew by heart—why should Tolstoy manage to make so little of him? It is unfortunate, for when Anna is stirred by the sight of him and his all-conquering speciosity, any reader is sure to protest. Tolstoy should have created Vronsky with a more certain touch before he allowed him to cause such a disturbance. But this is a minor matter, and it would count for little if the figure of Anna were all it should be. Vronsky's importance in the story is his importance to Anna, and her view of him is a part of *her;* and he might be left lightly treated on his own account, the author might be content to indicate him rather summarily, so long as Anna had full attention. It returns upon that again; if Anna's own life were really fashioned, Vronsky's effect would be *there,* and the independent effect he happens to make, or to fail to make, on the reader would be an irrelevant affair. Tolstoy's vital failure is not with him, but with her, in the prelude of his book.

It may be that there is something of the same kind to be seen in another of his novels, in *Resurrection,* though *Resurrection* is more like a fragment of an epic than a novel. It cannot be said that in that tremendous book Tolstoy pictured the rending of a man's soul by sudden enlightenment, striking in upon him unexpectedly, against his will, and destroying his established life—and that is apparently the subject in the author's mind. It is the woman, the accidental woman through whom the stroke is delivered, who is actually in the middle of the book; it is *her* epic much rather than the man's, and Tolstoy did not succeed in placing him where he clearly meant him to be. The man's conversion from the selfishness of his commonplace prosperity is not much more than a fact assumed at the beginning of the story. . . . But *Resurrection,* no doubt, *is* a fragment, a wonderful shifting of scenes that never reached a conclusion; and it is not to be criticized as a book in which Tolstoy tried and failed to carry out his purpose. I only mention it because it seems to illustrate, like *Anna Karenina,* his instinctive evasion of the matter that could not be thrown into straightforward scenic form, the form in which his imagination was evidently happiest. His great example, therefore, is complementary to that of Balzac, whose genius looked in the other direction, who was always drawn to the general picture rather than to the particular scene. (pp. 236-50)

> *Percy Lubbock, in a chapter in his* The Craft of Fiction, *1921. Reprint by The Viking Press, 1957, pp. 236-50.*

D. H. LAWRENCE (essay date 1936)

[*Lawrence was one of the first English novelists to introduce themes of modern psychology into his fiction. In his lifetime he was a controversial figure, both for the explicit sexuality he portrayed in his novels and for his unconventional personal life. Much of the criticism of Lawrence's work concerns his highly individualistic moral system, which was based on absolute freedom of expression, particularly sexual expression. Human sexuality was for Lawrence a symbol of the Life Force, and is frequently pitted against modern industrial society, which he believed was dehumanizing. His most famous novel,* Lady Chatterley's Lover *(1928), was the subject of a landmark obscenity trial in Great Britain in 1960, which turned largely on the legitimacy of Lawrence's inclusion of hitherto forbidden sexual terms. In the following excerpt from an essay published in 1936, Lawrence castigates Tolstoy for his later philosophy of self-denial and for his renunciation of* Anna Karenina.]

It is the novelists and dramatists who have the hardest task in reconciling their metaphysic, their theory of being and knowing, with their living sense of being. Because a novel is a microcosm, and because man in viewing the universe must view it in the light of theory, therefore every novel must have the background or the structural skeleton of some theory of being, some metaphysic. But the metaphysic must always subserve the artistic purpose beyond the artist's conscious aim. Otherwise the novel becomes a treatise.

And the danger is, that a man shall make himself a metaphysic to excuse or cover his own faults or failure. Indeed, a sense of fault or failure is the usual cause of a man's making himself a metaphysic, to justify himself.

Then, having made himself a metaphysic of self-justification, or a metaphysic of self-denial, the novelist proceeds to apply the world to this, instead of applying this to the world.

Tolstoi is a flagrant example of this. Probably because of profligacy in his youth, because he had disgusted himself in his own flesh, by excess or by prostitution, therefore Tolstoi, in his metaphysic, renounced the flesh altogether, later on, when he had tried and had failed to achieve complete marriage in the flesh. But above all things, Tolstoi was a child of the Law, he belonged to the Father. He had a marvellous sensuous understanding, and very little clarity of mind.

So that, in his metaphysic, he had to deny himself, his own being, in order to escape his own disgust of what he had done to himself, and to escape admission of his own failure.

Which made all the later part of his life a crying falsity and shame. Reading the remniscences of Tolstoi, one can only feel shame at the way Tolstoi denied all that was great in him, with vehement cowardice. He degraded himself infinitely, he perjured himself far more than did Peter when he denied Christ. Peter repented. But Tolstoi denied the Father, and propagated a great system of his recusancy, elaborating his own weakness, blaspheming his own strength. "What difficulty is there in writing about how an officer fell in love with a married woman?" he used to say of his *Anna Karenina;* "there's no difficulty in it, and, above all, no good in it."

Because he was mouthpiece to the Father in uttering the law of passion, he said there was no difficulty in it, because it came naturally to him. Christ might just as easily have said, there was no difficulty in the Parable of the Sower, and no good in it, either, because it flowed out of him without effort. (pp. 188-89)

> *D. H. Lawrence, "From 'Study of Thomas Hardy'," in his* Selected Literary Criticism, *edited by Anthony Beal, The Viking Press, 1956, pp. 166-228.**

VLADIMIR NABOKOV (essay date 1958?)

[*A Russian-born American man of letters, Nabokov was a prolific contributor to many literary fields, who produced works in both Russian and English and distinguished himself in particular as the author of the novels* Lolita *(1955) and* Pale Fire *(1962). Nabokov was fascinated with all aspects of the creative life: in his works he explored the origins of creativity, the relationships of artists to their work, and the nature of invented reality. Considered a brilliant prose stylist, Nabokov wrote fiction that entertains and sometimes exasperates readers in its preoccupation with playing intellectual and verbal games. Nabokov's technical genius as well as the exuberance of his creative imagination mark him as a major twentieth-century author. In the following excerpt, Nabokov examines the moral code implied by Anna's tragic love and death, then goes on to analyze some of the recurring motifs which support the artistic structure of Tolstoy's novel. For further discussion of the presentation of moral problems in* Anna Karenina, *see the excerpts by Prince P. A. Kropotkin (1901), Boris Eikhenbaum (1959), J. P. Stern (1964), R. F. Christian (1969), and Angus Calder (1976). For further discussion of the narrative structure of* Anna Karenina, *see the excerpts by Tolstoy (1876 and 1878), Percy Lubbock (1921), Louis Auchincloss (1961), and Elizabeth Stenbock-Fermor (1975).*]

Though one of the greatest love stories in world literature, *Anna Karenin* is of course not just a novel of adventure. Being deeply concerned with moral matters, Tolstoy was eternally preoccupied with issues of importance to all mankind at all times. Now, there is a moral issue in *Anna Karenin,* though not the one that a casual reader might read into it. This moral is certainly not that having committed adultery, Anna had to pay for it (which in a certain vague sense can be said to be the moral at the bottom of the barrel in *Madame Bovary*). Certainly not this, and for obvious reasons: had Anna remained with Karenin and skillfully concealed from the world her affair, she would not have paid for it first with her happiness and then with her life. Anna was not punished for her sin (she might have got away with that) nor for violating the conventions of a society, very temporal as all conventions are and having nothing to do with the eternal demands of morality. What was then the moral "message" Tolstoy has conveyed in his novel?

We can understand it better if we look at the rest of the book and draw a comparison between the Lyovin-Kitty story and the Vronski-Anna story. Lyovin's marriage is based on a metaphysical, not only physical, concept of love, on willingness for self-sacrifice, on mutual respect. The Anna-Vronski alliance was founded only in carnal love and therein lay its doom.

It might seem, at first blush, that Anna was punished by society for falling in love with a man who was not her husband. Now such a "moral" would be of course completely "immoral," and completely inartistic, incidentally, since other ladies of fashion, in that same society, were having as many love-affairs as they liked but having them in secrecy, under a dark veil. (Remember Emma's blue veil on her ride with Rodolphe and her dark veil in her rendezvous at Rouen with Leon.) But frank unfortunate Anna does not wear this veil of deceit. The decrees of society are temporary ones; what Tolstoy is interested in are the eternal demands of morality. And now comes the real moral point that he makes: Love cannot be exclusively carnal because then it is egotistic, and being egotistic it destroys instead of creating. It is thus sinful. And in order to make his point as artistically clear as possible, Tolstoy in a flow of extraordinary imagery depicts and places side by side, in vivid contrast, two loves: the carnal love of the Vronski-Anna couple (struggling amid their richly sensual but fateful and spiritually sterile emotions) and on the other hand the authentic, Christian love, as Tolstoy termed it, of the Lyovin-Kitty couple with the riches of sensual nature still there but balanced and harmonious in the pure atmosphere of responsibility, tenderness, truth, and family joys.

A biblical epigraph: Vengeance is *mine; I* will repay (saith the Lord).

(*Romans* XII, verse 19)

What are the implications? First, Society had no right to judge Anna; second, Anna had no right to punish Vronski by her revengeful suicide.

Joseph Conrad, a British novelist of Polish descent, writing to Edward Garnett, a writer of sorts, in a letter dated the 10th of June, 1902, said: "Remember me affectionately to your wife whose translation of Karenina is splendid. Of the thing itself I think but little, so that her merit shines with the greater lustre." I shall never forgive Conrad this crack. Actually the Garnett translation is very poor.

We may look in vain among the pages of *Anna Karenin* for Flaubert's subtle transitions, within chapters, from one character to another. The structure of *Anna Karenin* is of a more conventional kind, although the book was written twenty years later than Flaubert's *Madame Bovary*. Conversation between characters mentioning other characters, and the maneuvers of intermediate characters who bring about the meetings of main participants—these are the simple and sometimes rather blunt method used by Tolstoy. Even simpler are his abrupt switches from chapter to chapter in changing his stage sets.

Tolstoy's novel consists of eight parts and each part on the average consists of about thirty short chapters of four pages. He sets himself the task of following two main lines—the Lyovin-Kitty one and the Vronski-Anna one, although there is a third line, subordinate and intermediary, the Oblonski-Dolly one that plays a very special part in the structure of the novel since it is present to link up in various ways the two main lines. Steve Oblonski and Dolly are there to act as go-betweens in the affairs of Lyovin and Kitty and in those of Anna and her husband. Throughout Lyovin's bachelor existence, more-

over, a subtle parallel is drawn between Dolly Oblonski and Lyovin's ideal of a mother which he will discover for his own children in Kitty. One should notice, also, that Dolly finds conversation with a peasant woman about children as fascinating as Lyovin finds conversation with male peasants about agriculture.

The action of the book starts in February 1872 and goes on to July 1876: in all, four years and a half. It shifts from Moscow to Petersburg and shuttles among the four country estates (because the country place of the old Countess Vronski near Moscow also plays a part in the book, though we are never taken to it).

The first of the eight parts of the novel has as its main subject the Oblonski family disaster with which the book starts, and as a secondary subject the Kitty-Lyovin-Vronski triangle.

The two subjects, the two expanded themes—Oblonski's adultery and Kitty's heartbreak when her infatuation for Vronski has been ended by Anna—are introductory notes to the tragic Vronski-Anna theme which will not be so smoothly resolved as are the Oblonski-Dolly troubles or Kitty's bitterness. Dolly soon pardons her wayward husband for the sake of their five children and because she loves him, and because Tolstoy considers that two married people with children are tied together by divine law forever. Two years after her heartbreak over Vronski, Kitty marries Lyovin and begins what Tolstoy regards as a perfect marriage. But Anna, who becomes Vronski's mistress after ten months of persuasion, Anna will see the destruction of her family life and will commit suicide four years after the book's start.

"Happy families are all alike; every unhappy family is unhappy in its own way." (pp. 146-50)

Although he is mentioned earlier, Vronski makes his first appearance in part one, chapter 14, at the Shcherbatskis. Incidentally, it is here that starts an interesting little line, the line of "spiritualism," table tilting, entranced mediums, and so on, a fashionable pastime in those days. Vronski in a lighthearted mood wishes to try out this fashionable fad; but much later, in chapter 22 of part seven, it is, curiously enough, owing to the mediumistic visions of a French quack who has found patrons among Petersburg society people, it is owing to him that Karenin decides not to give Anna a divorce—and a telegram to that effect during a final period of tragic tension between Anna and Vronski helps to build up the mood that leads to her suicide.

Some time before Vronski met Anna, a young official in her husband's department had confessed his love to her and she had gaily relayed it to her husband; but now, from the very first look exchanged with Vronski at the ball, a fateful mystery enfolds her life. She says nothing to her sister-in-law about Vronski's giving a sum of money for the widow of the killed railway guard, an act which establishes, through death as it were, a kind of secret link between her and her future lover. And further, Vronski has called on the Shcherbatskis the evening before the ball at the exact moment when Anna remembers so vividly her child from whom she is separated for the few days she has spent in Moscow smoothing her brother's troubles. It is the fact of her having this beloved child which will later constantly interfere with her passion for Vronski.

The scenes of the horse race in the middle chapters of part two contain all kinds of deliberate symbolic implications. Firstly there is the Karenin slant. In the pavilion at the races a military man, Karenin's social superior, a high-placed general or a member of the royal family, kids Karenin, saying—and you, you're not racing; upon which Karenin replies deferentially and ambiguously, ''the race I am running is a harder one,'' a phrase with a double meaning, since it could simply mean that a statesman's duties are more difficult than competitive sport, but also may hint at Karenin's delicate position as a betrayed husband who must conceal his plight and find a narrow course of action between his marriage and his career. And it is also to be marked that the breaking of the horse's back coincides with Anna's revealing her unfaithfulness to her husband.

A far deeper emblematism is contained in Vronski's actions at that eventful horse race. In breaking Frou-Frou's back and in breaking Anna's life, Vronski is performing analogous acts. You will notice the same ''lower jaw trembling'' repeated in both scenes: the scene of Anna's metaphysical fall when he is standing over her adulterous body, and the scene of Vronski's physical fall when he is standing over his dying horse. The tone of the whole chapter of the race with the building up of its pathetic climax is echoed in the chapters relating to Anna's suicide. Vronski's explosion of passionate anger—anger with his beautiful, helpless, delicate-necked mare whom he has killed by a false move, by lettng himself down in the saddle at the wrong moment of the jump—is especially striking in contrast to the description that Tolstoy gives a few pages earlier, when Vronski is getting ready for the races—''he was always cool and self-controlled''—and then the terrific way he curses at the stricken mare.

> Frou-Frou lay gasping before him, bending her head back and gazing at him with her exquisite eye. Still unable to realize what had happened, Vronski tugged at his mare's reins. Again she struggled like a fish, and making the saddle flaps creak, she freed her front legs but uable to lift her rump, she quivered all over and again fell on her side. With a face hideous with passion, his lower jaw trembling and his cheeks white, Vronski kicked her with his heel in the stomach and again fell to tugging at the rein. She did not stir, but thrusting her nose into the ground, she simply gazed at her master with her speaking eye.
>
> 'A—a—a!' moaned Vronski, clutching at his head. 'Ah! what have I done! The race lost! And my fault! shameful, unpardonable! And this poor, lovely creature killed by me!'

Anna almost died giving birth to Vronski's child.

I shall not say much about Vronski's attempt to kill himself after the scene with Anna's husband at her bedside. It is not a satisfactory scene. Of course, Vronski's motives in shooting himself may be understood. The chief one was injured pride, since in the moral sense Anna's husband had shown himself, and had seemed to be, the better man. Anna herself had called her husband a saint. Vronski shoots himself much for the same reason as that for which an insulted gentleman of his day would have challenged the insulter to a duel, not to kill his man, but on the contrary to force him to fire at him, the insulted one. Exposing himself to the other man's forced fire would have wiped away the insult. If killed, Vronski would have been revenged by the other's remorse. If still alive, Vronski would have discharged his pistol in the air, sparing the other man's life and thus humiliating him. This is the basic idea of honor

behind duels, although of course there have been cases when both men were out to kill each other. Unfortunately, Karenin would not have accepted a duel, and Vronski has to fight his duel with his own self, has to expose himself to his own fire. In other words, Vronski's attempt at suicide is a question of honor, a kind of hara-kiri as understood in Japan. From this general point of view of theoretic morals this chapter is all right.

But it is not all right from the artistic viewpoint, from the point of view of the novel's structure. It is not really a necessary event in the novel; it interferes with the dream-death theme that runs through the book; it interferes technically with the beauty and freshness of Anna's suicide. If I am not mistaken, it seems to me that there is not a single retrospective reference to Vronski's attempted suicide in the chapter dealing with Anna's journey to her death. And this is not natural: Anna ought to have remembered it, somehow, in connection with her own fatal plans. Tolstoy as an artist felt, I am sure, that the Vronski suicide theme had a different tonality, a different tint and tone, was in a different key and style, and could not be linked up artistically with Anna's last thoughts.

The Double Nightmare: A dream, a nightmare, a double nightmare plays an especially important part in the book. I say ''*double* nightmare'' because both Anna and Vronski see the same dream. (This monogrammatic interconnection of two individual brain-patterns is not unknown in so-called real life.)

Vladimir Nabokov's sketch of Anna's ice-skating costume. From Vladimir Nabokov: Lectures on Russian Literature. *Copyright © 1981 by the Estate of Vladimir Nabokov. Reprinted by permission of Harcourt Brace Jovanovich, Inc.*

You will also mark that Anna and Vronski, in that flash of telepathy, undergo technically the same experience as Kitty and Lyovin do when reading each other's thoughts as they chalk initial letters on the green cloth of a card table. But in Kitty-Lyovin's case the brain-bride is a light and luminous and lovely structure leading towards vistas of tenderness and fond duties and profound bliss. In the Anna and Vronski case, however, the link is an oppressive and hideous nightmare with dreadful prophetic implications.

As some of you may have guessed, I am politely but firmly opposed to the Freudian interpretation of dreams with its stress on symbols which may have some reality in the Viennese doctor's rather drab and pedantic mind but do not necessarily have any in the minds of individuals unconditioned by modern psychoanalytics. Hence I am going to discuss the nightmare theme of our book, in terms of the book, in terms of Tolstoy's literary art. And this is what I plan to do: I shall go with my little lantern through those murky passages of the book where three phases of Anna's and Vronski's nightmare may be traced. First: I shall trace the formation of that nightmare from various parts and ingredients that are found in Anna's and Vronski's conscious life. Second: I shall discuss the dream itself as dreamed both by Anna and Vronski at a critical moment of their intertwined lives—and I shall show that although the ingredients of the twinned dream were not all the same with Anna and with Vronski, the result, the nightmare itself, is the same, although somewhat more vivid and detailed in Anna's case. And third: I shall show the connection between the nightmare and Anna's suicide, when she realizes that what the horrible little man in her dream was doing over the iron is what her sinful life has done to her soul—battering and destroying it—and that from the very beginning the idea of death was present in the background of her passion, in the wings of her love, and that now she will follow the direction of her dream and have a train, a thing of iron, destroy her body.

So let us start by studying the ingredients of the double nightmare, Anna's and Vronski's. What do I mean by the ingredients of a dream? Let me make this quite clear. A dream is a show—a theatrical piece staged within the brain in a subdued light before a somewhat muddleheaded audience. The show is generally a very mediocre one, carelessly performed, with amateur actors and haphazard props and a wobbly backdrop. But what interests us for the moment about our dreams is that the actors and the props and the various parts of the setting are borrowed by the dream producer from our conscious life. A number of recent impressions and a few older ones are more or less carelessly and hastily mixed on the dim stage of our dreams. Now and then the waking mind discovers a pattern of sense in last night's dream; and if this pattern is very striking or somehow coincides with our conscious emotions at their deepest, then the dream may be held together and repeated, the show may run several times as it does in Anna's case.

What are the impressions a dream collects on its stage? They are obviously filched from our waking life, although twisted and combined into new shapes by the experimental producer who is not necessarily an entertainer from Vienna. In Anna and Vronski's case the nightmare takes the form of a dreadful-looking little man, with a bedraggled beard, bending over a sack, groping in it for something, and talking in French—though he is a Russian proletarian in appearance—about having to beat iron. In order to understand Tolstoy's art in the matter, it is instructive to note the building up of the dream, the accumulation of the odds and ends of which that nightmare is

going to consist—this building up starts at their first meeting when the railway worker is crushed to death. I propose to go through the passages where the impressions occur of which this common nightmare will be formed. I call these dream-building impressions the ingredients of the dream.

The recollection of the man killed by the backing train is at the bottom of the nightmare that pursues Anna and that Vronski (although with less detail) also sees. What were the main characteristics of that crushed man? First, he was all muffled up because of the frost and thus did not notice the backward lurch of the train that brought Anna to Vronski. This "muffled up" business is illustrated before the accident actually happens by the following impressions: these are Vronski's impressions at the station as the train bringing Anna is about to come:

Through the frosty haze one could see railway workers in winter jackets and felt boots crossing the rails of the curving lines, and presently as the engine puffs in one could see the engine driver bowing in welcome—all muffled up and gray with frost.

He was a wretched, poor man, that crushed fellow, and he left a destitute family—hence a tattered wretch.

Mark incidentally the following point: this miserable man is the first link between Vronski and Anna, since Anna knows that Vronski gave money for the man's family only to please her—that it was his first present to her—and that as a married woman she should not accept gifts from strange gentlemen.

He was crushed by a great weight of iron.

And here are some preliminary impressions, Vronski's impression as the train draws in: "One could hear the rolling of some great weight." The vibration of the station-platform is vividly described.

Now we shall follow up these images—muffled up, tattered man, battered by iron, through the rest of the book.

The "muffled up" idea is followed up in the curious shifting sensations between sleep and consciousness that Anna experiences on her way back to Petersburg on the night train.

The muffled up conductor covered with snow on one side and the stove-heater whom she sees in her half-dream gnawing the wall with a sound as if something were torn apart, are nothing but the same crushed man in disguise—an emblem of something hidden, shameful, torn, broken, and painful at the bottom of her new-born passion for Vronski. And it is the muffled man who announces the stop at which she sees Vronski. The heavy iron idea is linked up with all this during these same scenes of her homeward journey. At that stop she sees the shadow of a bent man gliding as it were at her feet and testing the iron of the wheels with his hammer, and then she sees Vronski, who has followed her on the same train, standing near her on that station platform, and there is the clanging sound of a loose sheet of iron worried by the blizzard.

The characteristics of the crushed man have by now been amplified and are deeply engraved in her mind. And two new ideas have been added, in keeping with the muffled-up idea, the tattered element and the battered-by-iron element.

The tattered wretch is bending over something.

He is working at the iron wheels. (pp. 171-77)

Vladimir Nabokov, "Leo Tolstoy," in his Lectures on Russian Literature, *edited by Fredson Bowers, Harcourt Brace Jovanovich, Publishers, 1981, pp. 137-244.*

JOYCE CARY (essay date 1958)

[*Cary was an Anglo-Irish novelist, poet, and critic. His extensive studies in philosophy, history, and economics, and his experiences in the Balkan War of 1912-13 and as a colonial administrator in Nigeria served as background for novels in which he combined fiction with social commentary. In the following excerpt, Cary examines Tolstoy's use of the horse race in* Anna Karenina *as an allegory of Vronsky's relations with Anna, and concludes that the device is distracting and unsuccessful because the reader has not been prepared to accept the mare that Vronsky destroys as a symbol for Anna herself.*]

Tolstoy is a master of form and *Anna Karenina* was his masterpiece in formal perfection. How was he tempted into allegory? The professional answer is that he was haunted by his theme. Necessarily so. It was his form, and *Anna Karenina* is a masterpiece because every detail belongs to the formal unity of Tolstoy's meaning. Here he had organised a race meeting, to bring all his characters in play. And it takes no less than ten chapters. It's true that all these chapters carry the story forward and illustrate the theme. They show us the relations between the husband, Alexei and Anna, and between Anna and Vronsky in a new development. Anna's agitation when she sees Vronsky's fall during the race produces the critical interview with her husband when she declares that she hates him. All the same, this long succession of scenes has a certain monotony, and we know from Tolstoy's diary that this is exactly what he dreaded at this part of the book. He may well have thought that the race itself, which is the ostensible excuse for the whole ten chapters, would be an anti-climax unless it provided some dramatic peak, some new light upon the theme. So he builds up the dramatic climax of the race as an allegory of Vronsky's relations with Anna and a premonition of her fate when she too is physically unable to serve his will.

He does not make it too obvious an allegory. He realises for us all the details with his usual marvellous skill—the mare, the trainer, the whole racing background are from actual life, so is the race. And he hopes, no doubt, that we shall be carried along by our delighted sense of this brilliant art with such force that we will accept the intrusion of a conceptual idea without noticing its falseness. We will simply feel it subconsciously, in horrified sympathy for the innocent mare, as a vague but strong sense of the tragic relations between the wilful impatient egotism of the man and the patient feminine devotion of his victim. But unluckily our critical mind jumps up at once. We feel uneasy probably for the very reason that Tolstoy has succeeded in giving us the emotional effect that he intended—but an effect not congruent with the situation of the moment, involving characters we have accepted as actual in an actual world. We are checked by a false note.

Perhaps we are already uneasy. We have heard much of Vronsky's love of this mare, of her beauty, her high breeding. Tolstoy describes her as a creature so sensitive that we wonder she can't speak. Now we see her lying at his feet, she bends her head back and gazes at him with her speaking eyes. The very suspicion of allegory destroys the validity of the scene. Suddenly the characters become mere concepts invented to illustrate a theme, and the theme itself a precept out of a copybook. (pp. 161-62)

It is easy to see that [D. H.] Lawrence's *St Mawr,* so close to allegory, is a triumph, but why does Tolstoy, a far greater artist than Lawrence, fail? Where is his miscalculation? I suggest simply in a forgetfulness of character. Vronsky's rage startles us, and always seems to me untrue to that well-disciplined

guardsman. And the mare is made to act out of character. This is an important and interesting point. For the mare is true to her own character, to horse character. I have myself had such a horse, with the same sensibility, the same loyalty. But in the story, she is suddenly made to represent the feminine principle as Tolstoy conceived it.

A character in a story is part of the meaning. Anna is representative of womanhood and we accept her as a real woman, in Tolstoy's sense. Because she is true also to our sense. We would accept women as women that Tolstoy would describe as unwomanly. We have a wider idea of what women can do in the world and still be essentially women, good wives, good-mothers. But Tolstoy has not raised any such larger questions. He has given us a woman who is woman to us as well as to him, at once a living individual and a typical woman.

The mare is a real mare, but we have not received her as representative of the feminine character in the book. She appears simply as a part of the background of Vronsky's life which, for Tolstoy, represents the artificial structure of that high society in which Anna is corrupted. His sudden change of meaning is a false note. I use the word deliberately. For the effect is analogous to that of the false note in music which interrupts suddenly the recreation of the structure of our subconscious and causes our critical judgment to start up and say 'What's happened—what's wrong?'

And what's wrong in this case is simply that the meaning of a note, or phrase, the mare, has been forced into a context that doesn't belong to it. So she loses even her own character as a mare—she becomes like a performing animal, a puppet, manipulated by Tolstoy. (p. 166-68)

For we must remember always a tale is not life, it is art and subject to the limitations of art, in this case, to the logic of the subconscious, allotting by association a meaning to each character, to each development, in a construction that is fundamentally As If. (p. 168)

> *Joyce Cary, "Means and Ends" and "The Form of Allegory," in his* Art and Reality: Ways of the Creative Process, *Harper & Brother, Publishers, 1958, pp. 161-66, 166-72.**

BORIS EIKHENBAUM (essay date 1959)

[*Eikhenbaum was one of Tolstoy's most important critics, and his multi-volume biographical and critical study* Leo Tolstoy *(1928-1931) is considered a landmark in the study of the Russian author. In the following excerpt, Eikhenbaum discusses the meaning of the epigraph quoted by Tolstoy in* Anna Karenina: *"Vengeance is mine. I will repay." He notes that Tolstoy himself explained the epigraph as meaning that "the bad things that man does have as their consequence all the bitter things which come not from people, but from God." However, Eikhenbaum maintains that this does not illuminate the relationship of the epigraph to the moral problems presented in the novel, the key to which Eikhenbaum believes lies in Tolstoy's reading of the fourth book of Schopenhauer's the* World as Will and Idea. *For further discussion of the presentation of moral problems in* Anna Karenina, *see the excerpts by Prince P. A. Kropotkin (1901), J. P. Stern (1964), R. F. Christian (1969), Angus Calder (1976), and Vladimir Nabokov (1958).*]

Anna Karenina differs from *War and Peace* in its incomparably greater objectivity both of tone and illumination. The whole novel, with the exception of a few places, is written with an attentive but cold tone (to the point of cruelty, Strakhov wrote) like that of observing from outside. Tolstoy does not intrude his judgments and estimations. He watches life from on high and only rarely makes a remark similar to a scientific generalization: "All happy families are like each other, every unhappy family is unhappy in its own way." . . .

> Well, you think I'm on the side of Levin, and today Father Ambrose told me that somebody had been to see him to ask to be accepted into the monastery. This man said that my account of the confession had made a very strong impression on him.
>
> (p. 815)

The closest immediate stimulus to start writing a love novel was evidently Dumas' book *Man-Woman*, but the germ for it had existed even earlier. Dumas' book "struck" Tolstoy particularly because he often thought about this theme and found in Dumas many like ideas and conclusions. However, Dumas' concluding thesis about a woman who deceives her husband and leaves him and her children ("kill her!") contradicted Tolstoy's views and necessarily aroused his objections. The biblical epigraph, "Vengeance is mine, I shall repay," which appeared in the earliest versions of the novel, is an answer to Dumas' thesis. It is not necessary to kill her, because the guilty woman will perish, not by the hand of man, but by that of God. The plot of the novel and the images changed, becoming more complicated and freeing themselves from connection with Dumas' tract. But the epigraph remained and became somewhat puzzling. Anna changed from the "repulsive woman," the "Cain-like female destroying life and the activity of her husband," into another unhappy, suffering woman, "who lost herself." How could the epigraph remain and what does it signify? (pp. 816-17)

Tolstoy's idea expressed in this epigraph is that the unavoidable consequences of "the bad" are not vengeance by people, but one's own sufferings, which come "not from people." Anna's suicide is only a natural conclusion resulting from all the "bitter things" which Anna experienced. The point is not in her suicide itself (nor in Vronsky's attempt at suicide), but precisely in the fact that passion led her to suffering.

In an early version (1873) the epigraph read, "Vengeance belongs to me." This is evidently an abbreviated, rough note made by Tolstoy for himself. Where could this version have come from, different as it is from the Old Testament or the Gospel—or from Church Slavic and Russian? In the fourth book of Schopenhauer's *The World as Will and Idea*, there is a chapter which deals with juridical concepts—injustice, force, laws, state, and so on. Here he speaks also about the concepts of punishment and revenge. Schopenhauer asserts that "outside the state, the right to punish does not exist." Punishment differs from vengeance by being directed to the future and seeming predestined, whereas vengeance is directed only to the past and is motivated by what has happened. ". . . No man is entitled to act in the role of a purely moral judge and retributor and to punish the actions of another man by the pain which he causes him; consequently, to mete out penance to him for it. That would be extremely excessive self-confidence. Hence the biblical, 'Vengeance is mine, I shall repay.'"

Tolstoy doubtlessly read these pages. We must conclude that he took the epigraph from here and not directly from the Gospel. He read Schopenhauer in the original (there was no Russian translation at that time; Fet's translation appeared in 1881), and in German the statement reads "Meine ist die Rache, spricht der Herr, und ich will vergelten." Without looking it up in the Gospel and not recalling the Russian text by heart, Tolstoy simply translated the beginning of the saying from the German as "Vengeance belongs to me."

In the early version of *Anna Karenina*, Tolstoy, with the help of Schopenhauer's ethics, argued against Dumas' thesis. Taking as his starting point not only Dumas, but also Schopenhauer, he at first made woman the embodiment of evil and sin. But the novel moved beyond its original narrow confines and grew more complicated. Tolstoy clearly hesitated in his solution to the problem of evil and sin. Theories moved to the background under the pressure of artistic material, and Anna ceased to be guilty in the sense in which she was in the 1873 version. "Your Anna Karenina will arouse endless pity, and still, every lady will see clearly that she is guilty," Strakhov wrote in 1875. The nearer the novel came to completion, the less clear Anna's guilt grew, and the epigraph left over from the earlier version became more and more puzzling. From a transgressor, Anna turned into a victim, and the natural question arose—how did "Vengeance is mine, and I shall repay" apply here?

From Tolstoy's point of view, however, which was based on Schopenhauer's ethics, Anna and Vronsky nevertheless are guilty, not before society or social opinion (as Gromeka asserted), but before life, before "eternal justice." Both of them live a life which is not real because they are guided only by a narrow concept of "will" as desire. They do not, as Levin does, think deeply about the meaning of life. In that sense they are not real people, but slaves of their passion, and egoism. Their love, therefore, transforms itself into suffering—boredom, hate, jealousy. Anna begins to suffer because she makes "the eternal error men make by imagining that happiness consists in the gratification of their wishes." Tolstoy writes about Vronsky: "Soon he felt rising in his soul a desire for desires—Involuntarily he began to snatch at every passing caprice, mistaking it for a desire and a purpose." Anna begins to suffer from jealousy which then grows into the desire for revenge and punishment: "Death stood before her imagination clearly and vividly as the sole means to regenerate love for her in his heart, to punish him, and to win victory in that struggle which the evil spirit that had moved into her heart carried on with him. Now everything was all the same: to go to Vozdvizhenskoe or not, to receive a divorce from her husband or not, everything was unnecessary. Only one thing was necessary—to punish him." Critics have not paid attention to this passage, but it is very important. Here it is emphasized that Anna suffers and perishes not from external causes—not because society condemned her and her husband will not give her a divorce, but from passion itself, from the "evil spirit" which moved into her. Passion turns into a struggle, a "fateful duel," in Tiutchev's words. This passion is that "bad thing" about which Tolstoy spoke to Sukhotin, and Anna's and Vronsky's sufferings are "that bitter thing which comes not from people but from God." The Gospel saying which Tolstoy understood in the context of Schopenhauerian ethics kept its general meaning even after the shift of the original plot, without of course covering the entire meaning of the novel.

Thus the epigraph refers to Anna's and Vronsky's fate. "And what about Betsy Tverskaya and Stepan Oblonsky?" the reader who has read M. Aldanov's book will ask. Why do they continue to live cheerfully? This is the question of a man who judges Tolstoy's novel from a legal point of view, not by its essence. Tolstoy was not a lawyer and he did not write his novel for legal study. Here there is no "criminal material"—neither prosecutors nor defense attorneys have anything to do with it. Here is a problem of higher ethics. Betsy Tverskaya and Stepan Oblonsky, like all worldly society, live outside all ethics or morality and therefore stand outside of this problem. Anna and Vronsky became subject to moral judgment ("eternal justice") only because, in the grip of genuine passion, they rose above this world of utter hypocrisy, lying, and emptiness, and entered into the world of human feelings. In the world in which Levin, Anna, and Vronsky live, there Tolstoy and his God have nothing to do with Betsy and other "professional sinners": they exist in the novel as real social evil, which is subject to the verdict of history. Tolstoy, as a genuine realist, was not writing a moralistic novel on the theme of "higher justice," but something else. His epigraph cannot be understood either as a sermon preaching bourgeois morality or as a speech of a confused lawyer who began by accusing and ended by defending.

The characters in *Anna Karenina* (partly as the characters in *War and Peace*) are distributed on a kind of moral ladder. Stiva Oblonsky and Betsy Tverskaya and the like stand near the bottom of society, the inhabitants of which know no moral laws; Anna and Vronsky are higher, but they are slaves of a blind, egoistic passion and, for that very reason, subject to moral judgment; Levin, who also stands on the edge of the precipice, is saved, because he lives in all the fullness of life and aims towards the realization of the moral law. Such is Tolstoy's verdict on his age. (pp. 819-21)

> Boris Eikhenbaum, "The Puzzle of the Epigraph, N. Schopenhauer," translated by George Gibian, in "Anna Karenina" by Leo Tolstoy: The Maude Translation, Backgrounds and Sources, Essays in Criticism, edited by George Gibian, W. W. Norton & Company, Inc., 1970, pp. 815-21.

J. B. PRIESTLEY (essay date 1960)

[*A highly prolific English man of letters, Priestley was the author of numerous popular novels that depict the world of everyday, middle-class England. In this respect, Priestley has often been likened to Charles Dickens, a critical comparison that he dislikes. His most notable critical work is* Literature and Western Man *(1960), a survey of Western literature from the invention of movable type through the mid-twentieth century. In the following excerpt, Priestley discusses how Anna's tragic fate mirrors Tolstoy's own subconscious state during the spiritual crisis that he underwent while working on the novel. For another biographical reading of* Anna Karenina, *see the excerpt by Edward Wasiolek (1978).*]

To suggest, as many critics do, that *Anna Karenina* is a kind of continuation of *War and Peace,* is misleading. Tolstoy's literary method is almost the same, especially in the earlier part of the story; he brings to it the same handling of significant detail, the same power (perhaps rather heightened) of rapid and sure analysis of character, the same piercing sense of reality. But everyting else is different. *Anna Karenina* is no epic, no river of life, and time in it is not simply passing but conniving, shaping, and striking. It is not another panorama of instinctive life, in which the scene, however dark and tragic in the foreground, seems to vanish in the distance into a misty brightness. This may be a drama on an epic scale, but a drama it is, not an epic. How it came to be written is important. After *War and Peace,* Tolstoy began work on an historical novel about the Russia of Peter the Great, but then abandoned it in

disgust. A woman called Anna, the mistress of a neighbouring landowner, had committed suicide by throwing herself in front of a train; and Tolstoy had attended the inquest. Here was matter for a novel of contemporary life. The mastery and brilliance of the early chapters of *Anna Karenina* probably owe something to his feelings of relief after discarding the historical novel. But the Tolstoy behind the huge darkening tale of Anna and her lover, Vronsky, and her husband, Karenin, is not quite the same man who wrote *War and Peace.* The total creative personality is just beginning to crack, though still not ready for the 'conversion'. Levin, the only major character in this marvellous gallery of portraits that is not entirely successful, wears a thin mask and his voice is too often not his own. But on the whole the conflict in the depths of Tolstoy's personality, though it begins to darken the story, only seems to heighten the marvellous force and precision of his handling of Anna and her growing tragedy. So real are these people, especially Anna and Vronsky, that we can argue about them and what they did and what happened to them, just as we do about people we know and their affairs. The fatal flaw in the relationship between Anna and Vronsky, so sharply contrasted with that between Kitty and Levin, seems to have unfathomable depth, beyond the measure of any conscious purpose Tolstoy may have had; and her tragedy (which we sense, at our first reading, from the very beginning) certainly cannot be explained in ordinary social and moral terms, as a punishment for leaving her husband, a failure in courage, and so forth; and it may be—to hazard one guess—that the relationship is doomed because Anna herself is too feminine while Vronsky like Karenin, though otherwise so entirely different, is too masculine. What is certain is that Anna is so wonderfully alive and real and moving because to Tolstoy's unconscious, the source of his creative energy, she is symbolic archetypal Woman, whom consciously, with all the values she symbolises, now that he is nearing the break-up, he has to destroy. And we might risk adding that it is the defiant unconscious, working at full pressure before the lid comes down on it, that gives a curious feverish brightness to so many of the scenes in this very great novel.

There was to be nothing like it again, though the artist in Tolstoy, denounced and imprisoned by the prophet, was to break out several times, to add colour and depth to some of the later moral tales. (pp. 253-55)

> J. B. Priestley, "The Novelists," in his Literature and Western Man, Harper & Brothers, 1960, pp. 222-73.*

LEON EDEL (essay date 1961)

[*An American critic and biographer, Edel is a highly acclaimed authority on the life and work of Henry James. His five-volume biography* Henry James *(1953-73) is considered the definitive life and brought Edel critical praise for his research and interpretive skill. John K. Hutchens has summarized Edel's views on the ideal literary biographer as follows: "He is . . . a sensitive critic as well as a scrupulous collector of facts, searches a writer's work not only for its own esthetic sake but for what it says about the writer's inner life, uses the psychoanalyst's techniques but is not confined by them, and by-passes the orthodox biographer's subservience to chronology in favor of grouping for dramatic emphasis outside a fixed-time schedule." Edel himself has added, "My aim in biography is to achieve tightness of synthesis and a clear narrative 'line.' In criticism I like directness and lucidity." In the following excerpt, Edel discusses the manner in which the techniques that Tolstoy employed to depict the psychological states of his characters anticipated the stream of consciousness tech-*

nique more commonly associated with such writers as James Joyce and Virginia Woolf. Using Anna's disordered thoughts on her final day as an example, Edel explains that, although Tolstoy remained the omniscient author, rather than adopting Anna's point of view, his portrayal of her inner condition "has a sharpness and a reality that is very close to Mrs. Bloom's monologue or Mrs. Dalloway's reveries in the London streets." For further discussion of Tolstoy's psychological portraiture in Anna Karenina, see the excerpts by Konstantin Leontiev (1890) and Edward Wasiolek (1978).]

It is a measure of the genius of Tolstoy that he can be invoked not only for his great murals and his panoramas of outer reality, but for his close and observant exploration of the subjective life of his characters as well. In certain respects he anticipated Joyce; indeed he may yet come to be judged as the most significant precursor of the modern psychological novel and the stream of consciousness. Long before [Édouard] Dujardin, he sought to record perceptual experience; he was aware of association, point of view, simultaneity. The difference between him and Dujardin, on the experimental level, was that he continued to function as an omniscient author. We remain "outside" his characters; but his picture of their inner condition has a sharpness and a reality that is very close to Mrs. Bloom's monologue or Mrs. Dalloway's reveries in the London streets. The Russian critic Chernyshevsky, who recognized this early in Tolstoy's work, called it his "dialectic of the mind." Gleb Struve has shown that this critic was the first to use the term "internal monologue" to characterize the phenomenon. Chernyshevsky's description of the dialectic in Tolstoy, as quoted by Professor Struve, could be applied to any of the subjective novels of our time. Tolstoy, he said, was "interested in observing how an emotion, arising spontaneously from a given situation or impression, and succumbing to the influence of memories and the effect of combinations supplied by imagination, merges into other emotions, returns again to its starting point and wanders on and on along the whole chain of memories; how a thought, born of a primary sensation, is carried on and on, fusing dreams with actual sensations, and anticipations of the future with reflections about the present." This is an admirable statement and does honor to the critic who recognized the problem of subjectivity in fiction even before Tolstoy had written *War and Peace* and *Anna Karenin*.

It is possible to discover many passages in Tolstoy illustrative of Chernyshevsky's observations, for the Russian novelist is particularly alert to the life of the senses. In the final chapters of *Anna Karenin*, when Tolstoy wishes to convey the profound despondency of his heroine—in the very last moments of her life—it is to record the vividness with which sights and smells impinge upon her consciousness even while she is retreating in memory to the past, to far-away things that will hide from her the dispersed state of her feelings—her swing from despair to hate, to the wish to obliterate all experience. As she sits in her carriage, aware of its elastic springs and the trot of the horses, she falls to reading the signboards:

> Office and warehouse . . . Dental surgeon . . . Yes, I will tell Dolly everything. She doesn't like Vronsky. It wil be painful and humiliating, but I'll tell her all about eveything. She is fond of me and I will follow her advice. I won't give in to him. I won't allow him to teach me . . . Filippov, pastry-cook—I've heard he sends his pastry to St. Petersburg. The Moscow water is so good. Ah, the springs at Mitishchen, and the pancakes!

From her tragic love-affair with Vronsky, to taking counsel with Dolly, her consciousness has shifted (in the manner of Molly Bloom half a century later) to pastry and water, to pancakes and the springs of Mitishchen. And a moment later, as her carriage passes a building:

> . . . How nasty that paint smells! Why is it they're always painting and building? *Dressmaking and millinery*, she read. A man bowed to her. It was Annushka's husband. Our parasites, she remembered the words Vronsky had used. 'Our?' Why our? What's so dreadful is that one can't tear up the past by its roots. Yes but I can try not to think of it. I must do that.

Tolstoy recognized, and his succesors were to go still further, that nothing could convey the anguish of Anna and her distracted thought more vividly than direct quotation from her sensory as well as mental experience at this particular moment. And the smell of paint, the taste-memory of pastry and springwater, are as relevant as her remembering what Vronsky said. The state of diffused consciousness will continue to the moment when she will let herself fall under the wheels of the train, and her last thought will be the classic one of psychoanalysis of a later generation—the self-destruction that is at the same time destruction of the loved one, "and I shall punish him and escape from them all and from myself." (pp. 147-49)

Leon Edel, "Dialectic of the Mind: Tolstoy," in his The Modern Psychological Novel, *revised edition, 1961. Reprint by Grosset & Dunlap, 1964, pp. 147-53.*

LOUIS AUCHINCLOSS   (essay date 1961)

[An American man of letters, Auchincloss is known primarily as the author of novels of manners in the tradition of Edith Wharton and C. P. Snow. He is also a respected critic who has written major studies of such authors as Henry James, Ellen Glasgow, Henry Adams, and Wharton. Of his own literary scholarship Auchincloss has written: "I find in writing criticism I write more about novelists of the past, and I never write with any other object but to induce my reader to revisit them. This is not to say that I do not read my contemporaries—I do—but I feel less division than many of them do between past and present." In the following excerpt Auchincloss considers Anna Karenina *from the perspective of Henry James's criticism that Tolstoy's novels are "loose" and unstructured. While Auchincloss finds two specific flaws in the novel's narrative structure—the intrusion of Levin's agricultural theories and the abrupt introduction of Anna's adultery—he concludes that overall* Anna Karenina *is a subtle, complex, and well-organized work. For further discussion of the narrative structure of* Anna Karenina, *see the excerpts by Tolstoy (1876 and 1878), Percy Lubbock (1921), Elizabeth Stenbock-Fermor (1975) and Vladimir Nabokov (1958).]*

James usually spoke of Tolstoy in terms of guarded respect. . . . Neither Tolstoy nor Dostoyevsky was very much to his taste, and he regarded their effect on other writers as little short of disastrous. Turgenev, on the other hand, he loved and admired, both as a friend and a writer, but then Turgenev was a sort of Russian Henry James, an expatriate who cultivated the French novelists and was regarded as an equal by Flaubert himself. His concern, like James's, was with the fine details of craftsmanship; he was, in the latter's phrase, the novelist's novelist, "an artistic influence extraordinarily valuable and ineradicably established." Too many of Turgenev's rivals, James complained, "appear to hold us in comparison by violent means, and introduce us in comparison to vulgar things."

Did he mean to include Tolstoy among these rivals? It seems likely. For observe how he contrasts him with Turgenev:

> The perusal of Tolstoy—a wonderful mass of life—is an immense event, a kind of splendid accident, for each of us: his name represents nevertheless no such eternal spell of method, no such quiet irresistibility of presentation, as shines, close to us and lighting our possible steps, in that of his precursor. Tolstoy is a reflector as vast as a natural lake; a monster harnessed to his great subject—all human life!— as an elephant might be harnessed, for purposes of traction, not to a carriage, but to a coach house. His own case is prodigious, but his example for others dire: disciples not elephantine he can only mislead and betray.

The compliment, if one was intended, fades under the words "monster" and "elephant." (pp. 157-58)

[In a letter to Hugh Walpole, James] dropped the last pretense of admiration for Tolstoy. . . .

> I have been reading over Tolstoy's interminable *Peace and War*, and am struck with the fact that I now protest as much as I admire. He doesn't *do* to read over, and that exactly is the answer to those who idiotically proclaim the impunity of such formless shape, such flopping looseness and such a denial of composition, selection and style. He has a mighty fund of life, but the *waste,* and the ugliness and vice of waste, the vice of a not finer *doing* are sickening. For me he makes "composition" throne, by contrast, in effulgent lustre!

(p. 160)

To me there is "flopping looseness" in *War and Peace* only in Tolstoy's essays on military and historical theory. I find these as intrusive and boring as commercials in a television play, but they are easily skipped, so long as one is careful not to skip with them the chapters dealing with the personalities of the war leaders and the battle scenes, which are of the essence of Tolstoy's scheme. (p. 162)

In *Anna Karenina* I find only Levin's agricultural theories "floppingly loose." They are as irrelevant to the story as the historical asides in *War and Peace,* and much more difficult to skip, being more deeply imbedded in the plot. But a graver fault in the structure of the novel is Tolstoy's failure to prepare us for Anna's adultery. We meet her first as a charming and deeply understanding sister-in-law who, by consummate tact, saves her brother's crumbling marriage, but we pass with a dizzy speed over the year which elapses between her meeting Vronsky and her succumbing to him. We grasp Anna's character at last—or a good deal of it—but the hole in this part of the book is never quite filled. We never know why such a woman should have married a man like her husband or why, having done so, she should have been unfaithful to him. But aside from being occasionally bored by Levin and occasionally confused by the early Anna, I find no other looseness in the novel. It is like a well-organized English novel of its period: it has two plots, constantly interwoven and always in dramatic contrast, and in the end married love brings happiness and adultery despair. Even James could not have said that it contained the vice of waste.

Tolstoy liked to accomplish a great many obvious as well as a great many subtle things, and he was not afraid of old and well-worn formulas. What he needed for war was a burning capital and what he needed for a drama of love was a married and an unmarried couple. He never hesitated to hammer in his contrasts with heavy strokes. On the side of Kitty and Levin and lawful love are the rolling acres of a well-managed farm, and Moscow, no longer the capital, but still the center of the oldest, truest Russian values. On the side of Anna and Vronsky and illicit passion are the superficial court society of St. Petersburg and a motley pile of borrowed notions from Paris and London. The great columns of the two plots stand up before us, massive, conventional, imposing and trite, but on closer examination we find that the bas-reliefs that gird them have been carved with the greatest delicacy and skill. Whatever assumptions we make as we go along, we will find that we must qualify, until we begin to wonder if the two columns are twins or opposites.

Levin and Kitty, for example, may be depicted as the young couple on whose love we may properly smile, but in contrast to Anna and Vronsky they are frequently ridiculous. Levin is absurdly and irrationally jealous, and his nervousness on the birth of his child seems almost a caricature of the traditionally nervous father. He is violent, rude and ill-tempered, and Kitty is excitable and possessive. It is true that Tolstoy obviously likes Levin and considers his faults as rather lovably Russian,

Tolstoy's wife, Sonya, and children Tatyana and Seryozha.

but he is careful at the same time to show us that the other characters consider him a bull in a china shop. Vronsky, on the other hand, leads a St. Petersburg society life of which his creator disapproves to such an extent that it has become traditional to regard him as a shallow gadabout who is unworthy of the passion that he has inspired in Anna. But consider him more closely. Vronsky may be irresponsible in seducing Anna, but after that he behaves with the greatest possible style. He is never unfaithful to her, never deserts her, always tries to spare her pain, does everything he can to legalize their relationship and even attempts suicide when none of his plans for her happiness work out. There are moments in the book when he and Anna seem a couple unjustly condemned by a censorious and hypocritical society, while Kitty and Levin seem like spoiled youngsters who cannot find happiness in a veritable flood of good fortune.

For Tolstoy is not really condemning Anna, any more than he is praising Kitty. Anna is, indeed, the more high-minded of the two. He is rather proving that for women of their background and position (Levin's brother's mistress is quite happy as such), cohabitation outside of marriage is impossible. Kitty and Anna are both intensely female in their possessiveness. Levin feels, when Kitty wishes to accompany him to his brother's deathbed, that it is intolerable to be so shackled. Yet she comes and is a great help. Within the framework of a happy marriage such matters can always be adjusted. Kitty becomes absorbed in her babies, and Levin can then attend all the agricultural conventions he wants. But no such adjustment is possible for Anna. She destroys her life with Vronsky by her mad jealousy and her need to be with him every moment. Anna turns into a kind of monster, making scenes over everything, crazed by the thought that her lover should have any life or interest outside the dull and lonely house where she rants at him. Vronsky is a model of patience and restraint, but he is helpless to arrest her insane course of self-destruction. Anna has been idle and restless in St. Petersburg society, but she is utterly shattered when its doors are closed to her but not to him. It is ridiculous; it is pathetic; it is nineteenth century but it is very feminine. Kitty would have been just as bad. (pp. 164-67)

> Louis Auchincloss, ''James and the Russian Novelists,'' in his *Reflections of a Jacobite, Houghton Mifflin Company,* 1961, pp. 157-71.*

J. P. STERN (essay date 1964)

[*In the following excerpt, Stern finds that the moral code implied by Anna's suicide, and Tolstoy's acceptance of this code, is crucial to an understanding of the novel. For further discussion of the presentation of moral problems in* Anna Karenina, *see the excerpts by Prince P. A. Kropotkin (1901), Boris Eikhenbaum (1959), R. F. Christian (1969), Angus Calder (1976), and Vladimir Nabokov (1958).*]

Tolstoy, it has been said, has an 'almost sexual love for his heroine', and it is this love for her . . . which informs almost every phase of Tolstoy's presentation of Anna. Turgenyev, Matthew Arnold and a host of less distinguished critics have all given the novel that highest praise which is traditionally associated with the names of Homer and Shakespeare: it is Life, not Art, they exclaimed. And they meant by this, I think, that the experience encompassed in the novel, and the novelist's criterion of selection and presentation, are uniquely generous, uniquely wide. Yet the compass is meaningfully (not haphazardly) limited, and the criterion of selection is still strict. Take

the Levin story. It is very far from being a Utopian self-indulgence on Tolstoy's part, as some critics have condescendingly called it. On the contrary, it dovetails with and complements the story of Anna's own life, for through his marriage and his work with his peasant community Levin has at least a glimpse of that good life which Anna cannot attain. And the fact that Tolstoy views Levin's 'moment of truth' with irony and shows it to be brief and unsustained—that he sees Levin realistically—should not deceive us about the importance of Levin's insight for the balance of the novel as a whole: it is a moment in a moral development which goes in the opposite direction to Anna's. When he shows Anna flirting with Levin (during one of his rare visits to town), Tolstoy leaves us in no doubt as to the precariousness of Levin's hard-won virtue; more than that, he points to the potential danger that lurks at the intersection of the two opposing lines of moral development.

And with this term, moral developmant, we are at the centre of Tolstoy's preoccupation in *Anna Karenina.* It is neither social nor psychological, though both these narrative modes play important rôles in the unfolding of the story. If the novel is 'like Life', it is not the 'life' of Naturalism, it is an image of life shot through with morality. The development which Anna experiences . . . takes a moral form. The development consists in Anna's gradual realisation that the life she leads with Vronsky is unjustifiable on moral grounds, that almost all that presses in upon her embodies the morality from which she has defected. Take Alexei Karenin himself. . . . [He] is a bit of a schoolmaster, and has a great deal of the inhuman bureaucrat. Beyond this, he fails his wife in her emotional and erotic demands, he is unable to respond to her yearning for love. . . . In the face of the authentic demands which he cannot meet he does what men in such situations are prone to do— he shelters behind a façade of righteousness. He becomes a hypocrite, anxious to keep up appearances, he turns religiose and 'holier than thou'—and yet, for all that, imperfectly and intermittently he does represent the morality of family life against which Anna has offended. It is because she knows this that Anna speaks to their son of Karenin only charitably and without reproach; and her words move us because they have the ring of passionate sincerity. Tolstoy . . . is unable to portray a single character as wholly unlovable. And this implies, not a lack of moral discrimination, but on the contrary Tolstoy's innermost moral belief that all manner of people, simple and sophisticated, innocent and foolish (like Dolly) and corrupt (like Anna's brother Stiva) are, in spite of all their feelings, capable of *some* degree of moral goodness; that the moral commandment remains valid even when it is enforced through such a dessicated character as Karenin; and that the divergent insights all go to prove that life is what it is: a highly moral affair. This absolute anti-gnosticism of Tolstoy's has caused some misunderstanding and censure among his critics, beginning with Peter Kropotkin [see excerpt dated 1901] and ending with the Soviet critics of our own times. They make the same accusation against him, roughly speaking, as that which Hebbel had made against the author of *Die Wahlverwandschaften:* that he conforms to the social taboos of his day. Yet all that Tolstoy (and, incidentally, Goethe) does here is to express a subtlety and a wisdom of which a writer like Lawrence was not capable. The wisdom lies in the belief that society—the society of his day—and institutions—the institutions of marriage—are not wholly incapable of showing forth the moral law, the highest governance that men have set up above themselves; that it is not—or not only—the unversal historical process or some other large abstraction which embodies this law, but certain facets of our own conscious lives within the concrete limitations of a given society.

Of course, to single out the moral strand of the novel is to do violence to Tolstoy's design, which shows the moral embedded in the social. Yet it is hard to see how without such a distinction we can ever come close to the fullness of his achievement. (pp. 324-27)

'Vengeance is mine: I will repay', is the motto that Tolstoy takes for his book from St Paul's letter to the Romans. Yet the critics, in their eagerness to point to the 'life' of Tolstoy's novel, have been curiously reticent about the moral theme. 'It is difficult to believe', writes one of them, 'that Tolstoy considered Anna's unhappy end to be the righteous dispensation of an avenging diety. In fact, Tolstoy leaves the question of a supernatural sanction for the moral law unasked. Another critic confines himself to saying that 'Anna defied the laws of nature—nature quietly extracted retribution'. Again, it was her *nature* which remained unsatisfied in her marriage with Karenin, it was natural inclination and longing which found their fulfilment in her life with Vronsky. Not nature but her innermost awareness of the moral law—wholly concrete, never (in her) explicit or abstract, always sustained by actual, living situations—it is her growing inward preoccupation with her moral guilt which first imperils her love and finally disables her for life itself. Her 'unhappy end' is intimated again and again throughout the story by *leitmotif*, symbol and anticipation, the moral law is terribly vindicated in that anguish which is born with her love for Vronsky, which becomes inseparable from it and which grows as that love becomes impossible. Percy Lubbock has criticised the book by saying that Anna's crisis—that is, her falling in love with Vronsky—comes too early in the story, before we know her well enough [see excerpt dated 1921]. Yet surely such criticism presupposes a complexity of character and outlook which we do not look for in Anna at all. When she married Karenin, she was presumably an 'average' society lady. After that, all we need to know of her is in fact all we are told: that she is now a full-grown, normal, passionate woman, capable of a human relationship fundamentally different from that of her marriage. The rest—and it is virtually the whole story—follows on directly from that original and utterly normal situation.

The *form* af Anna's death, suicide, is determined by her psychological and social situation. . . . Anna's suicide is an instrument of punishment, the only form of expiation open to her.

But how can Anna's suicide be a *morally* motivated act? To see it as a form of punishment is not to say that it is the form decreed for her by God. (Anyway, the 'I' of the Pauline motto is for Tolstoy not God but the moral universe, whose relation to God Tolstoy here leaves unexplored.) Nor is this form decreed for her by morality. The matter is less abstruse: This is how (Tolstoy is saying) the voice of conscience speaks in *that* human soul, this is what, in her particular circumstances, *she* chooses, how *she* understands her moral situation. (And the fact that she intends her deed also to bring punishment of others, especially Vronsky, is further proof of its particularity.) In decreeing her punishment, Tolstoy never goes beyond the *human* view of the moral-spiritual law. Morality is his narrative mode. He 'judges' her only in the sense of showing the consequences of her conduct according to the logic of the novel's morality—as a painter 'judges' the distances in his picture according to the logic of his composition. It is an ironical thought that Tolstoy . . . was not much concerned with the final

form of his work, that by the time he had finished it, in 1877, he was already off to his 'religious crisis', and left the final pruning to his friend, the philosopher Strakhov. The style is discursive, apparently loose and undisciplined, apparently without any other distinction than that it traces out, unemphatically and without any conceits, one event of the story after another. Yet this very accumulation of words is organised and shot through with a moral purpose, the descriptive words and symbols being kept in their proper relation to the theme unobtrusively, the precision and sharpness of outline heightening into brief moral judgements at the points where the story's narrative structure is most firmly established.

The 'law' is to Tolstoy palpable and palpitating reality—a fact, out there in life and in the 'life' of his novel. (pp. 332-34)

Given Tolstoy's deep involvement in Anna's life *and* in the working out of the moral law, it is not surprising that his attitude towards Anna changes in the course of the novel. Many of the things she does—she rides in a man's habit, smokes, plays tennis, practices birth control, takes morphine against insomnia, keeps a disreputable English nurse, discusses Zola and Daudet—he strongly disapproves of. And his judgments on all these iniquities are reflected in her moral disintegration. While she, at first imperfectly aware of the moral implications of her adultery, comes gradually to recognise the law and ultimately (with these implications ever more clearly before her) to detest herself, Tolstoy's attitude too changes and returns to compassion: so that at last his love meets her self-hate, his concern with the moral theme finds its echo in her matured conscience, and she comes as it were to understand his mind. The measure of Tolstoy's achievement is simple enough: he cannot save her, but he never abandons her. His love *and* his judgement make for the same tension as that which informed the Paolo and Francesca story. (p. 335)

J. P. Stern, "Realism and Tolerance: Theodor Fontane," in his Re-interpretations: Seven Studies in Nineteenth-Century German Literature, *Basic Books, Inc., Publishers, 1964, pp. 301-47.**

S. P. BYCHKOV (essay date 1965)

[*In the following excerpt from an essay originally published in a 1965 Soviet anthology of criticism on Tolstoy, Bychkov discusses* Anna Karenina *from a Soviet perspective and demonstrates how the novel may be read as Tolstoy's denunciation of Russia in the period following the emancipation of the serfs in 1861. For a contrasting reading of* Anna Karenina, *see the excerpt by S. E. Sevitch (1879).*]

Tolstoy—"the writer of ideas," as Turgenev rightfully called him—was devoted in **Anna Karenina** to a profound understanding of Post-Emancipation social life in Russia, with all its complex contradictions. (pp. 822-23)

[Tolstoy] succeeds in ruthlessly condemning the corrupt ethics of private ownership and the hypocrisy of the "upper strata" of the bourgeois nobility.

[In Petersburg] all traditional duties in relation to family, children and work were subject to debasement and slander. Wives were unfaithful to husbands and vice versa. Princess Myagkaya speaks to Stiva about Anna's relationship with Vronsky: "She has done what everyone except me is doing secretly; but she did not want to lie, and she did a fine thing."

A typical representative of this society is Betsy Tverskaya. Deceitful and lewd woman that she was, continually and openly deceiving her husband, she not only feels no sense of remorse, but she is an equally distasteful bigot, as are many others. The Christian "goodness" of this sanctimonious woman, with her sweet words about God and faith, is exposed in the episode where she persistently prompts Karenin to refuse Anna a meeting with her son.

The extent of the moral and spiritual collapse of the higher strata of the nobility and aristocracy is vividly characterized by the success of the "clairvoyant" Zhyulya Landau in these circles. Landau—a salesman from Paris, both a cheat and a fraud—became the idol of some of the Bezzubov countesses. What extent of decay had the so-called "worldly" people reached if they make a swindler with "clammy hands" into an idol and turn to him for answers to the most important problems of their lives. It is Landau who in his delirious half-sleep denies Anna a divorce. Sensible people could not help but be horrified by this. Stiva is "stunned" by everything he sees and hears at the séance of the "clairvoyant one," and he runs out of Lydia Ivanovna's house "as though it were contaminated." But the entire aristocracy was "contaminated"—all of autocratic Russia was "contaminated."

In *Anna Karenina,* Tolstoy angrily attacks the czarist state machinery, the startling bureaucratism of various ministries, commissions, and committees, and the enormous amount of embezzlement of state property by officials of the highest ranks. Thus, the irrigation of the fields in Zarayskaya province, which dragged on for many years, serves to make a number of people richer. "Many people were fattened by this project, especially one very moral and musical family," the author satirically points out. Serpukhovskoy speaks to Vronsky about the mercenariness of prominent dignitaries: "They can be bought by either money or caresses"; the political attitudes of such "statesmen" are subordinate to their mercenary interests and serve as a means for "having a house provided by the government and a salary." Vivid is the image "of a famous St. Petersburg lawyer" who is basically indifferent toward people and who brightens up only when he gets a "profitable deal"; the misfortunes of his clients arouse "joy and delight" in him. And how many ordeals does Levin have to go through in order to get a decision on the simplest matter in the Kashin province offices.

Tolstoy makes cutting remarks about the way in which the committee for the investigation of the life of foreigners procures exact and unquestionable information, which is based on reports by governors and bishops who in turn rely on reports of district heads and priests, and so on down to the lowest level of the official step-ladder. "Answers were given perfectly well to all the inquiries and were not questioned because they were not subject to human error, being the product of an official process." This is indeed a devastating description of czarist bureaucracy.

Alexey Alexandrovich Karenin is a typical example of a czarist bureaucrat. A prominent dignitary with an "unpoetical" appearance, a conservative in his political convicions, devoid of the ability to manifest natural and normal feelings, he is the personification of "cold self-confidence." Right after graduating from the university, Karenin "devoted himself solely to his career ambitions," which dries up his soul and covers it with a protective coating of reason, though even by nature he does not distinguish himself for any particular depth of emotion. He subordinates all his emotions, desires, and thoughts to his career; his passion for success absorbs everything else. "Ambition and the desire to succeed alone fill his heart,"

thinks Anna. "Alexey Alexandrovich has spent his whole life working at a job which requires rejecting real life. Every time he has confronted life, he has pushed it aside."

"A slow delicate voice," "fixed dull eyes" and other physical details express Karenin's deadliness and the absence of any real life in him; this is not a person but a dummy, a wicked "ministerial machine" busy making bureaucratic circulars. Such personalities emerged in autocratic Russia, where the czarist government, cut off from real life and deeply hostile toward the masses, crippled people by fostering careerism and heartlessness in them.

A hardened bureaucrat devoid of "emotion," Karenin tries to manage his relationship with his wife in his habitual intellectual manner, coming up with the appropriate "reasonable" arguments for convincing Anna to observe an outward appearance of decency in her conduct. A slave to social proprieties, he is accustomed to lies and reconciles himself to the fact that Anna is an "unfaithful" wife; the only thing that alarms him is the thought of a possible scandal "in society" and that it could reflect unfavorably on his career. Karenin thinks only about himself and does not want to think about Anna or her thoughts and feelings; he is very indifferent to the emotional side of another person's life and he considers the urge to understand this side of life "a harmful and dangerous fancy." This is one of the expressions which characterizes his spiritual and moral abnormality. "The question of her feelings, of what goes on or could go on in her heart, is not my business—that is a matter of her own conscience and of religion." Such is Karenin's hypocritical reasoning.

This "artificial" person turns out to be a pauper next to Anna, who is the incarnation of real life. She is justly indignant: "He love? Is he capable of love? . . . He does not know what love is." Addressing Karenin's society friends in her own mind, Anna speaks with anger: "They say he is a religious, moral, clean, intelligent person, but they do not see what I have seen. They do not know how he has stifled my life for eight years, how he destroyed everything that was alive in me, how he did not once think of the fact that I am a living woman who needs love . . ."

Karenin's deliberate and cold inhumanity is particularly apparent in his decision not to grant his wife a divorce but to leave everything as it is. Of course, he finds a suitable "religious sanction" to justify this: it is necessary to hold Anna back so that she would have a chance for moral "reform." Thus, the ugly hypocrisy of this wicked bureaucrat is apparent to the very end. Karenin personifies the heartlessness and cruelty of the czarist regime.

Tolstoy, however does not limit himself to exposing Karenin's emotional poverty. In accordance with his religious convictions, Tolstoy tries to show that even Karenin is capable of emotional change and magnanimity. Thence the scene where Karenin is at the deathbed of Anna emerges. Here for the first time in his life, he experiences "the joy in forgiveness." He forgives Anna and makes up with Vronsky, which gives him complete "emotional peace." "He suddenly felt that what had been the source of his sufferings had become the source of his spiritual joy; that what seemed unsolvable when he condemned and hated became simple and clear when he forgave and loved."

Tolstoy skilfully chose the proper situation for showing that one of the basic dogmas of the Christian religion—that of forgiving one's enemy—should be preserved. At the bedside of a dying person, it is easier to forgive than to retain one's bitterness. The artistic truth of the scene, however, in no way detracts from the deeply reactionary ideas which are basic to it. It is no mere coincidence that it provoked tears of emotion in reactionary critics. It truly poeticizes the Christian religion, making it the only possible source of redemption and moral and spiritual elevation. Karenin is unfamiliar with compassion, but he is able to forgive his enemies and to love the newly-born little girl who is not his daughter. And the fact that he subsequently regrets doing this does not make false the Christian law of "universal" love: no—Karenin, it is possible, would have continued his role as a "true Christian" had he found some support, but he didn't.

In the way of the spiritually "reformed" Karenin stood the "brute force" of reality—"society." He rises above society with his great "deed" of forgiving Anna, but all the people around him continue to live as they always did and do not recognize religious truths; they renounce the dogmas of the Christian religion and lie and cheat and are hypocritical and laugh at him and at his new feelings. And Karenin is left alone—"disgraced, mocked, unneeded by anyone and held in contempt by everyone." He becomes close to Lydia Ivanovna, an advocate of the new mystical teachings. This is already the end. Karenin goes on to reach complete spiritual decay. This sequence of events testifies to the inability of this heartless bureaucrat to achieve any real rebirth of truly human feelings.

Vronsky—"one of the best examples of St. Petersburg's gilded youth"—is educated and intelligent and is not without good motives and noble impulses. Tolstoy could not have portrayed him differently; he could not have failed to give him a certain amount of charm—otherwise Anna's love could not have been justified. Nevertheless, he is a negative character, and although his character is developed differently than, say, that of Karenin, it is done so with no less consistency. Vronsky's very first appearance in the novel is accompanied by a harsh remark from Prince Shcherbatsky: "This one is a St. Petersburg dandy. They are all machine-made, all the same and all rubbish." This remark is not an accidental slip of the tongue by an irritated person; it will come to characterize Vronsky.

Vronsky is a typical product of aristocratic society. Much of his behavior is motivated by selfishness and by the desire for pleasure regardless of its moral quality. He does not find anything "bad" in his behavior toward Kitty, although it has a "definite name": "enticing young ladies without the intention of marriage." Vronsky does not understand this, because seducing young ladies and other "bad deeds" are widespread occurrences "among brilliant young people like him" and do not give rise to any sense of remorse or repentance.

Vronsky and the "real" members of his circle despise those "old-fashioned and ridiculous" people who remain faithful to definite moral principles. They consider that the main thing in life is to be "elegant, beautiful, magnanimous, brave, and gay, and to submit to any passion without blushing, and to laugh at everything else." This leads to the breakdown of all moral principles, for laughing "at everything else" means laughing at the faithfulness of someone else's wife, at the innocence of a young girl, at a man's self-control, as well as despising the upbringing of children and honesty in money matters, and mocking honest workers.

The cruel truth about capitalistic society with everyone fighting each other and with its inhuman exploitation and competition comes to light before Anna. In this society, where hostility, hate, and careerism are firmly established, where everything is subordinate to ruthless money-making, and where the appalling "dog eat dog" philosophy is the law, real humanity and noble and pure feelings cannot exist. In this society, the sincere and honest Annas cannot survive: it is saturated from top to bottom with lies. The Church is also deceitful, because it casts on this savage life a coating of Christian preachings for "universal" love and forgiveness, thereby sanctifying the existing evil and iniquity.

Anna dies uttering words of damnation and condemning everything around her. Her tragic death is a stern indictment of this whole world of violence and lies. Anna's life is stifled not only by Karenin and Vronsky but by all of society. She is therefore unable to move in with her aunt or with Dolly as she had intended—it is the same everywhere, for a truly humane life could not be found anywhere. In this society, she is unable to find recognition of her human dignity or to exercise her right for true happiness. And therein lies her tragedy—irresolvable under the conditions of a bourgeois society.

Thus, although Tolstoy tries to relate Anna's fate in religious and ethical terms he gives a deeply social basis to her tragic death. G. A. Rusanov expressed to Tolstoy the opinion that "he treated Anna Karenina very cruelly by making her die under the wheels of a train," to which the writer replied: "This opinion . . . reminds me of an incident that happened to Pushkin. Once he said to one of his friends, 'Imagine what my Tatiana did to me! She got married.' I can say the same thing about Anna Karenina. In general, my heroes and heroines sometimes do things which I would not have wanted them to do: they do what they would have to do in real life, according to the way things are, not just the way I would want them to be."

Tolstoy tries to present Anna "as pitiful" and to show the "criminal" nature of her behavior; he therefore introduces to the novel a whole series of artistic details written with ascetic severity: her "devilish and lovely" appearance, her confusion at the moment when she meets Vronsky at the railroad station, her lowered "shameful" head, her "wretched" face, and the feeling of "horror" which seizes her over what had happened—all this has something to to with the cruel meaning of the inexorable, "Divine" law, stated in the novel's epigraph: "Vengeance is mine, I shall repay."

But these traits and details become secondary before the real significance of the character of Anna. The author focuses his attention on the social causes of her tragic death; he makes his heroine "not guilty"—on the contrary, his Anna comes forth as the accuser of bourgeois-aristocratic society. That's why Anna and her tragic fate deeply move the Soviet reader. And the more he shares her passion for true human happiness, the greater the strength with which he hates proprietary bourgeois society, which bears the destruction of real humanity. (pp. 830-35)

> *S. P. Bychkov, "The Social Bases of 'Anna Karenina'," translated by Tanya E. Mairs, in ""Anna Karenina" by Leo Tolstoy: The Maude Translation, Backgrounds and Sources, Essays in Criticism, edited by George Gibian, W. W. Norton & Company, Inc., 1970, pp. 822-35.*

HENRI TROYAT (essay date 1965)

[*Troyat is a Russian-born French novelist, biographer, and critic. In the following excerpt from his biographical and critical study of Tolstoy, Troyat discusses* Anna Karenina *as a tragedy. Com-*

paring Anna Karenina *with the earlier* War and Peace, *Troyat notes that* War and Peace, *for all its numerous corpses, "seems a broad, optimistic, sun-filled work." In contrast, in* Anna Karenina *none of the characters is spared encounters with death and darkness, and the entire novel is weighted down with "ominous dreams, forebodings, hallucinations, and supernatural presences." For further comparison of* Anna Karenina *and* War and Peace, *see the excerpts by Konstantin Leontiev (1890) and Elizabeth Gunn (1971).]*

At first, Tolstoy thought of calling his novel *Two Couples* or *Two Marriages,* since in an early version Anna Karenina was supposed to get her divorce and marry Vronsky. Then, when the characters began to impose their own wills on the author, the theme veered off in another direction. But it was a theme of the utmost simplicity. (p. 376)

[Tolstoy's] attitude toward Anna Karenina, moreover, changed in the course of the book, almost as though the creator had gradually been seduced by his creature. Behind the love story of Anna and Vronsky lay the love story of Tolstoy and Anna. At first, Tolstoy did not like his heroine: he condemned her in the name of morality. He saw her as an incarnation of lechery and, oddly enough, did not even make her beautiful. His first notes on the woman who has become the quintessence of charm and elegance for generations of readers describe her in the following terms: "She is unattractive, with a narrow, low forehead, short, turned-up nose—rather large. If it were any bigger, she would be deformed. . . . But, in spite of her homely face, there was something in the kindly smile of her red lips that made her likable." So much for appearance. Her personality is that of a man-killer. One whole chapter in one of the early drafts of the book, devoted to a description of Anna, is entitled "The Devil." She is the agent of evil in the world. Both husband and lover are her victims. Hence Karenin, the government official, is initially portrayed as a warm, sensitive soul, cultivated and kind. His main fault is sentimentality. When he suspects his wife of infidelity, he tells his sister, "I feel like sobbing, I want sympathy, I want to be told what to do!" And the first model of Vronsky is "firm, kindhearted and sincere." In a word, two choice characters, in contrast to whom the diabolical Anna stands out blacker than ever.

However, Tolstoy unconsciously begins to be intrigued by his sinner. She moves him, disturbs him, disarms him. He is on the verge of declaring his love. Suddenly he can no longer deprive her of beauty. Plastic surgery is called for: the operation is a resounding success. The troll with the turned-up nose emerges a *sylphide:* "Vronsky was drawn, not by her beauty, although she was a very beautiful woman, nor by the unobtrusive elegance she radiated, but by the expression of utter sweetness in her charming face." . . . (pp. 377-78)

But Anna Karenina is not the conscious cause of the tragedies brought about by her implacable beauty: she was born under an evil spell, and at a moment chosen by fate, the spell simply begins to work. As the author continued, with infinite pains, to model each contour of this lost soul, he became increasingly irritated by the healthy, ordinary mortals around her. In the beginning she was the assassin and Karenin and Vronsky her victims. Now the tables were turned. Neither of the two men was worthy of her. With cold rage Tolstoy divested them, one by one, of the qualities he had freely bestowed upon them. He debased them in order to elevate and justify Anna.

Karenin becomes a dried-up, self-centered, narrow-minded man, a pure product of Petersburg bureaucracy. Life is hidden from him by administrative regulations; every gesture he makes is an expression of the law, of convention; he paralyzes and disfigures everything he touches; for him, his wife is simply one item of his establishment. Not until the storm is about to break does he actually concede that she "might have her own destiny, thoughts, desires," and as this possibility terrifies him, he prefers to dismiss it from his mind. Just as some people hate the countryside and can only walk on concrete pavement, so Karenin, when life rushes in upon him in all its brutal nakedness and no longer in the form of an official report, utterly loses his grip. . . . A mixture of sham dignity, official piety, self-righteousness, cowardice, rectitude and sanctimoniousness, the reactions he causes in people are the exact opposite of those aroused by his wife. The mere sight of Anna warms people's hearts; he, involuntarily, chills them. At a dinner at the Oblonskys, "he was the chief reason for the pall that fell over the party."

Faithful to his style of "contrasts," however, Tolstoy refuses to cut any character out of a single piece of cloth. When his wife is ill, Karenin suddenly becomes human. His carapace cracks. He becomes drunk with sympathy, dazzled by his own generosity. He even allows Anna's lover inside his house. "Remorse at having wished for Anna's death, the compassion she inspired in him and, more than anything else, the joy of forgiving had transformed his moral torments into a profound sense of peace." The lull is short-lived. As soon as Anna recovers, he becomes as hard as before. What was sublime at the bedside of a dying woman is ridiculous in the presence of a healthy one. As a member of society, he does what society demands. Thus he can have nothing to reproach himself with afterward. But she wants "to tear apart this spiderweb, sticky with lies, in which he was keeping her prisoner." "Whatever happens," she says, "anything is better than dissimulation and deceit."

She believes that in Vronsky she has found an ally as well as a lover. But he, whose heart was crystal-pure in the first draft, is subjected to the same process of degradation as Karenin, in order to highlight the figure of Anna. Tolstoy's dislike of his hero grows with his infatuation for his heroine. True, he is not just a handsome, vain and foolish officer, he belongs to the "gilded youth" of the capital for whom amorous intrigue is closely akin to the pleasures of the hunt. "In his Petersburg universe," wrote Tolstoy, "people were divided into two totally different types. The lower type was composed of vulgar, stupid and ridiculous people who believed that a husband should sleep only with his wife, a maiden should be pure, a married woman chaste, one must bring up one's children, make money, pay one's debts and other nonsense of that sort." On the other side there was "a world in which the rule was to appear elegant, handsome, free with money, bold and high-spirited, to abandon oneself without scruple to every passion, and to laugh at everything else." Vronsky, a bachelor, feels much more at home in the second. But when he meets Anna his self-assurance falters; he is gripped by a passion of unwonted violence. Even after the charm of novelty has worn off, he sometimes feels a superstitious fear of her grace and elegance and the intensity of the emotions that course through her. The thing he is least able to understand is her aching love for the son from whom she is separated. He refuses to think of her as a mother, and she is so aware of this that she prefers to hide from him the almost physical pain she suffers after seeing her little Sergey again. Vronsky's failure to understand this condemns her to solitude. (pp. 378-80)

With clinical exactitude, Tolstoy observes the slow poisoning of their liaison. Every phase of the disease is exhaustively described. More than their relations as lovers, the very structure of their personalities is infected, unable to withstand the trial of living together. They are ostracized by society, which will not forgive them for flaunting its rules, and they float in an artificial vacuum, with nothing to support them, no friends, nothing to plan for. Though she was strong enough to brave public opinion, Anna feels that a moral structure she has possessed since childhood is bending and giving way beneath her, and she had never realized how useful it could be. Of her two sources of support, her son and her lover—the first has been taken away from her and she may lose the second as well if she is not careful. She becomes anxious, she convinces herself that Vronsky must be pining for his carefree life of old, she accuses him of secretly seeing people whose doors are closed to her; she begins to think he has tired of her and is being unfaithful; she is tortured by jealousy; soon her only aim in life is to keep her hold over her lover, and as her fear that he will desert her increases, her efforts become more and more strained, nagging, awkward. Before long, her beauty and the physical pleasure she gives him are all she can rely upon to hold him. But Vronsky is no longer affected, even by her beauty. When he looks at her, magnificently attired on her way to the theater, a shudder of repulsion runs through him. "He raised his eyes," wrote Tolstoy, "and saw her beauty and the adornment that set it off so well; but just then it was her very beauty and elegance that irritated him." (pp. 380-81)

When shading his vast composition, Tolstoy wanted to save the brightest light for the legitimate couple, Kitty and Levin. Kitty is a pure, ardent and secretive girl in whom marriage suddenly reveals practical qualities of the highest order. . . .

As he progressed in life, he identified himself more and more with his own characters. After disguising himself as Nicholas Irtenyev, Nekhlyudov, Olenin and Pierre Bezukhov, here he was again, body and soul—and with what gusto!—in Konstantin Levin. He shamelessly attributed to him the events of his own blood. The relationship between Levin and Kitty—the declaration scene using the first letters of words, the wedding ceremony, including the last-minute hesitation and the incident of the forgotten shirt in the trunk, the young couple's first days in their country home, the birth of their first child—were one and all transposed from the author's past. (p. 381)

Levin personifies the quandary of the landowner. With his democratic turn of mind, it seems only fair to him that the peasants should have the land, "since the lord does nothing and his muzhiks work—thereby eliminating one unproductive element from the soil." But the aristocrat in him will not die and it hurts him to see the great estates breaking up, the nobility fleeing to Nice and abandoning priceless fields and forests behind them in the heart of Russia for a mere pittance, and crafty stewards speculating at both their employers' and the farmers' expense, as, "inexorably, on all sides, the impoverishment of the nobility pursued its course." He seeks to reconcile the interests of both parties, for he has "the love of the muzhik in his blood." The entire agricultural system must be reorganized, and the living conditions of the people changed in every respect," he thinks. "In place of poverty, prosperity for all; in place of mutual animosity, understanding in the interest of all. In a word, a revolution, bloodless but on a grand scale, beginning in the little circle of our district and widening to include our government, then Russia, then the whole world."

However, it is a far cry from theory to practice. When more and more flesh and blood beings lean with all their weight against the current of ideas, the stream is finally blocked; piled

on top of each other, one hundred exceptions ultimately disprove a rule. In spite of his enormous effort, Levin fails to give his peasants a share in their master's profits.

In addition to his problems as a landowner, there are his metaphysical doubts. In the early days of his marriage he thinks he has gone beyond the reach of sorrow and fear. But love is a frail bulwark against the specter of death. After witnessing his brother's death agony, Levin becomes obsessed by his own ignorance of the most urgent problem of all, the end of life on earth. The birth of his child renews his fascination with the unfathomable mystery. It seems to him that, by living like other people, he is neglecting the essential for the trivial. "Like a man who trades a warm fur coat for a muslin shirt in midwinter," Tolstoy wrote, "Levin felt naked, not in his mind but in his whole being, and condemned to perish miserably." He read the Bible and the philosophers and hovered between doubt and prayer, and added to his distress by attempting to explain it. While everyone else sees him as a strong, well-balanced man and a happy father, he turns away at the sight of a piece of rope and leaves his gun behind when he goes walking, for fear of yielding to the temptation of suicide. To escape from such depressing meditations, there is only one remedy: manual labor, and he hurls himself into it. Fatigue prevents him from thinking. "Now, against his will, he sank deeper and deeper into the ground like a plowshare, until he could not pull himself out without first plowing his furrow," Tolstoy went on. From associating with the peasants, Levin gradually absorbs their wisdom. One of them says to him, "Some people live only for their bellies, and others live for God and their soul." These simple words strike the young lord at his sorest point, and all his doubts are dispelled. What no philosopher or Church Father had been able to accomplish, a humble peasant does unwittingly: he brings a lost soul back to God. To what God? Levin doesn't know: "Just as the conclusions of the astronomers would be useless and inaccurate," he thinks, "if they were not reached through observation of the visible sky in relation to a fixed meridian and a fixed horizon, so would all metaphysical deductions be absurd if I did not base them on this knowledge of the innate goodness of every human heart which Christianity has revealed to me and of which I shall always be able to find proof in my own soul." At this point, he believes he has attained the inner peace he has so long aspired to, but the ambiguity of his religious feelings is a warning of fresh storms ahead.

During the four years (1873-77) it took him to write *Anna Karenina,* Tolstoy debated every one of the questions that were bothering him in his book. On the slightest pretext the novelist hands over the pen to the essayist, and the action halts to let the author express his views on rural husbandry, the meaning of life, the education of children or the relations between psychology and physiology. In the world of Levin and Anna, as in Tolstoy's own world, conversation centers on Gustave Doré's illustrations of the Bible, the novels of Daudet and Zola, the physicist Tindall's theories on radiant heat, the teachings of Spencer and Schopenhauer, Lassalle's scheme for workers' unions. Anna dips into Taine's *Ancien Régime,* her husband reads an article by Bréal in the *Revue des Deux Mondes,* there is a debate at Princess Betsy's on compulsory military service. . . . Tolstoy might be said to have used the novel as an outlet for his own intellectual preoccupations. (pp. 382-83)

Unlike *War and Peace,* however, where the author intercedes directly to present his view of some point of history, strategy or politics, in *Anna Karenina,* he hides behind his characters and attributes to them the opinions he holds himself. For the sake of impartiality, he even invents contradictions for them. One day, telling a friend of the difficulties he was encountering in his work, he said he had rewritten the conversation between Levin and the priest (Part V, Chapter I) four times, so that it would be impossible to tell which of the two he favored. . . . He also became increasingly aware of the interdependence of the parts of the book. In a mass of such dimensions everything hung together, the glitter and the tarnish were equally essential. As to the progression of the scenes, he believed it was the result of some mysterious process over which the author had no control. . . . To his close friends he also said, "Do you know, I often sit down to write some specific thing, and suddenly I find myself on a wider road, the work begins to spread out in front of me. That was the way it was with *Anna Karenina.*"

It is precisely this "spreading out," these digressions, this profusion of gratuitous ideas that an impatient judge might hold against Tolstoy. Some passages are difinitely too long: the descriptions of the Levins' life in the country, the debates on serfdom and emancipation, the rut in which the peasants live and their unwillingness to change, the county justices of the peace. But the author's skill as a storyteller is so great that just when the reader is about to lose patience, he is caught up and delighted anew. Scenes such as the hay mowing, drenched in sunlight and pagan joy, or the race and the fall of the mare Froufrou, or Anna's secret meeting with her son, or the death of Nicholas, or the suicide in the little railway station, are marvels of precision, fullness of design and controlled emotion.

Here, as in *War and Peace,* it is accuracy of psychological observation combined with a felicitous choice of detail that carries conviction. Returning to St. Petersburg after first meeting Vronsky, Anna suddenly notices that her husband's ears are very big, and she is annoyed because his habit of cracking his knuckles seems to be growing worse. On her wedding day, Kitty's friends find her "much less pretty than usual" in her white dress. Under the strain of her false position after she has left her husband, Anna acquires a habit of screwing up her eyes slightly when she speaks. (pp. 383-84)

But although the same description process is used in *Anna Karenina* and *War and Peace,* the general tone of the two works is very different. After dealing with a historical conflict between peoples in *War and Peace* Tolstoy narrowed his field of vision in *Anna Karenina,* to concentrate on a few persons and forage into their darkest recesses. What the picture loses in scope, it gains in depth. The epic is no longer played out in the open air, but within, in the dark shadows of the conscience. The battles are those of emotions, and they rage with the same incoherence and fury as the others.

Just as the outcome of military encounters is not determined by the strategists, so the fate of the individual most often escapes his own will. Actions are determined by circumstance, by the circles in which people move, the friends around them, a thousand imponderables collected together under the name of fatality. The fatality that presides over *Anna Karenina* is not, as in *War and Peace,* the god or war, bloated by politics and reeking of carrion and gunpowder, but the breathless god of passion. There are a hundred times more corpses in *War and Peace* than in *Anna Karenina,* yet the first seems a broad, optimistic, sun-filled work, while *Anna Karenina* is enveloped in gray, troubled clouds. *War and Peace* is an act of faith in life, a poetic glorification of the couple, the family, patriarchal traditions, a hymn to the triumph of the Russian armies over

the invader. Victory ennobles all the sacrifices made to obtain it, and the heroes emerge purified by the sufferings they have undergone in the defense of their native soil. None of this is true of *Anna Karenina,* where the air is weighted down with ominous dreams, forebodings, hallucinations and supernatural presences. The very first meeting between Vronsky and Anna at the Moscow railway station is marked by the death of a switchman, crushed beneath a train. After the accident, Oblonsky sees his sister's lips quivering and tears glittering in her eyes.

"What's the matter, Anna?" he asks.

And she answers:

"It's a bad omen."

Later, leaving the train, she is seized by a feeling of anguish and chaos as she steps out onto the platform in the snowstorm. After Vronsky's decisive words—"I am going to St. Petersburg to be where you are!"—the night, the cold and noise and the fleeting silhouettes of the passengers all conspire to plunge the young woman into a world of fantasy. "The wind, as though it would overcome all obstacles, beat the snow from the carriage roofs and triumphantly brandished a sheet of metal it had ripped loose, and the locomotive's whistle emitted a demented howl. Anna became even more exhilarated by the tragic splendor of the storm: she had just heard the words her reason dreaded and her heart longed for."

A still more awesome menace is Anna's famous dream, in which a little muzhik in rags appears, bending over an iron plate and mumbling incomprehensible words in French, "and she sensed that he was performing some strange ritual over her with this piece or iron, and awoke drenched in cold sweat." She had this nightmare several times; Vronsky himself was affected by it through a kind of telepathy; and the moment Anna throws herself under the wheels of the train, she sees, in a flash, "a little man, muttering to himself and tapping on the iron above her."

Another symbol: the death of the mare Froufrou. Through Vronsky's fault, she falls and breaks her back during the steeplechase, prefiguring Anna's suicide, to which she was driven by her lover's indifference. Even the words Tolstoy chooses to describe the fallen mare and the fallen woman are oddly similar. (pp. 385-86)

The evil omens become more clearly defined when Anna, returning to the hotel after her meeting with her son, removes from an album the photographs she had kept of him: "There was only one left, the best. . . . Her quick fingers, more nervous that ever, vainly tried to prize it out of the frame; there was no paper cutter nearby, so she poked at the stiff paper with another photograph she had picked up without looking, a portrait of Vronsky, taken in Rome." This incident strikes her as a warning from God: her lover driving out her son. . . .

Equally significant is the symbol of the candle that burns brighter just before going out. The first time she watches the wavering flame, Anna is seized by an irrational, morbid dread, and quickly, her heart pounding, lights another candle as though by doing so she might ward off the shadow of death. The second time is in the instant she loses consciousness under the wheels of the train: "And the candle by whose light she had read the book of life, full of conflict, treachery, sadness and horror, flared up more brightly than ever, lighting all the pages that had remained in darkness before, and then sputtered, flickered and went out forever."

Tolstoy's estate Yasnaya Polyana. Inge Morath/Magnum Photos, Inc.

Anna is not the only person to be affected by dread. Oblonsky's wife Dolly fears for her children's future; Princess Sherbatsky is beset by funereal presentiments at night; Levin's brother Nicholas is haunted by fear of what lies beyond life; the only chapter in the book that bears a title is Chapter XX of Part V: *Death*. All the characters' struggles to achieve happiness end in failure. Even Kitty and Levin are not exempt from the curse hanging over all couples who are bound by the flesh. In telling their story, the author tried to contrast the blessings that grow from conjugal love and the havoc caused by unsanctified love; but even the bliss of family life proves to be only a snare and a delusion. The happily married Levin is equally consumed by doubt. All his efforts at social improvement fail, and he saves himself *in extremis* only by grasping at the primitive faith of the muzhik. All in all, the hell of forbidden passion in which Anna and Vronsky are consumed is scarcely less perilous than the heaven of family affection in which Kitty and Levin slowly decompose.

One strange thing: in both *Anna Karenina,* and *War and Peace,* it is the exceptional, glittering beings, those marked by some metaphysical sign, who disappear, and the average, even insignificant ones who survive and trudge on along their little paths, halfway between good and evil. After the death of Prince Andrey—with his dreams, his doubts, his pride—we are left with the placid Bezukhov and Rostov families, for whom every imaginable felicity lies in store if they will only be content to

stay out of the limelight. Anna Karenina and Vronsky are swept from the scene, leaving behind them the mighty conquerors in the battle of life: Kitty and Levin, fine, upstanding, dull young folk, held up as an example by all their neighbors. Is this Tolstoy's plea for mediocrity? No; he simply feels that mankind needs, now and then, these extraordinary beings to shake up the dozing masses; but in the final analysis, it is the conjunction of innumerable ordinary destinies that carries history forward. Whether we like it or not, the future belongs to the Rostovs and Bezkhovs and Levins, to the shuffling mob of men of good-will. As landowner and father, Tolstoy considers himself among their number. In justifying them, he justifies himself. And even if he is occasionally tempted to desert to the camp of the idealists-in-revolt, he never tarries there. He is still at the stage of condemning private property with one hand while buying more land with the other, and inviting judges to his home while he reviles capital punishment.

But, contrary to his intentions, it is the damned, in this bitterly pessimistic novel, who arouse our sympathy and the virtuous who disappoint us. Saddled with every curse that could be laid upon her, Anna Karenina towers so far above all the other characters that the author was forced to give the book her name. The inscription, ''Vengeance is mine; I will repay,'' bears out the idea that Anna's fall proceeds from a decision by some higher authority, divine and without appeal. Everything in this superficially realistic tale is magical. Even objects—the candle, the snowy windowpane, Anna's little red bag—are invested with occult powers. Tolstoy invited his readers to contemplate the implications of a vast, disturbing, gloomy tragedy. (pp. 386-88)

> *Henri Troyat, in his* Tolstoy, *translated by Nancy Amphoux, Doubleday & Company, Inc., 1967, 791 p.*

R. F. CHRISTIAN (essay date 1969)

[*Christian is an English critic specializing in Russian language and literature. In the following excerpt, he discusses the meaning of the epigraph to* Anna Karenina *and examines the tragic nature of the novel. For further discussion of the presentation of moral problems in* Anna Karenina, *see the excerpts by Prince P. A. Kropotkin (1901) Boris Eikhenbaum (1959), J. P. Stern (1964), Angus Calder (1965), and Vladimir Nabokov (1958).*]

[The] meaning of the epigraph to *Anna,* . . . has perhaps attracted more critical attention than it really deserves. Tolstoy originally borrowed it from Schopenhauer, and it appeared in an early draft in the unbiblical form 'Mine is the Vengeance', an obviously literal translation of the German original 'Mein ist die Rache'. Tolstoy mistakenly thought it came from Solomon. What is now believed to have been the fifth version of the early chapters was headed by the same epigraph, although the first chapter was itself introduced by another thematic statement: 'For some, marriage is the most difficult and important thing in life; for others it is a trivial diversion.' Ultimately the familiar and definitive epigraph—'Vengeance is mine, I will repay'—assumed the form in which it was first used in Deuteronomy and by St Paul, and unfortunately rendered in an early German translation as 'Vengeance is mine. I play the ace!' What did Tolstoy mean by this?

One possibility is that he understood the words to emphasise the person, rather than the thing. Vengeance is *mine*, saith the Lord. It is the prerogative of God, not men. If this is so, he was no doubt influenced by his reading of *The World as Will and Idea* in which Schopenhauer advanced the argument that it would be the height of presumption for a man to act as a moral judge over his fellow men and to exact retribution for a wrong done to him, quoting the passage from Deuteronomy in support of his contention that it is the Lord who will repay. The Christian idea that there is an eternal justice beyond man's control, which Schopenhauer refers to in the context of the same passage, certainly commanded Tolstoy's respect. He was later to develop it by his vehement opposition to secular courts of law and by the prominence he gave to Christ's words: 'Judge not.' His later beliefs were clearly present in his thoughts on at least three occasions when he tried to explain what his intention was in choosing the epigraph he did. First he endorsed the interpretation proposed by the critic Gromeka that there can be no absolute freedom in sexual love, but that there are laws which man is free to accept or reject, and on his choice depends his happiness or unhappiness. The family cannot be broken up without causing unhappiness and a new happiness cannot be built on its ruins. Gromeka's apologia for the family as the only satisfactory basis for love, coupled with his condemnation of extra-marital sexual indulgence certainly had Tolstoy's approval at this stage of his life. But it is hardly an explanation of the epigraph, whether or not it explains (as Tolstoy said it did) 'what he unconsciously put into his work'.

Secondly he made it clear to his son-in-law, Sukhotin, in 1907 that he disagreed with Veresaev's interpretation that Anna came

to grief because she would not surrender herself entirely to her new life and love, but worried about her position in society and became a jealous mistress; because she would not heed the promptings of her own heart; but did violence to her deepest and inmost feelings—for which offence 'the natural laws of life' wrought their vengeance. In rejecting this reading Tolstoy said: 'I chose this epigraph simply in order to express the idea that the wrong which a person does leads to all the bitter consequences which stem, not from other people but from God, and which Anna Karenina experienced too.' This is an unambiguous declaration of intent (although it came thirty years after the novel was completed), but it takes no account of the fact that if Anna's conduct was wrong, so too was that of Oblonsky and Princess Betsy, who suffered no bitter consequences. On yet another occasion he recorded his opinion about the meaning of the epigraph when, in reply to a letter from two schoolgirls who put the question to him and offered their own answer 'that a person who has violated moral laws will be punished', he write back, 'You are right.' But this too was nearly thirty years after the event.

It would be wrong to attach too much importance to these retrospective pronouncements, and one is tempted to agree that Tolstoy originally meant no more by his epigraph than a simple statement of belief, following Schopenhauer, that it is not for men and women to cast the first stone—a point which it made explicitly on more than one occasion in the novel. 'It's for God to judge them, not us,' says the Princess Varvara to Dolly; 'it's not for us to judge'—Koznyshev echoes her words after Anna's death. More important, however, is the fact that Tolstoy chose his text with *only* the Anna-Vronsky-Karenin plot in mind, at a time when Anna was a worse and Karenin a better person, and that it remained unchanged while the conception of the characters altered. There is no doubt that the rational side of him strongly disapproved of adultery, and his devotion to the 'idea of the family' in *Anna,* in his wife's words, is amply documented. It seems to be the case that Tolstoy intended to pronounce Anna guilty, but refused to tolerate her condemnation by other mortals. As the novel progressed and as Anna changed for the better, the gap between intention and realisation grew wider, and we are not asked to condemn her, as we might have been if the first draft, for which the epigraph was written, had been the last. The novel as we have it passes no explicit judgment on Anna. For this reason critical reactions to her predicament (as opposed to what may have been Tolstoy's original *intentions* about her fate) have differed widely from writer to writer and from generation to generation. There have always been those who have argued that whatever the extenuating circumstances Anna was wrong to commit adultery, and that the consequences for her, *being the sort of person she was*, would inevitably be tragic. In Britain Matthew Arnold [see *TCLC*, Vol. II] was the first to set the moral tone, and while stressing the undoubted superiority of Anna over Madame Bovary, recorded his predictable Victorian belief that 'an Engligh mind will be startled by Anna's suffering herself to be so overwhelmed and irretrievably carried away by her passion, by her almost at once regarding it as something which it was hopeless to fight against'. This point of view, which draws support from Anna's undoubted moral deterioration and almost hysterical possessiveness, is less commonly voiced today, and Tolstoy's alleged 'punishment' of Anna is inevitably contrasted with his treatment of Princess Betsy and Oblonsky, whose easy infidelities lead to no tragic consequences for themselves. Absolute standards of morality are less interesting than relative standards of justice. But Tolstoy's experience of life told him that some people suffer while others who behave in the same way do not. What interests him is not absolute categories of justice. But Tolstoy's experience of life told him that some people suffer while others who behave in the same way do not. What interests him is not absolute categories of justice (the same punishment for the same offence), but individual people and their own sense of what is right and wrong. Anna has a conscience and she suffers for it. Betsy has no conscience, or is not shown to have, and she neither feels that adultery is wrong nor experiences unhappiness because of it. It is not for men to judge between them, for men did not implant that conscience. God has the right, so the epigraph may be taken to imply. But why should you suffer if you have a conscience and disregard it, but be happy if you have none, if the responsibility for the conscience or the lack of it does not rest with you alone? Tolstoy does not have to answer this question, but it is an essential part of his purpose that Anna should be a morally superior person to Betsy or Oblonsky, and should be capable of experiencing shame, horror and remorse.

It is fashionable nowadays to transfer the blame from Anna to society, and to attribute her tragedy to outmoded social conventions and antiquated divorce laws. D. H. Lawrence linked Anna's name with Tess of the D'Urbervilles as being at war with society, not God. 'And the judgement of men killed them, not the judgement of their own souls or the judgement of Eternal God. Or, in the very similar words of a Soviet critic. 'It was people, not God, who threw Anna under the train.' One can make out a plausible case for this point of view, without reference to the novel, although Tolstoy would not have agreed with it and had certainly no intention of giving it any prominence. There is no evidence that Tolstoy himself believed, or expected his readers to infer, that, had Anna obtained a divorce and been received back into society, all her troubles would have been over, or that she would have felt no shame, jealousy or alienation. It is Tolstoy's strength as an artist that he does not attempt to shift the blame from the shoulders of the individual to the impersonal forces of the law. If he had shown Anna, duly divorced from her husband, living happily with Vronsky and bringing up a new family while seeing Seriozha at legally prescribed intervals, his novel would have been immeasurably weaker as a novel, whatever its contribution may have been to the literature of divorce law reform.

But there is a sense in which society *was* for Tolstoy the villain of the piece—and not simply because the divorce laws were unjust or because Russia of the 1870s happened to be a bourgeois, capitalist society with semi-feudal agrarian roots, and not, let us say, a society which rewarded men according to their work, or according to their needs. As he grew older the whole concept of organised society, the whole apparatus of state organisation—legal, military, administrative and executive—became increasingly distasteful to him. Of course he had not arrived at the stage of utopian anarchism when he was writing *Anna Karenina*. And yet it is already possible to sense in the novel a rooted dissatisfaction with society in the widest sense of the word, an aversion to materialism and a groping towards spiritual values, which is hinted at, almost as an afterthought, in Levin's monologues in the final chapters. One could argue that a feeling of claustrophobia pervades the novel, a sense that there is no *institutional* way out, that the only hope for man is a discovery of his spiritual self, beside which the actual form of social organisation is an irrelevancy. To some extent Levin, for all his blundering egoism, is a liberating force, and his searching individualism, irritating as it can be, adds a new dimension to the story, much as the war in *War and Peace* releases the characters from their constricting social bonds.

Yet another approach to Anna's tragedy is to see it as the result of leaving one inadequate man for another, and failing to find in Vronsky a lover equal to her demands and her deserts. This line of argument stresses Vronsky's inability to satisfy 'a woman grown to passion and demanding it as the continuing centre of her life'. Anna, once awakened, must live her feelings right through; with Karenin she could live on a 'limited commitment'. She becomes a wife and mother without having been a girl in love. Vronsky brings out the girl in love, but by this time she is a guilty wife and mother. She has to give herself wholly . . . even her death is a revengeful move to make Vronsky love her more. By this argument Anna's tragedy is the inadequacy of her lover—and, needless to say, Tolstoy would not have been impressed by it. If adequacy means the total subordination of one's life to a woman's obsessive passion, no man can be deemed adequate. Anna, at a very early stage, comes to believe that she has certain claims on life, certain legimate needs and the right to satisfy them. She is like a hungry person, she says, who has been given a piece of bread, and she stubbornly clings to the belief that she is entitled to it. As it turns out, the bread does not nourish, but poisons her, and we can only speculate whether she was mistaken in thinking she could not have survived without it or in believing that it was hers by right. As a starving creature, Anna at first gratefully accepts her piece of bread, but her appetite grows beyond her power to control it. She becomes a parasite, exploiting her lover. In the last resort it could be said that Anna's plight is the tradedy of living by and off another person, the tragedy of exploitation.

None of these approaches is wholly satisfactory, nor yet completely wide of the mark. There can be no 'impartial' attitude to Anna's conduct. One can try to say what Tolstoy thought about it, and if we agree with him we can contrive to draw the same 'message' from his novel. But if our conclusions are different from his intentions and different from one another's, this fact has little to do with the literary merits of the book except in so far as the greatest works of art seem to share the property of also being the most controversial. The literary merits of a thought-provoking novel must lie in the posing of the problems, not their solutions, as Chekhov realised when he wrote: 'Not a single problem is solved in *Anna Karenina,* but it satisfies completely because all the problems are correctly stated.' If we leave aside for the moment the topical social issues and confine ourselves to the more universal problem of marriage and the family, we can appreciate what Chekhov meant.

One aspect of this central problem is illustrated by the theme of the unhappy family, the Karenins. Here the effect is achieved by balancing as nearly as possible the moral dignity and charm of Anna's character against her offence, and Karenin's bureaucratic coldness against his rectitude. The family background of the protagonists is important. Little or nothing is known about Anna's home life except that she was brought up and married off by an aunt. Karenin lost his parents when he was young, and was brought up by an uncle. Vronsky could not remember his father; his mother was involved in numerous liaisons. In all cases parental influence was minimal. There is no evidence of a happy and united home life. While this is not the fault of the younger generation, there is for some readers the implication in the statement of the theme that Anna and Vronsky were wrong to recreate a situation in which they themselves as children had been the innocent victims—the lack of a stable home environment.

It has been argued that Anna's marriage was not really a marriage, since it was not of her own making. Tolstoy, in stating the problem of the unhappy family, does not use this argument at all. She *is* married, and perhaps it was not such an unpleasant experience as she later persuaded herself to believe. Nothing is seen or known of her married life until Vronsky appears on the scene except for her reflections on returning from Moscow to Petersburg: 'Thank goodness, tomorrow I'll see Seriozha and Aleksei Aleksandrovich and my life—my nice, everyday life—will go on as before.' As a married woman she has to bear the terrible responsibility of choosing between a lover and a son. The choice made, she is shown to be unable to love her daughter by Vronsky as she loves Karenin's son. Now she is the victim of her own actions, and the inference is there to draw that if you behave as Anna does, you not only risk losing your legitimate son; you may also find that your illegitimate child can never be a substitute. For some readers the tragedy of Anna is the tragedy of a mother cut off from the son she loves, and not of a wife separated from a cold husband or a mistress jealous of an inadequate lover.

From time to time one senses the temptation on Tolstoy's part to weight the statement of his theme against his heroine, especially in the emphasis he places on Anna's growing moral deterioration. When Karenin sums up his objections to his wife's conduct under four headings: the flouting of public opinion, the violation of the religious sanctity of marriage, the unfortunate consequences for her son, and the unfortunate consequences for herself, the order is significant. With Tolstoy it is reversed. He shows the ripening of jealousy and rancour. Anna is ready to tell Dolly that in her place she would forgive Oblonsky's infidelity, even it it should occur again. But when she herself is the victim, even the suspicion of Vronsky's cooling ardour is enough to make her incapable of forgiveness. She becomes more and more selfish. She becomes increasingly the slave of her passions (the 'animal relationships' of an early draft). She is determined to punish Vronsky. She resorts to contraception and drugs. She is the first of Tolstoy's heroines to smoke! In these different ways Tolstoy is suggesting that her choice was the wrong one for her. But if his rational prejudices steer him in one direction, his heart is quick to correct him. It is not merely Anna's physical attractiveness, her charm as a woman, which has to be offset against her fall from grace. It is her dignity, her compassion, the vitality, warmth and sincerity of her character, and the enormity of her suffering which tip the scales back again and leave the problem so delicately poised in the balance. In comparing Anna Karenina, Effi Briest and Madame Bovary, one critic described Anna as the only wholly adult character of the three, and happily contrasted Fontane's tolerant compassion and Flaubert's detached psychological knowledge with Tolstoy's genuine love of his heroine. Loving Anna, he fought against his rational urge to condemn her for breaking the rules; so too did he resist his reason when it told him that Karenin was right to keep them. Karenin has his redeeming features, but his heart is cold. It is his head which predominates, as symbolised by his surname (if we are to believe his son, who claimed that it was derived from the Homeric Greek καρψηνου (karēnon)), his constant ratiocinations, or simply his obtruding ears.

Is is impossible to believe that Tolstoy's answer to the problem of marriage and the family as demonstrated through Anna and her husband was that divine retribution inevitably overtakes the adulterer; or that Anna could ever have found happiness with Karenin. Perhaps Tolstoy himself believed that a loveless marriage for Anna was the better of two evils, and it is possible to draw this inference from the novel to provide a 'solution', albeit an unhappy one. But so finely is the balance held that it is equally possible to draw many other inferences. Professor Poggioli can say with plausibility that Tolstoy sided with the person against the group (but not as Anna's destiny shows, against a morality standing higher than both the person and the group). And yet the final word must be that we are not asked to accept anything definitive about passion'. The charge of moral bullying cannot be laid at the author's door. (pp. 170-79)

> R. F. Christian, in his Tolstoy: A Critical Introduction, *Cambridge at the University Press, 1969, 291 p.*

ELIZABETH GUNN   (essay date 1971)

[*Gunn is an English novelist, poet, and critic. The following excerpt is taken from her study* A Daring Coiffeur: Reflections on "War and Peace" *and* "Anna Karenina." *In her discussion of* Anna Karenina, *Gunn calls the novel, in contrast to the earlier* War and Peace, *a "fully adult work" for its treatment of sexual love, death, and tragic human relationships. For further comparison of* Anna Karenina *and* War and Peace, *see the excerpts by Konstantin Leontiev (1890) and Henri Troyat (1965).*]

[*Anna Karenina*] is a book about human isolation, interlocking human isolations. The totality of this isolation is such that all relationships within it even are a form of torture; they are merely a jarring on, an intrusion, an infringement of one isolation by another.

And yet it is true that the book, despite its subject-matter, opens on a great wave of happiness—the irrepressible happiness of Stepan Arkadyevitch (it is easy to shut the door on Dolly), of Levin with his lover's hopes. It is a bachelor lunch; we are carried away by the sense of our well-being. This we feel is what life should be like! We feel it as we tuck in our starched napkins, reflecting that we have never liked oysters and how unwell we shall be for days after eating such a meal. This is what it is to be, as we are far from being, in a right relation to the world! The sheer goodness of life emerges from these pages like the smell of freshly baked bread. Yet Levin, and Oblonsky too, are isolated; each disapproves of the other. But this is smoothed over by Stiva's imperturbable good humour. His charm is an infectious quality. We ourselves fall on his neck when he comes to shoot with Levin. We have never been better pleased to see a guest. We open the book with him waking on the sofa in his study. He has been dreaming of little decanters like women on tables made of glass which sang *Il Mio Tesoro*—no, not that, perhaps *O Sole Mio.* . . .

The point I am making here, is that Oblonsky, the roué, is the only happy person in the book. And how, we may ask, does he contrive to achieve happiness? 'The answer is . . . love from day to day; in other words forget, but as he could not find forgetfulness in sleep, at least not until bedtime, nor return to the music sung by the little decanter women, he must therefore lose himself in the dream of life.'

To this extent, no more, Stepan Arkadyevitch may be said to prepare the way for Anna. But no, there is one other sentence. He is thinking of his unfaithfulness, of Dolly. '"No she will never forgive me—she cannot forgive me. And the worst of it is that I am to blame for everything—I am to blame and yet I am not to blame. That is the whole tragedy," he mused.'

This is an adult tragedy, by which I do not mean that Stepan Arkadyevitch is himself adult; but merely that when we are adult there is no one else to blame. We are both to blame and not to blame. We are what we have unconsciously, unthinkingly become. Not only are we not in control—we are no longer, as youth assumes, allowed the illusion of being so. The very qualities which go to make the enjoyment of Stepan Arkadyevitch are the identical qualities which create Anna's suffering.

The very buoyancy which has enabled Anna to survive her marriage to Karenin has allowed her to come through life too easily, without a struggle, without developing strength of character. She has lacked the compulsive streak which forges such a strength. She is, without being aware of it, rudderless. Moreover, all her life she has lacked passionate love. She has never been adored by her parents. She had none. Is this her fault? What woman in a similar position would not be conquered by such love, tenderness, passion, as Vronsky's?

If we stand back and pause with Matvey, his valet, to admire the blooming form of Stepan Arkadyevitch, inhaling the smell of coffee and fresh croissants, we may experience something of that same nostalgia which Tolstoy plainly felt for the social world, viewed not as in *War and Peace* as brutal and depraved but rather as if looking back on childhood—to a world where people were still, as he, Tolstoy, had once been, content to be thus childishly occupied absorbed, their trivial lives unshadowed by thoughts of death. Some clue to the reason why Tolstoy chose to write, to identify with *Anna*, is provided by the chapter describing Levin's visit to the club—where people leave their troubles behind with their hats in the hall, where everyone is accepted and relaxed. We smell the leather chairs and feel the relief of it all, of this milieu where no women are admitted, where time and money are gambled away, where we see—can it really be true?—the same old faces behind the newspapers.

'Vengeance is mine. I will repay' is the motto of the book. Unlike its predecessor *War and Peace, Anna Karenina* is a fully adult work. Its themes are those of sexual love and death, and, too, that actions have consequences which we can no longer, as when young, lightly leave behind. Later our acts become our lives. We are to blame but we are not to blame. It is this new restraint, a new complexity, that sets the second book above the first.

The motto, the threat itself is an impersonal one. As such it is far more terrible, more effective than Tolstoy himself could be, reading the riot act to us. Similarly we see him incognito, sliding out of sight behind his characters. It is this latter aspect, tone and style, that in the last resort distinguishes the book. We are to blame and we are not to blame. We see this. We see it clearly; we see that the matter is complex. We understand that we cannot, dare not judge. (pp. 92-5)

> *Elizabeth Gunn, in her* A Daring Coiffeur: Reflections on "War and Peace" and "Anna Karenina", *Rowman and Littlefield, 1971, 146 p.*

ELIZABETH STENBOCK-FERMOR (essay date 1975)

[*The following excerpt is taken from Stenbock-Fermor's* The Architecture of "Anna Karenina": A History of Its Writing, Structure, and Message. *After examining some of the elements that make up the structural "linkage" of Tolstoy's novel, as well as providing a discussion of Tolstoy's thoughts on "messages" in literature, Stenbock-Fermor finds that the message of* Anna Karenina *is related to love and family life, which were among the concerns which preoccupied Tolstoy at the time of writing this*

novel during the 1870s. For further discussion of the narrative structure of Anna Karenina, *see the excerpts by Tolstoy (1876 and 1878), Percy Lubbock (1921), Louis Auchincloss (1961), and Vladimir Nabokov (1958).*]

In architecture, elaborate workmanship and ornamentation enhance the beauty of the building and bestow on it its full artistic value, though they may conceal the main structural lines and even, too some extent, the purpose of the masterpiece. Yet the building would not be a masterpiece without these sculptured or carved ornaments; it would be a skeleton with a different meaning, and the ornaments in turn, would have a different meaning if viewed separately from the main structure, even if they preserved their individual beauty. These are passages in *Anna Karenina* which can be enjoyed even if one is totally ignorant of the plot. But for the author, everything was an inseparable part of the whole. (p. 14)

As early as April 1876, when working on Part Five, Tolstoj wrote to Straxov: "If I wanted to express in words everything I planned to express through my novel, I would have to rewrite anew from the beginning the very same novel I wrote." This was his belief concerning literature in general, not only his own creations. In September of the previous year, in a letter to a friend who was also a writer, though of a very different kind, he expressed the same opinion: "If you had been able, in conversation, to tell people what you wanted to express in your play—there would be no need for you to write the play." Therefore, for our investigation, the seemingly unimportant details are as worthy of analysis and interpretation as the intricacies of the plot and the relationships, or the basic structure. We will have to look at everything as part of the ultimate whole. (pp. 14-15)

[On] March 16, 1870, soon after the first conception of the plot which was to become *Anna Karenina* appeared to him, Tolstoj wrote in his notebook that the task of literary criticism should not be evaluation, but interpretation, meaning that a literary work ought to awaken thoughts and be judged by its content.

In April 1876, he at first expressed (in his very important, previously quoted letter to Straxov) a denial of the importance of thoughts and stressed the supreme importance of structure:

> Men are needed in the criticism of art who would show the nonsense of searching for thoughts in a work of art, who would constantly direct the readers through the endless labyrinth [maze] of linkage which forms the essence of art in accordance with laws which are the foundation of that linkage.

But in the same letter:

> In everything, almost in everything I have written, I was led by the necessity of putting together thoughts which were linked with each other in order to express myself; however, every thought expressed separately in words loses its meaning, it is dreadfully lowered when taken independently of the linkage in which it stands. The linkage itself, I believe, is not achieved through thinking, but in some other way, and it is absolutely impossible to express the essence of that linkage directly, using words; one can only do it indirectly—describing with the help of words, images, actions, situations.

And a few days later in a letter to the poet Fet, who had been very sick and had written that he wanted to ask Tolstoj to come and witness his "departure" (meaning death), Tolstoj developed his ideas on the attitude one should have towards death, on the inadequate role of organized religion in the presence of death, and suddenly concluded: "I have tried to express much of what I was thinking in the last chapter of the April issue." These words refer to Chapter 20 of Part Five, in which the agony of Levin's brother is described, and Levin's thoughts and behavior at his brother's deathbed are contrasted with the attitude of his wife, a believer and follower of the precepts of the Orthodox church. As the chapter ends with the discovery of Kitty's pregnancy, it is impossible not to see the deliberate insertion of the author's thoughts by means of a new situation: in it life and death become part of a natural process they somehow compensate each other and are closely linked—for many years the basis of his philosophy.

Thus, we have on one hand Tolstoj's opinion that searching for thoughts in a literary work is nonsense, and on the other that it is not evaluation but interpretation (the Russian word is *tolkovanie* which implies searching for a meaning which has not been clearly expressed) which is all-important. And then we are told that thoughts should be conveyed indirectly, through images, actions, and situations which are linked in a mysterious, inexplicable manner, and that it is the links and the manner which are the essence of art, and not the situations, plots, and relationships. (pp. 15-16)

We don't know whether Tolstoj ever had in mind the song from Oliver Goldsmith's *The Vicar of Wakefield*. We know that he admired the book, and the song outlines in simplified form the tragedy of Anna.

> When lovely woman stoops to folly
> And finds too late that men betray,
> What charm can soothe her melancholy,
> What art can wash her guilt away?
>
> The only art her guilt to cover,
> To hide her shame from every eye,
> To give repentance to her lover,
> And wring his bosom—is to die.

He finally offered to the public the life stories of several people struggling with a highly controversial contemporary problem which he defined later as the 'family idea'. The opening lines of the novel, which at first were meant to be only a second epigraph—"All happy families are like one another, each unhappy family is unhappy in its own way"—prove that the novel was growing in scope, taking in more than one couple. From the individual case of one unfaithful wife it developed into a discussion of marriage as a social and religious institution in the last quarter of the 19th century, when the words 'women's rights' implied first of all the right to love outside marriage.

To offset the individual case of Anna's tragic love, Tolstoj incorporated into the plot or connected with it several instances of love between married and unmarried couples belonging to various social groups, and even deviations from normal sex patterns. He also showed sex without love and love without sex. And as sex and procreation were for him the foundations of continuity in all of nature and therefore involved philosophical problems concerning the meaning and aim of life, he wove into the novel, as an integral part of it and not as independent digressions, the dilemma of faith opposed to reason and the possibility of reconciling them in order to live in peace with oneself and according to the laws of nature. We know

from his letters that this was a acute personal problem at that time. He described situations where class struggle was at work and suggested approaches to the labor problems of the day. He produced arguments for and against war between nations. He aired his opinions on radical ideas, education and child psychology, painting and contemporary music, the role of administration and philosophical writing. And he made clear his constant preoccupation with the meaning of human life when confronted with unavoidable and senseless death. How close all these problems were to the author's heart can be seen from his diaries and correspondence. They connect the novel with events of the day and with Tolstoj's personal experience. (pp. 20-1)

The majority of the Russian language commentaries on Tolstoj have not been translated, but English and other non-Russian biographers and essayists have used them and have described—with fewer details of course—how the novel was conceived and written.... Each author has his own explanation of the 'linkage' in the novel. (p. 22)

There are many . . . links which bind seemingly unconnected characters and events. At the beginning of the novel Levin declares that he feels only disgust towards fallen women, and adds that he never met any "charming fallen creature", pointing to the French woman at the buffet and hinting at Oblonskij's extamarital entanglements . . . ; so Tolstoj forces him to appreciate the qualities of devotion of his brother's mistress, a woman from a brothel, and later tells us that he had almost fallen in love with Anna "who could only be called a fallen woman".... Another such link is created when Nicholas declares to his brother that he considers his mistress "as his wife" . . . , and again when Vronskij uses exactly the same words about Anna, when he speaks of her to *his* brother.

All these links are part of the structure: they hold the edifice together, and because of them otherwise unrelated characters and events acquire a new meaning. This is the kind of linkage Tolstoj had in mind when he wrote to Račinskij that "the links in the structure are not in the plot and not in the relationship (acquaintance) of the characters, but in the inner linkage". Besides being important as details in subplots or ornamentation, they also become part of a message. But the work was not, as Račinskij wanted it to be, "limpid, like Alpine waters".

The message was not always clear, because the matter was not absolutely clear to Tolstoj himself. Tolstoj, who was by nature a fox in Isaiah Berlin's definition [see excerpt dated 1966 in *TCLC*, Vol. 4], "his thoughts moving on many levels", was more and more trying to think and live as a hedgehog "with a single, universal, organizing principle" in mind.

The message is about the family idea, and love is the foundation of the family, and the novel was conceived as a love story.

As she was leaving Betsy's party, in what at first was the beginning of the novel, Anna said to Vronskij: "Love. . . . The reason I dislike the word is because it means too much to me, much more than you can understand." . . . She was foretelling her own future, unwittingly of course. In her mind she was only warning Vronskij and illustrating for his benefit the statement she had made earlier, when in reply to Betsy's challenging question, she said: "There are as many kinds of love as there are hearts."

The novel depicts all kinds of hearts and all kinds of loves. They may not be connected by the plot: in fact, the connection exists only because they are all 'love-cases'. We sense who has Tolstoj's sympathy, but there is no definite condemnation of those he considers to be on the wrong path; rather there is irony and pity, as in the case of Oblonskij, or the innocent and perverted Liza Merkalov.... The novel is not a glorification of love in the romantic sense: it is exactly the opposite. It is a condemnation of violent love-passion and also of love as a pleasurable pastime; it does not advocate spectacular sacrifice, and it does not approve of sublimation and platonic love. The virtuous Varenka, the noble-minded Koznyšev, who love in the fond memory of their first unhappy loves, are not presented as examples to be followed. There is, for instance, the strange love of Lydia Ivanovna for Karenin. Tolstoj's sarcastic description of that woman and her repeated infatuations, together with her complete failure as a wife, indicate that this is something Tolstoj considers to be against nature, a kind of perversion. Towards frustrated females like Lydia Ivanovna and Madame Stahl, Tolstoj was unable to feel even pity. (pp. 108-09)

The novel certainly has a message, yet it is not the peremptory teaching of Tolstoj's later period; there is no absolute certitude as to what man should do. Rather it tells the reader where the evil and the danger lie in wait for him, what to avoid, what not to do. It is a negative attitude.

In the seventies, Tolstoj was still willing to accept the beliefs, and even many of the conventions, of the civilization which surrounded him, but on his own terms, his "sole wish being to be left alone as I leave the entire universe alone". But he was beginning to change his mind as to his own appointed role in life. He believed that he had an important role to play. In December 1874 he wrote to A. A. Tolstoj, who had mentioned her own charitable occupations (rehabilitation of young prostitutes) and social duties as being of little importance: "I, at least, whatever I may do, always feel convinced that forty centuries look down upon me from the heights of these pyramids [Napoleon's words to his soldiers in Egypt], and that the world will perish if I ever stand still." This alluded to both *Anna Karenina,* just sold to Katkov's [*Russian Messenger*], and to the publication of primers for schools. He had written in 1872 to his cousin that his ambition was to see his primer become "the only textbook for two generations of *all* Russian children, from the tsar's to the peasants' children, and that they would get their first poetic impressions from it".

Though this statement concerned only educational material, art indeed had an important place in it, and Tolstoj closely supervised the printing of every word and illustration. Soon education and art would fuse for him, and art would become the means of education not only of children but of adults. He knew that a work of art could be more effective than a sermon.

In the summer of 1865 he had written, but did not mail, a letter to the writer Boborykin. In it he said, enumerating the weak points of the latter's novels:

> Most important. Your two novels are written on a contemporary subject. Problems of the *zemstvo,* literature, women's emancipation, etc., are brought to the forefront in your novels, while in the realm of art, they do not exist. Problems of women's emancipation and literary parties necessarily seem important to you in your literary environment in Petersburg, but these problems just quiver in a small puddle of dirty water, mistaken for an ocean only by those who have been placed in it's center by fate. The aims of art are incommensurable (as math-

ematicians say) with social aims. The aim of an artist is not to solve a problem irrefutably, but to make people love life in all its innumerable, inexhaustible manifestations. If I had been told that I could write a novel in which I would irrefutably establish the opinion I consider right on all social problems, I would not devote even two hours of work to such a novel, but If I had been told that what I will write would be read in 20 years' time by people who are now children, and that they would weep and laugh while reading, and learn to love life, I would devote to it all my life and all my strength.

> (pp. 111-13)

In most cases when Tolstoj discussed in *Anna Karenina,* political and social problems—the *zemstvo,* the new courts, the elections, women's rights, and all the contemporary questions which ten years earlier he considered unfit for a novel—he did it through 'images, actions, situations', but in such a way that there could be little doubt concerning his personal opinion, when it was a negative one. (pp. 114-15)

In *Anna Karenina,* Tolstoj was trying to unite the two aims he considered incommensurable in 1865: promoting by his novel love of life (but no longer of everything in life) and offering a solution to certain social problems, the most important being in his opinion the family, and with it the institution of marriage, both under strong attack at that time.

There were several problems he had not quite yet solved for himself, and therefore he merely hinted at them, but did so several times, thus creating a secondary chain of links throughout the structure.

A family is not thinkable without children, and the main object of the family is to educate these children in the right spirit, for the continuation of family life.

How children should *not* be educated he made clear through scenes involving Dolly's children . . . , the L'vov's . . . , and particularly Sereža Karenin . . . , and through their lessons and textbooks. We know that Tolstoj read the latest books on education to write the chapters on Sereža's lessons, and asked for the kind of books Karenin might have read when organizing his son's life after Anna left. He ridiculed the contemporary methods of teaching grammar, Latin and religion, but how they should be taught and even what should be taught is not stated, except for hints that an association with the old and loyal doorman was more beneficial and important for Sereža's development than lessons with his teachers and, of course, with his father.

Although the novel ends with the religious conversion of the hero, there is no intimation that Levin's newly acquired faith is—in the author's opinion—the only true religion. There are almost as many kinds of religious attitudes in the novel as there are kinds of love, but while Tolstoj's principles on the importance of fidelity in love and marriage are plainly stated, he does not state whether there is an irrefutably right religious teaching. (pp. 115-16)

A letter Tolstoj wrote to Fet in 1873, as he was starting to write *Anna Karenina,* may serve as a guideline for his purpose and state of mind at that time. He speaks of the death and burial of his brother's infant son.

What do I mean by religious respect? This. Some time ago I was at my brother's. His child died and they were burying him. The clergy came, and a tiny pink coffin, and all as it should be. My brother and myself were of the same opinion as you on religious rites, and getting together we told each other that we felt almost disgusted by rituals. But then I thought: Well and what would my brother do to carry out of the house the decaying corpse of the child? How to do it? Have the coachman take it out in a sack? And where to put it, how to bury it? . . . And I at least could not think of anything better than the Requiem, incense, etc. . . . One feels the desire to express outwardly the importance and solemn meaning, and the religious awe at this greatest event in the life of every man. . . . And I can not devise anything more appropriate . . . than religious surroundings. In me at least, these Church Slavic words evoke the same metaphysic rapture as when I think of the Nirvana. . . .

And he goes on trying to understand why religion—a human invention and a senseless one—has been such an important service to humanity. And he ends with the words: ''There is something in it.'' These last words are the same he attributes to Levin after his confession.

We also have letters from Tolstoj written (in 1879) a year after he completely finished *Anna Karenina,* the year coinciding with the beginning of his most acute religious crisis. In these letters he speaks of praying for the souls of the dead, and addressing them in his prayers, and he uses the traditional church wording. There is no mention of such beliefs in the conversion of Levin. In the novel, Tolstoj did not discuss Church dogma, a problem which would cause him so much intellectual torment soon afterwards, when his reason rebelled against the requirement of blind faith in those mysteries of religion which his thinking mind could not accept either as realities or as symbols.

While ridiculing certain superstitions of the peasantry, together with those of the upper classes . . . , Tolstoj treated the religious beliefs of the Russian peasant with respect and sympathy throughout the entire novel, stressing that moral values were inseparably linked, for them, to sacraments and quotations from the Gospel. His hero's conversion proceeded from the realization that the moral standards of mankind (personified by peasants in this case) which are alive and at work in the human conscience were in opposition to physical impulses or rational behavior which is prompted by personal interests. The latter were earlier brought up by Levin as being the only movers of mankind. . . . Non-profitable moral standards, i.e., the dictum of the human conscience, could have been implanted in man only by something absolutely independent of material laws and more important than matter—divine revelation. As faith in a supernatural spiritual reality coincided with the teachings of the Church, and was shared by people he considered to be 'good', he accepted other basic teachings of the Church: the existence of an immortal soul, which meant that he need no longer dread physical decay and death, and of a Supreme Being— God—whom he could address in prayer and gratitude, something he previously did against his better judgment, in moments when he felt utterly helpless.

It also brought him deliverance from the nightmare of being nothing but an insignificant (in Nature's eyes) bit of matter,

submitted to physical laws and therefore deprived of freedom of will, as taught by determinism. The novel ends with the proclamation of human freedom of will towards good or against it, and freedom of choice, another of the main teachings of the Church. Having thus brought his hero to the happy end of his quest for the meaning of life, Tolstoj considered that the interest of the readers in him would stop. . . . (pp. 119-20)

But some readers were not satisfied. And ten years later Gromeka, at the end of his critical review of the novel, imagined that he visited Levin on his estate and had a long conversation with him. (p. 120)

Karenin's personality was later resurrected by Andrej Belyj in his novel *Petersburg,* and incarnated in A. A. Ableuxov, whose son joins a group of revolutionaries and is ordered to kill his father. Though Tolstoj had condemned his own great novels as being 'bad art', their heroes continued to be treated by readers as real people. He had started the tradition himself. (pp. 120-21)

In his old age, when anyone praised *Anna Karenina* in front of him, he would say:

> As if there were something difficult in describing how an officer fell in love with a lady, there is nothing difficult about it, and above all, nothing good. Bad and useless.

This was said at a time when he had renounced all writing that could not be labeled 'good', i.e., edifying, in accordance with the principles expounded in *What is Art?* (1898). But once, in 1902, talking to a writer who told him that he was forty-eight years old, he recalled with yearning the time when he was forty-eight himself, and writing *Anna Karenina,* and he said that it was the best period in his work. (p. 124)

Elisabeth Stenbock-Fermor, in her The Architecture of ''Anna Karenina'': A History of Its Writing, Structure, and Message, *The Peter De Ridder Press, 1975, 127 p.*

ANGUS CALDER   (essay date 1976)

[*Calder is an English author and critic whose works include* The People's War: Britain, 1939-1945 *(1969) and* Russia Discovered: Nineteenth Century Fiction from Pushkin to Chekhov *(1976). Commenting on the aims and basis of his writing, Calder has stated:* ''I try to express, as well as I can, my humanist values, which commit me to international, libertarian, revolutionary socialism. This is not narrowly 'political,' and I doubt if writers should get mixed up in political parties. My humanism involves every aspect of life which prose and poetry can cover. Ideology is, precisely, the writer's medium and his business. Writing is a form of action designed to affect the way people think. But it is also a form of exploration and research, and I think the acceptance as binding of any received set of ideas (Methodism, say, or a party political programme) is bound to hamper exploration and research.'' *In the following excerpt, Calder emphasizes the problematical nature of the moral questions raised by Tolstoy in* Anna Karenina. *Calder believes that because, in this novel, Tolstoy managed to contain his ideas and his penchant for philosophical discourse, he came closer to a purely aesthetic approach to writing than anywhere else in his works. Calder finds that Tolstoy only posed moral problems, without proposing exact solutions. For further discussion of the presentation of moral problems in* Anna Karenina, *see the excerpts by Prince P. A. Kropotkin (1901), Boris Eikhenbaum (1959), J. P. Stern (1964), R. F. Christian (1969), and Vladimir Nabokov (1958).*]

[*Anna Karenina*] is an unusually complex novel which at the same time appeals to us by its (real) clarity and its (apparent) simplicity. It is a book which touches on many aspects of life and which is loved and remembered for its flow of intimate details—but also because it concentrates our attention with prodigious force on its heroine, the doomed adulteress. Even more than *War and Peace,* it seems 'like life itself', so that Tolstoy is praised by some for removing himself altogether from his novel, yet attacked by others for 'killing' Anna. The critic's professional ingenuity seems more than usually inadequate. It would take an analysis three times as long as the novel itself to begin to do justice to it. No Russian novel has been better served by critics writing in English, yet none so consistently prompts the response, yes, Critic X is on to something there but somehow, the way he puts it, it's not quite right. Like Levin himself, we stumble from partial revelation through confusion to a new, still incomplete, illumination. *War and Peace,* as we re-read it, settles into patterns and seems to reveal its intentions. *Anna* won't settle and won't tell us what it 'means'.

So convincing is *Anna's* reality that we miss major inconsistencies until R. F. Christian tells us:

> that Kitty and Levin spend a year longer on their journey than Anna and Vronsky, while Dolly's story is at least six years out of step: that ages are muddled, that distances do not tally and that the day on which the novel begins is both a Thursday and a Friday.

The interweaving of two stories—or, we should perhaps say, of three marriages—is responsible for these discrepancies. There are plenty of novels with two or more stories. There can be no other in which the connections between the episodes seem so tenuous in summary and are in fact, from chapter to chapter, so profound and persistent. (pp. 212-13)

Very few scenes directly link Anna's story with Levin's. Levin is Vronsky's rival for Kitty, and meets Vronsky several times; furthermore, he is closely connected to Stiva by friendship and marriage. But before and after their brief meeting, Anna plays no part in his life, nor he in hers. And their stories are radically different in character. Anna's is taut with emotion throughout and full of dramatic confrontations. Levin's, by contrast, is a string of 'slices of life', reaching a kind of climax with his marriage to Kitty and always given interest by his sharply conceived character and his earnest strivings for truth and virtue. The great 'scenes' in Levin's story, except for his trip to succour his dying brother, are not intensive and dramatic but extensive and either humorous or lavishly descriptive. He lives at a pretty even pace the life of a country squire, albeit an eccentric one, and the marvellous passages where he mows with the peasants or hunts with Stiva are the most memorable ones in which he figures. Readers sometimes complain that the Levin story is mostly boring. Why must we be distracted from Anna's absorbing fate by a rather graceless landowner worrying over his relationship with his peasants?

The answer is one of the few points about the book on which we may be reasonably certain. Levin's slowly growing life brings him—and us with him—into touch with the lives of the peasants who produce the food which the other characters eat, and into touch with talkers who are concerned with important arguments about the modernization of Russia, the emancipation of women and the discoveries of natural science. Not only does this sharpen, but contrast, our image of the wealthy 'Peters-burg' world in which Vronsky and Anna move, it forces us to view the tragic lovers in the context of much wider reality than either of them recognizes. The shallow, if amiable, Veslovsky, is hopeless as a shooting companion for Levin in the marshes and outrages him by flirting with Kitty—but a little later we meet him flirting with Anna and very much at home in the rarefied, gadget-ridden life which she and her set maintain even in the countryside. With a gun, Veslovsky is a bungler. On Vronsky's tennis court, he is in his element.

As this example shows the two stories meet in an unbreakable continuum. Common social contacts draw them together into a single flow. Karenin is present at the dinner party where Levin and Kitty decide to get married. It is Levin's half-brother, the writer Koznyshev, through whom we meet Vronsky on his way to the Balkans. Stiva pops up everywhere, and without the knowledge of him which we gain through seeing him with Levin, we would not understand so well his sister Anna.

When Anna and Vronsky are in Italy, they meet Mikhailov, a Russian artist who is painting a figure-thronged picture of 'Christ Before Pilate'. They view this work in the company of a silly theorist named Golenischev. Mikhailov has every reason to ignore the judgment of such people, but when Golenischev praises his Pilate—'an official to his very backbone'—he is pleased. This was 'the very idea' he had meant to convey—although Golenischev's remark is 'only one reflection in a million that might have been made, with equal truth.' Much more could be said about this scene—how Mikhailov's subject, the judging of Christ, emphasizes a theme which we cannot miss in the novel, that of the fallibility of men presuming to weigh up the sins of their fellows; how Vronsky's reactions express that interest in superficial 'technique' rather than in profounder matters, which characterizes his outlook on life in general; and so on. There are as many 'meanings' in this passage as there are in Mikhailov's painting, and when we fish for significances in Tolstoy's continuum of life we can catch only a few and must leave behind others equally important. ('An official', for instance: we think of Karenin, as Pilate.)

Mikhailov paints Anna. This portrait is only one of three mentioned in the book. A fine one hangs in Karenin's study. Its expression, after he has learnt of her infidelity, seems to him 'unbearably insolent and challenging.' Vronsky, as a dabber in painting, attempts one of her in Italian costume. But she is not an Italian; she is a Russian, and Vronsky puts his own aside when he sees Mikhailov's portrait. When Levin visits Anna in Moscow his face is flushed although he himself doesn't think (what drunk man does?) that he has drunk too much. In this unreliable state, he looks at Mikhailov's picture:

> He even forgot where he was and did not hear what was being said: he could not take his eyes off the marvellous portrait. It was not a picture, but a living, lovely woman with black curling hair, bare shoulders and arms, and a dreamy half-smile on her soft, downy lips: triumphantly and tenderly she looked at him with eyes that disturbed him. The only thing that showed the figure was not alive was that she was more beautiful than a living woman could be.

But when Anna comes in she has the 'same perfection of beauty'. The reality is 'less dazzling', but there is 'something fresh and seductive in the living woman' which the portrait lacks.

Perhaps we remember at this point how Kitty saw Anna on the night of the ball when she conquered Vronsky. There were pansies in her black hair, with its 'wilful little curls that always escaped at her temples and on the nape of her neck.' Kitty had thought that a lilac dress would suit Anna. But she realized when she saw her, with her 'full shoulders and bosom, that seemed carved out of old ivory, and her rounded arms with their delicate tiny wrists' displayed and set off by a black gown richly trimmed with lace, that Anna's charm lay precisely in the fact that she stood out from whatever she was wearing. The dress 'was not at all conspicuous, but served only as a frame. It was Anna alone, simple, natural, elegant, and at the same time gay and animated, whom one saw.'

Her dress is a 'frame' as if she were a painting. She is aware of herself as an object of beauty. Just before her suicide, she sees her own feverish face with its glittering eyes in the mirror, recognizes herself, seems to feel Vronsky's kisses on her, and lifts to her lips her own hand and kisses it. In love with the idea that a man should be in love with her, she has become self-infatuated—or rather infatuated with a glamorous object-Anna external to her true self. Even at the ball, Kitty saw 'something terrible and cruel' in her, but Kitty was of course jealous. What we have met, in the Anna framed by her black dress, is someone both forthright and elusive. She seens 'simple', but her dress is luxurious, 'natural' although she must have taken trouble with the pansies which Nature has grown for her. Her wrists are delicate, her whole air elegant, she is Petersburg incarnate; yet she is a solid, full-blooded animal, as passionate as any peasant, and her ungovernable curls suggest both wantonness and 'naturalness'. She is self absorbed, pre-eminently 'herself'. But she is also the vulnerable plaything of the society which she moves in and whose values her way of dressing mirrors. Her vitality strains and pushes against that society, but since she belongs so much to that society, she is thereby set at war with herself. She is both supremely and singly her own self, and 'double', her natural self at odds with her 'social' self. Rousseau's distinction between the 'man of nature' and the 'man of society' is as fundamentally important in *Anna* as in *War and Peace*.

The frame cannot hold Anna. She is always in motion. What Vronsky first sees in her as she alights at the Moscow station is 'the suppressed animation which played over her face and flitted between her sparkling eyes and the slight smile curling her red lips. It was as though her nature were so brimming over with something that against her will it expressed itself now in a radiant look, now in a smile.' She moves like a pool, brimming over, renewed. Her expression cannot be captured except as one in movement between her eyes and her lips. No other woman in the book has such ample vitality. The powdered Princess Betsy with her long pale countenance, Dolly with her thin little braids of hair, and even Kitty—whom Levin first glimpses doll-like from afar at the skating ground, a pretty but slight creature—are all meagre beside her, fully 'real' though they are. Nor is it purely Anna's physical life which is in motion. As she reads an English novel, she envies the Member of Parliament in it making a speech—she would like to make that speech herself.

Of course, this implies that she is imitative, and we may link this moment with Vronsky's mimicry, at different times, of the manner of Italian Renaissance painting and of the life-style of the English country gentleman. But when Anna takes up the study of architecture, she surpasses Vronsky, and it is very significant that her frustration over her situation boils over when he is away playing at Parliaments at the Nobility elections. Not only does Russia have no parliament, women aren't at this time allowed to speak in the English one. When Petersburg ostracizes her and even the immoral Betsy explains that she can't call on her, Vronsky is still free to lead an active life in the open and indeed is welcomed wherever he goes. At the opera, he is courted while she is humiliated.

The fascination of Anna is that she is, we feel, capable of almost anything. In one important perspective, her tragedy is that she is unable to lead even the limited 'full life' open to women, and, more profoundly and simply, that she is a woman. Having become Vronsky's 'mistress' she is consigned to a role in which her sexual attractiveness is her only means of self-satisfaction; if she loses Vronsky, she loses everything. Dolly's situation in the home of the philandering Stiva shows how even the woman who finds satisfaction in the socially acceptable role of mother and housewife is at the mercy of men in a male world, but Anna has moved beyond such a role into one much more narrowing. Since she can only be sure of Vronsky when he is with her and making love to her, she must fascinate him sexually. Committing herself to him, she has in effect dedicated herself to her own body, as we infer when she kisses her own hand. She is developing the mentality of a courtesan. She tries to enchant Levin when he calls, and she succeeds. But there is still more to her than that. Levin finds her intelligent and sincere. These and other qualities which we know she really possesses are now shut into a house where no respectable woman calls.

But then, even if she were still Karenin's wife, they would have no outlet. Russia has no role for such a woman, unless it is throwing bombs at the Tsar. Tolstoy's genius makes us fcel the waste of her. No character in fiction is less 'idealized'. She is in the end a frightening, quarrelsome creature obsessed with herself and her own frustration and, like the patient, honourable Vronsky we may find it hard not to recoil from her. Yet she is still a woman of energy and charm, of real capacity and endless potentiality. We loathe and admire her. We cannot merely 'pity' her, though pity is all she gets, even from Levin and Dolly. We have to *become* her, as Tolstoy has become her, and not only watch but participate as her life narrows from the abundance of promise displayed in the early scenes to the treadmill of jealous copulation which she escapes from only to self-destruction.

But we must also pity her, because Levin and Dolly do. We are made to see her not only from her point of view, but from theirs. We could not be more 'inside' a character than we are 'inside' Anna when she takes her last journey to death and Tolstoy uses methods which anticipate the 'stream of consciousness' in Joyce and Faulkner. But the novel goes on for fifty pages after her death and in those pages Levin, in spite of temptation, does *not* commit suicide. Nor do he and his friends brood over Anna.

We don't know if Mikhailov is a good painter. We only know that his work impresses Anna, Vronsky and Levin. We can't say that Anna is really a great woman lost to the ranks of greatness. We only know that Kitty is infatuated by her, that Vronsky is enslaved by her, that Karenin, who takes her for granted, misses her in her absence, that her son adores her and that Levin admires her when he is pretty tight. We know also that she is the sister of Stiva, that sensualist who is so much 'himself' when he sprays his body with scent, tears quivering oysters from their pearly shells, whispers wicked things to Betsy and sniffs the leather of a new cigarette case. Stiva, of

Tolstoy on his estate Yasnaya Polyana in 1908.

course, is delightful. We are as relieved as Levin when a guest arrives and it proves not to be the agonized Nikolai but cheerful old Stiva, everyone's favourite, smoothing the movements of society's wheels with his 'almond-oil' smile. But Stiva is also supremely selfish. And Anna, too, is an Oblonsky.

We see Anna as part of a thronging world, and from many viewpoints. Her situation at every point is relative. She is jealous. So is Kitty. She loves Vronsky. So did Kitty. She 'commits adultery' and suffers terribly. Betsy does so too, and is unscathed. Stiva has nothing to fear from the judgements of society; his liaisons, like Levin's wild oats, are accepted as normal for a man. Vronsky only suffers (but less than Anna) because he contracts what his own immoral mother so much dislikes—a serious passion. Vronsky and Anna suffer because they are committed to each other so fully that a 'normal', discreet liaison is impossible. But this doesn't prove that their behaviour is justified.

The dogged Dolly, losing her grief in her housework but still somehow remaining independent, is an even more important counterweight to Anna than the growing, but still girlish, Kitty. No matter how much we may believe that Anna deserves fulfillment, when we see her country household and her unhappiness through the eyes of Dolly we are left in no doubt that Dolly the busy mother is both a luckier and a more valuable woman—in sober fact, in Russia, in the 1870s—than the Anna who is so indifferent to her child by Vronsky. And the husband she has left invites, in his narrower way, the same kind of double response as Anna does. We may loathe in him the consummate bureaucrat altogether adapted to his anti-human work, and yet feel for him as the vulnerable, unloved man who

has been unable to give way to his feelings and finds out their value only too late. Anna may see, and make us feel, that with him she lives in a cold world of lies. But she herself lies to him, and hates him.

Anna cannot transcend the life of the book, which is the life of a 'society'. She is trapped in a web of relativities and cannot fly out to stand before us as a clear and simple moral symbol. We may locate her tragedy in this fact; she is only what she can be in the world which she lives in, and she wants to be much more. She cannot help feeling guilty about her adutlery. She must still hanker for her beloved son and weigh Serezha against Vronsky. She can't write great books, when she starts to write, because she doesn't have the experience to be a great writer, and she couldn't be a great architect because her education, like that of most women of her time, is so imperfect. Even if she had been a man and a politician, she could only have followed Karenin into the aridities of bureaucracy, or Vronsky into the inanities of 'nobility politics'. The laws of history which govern her existence, like those which governed the war of 1812, are inflexibly limiting. Yet Tolstoy as he wrote about her knew that the world was changing—mostly in directions he didn't like—and doesn't attempt any lordly clarification of the Russian scene in the mid 1870s to match his second Epilogue to *War and Peace*. From the flux of values and conventions, different circumstances could emerge in which she might realize more of what is in her. She is free, as Pierre was, and her freedom like his includes the capacity to imagine a world transformed. As she reads her English novel in the train, she thinks of a different society, of a different world, and of herself taking part in it.

But Levin is free. Vronsky is free. They too pitch hope against limitation. And Anna, for Vronsky, becomes a limitation.

Anna is always insisting that she is not to blame, and after her humiliation at the opera she cries to Vronsky, 'it's all your fault', though in fact he appealed to her not to go. It is the most impressive feature of Vronsky's sharply limited personality that, until just before the end, he does accept the blame for what goes wrong. No one can miss the parallel Tolstoy sets up between Anna and the horse whose back Vronsky breaks in a race. He admits to himself at once that the loss of the race is his own fault. With ironic significance, he is busy selling a pedigree horse when, for the first time, he abdicates responsibility and tells himself that he is 'not to blame in any way' for what proves to be the final crisis of his relationship with Anna.

Men are on top in this world; they ride women like horses. If Vronsky is so ready to accept responsibility, this is in tune with his male confidence and arrogance. If Anna shirks it, this reflects the fact that she has never been educated to see herself as someone accountable for what happens to her. And Tolstoy never explicitly moralizes against Anna.

It might be objected here that the book's epigraph—'Vengeance is mine and I will repay'—implies that Anna gets what she deserves. But in that case, why doesn't Tolstoy punish Stiva and Betsy? He clearly isn't implying—he simply couldn't imply—that sin leads inevitable to punishment on this earth. The motto would seem to suggest, rather, that God has the right to punish, men don't. The 'society' of forty or so exalted people in Petersburg which ostracizes Anna is so amoral, or immoral, in its own standards that it above all has no right to judge her. Levin and Dolly, who might seem to have such a right are, on the contrary, very sympathetic to her. More than once, phrases in the novel remind us of the biblical verdict that only those without sin have a right to cast stones. After Anna's death, that persistent adulteress, Vronsky's mother, proclaims that 'she ended as such a woman deserved to end. Even the death she chose was low and vulgar.' But the likeable Koznyshev retorts, with a sigh, 'It is not for us to judge, countess.

The judger of *War and Peace* has given way to a novelist who presents moral riddles but can't presume to solve them. Perhaps only the squawk of sour rhetoric he directs against the doctor who examines Kitty at the beginning of the second book can be clearly shown to be in the vein of his assault on Napoleon in *War and Peace.* We can't justly accuse him of 'murdering' Anna to satisfy a moralist's prejudice against adultery. If we leave out of account certain things he said about her outside the book, and concentrate only on the text itself, we must conclude that Anna is presented with full compassion as a woman destroyed by forces within herself which are both created by, and in reaction against, the society in which she moves. Tolstoy's very methods in this novel preclude decisive moral judgement. (pp. 214-20)

Angus Calder, "Man, Woman and Male Woman: Tolstoy's 'Anna Karenina' and After," in his Russia Discovered: Nineteenth-Century Fiction from Pushkin to Chekhov, *Barnes and Noble Books, 1976, pp. 211-36.*

EDWARD WASIOLEK   (essay date 1978)

[*Wasiolek is an American critic and translator specializing in Russian literature, particularly the work of Fedor Dostoevski. In the following excerpt, Wasiolek examines Tolstoy's characteriza-tion of Anna and finds her passionate, troubled nature a reflection of the crisis Tolstoy himself was experiencing at the time he was writing his novel. For further discussion on Tolstoy's psychological portraiture, see the excerpts by Konstantin Leontiev (1890) and Leon Edel (1961). For another biographical reading of the novel, see the excerpt by J. B. Priestley (1960).*]

Anna Karenina is two novels, Anna's and Levin's. The novel about Kitty's and Levin's love is a familiar cartography, populated with people, situations, and values that we have met before [in Tolstoy's works]. We are not surprised that the peasants resist Levin's attempts at agricultural reform, that conscious goodness such as Mme Stahl's will be disapproved, that the abstract intellectualism of Koznyshev, especially when it is used in the service of the public good, will be caricatured, and that true love will have something to do with bearing and bringing up children. Levin's novel has a pastoral quality, not unlike some of the scenes in *War and Peace.* The mowing scene reminds us of the hunt scene in *War and Peace;* like the hunt scene it celebrates mysterious self-absorption in immediate reality and the at-one-ness with others by way of that self-absorption. Levin's novel is a continuation of Tolstoy's art and a reaffirmation of his vision. The novel about Anna's and Vronsky's love is something we have not met before in Tolstoy's work. Anna and the destructive passions that she embodies are enigmatic. Her love is an eruption of something almost demonic into the calm world of Tolstoy. Her appearance at this juncture of Tolstoy's work and the persuasiveness with which she dominates the novel comes from something unsettling in Tolstoy's horizon—something he was loath to confront.

Anna Karenina was written at a time when Tolstoy was going through a series of personal crises. There were three deaths in his family in the early 1870s; there was the feel of death at Arzamas; and there was the fact that he was in his middle years with all the reassessment and changed consciousness that the diminution of sensuous vitality brings. We know from his letters and diaries that he found the writing of *Anna Karenina* difficult to sustain; he found the work unpleasant, he was impatient to finish it, and he considered the end product to be repulsive. All the evidence seems to indicate that he was writing something that went against the grain of his conscious beliefs but which was nevertheless true. It was about this time that he stated in a letter to Strakhov (his close friend and a sympathetic critic) about *Anna Karenina* that it was impossible to lie in art without destroying the art. He may have told the truth in *Anna Karenina,* but he didn't like the truth. What appalled him about Anna's fate and what appalls us in its reading is the change that occurs in her person. She changes from a beautiful, warm person to one who becomes increasingly querulous, petty, and vicious. We are so moved by compassion for her suffering that we tend to overlook the fund of sheer nastiness in her by the end of the novel. Something in the love she bears Vronsky turns her from life to death and from love to hate. It is this something that constitutes the chief problem for explication in the novel. And it was this something that constituted a threat to everything that Tolstoy had believed up to this point.

Tolstoy had, of course, depicted love and physical passion in the works before *Anna Karenina:* there are seductions, romantic flights, and even irrational actions following on the impulses of physical passion. But they are treated lightly, as if whatever interference they posed in the good life could be easily disposed of. Masha in *Family Happiness* is estranged from her husband by the unnatural life she leads in the city. Among the banalities she experiences and finally discerns is the banality of romantic love, but no tragic consequences ensue; she feels only repulsion for the passionate Italian and ends up wiser and happier in the embraces of her middle-aged husband. The seduction of the mother and the near seduction of the daughter in **The Two Hussars** are both trivial and foolish—in different ways—and both are treated as escapades rather than personal crises. Indeed, the sex is incidental. The important point is the depiction of the virtues of one generation and the decay of those virtues in another generation. Even in **War and Peace** Tolstoy shows no consciousness of the destructive consequences of passion. Natasha's head is turned by Anatole, and she suffers disgrace; but time and the ministrations to the needs of others bring her to "natural" health and the dissipation of further romantic fantasies. Tolstoy depicts Natasha's love for Anatole as momentary foolishness, not as a tormenting part of her makeup. Physical passion and the temporary derangements of orderly life that it entails are treated in the early works as "errors" that experience, proper conditions, and the counsel of others correct. Princess Ellen and the coarse sensuality she embodies would seem to be an exception. But that is precisely what she is, an exception—an evil, coarse very stupid woman who has little place in Tolstoy's conception of life. He makes his nod to the existence of such creatures, showing his impatience with her by the sudden, unmotivated way in which he eliminates her from the novel and from his world.

There is no indication in Tolstoy's early works that a woman who lived in essentially beneficent conditions and one that was warm, intelligent, vital, sincere, and honest could be carried away by physical passion to the point of sacrificing her reputation, peace of mind, son, and even her life for the satisfaction of that passion. Tolstoy made his peace with the Betsy Tverskoys and Liza Merkalovs before **Anna Karenina,** but Anna herself was something new. Significantly, the early drafts of **Anna Karenina** show her to be a foolish, coarse woman. It is only reluctantly that Tolstoy comes to give her the redeeming moral traits that loom so large in the novel and which provoke so powerfully our sympathy. Yet it is as if in writing **Anna Karenina** Tolstoy perceived, as he had not done before, the full force of physical passion. Before she is carried away by her passion for Vronsky, Anna has been able to preserve her integrity in a corrupt society. Indeed, her passion is expressly differentiated from the banal passions of others in society, indicating that it is of a different order. If this is so, then nature itself, uncorrupted by false education, does not—contrary to what Tolstoy had long believed—automatically assure true forms of feeling. It appears, then, that it is not bad conditions that create false passion, but passion that creates false conditions. It is only after she is swept away by physical passion that the "unnatural" forms invade her life; that she flirts, lives abroad, exposes herself to foreign influences, disregards her maternal duties, uses birth control, and becomes dishonest, hypocritical, evasive, insensitive, and ugly in character. The very things that in other works would have explained why she had been swept away by physical passion become themselves the consequences and not the causes of the passion.

If then Anna's fate has not been caused by the corrupting influences around her, then the physical passion must have another source. But if the physical passion and its destructive attributes are something innate, something given, then they must be something in the order of nature. If this is so, then much of Tolstoy's edifice comes crashing down. It will not be enough to peal off the leaves of the onion to find the magic core; the core itself may be rotten. Tolstoy in the writing of **Anna Karenina** is at the point of a truly tragic stance, the acknowledgment that evil exists and is inextirpable from human nature. Up to this point Tolstoy had been an optimistic writer. No matter how much corruption and disorder he had found in human life, truth, happiness, and plenitude were in the order of things. It was only human stupidity and the cumulative codification of that stupidity in the conventions by which men lived that had clogged the pure springs of life. Is it any wonder, if the writing of **Anna Karenina** forced him to confront a situation that belied something essential in his world outlook that he would feel a profound disgust with its writing and with art in general? He had, of course, almost from the beginning of his artistic career shown a suspicion of the ends of art and a distaste for his own part in furthering its ends. But never before had those feelings beset him with such intensity.

I am aware of course that, in the various explanations of why Anna degenerates as a person and commits suicide, the influence of a corrupt society is often put forth as a cause, as has been the tragic irreconcilability of love for both son and lover. But it is part of Tolstoy's magnificent art that he is able to engage our belief in what appear to be persuasive explanations, which nevertheless turn out to be untenable. Anna does not kill herself because God punishes her or because society punishes her, or because she cannot have both son and lover. She kills herself for reasons more obvious yet more mysterious than these. What makes her kill herself is the same force that at this point has such an unsettling and profound effect on Tolstoy's life and art. (pp. 129-32)

Why does Anna kill herself? The question asks why Anna degenerated from the life-loving, generous and humane person we first meet to the tormented, punishing, strife-ridden and strife-giving person she becomes at the end. One will want to exonerate Anna—to blame society, her husband, Vronsky, and surely to blame the conditions of her love. Good reasons can be found to exonerate her; Tolstoy gives us many. But although he loves Anna and weeps for her, Tolstoy is convinced that she is wrong and that the love she bears for Vronsky is wrong. To show that she is wrong he gives us a picture of the right kind of love in Kitty's and Levin's love. The contrast between those two loves embraces the structure of the novel. Tolstoy has worked out the contrast in a deliberate way. While Anna is falling in love with Vronsky, Levin is being rejected by Kitty. When Kitty and Levin are falling in love, Anna is on her deathbed, attempting to reconcile herself to Karenin, struggling to give up Vronsky. As Anna and Vronsky leave Russia to begin their restless and aimless travels, Kitty and Levin are married. When Anna and Vronsky return to Moscow to make one desperate attempt to get a divorce and resolve their situation, Kitty is having a baby, finding new bonds of love and companionship with Levin. When Anna kills herself, Levin finds the secret of life in the words of an ignorant peasant. By and large the novel describes the deterioration of Anna's and Vronsky's love and the growth toward maturity of Kitty's and Levin's love. Both couples face some of the same situations, but the situations separate Anna and Vronsky and they bring Kitty and Levin together. Kitty, like Anna, experiences irrational outbursts of jealousy; like Anna, she feels unloved at times. Levin, like Vronsky, feels put upon by the demands of his beloved. Yet, while jealous outbursts increase the strife between Vronsky and Anna, they give Levin insight into the complexities of Kitty's soul. After Levin returns late and tells Kitty that he has been drinking at the club with Oblonsky and Vronsky and has met Anna, Kitty is convinced irrationally that her husband is in love with Anna. But the assurances of Levin assure Kitty, and the assurances of Vronsky that he is not in love with Princess Sorokin do not assure Anna. Later that night, when Kitty begins her labor, one of the important bonds between the couple becomes manifest.

To account for the difference between Kitty's and Levin's "right" love, and Anna's and Vronsky's "wrong" love, one may say that the former is "natural" and the latter "unnatural." But it is not so easy so say why one is natural and the other is unnatural. The good marriage for Tolstoy is free of the vanities of social life, fixed in mutual obligation of practical work, characterized by devotion of the partners to each other; most of all it is based on the birth and rearing of children. Levin's and Kitty's union fulfills, or at least comes to fulfill, all of these conditions. But in large measure so does the union of Vronsky and Anna. They are surely devoted to each other, at least before the union begins to sour; Anna has a contempt for society and Vronsky comes to say that he has; they have a child; and for a time at least they are both engaged in practical work—Vronsky, like Levin, with the circumstances of agricultural work, and Anna in helping him in his work. Yet each of these conditions comes to separate them rathr than to unite them. Some incalculable element converts some of the same things into a warm, growing relationship for Kitty and Levin, and some incalculable element converts the love of Anna and Vronsky into a destructive, humiliating relationship. Kitty's and Levin's love ends, of course, in marriage and enjoys the approval of the society about them. There can be no doubt that the illicit relationship makes the love of Anna and Vronsky harder to maintain. But it is inconceivable that the legality of the one and the illegality of the other should explain the rightness and wrongness of the loves. Tolstoy makes it amply clear that he has nothing but contempt for much of what is approved by society. It is equally clear in his description of Anna's love that something deeper than the violation of convention lies at the basis of the destruction which overcomes that love.

This incalculable element cannot be the cruelty of the society in which Anna lives, nor the condition of irreconcilable love of son and lover, for the reasons I have already explained. Even less can it be what the epigraph suggests: that Anna suffers because she has sinned. Karenin thinks about God, but Anna does not. During her last day on earth Anna does not think about society, divorce, sin, or her son; she thinks only about Vronsky and his lack of love for her. Her last words are: "I will punish him and escape from everyone and from myself." She kills herself, at least as she explains it to herself, in order to punish Vronsky. This is not the first time that the thought of death has been linked in her mind with punishing Vronsky. It is, in fact, a repeated refrain. At the time of the quarrel about when to leave for the country, she solaces her "horrible shame" with the thought of death: how, if she died, Vronsky would repent, pity her, love her, and suffer for her. (pp. 150-52)

The shame, as well as the desire to punish Vronsky and herself, come for Tolstoy from the nature of the love itself. It is the love that is wrong, not Anna or Vronsky or Karenin or society. And what is wrong with the love, for Tolstoy, is that it is contaminated and corrupted by sexual passion, whereas Kitty's and Levin's love is not so contaminated. Tolstoy insists rather coarsely on the physical basis of Anna's love. The imagery used to describe the suicide is sexual: the huge railway car throws Anna on her back; the peasant who appears at this point and who has appeared in her dreams is probably a symbol of the remorseless, impersonal power of sex. As he beats the iron, he pays no attention to her. In an early instance of the dream that she recounted to Vronsky, the bearded peasant (who mutters French phrases) runs into her bedroom. Vronsky too associates his dream of the peasant with the hideous things that he had to witness in conducting the visiting foreign prince about town. The last agonizing hours she spends on earth are also filled with sexual references. There is the explicit acknowledgment that she cannot live without Vronsky's caresses; she shudders with the imaginary physical caresses on her back as she stands in front of a mirror examining her hair. She sees the world about her as dirty, and such dirt is associated with shame and with the self-hate resulting from the slavery of sex. She reacts to children buying ice cream by the bitter acknowledgment that she has lived only for her dirty appetites, as do all people. On the train she mentally undresses a stout woman dressed in a bustle and finds her hideous.

It is the nature of physical passion that works for the destruction of Anna's and Vronsky's love, brings them to hatred of each other, brings Anna to hatred of herself, makes their relationship more and more spectral, breaks down the communication between them, brings them into a situation where they cannot speak frankly to each other, makes them avoid certain subjects, and forces them to surround themselves with other people so as to make each other's presence tolerable. Kitty's and Levin's relationship, on the other hand, is free of passion: they argue, work together; they feel close and at moments drift apart; they love each other and the love grows and prospers, but there is no indication on the part of either that the body of each is in some way the basis of their closeness. Kitty's and Levin's union is uncontaminated by sex. (pp. 152-53)

Tolstoy sees sex as a massive intrusion on a person's being and a ruthless obliteration of the sanctity of personhood. Both Anna and Vronsky feel coerced and manipulated by the other. The stronger Anna loves, the more she coerces and the more she alienates. The corrupting power of sex seems to be an extreme example of what Tolstoy has always been against: the attempt of the individual to make the world one's own and the consequent impoverishing and desiccating effect that such coercion has on the world about one. The truth he reaches in *War and Peace* consists of the consciousness of the plenitude of life that one attains when one gives up one's control of the world. The centers of being of others with all their radical uniqueness come into consciousness only when one permits them to so arise. The right love also, for Tolstoy, comes into being under the same conditions. And although it happens for Kitty and Levin, one cannot avoid the feeling that the love is there to assure Tolstoy that what he has believed in is still valid: that one can find wisdom, happiness, peace, fulfillment, no matter how powerfully Anna's story seems to argue the existence of something in nature that makes these things impossible.

Such an explanation of Anna's deterioration and death is consistent both with Tolstoy's view of life and with the course of Anna's actions in the novel. Anna's is a possessive love. Feeding on its possession, the love alienates or destroys what it attempts to possess. Tolstoy signals this in the seduction scene, when he compares the act of physical love to an act of murder; this is for him no idle conceit, for possessive love does kill what he considers to be the fount of a person's being—something sacrosanct, radically individual, belonging to no man but only to the self-in-God. Vronsky resents Anna's invasions of his personality, reacts unfavorably to her attempts to coerce him into undivided attention to her; yet his very resistance provokes Anna to demand more and more. The duel of control and resistance leads Anna to more and more hysterical attempts and to resentment too, because of his refusal to give himself entirely to her. Suicide thus becomes the final attempt to control his being by way of guilt. Tolstoy has built into the structure of the novel a fairly probable course for Anna'a actions that is in keeping with his personal distaste for sexual love. He has in short been able to generalize what is personal and for many a bizarre view of sexual love, and to incorporate it into his general views about what desiccates life and what makes it flourish.

What is more, with his immense talent he has been able to dramatize the course of such a love so that it appears persuasive in its consequences. All this is Tolstoy's reading; yet it is not the only reading that the text will support. There is, of course, a presumptive validity to what the author has on some discernible level of structure led the reader to believe; yet the reader is not bound to accept—and, indeed, in some cases must not accept—the author's intentional structure as the definitive structure of the novel. I am talking about an intentionalism that one can discern in the novel, not one pronounced by the author in letter or diary. Wimsatt and Beardsley disposed of the latter some decades ago, but the "intentional fallacy" disposed of one kind of intentionalism and obscured another. The personal predilections, even eccentricities, shape the inner relations of the text in an inescapable way. The author's text is only one of many. Otherwise the text would be the prisoner of a special personality; no matter how great, it would still be limited and fixed in a special time. Anna's fate continues to provoke in us powerful feelings of compassion and mystery for reasons other than those Tolstoy has worked into the structure of the novel. Tolstoy has drawn a powerful portrait of a woman tortured and torturing, loving and hurting and being hurt. The portrait moves us as powerfully as it did Tolstoy's contemporaries, but for different reasons—reasons supported by structures in the text. Tolstoy's views on sex were already extreme at the time he wrote *Anna Karenina;* they are bizarre today. If Anna's terrible fate is the consequence of her sexual love and its evil nature, as Tolstoy would have us believe, and if this were the only explanation that the text could support, then I do not believe the novel would continue to move us as deeply as it does. There seems little doubt that in reading *Anna Karenina* we are in the presence of one of those great texts, the structure of which is multiple and which in its richness can support a great number—perhaps an inexhaustible number—of explanations. (pp. 154-55)

After *Anna Karenina* and the ten-year hiatus in his creative work which followed upon his religious conversion, Tolstoy wrote principally only about two things: sex and death. The two were associated in his mind. Sex for him serves death, as it does in *Anna Karenina,* almost in eerie anticipation of the Marcusian interpretation of Freud, in which the sexual impulse is seen to be in the service of the death instinct. Tolstoy saw sexual passion as degrading, and destructive of man's spiritual self. Many of his works after the conversion, at the time of his renewed interest in creative writing, are campaigns against the corrupting attributes of sex, as *The Devil, Father Sergius* and *The Kreutzer Sonata* eloquently show.

The Kreutzer Sonata was to summarize Tolstoy's feelings of disgust with sex. Absent from this novel is the sympathy Tolstoy had felt for Anna in the grip of passion. The dogmatism and intractability always just under the surface of his views burst forth to bludgeon the reader. Love, or what the world called love, was for him not only stupid but degrading and repulsive. It was more than that: it destroyed everything human in people and in the end destroyed the people themselves. There are hints of this in *Anna Karenina,* though the compassion with

which Tolstoy treats Anna's life mitigates what she does to herself. Anna is wrong and Levin is right; there can be no doubt about that; but even if wrong, she is still to be loved and pitied. In *The Kreutzer Sonata,* however, there are no such mitigations: those who give themselves to sex are lunatics and ugly, vicious people, and the world which encourages such love is ugly and vicious. Even in marriage, sex is repulsive and destructive. (pp. 162-63)

In *Anna Karenina* Tolstoy perceived for the first time the destructive power of physical passion. His inability to explain its place in the world he had created up to then produced that troubling ambiguity of attraction and fear that we feel in the presence of Anna's enigmatic fate. It was Tolstoy's incertitude that abetted the peculiar suspension of judgment characteristic of the novel. By the time he wrote *The Kreutzer Sonata* he had come to terms with the new force and was once again the dogmatist bent on annihilating what he could not answer. (pp. 163-64)

> *Edward Wasiolek, in his* Tolstoy's Major Fiction, *The University of Chicago Press, 1978, 255 p.*

MARTIN GREEN (essay date 1983)

[*Green is an English critic who has been praised for his expertise in blending non-literary perspectives—including anthropology, science, religion, and politics—into studies focusing on literature and literary figures. In his* Tolstoy and Ghandi: Men of Peace, *Green offers an extensive consideration and comparison of the life and works of two different men who ultimately arrived at remarkably similar ethical and philosophical conclusions. Setting the ascetic world-renunciation of Tolstoy and Mohandas Ghandi in opposition to the possessiveness of modern economic and military imperialism, Green finds that "the only men who, in their time, said no to life with authority were Tolstoy and Ghandi." "Tolstoy and Ghandi's faith," Green further states in the introduction to his study, "was essentially antihumanist. They saw humanism as the self-indulgent world view of the ruling classes of great empires." In the following excerpt, Green examines how the beginnings of the negative, antivitalist doctrine developed by Tolstoy later in his life may be seen in* Anna Karenina.]

In *Anna Karenina,* as Tolstoy said, the main "idea" is the family. The hero becomes himself, saves himself from tormenting problems, by marrying, and marriage attracts him because it means family:

> Strange as it may seem, Konstantin Levin was definitely in love with the whole family, and especially the feminine half of it. Levin himself did not remember his mother, and his only sister was older than himself, so that in the home of the Shcherbatskys he found himself for the first time in the environment of a cultured and honorable old aristocratic family, of which he had been deprived by the death of his own father and mother.

Levin's own house (recognizably [Tolstoy's estate] Yasnaya Polyana) was a whole world to him. "It was the world in which his father and mother had lived and died. They had lived the sort of life which seemed to Levin the ideal of perfection, and which he had dreamed of restoring with a wife and family of his own." These passages are obviously autobiographical. They also ally marriage and family to tradition and the aristocratic caste, and so defy the most powerful current of opinion in Russia when Tolstoy was writing. *Anna Karenina* celebrated the family in defiance of radicals, revolutionaries, and nihilists.

The story of Levin and Kitty carries this theme; and contrastive but consonant in the meaning is the story of unmarried love, embodied in Anna and Vronsky. This is the material which was new, both new because it was not to be found in *War and Peace,* and generically "modern" in that the story involves modern social features like divorce, birth control, contemporary fashions; and new in the sense that it resembled European modern novels, especially French ones. This meant, for instance, an exploration of the ways hatred can be involved with love, desire with repulsion, as it is between Anna and Vronsky at the end, and the ways the body itself speaks against the mind and the soul—forbidding Anna, for instance, to feel anything but hatred for her husband even when he is being generous.

It is then primarily an erotic novel. There are other elements, but they are subordinate. And seen as an erotic novel, the two poles of its emotional current are pride and humiliation. Certain qualities—calm, pride, gaiety, strength, beauty, goodness, love—are stressed and interlinked as values. Kitty early thinks of Vronsky's "strong manly face, his great calm, and his goodness that came out in everything he did." These are all different aspects of manly vitality, the animating energy of life values. Correspondingly, Vronsky noted Anna's animation, ". . . which seemed to flutter between her brilliant eyes and the barely perceptible smile that curved her red lips. It was as though her entire being were brimming over with something that against her will expressed itself now in the sparkle of her eyes, now in her smile." At the opposite pole to that are the images of humiliation, of suicide, shame, deceit, jealousy, hatred, of something broken and hanging down, as in Levin's feeling when his proposal is rejected, or Kitty's reaction when she realizes that Vronsky is in love with Anna and is overcome with terror and despair.

On the whole, the images of pride are associated primarily with the illicit lovers, and humiliation with those who seek marriage. But there is a dialectic of progression, for if the former association makes a clear pattern at the beginning of the book, by the end it is Kitty who is proud, calm, happy, strong, and so on, and Anna who is broken and humiliated in every way.

However, there is a third set of images, associated with other characters in the book, which are described in terms like flat, thin, dry, clumsy, cold. The most obvious case of a personality summed up in those terms is Karenin, and they clearly convey his failure in eroticism. Eros can find no lodging within him, cannot inhabit and animate his body; this Rhadamanthine truth is embodied in his ears, fingers, voice, thighs,—things he cannot change—as well as in the behavior he is morally responsible for. But the same terms are applied to another character who is yet ranked as being somehow on the side of life—Dolly, Anna's sister-in-law. Eros, or Venus, has had but a brief lodging in her and will never return; that is what her thin hair and wrinkles tell us, but Magna Mater (motherhood) has replaced Eros. Dolly does not, like Karenin, lack all grace and warmth in personal relations. She in fact, visiting Anna in the country, comes off best in the contrast. Another pair characterized by the same polar terms, though less completely contrasted, are Levin's brother Sergei, whose mind is completely rational; and Kitty's friend Varenka, who is religious. There is the same contrast; in the woman's case the condemnation by Eros is softened or blurred by a suggestion that she may have gained more than she lost by becoming the temple of agape instead. The characterization of the man, on the other hand, suggests that Eros is an all-dominant deity, and his is the final judgment.

This conflict of values is not resolved within the novel, no doubt because it was far from resolved within the writer. The novel's dominant scheme of meaning is erotic, and all of the four characters just discussed are harshly treated at one point or another, while the four main and dominant characters are all characterized by their eroticism, Kitty and Levin as much as Anna and Vronsky. We are told that Varenka is good-looking but not attractive to men. "She was like a beautiful flower which, though its petals had not yet begun to droop, was already faded and without fragrance. Besides, she could not be attractive to men because she lacked that which Kitty had too much of—the suppressed fire of life and the consciousness of her own attractiveness." In that "too much," brushed aside in a first reading as a mere intensifier, lies the seed of Tolstoy's later judgments. Levin says that his brother "can't come to terms with reality, and Varenka is after all a reality." This is very like the harsher judgment of Karenin: "Karenin was face to face with life. . . . And every time he had come up against life itself, he had kept aloof from it." Thus Koznishev and Varenka do not marry, and Kitty explains why to her husband in the metaphor of two kinds of kissing:

> 'This is what I mean,' she said, taking her husband's hand, raising it to her mouth and just touching it with closed lips. 'The way one kisses a bishop's hand.' 'Who isn't biting?' he said, laughing. 'Neither. This is how it should have been. . . .' 'Some peasants are coming. . . .' 'They didn't see. . . .'

This is one of the moments the later Tolstoy must have considered vulgar, both in its elliptical and suggestive technique, and in its triumphal preference for the appetitive.

The world of the novel is erotic, and while within it the reader is bound to sympathize with Anna when he reads:

> 'He's in the right! In the right!' she said. 'Of course, he's always in the right! He's a Christian! He's magnanimous! Yes, the mean disgusting man! And no-one understands it except me. . . . They don't know how for eight years he has crushed my life, crushed everything alive in me, that he has never once thought that I was a live woman in need of love. . . . But the time came when I realized that I couldn't deceive myself any longer, that I was alive, that I couldn't be blamed if God had made me so, that I have to love and live.'

And this is exactly what Kitty says to Varenka: "'I can't live except as my heart dictated, but you live according to rules. I have grown fond of you just because I felt like it, but I expect you did so only in order to save me, to teach me.'" Kitty and Anna are sure they are right, because their drives come from the unconscious.

The treatment of the religious life, as embodied in Madame Stahl and Lidia Ivanova, is cruelly satirical and hostile; it is erotic values that are accepted and the rest of life is seen from that point of view. Of course eroticism extends to more than sensuality—Eros is the son of Magna Mater, the goddess of fertility and the love of children. Dolly is glad that Levin could see her with her children—"in all her glory. No-one could appreciate her splendour better than Levin." This is the im-

perialism of the world of women. Eros also implies the glorification of the body, as a way of knowing as well as a thing
known. Levin is like Anna and Stiva (and Kitty) in forwarding
his physical sensations. His brother is sitting indoors when
Levin bursts in, "his matted hair clinging to his perspiring
forehead and his back and chest black with moisture. 'We've
mown the whole meadow!' he cried joyfully. 'Oh, I feel so
good, so wonderful! And how did you spend your time?' he
inquired, completely forgetting their unpleasant conversation
of the previous day." He imposes his physical sensations upon
his brother as a charter to his personality and to the life he will
share with him. He brings his sensations to the other person
as wealth, as achievement. Similarly, Stiva had "a physical
impact that cheers people up," and the old prince, Kitty's
father, "communicated his high spirits to everyone."

These sensations derive their value from their freshness, from
their recent emergence from the unconscious. During the mowing we are told that:

> . . . more and more often now came those mo-
> ments of insensibility when it was possible not
> to think about what one was doing. The scythe
> cut of itself. Those were happy moments . . .
> it was not that his arms swung the scythe, but
> that the scythe itself made his whole body, full
> of life and conscious of itself, move after it,
> and as though by magic the work did itself, of
> its own accord and without a thought being
> given to it, with the utmost precision and reg-
> ularity. Those were the most blessed moments.

A natural extension of this is the character of Levin's sincerity,
which rejects all conscious system and stability, whether in the
world or in a man's beliefs. "'Well, you see,' said Oblonsky,
'You are a thoroughly earnest and sincere man. This is your
strength and your limitation . . . you want life to be earnest
and sincere too, but it never is.'" Thus, Levin always reacts
against established truths, and is a negative and critical mind
despite his naiveté. This is what we might call his authenticity—he is like Rousseau or Alceste—and it depends on his
staying dissatisfied. His search for values delights us as readers,
like the instinctive behavior of an animal, for example, Keats's
stoat. But a rational, and even an irrational, philosophy, when
completely worked out, is bound to seem inferior, as it does
in figures like Koznyshev. The reader contemplates the characters from the heights of Olympus (as Keats suggests) and
he/she is bored or offended by men who are not "graceful and
instinctive" like the stoat, but dead certain. The reader is both
naive and dialectical. He knows that indirect evocation and
even inarticulacy are better than analysis and rhetoric. (Readers
who have been taught this are proportionately disappointed by
Tolstoy's religious writings after 1881.)

This dominant scheme of values is all a defense and glorification of the marriage and family scene at Yasnaya Polyana.
But there are manifestations of other feelings, rebellions against
that scheme. The most important occur in the treatment of
Karenin's repentance, and his humiliation, and self-sacrifice.
Karenin's tragedy is summed up in terms of two laws. "He
felt that in addition to the beneficent spiritual force that governed his heart, there was another force, harsh and powerful,
if not indeed more powerful, which governed his life, and that
this force would not let him have the humble peace he longed
for." This force emanates, of course, from institutionalized
Eros—that socially though tacitly prescribed animality which
drives the social world, and on whose behalf that world was

punishing Karenin. "Never before had the impossibility of his
position in the eyes of the world, and his wife's hatred of him,
and altogether that harsh mysterious force which, contrary to
his inner mood, governed his life and demanded fulfillment of
its decrees and a change in his attitude to his wife, appeared
as evident as it did now."

It is of course possible for the reader to leave that problem,
that conflict of laws, merely as "tragedy"; or to regard the
novel's motto ("Vengeance is mine, sayeth the Lord") and
the sinister glow of love happiness on Anna's face ("the terrible
glow of a fire on a dark night,") as merely marking unmarried
love off from married. But the distinction between the two is
not an important one within the scheme of erotic values, and
so to build large emotions upon it seems intellectually external
here, and morally vulgar. The novel is saved from that reproach
only when one realizes that Tolstoy was deeply ambivalent
about this question and was in fact half ready to reject Anna
and prefer Karenin.

The novel is in fact conservative in its technique and erotic
philosophy, and allied to this is Tolstoy's conservative feeling
about the peasants and about history. Levin believes that:

> Russia's poverty was not only caused by a wrong
> distribution of land and a false agricultural pol-
> icy, but that of late years it was fostered by an
> alien civilization artificially grafted on Russia,
> particularly by the means of communication,
> that is, the railways . . . [which] had come pre-
> maturely, and instead of promoting agriculture,
> as had been expected, had outstripped it, and
> by stimulating the development of industry and
> credit facilities had arrested its progress. . . .

This is in line with the Gandhi criticism of capitalist development, of course. But it was as yet allied to quite imperialist
ideas about the expanding power of the Russian people:

> In his opinion, the Russian people, whose des-
> tiny it was to populate and cultivate enormous
> unoccupied tracts of land consciously, till all
> those lands had been occupied, kept to the
> methods best suited for that purpose, and those
> methods were not by any means as bad as was
> generally thought.

Of course, this was not state or government imperialism, and
Tolstoy took a different view of that. In the final chapters, he
satirized the contemporary Russian enthusiasm for a war against
Turkey in the Balkans, to liberate fellow Slavs and create a
new sphere of influence for Russia. His attitude was so "unpatriotic," so anti-imperialist, that Katkov refused to publish
those chapters as part of the novel (which was being serialized
in his magazine). But the grounds of Tolstoy's opposition to
the war were not radical but conservative, not passionate but
skeptical.

This skeptical conservatism is embodied in the figure of the
old prince Shcherbatsky, Kitty's father, a minor character but
important in the value structure of the novel. Dostoevsky pointed
out the unacceptable moral prominence of this figure, to whom
Tolstoy ascribes importance on the grounds of hearty healthi-
ness (that is, a determination to be ordinary) and a shrewd
though limited judgment (a shrewd insistence on accepting
ordinary limits). On these scanty grounds, Tolstoy asks us to
accept the old prince's judgments on war and politics, on Madame Stahl and Varenka, on intellectuals, and history. He

associates Kitty with her father, in the scene where she condemns Koznishev and Varenka as unerotic, as a way to endorse the former pair. The prince's is the voice of a seasoned eroticism on public matters. This aspect of the novel is indeed vulgar.

In *A Confession* (written 1879-1880, immediately after the novel) Tolstoy explained why he turned away from the kind of art that *Anna Karenina* represented: "It was plain to me that art is an adornment to life, an allurement to life. But life had lost attraction for me—so how could I attract others." "The power which drew me away from life was stronger, fuller, and more widespread than any mere wish. It was a force similar to the former striving to live, only in a contrary direction. All my strength drew me away from life." (pp. 148-55)

> *Martin Green, "Manhood," in his* Tolstoy and Gandhi, Men of Peace: A Biography, *Basic Books, Inc., Publishers, 1983, pp. 105-71.**

ADDITIONAL BIBLIOGRAPHY

Black, Michael. *"Anna Karenina."* In his *The Literature of Fidelity,* pp. 103-24. New York: Barnes and Noble, 1975.
Explores Tolstoy's use of the theme of the search for self-fulfillment in *Anna Karenina.*

Boyd, Alexander F. "An Anatomy of Marriage: Leo Tolstoy and *Anna Karenina.*" In his *Aspects of the Novel,* pp. 87-108. Totowa, N.J.: Rowan and Littlefield, 1972.
Discussion of Tolstoy's views on marriage and the role of women in society, with particular reference to how these ideas are reflected in his novel *Anna Karenina.*

Gifford, Henry. "D. H. Lawrence and Anna Karenina: Anna, Lawrence and 'The Law'." In *Russian Literature and Modern English Fiction,* edited by Donald Davie, pp. 148-63. Chicago: University of Chicago Press, 1965.
Review of Lawrence's criticisms of *Anna Karenina.* Gifford explains that Lawrence found fault with Tolstoy for his condemnation of Anna and Vronsky's "true and natural" love. Lawrence contended that Tolstoy's only reason for condemning the lovers was that their affair violated his philosophical principles.

Gorodetzky, Nadezhda. *"Anna Karenina."* The Slavic and East European Review XXIV, No. 63 (January 1946): 121-26.
Discussion of the theme of family life and the meaning of Anna's "homelessness" in *Anna Karenina.*

Grossman, Joan Delaney. "Tolstoy's Portrait of Anna: Keystone in the Arch." *Criticism* XVIII, No. 1 (Winter 1976): 1-14.
Discussion centered on the significance of Anna's meeting with Levin in *Anna Karenina.* Grossman analyzes the components of the scene when Anna and Levin meet, and its structural importance in the novel, noting especially the part that Anna's portrait plays in shaping Levin's response to her.

Hardy, Barbara. "Form and Freedom: Tolstoy's *Anna Karenina.*" In her *The Appropriate Form,* pp. 174-211. London: Athlone Press, 1964.
Structural analysis of *Anna Karenina.* Hardy examines the structure of Tolstoy's novel in relation to the works of such novelists as Henry James, D. H. Lawrence, and George Eliot.

Jahn, Gary R. "The Image of the Railroad in *Anna Karenina.*" *Slavic and East European Journal* 25, No. 2 (Summer 1981): 1-10.
Examines Tolstoy's use of the railroad as both an image and a structural device in *Anna Karenina.* Jahn postulates that the railroad functions in the novel as a symbol for "the social aspect of human existence."

Jones, Malcolm V. "Problems of Communication in *Anna Karenina.*" In *New Essays on Tolstoy,* edited by Malcolm Jones, pp. 85-108. New York: Cambridge University Press, 1978.
Analysis of the role that non-verbal communication plays in *Anna Karenina,* and the way in which the inadequacy of this type of communication contributes to the novel's tragic outcome.

Jones, Peter. "Action and Passion in *Anna Karenina.*" In his *Philosophy and the Novel,* pp. 70-111. London: Clarendon Press, Oxford University Press, 1975.
Analysis of the active and passive responses of the characters in *Anna Karenina.* Jones's essay measures the appropriateness of the characters' responses to two questions: "What is to be done?" and "What is the meaning of the situation in which I find myself?"

Knowles, A. V. "Russian Views of *Anna Karenina,* 1875-1878." *Slavic and East European Journal* 22, No. 3 (Fall 1978): 301-12.
Summary of the earliest critical responses to *Anna Karenina.* Knowles explains the political considerations that prompted some of the unfavorable early reactions to the novel.

Konick, Willis. "Tolstoy's Underground Woman: A Study of *Anna Karenina.*"In *Russian and Slavic Literature,* edited by Richard Freeborn, R. R. Milner-Guland, and Charles A. Ward, pp. 92-112. Cambridge, Mass.: Slavica Publishers, 1976.
Review of Harry J. Mooney, Jr.'s, discussion of *Anna Karenina*'s epic qualities in his *Tolstoy's Epic Vision: A Study of "War and Peace" and "Anna Karenina"* [see Additional Bibliography]. Konick concludes that the epic qualities of which Mooney is speaking are the characters "profound commitment to land and nature, family and society."

Lovett, Robert Morss. *"Anna Karenina."* In his *Preface to Fiction,* pp. 26-40. Chicago: Thomas S. Rockwell Co., 1931.
Discussion of the historical importance of *Anna Karenina* as the first Russian novel to be widely read and admired in the West.

Manning, Clarence Augustus. "Tolstoy and *Anna Karenina.*" *PMLA* XLII (June 1927): 505-21.
Analysis of the moral issues raised by Tolstoy in *Anna Karenina.* Manning attempts to illustrate that Tolstoy himself found the moral questions that arose as he wrote *Anna Karenina* nearly insoluble.

Merejkowski, Dmitri. *Tolstoy as Man and Artist: With an Essay on Dostoievski.* Westport, Conn.: Greenwood Press Publishers, 1970, 310 p.*
Discussion of Tolstoy's art in relation to the events of his life and his changing religious beliefs. Merejkowski's book contains scattered references to *Anna Karenina* throughout.

Mihajlov, Mihajlo. "A New Approach to *Anna Karenina.*" In his *Underground Notes,* pp. 153-68. Kansas City: Sheed Andrews and McMeel, 1976.
Discusses Anna's guilt and her own share of responsibility for her fate in the novel.

Mooney, Harry J., Jr. *Tolstoy's Epic Vision: A Study of "War and Peace" and "Anna Karenina."* Tulsa: University of Oklahoma Press, 1968, 88 p.
Discusses the Homeric qualities found in *Anna Karenina.* Mooney argues that the unique qualities of Tolstoy's two great novels can be best appreciated with reference to the epic tradition. For a review of Mooney's study, see the Willis Konick entry in the Additional Bibliography.

Muchnic, Helen. "The Steeplechase in *Anna Karenina.*" In her *Russian Writers: Notes and Essays,* pp. 126-38. New York: Random House, 1971.
Analysis of the steeplechase scene in *Anna Karenina.* Muchnic argues that the scene at the races illuminates the entire design of the novel.

Noyes, George Rapall. *"War and Peace* and *Anna Karenina."* In his *Tolstoy,* pp. 158-204. New York: Dover Publications, 1968.
Discussion of many facets of *Anna Karenina,* including its structure, its moral perspective, Tolstoy's attitude toward his heroine, and the meaning of the epigraph.

Peck, Harry Thurston. "Tolstoi's *Anna Karenina*." In his *Studies in Several Literatures*, pp. 227-37. New York: Dodd, Mead and Co., 1909.

   Discussion of the differing techniques that Tolstoy employed to tell Anna's and Levin's stories in *Anna Karenina.*

Reeve, F. D. *"Anna Karenina."* In his *The Russian Novel*, pp. 236-73. London: Frederick Muller, 1967.

   Discussion of the autobiographical nature of the character Levin in *Anna Karenina*. Reeve also discusses Tolstoy's ironic treatment of Russian high society in the novel.

Steiner, George. *Tolstoy or Dostoevsky: An Essay in the Old Criticism*. New York: Alfred A. Knopf, 1971, 354 p.*

   Analysis of the structure of *Anna Karenina*. Steiner disputes Matthew Arnold's claim that *Anna Karenina* represents not so much a work of art as a "piece of life." Steiner compares the novel's structure to that of a musical composition, and argues that it possesses every quality that Henry James felt was essential to "the deep-breathing economy of an organic form." References to *Anna Karenina* recur throughout the book.

Trilling, Lionel. *"Anna Karenina."* In his *The Opposing Self,* pp. 66-75. New York: Viking Press, 1955.

   Discussion of the classic status of *Anna Karenina*. Trilling notes that Tolstoy set the standards by which other realistic works are judged.

Van Kaam, Adrian and Healy, Kathleen. "Anna in Tolstoy's *Anna Karenina*." In their *The Demon and the Dove*, pp. 169-97. Pittsburgh: Duquesne University Press, l967.

   Study of the development of Anna's character and its eventual disintegration in the midst of crisis in Tolstoy's *Anna Karenina*.

Weitz, Morris. *"Anna Karenina:* Philosophy and the Word." In his *Philosophy in Literature*, pp. 23-40. Detroit: Wayne State University Press, 1963.

   Discussion of the manner in which philosophy and art are combined in *Anna Karenina* "to their mutual enrichment."

Stefan Zweig

1881-1942

Austrian biographer, short story and novella writer, novelist, dramatist, autobiographer, poet, essayist, critic, librettist, and translator.

Zweig was the author of popular biographies and psychological novellas that were among the first to venture into the field of analytic psychology. Also a humanist and fervent internationalist, Zweig upheld an ideal of a Europe undivided by political borders, and this goal dominated his life and work. Through numerous translations, tributes, adaptations, critical essays, lecture tours, and voluminous personal correspondence, Zweig endeavored to promote the works of foreign authors in German-speaking countries and eliminate barriers of language and culture in the world of letters. Commentary on Zweig has centered as much on his prominent place in European intellectual life as on the merit of his works; his Judaism, pacifism, and suicide have all served as points of controversy in the evaluation of his career.

Zweig was born into an upper-class Viennese family in 1881. His father was a self-made millionaire industrialist, his mother the daughter of a family of bankers whose clients had at one time included the Vatican. Although Jewish, the Zweigs considered themselves members of cosmopolitan Europe, with their Jewishness of secondary importance. As a child Zweig came to loathe the authoritarian Austrian school system, a hatred which he believed led to his lifelong obsession with personal freedom and resentment for authority. He began writing at an early age, publishing poems in leading literary magazines at sixteen and seeing his first poetry collection, *Silberne Saiten*, published when he was nineteen. These early efforts demonstrate the influence of "Young Vienna," a group that dominated the literary world of turn-of-the-century Vienna and which included Hugo von Hofmannsthal, Rainer Maria Rilke, and Arthur Schnitzler. A meeting with the Belgian poet Emile Verhaeren in 1902 provided Zweig with his first great role model; he later wrote, "In the very first hour of our meeting I had come to a decision: to serve this man and his work." Verhaeren influenced Zweig's literary style by turning him away from the aestheticism of "Young Vienna," but, more importantly, he imparted to the younger writer his philosophy of humanism and his enthusiasm for life. Before completing his university studies, Zweig devoted two years to the translation of Verhaeren's works, then continued to visit the poet yearly to translate his most current works into German. Between the completion of his studies at the University of Vienna in 1904 and the outbreak of World War I, Zweig spent a great deal of time traveling to North America, China, India, Africa, and the capitals of Europe, where he met regularly with leading members of Europe's intellectual community. His discovery of the works of the French novelist Romain Rolland in 1913 was another landmark in Zweig's moral and intellectual development; Rolland's appeal to brotherhood and European unity in his novel *Jean Christophe* became the inspiration for Zweig's cosmopolitan humanism. After serving in the Austrian War Archives during most of World War I (a period when he was temporarily and inexplicably caught up in the war fever of the times, composing violently pro-German propaganda), Zweig

Frau Friderike M. Zweig

wrote his first explicitly anti-war drama, *Jeremias (Jeremiah)*. He was permitted to attend the play's premiere in 1917 in neutral Switzerland, where he remained until after the war. Zweig returned to Austria in 1918 and spent the next twenty years writing prolifically, assembling a world-famous manuscript collection, and associating with such figures as Sigmund Freud, Hermann Hesse, and Arturo Toscanini.

With the completion in 1934 of *Die schweigsame Frau*, an opera libretto written at the request of German composer Richard Strauss, Zweig became the unwitting focal point of an international controversy. Although performance of a work by a Jewish author was forbidden in Nazi Germany, government officials were reluctant to offend Germany's foremost composer by an outright ban on production. At the same time, they were unwilling to take responsibility for its sanction. The issue became an affair of state, with officials at all levels examining Zweig's libretto, as well as his other works and his personal life, for any pretext on which to condemn him as an enemy of the German people. When none was forthcoming, the work was submitted to Adolf Hitler for personal approval, which he granted. The opera, however, was withdrawn from the stage after only two performances. Zweig received a great deal of censure from those who saw his collaboration with Strauss, the president of the Nazi's Reich Music Chamber, as tacit approval of the regime and disregard of his responsibility to the Jewish people and the rest of humanity. Zweig eventually severed his collaboration with Strauss, which some critics have interpreted as a political protest, and therefore a violation of Zweig's belief that an artist should remain uninvolved in politics of any kind. Others, however, believe that Zweig took this action to avoid the issue entirely, thus affirming his apolitical principles. Many critics note that throughout his life, Zweig was unable to reconcile his ardent pacifism with his concomitant belief that a writer's art should be free of all political influences, including pacifism. By the time of the German annexation of Austria in 1938, the political situation and a series of personal traumas had left Zweig despondent and exhausted. He emigrated to England, and was granted British citizenship in 1940. Zweig believed the Second World War signaled the collapse of European civilization and the destruction of his ideals of humanism and internationalism. As the war intensified and rumors of German concentration camps began to reach the world, Zweig entered a state of deep depression. In early 1942 Zweig and his wife committed suicide in Petropolis, Brazil.

While Zweig wrote successfully in many genres, most critics agree that it was the interpretive biography that best suited his talents. His stated goal was to humanize rather than deify his subjects, and it was this personal approach that made his biographies so appealing to readers. In studies of such figures as Ferdinand Magellan and Sigmund Freud, Zweig emphasized the theme that individuals possessed by a creative idea will often be in conflict with the powerful defenders of orthodoxy. Zweig favored the method of antithesis, often portraying two contrasting figures in opposition in order to highlight particular qualities, and always chose as his hero the individual who was ultimately defeated. In *Castellio gegen Calvin; oder, Ein Gewissen gegen die Gewalt (The Right to Heresy: Castellio against Calvin)* Zweig contrasted Sebastian Castellio, humanist and proponent of religious tolerance, with John Calvin, who is portrayed as a theocrat and tyrant. Despite their physical defeat, many of Zweig's protagonists, like Castellio, achieve a moral victory over their conquerors by championing humanistic values that outlive temporary political trends. In *Triumph und Tragik des Erasmus von Rotterdam (Erasmus of Rotterdam)*, which Zweig called "a quiet hymn of praise to the antifanatical man" and a veiled self-portrait, Zweig depicted Erasmus the idealist in opposition to Martin Luther, who is portrayed as a fanatic. In the opinion of many critics, Zweig identified with the humanist's unwillingness or inability to take a stand in a time of political crisis, and he saw a spiritual victory in Erasmus's defense of mankind's highest ideals. Zweig was also fond of making explicit correspondences, which Thomas Mann called "cheap parallels," between historical situations in his biographies and contemporary events; in the preface to *Erasmus*, written in 1934, Zweig wrote, "It is the duty of each of us to keep a cool head until the disaster is over."

Zweig's historical writings involved a tremendous amount of research. For his study of Honoré de Balzac, one of his literary heroes, Zweig collected material for over twenty years. In compiling information for *Marie Antoinette*, Zweig wrote that he "literally examined every bill to establish her personal expenses." Much of the detail accumulated in this way never appeared in published works. According to his autobiography *Die Welt von Gestern (The World of Yesterday)*, Zweig's creative method involved writing two to three times as much material as was necessary, then carefully pruning the work of every nonessential detail. This process of distillation was taken to its extreme in a series of biographical essays collected in

the volume *Baumeister der Welt (Master Builders)*, in which Zweig's exclusion of complicating detail enabled him to group historical figures by type. Critics have objected to this reduction of complex personalities such as Fedor Dostoevski and Friedrich Nietzsche to "types" as a vast oversimplification. Similar in scope to the biographical essays in *Master Builders* are the historical essays of *Sternstunden der Menschheit (The Tide of Fortune)*. These essays, which relate moments of destiny in the lives of individuals who have influenced history, reveal a particular interest in the effect of fate on the individual and the strengthening effect of adversity on character. While Zweig's biographies have generally been praised for their imaginative reconstruction of personalities and their narrative force, they have also been criticized for excessive interpretation of persons and events, a tendency toward melodrama, and a naive political viewpoint.

Zweig's works on his contemporaries, such as *Romain Rolland* and *Emile Verhaeren*, are less biographical and critical studies than personal tributes to these authors, and Zweig has been criticized for his almost unqualified adoration of the great minds of his day. Zweig's autobiography, *The World of Yesterday*, reveals very little of his own life, dealing instead with the secure world he knew during his youth, a world that was destroyed by World War I. Although some critics consider the work a brilliant evocation of the atmosphere of the last days of imperial Vienna and Europe between the wars, others find it overwhelmingly naive in its depiction of upper middle-class cultural life to the complete exclusion of political and social realities of the time.

With his fiction, Zweig gained a reputation for sensitive exploration of states of mind and psychological situations. He earned praise from Sigmund Freud for "Vierundzwanzig Stunden aus dem Leben einer Frau" ("Twenty-Four Hours from the Life of a Woman"), which Freud called a "little masterpiece" of psychological insight. Most of Zweig's fiction deals with violent emotions, and many of his protagonists are individuals in the grip of an obsession. Typical of these is the woman in "Brief einer Unbekannten" ("Letter from an Unknown Woman"), who is obsessed with a man only vaguely aware of her existence. Despite almost unanimous praise for Zweig's insight into the sufferings of his characters, critics have expressed disappointment at the unsatisfactory resolutions to his stories, which tend to be either contrived "happy endings" or maudlin appeals to the reader's sympathy. Critics often disparage Zweig's fiction for its exclusive focus on the character of the individual and its neglect of political or social issues. In *Die Augen des Ewigen Bruders (Virata)*, however, Zweig carefully examined the choice between political involvement and noninvolvement. According to critic Gertrude Teller, the story demonstrates a subtle understanding of the terms and alternatives of a conflict that Zweig was unable to resolve in his own life. "Der begrabene Leuchter" ("The Buried Candelabrum") has received critical attention as one of the few stories in which Zweig dealt with a specifically Jewish theme. Many critics have faulted Zweig for neglecting his Jewish heritage and showing no interest in the fate of his people, and critic Solomon Liptzin writes that even in "The Buried Candelabrum," a story of the Jewish struggle for existence in the Roman Empire, "Zweig's affirmation of Judaism is unconvincing." Other critics, however, feel that while Zweig was anything but indifferent to the fate of the Jews, he considered their tragedy merely a symptom of the decay of Europe as a whole, and it was to Europe that he owed his first allegiance. *Ungeduld des Herzens (Beware of Pity)*, Zweig's only full-length novel, is regarded by critics as being among his least successful works. In portraying an army lieutenant whose excessive pity for a crippled girl results in tragedy, Zweig falls victim to the melodrama and sentimentality that critics find repellent in his biographies and shorter fiction. The novel also demonstrates Zweig's concern with the individual psyche at the expense of greater social issues. Critic C. E. Williams notes: "It is characteristic of Zweig's writing that while the rest of the Empire is agog with the news of Sarajevo, his fictional hero is entirely absorbed in his personal dilemma."

Zweig's last and most highly acclaimed work of fiction, *Schachnovelle (The Royal Game)*, is also his most controversial, with critics debating whether it represents a continuation of, or a departure from, the author's earlier focus on individual psychology and his affirmation of humanist ideology. The novella concerns a sensitive intellectual, Dr. B., who survives solitary confinement at the hands of the Nazis by learning to play chess against himself. As a result of this, he becomes schizophrenic. Although warned by doctors after his release that further involvement with chess could lead to mental collapse, he cannot resist the opportunity to challenge a world master, who defeats the doctor only through manipulation of his delicate mental condition. Some critics consider *The Royal Game* a commentary on the conflict between the humanist Dr. B. and his anti-humanist opponent, a monomaniac whose brilliance at chess belies his crude and ignorant character, while others argue that the story is purely a psychological experiment and character study with no parallels to political situations. The ending has been variously interpreted as a pessimistic view of the effectiveness of humanist intervention in politics and an optimistic view of the survival of humanism in the face of political opposition. Despite contradictory interpretations, most critics agree that *The Royal Game* is among Zweig's most masterful works.

Zweig's career as a dramatist was plagued by tragedy. Four major theatrical figures died unexpectedly during the production of his plays, coincidences which devastated the sensitive Zweig and led him to avoid writing for the theater. His eight plays were popular and critical successes during his lifetime; however, most have not been translated into English and have been largely ignored by English-language critics. Zweig's first play, *Tersites*, is a neoclassical tragedy on a theme that recurs in some form in most of his plays, a theme he described as "how great griefs can refine a soul while happiness merely hardens it." *Jeremiah*, written during World War I, advocated peace at any cost and extolled the spiritual superiority of the defeated; Zweig wrote that Jeremiah was "not a specifically pacifist play—rather, an apotheosis of defeat," and that he considered *Jeremiah* to be among his most personal works. Zweig departed from the serious themes of his earlier plays with *Volpone*, an adaptation of Ben Jonson's play of the same name. *Volpone* revealed Zweig's considerable talent for writing comedy, and became a worldwide success. Zweig's dramas exhibit the influence of a variety of literary schools, including Impressionism, Expressionism, and Naturalism, but are notable primarily for their lyrical and highly declaimable dramatic lines.

Since the 1920s and 1930s Zweig's works have declined in popularity, with modern critics praising Zweig's insight into character and polished prose style, yet criticizing his works for their sentimentality and frequent superficiality. Serious examination of Zweig's works was for a time nearly overshadowed by the numerous personal tributes of those who knew him and by general assessments of his prominent role in European intellectual life. Since his death, a great deal of strongly opinionated commentary has been devoted to his suicide and the light it sheds on his life and work. Views range from that of Hannah Arendt, who has claimed that Zweig, "who had never concerned himself with the affairs of his own people, became nevertheless a victim of their foes—and felt so disgraced that he could bear life no longer," to that of Raoul Auernheimer, who has countered that "Zweig's weapon was the martyr's death which he courageously chose." While the value of Zweig's work remains controversial, the recent reissue of his fiction, along with collections of essays devoted to his life and works, indicate a continuing interest in an author who was a leading figure in one of the most creative and crisis-ridden eras in European history.

*PRINCIPAL WORKS

Silberne Saiten (poetry) 1901
Die Liebe der Erika Ewald (novellas) 1904
Paul Verlaine (biography) 1905
   [*Paul Verlaine*, 1913]
Tersites (drama) 1908
Emile Verhaeren (biography) 1910
   [*Emile Verhaeren*, 1914]
Brennendes Geheimnis (novella) 1911; published in
   Erstes Erlebnis
   [*The Burning Secret*, 1919]
Erstes Erlebnis (short stories and novellas) 1911
Das Haus am Meer (drama) 1912
Der verwandelte Komödiant (drama) 1912
Jeremias (drama) 1918
   [*Jeremiah*, 1922]
Legende eines Lebens (drama) 1919
Angst (novella) 1920
   [*Fear* published in *Kaleidescope*, 1934]
**Drei Meister: Balzac, Dickens, Dostojewski* (biography)
   1920
   [*Three Masters: Balzac, Dickens, Dostoeffsky*, 1930]
Der Zwang (novella) 1920
   [*Compulsion* published in *Passion and Pain*, 1924]
Romain Rolland (biography) 1921
   [*Romain Rolland*, 1921]
Amok (novellas) 1922
   [*Amok* (partial translation), 1931]
Die Augen des Ewigen Bruders (novella) 1922
   [*Virata* published in *Passion and Pain*, 1924]
Die gesammelten Gedichte (poetry) 1924
Passion and Pain (short stories and novellas) 1924
**Der Kampf mit dem Dämon: Hölderlin, Kleist, Nietzsche*
   (biography) 1925
   [*The Struggle with the Demon: Hölderlin, Kleist,*
   Nietzsche published in *Master Builders*, 1939]
Volpone [adaptor; from a drama by Ben Jonson] (drama)
   1926
   [*Volpone*, 1928]
Abschied von Rilke (essay) 1927
   [*Farewell to Rilke*, 1975]
Die Flucht zu Gott (drama) 1927
Verwirrung der Gefühle (novellas) 1927
   [*Conflicts*, 1927]
**Drei Dichter ihres Lebens: Casanova, Stendhal, Tolstoi*
   (biography) 1928
   [*Adepts in Self-Portraiture: Casanova, Stendhal, Tolstoy*,
   1928]

Joseph Fouché　(biography)　1929
　[*Joseph Fouché*, 1930]

*Die Heilung durch den Geist: Franz Anton Mesmer, Mary
　　Baker Eddy, Sigmund Freud*　(biography)　1931
　[*Mental Healers*, 1932]

Marie Antoinette　(biography)　1932
　[*Marie Antoinette*, 1933]

Triumph und Tragik des Erasmus von Rotterdam
　　(biography)　1934
　[*Erasmus of Rotterdam*, 1934]

Baumeister der Welt　(biography)　1935
　[*Master Builders*, 1939]

Maria Stuart　(biography)　1935
　[*Mary, the Queen of Scots*, 1935]

Die schweigsame Frau [adaptor; from a drama by Ben
　　Jonson]　(libretto)　1935

Der begrabene Leuchter　(novella)　1936
　[*The Buried Candelabrum*, 1937]

*Castellio gegen Calvin; oder, Ein Gewissen gegen die
　　Gewalt*　(biography)　1936
　[*The Right to Heresy: Castellio against Calvin*, 1936]

Kaleidoskop　(short stories and novellas)　1936
　[*Kaleidoscope*, 1934]

Begegnungen mit Menschen, Büchern, Städten　(essays and
　　criticism)　1937

The Old-Book Peddler, and Other Tales for Bibliophiles
　　(short stories)　1937

Magellan　(biography)　1938
　[*Conqueror of the Seas*, 1938]

Ungeduld des Herzens　(novel)　1939
　[*Beware of Pity*, 1939]

Brasilien: Ein Land der Zukunft　(travel)　1941
　[*Brazil, Land of the Future*, 1941]

Schachnovelle　(novella)　1942
　[*The Royal Game*, 1944]

Amerigo　(biography)　1944
　[*Amerigo*, 1942]

Die Welt von Gestern　(autobiography)　1944
　[*The World of Yesterday*, 1943]

Sternstunden der Menschheit　(historical essays)　1945
　[*The Tide of Fortune*, 1940]

***Balzac*　(biography)　1946
　[*Balzac*, 1946]

Briefwechsel: Stefan Zweig-Friderike Maria Zweig, 1912-42
　　(letters)　1951
　[*Stefan Zweig and Friderike Maria Zweig: Their
　　Correspondence*, 1954]

Stories and Legends　(short stories and novellas)　1955

Briefwechsel zwischen Richard Strauss und Stefan Zweig
　　(letters)　1957
　[*A Confidential Matter: The Letters of Richard Strauss
　　and Stefan Zweig, 1931-1935*, 1977]

*Several of Zweig's works appeared in English translation previous
to their German publication.

**These works were published as *Baumeister der Welt* in 1935.

***This work was completed by Richard Friedenthal.

AMELIA VON ENDE　(essay date 1913)

[*In the following excerpt, Von Ende praises Zweig's enthusiasm,
taste, and insight.*]

Among the writers whose name is of frequent occurrence in
the German magazines is that of Dr. Stefan Zweig, a lyric
poet, critic and translator of unusual gifts. He is an enthusiast
and a hero-worshipper of a type rather rare among the young
intellectuals of the present. He introduced to German readers
Emile Verhaeren, the Belgian poet, about whom he has written
a monograph and of whom he has translated a selection of
poems and some dramas. Another writer whom he profoundly
admires is Romain Rolland, and of our Walt Whitman he speaks
with something like reverence. These three names are proof
of his catholic taste and fine discernment. . . . [Zweig] has been
in America as a visitor to the Panama Canal, which he considers
a stupendous achievement and has celebrated in a feuilleton
which reads like a prose poem. In an essay on the rhythm of
New York he has pointed out some striking features that distinguish American cities from those of the Old World. He says
that the latter are most beautiful at rest, the former most repulsive, because their attractiveness is founded upon their stirring reality, their power upon the rhythm of their life. They
were dead heaps of stones to him on Sundays, but on weekdays
they resounded with a music of barbarous grandeur. "The
rhythm of New York is the first manifestation of the American
feeling of life; whoever can sense it, understands the tense
will-power that vibrates in all nerves of this unlimited country." A tribute which shows a penetrative insight uncommon
among the foreign literati that visit our shores. (p. 153)

> Amelia Von Ende, "Literary Vienna," in The Book-
> man, *New York*, Vol. XXXVIII, No. 2, October, 1913,
> pp. 141-55.*

THE NEW YORK TIMES BOOK REVIEW　(essay date 1915)

[*In the following excerpt from a favorable review of Emile Verhaeren, the critic finds Zweig's enthusiasm for his subject somewhat overzealous, yet praises his vivid portrayal of Verhaeren's
personality and works. For an excerpt from Zweig's work, see
the entry on Emile Verhaeren in TCLC-12, excerpt dated 1910.*]

The modern zest for timeliness is responsible for the impending
discovery of Emile Verhaeren by the English-reading public. . . . No translator other than Stefan Zweig has arisen for
the gigantic lyrics of this "Walt Whitman of Belgium," as he
will probably be misunderstood in the near future. Herr Zweig
alone has accomplished the large task of getting over into
another language practically all of M. Verhaeren's work.

It is Herr Zweig's appreciation of this suddenly-rising poet-
philosopher, now done into English, which will probably serve
as his formal introduction to England and America. There is
none better fitted to the task by reason of intimate knowledge
than the brilliant Viennese lyrist. Himself a poet of no small
attainment, he has been the Belgian's fervent, almost feverish,
disciple; he has followed step by step his master's progress;
he is fairly saturated with his message. The resulting estimates
are by no means lukewarm; they have caught much of the
stupendous energy, much of the overflow of M. Verhaeren's
prolific endeavor. . . .

[Zweig's] volume of appreciation reflects its subject matter in
very form. The book is whipped up to a high speed; it scorns
the blue pencil and the pruning shears and all the other implements of edition; adjective tumbles over adjective; simile
climbs upon metaphor. Here and there are moments of over-
strain; again points of absurdity, as when his zeal endeavors
to find something symbolic in the master's disorder of the
stomach or his hay fever. The whole is unavoidably Teutonic

in its glorious inconsistencies, in its earnestness, its bulky profusion, its eternal search for infinites, ultimates, and essentials, with the conscious drop into that glib vernacular with which the German philosophers have burdened speech. . . .

To Herr Zweig . . . belongs honest praise for a rich, vivid impression, much as it may be colored by his personal admiration of a man who is undoubtedly one of the looming figures of the day, and the fact that he mixes with his critical estimate some very noble poetic feeling is rather to his lasting credit than otherwise.

> *"Verhaeren," in* The New York Times Book Review, *January 3, 1915, p. 2.*

HANS REISIGER (essay date 1923)

[*In the following excerpt Reisiger, a prominent author and translator, maintains that Zweig's psychological insight enables him to represent emotional experiences in poetry that appeals to the reader by virtue of its universality.*]

Collected Poems [*Die gesammelten Gedichte*], which Stefan Zweig has just published, is the product of twenty-three years (1900-1923). Some poems are taken from the volumes *Silver Strings* [*Silberne Saiten*] and *Early Garlands* [*Die Frühen Kränze*], which are deliberately not being reprinted. There is an inner nobility and a fine austere humility in this critical attitude of Zweig towards his earlier poems. As befits a poet so cool, virile and free, he is not carried away by enthusiasm for the achievements of his own youth. Like Walt Whitman, he is opposed to the solemn and the priest-like, and for that very reason capable of true artistic discipline.

This being so, these voluptuously youthful silver chords, struck once again with a gentle smile, form a delightful prelude to the book itself. There is something lonely and melancholy about them as they take their place with the other poems in this volume. One is tempted, in view of the remaining contents of the book, particularly some of the powerful ballads, to wish that these early poems were in a place by themselves, but that would not be doing justice to its charm as a survey of the poet's development. For there is all the difference in the world between its end and its beginning! The language, which before was merely a finely-wrought casket for an inherited treasure, gradually rids itself of all conventionality. It takes its tone more and more from the language of the heart, from the still accents of the inner voice, and is animated by that only genuine and legitimate pathos, born of a passionate response to all things and all presences both without and within.

Stefan Zweig's special forte is the transmuting of emotional experiences, whether arising from the contemplation of great human types or from the depths of his own spirit, into poetry with all the dramatic tension of a ballad. The fine declamatory rhythm is never allowed to drop into mere ranting or pomposity but remains unerringly on the plane of the unceremonious, the entirely natural, the conversational. It is controlled by a penetrating psychological insight; and the special significance of these poems is that they succeed in pressing highly-differentiated and complex impressions of the human spirit into a mould that one would like to call popular, if popular can be understood to denote that quality in a work of art which makes it generally attractive, brilliant and colourful—in a good sense, marketable. And this can be achieved only by the artist so gifted that his visions and experiences become typical rather than individual. The individual spirits that Zweig conjures up—the 'singer,'

Cover of Zweig's first poetry collection.

the 'conductor,' the 'tempter,' the 'aviator,' the 'painter,' the 'sculptor'—are really the *typical* singer, conductor, sculptor; and the fact that they have been experienced in the first instance as *particular* personalities, long labelled by name and fame (Gustav Mahler, Rodin, Madame Cahier and others), does not reduce the poems to the level of anecdotes, because everything is controlled and universalised by the poet's vision.

Yet, in my view, Stefan Zweig's work is most characteristic when he keeps entirely within the sphere of dreams. The pleasurable sense of horror, the exaggerated loneliness that one experiences in dreams, seems to me to be one of his peculiar domains. The fine **"Ballad of a Dream"** (written in 1923) at the end of the book is alive with the same pulsing rhythm that stirs us so deeply in, let us say, Edgar Allan Poe's *The Raven*. It is actually as if the lonely beating of the blood had entered into the very words. The rhythms, too, take on something demonic which affects us urgently, persuasively. The diction is fiercely direct, like a soliloquy, and the whole atmosphere is shot with the bitter-sweet humour that marks one's most private relations with oneself. The theme of this moving ballad (which incidentally must be a veritable gift to the reciter) is the horror of finding ourselves stripped, in a dream, of all that masks us from ourselves and others in waking life, and the urgent desire to remain unrecognised after we have emerged from the nightmare pursuit, and everywhere the threatening, mocking words are yelled 'Du bist erkannt! Du bist erkannt!'

(You're recognised! You're recognised!). This poem is the one that makes us wish ardently that Stefan Zweig would enrich the modern spirit with more, with a complete cycle of such ballads, imbued with the essential magic of living! (pp. 47-9)

> *Hans Reisiger, in an extract from an introduction to "Die gesammelten Gedichte" ("Collected Poems"), in* Stefan Zweig: A Tribute to His Life and Work, *edited by Hanns Arens, translated by Christobel Fowler, W. H. Allen, 1951, pp. 47-9.*

SIGMUND FREUD (essay date 1928)

[*An Austrian neurologist, Freud was the father of psychoanalysis. The general framework of psychoanalytic thought, explained in his seminal work* The Interpretation of Dreams (1900), *encompasses both normal and abnormal behavior and is founded on the tenet that one's early experiences profoundly affect later behavior. Freud's interrelated theories on the unconscious (primitive impulses and repressed thoughts), the libido (sexual energy that follows a predetermined course), the structure of personality (id, ego, superego), and human psychosexual development (sequential stages of sexual development) have been widely used in the treatment of psychopathy. Freud was sometimes harshly criticized for his innovative theories, especially his insistence that sexual impulses exist in very young children and his definition of the Oedipus and Electra complexes. Nonetheless, he was for the most part greatly respected as a thinker and teacher. In addition, Freudianism has had significant influence on various schools of philosophy, religious and political ideas, and artistic endeavors such as surrealism in art, atonal music, and stream of consciousness in literature. Thus, along with such important thinkers as Karl Marx, Friedrich Nietzsche, and Albert Einstein, Freud is considered one of the most important shapers of modern thought. In the following excerpt, Freud argues that the plot of Zweig's story "Twenty-Four Hours from the Life of a Woman" is a veiled version of a boy's wish that his mother initiate him into sexual life to save him from the dangers of masturbation.*]

What part of a gambler's long-buried childhood is it that forces its way to repetition in his obsession for play? The answer may be divined without difficulty from a story by one of our younger writers. Stefan Zweig . . . has included in his collection of three stories *Die Verwirrung der Gefühle* . . . one which he calls **'Vierundzwanzig Stunden aus dem Leben einer Frau'** ['**Four-and-Twenty Hours in a Woman's Life**']. This little masterpiece ostensibly sets out only to show what an irresponsible creature woman is, and to what excesses, surprising even to herself, an unexpected experience may drive her. But the story tells far more than this. If it is subjected to an analytical interpretation, it will be found to represent (without any apologetic intent) something quite different, something universally human, or rather something masculine. And such an interpretation is so extremely obvious that it cannot be resisted. It is characteristic of the nature of artistic creation that the author, who is a personal friend of mine, was able to assure me, when I asked him, that the interpretation which I put to him had been completely strange to his knowledge and intention, although some of the details woven into the narrative seemed expressly designed to give a clue to the hidden secret.

In this story, an elderly lady of distinction tells the author of an experience she has had more than twenty years earlier. She had been left a widow when still young and is the mother of two sons, who no longer need her. In her forty-second year, expecting nothing further of life, she happens, on one of her aimless journeyings, to visit the Rooms at Monte Carlo. There, among all the remarkable impressions which the place produces, she is soon fascinated by the sight of a pair of hands which seem to betray all the feelings of the unlucky gambler with terrifying sincerity and intensity. These hands belong to a handsome young man—the author, as though unintentionally, makes him of the same age as the narrator's elder son—who, after losing everything, leaves the Rooms in the depth of despair, with the evident intention of ending his hopeless life in the Casino gardens. An inexplicable feeling of sympathy compels her to follow him and make every effort to save him. He takes her for one of the importunate women so common there and tries to shake her off; but she stays with him and finds herself obliged, in the most natural way possible, to join him in his apartment at the hotel, and finally to share his bed. After this improvised night of love, she exacts a most solemn vow from the young man, who has now apparently calmed down, that he will never play again, provides him with money for his journey home and promises to meet him at the station before the departure of his train. Now, however, she begins to feel a great tenderness for him, is ready to sacrifice all she has in order to keep him and makes up her mind to go with him instead of saying goodbye. Various mischances delay her, so that she misses the train. In her longing for the lost one she returns once more to the Rooms and there, to her horror, sees once more the hands which had first excited her sympathy: the faithless youth had gone back to his play. She reminds him of his promise, but, obsessed by his passion, he calls her a spoil-sport, tells her to go and flings back the money with which she has tried to rescue him. She hurries away in deep mortification and learns later that she has not succeeded in saving him from suicide.

The brilliantly told, faultlessly motivated story is of course complete in itself and is certain to make a deep effect upon the reader. But analysis shows us that its invention is based fundamentally upon a wishful phantasy belonging to the period of puberty, which a number of people actually remember consciously. The phantasy embodies a boy's wish that his mother should herself initiate him into sexual life in order to save him from the dreaded injuries caused by masturbation. (The numerous creative works that deal with the theme of redemption have the same origin.) The 'vice' of masturbation is replaced by the mania for gambling; and the emphasis laid upon the passionate activity of the hands betrays this derivation. The passion for play is an equivalent of the old compulsion to masturbate; 'playing' is the actual word used in the nursery to describe the activity of the hands upon the genitals. The irresistible nature of the temptation, the solemn resolutions, which are nevertheless invariably broken, never to do it again, the numbing pleasure and the bad conscience which tells the subject that he is ruining himself (committing suicide)—all these elements remain unaltered in the process of substitution. It is true that Zweig's story is told by the mother, not by the son. It must flatter the son to think: 'if my mother only knew what dangers masturbation involves me in, she would certainly save me from them by allowing me to lavish all my tenderness on her own body.' The equation of the mother with a prostitute, which is made by the young man in the story, is linked up with the same phantasy. It brings the unattainable within easy reach. The bad conscience which accompanies the phantasy brings about the unhappy ending of the story. It is also interesting to notice how the *façade* given to the story by its author seeks to disguise its analytic meaning. For it is extremely questionable whether the erotic life of woman is dominated by sudden and mysterious impulses. On the contrary, analysis reveals an adequate motivation for the surprising behaviour of this woman who had hitherto turned away from love. Faithful to the memory of her dead husband, she had armed herself against all similar attractions; but—and here the son's phantasy is right—she did not, as a mother, escape her quite unconscious transference of love on to her son, and fate was able to catch her at this undefended spot. (pp. 239-41)

> Sigmund Freud, *"Dostoevsky and Parricide," trans-*
> *lated by D. F. Tait, in his* Collected Papers: Mis-
> cellaneous Papers, 1888-1938, Vol. V, *edited by James*
> *Strachey, 1950. Reprint by Basic Books, Inc., Pub-*
> *lishers, 1959, pp. 222-42.**

NORMAN A. BRITTIN (essay date 1940)

[*In the following excerpt, Brittin argues that Zweig's approach to biography is that of a liberal humanist and moralist rather than that of a historian.*]

As a biographer, Zweig is unusual; but he is more than a biographer; he is a teacher. And since he is now advertised as "the most translated of living authors", a consideration of his ideas and methods has some significance. (p. 245)

Until the World War upset him, Zweig was a traveller and a man of letters, not a biographer. He wrote verse, short stories, and literary criticism. He became a friend and disciple of the Belgian poet Verhaeren, whose work he translated and interpreted. A pacifist during the War, he associated himself with Romain Rolland in Switzerland, and from Rolland received an enduring inspiration for his life and work.... After the War, Zweig retired to Salzburg, where, an intellectual in arms against a world of force, he proceeded to carry out a planned literary program. For, as befits a disciple of Verhaeren and Rolland, Zweig is an idealist, a lover of creativity, a humanitarian, an internationalist, an ardent supporter of free conscience, and a stubborn opponent of all that blocks man's development, of all that breaks bonds of brotherhood, leading men to hatred, of all that coerces the spirit. This exaltation for spiritual independence, fired by Rolland's example, provided Zweig with the purpose which informs most of his work.

This purpose is dramatically to revive for the present world the personalities of men and women who have contributed to the body of belief which is ours; to explain, through the form of interpretive biography, how man, symbolized in typical examples, has handled the recalcitrant world into which he was born, or how that world has handled him; to explain what patterns man has made "of the amazing kaleidoscope presented to him by life." Though Zweig constantly engages in psychological analysis, his biographies have a strong ethical basis, unusual in our age of "debunkery", so that he deserves more, perhaps, the title of spiritual biographer than that of psychological biographer. (pp. 245-46)

[In] his series of *Master Builders* Zweig is not a biographer *pur sang* ["purely"] but rather, a special blend of psychologist and historian of culture, interested less in his subjects for themselves than in certain types of character which, in his view, they represent. He is most successful, I believe, in his studies of Dostoeffsky, Hölderlin, and Stendhal, where, such is the force of his imaginative reconstruction, he seems practically to identify himself with the inner lives of the men he represents.

I speak, properly, I believe, of the force of his imaginative reconstruction. For biography is an art; and we should not be misled by Zweig's solemn terminology into thinking that his work is more "scientific" than that of any other biographer. Psychology, as a science, must deal with living people. Dealing with subjects out of the past, Zweig is employing the deductive

method upon material which does not lend itself to any experimental check of his results. As an anthropologist might pick members of a class to illustrate such human types as the Mediterranean, the Nordic, and the Alpine, so Zweig tries to show, by use of typical examples (but according to his own conception of the types) certain kinds of personalities that have been creative.

Zweig's work in *Master Builders* resembles that of Gamaliel Bradford. His studies are not intended as full-length biographies: "my essays are not meant as an introduction but as a sublimation, a condensation, an essence." The whole series is a group of "psychographs"—those soul-portraits, studies of the essential personality, which Bradford was at so much pains to perfect. Like Bradford, too, Zweig usually writes out of admiration.

His great emphasis upon some single characteristic, which enables him to group his subjects according to types, reminds one of the Comedy of Humors, and his fondness for the general as against the particular makes his *Master Builders,* in comparison with most biography, seem overly schematized. In fact, this endeavor to "type" his subjects persists throughout most of Zweig's work.

We gain further understanding of his purposes from his introduction to *Mental Healers:*

> My only desire is to portray ideas as embodied
> in certain human lives. A thought grows in a
> man's brain, and then leaps from this man to
> invade the whole world.... Nothing is to be
> compared to the dramatic power which is to be
> witnessed when one puny and isolated human
> being sets himself in opposition to a world-
> embracing organization.

This last sentence expresses Zweig's favorite theme: the struggle for independence of the one against the overbearing many.... Not only does this theme dominate the careers of Rolland, Mesmer, Mrs. Eddy, and Freud, but it is also evident in *Erasmus of Rotterdam* and *The Right to Heresy,* which, with its subtitle Castellio Against Calvin, is particularly significant for interpretation of Zweig's ideas and methods.

Sebastian Castellio, Swiss humanist and perhaps the most learned man of his time, was another Rolland, though lacking Rolland's fame: the only man in Europe who dared attack John Calvin, theocrat of Geneva, when Calvin, leader of those who had originally declared for liberty of interpretation, illegally caused Miguel Servetus to be burned at the stake for heresy.... On the physical plane Castellio did not triumph—did not overthrow Calvin, did not establish his ideal of toleration. Indeed, he was persecuted by the fanatical Genevese; his works were known to very few, for Calvin's heavy censorship stifled them; and Castellio himself, facing trial for heresy, escaped probable death at the stake only through merciful heart-failure.... But Castellio's books enjoyed "a life beyond life". Fifty years after his death, Dutch liberals resisting Calvinist theocracy had his works reprinted, and they furnished ammunition to Arminius.

In Zweig's view, man at his best is the instrument of the ideal; and though man's body perish and his name be reviled, yet the ideal is timeless.... Zweig, then, is a tireless warrior in the cause of individualism and in the cause of toleration, which alone can make individualism possible. He is more than a biographer; he is an ethical leader; and *The Right to Heresy,* though in it no person of our day is mentioned, is one of the finest tracts for the times that have recently been published.

Erasmus of Rotterdam is a companion piece of ***The Right to Heresy***. The life of Erasmus Zweig considers "a meagre subject for a biographer". But Erasmus as a symbol of the humanistic ideal is highly significant, for he was, Zweig asserts,

> of all the writers and creators in the West, the first conscious European, the first to fight on behalf of peace, the ablest champion of the humanities and of a spiritual idea.

More than any other method Zweig favors the method of antithesis; and just as *The Right to Heresy* is concentrated by the symbolic opposition of Castellio and Calvin, so, in *Erasmus of Rotterdam,* a chapter in the history of thought is made vivid by the dramatic antithesis of Erasmus and Luther—Erasmus the urbane, like "lucent syrops tinct with cinnamon", and Luther the fanatic, like "thunder, winged with red lightning and impetuous rage". The old story is repeated: the man of action has his way; the intellectual's voice, inept at emotional appeals, is lost in the blare of trumpets. But the ideal remains to challenge the twentieth century no less than the sixteenth. (pp. 247-50)

Zweig's *Fouché* is in some ways his best biography, being more the life-story of a man than an essay about him. Even here, however, the limitation of Zweig's method is apparent; for Fouché seems less an individual than a type, less a man than a slinking lust for power. Indeed, the biography is a sort of symphony on the theme of power. Fouché was the quintessence of the *genus* politician; and as Fouché was, so, Zweig would have us believe, are, in their varying degrees, all politicians. The biography is another lesson for our age.

In . . . *Conqueror of the Seas: The Story of Magellan,* Zweig reverts to the theme of the one versus the many. He sees Magellan as a man possessed by a creative idea, doomed to disappointment through most of his life because of the short-sighted opposition of the orthodox, the powerful, and the cowardly. It is another heroic biography, written, Zweig says, out of admiration for a man who is symbolic of the great discoverers without whose efforts the smooth, far-flung transportation system of the modern world would not exist.

Reading this biography, one becomes uncomfortably aware of an element in Zweig's writing which, though not usually so obtrusive, is present in all his work: his frequent mention of Fate, or Destiny. It is fairly common for a writer to personify fate for purposes of irony, and Zweig sometimes uses fate thus merely as a literary convention. But for him Fate has further significance. The following passage is typical.

> From among millions upon millions, Destiny had selected for a great deed this . . . navigator. . . . Others received the credit for his work . . . ; for strict as he himself had been throughout, Destiny was even stricter. . . . He was not permitted to finish his course. He could only look on, could only stretch out his hand towards the garland of victory; for when he wished to place it on his brow, Fate said: 'Enough,' and struck down the extended hand. . . .

There are many similar references in Zweig's work. Mary Baker Eddy "could not enter the stage until her cue was spoken." Heinrich von Kleist was hunted by the hounds of Fate. A

"sombre Will brooded over" Dostoeffsky's life. This Will is called not only Fate, but God. . . . Though Zweig has not stated his position explicitly, it is evident that he believes strongly in a purposive force which rules men, tests them, imposes upon them all manner of harsh experience, that they may live more fully, that they may develop their latent powers. Apparently this force is something supernatural, quite outside of man and beyond his control. To all appearances often malevolent, the force is actually beneficent, for Zweig holds constantly that "thro' the ages one increasing purpose runs." He speaks of "the great plan which mankind fulfils", and declares that "the spirit of development knows how to modify its creatures for its own mysterious purposes." Believing thus in a spirit of Progress which will utimately conduct man to "one far-off, divine event", he stands in contrast to the many contemporary intellectuals who have quite rejected the idea of Progress.

As Zweig sees his subjects, they are moulded by a shaping force that makes works of art out of their careers. Thus he is unusual among biographers, for he identifies his own dramatic purposes with the laws of life. This purposive doctrine may be dangerous to a historian, for if he frequently superimposes it upon his material, his work may become over-generalised and therefore over-simplified. But Zweig's biographies are not products of a historian. Considered as history, they contain an overplus of interpretation which clogs the narrative. They are products of an essayist and critic who uses the psychological method. Zweig is intent upon classifying his subjects into types and upon solving intimate problems of personality, upon discovering the psychological formulae which will make his subjects credible as human beings under the stress of special circumstances. It is this complete humanizing of his characters—his exposure of their inner lives: their urges, doubts, problems, passions, and sufferings—which has given Zweig's biographies their great popularity. He proceeds through moment after moment of lives, dwelling long upon the climaxes, continually explaining, explaining. He is always reading the barometer of souls, reporting their psychological weather. He is to his subjects, one may say, what A. C. Bradley was to Shakespeare's characters, for his biographers may well be compared to an elaborate analytical commentary on a play. Though we may wonder sometimes whether the play can stand the burden of the commentary, the commentary is, nevertheless, valuable.

The obtrusion into his work of his own view of life detracts, very likely, from the perfection of that work as sheer artistry; but it makes one increasingly aware of Zweig not as biographer merely, but as humanist; not as entertainer but as teacher. For his faith in the ideal of liberalism permeates his work, and it is to be hoped that it will permeate the world, encouraging men to value their would-be leaders for spiritual valor and truly creative strength. (pp. 252-54)

Norman A. Brittin, "Stefan Zweig: Biographer and Teacher," in The Sewanee Review, *Vol. XLVIII, No. 2, Spring, 1940, pp. 245-54.*

STEFAN ZWEIG [AS REPORTED BY ROBERT VAN GELDER] (essay date 1940)

[The following was excerpted from an interview with Robert Van Gelder that appeared in the New York Times Book Review *on July 28, 1940. Zweig discusses the difficulties of a writer in wartime, and speculates that the dramatic events of the time and the social transformation brought about by the war will result in a change in the nature of literature.]*

"The artist has been wounded," said Stefan Zweig, "in his concentration." He rapped his breast with the knuckles of his left hand. "How can the old themes hold our attention now? A man and woman meet, they fall in love, they have an affair—that was once a story. Sometime again it will be a story. But how can we lovingly live in such a trifle now?

"The last months have been fatal for the European literary production. The basic law of all creative work remains invariably concentration, and never has this been so difficult for the artists in Europe. How should complete concentration be possible in the midst of a moral earthquake? Most of the writers in Europe are doing war work of one kind or another, others had to flee from their country and live in exile, wandering about, and even the happy few who are able to continue working at their desks cannot escape the turmoil of our time.

"Reclusion is no more possible while our world stands in flames; the 'Ivory Tower' of esthetics is no more bomb-proof, as Irwin Edman has said. From hour to hour one waits for news, one cannot avoid reading the papers, listening to the wireless, and at the same time one is oppressed by the worries about the fate of near relatives and friends. Here flees one without home in the occupied area, others are interned and ask for freedom, others wander about begging from one consulate to another to find a hospitable country which will accept them. From all sides every one of us who has found a haven is daily assailed by letters and telegrams for help and intervention; every one of us lives more the lives of a hundred others than his own."

He spoke of external hindrances occasioned by blackouts, by lack of freedom of movement, by inability to obtain access to research materials.

"For instance, I was just about to lay the last hand to my favorite book on which I had been working for twenty years, a large and really the first comprehensive biography of the great genius Balzac. Reluctantly I had to abandon this nearly finished volume because the library of Chantilly which contains all of Balzac's manuscripts had been closed for the duration of the war and brought away to an unknown and inaccessible place; on the other hand, I could not take with me the hundreds and thousands of notes because of the censorship. Just as in my case, for thousands of artists and scientists work of many years has been stopped, perhaps for a long time, by purely technical difficulties.

"And the internal difficulty—what means psychology, what artistic perfection at such an hour, where for centuries the fate of our real and spiritual world is at stake? I, myself, had soon after completing my last novel, **'Beware of Pity,'** prepared the sketch for another novel. Then war started and suddenly it seemed frivolous to represent the private fate of imaginary persons. I had no more the courage to deal with private psychological facts and every 'story' appeared to me today irrelevant in contrast to history."

He said that most of the other writers he knew had experienced this same distraction in their own work. Paul Valéry, Roger Martin du Gard, Duhamel and Romains all had confessed to him that they could no longer concentrate on their work. "I would be suspicious against any European author who would now be capable to concentrate on his own, his private work. What was allowed to Archimedes, the mathematician, to continue his experiments undisturbed by the siege of his town, seems to me quasi inhuman for the poet, the artist, who does not deal with abstractions but whose mission it is to feel with the greatest intensity the fate and sufferings of his fellow beings."

Yet out of this war will come vast realms of experience in which the artist may work, and Mr. Zweig paced the floor excitedly as he talked of this:

"On each ship, in each travel bureau, in each consulate, one may hear from quite unimportant, anonymous people the stories of adventures and pilgrimages which are no less dangerous and thrilling than those of Odysseus. If any one would print, without altering a single word, the documents of the refugees which are now kept in the offices of charity organizations, by the Society of Friends, in the Home Office in London, it would make a hundred volumes of stories more thrilling and improbable than those of Jack London or Maupassant.

"Not even the first World War drove so many lives to such crises as this one year, never has human existence known such tensions and apprehensions as today—too much tension to be dissolved immediately into artistic form. That is why, in my opinion, the literature of the next years will be more of a documentary character than purely fictional and imaginative.

"We assist at the most decisive battle for freedom that has ever been fought, we will be witnesses of one of the greatest social transformations the world has ever gone through, and we writers before all have the duty to give evidence of what happened in our time. If we reproduce faithfully but our own life, our own experiences—and I intend to do so in an autobiography—we have perhaps done more than by an invented novel.

"No genius can nowadays invent anything which surpasses the dramatic events of the present time, and also the best poet has again to become student and servant of the greatest master of us all; of history."

Mr. Zweig says that the one thing he can work on now is his autobiography, which will carry the title "Three Lives."

"My grandfather lived a life, my father lived a life. I have lived at least three. I have seen two great wars, revolution, the devaluation of money, exile, famine. The period of the French Revolution and the Napoleonic wars, the period of the Reformation—they were times not unlike this. No other times can equal the change we who are of middle age now have seen." (pp. 86-9)

He said that he is writing his autobiography as he writes everything else—"four times too long."

"I write the first time to please myself. I put in everything that I think of. I am a contented writer who can write all day and be happy. So the early drafts of my books are very, very long.

"On the other hand, I am a nervous reader. I become very impatient when any author—including myself—strays from his point. So when I read what I have written I cut it in great chunks. I chop and chop until there is not a spare word, a sentence that can be done without." (p. 89)

Stefan Zweig [as reported by Robert van Gelder], "The Future of Writing in a World at War," in Writers and Writing *by Robert van Gelder, Charles Scribner's Sons, 1946, pp. 86-9.*

JULES ROMAINS (essay date 1941)

[*Romains was a French novelist, dramatist, poet, and critic. His best-known work,* Les hommes de bonne volonté *(1932-46), is a series of twenty-seven novels depicting French life and thought. Romains is noted for his part in founding Unanimism, a movement of young writers devoted to the principle of universal brotherhood and the belief that individual character is dependent upon and subordinate to the collective identity of the group. In the following excerpt, Romains contends that although Zweig's emphasis upon particular themes often becomes overly repetitive, his intense curiosity about human beings and clarity of vision result in works that are deeply personal for the reader.*]

Zweig's writings . . . are abundant and diversified, but the same intellect is always clearly perceptible through all of them. They include a small number of plays, a slightly larger number of novels, and many long *nouvelles.* Certain of these are deservedly famous: *Four-and-Twenty Hours in a Woman's Life; Conflicts; Letter from an Unknown Woman.* But the most considerable group consists of essays, some of which may be described as critical, some biographical, some historical. This does not mean that they may be divided into three distinct categories. It means only that they present an unequal mingling of the same elements, and that by means of the tone, the mechanism of learning which they set in motion, they resemble sometimes critical and philosophical studies, sometimes biographies—not romanticized, if you like, but vividly animated and glowing, of the kind which was so greatly admired— sometimes a genuine historical work. Thus there would be at one extremity his *Dickens* or his *Balzac,* for instance, and at the other his *Fouché* or his *Mary Queen of Scotland and the Isles.* But all these works are fundamentally related. What have they in common? And what is there in them that prevents confusion, even in their opening pages, with those of two other eminent writers whose names are in this case inevitably evoked by his, André Maurois and Emil Ludwig?

We cannot say: "The intense curiosity about human beings in their authentic diversity," for Maurois and Ludwig have this intense curiosity too. Perhaps in the case of Zweig it merely acquires an accent which is more affecting, more anxious. Yes, it ceases almost entirely to be objective curiosity, except in a very few cases. It is rather like a deeply personal interrogation: "In what way do those men resemble me? In what way do I resemble those men, those women? Isn't their life, their destiny, one of the satisfactions that I myself wanted to acquire? Was I wrong or right not to live as they have done? Have they or have I made the better choice?"

Hence this gesture of dramatic confession, this complete lack of detachment, of disinterestedness; hence also his readers' feeling that they themselves are concerned, that they are asking these anxious questions of themselves, questions which involve an examination of their whole lives.

It follows that Zweig's writings, even those which are the most replete with objective facts and, as we say, of historical material, are always meditative in the fullest sense of the word. Zweig is not satisfied merely to show us how Nietzsche, Erasmus, and Mary Stuart lived. He contemplates and asks us to contemplate the destiny of Nietzsche, Erasmus, and Mary Stuart. Probably without being aware of it, he more than once adopts Bossuet's attitude and even his accent in the *Oraisons Funèbres.* More than once he seems to us to exclaim: "And now, my brothers, let us meditate upon the amazing teachings which God has engraved upon the destiny of this man," "of this woman," "of this great queen."

Another peculiarity of Zweig's gift, which greatly helps him to endow his meditations with such power over our souls, is his virtuosity in marshalling his ideas and orchestrating great ideological themes. Like no one else he can extract a fundamental theme, even two or three of them, from a man's destiny, the subject of a biography, or a historical situation. He does not introduce his chosen theme gradually, but at the very beginning and with the maximum amount of brilliant argument. Then he develops it with an abundance of power and effect. He repeats it virtually unchanged and to the point of obsession; and one occasionally recalls certain amplifications of Hugo's prose or the methods of Wagner. Take, for instance, the theme of spices which forms the introduction to his *Magellan.*

This seeking after effect and this insistence seem to us French people of today slightly marked with Romanticism, or, if you prefer, a little too carefully designed to impress the thousands of minds that care more for simple, powerful ideas that are quickly absorbed than for delicate shades of meaning and complexities—the numberless minds for which propangandist formulas, publicity slogans, and the huge posters in our modern streets are designed.

So many others have recourse to this art of simplification to express unsound ideas or whims! But Zweig possesses an amazingly sure flair for appropriateness. Of someone else one might say: "His idea was amusing, his paradox stimulating, but here he is at it again. That's enough. He's a bore. He makes us want to shout the contrary." Of Zweig one says: "He insists a little too much, perhaps, and he seems to think that we have failed to understand. But how true it all is! How far his vision reaches!" (pp. 53-8)

Jules Romains, in his Stefan Zweig: Great European, *translated by James Whitall, The Viking Press, 1941, 64 p.*

HANNAH ARENDT (essay date 1943)

[*Arendt was a prominent Jewish political scientist and philosopher who fled Nazi Germany in 1933. She earned a reputation as a brilliant and original thinker and an authority on anti-Semitism with articles in scholarly periodicals and with her first book,* The Origins of Totalitarianism *(1951). Her best-known work,* Eichmann in Jerusalem: A Report on the Banality of Evil *(1963), provoked a storm of controversy by raising questions about the conduct of the Eichmann trial and the behavior of the Jewish community during the Holocaust. Like Solomon Liptzin (1944), Arendt is critical of Zweig's apparent indifference to his Jewish heritage and to the plight of European Jews in the twentieth century. In addition, Arendt attributes Zweig's suicide to his feeling of disgrace at being ostracized from European society and considers his lack of overt political commitment during his life the result of cowardice.*]

[In *The World of Yesterday: An Autobiography*] Stefan Zweig describes a part of the bourgeois world—the world of the *literati,* which had given him renown and protected him from the ordinary trials of life. Concerned only with personal dignity and his art, he had kept himself so completely aloof from politics that in retrospect the catastrophe of the last ten years seemed to him like a sudden monstrous and inconceivable earthquake, in the midst of which he had tried to safeguard his dignity as long as he could. He considered it unbearably humiliating when the hitherto wealthy and respected citizens of Vienna had to go begging for visas to countries which only a few weeks before they would have been unable even to find on the map. That he himself, only yesterday so famous and welcome a guest in foreign countries, should also belong to this miserable host of the homeless and suspect was simply hell on earth to him. But deeply as the events of 1933 had changed his personal existence, they could not touch his standards or his attitudes to the world and to life. He continued to boast of his unpolitical point of view; it never occurred to him that, politically speaking, it might be an honor to stand outside the law when all men were no longer equal before it. On the contrary, he found himself "one rung lower," he "had slipped down to a lesser . . . category." All he realized was that during the 1930's the better classes in Germany and elsewhere were steadily yielding to Nazi precepts, and discriminating against those whom the Nazis proscribed and banned: this, in his eyes, meant personal disgrace.

Not one of Stefan Zweig's reactions during all this period was the result of political convictions; they were all dictated by his supersensitiveness to social humiliation. Instead of hating the Nazis, he just wanted to annoy them. Instead of despising those of his coterie who had been *gleichgeschaltet* ["brought into line"], he thanked Richard Strauss for continuing to accept his libretti. Instead of fighting he kept silent, happy that his books had not been immediately banned. And later, though comforted by the thought that his works were removed from German bookstores together with those of equally famous authors, this could not reconcile him to the fact that his name had been pilloried by the Nazis like that of a "criminal," and that the famous Stefan Zweig had become the Jew Zweig. He failed to perceive that the dignified restraint, which society had so long considered a criterion of true culture, was under such circumstances tantamount to plain cowardice in public life.

Before Stefan Zweig took his own life he wrote down what the world had given him and then done to him—"the fall into the abyss . . . [and] the height from which it occurred"—with the pitiless accuracy which springs from the calm of absolute despair. He records the pleasures of fame and the curse of humiliation. He tells of the paradise of cultural enjoyments, of meeting men of equal renown. He describes his endless interest in the dead geniuses of history; penetrating their private lives and gathering their personal relics was the most enjoyable pursuit of an inactive existence. And then he tells how he suddenly found himself facing a reality in which there was nothing left to enjoy, in which those as famous as himself either avoided him or pitied him, and in which cultured curiosity about the past was continually and unbearably disturbed by the tumult of the present, the murderous thunder of bombardment, the infinite humiliations at the hands of authorities.

Gone, destroyed forever, was that other world in which, *"früh-gereift und zart und traurig"* ["precocious and delicate and melancholy"] (Hofmannsthal), one had established oneself so comfortably; razed was that "reservation" for the chosen few connoisseurs who had devoted their lives to the idolatry of Art; broken were the trellises that barred out the *profanum vulgus* ["vulgarity"] of the uncultured more effectively than a Chinese wall. With that world had passed also its counterpart, the poverty-stricken clique of bohemians. For the young son of a bourgeois household, craving escape from parental protection, bohemians who endured the hardships of ill-success and lack of money became identified with men experienced in the adversities of real life. The "unarrived," dreaming only of large editions of their works, became the symbol of unrecognized genius, and the reflection of the dreadful *dénouement* which destiny might have in store for hopeful and gifted young men.

Naturally, the world which Zweig depicts was anything but *the* world of yesterday; the author of this book lived only on its rim. The gilded trellises of this reservation were very thick, depriving the inmates of every view and every insight that could mar their bliss. Not once does Zweig mention the most ominous manifestation of the postwar period, which struck his native Austria more violently than any other European country—unemployment. But the rare value of his document is nowise lessened by the fact that for us today the trellises behind which these people spent their lives, and to which they owed their extraordinary feeling of security, seem singularly like prison or ghetto walls. It is astounding that there were still men among us whose ignorance was so profound, and whose conscience was so clear, that they could continue to look on the prewar period with the eyes of the nineteenth century. They could regard the impotent pacifism of Geneva and the treacherous lull before the storm, between 1924 and 1933, as a return to normalcy!

It is wryly gratifying that at least one of these men had the courage to record it all in detail, without hiding or prettifying anything. For Zweig finally realized what "chronic fools" they all had been—though the connection between their tragedy and their folly he hardly recognized. (pp. 307-09)

Sefan Zweig's knowledge of history preserved him from adopting without qualms the worldly yardstick of success. Yet, despite his connoisseurship, he ignored the two great postwar poets in the German language, Franz Kafka and Bert Brecht, neither of whom was ever successful. More than that, Zweig confounded the historical significance of writers with the size of their editions. He avers: "Hofmannsthal, Arthur Schnitzler, Beer-Hofmann and Peter Altenberg gave Viennese literature European standing such as it had not possessed under Grillparzer and Stifter."

Precisely because Zweig was modest about himself, discreetly glossing over as uninteresting the personal data in his autobiography, the repeated enumerations of famous people he met is especially striking. It seems like proof that even the best of those cultured Jews could not escape the curse of their time—the worship of that great leveler Success. (p. 312)

While the turn of the century brought economic security to the Jews and recognized their civic rights as a matter of course, it also made their social position less tenable and their social attitude uncertain, ambiguous. Socially they were pariahs, except when they used extravagant methods (of which fame was one) to enforce their social possibilities. In regard to a *famous* Jew, society would forget its unwritten laws. "The radiant power of fame" was a very real social force, in whose aura one could move freely and even have antisemites for friends, such as Richard Strauss and Karl Haushofer. (p. 313)

And fame brought also another privilege which, according to Zweig, was at least equally important—the suspension of anonymity, the possibility of being recognized by unknown people, of being admired by strangers. There is no doubt that Zweig feared nothing more than to sink back into obscurity where, stripped of his fame, he would become again what he had been at the beginning of his life. He would be no more than one of the many unfortunates confronted with the almost insuperable problem of conquering a strange world.

Fate, in the form of a political catastrophe, eventually did almost thrust him into this very anonymity. He knew—better than many of his colleagues—that a writer's fame flickers out when he becomes "homeless in borrowed languages." Furthermore, his collections were stolen from him, and with them his intimacy with the famous dead. His house in Salzburg was seized, and with it his bond with the famous men among the living. Taken finally, too, was the invaluable passport, which had not only enabled him to represent his native land in other countries; it had also helped him evade the dubiety of his civic existence in that native land itself.

But again, as during the first World War, it is to Zweig's credit that he did not yield to hysteria, nor take too seriously his newly acquired British citizenship. He could hardly have represented England in other countries. And since the international society of the famous disappeared completely with the second World War, this homeless man lost the only world in which he had once had the delusion of a home.

In a last article, **"The Great Silence,"** . . . written shortly before his death—an article which seems to me to belong with the finest of Stefan Zweig's work—he tried to take a political stand for the first time in his life. But the word Jew still did not occur to him; Zweig strove once more to represent Europe, at least Central Europe, now choked in "the great silence." Had he spoken about the terrible fate of his own people, he would have been closer to all the European peoples who are today, in the battle against their oppressor, struggling against the persecutor of the Jews. The European peoples know, better than did this self-appointed spokesman who had never in his whole lifetime concerned himself with their political destiny, that yesterday is not detached from today "as if a man had been hurled down from a great height as the result of a violent blow." To them yesterday was neither "an age of reason" nor that "century whose progress, whose science, whose arts, whose magnificent inventions were the pride and the faith of us all."

Now, without the protective armor of fame, Stefan Zweig was confronted with the reality all-too-familiar to the Jewish people. There had been various escapes from social pariahdom, including the ivory tower of fame. But only flight around the globe could offer salvation from political outlawry. Thus the Jewish bourgeois man of letters, who had never concerned himself with the affairs of his own people, became nevertheless a victim of their foes—and felt so disgraced that he could bear life no longer. Since he had wanted all his life to live in peace with the political and social standards of his environment, he could put up no fight against a world that brands the Jew. When finally the whole structure of his life, with its aloofness from civic struggle and politics, broke down, and he experienced disgrace, he was unable to discover what honor can mean to men.

For honor never will be won by the cult of success or fame, by cultivation of one's own self, nor even by personal dignity. From the "disgrace" of being a Jew there is but one escape— to fight for the honor of the Jewish people as a whole. (pp. 313-14)

Hannah Arendt, "Portrait of a Period," in The Menorah Journal, *Vol. XXXI, No. 3, Autumn, 1943, pp. 307-14.*

RAOUL AUERNHEIMER (essay date 1943)

[*Auernheimer was an Austrian novelist, playwright, and critic. As chairman of the Austrian PEN Club before World War II, Auernheimer opposed nazism in the field of literature, an effort for which he was later imprisoned in a German concentration camp. In the following excerpt, Auernheimer discusses the autobiographical nature of* Erasmus *and finds that Zweig, like the subject of this biography, upheld the values of humanism in his life and his work. Auernheimer views Zweig's suicide as the act of a martyr who elected death as an expression of personal freedom and the freedom of humanity.*]

Among all the biographies of Stefan Zweig his *Erasmus* is the most autobiographical. Generally speaking, Zweig concealed rather than revealed himself in his writings, and did not poetically express his inner experiences. . . . [He] escapes the rebuke of the American playwright, N. Behrman, who has coined the pointed phrase of the "loudspeaker in the confessional." Zweig had exposed himself to the danger of loud or half-loud confession only during his lyrical beginnings, when he was still counted as a member of the literary group called "Young Vienna"—merely because he was young and lived in Vienna.

Then came the First World War, an experience that gave an entirely different direction to his whole work. It was then that he wrote *Jeremiah*, his first creation permeated by the idea of humanity. Here, relinquishing a pretentious individualism, he allowed his war-weary self to be consumed by the oratorical fire of the Biblical prophet so that he might express what not only he but millions of his contemporaries were burning to utter. After the war he continued in the same direction, pursuing, with passionate realism, the path which leads from the ego to the fellow man, in a series of broadly conceived biographies. All these life portraits, drawn from the most diverse times and regions, have one thing in common: in them a creative artist, eliminating his own person—though by no means his own personality—penetrates and transposes himself into a foreign ego. And only once do we see Zweig deviate from this direction which he had seemingly chosen and intended to maintain constantly—in the *Erasmus*. This is a portrait, but also a confession.

Of exactly the same age as Erasmus when Erasmus wrote to a friend, "Why are they trying to thrust me into a party?" Stefan Zweig could have made this sentence the motto of his book which betrayed, in its successive headings, the nature of autobiographical confession and apology. Especially toward the end, the titles of single chapters become uncannily allusive and frighteningly candid.

In one of the main sections, most significantly entitled "The Titanic Adversary," Zweig confronts Erasmus' European outlook with German nationalism. For the great humanist is not so much concerned with the Lutheran religious reform as with the political fanaticism into which it degenerated and which finally drove even Erasmus out of the country. "Settlement and Account," the heading of the third chapter before the last, signifies Erasmus-Zweig's futile attempt at a temporary compromise.

This is followed by the penultimate chapter, called "The End." Zweig knew already then that this end would be, could be, no end. The final section, called "Erasmus' Legacy," adds an inspiring note. Here again Erasmus' legacy coincides with that of his biographer. Both hand down, as an eternal bequest, the idea of humanity which each had shaped and carried onward in his thoughts.

Accompanying the biographer on his simultaneously autobiograpical path in this prescient book, one repeatedly encounters glimpses which seem like mirror images of uncanny timeliness. This becomes apparent when Zweig describes Erasmus' facial expression in the great Holbein portrait with these words: "Fine, reflective, shrewdly apprehensive."

It is not certain whether Erasmus looked exactly like this, but it is certain that Zweig did while writing his book on Erasmus in his early fifties. He, too, was an "Epicurean by nature," as he calls the great humanist who liked to sample choice wines. At the same time his industry was remarkable—to call it love of work would be an understatement—as on Zweig's hand, too, "sat the pen like a sixth finger." He, too, safeguarded himself "behind a barricade of books above the fight between God and Lucifer, too prudent to be a hero." The demand to join the rank of fighters he repudiated by quoting from the *Letters to Obscurantists:* "Erasmus est per se!"

But, in order to excuse himself *and* Erasmus, he adds, slightly embarrassed, that this desire to remain independent of both right and left, of the emperor and Luther, constituted the foundation stone in Erasmus' character—"A foundation concealed beneath the completed edifice." And then, harmonizing the character portrait with the hero's destiny, he condenses—here, too, with prescience—Erasmus' tragedy into one sentence: "The tragedy of his life, and one which binds him to us in closer brotherly affection, was that he sustained defeat in the struggle for a juster and more harmonious world."

Characteristic of Zweig's viewpoint at that time is this "more harmonious," visualizing, quite in the spirit of the more or less heedless English appeasers, an understanding as being still possible and desirable. And this fully agrees with the following character description: "Erasmus loved many things we are fond of—books and arts and languages and peoples, without distinction of race and color." All this is the Zweig of 1934— and the final statement that he (Erasmus) negated only one thing, fanaticism, sounds again like self-defense. "It is the duty of each of us to keep a cool head until the disaster is over." So runs a warning sentence in the preface of this book, written in 1934, immediately after Hitler had invaded humanity's front.

Still the author seems inclined to ask himself: Is there not something higher than the quarrel of parties? And is not reason, the supreme judicial court of liberal thinking, this something higher? It is "reason," of which Zweig says expressly in this connection: "Often, while the drunkenness is at its height, she [reason] must needs lie still and mute. But her day dawns and ever and again she comes into her own anew."

Erasmus did not live to see this day, neither did Zweig. He too preferred, like his admired Erasmus, to seek refuge in work: "He retained his independence. He was free." Separated from his friends, Erasmus-Zweig consoled himself with a last friend who had remained faithful to him during his whole life: "One friend alone, his oldest, best and trustworthiest friend, shared study and writing table with him: Dame Work."

And again it is his own fate that this Dame Work, a poetically imagined half sister of Dürer's Melancholia, presages with sorrowful foresight, although our friend could not know and could hardly foresee that he, too, would have to die "outlawed and alone." In spite of the pessimism inborn in this man spoiled by fortune—like the pessimism in all late descendants of a prosperous European bourgeoisie—Zweig, looking down on the events in Germany from a high London rampart, still believed in the mild possibility of Erasmian solutions.

Seven years later, in Petropolis, Brazil, we see him so thoroughly cured of this delusion that he erased his life like an untenable sentence in an earlier manuscript: "The exalted dream of a spiritually united Europe had come to an end." This was written in 1934, in the preface to *Erasmus.*

There are barricade fighters without barricades, and as such the Erasmian appeaser Stefan Zweig finally revealed himself. (pp. 412-15)

Before killing himself he had to kill the Erasmian nature within him and he did; this was his great development, human as well as biographical.

"Before I depart from life by my own free will I want to do my duty," he wrote to a friend; and to another: "After one's sixtieth year unusual powers are needed in order to make a new beginning. Those that I possess have been exhausted by long years of homeless wandering. So I think it better to conclude in good time and in erect bearing a life in which intellectual labor meant the purest joy and *personal freedom the highest good on earth.*" What an unheard-of, new tone on his lyre, a heroic, Fidelio tone. In sounding it, he had fought his way to the final realization that delay was mutiny, and that everyone, in order to defend freedom, must join the rank and file: each with the weapons at his disposal.

Zweig's weapon was the martyr's death which he courageously chose. There are two kinds of torchbearers in history: some carry it onward, the others convert their own person into a torch. Stefan Zweig did the latter. In the afterglow of this image he will live on. (pp. 425-26)

> *Raoul Auernheimer, "Stefan Zweig," in* The Torch of Freedom: Twenty Exiles of History, *edited by Emil Ludwig and Henry B. Kranz, Farrar & Rinehart, Inc., 1943, pp. 407-26.*

SOLOMON LIPTZIN   (essay date 1944)

[*Liptzin is a Russian literary historian specializing in Jewish and German literature. He has held professorships at numerous universities in the United States and Israel. In the following examination of* "The Buried Candelabrum," *Liptzin concurs with Hannah Arendt (1943) that Zweig was indifferent to the fate of the Jewish people, and also views Zweig's suicide as an act of despair.*]

Zweig's intellectual life was rooted in *Young Vienna,* a circle of patricians, dandies, thinkers, and scoffers, who at the turn of the century dominated the literary, theatrical, and journalistic activities of the bustling Danubian metropolis. (p. 212)

The fame of the Viennese aesthetes was already well established when Theodor Herzl, at the turn of the century, discovered in Stefan Zweig, the nineteen-year-old son of a prosperous Jewish merchant, literary talent of a high order. As editor of the *Neue Freie Presse,* Herzl accepted for publication one of Zweig's earliest short stories and was the first person to write an appreciation of the unknown author. Herzl even hoped to win his protégé for the young Zionist movement; but in this he was unsuccessful. Reared in an assimilationist home that had profited from the fruit of emancipation, Zweig was unwilling to revert to the narrow confines of Jewish nationalism. For the ambitious youth not even the multi-national Austro-Hungarian Empire was sufficiently cosmopolitan and he was almost as much at home outside of its boundaries as within its many provinces. . . . Soon he began to envisage a Pan-Europe, in which political boundaries would be meaningless, and he projected himself the rôle of sympathetic intermediary between the great European literary personalities. His Jewish background, which prevented him from taking too seriously dynastic rivalries and local superpatriotism, also enabled him to view optimistically a future of constructive work in behalf of a common European culture, the final synthesis of Hellenism and Hebraism. He drew upon Hellenic sources for his drama *Tersites* and upon Hebraic sources for his drama *Jeremias*. The latter was written in 1916 and voiced not only horror at the unnecessary holocaust of the First World War but also the comforting hope that suffering and defeat would purge the European soul of its deeply embedded imperialistic dross and bring to the fore the unadulterated gold of brotherhood, mutual tolerance, and universal enlightenment. This hope was the basis for Zweig's activity in the 1920's and 1930's. In studies on Dostoyevsky and Tolstoy, he tried to make the Russian soul more intelligible to the West at a time when Russia was regarded as a pariah among the nations. In studies on Romain Rolland, Balzac, Stendhal, Joseph Fouché, and Marie Antoinette, he continued his efforts to bring to German-speaking peoples a better understanding of their French neighbors. In studies on Dickens, Mary Baker Eddy, Erasmus of Rotterdam, Amerigo Vespucci, and others, he appraised sympathetically the achievements of diverse peoples and ages.

In this period, when at the height of his popularity, he avoided Jewish themes, Jewish characters, and Jewish problems. To his palatial villa, atop the Capuchin Mountain overlooking Salzburg, European intellectuals made pilgrimages and came away with the impression that in him the transformation of the Jew and the Austrian into the good European seemed to have been successful.

By 1933, however, this good European was subjected to no less venomous attacks than his unassimilated coreligionists of the ghetto. (pp. 216-18)

It was then, in the sixth decade of his life, as loneliness gathered about him amidst the noise of cities and the bustle of busy

Dust jacket for a book publication of Zweig's drama Jeremias.

admiring gapers, that Zweig sought to find his way back to ancestral roots. In 1937 he published *The Buried Candelabrum,* as sad an affirmation of Jewishness as ever was penned in our century.

The events of this short novel are laid in Rome and Byzantium during the fifth century. It begins with the sacking of the capital of the Western Roman Empire by the Vandals in 455. Zweig has the marauders carry off, as part of their immense booty, a candelabrum, the most sacred treasure of Rome's Jewish community. (pp. 218-19)

The Menorah—the most precious relic of a glorious past, a relic linking Solomon's temple with its latest descendants, a relic that had been dragged from country to country along with the people whose shrine it had once adorned—the Menorah had to resume its wanderings once again. Because of the supreme value of this symbol, the elders of Israel set out from Rome in the night to accompany it on its way to the galleys of the Vandals. A child went with them so that in later years it might bear testimony to the events of the fateful night. Rabbi Eliezer, the leader of this strange pilgrimage, interpreted to the young boy during the mournful hours the meaning of Israel's destiny on the stage of history. (p. 221)

To the puzzled question of the boy as to why the Jews permitted their most valuable treasures to be taken from them again and again without offering physical resistance, Zweig's spokesman replied that in this world right adhered to the powerful and not to the just. Might was ever triumphant on this imperfect sphere and mere goodness was ineffective. The Jews received from God the capacity to endure suffering, but not the iron fist to enforce their right. Why then did not God, the all-just and all-powerful, assist them in their struggle against brute force? Why was He apparently on the side of the robbers and not on the side of the righteous? Zweig reached a height of eloquence in posing this question through the lips of both the boy and the graybeard and a depth of obscurity in venturing a tentative reply. The acts of the contemporary Nazis no less than of the ancient Vandals were obviously before Zweig's vision when he formulated what he called the ancient Jewish outcry: "Why is God especially severe towards us among all the peoples, towards us who serve Him as no others do? Why does He cast us under the soles of others so that they step on us, who were the first to acknowledge Him and to praise Him in His inconceivable essence? Why does He tear down what we build? Why does He dash our hopes? Why does He refuse to let us rest anywhere? Why does He stir up against us one people after another in ever-renewed hate? . . . '' (pp. 221-22)

Zweig's only answer to these outcries is faith: since God's plans are unknown to us and God's thoughts inconceivable to mortals, comfort may be found in the hope that there is meaning in all suffering and that all pain is atonement for guilt. Though God's people still wanders from exile to exile, it may perhaps find itself anew some day and know peace and rest in some distant future.

Despite this vague hope, voiced on the brink of despair, Zweig's affirmation of Judaism is unconvincing. It seems as though the Viennese aesthete who had remained indifferent to Jewish fate throughout the first third of the twentieth century, neither severing his connection with the Jewish community nor participating actively in its affairs, wished to record his faith in its continued survival at a time when this survival was being questioned by many. But once this literary document was completed, Zweig resumed his attitude of aloofness from the contemporary Jewish currents. It was the survival of European culture that he despaired of during the last months of his life and it was Europe's tragedy that drove him to suicide. Because Europe was dying, he was homeless. Jewry would survive, but he was not primarily of it. The cosmopolitanism of *Young Vienna*, to which he remained ever faithful, had made way for the brutal chauvinism of Hitler's minions. Zweig was too tired to live on. (pp. 222-23)

> Solomon Liptzin, "Stefan Zweig," in his Germany's Stepchildren, *The Jewish Publication Society of America, 1944, pp. 211-25.*

GERTRUDE E. TELLER   (essay date 1952)

[*In the following excerpt, Teller outlines Zweig's examination of the consequences of involvement and noninvolvement in the novella "Virata," maintaining that Virata's ultimate acquiescence to determinism was a course of action Zweig would have found intolerable; instead, he chose suicide. The abstracts of* Virata *included in the text are the critic's own.*]

Stefan Zweig's legend *Virata or The Eyes of the Undying Brother* deserves our special attention and interest. Although the story contains much of the thought of Zweig, whose ethical note is familiar to us from his major writings, it is ultimately designed to prove the philosophical untenability of Zweig's most cherished ideas. The legend brings us therefore face to face with the intricate question of how we can interpret Zweig's apparent breach of faith with his ethics, and thereby it seems to reveal the mental and spiritual personality of the author.

Five lines from the *Bhagavatgita* open the story and strike its keynote. They read:

> It is not by shunning action that we can really be freed from action. Never can we be freed from all activity, even for a moment.
> —*Bhagavatgita,* Third Song.

> What is action? What is inaction?—These questions have long puzzled the sages. For we must pay heed to action, must pay heed to forbidden action. Must pay heed likewise to inaction.—
> The nature of action is unfathomable.
> —*Bhagavatgita,* Fourth Song.

To Hindu philosophy, seeing as it did true spirituality in the negation of life and the world, the meaning of action or, more particularly, the justification of human activity, was the most crucial problem to be solved, the most vital question to be answered, if India was to survive and progress. The *Bhagavatgita*, "India's New Testament," undertook this difficult task. Its hero Aryuna, troubled by the apparent immorality of a war in which he must fight his own brothers and kill them if he is to be the victor, is inducted by the God whom he questions into the divergence of ethics, human and divine. He is induced to apprehend that not the visible consequences of the action but the spirit in which it is performed makes any human activity ethical and right. Zweig's hero Virata takes cognizance of the same truth. Only he is not indoctrinated by a God, but—to anticipate here the basic idea of Zweig's story— he arrives at this wisdom from his own experience with the world—that is to say, the experience of his inability to act in accordance with the ethical laws of human conduct toward man.

We shall see later how greatly Virata's striving for the fulfillment of these laws provided Zweig with the welcome opportunity to expound once again his own ethical creed. Literary criticism, so far as it has dealt at all with this story, has been able therefore to regard it with the same attitude Albert Schweitzer felt it displayed toward the *Bhagavatgita*. This book "contains," he states, "such marvellous phrases about inner detachment from the world, about the attitude of mind which knows no hatred and its kind, and about loving self-devotion to God, that *we are wont to overlook its non-ethical contents*." Similarly, [Zweig's] biographer was able to insist that "Virata . . . is united in brotherly union with Jeremiah, Erasmus, Castellio, Cicero and—Stefan Zweig himself," and that Virata's ethics are "the meaning of Zweig's timeless, ever recurring melody." Yet we propose to show how discordant a note is struck in that melody by Virata's conversion to Hindu determinism, and to reveal where Virata ceases to be Zweig himself. For from this recognition we are able to arrive at an understanding of Zweig's own inner struggle with a non-ethical world.

The way to this understanding leads through Virata's experience with his own ethical conscience—"the eyes of the undying brother." Yet before we turn to the high ethics of Virata-Zweig and their compelling influence upon Virata's life, it is well to recall here the basic reason for the divergence of those ethics from those of the East, a divergence which plays so important a part in Zweig's story.

The current of thought which has been most influential in the formation of occidental culture, having grown out of the synthesis of its Hellenic-Hebraic-Christian heritage, is dualistic. It conceives of the universe as a compound of two basically incongruous principles such as mind (or spirit) and matter, or creator and creation, which are in constant conflict with each other, the one being highest perfection and supreme ethical law, the other inert and imperfect. In this general concept man's soul becomes the battleground upon which these two conflicting principles fight their never-ceasing war, in which man is called upon to overcome his animal nature—that is to say, the laws of matter—and to live in accordance with the laws of the spirit, creator, or God, who, as Kant formulated it, is the highest ethical ideal.

Hindu philosophy, on the other hand, is monistic. It conceives of the universe not as a compound of two incompatible principles but as identical with the force that brought it into being, moves it on, and absorbs everything that exists back again into itself. Brahman, this omnipresent force, and Atman, its incarnation in man, thus are but two forms of the same principle that is one in kind. This is the meaning of the great words, *Tat tvam asi,* "That is you," which insist that man and the world spirit are one. Man's spiritual obligation is to live in constant mystical contemplation of this force and, by killing in himself the will to live, to speed up the innate desire of his soul to leave its individuation and to return to its source—the desire to become absorbed again into the force from which it came.

In later phases of Hindu philosophy Brahman became identified with God and creator, expecting love and devotion of man; and the demand for inactive mystical contemplation of the world spirit gave way to the conviction that its laws can, and even must, be fulfilled in an active life, in which, as Buddha taught, all actions must be performed in the "right attitude of mind." This Eastern concept of "right attitude of mind" has no analogue in Western ethics. This last fact cannot surprise us if we realize that the world spirit, or the cause of all being— by whatever name that it may be designated—can hardly be conceived of as an ethical force if it is identified in monistic thought with life or being itself. Thus, with Buddha and the *Bhagavatgita,* to act "rightly" means to conduct one's activity in awareness of the fact that no action is in itself a goal of life, but only a means by which the laws of life become fulfilled. "Wrong" action, or—as it is phrased in the lines from the *Bhagavatgita* which served Zweig as his motto—"forbidden" action, is activity performed in forgetfulness of the fact that all life, including man's own, is in constant flux. In other words, it is activity executed in an attitude of mind in which the action becomes the indulgence of man's own desires and the expression of his will to live. For such activity must needs produce a new *Karma* that will lead to man's rebirth, and thus to the continuation of life, instead of to the liberation from its mere suffering and pain for which his soul yearns.

If with this basic difference between occidental and oriental thought in mind we turn now to Zweig's hero Virata, we become immediately aware of the fact that this Indian is spiritually at home in the West:

> A great warrior and the prototype of courage and justice, Virata is called on by his king to defend his rights against an usurper. Virata's intrepidity turns the monarch's imminent defeat into victory. Yet this victory becomes the most fateful event in the hero's life. Among those whom he has slain with his sword he recognizes his own brother, whose broken eyes stare at him with terror. Their accusing look awakens in Virata an understanding of the immorality of his action and the responsibility of man in an ethical world. From this minute on, Virata's entire life will be an effort to avoid the confounding accusation that stares at him with the eyes of his slain brother. Yet he will not succeed, and the accusing eyes will stare at him again and again.
>
> Virata drops his sword into the river and renounces his warfaring life. "The Invisible One," he says, "has sent me a sign, and my heart has understood. I have slain my brother, and this has taught me that everyone who slays another human being kills his brother. I cannot lead the armies in war, for the sword is the embodiment of force, and force is the enemy of right."

Virata's mystical experience with the eyes of his slain brother apparently takes its starting point with the *Bhagavatgita* and Aryuna's hesitancy to kill his own brothers in war. Yet with Zweig this biological brotherhood becomes the spiritual brotherhood of mankind. The great significance of this change is but the expression of the essential difference between Western and Eastern thought, between the maxim Aryuna is made to understand and that of the words (Matt. 22:37-40): "Thou shalt love the Lord thy God. . . . This is the first . . . commandment. And the second is *like unto it, thou shalt love thy neighbor as thyself.* On these two commandments hang *all the law. . . .*" (Italics mine.)

This basic Western creed has found its eager exponent in Zweig, the untiring warrior against war and the use of force. His biographer implies that the mood conveyed in the opening scenes of Zweig's legend suggests the feeling of one of the author's best Italian friends when he realized, at some time during the First World War, that Zweig stood within reach of his friend's gun. Be this as it may, it is clear that Zweig's

horror of seeing Europe divided by that war into two enemy camps, and its soil turned into the battleground of fratricide, heightened the responsibility which his ethical beliefs and convictions placed upon him—the responsibility of opening the eyes of his fellow men to the madness and criminality of war, the immorality of man's conduct, and the true spirituality that his times lacked.

If it is thus true that Virata's first esoteric experience with the eyes of the undying brother is rooted in Zweig's own fight against an immoral world, Virata's second meeting with their accusing stare is no less intertwined with Zweig's own ethical creed:

> Virata, who has exchanged the sword of the warrior for the robe of the judge and who has been living in peace with his conscience for many years, is called upon one day to judge a man who has killed eleven people. The murderer, however, insists that he has done no wrong but only justice to a man who had sold the girl he loves to a rich merchant, and to his tribe. With mocking words he challenges Virata's wisdom and the justice of his verdict condemning him to spend eleven years in the darkness of the dungeon and to receive one hundred lashes each month. Virata would not have heeded the murderer's offending behavior and words, had there not been in his eyes the same condemning accusation that Virata had seen once before in the eyes of his slain brother. Shaken in his belief in the infallibility of his wisdom and justice by this new and frightening reminder, Virata knows that he must find out for himself whether his verdicts are really wise and just. Secretly he thus takes for but a month the murderer's place in the dungeon. The frightful experience of these thirty days teaches Virata that "he who passes judgment on another does injustice and grievous wrong" and that "the law of retaliation is itself unjust. . . . No one can judge another."

Virata's pronouncement will probably call to mind the words (John 8:7): "Let him who is without sin throw the first stone." However, Zweig's demand to abstain altogether from judging and punishing others goes beyond Christ's demand for the examination of one's own conscience before judging and condemning others. To some extent, Zweig seems here a disciple of Freud, whose discovery of the important role played by the unconscious in the life of man has curbed moral indignation in the face of crime and has taught man to refrain from judging others. Yet this Freudian aspect of Virata's words is but another side of the thoughts they suggest and, again, does not cover the full significance of Virata's experience in the dungeon. Rather, it seems that from this experience—that is to say, the deprivation of light, the deadening pain of the lashes, the agonizing solitude of the prison, and his own burning desire for the allurements of life—Virata arrived at an understanding of the manifest accessional cruelty of every punishment compared to that of the crime. In other words, he came to see the drastic inequality and incompatibility of their two spheres. Punishment is dealt in cold blood, crime in the heat of life, however premeditated it may have been. No criminal situation can ever be precisely reversed by punishment, and man can never do to the criminal what the criminal has done to others. Through the mouths of the murderer and of his protagonist, Zweig suggests that there is no measuring stick by which it is possible to measure the greatness of a crime, no mathematical table which permits us to find the correct equation between punishment and guilt, no coin with which the criminal can be made to pay for his offense and which is not an extortion. Therefore he who wishes to be just, he says, must neither punish nor judge.

> Zweig's hero Virata thus takes off forever the robe of the judge, withdrawing from all public activity into the confinement of his home. Yet he must learn again that the peace with his conscience that he had thus hoped to find is illusive. One day a slave is lashed by his sons. The unmistakable likeness of that slave's eyes to those of the slain brother leaves Virata awe-stricken. He orders his sons to return their freedom to all the slaves belonging to his household, since "freedom is the most intimate right of human beings." His sons, however, refuse to obey. Force, they insist, is the law of this earth. By force only the earth itself is made to yield fruit. By force only man can be master and owner. Moreover, he who orders others to do what they do not wish to do out of their own free will, encroaches no less upon the freedom of others than any master infringes upon that of his slaves.

> To this Virata knows no answer. Yet he understands that he must neither force his will on others, however justified his request may seem, nor have any part in the law of force which, as his sons claim, is the law of this earth. He thus divides his earthly possessions among his sons and departs from the community of men into the solitude of the woods, where he will be able to live outside the law of force in contemplation of the eternal spirit.

The implications of the thought underlying this narrative point in two directions. The true liberal, Zweig seems to say first, must not use force to make others accept his point of view. Believing in freedom as "the most intimate right of human beings," he refuses to infringe upon the freedom of others, and, since he grants everyone the right to his own opinion, he does not fight the opinion of others. Where he cannot convince, he must needs withdraw.

Second, however, Zweig implies that man has based his collective life not upon right, but upon might, not upon ethics, but upon force. Thus Virata's sons are right when they insist that the law of this earth is force, which is the law of matter. It operates no less in the earth itself than in man's striving to be master and owner and in the enslavement of man by man. Yet it remains alien to the one who adheres to the spirit.

Norman Brittin has made the true observation that "more than any other method Zweig favors the method of antithesis" [see excerpt dated 1940]. Yet, with Zweig the antithesis is more than a mere method. It is the expression of his antithetical philosophy—that is to say, of his dualistic concept of the world. Jeremiah, Erasmus, Castellio, Cicero, Virata are Zweig's heroes of the spirit, each of them symbol and representative of the ethical and spiritual life of man. In their opposites—be it one opponent or many, as, for example, a whole people in *Jeremiah*—the forces of matter are at work. By this emphatic

repetition of the same basic idea, expressed with so much emotional force and in such great variety, Zweig seems to say: The times may be Biblical or historical, the scene the East or the West, the same fundamental struggle between spirit and matter, love and hatred, ethics and force, can be detected everywhere and at all times. For this struggle is timeless and ageless; it is in fact as old as conscious and civilized man.

Thus, to hold the mirror up to his own twentieth century, Zweig did not need to speak of men of his day. Whatever the particular phase of human life with which he deals, from it emerges unmistakably the contemporary scene and its threat to liberal living, in particular, and to the ethical and spiritual values of Western civilization, in general.

Yet Zweig's reiterated interpretation of the world as the same basic conflict between the forces of good and evil is also of momentous significance for the author himself. It shows how deeply the clash between materiality and spirituality, between amorality and ethicality, has stirred his mind, and that he was unable to make his peace with this disturbing reality. In other words, it betrays Zweig's own mental and emotional struggle and wrestling with the perturbing problem, his own mental agony in the face of the antithetical universe.

Whereas in his biographies Zweig has made this conflict the leitmotiv, so to speak, of his heroes' lives, without attempting to present a solution to this problem, in his legend *Virata or The Eyes of the Undying Brother* he groped for an answer to the intricate and exciting question. Here where imagination and philosophical thought alone, independent of established historical facts, could determine the course of the action and the fate of his hero, it seemed possible to him, at least, to come to grips with the riddle of life, the great enigma, to which the historical lives of men offered no clue and yielded no answer. Yet, was it really possible to find a satisfactory philosophical solution to the perturbing complexity of life?

It was clear to Zweig as a European that, if there was a solution at all, it was certainly not the one which his hero Virata proposed by retiring from the world to a solitary life of philosophical speculation and mystical contemplation of the spirit—just as Hindu philosophy has come to see this truth. He knew that man, being matter *and* spirit, cannot escape the nexus of life; that detachment from it is virtually impossible, and thus any attempt at isolation can be nothing but selfishness and pride. Had not his social conscience already convinced him of this fact, philosophical thought would have affirmed to Zweig anew that not in solitude, but in union, must man fulfill the eternal circle of life and his individual existence.

> Indeed, Virata must meet again the accusing eyes of the undying brother, and he must learn from this last encounter that his very offense to the ethical laws of life consisted in shunning the world and in placing himself outside life and the community of men. The attempt was vain, since—as Virata now understands—"even the solitary lives in all his brethren."

> Thus, this prodigal son of life returns from the solitude of the jungle to the habitations of men. His hair is gray, his body weak, but his troubled heart and mind have found peace.

Yet it is a pitiable peace, and the price he has paid for it is dear. For the tranquillity of mind that Virata ultimately gains—it is but the peace of Hindu determinism. He knows now that man has no free will, and that "all human beings are but super-marionettes impelled by the inscrutable puppet-player of the universe." He has experienced that no one can "elude the eyes of the undying brother on whom our actions forever bear,"—that sad knowledge of the *Bhagavatgita,* which states that "all undertakings are surrounded by evil as fire is surrounded by smoke." Thus Virata has come to understand that all that man can do is to serve, blindly and without questioning. "For all willing is confusion, and all service is wisdom."

It is of comparatively little significance for the scope of this deterministic thought that Virata "serves" for the rest of his life as the keeper of the king's dogs, forgotten by men, and, when he dies after long, uneventful years, is buried in the servants' grave. Still, this end served Zweig well to show how great must needs become the humility of man upon recognizing the inscrutability of the plan upon which life and the universe are based, and the futility of every human attempt to understand the laws of life or to change their predetermined course. Yet the implications of this deterministic world view are of far greater significance than Virata's extreme humility permits us to see.

If, for the purpose of exposing the significance of Virata's ultimately acquired peace of mind, it is permitted here to take some liberty with Zweig's story, let us assume that the king, whom Virata approaches for service upon his return from the jungle, was as wise as proverbial kings commonly are. If so, he would hardly have taken offense at Virata's abstruse words that only he who serves is free, while he who commands is not. Nor would his kingly pride have been hurt by Virata's statement that all human deeds have the same value with God as long as they are performed in the true spirit of service. Such a wise king, instead of scorning and mocking Virata by offering to make him the keeper of his dogs, might have asked him to lead again his armies in war. Then Virata would once more have wielded the sword, "the embodiment of force," undisturbed by the fact that he must kill his brother anew. Or he would have condemned his brother again to the darkness of the dungeon and to scourges, had he been asked by this wise king to be once more his country's highest judge.

Enough of this speculation. It must suffice that Virata has succeeded in banishing forever the eyes of the undying brother. This burning and confounding accusation will, indeed, no longer be back to disturb the peace of his mind and the tranquillity of his soul. He has lulled forevermore his once wakeful conscience to sleep.

At this point we have arrived at the crucial problem which Zweig's legend presents to the critic. For from this end arises the question what the complete negation of all ethical values professed by the hero can mean in a work of Zweig, who seems here to reverse his position and to renounce his own fight and creed. In trying to answer this question we must not forget that the negativistic determinism of the Orient to which Virata ultimately submits, precisely because it dispenses with an ethical world, is able to solve the complexity of life and to set man's mind at ease. For here, as we have seen, the opposites of good and evil no longer exist, and the dualism of matter and spirit disappears. The antithetical world becomes synthesized as the expression of one single force, one idea, one will, whereby God ceases to be an absolute and objective reality with definite ethical attributes but is bound up with the human soul no less than the soul is bound up with him.

It seems that in the poetic intuition of a creative moment, Zweig grasped the profundity of this esoteric mysticism of Hindu philosophy and the possibility that its deterministic thought held for acquiescence of the mind in the perplexing reality of life. Yet I make bold to believe that with him this understanding remained the solitary philosophical experience of an elated hour and never grew into a permanent attitude of mind or a convincing concept of the universe. For this, Zweig was too deeply rooted in Western thought and ethics. To him, this world remained spirit and matter, ethics and force, opposites which could never make peace, and thus this earth and battleground upon which the ideals of human ethics, of the spiritual brotherhood of man, humanism and humanitarianism, liberalism and freedom, continued to be in constant conflict with the dark, non-ethical drives of man's own nature. If his hero Virata proposed that the battle was hopeless and senseless, and inner peace possible only by accepting without question the existing conditions of life, Zweig himself saw in the realization of these ethical ideals life's only true goal and in man's striving for their attainment his only claim on eternity.

The realization of Zweig's unchanged mental attitude toward the ethical problem of the world, in contrast to the *volte-face* of his hero, clarifies, we hope, the perplexing end of his story. At the same time, we suggest that this ending bears some analogy, at least, to the even more bewildering end of the author's life. It may, therefore, be helpful in casting light on this unhappy event. Zweig's suicide, committed in his Brazilian exile . . . has called forth many comments from the author's personal friends. If another comment may be added here, Zweig's desperate act, when seen in the light of *Virata,* will probably appear as the counterpart to his hero's solution to the ethical question of life—that is to say, its other extreme. To accept for himself—in the face of the last world events that he witnessed and the intense anguish that the spiritual regression of his time caused him—Virata's proposition of philosophical acquiescence in the unchangeable course of life and his esoteric insight into the harmonizing truth of the *Tat tvam asi,* no doubt, would have meant a form of spiritual suicide to Zweig's European mind. He chose therefore what must have seemed to him a spiritually more dignified way out of his inner torment—a way which we deeply regret, but from which we cannot withhold our sympathy.

Gertrude E. Teller, "'Virata or The Eyes of the Undying Brother' and Stefan Zweig's Thought," in The Germanic Review, *Vol. XXVII, No. 1, February, 1952, pp. 31-40.*

JOSEPH LEFTWICH (essay date 1958)

[*Leftwich was a Dutch-born writer and compiler of many works on Jewish and Yiddish subjects, and the translator of works from German and Yiddish into English. In the following excerpt, he defends Zweig against allegations that Zweig was indifferent to the plight of the Jews and that his avoidance of political action was the result of cowardice.*]

'The dead ride swiftly' out of the memory of the living. 'Does anyone still read Hardy?' was a comment I read when the new Hardy biography appeared. 'I am 28', said a young writer in a London periodical, 'and if it be my contribution to understanding my generation let me say that the world seen by and represented by Shaw and Wells, Chesterton and Belloc is a world not only alien but also incomprehensible to me.' So I was not surprised to be told that Stefan Zweig, who died in the midst of the war, and whose mind belonged to the pre-war world, is little more than a name to this post-war generation.

Zweig felt it in his lifetime. He said so in his autobiography, where he described his world aptly in the title he chose for the book: **'The World of Yesterday.'** 'My feeling', he wrote, 'is that the world in which I grew up and the world of to-day are entirely separate worlds. Whenever in conversation with younger friends I relate some episode of the time before the First War, I notice from their astonished questions how much that is still obvious reality to me has already become historical and incomprehensible to them.'

Zweig knew he was living through a period in which the world was changing. 'I saw the great mass ideologies grow and spread before my eyes', he wrote—'Fascism, National-Socialism, Bolshevism.' And he felt his personal tragedy in the midst of it: 'I was forced to be a defenceless, helpless witness.'

He had grown up to believe his world, the world of yesterday, secure. He came 'to know finally that this world of security was nothing but a castle of dreams.' He had not seen it till 'the great storm smashed it.' But others had been more perceptive. Wickham Steed told us that when he was the Vienna correspondent of 'The Times' before the First War, 'I who lived in Austria from the end of 1902 until the summer of 1913 was so penetrated by this sense of doom that I left the Austrian capital with the relief a man may feel when he escapes from a vast edifice that is tottering to its fall.'

Stefan Zweig in common with German-speaking Jewry as a whole felt none of that sense of doom. On the contrary, he called that period 'prior to the First World War'—Wickham Steed's period 'until the summer of 1913'—'The Golden Age of Security. Everything in our almost thousand-year-old monarchy seemed based on permanency', he wrote, 'and the State itself was the chief guarantor of this stability.'

The First World War in 1914 disturbed Stefan Zweig's sense of stability. In **'The World of Yesterday'** he recalls that in the First War he had been 'at the German front.' Before he escaped to Switzerland to join Romain Rolland's peace campaign, Stefan Zweig had been in the Austrian army. A friend of Zweig's of those days gave me a letter Zweig wrote to him from Vienna in 1915: 'I am a military person—*Zugsführer*. I work every day seven to eight hours at my war service. My nerves are torn', he went on, however, 'I feel very much diminished in my entire sense of life. For those who believe in Europe, the one, indivisible Europe, these days have become a catastrophe. I have much on my heart, but the words all stay within and wound my soul.'

With the end of the First War, Zweig thought stability had returned. 'We greeted the ascendance of order as the beginning of lasting peace. Again we thought we had risen above war, chronic fools that we had always been. Viewed from to-day the short decade between 1924 and 1933 represents an intermission in the catastrophic sequence of events whose witness and victims our generation has been since 1914.'

Yet the 'chronic fools' lived with their illusion that stability had returned. When the great storm of 1933 smashed the illusion, the older generation of German-speaking Jewry found, as Stefan Zweig did, that their reality had become incomprehensible to the younger generation, even of German-speaking Jewry. The older people who escaped became mostly refugees, emigrés, living with memories of the past, living, as Zweig put it, 'without solid ground under our feet.' The younger generation did not become refugees but immigrants, settlers in new lands, in Britain or America, or as Zionists builders in Israel. They found solid ground under their feet. The older

people retained their German speech, and German ways, and their hopes of an early return to Germany. I remember an afternoon at my house in 1934, with Stefan Zweig and several other German Jews, when the news arrived of the Roehm blood-bath. It was pathetic to see the stirring of hope among them. They were eager to get away, to go home and pack for their journey. Zweig was not so trustful as the others. His world had turned upside down, and he could not believe that he would live to see it right itself. He put something of his own feeling into an essay he wrote about Ernst Lissauer, who after the First War had found himself driven into the wilderness because of the 'Hymn of Hate' (against England) he had written during the war. 'After this first excommunication came another. National-Socialist German banned his writings. The man who was outlawed first because he had been too German was cast out a second time because he was not German enough.' Stefan Zweig clung to his German language. Though widely translated into English and other languages he was unhappy because his German words, the words he wrote—his words and not those of the translator—were not printed. 'Now I have only translations', he complained.

Language means much to a writer, especially one so fastidious about style as Stefan Zweig was. He felt cut off from the soil and atmosphere of his language, hearing round him a different tongue than that in which he thought and wrote, which was the medium of his work. It must have caused him anguish to read in Dr. Ernest Barker's review in the 'Observer' of his **'Erasmus':** 'Perhaps some of the errors are errors of the translators.' As one of Stefan Zweig's translators (in a note to me he said: 'Many thanks, dear friend, for the translation—excellent as always'), I am aware what variance of thought the different mind of the translator can unwittingly introduce. Translation is a very important activity. Stefan Zweig did a lot of translation himself, and much of his original work was a form of translation, to acquaint readers in German with the work and the mind of Balzac, Dickens, Dostoevsky, Verhaeren, Ben Jonson and others. The translator, by making accessible the work of other peoples and other ages, influences the whole course of civilisation, as did the translators of the Bible, and as the translators of the works of antiquity did in the Renaissance. Yet the existence of so many different styles of the same author through the minds of the different translators shows that however close the translation is, it is not the work of his own pen.

It certainly must have startled this European to read in that same review that the book was 'written in high and gorgeous style, often with an exotic orientalism of style.' Is there an underlying oriental streak in all Jews?

Stefan Zweig shared with other established German writers in exile the difficulties common to all emigrés, and to emigré writers most of all. One of the chief difficulties is nostalgia, homesickness. The younger generation not having the accumulated memories of the old, were able to assimilate. The younger people learnt English in England and America, and Hebrew in Israel, and took their place in the new life. In Zweig's own phrase, 'all the bridges have been burnt.' The reality of Stefan Zweig and his contemporaries has become 'incomprehensible' to the young people to-day.

Yet the younger writer of 28 who said he found Shaw and Wells, Chesterton and Belloc 'not only alien but also incomprehensible' ended his essay with these words: 'But a new humanism, which some are calling romanticism, is beginning to inspire us,' which he thinks will bring an understanding of those writers of the recent past who now seem 'alien and incomprehensible'. The point is that 'modern times' keep receding into the past, and in another generation the day of this young writer and that of Shaw, Wells, Stefan Zweig and the rest of their generation will merge, and to the succeeding generation they will both seem the same.

It has happened before. Dr. Needham begins his book 'Taste and Criticism in the Eighteenth Century' with the observation: "Twentieth century disillusionment may sometimes be heard comforting itself with the ironical remark that 'after all, European civilisation came to an end with the French Revolution'." Neither did it, in spite of our 'angry young men' and as Stefan Zweig feared it would, come to an end with Hitler. 'In all epochs', said Anatole France, 'people are alarmed by the same signs.' Yet, he concludes, 'if we are not precisely similar to our fathers we resemble them more than we think, and sometimes more than we like.'

I suppose it is true that most of the people who have recently formed the *Stefan Zweig Gesellschaft* are of his own generation, his contemporaries and friends. Yet there are some younger men among them. . . . Just as Zweig found in the medieval Erasmus something so 'strangely modern' that he seemed to speak to him in his own thoughts and words about the crisis of his own life and time, so Zweig may still have something to say to the younger people who were children when he died. We can carry this idea of the gulf between the generations too far. After all, we do not always keep starting our literature afresh. The Bible and Homer, Shakespeare, Goethe, Tolstoy and Dickens, and lesser writers of a century and more ago, still have meaning for us. There is an underlying element of all-humanness in them that is as modern—in the sense of facing our problems of to-day and depicting people who are as real as those we know—as anything now written. It is true that Ruth, gleaning in the field of Boaz, is as near to our minds as Hardy's Tess. The line that links all our literature from the first recorded story in Genesis till to-day is continuous and unbroken. It was not chance that decided Stefan Zweig to choose Jeremiah when, during the First World War, he wanted to write an anti-war play. 'In choosing a biblical theme', he said, 'I had unknowingly touched upon something that had remained unused in me up to that time.'

Certainly in Israel there is something that can appeal in Zweig's works. I have in front of me the words written by one of his younger admirers: 'The author of **'Jeremiah'** remains in us and with us, in the age-old tragedy of the Jewish people who, in our day, are reconstructing our ancient country in the land of the Prophets.' (pp. 81-6)

I have seen it said that Stefan Zweig was at best 'a Hitler Jew'—not a Jew by choice, not a positive Jew, but one driven by Hitlerism into the acceptance of an unpleasant and uncomfortable fact he had tried to forget, and that he therefore was an outsider with 'no inner relationship with Jewish life.' 'Not to him', said one writer, 'was given that faith in a divine providence which sustains the humble orthodox Jew even inside the German dungeon, nor the ardent belief of the Zionist, who knows which way salvation lies. Like so many contemporaries he lived in a world that is gone, and he could not readjust himself, as we, the Jews, must do.'

But others remembered that Stefan Zweig as a young man had been with Herzl and with the Zionist movement in Vienna. He himself said that he had been driven out of the Zionist movement because of the way in which the Zionists treated Herzl,

Zweig as a younger man.

by 'the hardly imaginable disrespect of even the foremost of his followers towards Herzl, it made me instinctively avoid those people. I knew how badly Herzl needed the help of devoted men, young men who would, without hesitation, work with him, even in opposition to their own private views; and the quarrelsome, contentious spirit of the internal revolt against Herzl made me turn away immediately from the movement to which I was drawn only because of Herzl.' Stefan Zweig spoke to me several times about Herzl and he often reverted to that central fact, how Herzl's followers had estranged him and driven him away from Herzl's movement. (pp. 90-1)

Later he 'turned away' as he expressed it, 'from Dr. Herzl's ideal in Zion.' He came to feel that the Jews were 'greater as thinkers and artists when they lived amidst the clash of the outside world than when they were isolated in a Jewish land.' (p. 91)

I doubt whether a man of Stefan Zweig's way of thinking about people and about the world would have stayed in the Zionist movement even if there had not been that difficulty over Herzl. He had once been a devoted follower of Martin Buber, and he told me that he could not understand how he had ever found it possible to agree with Buber. He was not, he said, a party man. 'Joining a Party you must overlook all the injustices of the Party, sacrifice your personal freedom, which is too great a sacrifice for an artist. It is impossible to be a good politician without telling lies. And the intellectual who endeavours to be just, to understand the opponent, can never be a fanatic, convinced only of the rightness and righteousness of his own Party. That is why the intellectual, that is why the artist can never be a good Party man.' (p. 92)

It was part of Zweig's misfortune that people had acquired the habit of attributing his shrinking withdrawal from anything strident and assertive to personal cowardice. Professor Jack Isaacs, of London University, who knew Zweig well, wrote to me about this article: 'I think there is a good deal to be said for Zweig's point of view—purely as expediency—though I fear there is a strong element of inner cowardice in it.'

At the New York Press Conference in 1935, where Zweig tried to explain his idea of an international Jewish periodical, the Pressmen tried to draw him into a denunciation of Hitler, and expressed their disappointment and distaste at the way he refused to be drawn. Joseph Brainin, who was there, said in an article published at the time: 'His reluctance to speak out against Hitlerism exasperated me. Persistently I tried to draw him out of his shell, intent on extracting from him a quotable condemnation of Hitler's barbaric persecution of the Jews. My efforts proved vain.' But Brainin went on: 'It was only a few days later, when I met him privately that I caught a glimpse of his tortured soul.'

In one of his letters to me Zweig said that he could not forget how his words might affect the fate of the Jews still left in Germany. 'They are hostages', he wrote, 'and anything we who are free say or do will be revenged on these defenceless people. We must do nothing now that involves a personal polemical demonstration.'

I know he had pangs of conscience about it. Brainin saw rightly when he 'caught a glimpse of his tortured soul.' Zweig was thinking of himself when he wrote in 'Erasmus': 'In political times it is harder to remain outside than to take a party stand.'

Zweig was fastidious, in his style of writing, in his home surroundings, and in his way of living. He liked good food, good wine and good cigars, no car of his own (not in London) but taxis wherever he had to go. That too was an Erasmian affinity. Zweig made a point of the fact that Erasmus could wear 'only fine and warm stuffs, sleep only in clean beds, he avoided smelly streets; he loved well-prepared food; he liked good wine—if it was the least bit acid his stomach turned.' And again, speaking of Erasmus: 'Any bad smell, noise, tumult, crudeness was an offence to his sensibility, a murderous torment of his spirit.' 'With such fearsome nerves', he concluded, 'with such over-sensitiveness of his organs it is hard for a man to be a hero.' Of course, as Zweig admitted, he had drawn his picture of Erasmus from himself.

It was his dislike of tumult and disturbance that made him anxious to avoid argument, denunciation and insistence on a particular point in a controversy. He slunk unheroically away. There were many people—especially Jewish writers who wanted a more active participation in the battle against Hitler—who did not like him, and sneered at him as a coward. Why didn't he stand up and fight, like Victor Hugo and Zola? Zweig tried to explain several times, as for instance in his message to Max Brod on his 50th birthday, where he spoke about the conflict in a writer, who, in order to write, must stand aside, concentrate on his work, keep away from active partisanship. But he was never in doubt about which side he was on. And if there was anything positive he could do with his word or pen to help those who suffered he was eager to do it. (pp. 97-8)

One could guess from his writings that Zweig was such a shrinking, hypersensitive man, who preferred to be alone with his thoughts or with one or two friends of his own kind. There is a variant I have in Zweig's hand-writing of the last page of his novel '**Beware of Pity**', a slightly different ending from that in the published book—I am struck by a sentence there: 'Somewhere to escape from the spectre.' When you read his stories you find that nearly all deal with souls in torment, trying to escape from a spectre. And you realise with a shock how many of his stories end with suicide. The way he describes Kleist's decision to commit suicide made me wonder how much of that description was Zweig's own feeling about death and suicide. Even Kleist's search for the woman who will die with him, who dies with him, brings to mind Stefan Zweig's second wife, Lotte Altmann, who died with him. 'The day no longer hurts him, his taut soul already breathes eternity, the painful vulgarity becomes remote, and he blissfully lives his own ego.'

To escape from something hateful and hostile which was pursuing, hunting him, became an obsession. . . .

Stefan Zweig had absorbed with his European humanism much humanistic doubt. The intellectual in him did not scoff and deny; but he lacked conviction. 'God was silent', he wrote in his story '**Rachel Strives with God**'. 'And nothing is more terrible on earth and in the heavens and in the suspended clouds between them than God's silence. When God is silent time ends, and the light goes out.' (p. 99)

Joseph Leftwich, "Stefan Zweig and the World of Yesterday," in Year Book of The Leo Baeck Institute, Vol. III, edited by Robert Weltsch, East and West Library, 1958, pp. 81-100.

DONALD G. DAVIAU AND **HARVEY I. DUNKLE** (essay date 1973)

[*Daviau is an American critic and educator, and the editor of the journal* Modern Austrian Literature. *He has also written and edited several works on German and Austrian literary figures. In the following excerpt, Daviau and Dunkle examine the two main characters of* Schachnovelle (The Royal Game), *and maintain that the story's conclusion is optimistic because Dr. B. survives his ordeal to keep the humanistic spirit alive. For a contrasting interpretation, see the excerpt by D. B. Douglas (1980).*]

Stefan Zweig's **Schachnovelle**, one of his most enduring and best known works, has been acclaimed as a masterpiece and as his finest *Novelle*. (p. 370)

In **Schachnnovelle** Zweig employs the traditional form of the *Rahmennovelle* with the unique feature that he himself appears both in the "frame" story and in the one inner story as narrator of Czentovic's background. The other inner story is told directly by Dr. B., the main protagonist, to the narrator. By this means Zweig avoids repetition in the manner of presenting his two principal characters and also establishes clearly that Dr. B. is more important than Czentovic. Zweig's aim is to contrast the emotional responses of these two unusual psychological 'specimens' before, while, and after they engage each other in a chess match. **Schachnovelle** is not primarily an attempt by Zweig to confront his age but instead may be considered a theoretical psychological experiment, intended to test under stress the emotional reactions of two men with unique backgrounds. More specifically, since Czentovic is a more or less psychologically stable entity, the story centers on the reactions of the sensitive and vulnerable Dr. B.

While the beginning of *Schachnovelle* may lead the reader to assume at first that Czentovic is the author's main interest, the gradual shift of emphasis from Czentovic to McConnor to Dr. B. expands the story beyond the usual scope of a novella to a representation of three distinctly different kinds of monomaniacs: Czentovic by accident of birth, McConnor because of intellectual limitations and egotism, and Dr. B., who has been artificially deformed in one specific area of life by imprisonment and mistreatment.

The story divides into distinct parts, which, when viewed separately, illustrate the distributions of emphasis. It begins with approximately eleven pages of detailed description of Czentovic, as though the author intended to make a study of this freakish character. A brief paragraph expressing Zweig's interest in monomaniacs connects this section with the following fourteen pages, which deal with shipboard events prior to the introduction of Dr. B. In these transitional pages Zweig digresses on the subject of chess in general and his personal, basically negative, attitude toward it. Dr. B. is introduced in the next eight pages, followed by forty additional pages relating Dr. B.'s personal history. This section shows him as a victim of political tyranny and describes how through chance he became involved with chess. The final fourteen pages build to the climax of the story, as the two monomaniacs, the one created by accident of nature and the other by chance and the effects of dehumanizing treatment, are pitted against each other. The suspenseful action is resolved only on the last page by Dr. B.'s ostensible "defeat."

This unequal distribution shows that Dr. B. rather than Czentovic is the character of primary interest to the narrator, namely to Zweig, because he represents a new type of monomaniac, one created artificially. Czentovic, whose nature is as unchanging as it is unyielding, serves as a means of testing Dr. B.'s self-control and mental stability, just as a control group does in a psychological experiment. Since Czentovic is capable of only a minimal range of psychological responses, he offers little opportunity for the writer. By contrast, Dr. B., who is described as an intellectual, contains a number of possibilities, particularly in view of the psychological torture and conditioning that he has endured. Thus, in both form and subject matter the story is a psychological novella, Zweig's favorite genre. Its primary purpose is to demonstrate the effects of brainwashing, a relatively new and unfamiliar technique at the time, which was bound to fascinate Zweig because of his interest in psychology. (pp. 371-72)

Zweig's interest in different kinds of monomaniacs was of a scientifically detached nature. He did not make moral distinctions between "good" and "bad" monomaniacs but stressed that accomplishment in life is often achieved by individuals who dedicate all of their energies to a single idea, as in the case of Freud or Mary Baker Eddy or Magellan. Such single-minded determination can produce tragic results when strong-willed individuals like Mary Stuart collide with even stronger external circumstances and cannot find the flexibility of mind and heart necessary to ward off disaster. However, Zweig also shows repeatedly that the man of action who focuses on a single goal always triumphs temporarily over humanists, who tend to be passive intellectuals or dreamers. For example, Castellio, the pure intellectual, is sacrificed to Calvin's ambition, while Erasmus' efforts to prevent violence are thwarted by Luther. In short, one of Zweig's major concerns throughout his career is the typically Austrian theme of the conflict between reflection and action.

However, Zweig's scholarly detachment with regard to monomaniacs became a more personal matter with the rise of Hitler in Germany. Although Zweig had already shown in *Erasmus* and *Castellio gegen Calvin* how monomaniacs pose a serious threat to mankind when their objectives oppose the best interests of society and destroy the freedom of other individuals, the idea gained heightened personal significance when it moved from the theoretical and historical realm into the practical, real world of personal experience. Zweig, who had already warned his contemporaries of the potential danger of Hitler in *Erasmus,* saw his worst fears realized when his own privacy was invaded in Salzburg under the pretext of a search for alleged weapons. . . .

Nevertheless, despite this background and although the story does contain allusions to contemporary events, they are peripheral and not central to its purpose. *Schachnovelle,* as will be shown, is primarily a character study. The plot could be set in any historical period without detriment to the effectiveness of the narrative. (p. 373)

Since the resolution of the chess game forms the climax of the story, the relationship in the story between chess and the characters can best be shown by analysing the ending, and particularly the reasons for Dr. B.'s collapse and "defeat." Does Dr. B. lose the game because he is not really a chess player after all or does the deterioration of his mind during the game, as he reverts to the horrible conditions under which he learned to play, so disorient him that he cannot continue playing? Is Dr. B. really the chess master that he appears to be? Before the first game he himself questions his ability to play real games despite his memorization of fifty master games and despite innumerable improvised games that he played against himself while in solitary confinement. His one expressed motivation in agreeing to play Czentovic, despite the doctor's order to avoid chess, is his own intellectual curiosity to discover whether his former games were "real." . . . (p. 374)

Despite his self-doubts, the evidence indicates that Dr. B. can play chess in superior fashion, for otherwise it would be difficult to explain how he could first stalemate and then defeat the world champion. This achievement can not be attributed to beginner's luck in a game as complex as chess and against a champion who always plays to win. If Dr. B. is not a good player, the story contains a fatal weakness and becomes contrived rather than psychologically convincing. (pp. 374-75)

Does the unusual manner in which Dr. B. allegedly masters the game of chess violate the laws of learning probability? Certainly Zweig has presented an unusual situation, but not one that is either completely impossible or implausible. Thus, the story remains within the context of reality and does not shift to the level of unreality. . . . Although Zweig undoubtedly developed the psychological aspects of the story on the basis of his own intuition, nothing in his descriptions of Dr. B.'s reactions to solitary confinement, his subsequent learning of chess, and finally his inadvertently self-induced schizophrenia and mental collapse contradicts the findings of research on sensory deprivation. These details, however, are only incidental to the main thrust of the work, which is intended to show that a man, so "conditioned," will revert to his former state if subjected again to the same circumstances that originally induced this state.

To accomplish Zweig's purpose Dr. B. has to be a superior chess player. His strategic skill, at first as adviser to the group opposing Czentovic and then singly, demonstrates his thorough knowledge of the game and stresses particularly his ability to anticipate many moves. After two moves are made on Dr. B.'s advice, even Czentovic, who has been coasting to an easy victory, sees that a new opponent has entered the contest and looks around to identify him. As further testimony to Dr. B.'s ability, Czentovic insists in the final game on taking the full ten minutes allowed per move. Although he defends this tactic as a matter of principle, he has not employed it in the previous games, and it must be considered an extraordinary precaution for a champion facing an amateur, unless he regards the latter as a genuine threat. Having been forced to a draw and then defeated by Dr. B., Czentovic, whose entire existence depends on winning, clearly recognizes the seriousness of the challenge.

Czentovic's precaution is motivated by a practical consideration that provides a clue to his character. Possessing an innate capacity to sense his opponent's weakness, Czentovic has shrewdly observed that Dr. B.'s anxiety increases the longer he waits for his turn. Thus, he does not defeat Dr. B. by skillful playing but causes Dr. B. to defeat himself through his psychological vulnerability. While Dr. B. is shown to possess skill equal to Czentovic's, his "defeat" is inevitable and psychologically convincing.

Having demonstrated that the two men are worthy chess opponents, the story takes on a second level of meaning, which recurs often in Zweig's works: namely, the eternal conflict between monomaniacal brute force (tyrannical political power) and the humanist. Although the story is primarily a character study, it is also invested with the additional symbolic significance not merely of the contemporary events but of a struggle that has existed throughout history. (pp. 375-76)

If *Schachnovelle* is to be viewed in the symbolic terms discussed above, then one must question to what degree Dr. B. can serve as a legitimate symbol of the humanist. Since he has suffered a collapse, his mental health is more precarious than it normally would or should be. Thus, if he exemplifies the humanist, as seems clearly intended, the symbolism is weakened substantially by Dr. B.'s specialized and unique conditioning, unless Zweig intended to show that the humanist has hidden psychological weaknesses which emerge to incapacitate him at times of stress. Under normal conditions (situations not involving chess), Dr. B. can function unimpaired. Only in playing chess does he revert to the dangerous mental state that leads to collapse. If one interprets the story as showing that humanists lead brilliant lives and careers in peaceful times when they can live on the level of words and theories, but succumb to their inner weaknesses in times of chaos, when they should act, then it would become a pessimistic commentary on the humanist and on his capability of contributing to the shaping of society. It might also tempt one to conclude that Zweig's natural pessimism, reinforced by this conclusion, led to his suicide. However, we do not feel that the story proceeds in this pessimistic direction, which goes against the grain of all of Zweig's other works.

Zweig's basic attitude is perhaps best illustrated by his study of Erasmus. . . . (pp. 376-77)

The study of Erasmus, like the parallel work *Castellio gegen Calvin,* is basically an essay on the contrast between the humanist and the monomaniac of strong will. The same confrontation is the essence of *Schachnovelle,* where the struggle is symbolized by the chess game. Since Zweig tended to reflect his personal views in his biographical studies, often confronted humanists with fanatics, and frequently symbolized the world

of struggles as a chessboard, it is possible to view *Schachnovelle* as a poetic statement representing the eternal competition of these two types. As such the story fits into the direct line of his work (e.g., *Magellan, Jeremiah, Mary Stuart, Mary Baker Eddy, Castellio gegen Calvin,* and *Triumph und Tragik des Erasmus von Rotterdam*) and does not represent any change of viewpoint on his part. (p. 377)

A simple contrast between Dr. B. as the humanist and Czentovic as the willful monomaniac is, however, untenable, because Dr. B.'s condition is produced by extraordinary circumstances, so that he is at best an inadequate symbol of the humanist. During the game Dr. B.'s mind reverts to the conditions immediately preceding his mental collapse in solitary confinement, and he loses all sense of balance, perspective, and reasoning powers that characterize the humanist. He becomes the opposite of a rational human being with a sense of values and regresses to his former state of a dehumanized robot intent on self-destruction. If *Schachnovelle* is interpreted to mean the defeat of the humanistic idea by a monomaniac exerting his will upon the world, this means that, in addition to the appearance of a totally new outlook in his last completed work, the story is contrived and lacks the inner integrity that a convincing use of symbols would provide. But the story does not represent any change of outlook, for, although Dr. B. is defeated in chess, he has survived his ordeal and will live to see the collapse of the tyrant.

Similarly, it would also be a mistake to regard Czentovic as a symbol of tyranny. Zweig's portrait of Czentovic (which may have been suggested by the humble origins of a real chess champion, Capablanca) makes it evident that he could not adequately represent a dictator. Czentovic, who is a chess genius despite his intellectual inferiority, is in every sense just as unusual a case as Dr. B. Chess holds unique importance for both men: for the one as the only means to be somebody, for the other as the means he has used to preserve his sanity. In both cases chess becomes a matter of life and death. Both play chess to win and both become robots when involved in the game.

Czentovic is described as "dieser unmenschliche Automat" ["that inhuman automaton"] who never plays for enjoyment but is always ready to play for money. He considers himself the greatest man in the world for having defeated all of the clever intellectual speakers and writers in their own field and for earning more money than they do. . . . He resents educated people and finds enjoyment in defeating learned men in the game which they claim as their own. Czentovic, who has no personal appeal and is an ungraceful performer even at chess, relies heavily on his peasant cunning and enormous patience. That he can be so enormously successful is a commentary on the nature of chess, which . . . Zweig does not hold in high esteem.

Czentovic serves incidentally as an example of the materialists like McConnor, whose only standard of measurement is the form of success rewarded by money. Zweig, who lived before the days of high-priced athletes, seems to be deploring the ability to acquire large sums for performing a skill without regard to its value to society and particularly without regard for the intellectual qualities of the performer. He did not place this kind of specific talent into the same category with creative accomplishment. However, Zweig recognized the reasons for Czentovic's shortcomings, and his portrait, while not flattering, is also not entirely unsympathetic. He does not ridicule Czentovic but describes him realistically, as a means of illustrating the false values of the age.

In complete contrast with Czentovic, Dr. B. is presented as the humanist, a man of intellect and imagination, dedicated to books and the arts, to everything that lies beyond Czentovic's awareness. Yet his very sensitivity becomes a two-edged sword during his solitary confinement. His mind, accustomed to absorbing and feeding on external stimuli, is in danger of collapse when deprived of sustenance. For both men chess becomes the means of survival, but, ironically for Dr. B., the very means of preventing madness ultimately induces it and causes his total collapse. Dr. B. illustrates Zweig's belief that a man of intellect could not devote himself to chess unremittingly without going mad . . . , although the special circumstances limit the possibility of generalizing further from Dr. B.'s case.

Thus far we have eliminated the possibilities that *Schachnovelle* represents a new artistic outlook for Zweig, that it is a reflection of a pessimistic mood that led to his suicide, and that the chess match is intended primarily to symbolize the confrontation between the humanist and tyranny in any form, and specifically between himself and Hitler. Instead, *Schachnovelle* is a psychological study of unique, individual characters, and as such parallels other such stories written throughout his career.

In preparing the reader for the confrontation of Dr. B. and Czentovic, Zweig makes the important point that a man reveals his character in the game of chess. This is indicated first in the game between the narrator and McConnor . . . and again in the contest of wills between Czentovic and Dr. B. during their final game. In the latter game the single-minded purpose of Czentovic and the hidden weakness of Dr. B. convert the game into a deadly serious attempt to destroy each other. . . . Czentovic cannot afford a defeat, for without chess he might still be the village idiot in his original environs. For Dr. B., however, chess is only peripheral to his existence. He can function without ever touching a chessboard, just as Zweig, though inconvenienced by his exile from Austria, could continue his life and literary career unimpeded. However, because of his chess poisoning, once Dr. B. begins to play, he becomes obsessed and, if not stopped in time, would collapse mentally again, just as the prison doctor has warned him. . . . (pp. 378-79)

All of the background information about Czentovic, Dr. B., and, to a lesser extent, McConnor, material that forms a large segment of the story, has the specific purpose of explaining the types of personalities involved in the several games. These detailed characterizations strengthen the view that the story is essentially a character study. Zweig is slowly setting the stage for the final confrontation, which becomes understandable only through the interrelation of three characters who are brought together by chance, a motif that runs throughout the story. Chance has brought these characters together on the same ship; chance is responsible for Czentovic's rise to chess supremacy; chance has brought Dr. B. to his expertise in chess; and chance causes Dr. B. to appear at the exact moment to offer useful advice to the group challenging Czentovic.

The line between chance (that is, probability) and contrivance on the part of the author is a narrow one. The crucial distinction is that chance as it occurs here is so logical, plausible, and convincing that it can be accepted without suspension of one's reasoning faculties, while the synthesis of chance and characterization keeps the story suspenseful. Zweig's postponement of the game between the two experts is a necessary device to inform the reader of Dr. B.'s past, while at the same time it

serves an additional practical function in the psychological motivation of the story, for it adds to the strain on Dr. B.'s nerves as he relives in narration the torture of his solitary confinement.

The fate of an intelligent, decent, and competent man who has been mistreated and exiled by the Nazi invaders of Austria parallels the fate of many Austrian intellectuals and creative artists, including Zweig. Zweig's vagueness about such details as the nature of the undercover work which led to Dr. B.'s arrest and the reason for Dr. B.'s release indicates that he is not seriously interested in Dr. B.'s political involvement. By contrast the insidious psychological torture of isolation, which interests Zweig above all else, is described in considerable detail. Here Zweig is anticipating later research in sensory deprivation "In the softening-up process and in S.D. [sensory deprivation] the confined individual experiences dreadful monotony and boredom, so much so that he will actively seek almost any form of novelty." Dr. B.'s breaking point, which is reached in four months, is temporarily postponed by the fortuitous theft of the book of chess games, which permits him to play the games in his mind and subsequently to invent his own games as he plays both black and white. In this self-induced schizophrenic state and without the encumbrance of a board and chess pieces, his imaginary games move faster and faster as each side demands that the opponent move ever more rapidly. After this obsession leads to his complete mental breakdown, a sympathetic doctor effects his release from prison. Again, Zweig's omission of explanatory details shows that Dr. B.'s conditioning and subsequent mania are the main points of interest.

After Dr. B. returns from his narrative to the present, the story pursues its inevitable and inexorable course. With his knowledge of psychology Zweig describes how Dr. B.'s nervous symptoms reappear during his first game with Czentovic, and how in the final game Czentovic's delaying tactic unnerves Dr. B., whose mind races far ahead of the action on the board, and who must be recalled to the present for each move. His incipient relapse into his former psychotic state proves to be his undoing in the contest.

Dr. B. has to fill the seemingly interminable intervals between moves by retracing in his mind other games that he has played. When he announces a checkmate that is not apparent on the chess board, it becomes evident that he has been playing a different game in his imagination. As Dr. B. is led away, Czentovic concludes the story with the comment that the former does not play badly for an amateur. . . . Although this remark may seem ironic and condescending, it is more likely that Zweig was intending to show a trace of human feeling in Czentovic, which can emerge after the threat to his status has vanished. In consideration of his temperament and character, as Zweig has portrayed him, he would be incapable of irony. Dr. B. is in fact a dilettante; furthermore, Czentovic has no way of knowing about Dr. B.'s peculiar condition that has caused his defeat. Thus, by making his statement *großmütig* ["magnanimous"], . . . the champion intends his remark as a compliment and not as an insult. This conclusion attests to a positive quality in Czentovic, whom Zweig has not portrayed as a vicious or evil man, but only as one who must survive by making the most of his single talent.

a symbol Czentovic suffers from the same limitations as Dr. B., for, like the latter, his unique condition stemming from his birth defects makes him atypical. Both Dr. B. and Czentovic are specialized cases which cannot be generalized. Thus, Zweig's use of the chess game as a symbol of the world situation at the time seems untenable on the basis of textual analysis. Since the element of evil does not enter into Czentovic's character, it seems certain that he is not intended as a symbol of the tyrant. The symbolism breaks down further if it is applied to the politics of the time, for Dr. B. has no opportunity of challenging Czentovic again without destroying himself. To interpret the story in terms of political symbolism, apart from violating the spirit of the characters, would also force the impossible conclusion that the world will be turned over to the tyrants irretrievably. The evidence in the story does not support this view. Dr. B. is not defeated in any essential way, for he can live a useful and productive life without ever playing chess. His spirit is undamaged and he does not express any negativism about beginning a new life. He remains alive and apparently healthy except in one detail. He has actually won the game against the Nazis, who were forced to release him without obtaining a confession. Having won once by remaining true to his ideals, there is nothing to deny that he can win again.

Dr. B. does not betray the slightest hint of self-pity or pessimism about his future. Zweig remains silent on these issues. He ends the narrative with Dr. B.'s defeat and makes no attempt to show how the latter will recover from his experience. On this basis it seems clear that the story is primarily a psychological study of the effects of brainwashing with the emphasis on the final chess game, which demonstrates the psychological aftereffects of Dr. B.'s mistreatment. Any attempt to view Dr. B.'s defeat as a portrayal of Zweig's pessimism or to relate *Schachnovelle* to Zweig's suicide is unsupported by the facts of the story. Admittedly, the sequence of events creates a tempting parallelism, which, however, cannot be twisted into a pattern of cause-and-effect.

Schachnovelle contains two layers of meaning and a relevancy on both levels that raises it above ordinary *Novellen* to true literary quality. On the personal psychological level and on the abstract level of suggesting individuality coerced by tyranny the story has a timelessness that earns it a place among Zweig's more lasting works. Although Dr. B. is ostensibly defeated on the field of battle, he is preserved for the world to keep the humanistic attitude alive. The conclusion echoes other expressions of the belief that the way to defeat the tyrant is not through confrontation but through the more subtle procedure of staying alive to defeat him eventually on other grounds. By giving no indication of Dr. B.'s future course of action, Zweig leaves the possibilities open.

If there is a weakness in *Schachnovelle,* it is the fact that Zweig describes the psychological processes of his characters too explicitly. Rather than allowing the reader to interpret the characters on the basis of their actions, he spells out in detail what the reader should conclude. Also at points of suspense Zweig does not allow the action to carry the reader but employs passionate language to create tension. . . . However, these are only minor flaws in a story that is structurally admirable and that deserves its reputation as Zweig's narrative masterpiece. (pp. 380-82)

> *Donald G. Daviau and Harvey I. Dunkle, "Stefan Zweig's 'Schachnovelle',"* in Monatshefte, *Vol. LXV, No. 4, Winter, 1973, pp. 370-84.*

C. E. WILLIAMS   (essay date 1974)

[*In the following excerpt, Williams discusses the development of Zweig's attitude toward politics, from his indifference in the years before World War I to his postwar distrust of political activity.*]

The memory of those anonymous forces that had controlled his fate during the War remained with Zweig long after he had reasserted his individual freedom of conscience, and inspired several stories. In *Episode vom Genfer See* . . . the Russian soldier, Boris, cannot grasp the political factors which determine the conditions of his existence and prevent him from living his own life according to his simple desires. Now that the Czar whom he once served has been deposed, he sees no more reason to fight and wishes to return to his home and family. But on escaping from a French camp he discovers that the only road open to him leads to a Swiss internment camp. Unable to communicate with people around him because he cannot speak French or German, and unable to comprehend his situation, he commits suicide. The hero of another story, *Buchmendel* . . . , is technically a Russian citizen but in spirit an Austrian. His birthplace only becomes important when war breaks out and an accident of geography leads him into an internment camp for enemy aliens. Soon after the end of the War Mendel dies, a broken man. Again a completely apolitical individual is caught up in the impersonal machinery of war and destroyed by it. In *Der Zwang* . . . one of the central issues is the struggle of the protagonist to resist the compulsive influence of wartime bureaucracy. He is on the verge of succumbing to its pressures when he is saved by the sight of sick and wounded French prisoners of war who restore his feelings of common humanity. The moral of the story is vitiated by the fact that the hero's dilemma is artificial; it is not the authentic problem of the conscientious objector, but the fabricated conflict of a man who is already safe in Switzerland and who simply has to decide whether or not to return to Vienna for a further medical examination. The lesson is still, however, clear: Zweig feels that even if one cannot control one's material fate, one can still resist the moral blandishments of political forces. (pp. 119-20)

Zweig's conception of political action was rudimentary—and in the postwar period he disavowed all forms of political organisation on the grounds that they were conducive to fanaticism and dogmatism, and encroached upon the moral freedom of the individual. He was drawn to actions which, though ineffective, represented the moral triumph of a solitary individual protester.

Such is the situation in *Jeremias:* a lone voice crying in a wilderness of chauvinism and selfish passions. The plot and setting owe much to the Biblical account given in the Book of Jeremiah, but Zweig has modified the traditional story in two important respects. In the first place, the Biblical model prophesies doom because the Jews turned away from God; their guilt lies in their sinfulness, and the prophet summons them to renounce their evil ways and to do penance for their sins by surrendering to the Chaldeans who are besieging the city of Jerusalem. In Zweig's play the guilt of the Jews is that they sue for war in a vain desire for conquest, booty and glory; it is their war-mongering which leads to their being punished at the hands of Nebuchadnezzar. In the second place the Bible narrative ends with a laconic statement of fact—that the Jews were driven into exile. Zweig, elaborating on this, shows them leaving as though in triumph, resolved to rebuild the razed city in their hearts. The story of Jeremiah and of the Jewish king Zedekiah is transformed into a vehicle of protest against the First World War. The *leitmotiv,* 'Jerusalem shall endure for ever!' changes its significance as the play proceeds. At first a sign of security and self-confidence, of defiance and self-assertion, it becomes by the end of the play an expression of trust in God and of faith in the integrity of man. Zweig com-

Playbill for Zweig's drama Das Haus am Meer.

mented on the peculiar aptness of an episode from Jewish history to illustrate the theme of 'victory in defeat': the whole history of the Jews, he felt, the centuries of suffering and tribulation, persecution and dispersion, revealed how spiritual values could be cherished and preserved amid the most terrible adversity.

Jeremias is not a subtle drama. Its highly coloured rhetoric does not allow of intellectual argument, and the main issue is reduced to the simplest of terms: should the Jews wage war upon Assyria for material gain, or not? There is no provocation, no urgent pressure in favour of war. Aggression is suggested by the Egyptians as a profitable course of action; all that remains for the Jews to do is to decide whether they should accept the offer. Politically the situation is unreal because it is oversimplified. This is partly due to Zweig's polemical purpose, the desire to present the crux of the problem in the clearest possible terms. But it is also symptomatic of his lack of sympathy with, or appreciation of the complexities of political life. His intention is not to castigate one nation in particular but to condemn the phenomenon of war and to show the suffering and destruction which it brings in its train, irrespective of the specific political circumstances. He argues that if only ordinary men and women would communicate across the international frontiers, they would discover their common humanity and forthwith put an end to war and aggression. Zweig's attitude is one of humanitarian individualism: his model is an archetypal individual free from social ties and political pressures, humanity in limbo.

The construction of *Jeremias* is untidy, its prose turgid, its passages of verse uninspired. The argument is emotional and unrealistic. As the play avoids identification with specific details of the contemporary situation, the polemic loses a good deal of force. Zweig is a victim of the time lag between the situation in which he began writing and the less repressive conditions in which *Jeremias* eventually appeared. (pp. 121-23)

The key to Zweig's attitude towards the political situation of the postwar years is his renewed emphasis on the need for European cooperation and unity. He was aware that in some circles 'internationalism' had become a convenient slogan: he pointed out that in fact it was a radical commitment demanding the renunciation of patriotism. Only through the success of the European movement, Zweig maintained, would it be possible to keep the militarists and their supporters in check.... He was under no illusion about the difficulties facing the movement, but to him the important thing was to keep its spirit alive. (p. 124)

In Zweig's biography of the great humanist [*Erasmus of Rotterdam*], published in 1934, Erasmus shares several of Zweig's characteristics—his reluctance to brave the storm of fanaticism while this was at its height, his cavilling and his weakness. Zweig was aware of his hero's shortcomings as he was aware of his own. He offset them, however, by indicating that Erasmus survived to argue the case for reason and humanity when the clamour had died down. By being prudent, he preserved intact his spiritual resources and his faith in mankind. There was here consolation for the setback and failure which Zweig himself had experienced. (In an analogous position Brecht's Galileo cannot acquit himself so easily.) Zweig knew that the aggressive instinct was deep-rooted in man; he held out the tenuous hope that this aggression might eventually be curbed through a lengthy process of education. But he distinguished between primitive instinct on the one hand, and its exploitation for political ends on the other. The targets of Zweig's criticism were the chauvinist, the war-monger, the irresponsible or incompetent diplomat and the unscrupulous propagandist, for without their manipulation, he argues, human aggression would be more limited in its extent and less pernicious in its effects. By transforming the climate of opinion, Zweig hoped that one could minimise the consequences of violence.

Before 1914 Zweig had been indifferent to politics, but with the coming of war he was compelled to acknowledge that politics was indeed relevant to the life of the individual. At the same time his contact with the machinery of state and his glimpse of wartime politics confirmed his profound distrust of political activity. His moral condemnation of politics was overwhelming. He equated it with both stupidity and cunning, incompetence and cleverness, cynicism and fanatical idealism, the manipulation of will-less masses by power-hungry leaders and the tyrannical control of their leaders by power-hungry masses. Zweig's biography *Joseph Fouché* . . . , subtitled 'Portrait of a Political Man', attempts to present the French statesman as an object lesson in political behaviour. This man who served in turn the French Revolution, the Directorate, the Consulate, the Empire and the restored Monarchy, is depicted as opportunistic, ruthless and unprincipled. Loyalty to persons or causes is alien to his nature. Occasional references in the text underline the relevance of his dubious career to the present age. Zweig wrote to Emil Ludwig in 1928 that Fouché was to serve as a warning of the dangers of the professional politician for the peoples of Europe.... His purpose in writing the biography of Fouché was too didactic to permit any noteworthy insight into the political history of the period with which he deals. His narrative assumes that history is entirely the work of individuals and their private motives. He avoids analysing social and economic forces, all the wider pressures to which individuals are subject in society. History for Zweig was largely applied psychology.

There are many other instances in Zweig's postwar writing of his distaste for politics. He alluded scathingly to the 'hired labourers of politics' and asserted that morality and political power were usually irreconcilable. He condemned the League of Nations as the last refuge of secret diplomacy and intrigue, wholly invidious to the European movement proper. In his biography of Erasmus the repeated warnings against fanaticism apply no less to contemporary politics than to the ostensible subject, religion. Apart from such admonitions Zweig shied away from any gesture or statement which might have carried party-political implications. He avoided associations of a political character because he felt that his moral independence would thereby be compromised. (pp. 124-26)

Unlike many contemporary writers, Zweig remained indifferent to the Habsburg Empire and the Austrian heritage. His memories of his upbringing in an upper middle class family in Vienna, as recalled in his autobiography, were somewhat ambivalent. He criticised the hypocrisy, shallowness, monotony and misguided pedagogic ideas of *fin de siècle* Vienna, while at the same time admiring its faith in human reason, its respect for the liberty and privacy of the individual, and its belief in progress. Its notions, even if excessively optimistic, frequently served a humane and constructive purpose. Above all he remembered fondly the illusion of security and solidity in which he had spent his youth. Where Zweig nostalgically evoked the world before 1914, he had in mind a whole era of European civilisation rather than any qualities unique to the Habsburg Monarchy. As in Schnitzler's work, there was little indication in Zweig's memoirs that beyond Vienna lay the hinterland of a great empire. One of Zweig's last books, *Ungeduld des Herzens* . . . , ventures into the Imperial provinces for its setting: the backcloth of the novel is a garrison town on the Hungarian-Slovak border. But despite the introduction of a Magyar country house, Ruthenian conscripts, a peasant wedding, the background remains rudimentary and conventional, lending a touch of local colour but of no intrinsic interest. Zweig too was a Viennese, not an Austrian, in his indifference to the ways of thinking, feeling and behaving of the Imperial peoples. In his memoirs he claimed that the theatre, not the problems of the Monarchy, provided the focus of attention among the Viennese bourgeoisie in the last years of the Empire. In retrospect he saw that theirs had been an inward-looking world where imagination and creativeness were expended in 'aesthetic' pursuits. Zweig's own character was moulded in the image of the society he described. His indifference to politics before 1914, his one-sided individualism, his dilettante probing of the psyche, his inability to comprehend or accept the necessary limitations of political activity—all this is strongly reminiscent of the Viennese intelligentsia at the turn of the century. That early environment shaped his work to the end: although *Ungeduld des Herzens* suggests that for certain men the First World War provided an escape from intolerable problems, the idea is stated in purely private terms. There is no attempt to attach any wider historical significance to this rather mawkish story of a young cavalry officer who—out of pity—becomes deeply embroiled with a crippled girl and her wealthy Jewish father. . . . It is characteristic of Zweig's writing that while the rest of the

Empire is agog with the news of Sarajevo, his fictional hero is entirely absorbed in his personal dilemma.

Zweig tried to flee from the conflagration that consumed the last vestiges of the 'world of yesterday'. Shortly after his final autobiographical tribute to the culture and society of Edwardian Europe appeared under that title in 1941, he committed suicide in his Brazilian exile. (pp. 130-31)

> C. E. Williams, "Stefan Zweig: Pacifist Extraordinary," in his The Broken Eagle: The Politics of Austrian Literature from Empire to Anschluss, *Barnes & Noble Books, 1974, pp. 113-31.*

D. B. DOUGLAS (essay date 1980)

[*In the following excerpt, Douglas examines the two main characters of* Schachnovelle (The Royal Game). *In particular, Douglas contends that Dr. B represents the unfortunate humanist who is forced to participate in political activities by circumstances. In contrast to Donald G. Daviau and Harvey I. Dunkle (see excerpt dated 1973), Douglas maintains that Dr. B's defeat is a representation of Zweig's pessimism concerning humanist intervention in politics.*]

To the reader already acquainted with Stefan Zweig's oeuvre, the *Schachnovelle,* completed shortly before Zweig's suicide in 1942, does not readily conform to a familiar pattern. *Triumph und Tragik des Erasmus von Rotterdam,* exemplary of the tendency of Zweig's later production, had depicted the struggle of the humanist Erasmus against the fanaticist Luther, a struggle of great political significance. This antagonism does in fact recur in the *Schachnovelle.* But it takes place at a private, individual level, between the chess-players Czentovic and Dr B. There is also a dispute, however, on the broad political plane between Dr B. and the Nazi invaders of Austria. But it cannot be interpreted as a symbolical reflection of the humanist-fanaticist conflict.

How is this problem to be explained? Perhaps it is a result of the work of art left in unpolished form by the author and published posthumously. Or perhaps it is proof of the difference between the literary creation, with its ultimately indefinable poetical residue, and the precise philosophico-biographical portrayal. Conversely, as the present writer contends, the solution to this dilemma lies in a more generous conception of the Novelle's action: for the *Schachnovelle* is a psychologically-oriented examination of the plight of Dr B., confronted both as a political figure and as a private individual with forces which threaten to crush his humanism. Although both the struggle against Nazi inhumanity and against fanaticism are allotted the same proportion of narrative time (each receiving approximately one half of the published text), it is clear that the thematic area of politics and humanism is of greatest concern. The private sphere serves as the testing-ground of the politically scarred Dr B.

Chess is the novelistic 'falcon', the unifying element within this thematic framework. The functions of the game must be carefully differentiated. Firstly, it acts catalytically in the psychological scrutiny of monomania. It becomes for Dr B., secondly, a weapon in his altercation with the anti-humanism of National Socialism, a weapon which is to turn against its wielder. Lastly, and in greater accordance with its essentially bellicose nature, the chess-board becomes the battleground for the encounter between two opposing forces: humanism and fanaticism. They are embodied in the central figures of Dr B. and Mirko Czentovic. A character-analysis of both is needed before the meaning of the three 'battles' in the Novelle—Dr B.'s struggle with the Nazi regime and his two self-initiated chess-games with Czentovic—can be fully elucidated.

Stefan Zweig defines humanism in his study of Erasmus of Rotterdam. According to this work, those individuals may be termed humanists who maintain a psychic balance which enables them to stand beyond heated conflict, view it impartially and act in a mediating, non-violent fashion to resolve it. This inner, emotional stability must be complemented with intellectual and idealistic, moral qualities developed and refined through the study of literature, music and the arts. The tragic dilemma of the humanist lies in his refusal to participate actively in the discord and friction which typify human existence. The violence of fanaticists like Luther demands violent reaction and disregards conciliatory manoeuvres. The humanist remains on principle a powerless spectator of the life-struggle.

Dr B., who makes his first appearance in the course of the second match against Czentovic played by the shipboard enthusiasts, is the fictional embodiment of the humanist. The chalky pallor of his skin remarked upon by the narrator suggests, if not the décadent, at least the intellectual: he does indeed possess highly developed intellectual faculties, main evidence of which are his brilliant chess achievements. His interest in literature is revealed by his yearning in prison for Goethe or Homer, and a possible musical propensity or appreciation is intimated by the reference to Schubert. Above all, his cultured, aristocratic background and his professional qualifications infer extensive education and learning, which have instilled in him not only an awareness of ethical requisites in social behaviour, but also a receptivity to values alien to Mirko Czentovic, the world's master chess player.

The dominant feature of Czentovic's character is the monomaniacal or fanatical ability to concentrate his entire intellectual energy upon a solitary object, the royal game of chess. Unlike the majority of chess-experts, generally of mathematical or philosophical nature, Czentovic is an ignorant peasant whose strength lies in the monomaniacal efficiency of his memory. He lacks completely the power of imaginative visualization, for he cannot play 'blindly', that is, without the chess-board. . . . He possesses no original creative talent (he must, for instance, mechanically learn the Sicilian Opening) and certainly betrays no interest in literature or the arts. He is, however, a specific type of monomaniac. Quite unlike the violent Luther, for example, he is an emotionless, coldly calculating mechanism. . . . The reason for this must lie in Zweig's desire for artistic truth. Without this quality, the reader could never accept Czentovic's chess-ability. Further, Czentovic functions in the Novelle as a form of control in the psychological experiment the narrator conducts: his cold reason serves to delineate the extent of change Dr B. undergoes when he succumbs to monomania.

Czentovic's chess-fanaticism is referred to by the narrator in a series of reflections on monomania. Like Stefan Zweig himself, he is particularly fascinated by the phenomenon of the monomaniac because the more such individuals confine their talent or special faculty, the closer they approximate to the infinite, the perfect. The narrator is hesitant, though, when he discusses the exceptional case of chess-monomania. He does consider chess an art-form and includes it in the category of art and painting; but he has difficulty in understanding the cerebrally capable person who values the chess-board to the exclusion of all else, for the game is judged a sterile pursuit. . . . Czentovic cannot be included in the select group of monomaniacs such as Mary Baker Eddy, or Magellan, whom Zweig

held in grudging respect because they had as their ultimate goal the advancement of humanity. . . . Ignorance and monomania have bred the materialism and misanthropy Dr B.'s counterpart displays.

Clearly, his character stands in stark contrast to that of Dr B., who, as is implicit in the character antagonism, would champion opposing values. However, the thematic interest of Stefan Zweig's *Schachnovelle* is focused primarily upon the core of the humanist's being, spiritual equilibrium, not upon the scale of values espoused by the humanist. Of course, humanist values, philanthropic ideals such as tolerance, freedom of thought or selflessness, can only be promoted by those who defend the supreme value of psychic stability with its stress upon totality and equality, not upon one-sidedness or prejudice. The importance Dr B. assigns to this nucleus of humanism, and his efforts to defend it, are portrayed in the three 'battles' in which he participates.

Dr B. describes the first 'battle' in the story he narrates to resolve the contradiction of his ability at chess. He commences his story by informing the narrator of his activities before the Nazi invasion of Austria as a counsellor and executor for the large monasteries, as well as financial advisor to members of the Imperial family. His law-firm had made transactions across the border to safeguard at least the movable property from confiscation, but a spy infiltrated the organization and Dr B. had been arrested and incarcerated in the Hotel Metropole, where each prisoner had received his own room. He was then confronted with a refined method of torture—the perfect void, a hermetic condition intended to torment the psyche. Zweig does not discuss brutality in physical terms, but rather as the disturbance or attempted destruction of inner stability. Dr B. is on the verge of 'breaking', when he is able to steal a book, not by Goethe or Homer as desired, but filled with famous chess-tournaments. Dr B. understands the meaning of the book— it is a weapon in the struggle against the void. At first he constructs a crude chess-board and pieces; but he is soon able to dispense with these empirical aids and to visualize situations through the power of his imagination. He is able to play 'blindly'. . . . Dr B. is constantly contrasted with Czentovic in this section treating the encounter with the Nazi terror. Like the narrator, Dr B. is able to perceive the artistic possibilities of chess and ceases mere reconstruction of the games. He wants to invent new games: as he realizes, though, this means that he must play against himself. . . . He has been forced into an absurd situation which can only result in divided personality, the inner strife of schizophrenia, for he must think from two opposing viewpoints. . . . This psychic disunity distinguishes Dr B.'s monomania from that of Czentovic. Dr B. is thus faced with a crucial decision. If he does not attempt to play against himself, total spiritual collapse and the personal betrayal of his twelve colleagues and their secrets must be his fate—the victory will belong to the Nazis. If he does play against himself, then a split personality in the form of schizophrenic monomania, the relinquishment of the humanist ideal, will result, but the void and the Nazis will be overcome. Both from a humanist and the political standpoint, there can be no hesitation: Dr B. must submit himself to chess-monomania. The process is recounted at length: gradually and inevitably the obsession with the game in the form of a maniacal, frenetic anger overwhelms him. Outer symptoms of his condition are an extreme thirst and a constant pacing in his cell. His torture ends finally, and he wakes in a hospital bed. The doctor informs him that the guard had heard his shouts, as though Dr B. were quarrelling with somebody. Dr B. had then tried to strangle the warden while demanding that he make a chess-move. Taken away for treatment, Dr B. had torn free and smashed a window with his bare fist.

Dr B. defeats the anti-humanism of National Socialism by neither surrendering to the void nor betraying what he knows of the Church and Imperial finance transactions: he gains a victory in the political arena. The renunciation of the aloof humanist position through the self-debasement to the machine-like monomania of a Czentovic and the subsequent loss of inner balance marked by the passionate perpetration of violent deeds—these are part of the great price the humanist must pay for mastery in the political mêlée.

It is now necessary to reflect upon the two games which conclude the Novelle, the first of which begins on the day following Dr B.'s recollections. The narrator notices the difference between the two players: Czentovic remains the ignorant peasant monomaniacally devoted to chess, but Dr B. is a dilettante, a player who enjoys and treats chess purely as a game. As the match advances, though, this posture is slowly replaced by a restlessness, by, in actuality, the incipient repetition of his prison monomania, which his growing thirst and constant pacing indicate. The monomaniac in mild form becomes apparent. . . . Yet he maintains his inner equilibrium and achieves a victory against his opponent. Stefan Zweig celebrates here the accomplishment of reason and intellect, the outlook and strength of the humanist. Dr B. has emerged fortified from the conflict with the Nazis in one respect: he possesses brilliant chess-ability and must be considered the true world-champion. His play betrays great skill and even attains the level of art (the narrator laments that the pattern of the game, like Beethoven's improvisations for the piano, has been lost to posterity).

But the Novelle does not end with this defeat of Czentovic, who immediately demands a return match. Ominous signs of monomania appear more frequently in Dr B.'s behaviour in the course of this second match. Czentovic cunningly employs delay-tactics to aggravate his opponent's condition. The now delicate poise of his psyche is again disturbed. His former customary politeness and respect are supplanted by rudeness and sarcasm aimed at his rival. Violence and hatred, the characteristic symptoms of fanaticism, overwhelm him. Chess is no longer a game, but a vicious life-and-death encounter. . . . A climax is reached when Dr B., in a totally uncontrollable state, announces a check on Czentovic's king, a move which does not coincide with the actual situation. Dr B. is again playing an unreal game, for the check is a figment of his imagination: the prison circumstances recur. Reminded by the narrator of his danger, Dr B. terminates the game and awards it as is proper to Czentovic. Czentovic will remain the world-champion—his values will predominate in the sphere of chess as those of the Nazis in the political. This second match does not only take place between Czentovic and Dr B., but also between the humanist Dr B. and the monomaniac Dr B. The fanatical Czentovic does, however, use ploys designed to stimulate Dr B.'s monomania, and may therefore be termed an anti-humanist, seeking to debase and defeat his rival. Dr B. makes the decision not to persist in the 'battle' at the cost of his own humanism. Whereas during the Nazi terror he had been forced into monomania, he is, as a private individual on board the ship, physically at liberty and so capable of retaining his inner freedom. The humanist laurels belong to the doctor.

It is timely to cite the hypothesis proffered by D. G. Daviau and H. I. Dunkle that, had the Novelle possessed a symbolic

perspective, it would imply that the world will be governed by the anti-humanists [see excerpt dated 1973]. They contend that Dr B. is not an adequate symbol of the humanist because he submits to monomania. But Zweig's outlook, as expressed in the *Schachnovelle,* is indeed of a pessimistic nature. To participate in the political skirmish is not the duty of the humanist . . . but Dr B. is constrained to do so by political circumstance. He is victorious on the political level, but only to a certain degree, for he cannot continue to fight, or rather he should not. Had Dr B. been able to steal a work by Goethe or Homer, as he had wished to, the humanist could have won the political battle and not sacrificed his stability. Zweig's utilization of a chess-book (thus the necessity for monomania) betrays his belief in the impossibility of the successful intervention of humanism in politics. Dr B. must retire permanently from the battlefield, too badly scarred to be able to persevere. He had to abandon his humanism to secure a triumph: the humanist, as a humanist, cannot emerge victorious. Despite its depressing political ineffectiveness, Zweig advocates the preservation of what Klaus Jarmatz calls contemplative humanism. Dr B. resolves never again to sit before the chessboard—ultimately the day belong to anti-humanist forces. Any optimism for the future, as expressed in *Triumph und Tragik des Erasmus von Rotterdam,* remains unvoiced and without foundation in the *Schachnovelle.* (pp. 17-23)

> D. B. Douglas, "The Humanist Gambit: A Study of Stefan Zweig's 'Schachnovelle'," in AUMLA, No. 53, May, 1980, pp. 17-24.

ADRIAN DEL CARO   (essay date 1981)

[*In the following excerpt, Del Caro examines the influence of the writings of Friedrich Nietzsche on Zweig's novel* Ungeduld des Herzens (Beware of Pity).]

Zweig's fascination with Nietzsche cannot be disputed. Not only do we have the famous essay from *Baumeister der Welt,* quoted by Walter Kaufmann in his introduction to the Penguin edition of *Thus Spoke Zarathustra,* but several observations on Nietzsche as well, such as the letter to Romain Rolland in which Nietzsche is referred to as "the first European." . . . Zweig the "European of yesterday" clearly identified with Nietzsche's concept of the European who transcends nationalism. And in a more human way, the Nietzschean influence was bound to make its mark on Zweig or almost *any* writer growing up at the close of the nineteenth century. . . . In the case of Stefan Zweig, the work of fiction which best depicts his understanding of the controversial Nietzsche is *Ungeduld des Herzens.*

Zweig's novel is a protracted study of the concept of pity, its motivations and its repercussions. Primarily it is a psychological analysis of four main characters who are caught up in the syndrome of pity; Edith the crippled daughter, Kekesfalva her adoring father, Lt. Hofmiller who pities Edith and finally Dr. Condor, who is the family physician, himself married to an incurably blind and neurotic woman. When he chose the concept of pity as the nucleus of his story, Zweig took on one of the fundamental targets of Nietzsche's war on Christianity. . . . Zweig was extremely well-read in Nietzsche, and made no pretense of circumventing Nietzsche's thoughts on pity. This is attested to by the fact that Dr. Condor, in discussing Edith's condition with Hofmiller, quotes almost verbatim from *Zarathustra.* This study, however, does not intend to prove that Zweig, like Nietzsche, used the analysis of pity to blast Christianity. Zweig's contribution lies in having juxtaposed the life of a young man with the "object" of that individual's pity, namely Edith, and the attending situation embarks not so much upon an attack of Christianity, as upon a theoretical investigation of how existentially dangerous *nihilistic* values such as pity can be. That Zweig reserves his own view on pity will become apparent.

Hofmiller is edged into a vulnerable position vis-à-vis Edith and her family when he thoughtlessly asks the crippled girl to dance. Though he had no way of knowing the girl's condition beforehand, Hofmiller allows her hysterical reaction to evoke strong feelings of guilt in him. From here he mires himself more deeply by over-reacting to his blunder; he begins to pity the girl and her soft-hearted, devoted father. Zweig makes this development credible by first drawing a portrait of Hofmiller.... [Zweig's] unflattering picture of the weak-willed lieutenant is important for establishing criteria by which a well-meaning individual may become ensnared, and the dramatic crisis culminating in Edith's suicide and her father's consequent death rests heavily on Hofmiller's lack of true character.... If Hofmiller had nurtured any strong existential goals, or embarked upon "his own way," he could not have been ripe for the plunge into pity which Edith and her father precipitate.

Zweig carefully describes the geographical and psychological milieu of Hofmiller, so that we are presented with a potential Emma Bovary. The garrison where Hofmiller lives and traffics with his dull comrades offers two sources of diversion [a coffee house and a pastry shop].... In addition to defining Hofmiller's life as one motivated by the conquest of daily ennui, Zweig attempts also to describe his hero as insecure, average, and in most respects, a nobody. Hence when Hofmiller's life *is made eventful* by the *faux pas* committed at Kekesfalva's *soirée*, he succumbs to the novelty of the situation and becomes hooked. Nietzsche enumerates some unconscious motivations for pitying, and among them are: a) exercising the option of pitying someone and enjoying that option, b) winning traditional approval, c) overcoming boredom with oneself, d) escaping oneself and e) gloating, as it were, over one's own good fortune.... As the unmotivated person that he truly is, Hofmiller fits the bill as the kind of individual who might feel elevated by conferring his pity on another. (pp. 195-98)

Apart from providing a diversion from his routine, Hofmiller's frequent visits to the home of Kekesfalva, where he is royally treated, provide a second source of satisfaction.... In pitying Edith, in providing her with his company, his attention and his courtesy, Hofmiller derives a benefit for himself. Soon he has learned how to tap this well of satisfaction with some skill.... Hofmiller is intrigued by his new and sudden position of authority; at the garrison he is not appreciated and certainly not recognized as an outstanding personality. He has neither patent nor money. At the Kekesfalva home, on the other hand, everyone welcomes him with obvious warmth and respect. He has succeeded in making the gloomy household cheerful, and Edith is ready to laugh at his benevolent, if unimaginative jokes. Hofmiller scarcely realizes that he has brought happiness to the household at the expense of his freedom, for Edith has construed his clumsy pity as a sign of love.

The height of his newly won power is manifest on the evening in which Hofmiller, essentially in order to prove his "true respect" for the crippled girl, becomes engaged to her.... Almost euphoric in his triumph, inspired as the Creator on the seventh day, Hofmiller revels in the sensation of power. It must be remembered that being able to confer pity on someone has opened this channel of fulfillment; overnight one has transcended the mundane and become a hero.

It is Zweig's intention to draw the hero more securely into the snare of pity. In order to do this, another character and his involvement with Hofmiller come into play, namely the father. If at any moment before the irreversible climax the hero sobers long enough to sense doubt, it is whenever Kekesfalva abandons his lofty station as nobleman-merchant and demeans himself before young Hofmiller. Kekesfalva actually begs and cajoles the young officer to continue in his benevolent pursuits: he buys him expensive gifts, and does not relent in hounding the suitor, at one point even waiting for hours in the dark street below the soldier's room, in order to waylay him and solicit help for the daughter. Hofmiller begins to perceive of the old man as a greedy, maniacal demon, indeed as the Djinn who climbs atop the all-too-helpful hero from the *Tales of the Arabian Knights*. He is at once repulsed by the old man, yet feels pity for him; mostly, however, he is made uncomfortable by the father's fanatic will to believe in the restoration of the daughter's health. Kekesfalva is motivated by love for his daughter, and this type of sincerity, with its attending joy in sacrifice and hope, is too much for the superficial Hofmiller.

The power and uplifting derived from bestowing pity and reaping the rewards are a mixed blessing. Zweig demonstrates this by staying one step ahead of his hero, by demanding ever new sacrifices on his part. Proportionate to the surge in power which Hofmiller feels vis-à-vis the crippled girl, Kekesfalva with his beseeching omnipresence and devouring gratitude affords the hero less room for maneuvering. Nietzsche speculated that pity is an extremely negative concept, which proliferates negativity rather than arresting it.... This Hofmiller only begins to understand when he finds himself cornered by the inflated assurances of good will which he makes to Edith, her father and to Dr. Condor. By the time war breaks out (reminiscent of the fate of Hans Castorp in *Zauberberg*) and Hofmiller is "liberated" from his dilemma, he has already lied seriously and misled Edith, Kekesfalva, Dr. Condor and his comrades, mainly because he is unable, when confronted, to assert himself. He is a totally "selfless" man, a caricature, of sorts, of the type which Nietzsche consigned to the herd. By having to yield to the needs of those around him without regard for his own stand on the respective problem, he has projected a pseudo-existence into the lives of others, feeding only off the brief pleasure which is rendered him by their approval. This condition of altruism carried *ad absurdum* results for Hofmiller in flight, for Edith in suicide, for Kekesfalva in death by heart break.

One positive note is sounded by Zweig throughout the novel, and this in the character of Dr. Condor, the family physician. When Hofmiller first views him, he is somewhat jealous and repulsed by the pudgy little man's appearance and lack of ceremony, though later on he must admit Condor's superiority. The doctor's words are those isolated by Zweig and placed before the text of the novel, and wherever a spark of personal integrity flares up in the story, Condor is the agent. He quotes Nietzsche, but not religiously, for Condor has conceived of two kinds of pity:

> Mitleid—schön! Aber es gibt zweierlei Mitleid. Das eine, das schwachmütige und sentimentale, das eigentlich nur Ungeduld des Herzens ist, sich möglichst schnell freizumachen von der peinlichen Ergriffenheit vor einem fremden Unglück, jenes Mitleid, das gar nicht Mit-leiden ist, sondern nur instinktives Abwehr des

fremden Leidens von der eigenen Seele. Und
das andere, das einzig zählt—das unsentimen-
tale, aber schöpferische Mitleid, das weiß, was
es will, und entschlossen ist, geduldig und mit-
duldend durchzustehen bis zum Letzten seiner
Kraft und noch über dies Letzte hinaus.

[''Pity—that's all right! But there are two kinds
of pity. One, the weak and sentimental kind,
which is really no more than the heart's impatience to be rid as quickly as possible of the
painful emotion aroused by the sight of another's unhappiness, that pity which is not compassion, but only an instinctive desire to fortify
one's own soul against the sufferings of another; and the other, the only kind that counts,
the unsentimental but creative kind, which knows
what it is about and is determined to hold out,
in patience and forbearance, to the very limit
of its strength and even beyond.'' (translation
by Phyllis and Trevor Blewitt)]

Condor reserves a place for pity, but he takes an aggressive,
Nietzschean point of view; words like *unsentimental, schöp-
ferisch, entschlossen, Kraft* and *noch über dies . . . hinaus*
[''unsentimental,'' ''creative,'' ''determined,'' ''strength,'' and
''even beyond''] indicate the Nietzschean semantic field, and
are not traditionally associated with the humble virtue of pity.
In one breath Zweig admits the possibility of nihilistic pity as
defined by Nietzsche, and to this he ascribes the term ''Ungeduld des Herzens'' [''impatience of the heart'']; Condor represents the other pity, *which is creative and therefore the opposite* of ''Nihilismus in Praxis'' [''nihilism in practice'']. At
this point Zweig is no longer a disciple of Nietzsche, i.e., he
has learned from the master and ventured forth on his own.
Applying the affirmative thought associations which Nietzsche
might use, Zweig makes of Dr. Condor an aggressively creative
individual who, on the basis of superior will and resolve, *chooses*
to apply the Christian concept and does not harm himself or
others. In fact, Condor is the only stable, reliable character in
the novel, and this Zweig demonstrates by allowing the others
to succumb to the vices of their virtues, while Condor enters
and exits as the supportive husband of a blind wife.

In a manner of speaking, Hofmiller illuminates Nietzsche's
thesis that pity is a nihilistic concept, but Condor represents a
Nietzscheanized Christian who overturns the judgment. Another instance in which Zweig chose to disagree is evidenced
in Condor's stand on incurability.

Ich weiß, der gescheiteste Mensch des letzten
Jahrhunderts, Nietzsche, hat das furchtbare Wort
hingeschrieben: Am Unheilbaren soll man nicht
Arzt sein wollen. Aber das ist so ziemlich der
falscheste Satz unter all den paradoxen und ge-
fährlichen, die er uns zum Auflösen gegeben.
Genau das Gegenteil ist richtig, und ich be-
haupte: gerade am Unheilbaren bewährt sich
ein Arzt. .

[''I know that it is to the most brilliant man of
the last century, Nietzsche, that we owe the
horrible aphorism: a doctor should never try to
cure the incurable. But that is about the most
fallacious proposition of all the paradoxical and
dangerous propositions he propounded. The exact opposite is the truth. I maintain that it is

precisely the incurable one should try to cure,
and, what is more, that it is only in so-called
incurable cases that a doctor shows his mettle.''
(translation by Phyllis and Trevor Blewitt)]

This is Nietzschean defiance of a Nietzschean tenet, or a transvaluation of a transvaluation. As in many cases where Nietzsche
reversed the priority of a given value, what is overlooked is
the possibility of infusing the decadent value with life and
meaning. Essentially, this is just what Nietzsche can count on
in his transvaluation, viz. a reappraisal as it is rendered for
example by Zweig through Condor. Pity is not denounced
entirely by Zweig, but the negative side is illuminated. As an
alternative we are given Dr. Condor, the unsentimental but
strong altruist whose faith in his work does not permit him to
back out, or to lead another on—in short, Condor is the consequential Christian envisioned by Kierkegaard, perhaps, but
not retained as a possibility by Nietzsche.

Of the novel Rolland is quoted by [Zweig's biographer Donald]
Prater as saying it was ''too long by half,'' and this view,
though somewhat exaggerated, can be defended. Prater mentions eleven volumes of notes, manuscripts and successive drafts,
which suggest that Zweig had some difficulty in managing
these copious materials. As usual when too much material is
pruned too hastily, repetition occurs. But Zweig obviously
intended the work to be a major one, and from a reader's
standpoint it is; the plot is strong, the characters are psychologically consistent and the underlying theme, set against the
backdrop of the Great War, is worthy of treatment in the novel
form.

Additional touches are added by Zweig. The regimental colonel, Bubencic, represents the military honor of the *ancien regime;* he destroys himself after losing in battle, but Hofmiller,
the ''new man,'' has no honorable way out. This and other
elements which juxtapose the old with the new, nihilistic Europe, predicted by Nietzsche, add to the plot. Not only is the
concept of pity subjected to close scrutiny, from the perspectives of Zweig and Nietzsche, but other concepts such as courage and honor are at stake, also. Hofmiller narrates the story
from the standpoint of a celebrated war hero whose desperate
battlefield courage was an escape from his real dilemma. Zweig
delves into the issue of *Massenmut* [''mass courage''] versus
Individualmut [''individual courage'']. . . . Hofmiller represents the times as someone incapable of asserting *Individualmut,* and this more than anything drives him to seek approval
from others for his actions, and to allow pity to become the
basis for his own existence. Hence in addition to presenting
an analysis of pity, Zweig has commented on the emerging
nihilistic Europe. Condor provides hope for the future, and the
blind woman still clings to his arm when he is last portrayed
in the novel.

Ungeduld des Herzens stands with the fictional works of other
early twentieth century authors who in some way acknowledged
their debt to Nietzsche. The novel is a critical investigation
into a difficult area of Nietzsche's thought, analyzing the concept of pity and raising questions on motivation, courage, free
will, and ''herd'' values. It is not too much to maintain that
the novel is in many ways a critique of the new nihilistic
Europe; Zweig shows his ironic view of the new European by
allowing his narrator, the cowardly ''war hero'' and veteran
of the war to end all wars, to recount his own tale. But there
is a further element of tragic irony, and this can be understood
by returning to Dr. Condor's defiant anti-Nietzschean stand.
Condor maintains ''gerade am Unheilbaren bewährt sich ein

Holograph copy of Zweig's last poem. Frau Friderike M. Zweig.

Arzt'' [''it is only in incurable cases that a doctor shows his mettle''], but this particular rebuttal of Zarathustra's speech has a different ending in Nietzsche's text: ''Aber es gehört Mehr Mut dazu, ein Ende zu machen, als einen neuen Vers: das wissen alle Ärzte und Dichter'' [''But it takes more courage to make an end than a new verse: all doctors and poets know that'']. (pp. 198-203)

> Adrian Del Caro, ''Stefan Zweig's 'Ungeduld des Herzens': A Nietzschean Interpretation,'' in Modern Austrian Literature, *Vol. 14, Nos. 3 & 4, 1981, pp. 195-204.*

PETER J. MACRIS   (essay date 1981)

[*In the following excerpt from an essay that originally appeared in 1981, Macris examines the themes and techniques of Zweig's dramas.*]

The world of the theater was an integral part of Zweig's life as a young, cultivated Viennese. He did express some doubts about the artistic fulfillment to be found in ''the cult of the theatre, as opposed to that of the book,'' . . . but this did not keep him from creating in August of 1905 as his most complete and comprehensive early work—of any genre—a serious drama on a Greek theme, *Tersites*. . . . Zweig continued to return to the drama often enough to have left a legacy that clearly testifies to a natural proclivity to write—and write extremely well—for the stage, despite the fact that in our time even the educated community doesn't tend to think of him as a playwright.

D. A. Prater has written of *Tersites,* in which Zweig presents the fate of the ugliest and most malicious of the Greeks before the walls of Troy, that ''it strikes today's readers as contrived, conventional in expression, and convincing only in rare snatches.'' . . . This criticism is, unfortunately, well founded. However, despite its lack of originality, the work possesses many important, positive characteristics that single it out and make understandable the keen interest which Ludwig Barnay, Director of the Königliches Schauspielhaus, and the renowned actors Adalbert Matkowsky and Joseph Kainz showed it it. Most notable among these are the richness and range of the potential acting postures provided by the leading characters, and the amazingly natural flow of its highly declaimable dramatic lines. Indeed, it was, to a large degree, precisely young Zweig's conventionalism which stimulated him to write the type of rippling free verse which appealed so directly and forcefully to these established giants of the German-speaking theater.

In other ways, too, the work displays a cautious and even reactionary approach to the impressionistic conventions then prevalent in a Vienna still under the clear literary dominance of Schnitzler and Hofmannsthal. For with its Greek theme, use of classical elements of structure, and refined, measured versification, it is basically a neo-classic tragedy. It is permeated, however, by a somewhat modern psychological and subliminal cast, created largely by the concentration on the dark broodings of the negative hero, Tersites. This new-old aspect to the work partially explains why Matkowsky and Kainz could both find the play attractive yet be interested in different roles. Matkowsky wanted to play Achilles, the old-fashioned hero type, a role he was preparing when he unexpectedly died, and Kainz tried, in vain, to convince the Burgtheater to mount a production of it, so that he could play the more modern, tortured character, Tersites. In truth this imperfect but highly promising drama often transcends its temperate traditionalism through exactly this means: the juxtaposition of the two different approaches to life embodied in Tersites and Achilles and the resultant dialectical friction. This confrontation also presents us with the play's most original concepts: ''how great griefs can refine a soul while happiness merely hardens it.'' . . . Tersites is what D. Daviau has called a victor in defeat . . . , [see Additional Bibliography], a type of hero we will see much more of in the later Zweig dramas, even if in various guises. (pp. 187-88)

It was the interest of Kainz in having another play from [Zweig] that encouraged him to then write *Der verwandelte Komödiant,* his first completed dramatic piece after *Tersites.* (p. 188)

Der verwandelte Komödiant has been described by Zweig himself as a ''featherweight rococo affair with two big lyrico-dramatic monologues.'' . . . It was this and more. For a still young writer, and one who had written only one full-length play up to that point, it exhibits a surprisingly firm command of dramatic tension and dialogue of a type not attempted in *Tersites.* In both plays Zweig was testing his ability to create dramas of different kinds, presenting different character types and historical settings. But in *Der verwandelte Komödiant* Zweig moves more directly into the impressionist camp of his fellow Austrians, both thematically and in the emphasis on psychological nuance in the consciously overrefined banter of his leading characters: the young actor gaining confidence in himself as he discovers the power of his calling and the no longer very young countess, with whom he shares deliberately precious but also engrossingly perceptive exchanges on subtle interrelationships between acting and loving, play and reality. (p. 189)

[Zweig's] third play, **Das Haus am Meer,** was completed in 1911 and was soon after accepted by the Burgtheater for a 1912 production. Here he again employed blank verse and produced a well-balanced and crafted web of theatrically tense and alive scenes, again using classical structural devices. The themes in this story, however, center on intense jealousy and vicious clashes of certain personality types, against an historical background of the activities of press gangs in the late eighteenth century. By effectively drawing all the major characters with the impressive psychological veracity and providing the clash of these finely chiseled character-types as the essential motor for the tragedy, Zweig has continued his bent for mixing the old and the new. Perhaps one should say the old and the not-so-old, since Impressionism with its powerfully Freudian overtones had been the prevailing Viennese literary movement for over twenty years, and this work brought Zweig closer to its main stream. In any event, Zweig's tendency to present sufferers as victors and his fascination with the malicious element in man led him to present a hero, Thomas, who after years of degradation and suffering set things somewhat aright by murdering the outrageously malevolent usurper of his place, Peter, who had reigned over Thomas' wife, and to some degree his daughter, with a demonic totality. (pp. 189-90)

[Zweig] did not turn to another major dramatic project during World War I. However, when he did return to the drama, the new work, **Jeremias,** was to be one of his greatest artistic successes.

With this tragic play on the biblical theme of the prophet Jeremiah and the destruction of Jerusalem by the Assyrians, Zweig reached his full maturity as a playwright. The play distinctly separates itself from the earlier works, not only through its refinement but in its type, structure, and style. It was written while Zweig was on military duty in Vienna during the war. His obligations required occasional visits to the battle front which engendered and inflamed in him the conviction that the real enemy against whom he had to struggle was not the "other side" in the war but rather, "false heroism that prefers to send others to suffering and death, the cheap optimism of the conscienceless prophets, both political and military, who boldly promising victory prolong the war." . . . For two years he worked with great intensity on the play whenever his military tasks permitted, referring to it later as the first of all his works to mean something to him. . . . Not only did he take up the obviously risky challenge of trying to write a "hymn of peace in the midst of war,' . . . but for the first time clearly addressed and recognized his heritage as a Jew.

Though it displays Zweig's continued affection for classical dramaturgic traditions and his interest in psychological motivation, **Jeremias** exhibits distinct expressionist tendencies, and this despite the author's professed distaste for the movement. . . . Instead of being divided into acts, for instance, the play is partitioned into nine scenes. Many of the characters surrounding Jeremiah are either two-dimensional or simply nondelineated types, such as a woman, the warrior, the speaker, the messenger, another one, the first one, the second one, a voice. . . . Further, Jeremiah's repeated long emotional effusions, often of an intense lyricism, are regularly countered by frenetic outbursts from the other characters which are almost always broken up into very brief sentence fragments divided among many speakers—a kind of telegraph style. Other times choral sections variously described as voices, brighter voices, serious voices, jubilating voices, exchange almost operatic statements and responses, lending a musical quality to the already highly lyric work. The expressionistic concept of the brotherhood of man is raised as a substantial issue, and the structural basis for presenting the major point of the drama, "the spiritual superiority of the vanquished," is Jeremiah's change or *Wandlung,* also a major formal element in the expressionist tradition. Indeed, the antiwar aspect of the piece also relates it to Expressionism, although as Zweig warned, **Jeremias** "is not specifically a pacifist play—rather, the apotheosis of defeat." (pp. 190-91)

The main theme is, of course, a more complex and finished handling of the same idea that infused **Tersites** and appears in some form in most of Zweig's plays. (p. 191)

Zweig's autobiography gives us little direct information about the motivation behind his next stage work, **Legende eines Lebens.** The work itself, however, is prefaced with a set of comments admitting to some slight and limited influence by Duhamel's *Dans l'ombre des statues* in one scene, and minor utilization of biographic elements from the lives of Hebbel, Wagner, and Dostoevski in the descriptions of the late poet, Karl Amadeus Franck, the invisible figure whose memory and following so dominate the leading characters of the play. The statement also warns, however, against giving any great importance to these original motivations. We are left to conjecture, then, as to why Zweig could go from a play whose theme is directly applicable and based upon the major concern of his life—the war—to one with which the war seems to have no discernibly explicit relationship. Most likely his recent release from the military, his new and rather pleasant life in a village outside of Zurich as well as the clear signs that the war would probably be over soon effected him not only to write another play but one whose positive and hopeful tone mirrored his own mood and situation at the time.

In any event, this is his first drama to deal with a contemporary subject and, if **Jeremias** represents Zweig's one largely expressionist creation, then **Legende eines Lebens,** with its emphasis on conscious and subconscious personality struggle, must be regarded as the closest he ever came to writing a stage work completely in the impressionist manner. The basic plot, for instance, concerns a young psychologically crippled writer, Friedrich Marius, who feels his personal and artistic development thwarted by the oppressive cult surrounding his father's life and art. The young artist's mother is not only locked in an emotional, psychic struggle with her son, but her attempts to dominate and manipulate everyone and everything associated with her former husband's life are the cause of the conflict in this well-made, taut play. The unraveling of the layers of control exerted by his father—and his mother—over his life, through the discovery of elements of dishonesty in the cult, enables the hero to free himself from the subconscious hindrances which had prevented his emotional and, ultimately, his artistic maturity.

But the extremely weighty role psychological forces are given in this piece is not the only characteristic which tends to align it with the impressionist movement. Zweig has left behind the neo-classic meters and the archaic forms, found in all his plays up to this time, for a more realistically reproduced language. However, it is not the exactly copied, dialectically precise language of the petty bourgeoisie or working classes, such as one would find in plays of the naturalistic tradition that we find in *Legende eines Lebens;* instead it is the smooth, often eloquent lines appropriate to aristocratic and artistic personages who are the major characters of the play. Here, too, Zweig is fitting in quite well with the proclivity of so many Austrian impressionists before him to deal with contemporary problems, but not those of the factory, the street, or the bread line. Rather, as in *Legends eines Lebens,* the problems tend to be those of sensitive, well-off, well-born individuals and take place in opera houses, concert halls, aristocratic villas. Occasionally the *Volk* ["populace"] enters into these plays also, as it does here in the characters of Friedrich's secret love and to some degree in Maria Folkenhof, but the tone-setting scene is always the aristocratic palace, or its equivalent.

Zweig's next play, *Volpone* . . . , is also a unique work among his collected plays. Stylistically it breaks new ground and shows Zweig as an absolute master of comic writing. It is an adaptation of the original by Ben Jonson. Zweig became familiar with the play in a seminar he attended on Elizabethan drama. But it is not a straight-forward translation, as was the case with the Verhaeren works he had put into German earlier in his career. Zweig changed, rearranged, dropped and added freely. He also took great liberties with the characters and their individual lines. The result was a masterpiece, more trenchant and focused than the original, displaying an outrageous wit akin to Dürrenmatt's today and a pointed use of the grotesque which reminds one of both Dürrenmatt and Brecht.

Zweig completed his "amusing farce about money" (Zweig's description of Jonson's original in a letter to Rolland—1925) in nine days. It became a sensational success, playing all over the world and he was "intensely proud" . . . of it. With it, he reached his zenith as a playwright and was to complete and publish only two more original plays, which, however, continued to show the hand of a superb craftsman and attest to his ability to create yet different dramatic moods and styles. *Die Flucht zu Gott* . . . is a brief piece, intended as an epilogue to Tolstoi's fragment, *Und das Licht scheinet in der Finsternis.* It moves closer toward being in the naturalistic style than Zweig normally was inclined to write, though it still keeps some distance from this movement. Based on serious study and documentation of Tolstoi's life, it amounts to a dramatic manifestation of his propensity to write historical works and an expression of his ideas on the Russian artist as a human being. *Das Lamm des Armen* . . . is a full-length play, also historical in its genesis, which moves even closer to Naturalism in its almost realistic recreation of the speech of Napoleon's troops in Egypt and the general salience given this group and its concerns. The subject is again a variation of Zweig's early displayed and constantly held concern for the vanquished—Napoleon's brutal misuse of his personal and executive powers to destroy the life of one of his soldiers by callously taking his much-loved wife from him. In this instance, however, the conquered individual is able to be a victor only by defacing a picture of Napoleon before he walks away from the whole situation. A weaker ending than one usually finds in a Zweig play, perhaps unavoidable due to the documentary nature of the work. The piece continues to show Zweig at the peak of his powers, however, demonstrating once again his adroitness at drawing three-dimensional, magnetic characters enmeshed in dramatically tense, riveting action. The drama was immediately and enthusiastically sought after, for, following the international success of *Volpone,* Zweig was treated not only

as a leading intellectual and writer, but specifically as a man of the theater, a highly successful playwright.

It was in this setting, in 1931, that Richard Strauss, following the death of Hugo von Hofmannsthal, requested that Zweig supply him with a comic libretto. The result was a long productive period of collaboration and rewarding communication which culminated in the opera, *Die schweigsame Frau.* . . . Again Zweig turned to Ben Jonson, and again he made liberal changes in the original, even more so than in the case of *Volpone.* Jonson's prose was changed to sleek, bubbling verse, characters and scenes were dropped and important concepts were greatly expanded or developed from scratch. Most notable was the notion of having a group of actor-friends and the actress-wife of Sir Morosus' nephew cooperate with the young man by playing roles in the feigned situation. This "play" helped the nephew to win back his inheritance and to keep the love of his wife, while also dispelling Sir Morosus' interest in finding "a Quiet Woman" and bequeathing all his wealth to her. The result was one of the most sparkling and charming comic libretti of our time. The fact that the work has not become a staple repertory item for opera companies in general is due mainly to Strauss' uneven composition and not to the libretto. (pp. 191-94)

Zweig's various plays showed the influence of a number of literary styles, though generally he must be considered a playwright who was and always remained conservative in style and form, except for occasional dazzling displays of controlled excess in *Volpone.* His plays, therefore, have not aged well. He was somewhat behind the times in his own day as far as dramatic structure and form are concerned—except for *Jeremias*—and today he is radically less modern. Yet neither in his time, nor today, has he been surpassed in his speciality: an awesome ability to spin mellifluous, flowing lines that just call out for declamation. . . . This is what will remain as their unique point of interest. (p. 194)

Peter J. Macris, "Zweig as Dramatist," in The World of Yesterday's Humanist Today: Proceedings of the Stefan Zweig Symposium, *edited by Marion Sonnenfeld, State University of New York Press, 1983, pp. 186-94.*

JOHN FOWLES (essay date 1981)

[*Fowles is a British novelist, short story writer, translator, essayist, and poet whose work is a blend of classical and mythical allusions presented in a modern context. Fowles consistently scrutinizes the importance of history in his novels, exploring how the past can influence the present. His novels—which include* The Magus *(1965) and* The French Lieutenant's Woman *(1969)—are distinguished by their narrative force, vital, resourceful characters, and by Fowles's ability to combine traditional literary techniques with his personal beliefs and methods to produce fresh and unusual perspectives. In the following excerpt from his introduction to* The Royal Game, and Other Stories, *Fowles provides a discussion of Zweig's short stories, which he considers praiseworthy. For a contradictory view, see the excerpt by Stephen Spender (1982).*]

Stefan Zweig has suffered, since his death in 1942, a darker eclipse than any other famous writer of this century. Even 'famous writer' understates the prodigious reputation he enjoyed in the last decade or so of his life, when he was arguably the most widely read and translated serious author in the world. Yet I suspect very few English-speaking readers who have grown up since the Second World War know anything of him at all, except the name. No one has been deeper drowned in the shade of his great German and Austrian contemporaries: Thomas Mann, Hesse, Rilke, Schnitzler, Hofmannsthal and the rest. Virtually all his books are long out of print in English. Even in Germany, where he is still read, there has been a marked lack of academic interest in his work. (p. vii)

A blame still attaches to his name for not declaring himself more openly in the 1930s; as also for being too prolific, too successful, too famous and too known by the famous, and thus implicitly guilty of a kind of élitism, the belief that the world can be changed by art and international colloquia, benign conspiracies of the celebrated. If in one way Zweig was the last of the nineteenth-century *poètes maudits,* in another he was (a little like Somerset Maugham) a victim of his own immense living reputation. And then, perhaps, he has an even worse fault in the eyes of our own age.

One of his less gifted biographers has written of him, with an infelicity bordering on the sublime, that 'No one has ever accused Zweig of a sense of humour.' He was not in fact without a dry humour in his letters, but it is true that he took life far too seriously, or anxiously, for his own eventual good. It is probably why he never really fathomed the British during his exile; and, one might hazard a guess, why he did not spend more time on the fiction for which, with his striking narrative powers and psychological insight, he had such an obvious natural bent. He wrote only one full-length novel. It was his seriousness, his sense of social and intellectual responsibility, that too often led him to disperse his tremendous energy in minor fields—in translations, tributes, commemorative essays, the pan-European gospel.

It is easy to dismiss all this side of his life, to say that it was often absurdly idealistic, that it was blown away like thistle-down before the reality of the storm-troopers, that Zweig ought to have seen there was only one option after 1933—total public opposition to Nazism. But to dismiss an idealist just because his ideal failed and finally went unheard seems to me distinctly unjust. . . . [The] inner Zweig was very far from being temperamentally suited to the public role of 'Great European', and his suicide proves the bitterness of the battle between the two sides of his personality.

It was also, of course, a battle between cultural reality and a cultural dream. Today we might think more of Zweig in terms of the former, as a representative—or victim—of those extraordinary last decades of Imperial, and Jewish, Vienna, the mother-city of Auden's Age of Anxiety. Certainly the psychological sign of the zodiac that dominated his life was *Angst.* (pp. xiii-xiv)

The two earliest stories in [*The Royal Game and Other Stories*], *The Burning Secret (Brennendes Geheimnis)* and *Fear,* were both written before 1914. In them we may already detect the unease, *Angst* indeed, behind the green and gold façade of Imperial Austria. It is in the very language, the recurrence of emotional key-words: German equivalents of passion, frenzy, shame, excitement, fear, stammering, blushing, nervousness, guilt. As in the disturbing undertones of the outwardly posed and carefully calculated art of the Secession, we sense a culture already in trouble, already predicating the later century, and far beyond Austria.

Though Zweig resented the common assumption that the *Novellen* were autobiographical, it is hard not to see personal echoes in *The Burning Secret.* His relationship with his mother, something of a frivolous socialite, was never too happy. A picture

of him exists when he was four. Even then there is something frighteningly precocious and knowing in the little boy's eyes: an unnatural inquisitiveness, an incipient rebellion. Edgar in the story is clearly foreshadowed, and it is surely significant that Zweig ends the story with Edgar safely returned to his family. This is well beyond where a Maupassant or a Schnitzler would have laid down the pen. They would have ended with the flight, not the reconciliation. Not for the last time, and despite Zweig's great gifts as a classic story-teller, an inner need was allowed to prevail—the therapeutic content, not an orthodox neatness of form.

The 1922 collection *Amok* . . . was Zweig's first great commercial success. Intended to portray adult passions (as opposed to the stories of childhood like *The Burning Secret*), the book was translated all over the world. One result was the enormous response from readers who saw him less as a writer than as a spare-time psychiatrist, a role Zweig found increasingly wearisome. Stories like *Amok,* with Conrad's literal typhoons carried over into the domain of the sexual, seemed both daring and decadent, and immensely revealing, to their first audiences.

Letter from an Unknown Woman, later to be filmed by Max Ophuls, is Zweig's most famous story. Its lasting power is a little mysterious, since in one way it is clearly a period piece. It comes not only from a past society—and a set of conventions about the relationship between the sexes—but deals with an almost vanished mode of feeling. An intelligent modern woman may well find the heroine's endless self-denial hideously improbable. Even the basic situation must seem implausible now, to any but the most resolute contemporary Casanovas—though perhaps less so in terms of *fin de siècle* city society, tacitly as permissive as our own, at least on the matter of prostitution and the middle-class male. In my view the hidden secret of the self-denial is precisely its endlessness. One has heard of mistresses who sob as they take lethal revenge; of lovers who foster the very crime a word from them might have avoided. There are countless other strange ambiguities in this memorable *conte.* As I have already mentioned, there is plenty of evidence that the author's own relationships with women were less than perfect in his always self-examining eyes. The masochism is not all on the female side; and what the 'unknown woman' and 'R.' stand for in Freudian terms is, I think, sufficiently obvious.

The Royal Game (Schachnovelle, or 'chess-nouvelle') was written in the last four months of his life. This fine story of a man who outwits the Gestapo and manages, though scarred, to find the courage to go on living—in other words a man who has neither run away nor given free course to despair—must be seen partly as an attempt to exorcize guilt and unhappiness through wish-fulfilment, a very common phenomenon in novelists. Never was there a clearer literary case of 'Doctor, cure thyself'.

We may also see a parallel between the mad, but saving, sanctuary the hero finds in 'imaginary' chess and Zweig's own habitual retreat into the imagination (or literary work) when domestic or political reality threatened him too closely. The mystery is how he failed to see that this last fiction, surely one of the most powerful ever based on the imagery of a game, proved the very contrary of what he persisted in believing: that his daimon was gone, he was 'written out'. It shows how tyrannical—one might almost say totalitarian—his pessimism had become at the end. (pp. xvi-xvii)

[Zweig's troubled, but always humane, spirit] has wandered much too far out of the English-speaking world's memory. It is time, on this centenary of his birth, that we read him again. (pp. xviii)

John Fowles, in an introduction to The Royal Game
& Other Stories *by Stefan Zweig, translated by Jill
Sutcliffe, Harmony Books, 1981, pp. vii-xviii.*

STEPHEN SPENDER (essay date 1982)

[*Spender is an English man of letters who rose to prominence
during the 1930s as a Marxist lyric poet and as an associate of
W. H. Auden, Christopher Isherwood, C. Day Lewis, and Louis
MacNeice. Like many other artists and intellectuals, Spender
became disillusioned with communism after World War II, and
although he still occasionally makes use of political and social
issues in his work, he is more often concerned with aspects of
self-knowledge and depth of personal feeling. His poetic reputation declined in the postwar years, while his stature as a prolific
and perceptive literary critic has grown. Spender believes that
art contains "a real conflict of life, a real breaking up and melting
down of intractable material, feelings and sensations which seem
incapable of expression until they have been thus transformed. A
work of art doesn't say 'I am life, I offer you the opportunity of
becoming me.' On the contrary, it says: 'This is what life is like.
It is even realer, less to be evaded, than you thought. But I offer
you an example of acceptance and understanding. Now, go back
and live!'" In the following excerpt, Spender takes issue with
John Fowles's sympathetic evaluation of Zweig's short stories
(see excerpt dated 1981). Spender maintains that while Zweig
demonstrates analytic power in his short fiction, the endings of
his stories are often unsatisfactory.*]

John Fowles's introduction to [*The Royal Game and Other
Stories* (see excerpt dated 1981)] begins:

> Stefan Zweig has suffered, since his death in
> 1942, a darker eclipse than any other famous
> writer of this century. Even "famous writer"
> understates the prodigious reputation he en-
> joyed in the last decade or so of his life, when
> he was arguably the most widely read and trans-
> lated serious author in the world.

I was in my twenties during the said decade and this seems a
considerable exaggeration. Perhaps Mr. Fowles meant to write
"famous German writer," since in his list of famous writers
then living which follows he mentions only Germans and Austrians—Mann, Hesse, Rilke, Schnitzler, Hofmannsthal—not
Joyce or Yeats or Gide. But in any case surely Thomas Mann
was incomparably better known and thought of than Zweig.

Whether Zweig was considered a writer of the first rank even
at the height of his fame seems to me a matter for doubt. I
asked two women recently—one a former Soviet citizen, the
other by origin French—whether they had read Stefan Zweig's
stories. They said yes, they had done so when they were adolescents, and that many other young girls of their acquaintance
in both their countries read them.

This certainly lends confirmation to Stefan Zweig's international fame. It also suggests that stories like **"Amok"** and
"Letter from an Unknown Woman" were peculiarly exciting
to adolescents forty or fifty years ago. There is every reason
why they should have been particularly so to the children of
European middle-class families. The setting of nearly all of
them is high-bourgeois *(hochbürgerliche)* Austrian family life
at the beginning of this century, an immense façade of respectability and polite manners. Young people were encouraged to believe that no life of passionate experience and sensuality existed beyond this façade. In fact, that life *was* the

façade. What Zweig's stories tell the reader—sometimes almost to the exclusion of everything else—is that behind the
façade of respectability there are hidden secrets of passion—
sex, terror, hysteria, mad infatuation. Naturally the more intelligent and sensitive adolescent children of respectable families were thrilled to be told that the dull respectability was a
false front.

One of the best stories in this book is about the situation of a
young boy finding out about the secret lives of the adults of
his family. **"The Burning Secret"** is revealing of Zweig's
strength as expounder of a psychological situation of extreme
tension, and his failure in being able to imagine a satisfactory
or true resolution to it, to end the story with any but the most
banal conclusion. It is worth considering here in some detail.

A rich Jewish lady ("slightly voluptuous," we are told) takes
her twelve-year-old son, who is physically weak, sensitive,
and an only child, to a luxurious hotel at the resort of Sem-
mering (the almost inevitable setting of a Zweig story is the
first-class hotel, the palatial Viennese house, or an ocean liner).
One of the guests at the hotel is a baron ("of an obscure
Austrian noble line") who is bored, in the manner of barons,
but who hopes to relieve the tedium of the hotel by having, in
the manner of barons, an affair with one of his fellow guests.

He soon sets eyes on the "slightly voluptuous" Jewish lady
and her little son. He quickly decides that the way to strike up
an acquaintance with the mother is by making himself agreeable
to the son. He does so with resounding success. The boy (who
enjoys the privilege, rarely exercised in this story, of having
a name—he is called Edgar) is enchanted by his new friend
the baron and the excursions that the baron proposes for them
both. He soon realizes, though, that the purpose of the baron
in arranging these outings has been to strike up an acquaintance
with the mother, of a kind which excludes the son.

Edgar's first reaction is to be furiously jealous but later on he
is seized with a passionate and malignant curiosity to discover
the secret of the baron and his mother's attraction for each
other. With fiendish cunning he spies on them wherever they
go, and finally discovers them in an embrace which he takes
to be a violent assault by the baron on his mother. There in
the hotel corridor he strikes out at the baron. The next day he
refuses to write, at his mother's dictation, a letter apologizing
to him. Then he runs away to the house of his grandmother in
Baden.

Before daring to break in on his grandmother, he spends an
hour or so sitting on a bench in the spa garden where through
the darkness he hears lovers whispering to each other. Sum-
moning up his courage he then goes to his grandmother's house,
where a maid discovers him on the doorstep and takes him
inside. There he is confronted by his father, who asks him why
he has run away, and whether anything happened to frighten
him that he should do so. At this his mother from the back of
the room makes him a covert sign and he realizes that he is
being implored not to betray her secret. He remains silent. The
story ends with his mother coming into his room and kissing
Edgar "good night." . . . (p. 7)

In his introduction John Fowles writes:

> It is surely significant that Zweig ends the story
> with Edgar safely returned to his family. This
> is well beyond where a Maupassant or a Schnit-
> zler would have laid down the pen. They would
> have ended with the flight, not the reconcilia-

tion. Not for the last time, and despite Zweig's great gifts as a classic storyteller, an inner need was allowed to prevail—the therapeutic content, not an orthodox neatness of form.

This seems evasive. If Maupassant or Schnitzler had ended the story with the boy seated alone in the darkness of the park, it would have been in the interest not of neatness but of the truth of the imagination as distinct from fact as it might have happened. Zweig shows here his complete failure to incorporate into the reconciliation the truth that Edgar knows himself to have been lied to, cheated, and betrayed by his mother and the baron. Even if he has learned the nature of the "burning secret" which caused the baron to embrace "Mama" in the corridor, he has also perceived the hollowness of their relationship. In making Edgar accept without any kind of revulsion his mother's conspiratorial good-night kiss, Zweig is really implying that what Edgar has learned about growing up is that he himself will someday become someone like the baron and have an affair with someone like his mother. Growing up means discovering the guilty secret of the high bourgeoisie and becoming part of a conspiracy of silence about goings-on that are not considered respectable.

Of course, it may well be that Zweig means exactly this, and that Edgar will become some latter-day version of the baron with his mother. In that case the lack of irony in the ending is remarkable. But irony about the high bourgeois society to which he himself belongs is exactly what Zweig lacks.

When John Fowles writes about Zweig's "inner need," which is allowed to prevail in his description of Edgar's reconciliation with his family—to which he also applies the word "therapeutic"—perhaps he means that Zweig for reasons of his own psychology wanted Edgar to be "cured" by reconciliation with his family and their bourgeois circumstances, at the price of his imaginative insight, his sense of truth. This would certainly go far to explain Zweig's limitations as an artist, and the hollowness of the endings of his stories, which often seem totally at odds with the analytic power shown in their beginnings. For this kind of cure has nothing to do with art.

In "Fear" Irene, the wife of a rich and clever lawyer called Fritz Wagner, has an affair with a rather fey pianist—a shadowy character "with interesting features." One day, as Irene is entering the door of the house where her lover has his apartment, a woman who is leaving the house runs into her. The woman is violently abusive. Irene immediately takes her to be the kept woman of the pianist who is trying to blackmail her. Terrified, she gives her some money. From then on she finds herself being blackmailed by this woman, who is of the so-called "lower orders."

Zweig, who was a friend of Freud, understands almost as well as the Viennese psychoanalyst the case of this rich woman, the center of her family, surrounded by comforts, living in a great house and waited on by servants, who finds her life unendurable.

> There is a flaccidity of atmosphere that affects the senses in a similar way to sultry weather or a storm, a well-regulated level of happiness that is more maddening than misfortune; and it is as disastrous for many women, because of their resignation to it, as a lasting discontent caused by despair. To have an overabundance is no less stimulating than to be hungry, and

the secure certainty of her life aroused her curiosity about having an affair.

So Irene has to have her affair, and Zweig describes all the agonies of her imagining she is being blackmailed. He puts his characters through the hoops of the extreme situations in which they find themselves. So much so that they almost cease to be characters. They just become minimal instances produced by the situation, whose names "Irene," "Fritz," are perfunctory labels. It turns out that Irene isn't being blackmailed at all. Her clever lawyer husband, noticing, between briefs, that his wife is unhappy, deduces that she has a lover. So he hires an actress to impersonate a blackmailer, thinking that this strategy will result in his wife confessing to him the cause of her unhappiness and effecting a reconciliation between them. While he is carrying out the experiment she is driven to the verge of suicide. Nevertheless in the nick of time she is redeemed for reconciliation with her husband. Again therapy is a substitute for imagination.

Zweig is preeminently a bourgeois writer who understands perfectly the life he is describing, who has great analytic gifts, and who, if he had any other values than those of that very society, might have written brilliant satires on it. But, like Galsworthy, just when he seems on the point of doing so he withdraws into those very values that he shares with the people whose cases he studies. We are left with someone cured or someone incurable. So what we have is a kind of casebook by a doctor dealing with rich patients who can be cured of everything but their circumstances: if they are troubled about these, they must learn to be reconciled with them. Instead of

Zweig's suicide note. Williams Verlag.

visions deriving from these extreme situations like the terrible "the horror!" in *Heart of Darkness*, we get precepts and warnings.

For instance, in **"The Burning Secret"** and **"Fear,"** if you are born or married into a millionaire's family and you are put into a situation where you see the utter hypocrisy of the values of those around you, whatever you do don't leave the family. Learn the truth that as long as the domestics can be trusted to keep secrets, the most horrifying passions can be wrapped in sables and buried under diamonds.

Or in the nauseating story **"Letter from an Unknown Woman"**: your case is hopeless if you are a woman who when you were a young girl made the mistake of falling in love with a world-famous novelist, every one of whose works you learned by heart, under the misapprehension that in doing so you were finding your way into *his* heart. He will scarcely be able to distinguish you from all his other innumerable fans, and having slept with you once when you were a girl, he will fail to recognize you when you inveigle him into sleeping with you again ten years later. After you have conceived his child on this second occasion he will merely use the letter you write from the room where you are sitting by the side of your child's coffin, another ten years later, for unacknowledged copy in his next novel. However, dear girl, your life has not been lived quite in vain. You have provided flowers in the vase on the desk of the world-famous author.

And in the case of **"Amok"**: whatever else you do, don't—having escaped the clutches of a woman in Europe who has forced you to commit, in her interest, a theft—go to the tropics and there become a doctor and do-gooder, though a bit alcoholic. Once there another European woman from the nearest city—wishing to conceal her condition from her absent husband on his return—will hunt you down at your remote outpost and ask you to perform an abortion on her, before the return of her husband. When as a reward you demand that she sleep with you, she will run away terrified, and you—given that this is the tropics—will run amok, confronting her with your scandalous sexual demands at a party given in Government House. And worse to come.

John Fowles quotes Zweig as writing about his own work:. . .

> A psychological problem is as attractive for me in a living man as a historical person. . . . In my endeavour to explain character or a problem to myself I write at first for my own pleasure. Then I begin to shorten, to leave out everything which is not strictly necessary.

The result of this method seems to be the paring down of his material to psychological models of behavior in particular given circumstances. The limitation of the method is that by the time he has engineered the material into nothing but the situation, the characters, as persons who have an existence apart from the situation, have almost disappeared: hence his perfunctoriness about the names he gives them. Also, in order to produce a psychological situation much as you set up an experiment in a laboratory, he can improvise a plot that exists only for the purpose of the demonstration—like the plot of **"Fear."**

The best story in the collection is that which provides its title: **"The Royal Game."** It does communicate something of the horror of the Nazi occupation of Vienna as it affected the particular circles of rich, privileged, aristocratic people whom Zweig—himself the son of a Jewish millionaire from that city—knew. (pp. 7-8)

This story has a quality different from the previous ones. Here the author has succeeded not just in describing symptoms in a given situation. He has achieved the very considerable feat of inventing, in his description of the game of chess, a metaphor for the terribly grim game he is playing with his Nazi tormentors. He does what he so signally fails to do in the other stories, transform the symptomatic behavior of characters in a given psychological situation into something quite other, the game of the imagination. Moreover the case history here is no longer that of individuals; it is the case history of Europe, and as a result, the author is not under pressure to provide some denouement which is either personal despair or else cure, by reconciling the individual to his unalterable circumstances. (p. 10)

> *Stephen Spender, "Guilty Secrets," in* The New York Review of Books, *Vol. XXIX, No. 4, March 18, 1982, pp. 7-8, 10.*

DONALD PRATER (essay date 1982)

[*Prater is the author of the first comprehensive biography of Zweig. In the following excerpt, Prater finds throughout Zweig's works a consistent affirmation of his devotion to the ideal of a united Europe. Although Prater acknowledges the possible validity of the arguments of such critics as Hannah Arendt (1943) and Solomon Liptzin (1944), who consider Zweig's avoidance of politics cowardly and his suicide an expression of weakness, Prater views these issues in the context of Zweig's passion for personal freedom, which Prater believes was more important to the author than the struggle for his humanitarian ideal.*]

Considering Zweig's character, "relevance" is the last thing we would expect to find in his work of the exile years, but it would nevertheless be reasonable to seek some evidence at least of his deep spiritual unease and of his vicarious experience of the sufferings, not only of his own people, but also of those of the whole world in war. With all due allowance, however, for his relative comfort in the material sense, after his uprooting from Salzburg and during his peregrinations in England and the Americas, it is remarkable how closely the work to which he "fled" in those last nine years follows the tradition of that which preceded it. With *Erasmus, Maria Stuart (The Queen of Scots), Castellio gegen Calvin (The Right to Heresy: Castellio against Calvin), Magellan, Amerigo,* and the almost completed "great *Balzac*," there is the same eager enthusiasm, though often now without the superheated and repetitive style that marked the earlier biographies, the same diligence in distillation of the source material (he had accumulated 2,000 pages of notes for the *Balzac*). Four further studies were added to the collection of historical miniatures *Sternstunden der Menschheit (The Tide of Fortune),* entirely in the model of the earlier—"between the report and *Novelle* . . . a new epic-dramatic genre," where "even the obvious . . . wears a mask of distinction." The legend of *Der begrabene Leuchter (The Buried Candelabrum)* followed that of *Rachel rechtet mit Gott (Rachel Arraigns God);* he translated Pirandello's *One Does Not Know How* in 1934, and, with Richard Friedenthal, Irwin Edman's *A Candle in the Dark* in the early months of World War II, just as he had collaborated with Rolland and Barbusse in World War I. The *Kleine Reise nach Brasilien (A Short Journey to Brazil),* written after his 1936 visit, is reminiscent of the 1919 essays entitled *Fahrten (Journeys).* The war found no reflection in his work, although in an interview for the *New York Times* in 1940 [see excerpt dated 1940] his concern was with its effect on literature—as it had been in the 1916 essay *Die Bücher und der Krieg (Books and the War)*. The four *Novellen*, finally, are (with the exception of *The Royal Game*) typical of the Zweig whom one rare critic had castigated ten years before: "everything false, impure . . . no matter how amusing his chatter, in the last resort this is only railway-carriage reading."

Surprisingly enough, in the United States and South America he was constrained for the first time in his life to write strictly for a living. Although his royalties from the Viking Press for the American editions of his works were not insignificant, the greater part of his wealth at this time was in Britain, and the wartime currency restrictions meant that his pen had to supplement his income, if the comfortable lifestyle to which he was accustomed was to be maintained. The nomadic life in New York and New Haven hotel rooms was costly, and even the small villa he rented at Ossining, New York, for the summer months of 1941 far from cheap. Therefore, whereas he continued in his own tradition with *Amerigo,* and prepared the reminiscences of *The World of Yesterday*, the *Novellen Fishermen of the Seine, Die spät bezahlte Schuld (The Debt)*, and *War er es? (Jupiter)* were little more than potboilers to bring in dollars from *Harpers, Colliers,* and the *Chicago Sunday Tribune*. That this was their object is clear from his total lack of interest in their translation, which, by unknown hands, resulted in considerable alteration and even abbreviation of the originals—a thing he would never have countenanced in normal times. He was not even above rehashing old material, as witness his essay on Rodin, **"Great Lesson from a Great Man."** The *Brazil* book, although the result of genuine enthusiasm for his subject as a land of the future, was written basically as repayment for government hospitality and to assure himself of a little local income. . . . He had already contributed to the *Reader's Digest* before leaving England, and renewed the association now with two contributions to a series entitled **"Profit from My Experience."** The spectacle of Zweig, of all people, in such company is sufficient commentary on this, for him, unprecedented situation.

The short article **"Hartrott and Hitler"** was a piece of journalism to which he would scarcely have turned his hand in earlier years, and is of interest as one of the very rare instances in Zweig's case of direct public comment on Hitlerism, which he describes here as the expression of the Germans' eternal subconscious dream of world domination. Typically, however, his theme is still a literary one: Julius von Hartrott, the caricature of the Pan-German, with strikingly Hitlerian views, is a minor character in Vicente Blasco Ibáñez' 1916 novel *Los cuatro jinetes del Apocalipsis (The Four Horsemen of the Apocalypse),* and Zweig concludes as we would expect of him: "Blasco Ibáñez' fiction has shown again that it is the poet who understands his time and the future better than the professors of politics." (pp. 322-24)

Whatever he may have said of Blasco Ibáñez and the superiority of the poet over the professors of politics, however, his own concept of the literary artist's role remained essentially that of the golden age of his youth, to which he now harked back in *The World of Yesterday;* and his ideal of the moral and intellectual unity of Europe and the world was not to be striven for with the journalist's pen in the public arena. *Erasmus,* the nearest he could come to literature of "relevance," had been his profession of faith, the condemnation of fanaticism by depicting the tragedy of the "gentle, weak man in the middle," "mirroring something of my own destiny." The last of the *Tide of Fortune* episodes, on the death of Cicero, which he

wrote in Bath in the summer of 1939, concerned "another who was killed by dictatorship, who dreamed of order and stood for justice" but drew no lessons for the modern struggle against the dictators. In *Castellio against Calvin,* two years after Hitler's rise to power, he had even seen hope for the future, asserting that moderation must eventually prevail over fanaticism, however entrenched the latter may appear. If Erasmus showed Zweig as he was, Castellio is his portrait as he would wish to have been; and in *The Royal Game,* too, his only work whose theme relates directly to current events, and the last to be completed, there is perhaps something of wish fulfillment in the Austrian lawyer's power of resistance to Gestapo pressure.

But the problem stated in *Castellio,* "how to unite freedom with order," remained with Zweig when he turned, in his refuge in Petropolis, to his "brother in destiny," Montaigne. With the world torn apart, and war sunk to the uttermost depths of brutality, in the twentieth century as in the sixteenth, he was faced, like Montaigne, with the supreme problem: how to remain free, how to preserve the inner self against the onslaughts of a world in chaos. The fragment on Montaigne that he left, almost completed, at his death concentrates only on this aspect of the great skeptic's philosophy and does not follow in its form the earlier *Master Builders* essays. That he left it unfinished is symptomatic of his own failure to achieve the solution that Montaigne's stoic determination offered.

He had broken new ground in the novel *Ungeduld des Herzens (Beware of Pity)*. It had long been his dream to write the "great Austrian novel," and the attempt was his refuge during the years that saw the Spanish Civil War, the annexation of Austria, and the Munich Pact. It is a sentimental theme, and its scene, the distant days of the Hapsburg Monarchy, is that of many of his earlier *Novellen*. The young Lieutenant Hofmiller, in fact, in his scarcely credible innocence, is strongly reminiscent of the student in *Verwirrung der Gefühle (Confusion of Feelings)*. Although the setting is that of the last years of Emperor Franz Joseph, as in Roth's *Radetzkymarsch,* Zweig's treatment concentrates on the narrower theme to the exclusion of the wider scene: Hofmiller's disastrous thoughtlessness remains a purely individual story, with 1914 significant only in the relief it offers from the burden of the tragedy he has brought about, and there is nothing of Roth's powerful evocation of the decay and collapse of a system.

Immensely long for its content, the book is no more than an expanded, overwritten *Novelle* of the Zweigian kind. . . . To write it had been an escape for Zweig, but it expressed something of his troubled spirit in exile—a deep nostalgia for his lost country, and the pity that played a large part in his regard for the woman who was to become his second wife.

The World of Yesterday was naturally also a new departure in his work. He had always shunned the limelight and had never been, despite his renown, the busy author constantly before the public view; but his feeling, when the war he had foreseen finally broke out, that it represented the end of the road for his generation, impelled him to set down his memories of what that generation had been through. It is not an autobiography in the accepted sense, and contains nothing beyond the most general allusions to his personal life. But the world of the mind, the historical picture of the Europe and the great Europeans he had known between 1880 and 1939, are drawn in with bold, broad strokes and in a sober style rare with Zweig. It combines, in masterly fashion, personal reminiscence with sensitive perception of the true current of events in that cataclysmic era. For his biographies he had always needed the source materials at hand, and in each case the final product had been the result of the most painstaking research. When he came to write his own story, in exile in the United States and Brazil and far from the home he had established in Bath, there were almost no aids to his memory—no notes, none of the vast correspondence he had received, and few contemporaries, apart from Friderike, whom he could consult. The talk he had prepared for the 1939 P.E.N. Club Congress in Stockholm— cancelled by the war—was on the theme "Die Geschichte als Dichterin" ["History as Artist"] and in it he had compared historical truth with an artichoke, from which successive layers can be peeled seemingly without ever reaching the inner core. Thus history, as he saw it, must always be to some extent artistic invention, *Gedichtetes*. The form of *The World of Yesterday* shows him a worthy instrument of history herself as artist; and its success in conveying the feel and atmosphere of the times lends it an extraordinary value, beyond that of a mere source book. "For the third time what I have built up has collapsed behind me," he wrote after completing the work in Brazil, "and it was a small satisfaction to have been able to preserve at least in written form the life that has gone. The main thing I could do for the old Austria was to evoke a picture of what it was and what it meant for European civilization." Although it was not his last work, there is little doubt that the dispatch of the manuscript to the publishing house of Bermann-Fischer in Stockholm in November 1941 was for Zweig the end of the last of his "three lives." (pp. 324-26)

Zweig strove all his life, against the demands of fame, loves, and friendships, to preserve his innermost privacy, what he calls . . . "Mein tiefstes Ich, mein Urgeheim" ["my inmost being, my most secret places"]. It was this that he meant by "personal freedom," "the finest thing on this earth." "Apostle of the religion of friendship," in Rolland's words, he could be the most sympathetic and gregarious of men, yet was ever on the move to escape even the closest of friends and, for all his nobility in charity, instinctively drew back from any relationship that threatened to make too great demands on him— *Ungeduld des Herzens* (literally, "impatience of the heart"), indeed, "to be rid as quickly as possible of the painful emotion aroused by the sight of another's unhappiness." . . . Zweig's withdrawal, exemplified by his silence in exile, was certainly often a cloak, even if not the deception implied by his "coat of false colors." It could be argued that his cleaving to the middle way was nothing more than fear of exposure if he took sides and that his humanism was merely a rationalization of the deep urge to personal freedom. Moreover, those who saw in him a streak of selfishness as the dominant motive for his suicide may not have been far from the truth. "Was he not conscious of any responsibility," wrote Thomas Mann to Friderike just after his death, "toward his many brothers in destiny the world over, for whom the bread of exile is so much harder than it was for him, who was celebrated and free of material cares? Did he regard his life as his own private affair, and simply say: 'I suffer too much. Look. I must go'?"

In his study on Verhaeren, written just before the outbreak of World War I, he had identified the sense of responsibility as the force that decides the effect of a man's work: to feel this was to look on one's whole life as a vast debt that one is bound to strive with all one's strength to discharge. His approach to his life's work showed at all times a clear feeling of responsibility in this sense, a consciousness of the obligation to devote all his effort to promote the moral and intellectual unity of the European community. That it failed him in the end, and that he had not the strength to see the struggle through, detracts in

no way from the genuineness of the ideal. But he had tried to meet the obligation without sacrificing his personal freedom, and at the last it was that which counted most. The draught of veronal was the only way he could see to preserve his "last essence": it was a final flight "to the uttermost depths of the being." (pp. 327-28)

> *Donald Prater, "Stefan Zweig," in* Exile: The Writer's Experience, *edited by John M. Spalek and Robert F. Bell, The University of North Carolina Press, 1982, pp. 311-32.*

ADDITIONAL BIBLIOGRAPHY

Allday, Elizabeth. *Stefan Zweig: A Critical Biography*. London: W. H. Allen, 1972, 284 p.
> Biographical and critical study.

Birkin, Kenneth W. "Strauss, Zweig, and Gregor: Unpublished Letters." *Music and Letters* 56, No. 2 (April 1975): 180-95.
> Reveals the extent of Zweig's role as an intermediary between Joseph Gregor and Richard Strauss, both in Zweig's advocacy of Gregor as a suitable librettist for Strauss and in his collaboration with Gregor on subsequent libretti.

Cap, Biruta. "Stefan Zweig as Agent of Exchange between French and German Literature." *Comparative Literature Studies* X, No. 3 (September 1973): 252-62.
> Biographical information and three previously unpublished letters from Zweig to Henri Ghéon concerning Zweig's desire to adapt Ghéon's play *Le Pain* for the German stage.

Daviau, Donald G. "Stefan Zweig's Victors in Defeat." *Monatshefte* LI, No. 1 (January 1959): 1-12.
> Examines Zweig's avoidance of the standard, triumphant hero in favor of a protagonist who is ultimately defeated in his aims, yet achieves a moral victory and is strengthened through suffering.

Fehn, Ann Clark and Rettig, Ulrike S. "Narrative Technique and Psychological Analysis in Two Novellas by Stefan Zweig." In *Stefan Zweig: The World of Yesterday's Humanist Today*, edited by Marion Sonnenfeld, pp. 168-76. Albany: State University of New York Press, 1983.
> Analyzes the psychological dimensions of the novellas *Angst* and *Brennendes Geheimnis*, concluding that despite their overtly happy endings, the stories depict disturbed relationships and conflicts that defy easy resolution.

Forsyth, Karen. "Stefan Zweig's Adaptations of Ben Jonson." *Modern Language Review* 76, No. 3 (July 1981): 619-28.*
> Compares Zweig's *Volpone* and *Die schweigsame Frau* to the works by Jonson (*Volpone* and *The Silent Woman*) on which they are based, and finds that in both cases Zweig simplified the plots, established moral heroes, and created happy endings, resulting in the transformation of Jonson's cynicism into an expression of Zweig's humanism.

Lucas, W. I. "Stefan Zweig." In *German Men of Letters*, Vol. II, edited by Alex Natan, pp. 227-48. London: Oswald Wolff, 1963.
> Provides biographical information and examines the themes and techniques of Zweig's biographies and short stories.

Mann, Klaus. "Stefan Zweig." In *Treasury for the Free World*, edited by Ben Raeburn, pp. 365-68. New York: Arco, 1946.
> Provides a personal interpretation of Zweig's character and his approach to life.

Mathis, Alfred. "Stefan Zweig as Librettist and Richard Strauss: Parts I and II." *Music and Letters* XXV, Nos. 3, 4 (July 1944; August 1944): 163-76, 226-45.*
> Part I examines the relationship and collaboration between Strauss and Hugo von Hofmannsthal. Part II provides background on the

adaptation of Ben Jonson's *Epicoene* as *Die schweigsame Frau* and on Zweig's collaboration with Strauss on the comic-opera, with an analysis of both Zweig's libretto and Strauss's musical score.

McClain, William H. and Zohn, Harry. "Zweig and Rolland: The Literary and Personal Relationship." *Germanic Review* XXVIII, No. 4 (December 1953): 262-81.*
  Contends that Rolland was the primary influence on the development of Zweig's cosmopolitan outlook.

Modern Austrian Literature, Special Stefan Zweig Issue 14, No. 3/4 (1981): 1-375.
  Essays in German and English devoted to various aspects of Zweig's life and works. Among the contributors are Donald Prater, Harry Zohn, and Joseph Strelka.

Prater, D. A. "Stefan Zweig and England." *German Life and Letters* XVI (1962): 1-13.
  Account of Zweig's various visits to England, which began in 1904 and culminated in his attaining British citizenship in 1940.

———. *European of Yesterday: A Biography of Stefan Zweig.* Oxford: Claredon Press, 1972, 390 p.
  First comprehensive biography.

Slochower, Harry. "In the Fascist Styx: Stefan Zweig and Ernst Toller; Richard Wright." In his *No Voice Is Wholly Lost: Writers and Thinkers in War and Peace,* pp. 75-91. New York: Creative Age Press, 1945.*
  Characterizes Zweig as a homeless traveller who "was unequal to the task of translating his esthetic internationalism into a social internationalism," and adds that "even as [Zweig] persisted in his passive resistance, he was apperceptive of its futility."

Sonnenfeld, Marion, ed. *Stefan Zweig: The World of Yesterday's Humanist Today.* Albany: State University of New York Press, 1983, 357 p.
  Proceedings of the Stefan Zweig Symposium. Examines various aspects of Zweig's life and career, including Zweig's humanism, Judaism, and interpretation of history.

Spitzer, Leo. "Assimilation and Identity in Comparative Perspective: André Rebouças, Cornelius May, Stefan Zweig, and the Predicament of Marginality." *Biography* 3, No. 1 (Winter 1980): 28-64.*
  Examines Zweig's life as a Jew in Viennese society in the context of the struggle for assimilation and acceptance by the individual who is the product of two or more social worlds, and concludes that Zweig's suicide was "a drastic but not uncommon response to marginality."

Steiman, L. B. "The Agony of Humanism in World War I: The Case of Stefan Zweig." *Journal of European Studies* 6, No. 22 (June 1976): 100-24.
  Posits that Zweig developed an aesthetic rather than a socio-political awareness of life because concern with political and social issues was discouraged in Viennese families of his class. Steiman views Zweig's vacillation during World War I between patriotism, pacifism and the determination to remain neutral as the consequence of his cultivation of spiritual values and lack of political understanding.

Turner, David. "Memory and the Humanitarian Ideal: An Interpretation of Stefan Zweig's *Buchmendel.*" *Modern Austrian Literature* 12, No. 1 (1979): 43-62.
  Argues that although the main character in *Buchmendel* is in the grip of an obsession, he differs from many of Zweig's other monomaniacs in that he falls far short of the author's humanitarian ideal and because there is no sign of moral victory in his defeat.

———. "The Function of the Narrative Frame in the 'Novellen' of Stefan Zweig." *Modern Language Review* 76, No. 1 (January 1981): 116-28.
  Explores Zweig's use of the narrative frame to set up analogies and contrasts within his stories in order to highlight certain characters, events, and issues.

Zohn, Harry. "Stefan Zweig and Verhaeren." *Monatshefte* XLII, No. 4-5 (April-May 1951): 199-205.*
  Examines Zweig's admiration for Verhaeren and devotion to the translation and promotion of Verhaeren's works. Zohn maintains that Zweig's most lasting contribution to world literature may be his work as a literary mediator between cultures and on behalf of little-known authors and works, in the form of translations, adaptations, critical essays, and introductions.

Zweig, Friderike. *Stefan Zweig.* New York: Thomas Y. Crowell, 1946, 277 p.
  Biographical and critical study by Zweig's first wife.

———. "Stefan Zweig." In her *Greatness Revisited,* pp. 79-104. Boston: Branden Press, 1971.
  Divided into three sections: 1) an anecdotal account of the Zweigs' journey to France and Spain; 2) a lecture given by Friderike Zweig at Brandeis University on the message of compassion and international understanding implied in Zweig's works; 3) thoughts on Zweig's suicide, partly in opposition to "the carping criticism leveled at what was an act of unbearable despair."

Appendix

The following is a listing of all sources used in Volume 17 of *Twentieth-Century Literary Criticism*. Included in this list are all copyright and reprint rights and acknowledgments for those essays for which permission was obtained. Every effort has been made to trace copyright, but if omissions have been made, please let us know.

THE EXCERPTS IN TCLC, VOLUME 17, WERE REPRINTED FROM THE FOLLOWING PERIODICALS:

The Academy, n. 585, July 21, 1883.

American Literary Realism 1870-1910, v. XVI, Spring, 1983. Copyright © 1983 by the Department of English, The University of Texas at Arlington. Reprinted by permission.

American Literature, v. 50, November, 1978. Copyright © 1978 Duke University Press, Durham, NC. Reprinted by permission.

The Athenaeum, n. 4672, November 14, 1919.

AUMLA, n. 53, May, 1980. Reprinted by permission.

Australian Letters, v. 3, March, 1961 for "The European View of Christopher Brennan" by Frank Kermode. Reprinted by permission of the author.

Biography, v. 7, Spring, 1984. © 1984 by the Biographical Research Center. All rights reserved. Reprinted by permission.

Book Week—World Journal Tribune, March 12, 1967. © 1967, *The Washington Post.* Reprinted by permission.

Book World—The Washington Post, August 19, 1984. © 1984, *The Washington Post.* Reprinted by permission.

The Bookman, New York, v. XXXVIII, October, 1913.

The Christian Science Monitor, April 29, 1933./ December 8, 1966. © 1966 The Christian Science Publishing Society. All rights reserved. Reprinted by permission from *The Christian Science Monitor.*

College English, v. 4, October, 1942.

College Literature, v. IX, Spring, 1982. Copyright © 1982 by West Chester University. Reprinted by permission.

The Criterion, v. X, July, 1931.

The Critic, London, v. X, November 15, 1851.

Delta, n. 11, Spring, 1957.

The Dial, v. LXXV, November, 1923.

The Drama, v. VI, May, 1916.

English Journal, v. XVIII, September, 1929.

The Explicator, v. 39, Summer, 1981; v. 42, Fall, 1983. Copyright 1981, 1983 by Helen Dwight Reid Educational Foundation. Both reprinted by permission of Heldref Publications.

Forum, v. LXXXI, March, 1929.

The Germanic Review, v. XXVII, February, 1952.

Harper's Monthly Magazine, v. CXXXI, September, 1915. Copyright © 1915, renewed 1942, by *Harper's Magazine.* Reprinted by special permission.

Hispania, v. XL, December, 1957 for "'La Voz a Ti Debida': An Appreciation" by Julian Palley; v. XLII, September, 1959 for "'Todo Más Claro': Salinas and the United States" by Julian Palley. © 1957, 1959 The American Association of Teachers of Spanish and Portuguese, Inc. Both reprinted by permission of the publisher and the author.

Horizon, v. V, February, 1942.

The Illustrated London News, March 19, 1932.

The Indiana University Bookman, n. 5, December, 1960 for "Vachel Lindsay across the Chasm" by Edwin H. Cady. Copyright 1960, by Indiana University, Bloomington, IN. Reprinted by permission of the publisher and the author.

Journal of American Studies, v. 2, October, 1968. © Cambridge University Press 1968. Reprinted by permission.

Judaism, v. 9, Winter, 1960. Copyright © 1960 by the American Jewish Congress. Reprinted by permission.

Ladies' Home Journal, v. LXXXIV, September, 1967 for "The Living Legacy of Anne Frank: The Memory Behind Today's Headlines" by Otto Frank. © 1967 Family Media, Inc., New York, NY. All rights reserved. Reprinted by permission of the ANNE FRANK-Fonds, Basle/Switzerland.

The Markham Review, v. 9, (Spring, 1980); v. 12, (Spring, 1983). © Wagner College 1980, 1983. Both reprinted by permission.

McCall's, v. LXXXV, July, 1958.

Meanjin Quarterly, v. 29, September, 1970. Reprinted by permission.

MELUS, v. 7, Spring, 1980. Copyright, MELUS, The Society for the Study of Multi-Ethnic Literature of the United States, 1980. Reprinted by permission.

The Menorah Journal, v. XXXI, Autumn, 1943.

Michigan Quarterly Review, v. XXI, Summer, 1982 for "What the Canon Excludes: Lindsay and American Bardic" by Donald Wesling. Copyright © The University of Michigan, 1982. Reprinted by permission of the publisher and the author.

Minnesota History, v. VIII, December, 1927.

Modern Austrian Literature, v. 14, 1981. © copyright International Arthur Schnitzler Research Association 1981. Reprinted by permission.

Modern Fiction Studies, v. 30, Summer, 1984. Copyright 1984 by Purdue Research Foundation, West Lafayette, IN 47907. Reprinted by permission.

Monatshefte, v. LXV, Winter, 1973. Copyright © 1973 by The Board of Regents of the University of Wisconsin System. Reprinted by permission.

The Nation, v. LXXXVIII, June 3, 1909; v. CXXVII, October 10, 1928.

The National Review, London, v. XIV, October, 1889.

The New Republic, v. I, December 5, 1914./ v. LXXXV, December 25, 1935 for "Lindsay and Masters" by Sherwood Anderson. © 1935 The New Republic, Inc. Renewed 1963 by Eleanor Copenhaver Anderson. Reprinted by permission of Harold Ober Associates Incorporated./ v. 145, November 13, 1961. © 1961 The New Republic, Inc. Reprinted by permission of *The New Republic*.

The New Statesman & Nation, n.s. v. IX, April 27, 1935; v. XLIII, May 17, 1952.

New York Herald Tribune Books, March 23, 1941. © 1941 I.H.T. Corporation. Reprinted by permission.

The New York Review of Books, v. III, November 19, 1964; v. XXIX, March 18, 1982; v. XXX, October 27, 1983. Copyright © 1964, 1982, 1983 Nyrev, Inc. All reprinted with permission from *The New York Review of Books*.

The New York Times, December 3, 1950. Copyright © 1950 by The New York Times Company. Reprinted by permission.

The New York Times Book Review, January 3, 1915; May 16, 1920; November 1, 1931; June 15, 1952; September 20, 1959; October 1, 1967; December 23, 1979. Copyright © 1915, 1920, 1931, 1952, 1959, 1967, 1979 by The New York Times Company. All reprinted by permission./ July 28, 1940. Copyright © 1940, renewed 1968, by The New York Times Company. Reprinted by permission.

The New Yorker, v. XLI, June 12, 1965. © 1965 by The New Yorker Magazine, Inc. Reprinted by permission.

Newsweek, v. XCIII, June 25, 1979. Copyright 1979, by Newsweek, Inc. All rights reserved. Reprinted by permission.

The Nineteenth Century and After, v. CXLI, April, 1947.

Nineteenth-Century Fiction, v. 38, December, 1983 for "William Dean Howells and the Irrational" by Ellen F. Wright. © 1983 by The Regents of the University of California. Reprinted by permission of The Regents and the author.

Nineteenth-Century French Studies, v. VIII, Spring & Summer, 1980. © 1980 by T. H. Goetz. Reprinted by permission.

The North American Review, v. CXXVIII, March 1879.

North Dakota Quarterly, v. 48, Autumn, 1980. Copyright 1980 by The University of North Dakota. Reprinted by permission.

Poet Lore, v. XLVI, Spring, 1940.

Poetry, v. XXIV, May, 1924; v. XXXII, July, 1928.

Prairie Schooner, v. 55, Spring-Summer, 1981. © 1981 by University of Nebraska Press. Both reprinted from *Prairie Schooner* by permission of University of Nebraska Press.

Quadrant, v. VII, Summer, 1963 for "Brennan's Stature As Critic" by Sybille Smith. Reprinted by permission of *Quadrant*, Sydney, Australia and the author.

The Review of English Studies, n.s. v. XVIII, February, 1967. Reprinted by permission of Oxford University Press.

Saturday Review, v. XLVII, November 7, 1964; v. L, December 2, 1967; v. LI, December 7, 1968. © 1964, 1967, 1968 *Saturday Review* magazine. All reprinted by permission.

The Saturday Review, London, v. 96, November 28, 1903; v. 142, December 11, 1926.

The Saturday Review of Literature, v. II, December 5, 1925.

Scandinavian Studies, v. 49, Winter, 1977 for "Rølvaag and Kierkegaard" by Harold P. Simonson. Reprinted by permission of the publisher and the author.

Scandinavian Studies and Notes, v. IX, August, 1926.

Scandinavica, v. 13, November, 1974 for "Stig Dagerman's 'Vår nattliga badort': An Interpretation" by Laurie Thompson. Copyright © 1974 by the Editor of *Scandinavica*. Reprinted with permission of the publisher and the author.

Scrutiny, v. IX, (1940-1941)./ v. VIII, September and December, 1939. Reprinted by permission of Cambridge University Press.

The Sewanee Review, v. XLVIII, Spring, 1940.

The South Dakota Review, v. 17, Spring, 1979. © 1979, University of South Dakota. Reprinted by permission.

Southerly, v. 14, 1953./ v. 18, 1957 for "Christopher Brennan's 1913 'Poems'" by Robert Ian Scott. Reprinted by permission of the publisher and the author./ v. 21 & 22, 1961 & 1962. Reprinted by permission.

The Spectator, v. XXXV, May 24, 1862; v. XXXV, June 7, 1862; v. LII, November 1, 1879; v. 115, December 4, 1915.

Studies in Short Fiction, v. 17, Fall, 1980; v. 20, Spring & Summer, 1983. Copyright 1980, 1983 by Newberry College. Both reprinted by permission.

Time, v. 123, January 30, 1984. Copyright 1984 Time Inc. All rights reserved. Reprinted by permission from *Time*.

Time, London, n.s. v. XII, May, 1885; March, 1890.

The Times Literary Supplement, n. 793, March 29, 1917; n. 860, July 11, 1918.

Western Humanities Review, v. XI, Winter, 1957. Copyright, 1957, University of Utah. Reprinted by permission.

THE EXCERPTS IN TCLC, VOLUME 17, WERE REPRINTED FROM THE FOLLOWING BOOKS:

Auchincloss, Louis D. From *Reflections of a Jacobite*. Houghton Mifflin, 1961. Copyright © 1951, 1960, 1961 by Louis Auchincloss. All rights reserved. Reprinted by permission of Houghton Mifflin Company.

Auernheimer, Raoul. From "Stefan Zweig," in *The Torch of Freedom: Twenty Exiles of History*. Edited by Emil Ludwig and Henry B. Kranz. Farrar & Rinehart, 1943. Copyright, 1943, by Farrar & Rinehart, Inc. Renewed 1971 by Elga Ludwig and Holt, Rinehart & Winston, Inc. All rights reserved. Reprinted by permission of Holt, Rinehart and Winston, Publishers and the Literary Estate of Emil Ludwig.

Beach, Joseph Warren. From *The Comic Spirit in George Meredith: An Interpretation*. Longmans, Green, and Co., 1911.

Bedell, R. Meredith. From *Stella Benson*. Twayne, 1983. Copyright 1983 by Twayne Publishers. All rights reserved. Reprinted with the permission of Twayne Publishers, a division of G. K. Hall & Co., Boston.

Beer, Gillian. From *Meredith, a Change of Masks: A Study of the Novels*. The Athlone Press, 1970. © Gillian Beer 1970. Reprinted by permission.

Bennett, Arnold. From *Books and Persons: Being Comments on a Past Epoch, 1908-1911*. George H. Doran Company, 1917.

Bennett, George N. From *The Realism of William Dean Howells: 1889-1920*. Vanderbilt University Press, 1973. Copyright © 1973 by Vanderbilt University Press. Reprinted by permission.

Benson, Stella. From "About My Books," in *Ten Contemporaries: Notes Toward Their Definitive Bibliography*. By John Gawsworth. Joiner and Steele Ltd., 1933.

Bernstein, Rabbi Philip S. From "The Book That Started a Chain Reaction: Later Reactions by Contemporaries," in *A Tribute to Anne Frank*. Edited by Anne G. Steenmeijer with Otto Frank and Henri van Praag. Doubleday, 1971. Translation copyright © 1970 by Doubleday & Company, Inc. Copyright © 1970 by Otto Frank. All rights reserved. Reprinted by permission of the publisher.

Berryman, John. From *The Freedom of the Poet*. Farrar, Straus and Giroux, 1976. Copyright © 1940, 1968, 1976 by John Berryman. All rights reserved. Reprinted by permission of Farrar, Straus and Giroux, Inc.

Bettelheim, Bruno. From *Surviving and Other Essays*. Knopf, 1979. Copyright © 1960 by Bruno Bettelheim and Trude Bettelheim as Trustees. All rights reserved. Reprinted by permission of Alfred A. Knopf, Inc.

Birstein, Ann and Alfred Kazin. From an introduction to *The Works of Anne Frank*. By Anne Frank. Doubleday, 1959. Copyright © 1952, 1959 by Otto Frank. All rights reserved. Reprinted by permission of Doubleday & Company, Inc.

Bogan, Louise. From a preface to *The Journal of Jules Renard*. By Jules Renard, edited and translated by Louise Bogan and Elizabeth Roget. Braziller, 1964. All rights reserved. Reprinted by permission of George Braziller, Inc., Publishers.

Brownell, William Crary. From "George Meredith," in *The Egoist: A Comedy in Narrative*. By George Meredith. Charles Scribner's Sons, 1901.

Burke, Kenneth. From *Counter-Statement*. Second edition. Hermes Publications, 1953.

Burne, Glenn S. From *Remy de Gourmont: His Ideas and Influence in England and America*. Southern Illinois University Press, 1963. Copyright © 1963 by Southern Illinois University Press. All rights reserved. Reprinted by permission of the publisher.

Bychkov, S. P. From "The Social Bases of 'Anna Karenina'," translated by Tanya E. Mairs, in *"Anna Karenina" by Leo Tolstoy: The Maude Translation, Backgrounds and Sources, Essays in Criticism*. A Norton Critical Edition. Edited by George Gibian. Norton, 1970. Copyright © 1970 by W. W. Norton & Company, Inc. Reprinted with the permission of W. W. Norton & Company, Inc.

Byrne, Madge E. Coleman. From "Introduction to the Aesthetic Theory of Remy de Gourmont," in *Papers of the Michigan Academy of Science, Arts, and Letters, Vol. XLIII*. Edited by Sheridan Baker. The University of Michigan Press, 1958. Copyright © 1958 by The University of Michigan. Reprinted by permission.

Cady, Edwin H. From "What Kind of Critic Was Howells?" in *W. D. Howells As Critic*. By W. D. Howells, edited by Edwin H. Cady. Routledge & Kegan Paul, 1973. Copyright Edwin H. Cady 1973. Reprinted by permission of Routledge & Kegan Paul PLC.

Calder, Angus. From *Russia Discovered: Nineteenth-Century Fiction from Pushkin to Chekhov*. Barnes & Noble, 1976. © Angus Calder 1976. By permission of Barnes & Noble Books, a Division of Littlefield, Adams & Co., Inc.

Cary, Joyce. From *Art and Reality: Ways of the Creative Process*. World Perspective Series, Vol. 20. Planned and Edited by Ruth Nanda Anshen. Harper & Brothers, Publishers, 1958. Copyright © 1958 by Arthur Lucius Michael Cary and David Alexander Ogilvie, Executors, Estate of Joyce Cary. All rights reserved. Reprinted by permission of Harper & Row, Publishers, Inc. In Canada by Curtis Brown Ltd, London.

Chesterton, G. K. From *The Uses of Diversity: A Book of Essays*. Fifth edition. Methuen & Co. Ltd., 1927.

Chisholm, A. R. From an introduction and epilogue to *A Study of Christopher Brennan's "The Forest of Night."* Melbourne University Press, 1970. © Alan Rowland Chisholm 1970. Reprinted by permission.

Christian, R. F. From *Tolstoy: A Critical Introduction*. Cambridge at the University Press, 1969. © Cambridge University Press 1969. Reprinted by permission.

Chuyko, V. V. From an excerpt from two articles in "Voice," translated by A. V. Knowles, in *Tolstoy: The Critical Heritage*. Edited by A. V. Knowles. Routledge & Kegan Paul, 1978. © A. V. Knowles 1978. Reprinted by permission of Routledge & Kegan Paul PLC.

Clark, Axel. From *Christopher Brennan: A Critical Biography*. Melbourne University Press, 1980. © Axel Clark 1980. Reprinted by permission.

Colcord, Lincoln. From an introduction to *Giants in the Earth: A Saga of the Prairie*. By O. E. Rölvaag, translated by Lincoln Colcord and O. E. Rölvaag. Harper & Row, 1927. Copyright, 1927, by Harper & Brothers. Renewed copyright © 1955 by Jennie Marie Berdahl Rölvaag. All rights reserved. Reprinted by permission of Harper & Row, Publishers, Inc.

Collins, Joseph. From *The Doctor Looks at Literature: Psychological Studies of Life and Letters*. Doran, 1923. Copyright, 1923, by George H. Doran Company. Renewed 1950 by the Literary Estate of Joseph Collins. Reprinted by permission of the Literary Estate of Joseph Collins.

Cooley, John R. From *Savages and Naturals: Black Portraits by White Writers in Modern American Literature*. University of Delaware Press, 1982. © 1982 by Associated University Presses, Inc. Reprinted by permission.

Crispin, John. From *Pedro Salinas*. Twayne, 1974. Copyright 1974 by Twayne Publishers, Inc. All rights reserved. Reprinted with the permission of Twayne Publishers, a division of G. K. Hall & Co., Boston.

Diggory, Terence. From *Yeats & American Poetry: The Tradition of the Self*. Princeton University Press, 1983. Copyright © 1983 by Princeton University Press. All rights reserved. Excerpts reprinted with permission of Princeton University Press.

Dussert, Pierre. From a foreword to *Springfield Town Is Butterfly Town and Other Poems for Children*. By Vachel Lindsay. The Kent State University Press, 1969. Copyright © 1969 Pierre Dussert. All rights reserved. Reprinted by permission.

Eble, Kenneth E. From *William Dean Howells*. Second edition. Twayne, 1982. Copyright 1982 by Twayne Publishers. All rights reserved. Reprinted with the permission of Twayne Publishers, a division of G. K. Hall and Co., Boston.

Edel, Leon. From *The Psychological Novel: 1900-1950*. Revised edition. R. Hart-Davis, 1961. Copyright © 1955, 1961, 1964 by Leon Edel. Reprinted by permission of William Morris Agency, Inc., on behalf of the author.

Ehrenburg, Ilya. From "Anne Frank's Diary," translated by Tatiana Shebunia and Yvonne Kapp, in his *Chekhov, Stendhal, and Other Essays*. Knopf, 1963. Copyright © 1963 by Alfred A. Knopf, Inc. All rights reserved. Reprinted by permission of the Literary Estate of Ilya Ehrenburg.

Eikhenbaum, Boris. From "The Puzzle of the Epigraph, N. Schopenhauer," translated by George Gibian, in *"Anna Karenina" by Leo Tolstoy: The Maude Translation, Backgrounds and Sources, Essays in Criticism*. A Norton Critical Edition. Edited by George Gibian. Norton, 1970. Copyright © 1970 by W. W. Norton & Company, Inc. Reprinted with the permission of W. W. Norton & Company, Inc.

Ellis, Havelock. From *From Rousseau to Proust*. Houghton Mifflin Company, 1935. Copyright, 1935, by Havelock Ellis. All rights reserved. Reprinted by permission of the Literary Estate of Havelock Ellis.

Foster, S. From "W. D. Howells: 'The Rise of Silas Lapham' (1885)," in *The Monster in the Mirror: Studies in Nineteenth-Century Realism*. Edited by D. A. Williams. Oxford University Press, 1978. All rights reserved. Reprinted by permission of Oxford University Press.

Fowles, John. From an introduction to *The Royal Game & Other Stories*. By Stefan Zweig, translated by Jill Sutcliffe. Harmony Books, 1981. Introduction copyright © 1981 by J. R. Fowles Ltd. All rights reserved. Used by permission of Harmony Books, a division of Crown Publishers, Inc.

Freud, Sigmund. From "Dostoevsky and Parricide," translated by D. F. Tait, in *Collected Papers: Miscellaneous Papers, 1888-1938, Vol. V*. Edited by Ernest Jones, M.D. and James Strachey. Basic Books by arrangement with The Hogarth Press Ltd. and The Institute of Psycho-Analysis, 1959. Reprinted by permission of Basic Books, Inc. Publishers: In Canada by The Hogarth Press, Ltd.

Goes, Albrecht. From ''The Book That Started a Chain Reaction: Prefaces to the Diary,'' in *A Tribute to Anne Frank*. Edited by Anna G. Steenmeijer with Otto Frank and Henri van Praag. Doubleday, 1971. Translation copyright © 1970 by Doubleday & Company, Inc. Copyright © 1970 by Otto Frank. All rights reserved. Reprinted by permission of the publisher.

Gorky, Maxim. From *Reminiscences of Leo Nikolaevich Tolstoy*. Translated by S. S. Koteliansky and Leonard Woolf. B. W. Huebsch, 1920. Copyright © 1920 by B. W. Huebsch, Inc. Renewed 1947 by S. S. Koteliansky and Leonard Woolf. Reprinted by permission of Viking Penguin Inc.

Gourmont, Remy de. From *The Book of Masks*. Translated by Jack Lewis. J. W. Luce and Company, 1921.

Green, Martin. From *Tolstoy and Gandhi, Men of Peace: A Biography*. Basic Books, 1983. Copyright © 1983 by Martin Green. Reprinted by permission of Basic Books, Inc., Publishers.

Guillén, Jorge. From ''Introduction: Pedro Salinas,'' translated by Elias L. Rivers, in *Reality and the Poet in Spanish Poetry*. By Pedro Salinas, translated by Edith Fishtine Helman. The Johns Hopkins University Press, 1966. Copyright © 1940, 1966 by The Johns Hopkins Press, Baltimore, MD 21218. Reprinted by permission.

Gunn, Elizabeth. From *A Daring Coiffeur: Reflections on ''War and Peace'' and ''Anna Karenina''*. Rowman and Littlefield, 1971. © Elizabeth Gunn 1971. Reprinted by permission.

Gustafson, Alrik. From *A History of Swedish Literature*. University of Minnesota Press, 1961. © copyright 1961 by the American-Scandinavian Foundation. All rights reserved. Reprinted by permission.

Habegger, Alfred. From *Gender, Fantasy, and Realism in American Literature*. Columbia University Press, 1982. © 1982, Columbia University Press. All rights reserved. Reprinted by permission.

Hardy, Barbara. From '''Lord Ormont and His Aminta' and 'The Amazing Marriage','' in *Meredith Now: Some Critical Essays*. Edited by Ian Fletcher. Barnes & Noble, 1971. © Ian Fletcher 1971. By permission of Barnes & Noble Books, a Division of Littlefield, Adams & Co., Inc.

Harrison, James. From *Rudyard Kipling*. Twayne, 1982. Copyright 1982 by Twayne Publishers. All rights reserved. Reprinted with the permission of Twayne Publishers, a division of G. K. Hall & Co., Boston.

Haugen, Einar. From *Ole Edvart Rölvaag*. Twayne, 1983. Copyright 1983 by Twayne Publishers. All rights reserved. Reprinted with the permission of Twayne Publishers, a division of G. K. Hall & Co., Boston.

Hochman, Stanley. From an introduction to *Poil de Carotte and Other Plays*. By Jules Renard, translated by Stanley Hochman. Ungar, 1977. Copyright © 1977 by Frederick Ungar Publishing Co., Inc. Reprinted by permission.

Howard, Richard. From an introduction to *Natural Histories*. By Jules Renard, translated by Richard Howard. Horizon Press, 1966. Copyright 1966. Reprinted by permission of the publisher, Horizon Press, NY.

Hughes, Randolph. From *C. J. Brennan: An Essay in Values*. P. R. Stephensen & Co. Limited, 1934.

Huneker, James. From *Unicorns*. Charles Scribner's Sons, 1917. Copyright 1917 Charles Scribner's Sons. Copyright renewed 1945 Josephine Huneker. Reprinted with the permission of Charles Scribner's Sons.

Johnson, R. Brimley. From *Some Contemporary Novelists (Women)*. Leonard Parsons, 1920.

Jorgenson, Theodore and Nora O. Solum. From *Ole Edvart Rölvaag: A Biography*. Harper & Brothers Publishers, 1939. Copyright, 1939, by Theodore Jorgenson & Nora O. Solum. Renewed copyright © 1967 by Theodore Jorgenson. All rights reserved. Reprinted by permission of Harper & Row, Publishers, Inc.

Kazin, Alfred. From *An American Procession*. Knopf, 1984. Copyright © 1984 by Alfred Kazin. All rights reserved. Reprinted by permission of Alfred A. Knopf, Inc.

Knodel, Arthur J. From a conclusion to *Jules Renard As Critic*, University of California Publications in Modern Philology, No. 3. University of California Press, 1951.

Kropotkin, Prince. From *Russian Literature*. McClure, Phillips & Co., 1905.

Lalou, René. From *Contemporary French Literature*. Translated by William Aspenwall Bradley. Knopf, 1924. Copyright 1924 and renewed 1952 by Alfred A. Knopf, Inc. Reprinted by permission of the publisher.

Lawrence, D. H. From *Phoenix: The Posthumous Papers of D. H. Lawrence*. Edited by Edward D. McDonald. The Viking Press, 1936. Copyright 1936 by Frieda Lawrence. Copyright renewed © 1964 by the Estate of Frieda Lawrence Ravagli. Reprinted by permission of Viking Penguin Inc.

Leftwich, Joseph. From "Stefan Zweig and the World of Yesterday," in *Year Book of The Leo Baeck Institute, Vol. III*. Edited by Robert Weltsch. East and West Library, 1958. © Leo Baeck Institute 1958. Reprinted by permission.

Leontiev, Konstantin. From "The Novels of Count L. N. Tolstoy: Analysis, Style, and Atmosphere," in *Essays in Russian Literature, the Conservative View: Leontiev, Rosznov, Shestov*. Edited and translated by Spencer E. Roberts. Ohio University Press, 1968. Copyright © 1968 by Spencer Roberts. Reprinted by permission of Spencer E. Roberts.

Lewisohn, Ludwig. From an introduction to *The Book of Masks*. By Remy de Gourmont, translated by Jack Lewis. J. W. Luce and Company, 1921.

Liptzin, Solomon. From *Germany's Stepchildren*. The Jewish Publication Society of America, 1944. Copyright, 1944, renewed 1971 by The Jewish Publication Society. All rights reserved. Used through the courtesy of The Jewish Publication Society.

Lowell, Amy. From *Six French Poets: Studies in Contemporary Literature*. The Macmillan Company, 1915.

Lubbock, Percy. From *The Craft of Fiction*. J. Cape, 1921.

Lynn, Kenneth S. From *William Dean Howells: An American Life*. Harcourt Brace Jovanovich, 1971. Copyright © 1970, 1971 by Kenneth S. Lynn. Reprinted by permission of Harcourt Brace Jovanovich, Inc.

Macris, Peter J. From "Zweig As Dramatist," in *The World of Yesterday's Humanist Today: Proceedings of the Stefan Zweig Symposium*. Edited by Marion Sonnenfeld. State University of New York Press, 1983. © 1983 State University of New York. All rights reserved. Reprinted by permission of the State University of New York Press.

McAuley, James. From *Christopher Brennan*. Oxford University Press, Melbourne, 1973. Copyright © 1973 by Oxford University Press, Inc. Reprinted by permission.

McClure, John A. From *Kipling & Conrad: The Colonial Fiction*. Cambridge, Mass.: Harvard University Press, 1981. Copyright © 1981 by the President and Fellows of Harvard College. All rights reserved. Excerpted by permission.

Mencken, H. L. From *Vachel Lindsay*. n.p., 1947. Copyright 1947 by John S. Mayfield. Renewed 1974 by Mercantile Safe Deposit and Trust Company. Used by permission of The Enoch Pratt Free Library of Baltimore in accordance with the terms of the will of H. L. Mencken.

Morris, C. B. From *A Generation of Spanish Poets 1920-1936*. Cambridge University Press, 1969. © Cambridge University Press 1969. Reprinted by permission.

Moss, Robert F. From *Rudyard Kipling and the Fiction of Adolescence*. St. Martin's Press, 1982. Macmillan, 1982. © Robert F. Moss 1982. All rights reserved. Reprinted by permission of St. Martin's Press Inc. In Canada by Macmillan, London and Basingstoke.

Nabokov, Vladimir. From *Lectures on Russian Literature*. Edited by Fredson Bowers. Harcourt Brace Jovanovich, 1981. Copyright © 1981 by the Estate of Vladimir Nabokov. Reprinted by permission of Harcourt Brace Jovanovich, Inc.

Papini, Giovanni. From *Four and Twenty Minds*. Edited and translated by Ernest Hatch Wilkins. Thomas Y. Crowell Company, Publishers, 1922.

Pound, Ezra. From *Instigations*. Boni and Liveright Publishers, 1920.

Prater, Donald. From "Stefan Zweig," in *Exile: The Writer's Experience*. Edited by John M. Spalek and Robert F. Bell. University of North Carolina Press, 1982. © 1982 The University of North Carolina Press. All rights reserved. Reprinted by permission.

Priestley, J. B. From *George Meredith*. The Macmillan Company, 1926.

Priestley, J. B. From *Literature and Western Man*. Harper & Brothers, 1960. Copyright © 1960 by J. B. Priestley. All rights reserved. Reprinted by permission of the Literary Estate of J. B. Priestley.

Prioleau, Elizabeth Stevens. From *The Circle of Eros: Sexuality in the Work of William Dean Howells*. Duke University Press, 1983. Copyright © 1983 by Duke University Press, Durham, NC. Reprinted by permission of the Publisher.

Pritchett, V. S. From *George Meredith and English Comedy: The Clark Lectures for 1969*. Chatto & Windus Ltd., 1970. Copyright © 1969 by V. S. Pritchett. All rights reserved. Reprinted by permission of A. D. Peters & Co. Ltd.

Proust, Marcel. From *Marcel Proust on Art and Literature 1896-1919*. Translated by Sylvia Townsend Warner. Meridian Books, 1958. Published in England as *By Way of Sainte-Beuve (Contre Sainte-Beuve)*. Chatto & Windus, 1958. © 1958 by Meridian Books, Inc. Reprinted by permission of Georges Borchardt, Inc., as agents for the author. In Canada by the Literary Estate of Sylvia Townsend Warner and Chatto & Windus Ltd.

Ransome, Arthur. From a preface to *A Night in the Luxembourg*. By Remy de Gourmont, translated by Arthur Ransome. The Modern Library Publishers, 1926.

Raskin, Jonah. From *The Mythology of Imperialism: Rudyard Kipling, Joseph Conrad, E. M. Forster, D. H. Lawrence, and Joyce Cary*. Random House, 1971. Copyright © 1971 by Jonah Raskin. All rights reserved. Reprinted by permission of Random House, Inc.

Reisiger, Hans. From an extract from an introduction to "Die gesammelten Gedichte" ("Collected Poems"), in *Stefan Zweig: A Tribute to His Life and Work*. Edited by Hanns Arens, translated by Christobel Fowler. W. H. Allen, 1951.

Romains, Jules. From *Stefan Zweig: Great European*. Translated by James Whitall. The Viking Press, 1941.

Romein, Jan. From "A Child's Voice," in *A Tribute to Anne Frank*. Edited by Anna G. Steenmeijer with Otto Frank and Henri van Praag. Doubleday, 1971. Translation copyright © 1970 by Doubleday & Company, Inc. Copyright © 1970 by Otto Frank. All rights reserved. Reprinted by permission of the publisher.

Romein-Verschoor, Annie. From "The Book That Started a Chain Reaction: Prefaces to the Diary," in *A Tribute to Anne Frank*. Edited by Anna G. Steenmeijer with Otto Frank and Henri van Praag. Doubleday, 1971. Translation copyright © 1970 by Doubleday & Company, Inc. Copyright © 1970 by Otto Frank. All rights reserved. Reprinted by permission of the publisher.

Roosevelt, Eleanor. From an introduction to *Anne Frank: The Diary of a Young Girl*. By Anne Frank, translated by B. M. Mooyaart-Doubleday. The Modern Library, 1952. Vallentine Mitchell, 1954. Copyright 1952, renewed 1980, by Otto H. Frank. All rights reserved. Reprinted by permission of Doubleday & Company, Inc. In Canada by Vallentine Mitchell & Co., Ltd. (London).

Salinas, Pedro. From a preface to *Lost Angel and Other Poems*. Translated by Eleanor L. Turnbull. The Johns Hopkins University Press, 1938.

Saurat, Denis. From *Modern French Literature: 1870-1940*. J. M. Dent & Sons Limited, 1946.

Schouw, Daniel L. From "The Book that Started a Chain Reaction: Later Reactions by Contemporaries," in *A Tribute to Anne Frank*. Edited by Anna G. Steenmeijer with Otto Frank and Henri van Praag. Doubleday, 1971. Translation copyright © 1970 by Doubleday & Company, Inc. Copyright © 1970 by Otto Frank. All rights reserved. Reprinted by permission of the publisher.

Smith, Henry Nash. From *The American Self: Myth, Ideology, and Popular Culture*. Edited by Sam B. Girgus. University of New Mexico Press, 1981. © 1981 by the University of New Mexico Press. All rights reserved. Reprinted by permission of the author.

Spindler, Michael. From *American Literature and Social Change: William Dean Howells to Arthur Miller*. Indiana University Press, 1983. Copyright © 1983 by Michael Spindler. All rights reserved. Reprinted by permission.

Stenbock-Fermor, Elisabeth. From *The Architecture of "Anna Karenina": A History of Its Writing, Structure, and Message*. The Peter De Ridder Press, 1975. © copyright Elisabeth Stenbock-Fermor. Reprinted by permission.

Stern, J. P. From *Re-interpretations: Seven Studies in Nineteenth-Century German Literature*. Basic Books, Inc., Publishers, 1964. © J. P. Stern, 1964. Reprinted by permission of the author.

Stern, G. B. From an introduction to *Tales from the House Behind: Fables, Personal Reminiscences and Short Stories*. By Anne Frank, translated by H.H.B. Mosberg and Michel Mok. The World's Work (1913) Ltd., 1962. All rights reserved. Reprinted by permission of William Heinemann Limited.

Suvorin, A. S. From an excerpt from "Russian News," translated by A. V. Knowles, in *Tolstoy: The Critical Heritage*. Edited by A. V. Knowles. Routledge & Kegan Paul, 1978. © A. V. Knowles 1978. Reprinted by permission of Routledge & Kegan Paul PLC.

Thibaudet, Albert. From *French Literature from 1795 to Our Era*. Translated by Charles Lam Markmann. Funk & Wagnalls, 1967. Translation copyright © 1967 by Harper & Row, Publishers, Inc. All rights reserved. Reprinted by permission of Harper & Row, Publishers, Inc.

Thompson, Laurie. From *Stig Dagerman*. Twayne, 1983. Copyright 1983 by Twayne Publishers. All rights reserved. Reprinted with the permission of Twayne Publishers, a division of G. K. Hall & Co., Boston.

Tolstoy, L. From a letter to N. N. Strakhov on April 23, 1876, in *Tolstoy's Letters: 1828-1879, Vol. I*. By Leo Tolstoy, edited and translated by R. F. Christian. Charles Scribner's Sons, 1978. English translation and editorial matter copyright © 1978 R. F. Christian. All rights reserved. Reprinted with the permission of Charles Scribner's Sons.

Tolstoy, L. From a letter to S. A. Rachinsky on January 27, 1878, in *Tolstoy's Letters: 1828-1879, Vol. I*. By Leo Tolstoy, edited and translated by R. F. Christian. Charles Scribner's Sons, 1978. English translation and editorial matter copyright © 1978 R. F. Christian. All rights reserved. Reprinted with the permission of Charles Scribner's Sons.

Trombly, Albert Edmund. From *Vachel Lindsay, Adventurer*. Lucas Brothers, 1929.

Troyat, Henri. From *Tolstoy*. Translated by Nancy Amphoux. Doubleday, 1967. Copyright © 1967 by Doubleday & Company, Inc. All rights reserved. Reprinted by permission of the publisher.

Turgenev, Ivan. From a letter to Alexander Vasilyevich Toporov on April 1, 1875, in *Turgenev's Letters*. By Ivan Turgenev, edited and translated by A. V. Knowles. Charles Scribner's Sons, 1983. Copyright © 1983 A. V. Knowles. All rights reserved. Reprinted with the permission of Charles Scribner's Sons.

Uitti, Karl D. From *The Concept of Self in the Symbolist Novel*. Mouton, 1961. © Mouton & Co., Publishers, The Hague, The Netherlands. Reprinted by permission of Mouton Publishers, a Division of Walter de Gruyter & Co.

Untermeyer, Louis. From *The New Era in American Poetry*. Holt, Rinehart and Winston, Publishers, 1919. Copyright © 1910 by Henry Holt and Company. Renewed 1947 by Louis Untermeyer. Reprinted by permission of Bryna Untermeyer.

Van Doren, Carl. From *Many Minds*. Alfred A. Knopf, 1924.

Viereck, Peter. From "Vachel Lindsay: The Dante of the Fundamentalists," in *A Question of Quality: Popularity and Value in Modern Creative Writing*. Edited by Louis Filler. Bowling Green University Popular Press, 1976. Copyright © 1976 Bowling Green University Popular Press. Reprinted by permission.

Wagenknecht, Edward. From *Cavalcade of the English Novel: From Elizabeth to George VI*. Holt, Rinehart and Winston, 1943. Copyright © 1943 by Henry Holt and Company, Inc. Renewed 1970 by Edward Wagenknecht. Reprinted by permission of the author.

Wasiolek, Edward. From *Tolstoy's Major Fiction*. University of Chicago Press, 1978. © 1978 by The University of Chicago. All rights reserved. Reprinted by permission of The University of Chicago Press and the author.

White, George Leroy, Jr. From *Scandinavian Themes in American Fiction*. University of Pennsylvania Press, 1937.

Whitney, Blair. From *The Vision of This Land: Studies of Vachel Lindsay, Edgar Lee Masters, and Carl Sandburg*. Edited by John E. Hallwas and Dennis J. Reader. Western Illinois University, 1976. Copyright © 1976 by Western Illinois University. Reprinted by permission.

Williams, C. E. From *The Broken Eagle: The Politics of Austrian Literature from Empire to Anschluss*. Barnes & Noble, 1974. Copyright © 1974 C. E. Williams. All rights reserved. By permission of Barnes & Noble Books, a Division of Littlefield, Adams & Co., Inc.

Williams, Charles. From *Poetry at Present*. Oxford at the Clarendon Press, Oxford, 1930.

Wilt, Judith. From *The Readable People of George Meredith*. Princeton University Press, 1975. Copyright © 1975 by Princeton University Press. All rights reserved. Excerpts reprinted with the permission of Princeton University Press.

Woodcock, George. From an introduction to *The Egoist*. By George Meredith, edited by George Woodcock. Penguin Books, 1968. Introduction and notes copyright © 1968 by George Woodcock. All rights reserved. Reprinted by permission of Penguin Books Ltd.

Woolf, Virginia. From *The Second Common Reader*. Harcourt Brace Jovanovich, 1932. Published in Britain as *The Common Reader, second series*. Hogarth Press, 1932. Copyright 1932 by Harcourt Brace Jovanovich, Inc. Renewed 1960 by Leonard Woolf. Reprinted by permission of Harcourt Brace Jovanovich, Inc. In Canada by the Literary Estate of Virginia Woolf and The Hogarth Press Ltd.

Woolf, Virginia. From a diary entry of December 7, 1933, in *A Writer's Diary: Being Extracts from the Diary of Virginia Woolf*. By Virginia Woolf, edited by Leonard Woolf. Hogarth Press, 1953. Harcourt Brace Jovanovich, 1954. Copyright 1953, 1954 by Leonard Woolf. Renewed 1981, 1982 by Quentin Bell and Angelica Garnett. Reprinted by permission of Harcourt Brace Jovanovich, Inc. In Canada by The Hogarth Press Ltd.

Wright, Judith. From *Preoccupations in Australian Poetry*. Oxford University Press, Melbourne, 1965. Reprinted by kind permission of the author.

Wright, Walter F. From *Art and Substance in George Meredith: A Study in Narrative*. University of Nebraska Press, 1953. © 1953 by University of Nebraska Press, Lincoln, NE. Renewed 1981 by Walter F. Wright. Reprinted by permission of University of Nebraska Press.

Zempel, Solveig. From an introduction to *When the Wind Is in the South and Other Stories*. By O. E. Rølvaag, edited and translated by Solveig Zempel. The Center for Western Studies, 1984. Reprinted by permission.

Cumulative Index to Authors

This index lists all author entries in the Gale Literary Criticism Series and includes cross-references to other Gale sources. References in the index are identified as follows:

AITN: *Authors in the News*, Volumes 1-2
CAAS: *Contemporary Authors Autobiography Series*, Volume 1-2
CA: *Contemporary Authors* (original series), Volumes 1-114
CANR: *Contemporary Authors New Revision Series*, Volumes 1-14
CAP: *Contemporary Authors Permanent Series*, Volumes 1-2
CA-R: *Contemporary Authors* (revised editions), Volumes 1-44
CLC: *Contemporary Literary Criticism*, Volumes 1-33
CLR: *Children's Literature Review*, Volumes 1-8
DLB: *Dictionary of Literary Biography*, Volumes 1-38
DLB-DS: *Dictionary of Literary Biography Documentary Series*, Volumes 1-4
DLB-Y: *Dictionary of Literary Biography Yearbook*, Volumes 1980-1984
LC: *Literature Criticism from 1400 to 1800*, Volumes 1-2
NCLC: *Nineteenth-Century Literature Criticism*, Volumes 1-10
SATA: *Something about the Author*, Volumes 1-39
TCLC: *Twentieth-Century Literary Criticism*, Volumes 1-17
YABC: *Yesterday's Authors of Books for Children*, Volumes 1-2

Author Index

Benson, Stella 1892-1933 .... TCLC **17**
See also DLB 36

Bentley, E(dmund) C(lerihew)
1875-1956................. TCLC **12**
See also CA 108

Bentley, Eric (Russell) 1916- ......CLC **24**
See also CANR 6
See also CA 5-8R

Berger, John (Peter) 1926-...... CLC **2, 19**
See also CA 81-84
See also DLB 14

Berger, Melvin (H.) 1927- ....CLC **12**
See also CANR 4
See also CA 5-8R
See also SATA 5

Berger, Thomas (Louis)
1924-............ CLC **3, 5, 8, 11, 18**
See also CANR 5
See also CA 1-4R
See also DLB 2
See also DLB-Y 80

Bergman, (Ernst) Ingmar
1918-.........................CLC **16**
See also CA 81-84

Bergstein, Eleanor 1938- ....CLC **4**
See also CANR 5
See also CA 53-56

Bernanos, (Paul Louis) Georges
1888-1948................... TCLC **3**
See also CA 104

Bernhard, Thomas 1931- .... CLC **3, 32**
See also CA 85-88

Berrigan, Daniel J. 1921-...........CLC **4**
See also CAAS 1
See also CANR 11
See also CA 33-36R
See also DLB 5

Berry, Chuck 1926-................CLC **17**

Berry, Wendell (Erdman)
1934 ....CLC **4, 6, 8, 27**
See also CA 73-76
See also DLB 5, 6
See also AITN 1

Berryman, John
1914-1972..... CLC **1, 2, 3, 4, 6, 8, 10,**
13, 25
See also CAP 1
See also CA 15-16
See also obituary CA 33-36R

Bertolucci, Bernardo 1940- ....CLC **16**
See also CA 106

Besant, Annie (Wood)
1847-1933................... TCLC **9**
See also CA 105

Bessie, Alvah 1904-................CLC **23**
See also CANR 2
See also CA 5-8R
See also DLB 26

Beti, Mongo 1932-................CLC **27**

Betjeman, John
1906-1984...........CLC **2, 6, 10, 34**
See also CA 9-12R
See also obituary CA 112
See also DLB 20
See also DLB-Y 84

Betti, Ugo 1892-1953.............TCLC **5**
See also CA 104

Betts, Doris (Waugh)
1932-....................CLC **3, 6, 28**
See also CANR 9
See also CA 13-16R
See also DLB-Y 82

Bidart, Frank 19??-................CLC **33**

Bienek, Horst 1930-............ CLC **7, 11**
See also CA 73-76

Bierce, Ambrose (Gwinett)
1842-1914?................TCLC **1, 7**
See also CA 104
See also DLB 11, 12, 23

Binyon, T(imothy) J(ohn)
1936-.......................CLC **34**
See also CA 111

Bioy Casares, Adolfo
1914-.................. CLC **4, 8, 13**
See also CA 29-32R

Bird, Robert Montgomery
1806-1854.................. NCLC **1**

Birdwell, Cleo 1936-
See DeLillo, Don

Birney (Alfred) Earle
1904-.................CLC **1, 4, 6, 11**
See also CANR 5
See also CA 1-4R

Bishop, Elizabeth
1911-1979...... CLC **1, 4, 9, 13, 15, 32**
See also CA 5-8R
See also obituary CA 89-92
See also obituary SATA 24
See also DLB 5

Bishop, John 1935-..............CLC **10**
See also CA 105

Bissett, Bill 1939-................CLC **18**
See also CA 69-72

Biyidi, Alexandre 1932-
See Beti, Mongo
See also CA 114

Bjørnson, Bjørnstjerne (Martinius)
1832-1910.................. TCLC **7**
See also CA 104

Blackburn, Paul 1926-1971 ....CLC **9**
See also CA 81-84
See also obituary CA 33-36R
See also DLB 16
See also DLB-Y 81

Blackmur, R(ichard) P(almer)
1904-1965................. CLC **2, 24**
See also CAP 1
See also CA 11-12
See also obituary CA 25-28R

Blackwood, Algernon (Henry)
1869-1951................. TCLC **5**
See also CA 105

Blackwood, Caroline 1931- ...... CLC **6, 9**
See also CA 85-88
See also DLB 14

Blair, Eric Arthur 1903-1950 .... TCLC **15**
See Orwell, George
See also CA 104
See also SATA 29

Blais, Marie-Claire
1939-............ CLC **2, 4, 6, 13, 22**
See also CA 21-24R

Blaise, Clark 1940- ....CLC **29**
See also CANR 5
See also CA 53-56R
See also AITN 2

Blake, Nicholas 1904-1972
See Day Lewis, C(ecil)

Blasco Ibáñez, Vicente
1867-1928................. TCLC **12**
See also CA 110

Blatty, William Peter 1928-.........CLC **2**
See also CANR 9
See also CA 5-8R

Blish, James (Benjamin)
1921-1975...................CLC **14**
See also CANR 3
See also CA 1-4R
See also obituary CA 57-60
See also DLB 8

Blixen, Karen (Christentze Dinesen)
1885-1962
See Dinesen, Isak
See also CAP 2
See also CA 25-28

Bloch, Robert (Albert) 1917-.......CLC **33**
See also CANR 5
See also CA 5-8R
See also SATA 12

Blok, Aleksandr (Aleksandrovich)
1880-1921................... TCLC **5**
See also CA 104

Bloom, Harold 1930-..............CLC **24**
See also CA 13-16R

Blume, Judy (Sussman Kitchens)
1938 ....CLC **12, 30**
See also CLR 2
See also CANR 13
See also CA 29-32R
See also SATA 2, 31

Blunden, Edmund (Charles)
1896-1974.....................CLC **2**
See also CAP 2
See also CA 17-18
See also obituary CA 45-48
See also DLB 20

Bly, Robert 1926- ..... CLC **1, 2, 5, 10, 15**
See also CA 5-8R
See also DLB 5

Bødker, Cecil 1927-................CLC **21**
See also CANR 13
See also CA 73-76
See also SATA 14

Boell, Heinrich (Theodor) 1917-
See Böll, Heinrich
See also CA 21-24R

Bogan, Louise 1897-1970 ....CLC **4**
See also CA 73-76
See also obituary CA 25-28R

Bogarde, Dirk 1921- ....CLC **19**
See also Van Den Bogarde, Derek (Jules
Gaspard Ulric) Niven
See also DLB 14

Böhl de Faber, Cecilia 1796-1877
See Caballero, Fernán

Böll, Heinrich (Theodor)
1917-........CLC **2, 3, 6, 9, 11, 15, 27**
See also Boell, Heinrich (Theodor)

Author Index

Duberman, Martin 1930- . . . . .CLC 8
See also CANR 2
See also CA 1-4R

Du Bois, W(illiam) E(dward) B(urghardt)
1868-1963. . . . . CLC 1, 2, 13
See also CA 85-88

Dubus, Andre 1936- . . . . .CLC 13
See also CA 21-24R

Duclos, Charles Pinot 1704-1772 . . . . . LC 1

Dudek, Louis 1918- . . . . CLC 11, 19
See also CANR 1
See also CA 45-48

Dudevant, Amandine Aurore Lucile Dupin
1804-1876
See Sand, George

Duerrenmatt, Friedrich 1921-
See also CA 17-20R

Dugan, Alan 1923-. . . . . CLC 2, 6
See also CA 81-84
See also DLB 5

Duhamel, Georges 1884-1966 . . . . . . .CLC 8
See also CA 81-84
See also obituary CA 25-28R

Dujardin, Édouard (Émile Louis)
1861-1949. . . . . TCLC 13
See also CA 109

Duke, Raoul 1939-
See Thompson, Hunter S(tockton)

Dumas, Alexandre, (*fils*)
1824-1895. . . . . NCLC 9

Dumas, Henry (L.) 1934-1968. . . . . . .CLC 6
See also CA 85-88

Du Maurier, Daphne 1907- . . . . . CLC 6, 11
See also CANR 6
See also CA 5-8R
See also SATA 27

Dunbar, Paul Laurence
1872-1906. . . . . TCLC 2, 12
See also CA 104
See also SATA 34

Duncan (Steinmetz Arquette), Lois
1934-. . . . . .CLC 26
See also Arquette, Lois S(teinmetz)
See also CANR 2
See also CA 1-4R
See also SATA 1, 36

Duncan, Robert
1919-. . . . . CLC 1, 2, 4, 7, 15
See also CA 9-12R
See also DLB 5, 16, 37

Dunlap, William 1766-1839. . . . . . . NCLC 2
See also DLB 30

Dunn, Douglas (Eaglesham)
1942-. . . . . .CLC 6
See also CANR 2
See also CA 45-48

Dunne, John Gregory 1932-. . . . . . . .CLC 28
See also CANR 14
See also CA 25-28R
See also DLB-Y 80

Dunsany, Lord (Edward John Moreton Drax
Plunkett) 1878-1957. . . . . TCLC 2
See also CA 104
See also DLB 10

Durang, Christopher (Ferdinand)
1949-. . . . . .CLC 27
See also CA 105

Duras, Marguerite
1914-. . . . . CLC 3, 6, 11, 20, 34
See also CA 25-28R

Durrell, Lawrence (George)
1912-. . . . . CLC 1, 4, 6, 8, 13, 27
See also CA 9-12R
See also DLB 15, 27

Dürrenmatt, Friedrich
1921-. . . . . CLC 1, 4, 8, 11, 15
See also Duerrenmatt, Friedrich

Dylan, Bob 1941-. . . . . .CLC 3, 4, 6, 12
See also CA 41-44R
See also DLB 16

East, Michael 1916-
See West, Morris L.

Eastlake, William (Derry) 1917- . . . . .CLC 8
See also CAAS 1
See also CANR 5
See also CA 5-8R
See also DLB 6

Eberhart, Richard 1904- . . . . CLC 3, 11, 19
See also CANR 2
See also CA 1-4R

Echegaray (y Eizaguirre), José (María
Waldo) 1832-1916. . . . . TCLC 4
See also CA 104

Eckert, Allan W. 1931-. . . . . .CLC 17
See also CANR 14
See also CA 13-16R
See also SATA 27, 29

Eco, Umberto 1932- . . . . .CLC 28
See also CANR 12
See also CA 77-80

Eddison, E(ric) R(ucker)
1882-1945. . . . . TCLC 15
See also CA 109

Edel, (Joseph) Leon 1907- . . . . . CLC 29, 34
See also CANR 1
See also CA 1-4R

Eden, Emily 1797-1869. . . . . NCLC 10

Edgeworth, Maria 1767-1849 . . . . . NCLC 1
See also SATA 21

Edmonds, Helen (Woods) 1904-1968
See Kavan, Anna
See also CA 5-8R
See also obituary CA 25-28R

Edson, Russell 1905-. . . . . .CLC 13
See also CA 33-36R

Edwards, G(erald) B(asil)
1899-1976. . . . . .CLC 25
See also obituary CA 110

Ehle, John (Marsden, Jr.)
1925-. . . . . .CLC 27
See also CA 9-12R

Ehrenbourg, Ilya (Grigoryevich) 1891-1967
See Ehrenburg, Ilya (Grigoryevich)

Ehrenburg, Ilya (Grigoryevich)
1891-1967. . . . . CLC 18, 34
See also CA 102
See also obituary CA 25-28R

Eich, Guenter 1907-1971
See also CA 111
See also obituary CA 93-96

Eich, Günter 1907-1971. . . . . .CLC 15
See also Eich, Guenter

Eichendorff, Joseph Freiherr von
1788-1857. . . . . NCLC 8

Eigner, Larry 1927- . . . . .CLC 9
See also Eigner, Laurence (Joel)
See also DLB 5

Eigner, Laurence (Joel) 1927-
See Eigner, Larry
See also CANR 6
See also CA 9-12R

Eiseley, Loren (Corey)
1907-1977. . . . . .CLC 7
See also CANR 6
See also CA 1-4R
See also obituary CA 73-76

Ekeloef, Gunnar (Bengt) 1907-1968
See Ekelöf, Gunnar (Bengt)
See also obituary CA 25-28R

Ekelöf, Gunnar (Bengt)
1907-1968. . . . . .CLC 27
See also Ekeloef, Gunnar (Bengt)

Ekwensi, Cyprian (Odiatu Duaka)
1921-. . . . . .CLC 4
See also CA 29-32R

Eliade, Mircea 1907-. . . . . .CLC 19
See also CA 65-68

Eliot, George 1819-1880. . . . . NCLC 4
See also DLB 21, 35

Eliot, T(homas) S(tearns)
1888-1965. . . . . . . CLC 1, 2, 3, 6, 9, 10,
13, 15, 24, 34
See also CA 5-8R
See also obituary CA 25-28R
See also DLB 7, 10

Elkin, Stanley L(awrence)
1930-. . . . . CLC 4, 6, 9, 14, 27
See also CANR 8
See also CA 9-12R
See also DLB 2, 28
See also DLB-Y 80

Elledge, Scott 19?-. . . . . .CLC 34

Elliott, George P(aul)
1918-1980. . . . . .CLC 2
See also CANR 2
See also CA 1-4R
See also obituary CA 97-100

Ellis, A. E. .CLC 7

Ellis, (Henry) Havelock
1859-1939. . . . . TCLC 14
See also CA 109

Ellison, Harlan 1934- . . . . CLC 1, 13
See also CANR 5
See also CA 5-8R
See also DLB 8

Ellison, Ralph (Waldo)
1914-. . . . . CLC 1, 3, 11
See also CA 9-12R
See also DLB 2

Elman, Richard 1934-. . . . . .CLC 19
See also CA 17-20R

Éluard, Paul 1895-1952 . . . . TCLC 7
See also Grindel, Eugene

Elvin, Anne Katharine Stevenson 1933-
See Stevenson, Anne (Katharine)
See also CA 17-20R

Author Index

Gilliam, Terry (Vance) 1940-
  See Monty Python
  See also CA 108, 113

Gilliatt, Penelope (Ann Douglass)
  1932-.................CLC 2, 10, 13
  See also CA 13-16R
  See also DLB 14
  See also AITN 2

Gilman, Charlotte (Anna) Perkins (Stetson)
  1860-1935..................TCLC 9
  See also CA 106

Gilroy, Frank D(aniel) 1925-........CLC 2
  See also CA 81-84
  See also DLB 7

Ginsberg, Allen
  1926-..........CLC 1, 2, 3, 4, 6, 13
  See also CANR 2
  See also CA 1-4R
  See also DLB 5, 16
  See also AITN 1

Ginzburg, Natalia 1916-........CLC 5, 11
  See also CA 85-88

Giono, Jean 1895-1970........CLC 4, 11
  See also CANR 2
  See also CA 45-48
  See also obituary CA 29-32R

Giovanni, Nikki 1943-........CLC 2, 4, 19
  See also CLR 6
  See also CA 29-32R
  See also SATA 24
  See also DLB 5
  See also AITN 1

Giovene, Andrea 1904-............CLC 7
  See also CA 85-88

Gippius, Zinaida (Nikolayevna) 1869-1945
  See also Hippius, Zinaida
  See also CA 106

Giraudoux, (Hippolyte) Jean
  1882-1944................TCLC 2, 7
  See also CA 104

Gironella, José María 1917-........CLC 11
  See also CA 101

Gissing, George (Robert)
  1857-1903...................TCLC 3
  See also CA 105
  See also DLB 18

Glanville, Brian (Lester) 1931-......CLC 6
  See also CANR 3
  See also CA 5-8R
  See also DLB 15

Glasgow, Ellen (Anderson Gholson)
  1873?-1945...............TCLC 2, 7
  See also CA 104
  See also DLB 9, 12

Glassco, John 1909-1981 ....CLC 9
  See also CA 13-16R
  See also obituary CA 102

Glissant, Edouard 1928-...........CLC 10

Glück, Louise 1943- ....CLC 7, 22
  See also CA 33-36R
  See also DLB 5

Godard, Jean-Luc 1930-...........CLC 20
  See also CA 93-96

Godwin, Gail 1937-.......CLC 5, 8, 22, 31
  See also CA 29-32R
  See also DLB 6

Goethe, Johann Wolfgang von
  1749-1832..................NCLC 4

Gogarty, Oliver St. John
  1878-1957.................TCLC 15
  See also CA 109
  See also DLB 15, 19

Gogol, Nikolai (Vasilyevich)
  1809-1852..................NCLC 5

Gökçeli, Yasar Kemal 1923-
  See Kemal, Yashar

Gold, Herbert 1924-..........CLC 4, 7, 14
  See also CA 9-12R
  See also DLB 2
  See also DLB-Y 81

Goldbarth, Albert 1948-............CLC 5
  See also CANR 6
  See also CA 53-56

Goldberg, Anato 19?-.............CLC 34

Golding, William (Gerald)
  1911-.......CLC 1, 2, 3, 8, 10, 17, 27
  See also CANR 13
  See also CA 5-8R
  See also DLB 15

Goldman, Emma 1869-1940 ..... TCLC 13
  See also CA 110

Goldman, William (W.) 1931-.......CLC 1
  See also CA 9-12R

Goldmann, Lucien 1913-1970......CLC 24
  See also CAP 2
  See also CA 25-28

Goldsberry, Steven 1949- ....CLC 34

Goldsmith, Oliver 1728(?)-1774 .... LC 2
  See also SATA 26

Gombrowicz, Witold
  1904-1969...............CLC 4, 7, 11
  See also CAP 2
  See also CA 19-20
  See also obituary CA 25-28R

Gómez de la Serna, Ramón
  1888-1963....................CLC 9

Goncharov, Ivan Alexandrovich
  1812-1891..................NCLC 1

Goncourt, Edmond (Louis Antoine Huot) de
  1822-1896
  See Goncourt, Edmond (Louis Antoine
  Huot) de and Goncourt, Jules (Alfred
  Huot) de

Goncourt, Edmond (Louis Antoine Huot) de
  1822-1896 **and Goncourt, Jules (Alfred
  Huot) de** 1830-1870 .... NCLC 7

Goncourt, Jules (Alfred Huot) de 1830-1870
  See Goncourt, Edmond (Louis Antoine
  Huot) de and Goncourt, Jules (Alfred
  Huot) de

Goncourt, Jules (Alfred Huot) de 1830-1870
  **and Goncourt, Edmond (Louis Antoine
  Huot) de** 1822-1896
  See Goncourt, Edmond (Louis Antoine
  Huot) de and Goncourt, Jules (Alfred
  Huot) de

Goodman, Paul
  1911-1972.............CLC 1, 2, 4, 7
  See also CAP 2
  See also CA 19-20
  See also obituary CA 37-40R

Gordimer, Nadine
  1923-.........CLC 3, 5, 7, 10, 18, 33
  See also CANR 3
  See also CA 5-8R

Gordon, Caroline
  1895-1981.............CLC 6, 13, 29
  See also CAP 1
  See also CA 11-12
  See also obituary CA 103
  See also DLB 4, 9
  See also DLB-Y 81

Gordon, Mary (Catherine)
  1949-....................CLC 13, 22
  See also CA 102
  See also DLB 6
  See also DLB-Y 81

Gordon, Sol 1923-...............CLC 26
  See also CANR 4
  See also CA 53-56
  See also SATA 11

Gordone, Charles 1925-.........CLC 1, 4
  See also CA 93-96
  See also DLB 7

Gorenko, Anna Andreyevna 1889?-1966
  See Akhmatova, Anna

Gorky, Maxim 1868-1936 .... TCLC 8
  See also Peshkov, Alexei Maximovich

Goryan, Sirak 1908-1981
  See Saroyan, William

Gotlieb, Phyllis (Fay Bloom)
  1926-.......................CLC 18
  See also CANR 7
  See also CA 13-16R

Gould, Lois 1938?- .... CLC 4, 10
  See also CA 77-80

Gourmont, Rémy de
  1858-1915.................TCLC 17
  See also CA 109

Goyen, (Charles) William
  1915-1983..............CLC 5, 8, 14
  See also CANR 6
  See also CA 5-8R
  See also obituary CA 110
  See also DLB 2
  See also DLB-Y 83
  See also AITN 2

Goytisolo, Juan 1931-.......CLC 5, 10, 23
  See also CA 85-88

Grabbe, Christian Dietrich
  1801-1836..................NCLC 2

Gracq, Julien 1910-...............CLC 11

Grade, Chaim 1910-1982..........CLC 10
  See also CA 93-96
  See also obituary CA 107

Graham W(illiam) S(ydney)
  1918-.......................CLC 29
  See also CA 73-76
  See also DLB 20

Graham, Winston (Mawdsley)
  1910-.......................CLC 23
  See also CANR 2
  See also CA 49-52

Granville-Barker, Harley
  1877-1946..................TCLC 2
  See also CA 104

Heine, Harry 1797-1856
See Heine, Heinrich

Heine, Heinrich 1797-1856....... NCLC 4

Heiney, Donald (William) 1921-
See Harris, MacDonald
See also CANR 3
See also CA 1-4R

Heinlein, Robert A(nson)
1907-............ CLC 1, 3, 8, 14, 26
See also CANR 1
See also CA 1-4R
See also SATA 9
See also DLB 8

Heller, Joseph 1923- .... CLC 1, 3, 5, 8, 11
See also CANR 8
See also CA 5-8R
See also DLB 2, 28
See also DLB-Y 80
See also AITN 1

Hellman, Lillian (Florence)
1905?-1984..... CLC 2, 4, 8, 14, 18, 34
See also CA 13-16R
See also obituary CA 112
See also DLB 7
See also DLB-Y 84
See also AITN 1, 2

Helprin, Mark 1947-.....CLC 7, 10, 22, 32
See also CA 81-84

Hemingway, Ernest (Miller)
1899-1961...... CLC 1, 3, 6, 8, 10, 13,
19, 30, 34
See also CA 77-80
See also DLB 4, 9
See also DLB-Y 81
See also DLB-DS 1
See also AITN 2

Henley, Beth 1952-...............CLC 23
See also Henley, Elizabeth Becker

Henley, Elizabeth Becker 1952-
See Henley, Beth
See also CA 107

Henley, William Ernest
1849-1903.................. TCLC 8
See also CA 105
See also DLB 19

Hennissart, Martha
See Lathen, Emma
See also CA 85-88

Henry, O. 1862-1909? .... TCLC 1
See also Porter, William Sydney

Hentoff, Nat(han Irving) 1925- .....CLC 26
See also CLR 1
See also CANR 5
See also CA 1-4R
See also SATA 27

Heppenstall, (John) Rayner
1911-1981...................CLC 10
See also CA 1-4R
See also obituary CA 103

Herbert, Frank (Patrick)
1920-................... CLC 12, 23
See also CANR 5
See also CA 53-56
See also SATA 9, 37
See also DLB 8

Herbert, Zbigniew 1924- ....CLC 9
See also CA 89-92

Herbst, Josephine 1897-1969.......CLC 34
See also CA 5-8R
See also obituary CA 25-28R
See also DLB 9

Herder, Johann Gottfried von
1744-1803.................. NCLC 8

Hergesheimer, Joseph
1880-1954................. TCLC 11
See also CA 109
See also DLB 9

Herlagñez, Pablo de 1844-1896
See Verlaine, Paul (Marie)

Herlihy, James Leo 1927-...........CLC 6
See also CANR 2
See also CA 1-4R

Herriot, James 1916-..............CLC 12
See also Wight, James Alfred

Hersey, John (Richard)
1914-.................CLC 1, 2, 7, 9
See also CA 17-20R
See also SATA 25
See also DLB 6

Herzen, Aleksandr Ivanovich
1812-1870.................. NCLC 10

Herzog, Werner 1942- ....CLC 16
See also CA 89-92

Hesse, Hermann
1877-1962...... CLC 1, 2, 3, 6, 11, 17,
25
See also CAP 2
See also CA 17-18

Heyen, William 1940-......... CLC 13, 18
See also CA 33-36R
See also DLB 5

Heyerdahl, Thor 1914-.............CLC 26
See also CANR 5
See also CA 5-8R
See also SATA 2

Heym, Georg (Theodor Franz Arthur)
1887-1912................. TCLC 9
See also CA 106

Heyse, Paul (Johann Ludwig von)
1830-1914.................. TCLC 8
See also CA 104

Hibbert, Eleanor (Burford)
1906-......................CLC 7
See also CANR 9
See also CA 17-20R
See also SATA 2

Higgins, George V(incent)
1939-................CLC 4, 7, 10, 18
See also CA 77-80
See also DLB 2
See also DLB-Y 81

Highsmith, (Mary) Patricia
1921-.................. CLC 2, 4, 14
See also CANR 1
See also CA 1-4R

Highwater, Jamake 1942-..........CLC 12
See also CANR 10
See also CA 65-68
See also SATA 30, 32

Hill, Geoffrey 1932-......... CLC 5, 8, 18
See also CA 81-84

Hill, George Roy 1922-............CLC 26
See also CA 110

Hill, Susan B. 1942- ....CLC 4
See also CA 33-36R
See also DLB 14

Hilliard, Noel (Harvey) 1929- ......CLC 15
See also CANR 7
See also CA 9-12R

Himes, Chester (Bomar)
1909-1984.............CLC 2, 4, 7, 18
See also CA 25-28R
See also obituary CA 114
See also DLB 2

Hinde, Thomas 1926- .... CLC 6, 11
See also Chitty, (Sir) Thomas Willes

Hine, (William) Daryl 1936- ....CLC 15
See also CANR 1
See also CA 1-4R

Hinton, S(usan) E(loise) 1950-......CLC 30
See also CLR 3
See also CA 81-84
See also SATA 19

Hippius (Merezhkovsky), Zinaida
(Nikolayevna) 1869-1945..... TCLC 9
See also Gippius, Zinaida (Nikolayevna)

Hiraoka, Kimitake 1925-1970
See Mishima, Yukio
See also CA 97-100
See also obituary CA 29-32R

Hirsch, Edward 1950-.............CLC 31
See also CA 104

Hitchcock, (Sir) Alfred (Joseph)
1899-1980...................CLC 16
See also obituary CA 97-100
See also SATA 27
See also obituary SATA 24

Hoagland, Edward 1932-..........CLC 28
See also CANR 2
See also CA 1-4R
See also DLB 6

Hoban, Russell C(onwell)
1925-.................... CLC 7, 25
See also CLR 3
See also CA 5-8R
See also SATA 1

Hobson, Laura Z(ametkin)
1900-.................... CLC 7, 25
See also CA 17-20R
See also DLB 28

Hochhuth, Rolf 1931-....... CLC 4, 11, 18
See also CA 5-8R

Hochman, Sandra 1936-......... CLC 3, 8
See also CA 5-8R
See also DLB 5

Hocking, Mary (Eunice) 1921- .....CLC 13
See also CA 101

Hodgins, Jack 1938- ....CLC 23
See also CA 93-96

Hodgson, William Hope
1877-1918................. TCLC 13
See also CA 111

Hoffman, Daniel (Gerard)
1923-.................CLC 6, 13, 23
See also CANR 4
See also CA 1-4R
See also DLB 5

Hoffman, Stanley 1944- ....CLC 5
See also CA 77-80

Author Index

Landis, John (David) 1950- ....CLC 26
See also CA 112

Landolfi, Tommaso 1908-.........CLC 11

Landwirth, Heinz 1927-
See Lind, Jakov
See also CANR 7

Lane, Patrick 1939-..............CLC 25
See also CA 97-100

Lang, Andrew 1844-1912....... TCLC 16
See also CA 114
See also SATA 16

Lang, Fritz 1890-1976 ....CLC 20
See also CA 77-80
See also obituary CA 69-72

Langer, Elinor 1939-.............CLC 34

Lanier, Sidney 1842-1881........ NCLC 6
See also SATA 18

Larbaud, Valéry 1881-1957...... TCLC 9
See also CA 106

Lardner, Ring(gold Wilmer)
1885-1933................ TCLC 2, 14
See also CA 104
See also DLB 11, 25

Larkin, Philip (Arthur)
1922-.....CLC 3, 5, 8, 9, 13, 18, 33
See also CA 5-8R
See also DLB 27

Larson, Charles R(aymond)
1938-.......................CLC 31
See also CANR 4
See also CA 53-56

Latham, Jean Lee 1902-...........CLC 12
See also CANR 7
See also CA 5-8R
See also SATA 2
See also AITN 1

Lathen, Emma ....CLC 2
See also Hennissart, Martha
See also Latsis, Mary J(ane)

Latsis, Mary J(ane)
See Lathen, Emma
See also CA 85-88

Lattimore, Richmond (Alexander)
1906-1984....................CLC 3
See also CANR 1
See also CA 1-4R
See also obituary CA 112

Laurence, (Jean) Margaret (Wemyss)
1926-................... CLC 3, 6, 13
See also CA 5-8R

Lavin, Mary 1912-.............. CLC 4, 18
See also CA 9-12R
See also DLB 15

Lawrence, D(avid) H(erbert)
1885-1930.........TCLC 2, 9, 16
See also CA 104
See also DLB 10, 19, 36

Laxness, Halldór (Kiljan)
1902-........................CLC 25
See also Gudjonsson, Halldór Kiljan

Laye, Camara 1928-1980...........CLC 4
See also CA 85-88
See also obituary CA 97-100

Layton, Irving (Peter) 1912- .... CLC 2, 15
See also CANR 2
See also CA 1-4R

Lazarus, Emma 1849-1887 .... NCLC 8

Leacock, Stephen (Butler)
1869-1944.................. TCLC 2
See also CA 104

Lear, Edward 1812-1888 .... NCLC 3
See also CLR 1
See also SATA 18
See also DLB 32

Lear, Norman (Milton) 1922- ......CLC 12
See also CA 73-76

Leavis, F(rank) R(aymond)
1895-1978...................CLC 24
See also CA 21-24R
See also obituary CA 77-80

Leavitt, David 1961?- ....CLC 34

Lebowitz, Fran 1951?- ....CLC 11
See also CANR 14
See also CA 81-84

Le Carré, John
1931-............. CLC 3, 5, 9, 15, 28
See also Cornwell, David (John Moore)

Le Clézio, J(ean) M(arie) G(ustave)
1940-.......................CLC 31

Leduc, Violette 1907-1972 ....CLC 22
See also CAP 1
See also CA 13-14
See also obituary CA 33-36R

Lee, Don L. 1942-.................CLC 2
See also Madhubuti, Haki R.
See also CA 73-76

Lee, (Nelle) Harper 1926-..........CLC 12
See also CA 13-16R
See also SATA 11
See also DLB 6

Lee, Lawrence 1903-..............CLC 34
See also CA 25-28R

Lee, Manfred B(ennington) 1905-1971
See Queen, Ellery
See also CANR 2
See also CA 1-4R
See also obituary CA 29-32R

Lee, Stan 1922- ....CLC 17
See also CA 108, 111

Lee, Vernon 1856-1935.......... TCLC 5
See also Paget, Violet

Leet, Judith 1935-................CLC 11

Le Fanu, Joseph Sheridan
1814-1873................... NCLC 9
See also DLB 21

Leffland, Ella 1931-..............CLC 19
See also CA 29-32R
See also DLB-Y 84

Léger, (Marie-Rene) Alexis Saint-Léger
1887-1975
See Perse, St.-John
See also CA 13-16R
See also obituary CA 61-64

Le Guin, Ursula K(roeber)
1929-................. CLC 8, 13, 22
See also CLR 3
See also CANR 9
See also CA 21-24R
See also SATA 4
See also DLB 8
See also AITN 1

Lehmann, Rosamond (Nina)
1901-........................CLC 5
See also CANR 8
See also CA 77-80
See also DLB 15

Leiber, Fritz (Reuter, Jr.)
1910-.......................CLC 25
See also CANR 2
See also CA 45-48
See also DLB 8

Leithauser, Brad 1953-...........CLC 27
See also CA 107

Lelchuk, Alan 1938-..............CLC 5
See also CANR 1
See also CA 45-48

Lem, Stanislaw 1921- .... CLC 8, 15
See also CAAS 1
See also CA 105

L'Engle, Madeleine 1918-.........CLC 12
See also CLR 1
See also CANR 3
See also CA 1-4R
See also SATA 1, 27
See also AITN 2

Lennon, John (Ono) 1940-1980
See Lennon, John (Ono) and McCartney,
Paul
See also CA 102

Lennon, John (Ono) 1940-1980 and
McCartney, Paul 1942- ....CLC 12

Lentricchia, Frank (Jr.) 1940-......CLC 34
See also CA 25-28R

Lenz, Siegfried 1926- ....CLC 27
See also CA 89-92

Leonard, Elmore 1925-....... CLC 28, 34
See also CANR 12
See also CA 81-84
See also AITN 1

Leonard, Hugh 1926 ....CLC 19
See also Byrne, John Keyes
See also DLB 13

Lerman, Eleanor 1952-.............CLC 9
See also CA 85-88

Lermontov, Mikhail Yuryevich
1814-1841................... NCLC 5

Lesage, Alain-René 1668-1747....... LC 2

Lessing, Doris (May)
1919-........CLC 1, 2, 3, 6, 10, 15, 22
See also CA 9-12R
See also DLB 15

Lester, Richard 1932-..............CLC 20

Levertov, Denise
1923-.........CLC 1, 2, 3, 5, 8, 15, 28
See also CANR 3
See also CA 1-4R
See also DLB 5

Levin, Ira 1929-................. CLC 3, 6
See also CA 21-24R

Levin, Meyer 1905-1981...........CLC 7
See also CA 9-12R
See also obituary CA 104
See also SATA 21
See also obituary SATA 27
See also DLB 9, 28
See also DLB-Y 81
See also AITN 1

MacDonald, George
    1824-1905................... TCLC 9
  See also CA 106
  See also SATA 33
  See also DLB 18

MacDonald, John D(ann)
    1916-..................... CLC 3, 27
  See also CANR 1
  See also CA 1-4R
  See also DLB 8

Macdonald, (John) Ross
    1915-1983............CLC 1, 2, 3, 14
  See also Millar, Kenneth

MacEwen, Gwendolyn 1941-.......CLC 13
  See also CANR 7
  See also CA 9-12R

Machado (y Ruiz), Antonio
    1875-1939.................. TCLC 3
  See also CA 104

Machado de Assis, (Joaquim Maria)
    1839-1908................. TCLC 10
  See also CA 107

Machen, Arthur (Llewellyn Jones)
    1863-1947.................. TCLC 4
  See also CA 104
  See also DLB 36

MacInnes, Colin 1914-1976..... CLC 4, 23
  See also CA 69-72
  See also obituary CA 65-68
  See also DLB 14

MacInnes, Helen 1907-...........CLC 27
  See also CANR 1
  See also CA 1-4R
  See also SATA 22

Macintosh, Elizabeth 1897-1952
  See Tey, Josephine
  See also CA 110

Mackenzie, (Edward Montague) Compton
    1883-1972....................CLC 18
  See also CAP 2
  See also CA 21-22
  See also obituary CA 37-40R
  See also DLB 34

Mac Laverty, Bernard 1942-.......CLC 31

MacLean, Alistair (Stuart)
    1922-..................... CLC 3, 13
  See also CA 57-60
  See also SATA 23

MacLeish, Archibald
    1892-1982............... CLC 3, 8, 14
  See also CA 9-12R
  See also obituary CA 106
  See also DLB 4, 7
  See also DLB-Y 82

MacLennan, (John) Hugh
    1907-..................... CLC 2, 14
  See also CA 5-8R

MacNeice, (Frederick) Louis
    1907-1963............ CLC 1, 4, 10
  See also CA 85-88
  See also DLB 10, 20

Macpherson, (Jean) Jay 1931-......CLC 14
  See also CA 5-8R

Macumber, Mari 1896-1966
  See Sandoz, Mari (Susette)

Madden, (Jerry) David
    1933-..................... CLC 5, 15
  See also CANR 4
  See also CA 1-4R
  See also DLB 6

Madhubuti, Haki R. 1942-..........CLC 6
  See also Lee, Don L.
  See also DLB 5

Maeterlinck, Maurice
    1862-1949.................. TCLC 3
  See also CA 104

Maginn, William 1794-1842...... NCLC 8

Mahapatra, Jayanta 1928-.........CLC 33
  See also CA 73-76

Mahon, Derek 1941-..............CLC 27
  See also CA 113

Mailer, Norman
    1923-......CLC 1, 2, 3, 4, 5, 8, 11, 14,
                             28
  See also CA 9-12R
  See also DLB 2, 16, 28
  See also DLB-Y 80, 83
  See also DLB-DS 3
  See also AITN 2

Mais, Roger 1905-1955........... TCLC 8
  See also CA 105

Major, Clarence 1936-......... CLC 3, 19
  See also CA 21-24R
  See also DLB 33

Major, Kevin 1949-...............CLC 26
  See also CA 97-100
  See also SATA 32

Malamud, Bernard
    1914-......CLC 1, 2, 3, 5, 8, 9, 11, 18,
                             27
  See also CA 5-8R
  See also DLB 2, 28
  See also DLB-Y 80

Mallarmé, Stéphane
    1842-1898.................. NCLC 4

Mallet-Joris, Françoise 1930-.......CLC 11
  See also CA 65-68

Maloff, Saul 1922-.................CLC 5
  See also CA 33-36R

Malouf, David 1934-..............CLC 28

Malraux, (Georges-) André
    1901-1976......... CLC 1, 4, 9, 13, 15
  See also CAP 2
  See also CA 21-24R
  See also obituary CA 69-72

Malzberg, Barry N. 1939- ....CLC 7
  See also CA 61-64
  See also DLB 8

Mamet, David 1947-........ CLC 9, 15, 34
  See also CA 81-84
  See also DLB 7

Mamoulian, Rouben 1898-.........CLC 16
  See also CA 25-28R

Mandelstam, Osip (Emilievich)
    1891?-1938?.............. TCLC 2, 6
  See also CA 104

Manley, Mary Delariviere ?-1724..... LC 1

Mann, (Luiz) Heinrich
    1871-1950.................. TCLC 9
  See also CA 106

Mann, Thomas
    1875-1955.............TCLC 2, 8, 14
  See also CA 104

Manning, Olivia 1915-1980 ..... CLC 5, 19
  See also CA 5-8R
  See also obituary CA 101

Mano, D. Keith 1942-......... CLC 2, 10
  See also CA 25-28R
  See also DLB 6

Mansfield, Katherine
    1888-1923................. TCLC 2, 8
  See also CA 104

Marcel, Gabriel (Honore)
    1889-1973....................CLC 15
  See also CA 102
  See also obituary CA 45-48

Marchbanks, Samuel 1913-
  See Davies, (William) Robertson

Marinetti, F(ilippo) T(ommaso)
    1876-1944................. TCLC 10
  See also CA 107

Markandaya, Kamala (Purnalya)
    1924-........................CLC 8
  See also Taylor, Kamala (Purnalya)

Markfield, Wallace (Arthur)
    1926-........................CLC 8
  See also CA 69-72
  See also DLB 2, 28

Markham, Robert 1922-
  See Amis, Kingsley (William)

Marks, J. 1942-
  See Highwater, Jamake

Marley, Bob 1945-1981 .... CLC 17
  See also Marley, Robert Nesta

Marley, Robert Nesta 1945-1981
  See Marley, Bob
  See also CA 107
  See also obituary CA 103

Marmontel, Jean-François
    1723-1799.................... LC 2

Marquand, John P(hillips)
    1893-1960................ CLC 2, 10
  See also CA 85-88
  See also DLB 9

Márquez, Gabriel García 1928-
  See García Márquez, Gabriel

Marquis, Don(ald Robert Perry)
    1878-1937.................. TCLC 7
  See also CA 104
  See also DLB 11, 25

Marryat, Frederick 1792-1848 .... NCLC 3
  See also DLB 21

Marsh, (Edith) Ngaio
    1899-1982....................CLC 7
  See also CANR 6
  See also CA 9-12R

Marshall, Garry 1935?- ....CLC 17
  See also CA 111

Marshall, Paule 1929-..............CLC 27
  See also CA 77-80
  See also DLB 33

Marsten, Richard 1926-
  See Hunter, Evan

Martin, Steve 1945?-..............CLC 30
  See also CA 97-100

Author Index

Saroyan, William
     1908-1981....... **CLC 1, 8, 10, 29, 34**
     See also CA 5-8R
     See also obituary CA 103
     See also SATA 23
     See also obituary SATA 24
     See also DLB 7, 9
     See also DLB-Y 81

Sarraute, Nathalie
     1902-.......... **CLC 1, 2, 4, 8, 10, 31**
     See also CA 9-12R

Sarton, (Eleanor) May
     1912-..................... **CLC 4, 14**
     See also CANR 1
     See also CA 1-4R
     See also SATA 36
     See also DLB-Y 81

Sartre, Jean-Paul
     1905-1980...... **CLC 1, 4, 7, 9, 13, 18, 24**
     See also CA 9-12R
     See also obituary CA 97-100

Saura, Carlos 1932-.............. **CLC 20**
     See also CA 114

Sauser-Hall, Frédéric-Louis 1887-1961
     See Cendrars, Blaise
     See also CA 102
     See also obituary CA 93-96

Sayers, Dorothy L(eigh)
     1893-1957................ **TCLC 2, 15**
     See also CA 104
     See also DLB 10, 36

Sayles, John (Thomas)
     1950-.................. **CLC 7, 10, 14**
     See also CA 57-60

Scammell, Michael 19?-........... **CLC 34**

Schaeffer, Susan Fromberg
     1941-.................. **CLC 6, 11, 22**
     See also CA 49-52
     See also SATA 22
     See also DLB 28

Scherer, Jean-Marie Maurice 1920-
     See Rohmer, Eric
     See also CA 110

Schevill, James (Erwin) 1920-....... **CLC 7**
     See also CA 5-8R

Schisgal, Murray (Joseph)
     1926-........................ **CLC 6**
     See also CA 21-24R

Schmitz, Ettore 1861-1928
     See Svevo, Italo
     See also CA 104

Schneider, Leonard Alfred 1925-1966
     See Bruce, Lenny
     See also CA 89-92

Schnitzler, Arthur 1862-1931 ..... **TCLC 4**
     See also CA 104

Schorer, Mark 1908-1977 .... **CLC 9**
     See also CANR 7
     See also CA 5-8R
     See also obituary CA 73-76

Schrader, Paul (Joseph) 1946-...... **CLC 26**
     See also CA 37-40R

Schreiner (Cronwright), Olive (Emilie
     Albertina) 1855-1920 .... **TCLC 9**
     See also CA 105
     See also DLB 18

Schulberg, Budd (Wilson) 1914-..... **CLC 7**
     See also CA 25-28R
     See also DLB 6, 26, 28
     See also DLB-Y 81

Schulz, Bruno 1892-1942 .... **TCLC 5**

Schulz, Charles M(onroe)
     1922-........................ **CLC 12**
     See also CANR 6
     See also CA 9-12R
     See also SATA 10

Schuyler, James (Marcus)
     1923-.................... **CLC 5, 23**
     See also CA 101
     See also DLB 5

Schwartz, Delmore
     1913-1966................ **CLC 2, 4, 10**
     See also CAP 2
     See also CA 17-18
     See also obituary CA 25-28R
     See also DLB 28

Schwartz, Lynne Sharon 1939-..... **CLC 31**
     See also CA 103

Schwarz-Bart, André 1928-...... **CLC 2, 4**
     See also CA 89-92

Schwarz-Bart, Simone 1938-........ **CLC 7**
     See also CA 97-100

Sciascia, Leonardo 1921-........ **CLC 8, 9**
     See also CA 85-88

Scoppettone, Sandra 1936-......... **CLC 26**
     See also CA 5-8R
     See also SATA 9

Scorsese, Martin 1942-............ **CLC 20**
     See also CA 110, 114

Scotland, Jay 1932-
     See Jakes, John (William)

Scott, Duncan Campbell
     1862-1947.................. **TCLC 6**
     See also CA 104

Scott, F(rancis) R(eginald)
     1899-1985................... **CLC 22**
     See also CA 101
     See also obituary CA 114

Scott, Paul (Mark) 1920-1978 .... **CLC 9**
     See also CA 81-84
     See also obituary CA 77-80
     See also DLB 14

Scudéry, Madeleine de 1607-1701..... **LC 2**

Seare, Nicholas 1925-
     See Trevanian
     See also Whitaker, Rodney

Sebestyen, Igen 1924-
     See Sebestyen, Ouida

Sebestyen, Ouida 1924-............ **CLC 30**
     See also CA 107
     See also SATA 39

Seelye, John 1931-................. **CLC 7**
     See also CA 97-100

Seferiades, Giorgos Stylianou 1900-1971
     See Seferis, George
     See also CANR 5
     See also CA 5-8R
     See also obituary CA 33-36R

Seferis, George 1900-1971 ...... **CLC 5, 11**
     See also Seferiades, Giorgos Stylianou

Segal, Erich (Wolf) 1937-....... **CLC 3, 10**
     See also CA 25-28R

Seghers, Anna 1900-................ **CLC 7**
     See Radvanyi, Netty

Seidel, Frederick (Lewis) 1936-..... **CLC 18**
     See also CANR 8
     See also CA 13-16R
     See also DLB-Y 84

Seifert, Jaroslav 1901- .... **CLC 34**

Selby, Hubert, Jr.
     1928-................... **CLC 1, 2, 4, 8**
     See also CA 13-16R
     See also DLB 2

Sender, Ramón (José)
     1902-1982................... **CLC 8**
     See also CANR 8
     See also CA 5-8R
     See also obituary CA 105

Serling, (Edward) Rod(man) 1924-1975
     See also CA 65-68
     See also obituary CA 57-60
     See also DLB 26
     See also AITN 1

Serpières 1907-
     See Guillevic, (Eugène)

Service, Robert W(illiam)
     1874-1958................. **TCLC 15**
     See also SATA 20

Seton, Cynthia Propper
     1926-1982................... **CLC 27**
     See also CANR-7
     See also CA 5-8R
     See also obituary CA 108

Settle, Mary Lee 1918-............ **CLC 19**
     See also CAAS 1
     See also CA 89-92
     See also DLB 6

Sexton, Anne (Harvey)
     1928-1974....... **CLC 2, 4, 6, 8, 10, 15**
     See also CANR 3
     See also CA 1-4R
     See also obituary CA 53-56
     See also SATA 10
     See also DLB 5

Shaara, Michael (Joseph)
     1929-........................ **CLC 15**
     See also CA 102
     See also DLB-Y 83
     See also AITN 1

Shaffer, Anthony 1926-............ **CLC 19**
     See also CA 110
     See also DLB 13

Shaffer, Peter (Levin)
     1926-.................. **CLC 5, 14, 18**
     See also CA 25-28R
     See also DLB 13

Shalamov, Varlam (Tikhonovich)
     1907?-1982................... **CLC 18**
     See also obituary CA 105

Shamlu, Ahmad 1925- .... **CLC 10**

Shange, Ntozake 1948-........ **CLC 8, 25**
     See also CA 85-88
     See also DLB 38

Shapiro, Karl (Jay) 1913-..... **CLC 4, 8, 15**
     See also CANR 1
     See also CA 1-4R

Shaw, (George) Bernard
     1856-1950................ **TCLC 3, 9**
     See also CA 104, 109
     See also DLB 10

Author Index

Shaw, Irwin 1913-1984...... CLC 7, 23, 34
See also CA 13-16R
See also obituary CA 112
See also DLB 6
See also DLB-Y 84
See also AITN 1

Shaw, Robert 1927-1978 ....CLC 5
See also CANR 4
See also CA 1-4R
See also obituary CA 81-84
See also DLB 13, 14
See also AITN 1

Sheed, Wilfrid (John Joseph)
1930-................. CLC 2, 4, 10
See also CA 65-68
See also DLB 6

Shepard, Lucius 19?- ....CLC 34

Shepard, Sam 1943- .....CLC 4, 6, 17, 34
See also CA 69-72
See also DLB 7

Sherburne, Zoa (Morin) 1912- .....CLC 30
See also CANR 3
See also CA 1-4R
See also SATA 3

Sheridan, Richard Brinsley
1751-1816................. NCLC 5

Sherman, Martin ....CLC 19

Sherwin, Judith Johnson
1936-.................... CLC 7, 15
See also CA 25-28R

Sherwood, Robert E(mmet)
1896-1955................. TCLC 3
See also CA 104
See also DLB 7, 26

Shiel, M(atthew) P(hipps)
1865-1947................. TCLC 8
See also CA 106

Shiga Naoya 1883-1971............CLC 33
See also CA 101
See also obituary CA 33-36R

Shimazaki, Haruki 1872-1943
See Shimazaki, Tōson
See also CA 105

Shimazaki, Tōson 1872-1943...... TCLC 5
See also Shimazaki, Haruki

Sholokhov, Mikhail (Aleksandrovich)
1905-1984................. CLC 7, 15
See also CA 101
See also obituary CA 112
See also SATA 36

Shreve, Susan Richards 1939-......CLC 23
See also CANR 5
See also CA 49-52

Shulman, Alix Kates 1932-...... CLC 2, 10
See also CA 29-32R
See also SATA 7

Shuster, Joe 1914-
See Siegel, Jerome and Shuster, Joe

Shute (Norway), Nevil
1899-1960...................CLC 30
See also Norway, Nevil Shute

Shuttle, Penelope (Diane) 1947-......CLC 7
See also CA 93-96
See also DLB 14

Siegel, Jerome 1914-
See Siegel, Jerome and Shuster, Joe

Siegel, Jerome 1914- and **Shuster, Joe**
1914-........................CLC 21

Sienkiewicz, Henryk (Adam Aleksander Pius)
1846-1916.................. TCLC 3
See also CA 104

Sigal, Clancy 1926-................CLC 7
See also CA 1-4R

Silkin, Jon 1930- .... CLC 2, 6
See also CA 5-8R
See also DLB 27

Silko, Leslie Marmon 1948-........CLC 23

Sillanpää, Franz Eemil
1888-1964...................CLC 19
See also obituary CA 93-96

Sillitoe, Alan 1928- .... CLC 1, 3, 6, 10, 19
See also CAAS 2
See also CANR 8
See also CA 9-12R
See also DLB 14
See also AITN 1

Silone, Ignazio 1900-1978..........CLC 4
See also CAP 2
See also CA 25-28
See also obituary CA 81-84

Silver, Joan Micklin 1935-.........CLC 20
See also CA 114

Silverberg, Robert 1935- ....CLC 7
See also CANR 1
See also CA 1-4R
See also SATA 13
See also DLB 8

Silverstein, Alvin 1933-
See Silverstein, Alvin and Silverstein,
Virginia B(arbara Opshelor)
See also CANR 2
See also CA 49-52
See also SATA 8

Silverstein, Alvin 1933- and **Silverstein,
Virginia B(arbara Opshelor)**
1937-........................CLC 17

Silverstein, Virginia B(arbara Opshelor)
1937-
See Silverstein, Alvin and Silverstein,
Virginia B(arbara Opshelor)
See also CANR 2
See also CA 49-52
See also SATA 8

Simak, Clifford D(onald) 1904-......CLC 1
See also CANR 1
See also CA 1-4R
See also DLB 8

Simenon, Georges (Jacques Christian)
1903-.............. CLC 1, 2, 3, 8, 18
See also CA 85-88

Simenon, Paul 1956?-
See The Clash

Simic, Charles 1938-......... CLC 6, 9, 22
See also CA 29-32R

Simms, William Gilmore
1806-1870.................. NCLC 3
See also DLB 3, 30

Simon, Carly 1945-...............CLC 26
See also CA 105

Simon, Claude 1913-........ CLC 4, 9, 15
See also CA 89-92

Simon, (Marvin) Neil
1927-.................. CLC 6, 11, 31
See also CA 21-24R
See also DLB 7
See also AITN 1

Simon, Paul 1941-.................CLC 17

Simonon, Paul 1956?-
See The Clash

Simpson, Louis (Aston Marantz)
1923-................. CLC 4, 7, 9, 32
See also CANR 1
See also CA 1-4R
See also DLB 5

Simpson, N(orman) F(rederick)
1919-.......................CLC 29
See also CA 11-14R
See also DLB 13

Sinclair, Andrew (Annandale)
1935-.................... CLC 2, 14
See also CANR 14
See also CA 9-12R
See also DLB 14

Sinclair, Mary Amelia St. Clair 1865?-1946
See Sinclair, May
See also CA 104

Sinclair, May 1865?-1946...... TCLC 3, 11
See also Sinclair, Mary Amelia St. Clair
See also DLB 36

Sinclair, Upton (Beall)
1878-1968............. CLC 1, 11, 15
See also CANR 7
See also CA 5-8R
See also obituary 25-28R
See also SATA 9
See also DLB 9

Singer, Isaac Bashevis
1904-........CLC 1, 3, 6, 9, 11, 15, 23
See also CLR 1
See also CANR 1
See also CA 1-4R
See also SATA 3, 27
See also DLB 6, 28
See also AITN 1, 2

Singh, Khushwant 1915-...........CLC 11
See also CANR 6
See also CA 9-12R

Sinyavsky, Andrei (Donatevich)
1925-........................CLC 8
See also CA 85-88

Sissman, L(ouis) E(dward)
1928-1976................. CLC 9, 18
See also CA 21-24R
See also obituary CA 65-68
See also DLB 5

Sisson, C(harles) H(ubert) 1914-.....CLC 8
See also CANR 3
See also CA 1-4R
See also DLB 27

Sitwell, (Dame) Edith
1887-1964.................. CLC 2, 9
See also CA 9-12R
See also DLB 20

Sjoewall, Maj 1935-
See Wahlöö, Per
See also CA 65-68

Sjöwall, Maj 1935-
See Wahlöö, Per

Author Index

Skelton, Robin 1925-..............CLC 13
  See also CA 5-8R
  See also AITN 2
  See also DLB 27

Skolimowski, Jerzy 1938-.........CLC 20

Skolimowski, Yurek 1938-
  See Skolimowski, Jerzy

Skrine, Mary Nesta 1904-
  See Keane, Molly

Škvorecký, Josef (Vaclav)
  1924-.......................CLC 15
  See also CAAS 1
  See also CANR 10
  See also CA 61-64

Slade, Bernard 1930- ....CLC 11
  See also Newbound, Bernard Slade

Slaughter, Frank G(ill) 1908- ......CLC 29
  See also CANR 5
  See also CA 5-8R
  See also AITN 2

Slavitt, David (R.) 1935-........ CLC 5, 14
  See also CA 21-24R
  See also DLB 5, 6

Slesinger, Tess 1905 1945........ TCLC 10
  See also CA 107

Slessor, Kenneth 1901 1971........CLC 14
  See also CA 102
  See also obituary CA 89-92

Smith, A(rthur) J(ames) M(arshall)
  1902-1980....................CLC 15
  See also CANR 4
  See also CA 1-4R
  See also obituary CA 102

Smith, Betty (Wehner)
  1896-1972....................CLC 19
  See also CA 5-8R
  See also obituary CA 33-36R
  See also SATA 6
  See also DLB-Y 82

Smith, Dave 1942-.................CLC 22
  See also Smith, David (Jeddie)
  See also DLB 5

Smith, David (Jeddie) 1942-
  See Smith, Dave
  See also CANR 1
  See also CA 49-52

Smith, Florence Margaret 1902-1971
  See Smith, Stevie
  See also CAP 2
  See also CA 17-18
  See also obituary CA 29-32R

Smith, Lee 1944-.................CLC 25
  See also CA 114
  See also DLB-Y 83

Smith, Martin Cruz 1942-.........CLC 25
  See also CANR 6
  See also CA 85-88

Smith, Martin William 1942-
  See Smith, Martin Cruz

Smith, Patti 1946-.................CLC 12
  See also CA 93-96

Smith, Sara Mahala Redway 1900-1972
  See Benson, Sally

Smith, Stevie 1902-1971...... CLC 3, 8, 25
  See also Smith, Florence Margaret
  See also DLB 20

Smith, Wilbur (Addison) 1933-.....CLC 33
  See also CANR 7
  See also CA 13-16R

Smith, William Jay 1918-...........CLC 6
  See also CA 5-8R
  See also SATA 2
  See also DLB 5

Smollett, Tobias (George)
  1721-1771..................... LC 2

Snodgrass, W(illiam) D(e Witt)
  1926-.................CLC 2, 6, 10, 18
  See also CANR 6
  See also CA 1-4R
  See also DLB 5

Snow, C(harles) P(ercy)
  1905-1980...... CLC 1, 4, 6, 9, 13, 19
  See also CA 5-8R
  See also obituary CA 101
  See also DLB 15

Snyder, Gary 1930-..... CLC 1, 2, 5, 9, 32
  See also CA 17-20R
  See also DLB 5, 16

Snyder, Zilpha Keatley 1927- ......CLC 17
  See also CA 9-12R
  See also SATA 1, 28

Sokolov, Raymond 1941-...........CLC 7
  See also CA 85 88

Sologub, Fyodor 1863-1927....... TCLC 9
  See also Teternikov, Fyodor Kuzmich

Solwoska, Mara 1929-
  See French, Marilyn

Solzhenitsyn, Aleksandr I(sayevich)
  1918-.....CLC 1, 2, 4, 7, 9, 10, 18, 26, 34
  See also CA 69-72
  See also AITN 1

Sommer, Scott 1951 ....CLC 25
  See also CA 106

Sondheim, Stephen (Joshua)
  1930-.......................CLC 33
  See also CA 103

Sontag, Susan
  1933-............ CLC 1, 2, 10, 13, 31
  See also CA 17-20R
  See also DLB 2

Sorrentino, Gilbert
  1929-................CLC 3, 7, 14, 22
  See also CANR 14
  See also CA 77-80
  See also DLB 5
  See also DLB-Y 80

Soto, Gary 1952- ....CLC 32

Souster, (Holmes) Raymond
  1921-.................... CLC 5, 14
  See also CANR 13
  See also CA 13-16R

Southern, Terry 1926- ....CLC 7
  See also CANR 1
  See also CA 1-4R
  See also DLB 2

Southey, Robert 1774-1843 .... NCLC 8

Soyinka, Wole 1934-......... CLC 3, 5, 14
  See also CA 13-16R

Spacks, Barry 1931- ....CLC 14
  See also CA 29-32R

Spark, Muriel (Sarah)
  1918-.......... CLC 2, 3, 5, 8, 13, 18
  See also CANR 12
  See also CA 5-8R
  See also DLB 15

Spencer, Elizabeth 1921- ....CLC 22
  See also CA 13-16R
  See also SATA 14
  See also DLB 6

Spencer, Scott 1945-..............CLC 30
  See also CA 113

Spender, Stephen (Harold)
  1909-.................CLC 1, 2, 5, 10
  See also CA 9-12R
  See also DLB 20

Spicer, Jack 1925-1965........ CLC 8, 18
  See also CA 85 88
  See also DLB 5, 16

Spielberg, Peter 1929-..............CLC 6
  See also CANR 4
  See also CA 5-8R
  See also DLB-Y 81

Spielberg, Steven 1947-............CLC 20
  See also CA 77-80
  See also SATA 32

Spillane, Frank Morrison 1918-
  See Spillane, Mickey
  See also CA 25-28R

Spillane, Mickey 1918- .... CLC 3, 13
  See also Spillane, Frank Morrison

Spitteler, Carl (Friedrich Georg)
  1845-1924.................. TCLC 12
  See also CA 109

Spivack, Kathleen (Romola Drucker)
  1938-........................CLC 6
  See also CA 49-52

Springsteen, Bruce 1949-..........CLC 17
  See also CA 111

Spurling, Hilary 1940- ....CLC 34
  See also CA 104

Staël-Holstein, Anne Louise Germaine
  Necker, Baronne de
  1766-1817.................. NCLC 3

Stafford, Jean 1915 1979 ..... CLC 4, 7, 19
  See also CANR 3
  See also CA 1-4R
  See also obituary CA 85-88
  See also obituary SATA 22
  See also DLB 2

Stafford, William (Edgar)
  1914-................... CLC 4, 7, 29
  See also CANR 5
  See also CA 5-8R
  See also DLB 5

Stanton, Maura 1946-..............CLC 9
  See also CA 89-92

Stark, Richard 1933-
  See Westlake, Donald E(dwin)

Stead, Christina (Ellen)
  1902-1983.............CLC 2, 5, 8, 32
  See also CA 13-16R
  See also obituary CA 109

Stegner, Wallace (Earle) 1909- ......CLC 9
  See also CANR 1
  See also CA 1-4R
  See also DLB 9
  See also AITN 1

Cumulative Index to Nationalities

AMERICAN
Adams, Henry **4**
Agee, James **1**
Anderson, Maxwell **2**
Anderson, Sherwood **1, 10**
Atherton, Gertrude **2**
Barry, Philip **11**
Baum, L. Frank **7**
Beard, Charles A. **15**
Belasco, David **3**
Benchley, Robert **1**
Benét, Stephen Vincent **7**
Bierce, Ambrose **1, 7**
Bourne, Randolph S. **16**
Bromfield, Louis **11**
Burroughs, Edgar Rice **2**
Cabell, James Branch **6**
Cable, George Washington **4**
Cather, Willa **1, 11**
Chandler, Raymond **1, 7**
Chapman, John Jay **7**
Chesnutt, Charles Waddell **5**
Chopin, Kate **5, 14**
Comstock, Anthony **13**
Crane, Hart **2, 5**
Crane, Stephen **11, 17**
Crawford, F. Marion **10**
Cullen, Countee **4**
Davis, Rebecca Harding **6**
Dreiser, Theodore **10**
Dunbar, Paul Laurence **2, 12**
Fisher, Rudolph **11**
Fitzgerald, F. Scott **1, 6, 14**
Forten, Charlotte L. **16**
Freeman, Douglas Southall **11**
Freeman, Mary Wilkins **9**
Gale, Zona **7**
Garland, Hamlin **3**
Gilman, Charlotte Perkins **9**

Glasgow, Ellen **2, 7**
Goldman, Emma **13**
Grey, Zane **6**
Harper, Frances Ellen Watkins **14**
Harris, Joel Chandler **2**
Harte, Bret **1**
Hearn, Lafcadio **9**
Henry, O. **1**
Hergesheimer, Joseph **11**
Howard, Robert E. **8**
Howells, William Dean **7, 17**
James, Henry **2, 11**
James, William **15**
Jewett, Sarah Orne **1**
Johnson, James Weldon **3**
Kornbluth, C. M. **8**
Kuttner, Henry **10**
Lardner, Ring **2, 14**
Lewis, Sinclair **4, 13**
Lindsay, Vachel **17**
London, Jack **9, 15**
Lovecraft, H. P. **4**
Lowell, Amy **1, 8**
Marquis, Don **7**
Masters, Edgar Lee **2**
McKay, Claude **7**
Mencken, H. L. **13**
Millay, Edna St. Vincent **4**
Mitchell, Margaret **11**
Monroe, Harriet **12**
O'Neill, Eugene **1, 6**
Rawlings, Majorie Kinnan **4**
Reed, John **9**
Robinson, Edwin Arlington **5**
Rogers, Will **8**
Rölvaag, O. E. **17**
Rourke, Constance **12**
Runyon, Damon **10**

Saltus, Edgar **8**
Sherwood, Robert E. **3**
Slesinger, Tess **10**
Stein, Gertrude **1, 6**
Stevens, Wallace **3, 12**
Tarkington, Booth **9**
Teasdale, Sara **4**
Thurman, Wallace **6**
Twain, Mark **6, 12**
Washington, Booker T. **10**
West, Nathanael **1, 14**
Wharton, Edith **3, 9**
White, Walter **15**
Wolfe, Thomas **4, 13**
Woollcott, Alexander **5**
Wylie, Elinor **8**

ARGENTINIAN
Lugones, Leopoldo **15**
Storni, Alfonsina **5**

AUSTRALIAN
Brennan, Christopher John **17**
Franklin, Miles **7**
Richardson, Henry Handel **4**

AUSTRIAN
Hofmannsthal, Hugo von **11**
Kafka, Franz **2, 6, 13**
Kraus, Karl **5**
Musil, Robert **12**
Schnitzler, Arthur **4**
Steiner, Rudolf **13**
Trakl, Georg **5**
Werfel, Franz **8**
Zweig, Stefan **17**

BELGIAN
Maeterlinck, Maurice **3**
Verhaeren, Émile **12**

BRAZILIAN
Machado de Assis, Joaquim Maria **10**

CANADIAN
Campbell, Wilfred **9**
Carman, Bliss **7**
Garneau, Hector Saint-Denys **13**
Grove, Frederick Philip **4**
Leacock, Stephen **2**
McCrae, John **12**
Nelligan, Émile **14**
Roberts, Charles G. D. **8**
Scott, Duncan Campbell **6**
Service, Robert W. **15**

CHILEAN
Mistral, Gabriela **2**

CHINESE
Liu E **15**
Lu Hsün **3**

CZECHOSLOVAKIAN
Capek, Karel **6**
Hašek, Jaroslav **4**

DANISH
Brandes, Georg **10**

DUTCH
Couperus, Louis **15**
Frank, Anne **17**

ENGLISH
Baring, Maurice **8**
Beerbohm, Max **1**

519

Nationality Index

Cumulative Index to Critics

Benn, Gottfried
  Friedrich Nietzsche 10:371

Bennett, Arnold
  Maurice Baring 8:31
  Joseph Conrad 1:196
  Theodore Dreiser 10:172
  Ford Madox Ford 15:68
  Anatole France 9:44
  John Galsworthy 1:292
  George Gissing 3:223
  Joris-Karl Huysmans 7:408
  George Meredith 17:264
  Olive Schreiner 9:396
  H. G. Wells 12:487

Bennett, Charles A.
  John Millington Synge 6:427

Bennett, D.R.M.
  Anthony Comstock 13:86

Bennett, E. K.
  Stefan George 14:202
  Paul Heyse 8:120

Bennett, George N.
  William Dean Howells 17:162

Bennett, Warren
  F. Scott Fitzgerald 14:181

Benoit, Leroy J.
  Paul Eluard 7:247

Bensen, Alice R.
  Rose Macaulay 7:430

Benson, Eugene
  Gabriele D'Annunzio 6:127

Benson, Ruth Crego
  Leo Tolstoy 4:481

Benson, Stella
  Stella Benson 17:22

Benstock, Bernard
  James Joyce 8:165

Bentley, C. F.
  Bram Stoker 8:388

Bentley, D.M.R.
  Wilfred Campbell 9:33
  Bliss Carman 7:149

Bentley, E. C.
  E. C. Bentley 12:15
  Damon Runyon 10:423

Bentley, Eric
  Stephen Vincent Benét 7:78
  Bertolt Brecht 1:98, 99; 6:40;
    13:47
  James Bridie 3:134
  Anton Chekhov 3:156
  Federico García Lorca 1:310
  Stefan George 14:198
  Henrik Ibsen 2:225
  Friedrich Nietzsche 10:377
  Eugene O'Neill 1:392
  Luigi Pirandello 4:337, 340
  August Strindberg 1:446
  Frank Wedekind 7:578
  Oscar Wilde 1:499
  William Butler Yeats 1:562

Berberova, Nina
  Vladislav Khodasevich 15:201

Berendsohn, Walter A.
  Selma Lagerlöf 4:231

Beresford, J. D.
  Dorothy Richardson 3:349

Bereza, Henryk
  Bruno Schulz 5:421

Berger, Dorothea
  Ricarda Huch 13:251

Berger, Harold L.
  C. M. Kornbluth 8:218

Bergin, Thomas Goddard
  Giovanni Verga 3:540

Bergmann, S. A.
  Stig Dagerman 17:85

Bergon, Frank
  Stephen Crane 11:161

Bergonzi, Bernard
  Hilaire Belloc 7:39
  Rupert Brooke 7:127
  G. K. Chesterton 1:180
  Ford Madox Ford 1:289
  John Galsworthy 1:302
  Wyndham Lewis 9:250
  Wilfred Owen 5:371
  Isaac Rosenberg 12:301
  H. G. Wells 6:541

Bergson, Henri
  William James 15:158

Berkman, Sylvia
  Katherine Mansfield 2:452

Berlin, Isaiah
  Osip Mandelstam 6:259
  Leo Tolstoy 4:463

Berman, Paul
  Emma Goldman 13:223
  John Reed 9:390

Bermel, Albert
  Guillaume Apollinaire 8:22
  Antonin Artaud 3:61

Bernhard, Svea
  Verner von Heidenstam 5:250

Bernstein, Melvin H.
  John Jay Chapman 7:198

Bernstein, Rabbi Philip S.
  Anne Frank 17:106

Berryman, John
  Isaak Babel 2:36
  Stephen Crane 11:139
  F. Scott Fitzgerald 1:240
  Anne Frank 17:116
  Ring Lardner 2:334
  Dylan Thomas 8:449
  William Butler Yeats 11:513

Bersani, Leo
  D. H. Lawrence 2:374

Bertaux, Felix
  Alfred Döblin 13:160
  Heinrich Mann 9:316
  Jakob Wassermann 6:512

Berthoff, Warner
  Ambrose Bierce 1:94
  Willa Cather 1:165
  Gertrude Stein 1:434

Bertocci, Angelo P.
  Charles Péguy 10:417

Besant, Annie
  Annie Besant 9:12

Best, Alan
  Frank Wedekind 7:590

Besterman, Theodore
  Annie Besant 9:17

Bethea, David M.
  Vladislav Khodasevich 15:210

Bettany, F. G.
  Arnold Bennett 5:22

Bettelheim, Bruno
  Anne Frank 17:111

Bettinson, Christopher
  André Gide 5:244

Bettman, Dane
  Marcel Proust 13:406

Beucler, André
  Léon-Paul Fargue 11:198

Bevington, Helen
  Laurence Housman 7:360

Bewley, Marius
  F. Scott Fitzgerald 1:260
  Isaac Rosenberg 12:304
  Wallace Stevens 3:450

Beyer, Edvard
  Henrik Ibsen 16:189

Beyer, Harald
  Bjørnstjerne Bjørnson 7:112
  Nordahl Grieg 10:207
  Alexander Kielland 5:279

Bhattacharya, Bhabani
  Rabindranath Tagore 3:494

Bhattacharyya, Birendra Kumar
  Saratchandra Chatterji 13:78

Biagi, Shirley
  Tess Slesinger 10:444

Biasin, Gian-Paolo
  Giuseppe Tomasi di Lampedusa
    13:296

Bien, Peter
  C. P. Cavafy 2:91
  Nikos Kazantzakis 2:315, 321,
    5:268

Bier, Jesse
  Ambrose Bierce 1:96

Bierce, Ambrose
  William Dean Howells 7:367
  Jack London 9:254

Bierstadt, Edward Hale
  Lord Dunsany 2:138

Bigelow, Gordon E.
  Marjorie Kinnan Rawlings
    4:362

Billington, Ray Allen
  Charlotte L. Forten 16:145

Bilton, Peter
  Saki 3:372

Binion, Rudolph
  Franz Kafka 6:221

Birchby, Sid
  William Hope Hodgson 13:233

Birchenough, M. C.
  Israel Zangwill 16:440

Birmingham, George A.
  John Millington Synge 6:425

Birnbaum, Marianna D.
  Géza Csáth 13:146

Birnbaum, Martin
  Miklós Radnóti 16:415
  Arthur Schnitzler 4:385

Birrell, Francis
  Alfred Sutro 6:422

Birstein, Ann
  Anne Frank 17:106

Bishop, Charles
  Christian Morgenstern 8:308

Bishop, Ferman
  Sarah Orne Jewett 1:365

Bishop, John Peale
  Sherwood Anderson 10:33
  Stephen Vincent Benét 7:69
  F. Scott Fitzgerald 6:160
  A. E. Housman 10:245
  Margaret Mitchell 11:371
  Thomas Wolfe 4:511

Bithell, Jethro
  Ricarda Huch 13:251
  Christian Morgenstern 8:307
  Emile Verhaeren 12:463

Bittleston, Adam
  Rudolf Steiner 13:447

Bixler, Julius Seelye
  William James 15:167

Björkman, Edwin
  Knut Hamsun 14:220
  Selma Lagerlöf 4:229
  Maurice Maeterlinck 3:323
  Władysław Stanisław Reymont
    5:391
  Arthur Schnitzler 4:388
  Sigrid Undset 3:510
  Edith Wharton 3:556

Bjørnson, Bjørnstjerne
  Georg Brandes 10:59
  Jonas Lie 5:325

Black, Hugo
  Charles A. Beard 15:32

Blackmur, R. P.
  Henry Adams 4:9
  Samuel Butler 1:135
  Hart Crane 2:113
  Ford Madox Ford 15:77
  Thomas Hardy 4:165
  Henry James 2:252, 258, 263
  D. H. Lawrence 2:351
  Wyndham Lewis 9:235
  Thomas Mann 2:421
  Edwin Muir 2:484
  Wallace Stevens 3:445
  Leo Tolstoy 4:471
  William Butler Yeats 1:565

Blair, Hector
  Mikhail Zoshchenko 15:507

Blair, Walter
  Robert Benchley 1:77, 79
  Will Rogers 8:333
  Mark Twain 6:463

Blake, Caesar R.
  Dorothy Richardson 3:355

Blake, George
  J. M. Barrie 2:46

Blake, Nicholas
  See also **Day Lewis, C.**
  E. C. Bentley 12:15

Critic Index

Critic Index

Gignilliat, John L.
Douglas Southall Freeman
11:231

Gilbert, Mary E.
Hugo von Hofmannsthal 11:303

Gilbert, Sandra M.
D. H. Lawrence 9:224

Gilbert, Stuart
Algernon Blackwood 5:73
James Joyce 3:265

Gilder, Rosamund
Montague Summers 16:427

Giles, James R.
Claude McKay 7:470

Gilkes, Michael
H. G. de Lisser 12:99

Gill, Brendan
Eugene O'Neill 1:407

Gillen, Charles H.
Saki 3:373

Gillespie, Diane F.
May Sinclair 11:417

Gilman, Charlotte Perkins
Charlotte Gilman 9:102

Gilman, Richard
Sholom Aleichem 1:26
Bertolt Brecht 1:121
Anton Chekhov 3:173
Henrik Ibsen 2:233
Eugene O'Neill 1:399
Bernard Shaw 3:402
August Strindberg 1:461
Italo Svevo 2:546

Gindin, James
F. Scott Fitzgerald 1:265
Virginia Woolf 1:544

Gingrich, Arnold
F. Scott Fitzgerald 1:238

Ginsburg, Mirra
Mikhail Bulgakov 16:82

Ginzburg, Lidija
Osip Mandelstam 2:407

Ginzburg, Natalia
Cesare Pavese 3:337

Giovanni, Nikki
Paul Laurence Dunbar 12:124

Gippius, Zinaida
Fyodor Sologub 9:433

Gittleman, Sol
Carl Sternheim 8:378
Frank Wedekind 7:583

Gladstone, W. E.
Annie Besant 9:14

Glasgow, Ellen
Ellen Glasgow 7:336
Joseph Hergesheimer 11:269

Glassco, John
Hector Saint-Denys Garneau
13:202

Glatstein, Jacob
Isaac Leib Peretz 16:392

Glenny, Michael V.
Mikhail Bulgakov 16:75, 91

Glicksberg, Charles I.
John Middleton Murry 16:339

Gloster, Hugh M.
Rudolph Fisher 11:205
Frances Ellen Watkins Harper
14:257
James Weldon Johnson 3:242
Wallace Thurman 6:448
Walter White 15:479

Goble, Danney
Zane Grey 6:184

Godwin, A. H.
W. S. Gilbert 3:211

Godwin, Murray
Damon Runyon 10:422

Goes, Albrecht
Anne Frank 17:104

Goetz, T. H.
Paul Bourget 12:75

Gogarty, Oliver St. John
Lord Dunsany 2:144
Oscar Wilde 1:501

Goist, Park Dixon
Zona Gale 7:287
Booth Tarkington 9:474

Gold, Herbert
Sherwood Anderson 1:49

Gold, Joseph
Charles G. D. Roberts 8:322

Goldberg, Isaac
Sholem Asch 3:65
Jacinto Benavente 3:97
Vicente Blasco Ibáñez 12:31
Rubén Darío 4:59
Havelock Ellis 14:110
Machado de Assis 10:278
Amado Nervo 11:393

Goldberg, S. L.
James Joyce 8:160

Golden, Bruce
Ford Madox Ford 1:285

Golding, William
Jules Verne 6:492

Goldman, Emma
Emma Goldman 13:211, 212

Goldsmith, Ulrich K.
Stefan George 2:154; 14:208

Goldstein, Sanford
Ishikawa Tabuboku 15:125

Golffing, Francis
Gottfried Benn 3:104
C. P. Cavafy 7:155

Gomme, Andor
Giuseppe Tomasi di Lampedusa
13:302

Gőmőri, George
Miklós Radnóti 16:413

Goodman, Anne L.
Walter White 15:479

Goodman, Paul
Franz Kafka 13:260

Gordon, Ambrose, Jr.
Ford Madox Ford 1:280, 286

Gordon, Caroline
James Joyce 3:266

Gordon, Ian A.
Katherine Mansfield 2:456;
8:281

Gordon, Jan B.
Arthur Symons 11:447

Gorky, Maxim
Leonid Andreyev 3:25
Isaac Babel 13:15
Anton Chekhov 3:145
Sergei Esenin 4:107

Gorman, Herbert S.
Sholem Asch 3:66
James Joyce 16:203
Katharine Tynan 3:504

Gosse, Edmund
Bjørnstjerne Bjørnson 7:105
Paul Claudel 10:122
Anatole France 9:42
André Gide 5:213
Thomas Hardy 4:149
Henrik Ibsen 8:141; 16:154
Henry James 11:321
Andrew Lang 16:255
Jonas Lie 5:323
Pierre Loti 11:354
George Moore 7:478
Henryk Sienkiewicz 3:421
Lytton Strachey 12:391
Emile Zola 1:585

Gottlieb, Annie
Tess Slesinger 10:442

Gould, George M.
Lafcadio Hearn 9:120

Gould, Gerald
May Sinclair 3.438

Gould, Jean
Amy Lowell 8:234

Gourmont, Rémy de
André Gide 12:142
Joris-Karl Huysmans 7:412
Jules Renard 17:301
Emile Verhaeren 12:458

Grabowski, Zbigniew A.
Stanisław Ignacy Witkiewicz
8:506

Graham, Eleanor
A. A. Milne 6:313

Graham, Kenneth
Henry James 11:342

Graham, Stephen
Valery Bryusov 10:78
Aleksandr Kuprin 5:296

Gramont, Sanche de
Antonin Artaud 3:54

Grandgent, Charles Hall
John Jay Chapman 7:187

Grant, Patrick
Rudolf Steiner 13:460

Granville-Barker, Harley
Laurence Housman 7:355

Granville-Barker, Helen
Gregorio Martínez Sierra and
María Martínez Sierra 6:275

Grass, Günter
Alfred Döblin 13:180

Grattan, C. Hartley
Ambrose Bierce 1:85
Jack London 9:259
H. G. Wells 12:500

Graver, Lawrence
Ronald Firbank 1:232

Graves, Robert
Samuel Butler 1:134
Alun Lewis 3:284
George Moore 7:488

Gray, Donald P.
Pierre Teilhard de Chardin
9:495

Gray, J. M.
Arthur Symons 11:426

Gray, James
Edna St. Vincent Millay 4:318

Gray, Ronald D.
Bertolt Brecht 6:35
Henrik Ibsen 16:186
Franz Kafka 6:222; 13:279
Thomas Mann 14:344

Gray, Simon
Tadeusz Borowski 9:20

Gray, Thomas A.
Elinor Wylie 8:532

Grayburn, William Frazer
Rebecca Harding Davis 6:152

Greacen, Robert
Oliver St. John Gogarty 15:105

Grebstein, Sheldon Norman
Sinclair Lewis 4:256

Green, Bonny
Damon Runyon 10:434

Green, Dorothy
Henry Handel Richardson 4:380

Green, Ellin
Laurence Housman 7:360

Green, Julian
Charles Péguy 10:406

Green, Martin
Dorothy L. Sayers 2:532

Green, Roger Lancelyn
Andrew Lang 16:263
David Lindsay 15:217

Greenberg, Clement
Bertolt Brecht 1:97

Greenberg, Eliezer
Isaac Leib Peretz 16:401

Greenberg, Martin
Franz Kafka 13:273

Greene, Anne
James Bridie 3:139

Greene, Graham
George Bernanos 3:126
Louis Bromfield 11:78
Samuel Butler 1:135
Havelock Ellis 14:124
Ford Madox Ford 1:282; 15:75
Henry James 2:256
Dorothy Richardson 3:353
Frederick Rolfe 12:270
Saki 3:366
Hugh Walpole 5:501
H. G. Wells 12:505

Critic Index

Critic Index

Critic Index

Critic Index

Critic Index

Critic Index

Critic Index